International Business

Environments and Operations

EIGHTH EDITION

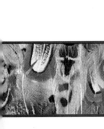

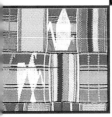

▲ **ADDISON-WESLEY**

An imprint of Addison Wesley Longman, Inc.

Reading, Massachusetts • Menlo Park, California • New York • Harlow, England
Don Mills, Ontario • Sydney • Mexico City • Madrid • Amsterdam

International Business

Environments and Operations

EIGHTH EDITION

John D. Daniels
E. Claiborne Robbins Distinguished Chair
University of Richmond

Lee H. Radebaugh
KPMG Peat Marwick Professor of Accounting
Brigham Young University

ANDREW FARLA   3RD COMM

WORLD STUDENT SERIES

Publishing Partner:	Michael Roche
Senior Project Manager:	Mary Clare McEwing
Production Supervisors:	Loren Hilgenhurst Stevens
	Mary Sanger
Production Services:	Kathy Smith
Art Editor:	Dale Horn
Illustrator:	Maryland CartoGraphics, Inc.
Text Design:	John Kane, Sametz Blackstone Associates
	Corey McPherson Nash
Cover Design:	Corey McPherson Nash
	Meredith Nightingale
Prepress Services Buyer:	Caroline Fell
Manufacturing Supervisor:	Hugh Crawford
Marketing Manager:	Jodi Fazio

Photo Credits: Part 1: fabric photo, Seth K. Sweetser Fund, courtesy Museum of Fine Arts, Boston; inset photo, © D. Farber, Woodfin Camp and Associates. Part 2: fabric photo, Gift of Mrs. Frederick L. Ames in the name of Frederick L. Ames, courtesy Museum of Fine Arts, Boston; inset photo, © Robert Azzi, Woodfin Camp and Associates. Part 3: fabric photo, The Textile Museum, Washington, D.C., 1985.41.1b, gift of Barbara Bischoff Hanzely; inset photo, © Robert E. Murowchick, Photo Researchers. Part 4: fabric photo, courtesy Peabody Essex Museum, Salem, Mass.; inset photo, © The Stock Market, Peter M. Fisher, 1994. Part 5: fabric photo, The Textile Museum, Washington, D.C., 1975.17.12, gift of Fred M. Fernald; inset photo, © Scott Daniel Peterson, The Gamma Liaison Network. Part 6: fabric photo, William A. Paine Fund, courtesy Museum of Fine Arts, Boston; inset photo, © 1990 Claus Meyer, Black Star. Part 7: fabric photo, in memory of J.S. and Sadyre Z. Gordon from Myron K. and Natalie G. Stone, courtesy Museum of Fine Arts, Boston; inset photo, © Tony Stone Images, Suzanne and Nick Geary.

ISBN 0-201-76733-3
1 2 3 4 5 6 7 8 9 10-RNT-01 00 99 98 97

About the Authors

John D. Daniels

John D. Daniels, the E. Claiborne Robbins Distinguished Chair at the University of Richmond, received his PhD at the University of Michigan. His dissertation won first place that year in the award competition of the Academy of International Business. Since then he has been an active researcher, publishing six books and over seventy articles and professional papers in such leading journals as the *Academy of Management Journal, California Management Review, Columbia Journal of World Business, Journal of International Business Studies,* and *Strategic Management Journal.* On its thirtieth anniversary in 1994, *Management International Review* referred to him as "one of the most prolific American IB scholars." He has served on the editorial board of eleven journals and has been a fellow of the Academy of International Business since 1985. He is currently Dean of the Fellows. Professor Daniels's international qualifications go well beyond his academic research. He has worked and lived a year or longer in seven different countries, worked shorter stints on six continents in about thirty other countries, and traveled in many more. His foreign work has been a combination of private sector, governmental, teaching, and research assignments; thus he is able to combine academic rigor with practical applications in this text. He has served as president of the Academy of International Business and as chairperson of the international division of the Academy of Management. He was formerly director of the Center for International Business Education and Research (CIBER) at Indiana University.

Lee H. Radebaugh

Lee H. Radebaugh is the KPMG Peat Marwick Professor of Accounting at Brigham Young University and co-director of the BYU–University at Utah Center for International Business Education and Research. He received his MBA and doctorate from Indiana University. He taught at the Pennsylvania State University from 1972 to 1980. He has also been a visiting professor at Escuela de Administracion de Negocios para Graduados (ESAN), a graduate business school in Lima, Peru. In 1985, Professor Radebaugh was the James Cusator Wards visiting professor at Glasgow University, Scotland. He was associate dean of the Marriott School of Management from 1984 to 1991. His other books include *International Accounting and Multinational Enterprises* (John Wiley & Sons, 4th edition) with S. J. Gray, *Introduction to Business: International Dimensions* (South-Western Publishing Company) with John D. Daniels, and seven books on Canada-U.S. trade and investment relations, with Earl Fry as co-editor. He has also published several other monographs and articles on international business and international accounting in journals such as the *Journal of Accounting Research,* the *Journal of International Business Studies*, and the *International Journal of Accounting.* His primary teaching interests are international business and international accounting. He is an active member of the American Accounting Association, the European Accounting Association, and the Academy of International Business, having served on several committees as the president of the International Section of the AAA and as the secretary-treasurer of the AIB. He is also active with the local business community as past president of the World Trade Association of Utah and member of the District Export Council.

Titles in International Business, International Economics, and International Finance

Contents

Each part opener displays
fabric from one of seven major regions
of international business. Part 1 shows
a mid-18th century U.S. colonial
fabric called "The Fishing Lady."

Part 2

Comparative
Environmental
Frameworks

Part 2 shows a northern
Indian Mughal carpet
from about 1600.

Part 3

Theories and
Institutions:
Trade and
Investment

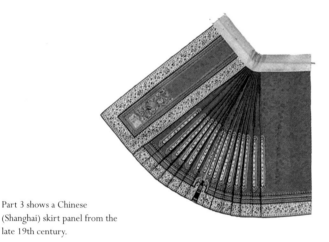

Part 3 shows a Chinese (Shanghai) skirt panel from the late 19th century.

Part 4

World Financial Environment

Part 4 shows a New Zealand
Maori cloak, circa 1930.

Part 5

The Dynamics of International Business-Government Relationships

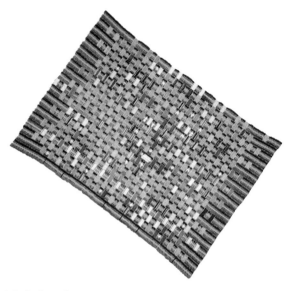
Part 5 shows a tribal robe from Ghana.

Part 6

Operations:
Overlaying
Tactical
Alternatives

Chapter 14
Collaborative Strategies   568

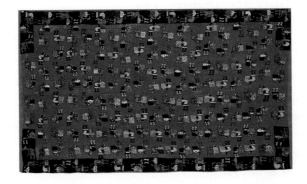

Part 6 shows a Peruvian mantle
from Paracas, circa 0-100 AD.

Chapter 15
Control Strategies   608

Part 7

Operations: Managing Business Functions Internationally

Part 7 shows an embroidered panel
designed by William Morris and worked
by his daughter, May Morris, from
England, circa 1900.

Chapter 21
Human Resource Management   861

List of Maps

Cases in the Eighth Edition

Preface

Toward the Twenty-first Century

Few texts (or their authors) have the vitality to reach an eighth edition; thus, for us this book is a cause for celebration. This edition also has symbolic significance because it will span the changeover from the twentieth to the twenty-first century.

Mention of the twenty-first century immediately brings to mind technology, especially as it delivers information through the World Wide Web (WWW). By connecting our eighth edition throughout to the Web, we are able to provide students and teachers with the means to update information in the text by linking to relevant sources through our Web site at http://hepg.awl.com/daniels/IB8. For each place in the text that we have Web linkages, we show the icon at left. All the chapter opening and closing cases feature Web links; thus, students can find additional up-to-date information on the companies and/or countries covered in every case. In addition, we have more generalized links for each chapter under the heading, "Web Connection." Finally, where appropriate in the text, we also have links to organizations that publish data on international transactions, such as on trade and investment. These links are principally important because all texts, especially those dealing with the fast-changing global environment, are quickly out of date. For example, throughout our first seven editions and this edition as well, we have always sought to include the latest published data for our tables and figures; however, we sometimes must go to press just weeks before newer data are published—a particularly frustrating situation for data published less frequently than once a year, such as census data that typically is collected every ten years. Even when we manage to include annual data just published, these data are often more than a year old because of the time organizations take to compile and tabulate what they collect. Fortunately, the technology leading us into the twenty-first century enables us to largely mitigate the obsolescence problem of the past because our Web site offers an efficient alternative for obtaining more recent information.

Enhancements for the Eighth Edition

To help guide us in the preparation of this eighth edition, we queried people who have taught international business courses in a variety of institutions. Based on their familiarity with the seventh edition, we asked what topics should be added, deleted, or emphasized to a different degree. We asked how materials could be better presented. We asked what additional enhancements would best assist in teaching the course. We were gratified that so many professors took the time to give us constructive suggestions.

Although there were too many suggestions to detail them all here, the major ones for the text are as follows:

- Develop a Web site to lead to updated and supplemental information
- Amplify and integrate the coverage of international business strategy throughout the text
- Explain for each section how companies' international operations evolve
- Add summary data on countries alongside their locations in the Map Atlas
- Update examples and add new cases
- Simplify the presentation by using more tables and figures
- Help students identify where places are geographically by maintaining and enhancing the large number of maps
- Use maps to a greater extent to convey information other than simply location
- Provide a framework for understanding and analyzing ethical issues
- Illustrate the countervailing forces that create uncertainties in international business management
- Integrate more coverage of the external environment as it affects business operations
- Present more examples of small company operations in international business
- Speculate more about the future

And, for the Instructor's Resource Manual, suggested improvements include:

- Update the section on audio-visual materials
- Refine and supplement the multiple-choice test bank
- Suggest supplementary reading materials to complement chapters
- Include creative learning ideas that instructors may use

We have implemented each of these suggestions in the eighth edition. A description of the major content and pedagogical features follows. The enhancements to the ancillary package, cases, and art are described later in this preface.

Content   Major content changes to the eighth edition are as follows:

- Chapter 1 introduces the strategic motives for companies to engage in international business and relates their tactics to the degree to which they have become international.

- Chapter 2 has explicit explanations of low- versus high-context cultures, monochronic versus polychronic cultures, the masculinity index, individualism versus collectivism, and uncertainty avoidance; it also references new studies comparing countries on their trust of others.

- Chapter 3 discusses the uses of new technology such as the Internet as part of the political process, especially in gathering information to help make decisions. In addition, we have added a new figure that shows how civil liberties and political rights intersect as measures of freedom.

- Chapter 4 contains a new discussion of economic freedom—freedom from government restraints and legal and institutional frameworks to safeguard economic freedoms—as a complement to political freedom in Chapter 3. The balance of payments discussion is moved to Chapter 10, and privatization is discussed in the context of budget deficits in a new section entitled Deficits and Privatization. A new case on Pizza Hut in Brazil is featured.

- Chapter 5 adds a section on strategic trade policy, expands examination of the Porter diamond, and delineates the place of trade in companies' strategies.

- Chapter 6 summarizes the comparable access arguments for protectionism, discusses the dispute settlement experience of the World Trade Organization, and adds a new ending case on United States–Cuban trade, which highlights the Helms-Burton bill.

- Chapter 7 contains a discussion of regionalism in the context of the World Trade Organization, which was discussed in Chapter 6. A discussion of the European monetary union is brought into the treatment of the EU instead of waiting until the foreign exchange chapters. We have expanded coverage of NAFTA, MERCOSUR, and APEC, and added a new case at the end of the chapter entitled "Crystal Lake Manufacturing: A NAFTA Dilemma."

- Chapter 8 expands the coverage of resource (including information) seeking motives for foreign direct investment and adds a new case on this subject dealing with a U.S.-owned cranberry growing operation in Chile.

- Chapter 9 contains a new version of the introductory case on the problems of foreign exchange when traveling overseas. We have also added a new figure on how foreign exchange transactions take place and a new case at the end of the chapter, "Ilusión Textiles and the Mexican Peso."

- Chapter 10 includes the discussion of the balance of payments that was contained in Chapter 4 in the seventh edition.

- Chapter 11 (formerly Chapter 12) has a new opening case on foreign direct investment in China, adds material on international efforts to limit bribery, and discusses differences among countries in acceptance of bribery.

- Chapter 12 (formerly Chapter 13) discusses the "compliance, circumvention, and avoidance" of governmental regulation by MNEs, alternative culturally responsive strategies in international negotiations, the 1995 U.S. voluntary code for the behavior of U.S. companies abroad, and the role of the WTO in international investment disputes.

- Chapter 13 (formerly Chapter 11) highlights the effects of recent economic growth on shifts in geographic emphasis by international companies, the concept of *liability of foreignness*, and the difference between micro and macro risk, and features a new ending case on Shell's operations in Nigeria.
- Chapter 14 (formerly Chapter 15) now differentiates reasons for collaborative arrangements in general from those that are unique to international operations, adds discussion of equity alliances, greatly expands the coverage of collaborative problems, and adds discussion of the alternatives for dissolving joint ventures.
- Chapter 15 (formerly Chapter 16) discusses why and what control is important for international companies, highlights evolving organizational forms (network, spinoff, and lead subsidiary organizations), strengthens the coverage of informal and transnational control, and adds a new ending case on GE's efforts to control a Hungarian acquisition, Tungsram.
- Chapter 16 (formerly Chapter 17) discusses the effect of infrastructure differences on the ability to standardize marketing programs globally and has a new ending case on Avon's international operations.
- Chapter 17 (formerly Chapter 14) is placed closer to the marketing chapter because of the obvious linkages between the two chapters. Coverage of trading companies is expanded to include the largest in the world, not just the Japanese trading companies, and a new letter of credit is introduced that is more consistent with the electronic age and the use of electronic transfer of documents.
- Chapter 18, now titled "Global Operations Management and Sourcing Strategies," features new material and existing material sequenced very differently from previous editions. It includes a new discussion on differences in characteristics between manufacturing and service organizations and on how such differences would affect operations management. There are also new sections on plant location, layout planning, and the global purchasing function.
- Chapter 19 includes the balance sheet of a British company so that students can compare format differences with those used in the United States and a new figure on the selection of translation methodology to help students get a better feel for the choice of translation methodologies under different conditions.
- Chapter 20 focuses on global capital markets and hedging foreign exchange exposures and features an expanded discussion of global bond issues and the conditions under which a foreign corporation might list and trade its securities on foreign markets, especially the New York Stock Exchange. There is also a new section on examples of foreign exchange strategies after the conceptual coverage of the issues to show students how different companies deal with hedging conditions.
- Chapter 21 relates the differences in subsidiary roles to differences in human resource needs and covers the ethical issue of using child labor.

Features   Each chapter now has a section relating the chapter's subject to a company's internationalization process. The framework for this discussion is set forth in Chapter 1. This feature provides an overview of the evolution from a company's having little or no international business activity to being highly dependent on its international operations. The new coverage should enhance an understanding that "one size does not fit all companies" because companies' needs evolve with their growth in international operations.

We have retained popular features from the seventh edition, such as "Looking to the Future." In some earlier editions we discussed the future in a separate, end-of-book chapter; however, much of the material was too far removed from the topics to which it related. Each chapter now ends with a section that relates its content to future scenarios of which students should be aware. Another retained feature, "Countervailing Forces," highlights the environmental conditions that pull companies in opposite directions. Countervailing forces add complexities to decision making in international business. The strength of one force relative to another will influence the choices available and the decisions made by companies competing internationally. Again, a framework for these sections is introduced in Chapter 1, and every chapter after that has a section related to its content. Finally, we have retained the popular feature, "Ethical Dilemmas," but have expanded and renamed the feature to include the concept of social responsibility. After introducing a framework in Chapter 1, we include a section in each of the other chapters that deals with ethical and social responsibility issues related to that chapter's content. For example, the "Ethical Dilemmas and Social Responsibility" in Chapter 8 covers direct investment issues, such as companies' responsibilities to displaced workers when they shift production abroad.

Our Approach to Teaching International Business

Since the first edition of this text we have started each revision with a "zero budget," that is, planning anew rather than depending on what we had written before. There has been nothing that could not be altered, no matter how much effort went into writing it originally. This approach undoubtedly helped us avoid overlooking the multitude of environmental changes that are the norm for international business. At the same time, we have agreed that our text should have strong theoretical underpinnings that are probably unaffected by international occurrences. We are fortunate that these give our text continuity and a backdrop against which we are able to explain recent global changes that are likely to be familiar to students.

We have started each edition with the same question to guide us: *What should be taught in a first course in international business when some of the students will thereafter have little or no direct classroom exposure to the subject, and others will use the course as background for more specialized studies in the area?* We continue to feel strongly that introductory students should be exposed to all the essential elements of international business. But what are these essential elements? Our queries indicated a near consensus that our coverage should continue to be as broad as possible. The pervasive feeling is that the field will continue to evolve too rapidly for anyone to know for sure what the future essentials will be. It is far better, our respondents reasoned, to risk covering too many things than to risk the omission of emerging issues and approaches that may well turn out to be essentials by the time students enter the workplace and need to be informed citizens. Such a broad coverage is a challenge.

The text has expanded and contracted throughout its lifetime in response to new information and because of added features, as well as our efforts to avoid an explosion in length. In this edition we have relocated two chapters, necessitating the renumbering of some other chapters. The basic content of the parts and their order of presentation are as follows: (1) an overview of the means of conducting international business, with an emphasis on what makes international business different from domestic business and the framework for the features we include in each chapter; (2) the effects of the social systems within countries on the conduct of international business; (3) the major theories explaining international business transactions and the institutions influencing those activities; (4) the foreign exchange systems and institutions that measure and facilitate international transactions; (5) the dynamic interface between countries and companies attempting to conduct foreign business activities; (6) the overlaying international operating concerns of where to go, whether and how to collaborate with other companies, and how to control the company as it expands internationally; and (7) the management of and strategy for concerns about international activities that fall largely within functional disciplines.

Our viewpoint, exemplified throughout the text, is that of real-world managers rather than the social science disciplines from which international business draws its theoretical underpinnings. For example, as we talk about trade policy, we discuss not only the effects of different policies on national objectives but also the courses of action that companies and industries can and do take in order to influence policy making and to react to policies that are implemented.

Why Students Will Learn Well by Using This Book

Our objective still is to provide more breadth and depth of coverage than any of the other international business texts do, while at the same time taking care not to overwhelm students.

Visuals   Many new charts and figures have been added to clarify the discussions (the total is now 144, including maps). The accompanying captions will aid students in grasping materials rapidly. Color is used throughout as a learning aid. For example, Map 2.2 in Chapter 2 shows countries colored to coincide with their principal languages, and Figure 6.2 in Chapter 6 uses color variations to demonstrate a shift in a supply curve. The part openers have photographs that highlight seven major regions of international business, set against a backdrop of fabric from that region.

Integrated case methodology   We provide detailed cases to begin and end each of the twenty-one chapters. Ten of the cases are entirely new; all others have been updated. Forty-one of the forty-two cases are real; all but one of those are identifiable situations.

The opening cases are designed to accomplish two objectives: (1) build the interest of the students so that they are motivated to read what is coming in the chapter, and (2) introduce problems and situations that will be explained further by theories and research findings presented within the chapter. For instance, the first chapter begins with a case dealing with the Walt Disney Corporation's decision to build a European theme park (Euro Disney) and the subsequent operation of that park. Almost all students should have some familiarity with and/or interest in this topic. Elements of the case are integrated into the chapter as examples to illustrate what makes international business different from its domestic counterpart and what types of adjustments Disney and other international businesses have to make. The closing cases are designed to serve a different purpose from the opening ones. They present situations for which students must analyze possible actions based on what they have learned in the chapter. In other words, the opening cases should enhance interest and the recall of essential facts; the closing cases should enhance the development of critical reasoning skills to apply the essential facts to necessary decision making.

Real-world examples   We have also continued the extensive use of updated real-world examples throughout the text to illustrate diverse approaches that individuals, companies, industries, and countries have taken in specific situations. (Examples of over 700 *different* companies are cited.) These examples not only help enliven the presentation, they also provide a practical and concrete counterpoint to the general discussion, which will help students understand the key concepts. Also, because most global employment growth has recently come from smaller companies and because students often think erroneously that international business is the domain of large enterprises, we have included many more examples about small companies. For example, Chapter 1 explains that small companies account for 20 percent of U.S.-manufactured exports. Further, one of the new cases, "Crystal Lake Manufacturing—A NAFTA Dilemma," deals specifically with a small business.

Study Support   To further emphasize key ideas (and to encourage students not to direct their study efforts too much to illustrative data), we continue to include the marginal notes that first appeared in the fourth edition. These notes highlight the text's major points in the margin for easy reference. They have been fully revised for this edition for the sake of emphasis and clarity. We have also highlighted new terms when they are introduced and included them in the expanded glossary. Chapter objectives are outlined clearly at the beginning of each chapter, and the summary's bulleted list recaps each chapter's major points.

An ample list of endnotes to aid students and instructors in digging deeper on the various subjects completes each chapter. Although we have omitted names of authors (except classics such as David Ricardo) within the text so that students would not think they had to remember those names, we reference almost 1600 *different* contributors. There are three indexes—subject, name, and company/trademarks. A glance at these and the endnotes will show that the content is up-to-date, worldwide, and easy to access. A map index keyed to the full-color atlas appears between Chapters 1 and 2 and is described below.

Maps   The maps for the seventh edition were well received, and we have retained the full-color atlas as a reference for students. The map index accompanying the atlas has been greatly enhanced in this edition as a learning tool. It now includes a pronunciation guide, geographical size, population, climate, major religion, main language, capital, currency, GNP for 1994, GNP per capita income for 1994, and where the countries can be located on the maps in the the atlas.

All other maps are placed adjacent to relevant text material. We have added many maps (for a total of 52 of them) and have illustrated more types of information via maps. For example, a map that accompanies the case on Blockbuster Video shows VCR equipment by region, and a map accompanying the Marks & Spencer case shows the company's operations by region, country, and type of operating venture.

We feel strongly that there is a need to improve students' geographic literacy without having them resort to the rote memorization of maps. A poll conducted by the Gallup Organization asked for the locations of sixteen seemingly not too obscure places on a world map: for example, the United States, Central America, France, Japan, and the Pacific Ocean. No nationality scored very well. Swedes did the best but averaged only 11.6 correct answers, or 70 percent. Regardless of nationality, people were better able to locate places closer to them. For example, respondents in Sweden scored higher than those in the United States at locating the six European countries on the list; but U.S. respondents scored better than Swedes in finding the United States, Canada, Central America, Mexico, and the Pacific Ocean. The Gallup/National Geographic poll also indicated possible differences among countries in educational philosophy, such as emphasis on rote memorization of information versus the use of tools to find information. For example, Swedes scored higher than any other group on factual geographic information, such as locating countries without an index and knowing population figures. However, U.S. respondents placed more emphasis than those of any other nationality on tool skills, including the importance of using computers and knowing how to interpret maps, such as by estimating distances from map scales. Because of these two approaches, we have included two types of maps. Those within the chapters are not indexed and are aimed primarily at presenting information of an interpretive nature. The full-color atlas is indexed so that students may look up locations.

Regrettably, we cannot present maps from all national perspectives; however, students should be aware that maps do differ among countries. An obvious difference is in the portrayal of disputed territories. Furthermore, most people put their own countries toward the middle, from west to east, of a flat map projection. They also divide global segments differently. For example, in the United States students are taught that there are seven continents and that North and South America are two continents divided at the border between Panama and Colombia. But the International Olympic Committee uses a flag with five rings to symbolize the five continents of the world. And Panamanians are taught that North and South America are divided between Costa Rica and Panama. In most other Latin American and Caribbean countries, students learn that the Western Hemisphere contains only one continent, America, with several subcontinental segments. Most people within these countries refer to everyone living in the Western Hemisphere as Americans and to people from the United States as either *estadounidenses* or *norteamericanos*—Spanish for "United Statesians" and "North Americans," respectively.

Maximizing the Learning Environment

A highly competitive set of ancillaries is available to adopters of this text.

Instructor's Resource Manual   The Instructor's Resource Manual contains many valuable materials for faculty. Suggestions are made for games, exercises, and projects suitable for classroom use. The manual also includes selected sources of published international business data. Chapter outlines, detailed lecture notes, and discussions of introductory and end-of-chapter cases have been revised for each chapter. Study questions complement the multiple-choice questions in the Test Bank and may be copied and distributed to students to help them focus on key elements for each chapter. The Instructor's Resource Manual also contains Transparency Masters of all the art in the book.

Test Bank   Included in the Instructor's Resource Manual, the Test Bank for the eighth edition is completely revised. Each multiple-choice question has the correct answer and the text page on which the answer is found. The questions are organized in sections that correspond to each chapter's learning objectives. Discussion questions that may be used either in essay exams or in class discussion are included in the Instructor's Resource Manual. The Test Bank includes 35–55 questions per chapter, and all have been reviewed and edited from a student's perspective.

Passport to the Web   Each new copy of this book contains a Passport to the Web that provides students with a guide for using the World Wide Web, directions to this book's Web site, and a place to log useful sites that they have visited.

Videos   A set of videos, selected from the MacNeil/Lehrer Business Reports News Hour and other sources, complements the text. Detailed summaries of each tape are provided on our Web site. This manual also includes a completely updated section on audio-visual materials. This section provides brief descriptions of approximately 300 videotapes, as well as information on where they may be purchased, rented, or borrowed.

Instructor's Resource CD-ROM   The Instructor's Resource CD-ROM contains instrumental tools to facilitate instructors' lectures and examinations. These include PowerPoint Electronic Transparency Masters—a complete set of figures and charts from the eighth edition, along with detailed outlines of each chapter. The instructor may customize these presentations and can print copies of individual slides for student handouts. The CD also includes Test Generator Software (TestGen-EQ with QuizMaster-EQ for Windows), which is fully networkable. TestGen-EQ's friendly graphical interface enables instructors to easily view, edit, and add questions; transfer questions to tests; and print tests in a variety of fonts and forms. Search and sort features let the instructor quickly locate questions and arrange them in a preferred order. QuizMaster-EQ automatically grades the exams, stores results on disk, and allows the instructor to view or print a variety of reports. The Instructor's Resource Manual has also been added to the Instructor's Resource CD-ROM.*

Both of us have diverse functional backgrounds, and we represent a gamut of opinions on the proper role of business and government in international affairs. In order to develop better coherence among the chapters, we read, criticized, and contributed to each other's work. John D. Daniels was charged with Chapters 1, 2, 5, 6, 8, 11, 12, 13, 14, 15, 16, and 21; Lee H. Radebaugh was charged with Chapters 3, 4, 7, 9, 10, 17, 18, 19, and 20. We welcome your comments and suggestions for the next edition.

J.D.D.
Richmond, Virginia
L.H.R.
Provo, Utah

*Because of legal and other restrictions, some ancillary items may not be available to adopters outside the United States.

Acknowledgments

We have been fortunate since the first edition to have colleagues who have been willing to make the effort to critique draft materials, react to coverage already in print, advise on suggested changes, and send items to be corrected. Because this book is the cumulation of several previous editions, we would like to acknowledge everyone's efforts. However, many more individuals than we can possibly list have helped. To those who must remain anonymous, we offer our sincere thanks.

Special thanks go to the faculty members who made detailed comments that contributed to the planning of this and previous editions:

Craig Woodruff	American Graduate School of International Management
Ann Perry	American University
Stan Fawcett	Brigham Young University
Ron Schill	Brigham Young University
Georgia White	Brigham Young University
Moonsong David Oh	California State University at Los Angeles
Ralph Gaedeke	California State University at Sacramento
Eldridge T. Freeman, Jr.	Chicago State University
Jean J. Boddewyn	City University of New York
Lucie Pfaff	College of Mt. St. Vincent
Urnesh C. Gulati	East Carolina College
George Sutija	Florida International University
Robert L. Thornton	Miami University of Ohio
Robert Buzzell	George Mason University
Phillip D. Grub	George Washington University
Fernando Robles	George Washington University
Michael J. Hand	United States Department of Commerce
Charles Mahone	Howard University

Victor E. Childers	Indiana University
Paul Marer	Indiana University
John Stanbury	Indiana University, Kokomo
Miriam K. Lo	Mankato State University
Arvind K. Jain	Concordia University
Heidi Vernon	Northeastern University
Roberto Garcia	The Ohio State University
Lee C. Nehrt	The Ohio State University
Michelle Govekar	Pennsylvania State University, Behrend Campus
Refik Culpan	Pennsylvania State University, Harrisburg
William A. Stoever	Seton Hall University
Thomas H. Bates	San Francisco State University
Leslie Jankovich	San Jose State University
Jeffrey T. Doutt	Sonoma State University
Van Wood	Texas Tech University
John Thanapoulos	University of Akron
Peter Walters	University of Arkansas, Little Rock
Kang Rae Cho	University of Colorado, Denver
Robert Grosse	Instituto de Empresa, Madrid
Jeffrey Krug	University of Memphis
Duane A. Kujawa	University of Miami
Srilata Zaheer	University of Minnesota
Klaus Sinai	University of Portland
Arnold Stebinger	University of South Carolina
Mark E. Mendenhall	University of Tennessee, Chattanooga
Karin Fladmoe-Lindquist	University of Utah
Richard W. Moxon	University of Washington
Jerry Ralston	University of Washington
Scott Kramer	University of Wisconsin, Madison
Peggy Chaudhry	Villanova University

We would also like to thank those individuals who have previously taken part in our market research and have helped us keep tabs on the changing nature of international business:

Golpira Eshegi	Bentley College
John Reed	Clarion University
David Grisby	Clemson College
Robert Spagnola	Colorado State University
Suhail Abboushi	Duquesne University
Jeffrey Rosensweig	Emory University
Thomas Becker	Florida Atlantic University
Charles Newman	Florida International University

Victor Cordell	George Mason University
Kamal Elsheshai	Georgia State University
John McIntire	Georgia Tech University
Keun Lee	Hofstra University
Ann Hackert	Idaho State University
Khairy Tourk	Illinois Institute of Technology
Alberto Ottaviani	Iona College
Robert L. Thornton	Miami University
Kenneth R. Tillery	Middle Tennessee State University
Patrick Bourman	National University
Fairalee Winfield	Northern Arizona University
Ann Marie Francesco	Pace University
Gregory Stephens	Texas Christian University
Douglas Ross	Towson State University
Hoon Park	University of Central Florida
George Gore	University of Cincinnati
Jack Nedell	University of Oregon
Denise Dimon	University of San Diego
Gerald Cox	University of Texas
Jerry Ralston	University of Washington
Scott Kramer	University of Wisconsin
Peggy Chaudhry	Villanova University

Several typists and graduate students gave us needed assistance during the preparation of this edition, and without this anonymous support we could not have made the necessary changes. Some others were so helpful that we cannot let them remain anonymous. They are Steven Hadley, Terri Hagler, Melanie Hunter, Adam and Elaine Schader, and Janaan Lake.

We would also like to thank Roberto Garcia of The Ohio State University and Nagarajan Gopalan, who did such a beautiful job on the Web site for our book.

Background for International Business

Tourism is one of the largest and fastest growing sectors of international business worldwide. Here a group of Buddhist monks from Asia enjoys a ride at Disneyland in the United States, the country that receives the largest amount of revenue from foreign visitors. The photo is set against a backdrop of a mid-18th century U.S. colonial fabric called "The Fishing Lady."

Chapter 1

International Business: An Overview

The world is a chain,
one link in another.
—Maltese Proverb

Objectives

- To define international business and describe how it differs from domestic business

- To define and discuss basic terms relating to international business

- To explain the major motives of companies for engaging in international business and why its growth has accelerated

- To introduce different means a company can use to accomplish its global objectives

- To illustrate the role social science disciplines play in understanding the environment of international business

- To provide an overview of the primary patterns for companies' international expansion

- To describe the major countervailing forces that affect the performance of international business

Case
Euro Disney[1]

Euro Disney's losses of almost $1.5 billion during its first three years of operations led to recurrent rumors that the theme park would close because of bankruptcy. But in 1995 and 1996 Euro Disney announced profits. Much of the turnabout was attributable to operating adjustments as Disney learned how to cope with an unfamiliar environment. Nevertheless, analysts have cautioned that Euro Disney's financial problems may have merely been delayed because of an agreement to defer large debt payments. Further, the company has rolled back some prices and deferred an increase in others in order to attract more customers; however, because of rising costs, there have been pressures on profits in spite of increased attendance.

Some of Euro Disney's problems began even before the park opened. Prior to Euro Disney's 1992 debut, a French writer expressed the hope that a fire would destroy the 4,800-acre theme park. Critics referred to the park, which lies twenty miles east of Paris and is about one fifth its size, as a "cultural Chernobyl"; Disney's chairman was pelted by eggs in Paris; and *le Nouvel Observateur* magazine showed a giant Mickey Mouse stepping on the rooftops of Parisian buildings. Disney sought to head off the criticism by explaining in the French press that Walt Disney was of French descent and his ancestors' name was originally D'Isigny. The company also agreed to make French the first language in the park (see Fig. 1.1) (although it would rely heavily on visual symbols).

Despite opposition to the park, Disney's management was optimistic about its success and some Disney executives wondered if the park's 50,000-person capacity would accommodate expected crowds. This optimism was partially based on the belief that criticism of the project emanated from only a small vocal minority. The late actor Yves Montand summarized the apparent majority French viewpoint when he said, "T-shirts, jeans, hamburgers—nobody imposes these things on us. We like them."

High expectations also were based on the success of Tokyo Disneyland, which exceeded attendance projections its first year, 1984. Map 1.1 shows that Tokyo Disneyland is the most visited amusement park in the world.

Figure 1.1
Source: The New Yorker, Vol. LXIII, No. 7, April 6, 1987, p. 34

Map 1.1
The Ten Most Visited Amusement Parks
Six of the ten most visited amusement parks in the world (those shown with mouse ears) are Disney or Disney-related parks. All ten parks are easily reached from highly populated areas. The five parks in the United States and the park in Indonesia are more suitable, climate-wise, for year-long outside activities than the other locations are.

Figures are 1996 estimates of attendance by *Amusement Business,* December 16, 1996, p. 79.

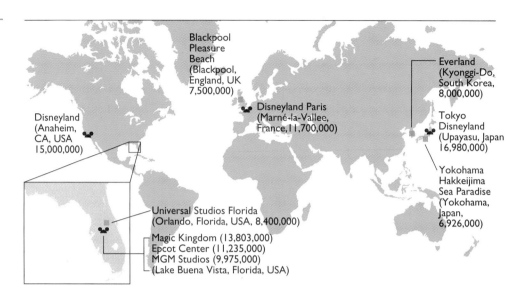

Blackpool Pleasure Beach (Blackpool, England, UK 7,500,000)

Everland (Kyonggi-Do, South Korea, 8,000,000)

Disneyland (Anaheim, CA, USA 15,000,000)

Disneyland Paris (Marné-la-Vallee, France,11,700,000)

Tokyo Disneyland (Upayasu, Japan 16,980,000)

Yokohama Hakkeijima Sea Paradise (Yokohama, Japan, 6,926,000)

Universal Studios Florida (Orlando, Florida, USA, 8,400,000)

Magic Kingdom (13,803,000)
Epcot Center (11,235,000)
MGM Studios (9,975,000)
(Lake Buena Vista, Florida, USA)

Disney announced in 1985 that it would open a park in either Spain or France. Because the park was estimated to provide about 40,000 permanent jobs and attract large numbers of tourists, the two countries courted Disney. The company, in turn, was likened to Scrooge McDuck as it played one country against the other in an attempt to get more incentives. The Spanish government offered to pay 25 percent of the construction costs and claimed that a park in Spain could attract 40 million tourists a year. The French government, although it estimated only 12 million visitors a year to a French park, offered even greater concessions: to extend the Paris railway to the park (thus linking the park to the rest of Europe) at a cost of almost $350 million, to make available cheaply land on which to build the park, and to lend Disney 22 percent of the funds needed to build it. Other factors also influenced Disney's decision in favor of France:

- Its central location, as shown on Map 1.2. About 109 million people live within a six-hour drive of the park.
- The number of tourists. The 26 million tourists in Paris each year make it Europe's most visited city.
- The popularity of Disney characters. The French are Europe's primary consumers of Disney products. For example, 10 million French children out of a total French population of about 56 million read the comic book *le Journal de Mickey* every week.

In addition, although the Spanish climate was more suited for winter attendance, Disney reasoned from its Tokyo experience that visitors would attend the park even in cold weather.

Disney's negotiations with the French government regarding who would own the park were heavily influenced by its experience with Tokyo Disneyland. On entering the Japanese market, the company, to avoid any risk of loss, made an agreement with the Oriental Land Company whereby Disney provided no financing and took no ownership in the park or the

**Map 1.2
Euro Disney's Central
Location**

Disney's park near Paris is located such that 109 million people can reach it in six hours or less by car.

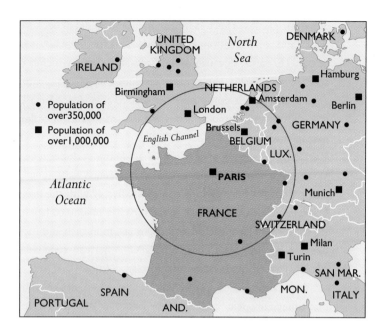

property on which it was built. Instead, Disney was paid to provide master planning, design, manufacturing, and training services during construction and consulting services after the park's completion. It also was to receive a 10-percent royalty from admissions and a 5-percent royalty from merchandise and food sales.

Because of the profitability of Tokyo Disneyland and research showing that 2.5 million Europeans visited Disney's U.S. parks in 1990, Disney opted for the maximum ownership stake allowed in its agreement with the French government (49 percent), which included investments in various satellite operations—hotels, shopping centers, campgrounds, and other facilities. (The entire operation is a company called Euro Disney; however, the park itself is now officially called Disneyland Paris, although generally referred to as Euro Disney as well.) Because most financing was through debt, this stake cost Disney only about $150 million. The remaining shares were sold to other investors, mainly in France and the United Kingdom, through an international syndicate of banks and securities dealers. In addition to equity, Disney agreed to accept a management fee of between 3 and 6 percent of gross revenue, a 10-percent royalty on admissions proceeds, and a 5-percent royalty on food sales.

The $5 billion Euro Disney looks very much like Disneyland and the Magic Kingdom in the United States. For instance, it includes Adventureland, Frontierland, Fantasyland, Mainstreet-USA, and *Le Chateau de la Belle au Bois Dormant* (Sleeping Beauty's Castle), plus six theme hotels outside the park. However, a number of changes were made to cater to European tastes, especially those of the French. Disney built a new attraction, Discoveryland, based on the science fiction stories of Jules Verne and the science fiction art of Leonardo da Vinci, as well as a movie theater featuring European history and French culture. The park emphasizes that Pinocchio was Italian, Cinderella was French, and Peter Pan flew over London. Sleeping Beauty's Castle is cartoon-like so as not to copy nearby authentic castles. There is more architectural detail because of the French penchant for depth and sophistication. For example, Mainstreet-USA is more ornate and Victorian than at the U.S. parks. Because of the Parisian climate, which is colder than that of Florida or southern California, the company included fireplaces, protected waiting lines, more indoor shows, plus a glass dome over the teacup ride. Also, Euro Disney at first sold alcohol only in its hotels and restaurants outside the main gates in order to uphold what Disney's U.S. management saw as the park's family image. However, about a year after opening, alcohol was added to menus of restaurants *inside* the park because visitors from Germany and the United Kingdom feel wine is part of the French experience. The large number of adaptations for Euro Disney contrasts sharply with the few that were made for Tokyo Disneyland. However, a few attractions are unique to Japan, such as a big-screen exploration of Japanese history. Signs are in English and most food is American-style because Japanese youth have embraced American-style culture. In Japan, there has been no criticism about the invasion of a foreign culture.

Euro Disney hired 12,000 employees. All employees must speak French plus at least one other European language; they wear flag lapel pins to indicate which languages they speak. Except for a handful of top managers, all employees are required by French law to have European Union (EU) passports or permits to work in France. To attract applicants, Disney advertised and/or held recruitment meetings in France, Ireland, the Netherlands, Germany, the United Kingdom, Canada, and the United States. Because of French individualism, Disney had to relax some of its U.S. grooming codes to entice French applicants to accept positions.

Certain European customs and attitudes make operating Euro Disney easier than operating U.S. parks. For example, in the United States, Disney plans events at different times in order to stagger the hours when people use the restaurant facilities. At Euro Disney, the British are usually finished with lunch before 1 p.m., when the French begin theirs; and the Italians and Spaniards arrive at about the time the French leave.

Euro Disney spent $220 million on a marketing blitz for its opening. Despite this massive effort, the first year's attendance was 20 percent below projections, which was caused in part by the lukewarm attendance of the French (only 29 percent of total attendance, rather than the forecast 50 percent) and which resulted in the 1100-room Newport Hotel closing for the winter because of low bookings. The dismal performance was intensified by lower-than-expected spending by the average visitor for food and souvenirs. Further, a slump in the French property market prompted Euro Disney to delay development of property around the park, including the planned MGM Studio tour park. Within five months of the opening, the price of Euro Disney stock fell from 164 to 68 French francs, prompting some securities analysts to compare the drop in the stock price to a ride on a roller coaster. The subsequent Euro Disney losses made the park the butt of jokes in the press, which called it "Mousechwitz" and "Eurodismal."

Euro Disney's early problems were caused by several factors:

- The leisure habits of Europeans
- Competition

- The cost of visiting the park
- U.S.-French agricultural trade animosity
- Slow-moving and chaotic lines at the park

Typically, Europeans are not very enthusiastic about amusement parks; the adults find it trying to act like children for an entire day. They prefer other types of leisure outings, especially in the winter. (No European amusement park has made money by staying open year-round.) For example, although an estimated 88 percent of people in the United States and Canada visited an amusement park in 1991, only 18 percent in Western Europe did. As a result, several European theme parks—the Mirapolis, Zygofolies, and Magic Planet— failed within the five years preceding Euro Disney's opening. And whereas Disney's U.S. and Tokyo parks opened when visitors to them were seeking ways to fill newly available leisure time, European leisure habits were already well formed.

Many potential Euro Disney customers instead visited the 1992 Olympics and World's Fair in Spain or other European amusement parks that recently sprang up or were refurbished. For example, Walibi, the world's fifth largest amusement-park operator, with headquarters in Belgium, built parks in locations from Amsterdam to Bordeaux. Parc Astérix, a theme park north of Paris modeled after a favorite European comic strip, was renovated and expanded just prior to Euro Disney's opening.

The cost of visiting Euro Disney also was a significant factor for potential visitors. European gasoline prices run as much as five times those in the United States, making family automobile vacations expensive. In addition, Euro Disney's entry and restaurant prices were set well above those in Disney's U.S. parks because the company had to offset the high wages necessary to attract workers to the area, which was plagued by insufficient and high-priced housing. European families, caught in a recession, were leery of spending so much on a day's outing.

Foreign visitors faced additional barriers. Because prices at Euro Disney were set in French francs, the exchange rate of other currencies into francs was an important factor affecting the cost. For example, in 1992, the year Euro Disney opened, European currencies were generally strong relative to the U.S. dollar. Consequently, British tourists could fly to Disney's parks in Florida on packages that included transportation, hotel, and park entry for a lower cost than a similar package to Euro Disney. Further, because European currencies could fluctuate substantially in value relative to each other, potential foreign visitors were wary of unexpectedly higher prices.

Another problem that affected Euro Disney's profitability was animosity in France over trade with the United States. In the fall of 1992, many French farmers went on strike to protest agricultural trade agreements that were being negotiated between the two countries and that they felt would unfavorably affect them. They seized the opportunity to treat Euro Disney as a symbol of the United States by partially blocking transportation to and entry into the park. They were joined by beet farmers whose land had been taken by the French government as the site for Euro Disney.

To complicate matters, if tourists managed to get past the striking farmers, they then faced slow-moving lines for security checks at the park's entry because of political unrest in several European countries. Finally, although Europeans, in accordance with U.S. custom, line up in orderly queues when visiting Disney's U.S. parks, they typically don't do the same in their home countries (such as at ski resorts). Whoever can best shove into a line wins. Hence, the complaint heard most often regarding Euro Disney concerned chaotic lines throughout the park.

To increase attendance, Euro Disney cut prices by as much as 20 percent for tickets, hotel rooms, and food. It also added the Space Mountain roller coaster. These moves apparently succeeded; Euro Disney had 11.7 million visitors in 1996, up 9 percent from the year before. Euro Disney now has more visitors than any other attraction in France, for example, more than twice as many visitors as the Louvre. To counter financial problems, Euro Disney worked out a financial rescue plan in 1994. A Saudi Arabian investor put up almost $400 million for about a 25-percent ownership stake (the result is that Disney now owns about 39 percent and the general public about 36 percent), and lenders agreed to defer receipt of interest on about $3.6 billion of debt until 1997 and beyond.

Disney remains openly optimistic about its future in Europe as well as in Japan. Disney's master plan, which extends far into the twenty-first century, calls for another park in each of those regions. And whatever Disney does will be noticed by competitors who have theme parks either in planning stages or under way all over Europe and Asia.

WEB CONNECTION

As students of international business, you will want to become aware of the tremendous number of resources available to do further research and to stay current with events that will have an impact on doing business abroad. One of the best ways to accomplish this goal is through the World Wide Web. To help you navigate through the vast cyberspace of the Web, we've constructed a Web home page that will link you to many useful sites. Throughout this text, you will see icons like the one at left, which indicate that a set of links exists on the website for this text at http://hepg.awl. com/daniels/IB8. At this URL, you will find a set of links leading you to related URLs for all opening and closing cases of the book and other chapter topics. You may want to bookmark this address. Addison Wesley Longman's main home page address is http://www.awl.com. Come and visit!

Introduction

The Field of International Business

International business is all business transactions—private and governmental—that involve two or more countries. Private companies undertake such transactions for profit; governments may or may not do the same in their transactions.

Why should you study international business? A simple answer is that international business comprises a large and growing portion of the world's total business. Today, almost all companies—large or small—are affected by global events and

The goal of private business is to increase or to stabilize profits. Success is influenced by
• Foreign sales
• Foreign resources

Government business may or may not be profit-motivated.

competition because most sell output to and/or secure supplies from foreign countries and/or compete against products and services that come from abroad.

A more complex answer is that a company that enters the international business field probably will engage in modes of business, such as exporting and importing, that differ from those it is accustomed to on a domestic level. To operate effectively, managers must understand these different modes. In addition, international business usually takes place within a more diverse external environment (the environment outside the company as opposed to its internal one) than is found domestically. The conditions within this external environment—physical, societal, and competitive—affect the way business functions such as marketing are carried out. These relationships are illustrated in Fig. 1.2.

Even if you never have direct international business responsibilities, you may find it useful to understand some of the complexities involved. Companies' international operations and governmental regulation of international business affect company profits, employment security and wages, consumer prices, and national security. A better understanding of international business may help you to make more informed decisions, such as where you want to work and what governmental policies you want to support.

Why Companies Engage in International Business

In operating internationally, a company should consider its **mission** (what the company will seek to do and become over the long term), its objectives (specific performance targets to fulfill its mission), and **strategy** (the means to fulfill its objectives). As shown in the objectives section of Fig. 1.2, there are four major operating objectives that may influence companies to engage in international business. They are:

- To expand their sales
- To acquire resources
- To diversify their sources of sales and supplies
- To minimize competitive risk

Expand sales Companies' sales are dependent on two factors: the consumers' interest in their products or services and the consumers' willingness and ability to buy them. The number of people and the amount of their purchasing power are higher for the world as a whole than for a single country, so companies may increase their sales by defining certain markets in international terms.

Ordinarily, higher sales mean higher profits, assuming each unit sold has the same markup. For example, Disney promotes its U.S. theme parks in Latin America in order to increase the number of park visitors, and Disney's revenues increase with each additional admission or hotel space that is sold to Latin American tourists. Profits per unit of sales may even increase as sales increase. For example, Disney films such as *The Lion King* and *The Hunchback of Notre Dame* cost millions of

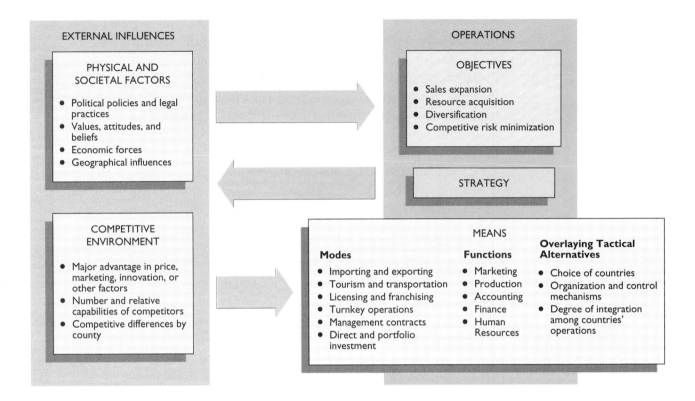

Figure 1.2
International Business: Operations and Influences
The conduct of international operations depends on companies' objectives and the means with which they choose to carry them out. The operations affect, and are affected by, the physical and societal factors and competitive environment encountered. The sizes of the arrows reflect that companies usually affect the external environment less than they are affected by it.

dollars to produce; but as more people see the films, the average production cost per viewer decreases.

Increased sales are thus a major motive for a company's expansion into international business. Many of the world's largest companies derive over half of their sales from outside their home country. These companies (with their home country in parentheses) include BASF (Germany), Electrolux (Sweden), Gillette (the United States), Michelin (France), Nestlé (Switzerland), Philips (the Netherlands), and Sony (Japan). However, smaller companies also may depend on foreign sales. For example, Maddox Metal Works, a U.S. manufacturer of equipment used in snack-food processing, makes about 65 percent of its $18 million-a-year sales abroad; and the U.S. Department of Commerce estimates that small companies account for 30 percent of U.S. exports.[2] Many small companies also depend on sales of components to large companies, which in turn sell finished products abroad.

Acquire resources   Manufacturers and distributors seek out products, services, and components produced in foreign countries. They also look for foreign capital, technologies, and information they can use at home. Sometimes they do this to reduce their costs; for example, Disney relies on cheap manufacturing bases in China and Taiwan to supply clothing to its souvenir outlets.[3] The potential benefits of this practice are obvious: Either the profit margin may be increased or the cost savings may be passed on to consumers, who will in turn buy more products, thus producing increased profits through greater sales volume. Sometimes a company buys abroad in order to acquire a service not readily available within the company's home country. For example, Disney buys from the U.K.'s Staffordshire Tableware because the company has developed automated techniques for putting complicated patterns on mugs, which Disney sells in its outlets.[4] Such a strategy may enable a company to improve its product quality and/or to differentiate itself from its competitors—in either case potentially increasing its market share and profits. Whereas a company may initially use domestic resources to expand abroad, once the foreign operations are in place, the foreign earnings may then serve as a source of resources for domestic operations. For example, McDonald's has recently relied on the strong financial performance of its foreign operations to pour more resources into domestic expansion.[5]

Diversify sources of sales and supplies   To help avoid wild swings in sales and profits, companies may seek out foreign markets and sources of supplies. Many companies take advantage of the fact that the timing of business cycles—recessions and expansions—differs among countries; that is, sales decrease in a country that is in a recession and increase in one that is expanding economically. In addition, by obtaining supplies of the same product or component from different countries, companies may be able to avoid the full impact of price swings or shortages in any one country.

Minimize competitive risk   Many companies move internationally for defensive reasons. In other words, they seek to counter advantages that competitors or potential competitors might gain from foreign operations that, in turn, could be used against them domestically. For example, a company may fear that another firm might generate large profits from a given foreign market if it is left alone to serve that market. Those profits may then be used in various ways (such as additional advertising or development of improved products) to improve its competitive position. The company harboring such a fear may thus enter foreign markets primarily to prevent a competitor from gaining such advantages.

Reasons for Recent International Business Growth

The amount of international business conducted over time is difficult to determine on a long-term historical basis because early records comparing like data are not available. Even in recent times, gathering data that can be used to make accurate comparisons can be difficult. For example, whether business is transacted across or within national boundaries determines whether business is international or domestic; shifting boundaries may cause what were domestic transactions to become international transactions, or vice versa. When the former Soviet Union disbanded in 1991, business transactions between Russia and Ukraine changed from domestic to international.

Regardless of these and other problems that impede accurate comparisons, it is generally concluded that international business has been growing recently at a faster pace than it did in earlier years and also at a faster pace than domestic business has been recently. For example, global merchandise exports grew faster than global production in eleven of twelve years in the 1984–1995 period.[6] Further, the portion of world output accounted for by foreign-owned facilities has been growing substantially.[7]

It seems the reasons companies pursue international business—to expand sales, to acquire resources, to diversify sources of sales and supplies, and to minimize competitive risk—would have applied in earlier periods as well. So what has happened in recent years to bring about the increased growth in international business? The answer can be found by examining the following four, sometimes interrelated, factors:

1. Rapid increase in and expansion of technology
2. Liberalization of governmental policies regarding cross-border movement of trade and resources
3. Development of the institutions needed to support and facilitate international trade
4. Increased global competition

Expansion of technology   Much of what we take for granted today results from technology that has been developed only within the last century. Before then, change occurred slowly. For example, it was only about a century ago when Jules Verne fantasized that people might go around the world in only eighty days. In recent years, however, the pace of technological advances has accelerated at a dizzying rate, while knowledge of products and services is available more widely and quickly because of tremendous strides in communications and transportation technology. As recently as 1970, there was no commercial transatlantic supersonic travel, faxing, e-mailing, Internet, teleconferencing, or overseas direct-dial telephone service. Today, the situation is radically different. A traveler can fly from New York to London by Concorde in only three and a half hours (although most people take the customary six-and-a-half-hour flights), and communications are almost instantaneous. Further, the cost of the improved communications and transportation have risen less fast than costs in general. For example, a three-minute phone call from London to New York in 1996 cost £0.52; whereas the same call in 1970 cost £1.50 in current prices and £12.46 in 1996 prices.[8]

By increasing the demand for new products and services, technology has tremendous impact on international business. As the demand increases, so do the number of international business transactions. But conducting business on an international level usually involves greater distances than does conducting domestic business, and greater distances increase operating costs and make control of a company's foreign operations more difficult. Improved communications and transportation speed up interactions and improve managers' ability to control foreign operations. Disney, for example, probably would be less willing to commit resources to its foreign operations without this ease of interaction.

Business is becoming more global because
• **Transportation is quicker**
• **Communications enable control from afar**
• **Transportation and communications costs are more conducive for international operations**

Lower governmental barriers to the movement of goods, services, and resources enable companies to take better advantage of international opportunities.

Liberalization of cross-border movements   Every country restricts the movement across its borders of goods and services and the resources, such as workers and capital, to produce both. To build Euro Disney, Disney had to negotiate with the French government, and the final agreement between the two parties prevented the company from owning a majority stake in the park as well as restricted the number of employees with experience at the company's U.S. parks who could work at Euro Disney. Disney also must contend with import restrictions, such as taxes, when its Chinese-produced souvenirs cross a border to be sold in its shops in other countries. Such restrictions make international business more expensive to undertake. Because the regulations may change at any time, international business also is riskier.

Generally, governments today impose fewer restrictions on cross-border movements than they did a decade or two ago, but more than during the late nineteenth and early twentieth century until World War I.[9] With the enactment of the World Trade Organization in 1995 (to be discussed in Chapter 6), there has been optimism that restrictions will continue to diminish. Although the past decrease in restrictions has been erratic, governments have lowered them for the following reasons:

1. Their citizens have expressed the desire for better access to a greater variety of goods and services at lower prices.
2. They reason that their domestic producers will become more efficient as a result of foreign competition.
3. They hope to induce other countries to reduce their barriers to international movements.

Fewer restrictions enable companies to take better advantage of international opportunities.

Institutional arrangements
• Are made by business and government
• Ease flow of goods
• Reduce risk

Development of supporting institutional arrangements   Much of what we now take for granted has resulted not only from expanding technology but also from the development by businesses and governments of institutions that enable us to effectively apply that technology. Disney can easily distribute films in foreign countries because of advances in transportation facilities as well as the evolution of various institutional arrangements that facilitate trade. For example, as soon as the films arrive in French customs, a bank in Paris can collect the distribution fee, in francs, from the French distributor and then make payment to Disney, in U.S. dollars, at a bank in the United States. In contrast, if business were still being conducted as in the era of early caravan traders, Disney probably would have to accept payment in the form of French merchandise, such as perfume or wine. The merchandise then would need to be shipped back to the United States and sold before Disney could receive a usable income.

Although barter accounts for about 10 percent of world trade,[10] it is not common because it can be cumbersome, time-consuming, risky, and expensive. Increasingly, business relies on the institutions that facilitate international trade, among them banks, postal services, and insurance companies. Today, most producers can be paid relatively easily for goods and services sold abroad because of, for example, bank credit agreements, clearing arrangements that convert one country's currency into another's, and insurance that covers damage en route and nonpayment by the buyer.

Consider, for example, the transport of mail internationally. Until the sixteenth century, when the first international postal agreement was enacted (between France and part of what is now Germany), there was no postal system as we know it today; separate arrangements had to be made for payment and shipment of each piece for each country through which it would pass. Today you can mail a letter to any place in the world using only stamps from the country where you mail it, regardless of how many countries the letter must pass through to get to its destination and regardless of the nationality of the company carrying it. For example, Disney can use U.S. postage stamps for a letter sent to its French distributors, even though the letter might be carried on an Indian airline that en route makes a stop in the United Kingdom.

More companies operate internationally because
- **New products quickly become global**
- **Companies can produce in different countries**
- **Domestic companies' competitors, suppliers, and customers become international**

Increase in global competition   The pressures of increased foreign competition can persuade a company to expand its business into international markets. It can do this more easily because of the technological, governmental, and institutional developments just discussed. Today, companies can respond rapidly to many foreign sales opportunities. They can shift production quickly among countries because of their experience in foreign markets and because goods can be transported efficiently from most places. Companies also can distribute component and/or product manufacturing among countries to take advantage of cost differences. For example, Kenner carries out some of the more automated parts of its toy production in the United States, with the more labor-intensive production done in Mexico. Also, some Japanese and South Korean companies produce part of their product lines at home and part of their product lines in the United States and then export from each production location.

Once a few companies respond to foreign market and production opportunities, others may see that there are foreign opportunities for them as well. For example, Lego Systems, a Danish theme park operator, saw that its revenues did not suffer from competition with Euro Disney and announced that it would open fifteen foreign theme parks by 2050.[11] Many other firms have to become more global to maintain competitiveness; failure to do so could be catastrophic for them.

Modes of International Business

The choice of operating mode is an important alternative in international strategy. Figure 1.3 shows that a company has a number of modes from which to choose. The following discussion introduces these modes. The first three categories in the discussion (merchandise exports and imports, service exports and imports, and investments) correspond closely to the categories in which countries aggregate

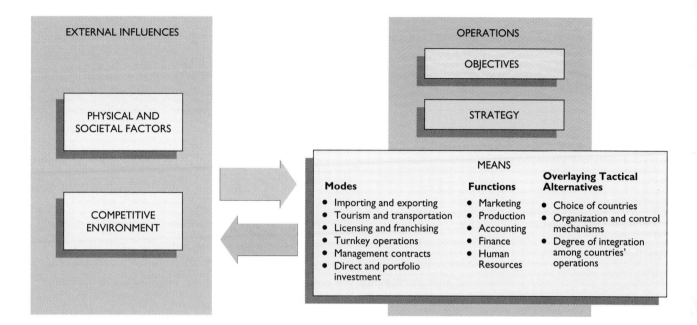

**Figure 1.3
Means of Carrying
Out International
Operations**

statistics of all the economic transactions involving their residents and residents of
foreign countries. These statistics are included in what are known as *balance of payments accounts.* The last category (other operational definitions) covers commonly
used terms for international business activities that may involve using any of the
modes in the first three categories.

Merchandise Exports and Imports

Merchandise exports are tangible goods sent out of a country; **merchandise
imports** are tangible goods brought in. Because these goods can be seen to leave
and enter, they sometimes are referred to as *visible* exports and imports. The terms
exports and *imports* frequently are used to refer only to *merchandise,* not *service,*
exports and imports. In Disney's case, souvenirs are merchandise exports for China
or Taiwan when they are sent to the United States or France and merchandise
imports for the United States or France when they arrive. For most countries,
exporting and importing of goods are the major sources of international revenue
and expenditures.

   More companies that engage in some form of international business are involved
in exporting and importing than in any other type of business transaction. This is
especially true of smaller companies, even though they are less likely than large
companies to engage in exporting. (Large companies are also more apt to engage in
other forms of foreign operations in addition to exporting and importing.) Nevertheless, many small companies are highly successful exporters, especially in growing export sectors.[12]

*Merchandise exports and
imports usually are a
country's key international
economic transaction*

Service Exports and Imports

Service exports and imports are international earnings other than those derived from the exporting and importing of tangible goods. Earnings received are **service exports;** earnings paid are **service imports.** Because services are not goods that can be seen, they also are referred to as *invisibles.* Service exports and imports take many forms. In this section, we discuss the following sources of such earnings:

- Tourism and transportation
- Performance of services
- Use of assets

Tourism and transportation   When Disney exports films from the United States, the films travel internationally, as do Disney executives when they visit Euro Disney on business. International tourism and transportation are important sources of revenue for airlines, shipping companies, travel agencies, and hotels. Some countries' economies, too, depend heavily on revenue from these economic sectors; for example, in Greece and Norway, a significant amount of employment, profits, and foreign exchange earnings comes from foreign cargo that is carried on ships owned by citizens of those countries. Earnings from foreign tourism are more important for the Bahamian economy than are earnings from the export of merchandise. Similarly, the United States has in recent years earned more from foreign tourism than from its exports of agricultural goods.[13]

Performance of services   Some services—such as banking, insurance, rentals (such as of Disney films), engineering, and management services—net companies earnings in the form of **fees,** that is, payments for the performance of those services. On an international level, for example, fees are paid for engineering services that often are handled through **turnkey operations**—construction, performed under contract, of facilities that are transferred to the owner when they are ready to begin operating. Fees also are paid for management services that often result from **management contracts**—arrangements whereby one company provides personnel to perform general or specialized management functions for another company; for example, part of Disney's revenues from Euro Disney comes from management fees.

Use of assets   The use of assets such as trademarks, patents, copyrights, or expertise under contracts, also known as **licensing agreements,** generates earnings called **royalties.** On an international level, for example, Disney has licensed Vigor International, a Taiwanese trading company, to use Disney trademarks for a chain of twenty Mic-Kids retail outlets.[14] Royalties also are paid for franchise contracts. **Franchising** is a way of doing business in which one party (the franchisor) allows another party (the franchisee) the use of a trademark that is an essential asset for the franchisee's business. The franchisor also assists on a continuing basis in the operation of the business, such as by providing components, management services, and/or technology.

Dividends and interest paid on foreign investments are also treated as service exports and imports because they represent the use of assets (capital). However, the investments themselves are treated separately in countries' balance of payments accounts.

Investments

Foreign investment involves ownership of foreign property in exchange for financial return. Disney's ownership in Euro Disney is an example of foreign investment. Foreign investment takes two forms: direct and portfolio.

Key features of direct investment are
• **Control**
• **Access to foreign markets**
• **Access to foreign resources**
• **Higher foreign sales than exporting (often)**
• **Partial ownership (sometimes)**

Direct investment   A **direct investment** is one that gives the investor a controlling interest in a foreign company. Such a direct investment also is called a **foreign direct investment (FDI),** a term frequently used in this text. Control need not be a 100-percent or even a 50-percent interest. For example, Disney can control Euro Disney with only a 39-percent stake because the remaining ownership is too widely dispersed to counter the company effectively. When two or more companies share ownership of an FDI, the operation is called a **joint venture.** When a government joins a company in an FDI, the operation is called a **mixed venture,** which is a type of joint venture.

FDI can provide the controlling company with access to certain resources or to a market. For example, through Disney's direct investment in China, the company can access that country's cheap labor to make clothing, for example, for its Mic-Kids outlets. In addition, its direct investment in Euro Disney enables Disney to service a market it could not otherwise tap: European customers who are unlikely to visit the company's U.S. parks.

Today, about 39,000 companies worldwide have FDIs that encompass every type of business function—extracting raw materials from the earth, growing crops, manufacturing products or components, selling output, providing various services, and so on. The 1995 value of these investments was about $2.7 trillion. The sales from the investments were about $8.1 trillion, which were more than the $6-trillion value of the world's exports of goods and services.[15] FDI is not the domain of large companies only. For example, many small companies maintain sales offices abroad to complement their export efforts. However, because large companies tend to have larger foreign facilities and operate in more countries, they own most FDI in terms of value.[16]

FDI may take place even though most or all of the capital is raised abroad. For example, the small U.S. computer manufacturer Momenta raised foreign capital within only six months of its founding. This capital funded the company's expansion into Japan, Taiwan, and Singapore.[17]

Key components of portfolio investment are
• **Noncontrol of foreign operation**
• **Financial benefit (for example, loans)**

Portfolio investment   A **portfolio investment** is an investment that gives the investor a noncontrolling interest in a company or ownership of a loan to another party. Usually a portfolio investment takes one of two forms: stock in a company or loans to a company or country in the form of bonds, bills, or notes that the investor purchases.

Foreign portfolio investments are important for most companies that have extensive international operations. They are used primarily for short-term financial gain, that is, as a means for a company to earn more money on its money with relative safety. For example, company treasurers routinely move funds among countries to get higher yields on short-term investments.

Other Operational Definitions

Many of the commonly used terms in international business are confusing because different writers, both in the popular media and in governmental and academic reports, use them to mean very different things. This discussion will highlight the variety of meanings and usage throughout this textbook.

There are numerous ways that companies may work together in international operations, such as through joint ventures, licensing, management contracts, minority ownership in each other's company, or long-term contractual arrangements. Tokyo Disneyland is an example of a strategic alliance between the Oriental Land Company and Disney that has involved turnkey operations, management contracts, and franchising. An all-encompassing term to describe these operations is **collaborative arrangements,** the term that we shall use throughout this text. Another term, **strategic alliance,** is sometimes used to mean the same thing, but sometimes used more narrowly—to indicate an agreement that is of critical importance to the competitive viability of one or more partners. We shall use strategic alliance only in its narrower meaning.

The **multinational enterprise (MNE)** is a company that takes a global approach to foreign markets and production; thus, it is willing to consider market and production locations anywhere in the world. The true MNE usually utilizes most of the operating forms discussed so far. However, it can be difficult to determine whether a company takes this global approach, so narrower definitions of the term *multinational enterprise* have emerged. For example, some say a company, to qualify as an MNE, must have production facilities in some minimum number of countries or be of a certain size. Under this definition, an MNE usually would have to be a giant company. However, a small company also can take a global approach within its resource capabilities and might use most of the operating forms we have discussed; therefore, most writers today use the term to include any company that has operations in more than one country—the way that we use the term in this text.

The term **multinational corporation (MNC)** also is commonly used in the international business arena and often is a synonym for MNE. We prefer the MNE designation because there are many internationally involved companies, such as accounting partnerships, that are not organized as corporations. Another term sometimes used interchangeably with MNE, especially by the United Nations, is **transnational company (TNC).** However, this term also is used in two other contexts. The first (and the earliest use) is to refer to a company owned and managed by nationals in different countries. For example, Royal Dutch Shell is a company that is jointly owned in the United Kingdom and the Netherlands, and its corporate management is split between the two countries. However, this type of company is uncommon; therefore the term

A company that has a worldwide approach to markets and production is known as an MNE or TNC. It usually is involved in nearly every type of international business practice.

is not often used in this respect. Today, the most common usage of the term (and the one we use throughout this text) has come from writers on international business strategy. They use the term to mean an organization in which capabilities and contributions may differ by country; however, they are developed and shared in integrated worldwide operations as companies learn from all the environments in which they operate and appropriate the knowledge for use throughout their global operations.[18]

MNEs as well as any companies with international operations can be separated into two categories: global companies and multidomestic companies. A **global company,** sometimes called a **globally integrated company,** integrates its operations that are located in different countries. For example, it might design a product or service with a global market segment in mind. Or it might depend on its operations in different countries to produce the components used in its products and services. In this type of company, the development of capabilities and the decisions to diffuse them globally are essentially made in the company's home country. A **multidomestic company,** sometimes called a **locally responsive company** and sometimes called a multinational company, allows each of its foreign-country operations to act fairly independently, such as by designing and producing a product or service in France for the French market and in Japan for the Japanese market. These categories also can be combined; for example, production may be global, whereas marketing is multidomestic. The TNC differs from both the global and the multidomestic company in that (1) it leverages the capabilities of both the home country and the foreign countries where it operates *and* (2) the main location of power within the organization may be geographically dispersed.

External Influences on International Business

A company's external environment is the aggregate of conditions outside the company that influence its success. A company also influences its external environment, but usually to a lesser degree. The external environment is the main focus of Part 2, Chapters 2–4 of the text. A company should form its strategies and the means to implement them by examining the interactions among the external environment, its objectives, and the resources it has to carry out these objectives. As shown in Fig. 1.4, the external environment includes physical factors, such as a country's geography, and societal factors, such as a country's politics, economy, law, and culture; it also includes competitive factors, such as the number and strength of suppliers, customers, and rival companies.

Managers in the worldwide environment must understand
- **Social science disciplines**
- **All functional business fields**

Understanding a Company's Physical and Societal Environments
To operate within a company's external environment, its managers must have, in addition to knowledge of business operations, a working knowledge of the basic social sciences: political science, law, anthropology, sociology, psychology, economics, and geography.

Politics has played and will continue to play an important role in shaping business worldwide. *Political science,* in part, describes the relationships between business and government and explains how the two interact with each other and react when their interests conflict. The political leadership in each country controls whether and how international business will occur in that country. For example, the French government's decision to court Disney enabled the company to buy cheap land, which the government had taken by eminent domain. More recently, Chinese authorities warned Disney that if it released its film *Kundun,* about the Dalai Lama, it would imperil the company's expansion into China. (China considers the Dalai Lama a threat to its control over Tibet.) Disney has been negotiating a theme park in China, and its ABC division covers China; therefore, if China carries out its threats, Disney's expansion could be greatly curtailed for political reasons.[19] Political disputes, particularly those that result in military conflicts, can disrupt trade and investment; even localized conflicts can have far-reaching effects. For example, political unrest elsewhere in Europe, along with anti-U.S. feelings in France, caused lower than projected attendance at Euro Disney.

Each country has its own laws regulating business. Agreements among countries set international law.

Domestic and international *law* determines largely what a manager of a company operating internationally can do. Domestic law includes regulations in both the home and host countries on such matters as taxation, employment, and foreign-exchange transactions. For example, French law determines how Euro Disney revenues are taxed and how they can be exchanged from francs to U.S. dollars. U.S. law, in turn, determines how and when the losses or earnings from France are treated for tax purposes in the United States. International law in the form of legal agreements between the two countries tempers how the earnings are taxed by both. International law may also determine how and whether companies can operate in certain locales. For example, Disney ceased selling cartoons and comic books in Serbia because of U.S. compliance with United Nations trade sanctions.[20] How laws are enforced also affects operations. For example, Disney and other U.S. movie companies long avoided distribution in China because of fear that the Chinese authorities would not enforce their laws against the copying and sale of films.[21]

Figure 1.4
Physical and Societal
Influences on
International Business

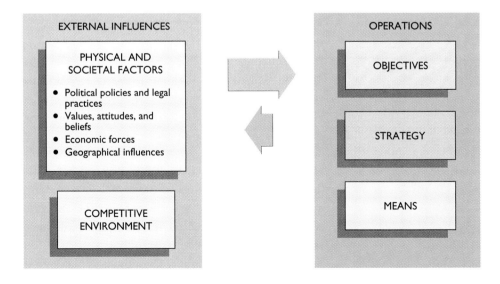

Only by understanding the treaties among countries and the laws of each country in which a company may want to operate, as well as how laws are enforced, can that company determine where it might profitably operate abroad.

The related sciences of *anthropology, sociology,* and *psychology* describe, in part, people's social and mental development, behavior, and interpersonal activities. By studying these sciences, managers can better understand societal values, attitudes, and beliefs concerning themselves and others. This understanding can help them function better in different countries. Recall that Disney had to counter adverse opinion that held that its new park in France would undermine the integrity of French culture. It also tailored certain aspects of Euro Disney to accommodate the tastes of French visitors.

Economics explains, among other concepts, why countries exchange goods and services with each other, why capital and people travel among countries in the course of business, and why one country's currency has a certain price relative to another's. By studying economics, managers can better understand why, where, and when one country can produce goods or services less expensively than another can. In addition, managers can obtain the analytical tools needed to determine the impact of an MNE on the economies of the host and home countries and the effect of a country's economic policies and conditions on the company. For example, Disney's decision to establish a theme park in France rather than, say, Haiti was based on the belief that the French population and that of other nearby countries could better afford the cost of visiting such a park. The decision also was based on the expectation that the French francs earned from visitors would buy enough U.S. dollars to make Euro Disney profitable.

Managers who know *geography* can better determine the location, quantity, quality, and availability of the world's resources, as well as the best means to exploit them. The uneven distribution of resources results in different products and services being produced or offered in different parts of the world. In the case of Euro Disney, France's colder climate prompted changes in the park's design that weren't needed in the warmer climates in which Disney's U.S. parks are located. Geographical differences also caused problems when Euro Disney imported reindeer from Finland for its first winter holiday season: The reindeer refused to drink the local water, and the wetter weather of France caused some to shed their antlers.[22] Geographical barriers such as high mountains, vast deserts, and inhospitable jungles affect communications and distribution channels for companies in many countries. The probability of natural disasters and adverse climatic conditions such as hurricanes, floods, or freezing weather make it riskier to invest in some areas than in others. These factors also affect the availability of supplies and the prices of products. For example, the 1995 earthquake in Kobe, Japan, caused shortages of certain specialized steel, affecting automobile production worldwide.[23] In addition, human population distribution around the world and the impact of human activity on the environment exert a strong influence on international business relationships. For example, concern about destroying the world's rain forests may lead to regulations or other pressures that may prompt companies to change the place or method of conducting business activities.

Physical and societal environments affect how a company operates and the amount of adjustment it must make to its operations in a particular country, for example, how it produces and markets its products, staffs its operations, and maintains its accounts. In fact, as shown in Fig. 1.4, each functional area may be influenced by the local external environment. The amount of adjustment is influenced by how much the environments of home and host countries resemble each other. In the case of Euro Disney, the company had to alter some of the attractions and require that employees be bilingual. It also undoubtedly must deal with French labor and accounting regulations that differ from those in the United States. These factors and the adjustments companies must make are examined in greater detail in Part 7, Chapters 16–21 of the text.

The Competitive Environment

In addition to its physical and societal environments, each company operates within its competitive environment. The competitive environment varies by industry, company, and country; therefore, international strategies differ substantially from one company to another and the means to implement them from one place to another for a given company. For example, companies in industries with relatively homogenous products, such as copper tubing or newsprint, compete more on price than companies in industries that compete more on differentiated and/or innovative products, such as branded toothpaste or state-of-the-art computer chips. Thus operating strategies for the former are usually more influenced than the latter by cost savings, such as developing more productive equipment and operating methods, producing on a large scale to allocate fixed costs over more units, and locating to secure cheap labor materials. But companies within the same industry also differ in their strategies, such as Volkswagen being more concerned with reducing costs of automobiles than Rolls-Royce; thus explaining why the former has recently moved much of its automobile production to Brazil to take advantage of lower labor costs, whereas the latter has not. Still another factor is the size of company and the resources it has relative to its competitors. For example, a market leader, such as Coca-Cola, has resources for many more international options than a much smaller competitor such as Royal Crown. But being a leader in one market does not guarantee leadership in all. For example, in most markets Coca-Cola is the leader, with Pepsi-Cola in a strong second position; however, Pepsi outsells Coke in India, and Inca Kola outsells both of them in its native Peru.[24]

The competitive environment also varies in other ways among countries. For example, a large domestic market exists in the United States but not in Sweden. One result is that Swedish producers have had to become more highly dependent than U.S. producers are on foreign sales in order to spread fixed costs of product development and production. The Swedish company Electrolux, for instance, had to promote exports very early in its history and depends much more on foreign sales of household appliances than do its main U.S. competitors, GE and Whirlpool. Another result of the larger U.S. market is that foreign companies have to invest much more to gain national distribution in the United States than they do in Sweden. Still another competitive difference is whether companies face international or local competitors. On the one hand, Boeing and Airbus compete with each other everywhere they try to sell commercial aircraft; therefore, what they learn about each other in one country is useful in predicting competitive behaviors in all the other countries in which they operate. On the other hand, Kmart faces different retailers as competitors in each of the foreign countries where it operates; thus, it must adjust to multiple competitive reactions differing by country.

These and other competitive differences enable some companies to take better advantage of foreign opportunities. Competitive factors influence whether companies follow multidomestic, global, or transnational strategies. They also can cause companies to choose different modes of operating, depending on the country or the product. For example, a company may elect to serve one country by exporting to it and another country with output from a direct investment there. Some of the most important competitive factors are shown in Fig. 1.5. They will be discussed in later chapters as alternate strategies are examined in depth.

Evolution of Strategy in the Internationalization Process

When one thinks of multinational enterprises, one often thinks of giant companies like IBM or Nestlé, which have sales and production facilities in scores of countries. But companies do not start out as giant entities, and few think globally at their inception. Therefore, as we discuss strategies throughout this text, we shall note that companies are at different levels of internationalization and that their current status affects the optimal strategic alternatives available to them. Although there are variations in how international operations evolve, some overall patterns have been noted. These are shown in Fig. 1.6. Most of these patterns relate to risk minimization behavior. In other words, most companies view foreign operations as being riskier than domestic ones because they must operate in environments which are less familiar to them. Thus, they initially undertake international activities reluctantly and follow practices to minimize their risks. But as they learn more about foreign operations and experience success with them, they move to deeper foreign commitments that now seem less risky to them.

Strategies for heavy international commitments usually evolve gradually from
- **Passive to active pursuit of opportunities**
- **External to internal handling of the business**
- **Limited to extensive modes of operations**

Patterns of Expansion

As you examine Fig. 1.6, note that the farther a company moves from the center on any axis, the deeper its international commitment becomes. However, a company does not necessarily move at the same speed along each axis. A slow movement along one axis may free up resources that allow faster expansion along another. For example, a company may lack initial capacity to own facilities wholly in multiple

**Figure 1.5
The Competitive
Environment and
International Business**

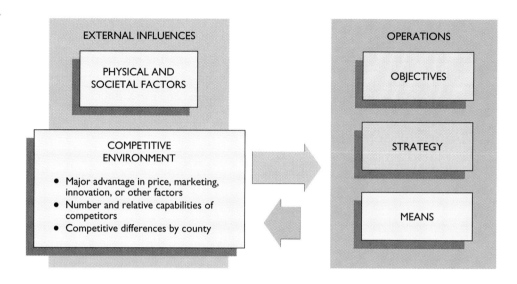

- Few to many foreign
  locations
- Similar to dissimilar
  environments

foreign countries; thus it may choose either to limit its foreign capital commitment by moving slowly along axis C in order to move rapidly along axis D (to multiple foreign countries), or vice versa.

Passive to active expansion   The impetus of strategic focus is shown on axis A in Fig. 1.6. Most new companies are established in response to observed domestic needs, and they frequently think only of domestic opportunities until a foreign opportunity is presented to them. For example, companies commonly receive unsolicited export requests because someone has seen or heard of their products. Often these companies have no idea of how their products became known abroad, but at this juncture, they must make a decision to export or not. Many decide not to because they fear they will not be paid or they know too little about the mechanics of foreign trade. Those that do fulfill the unsolicited export orders and then see that opportunities are available to them abroad are apt later to seek out other markets to sell their goods. Even large companies may move from passive to active involvement with aspects of their business. For example, although Tokyo Disneyland was proposed by a group of Japanese businessmen, the success of that venture led Disney to actively seek out a European location for another park.

External to internal handling of operations   The use of intermediaries to handle foreign operations is common during early stages of international expansion because this method may minimize risk through commitment of fewer of one's own resources to international endeavors and because of reliance on another company that already knows how to operate in foreign environments. But if the business grows successfully, the company will usually be more willing to handle the operations with its own staff. This is because it has learned more about foreign

Figure 1.6
The Usual Pattern of Internationalization
The farther out a company moves from the center of the diagram along any of the axes (A, B, C, D, or E), the deeper its commitment is internationally. The moves need not be at the same speed along each axis.

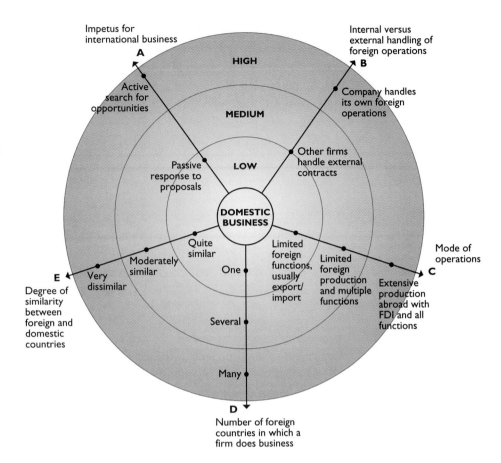

operations, sees them as being less risky than at the onset, and realizes the volume of business may justify the development of internal capabilities by hiring additional trained personnel, for purposes such as to maintain a department to carry out foreign sales or purchases. This evolution is shown on axis B in Fig. 1.6.

Deepening mode of commitment   Axis C in Fig. 1.6 shows that importing or exporting is usually the first type of foreign operation a company undertakes. At an early stage of international involvement, importing or exporting requires the least commitment of and the least risk to the company's resources, such as capital, personnel, equipment, and production facilities. For example, a company could engage in exporting by using excess production capacity to produce more goods, which then would be exported. By doing this, it would limit its need to invest more capital in additional production facilities such as plants and machinery. Further, the engagement only of importing and exporting limits the functions with which the company is responsible abroad. For example, it does not have to manage a foreign work force.

Companies often move into some type of foreign production after successfully building exports to that market. Initially this foreign production is apt to minimize the use of one's own resources by licensing a company to handle the production abroad, by sharing ownership in the foreign facility, or by limiting the amount of manufacture—such as simply packaging or assembling output abroad. Nevertheless, this foreign production usually involves a greater international commitment of the company's resources than does exporting or importing. The greater commitment results primarily because the company has to send qualified technicians to the foreign country to establish and help run the new operation. Further, it must be responsible for multifunctional activities abroad, such as sales and production. Later, companies are apt to make an even higher commitment through foreign direct investments that involves more than packaging and assembly. Their infusion of capital, personnel, and technology are highest for these operations.

A company typically does not abandon its early modes of operating abroad, such as importing and exporting, when it adopts other means of operating internationally. Rather, it usually either continues them by expanding its trade to new markets or complements them with new types of business activities.

Geographic diversification   When companies first move internationally, they are most apt to do business in only one or very few foreign locations. Axis D in Fig. 1.6 shows that over time, the number of countries in which they operate increases. The initial narrow geographic expansion parallels the low early commitment of resources abroad. It also minimizes the number of foreign environments with which the company must be familiar. The choice of countries in this geographic expansion also tends to follow certain patterns, as shown on Axis E. Initially, companies tend to go to those locations that are geographically close and/or perceived to be similar. For example, when beginning foreign operations, most U.S. companies have gone first to Canada, and Canadian companies have gone first to the United States. The closeness eases the process of control because of ease in moving personnel. There is also a perception of less risk because of greater familiarity with nearby areas and because of a perception of similarity of environments because of common languages and levels of economic development. However, this perception of similarity often masks subtle differences among countries, lulling them into costly operating mistakes.[25] Later, companies move to more distant countries, including those that are perceived to have less similar environments to those found in the home country.

Leapfrogging of Expansion

The patterns that most companies have followed in their international expansion are not necessarily optimal for their long-range performance. For example, the initial movement into a nearby country, such as movement by a U.S. company into Canada, may delay entry into faster growing markets, such as some of those in Southeast Asia. There is, however, evidence that many new companies are starting out with a global focus because of the international experience and education of their founders. Further, because of technological advancements, especially in communications (for example, posting product information on the World Wide Web), these start-up companies have a better idea of where their markets are globally and how they may gain resources from different countries. For example, II, a United Kingdom software designer, received initial financing from the United Kingdom, Germany, Austria, and Japan, and its first three customers were multinational companies in the United States and Japan.[26] In another case, the U.S. company Ecology Pure Air International sold its technology in Malaysia before selling in the United States because of U.S. federal and state requirements for extensive testing that slowed its domestic entry.[27]

COUNTERVAILING FORCES

In addition to the effect of external and competitive environmental factors, countervailing forces complicate decision making in international business. The strength of one force versus the strength of another influences the choices available to and the decisions taken by companies that compete internationally. For each chapter in this book, these forces are discussed in the section entitled Countervailing Forces. The following discussion highlights this contextual framework.

Globally Standardized versus Nationally Responsive Practices

Any company operating internationally must make trade-offs between the advantages of globally standardized practices and those practices that respond to different national preferences. These advantages may vary by product, function, and/or country of operation.[28]

Globally standardized practices tend to lower costs.

Nationally responsive practices enable companies to adjust to unique local conditions.

The trends that have influenced the recent worldwide growth in international business—rapid expansion of technology, liberalization of governmental trade policies, development of the institutions needed to support and facilitate international trade, and increased global competition—also usually favor a globally standardized approach. One advantage is that the company can reduce costs. For example, by designing a product or service to suit multiple countries, a company can avoid duplicating developmental expenses. It also may reduce manufacturing costs by serving multiple markets from a single production unit. In either case, the company gains from **economies of scale,** that is, a situation in which the cost per unit is lowered as output increases because fixed costs are allocated over more units of production.

However, when a company goes abroad, it faces conditions very different from those it encounters at home—as was amply demonstrated in the Euro Disney case. The company may need to engage in **national responsiveness,** that is, make operating adjustments in order to reach a satisfactory level of performance. In such situations, a multidomestic approach often works better because the company managers abroad are best able to assess and deal with the environments of the foreign countries in which the company operates. As a result, they are given a great deal of independence in running facilities in those countries.

Country versus Company Competitiveness

So far we have addressed competition from the viewpoint of companies. Companies, at least those that are not government-owned, may compete by seeking maximum production efficiency on a global scale. To accomplish this goal, production would be done using the best inputs for the price, even if the production location moved abroad. The output would then be sold wherever it would fetch the best price. Such practices should lead to maximum performance for the company.

But countries also compete with each other. They do so in terms of fulfilling economic, political, and social objectives. Countries are concerned not only with the absolute achievement of these objectives but also with how well they do relative to other countries. In fact, relative performance might be the overriding concern.

At one time, the performance of a country and that of companies headquartered in that country were considered to be mutually dependent and beneficial; that is, they rose and fell together. For example, consider the once-popular expression "What's good for General Motors is good for the country." The idea was that if General Motors (GM) increased its global share of automobile production, the United States would benefit also—from more automobile sales, tax collections, and jobs, both production and managerial. This benefit was considered possible because almost all of the company's production and sales at the time were in the United States. But today, the relationship between country performance and company performance is not as clear-cut. GM could elect to improve its global or even its domestic market share by producing more cars in its foreign manufacturing units and fewer in the United States. What would this mean for the U.S. competitive performance?

Keep in mind that competition among countries is the means to an end—the end being the well-being of a country's citizens. However, there is no consensus on how to measure well-being. Further, accepted indicators of current prosperity actually may foretell longer-term problems; for example, high current consumption may occur at the expense of investment for future production and consumption.[29]

These measurement problems are at the heart of the controversy regarding how the performance of companies affects the national competitiveness of the countries in which they are headquartered. Consider the hypothetical GM example. Some people would argue that the important indicator is the location of **high-value activities,** that is, activities that either produce high profits or are done by high-salaried employees such as managers. So GM's move to produce more cars abroad could improve the U.S. competitive position by increasing high-value activity at headquarters, in the form of more jobs for managers and executives, while reducing low-value activity in production, in the form of fewer jobs for U.S. assembly-line workers. In fact, there is evidence that the demand and income for higher-paid employees in the United States has increased as a result of U.S. companies' outsourcing to low-labor-cost countries.[30] However, other people would argue that U.S. competitiveness would deteriorate if there were a net loss in the number of U.S. jobs.[31] Closely related to this controversy is another regarding whether the nationality of a company's ownership makes any difference. For example, should it matter whether U.S. auto production is owned by Honda in Japan instead of GM

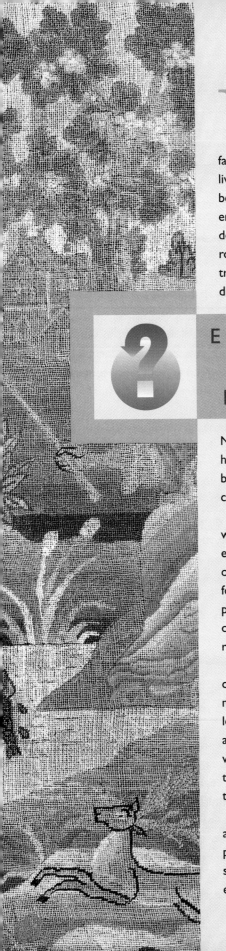

We all have our own beliefs as to what is right and wrong based on family and religious teachings, the laws and social pressures of the societies in which we live, our observations and experiences, and our own economic circumstances. Our ethical beliefs tend to be deep-seated; thus our debates with people of opposing views tend to be emotional. Even within a country, vastly opposing viewpoints frequently exist. This is demonstrated in the United States by the recent controversies on abortion, women's roles, gay rights, flag burning, capital punishment, gun control, euthanasia, organ transplants, marijuana usage, and welfare payments. Our own values on given issues may differ from the policies or practices of the companies for which we work, and any of these may differ from the prevalent societal norms or laws.

ETHICAL DILEMMAS & SOCIAL RESPONSIBILITIES

An MNE can encounter situations that give it either narrower or greater latitude in making decisions than it may have in its home country. Normal practices in a given foreign country will be based on that country's ethics; these host-country practices may conflict with the company's domestic practices or with the beliefs of its domestic constituencies. For example, U.S. companies must contend with child labor laws at home that they probably wouldn't encounter in Indonesia.

On the one hand, a company can face pressures to be socially responsible by complying with the norms in the foreign country. These pressures may include laws that permit or even require certain practices, competitive advantages for rivals who adapt to local norms, or accusations of meddling if a company tries to impose its home-country practices in the foreign country. On the other hand, companies can face pressures not to comply. These pressures can come from a company's own ethical values, its home-country government, or constituencies that threaten to boycott its products or to spread adverse publicity regarding it or its products.

Despite MNEs' efforts to comply with foreign laws and adhere to foreign customs, they continue to be targets of criticism. Many individuals and organizations have laid out various minimum levels of business ethics that they say a company must follow regardless of the legal requirements or ethical norms prevalent in a location in which it operates.[32] They argue that *legal* permission for some action may be given by uneducated or corrupt leaders who either do not understand or do not care about the consequences. They argue further that ethical norms are based on a long history of learned behavior and MNEs are obligated to affect that learning process by setting good examples.

From a business standpoint, two possible objectives are to create competitive advantages through socially responsible behavior and to avoid negative consequences from perceived irresponsibility. In terms of the former, it is argued that equitable acts lead to strategic and financial success because they lead to trust, which leads to commitment.[33] For example, the CEO of Levi Strauss has argued that its practices (including the refusal to operate where there are substantial human rights violations or to buy from suppliers whose worker safety measures are poor) has enabled the company to attract and maintain better employees and suppliers, to gain more consumer loyalty, and to maintain credibility during times of crisis. In terms of the latter, the same CEO said, "In today's world, an exposé on *60 Minutes* can undo years of effort to brand loyalty. Why squander an investment when, with foresight and commitment, reputational problems can be prevented?"[34]

In practice, governments may be forced into trade-offs among the objectives of their societies, and their actions can lull companies into thinking that society at large will not blame them for governmental decisions. This is not always the case. For example, the French government willingly allowed the incursion of U.S. culture into France and provided Disney with agricultural land at below market prices in order to gain what seemed to be overriding economic benefits for France. In return, however, Disney has suffered heavy criticism for undermining French culture and displacing French farmers.

Within lower-income countries, both societies and companies often must choose between the lesser of two evils. For example, higher-income countries banned the use of the pesticide DDT in order to protect the environment. Companies from those countries subsequently have been criticized for selling DDT to lower-income countries, whose leaders say that without it they cannot feed their populations.[35]

Another dilemma is whether MNEs should abandon markets in which they are not allowed to operate according to their own or an external concept of social responsibility. Some people argue that MNEs are so powerful and important that, if they cease operations in such a market, change in the country's policies will result. Others argue that MNEs are better able to bring about change by working within the system.[36] For example, because of apartheid policies, international companies were pressured through boycotts to leave South Africa. Many did, but many stayed as well. Apartheid policies, such as disallowing equal pay for equal work, were discontinued, but the effect of international companies' practices on the change is debatable. More recently, Carlsberg, a Danish brewery, reluctantly gave in to pressure by Danish trade unions and consumers to drop out of a joint venture in Myanmar because of the country's military dictatorship. A company spokesman pointed out that Carlsberg was not in business to pursue a foreign policy and the decision might weaken its future business possibilities in Myanmar in relationship to its competitors.[37] Anheuser-Busch, for example, continued its operations there.

Social responsibility requires judgment, which makes it relative and subjective. However, many multilateral agreements exist that can help a company understand the evolving global ethic and make ethical decisions. These agreements deal primarily with employment practices, consumer protection, environmental protection, political activity, and human rights in the workplace.[38] Further, the U.S. government issued a voluntary code in 1995 for U.S. companies' operations abroad, including recognition of workers' rights to organize and the avoidance of using child or forced labor. Interestingly, this code calls for U.S. companies to publicize their positive accomplishments in the workplace abroad.[39] Despite this growing body of agreements and codes, no set of workable corporate guidelines is universally accepted and observed. Clearly, many aspects of doing business internationally involve ethical questions. Thus ethical dilemmas and social responsibility related to that chapter's subject matter will be discussed in each chapter of this text.

in the United States? Some would argue that it would make no difference because the United States gains the jobs and production either way; others would argue that the high-value activity jobs would more likely be in Japan if Honda were the owner.[40] In actuality, there is little hard evidence to support any conclusion regarding the relationship between company and country performance.

Regardless of these unresolved controversies, countries continue to entice companies to locate company headquarters and production facilities within their borders. They do this through regulations and persuasion and by addressing the underlying factors that companies consider when they choose operating locations. In the hypothetical GM example, the U.S. government might enact regulations to prevent GM from expanding abroad, such as by limiting the capital it could send out of the country. Or the government could restrict imports of foreign-produced automobiles. It might try to persuade GM by holding out the possibility of future defense contracts (for companies acting in the "national interest") or simply by appealing to nationalism. To improve the country's investment-worthiness, the U.S. government might seek to address underlying factors of concern to companies in general. It could do so by improving the availability and quality of education, building roads and port facilities, or enacting measures to lower taxes. Any of these incentives could apply only to U.S.-based companies or to any auto company, regardless of nationality.

Business managers need to understand these complexities so they can argue logically and effectively regarding legislation that may affect their operations and so they can adjust to changing governmental regulations and incentives that can affect whether and how companies enter a foreign market. At the same time, they must balance dual roles: In one, they are managers with global efficiency objectives; in the second, they are members of a given society that has national rather than global objectives.

Sovereign versus Cross-National Relationships

Countries reluctantly cede some sovereignty because of
- **Coercion**
- **Military conflicts**

Countries compete; they also cooperate. We live in a world of countries that exist primarily because groups of people share a common sense of national identity that sets them apart from and causes them to prefer independence from other people. Countries sometimes cede sovereignty reluctantly because of coercion and international conflicts. However, countries willingly cede sovereignty through treaties and agreements with other countries for the following reasons:

Countries willingly cede some sovereignty to
- **Gain reciprocity**
- **Attack problems jointly**
- **Deal with extraterritorial concerns**

1. To gain reciprocal advantages
2. To attack problems that cannot be solved by one country acting alone
3. To deal with areas of concern that lie outside the territory of all countries

Countries want to ensure that companies headquartered within their borders are not disadvantaged by foreign-country policies, so they enter into reciprocal treaties and agreements with other countries on a variety of commercially related activities, such as transportation and trade. Treaties and agreements may be bilateral (involving only two countries) or multilateral (involving a few or many). For example, countries commonly enter into treaties whereby each allows the other's commercial ships and planes to use certain of its seaports and airports in exchange for reciprocal port usage. They may enact treaties that cover commercial aircraft safety standards and fly-over rights or treaties to protect property such as direct investments, patents, trademarks, and copyrights in each other's territory. And they may enact treaties for reciprocal reductions of import restrictions (and then retaliate when others raise barriers by, for example, raising barriers of their own or cutting diplomatic ties).

Countries enact treaties or agreements to coordinate activities along their shared borders, such as building connecting highways and railroads or hydroelectric dams that serve all parties. They also enact treaties to solve problems they either cannot or will not solve alone because of one or both of two reasons:

1. The problem is too big or widespread.
2. The problem results from conditions that spill over from another country.

In the first case, the resources needed to solve the problem may be too large, or one country does not want to pay all the costs for a project that also will benefit another country. For example, countries may enact a treaty whereby they share the costs of joint technology development, such as Europe's Esprit program in electronics. In the second case, conditions that involve spill-over effects can occur because one country's economic and environmental policies affect another country or countries. For example, high real interest rates in one country can attract funds from countries in which interest rates are lower, which can disrupt economic conditions in the latter countries. This is why the seven largest industrialized countries (known as the G-7 countries)—Canada, France, Germany, Italy, Japan, the United Kingdom, and the United States—meet regularly to coordinate economic policies. In addition, most environmental experts agree that cooperation among most countries will be needed to achieve meaningful environmental policies that will protect our planet. So far, agreements have been made among some countries on such issues as restricting harmful emissions, keeping waterways unpolluted, preserving endangered species, and banning the use of certain pesticides. Despite these agreements, however, discussions among countries continue on these, and other, issues.

Three areas remain outside the territories of countries—the noncoastal areas of the oceans, outer space, and Antarctica. Until their commercial viability was demonstrated, these areas excited little interest in multinational cooperation. The oceans contain food and mineral resources. They also are the surface over which much international commerce passes. Today, treaties on ocean use set out the amounts and methods of fishing allowed, international discussion attempts to resolve who owns oceanic minerals,[41] and agreements detail how to deal with pirates (yes, pirates are still a problem).[42] In space, radio and television signals are transmitted. Also, specialized manufacturing may soon be feasible in space stations that have germ-free conditions. But much disagreement still exists on who should reap commercial benefits from space. Antarctica has minerals and abundant sea life along its coast and attracts thousands of tourists each year. Consequently, a series of recent agreements have been made that limit its commercial exploitation.

LOOKING TO THE FUTURE

Companies must make decisions today about an uncertain future. If a company waits to see what happens on political and economic fronts, it may already be too late because investments in research, equipment, plants, and personnel training can take many years to complete. The company that correctly guesses now where future opportunities lie will be the one that produces and sells the goods and services consumers want at a price they are willing to pay—and does so in conformity with the rules of the societies in which it operates.

Guessing correctly is not always possible. However, by envisioning different ways in which the future may evolve, a company's management may better avoid unpleasant surprises. Accordingly, each chapter of this text ends with a section that discusses foreseeable ways in which topics covered in the chapter may develop.

WEB CONNECTION

Check out our home page for links to newspapers and periodicals that can be key resources for you in your study of international business.

Summary

- Companies engage in international business to expand sales, acquire resources, diversify their sources of sales and supplies, and minimize competitive risk.

- International business has been growing rapidly in recent decades because of technological expansion, liberalization of governmental policies on trade and resource movements, development of institutions needed to support and facilitate international transactions, and increased global competition. Because of these factors, foreign countries increasingly are a source of both production and sales for domestic companies.

- When operating abroad, companies may have to adjust their usual methods of carrying on business. This is because foreign conditions often dictate a more appropriate method and because the operating modes used for international business differ somewhat from those used on a domestic level.

- A company can engage in international business through various means, including exporting and/or importing of merchandise and services, direct and portfolio investments, and strategic alliances with other companies.

- Multinational enterprises (MNEs) take a global approach to markets and production. They sometimes are referred to as multinational corporations (MNCs) or transnational corporations (TNCs).

- To operate within a company's external environment, its managers must have not only knowledge of business operations but also a working knowledge of the basic social sciences: political science, law, anthropology, sociology, psychology, economics, and geography.

- Few companies include a high commitment to international operations as part of their start-up strategy; however, the inclusion of this commitment within their growth and operating strategies evolves over time.

- Countervailing forces influence the conditions in which companies operate and their options for operating internationally. A company's quest for maximum global profits is inhibited by different conditions in foreign countries, rivalry among countries, cross-national treaties and agreements, and ethical dilemmas.

Case
Blockbuster Video[43]

Blockbuster Video, by far the biggest video rental chain in the United States with about 4000 U.S. stores, announced in 1995 that it would open 1000 stores in the Asia-Pacific region by the year 2000. Most of Blockbuster's domestic growth occurred between 1987 and 1992; during that time the number of its stores increased from 238 to 2989. This increase was partially the result of growth in the video rental market as more people rented tapes for home entertainment on their newly acquired VCRs. Much of it came at the expense of thousands of mom-and-pop-type stores that stocked a small supply of tapes along with their other merchandise.

Blockbuster's primary growth strategy has been to attract customers by offering a large selection of tapes. It rents these videos in very large stores that can accommodate 7000–13,000 tapes representing 5000–8500 different titles. By expanding rapidly, Blockbuster has been able to gain economies of scale to offset the more than $100 million it spends per year on advertising. It buys vast numbers of tapes, which gives it buying clout with the film studios that sell tapes.

To finance its growth in the United States, Blockbuster has relied on acquisitions in exchange for Blockbuster stock, has franchised about half of its stores rather than obtaining ownership, and has raised equity capital for company-owned stores. Philips Electronics of the Netherlands became one of Blockbuster's largest equity sources when it invested $149 million in two stages for a 7.9-percent ownership in the company. Although this amount falls far short of giving Philips a controlling interest, Philips still owns enough shares to have a say in some of Blockbuster's practices; for example, the stores have been used to test-market Philips's compact disc interactive (CDI) technology.

Despite its impressive growth, by 1992 Blockbuster had acquired only a 13-percent share of the $11 billion U.S. home video market. Although there was room to grow in the United States, the company announced plans to focus on expanding abroad during the 1990s.

The shift in market emphasis from domestic to foreign resulted for three reasons: the maturing of the U.S. market for sales of VCRs, the threat of competition from pay-per-view movies, and the growth in retail sales of videotapes for home use—the sell-through market—as opposed to rentals. Blockbuster was slow to enter the sell-through market, hence retailers such as Kmart got a head start on gaining market share. Further, because film distributors typically sell rental tapes for about $65 and sell-through tapes for about $14, many more retailers can afford to compete against Blockbuster for tape sales than for tape rentals.

Initially, Blockbuster's major foreign expansion was to the world's higher-income, industrial areas—Canada, Europe, and Japan. This was a logical move, since the market for video rentals is limited by the number of VCRs owned by consumers, a number that varies widely among countries (see Map 1.3). Among countries with high incomes, the percentage of TV-owning households having VCRs varies substantially (for example, 47.5 percent for Italy versus 74.5 percent for the United Kingdom). The new emphasis on the Asia-Pacific area is the result of rapid economic growth in the area, which has led to more VCR ownership. For example, the number of VCRs in China grew from 1.2 million in 1990 to 14.8 million in 1994. Within lower-income countries, most households with VCRs use them to record television shows rather than to view rented videotapes. Two other factors limit the market in lower-income countries: the low cost of movie tickets, which makes videotapes a higher-cost rather than a lower-cost alternative, and competition from stores that rent cheap and unauthorized videotapes, which are sometimes copied directly from television-movie channels in the United States.

Blockbuster entered the British market in 1990 and by the end of 1991 had built fifteen stores. All were company-owned because of difficulty in selling franchises. This difficulty arose for two reasons. First, franchising was not yet developed in the United Kingdom video store market. Second, with only fifteen stores, Blockbuster could not justify large advertising outlays; such advertising is an incentive for investors to buy into franchises. To increase its presence in that country, Blockbuster in 1992 bid on Cityvision, the largest video store chain in the United Kingdom with 775 stores in the United Kingdom and 23 in Austria. To finance this purchase, Blockbuster induced Philips to back its bid in exchange for an option either to buy more Blockbuster stock or to become a joint-venture partner in the U.K. operation. Philips opted for the former. Cityvision's stockholders were offered, in exchange for one share of Cityvision stock, the choice of either 48 pence cash or a share of Blockbuster stock, valued then at 50 pence. The acquisition's total cost was $135 million—about $81 million in cash and the rest in the exchange of stock. The stores initially were operated under the Cityvision name for its stores, Ritz. The stores later were to be converted to Blockbuster stores as a springboard for the company's expansion into France, Germany, and Italy via joint ventures.

In 1991, Blockbuster bought a chain of twenty-five Major Video stores in Canada for conversion into Blockbuster stores. This move brought the company additional economies

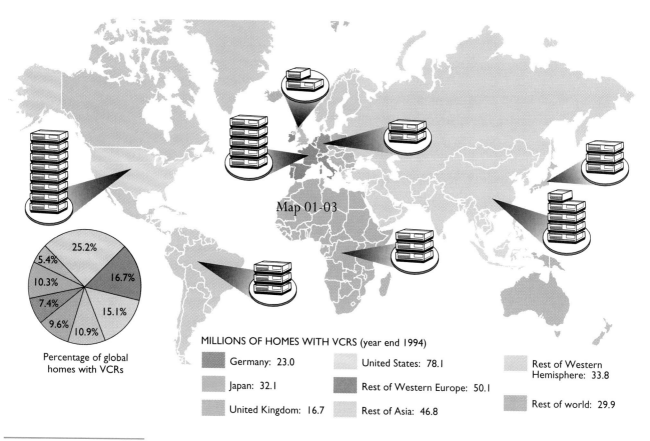

Map 01-03

MILLIONS OF HOMES WITH VCRS (year end 1994)

Germany: 23.0   United States: 78.1   Rest of Western Hemisphere: 33.8

Japan: 32.1   Rest of Western Europe: 50.1

United Kingdom: 16.7   Rest of Asia: 46.8   Rest of world: 29.9

Percentage of global homes with VCRs

25.2% | 5.4% | 10.3% | 7.4% | 9.6% | 10.9% | 15.1% | 16.7%

Map 1.3
Numbers of Homes with VCRs Worldwide, 1994

Note that four countries—Germany, Japan, the United Kingdom, and the United States—have 47 percent of the world's homes with VCRs but only about 9 percent of the world's population.

Source: Data from *Screen Digest*, August 1995, pp. 177–180.

of scale because much of the Canadian population lives within reception range of TV broadcasts from the United States and hence within range of Blockbuster's advertising. Blockbuster also set up franchise operations in Chile, Mexico, Australia, Spain, Venezuela, and Ireland. The move into Ireland was largely in response to a move into the U.S. market by Xtra-vision, Ireland's largest video chain. By 1990, Xtra-vision had fifty U.S. stores under the Videosmith and Video Library names.

In 1991, Blockbuster decided to enter Japan. It decided on a 50/50 joint venture in order to gain know-how about the market from a knowledgeable Japanese partner, Fujita Shoten. (Fujita Shoten's chairman had established an earlier 50/50 joint venture with McDonald's, which now has about 800 restaurants in Japan. Fujita Shoten also has a stake in Toys 'R Us Japan.) Blockbuster planned to expand through franchising its outlets and expected to have a thousand Japanese stores by the year 2000. In deciding to move into Japan, company executives saw the following conditions that afforded opportunities for Blockbuster:

- There were no major video rental chains in Japan. The largest rental chain, the Culture Convenience Club, had only small-scale outlets.
- There were only 1800 movie theaters in Japan, fewer than one tenth the number in the United States. They were controlled by Japanese film studios that limited distribution of foreign films to about 100 theaters. Despite distribution problems, however, U.S. films had 60 percent of the Japanese film market.

- Existing video stores catered mainly to Japanese males under 25 years of age by renting tapes of pornographic and violent films. Blockbuster would target an older and more family-oriented market and would rent no adult videos.

Blockbuster's management reasoned that there was a big, unfulfilled demand for U.S. videos and that it could introduce these more rapidly into the Japanese market than Japanese competitors could (at the time, the wait for U.S. releases was about a year).

When Blockbuster entered Japan, it planned to earn 12–15 percent of its income from game rentals, as it does in the United States. However, it was unable to meet this goal. Japanese law requires permission from the author of copyrighted material before anyone can sell or rent the material. Of the two giants in the video game industry, Sega Enterprises gave its permission but Nintendo refused.

Because space is so limited and expensive in Japan, Blockbuster had to reduce the size of its stores. However, redesigning the stores' interiors allowed them to carry about 8000 titles and 10,000 tapes. Aside from its ban on adult videos, Blockbuster allows each country's managers to decide which tapes to buy for their stores. All tape purchases are made locally through distributors representing film studios. This arrangement is necessary because the local distributors can perform certain tasks more easily, such as arranging for subtitles or dubbing, dealing with local censorship issues, converting films to the tape format (for example, VHS, Beta, or Secam) preferred in that country, and acquiring local films to meet local demand. On this last point, Hollywood productions dominate markets worldwide; however, where there is a strong local film industry, such as in the United Kingdom and France, there is market demand for more tapes made from local films.

Blockbuster also used its foreign experience to help it grow in the United States. For example, in 1992, the company acquired a 50-percent interest in the Virgin Retail Group, whose stores sell recorded music. This U.K. company owns megastores in the United Kingdom, France, Germany, Italy, Austria, the Netherlands, and Australia. The operations continued to be managed by Virgin, and there were plans for major expansion into the U.S. market. The first store, in Los Angeles, was modeled after Virgin's megastores, which offer 200 listening booths, a stage for live performances, and specialty rooms so classical music lovers needn't mix with heavy metal fans.

Questions

1. Why do you think Blockbuster has used various operating forms (company-owned operations, joint ventures, and franchises) for the different foreign markets it has entered?
2. What are the advantages and disadvantages of Blockbuster's expanding abroad rather than concentrating its efforts on the U.S. market?
3. Blockbuster's earliest and primary foreign thrust was into the British market. Do you agree with this expansion priority?
4. Blockbuster bought video store chains abroad that already had well-known names. Why should the company change these stores to Blockbuster stores?

5. What factors other than those presented in the case might inhibit Blockbuster's expansion into lower-income countries?

6. Why would many Cityvision stockholders sell for cash rather than Blockbuster stock?

Remember that the icon at the left indicates that links exist from our home page to relevant sites for the case (in this instance, Blockbuster). Look for these icons at the end of all cases in the book.

Chapter Notes

1. Data for the case were taken from Michael Dobbs, "Mickey Mouse Storms the Bastille," *Across the Board,* Vol. 23, No. 4, April 1986, pp. 9–11; Stewart Toy, Mark Maremont, and Ronald Grover, "An American in Paris," *Business Week,* March 12, 1990, pp. 60–64; Robert Wrubel and Phyllis Feinberg, "Breaking Out of the Mousetrap," *Financial World,* Vol. 157, No. 3, January 26, 1988, pp. 20–22; Steven Greenhouse, "Playing Disney in the Parisian Fields," *New York Times,* February 17, 1991, p. F1; "Trouble at Euro Disney: The Not-So-Magic Kingdom," *Business Week,* September 26, 1992, p. 87; William E. Schmidt, "Visiting Disney's French Kingdom," *New York Times,* May 24, 1992, p. 8; Richard Turner, "Disney Hits Bad Patch After Eisner's Six Years of Giddy Expansion," *Wall Street Journal,* November 12, 1991, p. A1; Martin du Bois, "Meeus Goes After the Mouse for Theme Park Visitors," *Wall Street Journal,* December 3, 1992, p. B4; Roger Cohen, "Resisting Disney: Unmitigated Gaul," *New York Times,* April 9, 1992, p. C1; Peter Gumbel and David J. Jefferson, "Disney Continues Drive to Expand World-Wide," *Wall Street Journal,* November 20, 1992, p. B4; Judson Gooding, "Of Mice and Men," *Across the Board,* March 1992, pp. 40–44; Alan Riding, "Only the French Elite Scorn Mickey's Debut," *New York Times,* April 13, 1992, p. A1; "The Mouse Isn't Roaring," *Business Week,* August 24, 1992, p. 38; Andrew Marton, "Le Monde According to Mickey," *New York Times,* April 12, 1992, p. H33; Shawn Tully, "The Real Estate Coup at Euro Disneyland," *Fortune,* April 28, 1986, p. 172; "Euro Disney Adding Alcohol," *New York Times,* June 12, 1993, p. 24; Martin Fletcher, "The Mouse That Snored," *Travel & Leisure,* September 1993, p. 34; William Echikson, "Winter Is Putting Chill in France's Magic Kingdom," *Boston Globe,* January 1, 1993, p. 71; Roger Cohen, "Euro Disney Trying to Warm Up Winter," *New York Times,* December 12, 1993, Sec. 5, p. 3; Nicholas D. Kristof,

   "Disney's Tokyo Kingdom," *New York Times,* August 27, 1995, p. 10; James Sterngold, "Tokyo's Magic Kingdom Outshines Its Role Model," *New York Times,* March 7, 1994, p. C1; Peter Gumbel and Richard Turner, "Fans Like Euro Disney But Its Parent's Goofs Weigh the Park Down," *Wall Street Journal,* March 10, 1994, p. A1; Sharon Waxman, "Le Mouse That Roared Back," *Washington Post,* July 27, 1995, p. B9; Andrew Jack, "Euro Disney Net Income Falls 14% in Third Quarter," *Financial Times,* July 24, 1996, p. 17; Douglas Lavin, "Euro Disney Claims Success at Theme Park," *Wall Street Journal,* November 21, 1996, p. A4; Andrew Jack, "Euro Disney Up 11% But Warns on 1997," *Financial Times,* January 23, 1997, p. 20. For up-to-date information on Euro Disney, see its home page on the World Wide Web (http://www.informatik. tu-muenchen.de/cgi-bin/nph-gateway /hphalle11/~schaffnr/etc/disney/).

2. Stephanie N. Mehta, "Export Drive by Small Firms Creates Jobs," *Wall Street Journal,* September 20, 1996, p. B2.

3. Michael Duckworth, "Disney Plans to Reenter China Market As Beijing Promises Copyright Reforms," *Wall Street Journal,* March 24, 1992, p. C19.

4. Peter Marsh, "Disney Shifts Output from Asia," *Financial Times,* March 2–3, 1996, p. 4.

5. Richard Tomkins, "McDonald's Makes Skeptics Eat Their Words," *Financial Times,* March 11, 1996, p. 17.

6. "World Trade Expanded Strongly in 1995 for the Second Consecutive Year," *Focus* (World Trade Organization Newsletter), No. 10, May 1996, p. 1.

7. Robert Lipsey, Magnus Blömstrom, and Eric Ramstetter, *Internationalized Production in World Output* (NBER Working Paper No. 5385), 1996 estimate that the portion of global output was 4.5 percent in 1970 and almost 7 percent in 1990.

8. Alan Cane, "Why Talk Today Is Relatively Cheap," *Financial Times,* December 23, 1996, p. 15.

9. Paul Hirst and Grahame Thompson, *Globalization in Question* (London: Blackwell, 1996).

10. United States Information Agency, "Barter and Countertrade Appear to Be on the Increase Again," *Washington Economics Reports,* No. 89, November 2, 1994, p. 1.

11. Richard C. Morais, "Babes in Toyland," *Forbes,* January 3, 1994, p. 70; and Andrew Jack, "Euro Disney Net Income Falls 14% in Third Quarter," *Financial Times,* July 24, 1996, p. 17.

12. Andrea Bonaccorsi, "On the Relationship Between Firm Size and Export Intensity," *Journal of International Business Studies,* Vol. 23, No. 4, Fourth Quarter, 1992, pp. 605–635.

13. *Survey of Current Business,* July 1996, pp. 80–86.

14. Duckworth, loc. cit.

15. FDI information is taken from Karl Sauvant, "[U.S.] State Department Briefing," *Federal News Service,* September 24, 1996, n.p. The trade figures used cited are from *Focus,* World Trade organization Newsletter, No. 10, May 1996, p. 1.

16. Fred R. Bleakly, "Smaller U.S. Firms Trail in Setting Up Operations Abroad," *Wall Street Journal,* August 24, 1993, p. A14, citing a report by Masataka Fujita at a UN conference on small and medium-sized firms; and United Nations Conference on Trade and Development Programme on Transnational Corporations, op. cit., p. 4.

17. Udayan Gupta, "Small Firms Aren't Waiting to Grow Up to Go Global," *Wall Street Journal,* December 5, 1989, B2.

18. Christopher A. Bartlett and Sumantra Ghoshal, *Managing Across Borders* (Boston: Harvard Business School Press, 1989), pp. 63–64; and Christopher A. Bartlett and Sumantra Ghoshal, *Transnational Management* (Homewood, IL: Irwin, 1992), pp. 117–119.

19. Tony Walker and Christopher Parkes, "China Warns Disney on Dalai Lama Film," *Financial Times,* November 22, 1996, p. 1; Bernard Weinraub, "Disney

Will Defy China on Its Dalai Lama Film," *New York Times,* November 27, 1996, p. B1+; and Christopher Parkes, "Disney Risks Beijing's Ire Over Tibetan Film," *Financial Times,* November 28, 1996, p. 7.

20. Roger Thurow, "Amid Their War, Serbs Bid Goodbye to Donald Duck," *Wall Street Journal,* January 27, 1993, p. A1.

21. "Film Giants Scramble for China Screenings," *South China Morning Post* [Hong Kong], May 14, 1995, money section, p. 1.

22. "The Horns of a Dilemma," *The Economist,* Vol. 325, No. 7787, November 28, 1992, p. 80.

23. "Disruption at Kobe Steel Imperils Global Car Output," *Asian Wall Street Journal,* March 3–4, 1995, p. 1.

24. Sally Bowen, "Inca Kola Ahead of U.S. Rivals in 'Cola Wars,'" *Financial Times,* January 26, 1996, p. 15.

25. Shawna O'Grady and Henry W. Lane, "The Psychic Distance Paradox," *Journal of International Business Studies,* Vol. 27, No. 2, Second Quarter 1996, pp. 309–333.

26. Benjamin M. Oviatt and Patricia Phillips McDougall, "Global Start-Ups: Entrepreneurs on a Worldwide Stage," *Academy of Management Executive,* Vol. 9, No. 2, 1995, pp. 30–44.

27. "Enterprise," *Wall Street Journal,* July 16, 1996, p. B2.

28. For a coverage of the various countervailing forces affecting global versus multidomestic practices, see Christopher A. Bartlett and Sumantra Ghoshal, *Transnational Management* (Homewood, Ill.: Irwin, 1992), Chapter 2.

29. John D. Daniels, "The Elusive Concept of National Competitiveness," *Business Horizons,* November-December 1991, pp. 3–6.

30. Robert Feenstra and Gordon Hanson, *Foreign Investment, Outsourcing, and Relative Wages* (Cambridge, MA: National Bureau of Economic Research Working Paper No. 5121, 1995).

31. For examples of different views on the relationship of location of headquarters and production with national well-being, see Kenichi Ohmae, *Triad Power: The Coming Shape of Global Competition* (New York: Free Press, 1985); Michael E. Porter, *The Competitive Advantage of Nations* (New York: Free Press, 1990); and Robert B. Reich, *The Work of Nations: Preparing Ourselves for 21st Century Capitalism* (New York: Alfred A. Knopf, 1991).

32. See, for example, Thomas Donaldson, "Can Multinationals Stage a Universal Morality Play?" *Business & Society Review,* Spring 1992, pp. 51–55; and Richard T. De George, *Business Ethics* (New York: Macmillan, 1990), Chapters 19 and 20.

33. Larue Tone Hosmer, "Response to 'Do Good Ethics Always Make for Good Business?'" *Strategic Management Journal,* Vol. 17, 1996, p. 501.

34. Robert D. Haas, "Ethics in the Trenches," *Across the Board,* Vol. 31, No. 5, May 1994, pp. 12–13.

35. K. Getz, "International Codes of Conduct: An Analysis of Ethical Reasoning," *Journal of Business Ethics,* Vol. 9, 1990, pp. 567–577; and Michael Harvey, "Marketing of Banned Pesticides and Unapproved Pharmaceuticals to Developing Countries," *Journal of Global Marketing,* Vol. 93, No. 3, 1996, pp. 67–93.

36. John Delaney and Donna Sockell, "Ethics in the Trenches," *Across the Board,* October 1990, pp. 15–21.

37. Hilary Barnes, "Carlsberg Drops Burma Project," *Financial Times,* July 7, 1996, p. 4.

38. The agreements are outlined in William C. Frederick, "Moral Authority of Transnational Corporate Codes," *Journal of Business Ethics,* March 1991, pp. 165–176; and David M. Schilling and Ruth Rosenbaum, "Principles for Global Corporate Responsibility," *Business and Society Review,* Vol. 94, Summer 1995, pp. 55–56.

39. Robert S. Greenberger, "Clinton to Unveil Voluntary Business Code," *Asia Wall Street Journal,* March 27, 1995, p. 12.

40. Paul Magnusson, "Why Corporate Nationality Matters," *Business Week,* July 12, 1993, pp. 142–143.

41. Canute James, "'Dead Sea Scroll' Shows Signs of Life," *Financial Times,* April 19, 1996, p. 23.

42. See, for example, G. Pierre Goad, "Strait of Malacca Spill Raises Safety Issue," *Wall Street Journal,* January 25, 1993, p. A10; Marcus W. Brauchli, "Pirates Off China Reportedly Attack North Korean Ship," *Wall Street Journal,* July 15, 1993, p. A10; and Marcus W. Brauchli, "Russia and Japan Move to Curb Piracy Off China," *Wall Street Journal,* July 12, 1993, p. A10.

43. We wish to acknowledge the cooperation of Mr. Joseph R. Baczko, President and Chief Operating Officer of Blockbuster Entertainment Corporation, for granting information in an interview. Supplementary data were taken from Ken Stewart, "Turf Battle Looms in Emerald Isle; Blockbuster Opening Threatens Xtra-vision," *Billboard,* September 29, 1990, p. 49; Terry Ilott, "Blockbuster Clinches Cityvision Brit Vid Bid," *Variety,* January 27, 1992, p. 69; "Blockbuster Acquires 25 Stores in Canada," *Supermarket News,* Vol. 41, No. 27, July 1, 1991, p. 24; Jeff Clark-Meads, "Philips Elects to Purchase 6 Million Blockbuster Shares," *Billboard,* April 18, 1992, p. 6; Steve McClure, "Blockbuster Hits Japan With Hopes for 1,000 Stores," *Billboard,* April 6, 1991, p. 89; Garth Alexander, "Blockbuster Bends Japan's Video Rules," *Variety,* Vol. 345, No. 2, October 21, 1991, p. 57; Terry Ilott, "Blockbuster's Bid Could Boost U.K. Vid Biz," *Variety,* Vol. 345, No. 8, December 2, 1991, p. 66; Leslie Helm, "Selling Hollywood in Japan," *Los Angeles Times,* September 21, 1992, p. D1; Eleena de Lisser, "Blockbuster's Baczko Quits Two Posts Amid Reorganization and Expansion," *Wall Street Journal,* January 5, 1993, p. B7; Richard Turner, "Disney Leads Shift From Rentals to Sales in Videocassettes," *Wall Street Journal,* December 24, 1991, p. A1; Helene Cooper, "Blockbuster Entertainment, U.K. Firm Plan a Chain of 'Megastores' in the U.S.," *Wall Street Journal,* November 17, 1992, p. B7; Gail De George, Jonathan B. Levine, and Robert Neff, "They Don't Call It Blockbuster For Nothing," *Business Week,* October 19, 1992, pp. 113–114; Johnnie L. Roberts, "Blockbuster Officials Envision Superstores For Music Business," *Wall Street Journal,* October 28, 1992, p. B7; and "Blockbuster's Foreign Strategy," *Wall Street Journal,* October 6, 1995, p. A11.

International
Business
Environment

An Atlas

Satellite television transmission now makes it commonplace for us to watch events as they unfold in other countries. Transportation and communication advances and government-to-government accords have contributed to our increasing dependence on foreign products and markets. As this dependence grows, updated maps are a valuable tool. They can show the locations of population, economic wealth, production, and markets; portray certain commonalities and differences among areas; and illustrate barriers that might inhibit trade. In spite of the usefulness of maps, a substantial number of people worldwide have a poor knowledge of how to interpret information on maps and even of how to find the locations of events that affect their lives.

We urge you to use the following maps and tables of demographic data to locate areas you study in order to build your geographic and cultural awareness. Such awareness will help you identify viable international alternatives when you are a business decision maker.

WEB CONNECTION
We also encourage you to visit the atlas section of our Web page for links to many map-related Web sites and indexes of such sites.

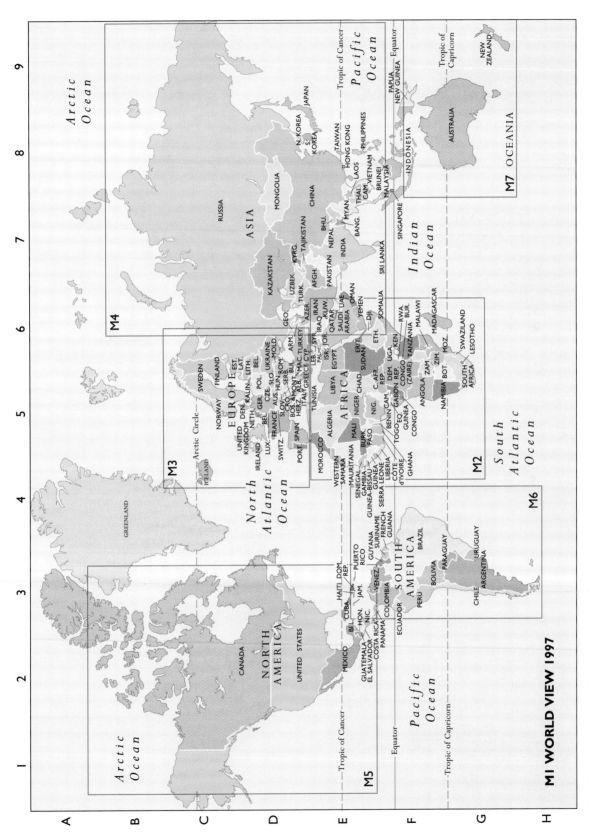

M1 WORLD VIEW 1997

This global view, which forms the main reference for subsequent maps in the Atlas, covers the Earth continent by continent. Rectangles indicate enlarged views of the following areas: M2 Africa, M3 Europe, M4 Asia, M5 North America, M6 South America and M7 Oceania.

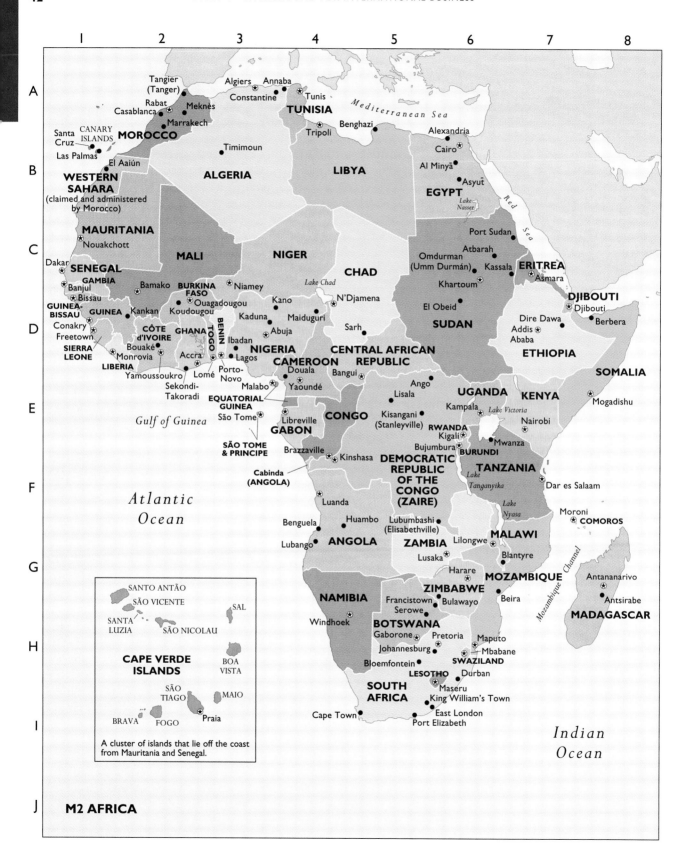

M2 AFRICA

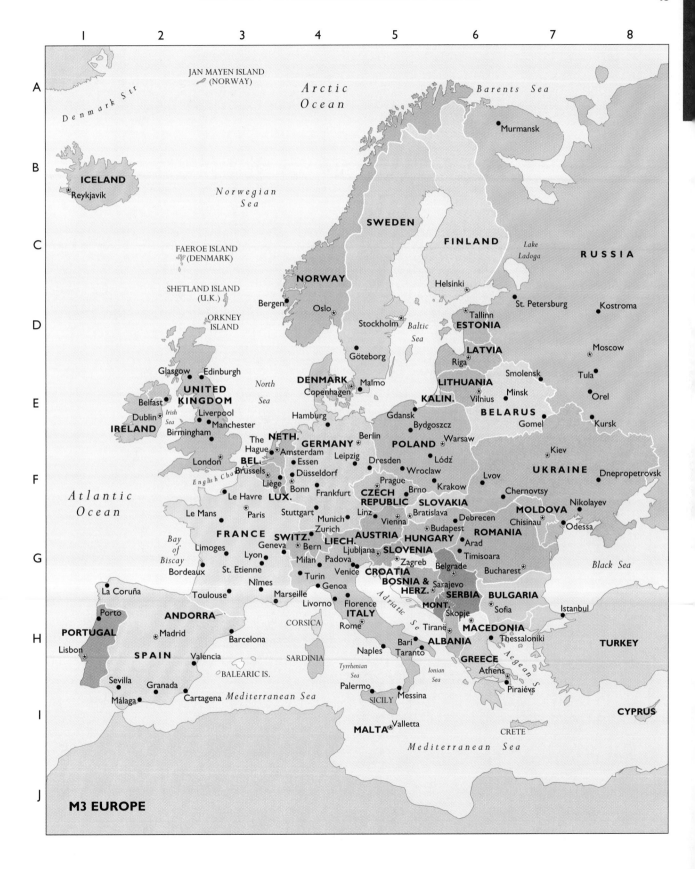

M3 EUROPE

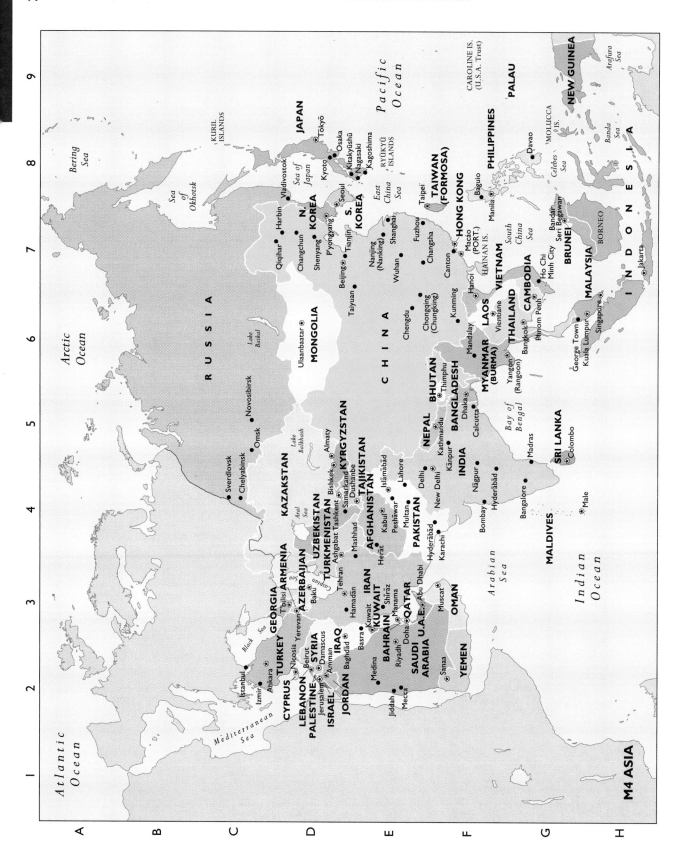

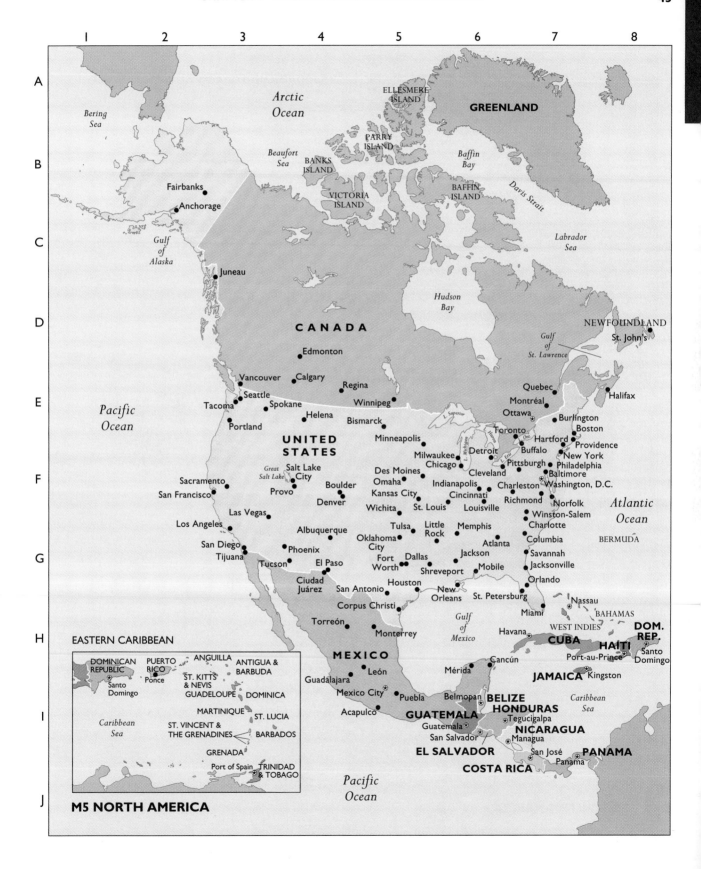

M5 NORTH AMERICA

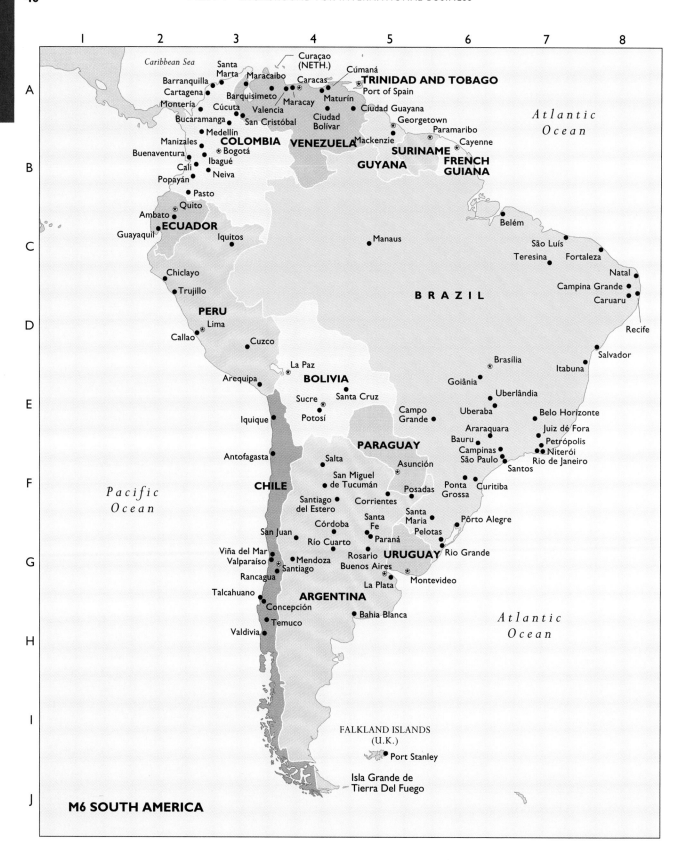

M6 SOUTH AMERICA

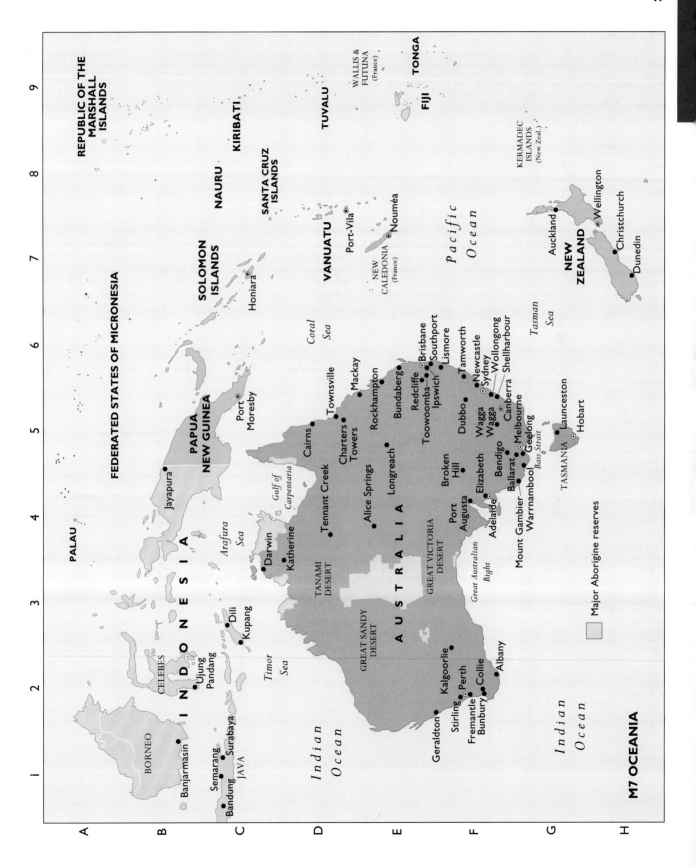

M7 OCEANIA

Map Index

Country	Pronunciation	Area (Km²)	Climate	Population *	Major Religion
Afghanistan	af-'gan-ə-,stan	647,500	Arid/Semiarid	18,879	Sunni Muslim
Albania	al-'bā-nē-ə	28,750	Mild temperate	3,414	Muslim
Algeria	al-'jir-ē-ə	2,381,740	Arid/Semiarid	27,325	Muslim
Andorra	an-'dȯr-ə	450	Temperate	64	Roman Catholic
Angola	an-'gō-lə	1,246,700	Semiarid (south)	10,674	Indigenous Belief
Antigua & Barbuda	an-'tē-g(w)ə / bär-'büd-ə	440	Tropical, marine	65	Anglican
Argentina	,är-jen-'tē-nə	2,766,890	Mostly temperate	34,180	Roman Catholic
Armenia	är-'mē-ne-ə	29,800	Continental	3,773	Armenian Orthodox
Australia	ȯ-'strāl-yə	7,686,850	Arid/Semiarid	17,841	Anglican
Austria	'ȯs-trē-ə	83,850	Temperate	7,915	Roman Catholic
Azerbaijan	,az-ər-,bī-'jän	86,600	Dry, semiarid steppe	7,472	Muslim
Bahrain	bä-'rān	620	Arid	548	Muslim
Bangladesh	,bäŋ-glə-'desh	144,000	Tropical	117,789	Muslim
Barbados	bär-'bād-əs	430	Tropical	261	Protestant
Belarus	,bē-lə-'rüs	207,600	Mild & Moist	10,163	Russian Orthodox
Belgium	'bel-jəm	30,510	Temperate	10,080	Roman Catholic
Belize	bə-'lēz	22,960	Tropical	210	Roman Catholic
Benin	bə-'nin	112,620	Tropical	5,246	Indigenous Belief
Bermuda	(,)bər-'myüd-ə	50	Subtropical	63	Anglican
Bhutan	bü-'tan	47,000	Varies with altitude	675	Lamaistic Buddhism
Bolivia	bə-'liv-ē-ə	1,098,580	Varies with altitude	7,237	Roman Catholic
Bosnia & Herzegovina	'bäz-nē-ə / ,hert-sə-gō-'vē-nə	51,233	Hot summer, cold winter	NA	Slavic Muslim
Botswana	bät-'swän-ə	600,370	Semiarid	1,443	Indigenous
Brazil	brə-'zil	8,511,965	Mostly tropical	159,143	Roman Catholic
Bulgaria	,bəl-'gar-ē-ə	110,910	Temperate	8,818	Bulgarian Orthodox
Burkina Faso	bùr-'kē-nə-'fä-sō	274,200	Tropical	10,046	Indigenous
Burundi	bu-'rün-dē	27,830	Temperate	6,209	Roman Catholic
Cambodia	kam-'bōd-ē-ə	181,040	Tropical	9,968	Buddhism
Cameroon	,kam-ə-'rün	475,440	Varies with terrain	12,871	Indigenous
Canada	'kan-əd-ə	9,976,140	Subarctic/arctic	29,121	Roman Catholic
Cape Verde Islands	'vard	4,030	Temperate	381	Roman Catholic
Central African Rep.		622,980	Tropical	3,235	Indigen. Protestant
Chad	'chad	1,284,000	Tropical, desert	6,183	Muslim
Chile	'chil-ē	756,950	Temperate	14,044	Roman Catholic
China	'chī-nə	9,596,960	Diverse	1,190,918	Atheist (Various)
Colombia	kə-'ləm-bē-ə	1,138,910	Tropical, cooler (higher elev.)	36,330	Roman Catholic
Congo Republic	'käŋ(,)gō	342,000	Tropical	2,516	Christian
Costa Rica	,käs-tə-'rē-kə	51,100	Tropical	3,304	Roman Catholic
Croatia	krō-'ā-sh(ē)ə	56,538	Mediterranean	4,780	Catholic
Cuba	'kyü-bə	110,860	Tropical	10,951	Roman Catholic
Curaçao	'k(y)ür-ə-'sō	9,250	Temperate	716	Greek Orthodox
Cyprus	'sī-prəs	127,850	Mediterranean	734	Greek Orthodox
Czech Republic	,chek	43,070	Temperate	10,295	Roman Catholic
Denmark	'den-,märk	43,070	Temperate	5,173	Evangelical Lutheran
Djibouti	jə-'büt-ē	22,000	Desert	566	Muslim
Dominica	,däm-ə-'nē-kə	750	Tropical	71	Roman Catholic
Dominican Republic	də-,min-i-kən	48,730	Tropical, maritime	7,684	Roman Catholic
Ecuador	'ek-wə-,dȯ(ə)r	283,560	Tropical	11,220	Roman Catholic
Egypt	'ē-jəpt	1,001,450	Desert	57,556	Muslim
El Salvador	el-'sal-və-,dȯ(ə)r	21,040	Tropical	5,641	Roman Catholic
Equatorial Guinea	ē-kwa'-tōr-ēal ġi-nē	28,050	Tropical	389	Roman Catholic
Eritrea	,er-ə-'trē-ə	121,300	Hot, dry desert	3,578	Muslim
Estonia	e-'stō-nē-ə	45,100	Maritime	1,541	Lutheran
Ethiopia	,ē-thē-'ō-pē-ə	1,221,900	Tropical, monsoon	53,435	Muslim
Falkland Islands	'fȯ(l)-klənd	12,170	Cold marine	19	Anglican

* in thousands
⁺ in millions of U.S. dollars
** in U.S. dollars   [NA = Not Available]

Main Language	Capital	Currency	GNP 1994+	GNP per Capita** 1994	Map 1	Maps 2-7
Pashtu, Dari	Kabul	Afghani	NA	NA	E6	Map 4, E4
Albanian	Tirane	Lek	1,229	360	D5	Map 3, H6
Arabic	Algiers	Algerian dinar	46,115	1,690	E5	Map 2, B3
Catalan	Andora la Vella	French franc	NA	NA		Map 3, H2
Portuguese	Luanda	Kwanza	NA	NA	F5	Map 2, G4
English	Saint John's	E. Carib. dollar	453	6,970		Map 5, H3
Spanish	Buenos Aires	Peso	275,657	8,060	G3	Map 6, G4
Armenian	Yerevan	Ruble	2,532	670	D6	Map 4, D3
English	Canberra	Aust. dollar	320,705	17,980	G8	Map 7, E4
German	Vienna	Aus. schilling	197,475	24,950	D5	Map 3, G5
Azeri	Baku	Ruble	3,730	500	E6	Map 4, D3
Arabic	Manama	Bah. dinar	4,114	7,500		Map 4, E3
Bangla, English	Dhaka	Taka	26,636	230	E7	Map 4, F5
English	Bridgetown	Barb. dollar	1,704	6,530		Map 5, I3
Byelorusian	Minsk	Ruble	21,937	2,160	D6	Map 1, D6
Flemish (French)	Brussels	Belgian franc	231,051	22,920	D5	Map 3, F3
English	Belmopan	Belizean dollar	535	2,550	E3	Map 5, I6
French	Porto-Novo	C.F. Afri. franc	1,954	370	E5	Map 2, D3
English	Hamilton	Berm. dollar	NA	NA		Map 5, G8
Tibet & Nepalese	Thimphu	Ngultrum	272	400	E7	Map 4, F5
Spanish	La Paz	Boliviano	5,601	770	F3	Map 6, E4
Serbo-Croatian	Sarajevo	Yugoslavian new dinar	NA	NA	D5	Map 3, G5
English	Gaborone	Pula	4,037	2,800	F5	Map 2, H5
Portuguese	Brasilia	Cruzeiro	536,309	3,370	F4	Map 6, D6
Bulgarian	Sofia	Lev	10,255	1,160	D6	Map 3, H6
French	Ouagadougou	C.F.A. franc	2,982	300	E5	Map 2, D2
Kirundi, French	Bujumbura	Burundi franc	904	150	F6	Map 2, E6
Khmer	Phnompenh	Riel	NA	NA	E8	Map 4, G6
English, French	Yaounde	C.F.A. franc	8,735	680	F5	Map 2, D4
English, French	Ottawa	Canadian dollar	569,949	19,570	C2	Map 5, D5
Portuguese	Praia	Cape Verdean	346	910		Map 2, H2
French	Bangui	C.F.A. franc	1,191	370	F5	Map 2, D5
French, Arabic	N'Djamena	C.F.A. franc	1,153	190	E5	Map 2, C5
Spanish	Santiago	Chilean peso	50,051	3,560	G3	Map 6, G3
Mandarin, Cantonese	Beijing	Yuan	630,202	530	E7	Map 4, E6
Spanish	Bogota	Colombian peso	58,935	1,620	F3	Map 6, B3
French	Brazzaville	C.F.A. franc	1,607	640	F5	Map 2, E4
Spanish	San Jose	Costa Rican colon	7,856	2,380	F3	Map 5, I7
Serbo-Croatian	Zagreb	Croatian dinar	12,093	2,530	D5	Map 3, G5
Spanish	Havana	Cuban peso	NA	NA	E3	Map 5, H7
Dutch, Papiamento	Willemstad	Netherlands guilder	NA	NA		Map 6, A4
Greek	Nicosia	Cypriot pound	NA	NA		Map 3, I8
Czech & Slovak	Prague	Koruna	33,051	3,210	D5	Map 3, F5
Danish	Copenhagen	Danish krone	145,384	28,110	D5	Map 3, E4
French & Arabic	Djibouti	Djiboutian franc	NA	NA	E6	Map 2, D7
English	Roseau	East Caribbean dollar	201	2,830		Map 5, I3
Spanish	Santo Domingo	Dominican peso	10,109	1,320	E3	Map 5, H8
Spanish	Quito	Sucre	14,703	1,310	F3	Map 6, C2
Arabic	Cairo	Egyptian pound	40,950	710	E6	Map 2, B6
Spanish, Nahua	San Salvador	Salvadoran colon	8,365	1,480	E3	Map 5, I6
Spanish	Malabo	CFA franc	167	430	F5	Map 2, E3
Toger, Kunama	Asmara	Ethiopian	NA	NA	F6	Map 2, C7
Estonian	Tallinn	Kroon	4,351	2,820	D5	Map 3, D6
Amharic	Addis Ababa	Birr	6,947	130	F6	Map 2, D7
English	Stanley	Falkland pound	NA	NA		Map 6, I5

Country	Pronunciation	Area (Km^2)	Climate	Population *	Major Religion
Fiji	ˈfē-jē	18,270	Tropical, marine	771	Christian
Finland	ˈfin-lənd	337,030	Cold temperate	5,083	Evangelical Lutheran
France	ˈfran(t)s	547,030	Mediterranean	57,726	Roman Catholic
French Guiana	gē-ˈan-ə	91,000	Tropical	140	Roman Catholic
Gabon	ga-ˈbōn	267,670	Tropical	1,035	Christian
Gambia	ˈgam-bē-ə	11,300	Tropical	1,081	Muslim
Georgia	ˈjȯr-jə	69,700	Warm & pleasant	5,450	Russian Orthodox
Germany	ˈjerm-(ə-)nē	356,910	Temperate, marine	81,141	Protestant
Ghana	ˈgän-ə	238,540	Tropical	16,944	Indigenous beliefs
Greece	ˈgrēs	131,940	Temperate	10,408	Greek Orthodox
Greenland	ˈgrēn-lənd	2,175,600	Arctic to subarctic	58	Evangelical Lutheran
Guatemala	ˌgwät-ə-ˈmäl-ə	108,890	Tropical	10,322	Roman Catholic
Guinea	ˈgin-ē	245,860	Generally hot & humid	6,501	Muslim
Guinea-Bissau	ˌgin-ē-bis-ˈau̇	36,120	Tropical	1,050	Indigenous beliefs
Guyana	gī-ˈan-ə	214,970	Tropical	825	Christian
Haiti	ˈhāt-ē	27,750	Tropical	7,035	Roman Catholic
Honduras	hän-ˈd(y)u̇r-əs	112,090	Subtropical	5,493	Roman Catholic
Hong Kong	ˈhäŋ-ˌkäŋ	1,040	Tropical, monsoon	5,833	Eclectic mixture
Hungary	ˈhəŋ-g(ə)rē	93,030	Temperate	10,161	Roman Catholic
Iceland	ˈī-slənd	103,000	Temperate	266	Evangelical Lutheran
India	ˈin-dē-ə	3,287,590	Tropical, monsoon	913,600	Hindu
Indonesia	ˌin-də-ˈnē-zhə	1,919,440	Tropical	189,907	Muslim
Iran	i-ˈrän	1,648,000	Mostly arid or semiarid	65,758	Shi'a Muslim
Iraq	i-ˈräk	436,245	Mostly desert	19,951	Muslim
Ireland	ˈī(ə)r-lənd	70,280	Temperate maritime	3,543	Roman Catholic
Israel	ˈiz-rē-əl	20,770	Temperate	5,420	Judaism
Italy	ˈit-ᵊl-ē	301,230	Mediterranean	57,154	Roman Catholic
Jamaica	jə-ˈmā-kə	10,990	Tropical	2,496	Protestant
Japan	jə-ˈpan	377,835	Tropical, temperate	124,782	Shinto
Jordan	ˈjȯrd-ᵊn	91,880	Mostly arid desert	4,217	Sunni Muslim
Kazakhstan	kə-ˌzak-ˈstan	2,717,300	Dry continental	17,027	Muslim
Kenya	ˈken-yə	582,650	Tropical, arid	26,017	Protestant
Kiribati	ˈkir-ə-bas	717	Tropical	77	Roman Catholic
Korea, North	kə-ˈrē-ə	120,540	Temperate	23,472	Buddhism & Confucianism
Korea, South	kə-ˈrē-ə	98,480	Temperate	44,563	Strong Confucian
Kuwait	kə-ˈwāt	17,820	Dry desert	1,651	Muslim
Kyrgyzstan	kîr-gē-stän	198,500	Dry continental	4,667	Muslim
Laos	ˈlau̇s	236,800	Tropical, monsoon	4,742	Buddhist
Latvia	ˈlat-vē-ə	64,100	Maritime	2,583	Lutheran
Lebanon	ˈleb-ə-nən	10,400	Mediterranean	3,930	Muslim
Lesotho	lə-ˈsō-(ˌ)tō	30,350	Temperate	1,996	Christian
Liberia	lī-ˈbir-ē-ə	111,370	Tropical	2,941	Traditional
Libya	ˈlib-ē-ə	1,759,540	Mediterranean	5,222	Sunni Muslim
Lithuania	ˌlith-(y)ə-ˈwā-nē-ə	65,200	Maritime	3,706	Roman Catholic
Luxembourg	ˈlək-səm-ˌbərg	2,586	Continental	401	Roman Catholic
Macedonia	ˌmas-ə-ˈdō-nyə	25,333	Hot, dry	2,093	Eastern Orthodox
Madagascar	ˌmad-ə-ˈgas-kər	587,040	Tropical	13,101	Indigenous beliefs
Malawi	mə-ˈlä-wē	118,480	Tropical	10,843	Protestant
Malaysia	mə-ˈlā-zh(ē-)ə	329,750	Tropical	19,498	Muslim, Buddhist
Mali	ˈmäl-ē	1,240,000	Subtropical to arid	9,524	Muslim
Malta	ˈmȯl-tə	320	Mediterranean	364	Roman Catholic
Mauritania	ˌmȯr-ə-ˈtā-nē-ə	1,030,700	Desert	2,217	Muslim
Mexico	ˈmek-si-ˌkō	1,972,550	Tropical, desert	91,858	Roman Catholic
Moldova	mäl-ˈdō-və	33,700	Mild/warm	4,420	Eastern Orthodox
Mongolia	män-ˈgōl-yə	1,565,000	Desert/continental	2,363	Tibetan Buddhist

* in thousands
+ in millions of U.S. dollars
** in U.S. dollars   [NA = Not Available]

Main Language	Capital	Currency	GNP 1994[+]	GNP per Capita** 1994	Map I	Maps 2-7
English, Fijian	Suva	Fijian dollar	1,785	2,320		Map 7, E9
Finnish	Helsinki	Markka	95,817	18,850	C6	Map 3, C6
French	Paris	French franc	1,355,039	23,470	D5	Map 3, G3
French	Cayenne	French franc	NA	NA	F4	Map 6, B6
French	Libreville	CFA franc	3,669	3,550	F5	Map 2, E4
English	Banjul	Dalasi	384	360	E5	Map 2, C1
Georgian	Tbilisi	Ruble (1992)	NA	NA	D6	Map 4, C3
German	Berlin	Deutsche mark	2,075,452	25,580	D5	Map 3, F4
English	Accra	Cedi	7,311	430	F5	Map 2, D2
Greek	Athens	Drachma	80,194	7,710	E5	Map 3, H6
Eskimo dialects	Nuuk	Danish krone	NA	NA	B4	Map 5, A6
Spanish	Guatemala	Quetzal	12,237	1,190	E3	Map 5, I6
French	Conakry	Guinean franc	3,310	510	F5	Map 2, E4
Portuguese	Bissau	Guinea-Bissauan peso	253	240	F4	Map 2, D1
English	Georgetown	Guyanese dollar	434	530	F3	Map 6, B5
French	Port-au-Prince	Gourde	1,542	220	E3	Map 5, H7
Spanish	Tegucigalpa	Lempira	3,162	580	E3	Map 5, I6
Chinese, English	Victoria	Hong Kong dollar	126,286	21,650	E8	Map 4, F7
Hungarian	Budapest	Forints	39,009	3,840	D5	Map 3, G5
Icelandic	Reykjavik	Krona	6,545	24,590	C4	Map 3, B1
Hindu, English	New Delhi	Indian rupee	278,739	310	E7	Map 4, F4
Bahasa Indonesia	Jakarta	Indonesian rupiah	167,632	880	F8	Map 7, B3
Persian	Tehran	Iranian rial	NA	NA	E6	Map 4, E3
Arabic	Baghdad	Iraqi dinar	NA	NA	E7	Map 4, D3
Irish & English	Dublin	Irish pound	48,275	13,630	D5	Map 3, E2
Hebrew	Jerusalem[++]	New Israeli shekel	78,113	14,410	E6	Map 4, D2
Italian	Rome	Italian lira	1,101,258	19,270	D5	Map 3, H5
English, Creole	Kingston	Jamaican dollar	3,553	1,420	E3	Map 5, H7
Japanese	Tokyo	Yen	4,321,136	34,630	E8	Map 4, D8
Arabic	Amman	Jordanian dinar	5,849	1,390	E6	Map 4, D2
Kazakh	Alma-Ata	Ruble	18,896	1,410	D6	Map 4, D4
English & Swahili	Nairobi	Kenyan shilling	6,643	260	F6	Map 2, E7
English, Gilbertese	Tarawa	Australian dollar	56	730		Map 7, C9
Korean	P'yongyang	North Korean won	NA	NA	E8	Map 4, D7
Korean	Seoul	South Korean won	366,484	8,220	E8	Map 4, E7
Arabic	Kuwait	Kuwaiti dinar	31,433	19,040	E6	Map 4, E3
Kirghiz	Bishkek	Ruble	2,825	610	D7	Map 4, D4
Lao, French, English	Vientiane	New kip	1,496	320	E7	Map 4, F6
Latvian	Riga	Ruble	5,920	2,290	D6	Map 3, E6
Arabic, French	Beirut	Lebanese pound	NA	NA	E6	Map 4, D2
Sesotho	Maseru	Loti	650	700	G6	Map 2, I5
English	Monrovia	Liberian dollar	NA	NA	F5	Map 2, D1
Arabic	Tripoli	Libyan dinar	NA	NA	E5	Map 2, B4
Lithuanian	Vilnius	Ruble	4,992	1,350	D6	Map 3, E6
Luxembourgisch	Luxembourg	Luxembourg franc	15,973	39,850	D5	Map 3, F3
Macedonian	Skopje	Denar	1,653	790	D5	Map 3, H6
French & Malagasy	Antananarivo	Malagasy franc	3,058	230	F6	Map 2, G8
English & Chichewa	Lilongwe	Malawian kwacha	1,560	140	F6	Map 2, G6
Malay, English	Kuala Lumpur	Ringgit	68,674	3,520	F7	Map 4, G6
French	Bamako	CFA franc	2,421	250	E5	Map 2, C2
Maltese, English	Valletta	Maltese lira	NA	NA		Map 3, I5
Hasaniya Arabic	Nouakchott	Ouguiya	1,063	480	E4	Map 2, C1
Spanish	Mexico City	Mexican peso	368,679	4,010	E2	Map 5, H4
Romanian	Chisinau	Ruble	3,853	870	D6	Map 3, G7
Khalkha Mongol	Ulaanbaatar	Tughrik	801	340	D7	Map 4, D6

Country	Pronunciation	Area (Km²)	Climate	Population *	Major Religion
Morocco	mə-'räk-(,)ō	446,550	Mediterranean	26,488	Muslim
Mozambique	,mō-zəm-'bēk	801,590	Tropical	16,614	Indigenous beliefs
Myanmar	'myän-,mär	678,500	Tropical, monsoon	45,555	Buddhist
Namibia	nə-'mib-ē-ə	824,290	Desert	1,500	Christian
Naura	nä'-ü-rü	21	Tropical	10	Christian
Nepal	nə-'pȯl	140,800	Variable	21,360	Hindu
Netherlands	'ne<u>th</u>-ər-lən(d)z	37,330	Temperate	15,391	Roman Catholic
New Caledonia	,kal-ə-'dō-nyə	19,060	Tropical	178	Roman Catholic
New Zealand	'zē-lənd	268,680	Temperate	3,531	Anglican
Nicaragua	,nik-ə-'räg-wə	129,494	Tropical	4,275	Roman Catholic
Niger	'nī-jər	1,267,000	Desert	8,846	Muslim
Nigeria	nī-'jir-ē-ə	923,770	Variable	107,900	Muslim
Norway	'nȯ(ə)r-,wā	324,220	Temperate	4,318	Evangelical Lutheran
Oman	ō-'män	212,460	Dry desert	2,073	Ibadhi Muslim
Pakistan	,pak-i-'stan	803,940	Hot, dry desert	126,284	Muslim
Palestine	pa-lə-'stīn	360	Temperate	813	Muslim
Panama	'pan-ə-,mä	78,200	Tropical	2,585	Roman Catholic
Papua New Guinea	'pap-yə-wə	461,690	Tropical	4,205	Roman Catholic
Paraguay	'par-ə-,gwī	406,750	Variable	4,830	Roman Catholic
Peru	pə-'rü	1,285,220	Variable	23,331	Roman Catholic
Philippines	,fil-ə-'pēnz	300,000	Tropical, marine	66,188	Roman Catholic
Poland	'pō-lənd	312,680	Temperate	38,341	Roman Catholic
Portugal	'pȯr-chi-gəl	92,080	Maritime temperate	9,832	Roman Catholic
Puerto Rico	,pȯrt-ə-'rē(,)kō	9,104	Tropical, marine	3,645	Roman Catholic
Qatar	'kät-ər	11,000	Desert	537	Muslim
Romania	rō-'mā-nē-ə	237,500	Temperate	22,736	Romanian Orthodox
Russia	'rəsh-ə	17,075,200	Variable	148,366	Russian Orthodox
Rwanda	rü-'än-də	26,340	Temperate	7,750	Roman Catholic
St. Kitts & Nevis	'kits / 'nē-vəs	269	Subtropical	41	Anglican
St. Lucia	sānt-'lü-shə	620	Tropical	145	Roman Catholic
Saudi Arabia	,sau̇d-ē	1,945,000	Harsh dry	17,498	Muslim
Senegal	,sen-i-'gȯl	196,190	Tropical	8,102	Muslim
Serbia	'sər-bē-ə	102,350	Variable	10,642	Orthodox
Sierra Leone	sē-,er-ə-lē-'ōn	71,740	Tropical	4,587	Muslim
Singapore	'siŋ-(g)ə-,pō(ə)r	632.6	Tropical	2,819	Buddhist
Slovakia	slō-'väk-ē-ə	48,845	Temperate	5,333	Roman Catholic
Slovenia	slō-'vēn-ē-ə	20,296	Mediterranean	1,995	Roman Catholic
Solomon Islands	'säl-ə-mən	28,450	Tropical, monsoon	366	Christian
Somalia	sō-'mäl-ē-ə	637,660	Desert	9,077	Sunni Muslim
South Africa	'a-fri-kə	1,221,040	Semiarid	41,591	Christian
Spain	'spān	504,750	Temperate	39,551	Roman Catholic
Sri Lanka	(')srē-'läŋ-kə	65,610	Tropical	18,125	Buddhist
Sudan	sü-'dan	2,505,810	Tropical	27,361	Sunni Muslim
Suriname	su̇r-ə-'näm-ə	163,270	Tropical	418	Hindu
Swaziland	'swäz-ē-,land	17,360	Variable	906	Christian
Sweden	'swēd-ᵊn	449,964	Variable	8,735	Evangelical Lutheran
Switzerland	'swit-sər-lənd	41,290	Temperate	7,127	Roman Catholic
Syria	'sir-ē-ə	185,180	Desert, hot	14,171	Sunni Muslim
Taiwan	'tī-'wän	35,980	Tropical	20,878	Buddhist Confucian
Tajikistan	tä-,ji-ki-'stan	143,100	Midlatitude semiarid	5,933	Sunni Muslim
Tanzania	,tan-zə-'nē-ə	945,090	Variable	28,846	Christian
Thailand	'tī-land	514,000	Tropical	58,718	Buddhism
Togo	'tō(,)gō	56,790	Tropical	98	Indigenous beliefs
Tonga	'tän-gə	748	Tropical	98	Christian
Trinidad & Tobago	'trin-ə-,dad / tə-'bā-(,)gō	5,130	Tropical	1,292	

* in thousands
⁺ in millions of U.S. dollars
** in U.S. dollars   [NA = Not Available]

Main Language	Capital	Currency	GNP 1994+	GNP per Capita** 1994	Map I	Maps 2-7
Arabic	Rabat	Moroccan dirham	30,330	1,150	E5	Map 2, A2
Portuguese	Maputo	Metical	1,328	80	G6	Map 2, G6
Burmese	Rangoon	Kyat	NA	NA	E7	Map 4, F6
English, Afrikaans	Windhoek	South African rand	3,045	2,030	G5	Map 2, H4
Nauruan	Yaren district	Australian dollar	NA	10,000		Map 7, C8
Nepali	Kathmandu	Nepalese rupee	4,174	200	E7	Map 4, F5
Dutch	Amsterdam	Netherlands guilder	338,144	21,970	D5	Map 3, F3
French	Noumea	CFP franc	NA	NA		Map 7, E7
English, Maori	Wellington	New Zealand dollar	46,578	13,190	G9	Map 7, G7
Spanish	Managua	Cordoba	1,395	330	E3	Map 5, I7
French, Hausa	Niamey	CFA franc	2,040	230	E5	Map 2, C3
English	Abuja	Naira	29,995	280	F5	Map 2, D3
Norwegian	Oslo	Norweigan krone	114,328	26,480	C5	Map 3, C4
Arabic	Muscat	Omani rial	10,779	5,200	E6	Map 4, F3
Urdu, English	Islamabad	Pakistani rupee	55,565	440	E6	Map 4, E4
Arabic, Hebrew	NA	New Israeli shekel	NA	2,400		Map 4, D2
Spanish	Panama	Balboa	6,905	2,670	F3	Map 5, J7
Indigenous	Port Moresby	Kina	4,857	1,160	F8	Map 7, B5
Spanish	Asuncion	Guarani	7,606	1,570	G3	Map 6, F5
Spanish	Lima	Nuevo sol	44,110	1,890	F3	Map 6, D3
Philippino	Manila	Philippine peso	63,311	960	F8	Map 4, F8
Polish	Warsaw	Zloty	94,613	2,470	D5	Map 3, F5
Portuguese	Lisbon	Portuguese escudo	92,124	9,370	D5	Map 3, H1
Spanish	San Juan	US currency	NA	NA	E3	Map 5, H2
Arabic	Doha	Qatari riyal	7,810	14,540	E6	Map 4, E3
Romanian	Bucharest	Leu	27,921	1,120	D5	Map 3, G6
Estonian, Russian	Moscow	Ruble	392,496	2,650	C7	Map 3, C8; Map 4, C6
Kinyarwanda	Kijali	Rwandan franc	NA	NA	F6	Map 2, E6
English	Basseterre	East Caribbean dollar	195	4,760		Map 5, I3
English	Castries	East Caribbean dollar	501	3,450		Map 5, I3
Arabic	Riyadh	Saudi riyal	126,597	7,240	E6	Map 4, E2
French	Dakar	CFA franc	4,952	610	E4	Map 2, C1
Serbo-Croatian	Belgrade	Yugoslav new dinar	NA	NA	D5	Map 3, G6
English	Freetown	Leone	698	150	F5	Map 2, D1
Chinese	Singapore	Singapore dollar	65,842	23,360	F8	Map 4, H6
Slovak	Bratislava	Koruna	11,914	2,230	D5	Map 3, F6
Slovenian	Ljubljana	Solvene tolar	14,246	7,140	D5	Map 3, G5
Indigenous	Honiara	Solomon Islands dollar	291	800		Map 7, B7
Somali	Mogadishu	Somali shilling	NA	NA	F6	Map 2, D8
Afrikaans	Pretoria	Rand	125,225	3,010	G5	Map 2, I5
Castilian Spanish	Madrid	Peseta	525,334	13,280	E5	Map 3, H2
Sinhala	Colombo	Sri Lankan rupees	11,634	640	F7	Map 4, G5
Arabic	Khartoum	Sudanese pound	NA	NA	F6	Map 2, D6
Dutch	Paramaribo	Surinamese guilder	364	870	F3	Map 6, B5
English, Siswati	Mbabane	Lilangeni	1,048	1,160	G6	Map 2, H6
Swedish	Stockholm	Swedish kronor	206,419	23,630	C5	Map 3, C5
German	Bern	Swiss franc	264,974	37,180	D5	Map 3, G4
Arabic	Damascus	Syrian pound	NA	NA	E6	Map 4, D2
Mandarin	Taipei	New Taiwan dollar	NA	12,070	E8	Map 4, F7
Tajik	Dushanbe	Ruble	2,075	350	D7	Map 4, E4
Swahili, English	Dar es Salaam	Tanzanian shilling	NA	NA	F6	Map 2, F7
Thai	Bangkok	Baht	129,864	2,210	F7	Map 4, G6
French	Lome	CFA franc	1,267	320	F5	Map 2, D3
Tongan, English	Nuku'alofa	Pa'anga	160	1,640		Map 7, E9
English	Port-of-Spain	Trinidad & Tobago dollar	4,838	3,740		Map 5, J3

Country	Pronunciation	Area (Km²)	Climate	Population *	Major Religion
Tunisia	t(y)ü-'nē-zh(ē-)ə	163,610	Temperate	8,815	Muslim
Turkey	'tər-kē	780,580	Temperate	60,771	Muslim
Turkmenistan	tûrk'-mĕn-ĭ-stăn'	488,100	Subtropical	4,010	Islam
Tuvalu	tü'-vä-lü	26	Tropical	9.9	Church of Tuvalu
Uganda	(y)ü-'gan-də	236,040	Tropical	18,592	Roman Catholic
Ukraine	yü-'krān	603,700	Temperate	51,465	Ukrainian Autonom
United Arab Emirates	yoo-nī'tĭd ăr'əb ĭ-mîr'its	83,600	Desert	1,855	Muslim
United Kingdom	kĭng'dəm	244,820	Temperate	58,088	Anglican
United States	yü-,nīt-əd-'stāts	9,372,610	Temperate	260,529	Protestant
Uruguay	'(y)ùr-ə-gwī	176,220	Warm temperate	3,167	Roman Catholic
Uzbekistan	(,)ùz-,bek-i-'stan	447,400	Midlatitude semiarid	22,349	Muslim
Vanuatu	van-ə-'wät-(,)ü	14,760	Tropical	165	Presbyterian
Venezuela	,ven-əz(-ə)-'wā-lə	912,050	Tropical	21,378	Roman Catholic
Vietnam	vē-'et-'näm	329,560	Tropical	72,500	Buddhist
Western Sahara	sə-hâr'ə	266,000	Hot, dry	201	Muslim
Yemen	'yem-ən	527,970	Desert, dry	13,873	Muslim
Zaire (Dem. Rep. Congo)	'zī(ə)r	2,345,410	Tropical	42,552	Roman Catholic
Zambia	'zam-bē-ə	752,610	Tropical	9,196	Christian
Zimbabwe	zim-'bäb-wē	390,580	Tropical	11,002	Syncretic

* in thousands
⁺ in millions of U.S. dollars
** in U.S. dollars   [NA = Not Available]
++ Most countries maintain their embassies in Tel Aviv.

Source: The World Factbook 1993–1994, Central Intelligence Agency, Brassey's (US) A Maxwell Macmillan Company, First Brassey's Edition 1993; World Tables 1995.
Published for the World Bank, The Johns Hopkins University Press, Baltimore & London. First printing May 1995; and Web http://www.city.net/countries.

Main Language	Capital	Currency	GNP 1994+	GNP per Capita** 1994	Map I	Maps 2-7
Arabic	Tunis	Tunisian dinar	15,873	1,800	E5	Map 2, A4
Turkish	Ankara	Turkish lira	149,002	2,450	E6	Map 4, D2
Turkmen	Ashgabat	Ruble	NA	NA	E6	Map 4, D3
Tuvaluan, English	Funafulti	Tuvaluan dollar	NA	800		Map 7, D9
English	Kampala	Ugandan shilling	3,718	200	F6	Map 2, E6
Ukrainian	Kiev	Ruble	80,921	1,570	D6	Map 3, F7
Arabic	Abu Dhabi	Emirian dirham	NA	NA	E6	Map 4, F3
English	London	British pounds	1,069,457	18,410	D5	Map 3, E2
English	Washington, DC	U.S. dollar	6,737,367	25,860	D2	Map 5, G5
Spanish	Montevideo	New Uruguayan pesos	14,725	3,960	G3	Map 6, G5
Uzbek	Tashkent	Ruble	21,142	980	E6	Map 4, D4
English & French	Port-Vila	Vatu	189	1,150		Map 7, D7
Spanish	Caracas	Bolivar	59,025	2,760	F3	Map 6, B4
Vietnamese	Hanoi	New dong	13,775	190	F8	Map 4, F6
Hassaniya Arabic	NA	Moroccan dirham	NA	NA	E4	Map 2, B1
Arabic	Sanaa	North Yemeni riyal	3,884	280	F6	Map 4, F2
French	Kinshasa	Zaire	NA	NA	F5	Map 2, E5
English	Lusaka	Zambian kwacha	3,206	350	F5	Map 2, G5
English	Harare	Zimbabwean dollar	5,424	490	F5	Map 2, G6

2 Comparative Environmental Frameworks

International air transportation for tourists, business travelers, and cargo has increased rapidly in recent years, leading to the development of new international airport facilities, such as the one shown in the photo of the New Riyadh Airport in Saudi Arabia. The photo is set against a backdrop of a northern Indian Mughal carpet from about 1600.

Chapter 2

The Cultural Environments Facing Business

*To change customs is
a difficult thing.*
—Lebanese Proverb

Objectives

- To demonstrate problems and methods of examining cultural environments

- To explain the major causes of cultural difference and change

- To examine major customs that differentiate business practices among countries

- To present guidelines for companies that operate internationally

Case
Parris-Rogers
International (PRI)[1]

In June 1996, a car bomb in Saudi Arabia killed nineteen American servicemen. The victims were among approximately 9000 U.S. troops remaining in Saudi Arabia, Kuwait, Bahrain, and the United Arab Emirates since the end of the 1991 Persian Gulf War to liberate Kuwait from Iraq. Although no group claimed responsibility for the blast, most analysts reasoned that cultural conflict was an underlying cause. Traditionalists wanted to rid the area of Western influences, such as music, entertainment, and dress, that they considered immoral. At the same time, a Western-educated middle class was questioning many of the traditional rules. The cultural conflict and accommodation is illustrated by the rules imposed by the U.S. army on female troops during the war. They were not permitted to jog, drive, or show their legs outside the military base. In deference to U.S. sensitivities, Saudi Arabia suspended beheadings in central squares during the Gulf crisis.

A few years earlier, Parris-Rogers International (PRI), a British publishing house, sold its floundering Bahraini operations. This branch had been set up to edit the first telephone and business directories for five Arab states on or near the Arabian peninsula, plus the seven autonomous divisions making up the United Arab Emirates (the region is shown in Map 2.1). Although the U.S. Army had protocol officers to advise it on accepted behavior, PRI had no such guidance. Further, although the Saudis were willing to make some accommodations to assure the defense of their country, PRI's directories were less

Map 2.1
The Scope of PRI's
Business Contract
PRI's contract included Bahrain, Kuwait, Oman, Qatar, Saudi Arabia, and the United Arab Emirates (Abu Dhabi, Ajman, Dubai, Fuzaira, Ras al-Khaimah, Sharjah, and Umm al-Qaiwain).

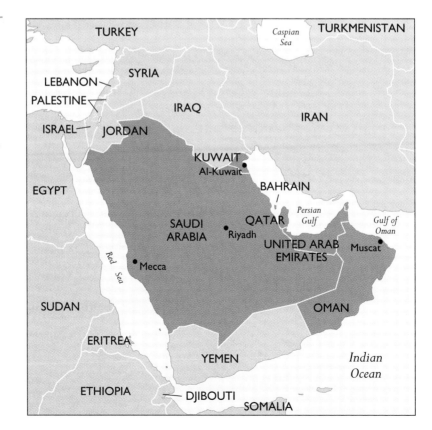

important to the twelve Arab states. The ensuing lack of understanding between the Arab states and PRI and PRI's failure to adapt to a different culture contributed directly to the company's failure.

Most Middle Eastern oil-producing countries have an acute shortage of local personnel, so many foreign workers have been hired. They now make up a large portion of the population in those countries. In the United Arab Emirates in 1995, for example, 70 percent of the population was foreign, mainly from India and Pakistan. In Saudi Arabia, about 40 percent was foreign. Thus when PRI could not find sufficient qualified people locally, it filled four key positions through advertisements in London newspapers. Angela Clarke, an Englishwoman, was hired as editor and researcher, and three young Englishmen were hired as salesmen. The four new hires left immediately for Bahrain. None had visited the Middle East before; all expected to carry out business as usual.

The salesmen, hired on a commission basis, expected that by moving aggressively they could make the same number of calls as they normally could in the United Kingdom. They were used to working about eight hours a day, to having the undivided attention of potential clients, and to restricting most conversation to the specifics of the business transaction.

The salesmen found instead an entirely different situation. There was less time to sell, first, because the Muslims were required to pray five times a day and, second, because the workday was reduced even further during the sacred ninth month of the Muslim year, Ramadan, when there is fasting from sunrise to sunset. The Muslim year is based on a lunar rather than a solar calendar; thus Ramadan may begin in different solar months, such as in January for 1997, or December 1997 for 1998. Moreover, the start of Ramadan is based on the sighting of a new moon; thus longitudinal, latitudinal, and weather conditions usually cause the start to vary by a day or two among countries and cannot be determined in advance. The salesmen also felt that the Arabs placed little importance on appointments. Appointments seldom began at the scheduled time. When the salesmen finally got in to see Arab businessmen, they were often expected to go to a café where the Arabs would engage in what seemed to them to be idle chitchat. Whether in a café or in the office, drinking coffee or tea seemed to take precedence over business matters. The Arabs also frequently diverted their attention to friends who joined them at the café or in the office.

Angela Clarke, too, encountered considerable resistance as she sought to do her job. And, since she was paid a salary instead of a commission, PRI had to bear all of the expense resulting from her work being thwarted in unexpected ways. PRI had based its budgets for preparing the directories on its English experience. In Bahrain, however, preparing such books turned out to be more time-consuming and costly. For example, in the traditional Middle Eastern city, there are no street names or building numbers. Thus, before getting to the expected directory work, Clarke had to take a census of Bahraini establishments, identifying the location of each with such prepositions as "below," "above," or "in front of" some meaningful landmark.

Clarke encountered other problems because she was a single woman. She was in charge of the research in all twelve states and had planned to hire freelance assistants in most of them. But her advertisements to hire such assistants were answered by personal harassment and obscene telephone calls. In addition, Saudi authorities denied her entry to Saudi Arabia, while her visa for Oman took six weeks to process *each time she went there*. These experiences were particularly frustrating for her because both Saudi Arabia and Oman sometimes eased the entry of a single woman when her business was of high local priority and/or when she would be serving as a housemaid or nanny where her only contact would be with women and children. In the states she could enter, Clarke sometimes was required to stay only in hotels that government officials had approved for foreign women, and even there, she was prohibited from eating in the dining room unless accompanied by the hotel manager.

PRI's salesmen never adjusted to working in the new environment. Instead of pushing PRI to review its commission scheme, they tried to change the way the Arab businessmen dealt with them. For example, after a few months they refused to join their potential clients for refreshments and began showing their irritation at "irrelevant" conversations, delays, and interruptions from outsiders. The Arab businessmen responded negatively. In fact, PRI received so many complaints from them that the salesmen had to be replaced. By then, however, irrevocable damage had been done to PRI's sales.

Clarke fared better, thanks to her compromises with Arab customs. She began wearing a wedding ring and registering at hotels as a married woman. When traveling, she ate meals in her room, conducted meetings in conference rooms, and had all incoming calls screened by the hotel operators. To avoid arrest by decency patrols, she wore long-sleeved blouses and below-the-knee skirts in plain blue or beige. Still, in spite of her compromises, her inability to enter Saudi Arabia caused PRI to send in her place a salesman, who was not trained to do the research.

The rapidly growing number of foreigners in the Middle East has created adjustment problems for both the foreigners and the local societies. In many cases, foreigners are expected to conform; in others, they are allowed to pursue their own customs in isolation from the local populace. For example, according to traditional Islamic standards, most Western television programming is immoral. However, in some places foreigners are permitted to acquire unscramblers to view Western programs; local people may not. At the same time, although satellite dishes are technically illegal in Saudi Arabia, these "devils' dishes"—a term used by hard-line Islamic fundamentalists—are seen on rooftops everywhere. Nevertheless, the BBC axed its Arabic Television Service in 1996 because of disagreements over program content. This led a BBC executive to remark, "Looking at the partners involved, the Saudis and the BBC, who would have thought two such different cultures could comfortably coexist?"

The Saudi government also has had second thoughts about some of its culture's double standards. For example, at one time, male and female hotel guests were allowed to swim in the same pools in Saudi Arabia. This permission was rescinded, however, because Saudis frequent the hotels. It was feared they might be corrupted by viewing "decadent" behavior. Also, when Angela Clarke and the salesmen first arrived in Bahrain, there were prohibitions on the sale of pork products, including imported canned foods. This prohibition was later modified, but grocers had to stock pork products in separate rooms in which only non-Muslims could work or shop.

These dual and changing standards for foreigners and citizens hamper foreign efforts to adapt. This situation has been further complicated because the Middle East is going through a period of substantial, but uneven, economic and social transformation. As contact increases between Arabs and Westerners, cultural borrowing and meshing of certain aspects of traditional and modern behavior will increase. These changes are apt to come slowly, perhaps more so than many think.

Introduction

The PRI case illustrates how behavioral differences give rise to different business practices in various parts of the world. Understanding the cultures of groups of people is useful because business employs, sells to, buys from, is regulated by, and is owned by people. An international company must consider these differences in order to predict and control its relationships and operations. Further, it should realize that its accustomed way of doing business may not be the only or best way. When doing business abroad, a company first should determine whether a usual business practice in a foreign country differs from its home-country experience or from what its management ideally would like to see exist. If the practice differs, international management then must decide what, if any, adjustments are necessary to operate efficiently in the foreign country. When individuals come in contact with groups whose cultures differ from their own—abroad or within their own countries—they must decide if and how they can cope.

Some differences, such as those regarding acceptable attire, are discerned easily; others may be more difficult to perceive. For example, people in all cultures have culturally ingrained responses to given situations. They expect that people from other cultures will respond the same ways as people in their own culture do and that people in similar stations or positions will assume similar duties and privileges. All of these expectations may be disproved in practice. In the PRI case, the British salesmen budgeted their time and so regarded drinking coffee and chatting about nonbusiness activities in a café as "doing nothing," especially if there was "work to be done." The Arab businessmen, on the other hand, had no compulsion to finish at a given time, viewed time spent in a café as "doing something," and considered "small talk" a necessary prerequisite for evaluating whether they could interact satisfactorily with potential business partners. The Englishmen, because of their belief that "you shouldn't mix business and pleasure," became nervous when friends of the Arab businessmen intruded. In contrast, the Arabs felt "people are more important than business" and saw nothing private about business transactions.

After a company successfully identifies the differences in the foreign country in which it intends to do business, must it alter its customary or preferred practices in order to be successful there? There is no easy answer. Although the PRI case illustrates the folly of not adjusting, international companies nevertheless sometimes have been very successful in introducing new products, technologies, and operating procedures to foreign countries. At times, these introductions have not run counter to deep-seated attitudes. At others, the host society is willing to accept unwanted change as a trade-off for other advantages. In addition, in some cases the local society is willing to accept behavior from foreigners that it would not accept from its own citizens. For example, Western female managers in Hong Kong have expressed that they are seen by local people primarily as foreigners, not as women; thus, they are not subject to the same operating barriers that local females face as managers.[2] Members of the host society may even feel they are being stereotyped in an uncomplimentary way when foreigners adjust too much.[3] For example, Angela Clarke might have been even less effective for PRI if she had worn the traditional Arab woman's dress with veil.

The Nation as a Definition of a Society

The nation is a useful definition of society because
- **Similarity among people is a cause and an effect of national boundaries**
- **Laws apply primarily along national lines**

There is no universally satisfactory definition of a society, but in international business the concept of the nation provides a workable one, since basic similarity among people is both a cause and an effect of national boundaries. The laws governing business operations apply primarily along national lines. Within the bounds of a nation are people who share essential attributes perpetuated through rites and symbols of nationhood—flags, parades, rallies—and a subjective common perception of and maintenance of their history, through the preservation of national sites, documents, monuments, and museums. These shared attributes do not mean that everyone in a country is alike. Neither do they suggest that each country is unique in all respects; in fact, nations may include various subcultures, ethnic groups, races, and classes. However, the nation is legitimized by being the mediator of the different interests.[4] Failure to serve adequately in this mediating role may cause dissolution of the nation, as occurred recently in the former Soviet Union and the former Yugoslavia and almost in Canada through a Quebec separatist movement. In the mid-1990s there was ethnic unrest in the form of violence or strong separatist movements in about a third of nations; thus the boundaries of countries as we know them are far from secure.[5] Nevertheless, each country possesses certain characteristic physical, demographic, and behavioral norms that constitute its national identity and that may affect a company's methods of conducting business in that country.

Country-by-country analysis has limitations because
- **Not everyone in a country is alike**
- **Variations within some countries are great**
- **Similarities link groups from different countries**

In using the nation as a point of reference, remember that some countries have much greater internal variation than do others. Geographical and economic barriers in some countries can inhibit people's movements from one region to another, thus limiting their personal interactions. Decentralized laws and government programs may increase regional separation, and linguistic, religious, and ethnic differences within a country usually preclude the fusing of the population into a homogeneous state. For example, for all the reasons just given, India is much more diverse than Denmark.

Of course, nationality is not the only basis on which to group people. Everyone belongs to various other groups—for example, those based on profession, age, religion, and place of residence. Many similarities exist that in some ways can link groups from different countries more closely than groups within a country. For instance, regardless of the country examined, people in urban areas differ in certain attitudes from people in rural areas, and managers have different work-related attitudes than production workers do.[6] When you compare countries, therefore, you must be careful to examine relevant groups.

There are thousands of possible relationships between human variables and business functions—too many to discuss exhaustively in one chapter.[7] However, keep in mind that different attitudes and values affect how any business function may be conducted, such as what and how products will be accepted, how they are best produced, and how the operation should be organized, financed, managed, and controlled. This chapter first concentrates on just a few of the variables that have been found to influence business practices substantially. It then highlights alternative approaches for determining and dealing with differences in foreign countries as well as the changes that may occur in international companies as they come in contact with new human environments.

The Concept of Culture

Businesspeople agree that cultural differences exist but disagree on what they are.

Culture consists of specific learned norms based on attitudes, values, and beliefs, all of which exist in every society. Visitors remark on differences; experts write about them; and people managing affairs across countries find that they affect operating results.[8] Great controversy surrounds these differences because there is an acknowledged problem with measuring variances.[9] Culture cannot easily be isolated from such factors as economic and political conditions and institutions. For example, an opinion survey may reflect a short-term response to temporary economic conditions rather than basic values and beliefs that will have longer-term effects on managing business. Further, some national differences in specific work behavior that have generally been attributed to culture may be due to other factors, such as climatic differences.[10]

Despite these problems, considerable evidence indicates that some aspects of culture differ significantly across national borders and have a substantial impact on how business is normally conducted in different countries. Some evidence is derived by anthropologists or so-called country experts who rely on qualitative techniques, such as interviews and observations, used to uncover people's ideas, attitudes, and relationships to other people in the society. They then interpret processes and events and describe national character. Other evidence is derived by researchers who compare the opinions of carefully paired samples of people in more than one country. For example, questionnaires may be used to determine attitudes toward specific business practices, such as an advertising message or shared decision making in the workplace.[11]

Causes of Cultural Difference and Change

Cultural value systems are set early in life and are difficult to change, but change may come through
• Choice or imposition
• Contact with other cultures

Culture is transmitted by various patterns, such as from parent to child, from teacher to pupil, from social leader to follower, and from one age peer to another. Studies among diverse societies indicate that the parent-to-child route is especially important in the transmission of religious and political affiliations.[12] Developmental psychologists believe that by age 10 most children have their basic value systems firmly in place, after which changes are difficult to make. These basic values include such concepts as evil versus good, dirty versus clean, ugly versus beautiful, unnatural versus natural, abnormal versus normal, paradoxical versus logical, and irrational versus rational.[13] The relative inflexibility of values helps explain the deeply rooted opinions of an American female soldier and Saudi female doctor during the Persian Gulf War. The soldier said, "I'm thankful I'm not a Saudi woman. I just don't know how they do it." The doctor said, "It is so strange, I am glad not to be an American woman. Women are not made for violence and guns."[14]

However, because of multiple influences, individual and societal values and customs may evolve over time. Change may come about through choice or imposition.[15] Change by choice may take place as a by-product of social and economic change or because of new contacts that present reasonable alternatives. For example, the choice of rural people in many places to accept factory jobs changed their previous customs by requiring them to work regular hours and to forgo social activities with their families during work hours. A person's choice to embrace a different religion requires acceptance of a new set of values and beliefs. Change by imposition, sometimes called *cultural imperialism,* has occurred, for example, when colonial powers introduced their legal systems abroad by prohibiting established practices and defining them as being criminal.[16] The process of introducing some, but not all, elements of an outside culture often is referred to as *creolization, indigenization,* or *cultural diffusion.*

Isolation tends to stabilize a culture, whereas contact tends to create cultural borrowing. In addition to national boundaries and geographical obstacles, language is a major factor that affects cultural stability. Map 2.2 shows the world's major language groups. When people from different areas speak the same language, culture is transmitted from one area to another much more easily. Thus more cultural similarity exists among English-speaking countries or among Spanish-speaking ones than between English-speaking and Spanish-speaking countries. This is due partially to heritage and partially to the ease of communicating. Map 2.2 does not include the hundreds of languages that are spoken in limited areas. When people speak only one of those languages, they tend to adhere to their culture because meaningful contact with others is difficult. For example, in Guatemala, the official language is Spanish; however, there are twenty-two ethnic groups, three main ethnic languages, and derivations of those three. These groups have cultures that are much the same as those of their ancestors hundreds of years ago. The Guatemalan Nobel Peace Prize winner Rigoberta Menchú is from the Quiché group. She recounted that parents in that group do not permit their children to go to school, because all public schools

Map 2.2
Major Languages of the World

Hundreds of languages are spoken globally, but a few dominate. This map shows the eleven major ones. Note that English, French, or Spanish is the primary language in over half of the world's countries. Some other languages, such as Mandarin and Hindi, are prevalent in only one country but are important because of the number of native speakers.

Source: From *The Economist World Atlas and Almanac,* The Economist Books/Henry Holt & Co., Inc., pp. 116–117. Reprinted with permission. The number of native speakers is taken from *The World Almanac and Book of Facts, 1995,* Funk & Wagnalls, p. 598.

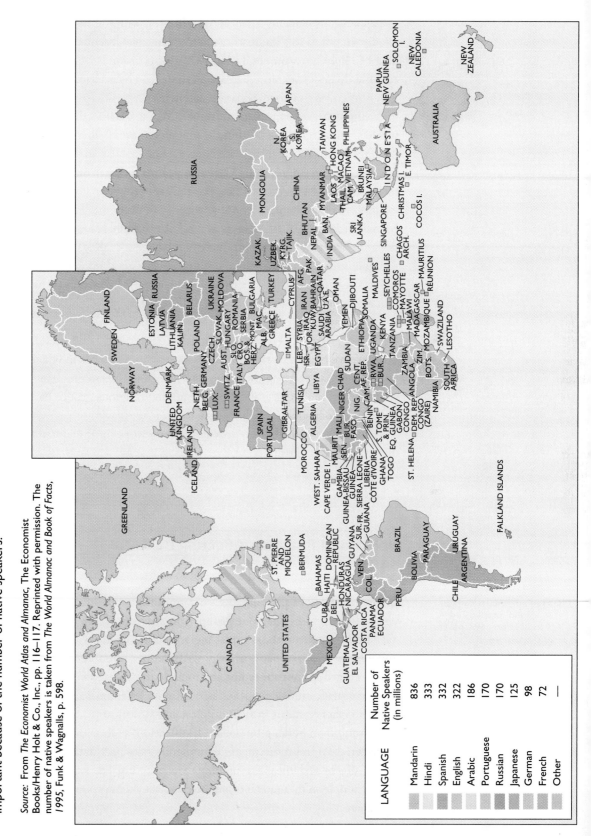

LANGUAGE	Number of Native Speakers (in millions)
Mandarin	836
Hindi	333
Spanish	332
English	322
Arabic	186
Portuguese	170
Russian	170
Japanese	125
German	98
French	72
Other	—

use Spanish; by learning Spanish, the children will lose their values and customs. She broke out of this linguistic isolation when she learned Spanish as an adult in order to fight governmental policies.[17] Her position has been to promote the multi-cultural diversity within Guatemala rather than have ethnic groups either embrace a different culture or form separate countries.[18]

Religion is a strong shaper of values. Map 2.3 shows the distribution of the world's major religions. Within the major religions—Buddhism, Christianity, Hinduism, Islam, and Judaism—are many factions whose specific beliefs may affect business. For example, some Christian groups forgo alcohol, but others do not. Differences among nations that practice the same religion also can affect business. For example, Friday is normally not a workday in predominantly Muslim countries because it is a day of worship; however, Tunisia adheres to the Christian work calendar in order to be more productive in business dealings with Europe.[19] When a religion is dominant in an area, it is apt to have great influence on laws and governmental policies. It also is apt to limit acceptance of products or business practices that are considered unorthodox (recall the Bahraini prohibition of pork in the PRI case). Consequently, foreign companies may have to alter their usual business practices. For example, because of criticism from fervent Hindus, McDonald's agreed not to serve beef in its restaurants in India.[20] In countries in which rival religions vie for political control, the resulting strife can cause so much unrest that business is disrupted. In recent years, violence among religious groups has erupted in India, Lebanon, Northern Ireland, and the former Yugoslavia.

The following discussion provides a framework for understanding how cultural differences affect business.

Behavioral Practices Affecting Business

Group Affiliations

Group affiliations can be
- Ascribed or acquired
- A reflection of resources and position

The populations of all countries are commonly subdivided into groups, and individuals belong to more than one group. Affiliations determined by birth—known as **ascribed group memberships**—include those based on gender, family, age, caste, and ethnic, racial, or national origin. Affiliations not determined by birth are called **acquired group memberships** and include those based on religion, political affiliation, and professional and other associations. A person's affiliations often reflect that person's class or status in a country's social-stratification system. And every society uses group membership for social stratification, such as by valuing members of managerial groups more highly than members of production groups. Social stratification affects such business functions as marketing. For example, companies choose to use people in their advertisements who are from groups admired by their target audience.

Map 2.3
Major Religions of the World

Almost all areas have people of various religious beliefs, but the culture of a region is most influenced by the dominant religion. Note that some countries have different dominant religions in different areas and that religions' areas of dominance transcend national boundaries.

Source: Mapping © Bartholomews, 1990. Extract taken from Plate 5 of *The Times Comprehensive Atlas of the World*, 8th Edition. Reprinted with permission of HarperCollins. MM-0397-300. Numbers are taken from *The World Almanac and Book of Facts*, 1995, Funk & Wagnells, p. 731.

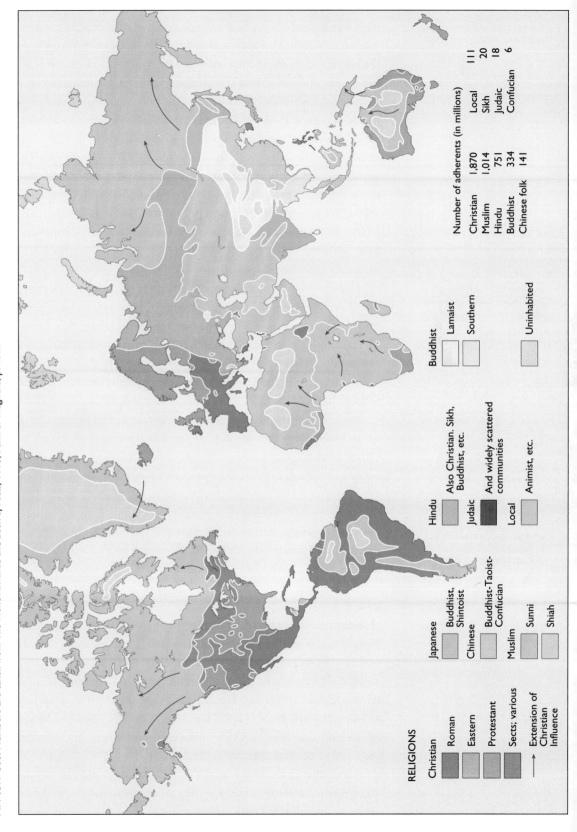

RELIGIONS

Christian
- Roman
- Eastern
- Protestant
- Sects; various

→ Extension of Christian Influence

Japanese
- Buddhist, Shintoist

Chinese
- Buddhist-Taoist-Confucian

Muslim
- Sunni
- Shiah

Hindu
- Also Christian. Sikh, Buddhist, etc.

Judaic
- And widely scattered communities

Local
- Animist, etc.

Buddhist
- Lamaist
- Southern

Uninhabited

Number of adherents (in millions)

Christian	1,870	Local	111
Muslim	1,014	Sikh	20
Hindu	751	Judaic	18
Buddhist	334	Confucian	6
Chinese folk	141		

Competence is rewarded
highly in some societies.

Role of competence   In some societies, such as that of the United States, a person's acceptability for jobs and promotions is based primarily on competence. Thus the workplace is characterized more by competition than by cooperation. This does not mean, of course, that U.S. society has no discrimination against people on the basis of group affiliation. However, the belief that competence should prevail is valued highly enough in the United States that legislative and judicial actions have aimed at preventing discrimination on the basis of sex, race, age, and religion. This value is far from universal. In many cultures, competence is of secondary importance, and the belief that it is right to place some other criterion ahead of competence is just as strong in those cultures as the belief in competence is in the United States. Whatever factor is given primary importance—whether seniority, as in Japan (where the workplace is characterized more by cooperation than by competition), or some other quality—will largely influence a person's eligibility for certain positions and compensation.[21]

Egalitarian societies place
less importance on ascribed
group memberships.

The more egalitarian, or open, a society is, the less difference ascribed group membership makes for access to rewards; however, in less open societies, legal proscriptions sometimes enforce distinctions on the basis of ascribed group memberships. In other cases, group memberships prevent large numbers of people from getting the preparation that would equally qualify them. For example, in countries with poor public education systems, elite groups send their children to private schools but other children receive inferior schooling.

Local attitudes may force
hiring according to local
norms or opinions.

Even when individuals qualify for certain positions and there are no legal barriers to hiring them, social obstacles may make companies wary of employing them. Other workers, customers, local stockholders, or governmental officials may oppose certain groups, making it even more difficult for their members to succeed.

Country-by-country
attitudes vary toward
• Male and female roles
• Respect for age
• Family ties

Importance of different group memberships   Although there are countless ways of defining group memberships, three of the most significant are in terms of gender, age, and family. An international comparison reveals the wide differences in attitudes concerning these memberships and how important they are to business considerations.

Gender-based groups   There are strong country-specific differences in attitudes toward males and females. The Chinese and Indians show an extreme degree of male preference. Because of governmental and economic restrictions on family size and the desire to have a son to carry on the family name, the practices of aborting female fetuses and killing female babies are widespread despite governmental opposition to the practices.[22] In Afghanistan, the 1996 takeover by religious fundamentalists led to prohibitions of women to attend school and to work. They were also required to be shrouded from head to toe.[23]

Recall that in the PRI case the female editor could not get permission to enter Saudi Arabia, a country that exhibits an extreme degree of behavioral rigidity related to gender. Schools are separate, as is most social life, such as wedding parties and zoo outings. Women are legally prohibited from driving cars and socially restricted from riding in a taxi without a male relative. Only about 10 percent of women work outside the home, and those who do remain separate from men. Most jobs for women are in professions that entail little or no contact with males, such as teaching or providing medical treatment to other women. When women do work in integrated organizations, the Saudis place partitions between them and male employees.

Even among countries in which women constitute a large portion of the working population, vast differences exist in the types of jobs regarded as "male" or "female." For example, in the United States, more than 40 percent of administrative and managerial positions are filled by women; in Japan, that figure is less than 10 percent.[24]

Culturally mandated male and female behaviors may carry over to other aspects of the work situation. For example, Molex, a U.S. manufacturing company in Japan, invited its Japanese workers and their spouses to a company dinner one evening. Neither wives nor female employees appeared. To comply with Japanese standards, the company now has a "family day," which the women feel comfortable attending.[25]

Age-based groups   Attitudes toward age involve some curious variations. Many cultures assume that age and wisdom are correlated. These cultures usually have a seniority-based system of advancement. In the United States, retirement at age 60 or 65 was mandatory in most companies until the 1980s, and relative youthfulness has been a professional advantage. However, this esteem for youthfulness has not carried over into the U.S. political realm, where representatives must be at least 25, senators 30, and the president 35—none of which carries a mandatory retirement age.

Barriers to employment based on age or gender are changing substantially in many parts of the world. Thus statistical and attitudinal studies that are even a few years old may be unreliable. One change has involved the growing numbers of women and men in the United States employed in occupations previously dominated by the other gender. For example, recently the proportion of male secretaries, telephone operators, and nurses has risen substantially, as has the proportion of female architects, bartenders, and bus drivers. Further, the proportion of the workforce made up by women has been increasing throughout most of the world; however, the increase is largely in part-time employment, where women dominate.[26]

Family-based groups   In some societies, the family constitutes the most important group membership. An individual's acceptance in society is largely based on the family's social status or respectability rather than on the individual's achievement. Because family ties are so strong, there also may be a compulsion to cooperate closely within the family unit while distrusting links involving others. In societies where there is low trust outside the family, such as in China and southern Italy, family-run companies are more successful than large business organizations, where people are from many different families. The difficulty of sustaining large-scale companies retards these countries' economic development.[27]

Importance of Work

In industrial countries, most people work more than they would need to simply to satisfy basic needs.

People work for a number of reasons. Many, especially in industrial societies, could satisfy their basic needs for food, clothing, and shelter by working fewer hours than they do. What motivates them to work more? The reasons for working and the relative importance of work among human activities may largely be explained by the interrelationship of the cultural and economic environments of the particular country. The differences in motivation help to explain management styles, product demand, and levels of economic development.

The motives for working are different in different places.

Protestant ethic   Max Weber, a German sociologist, observed near the beginning of the twentieth century that the predominantly Protestant countries were the most economically developed. Weber attributed this fact to the attitude toward work held by most of those countries, an attitude he labeled the *Protestant ethic*. According to Weber, the Protestant ethic was an outgrowth of the Reformation, when work was viewed as a means of salvation. Adhering to this belief, people preferred to transform productivity gains into additional output rather than into additional leisure.[28]

Although Weber's conclusions on the relationship between work and Protestantism were simplistic, there is evidence that some societies have more leisure than others. For example, on average, the Japanese take less leisure than do people in any other industrial country. But in a survey of over 1,200 companies in more than 60 countries covering about 26,000 employees, the Japanese were the least satisfied with both their jobs and employers. (The Swiss were the most satisfied.) Thus it is unclear why the Japanese take so little leisure. In the United States, another country where incomes probably allow for considerably more leisure time than most people use, there is still much disdain, on the one hand, for the millionaire socialite who contributes nothing to society and, on the other hand, for the person who lives on welfare. People who are forced to give up work, such as retirees, complain strongly of their inability to do anything "useful." This view contrasts with those that predominate in some other societies. In much of Europe, the highest place in the social structure is held by the aristocracy, which historically has been associated with leisure. Therefore, upward mobility is associated with more leisure activities, but only those that are broadening, such as trips, reading, or sports endeavors, and not household-related activities, such as gardening and taking care of children.[30] In rural India, living a simple life with minimum material achievements still is considered a desirable end in itself.

Attitudes toward work may change as economic gains are achieved.

Today, personal economic achievement is considered commendable not only in industrial countries but also in most rapidly developing ones. Some observers note that many economies, in contrast, are characterized by limited economic needs that

are an outgrowth of the culture. If incomes start to rise, workers in these economies tend to reduce their efforts, and thus personal income remains unchanged.
This cultural trait has been noted as an essential difference that underpins national
self-identity in many lower-income countries. Rather than rejecting the labels of
"traditional" for themselves and "progressive" for the higher-income nations, leaders
of these countries have stressed the need for a superior culture—one that combines
material comforts with spirituality.[31] Other observers, however, have argued that
limited economic needs may be a very short-lived phenomenon because expectations rise slowly as a result of past economic achievement. Most of us believe we
would be happy with just "a little bit more," until we have that "little bit more,"
which then turns out to be not quite enough.

People are more eager to work if
- **Rewards for success are high**
- **There is some uncertainty of success**

Belief in success and reward   One factor that influences a person's attitude
toward working is the perceived likelihood of success and reward. The concepts of
success and reward are closely related. Generally people have little enthusiasm for
efforts that seem too easy or too difficult, that is, where the probability of either
success or failure seems almost certain. For instance, few of us would be eager to
run a foot race against either a snail or a racehorse because the outcome in either
case is too certain. Our highest enthusiasm occurs when the uncertainty is high—in
this example, probably when racing another human of roughly equal ability. The
reward for successfully completing an effort, such as winning a race, may be high or
low as well. People usually will work harder at any task when the reward for success is high compared with the reward for failure.

The same tasks performed in different countries will have different probabilities
of success and different rewards associated with success and failure. In cultures
where the probability of failure is almost certain *and* the perceived rewards of success are low, there is a tendency to view work as necessary but ungratifying. This
attitude may exist in harsh climates, in very poor areas, or in subcultures that are
the objects of discrimination. At the other extreme, in areas such as Scandinavia,
where the tax structures and public policies redistribute income from higher earners to low earners, there also is less enthusiasm for work. In this case, the probability of success is high and rewards tend to be high, but the rewards are similar
regardless of how hard one works. The greatest enthusiasm for work exists when
high uncertainty of success is combined with the likelihood of a very positive
reward for success and little or no reward for failure.[32]

The work ethic is related to habit.

Work as a habit   Another factor in the trade-off between work and leisure is that
the pursuit of leisure activities may itself have to be learned. After a long period of
sustained work, a person may have problems deciding what to do with free time.
This insight helps to explain the continued drive for greater achievement seen in
some societies in which most people already have considerable material comforts.
One study that attempted to determine why some areas of Latin America developed a higher economic level and greater desire for material achievement than

others attributed differences to the fact that some Spanish settlers worked themselves rather than using slave or near-slave labor. In such areas as Antioquia in Colombia, the Spanish settlers who labored themselves developed a work ethic and became the industrial leaders of the country.[33] Clearly, when comparing the importance of work from one country to another, the effects of habit cannot be overlooked. An international company thus may find it easier in some societies than in others to motivate its workforce with shorter hours or longer vacation periods.

High-need achievement   The **high-need achiever** is a person who will work very hard to achieve material or career success, sometimes to the detriment of social relationships or spiritual achievements.[34] Three attributes distinguish high-need achievers:

High-need achievers want
- **Personal responsibility**
- **To take calculated risks in order to achieve reasonable goals**
- **Performance feedback**

Lower-need achievers often prefer smooth social relationships.

1. They like situations that involve personal responsibility for finding solutions to problems.
2. They set moderate achievement goals and take calculated risks.
3. They want concrete feedback on performance.

The average manager's interest in material or career success varies substantially among countries. For example, one study compared the attitudes of employees from 50 countries on what was called a *masculinity index.* Employees with a high masculinity score were those who had (among other attributes) more sympathy for the successful achiever than for the unfortunate, preferred to be the best rather than like others, more of a money-and-things orientation than a people orientation, a belief that it is better "to live to work" than "to work to live," and a preference for performance and growth over quality of life and the environment. The masculinity index also included attitudes toward gender roles, with higher scores going for beliefs that roles should be differentiated by gender and that men should dominate. The countries with the highest masculinity scores were Japan, Austria, Venezuela, and Switzerland. Those with the lowest scores were Sweden, Norway, the Netherlands, and Denmark.[35] These attitudinal differences help explain situations in which the local manager reacts in ways that the international management may neither expect nor wish. For instance, a purchasing manager with a high need for smooth social relationships may be much more concerned with developing an amiable and continuing relationship with suppliers than with reducing costs and speeding delivery. Or local managers in some countries may place such organizational goals as employee and social welfare ahead of the foreign company's priorities for growth and efficiency.

Need hierarchy   The **hierarchy of needs** is a well-known motivation theory, which is shown schematically in Fig. 2.1. According to the theory, people try to fulfill lower-order needs sufficiently before moving on to higher ones.[36] People will work to satisfy a need, but once it is fulfilled, it is no longer a motivator. This fulfill-

**Figure 2.1
The Hierarchy
of Needs and
Need-Hierarchy
Comparisons**
The lower hierarchy on the
right has a wider affiliation
bar (3) and a narrower
self-actualization bar
(5) than the upper one.
People represented by the
lower hierarchy require
more affiliation needs to be
fulfilled before a self-
esteem need (4) will be
triggered as a motivator.
These people would be
less motivated by self-
actualization than would
those represented by the
upper hierarchy.

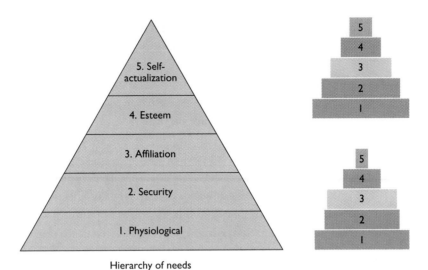

Hierarchy of needs

ment is not an all-or-nothing situation. However, because lower-order needs are
more important than higher-order ones, they must be nearly fulfilled before any
higher-order need becomes an effective motivator. For instance, the most basic
needs are physiological, including the needs for food, water, and sex. Physiological
needs may have to be nearly satisfied (say, 85-percent satisfied), before a security
need becomes a powerful motivator. The security need, centering around a safe
physical and emotional environment, may have to be nearly satisfied before trigger-
ing the influence of the need for affiliation, or social belongingness (acceptance by
peers and friends). After the affiliation need is sufficiently satisfied, a person may be
motivated by an esteem need, the need to bolster one's self-image through receipt
of recognition, attention, and appreciation for one's contributions. The highest-
order need is that for self-actualization, which refers to self-fulfillment, or becoming all that it is possible for one to become. The relative fulfillment requirements
are shown by the horizontal bars in Fig. 2.1.

The ranking of needs differs
among countries.

   The hierarchy of needs theory is helpful for differentiating the reward preferences of employees in different countries. In very poor countries, most workers
may be so deprived that a company can motivate them simply by providing enough
food and shelter. Elsewhere, other needs have to be addressed to motivate workers.
Researchers have noted that people from different countries attach different
degrees of importance to various needs and even rank some of the higher-order
needs differently. For example, studies have compared employees on *individualism
versus collectivism*. Countries with the highest individualism scores are the United
States, Australia, the United Kingdom, Canada, and the Netherlands. Attributes of
high individualism are low dependence on the organization and a high desire for
personal time, freedom, and challenge. Countries with the highest collectivism
scores (opposite to individualism) are Guatemala, Ecuador, Panama, Venezuela, and
Colombia. Attributes of high collectivism are high dependence on the organization

and a high desire for training, physical conditions, and benefits.[37] In those countries with high individualism scores, one should expect that self-actualization will be a workable motivator because employees want challenges; however, in countries with high collectivism scores, one may expect that the provision of a safe physical and emotional environment (security need) will be a workable motivator because employees depend more on the organization.

Importance of Occupation

The perception of what jobs are "best" varies somewhat among countries.

In every society, certain occupations are perceived to bring greater economic, social, or prestige rewards than others do. This perception to a great extent determines the numbers and qualifications of people who will seek employment in a given occupation. Although overall patterns are universal (for example, professionals are ranked ahead of street cleaners), there are some national differences. For instance, university professors are more influential as opinion leaders in Korea and Japan than in the United States and the United Kingdom.[38] The importance of business as a profession also is predictive of how difficult it may be for an international company to hire qualified managers. If jobs in business are not held in high esteem, a company may have to spend more to attract and train local managers, or it may have to rely more on managers transferred from abroad.

Another international difference involves the desire to work for an organization rather than to be one's own boss. For example, the Belgians and the French, more than most other nationalities, prefer, if possible, to go into business for themselves. Thus Belgium and France have more retail establishments per capita than most other countries do. One reason for this is that owning a small or medium-sized enterprise, rather than earning more income, is a means for Belgian and French people to get out of the working class and to move up socially. Further, psychological studies show that Belgian and French workers place a greater importance on personal independence from the organizations employing them than do workers in many other countries.[39]

Jobs with low prestige usually go to people whose skills are in low demand. In the United States, for example, such occupations as babysitting, delivering newspapers, and carrying groceries traditionally have been largely filled by teenagers, who leave these jobs as they age and gain additional training. In most less-developed countries, these are not transient occupations; rather, they are filled by adults who have very little opportunity to move on to more rewarding positions. (In the United States, there is rising concern that many low-paying menial jobs are becoming more permanent, thus perpetuating income disparities.)

Self-Reliance

Superior-subordinate relationships   In some countries, an autocratic style of management is preferred; in others, a consultative style prevails. Studies on what is known as *power distance* show that in Austria, Israel, New Zealand, and the Scandina-

There are national variations in
- Preference for autocratic versus consultative management
- Degree of trust among people
- Attitudes of self-determination versus fatalism

vian countries, the consultative style is strongly preferred, but in Malaysia, Mexico, Panama, Guatemala, and Venezuela, the autocratic style is favored. Interestingly, those preferring an autocratic style are also willing to accept decision making by a majority of subordinates. What they don't accept is the interaction between superiors and subordinates in decision making. Clearly, it may be easier for organizations to initiate certain types of worker-participation methods in some countries than in others.

Uncertainty avoidance   Studies on what is known as *uncertainty avoidance* show that in Greece, Portugal, Guatemala, Uruguay, El Salvador, and Belgium employees prefer that rules should be set out and that they should not be broken—even if breaking them is in the company's best interest. Further, these employees plan to work for the company a long time. At the opposite end of the spectrum are Singapore, Jamaica, Denmark, Sweden, Hong Kong, the United Kingdom, and Ireland.[40] When uncertainty avoidance is high, superiors may need to be more precise and assured in the directions they give to subordinates.

Trust   Surveys that measure trust among countries by having respondents evaluate such statements as "Most people can be trusted" and "You can't be too careful in dealing with people" indicate substantial national differences. For example, 61.2 percent of Norwegians think that most people are trustworthy, but only 6.7 percent of Brazilians feel that way. Where trust is high, there tends to be a lower cost of doing business because managers do not have to spend time trying to write contracts foreseeing every possible contingency and then monitoring every action for compliance. Instead, they can spend their efforts on investing and innovating.[41]

Degree of fatalism   If people believe strongly in self-determination, they may be willing to work hard to achieve goals and take responsibility for performance. A belief in fatalism, on the other hand, may prevent people from accepting a basic cause-effect relationship. In this regard, religious differences play a part: Conservative or fundamentalist Christian, Buddhist, Hindu, and Muslim societies tend to view occurrences as "the will of God." For example, Muslim mosques in the United States now generally rely on computer-generated programs to decide ahead of time when the new moon will be in the right place for Ramadan to begin; however, in conservative countries such as Saudi Arabia the view is, "How can you say six months before that it [the moon] will appear that day? You're not the one that controls the universe."[42] In a fatalistic atmosphere, people plan less for contingencies; for example, they may be reluctant to buy insurance. Studies have shown national differences in degree of fatalism even among managers in economically developed societies.[43]

Individual versus group   Japan has a much more collectivist culture than the United States does, one that values submergence of individual concerns to those of a group. For Japanese, the dominant group loyalty is to the work group."[44] For example, a U.S. scientist was invited to work in a Japanese laboratory; however, he was treated as an outsider until he realized he had to demonstrate his willingness to subordinate his personal interests to those of the group. He did so by mopping the lab floor for several weeks, after which he was invited to join the experiment.[45]

Although China and Mexico are also characterized as collectivist cultures, they differ from Japan in that the collectivism is based on kinship that does not carry over to the workplace.[46] Further, the concept of family in China and Mexico includes not only a nuclear family (a husband, wife, and minor children), but also a vertically extended family (several generations) and/or a horizontally extended one (aunts, uncles, and cousins). This difference affects business in several ways. First, material rewards from an individual's work may be less motivating because these rewards are divided among more people. Second, geographical mobility is reduced because relocation means other members of a family also have to find new jobs. Even where extended families do not live together, mobility may be reduced because people prefer to remain near relatives. Third, purchasing decisions may be more complicated because of the interrelated roles of family members. Fourth, security and social needs may be met more extensively at home than in the workplace.

Communications

All languages are complex and reflective of environment.

A common language within countries is a unifying force.

Language   Linguists have found that all societies have complex languages that reflect the environment in which their people live. Because of varying environments, translating one language directly into another can be difficult. For example, people living in the temperate zone of the Northern Hemisphere customarily use the word *summer* to refer to the months of June, July, and August. People in tropical zones may use that term to denote the dry season, which occurs at different times in different countries. Some concepts simply do not translate. For instance, in Spanish there is no word to refer to everyone who works in a business organization. Instead, there is one word, *empleados,* that refers to white-collar workers, and another, *obreros,* that refers to laborers. This distinction reflects the substantial class difference between the groups. Further, common language usage is constantly evolving. Microsoft purchased a thesaurus code for its Spanish version of Word 6.0, but many synonyms turned out to be too derogatory to be currently acceptable. The company corrected the software after newspapers and radio reports denounced the program.[47]

English, French, and Spanish have such widespread acceptance (they are spoken prevalently in forty-four, twenty-seven, and twenty countries, respectively) that native speakers of these languages generally are not very motivated to learn others. Commerce and other cross-border associations can be conducted easily with other nations that share the same language. When a second language is studied, it usually is chosen because of its usefulness in dealing with other countries. English and

French traditionally have been chosen because of commercial links developed during colonial periods. But English is gaining in relative importance as countries, such as Vietnam, are switching to English studies. Further, more young people in Europe are learning English than in the past.[48] In countries that do not share a common language with other countries (for example, Finland and Greece), there is a much greater need for citizens to study other languages in order to function internationally.

English, especially American English, words are being added to languages worldwide, partly because of U.S. technology that develops new products and services for which new words must be coined. When a new product or service enters another language area, it may take on an Anglicized name. For example, Russians call tight denim pants *dzhinsi* (pronounced "jeansy"); the French call a self-service restaurant *le self;* and Lithuanians go to the theater to see *moving pikceris.*[49] An estimated 20,000 English words have entered the Japanese language. However, some countries, such as Finland, have largely developed their own new words rather than using Anglicized versions.

Translating one language into another does not always work as intended. The following are examples of signs in English observed in hotels around the world:

France: "Please leave your values at the desk."
Mexico (to assure guests about the safety of drinking water): "The manager has personally passed all the water served here."
Japan: "You are invited to take advantage of the chambermaid."
Norway: "Ladies are requested not to have children in the bar."
Switzerland: "Because of the impropriety of entertaining guests of the opposite sex in the bedroom, it is suggested that the lobby be used for this purpose."
Greece (at check-in line): "We will execute customers in strict rotation."

Even within the same language there often are differences in usage or meaning. *Corn, maize,* and *graduate studies* in the United Kingdom correspond to *wheat, corn,* and *undergraduate studies,* respectively, in the United States. These are among the approximately 4000 words used differently in these two countries. Although the wrong choice of words usually is just a source of brief embarrassment, a poor translation may have tragic consequences. For example, inaccurate translations have been blamed for structural collapses and airplane crashes.[50] In contracts, correspondence, negotiations, advertisements, and conversations, words must be chosen carefully.

Silent language includes such things as color associations, sense of appropriate distance, time and status cues, and body language.

Silent language   Of course, formal language is not our only means of communicating. We all exchange messages by a host of nonverbal cues that form a *silent language.*[51] Colors, for example, conjure up meanings that are based on cultural experience. In most Western countries, black is associated with death; white has the same connotation in parts of Asia and purple in Latin America. For products to be successful, their colors and their advertisements must match the consumers' frame of reference.

Another aspect of silent language is the distance between people during conversations. People's sense of appropriate distance is learned and differs among societies. In the United States, for example, the customary distance for a business discussion is five to eight feet; for personal business, it is eighteen inches to three feet.[52] When the distance is closer or farther than is customary, people tend to feel very uneasy. For example, a U.S. manager conducting business discussions in Latin America may be constantly moving backward to avoid the closer conversational distance to which the Latin American official is accustomed. Consequently, at the end of the discussion, each party may inexplicably distrust the other.

Perception of time, which influences punctuality, is another unspoken cue that may differ across cultures and create confusion. In the United States, participants usually arrive early for a business appointment. For a dinner at someone's home, guests arrive on time or a few minutes late, and for a cocktail party, they may arrive a bit later. In another country, the concept of punctuality may be radically different. For example, a U.S. businessperson in Latin America may consider it discourteous if a Latin American manager does not keep to the appointed time. Latin Americans may find it equally discourteous if a U.S. businessperson arrives for dinner at the exact time given in the invitation.

Cues concerning a person's relative position may be particularly difficult to perceive. A U.S. businessperson, who tends to place a greater reliance on objects as prestige cues, may underestimate the importance of a foreign counterpart who does not have a large private office with a wood desk and carpeting. A foreigner may react similarly if U.S. counterparts open their own entry doors and mix their own drinks.

Body language or *kinesics* (the way in which people walk, touch, and move their bodies) also differs among countries. Few gestures are universal in meaning. For example, the "yes" of a Greek, Turk, or Bulgarian is indicated by a sideways movement of the head that resembles the negative headshake used in the United States and elsewhere in Europe. In some cases, one gesture may have several meanings: The joining of the index finger and thumb to form an O means "okay" in the United States, money in Japan, and "I will kill you" in Tunisia.[53]

Cues—especially those concerning time and status—are perceived selectively and differ among societies.

Perception and processing   We perceive cues selectively. We may identify what things are by means of any of our senses (sight, smell, touch, sound, or taste) and in various ways within each sense. For example, through vision we can sense color, depth, and shape. The cues people use to perceive things differ among societies. The reason for this is partly physiological; for example, genetic differences in eye pigmentation enable some groups to differentiate colors more finely than others can. It also is partly cultural; for example, a relative richness of vocabulary can allow people to notice and express very subtle differences in color.[54] Differences in vocabulary reflect cultural differences. For example, Arabic has more than 6000 different words for camels, their body parts, and the equipment associated with them.[55]

Regardless of societal differences, once people perceive cues, they process them. Information processing is universal in that all societies categorize, plan, and quantify. In terms of categorization, people bring objects together according to their major shared function: A piece of furniture to sit on is called a chair in English, whether it is large or small, wood or plastic, upholstered or not. The languages of all societies express the future and conditional situations; thus all societies plan. All societies have numbering systems as well. But the specific ways in which societies go about grouping things, dealing with the future, and counting differ substantially.[56] For example, in U.S. telephone directories, the entries are organized by last (family) names; in Iceland, they are organized by first (given) names. Icelandic last names are derived from the father's first name: Jon, the son of Thor, is Jon Thorsson, and his sister's last name is Thorsdottir (daughter of Thor).[57]

National norms differ in preference for
- **Focused versus broad information**
- **Sequential versus simultaneous handling of situations**
- **Handling principals versus small issues first**

Obtaining and evaluating information   In spite of vast differences within countries, some, such as those in northern Europe, are categorized as being **low-context cultures**—that is, most people consider relevant only information that they receive firsthand and that bears very directly on the decision they need to make. They also spend little time on "small talk" in business situations. However, other countries, such as in southern Europe, are **high-context cultures**—that is, most people consider that peripheral and hearsay information are necessary for decision making because they bear on the context of the situation. Northern Europeans are also called **monochronic,** which means that most prefer to deal with situations sequentially (especially those involving other people), such as finishing with one customer before dealing with another. On the other hand, **polychronic** southern Europeans are more comfortable in dealing simultaneously with all the situations facing them. For example, they feel uncomfortable when not dealing immediately with all customers who need to be served.[58]

There are also national norms that govern the degree to which people will try to determine principles before they try to resolve small issues, or vice versa. In other words, people will tend toward either **idealism** or **pragmatism.** From a business standpoint, the differences manifest themselves in a number of ways. The idealist sees the pragmatist as being too interested in trivial details, whereas the pragmatist considers the idealist to be too theoretical. In a society of pragmatists, labor tends to focus on very specific issues, such as a pay increase of a dollar per hour. In a society of idealists, labor tends to make less precise demands and to depend instead on mass action, such as general strikes or support of a particular political party, to publicize its principles.[59]

Reconciliation of International Differences

Cultural Awareness

Problem areas that can
hinder cultural awareness
are
• Things learned
subconsciously
• Stereotypes
• Societal subgroups

Where cultural differences exist, businesspeople must decide whether and to what extent they should adapt home-country practices to the foreign environment. But before making that decision, managers must be aware of what the differences are. As discussed earlier in this chapter, there is much disagreement about such differences. Thus building cultural awareness is not an easy task, and no foolproof method exists for doing so.

In any situation, some people are prone to say the right thing at the right time and others to offend unintentionally. Most people are more aware of differences in things they have learned consciously, such as table manners, than of differences in things they have learned subconsciously, such as methods of problem solving. Nevertheless, there is general agreement that awareness and sensitivity can be improved and that training about other cultures will enhance the likelihood of success in operating within those cultures, a subject discussed in detail in Chapter 21. This chapter has presented a framework of some of the human cultural factors that require special business adjustments on a country-to-country basis. By paying special attention to these factors, businesspeople can start building cultural awareness.

Reading about and discussing other countries and researching how people regard a specific culture can be very instructive. The opinions presented must be measured carefully. Very often they represent unwarranted stereotypes, an accurate assessment of only a subsegment of the particular country, or a situation that has since undergone change. By getting varied viewpoints, businesspeople can better judge assessments of different cultures. In a given society, managers can also observe the behavior of those people who are well accepted or those with whom they would like to be associated in order to become aware of and learn to emulate acceptable behavior. Samsung, Korea's largest company, is experimenting with a cultural awareness program that involves sending 400 junior employees abroad for a year. In the United States, for example, they don't work; rather, they idle at malls, watch people, and try to develop international tastes. The company is convinced this program will pay off in more astute judgments about what customers want.[60]

There are so many behavioral rules that businesspeople cannot expect to memorize all of them for every country in which business relations might be attempted. Wide variations exist even in form of address; for example, it may be difficult to know whether to use a given name or surname, which of several surnames to use, and whether a wife takes the husband's name.[61] Fortunately, there are up-to-date guidebooks that have been compiled for particular geographical areas, based on the experiences of many successful international managers.[62] A manager also may consult with knowledgeable people at home and abroad, from governmental offices or in the private sector.

A person who moves to a foreign country or who returns home after an extended stay abroad frequently encounters **culture shock.** "This is a generalized trauma one experiences in a new and different culture because of having to learn and cope with a vast array of new cultural cues and expectations, while discovering that your old ones probably do not fit or work."[63] People working in a very different culture may pass through stages. First, like tourists, they are elated with "quaint" differences. Later, they may feel frustrated, depressed, and confused—the culture shock phase—and their usefulness in a foreign assignment may be greatly impaired. Fortunately for most people, culture shock begins to ebb after a month or two as optimism and satisfaction improve.[64] Interestingly, some people also encounter culture shock when they return to their home countries—a situation known as **reverse culture shock**—because they have learned to accept what they have encountered abroad.

Grouping Countries

Some countries are relatively similar to one another, usually because they share many attributes that help mold their cultures, such as language, religion, geographical location, ethnicity, and level of economic development. In Map 2.4, countries are grouped by attitudes and values based on data obtained from a large number of cross-cultural studies. A company should expect fewer differences when moving within a cluster (a Peruvian company doing business in Colombia) than when moving from one cluster to another (a Peruvian company doing business in Thailand).[65] Such relationships must be used with caution, however. They deal only with overall similarities and differences among countries, and managers may easily be misled when considering specific business practices to use abroad. In fact, there is some tendency to expect that seemingly similar countries are more alike than they really are; thus a company may be lulled into a complacency that overlooks subtleties that are important for performance. For example, in the PRI case the company expected the twelve Middle Eastern Arab countries to be more similar than they turned out to be—and the PRI experience only touches the "tip of the iceberg" as far as national differences are concerned.[66]

Cultural Needs in the Internationalization Process

Not all companies need to have the same degree of cultural awareness. Nor must a particular company have a consistent degree of awareness during the course of its operations. As we discussed in Chapter 1 companies usually increase foreign operations over time. They may expand their knowledge of cultural factors in tandem with their expansion of foreign operations. In other words, they may increase their cultural knowledge as they move from limited to multiple foreign functions, from one to many foreign locations, from similar to dissimilar foreign environments, and from external to internal handling of their international operations. Thus, for example, a small company that is new to international business may have to gain only a minimal level of cultural awareness, but a highly involved company needs a high level.

Map 2.4
A Synthesis of Country Clusters

Not all countries have been studied extensively in terms of attitudinal variables that may have different effects on the efficient conduct of business. However, it has been noted that, of the countries that have been studied, some can be grouped together as having similar attitudes and values.

Source: Groupings taken from Simcha Ronen and Oded Shenkar, "Clustering Countries on Attitudinal Dimensions: A Review and Synthesis," *Academy of Management Review*, Vol. 10, No. 3, 1985, p. 449.

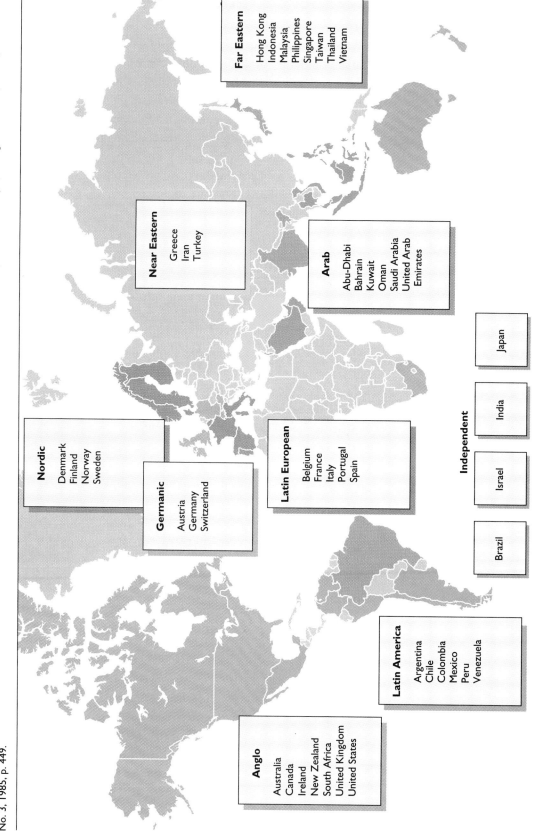

Far Eastern

Hong Kong
Indonesia
Malaysia
Philippines
Singapore
Taiwan
Thailand
Vietnam

Near Eastern

Greece
Iran
Turkey

Arab

Abu-Dhabi
Bahrain
Kuwait
Oman
Saudi Arabia
United Arab
Emirates

Nordic

Denmark
Finland
Norway
Sweden

Germanic

Austria
Germany
Switzerland

Latin European

Belgium
France
Italy
Portugal
Spain

Latin America

Argentina
Chile
Colombia
Mexico
Peru
Venezuela

Anglo

Australia
Canada
Ireland
New Zealand
South Africa
United Kingdom
United States

Independent

Brazil

Israel

India

Japan

When foreign functions are limited, for example, in a purely market-seeking operation, such as exporting from the home country, a company must be aware of cultural factors that may influence the marketing program. Consider advertising, which may be affected by the real and ideal physical norms of the target market, the roles of group membership in terms of status and buying decisions, and the perception of different words and images. A company undertaking a purely resource-seeking foreign activity can ignore the effects of cultural variables on advertising but must consider factors that may influence supply, such as methods of managing a foreign workforce. For multifunctional activities, such as producing *and* selling a product in a foreign country, a company must be concerned with a wider array of cultural relationships.

The more countries in which a company is doing business, the more cultural nuances it must consider. Think of the adjustments a manager from corporate headquarters who visits the company's foreign distributors would undergo. The more countries visited, the more cultural differences would be encountered on the trip and the more predeparture training time would be needed.

There is a relationship in the similarity between countries and the relative need for cultural awareness. For example, a U.S. firm starting a new business in Australia will find cultural differences that may be important enough to create operating problems; however, the number and intensity of these differences are apt to be less than if it were starting a new business in Japan.

A company may handle foreign operations on its own or contract with another company to handle them. The risk of making operating mistakes because of misunderstanding may effectively be reduced if foreign operations are turned over to another company at home or abroad that is experienced in the foreign country. If the operations are contracted to a company abroad, then some cultural awareness is necessary because of nuances that may influence the relationship between the two companies, such as the means of negotiating an agreement or the ordering of objectives for the operation. As a company takes on activities that had previously been contracted to another company, it will need to know much more about the cultures where it is doing business.

Polycentrism

Polycentrists are overwhelmed by national differences and risk not introducing workable changes.

In organizations characterized by **polycentrism,** control is decentralized so that "our manager in Rio" is free to conduct business in what he thinks is "the Brazilian way." When the concept is taken to extremes, a polycentric individual or organization is "overwhelmed by the differences, real and imaginary, great and small, between its many operating environments."[67] Since most discussions of international business focus on uniquenesses encountered abroad and the attendant problems that companies have experienced, it is understandable that many managers develop a polycentric view. Polycentrism may be, however, an overly cautious response. In reality, it is uncertain how much companies adjust when operating abroad and whether their practices abroad are any more prone to failure than those at home.

A company that is too polycentric may shy away from certain countries or may avoid transferring home-country practices or resources that may, in fact, work well abroad. For example, American Express assembled its worldwide personnel managers for an exchange of views. The complaints from the overseas managers centered on certain corporate directives that they claimed did not fit "their" countries. The impression was created that foreign operations were so unique that each overseas office should develop its own procedures. Further talks, however, revealed that the complaints really focused on only one particular personnel evaluation form. If the company had delegated procedural control, as these overseas managers were suggesting, it would have risked not introducing abroad some of its other standard forms and procedures that would work reasonably well. Furthermore, it would have risked duplicating efforts, which might have been more costly than trying to administer the ill-suited form. The additional discussions also generated for the first time comments from personnel managers in U.S. offices who had received the same corporate instructions. They indicated that they had had just as many problems with the form as their foreign counterparts had. Thus the problem, originally attributed to environmental differences, was seen to be universal.

To compete effectively with local companies, an international company usually must perform some functions in a distinct way. Polycentrism, however, may lead to such extensive delegation or such extensive imitation of proven host-country practices that innovative superiority is lost. Furthermore, control may be diminished as managers within each country foster local rather than worldwide objectives.

Ethnocentrism

Ethnocentrism is the belief that one's own group is superior to others. The term is used in international business to describe a company or individual so imbued with the belief that what worked at home should work abroad that environmental differences are ignored. Ethnocentrism can be categorized into three types:

1. Important factors are overlooked because management has become so accustomed to certain cause-effect relationships in the home country that differences abroad are ignored. To combat this type of ethnocentrism, managers can refer to checklists of human variables in order to assure themselves that all the major factors are at least considered.
2. Management recognizes both the environmental differences and the problems associated with change but is focused on achieving home-country rather than foreign or worldwide objectives. The result may be diminished long-term competitive viability because the company does not perform as well as its competitors and because opposition to its practices develops abroad.
3. Management recognizes differences but assumes that the introduction of change is both necessary and easily achieved. (The problems accompanying

Ethnocentrists overlook national differences and
- *Ignore important factors*
- *Believe home-country objectives should prevail*
- *Think change is easily introduced*

this type of ethnocentrism are discussed in the next subsection, "Geocentrism.")

Geocentrism

Between the extremes of polycentrism and ethnocentrism are hybrid business practices that are neither exactly like the international company's home operations nor exactly like those of the typical host-country company. When the host-country environment is substantially different, the international company must decide whether to persuade people in that country to accept something new (in which case, the company would be acting as a change agent) or to make changes in the company itself. **Geocentrism** refers to operations based on an informed knowledge of both home and host country needs, capabilities, and constraints.

Value system   It is much easier to adapt to things that do not challenge our value systems than to things that do. We usually can be flexible about whether we eat the salad before or after the main course, but we would probably think twice before exposing more of our bodies in public or paying bribes to government officials, actions that would require some moral adjustment if we do not do them in our country. For example, Eritreans eat only 175 grams of fish per capita per year (compared with 20 kilos in the United States and 70 kilos in Japan), despite having a long coastline rich in seafood and a recent experience with famine. The Eritrean government and the United Nations World Food Program have faced formidable opposition in trying to persuade Eritrean adults to eat more seafood because their value systems are too set. Many have religious taboos about eating insect-like sea creatures (such as shrimp and crayfish) and fish without scales, and most grew up believing that seafood tasted putrid. But there is little opposition among school children who are being fed seafood that adults find unpalatable. Simply, their value systems and habits are not yet set, so they can be easily influenced.[68] The important lesson here is that the more a change disrupts basic values, the more the people affected will resist it. When changes do not interfere with deep-seated customs, accommodation is much more likely.

Cost-benefit of change   Some adjustments to foreign cultures are costly to undertake; others are inexpensive. Some result in greatly improved performance, such as higher productivity or sales; others may improve performance only marginally. A company must consider the expected cost-benefit relationship of any adjustments it makes abroad. For example, Cummins Engine shuts down its plant in Mexico each December 12 so workers may honor the Virgin of Guadalupe. It throws a celebration in the company cafeteria for employees and their families that includes a priest who offers prayers to the Virgin at an altar.[69] The cost is small in relation to the resultant employee commitment to the company.

Resistance to too much change   When Germany's Gruner + Jahr bought the U.S. magazine *McCall's,* it quickly began to overhaul the format. Gruner + Jahr changed the editor, eliminated long stories and advice columns, increased coverage on celebrities, made the layouts more dense, initiated the use of sidebars and boxes in articles, and refused discounts for big advertisers. But employee turnover began to increase because of low morale, and revenues fell because the new format seemed too different to advertisers.[70] Acceptance by employees and advertisers might have been easier to obtain if Gruner + Jahr had made fewer demands at one time and had phased in other policies more slowly.

> Resistance to change may be lower if the number of changes is not too great.

Participation   One way to avoid undue problems that could result from change is to invite the prior participation of stakeholders, such as employees, who might otherwise feel they have no say in their own destinies. By discussing a proposed change with stakeholders in advance, the company may ascertain how strong resistance to the change is, stimulate in the stakeholders a recognition of the need for improvement, and allay their fears of adverse consequences resulting from the change. Managers sometimes think that delegation and participation are unique to highly developed countries, in which people have educational backgrounds that enable them to make substantial contributions. Experience with economic development and population control programs, however, indicates that participation may be extremely important even in countries with a preference for authoritarian leadership. However, participation is limited to the extent that proposed actions do not violate conditions in the prevailing value system and to the extent that participants are not so fatalistic that they believe they can have no control over the results of actions taken.

> People are more willing to implement change when they are involved in the decision to change.

Reward sharing   Sometimes a proposed change may have no foreseeable benefit for the people whose support is needed to ensure its success. For example, production workers have little incentive to shift to new work practices unless they see some benefits for themselves. A company's solution may be to develop a bonus system for productivity quality.

> People are more apt to support change when they expect personal or group rewards.

Opinion leaders   By discovering the local channels of influence, an international company may locate opinion leaders who can help speed up the acceptance of change. Opinion leaders may emerge in unexpected places. For example, in rural Ghana, government health workers frequently ask permission from and seek the help of village shamans before inoculating people or spraying huts to fight malaria. Doing this achieves the desired result without destroying important social structures. Characteristics of opinion leaders may vary by country, such as generally being more mature people in India and Korea, but not in Australia.[71]

> Managers seeking to introduce change should first convince those who can influence others.

How companies and businesspeople should react to cultural practices that run counter to their own values is itself a value judgment. On the one hand, *relativism* affirms that ethical truths are relative to the groups holding them; thus intervention would be unethical. On the other hand, *normativism* holds that there are universal standards of behavior that should be upheld; thus nonintervention would be unethical. Respect for other cultures is itself a Western cultural phenomenon that goes back at least as far as St. Ambrose's fourth-century advice: "When in Rome, do as the Romans do."

Neither international companies nor their employees are expected always to adhere to the norms of a host society. This would seem to remove ethical questions; however, exposure to certain practices may be traumatic to foreigners. For example, many practices that are considered "wrong" in home country cultures are elsewhere either customary or only recently abolished and liable to be reinstated—including slavery, polygamy, concubinage, child marriage, and the burning of widows.[72] Some companies have avoided operating in locales in which such practices occur; others have pressured a host country to change the "wrong" behaviors. For example, complaints from international business leaders induced Papua New Guinea, which depends on foreign investment, to abandon policies of payback killings.[73]

Although the preceding examples are extreme and seldom, if ever, encountered by international managers, many other behavioral differences may violate a manager's own ethical code to a lesser degree. It is easier to adjust in these cases, although dilemmas still exist. For example, using gifts and flattery to gain business advantages may seem unethical to some people. But in many countries, particularly in Asia, failure to bring a small gift may not only be considered a breach of etiquette but also be interpreted as indicating a lack of interest in doing business. The difference is due to the fact that most Westerners are conditioned to express gratitude verbally, and most Asians, particularly Chinese, are conditioned to express appreciation tangibly, such as with gifts.[74] Giving gifts to government officials may be particularly perplexing to Westerners. In many places such gifts or payments are customary to obtain governmental services or contracts. Although this practice may be condemned officially, it is so well embedded in local custom and precedent that it has nearly the prescribed enforcement of common law. In Mexico, for example, companies commonly give tips once a month to the mail carrier; otherwise, their mail simply gets lost.[75] The going rate of payment is rather easily ascertained and is usually graduated on the ability to pay. The practice of making payments to government officials is, in effect, a fairly efficient means of taxation in countries that pay civil servants poorly and do not have the means for collecting income taxes. Still, these payments are considered bribes by many MNEs, and the practice frequently is viewed by home-country constituents as so unethical that home-country laws against it are enforced in foreign operations.

In situations such as that of making payments to government officials, companies may incur operational inefficiencies or loss of business if they do not comply with local custom. This brings up the question of whether operational performance should be considered along with potential violation of ethical standards. For example, many people feel it is more acceptable to give payments to government officials when a large, rather than a small, amount of business is at stake and when small, rather than large, payments are expected.

Another thorny ethical question concerns practices by international businesses that do not clash with foreign values directly but that nevertheless may undermine the long-term cultural identity of the host country. Examples of such practices are the use of a company's home-country language and the introduction of products and work methods that effect changes in social relationships. Companies may face unexpected criticism that may affect their performance. For example, Finns have criticized MNEs for introducing non-Finnish architecture[76], Poles delayed McDonald's start-up because of its architecture[77], Greeks are resisting TVX Gold's building of a processing plant near a unique archeological site[78], and France fined Bodyshop for using English in its French stores and a branch of Georgia Tech for using English on the Internet.[79]

The Society for Applied Anthropology, which advises agencies on instituting change in different cultures, has adopted a code of ethics to protect foreign cultures with which such agencies interact. The code considers whether a project or planned change actually will benefit the target population. Because the definition of what constitutes a benefit depends on cultural value systems, implementing this code is a challenge. Further, there may be trade-offs to inducing changes, such as a trade-off between economic gains for the target population and the perpetuation of ways of life that have heretofore given that population great satisfaction. Thus, we often hear of "spiritual poverty in the midst of plenty" as aesthetic, philosophical, and human dimensions of development have been ignored or neglected.[80] Further, the concept of "quality of life" varies substantially among cultures.[81] The result is that an international company may be criticized as being socially irresponsible if it ignores the total spectrum of human needs for each place in which it operates.

Companies often lack complete information to guide them in advance of taking action abroad. There are many anecdotes about companies unwittingly violating a foreign country's values, even when they had sought advice from local managers or consultants. For example, consider the area of human rights. In 1948, before most of today's nations were in existence, the United Nations adopted the Universal Declaration of Human Rights. The Declaration has been criticized for having too Western an orientation, which does not consider distinctive values of specific countries or religions. Some provisions that lack universal acceptance include the right to individual ownership of property, the right to governance through universal secret elections, and the implicit statement that the nuclear family is the fundamental unit of society. In fact, not all countries have explicitly declared their concept of human rights. Without such an explicit delineation, there is uncertainty about the accuracy of descriptions of the human rights sentiments of many countries.[82] Further, any human rights code must enjoy cultural legitimacy for it to work as a normative (universal) system.[83]

Companies should time change to occur when resistance is likely to be lower.

Timing   Many good ideas are never applied effectively because they are ill timed. Change brings uncertainty and insecurity. For example, a labor-saving production method will create resistance because people fear losing their jobs, regardless of what management says will happen to employment. However, less resistance will occur if the labor-saving method is introduced when there is a labor shortage rather than a surplus. Attitudes and needs may change slowly or rapidly, so keeping abreast of these changes helps in determining timing.

International companies
- **Change some things abroad**
- **Change themselves when encountering foreign environments**
- **Learn things abroad that they can apply at home**

Learning abroad   The discussion so far has centered on the interaction between an international company and the host society. This interaction is a two-way street. The company not only affects the relationship but is affected by it. The company may change things abroad or alter its activities to fit the foreign environment; it also may learn things that will be useful in its home country or in other operations. This last point is the essence for undertaking transnational practices, in which the company seeks to capitalize on diverse capabilities among the countries in which it operates. In fact, the management within a given foreign country may serve effectively as the worldwide headquarters for a specific product or function.

The national practices most likely to be scrutinized for possible use in other countries are those found in the countries that are doing best economically.[84] For example, in the nineteenth century, when Britain was the world economic leader, interest focused on the British cultural character. At the turn of the century, such attention was diverted to Germany and the United States. More recently, it has shifted toward Japan and the newly industrialized countries of Asia. Whether a company is importing or exporting business practices, managers must consider the same factors when questioning whether and how change can be introduced.

Cultures are becoming more similar in some respects but not in others.

C O U N T E R V A I L I N G
F   O   R   C   E   S
Contact across cultures is becoming more widespread than ever. This should lead to a leveling of cultures, which, on the surface, is occurring. People around the world wear similar clothes and listen to the same recording stars. Competitors from all over the world often buy the same production equipment, the use of which imposes more uniform operating methods on workers. This globalization of culture is illustrated by the fact that Japanese tourists may hear a Philippine group sing a U.S. song in a hotel in Thailand.[85]

However, below the surface people continue to hold fast to their national differences.[86] In other words, although some tangibles have become more universal, the ways in which people cooperate, attempt to solve problems, and are motivated have tended to remain the same. Religious differences are as strong as ever. And language differences continue to bolster separate ethnic identities. These differences fragment the globe into regions and stymie global standardization of products and operating methods.

One factor that inhibits the leveling of cultures is nationalism. Without perceived cultural differences, people would not see themselves so apart from other nationalities; thus cultural identities are used to mobilize national identity and separateness. This is done by regulating and encouraging the so-called national culture.

Language is regulated in many ways, such as by designating an official language, preventing bilingual education, or requiring "Made in _____" labels printed in the language of the importing country. A religion may be designated a country's official one or made a requisite to holding certain governmental posts or to voting.

Those things that are part of the essential national heritage are perpetuated by marketing them to visitors at home and abroad, as the image of Britain is used in promotions to foreign tourists. They also may be off-limits to foreign ownership. For example, the French government has prevented foreign acquisition of vineyards for reasons based on heritage. Canada prevents foreign ownership in culturally sensitive industries. And, although the game of baseball has spread in popularity from the United States to Japan, when a Japanese group bought the Seattle Mariners team, there was an uproar in the United States—not on economic or national security grounds but on the basis of heritage. Maintaining a national identity may extend beyond heritage. For example, most countries have a national airline that is government subsidized so that there is a national identity associated with the flag painted on the aircraft.

As long as nations seek to perpetuate themselves through the promotion of separate cultural or national identities, companies will be constrained in their global competitive moves.

LOOKING TO THE FUTURE

International companies are likely to continue to face diverse cultural trends in different parts of the world and for different parts of their operations. In some areas, diversity will decrease as small cultural groups are absorbed into more dominant national ones. For example, in recent years such absorption has led to the extinction of many regional languages. Such extinction is sometimes expedited by governmental assimilation programs and by bans on religious groups or the use of anything except the official language.[87] At the same time, there is evidence of more powerful subcultures *within* countries because of the influx of people from other countries, the global rise in religious fundamentalism, and the growing belief of ethnic groups that they should be independent.

Three scenarios for future international cultures:
• Smaller cultures will be absorbed by national and global ones.
• Subcultures will transcend national boundaries.
• Cultural similarity will be used to mobilize a sense of national identity.

All of these factors might lead to future problems in defining culture along national lines. Subcultures may transcend borders, and the distinct subcultures within a country may have less in common with each other than they do with subcultures in other countries. Examples of transnational subcultures are the Inuits in Arctic lands and the Kurds of the Middle East. Simultaneously, cultural similarity will continue to be used to mobilize a sense of national identity, for example, religious separatism in Iran or the independence movement among the Québeçois in Canada and among the Tamils in Sri Lanka. Such activities may retard or even prevent the homogenization of cultures.[88]

An interesting potential scenario is that cultural competition—the promotion of ideas, attitudes, norms, and values—among nations will become more important.[89] With the termination of the Cold War, cultural competition may become a more important means to bring about economic growth as nations try to harness their distinctive human resource capabilities as a means of outperforming other countries.

WEB CONNECTION

Check out our home page for links to the Web of Culture (an index of links dealing with cultural issues such as cuisine, gestures, holidays, languages, religions, and so on) and the Multicultural Pavilion (another index of links to resources on multicultural issues, located at the University of Virginia).

Summary

- International companies must evaluate their business practices to ensure that national norms in behavioral characteristics are taken into account.

- A given country may encompass very distinct societies. People also may have more in common with similar groups in foreign countries than with different groups in their own country.

- Culture includes norms of behavior based on learned attitudes, values, and beliefs. Businesspeople agree that there are cross-country differences in these but disagree as to what the differences are.

- Cultural change may take place as a result of choice or imposition; however, isolation from other groups tends to stabilize cultures.

- Group affiliations based on gender, family, age, caste, religion, political preference, professional associations, and ethnic, racial, or national origin often affect a person's degree of access to economic resources, prestige, social relations, and power. An individual's affiliations may determine his or her qualifications and availability for given jobs.

- Some people work far more than is necessary to satisfy their basic needs for food, clothing, and shelter. The relative importance of work is determined largely by the interrelationship of the cultural and economic environments. People are motivated to work for various reasons, including the Protestant ethic, the belief that work will bring success and reward, habit, the need for achievement, and the fulfillment of higher-order needs.

- Different occupations bring different economic, social, and prestige rewards in different countries. People gravitate to jobs for which they perceive they will receive high rewards. The many differences among societies result in varied attitudes toward working for business organizations.

- National groups differ as to whether they prefer an autocratic or a consultative working relationship, in the degree to which individuals trust others, in attitudes toward self-determination and fate, and in the importance placed on group memberships, especially family-based ones.

- People communicate through both formal language and silent language based on culturally determined cues. Information processing is greatly affected by cultural background. The failure to perceive subtle distinctions can result in misunderstandings in international dealings.

- Companies can build awareness about other cultures. The amount of effort needed to do this depends on the similarity between countries and the type of business operation undertaken.

- People working in a foreign environment should be sensitive to the dangers of either excessive polycentrism or excessive ethnocentrism. Instead they should try to become geocentric.

- In deciding whether to try to bring change to home or host country operations or to develop new practices to fit conditions, an international company should consider several factors, including how important the change is to each party, the cost and benefit to the company of each alternative, the possibility of participation in decision making, the need to share the rewards of change, the use of opinion leaders, and the timing of change.

- There usually is more interest in studying and possibly adopting business practices from countries that are showing the greatest economic success. Cultural factors may determine whether the practices can work successfully in another society.

- Although increased contact among people is evoking more widespread cultural similarity among nations, people nevertheless tend to hold on to their basic values. These values are bolstered by efforts to protect cultural separateness and national identity.

Case
John Higgins[90]

Leonard Prescott, vice president and general manager of Weaver-Yamazaki Pharmaceutical of Japan, believed that John Higgins, his executive assistant, was losing effectiveness in representing the U.S. parent company because of an extraordinary identification with the Japanese culture. (Japan is shown in Map 2.5.)

The parent company, Weaver Pharmaceutical, had extensive international operations and was one of the largest U.S. drug firms. Its competitive position depended heavily on research and development (R&D). Sales activity in Japan started in the early 1930s when Yamazaki Pharmaceutical, a major producer of drugs and chemicals in Japan, began distributing Weaver's products. World War II disrupted sales, but Weaver resumed

Map 2.5
Japan
As a nation consisting of islands, Japan's relative historical isolation has led to less cultural borrowing than one finds in most other countries.

Japanese Work Customs

- Low employee turnover
- Advancement based primarily on longevity with the company
- Considerable after-work socializing among employees
- Group work assignments and rewards
- Bottom-up consensus building for decisions

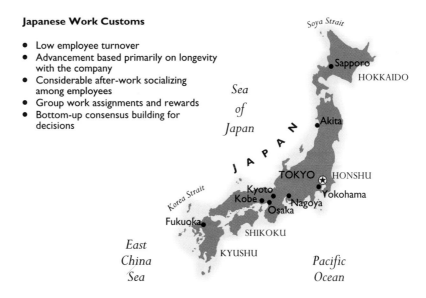

exporting to Japan in 1948 and subsequently captured a substantial market share. To prepare for increasingly keen competition from Japanese producers, Weaver and Yamazaki established in 1954 a jointly owned and operated manufacturing subsidiary to produce part of Weaver's product line.

Through the combined effort of both parent companies, the subsidiary soon began manufacturing sufficiently broad lines of products to fill the general demands of the Japanese market. Imports from the United States were limited to highly specialized items. The company conducted substantial R&D on its own, coordinated through a joint committee representing both Weaver and Yamazaki to avoid unnecessary duplication of efforts. The subsidiary turned out many new products, some of which were marketed successfully in the United States and elsewhere. Weaver's management considered the Japanese operation to be one of its most successful international ventures and felt that the company's future prospects were promising, especially given the steady improvement in Japan's standard of living.

The subsidiary was headed by Shozo Suzuki who, as executive vice president of Yamazaki and president of several other subsidiaries, limited his participation in Weaver-Yamazaki to determining basic policies. Daily operations were managed by Prescott, assisted by Higgins and several Japanese directors. Although several other Americans were assigned to the venture, they were concerned with R&D and held no overall management responsibilities.

Weaver Pharmaceutical had a policy of moving U.S. personnel from one foreign post to another with occasional tours in the home-office international division. Each such assignment generally lasted for three to five years. There were a limited number of expatriates, so company personnel policy was flexible enough to allow an employee to stay in a country for an indefinite time if desired. A few expatriates had stayed in one foreign post for over ten years.

Prescott replaced the former general manager, who had been in Japan for six years. An experienced international businessman who had spent most of his 25-year career at Weaver abroad, he had served in India, the Philippines, and Mexico, with several years in the home-office international division. He was delighted to be challenged with expanding Japanese operations. Two years later, he was pleased with the company's progress and felt a sense of accomplishment in having developed a smoothly functioning organization.

Born in a small Midwestern town, Higgins entered his state university after high school. Midway through college, however, he joined the army. Because he had shown an interest in languages in college, he was able to attend the Army Language School for intensive training in Japanese. Fifteen months later, he was assigned as an interpreter and translator in Tokyo and subsequently took more courses in Japanese language, literature, and history. He made many Japanese friends, fell in love with Japan, and vowed to return there. After five years in the army, Higgins returned to college. Because he wanted to use Japanese as a means rather than an end in itself, he finished his college work in management, graduating with honors, and then joined Weaver. After a year in the company training program, he was assigned to Japan, a year before Prescott's arrival.

Higgins was pleased to return to Japan, not only because of his love for the country but also because of the opportunity to improve the "ugly American" image held abroad. His language ability and interest in Japan enabled him to intermingle with broad segments of the Japanese population. He noted with disdain that U.S. managers tended to impose their value systems, ideals, and thinking patterns on the Japanese, believing that anything from the United States was universally right and applicable.

Under both Prescott and his predecessor, Higgins's responsibilities included troubleshooting with major Japanese customers, attending trade meetings, negotiating with government officials, conducting marketing research, and helping with day-to-day administration. Both general managers sought his advice on many difficult and complex administrative problems and found him capable. Prescott became concerned, however, with the notable changes in Higgins's attitude and thinking. He felt that Higgins had absorbed and internalized the Japanese culture to such a degree that he had lost the U.S. point of view. He had "gone native," resulting in a substantial loss of administrative effectiveness.

Prescott mentally listed a few examples to describe what he meant by Higgins's "complete emotional involvement" with Japanese culture. The year before, Higgins had married a Japanese woman who had studied in the United States and graduated from a prestigious Japanese university. At that time, Higgins had asked for and received permission to extend his stay in Japan indefinitely. This seemed to Prescott to mark a turning point in Higgins's behavior. Higgins moved to a strictly Japanese neighborhood, relaxed in a kimono at home, used the public bath, and was invited to weddings, neighborhood parties, and even Buddhist funerals. Although Weaver had a policy of granting two months' home leave every two years, with paid transportation for the employee and his family, Higgins declined to take trips, preferring instead to visit remote parts of Japan with his wife.

At work, Higgins also had taken on many characteristics of a typical Japanese executive. He spent considerable time listening to the personal problems of his subordinates, maintained close social ties with many of the men in the company, and had even arranged marriages for some of the young employees. Consequently, many employees sought out Higgins in order to register their complaints and demands with management. These included requests for more liberal fringe benefits, such as more recreational activities and the acquisition of rest houses at resort areas. Many employees also complained to Higgins about a new personnel policy, installed by Prescott, that involved a move away from basing promotions on seniority and toward basing them on superiors' evaluations of subordinates. The employees asked Higgins to intercede on their behalf. He did so, insisting their demands were justified.

Although Prescott believed it was helpful to learn the feelings of middle managers from Higgins, he disliked having to deal with Higgins as an adversary rather than an ally. Prescott became hesitant to ask his assistant's opinion because Higgins invariably raised objections to changes that were contrary to the Japanese norm. Prescott believed that there were dynamic changes occurring in traditional Japanese customs and culture, and he was confident that many Japanese were not tied to existing cultural patterns as rigidly as Higgins seemed to think. This opinion was bolstered by the fact that many Japanese subordinates were more willing than Higgins was to try out new ideas. Prescott also thought that there was no point in a progressive U.S. company's merely copying the local customs. He felt that the company's real contribution to Japanese society was in introducing new ideas and innovations.

Recent incidents had raised some doubts in Prescott's mind as to the soundness of Higgins's judgment, which Prescott had never questioned before. One example involved the dismissal of a manager who in Prescott's opinion lacked initiative, leadership, and general competency. After two years of continued prodding by his superiors, including Prescott, the manager still showed little interest in self-improvement. Both Higgins and the personnel manager objected vigorously to the dismissal because the company had never fired anyone before. They also argued that the employee was loyal and honest and that the company was partially at fault for having kept him on for the last ten years without spotting the incompetency. A few weeks after the dismissal, Prescott accidentally learned that Higgins had interceded on behalf of the fired employee, with the result that Yamazaki Pharmaceutical had taken him on. When confronted with this action, Higgins simply said that he had done what was expected of a superior in any Japanese company.

Prescott believed these incidents suggested a serious problem. Higgins had been an effective and efficient manager whose knowledge of the language and the people had proved invaluable. Prescott knew that Higgins had received several outstanding offers to go with other companies in Japan. And on numerous occasions, Prescott's friends in U.S. companies said they envied him for having a man of Higgins's qualifications as an assistant. However, Prescott felt Higgins would be far more effective if he took a more emotionally detached attitude toward Japan. In Prescott's view, the best international executive was one who retained a belief in the fundamentals of the home point of view while also understanding foreign attitudes. This understanding, of course, should be thorough or even instinctive, but it also should be objective, characterized neither by disdain nor by strong emotional attachment.

Questions

1. How would you contrast Higgins's and Prescott's attitudes toward the implementation of U.S. personnel policies in the Japanese operations?
2. What are the major reasons for the differences in attitude?
3. If you were the Weaver corporate manager responsible for the Japanese operations and the conflict between Higgins and Prescott came to your attention, what would you do? Be sure to first identify some alternatives and then make your recommendations.

Chapter Notes

1. Most data were taken from an interview with Angela Clarke, a protagonist in the case. Additional background information came from Samira Harfoush, "Non-Traditional Training for Women in the Arab World," *Bridge,* Winter 1980, pp. 6–7; "British Premier Visits Saudi Arabia," *New York Times,* April 20, 1981, p. A2; Karen Elliott House, "Modern Arabia," *Wall Street Journal,* June 4, 1981, p. 1; Geraldine Brooks, "Mixed Blessing," *Wall Street Journal,* September 11, 1990, p. A1; Tony Horwitz, "Thought Police," *Wall Street Journal,* May 2, 1991, p. A1+; Tony Horwitz, "Arabian Backlash," *Wall Street Journal,* January 13, 1993, p. A1; Robin Allen, "Imported Labour May Not Be Cheap for Gulf States," *Financial Times,* October 13, 1995, p.5; Macon Morehouse, "Western Influence Brings Wealth, Strain, to Saudi Society," *The Atlanta Journal,* June 26, 1996, p.10A; Sandra Mackey, "Perspectives on the Saudi Bombing," *Los Angeles Times,* June 28, 1996, p. B9; Thomas W. Lippman, "Mission to Bolster Saudi Security Also Provokes Rulers' Enemies," *Washington Post,* June 27, 1996, p. A24; Robin Allen, "Oil Price Alert on Saudi State Finances," *Financial Times,* June 26, 1996, p. 4; "The Shockwaves That Unsettle," *Financial Times,* July 26, 1996, p. 16; Mathew Horsman and Edward Waller, "The BBC's Arabian Plight," *The Independent,* April 16, 1996, p. 18; Daniel Pearl, "Moon Over Mecca: It's Tough to Pinpoint Start of Holy Month," *Wall Street Journal,* January 7, 1997, p. A1+.
2. R. I. Westwood and S. M. Leung, "The Female Expatriate Manager Experience," *International Studies of Management and Organization,* Vol. 24, No. 3, 1994, pp. 64–85.
3. June N. P. Francis, "When in Rome? The Effects of Cultural Adaptation on Intercultural Business Negotiations," *Journal of International Business Studies,* Vol. 22, No. 3, 1991, pp. 421–422.
4. Robert J. Foster, "Making National Cultures in the National Ecumene," *Annual Review of Anthropology,* Vol. 20, 1991, pp. 235–260, discusses the concept and ingredients of a national culture.
5. David Binder and Barbara Crossette, "As Ethnic Wars Multiply, U.S. Strives for a Policy," *New York Times,* February 7, 1993, p. A1+; Marcus W. Brauchli and David P. Hamilton, "Tensions in Asia," *Wall Street Journal,* August 18, 1995, p. A6; Bob Davis, "Global Paradox," *Wall Street Journal,* June 20, 1994, p. A1.
6. Marshall H. Segall, *Cross-Cultural Psychology: Human Behavior in Global Perspective* (Monterey, Calif.: Brooks/Cole, 1979), p. 143; and Luis R. Gomez-Mejia, "Effect of Occupation on Task Related, Contextual, and Job Involvement Orientation: A Cross-Cultural Perspective," *Academy of Management Journal,* Vol. 27, No. 4, 1984, pp. 706–720.
7. Richard N. Farmer and Barry M. Richman, *Comparative Management and Economic Progress,* rev. ed. (Bloomington, Ind.: Cedarwood, 1970), pp. 20–21, for example, list 15 behavioral variables relating to each of 36 business functions. George P. Murdock listed 72 cultural variables in "The Common Denominator of Culture," in *The Science of Man in the World Crises,* Ralph Linton, ed. (New York: Columbia University Press, 1945), pp. 123–142.
8. Ian Jamieson, *Capitalism and Culture: A Comparative Analysis of British and American Manufacturing Organizations* (Farnborough, England: Gower Press, 1980), Chapter 1.
9. Nancy J. Adler and Jill de Villafranca, "Epistemological Foundations of a Symposium Process: A Framework for Understanding Culturally Diverse Organizations," *International Studies of Management and Organization,* Winter 1982–1983, pp. 7–22.
10. Evert Van de Vliert and Nico W. Van Ypern, "Why Cross-National Differences in Role Overload? Don't Overlook Ambient Temperature!" *Academy of Management Journal,* Vol. 39, No. 4, 1996, pp. 986–1004.
11. Maureen J. Giovannini and Lynne M. H. Rosansky, *Anthropology and Management Consulting: Forging a New Alliance* (N.P.: National Association for the Practice of Anthropology, Bulletin 9, 1990), pp. 19–27. For discussion breaking techniques into four categories, see P. Christopher Earley, "International and Intercultural Management Research: What's Next?" *Academy of Management Journal,* Vol. 38, No. 2, 1995, pp. 327–340.
12. L. L. Cavalli-Sforza, M. W. Feldman, K. H. Chen, and S. M. Dornbusch, "Theory and Observation in Cultural Transmission," *Science,* Vol. 218, 1982, pp. 19–27.
13. Geert Hofstede, *Cultures and Organizations* (London: McGraw-Hill, 1991), p. 8.
14. James Le Moyne, "Army Women and the Saudis Shock One Another," *New York Times,* September 25, 1990, p. A1.
15. William H. Durham, "Applications of Evolutionary Culture Theory," *Annual Review of Anthropology,* Vol. 21, 1992, pp. 331–355.
16. Sally Engle Merry, "Anthropology, Law, and Transnational Processes," *Annual Review of Anthropology,* Vol. 21, 1992, p. 364.
17. Rigoberta Menchú, *I, Rigoberta Menchú: An Indian Woman in Guatemala* (London: Verso, 1984).
18. Rigoberta Menchú, "Asserting Our Dignity," *Harvard International Review,* Winter 1994-95, pp. 42–44+.
19. Vern Terpstra and Kenneth David, *The Cultural Environment of International Business,* 3rd ed. (Cincinnati: South-Western, 1991), p. 93.
20. "Big Mac vs. Sacred Cows," *Business Week,* March 1, 1993, p. 58.
21. Harry C. Triandis, "Dimensions of Cultural Variation as Parameters of Organizational Theories," *International Studies of Management and Organization,* Winter 1982–1983, pp. 143–144.
22. "China's Gender Imbalance," *Wall Street Journal,* June 7, 1990, p. A12.

23. Barbara Crossette, "Afghans Draw U.N. Warning Over Sex Bias," *New York Times,* October 8, 1996, p. A1.

24. "Comparing Women Around the World," *Wall Street Journal,* July 26, 1995, p. B1.

25. Kenneth Dreyfack, "You Don't Have to Be a Giant to Score Big Overseas," *Business Week,* April 13, 1987, p. 63.

26. Lin Leam Lin, *More and Better Jobs for Women—An Action Guide* (Geneva: International Labor Organization, 1996).

27. Francis Fukuyama, *Trust: The Social Virtues and the Creation of Prosperity* (New York: The Free Press, 1995).

28. Max Weber, "The Protestant Ethic and the Spirit of Capitalism," and Kember Fullerton, "Calvinism and Capitalism," both in *Culture and Management,* Ross A. Webber, ed. (Homewood, Ill.: Richard D. Irwin, 1969), pp. 91–112.

29. Robert Taylor, "Work Culture That Brings No Satisfaction," *Financial Times,* August 25, 1995, p. 8, referring to a study by ISR, International Survey Research.

30. Jean J. Boddewyn, "Fitting Socially in Fortress Europe: Understanding, Reaching, and Impressing Europeans," *Business Horizons,* November–December 1992, pp. 35–43.

31. R. Inden, "Tradition Against Itself," *American Ethnologist,* Vol. 13, No. 4, 1986, pp. 762–775; and P. Chatterjee, *Nationalist Thoughts and the Colonial World: A Derivative Discourse* (London: Zed Books, 1986).

32. Triandis, op. cit., pp. 159–160.

33. Everett E. Hagen, *The Theory of Social Change: How Economic Growth Begins* (Homewood, Ill.: Richard D. Irwin, 1962), p. 378.

34. David C. McClelland, *The Achieving Society* (Princeton, N.J.: Van Nostrand, 1961); David C. McClelland, "Business Drives and National Achievement," *Harvard Business Review,* July–August 1962, pp. 92–112; and M. L. Maehr and J. G. Nicholls, "Culture and Achievement Motivations: A Second Look," in *Studies in Cross Cultural Psychology,* Neil Warren, ed. (London: Academic Press, 1980), Vol. 2, Chapter 6.

35. Geert Hofstede, "National Cultures in Four Dimensions," *International Studies of Management and Organization,* Spring-Summer 1983, pp. 46–74.

36. Abraham Maslow, *Motivation and Personality* (New York: Harper, 1954).

37. Hofstede, op. cit., pp. 46–74; and for an earlier comparison among countries, see Mason Haire, Edwin Ghiselli, and Lyman Porter, *Managerial Thinking* (New York: Wiley, 1966), pp. 90–103.

38. Mary Jordan, "Respect Is Dwindling in the Hallowed Halls," *Washington Post,* June 20, 1994, p. A3, citing data collected by the Carnegie Foundation for the Advancement of Teaching in a survey of 20,000 professors in 13 nations and Hong Kong.

39. Hofstede, op. cit., pp. 54–55; Boddewyn, op. cit., p. 36.

40. Hofstede, loc. cit.

41. Stephen Knack, "Low Trust, Slow Growth," *Financial Times,* June 26, 1996, p. 12; and Francis Fukuyama, *Trust: The Social Virtues and the Creation of Prosperity* (London: Hamish Hamilton, 1995).

42. Pearl, loc. cit.

43. L. L. Cummings, D. L. Harnett, and D. J. Stevens, "Risk, Fate, Conciliation and Trust: An International Study of Attitudinal Differences among Executives," *Academy of Management Journal,* September 1971, p. 294, found differences among the United States, Greece, Spain, Central Europe, and Scandinavia.

44. R. M. Kanter, "Transcending Business Boundaries: 12,000 World Managers View Change," *Harvard Business Review,* May–June 1991, pp. 151–164.

45. Book review of Patricia Gercik, *On the Track with the Japanese* (Kodansha, 1992), by James B. Treece, *Business Week,* December 28, 1992, p. 20.

46. John J. Lawrence and Reh-song Yeh, "The Influence of Mexican Culture on the Use of Japanese Manufacturing Techniques in Mexico," *Management International Review,* Vol. 34, No. 1, 1994, pp. 49–66; P. Christopher Earley, "East Meets West Meets Mideast: Further Explorations of Collectivistic and Individualistic Work Groups," *Academy of Management Journal,* Vol. 36, No. 2, 1993, pp. 319–346.

47. Don Clark, "Hey, #@*% Amigo, Can You Translate the Word 'Gaffte'?" *Wall Street Journal,* July 8, 1996, p. B6.

48. Barry Newman, "Global Chatter: The World Speaks English, But Often None Too Well," *Asia Wall Street Journal,* March 23, 1995, p. 1+.

49. Vivian Ducat, "American Spoken Here—and Everywhere," *Travel & Leisure,* Vol. 16, No. 10, October 1986, pp. 168–169; Bill Bryson, *The Mother Tongue: English and How It Got That Way* (New York: Morrow, 1990).

50. Newman, op. cit.; Mark Nicholson, "Language Error 'Was Cause of Indian Air Disaster,'" *Financial Times,* November 14, 1996, p. 1.

51. This term was first used by Edward T. Hall, "The Silent Language in Overseas Business," *Harvard Business Review,* May–June 1960, and included five variables (time, space, things, friendships, and agreements).

52. Ibid.

53. Emmanuelle Ferrieux, "Hidden Messages," *World Press Review,* July 1989, p. 39.

54. For a survey of major research contributions, see Harry C. Triandis, "Reflections on Trends in Cross-Cultural Research," *Journal of Cross-Cultural Psychology,* March 1980, pp. 46–48.

55. Benjamin Lee Whorf, *Language, Thought and Reality* (New York: Wiley, 1956), p. 13.

56. Segall, op. cit., pp. 96–99.

57. Tony Horwitz, "Iceland Pushes Back English Invasion in War of the Words," *Wall Street Journal,* July 25, 1990, p. A8.

58. For an examination of subtle differences within northern Europe, see Malene Djursaa, "North Europe Business Culture: Britain vs. Denmark and Germany," *European Management Journal,* Vol. 12, No. 2, June 1994, pp. 138–146.

59. E. Glenn, *Man and Mankind: Conflict and Communication Between Cultures* (Norwood, N.J.: Ablex, 1981).

60. "Sensitivity Kick," *Wall Street Journal,* December 30, 1992, p. A1.

61. Peter Gosling, "Culture and Commerce: What's in a Name?" *Southeast Asia Business,* No. 6, Summer 1985, pp. 30–38; Frank L. Acuff, "Just Call Me Mr. Ishmael," *Export Today,* July 1995, p. 14.

62. A list of books appears in Katherine Glover, "Do's & Taboos," *Business America,* August 13, 1990, p. 5. See also Roger Axtell, *Do's and Taboos Around the World* (New York: John Wiley, 1992).

63. Philip R. Harris and Robert T. Moran, *Managing Cultural Differences* (Houston: Gulf, 1979), p. 88, quoting Kalervo Oberg.

64. Adrian Furnham and Stephen Bochner, *Culture Shock* (London: Methuen, 1986), p. 234.

65. Ben L. Kedia and Rabi S. Bhagat, "Cultural Constraints on Transfer of Technology Across Nations: Implications for Research in International and Comparative Management," *Academy of Management Review,* Vol. 13, No. 4, October 1988, pp. 559–571.

66. Two recent books that explain differences among these countries are Judith Miller, *God Has Ninety-Nine Names* (New York: Simon & Schuster, 1996); and Bernard Lewis, *The Middle East: 2000 Years of History from the Rise of Christianity to the Present Day* (London: Weidenfeld & Nicolson, 1996).

67. Hans B. Thorelli, "The Multi-National Corporation as a Change Agent," *The Southern Journal of Business,* July 1966, p. 5.

68. Geraldine Brooks, "Eritrea's Leaders Angle for Sea Change in Nation's Diet to Prove Fish Isn't Foul," *Wall Street Journal,* June 2, 1994, p. A10.

69. Marjorie Miller, "A Clash of Corporate Cultures," *Los Angeles Times,* August 15, 1992, p. A1.

70. Patrick M. Reilly, "Pitfalls of Exporting Magazine Formulas," *Wall Street Journal,* July 24, 1995, p. B1+.

71. Roger Marshall and Indriyo Gitosudarmo, "Variation in the Characteristics of Opin-

ion Leaders Across Cultural Borders," *Journal of International Consumer Marketing,* Vol. 8, No. 1, 1995, pp. 5–21.

72. Bernard Lewis, "Western Culture Must Go," *Wall Street Journal,* May 2, 1988, p. 18.

73. Merry, op. cit., pp. 366–367.

74. Boye de Mente, *Chinese Etiquette and Ethics in Business* (Lincolnwood, Ill.: NTC, 1989).

75. William Stockton, "Bribes Are Called a Way of Life in Mexico," *New York Times,* October 25, 1986, p. 3.

76. Pirkko Lammi, "My Vision of Business in Europe," in *Business Ethics in a New Europe,* Jack Mahoney and Elizabeth Vallance, eds. (Dordrecht, the Netherlands: Kluwer Academic, 1992), pp. 11–12.

77. "Golden Arches Raise Eyebrows in Poland," *The State* (Columbia, S.C.), September 10, 1993, p. 5A.

78. Kerin Hope, "Aristotle Provides Inspiration in Fight for Cultural Crock of Gold," *Financial Times,* June 16, 1996, p. 22.

79. Andrew Jack, "French Prepare to Repel English Advance," *Financial Times,* January 7, 1997, p. 2.

80. D. Paul Schafer, "Cultures and Economics," *Futures,* Vol. 26, No. 8, 1994, pp. 830–845.

81. William Kuyken, John Orley, Patricia Hudelson, and Norman Sartorius, "Quality of Life Assessment Across Cultures," *International Journal of Mental Health,* Vol. 23, No. 2, 1994, pp. 5–27.

82. Alison Dundes Renteln, "The Concept of Human Rights," *Anthropos,* Vol. 83, 1988, pp. 343–364.

83. Ingrid Mattson, "Law, Culture, and Human Rights: Islamic Perspectives in the Contemporary World," summary of a conference at Yale Law School (November 5–6, 1993) in *The American Journal of Islamic Social Sciences,* Vol. 11, No. 3, 1994, pp. 446–450.

84. Ian Jamieson, "The Concept of Culture and Its Relevance for an Analysis of Business Enterprise in Different Societies," *International Study of Management and Organization,* Winter 1982, pp. 71–72.

85. Foster, op. cit., p. 236.

86. J. D. Child, "Culture, Contingency and Capitalism in the Cross-National Study of Organizations," in *Research in Organizational Behavior,* L. L. Cummings and B. M. Staw, eds. (Greenwich, Conn.: JAI, 1981), Vol. III, pp. 303–356; Andre Laurent, "The Cross-Cultural Puzzle of International Human Resource Management," *Human Resource Management,* Vol.

25, No. 1, pp. 91–102.

87. See, for example, "Asians May Ban Islamic Sect," *Wall Street Journal,* August 4, 1994, p. A6; and Simone Veil, "Forging Cultural Unity: Assimilation and Integration in France," *Harvard International Review,* Summer 1994, pp. 30–31.

88. Lourdes Arizpe, "On Cultural and Social Sustainability," *Development,* Vol. 1, 1989, pp. 5–10.

89. J. Ørstrøm Møller, "The Competitiveness of U.S. Industry: A View from the Outside," *Business Horizons,* November–December 1991, pp. 27–34; Richard Tomkins, "US Tops Poll on Cultural Exports," *Financial Times,* December 4, 1996, p. 9.

90. The case is a condensed version of the original by M. Y. Yoshino. Reprinted with permission of Stanford University Graduate School of Business, ©1963 by the Board of Trustees of the Leland Stanford Junior University.

Chapter 3

The Political and Legal Environments Facing Business

Half the world knows not how the other half lives.

—English Proverb

Objectives	• To discuss the different functions that political systems perform
	• To compare democratic and totalitarian political regimes and discuss how they can influence managerial decisions
	• To describe how management can formulate and implement strategies to deal with the political environment
	• To study the different types of legal systems and the legal relationships that exist between countries
	• To examine the major legal issues in international business

Case
The Taipan's
Dilemma[1]

Peter Sutch, the chairman, or *taipan,* of Swire Pacific Ltd. is faced with important and pressing strategic decisions. As taipan of one of the major *hongs,* or family-controlled foreign trading houses, that figure prominently in Hong Kong business circles, Sutch must decide what to do when Hong Kong reverts to China's control in 1997.

The hongs began as British-owned, nineteenth-century traders to China. Although all have begun diversifying out of Hong Kong, they, and Swire in particular, still will depend greatly on the economy of Hong Kong and thus will need to reach some sort of accommodation with China.

As shown in Map 3.1, Hong Kong is a British Crown Colony that comprises Hong Kong Island, Kowloon Peninsula, and the New Territories. It is one of the world's major seaports. Why will Hong Kong's revised status be a problem to the hongs? The answer lies partly in the history of the region and partly in what it is today. Until the mid-seventeenth century, China sought to minimize its contact with foreigners by restricting foreign trade to the port at Macao, 75 miles south of Canton. These restrictions resulted from a long history of mutual distrust and misunderstanding between the Chinese and foreigners. In the late eighteenth century, the Chinese were persuaded to open up more of their ports, a decision they soon regretted. By the middle of the nineteenth century, they again sought to restrict foreign trade to Canton. Under one of the new regulations, Western traders had to deal exclusively with a group of Chinese merchants called "officially authorized merchants," who were charged with fixing prices, regulating trade volume, and policing the behavior of the Westerners.

Despite the history of restrictions, trade between China and the West flourished. And trade between Britain and China became particularly important: The British wanted Chinese tea; the Chinese wanted the opium British traders shipped in from India. Although opium was officially illegal in China, its use was widespread: By the 1830s an estimated 4–12 million Chinese were addicted to the drug. The Chinese government sought to halt its importation; not surprisingly, the British protested. The eventual results were three Opium Wars between the two countries within a period of twenty-one years (1839–1860). In all three, China emerged the loser. The First Opium War netted for the British permanent ownership of the island of Hong Kong and its harbor (among other concessions). From the Third Opium War, they gained Kowloon. The New Territories, which comprise 90 percent of the land area of Hong Kong, came under British control in 1898 under the terms of a 99-year lease that expired June 30, 1997.

In the middle of the nineteenth century, Hong Kong was barren, virtually uninhabited, and disease-ridden. Also one of the best harbors in the world, it served two purposes for the British: It was a secure base from which traders could manage their operations and a good deep-water port that could serve as a naval base. Its acquisition was largely due to the lobbying efforts of Jardine, Matheson and Company, the oldest of the Hong Kong hongs, whose owner, William Jardine, persuaded the British government that a permanent base on the China coast was needed.

Until the early 1980s, the issue of the expiration of the 99-year lease obtained in 1898 was largely ignored. However, real estate in Hong Kong tends to be leased on a 15-year

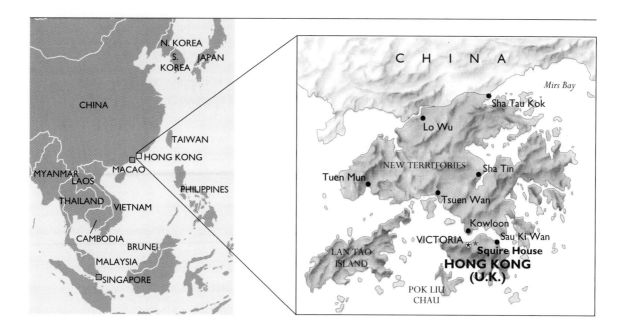

Map 3.1
Hong Kong
Hong Kong, situated at the mouth of the Pearl River, is a free-market economy surrounded by (and becoming more closely integrated with) China.

basis. In 1982, therefore, nervousness on the part of the Hong Kong business community led then British Prime Minister Margaret Thatcher to initiate talks with the Chinese government to determine the island's status beginning in 1997.

After prolonged negotiations, in 1984 the British and Chinese signed the Sino-British Joint Declaration on the future of Hong Kong. Under the agreement, China assumed control over Hong Kong on July 1, 1997, at which time Hong Kong became a Special Administrative Region of China. The agreement also calls for "one country, two systems." This provision provides that Hong Kong and China—together, "one country"—will have two governmental systems. China will continue its current economic structure, which involves heavy governmental control (a system that is, however, undergoing significant transition, as will be discussed in Chapter 4); Hong Kong will retain its separate political and economic status for fifty years and continue to enjoy the free-wheeling, free-market economy that historically has flourished so successfully there. The Joint Declaration along with the Basic Law, the post-1997 Hong Kong constitution developed by China, provides a sense of direction for economic and political change. Together, they call for Hong Kong's courts to have a judicial system separate from China's. This is a vital concern if Hong Kong is to remain an important international financial and commercial center; it means law will be based on British law, which, unlike China's, supports a free-market system.

Democracy has never been a major part of the political landscape in Hong Kong. Only once in the first 140 years of British rule was representative rule considered, and that was quashed by the local business elite, who even today are more sympathetic to China's point of view than to the democracy movement's point of view. Until Hong Kong reverted back to China, it was considered a British colony, presided over by a governor appointed by the Queen of England. Once the Joint Declaration of 1984 established a date for turnover of Hong Kong to China, the British began to push for democracy. The June 1989 massacre of pro-democracy demonstrators in Bejing caused confidence in Hong Kong to plunge. In 1990, political parties were allowed to exist, and in 1991 for the first time, the parties won the right to be represented in the Legislative Council (Legco). In 1995 elections, all Legco seats were chosen by direct election. Fewer than half of the seats were chosen by universal suffrage, while the rest were elected by small groups of professionals and other groups. Most of the contested seats went to members of the Democratic Party, which wants total democracy, including the election of the administrative officer that will replace the governor in 1997.

Legco and the democrats certainly did not get their wish. On December 11, 1996, a 400-person committee voted for Hong Kong shipping magnate C. H. Tung as the first chief executive to run Hong Kong beginning July 1, 1997. Although Tung has pledged to continue with the best of the West, he also hopes to reinforce traditional Chinese values, and it is also evident that Legco's short rein of power would end on June 30, 1997, to be replaced by something more acceptable to China. The provisional legislature which would replace Legco was appointed by the same 400-person committee that elected Tung.

The trend to democracy in Hong Kong is interesting. In 1981, 6,195 votes were cast out of 34,381 voters for the election of 15 government positions. In 1995, 3 million out of 3.698 million electors voted for 457 members elected to 4 different government bodies. However, the real power in Hong Kong resides with the Executive Council (Exco), which is the governor's cabinet, composed mostly of business interests. Exco advises the governor's civil servants who run Hong Kong. There is no clear indication what will eventually happen after China's takeover, but China is fighting democratic forces as hard as it can.

Given the political instability in Hong Kong, why don't more companies just leave? Mainly because Hong Kong is still important. Hong Kong is the world's eighth-largest trading nation, has more than $40 billion in foreign exchange reserves, boasts a higher per capita income than Britain, has one of the world's lowest tax rates, and has a gross domestic product equal to roughly 20 percent of mainland China, which has a population of 1.2 billion people, compared with 6 million in Hong Kong. (See Hong Kong in the Country Section of **http://international.byu.edu/ibd** for several Web sites with up-to-date information on Hong Kong). However, Hong Kong is slipping. It once was a haven for low-cost manufacturing, but times are changing. In 1984, more than 900,000 people had manufacturing jobs in Hong Kong, but that number had shrunk to just 400,000 people by 1995. Manufacturing jobs are moving to China and other low-cost areas of Southeast Asia. And 1.5 million people are working in services in Hong Kong. However, even service jobs are fleeing to China. Hong Kong is beset by competition on all sides. In particular, Singapore is trying to grab away business from Hong Kong. For example, while only 11.1 percent of Hong Kong's GDP comes from manufacturing, Singapore gets 27 percent of its GDP from manufacturing. Financial services in Hong Kong and Singapore are about equal (25.8 percent versus 29.5 percent of GDP), but Hong Kong generates far more of its GDP from other services. Singapore is now trying to convince companies to come to Singapore where labor, rents, and other expenses are significantly lower than they are in Hong Kong. Although companies like Unisys, Morgan Stanley, Goldman Sachs, ESPN, and HBO have moved from Hong Kong to Singapore, most companies are staying put. Hong Kong is still very much a *laissez-faire* economy, compared with Singapore's more government-directed and controlled economy.

However, even the hongs are affected by the events in Hong Kong and China. Hutchison Whampoa, one of the old hongs, was bought by Hong Kong businessman Li Ka-shing, while new hongs, such as China International Trust Investment Corporation (CITIC), which is backed by China, are moving in. The two remaining original noble houses, Swire Pacific and Jardine Matheson, are struggling with their future strategies and are taking different approaches. They are different companies, with Swire Pacific generating 65 percent of its revenues from aviation (primarily Cathay Pacific and Dragonair), and Jardine Matheson generating 81 percent of its revenues from retailing and distribution. Jardine Matheson moved its legal domicile to Bermuda in 1984 and moved its main stock market listing from Hong Kong to London in 1992 and delisted its securities from the Hong Kong Stock Exchange at the end of 1994. It is also moving the secondary listings of its major companies from Hong Kong to Singapore. Another complicating factor is Jardine's nineteenth century involvement in the opium trade.

Swire, on the other hand, is cooperating directly with China in a significant way. Swire even removed the Union Jack from its Cathay Pacific aircraft and repainted them an oriental jade color. The Swire family and their British-based parent company, John Swire & Sons, have some 90 percent of their assets in China. They are involved in joint ventures with CITIC and other Chinese entities, and they are constantly approached by Western investors who want to do business in China via Swire Pacific. However, Peter Sutch is still concerned about Swire's future in Hong Kong and China. As one Swire source described the difference between Swire and Jardine, "The Chinese hate us the least." Sutch is worried that China could seize its businesses, just as it did in Shanghai forty years ago. More importantly, however, he worries that his Chinese partners will become increasingly more influential and sophisticated and will need to rely less on Swire's partnership. Who is right? Is Peter Sutch right in pegging his future to that of China, or is Jardine's Alasdair Morrison right in diversifying Jardine Matheson from Hong Kong and China?

Introduction

As noted in the opening case, MNEs must operate in countries that are characterized by different political, legal, and economic frameworks, diverse levels of economic development, and a variety of economic conditions. To each of an infinite number of situations, the MNE brings a frame of reference based on its domestic experience as well as its lessons from foreign settings. For the company to be successful, its management must carefully analyze the interaction between corporate policies and the political, legal, and economic environments in order to maximize efficiency. This chapter discusses the political and legal systems that managers are likely to encounter and the factors they need to consider as they make strategic decisions about operations in different countries.

The Political Environment

Public institutions: the government, governmental agencies, and government-owned businesses

Nonpublic institutions: special interest groups, such as environmentalists

Figure 1.2 identified the environments that influence managerial decisions. The political environments in a company's home country and the countries in which it does business are important external influences on management.

Countries have both market and nonmarket environments. The market environment involves the interactions between households (or individuals) and companies to allocate resources, free from governmental ownership or control. The nonmarket, or political, environment refers to **public institutions** (such as the government, government agencies, and government-owned businesses) and **nonpublic institutions** (such as environmental and other special interest groups that represent specific individuals or groups).[2] Managers must establish corporate strategies for both the market and nonmarket environments, individually and combined. For example, the British-Chinese negotiations over the future of Hong Kong—a political issue—caused Jardine Matheson to move its legal domicile to Bermuda—a market strategy.

The Political System and Its Functions

The role of the political system is to integrate the society.

The political system is influenced by forces from within and outside a country.

The political system is designed to integrate the parts of a society into a viable, functioning unit. A country's political system has an enormous impact on how business is conducted domestically and/or internationally. It influences and is influenced by various factors. In Hong Kong, for example, political change was influenced by China because it took control of Hong Kong in 1997; by Britain because it had ruled Hong Kong and tried to institute more democracy before the takeover by China; and by the United States because of the strong trading relationship between it and Hong Kong as well as the ongoing debate with China over human rights issues. The political system is also influenced by a variety of internal factors, such as the nature of the population, the size and influence of corporations and governmental bureaucracies, and the strength of the politicians. For example, important factors influencing the political process in Hong Kong are the general population, the large companies that are investing and doing business there, and emerging politicians.

Political process functions are
- **Interest articulation**
- **Interest aggregation**
- **Policy making**
- **Policy implementation and adjudication**

Interest aggregation is the collection of interests in the political system.

Figure 3.1 illustrates the interaction of the process functions, inputs, and outputs in any political environment. The process functions in the figure are interest articulation and aggregation, formulation of policy alternatives, and implementation and adjudication of policies. Politicians, individuals, businesses, and interest groups provide inputs through the process of interest articulation, that is, making their desires known. These inputs then are aggregated through a process called **interest aggregation** so that policy alternatives can be formulated that stand a chance of making it through the political process. The alternatives are debated, and

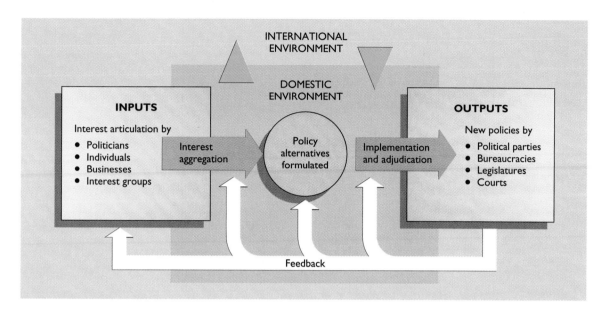

Figure 3.1
The Political System and Its Functions

Policy alternatives are formulated from the inputs of different foreign and domestic entities, and then implemented. Once implemented, the outputs of these policies are tested in the marketplace and revised as necessary.

Source: From *Comparative Politics Today: A World View,* 3rd Ed., by Gabriel A. Almond and G. Bingham Powell, Jr. Copyright ©1984 Gabriel A. Almond and G. Bingham Powell, Jr. Reprinted by permission Addison-Wesley Educational Publishers.

An ideology is the systematic and integrated body of constructs, theories, and aims that constitute a sociopolitical program.

Pluralistic societies are those in which a variety of ideologies coexist.

policies are made, usually by political structures such as political parties, governmental bureaucracies, state and federal legislatures, and courts. Next the policies are implemented, and any controversial features of them are adjudicated through the court process to determine if they are legal.[3]

These process functions occur regardless of whether a country is democratic. This is true, for example, of the United Kingdom and Hong Kong, which differ in this regard only in degree. There is much wider interest articulation in the United Kingdom than in Hong Kong (although this is changing), and the steps of interest aggregation, policy making, and implementation and adjudication involve more checks and balances in the U.K. than in Hong Kong.

Basic Political Ideologies

A political **ideology** is the systematic and integrated body of constructs (complex ideas), theories, and aims that constitute a sociopolitical program. Most modern societies are **pluralistic** from a political point of view; that is, different ideologies coexist within the society because there is no official ideology accepted by everyone. Pluralism is an outgrowth of the fact that groups within countries often differ significantly from each other in language (for example, the former Yugoslavia, with its many different languages and alphabets), ethnic background (for example, South Africa), or religion (for example, Northern Ireland). As noted in Chapter 2, these and other cultural dimensions strongly influence the political system.

The ultimate test of any political system is its ability to hold a society together despite pressures from different ideologies tending to split it apart. The more widely different and strongly held the articulated ideas are, the more difficult it is to

Map 3.2
Europe on the Eve of World War I
The German, Russian, Ottoman, and Austro-Hungarian empires dominate the continent.

Source: From *The Boston Globe Magazine,* 2/21/93. Reprinted courtesy of The Boston Globe.

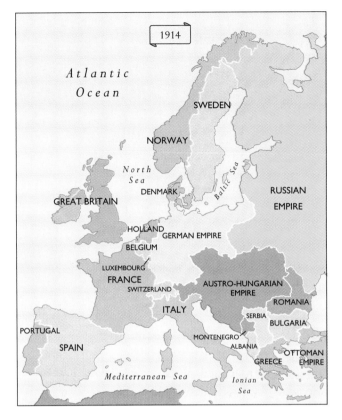

Ethnic differences are tearing apart many countries in Eastern Europe and the former Soviet Union.

aggregate them and formulate policies that everyone can accept. Ideologies already broke apart many countries in the 1990s, including the former Yugoslavia, the former Czechoslovakia, and the former Soviet Union.

However, ideologies, language, religion, and ethnic background play an important role in bringing countries together. In one example involving violence, Serbs in the former Yugoslavia initiated conflict in that region and brought together Serbs from different regions of Yugoslavia in an attempt to form a new country, a "Greater Serbia." Also, one reason China wants Hong Kong back is because of ethnic Chinese ties. In fact, the U.S. government refers to Mainland China, Taiwan, Hong Kong, and Singapore as the Chinese Economic Area.

An example of how such pressures affect national boundaries over time can be seen in Maps 3.2 through 3.5. The Austro-Hungarian Empire (see Map 3.2) was broken up (somewhat arbitrarily) after World War I, into Austria, Czechoslovakia, Hungary, Romania, and Yugoslavia (Map 3.3). With the advent of communist rule after World War II, countries often were formed from different ethnic groups held together by totalitarian rule rather than by any particular logic. Yugoslavia, for example, comprised peoples that were ethnically and religiously very different from each other (Roman Catholic Croats, Greek Orthodox Serbs, and Muslim Bosnians). Further, the Croats and Serbs were on opposite sides during World War II, and Croats were accused of murdering thousands of Serbs. (Some have termed the bloodshed by Serbs in recent years "a thousand years of payback" for earlier

Croat atrocities.) As shown in Map 3.5, the recent break-up of the communist bloc resulted in the disintegration of countries due to the loss of totalitarian control and to ethnic and other differences. Understanding historical roots is essential to understanding the political environment.

A Political Spectrum

The two extremes on the political spectrum are democracy and totalitarianism.

Political ideologies are many and varied, so it is difficult to fit them neatly into a continuum that represents degrees of citizen participation in decision making. Figure 3.2 presents a general schematic of the various forms of government. The two extremes in a theoretical sense are democracy and totalitarianism. From these two, various degrees of participation have evolved. Change continues to occur rapidly around the world, and many authoritarian regimes are being replaced by different types of democracies, as can be seen in East Germany's becoming a part of the new Germany, in former Eastern Bloc countries like Poland and the Czech Republic, and in former republics of the Soviet Union. Brazil, which had been ruled by the military since 1964, finally elected a president in 1984, although he died before taking office. Thus the first person to be elected President and to take office was President Collor in 1989.

Democracy

Democratic systems involve wide participation by citizens in the decision-making process.

In representative democracy, majority rule is achieved through periodic elections.

The ideology of pure democracy derives from the ancient Greeks, who believed that citizens should be directly involved in the decision-making process. According to the ideal, *all* citizens should be equal politically and legally, should enjoy widespread freedoms, and should actively participate in the political process. In reality, the complexity of society increases as the population increases, and so full partici-

Figure 3.2
The Political Spectrum
Although democratic and totalitarian governments are extremes, there are variations to each approach. For example, democratic governments range from radical on one side (advocates of political reform) to reactionary (advocates of a return to past conditions). The majority of democratic governments, however, lie somewhere in between.

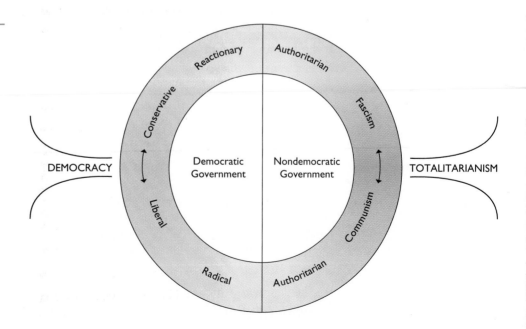

**Map 3.3
Europe after
World War I**
The empires have been broken up. Finland, Ukraine, and the Baltics are freed; Romania is enlarged; Poland, Czechoslovakia, Yugoslavia, and Turkey are created.

Source: From *The Boston Globe Magazine,* 2/21/93. Reprinted courtesy of The Boston Globe.

pation becomes impossible. Consequently, most modern democratic countries actually practice various forms of representative democracy, in which citizens elect representatives to make decisions rather than voting on every specific issue.

Contemporary democratic political systems share the following features:

1. Freedom of opinion, expression, and press, and freedom to organize
2. Elections in which voters decide who is to represent them
3. Limited terms for elected officials
4. An independent and fair court system with high regard for individual rights and property
5. A relatively nonpolitical bureaucracy and defense infrastructure
6. A relative accessibility to the decision-making process[4]

A key element of democracy is freedom in the areas of political rights and civil liberties. Each year, a list of countries ranked according to the degree to which these freedoms exist is published by Freedom House. The major indicators for political rights are

- The degree to which fair and competitive elections occur
- The ability of voters to endow their elected representatives with real power

Factors for evaluating freedom are
- **Political rights**
- **Civil liberties**

Political rights include
- **Fair and competitive elections**
- **Power for elected representatives**
- **Ability to organize**
- **Safeguards on rights of minorities**

**Map 3.4
Europe after
World War II**
Germany is divided. Eastern European nations come under Soviet control.

Source: From *The Boston Globe Magazine,* 2/21/93. Reprinted courtesy of The Boston Globe.

- The ability of people to organize into political parties or other competitive political groupings of their choice
- The existence of safeguards on the rights of minorities

The major indicators for civil liberties are

Civil liberties include
- **Freedom of the press**
- **Equal rights under the law**
- **Personal social freedoms**
- **Freedom from governmental indifference and corruption**

- The existence of freedom of the press
- Equality under the law for all individuals
- The extent of personal social freedoms
- The degree of freedom from extreme governmental indifference or corruption

Figure 3.3 illustrates how countries high in both political rights and civil liberties are classified as "free," countries quite low in both political rights and civil liberties are classified as "not free," and countries in between are classified as "partly free." See Appendix 1 for the list of countries according to a survey by Freedom House, a nonprofit organization in New York that was established in 1941 and that monitors political rights and civil liberties around the world.

The survey identifies the number of countries in each category as well as the percentage of the world's population in each category. In 1994, there were 114

Figure 3.3
Comparative Measures of Freedom
Countries classified as "free" in a political sense have a high degree of political rights and civil liberties. Those classified as "partly free" tend to be average to just below average in political rights and civil liberties. Those classified as "not free" tend to be quite low in both political rights and civil liberties. Examples of countries in each classification:
Free—Australia, Bahamas, Belgium, Canada, Chile, Czech Republic, Estonia, Japan, South Africa, South Korea
Partly Free—Brazil, Burkino Faso, Cambodia, Malaysia, Mexico
Not Free—Algeria, China, Egypt, Ethiopia, Iraq, Kenya, North Korea, Nigeria, Saudi Arabia

Source: Original art based on Freedom House survey. Adrian Karatnycky, *Freedom in the World* (New York: Freedom House, 1995).

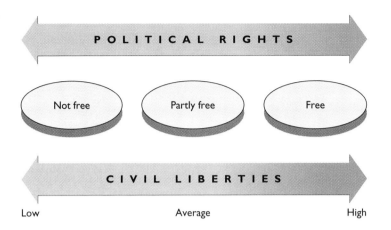

countries that could be classified as democracies, double the number of countries that were called democracies in the early 1970s. What some call the "third wave" of democratization started in the early 1970s and is still under way.[5] However, these democratic countries are considered a mixture of "free" and "partly free" countries. In fact, 37 of the democratic countries were considered "partly free" in 1995.[6]

The following identifies the percentage of the total population living in "free," "partly free," and "not free" conditions in 1981, 1990, and 1995.[7]

	1981	1990	1995
Free	35.9%	21.6%	42.5%
Partly Free	38.9%	21.6%	39.3%
Not Free	20.0%	40.0%	40.0%

The problem is that many of the democracies that have emerged since the early 1970s are fragile and are confronted by challenges to stability and cohesiveness. These stem from internal division, corruption, militaries and oligarchies (ruling power in the hands of a few), and destabilization from abroad. Although there is a certain euphoria in the number of democracies that have surfaced, there is still concern over whether or not the democracies will continue on the path to freedom in political rights and civil liberties.

Although pure democracy does not exist in modern countries, various forms of representative government exist in which citizens vote for individuals to represent them and to make collective decisions. Voting eligibility may be based on gender, religious affiliation, the attainment of a certain minimum age, or racial classifications. In South Africa, for example, the policy of apartheid resulted in only 12.6 percent of the population eligible to vote. In April 1994, after the fall of apartheid and the rise of new labor parties, a coalition government was elected with whites and blacks ruling together. The interim constitution guarantees "equality between men and women and people of all races, thus opening up the vote to all."[8] It is interesting to note that Freedom House now classifies South Africa as "free" and

**Map 3.5
Europe after
Communism**
Germany reunites, and the
Soviet Union, Yugoslavia,
and Czechoslovakia break
up, creating twenty-two
countries.

Source: From *The Boston Globe
Magazine,* 2/21/93. Reprinted
courtesy of The Boston Globe.

improving its political rights and civil liberties, an improvement over its previous
position as "partly free." In some democracies, such as the United States, voting is
optional; in others, such as Australia and Belgium, it is mandatory.

One form of democracy is **parliamentary government,** an excellent example
of which is found in the United Kingdom. The United Kingdom is divided into geographical districts, and a representative is elected to represent each district in the
House of Commons. General elections must be held at least every five years. After a
general election, the monarch asks the leader of the party that has the majority of
seats in the House of Commons to form a government. The party with the second-
largest number of seats becomes the opposition. Other parties can align with either
the majority party or the opposition party. The members of each party select the
person who leads that party. The leader of the majority party becomes the prime
minister and selects a cabinet.

Although the people vote for their representatives in the House of Commons,
also known as the Members of Parliament, the MPs select their own leader, who
becomes the Prime Minister. In November 1990, the conservative party in the
U.K., with Margaret Thatcher as Prime Minister, was undergoing turmoil, so the
conservative MPs held an election to select their leader, and Thatcher did not have
enough votes to continue. On the second ballot, John Major was elected as Prime

**In a parliamentary system,
the majority party forms the
government.**

Minister. In April 1992, a general election was held, and the conservatives won a majority of the seats in the Parliament, so Major continued on as Prime Minister. He was not directly elected by the people to be Prime Minister, but he did have to win reelection as an MP in his own district.[9]

The French form of parliamentary government involves the direct election of a president who is in power for seven years and selects a premier and, upon the recommendation of the premier, a Council of Ministers. A parliament composed of a National Assembly elected by the people and a Senate selected by the National Assembly is responsible for legislation. Despite having a parliament, France has a system of government more like that of the United States than that of the United Kingdom. For example, like the U.S. system, the French system separates the executive and legislative branches.

To illustrate the French process, the French elections for President were held on April 23 and May 7, 1995. Because there were so many candidates, a president was not elected on the first ballot. Lionel Jospin won 23 percent of the vote, Jacques Chirac won 21 percent of the vote, and the rest of the votes were split among several other candidates. On the second ballot, however, only Jospin and Chirac were on the ballot—the two highest vote-getters on the first ballot—and Chirac won the presidency with 53 percent of the vote.[10]

In most democratic countries, multiple political parties may participate in the election process. Many democracies have only a few dominant parties, so it usually is not difficult for them to form a government. The exceptions to this are Italy and Israel, in which there are so many political parties that the government in power is usually a minority government formed from a coalition of several minority parties. In these countries, whenever a vote of no confidence is taken, a new coalition must be formed before a new government can be formed. In 1996, the Israelis changed their election procedures and went to a direct vote of the prime minister for the first time, rather than have the prime minister automatically be the head of the party that can make a coalition work. In a run-off election, Benjamin Netanyahu was elected prime minister over Shimon Peres in the slimmest of margins, but he still won a majority of the votes. This allowed him to rule without having to form tricky coalitions with smaller, but even more radical parties.[11]

The United States is an example of a country that elects its president by a plurality vote of the electoral college instead of a majority vote. In 1984, Ronald Reagan was elected president with 59.2 percent of the popular vote, in 1988 George Bush was elected with 53.9 percent of the vote, but in 1992, Bill Clinton was elected with only 43 percent of the vote. In that election, Ross Perot won 18.9 percent of the vote as an independent, making it virtually impossible for either Clinton or Bush to win a majority of votes. If the system were the same as that in France, a run-off election between Clinton and Bush would have had to be held within a few weeks of the first ballot. That would have been interesting.

In some democracies, a single dominant party controls political power, for example, in Mexico. Mexico has been ruled by one political party, the Institutional

France has a presidential form of government with a separately elected parliament.

In a coalition parliamentary government, minority parties form a coalition to gain majority control and the power to form the government.

Mexico has a single-dominant-party democracy.

Revolutionary Party (PRI), since it acquired its independence from Spain. Its members are Mexico's elite, who are the most educated and the most experienced in government. The PRI does not have a particularly ideological thrust; it is mainly interested in keeping the country together. In 1994, however, that coalition faced severe difficulties as the hand-picked president was assassinated during campaigns, and another leader of the PRI was also assassinated. In the murder conspiracy, the brother of the sitting President was implicated, throwing the PRI into even more turmoil. And even though Mexico is considered to be a democracy, it is ranked only as "partly free" due to the relative power of the PRI and the concern over the lack of political freedom, and, to a lesser extent, the abuse of civil liberties. Ernesto Zedillo of the PRI was elected president in 1995, and he has moved ahead with electoral reforms to try to eliminate some of the abuses of the past, especially at the state and local levels. However, he has to deal with decades of graft and corruption, so change will not come easily.

Hong Kong is a quasi-democracy that is classified as a partly free, related territory.

Hong Kong is an interesting example of a quasi-democracy. Prior to the takeover by China, Freedom House classified Hong Kong as a partly free, related territory rather than as a free country. The British Parliament had served as the democratic check against any governor, who was selected by the Queen. However, the Chinese residents of Hong Kong had little real democratic power because although freedom of expression was guaranteed, freedom to select the government did not exist. Hong Kong's status should slip in future Freedom House surveys, because the Chinese government has made it very clear that freedom of expression in Hong Kong will be curtailed after July 1, 1997, and democratic institutions put into place by former Governor Patton will not be allowed to continue.

Democracies differ not only in the amount of citizen participation in decision making but also in the degree of centralized control. Canada, for example, gives significant political power to the provinces at the expense of its federal government. Thus a major difficulty in negotiating the Canada-U.S. Free Trade Agreement (FTA) was that many provinces had their own trade barriers that had to be considered. The provincial power and concern over lack of safeguards for French-speaking Canadians were two factors leading to the 1995 vote in Canada on whether or not to allow citizens of the province of Quebec to leave Canada and form their own country. Although the unity side won the election by 50.6 percent to 49.9 percent (only 53,498 votes), it was clear that Canadians are deeply concerned over the nature of their federal system and the role of the French-speaking province of Quebec.[12] The United States, in contrast, has always considered states' rights important as a counterweight to encroaching intervention and control by the central government, yet it has a stronger federal government than Canada does. Companies may have difficulty determining how to act in decentralized democratic systems because they face many sometimes conflicting laws. For example, because of different state tax systems in the United States, foreign companies need to locate their U.S. headquarters carefully. The states even differ in their approach to taxing income from different states. In contrast, the political and legal systems of France and Japan are more highly centralized. Companies consequently find it easier to deal with those countries' systems, since there is less variation from one part of the country to another.

Democracy is being radically affected by technology through the Internet. The essence of politics is communication, and the Internet has made communicating that much easier and cheaper. Government documents that used to be available only through hard copy or CD-ROM are now available on the Internet. Lobbying groups can easily set up distribution lists for sending out information quickly and cheaply. Elected representatives can now communicate faster and more cheaply with their constituents. President Clinton averaged 1,000–2,000 e-mail messages daily in 1995, making him the world's most e-mailed person. He relies on e-mail and other messages from external constituents as part of the interest articulation and interest aggregation process described in Fig. 3.1, averaging a total of 20,000 daily, whereas his predecessor, President Bush, only received on average 8,000 messages daily.[13] The information flow to the President is increasing at a rapid rate, and electronic mail is an important component of that flow. Not only are companies using the Internet to get their message across to potential investors and customers, but so are politicians and lobbyists. The Internet will not replace elected representatives, because democracy still needs specialists who can interpret and compromise, but the Internet makes it easier to find the information on which to base an informed decision, and it allows Congress to keep more in touch with constituents.

Totalitarianism

Democracy is at one end of the political spectrum, and totalitarianism is at the other. As noted in Fig. 3.2, totalitarianism takes several forms, including authoritarianism, communism, and fascism. Mussolini defined the fascist side of authoritarianism as

In a totalitarian system, decision making is restricted to a few individuals.

follows: "The Fascist conception of the state is all-embracing; outside of it no human or spiritual value may exist, much less have any value. Thus understood Fascism is totalitarian and the Fascist State, as a synthesis and a unit which includes all values, interprets, develops and lends additional power to the whole life of a people."[14] In a **totalitarian state,** a single party, individual, or group of individuals monopolizes political power and neither recognizes nor permits opposition. Only a few individuals participate in decision making. One famous construct of totalitarianism contains the following six interrelated and interdependent components or syndromes: "an ideology, a single party typically led by one man, a terroristic police, a communication monopoly, a weapons monopoly, and a centrally directed economy."[15] In Fig. 3.3, totalitarian regimes are in the "partly free" and "not free" categories.

Theocratic totalitarianism is the form prevalent in Muslim countries. With secular totalitarianism, control is often enforced through military power.

Totalitarian governments typically take one of two forms: theocratic or secular. In **theocratic totalitarianism,** religious leaders are also the political leaders. This form is best exemplified in Middle Eastern Islamic countries such as Iran. In **secular totalitarianism,** the government often imposes order through military power and is based on worldly rather than religious concepts. Examples of this form are found in Cambodia and Iraq.

Looking at totalitarianism slightly differently, Fig. 3.2 defines totalitarianism as being authoritarian, fascist, or communist. Examples of fascist totalitarianism in the past include Germany, Hungary, Romania, Portugal, and Spain. Examples of Communism include China, Cuba, Vietnam, and the former Soviet Union. Examples of authoritarian totalitarianism include Chile under Pinochet, and South Africa prior to the end of apartheid and the initiation of Black rule. Authoritarianism differs from Communism, fascism, or Islamic fundamentalism in that the former simply desires to rule people, whereas the latter desires to control people's minds and souls, to convert them to their own faith.[16]

Communism is a form of secular totalitarianism. Under communism, the political and economic systems are virtually inseparable. According to Karl Marx, the nineteenth-century German philosopher and political economist who founded world communism, economic forces determine the course taken by a society. He predicted that the capitalist societies eventually would be overcome by two types of revolution—political and social. The political revolution would precede and ignite the social revolution, which would be a long-term transformation based largely on eliminating economic inequities. This social revolution would be guided by what Marx called a dictatorship of the proletariat, that is, the working class. In theory, the proletariat dictatorship would remain in power only long enough to smooth the transition to communism. The government would be responsible for organizing society into groups in order to obtain as much input as possible for the decision-making process. Then, as the social revolution neared completion, the dictatorship would disappear and full communism would take its place.

Even casual observation reveals that real-world communism has differed markedly from theoretical communism. Marx's concept of democratic centralism gave way to totalitarian or autocratic centralism, with no general participation in decision making, especially from those with opposing viewpoints. In recent years communism has been discredited in most parts of the world. The Eastern European countries and the former Soviet Union have moved away from communism to various degrees. And, as communism moves toward democracy, the link between economics and politics in communist countries has been weakened, making "free" communist countries such as Estonia, Latvia, and Lithuania possible. China, North Korea, and Vietnam, however, are still communist countries with strong centralized authoritarian control over the political process.

Totalitarian regimes fit primarily in the "not free" category in Fig. 3.3. Freedom House notes that 90 percent of the "not free" countries share one or more of the following characteristics:

1. They have a majority Muslim population and frequently confront the pressures of fundamentalist Islam;
2. they are multi-ethnic societies in which power is not held by a dominant ethnic group, (one that represents more than two-thirds of the population);
3. they are neo-Communist or post-Communist transitional societies.[17]

> Communism is a form of secular totalitarianism that relates political and economic systems.

In fact, it is not uncommon to find at least two of the characteristics present in "not free" countries. For example, it is common for politicians in formerly totalitarian, including former Communist, countries to appeal to ethnic, religious, and racial differences to gain votes. This is very divisive and runs the risk of moving back to totalitarianism. Rwanda and Somalia are other examples of "not free" countries torn apart by ethnic strife.

Although some would argue that Islamic fundamentalism is a growing force for totalitarianism, there is no evidence that a single, unified fundamentalist movement will ever take place. Some of the countries where Islamic fundamentalism is growing, such as Algeria and maybe Saudi Arabia, are "not free" for other reasons. Islamic fundamentalism is trying to replace a more secular totalitarianism, but is not having great success on a broad scale. The Islamic movement has turned out to be different movements, often sowing seeds of conflict within nations, in addition to across nations. As noted by one expert, "In many cases, tensions between Islamists are greater than the conflict between them and the government they oppose.[18]

The Impact of the Political System on Management Decisions

Every political system struggles with the balance between decentralized decision making by individuals and centralized regulation and control of decisions by governments. Even democratic governments are faced with this dichotomy, but it is creating great conflict in the former totalitarian states of Eastern Europe and the former Soviet Union as their political systems evolve toward democracy and their economic systems toward free-market economies.

There is a dichotomy between governmental control and consumer control of the political system and the economy.

Managers must deal with varying degrees of governmental intervention and, as was brought out in the Hong Kong case, varying degrees of political stability. To do so, they must understand the critical functions that a democratic government performs in the economy, for example:

Managers need to understand the critical functions that a government performs in the economy.

1. Protect the liberty of its citizens
2. Promote the common welfare of its citizens
3. Provide for public goods such as national defense and transportation and communications systems
4. Handle market defects such as entry barriers and insufficient consumer knowledge and power
5. Deal with spillover effects and externalities[19]

One type of public good whose development currently is under debate in many industrial countries is an information highway—a mechanism for the rapid, widespread transmittal of electronic data. Market defects are barriers to the efficient and effective running of a market economy. They interfere with the supply and demand of products and with the ability of consumers to make rational choices. Examples of spillover effects are the many developments and applications that have commercial purposes the private sector can exploit. An example of a spillover effect is the U.S. Air Force's Global Positioning System, which is composed of the linkage of personal computers with 24 satellites equally divided among six orbits. The satellites emit a radio signal that can be used to determine the location of the receiver within 20 to 300 yards of the exact position. The system is now available for civilian uses such as air-traffic control, wilderness search and rescue, car dashboard navigation systems, and truck-fleet management.[20] Externalities refer to by-products of the manufacturing process, such as pollution. Some governments largely ignore polluting externalities in the name of economic development, whereas others control pollution very carefully.

The political process affects international business through regulation of cross-border transactions.

The political process also affects international business through laws that regulate business activity at both the domestic and international levels. Governments may deal with international transactions on a unilateral basis or through treaties and conventions. An MNE must be concerned with the laws in its home country that regulate cross-border transactions and must understand legal requirements in each country in which it operates.

Various U.S. government agencies deal with international issues.

In addition to understanding governmental functions, managers also must realize that governmental action is not always consistent. In the United States, for example, significant conflict exists within government regarding how and to what extent international business activities should be regulated. No specific government agency deals with international issues, so conflicting policies can be expected. For example, at least three different U.S. government agencies share responsibility for regulating nonagricultural exports: the State Department, the Department of Defense, and the Department of Commerce. State is responsible for the overall political relationships between the United States and other countries, Defense is responsible for national defense, and Commerce is responsible for facilitating commercial—including export—activities. These agencies also have three different viewpoints on how to regulate exports. For example, the Clinton administration announced in 1993 that it intended to remove most restrictions on the sale of high-technology products—especially computers—that have possible defense uses. Commerce and State had always favored liberalizing such restrictions, whereas Defense had always supported them.[21]

Formulating and Implementing Political Strategies

Formulating political strategies often is more complicated than formulating competitive marketplace strategies. Nonmarket issues attract different participants than

Formulating political strategies is complicated by the range of participants in the decision-making process, differences in logic, and institutional power.

do market issues. In addition, important components of political strategies are implemented in public view; such exposure can constrain the actions of companies. Further, the logic of collective and political action is different from that of market action. Unlike market issues, which are resolved by voluntary agreements, political issues are resolved by institutions that have the power to compel action, regulate activities, and structure the conditions under which market participants operate.[22]

Establishing a political strategy involves identifying and defining the political situation, important institutions, and key individuals.

Political action always is a sensitive area. However, there are certain steps that a company must follow if it wants to establish an appropriate political strategy:

1. Identify the issue. What is the specific issue facing a firm—protectionism, environmental standards, worker rights?
2. Define the nature of the politics of the issue.
3. Assess the potential political action of other companies and of special interest groups. Who are the parties that are affected and able to generate political pressure? What are their strategies likely to be?
4. Identify important institutions and key individuals—legislatures, regulatory agencies, courts, important personalities.
5. Formulate strategies. What are the key objectives, the major alternatives, and the likely effectiveness of alternative strategies?
6. Determine the impact of implementation. What will be the public relations fallout in the home and host countries if the action taken is unpopular?
7. Select the most appropriate strategy and implement.[23]

Lobbyists educate and persuade decision makers.

Implementing a strategy involves marshaling whatever resources are necessary to accomplish the company's political objectives. In the United States, lobbyists are hired by a company, whether domestic or foreign, to educate and persuade decision makers about the merits of the company's position. However, there has been heavy criticism of the practice of hiring lobbyists who have departed recently from the government agency that is likely to take action against the company. On the other hand, lobbyists also perform an important role in communicating ideas to decision makers. In a representative democracy, lobbyists represent constituencies and perform the important role of aggregating ideas and communicating them to decision makers. Without the freedom of expression, democracy could not exist. As the ethical dimensions of government-business relationships have gained prominence even in relatively totalitarian countries, companies have greater reason to examine carefully their policy formulation and implementation strategies.

Foreign companies often enlist the support of consumers to combat government restrictions on sales.

A company also can attempt to influence governmental action from the bottom up by using a grass-roots campaign or by building coalitions of different groups that share the company's interests. For example, to fight U.S. trade protectionism in the form of tariffs or quotas on imported automobiles, foreign automobile manufacturers might try to convince consumers that, as a result of such actions, they would be worse off because of higher prices or reduced availability.

The laws of democratic countries often are more flexible than those of totalitarian countries.

Part of the problem with establishing a political strategy is that democracies deal with companies differently than do totalitarian regimes. In general, democracies can be influenced through lobbying. However, companies sometimes abuse their power by engaging in bribery and other illicit activities. In a totalitarian regime, companies usually operate in a more stable environment. However, when such a regime is overthrown, the changes for business tend to be larger and more rapid than change typically is within a democracy. For example, when the Soviet Union broke up, companies that had entered into contracts with the former central government found that these contracts were not binding on the governments of the individual republics.

The Legal Environment

Closely related to the political system, the legal system is another dimension of the external environment that influences business. Managers must be aware of the legal systems in the countries in which they operate, the nature of the legal profession, both domestic and international, and the legal relationships that exist between countries. Both totalitarian and democratic countries have legal systems, but the independence of the law from political control may differ markedly from one to the other. In addition, some totalitarian systems, notably that of China, are not well equipped to deal with market economies in a legal sense, primarily because its legal system does not provide for issues that arise in such an economic environment.

Kinds of Legal Systems

A common law system is based on tradition, precedent, custom and usage, and interpretation by courts.

Legal systems usually fall into one of three categories: common law, civil law, and theocratic law. The United States and the United Kingdom are examples of countries with a **common law system.** Common law is based on tradition, precedent, and custom and usage, and the courts fulfill an important role in interpreting the law according to those characteristics. Because the United Kingdom originated common law in the modern setting, its former and current colonies, such as Hong Kong, also have common law systems.

A civil law system is based on a very detailed set of laws organized into a code.

The **civil law system,** also called a **codified legal system,** is based on a very detailed set of laws that are organized into a code. This code is the foundation for doing business. Over seventy countries, including Germany, France, and Japan operate on a civil law basis.

The two legal systems differ primarily in that common law is based on the courts' interpretations of events, whereas civil law is based on how the law is applied to the facts. An example of an area in which the two systems differ in practice is contracts. In a common law country, contracts tend to be very detailed, with all contingencies spelled out. In a civil law country, contracts tend to be shorter and less specific because many of the issues that a common law contract would cover already are included in the civil code. Also civil law tends to be less adversarial than common law, since judges rely on detailed legal codes rather than on precedent. This is one reason why British and U.S. law firms encounter so much resistance when they enter civil law countries. They are used to the competitive, adversarial approach that the common law system engenders, an approach that tends to shake up the more orderly systems.

The third type of legal system is the **theocratic law system,** which is based on religious precepts. The best example of this system is the Islamic one, which is found in Muslim countries. Islamic law, known as *Shair'a,* is based on the following sources:

- The Koran, the sacred text
- The Sunnah, or decisions and sayings of the Prophet Muhammad
- The writings of Islamic scholars, who derive rules by analogy from the principles established in the Koran and the Sunnah
- The consensus of Muslim countries' legal communities[24]

Since the tenth century A.D., Islamic law has been frozen; that is, it cannot be changed, modified, or extended, even though conditions have changed significantly. Islamic law is a moral rather than a commercial law and was intended to govern all aspects of life. Many Muslim countries have legal systems that are a unique blend of the Islamic law system and a common or civil law system derived from previous colonial ties.

An example of how Islamic law influences business can be found in banking. According to Islamic law, banks cannot charge interest or benefit from interest, which is viewed as usury, and investments in commodities such as alcohol or tobacco are forbidden.[25] There are approximately a hundred banks worldwide that offer Islamic banking, including the multinationals Citibank and Barclays. The Malaysian government, in an attempt to bring more Muslim Malays into the economic system, announced in 1993 that all commercial banks should offer Islamic banking services. However, it is sometimes difficult to determine just what Islamic banking involves. There is no uniform Islamic-correct formula to structure leasing and other products to take into account issues such as inflation, the rising costs of imported equipment, and exchange rate fluctuations.[26] Malaysia, though, is considered to be at the forefront of Islamic banking, with more than 30 institutions in Malaysia offering Islamic banking services by late 1995.[27]

More conservative Muslim countries such as Saudi Arabia also interpreted the *Shair'a* to mean that equity investments were not permitted. This occurred presumably because of the fear that many companies had involvement with non-Islamic practices, such as alcohol commerce and paying or receiving interest. Not all Islamic countries maintained the same position as Saudi Arabia. For example,

Malaysia has a much more relaxed interpretation of the *Shair'a,* and the Islamic banking services mentioned above include investment banking as well. In 1994, however, the Islamic jurisprudence academy in Saudi Arabia issued a decree that permitted equity investment under certain parameters. These investments can take place in screened mutual funds involving companies that avoid unIslamic activities. In addition, the decree requires investors to subtract from dividends any interest earned by the company from money on deposit. This interest is then donated to charities. As a result, a number of Islamic investment funds have been established, including fund initiated by Western banks.[28] Because of Islamic law's prohibitions against interest, those Muslims who save in these banks are paid a share of the profits made by the bank that uses the funds. The profit share is roughly the same as the current interest rate.[29]

Regardless of the legal system, the practice of law can be divided into criminal and civil. Although business practices can be found to violate criminal law, business issues more commonly are considered in the context of civil law. A study of civil law cases in the United States found that most involved small claims, divorces, and wills; only 14 percent involved contracts and 10 percent involved torts. Torts are wrongful acts; many tort cases are product-liability ones, in which an injured person tries to recover money for damages that are economic (such as medical expenses and lost wages) or noneconomic (such as pain and suffering). The number of suits involving torts has increased dramatically in the United States for a variety of reasons. Almost unique characteristics of the U.S. legal system are that lawyers take contingency fees (fees determined by a percentage of the final judgment if the case is won), groups can file class action lawsuits, pretrial "discovery" requires the submission of volumes of information by both sides, and juries, rather than judges, decide cases and set damages.[30] The cost of torts in the United States has reached 2.4 percent of GNP, compared with between 0.4 and 0.8 percent of GNP for most other industrial countries.

Different legal systems provide different safeguards for consumers. For example, it appears that consumers have less access to and assistance from the legal community in Japan than in the United States. The United States has 312 lawyers per 100,000 of population compared with only 101.6 lawyers per 100,000 in Japan. Also, the Japanese legal system differs from the U.S. system in that legal prices are set by the Japanese Federation of Bar Associations, foreign lawyers are prohibited from advising on local law or hiring domestic lawyers to do so, and consumer information about legal services is limited by advertising restrictions. In addition, in Japan consumers are discouraged from filing civil suits because of the high cost of legal services and the long delays in the legal process. A survey of 194 big Japanese manufacturers found that only 24 had ever faced a product-liability suit at home and, of those, only 7 had lost. Further, one auto company had been hit with 250 product-liability suits a year in the United States and only 2 in Japan.[31] Thus it appears that in Japan consumers have less legal protection and corporations have fewer legal problems than is the case in the United States.

Of U.S. civil law cases,
- **One quarter involve torts and contracts**
- **Three quarters involve small claims, divorces, or wills**

The United States has the most lawyers of any country in the world and is one of the highest in the number of lawyers per capita.

The Legal Profession

Recently, increased discussion has focused on the expanding number of lawyers and their impact on the world economy. MNEs must use lawyers for a variety of services, such as negotiating contracts and protecting intellectual property. Lawyers and their firms vary among countries in terms of how they practice law and service clients.

Most legal firms are small.

Large firms have surfaced in response to worldwide merger and acquisition activity.

Law firms that service international clients have changed over the years. In general, most law firms are quite small. In the United Kingdom and the United States, for example, 60 percent of lawyers are in firms of five persons or fewer.[32] Although the business expansion in the 1960s and 1970s, especially in the area of mergers and acquisitions, led to larger law firms, the 1980s slowdown in the world's economy resulted in a subsequent shrinking in firm size. There are still large firms servicing multinational clients, but many MNEs, concerned about upward-spiraling legal fees, have established their own in-house legal staffs and have begun to rely on outside firms primarily for specialized work. However, smaller companies involved in international business still rely on outside legal counsel for help with a wide variety of issues, such as agent/distributor relationships and the protection of intellectual property.

Foreign firms are barred from practicing law in some countries.

Just as MNEs have invested abroad to take advantage of expanding business opportunities, law firms have expanded abroad to service their clients. Laws vary from country to country, and legal staffs need to understand local practices. There definitely has been an expansion of legal services across national boundaries, even though law firms have had to overcome significant barriers as they have expanded abroad. Those barriers include restrictions on foreign firms from hiring local lawyers, from forming partnerships with local law firms, or even from entering the country to practice law.

Impact of laws on business:
• National laws affect all local business activities.
• National laws affect cross-border activities.
• International treaties and conventions govern cross-border transactions.

Key legal issues in international business:
• Trade and investment regulation
• Intellectual property protection
• Financial flows regulation
• Taxation
• Reporting requirements
• Ownership regulation
• Contractual relationships
• International treaties
• Dispute resolution

Legal Issues in International Business

National laws affect how critical elements of the management process are performed. They can relate to business within the country or business among countries. Some national laws on local business activity influence both domestic and foreign companies, for example, in the areas of health and safety standards, employment practices, antitrust prohibitions, contractual relationships, environmental practices, and patents and trademarks. Laws also exist that govern cross-border activities, such as the investment of capital, the repatriation of earnings, and customs duties on imports. Business activity also is governed by international laws, such as treaties governing the cross-border transfer of hazardous waste.

Several subsequent chapters discuss legal issues in international business, for example, different laws for the regulation of trade and investments, taxes, intellectual-property protection, regulation of financial flows and of ownership, reporting requirements, contractual relationships, extraterritoriality, international treaties, and dispute resolution.

Ethical dilemmas involve a balancing of means and ends. *Means* refers to the actions that are taken, which may be right or wrong; *ends* refers to the results of the actions, which may also be right or wrong. Ethics teaches that "people have a responsibility to do what is right and to avoid doing what is wrong."[33] Questions of right and wrong refer to intentions, which are a function of the various cultural issues that were discussed in Chapter 2. Some people argue that cultural relativism, or the belief that behavior has meaning only in its specific cultural or ethical context, implies that no specific method exists for deciding whether behavior is appropriate. However, we contend that individuals must seek justification for their behavior, and that justification is a function of cultural values (many of which are universal), legal principles, and economic practices.

ETHICAL DILEMMAS & SOCIAL RESPONSIBILITY

Some people also argue that the legal justification for ethical behavior is the only important one. By this standard, a person or company can do anything that is not illegal. However, there are five reasons why the legal argument is insufficient:

1. The law is not appropriate for regulating all business activity because not everything that is unethical is illegal. This would be true of many dimensions of interpersonal behavior, for example.
2. The law is slow to develop in emerging areas of concern. Laws take time to be legislated and tested in courts. Further, they cannot anticipate all future ethical dilemmas; basically they are a reaction to issues that have already surfaced. Countries with civil law systems rely on specificity in the law, and there may not be enough laws actually passed that deal with ethical issues.
3. The law often is based on moral concepts that are not precisely defined and that cannot be separated from legal concepts. Thus moral concepts must be considered along with legal ones.
4. The law is often in need of testing by the courts. This is especially true of case law, in which the courts establish precedent.
5. The law is not very efficient. A reliance on legal rulings on every area of ethical behavior would not be in anyone's best interests.[34]

In spite of the pitfalls of using the law as the major basis for deciding ethical disputes, there also are good reasons for at least complying with it:

1. The law embodies many of a country's moral beliefs and is thus an adequate guide for proper conduct.
2. The law provides a clearly defined set of rules. Following those rules at least establishes a good precedent. Some are afraid to go beyond the law because of the potential legal liability that could result if they did.

3. The law contains enforceable rules that all must follow; everyone is on an equal footing. Thus, everyone working for a company established in the United States must comply with the Foreign Corrupt Practices Act, which prohibits bribery of foreign governmental officials for business benefit. As long as everyone complies with the law, no one will have an edge due to bribery. Still, laws are subject to interpretation and often contain loopholes.

4. The law represents a consensus derived from significant experience and deliberation. It should reflect careful and wide-ranging discussions.[35]

The problem for companies that use a legal basis for ethical behavior is that laws vary among countries. For example, a major area of contention between industrial and developing countries during the GATT Uruguay Round was the protection of intellectual property, such as computer software. The industrial countries, which have strong laws concerning intellectual-property rights, argued that developing countries need to strengthen such laws and their enforcement. U.S. software manufacturers have noted that in some Asian countries it is possible to buy a heavily discounted pirated version of new software in one store and then go next door and purchase a photocopy of the documentation for the software. Using a legal basis for ethical behavior would mean that such purchases are ethical because they occur in countries that either do not have laws on intellectual-property rights or do not enforce the laws. Although the Agreement on Trade-Related Aspects of Intellectual Property Rights (TRIPs) of the World Trade Organization, which came about as a result of the Uruguay Round of GATT, provides for better protection of intellectual property, it is up to the member countries to implement the provisions, and that is proceeding at a very slow pace in those countries that are the traditional violators of intellectual property.

One could argue that the moral values that cross cultures will be embodied in legal systems, but, as the software example demonstrates, that is too simplistic. Not all moral values are common to every culture. In addition, strong home-country governments may try to extend their legal and ethical practices to the foreign subsidiaries of domestically headquartered companies—an action known as **extraterritoriality.** For example, a subsidiary of a U.S. company operating in China might be forced to follow some U.S. laws, even though China has no comparable laws and other companies operating there are not subject to the U.S. laws. In some cases, such as with health and safety standards, extraterritoriality should not cause problems. In other cases, such as with restrictions on trade with enemies of the United States, extraterritoriality may cause tension between the foreign subsidiary and the host-country government.

As noted, the law provides a clearly defined set of rules, which companies often follow strictly because of concerns about potential legal liability. However, a company may seek a loophole in order to accomplish some important objective. Evaluating potential liability and legality of actions varies between countries with civil law systems and those with common law ones. Civil law countries tend to have a large body of laws that specify the legality of various behaviors; common law countries tend to rely more on cases and precedents than on statutory regulations. A company must pay attention to laws to ensure the minimum level of compliance in each country in which it operates. When faced with conflicting laws, management must decide which applies. The forces of national sovereignty may encourage managers to follow the adage "When in Rome, do as the Romans do."

Evolution of Legal and Political Strategies in the Internationalization Process

Companies deal with political and legal issues at different levels as they become more international. If a company selects exporting as the mode of entry, management is not as concerned with the political process or with the variety of legal issues as would be the case with a foreign direct investment. There are laws that relate to international trade—both at the export country level (such as with the export of defense-related products to an enemy) as well as the import country level (such as tariffs and quotas on imports). In addition, exporters must worry about laws dealing with distributor relationships and how to settle disputes. The political process can have a direct impact on the company, but home-country management is usually fairly removed from that process. Since it has not committed significant assets to the foreign country, it is not quite as affected by political decisions as would be the case if it had established a foreign investment.

A major exception is for companies that generate a significant percentage of their earnings from exports. In the past two decades, there has been a lot of pressure on the foreign auto industry to reconsider its strategy to completely capture the U.S. market through exports. As a result, many exporters, such as Honda and Toyota, have invested significant assets in the United States as a way of mitigating the impact of tariffs and quotas on their market share, thus helping to preserve U.S. jobs.

As the company penetrates the foreign environment in increasingly more complex ways, such as through foreign direct investment, political and legal issues become more complex as well. As noted in Fig. 1.6, as the company moves out from the center of the diagram and operates in more countries in more complex ways, the dissimilarity of countries becomes more obvious and more important. For example, Japanese engaging in foreign direct investment in the United States become increasingly susceptible to questioning about their lobbying efforts, and they have to worry about another set of laws, such as equal employment laws, gender discrimination, OSHA, etc. Moreover, their U.S. entities are now taxable entities, according to U.S. tax laws.

From a political point of view, foreign investors need to be concerned about the impact of their investment on the local environment and have to figure out how to work with local and country-level government officials and agencies. In more traditional societies where democracy is not firmly entrenched, they need to be more aware of the importance of contacts and influence and the possibility that they will be asked to behave in ways inconsistent with the way they behave in their own political and legal context or in ways that might even be illegal.

Thus, as the degree of internationalization increases, the nature, complexity, and breadth of the company's political and legal interactions also increases.

Differences in legal and
political systems drive
companies to adopt
multidomestic strategies.

COUNTERVAILING

F O R C E S

Politics clearly affects corporate strategies through
national policies and governmental influence on cross-
border transactions. Because of differences in national
laws, legal practices are multidomestic. Acquiring good legal counsel in the countries in
which a company does business is essential. Global legal firms provide legal assistance for
MNEs doing business in different parts of the world, but their value is in having good
lawyers in different countries rather than a few lawyers that understand all laws in all
countries.

Some legal issues, however, are cross-border in nature. A good example is protecting
intellectual property. Although each country has its own intellectual-property laws, most
countries are part of cross-national treaties and conventions that allow firms to acquire
widespread protection for intellectual property. Although this issue will be discussed in
more detail in Chapter 11, it is important to note that there are international agreements
on the protection of intellectual property, such as the Paris Convention and the TRIPs
agreement of the World Trade Organization, and there are regional agreements such
as those that are part of the European Union and the North American Free Trade
Agreement (the EU and NAFTA will be discussed in more depth in Chapter 7). Thus
companies can establish multidomestic strategies on protecting intellectual property, or
they can use legal experts who are familiar with appropriate cross-national treaties and
conventions to establish global or regional strategies.

Differences in legal and political systems drive companies toward multidomestic or
transnational rather than global strategies. Local differences require managers to make
adjustments in virtually all areas of business—including marketing, finance, and human
resources.

Both political and legal dimensions are at the heart of sovereignty. Smaller countries
are very concerned that they could be dominated politically by larger countries. In many
international trade agreements, such as the European Union and the North American
Free Trade Agreement, smaller countries have attempted to protect their interests
against the larger countries. This has been true, for example, of Denmark within the EU
and of Mexico within NAFTA. In fact, Denmark nearly left the EU because it feared too
many decisions affecting Danish individuals and companies would be made by EU
bureaucrats.

Countries prefer to have their own laws enforced on their own soil. This is problematic
for foreign companies, whose managers and workers might not understand local laws.
Whether or not they have such understanding they usually must use local courts to
resolve local disputes. A country that tries to enforce its laws in another country through
extraterritoriality threatens that other country's national sovereignty. Such action is usually
met with significant resistance.

As a counterforce to sovereignty, treaties and conventions can modify or set aside
national laws. The very purpose of treaties is to subjugate national law to the greater good
of the group of countries that sign a treaty. If no national laws were to be changed, treaties
would not be needed. However, because treaties moderate sovereignty, they are difficult

to implement. For example, U.S. environmentalists have been concerned that NAFTA could result in U.S. environmental legislation being changed in such a way that could harm the environment. Despite these kinds of problems, treaties can be very useful in promoting better interaction between countries and a better operating environment for companies operating internationally.

LOOKING TO THE FUTURE

What will happen to the political situation in the world? Will democracy continue to grow, or will authoritarianism creep back? Winston Churchill once said that democracy is the worst form of government, except for all the others.[37] The next decade will test whether this hypothesis is true. The issue with democracy and totalitarianism involves two facets. The first is whether the 40 or so countries that have become democratic in the past two decades will remain democratic or slip back into totalitarianism. The second is what path the next wave of "not free" and "partly free" countries will take as they develop economically.

Some argue that the movement toward democracy involves preconditions, such as economic development. This thesis will be explored more in Chapter 4 as we discuss economic systems and how they interact with political systems. Most non-oil-producing, high-income or upper-middle-income countries are democratic, whereas most of the remaining non-democracies are poor, non-Western, or both.[38] Others argue that democracy is the product of political leaders with the will and skill to see democratization occur.[39] Some would argue that the move toward democracy in Russia occurred because of the wills of two men: Mikhail Gorbachev and Boris Yeltsin. When Gorbachev went as far as he could, Yeltsin was there for the next steps. After Yeltsin, someone else will hopefully fill the void and take Russia to the next democratic plateau, although there is no guarantee that Russia will continue to democratize and that Yeltsin's replacement and those that support him or her will continue to support the trend to greater democracy. In reality, the movement to democracy may require both preconditions and vision.

Democracy does not necessarily mean stability. In many elections in 1996, such as the one described earlier in the chapter in Israel and in India as well, established leaders were thrown out and new leaders ushered in. The newer democracies are still unstable enough to possibly threaten war. A war between two democracies has not happened in this century, but it could happen as the new democracies try to find their way. In addition, some countries such as Zambia are retreating from experiments in liberal democracy and its freedoms.

There is an alternative to democracy that is being tested in Asia. With the exception of Japan, and to a lesser extent India, most Asian countries are not democracies, and their leaders do not appear to want democracy. Instead, they are attempting to forge a link between strong economic growth and totalitarian political systems. This is clearly the case with China, and to only a slightly lesser extent in Singapore. However, encouraging signs are appearing for those who favor increased democracy, such as the elections in Taiwan that nudged that island nation closer to democracy and farther away from the autocratic policies of the past and from the encroachment of the People's Republic of China. So the key at the present time is to consolidate the gains of democracy, helping the fledgling democracies of Eastern Europe, Africa, and Latin America strengthen their political rights and civil liberties. In some respects, the elimination of strong central controls with the advent of democracy has created problems in terms of ethnic, tribal, religious, and other constituencies and the removal of individual moral constraints, resulting in crime, corruption, and an atmosphere of amoralism.[40] The threat to democracy could come from the return to communism, from the electoral victory of antidemocratic forces (such as Islamic fundamentalism), or from the concentration of power in a leader. The latter seems to be the approach in many of the countries of East Asia. The key, then, is to define democracy in different national contexts.

WEB CONNECTION

Check out our home page for links to various international political science and legal information resources.

Summary

- **To be successful, managers must learn to deal with public institutions (such as the government, government agencies, and government-owned businesses) and nonpublic institutions (such as environmental and other special interest groups) in addition to market forces.**

- **The political process involves inputs from various interest groups, articulation of issues that affect policy formulation, aggregation of those issues into key alternatives, development of policies, and implementation and adjudication of the policies.**

- **Most complex societies are pluralistic; that is, they encompass a variety of ideologies.**

- **The ultimate test of any political system is its ability to hold a society together despite pressures from different ideologies.**

- **In democracies, there is wide participation in the decision-making process; in totalitarian regimes, only a relative few may participate, although some are beginning to allow greater participation in the decision-making process. Totalitarian regimes can be either secular or theocratic.**

- Factors considered in measuring freedom include the degree to which fair and competitive elections occur, the extent to which individual and group freedoms are guaranteed, and the existence of freedom of the press.

- Managers of MNEs must learn to cope with varying degrees of governmental intervention in economic decisions, depending on the countries in which a company is doing business.

- As governments become more democratic, they influence their citizens and institutions by protecting liberty, promoting the common welfare of citizens, providing for public goods, handling market defects, and dealing with spillover effects and externalities.

- The political impact on international business activities is relatively complex because the domestic political process is subject to various influences and managers must deal with different political processes in different countries.

- In formulating political strategies, managers must consider the possible political actions that could affect the company, the different constituencies that might influence those political actions, the political strategies that would be in the best interests of the company, and the costs of implementing those strategies.

- Common law systems are based on tradition, precedent, and custom and usage. Civil law systems are based on a detailed set of laws organized into a code. Theocratic legal systems are based on religious precepts, as exemplified by Islamic law.

- Many law firms have increased their size in order to better service corporate clients in domestic and international mergers and acquisitions.

- There are national laws that govern local business activity of both domestic and foreign firms, national laws that govern cross-border activities, and international laws that govern cross-border activities.

- The legal environment can influence international companies in various ways, for example, by regulating trade and investment and protecting intellectual property.

- Although there is legal justification for some ethical behavior, the law is not an adequate guide for all such behavior. The legality of an action is one element that should be considered, but not the only one.

Case
Bata, Ltd.[41]

In 1996, Bata, Ltd. was struggling to determine its future, both in defining its long-term strategy and in finding a top management team who would move the company into the twenty-first century. And in doing so, it was being deeply effected by the dramatic political changes taking place in Eastern Europe, South Africa, and elsewhere.

As war swept across Europe in 1939, Tom Bata, Sr., was faced with a difficult situation. His father, the ninth generation of a family of Czechoslovakian shoemakers, had built a worldwide shoe network in twenty-eight countries, using machinery and the mass-production technology of the 1920s. On his father's death, Tom Bata, Sr., was left with the responsibility of expanding that empire during a period of great political uncertainty worldwide. Because of the Nazi invasion of Czechoslovakia and the uncertain future engendered by the resulting occupation, Tom Bata, Sr., sought to preserve his father's business by abandoning his Czechoslovakian operations and emigrating to Canada with a hundred of his managers and their families. His Czech operations were subsequently taken over by the communists after World War II.

Since that time, Bata's decision has been ratified through strong growth worldwide. The company is a family-owned business that is the world's largest manufacturer and retailer of footwear. Activities are carried out in over 60 countries on virtually every continent, employing more than 67,000 people worldwide. Bata operates 6,300 company-owned stores worldwide, and has over 100,000 independent retailers and franchisees. Bata owns over 70 manufacturing units worldwide, including shoe manufacturing plants, engineering plants producing molds, quality control laboratories, hosiery factories, and tanneries. Bata produces about 170 million pairs of shoes annually and sells about 270 million pairs worldwide (see Bata's Web page for current information).

It might appear that Bata is a multidomestic company where local managers are free to adjust operating procedures to local environments, within certain parameters. As one outsider noted, "wherever you had a strong Czech, you had a strong company. Where you had a lousy Czech, you had a lousy company." However, Bata's core philosophies and strategies are tightly controlled by Bata himself, who was 82 in 1996. In 1994, Bata hired the company's first non-family chief executive in an attempt to reinvigorate the paternalistic company, but disagreements over the future of the company forced the resignation of the CEO and two of the top members of his management team in October 1995. In announcing his resignation, the CEO stated that he had tried to balance the strong values of the company with the need for change. But he appeared to have overestimated his ability to operate independently of the family shareholders. As one executive stated, "Tom Bata is a charismatic personality who exerts an awful lot of personal authority."

The problem is that the shoe business is changing, and Bata is being affected like any other company. The key to Bata's success has traditionally been a low-cost manufacturing base tied to an extensive distribution network. But Nike and Reebok turned the footwear industry into one that was market-driven, not manufacturing-driven. Several of Bata's retail outlets began losing money, and Bata was forced to close down 20 percent of its retail outlets in 1995 and 1996.

Although Bata has factories and operations of various forms in many countries, it does not own all of those facilities. Where possible, it owns 100 percent of them. The governments of some countries, however, require less-than-majority ownership. In some cases, Bata provides licensing, consulting, and technical assistance to companies in which it has no equity interest.

The company's strategy for serving world markets is instructive. Some MNEs try to lower costs by achieving economies of scale in production, which means they produce as much as possible in the most optimally sized factory and then serve markets worldwide from that single production facility. Bata serves its different national markets by producing in a given market nearly everything it sells in that market. It does this in part because substantial sales volume in the countries in which it produces enable it to achieve economies of scale very quickly. It may seem difficult to believe that Bata can always achieve economies of scale, especially since the company has production facilities in some small African nations. However, Bata's management believes that the company can achieve scale economies very easily because its shoe production is a labor-intensive operation. It also tries to buy all its raw materials locally, although this is not always possible, especially in some poorer countries.

Bata also prefers not to export production; when possible, it chooses local production to serve the local market rather than imports. However, sometimes Bata becomes entangled with local governments when it imports some raw materials but does not export. In such cases, it must adjust to local laws and requirements for operation.

Bata avoids excessive reliance on exports partly to reduce its risks. For example, if an importing country were to restrict trade, Bata could possibly lose market opportunity and market share. In addition, Tom Bata, Sr., noted the benefit to a developing country of not exposing itself to possible protectionism:

> We know very well what kind of a social shock it is when a plant closes in Canada. Yet in Canada we have unemployment insurance and all kinds of welfare operations, and there are many alternative jobs that people can usually go to. In most of the developing countries, on the other hand, it's a question of life and death for these people. They have uprooted themselves from an agricultural society. They've come to a town to work in an industry. They've brought their relatives with them because working in industry, their earnings are so much higher. Thus a large group of their relatives have become dependent on them and have changed their lifestyle and standard of living. For these people it is a terrible thing to lose a job. And so we are very sensitive to that particular problem.

Bata operates in many different types of economies. It has extensive operations in both industrial democratic countries and developing countries. However, it was soundly criticized for operating in South Africa and thus tacitly supporting the white minority political regime. It also has been censured for operating in totalitarian regimes, such as that in Chile. In the latter case, Tom Bata, Sr., countered by pointing out that the company had been operating in Chile for over forty years, during which time various political regimes were in power.

Although Bata's local operations have not been nationalized often, the company has had some fascinating experiences with such actions. For example, in Uganda, Bata's local operations were nationalized by Milton Obote, denationalized by Idi Amin, renationalized by Amin, and finally denationalized by Amin. During that time, the factory continued to operate as if nothing had happened. As Tom Bata, Sr., explained, "Shoes had to be bought and wages paid. Life went on. In most cases, the governments concluded it really wasn't in their interest to run businesses, so they canceled the nationalization arrangements."

Despite Bata's ability to operate in any type of political environment, Tom Bata, Sr., prefers a democratic system. He feels that both democratic and totalitarian regimes are bureaucratic, but a democracy offers the potential to discuss and change procedures, whereas under totalitarianism it sometimes is wisest to remain silent.

Bata has a multifaceted impact on a country. Its product is a necessity, not a luxury. The company's basic strategy is to provide footwear at affordable prices for the largest possible segment of the population. The production of shoes is labor-intensive, so jobs are created, which increases consumers' purchasing power. Although top management may come from outside the country, local management is trained to assume responsibility as quickly as possible. Because the company tries to get most of its raw materials locally, sources of supplies usually are developed. Further, it likes to diversify its purchases, so it usually uses more than one supplier for a given product, which leads to competition and efficiencies.

South Africa presented unique challenges for Bata management. The size of the country's population is just under that of Nigeria, Egypt, or Ethiopia. Thus South Africa had long been considered a good place in which to invest because of its large market size. Further, South Africa's per capita GNP was the largest in Africa. However, the country's main attraction was the incredibly high rate of return that companies could earn, which was largely the result of low labor costs and extensive mineral wealth. The large market allowed companies to achieve economies of scale in production while exploiting the low labor costs.

But the situation deteriorated rapidly in the early 1980s. A relatively stagnant economy, political strife resulting from apartheid, including the policy of not granting political freedom and civil liberties to blacks, prompted foreign companies and governments to pressure the government for political reforms. The Canadian attitude toward South Africa was very negative. Canada's government issued very conservative voluntary guidelines on new investments in South Africa. As a result, Bata sold its holdings in South Africa in 1986. It did not identify the buyer or the sales price, and it denied that apartheid was the reason for its pulling out. Company personnel stated, "It really was a business decision that took into account all of the factors with respect to investment in South Africa at the present time." Under the terms of the sale, the Bata company name and trademark could no longer be used in South Africa, and all ties with Canadian headquarters were broken. In addition, the new buyer apparently assured that the jobs of the workers, most of whom are black, would be preserved.

Bata also faced problems trying to get back into Slovakia. As noted earlier, the Bata operations started in the former Czechoslovakia, and as Eastern Europe opened up, Bata immediately tried to recover lost investments in the Czech Republic and Slovakia. The problem was that the Czech and Slovak governments wanted compensation for the factories, but Bata (known as Tomas Baoa in his homeland) felt the factories were still his. He eventually opened one factory in the Czech Republic and 48 retail outlets where the company sold 3 million pairs of shoes in the first year, capturing 11 percent of the Czech shoe market.

However, things were not so rosy in Slovakia. Baoa said that the problem is that "his company's former Slovak properties ended up in the hands of the Slovak government, which isn't interested in giving them up. Instead, he is expected to rebuild his Slovak business using his own resources." He says that he is still waiting for the government to keep the promise it made when his 45,000-employee factory in Slovakia was nationalized. Compensation was promised by the communists but never paid. The official government position is that a new restitution law has been put into effect and that Bata has to raise his ownership claims with the new owner of the factory. If the two parties cannot agree to a joint solution to the problem, Bata is welcome to file a lawsuit against the new owner to be settled in Slovakian courts. Despite his success in the Czech Republic, Bata had not sold one pair of shoes in Slovakia by the beginning of 1996.

Questions

1. Evaluate the different ways in which Bata has interacted with foreign political systems in its investments and operations abroad.

2. Do you think Bata made the correct decision to pull out of South Africa? How do you think the political events in South Africa in the past few years might change Bata's strategy for South Africa? How should Bata formulate a strategy for determining whether or not to reenter South Africa?

3. What are the advantages and disadvantages to both Bata and the Republic of Slovakia of having Bata take over his former operations? Why do you think the Czech Republic allowed Bata to reenter the market, but Slovakia had not as of the end of 1995? Why do you think Bata is appealing for a political solution to his problems rather than go through the courts to get back his property? What type of political system do the Czech Republic and Slovakia have? How might that help explain Bata's problems?

4. Check the Web for country pages, the CIA Factbook, or other sources of information on South Africa, the Czech Republic, or Slovakia that will help you understand more about the changing political and economic climates in those countries.

5. Why do you think Tom Bata, Sr., has joined the list of entrepreneurs who cannot bear to loosen their grip on businesses they started? What is the risk to Bata, Ltd. if Tom Bata, Sr., cannot find a way to retire?

Chapter Notes

1. The major sources for the case are as follows: Pete Engardio, "In Asia, the Sweet Taste of Success," *Business Week,* November 26, 1990, p. 96; "The Dragon's Embrace," *The Economist,* August 26, 1989, pp. 51–52; John Newhouse, "Tweaking the Dragon's Tail," *The New Yorker,* March 15, 1993, pp. 89–103; Richard Meyer, "Hostage," *Fortune,* September 18, 1990, pp. 22–27; "Patten Sets the Path," *The Economist,* October 10, 1992, pp. 35–36; and "New Medicine for Hong Kong," *The Economist,* February 20, 1993, pp. 31–32; Henny Sender, "Fixed Assets; British Hongs Still Tied to the Colony," *Far East Economic Review,* July 8, 1993, p. 22; Mark Clifford, "Back to China," *Far East Economic Review,* January 27, 1994, pp. 38+; "Hong Gone," *The Economist,* March 26, 1994, p. 97; Jonathan Karp, "Island Hopping: Jardine Matheson Flees Hong Kong for Bermuda," *Far Eastern Economic Review,* April 7, 1994, pp. 73–74; Kathleen Morris, "There's No Place Like Home," *Financial World,* August 2, 1994, pp. 36+; "The Noble Houses Look Forward," *The Economist,* October 1, 1994, pp. 77–78; "The Taipan and the Dragon," *The Economist,* April 8, 1995, p. 62; Karen Elliott House, "Why Hong Kong Must Remain Hong Kong," *The Wall Street Journal,* June 6, 1995, p. A16; Bruce Einhorn, "This Tiger Has a Thorn in its Paw," *Business Week,* July 24, 1995, p. 48; "Hong Kong," *The Economist,* September 23, 1995, pp. 29–32; "The Swire Group: Thin Ice?" *The Economist,* September 23, 1995, p. 58; "A Great Way to Flee," *The Economist,* October 14, 1995, pp. 37–38; "Boarding for Beijing," *The Economist,* May 4, 1996, pp. 65; Mark Clifford and Joyce Barnathan, "Beijing Is Buying Hong Kong—But at Its Own Price" *Business Week,* May 13, 1996, p. 64; and Joyce Barnathan and David Lindorff, "Hong Kong's New Boss," *Business Week,* December 23, 1996, p. 50.
2. David P. Baron, *Business and Its Environment* (Englewood Cliffs, N.J.: Prentice-Hall, 1993), pp. 7–9.
3. Gabriel A. Almond and G. Bingham Powell, Jr., general editors, *Comparative Politics Today: A World View* (Boston: Little, Brown, 1984), pp. 1–9.
4. Robert Wesson, *Modern Government—Democracy and Authoritarianism,* 2nd ed. (Englewood Cliffs, N.J.: Prentice-Hall, 1985), pp. 41–42.
5. Samuel Huntington, "Democracy for the Long Haul," *The Strait Times,* September 10, 1995, p. 1+, Available: NEXIS Library: NEWS: CURNWS.
6. Adrian Karatnycky, *Freedom in the World* (New York: Freedom House, 1995), pp. 3–5.
7. Ibid., p. 4.
8. "South Africa: The Joys of Normality," *The Economist,* May 20, 1995, Survey pp. 1–26.
9. *Europa World Year Book* (London: Europa Publications Limited, 1995), pp. 3130–3131.
10. *Europa World Year Book* (London: Europa Publications Limited, 1996), pp. 1222–1223.
11. "Netanyahu's Day," *The Economist,* June 1, 1996, p. 39.
12. "That's That, Until Quebec Tries Again," *The Economist,* November 4, 1995, p. 45; "Canada May be Intact, But It Is Not United; Separatists Vow: 'Until Next Time,'" *News Services.* Available: Nexis Library: NEWS:
13. "Democracy and Technology," *The Economist,* June 17, 1995, pp. 21–23.
14. Jaroslaw Piekalkiewicz and Alfred Wayne Penn, *Politics of Ideocracy* (Albany, New York: State University of New York Press, 1995), p. 4.
15. Carl J. Friedrich, and Zbigniew K. Brzezinski, *Totalitarian Dictatorship and Autocracy* (New York: Praeger Publishers, 1965), as quoted in Piekalkiewicz and Penn, p. 9.
16. Piekalkiewicz and Penn, op. cit., p. 17.
17. Karatnycky, op. cit., pp. 6–7.
18. Daniel Pearl and Amy Dockser Marcus, "Political Islam's Hope of Unified Movement Has Failed to Solidify," *The Wall Street Journal,* July 3, 1996, p. A1.
19. Alfred A. Marcus, *Business & Society: Ethics, Government, and the World Economy* (Homewood, Ill.: Richard D. Irwin, 1993), p. 216.
20. John Markoff, "Finding Profit in Aiding the Lost," *The New York Times,* March 5, 1996, p. D1.
21. Andy Pasztor and John J. Fialka, "Export Controls to Be Relaxed," *Wall Street Journal,* September 20, 1993, p. 2.
22. Baron, op. cit., p. 162.
23. Baron, op. cit., pp. 177–179.
24. Ray August, *International Business Law: Text, Cases, and Readings* (Englewood Cliffs, N.J.: Prentice-Hall, 1993), p. 51.
25. Aline Sullivan, "Westerners Look at Risks and Rewards of Islamic Banking," *International Herald Tribune,* January 30, 1993, p. 1.
26. Robin Allen, "In Search of an Identity," *Financial Times,* November 28, 1995, p. iii.
27. Kieran Cooke, "Two Systems Exist Side by Side," *Financial Times,* November 28, 1995, p. iv.
28. Roger Taylor, "Western Funds Scent Rich Rewards in Islam," *The Financial Times,* February 13, 1996, p. 17.
29. "For God and GDP," *The Economist,* August 7, 1993, pp. 34–35.
30. "Survey: The Legal Profession," *The Economist,* July 18, 1992, p. 11.
31. Ibid., p. 14.
32. Ibid., p. 5.
33. Marcus, op. cit., pp. 49–52.
34. John R. Boatright, *Ethics and the Conduct of Business* (Englewood Cliffs, N.J.: Prentice-Hall, 1993), pp. 13–16.
35. Ibid., pp. 16–18.
36. Peggy E. Chaudhry and Michael G. Walsh, "An Assessment of the Impact of Counterfeiting in International Markets: The Piracy Paradox Persists," *Columbia Journal of World Business,* Fall 1996; Michael G. Walsh and Peggy E. Chaudhry, "Intellectual Property Rights," *Columbia Journal of World Business,* XXX, No. 2, 1995, pp. 80–92.
37. Huntington, op. cit., Library: NEWS:
38. Ibid.
39. Ibid.
40. Ibid.
41. The material for the case was taken from the following sources: Dean Walker, "Shoemaker to the World," *Executive,* January 1981, pp. 63–69; Gary Vineberg, "Bata Favors Free Trade but Tempers Asia Stance," *Footwear News,* Vol. 39, No. 24, June 13, 1983, p. 2+; Ira Breskin and Gary Vinesbert, "Parent Bata Looks After Far Flung Footwear Family," *Footwear News,* Vol. 39, No. 23, June 6, 1983, p. 1+; "After Sullivan," *The Economist,* June 13, 1987, p. 71; Robert Collison, "How Bata Rules Its World," *Canadian Business,* September 1990, pp. 28–34; Peter C. Newman, "The Return of the Native Capitalist," *Macleans,* March 12, 1990, p. 53; Tammi Gutner, "Bringing Back Bata," *International Management,* November 1990, pp. 41–43; "Faded Euphoria," *Fortune,* July 1, 1991; "Pulled Up by the Bootlaces," *Financial Times,* October 9, 1995, p. 23; James Anderson, "Bata Property Still Held by Slovak Government," *The Prague Post,* July 26, 1995, pp. 1+, Available: NEXIS Library: NEWS: CURNWS; Bernard Simon, "Bata Executives Quit in Strategy Row . . . ," *Financial Times,* October 9, 1995, p. 25; and Bernard Simon, "Footwear Goes Out of Fashion," *Financial Times,* June 6, 1996, p. 18.

Appendix 1
Comparative Measures of Freedom

Country	Political Rights	Civil Liberties	Country	Political Rights	Civil Liberties
Free			**Free**		
Andorra	1	1	Liechtenstein	1	1
Argentina	2	3	Lithuania	1	3
Australia	1	1	Luxembourg	1	1
Austria	1	1	Malawi	2	3
Bahamas	1	2	Malta	1	1
Barbados	1	1	Marshall Islands	1	1
Belgium	1	1	Mauritius	1	2
Belize	1	1	Micronesia	1	1
Benin	2	3	Monaco	2	1
Bolivia	2	3	Mongolia	2	3
Botswana	2	3	Namibia	2	3
Bulgaria	2	2	Naura	1	3
Canada	1	1	Netherlands	1	1
Cape Verde	1	2	New Zealand	1	1
Chile	2	2	Norway	1	1
Costa Rica	1	2	Palau	1	2
Cyprus	1	1	Panama	2	3
Czech Republic	1	2	Poland	2	2
Denmark	1	1	Portugal	1	1
Dominica	2	1	St. Kitts & Nevis	2	2
Ecuador	2	3	St. Lucia	1	2
Estonia	3	2	St. Vincent & The Grenadines	2	1
Finland	1	1	San Marino	1	1
France	1	2	Sao Tome and Principe	1	2
Germany	1	2	Slovakia	2	3
Greece	1	3	Slovenia	1	2
Grenada	1	2	Solomon Islands	1	2
Guyana	2	2	South Africa	2	3
Hungary	1	2	Spain	1	2
Iceland	1	1	Sweden	1	1
Ireland	1	2	Switzerland	1	1
Israel	1	3	Trinidad & Tobago	1	2
Italy	1	2	Tuvalu	1	1
Jamaica	2	3	United Kingdom	1	2
Japan	2	2	United States	1	1
Kiribati	1	1	Uruguay	2	2
Korea, South	2	2	Vanuatu	1	3
Latvia	3	2	Western Samoa	2	2
Partly Free			**Partly Free**		
Albania	3	4	Fiji	4	3
Antigua & Barbuda	4	3	Gabon	5	4
Armenia	3	4	Georgia	5	5
Bangladesh	2	4	Ghana	5	4
Belarus	4	4	Guatemala	4	5
Brazil	2	4	Guinea-Bissau	3	4
Burkina Faso	5	4	Haiti	5	5
Cambodia	4	5	Honduras	3	3
Central Africa Republic	3	4	India	4	4
Colombia	3	4	Jordan	4	4
Comoros	4	4	Kuwait	5	5
Congo	4	4	Kyrgyz Republic	2	3
Croatia	4	4	Lebanon	6	5
Dominican Republic	4	3	Lesotho	4	4
El Salvador	3	3	Macedonia	4	3

Appendix 1-continued
Comparative Measures of Freedom

Country	Political Rights	Civil Liberties	Country	Political Rights	Civil Liberties
Partly Free			**Partly Free**		
Madagascar	2	4	Russia	3	4
Malaysia	4	5	Senegal	4	5
Mali	2	4	Seychelles	3	4
Mexico	4	4	Singapore	5	5
Moldova	4	4	Sri Lanka	4	5
Morocco	5	5	Suriname	3	3
Mozambique	3	5	Taiwan (Rep of China)	3	3
Nepal	3	4	Thailand	3	5
Nicaragua	4	5	Tonga	5	3
Niger	3	5	Turkey	5	5
Pakistan	3	5	Uganda	5	5
Papua New Guinea	2	4	Ukraine	3	4
Paraguay	4	3	Venezuela	3	3
Peru	5	4	Zambia	3	4
Philippines	3	4	Zimbabwe	5	5
Romania	4	3			
Not Free			**Not Free**		
Afghanistan	7	7	Korea, North	7	7
Algeria	7	7	Laos	7	6
Angola	7	7	Liberia	7	6
Azerbaijan	6	6	Libya	7	7
Bahrain	6	6	Maldives	6	6
Bhutan	7	7	Mauritania	7	7
Bosnia-Hercegovina	6	6	Nigeria	7	6
Brunei	7	6	Oman	6	6
Burma (Myanmar)	7	7	Qatar	7	6
Burundi	6	7	Rwanda	7	7
Cameroon	6	5	Saudi Arabia	7	7
Chad	6	5	Sierra Leone	7	6
China (PRC)	7	7	Somalia	7	7
Cuba	7	7	Sudan	7	7
Djibouti	6	6	Swaziland	6	5
Egypt	6	6	Syria	7	7
Equatorial Guinea	7	7	Tajikistan	7	7
Eritrea	6	5	Tanzania	6	6
Ethiopia	6	5	Togo	6	5
Gambia	7	6	Tunisia	6	5
Guinea	6	5	Turkmenistan	7	7
Indonesia	7	6	United Arab Emirates	6	5
Iran	6	7	Uzbekistan	7	7
Iraq	7	7	Vietnam	7	7
Ivory Coast	6	5	Yemen	5	6
Kazakhstan	6	5	Yugoslavia (Serbia & Montenegro)	6	6
Kenya	6	6	Zaire	7	6

Note: 1 represents most free and 7 the least free category.

Source: From Adrian Karatnycky, *Freedom in the World* (New York: Freedom House, 1995), pp. 678–679. Reprinted with permission.

Chapter 4

The Economic Environment

Poverty does not destroy virtue,
nor does wealth bestow it.
—Spanish Proverb

Objectives

- **To discuss different economic systems**

- **To divide countries into different economic categories**

- **To discuss key economic issues that influence international business**

- **To assess the transformation process from central planning to market economy and how it affects international firms**

Case
McDonald's
Corporation[1]

Some historians trace the origin of the hamburger to Russia. Supposedly, sailors took a dish made of raw ground beef and hot spices from Russia to the port of Hamburg, where the recipe was altered, popularized, and given its name. Hamburgers eventually showed up in England and then North America. If this historical account is accurate, then when McDonald's Corporation opened its first Moscow restaurant in 1990, the hamburger's round-trip journey was complete.

McDonald's entry into Russia capped a long and involved negotiation process. During the 1976 Olympics in Montreal, George A. Cohon, president of McDonald's Canadian subsidiary, made the first contact with Soviet officials. This began lengthy negotiations that culminated in the signing of a protocol agreement in 1987, shortly after the Soviets enacted legislation permitting joint ventures with Western companies. After that, the pace of negotiations quickened, until in 1988 a formal agreement was signed. In the meantime, McDonald's had opened restaurants in Hungary and Yugoslavia, thus providing the company with valuable experience in operating in communist countries.

These moves were highly compatible with McDonald's growth strategy. By the mid-1980s, the company was expanding more rapidly outside the United States than inside, and company executives reasoned that if they were to meet the company's rapid growth objectives, that trend must continue. It did. By the end of 1995, McDonald's had 18,380 restaurants in over seventy-nine countries. Its foreign sales had reached 47 percent of total company sales—up from 37.2 percent in 1991 and 19 percent in 1981.

From 1990–1995, 56 percent of the new McDonald's restaurants have been opened outside of the United States. Of the 1,007 restaurants added in 1995, 42 percent were from the six largest foreign markets—Australia, Canada, England, France, Germany, and Japan—with Japan alone adding 313 of the new restaurants. This compared with 57 percent in 1992 and 51 percent in 1994 of the new additions coming from the big six, demonstrating the importance of new emerging markets. McDonald's hopes to increase its expansion outside of the United States by adding between 1,200 and 1,500 traditional restaurants and 350 to 500 satellite restaurants annually for the next few years. As noted in their 1995 *Annual Report,*

> At year-end 1995, 38 percent of Systemwide restaurants were outside of the U.S. compared with 36 percent in 1994 and 27 percent five years ago. Restaurants outside of the U.S. comprised 53 percent of traditional Company-operated restaurants and 27 percent of traditional franchised restaurants. About 29 percent of the traditional restaurants outside of the U.S. were Company-operated, 47 percent were franchised and 24 percent were operated by affiliates. Approximately 69 percent of traditional Company-operated restaurants were in England, Canada, Germany, Australia, Taiwan and Brazil. About 66 percent of traditional franchised restaurants were in Canada, Germany, Australia, France, England and the Netherlands. Restaurants operated by affiliates were principally located in Japan and other Asia/Pacific countries. Approximately 81 percent of satellite restaurants outside of the U.S. were operated by franchisees and affiliates at year-end 1995. The vast majority were located in Japan, Canada and Brazil. (p. 21)

The McDonald's-Russian joint venture is between McDonald's Canadian subsidiary and the Moscow City Council. McDonald's has a 49-percent interest, the maximum allowed by

Soviet law when the formal agreement was signed in 1988. (Since 1990, foreigners may own a 99-percent interest in a joint venture.) The minority ownership has not proved to be a problem, however, because Russian law requires at least a three-quarters majority vote to approve important decisions. Therefore, the representatives of McDonald's and the City Council must agree on all major decisions.

On the other hand, supply procurement was a major hurdle, as it has been for most foreign companies operating in Russia. The problem has several causes:

- The rigid bureaucratic system
- Supply shortages caused by distribution and production problems
- Available supplies not meeting McDonald's quality standards

Even with the Moscow City Council being majority owner in the venture, not to mention having the backing of the Kremlin, the company repeatedly ran into negative responses, such as "Sorry, you're not in my five-year plan," when it attempted to obtain such materials as sand or gravel to build the restaurant. The company had to negotiate to ensure it would be allocated, in the Soviet central plan, sufficient sugar and flour, which were in chronically short supply. Even for some products in sufficient supply, such as mustard, government regulations prevented Soviet manufacturers from deviating from standard recipes in order to comply with McDonald's needs. In other cases, strict allocation regulations dictated that Soviet plants sell all output to existing Soviet companies, thus leaving them no chance to produce products for McDonald's. Yet another problem was that some supplies simply were not produced or consumed in the Soviet Union, including iceberg lettuce, pickling cucumbers, and the Russet Burbank potatoes that are the secret behind McDonald's french fries.

To handle these problems, McDonald's scoured the country for supplies, contracting for such items as milk, cheddar cheese, and beef. To help ensure ample supplies of the quality products it needed, it undertook to educate Soviet farmers and cattle ranchers on how to grow and raise those products. In addition, it built a $40-million food-processing center about 45 minutes from its first Moscow restaurant. And because distribution was as much a cause of shortages as production was, McDonald's carried supplies on its own trucks. Some other needed supplies the company had to import. (Today, 98 percent of supplies come from the Commonwealth of Independent States, which comprises most of the former republics of the Soviet Union.)

The company placed one small help-wanted ad and received about 27,000 Russian applicants for its 605 positions. It sent 6 Russian managers to its Hamburger University outside Chicago for six months' training and another 30 managers for several months' training in Canada or Europe. The company translated training and operations manuals and videotapes into Russian so that trainees could learn everything from how to wash windows and mop floors to how to assemble a Big Mac.

In order to establish a Western image, McDonald's used its name and familiar golden arches in Moscow. However, in 1993 a law was passed in that city requiring all stores to have Russian names, or at least names transliterated into the Cyrillic alphabet. Just as

PepsiCo chose Cyrillic letters to convey the sound of "Pepsi" in Russian, McDonald's used the following Cyrillic letters that retain the sound of its name: **МАКДОНАЛДС** .

One problem McDonald's did not encounter was attracting customers. When the company opened its restaurant in Hungary, it quickly had to eliminate its advertising because of unexpectedly heavy consumer response. On the basis of this experience, McDonald's did no advertising prior to its Moscow opening. However, Russian television covered the upcoming event extensively. When the restaurant's doors opened for the first time in January 1990, it was almost impossible to accommodate the crowd, even though the restaurant's 700 indoor seats made it the largest McDonald's anywhere in the world. (An additional 200 seats outside could not be used because of cold weather.) An estimated 30,000 people were served the first day, eclipsing the previous daily record of 9,100 set in Budapest. The crowds continued to arrive, even though the price of a Big Mac, french fries, and soft drink equaled a Russian worker's average pay for four hours of work. In contrast, lunch at a state-run or private sector cafe cost 15–25 percent as much as a meal at McDonald's.

However, McDonald's was not satisfied with one restaurant in Moscow. In 1993, Moscow was the fourth largest city in the world with nearly 9 million people, following Cairo, São Paulo, and Seoul, and just above Mexico City. It was obvious to McDonald's management that Moscow's 3 million commuters who were used to poor, slow service would warm to McDonald's immediately. For example, the first Moscow McDonald's in Pushkin Square serves an average of 40,000 to 50,000 customers per day, whereas the restaurant that formerly occupied the space served only 200 customers per day. To illustrate the potential, the United States has a population of 240 million people and 8,500 McDonald's restaurants, whereas Russia had 149 million people and only 10 restaurants by the end of 1996 or early 1997. However, business was booming to such an extent in Moscow that McDonald's projected as many as 40 restaurants by 1998.

Since McDonald's joint venture partners are the Moscow city catering officials, it is relatively easy to get access to prime commercial property to open new sites. In most market economies, it would be considered a conflict of interest to have local government officials as partners in a commercial interest, but Russia's brand of capitalism involves significant state intervention.

The Pushkin Square McDonald's was so successful that they opened up a second restaurant on Ogareva Street on June 1, 1993; renovated two eighteenth century Arbat Street buildings to house their third restaurant which was opened July 3, 1993, seating up to 400 customers at once; opened a fourth restaurant at Prospect Mira that is able to seat 300 customers at once; and opened the Sokolniki restaurant next to Moscow's fire observation tower in 1995. When the Arbat Street McDonald's opened, 10,000 people lined up to get in, and 60,000 were served on the first day. Since then, the Arbat Street McDonald's has served 70,000 people per day, every day.

Although McDonald's is reinvesting its ruble profits in new stores, it has entered into a special barter arrangement with the Soviet government that allows it to earn some hard currency on its operations. It is hypothesized that McDonald's might be selling Soviet products like metals and other raw materials to help cover the cost of items like cups and restaurant equipment that it needs to import.

The employment record of McDonald's is impressive. Although McDonald's opened with 80–90 expatriates, it had replaced most with locals by the end of 1995. McDonald's employs 2200 Russians at the five McDonald's restaurants and its food processing and distribution center, McComplex. A reporter from *Pravda* noted that "people working in the service industry in the Soviet Union have a reputation for being lazy, slovenly, and a little like petty thieves. . . . All around us, no matter where you look, there is ruin, irresponsibility, laziness, boorishness, lack of professionalism and theft." However, McDonald's is very satisfied with the performance of its employees, who have excellent pay and benefits. As noted by Cohen, "There is no other restaurant in the world that could serve up the 55,000 people in a day. I could take the Soviet crew from the Pushkin Square restaurant, send them to any country, and be absolutely certain that they would do well anywhere." The strong investment in training has paid off.

What is the future of McDonald's in places such as the former Soviet Union, Eastern Europe, and China? Since opening its first restaurants in China and Russia, the company has opened more restaurants in those countries. It also is studying the feasibility of opening restaurants in Ukraine, St. Petersburg, and the Balkan states. The managing director of McDonald's Development Corporation said, "We'll do one store, one country at a time, and plans will be made as we grow and develop."

Several factors control McDonald's expansion abroad. Key among these are the size and growth rate of different economies. As noted above, most of the company's foreign restaurants are in high-income countries (those with per capita incomes of $8956 or more in 1994).

Although the main thrust of McDonald's expansion has been in the high-income countries, the developing countries have significant expansion potential. The following developing countries (those with per capita incomes of less than $8956 in 1994) already have restaurants: Brazil, Hong Kong, Taiwan, Philippines, Singapore, Puerto Rico, and Mexico. Working with these countries involves challenges very different from those connected with doing business in high-income countries, as you will see later in this chapter.

Introduction

As a company considers where in the world to build factories and sell products, it must analyze the countries in which it may do business. Understanding the economic and political environments of these countries can help the company predict how trends and events in those environments might affect its future performance there.

In this chapter, we discuss the economic environments of the countries in which a U.S. company may want to operate. However, we will not discuss the specific decision to invest in or do business with a specific country. Those decisions will be discussed more specifically in Chapters 8 and 11. This **country analysis** "examines the economic strategy of the nation state. It takes the holistic approach to understanding how a country, and in particular its government, has behaved, is behaving, and may behave."[2] Country analysis requires, in part, understanding national goals, priorities, and policies; we discussed these in Chapter 3. It also involves understanding economic performance as indicated by economic growth, inflation, and budget and trade deficits. We discuss these in the next several chapters as we lay the economic foundation for an analysis of international business. This chapter focuses on the various types of world economies and how differences in them affect managerial decisions. In particular, we will first classify economic systems into market economies, planned economies, and mixed economies; second, we will discuss different ways to classify countries according to per capita income and quality of life measures; third, we will discuss key macroeconomic factors that influence a country's competitive advantage vis-à-vis other countries; and finally, we will discuss the problems of transition or transformation from planned to market economies.

Classifying Economic Systems

In a market economy, resources are allocated and controlled by consumers, who "vote" by buying or not buying goods.

In a command economy, resources are allocated and controlled by governmental decision.

Economic systems usually are classified as capitalist, socialist, or mixed. The term *mixed* may be a little misleading in that all economies are really mixed. No country is purely market or purely command, but they tend to lean to one direction or another. If an economy is considered to be a market economy with private ownership (block A), it is so classified because the market and private ownership dominate the economy. There may be some government control of decision making and government ownership of resources, but not in a significant way. However, as the economy moves to more balance between market and command or between public and private ownership, it is considered mixed. France would be a mixed economy that is more weighted to public ownership than would be the United States, because the French government is much more actively involved in the ownership of large companies. It also is possible to classify economic systems according to two other criteria:

- Type of property ownership—private or public
- Method of resource allocation and control—a market economy or a command economy (in which resources are allocated and controlled by the government)

With private ownership, individuals own the resources.

These two criteria can be expanded to include mixed ownership and control. Figure 4.1 shows these classifications. Note that Hong Kong probably fits in block A, whereas China is best located in the upper left-hand corner of block I but may soon be in block E, B, or H. The United States probably lies in the upper part of block D.

With public ownership, the government owns the resources.

Ownership of the means of production in theory ranges from complete private ownership to complete public ownership. In reality, these extremes do not exist. Most countries lie somewhere in the mixed ownership range. For example, the

**Figure 4.1
Interrelationships
between Control of
Economic Activity and
Ownership of
Production Factors**
Although the most logical
combinations of ownership
and control are sectors A
and I, most countries in
the world have mixed
economies with a variety
of combinations of owner-
ship and control.

CONTROL \ OWNERSHIP	Private	Mixed	Public
Market	A	B	C
Mixed	D	E	F
Command	G	H	I

Control/Ownership	Control/Ownership	Control/Ownership
A. Market/Private	D. Mixed/Private	G. Command/Private
B. Market/Mixed	E. Mixed/Mixed	H. Command/Mixed
C. Market/Public	F. Mixed/Public	I. Command/Public

United States is considered to be the prime example of a private enterprise system,
yet the government owns some means of production and actively produces in such
sectors of the economy as education, national parks, the postal service (which is in
the quasi-public sector), and certain utilities. Similarly, the control of economic
activity in theory ranges from market to command.

The next several sections examine more closely market, centrally planned, and
mixed economies.

Market Economy

**The market mechanism
involves an interrelationship
of price, quantity, supply,
and demand.**

In a **market economy,** two societal units play important roles: the individual and
the company. Individuals own resources and consumer products; companies use
resources and produce products. The market mechanism involves an interaction of
price, quantity, supply, and demand for resources and products, as follows:

- Labor is supplied by the individual if the company offers an adequate wage.
- Products are consumed if the price is within a certain acceptable range.
- A company sets its wages on the basis of quantity of labor available to do a
  job.
- Resources are allocated as a result of constant interplay between individuals
  and companies, between individuals, and between companies (for example,
  when the output of one company is the input of another).

**Consumer sovereignty is the
freedom of consumers to
influence production by
exercising their power of
choice regarding purchases.**

The key factors that make the market economy work are **consumer sovereignty**—
that is, the right of the consumer to decide what to buy—and freedom of the enterprise to operate in the market. As long as both the individual and the company are
free to make economic decisions, the interplay of supply and demand should ensure
proper allocation of resources.

More specifically, a market economy implies a degree of economic freedom, which can be measured in a variety of ways. Freedom House, which developed the comparative measure of freedom from a political rights and civil liberties point of view as discussed in Chapter 3, has also developed a measure of economic freedom. Their feeling is that economic freedom involves two dimensions. The first is the freedom from government restraints on wages, prices, trade flows, and business formation. The second is the establishment of rules that govern the economic game. In particular, Freedom House measures the extent to which "government hinders or prevents its citizens from exercising their right to own property, earn a living, operate a business, invest one's earnings, trade internationally, and participate equally in all aspects of the market economy."[3] The key to the first dimension is the degree of state intrusion. The less the intrusion, the more likely the country is to have a free economy. The key to the second is the nature of the legal and institutional frameworks of a country in safeguarding the ability of all citizens, including women and minorities, "to enter the professions, open businesses, own and transfer property, and participate in the economy."[4]

Centrally Planned Economy

In a **centrally planned economy,** the government coordinates the activities of the different economic sectors. Goals are set for every enterprise in the country; the government determines how much is produced, by whom, and for whom. In this type of economy, the government is assumed to be a better judge of how resources should be allocated than are businesses or consumers. As a result of the recent political and economic changes in Eastern Europe and the former Soviet Union, however, few countries use strict central planning today. Most countries in this category have been moved into a new one called **historically planned economies (HPEs),** which comprises countries that previously used central planning as their primary economic system but may no longer do so.

Mixed Economy

In actuality, no economy is either purely market determined or completely centrally planned. Hong Kong and China represent opposite ends of the spectrum of mixed economies. In practice, however, what we call **mixed economies** generally have a higher degree of government intervention than is found in Hong Kong and a greater degree of reliance on market forces than is found in China. The two ends of the spectrum from the Freedom House point of view are "Free" and "Not Free." Countries in the mixed categories would be "Partly Free" and "Mostly Not Free." Examples of countries that are "Partly Free" are Hungary, Israel, and Taiwan; examples of countries that are "Mostly Not Free" are India, Mexico, Brazil, and Russia. Countries that are "Not Free" would not necessarily be central command economies, however. They might have a form of state capitalism where the market is severely impaired, such as in Haiti, Indonesia, and Saudi Arabia. In some cases, however, they might be central command, such as in Vietnam, China, Cuba, and North Korea. Countries that have historically classified themselves as central command are rapidly moving toward the market, as we will discuss later in the chapter. Government intervention can be regarded in two ways: government ownership of the means of production and government influence in economic decision making. Ownership is easy to quantify statistically; influence, however, is a matter of policy and custom and therefore is more difficult to measure precisely.

Many high-income countries such as Germany and Sweden have relatively low levels of government ownership but a strong tradition of social welfare supported by taxes and therefore high total expenditures as a percentage of gross national product (GNP). France has a similar system, although the government is more heavily involved in corporate ownership.

Japan offers an illustration of government intervention in the form of influence. At the close of World War II, Japan, unlike other countries involved in the war, such as France and Italy, decided to leave ownership of the means of production in the private sector rather than nationalizing key industries. Japanese policymakers focused on setting targets and using fiscal incentives to direct the flow of investment. The Ministry of International Trade and Industry (MITI) was organized to guide industrial development through "strategic planning and authority (both formal and informal) over investment and production priorities."[5] MITI was more concerned with developing a vision for the economy than with setting up a blueprint for it.

Table 4.1 summarizes the number of countries, population, and gross domestic product (GDP) of those countries according to economic freedom. Those in the "Free" category would be considered market economies, those in the "Partly Free" and "Mostly Not Free" categories would be considered mixed economies, and those in the "Not Free" category would be considered state capitalist and command economies. It is interesting to note that only 17 percent of the world's population lives in countries that are free economically, but they represent 81 percent of the

Japan's MITI has given strategic direction to that country's investment and production priorities.

Table 4.1
Economic Freedom

	Number of countries	Population (in millions)	Gross domestic product (trillions of U.S. $)
Free	27	942 (17%)	18.8 (81%)
Partly Free	22	395 (7%)	1.1 (5%)
Mostly Not Free	13	1,645 (30%)	1.9 (8%)
Not Free	20	1,974 (36%)	1.1 (5%)
Not Surveyed	109	546 (10%)	.2 (1%)
Total World	191	5,502	23.1

Source: R. E. Messick, "The World Survey of Economic Freedom," *Freedom Review*, Vol. 27, No. 2, March–April 1996, p. 10.

world's GDP. In contrast, 36 percent of the world's population lives in countries that are "Not Free," and they represent only 5 percent of the world's GDP.

Political-Economic Synthesis

Democratic governments usually mix best with private ownership and control of resources.

Except for central planning and communism, we have made no attempt to link an economic philosophy or system with a particular political philosophy or regime. A logical linkage is a democratic form of government with a market economy and private ownership of the means of production. The assumption is that voters, like consumers, are rational, understand their own self-interest, and prefer to make their own decisions. Japan, the United States, Switzerland, Germany, Canada, Colombia, Ecuador, and Argentina have this combination of political and economic systems.

Democratic socialists believe that elected governments should own resources and control the economic system.

Democratic socialists, however, have a different viewpoint. They believe that because economics and politics are so closely connected, voters should rely on their elected government to control the economic system; that is, the part of the economy not owned by the government should be regulated by the government. Democratic socialists reason that in order to have an economy that is democratically controlled and that provides the security necessary for liberty, resources and production factors must be owned or regulated by a welfare-oriented government. France, when controlled by the Socialists, was a good example of democratic socialism. Radical democratic socialists support a mix of government-owned companies, cooperatives, small-scale private companies, and "freelancers" (for example, journalists and artists).[6]

The extremes of political-economic combinations are converging in mixed economies.

Clearly, numerous combinations of political and economic systems are possible. Generally, the more a country leans toward political totalitarianism, the greater is its reliance on government intervention in the economy. However, most democratic countries have experimented with different degrees of government intervention in the economy, and many totalitarian countries have not resorted to ownership of the factors of production as a method of control. The extremes tend to converge to a mix of public and private interaction in matters of ownership and control. In the case of the industrial countries, the emphasis seems to be on control rather than on ownership.

The Freedom House survey found that with few exceptions, countries rated as economically "Free" were "Free" in terms of political rights and civil liberties. Similarly, those "Not Free" economically tended to be "Not Free" in terms of political rights and civil liberties. Seventy-nine percent of the countries were classified correctly in economic and political terms.[7] An example of a country that did not match up was South Korea, which was considered to be "Free" in political terms but "Mostly Not Free" in economic terms due to the government policy of encouraging the growth of the large *chaebol* (large Korean business groups that tend to be diversified into different businesses and which are held together by ownership, management, and family ties) at the expense of small firms. However, the political scandals of 1995 and 1996 are sure to break the influence of the *chaebol* and move South Korea closer to the "Free" economic category.

Classifying Countries

International competitive-
ness is a function of
• Factor conditions
• Demand conditions

The classification of countries is always a difficult proposition because of the different ways of classification. In Chapter 5, we will discuss Porter's diamond, which identifies the determinants of global competitive advantage. A country's international competitiveness is a function of several factors, including factor conditions and demand conditions, which are relevant to this chapter. **Factor conditions,** also known as production factors, include essential inputs to the production process such as human resources, physical resources, knowledge resources, capital resources, and infrastructure.[8] **Demand conditions** include three dimensions: the composition of home demand (or the nature of buyer needs), the size and pattern of growth of home demand, and the internationalization of demand.[9] The composition of demand is known as the *quality* of demand, and the size is known as the *quantity* of demand.

In this chapter, we will look at several economic indicators that are helpful to understand in describing the economic performance of a country. One of the challenges is getting access to good current data. At this point, it is impossible to identify all good sources of information on economic data, but the Internet is rapidly becoming one of the best places to get current data on a country. Searching for a specific country on the Internet using one of the many search engines will bring up country home pages by governments themselves as well as individuals and organizations that are interested in the country. We use the Internet heavily in the references at the end of the chapters, and there are also good references included in our book's home page. In addition to the Internet, there are a number of good on-line databases, such as LEXIS/NEXIS, that can be used to search for information on companies, countries, and special topics. CD-ROMS are being used to store large amounts of data. Two examples are the World Bank socioeconomic indicators and the National Trade Data Bank (NTDB) by the International Trade Administration of the U.S. Department of Commerce. The NTDB, which contains about 120,000 pages of information and is updated monthly, allows you to perform different types of searches, including searches by country. Be sure to check our home page for a more detailed description of these different databases and for some good Internet links that you can use to get updated country information.

Two important components of demand are population size and per capita income. Although it is hard to capture every concept in one measure, the two most widely used measures of categorizing countries are per capita gross national product and per capita gross domestic product.

GNP—the market value of
final goods and services
newly produced by domestic
factors of production,
whether at home or abroad

Gross national product (GNP) is the broadest measure of economic activity and is defined as "the market value of final goods and services newly produced by domestic factors of production."[10] Note that the production by domestic factors could take place at home or abroad. It comprises gross domestic product (see below) plus net factor income from abroad, which is the income residents receive

GDP—the value of produc-
tion that occurs within a
country's borders whether
done by domestic or foreign
factors of production

from abroad for factor services (labor and capital) less similar payments made to nonresidents who contribute to the domestic economy.[11]

Gross domestic product (GDP) measures the value of production that occurs within a country's borders without regard to whether the production is done by domestic or foreign factors of production. For most countries, GNP and GDP are very similar. However, GDP more accurately reflects economic activity within a country's borders. Of the two, per capita gross national product is the approach used by the World Bank for operational and analytical purposes.

Every economy is classified into one of the following categories according to their per capita GNP.[12]

Per Capita Income
Classifications
• High-income
• Middle-income (lower and
  upper)
• Low-income

Low-income	$725 or less in 1994
Middle-income	$726–$8,955
Lower-middle-income	$726–$2,895
Upper-middle-income	$2,896–$8,956
High-income	$8,956 or more

This classification has changed in recent years because of rapid changes in political and economic systems. In the 1985 issue of the *World Development Report,* for example, the categories were: low-income economies, middle-income economies, upper middle-income economies, high-income oil exporters, industrial market economies, and East European nonmarket economies.

Developing Countries—
middle- and low-income
countries

The low-income and middle-income countries are often known as **developing countries,** but the East European nonmarket economies are put into their proper per capita income classification rather than separated out. In the past, we have referred to countries like Cuba, China, and Russia as Second World, Socialist, or Communist countries. Today, it is more common to refer to these countries as

Countries with Economies in
Transition (CEIT)—Former
nonmarket economies

countries with economies in transition (CEIT), since most of them are moving in various degrees from central command to a market economy. The high-income countries are less likely to be known as industrial market economies, because most of them generate less than half of their GNP from industry. It is interesting to note that five of the high-income countries in terms of per capita GNP are referred to as developing countries by the United Nations: Israel, Hong Kong, Kuwait, Singapore, and United Arab Emirates.

Per Capita Income   In Table 4.2, countries are classified into different economic categories according to per capita GNP. As shown in Fig. 4.2 and Map 4.1, the world's wealth is located primarily in the high-income countries. The low- and middle-income countries where the vast majority of the world's population lives, do not have a proportional share of per capita income. It is interesting to note from the map that the high-income countries are north of the equator (except for Australia and New Zealand). Thus, the so-called North-South dialogue consists of dis-

Table 4.2
World Bank Categories for Economies

The industrial countries are in the high-income category, and the developing countries are in the middle- and low-income categories.

High-income economies (42 countries with 1994 per capita GNP of $8,956 or more)	Upper-middle-income economies (36 countries with 1994 per per capita GNP between $2,896 and $8,956)	Lower-middle-income economies (65 countries with 1994 per capita income between $726 and $2,895)	Low-income economies (65 countries with 1994 per per capita income of $725 or less)
Andorra	American Samoa	Algeria	Afghanistan
Aruba	Antigua and Barbados	Angola	Albania
Australia	Argentina	Belarus	Armenia
Austria	Azerbaijan	Belize	Azerbaijan
Bahamas, the	Bahrain	Bolivia	Bangladesh
Belgium	Barbados	Botswana	Benin
Bermuda	Brazil	Bulgaria	Bhutan
Brunei	Chile	Colombia	Bosnia and Herzegovina
Canada	Czech Republic	Costa Rica	Burkina Faso
Cayman Islands	French Guiana	Croatia	Burundi
Channel Islands	Gabon	Cuba	Cambodia
Cyprus	Greece	Djibouti	Cameroon
Denmark	Guadeloupe	Dominica	Cape Verde
Faeroe Islands	Guam	Dominican Republic	Central African Republic
Finland	Hungary	Ecuador	Chad
France	Isle of Man	El Salvador	China
French Polynesia	Korea, Rep.	Estonia	Comoros
Germany	Libya	Fiji	Congo
Greenland	Malaysia	Grenada	Côte d'Ivoire
Hong Kong	Malta	Guatemala	Egypt, Arab Rep.
Iceland	Martinique	Indonesia	Equatorial Guinea
Ireland	Mauritius	Iran, Islamic Rep.	Eritrea
Israel	Mayotte	Iraq	Ethiopia
Italy	Mexico	Jamaica	Gambia, the
Japan	New Caledonia	Jordan	Georgia
Kuwait	Oman	Kazakhstan	Ghana
Luxembourg	Puerto Rico	Kiribati	Guinea
Macao	Reunion	Korea, Dem. Rep.	Guinea-Bissau
Netherlands	Saudi Arabia	Latvia	Guyana
Netherlands Antilles	Seychelles	Lebanon	Haiti
New Zealand	Slovenia	Lithuania	Honduras
Norway	South Africa	Macedonia, FYR	India
Portugal	St. Kitts and Nevis	Maldives	Kenya
Quatar	St. Lucia	Marshall Islands	Kyguz Republic
Singapore	Trinidad and Tobago	Micronesia, Fed. Sts.	Lao PDR
Spain	Uruguay	Moldova	Lesotho
Sweden		Morocco	Liberia
Switzerland		Namibia	Madagascar
United Arab Emirates		Northern Mariana Is.	Malawi
United Kingdom		Panama	Mali
United States		Papua New Guinea	Mauritania
Virgin Islands		Paraguay	Mongolia
		Peru	Mozambique
		Philippines	Myanmar
		Poland	Nepal
		Romania	Nicaragua
		Russian Federation	Niger
		Slovak Republic	Nigeria
		Solomon Islands	Pakistan
		St. Vincent	Rwanda
		Suriname	Sao Tome and Principe
		Swaziland	Senegal
		Syrian Arab Republic	Sierra Leone

Table 4.2 continued

High-income economies (42 countries with 1994 per capita GNP of $8,956 or more)	Upper-middle-income economies (36 countries with 1994 per per capita GNP between $2,896 and $8,956)	Lower-middle-income economies (65 countries with 1994 per capita income between $726 and $2,895)	Low-income economies (65 countries with 1994 per capita income of $725 or less)
		Thailand	Somalia
		Tonga	Sri Lanka
		Tunisia	Sudan
		Turkey	Tajikistan
		Turkmenistan	Tanzania
		Ukraine	Togo
		Uzbekistan	Uganda
		Vanuatu	Viet Nam
		Venezuela	Yemen, Rep.
		West Bank and Gaza	Zaire
		Western Somoa	Zambia
		Yugoslavia, Fed. Rep.	Zimbabwe

Sources: World Bank, *World Development Report 1996* (New York: Oxford University Press, 1996), p. viii; International Bank for Reconstruction and Development/World Bank. *The World Bank Atlas 1996* (Washington, D.C.: The World Bank, 1995), pp. 18–19. The World Bank provides the data for both the *World Bank Atlas* and the *World Development Report,* and both sources are used for different discussions. The *Atlas* provides data for 209 countries, whereas the *World Development Report* provides data for 133 countries. The difference between the two is that the *World Development Report* tables do not include countries with populations of less than 1 million or those with incomplete data. Some of the categories in the *Atlas* contain countries for which data is estimated. In addition, data from the former USSR is preliminary. The classifications used in this table are from the *World Development Report,* but the countries listed in the table are from the more complete *World Bank Atlas.*

cussions on economic development between the rich Northern Hemisphere countries and the poorer Southern Hemisphere countries.

Most of the world's wealth is in the high-income countries.

It is interesting to note the relative importance of the high-income countries in the world economy. They represent only 21 percent of the number of economies and 15.2 percent of the population, but they generate 79.5 percent of the world's GNP. On the other hand, the low-income countries account for 30.6 percent of the number of economies in the world, 56.7 percent of the population, but only 4.9 percent of the GNP. The middle-income countries fit in between with 28.1 percent of the world's population and 15.6 percent of its GNP, while representing 48.3 percent of the total countries.[13]

Figure 4.2
Per Capita GNP by Income Category, 1994
The world's wealth is located primarily in the high-income countries. The majority of the world's population is underrepresented in per capita income.

Source: World Bank, *The World Bank Atlas* (Washington, D.C.: World Bank, 1996), p. 20.

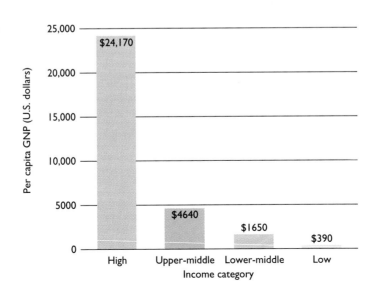

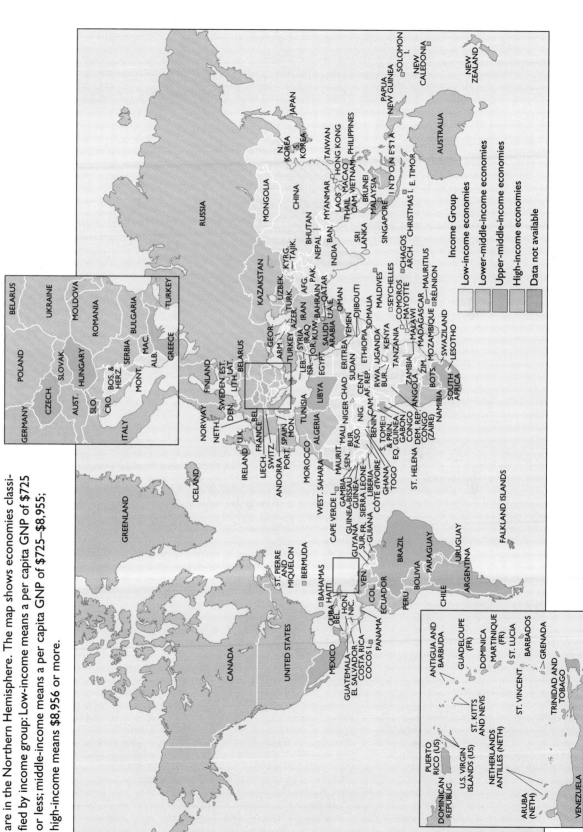

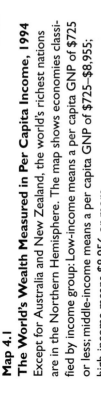

Map 4.1
The World's Wealth Measured in Per Capita Income, 1994
Except for Australia and New Zealand, the world's richest nations are in the Northern Hemisphere. The map shows economies classified by income group: Low-income means a per capita GNP of $725 or less; middle-income means a per capita GNP of $725–$8,955; high-income means $8,956 or more.

Income Group

Low-income economies

Lower-middle-income economies

Upper-middle-income economies

High-income economies

Data not available

Purchasing Power Parity—
the number of units of a
country's currency required
to buy the same amounts of
goods and services in the
domestic market as one
dollar would buy in the
United States

Purchasing power   Per capita GNP is an important measure of wealth, but it is not the only measure. In particular, the World Bank is quick to point out that per capita GNP does not measure welfare or success in development, nor does it measure factors such as the costs and benefits of development on the environment. An alternative measure of wealth is **purchasing power parity (PPP)** estimates of per capita GNP. The basic idea of PPP is to identify the number of units of a country's currency required to buy the same amounts of goods and services in the domestic market as one dollar would buy in the United States.[14] An example of this concept is the Big Mac comparison found in Chapter 10. We note that in dollar terms a Big Mac costs more in Tokyo than it does in the United States, so the yen is not able to buy as much in Japan as the dollar can buy in the United States (since things are so much more expensive). This means that the purchasing power of the yen is lower—at least in terms of Big Macs. Table 4.3 compares the traditional per capita GNP of several countries with their PPP per capita GNP. It is interesting to note that some countries, such as China, have a higher PPP per capita GNP, whereas others, such as Japan, have a lower PPP per capita GNP. Although there are several countries with a traditional per capita GNP that is higher than that of the United States, there is only one country—Luxembourg—that has a higher PPP per capita GNP than the United States. Thus, even though per capita GNP is the primary measure of wealth in a country, purchasing power GNP is an alternative way to measure wealth that is more indicative of the purchasing power of a country's currency.

Quality of life—human happiness, life expectancy, educational standards, individual
purchasing power, health,
sanitation, treatment of
women

Quality of life   Per capita income, as noted above, does not represent the **quality of life.** The United Nations publishes an annual *Human Development Report* in which it ranks countries according to various measures of human happiness, such as life expectancy, educational standards, individual purchasing power, health, sanita-

Table 4.3
Per Capita Income Measured Two Ways

Country	GNP per capita dollars 1994	PPP estimates of GNP per capita current international dollars 1994
Brazil	3,370	5,630
China	530	2,510
Czech Republic	2,710	7,910
France	23,470	19,820
Japan	34,630	21,350
Mali	250	520
Mexico	4,010	7,050
Russia	2,650	5,260
Thailand	2,210	6,870
U.S.	25,860	25,860

Source: The World Bank, *The World Bank Atlas 1996* (Washington, D.C.: The World Bank. 1995), pp. 18–19.

tion, and treatment of women and other important aspects of life. The top five countries in the 1996 survey are Canada, the United States, Japan, the Netherlands, and Norway. In that list of 174 countries, Russia ranks 57th, China 108th, and India 135th.[15] The 1996 survey also determines a **capability poverty measure,** which is an index that measures factors that could lead to poverty or result in conditions that can negatively affect the future of a country. The index includes measures such as the percentage of children under five who are underweight, the proportion of unattended births, the number of children in school, and the rate of female illiteracy.[16] The objective of this measure is to get countries to look at all factors that might affect a country's future and not focus strictly on income growth.

Another key issue in examining the wealth of a country is to note the widening gap between the rich and poor. The *Human Development Report* referred to above also notes that the gap between rich and poor is not only widening in the United States, but it is widening worldwide. An indication of this gap is where the national average per capital GNP is four times or higher than the average income of the poorest fifth of the country. The ratio of the top 20 percent of U.S. incomes to the poorest 20 percent is now 9 to 1, and the average income of the poorest fifth as a percent of the average per capita income as a whole is 24 percent. In contrast, the latter figure in Japan is 43.5 percent and the Netherlands 41 percent. Comparable numbers for the United Kingdom are 23 percent, basically the same as that of the United States, whereas it is only 10.5 percent in Brazil.[17] Some might argue, however, that equitable income distribution is not the most important issue. More important is whether the bottom fifth of the population has a good overall standard of living, not whether it is the same as the top fifth of the population. Equal distribution gets at the heart of a social welfare economic/political system, whereas a market system is concerned with overall economic gains in a country, not whether the gains are evenly distributed.

In a far less analytical approach to quality of life, the Gallup Poll conducted an international survey of eighteen countries to determine if people were satisfied with their lives, and in all but two of the countries surveyed (Mexico and Hungary), more people say they are satisfied than dissatisfied with their lives. The top five countries were Iceland, Canada, Germany, Thailand, the United States, and France. Although people tended to be more satisfied with their family situation and material possessions, they were least satisfied with their overall financial situation.[18] In explaining Iceland's top ranking, a Professor of Sociology at the University of Iceland feels that the secret of their success is their harsh environment, "Our culture is colored by the harshness of nature. That's why Icelanders have a more tolerant attitude to the problems of life. They don't expect the same sort of stability often expected in other nations."[19] Interestingly, the survey found that although respondents felt that the world in which they live today is better than the one in which their parents grew up, the world the next generation of children would live in would not be better than their own. Quality of life is an important way to compare countries, even though perceptions are relatively subjective.

Capability poverty measure—an index that measures factors that could lead to poverty or result in conditions that can negatively affect the future of a country

Widening gap between rich and poor; relationship between top and bottom fifth of the incomes in a country

Economic Objectives: Equal distribution of income or overall rise in the standard of living?

As per capita income rises, per capita income shifts from agriculture to industry to services.

Structure of production   A final way to classify countries is according to **structure of production,** which refers to the percentage of GDP generated by agriculture, industry, manufacturing (which is a subcategory of industry), and services. Table 4.4 provides this information for the World Bank country categories and a few illustrative countries per category. It is interesting to note that the data for high-income countries were not available in the 1996 *World Development Report* for 1994, but information was provided for a few representative countries. The key is to note that as income rises, the percentage of GDP devoted to agriculture falls, and the percentage devoted to services rises. This is also true across time. In 1980, for example, 34 percent of the GDP of low-income countries went to agriculture, whereas it was only 28 percent in 1994. Industry went from 32 percent to 34 percent, and services from 32 percent to 36 percent.

Key Macroeconomic Issues

Developing countries share many problems and characteristics, although they vary from region to region and country to country. Some of the most frequently mentioned problems are inflation, heavy external debt, weak currencies, shortage of skilled workers, political and economic instability, overreliance on the public sector for economic development, war and insurrection, mass poverty, rapid population growth, weak commodity prices, and environmental degradation. Some of these same problems plague the high-income countries. However, these countries tend to focus on other issues as well. Europeans, for example, have been overly concerned about high unemployment, excessive regulation, competition from the developing countries of Asia, and the assimilation of the former centrally planned economies of Eastern Europe. Economic growth in Europe and North America has also been relatively weak in recent years.

Key macroeconomic factors: economic growth, inflation, debt, and deficits

Table 4.4
Structure of the Economy—Distribution of Gross Domestic Product (%)

	Agriculture	Industry	Manufacturing	Services
Low-income	28	34	25	36
China	21	47	37	32
Tanzania	57	17	8	26
Middle-income	10	36	20	52
Brazil	13	39	25	49
Indonesia	17	41	24	42
Russia	7	38	31	55
High-income	NA	NA	NA	NA
Japan	2	40	27	58
United Kingdom	2	32	22	66

Source: World Bank, *The World Development Report 1996* (New York: Oxford University Press, 1996), pp. 210–211.

In any event, we cannot discuss all aspects of the economic environment in this chapter, and some issues, such as currency, will be discussed in other chapters. However, we will focus on a few important macroeconomic factors at this point: economic growth, inflation, and deficits and debt—both internal and external. Following this section, we will discuss some unique problems of countries in transition from planned to market economies.

A large and growing market is a location-specific advantage of a country.

Economic growth   Companies would like every country to have political stability, a low inflation rate, and a high real growth rate. If this were the case, even if a company did not expand its share in each market, it would still be able to increase revenues at the same pace as the general growth in the economy. However, there are significant differences in growth rates worldwide.

Figure 4.3 illustrates real growth in GDP for high-income and developing countries during the periods 1980–1990 and 1990–1994. In recent years, growth has been especially strong in East and South Asia, where it has been boosted by the region's tremendous market size; Asia's population is ten times North America's and six times Europe's. In contrast, the high-income countries have experienced relatively slower growth, a troublesome sign because they historically have tended to fuel growth in the rest of the world. Further, although high-income countries accounted for 80 percent of the world's GNP in 1994, compared with only 8 percent for Asia (excluding Japan), the *growth rates* in Asia today are averaging about 8 percent annually, compared with less than 2 percent in the high-income countries.

At current growth rates, developing countries could generate 60 percent of the world's GNP by 2020.

Projections of growth trends are dramatic. For example, the World Bank projects the growth of the high-income countries to be 2.7 percent for the period 1994–2003, whereas the developing countries are expected to grow at nearly twice that rate—4.8 percent. Within the developing countries, the greatest growth is expected to take place in East Asia and South Asia—7.6 percent and 5.3 percent, respectively. East Asia and South Asia, minus Japan, comprise 53 percent of the world's population but only 7 percent of its GDP. Using projected growth rates and measuring national income according to purchasing power parity, the high-income countries might account for less than half of the world output by the end of the decade, and less than 40 percent of the total by the year 2020. And by the year 2020, as many as 9 of the top 15 economies in the world could be from developing countries.[20] Thus, companies looking for greater sales and earnings will increasingly look toward the faster-growing economies of Asia rather than the slower-growing economies elsewhere.

This disparity in growth rates creates a major problem: High-income countries tend to invest in the fastest-growing economies, and such investment heightens the disparity. For example, of the total foreign investments in the developing world between 1986 and 1991, 55 percent went to six countries: Mexico, China, Malaysia, Argentina, Brazil, and Thailand. The poorest of the poor, such as Pakistan and Mali, received very little.[21]

Country group	1980 – 1990	1990 – 1994
Developing countries	3.1	1.9
Sub-Sahara Africa	1.7	0.9
East Asia and Pacific	7.9	9.4
South Asia	5.7	3.9
Europe and Central Asia	2.3	-7.5
Middle East and North Africa	0.2	2.3
Latin America and Caribbean	1.7	3.6
High-income countries	3.2	1.7

Figure 4.3
Real Rate of Growth of GDP
Economic growth in recent years has been especially strong in East Asia and South Asia. Developing countries provide large market potential and exhibit strong economic growth overall, but investing there tends to be riskier than in the industrial countries.

Source: World Bank, *World Development Report* (New York: Oxford University Press, 1996), pp. 208–209.

From 1985–1994,
• 68 countries suffered a decline in growth in per capita income
• 28 countries, mostly in East and South Asia, grew at 3 percent or more per annum

When economic and political crisis hit Mexico in late 1994 and early 1995, the instability rippled through Latin America and even other emerging markets outside of Latin America, causing some companies to pull back on their plans to expand in those markets. As economic growth began to pick up, so did their confidence, and the markets became more attractive again. However, during the period 1985–1994, 68 countries suffered a decline in per capita income, and most of those were in developing countries. At the same time, 28 countries enjoyed average annual growth rates of 3 percent or more, representing 30.5 percent of the world's population and 38.7 percent of its GNP. Those countries as a group, represented primarily in East and South Asia as noted in Map 4.2, are important markets for MNEs and prime locations for investment. Their size and growth rates are significant location-specific advantages that cannot be ignored by companies that want to establish global strategic advantage.

Inflation

Inflation is a dimension of the economic environment that affects interest rates, exchange rates, the cost of living, and the general confidence in a country's political and economic system. For example, the constitutional charge of the *Bundesbank,* the central bank of Germany, is to control inflation. When Germany began the assimilation of East Germany with West Germany after the fall of the Berlin Wall in 1989, inflation rose to 2.7 percent in 1990 and a high of 4.1 percent in 1993. The *Bundesbank* raised interest rates to try to bring inflation back into control, which precipi-

Map 4.2
GNP Per Capita Growth Rate, 1985–1994

Sixty-eight countries showed a decline in per capita GNP, whereas countries in South East Asia showed rapid growth.

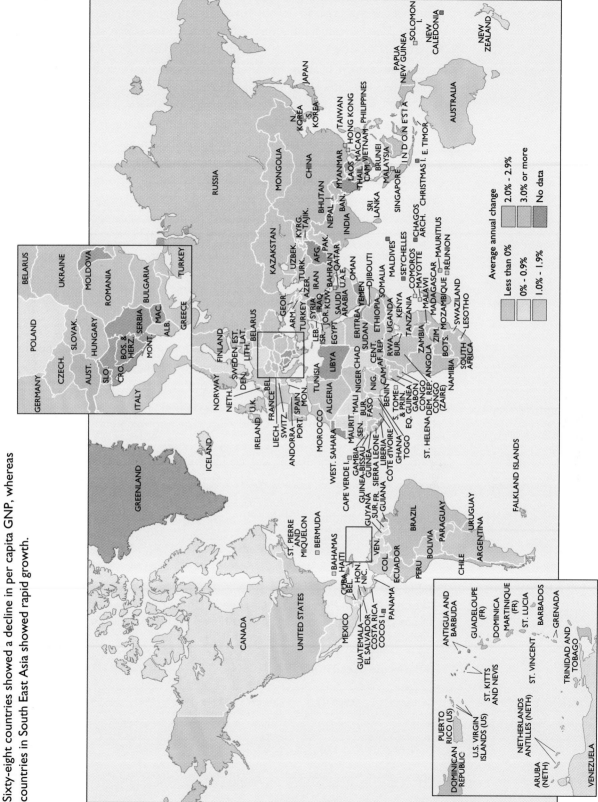

Average annual change

- Less than 0%
- 0% - 0.9%
- 1.0% - 1.9%
- 2.0% - 2.9%
- 3.0% or more
- No data

Inflation can be defined as an increase in the consumer price index from one period to another.

Inflation can cause an increase in interest rates
• to allow for a real return on interest-bearing assets
• to help slow down the economy and reduce inflation

Inflation in developing countries fell to 27.6 percent in 1995, reducing the number of countries considered highly inflationary.

tated a currency crisis in Europe that will be discussed in more detail in Chapters 7 and 10. However, high inflation tends to force interest rates up for two reasons. The first is that interest rates must be higher than inflation so that they can reflect a real return on interest-bearing assets. Otherwise, no one would hold those assets. Second, monetary authorities use high interest rates to bring down inflation. Thus companies must watch the governments of high-inflation countries to determine what economic policies will be used to counteract inflation. If the government uses high interest rates to try to wipe out inflation, economic growth could slow down as well, causing the market to be a less attractive place to do business.

A comparison of annual increases in the consumer price index for selected countries is shown in Tables 4.5 and 4.6. Table 4.5 provides a view of inflation for five-year time periods beginning in 1966 for the broad categories of the world, high-income countries, and developing countries. Table 4.6 provides the annual percentage change in the consumer price index for a sample of high-income and developing countries.

The oil price shocks of the 1960s and 1970s brought with them an increase in inflation, especially in the developing countries. Although inflation continued on a downward trend in the early 1990s, it picked up again in 1993 and 1994, due largely to an increase in inflation in the developing countries. At the beginning of the 1990s, the countries in the IMF survey with inflation of more than 100 percent per year were Sierra Leone, Zambia, Poland, Yugoslavia, Argentina, Brazil, Nicaragua, Peru, and Uruguay. The high-inflation countries at the end 1995 were Russia, Suriname, the Ukraine, and Zaire. The improvement was due to the overall drop in the inflation rate in the developing countries from 66 percent in 1994 to 27.6 percent in 1995. Russia and the Ukraine were not included in the 1990 IMF survey but were undoubtedly highly inflationary at that time as well. Brazil, a country that registered high inflation at 2,937.8 percent in 1990, improved to 84.4 percent for 1995, and was less than 30 percent on an annual basis for the first quarter of 1996. The government's resolve to control inflation seemed to be working.

Table 4.5

Average Annual Percentage Change in Consumer Price Index for Each Period
Inflation gradually rose over the period 1966–1990. In particular, the developing countries exhibited significantly higher inflation than the industrial countries over every time period, but the difference was greatest since the early 1980s when inflation began to come down in the industrial countries.

Category	1966–1970	1971–1975	1976–1980	1981–1985	1986–1990	1991–1995
World	5.9	10.1	13.2	15.0	20.6	18.3
High-income	4.1	8.6	9.4	6.5	3.8	3.0
Developing	13.0	13.1	20.4	31.3	54.6	47.4

Source: International Financial Statistics Yearbook, 1995 (Washington, D.C.: International Monetary Fund, 1994), p. 121; International Financial Statistics (Washington, D.C.: International Monetary Fund, July 1996), p. 69.

Table 4.6
Percentage Change in Consumer Price Index over Previous Year

In 1994, compared with the previous four years, inflation began to creep back up in the world in general and in the developing countries in particular. There was improvement in Argentina, a country that formerly experienced hyperinflation, but a worsening situation in Brazil until its new economic plan was put into effect in 1994. Inflation in Brazil reached an annual rate of over 4,000 percent in the 3rd quarter of 1994 before it began to improve. By 1995, inflation had begun to fall back in the developing countries as a whole, and some countries such as Brazil in particular.

Country or Category	Year					
	1990	1991	1992	1993	1994	1995
World	21.3%	12.7%	11.9%	19.7%	23.8%	11.7%
High-Income Countries	5.0	4.3	3.0	2.8	2.3	2.5
Canada	4.8	5.6	1.5	3.0	2.6	2.2
France	3.4	3.2	2.4	2.1	1.7	1.8
Germany	2.7	3.5	4.0	4.1	3.0	1.8
Japan	3.1	3.3	1.7	1.3	0.7	−0.1
United Kingdom	9.5	5.9	3.7	1.6	2.5	3.4
United States	5.4	4.2	3.0	3.0	2.6	2.8
Developing Countries	103.7	49.1	51.8	52.3	66.8	27.6
Argentina	2314.0	171.7	24.9	10.6	4.2	3.4
Brazil	2937.8	440.9	1008.7	2148.4	2668.5	84.4
Hong Kong	9.7	11.0	9.6	8.7	8.6	9.2
Korea	8.6	9.7	6.2	4.8	6.3	4.5
Mexico	3.7	4.0	1.4	9.8	7.0	35.0
Peru	7481.7	409.5	73.5	48.6	23.7	11.1
Russia	n/a	n/a	n/a	874.6	307.4	197.4

Source: International Financial Statistics (Washington, D.C.: International Monetary Fund, various issues).

Companies with dealings in high-inflation countries have difficulty planning for the future and running profitable operations. They must change prices almost daily in order to maintain sufficient cash flow to replace inventory and keep operating. Accurate inflation forecasting also is difficult, and so companies end up underpricing or overpricing products. This practice results in a cash-flow shortage or a price that is too high to allow the company to maintain market share.

Inflation of the magnitude seen in Brazil in the early 1990s and Russia also creates problems for companies that deal in imports and exports. If the exchange rate depreciates at the same pace as inflation rises, then the prices foreigners pay for the exports of the inflationary country will not change. However, an exchange rate that depreciates slower than inflation rises causes prices to increase in importing countries. The local companies soon find they cannot compete in world markets. A depreciating currency also causes the cost of inputs to rise, thus further fueling inflation. To keep its costs from being affected much by exchange-rate changes, the Moscow McDonald's developed a strategy of purchasing as many inputs as possible in Russia. However, inflation in Moscow is pushing up local costs and forcing McDonald's to raise prices as well.

Inflation causes political destabilization. If the government tries to control inflation by controlling wages, the real income of the population declines and frustration sets in. If the government decides to do nothing, the economy may deteriorate to the point that real incomes fall anyway. Instituting tighter fiscal controls when the government is already in a fragile position is very difficult. This is clearly the problem that faces both Brazil and Russia and strikes fear in the Chinese government. As mentioned earlier in this chapter, China has been experiencing rapid economic growth that began in the early 1990s. However, this growth, if allowed to get out of hand, could reignite inflation, thus devaluing the Chinese currency and forcing the government to slow down economic growth. Such instability concerns foreign investors, who hesitate to invest significant amounts of money in the country.[22]

Surpluses and Deficits—International Transactions

The transactions between the residents of one country and all other countries are captured in the balance of payments of that country. These transactions constitute either an export or an import. For each transaction, payment must either be received from a foreign resident (an export) or made to a foreign resident (an import). The major balance of active transactions (those for which payment must be received or made) included in the balance of payments is called the **current account balance,** and it is comprised of the following transactions:

- Merchandise trade account
- Services account
- Income receipts and payments on assets accounts
- Unilateral transfers account

The **merchandise trade account** measures the trade deficit or surplus. Its balance is derived by subtracting merchandise imports from merchandise exports. A negative result indicates a balance-of-trade deficit; a positive result, a balance-of-trade surplus. An export is considered positive because it results in a payment received from abroad—an inflow of cash. An import is considered negative because it results in a payment made to a seller abroad—an outflow of cash. For example, in 1995, the United States had a deficit in the balance of merchandise trade (also known as goods) of $174 billion, of which $59.3 billion was the deficit with Japan. In 1995, the deficit with China was $33.8 billion, and in June 1996, the deficit with China exceeded that of Japan.[23] In 1996, the merchandise trade deficit with Japan narrowed to $47.7 billion, and the deficit with China widened to $39.5 billion. The overall trade deficit (which includes both merchandise and services trade) widened from $105.06 billion to $114.23 billion. However, the deficit in 1996 was actually smaller than 1988's deficit of $115.52 billion.

The **services account** measures the following transactions: travel and transportation, tourism, and fees and royalties. For example, when a German tourist vacations in the United States, that person's total expenditures are considered to be a service *export*—that is, a cash inflow from Germany. When a U.S. tourist vacations in Germany, that person's total expenditures are considered to be a service *import*—that is, a cash outflow to Germany.

Income receipts and payments on assets accounts measure foreign investment in the United States and U.S. investment abroad. For example, a dividend received by a U.S. company from one of its subsidiaries in Brazil is considered to be an income *receipt*. A dividend sent by, for example, BMW of America to its parent company in Munich is considered to be an income *payment*.

Unilateral transfers are payments made to a country for which no goods or services are received. For example, to help defray the cost of the Gulf War in 1991, many countries made payments to the United States. These payments were represented by a positive entry under unilateral transfers in the U.S. balance-of-payments accounts.

In summary, the current account balance is the arithmetic sum of the exports and imports of goods, services, and income, and net unilateral transfers.

Balance-of-payments surpluses and deficits can influence trade policy and the value of currencies.

Impact of different balances on business What difference does it make whether a country has a current account surplus or deficit? There probably is no direct effect; however, the events that comprise the balance-of-payments data influence exchange rates (as discussed in Chapter 10) and government policy (as discussed in Chapter 6), which, in turn, influence corporate strategy. The size of the deficit can be measured in absolute terms or as a percentage of GDP. In 1994, for example, the current account deficit of the United States was $136.5 billion, whereas the current account surplus of Japan was $133.9 billion. These respective balances were by far the largest in the world. Closest to the United States was Mexico with a deficit of $28.9 billion, and closest to Japan was Italy with a surplus of $21.5 billion.[24] As a percentage of GDP, however, the United States was not so bad with a deficit of just 2.1 percent. There were 60 countries with deficits that were a larger percentage of GDP, including Mozambique with the largest at 71.4 percent.[25]

Deficit Measures: Size of Deficit, Percentage of GDP

The policy implications of current account deficits are illustrated in several countries in Southeast Asia, including Thailand and Malaysia, which were suffering current account deficits in 1996. Thailand's deficit was expected to reach 8 percent of GDP by the end of 1996, whereas Malaysia's deficit was expected to reach 10 percent.[26] Although the deficits were partly a result of slower export growth, the governments were focusing on policy issues to curtail imports. Malaysia's prime minister argued that "if Malaysians could not restrain themselves from buying imports, then duties should be raised and, if that did not work, quotas and import permits should be imposed on certain nonessential goods. This would be better than to try and stifle growth by increasing interest rates."[27]

Two ways to solve payments imbalance
- **restrict imports**
- **raise interest rates to slow down economic growth**

Thus it appears that two ways to help solve a payments imbalance are to restrict imports or slow down economic growth through raising interest rates so that demand for imports slows. In the first case, companies exporting to the country will suffer, as will foreign investors inside the country that rely on the import of essential materials and components. In addition, it might be more difficult to get access to foreign exchange to remit dividends to the parent company. In the second case, the general slowdown of the economy would affect demand, thus making the country a less attractive place as a market and a location for investment.

External Debt

The regions in which external debts are largest are Latin America and Africa.

One consequence of the rapid increase in oil costs during the 1970s was the equally rapid increase in many countries' external debt. This burgeoning debt resulted as developing countries sought help from foreign private or government institutions to finance oil imports and other products necessary for development. At the time, the two regions where the largest borrowing occurred were Latin America and Africa.

Figure 4.4 identifies the major debtors among the developing countries in 1994. Note the tremendous debt of Brazil and Mexico. It is interesting to observe that in 1986, South Korea was third; in 1994, it ranked tenth. A major problem with large debt is that countries find it difficult to pay even the interest, let alone the principal.

As noted in Table 4.7, there are at least four different ways to measure external debt: the actual amount, external debt as a percentage of GNP, external debt as a percentage of exports of goods and services, and the debt-service ratio. External debt as a percentage of GNP helps keep the size of debt in perspective. As noted in the table, this is quite high for Sub-Saharan Africa. For most countries in Africa, debt as a percentage of GNP exceeds 100 percent. The worst country is Nicaragua, however, with debt equal to 800 percent of GNP.[28]

Figure 4.4
External Debt of Selected Developing Countries, 1994
The two largest borrowing regions of the world were Latin America and Africa, led by Brazil and Mexico. The large amount of debt creates cash-flow problems for developing countries as they must use an increasing share of their export earnings to pay principal and interest.

Source: World Bank, *World Development Report* (New York: Oxford University Press, 1996), pp. 220–221.

Country	Abbreviation	Total debt, 1994 (in billions)
Brazil	BRZ	$151.1
Mexico	MEX	128.3
China	CHI	100.5
India	IND	99.0
Indonesia	INDO	96.5
Russia	RUS	94.2
Argentina	ARG	77.4
Turkey	TUR	66.3
Thailand	THA	61.0
Korea, Rep. of	KOR	54.5

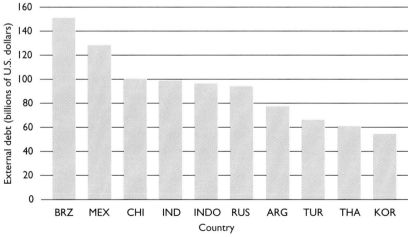

Table 4.7
External Debt Indicators, 1994

Developing country regions	External debt as a percentage of GNP	Exports of goods and services	Debt-service ratio
Sub-Saharan Africa	78.7	265.7	14.0
East Asia and Pacific	30.9	93.3	12.0
South Asia	42.0	271.6	25.6
Europe and Central Asia	32.8	153.7	14.6
Middle East and North Africa	41.7	148.5	15.4
Latin America and Caribbean	37.2	258.6	27.5

Source: World Development Report 1996 (Washington, D.C.: World Bank, 1996), p. 221.

Four Ways to Measure External Debt
- Absolute size
- As a percentage of GNP or GDP
- As a percentage of exports
- Debt-service ratio (ratio of interest payments plus principal amortization to exports)

High debt-service ratios hamper economic growth.

Current account deficits may lead to external debt.

The second measure is external debt as a percentage of exports of goods and services. This measure relates the size of the debt to the capacity of the company to generate foreign exchange to pay off the debt. Sub-Saharan Africa, South Asia, and Latin America and the Caribbean are about the same with debt over 200 percent of exports. In Nicaragua and Rwanda, debt is over 2000 percent of exports.[29]

The final measure is the debt-service ratio, which is the ratio of interest payments plus principal amortization to exports. South Asia and Latin America and the Caribbean are the two regions with the highest debt-service ratios, although all regions have countries with ratios in excess of 20 percent. An increasing share of many countries' export earnings are going to service their debt; thus, less is available for economic development. A total of 28 countries have to use at least one quarter of their export earnings just to service their external debt.[30] That really hampers local economic development. If the debt is invested in capital developments, it should help improve the location-specific advantage of the borrowing country. However, if the debt gets too big, it becomes a drag on the economy.

The interrelationship between deficits and debt is obvious, especially given the importance of linking exports to the ability to repay debt. As noted above, some countries in South Asia are suffering from current account deficits. Although Indonesia's deficit as a percentage of GDP was expected to be only 3.8 percent in 1996, compared with Thailand's 8 percent and Malaysia's 10 percent, there was still concern in Indonesia because of its nearly $100 billion of external debt. In 1994, Indonesia's external debt as a percentage of GNP was 57.4 percent, its external debt as a percentage of exports of goods and services was 211.3 percent, and its debt-service ratio was 32.4 percent, all well above the averages for East Asia and Pacific countries as noted in Table 4.7.[31] As a result, Indonesian President Suharto warned that "a surge in imports may have a far-reaching impact on growth and equitable distribution,"[32] encouraging people to buy local rather than imported products.

The debt crisis of the 1980s resulted in several defaults and reschedulings of loans.

In response to the increasing uncertainty regarding repayment of developing country loans, many banks began setting aside large reserves in case those debtors defaulted. A bank establishes reserves by funneling some of its earnings into a reserve account. Doing this allows it to reduce earnings a little each year, especially profitable years, rather than being surprised by a major default and having to reduce earnings all at once. However, the practice of setting aside large reserves is problematic because it weakens the bank's lending ability and financial strength.

The IMF provides economic advice to help countries solve debt problems and get new loans; it also has created controversy.

The International Monetary Fund (IMF), which will be discussed in greater detail in Chapter 10, has played a crucial role in helping debtor nations restructure their economies. In country after country, the IMF has recommended strong economic restrictions as a precondition to granting a loan. These restrictions typically have involved a combination of export expansion, import substitution, and drastic reductions in public spending. In many developing countries, IMF restrictions have touched off heated debate and sorely tested the political stability of the government.

In many cases, an IMF loan is a prerequisite for persuading international commercial banks to reschedule a country's debts. Usually, the IMF periodically monitors the targets it sets as a precondition to releasing funds. Private international banks often use the results of this monitoring to determine their lending policies regarding the monitored country.

Managers of MNEs are concerned about high debt because of the difficulty of operating in an environment that is politically and economically unstable. In such an environment, imports often are curtailed and hard currency is difficult to obtain. In addition, governments may institute a variety of macroeconomic measures to control debt, including slowing down economic growth, which could have a negative impact on companies' sales opportunities.

Deficits and Privatization

Two ways to measure internal deficits
• Absolute size
• As percentage of GDP or GNP

A constant struggle for governments, in high-income as well as in developing countries, in market as well as command economies, and at the federal, state, provincial, and local levels, is the balance between revenues and expenditures, with expenditures usually exceeding revenues. In 1994, for example, only two high-income countries—New Zealand and Singapore—had a central government surplus. A good measure of the size of the deficit is the ratio of the deficit to GDP or GNP. However, as noted by the World Bank, "Because of differences in coverage of available data, the individual components of central government expenditure and revenue shown may not be strictly comparable across all economies. Inadequate statistical coverage of state, provincial, and local governments requires the use of central government data; this may seriously understate or distort the statistical portrayal of the allocation of resources for various purposes, especially in countries where lower levels of government have considerable autonomy and are responsible for many economic and social services."[33]

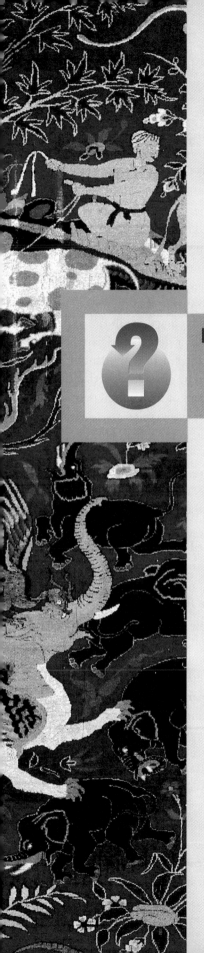

A major issue of social responsibility implied in this chapter concerns the obligations of high-income countries to assist developing ones. Some of the areas in which the high-income countries might be seen as having an ethical obligation to provide support are access to markets for developing countries' exports, foreign aid, and repayment of loans.

First, developing countries must have access to markets in high-income countries in order to sell products. Many developing countries have domestic markets of limited size, and their trade with each other is not significant. For example, Latin American countries on average export only about 10 percent of their products to other Latin American countries but almost 20 percent of them to the United States. However, during the recent period of relatively high unemployment in industrial countries, protectionism has threatened to cut off developing countries' access to industrial markets. If high-income countries discriminate against exports from developing countries, they are hurting those countries' prospects for further development.

ETHICAL DILEMMAS & SOCIAL RESPONSIBILITY

As for foreign aid, there has been increasing pressure in the United States to cut down the amount of such aid in order to put the funds to use in improving the domestic economy. However, the United States and other high-income countries benefit from trade with developing countries not only through gaining access to their markets but also through utilizing their resources. Some high-income countries view foreign aid as a means of putting resources back into developing countries. For example, the Scandinavian countries contribute a larger percentage of their GDPs to foreign aid than do the United States and Japan. And other high-income European countries, such as Germany and the Netherlands, provide funding to their developing neighbors Spain and Portugal to help them improve their infrastructure. In contrast, when the United States and Mexico were debating NAFTA in 1993, much of the opposition to the agreement came from people who wondered how it was going to be funded rather than how the United States could provide more resources to Mexico to help develop the economy.

A third ethical issue concerns the repayment of loans. Because of the overwhelming size of the external debt of many developing countries, one possible solution is forgiveness of some or all of such debt. Another possibility is to restructure it so that repayment is less burdensome to a developing country's economic growth. Forgiveness might be more appropriate for loans made by governments of high-income countries than for those made by private-sector banks. But, in any case, some feel the high-income countries need to make an effort to be part of the solution to the debt crisis rather than just part of the problem.

European Union Targets
• **Budget deficits less than 3 percent of GDP**
• **Debt not more than 60 percent of GDP**

However, the measure is still an important one to consider. The European Union identified several criteria that countries must meet as they move to establishing a common currency—which will be discussed more in Chapter 10—and two of the criteria refer to deficits and debt. National budget deficits must be less than 3 percent of GDP, and the public debt ratio (total debt to GDP) must not exceed 60 percent.[34] The World Bank measures a country's surplus/deficit as current revenue of the central government less current expenditure. Specifically excluded are grants and the capital account.[35] Seven of the 25 countries listed by the World Bank as high-income countries had deficits greater than 3 percent of GNP, including seven members of the European Union. Although there is serious political debate in the United States over the size of the budget deficit, it was only 2.2 percent of GNP in 1994. However, it was only 0.4 percent in 1980. The problem is that the size of the deficit is significant, even though it is a relatively small percentage of GNP.[36]

Financial markets have forced countries to reduce deficits.

It is clear that countries have been moving to reduce their deficits and have been successful in doing so. This has been due in large part to the reaction of financial markets to government fiscal policies and the recognition by governments that they need to bring their deficits under control. In the early years of the Clinton presidency, budget battles with Congress and the inability to forge a consensus to establish a balanced budget put significant downward pressure on the dollar. However, in fiscal year 1995, the average budget deficit of high-income countries in the Organization for Economic Cooperation and Development was expected to be only 3.4 percent of GDP. The United States was expected to have "the smallest budget deficit, the lowest level of government expenditure and the lowest tax burden, relative to economic size."[37]

Reasons for internal deficits
• **Poor tax collection system**
• **Huge government programs**
• **Government ownership of assets**

Major targets
• **Rightsizing government**
• **Setting spending priorities**
• **Better expenditure control and budget management**
• **Improving tax policy and administration**
• **Decentralization of some services**

Government internal deficits typically occur for one of several reasons: The tax system is so poor that the government cannot collect all the revenues it wants to, government programs such as defense and welfare are too big for the revenue side to adequately cover, and the government gets involved in the ownership of assets. In addition, there is the constant battle between liberals and conservatives as illustrated in the United States over whether cutting taxes will lead to greater personal freedom but higher budget deficits, or if it will result in the stimulation of growth and the collection of higher revenues, but at lower personal rates. Thus all governments, including those in transition from command to market, struggle with several issues, such as rightsizing government, setting spending priorities, working toward better expenditure control and budget management, improving tax policy and administration to close the revenue gap, and the degree to which services should be decentralized.[38]

Privatization: sale of state-owned assets

Privatization   As countries move to control expenditures and reduce their budget deficits, a major target is state-owned companies. The movement of ownership from the public to the private sector is known as **privatization,** and it involves all types of countries. There are many benefits to privatization, which include

Benefits of privatization

- improving enterprise efficiency and performance
- developing competitive industry that services consumers well
- assessing the capital, know-how, and markets that permit growth
- achieving effective corporate governance
- broadening and deepening capital markets, and
- securing the best price possible for the sale.[39]

However, privatization is not easy. It is a political as well as an economic process, and political objectives do not always result in the best economic results. In addition to political objectives are political impediments, such as the obstructive attitudes of existing managers and employees of state-owned enterprises.[40]

Industrial countries account for 15 percent of privatization but 65 percent of revenues.

The term "privatization" began with the sale of British Telecom in 1984, and most of the significant earlier privatization efforts took place in Britain. The process gradually spread to other high-income countries and eventually to the developing countries. After the fall of the Berlin Wall in 1989, the privatization effort moved to the countries of Eastern Europe and the former Soviet Union, which will be discussed more in the final section of the chapter. The privatization efforts in the noncommunist world took place primarily through cash sales. As noted by the International Finance Corporation, "a database of larger, [cash] sales records 2,655 transactions in 95 countries between 1988 and 1993, yielding US$271 billion in revenues. Industrialized countries accounted for US$175 billion of this, and 15 percent of the number of transactions, so over the period developing countries accounted for 85 percent of sales and 35 percent of all revenue generated."[41]

In the developing countries, the privatization movement began in Latin America and the Caribbean, with 57 percent of the value of total developing-country privatizations taking place there, followed by Europe and Central Asia with 18.7 percent, and only minimal privatizations in Sub-Saharan Africa, the Middle East, and North Africa.[42]

Key: availability of capital

The key to successful privatization is the availability of capital. Although privatization is a lofty goal preached by governments worldwide, Europeans alone will have to come up with more than $150 billion before the end of the decade to pay for numerous efforts ranging from automakers to banks to oil and telecommunications companies.[43] This implies solid capital markets and both domestic and foreign investors willing to purchase the state-owned companies.

France provides an example of the privatization experience. Most efforts at privatization in France have involved selling minority interests in state-owned enterprises, with little initial involvement by foreign investors. When the conservatives came into power in 1993, they vowed to privatize all banks, insurance companies, and competitive enterprises such as Renault, Elf Aquitaine, and Pechiney. To help fund the country's privatization effort, the conservatives have sought to attract significant foreign capital by encouraging increased foreign involvement and by allowing foreigners to hold a larger percentage of French companies.[44]

The problems that France has faced are no different from those of other European countries that are privatizing state-owned assets. Some of the factors that seem to have an impact on the success of privatization are: (1) the relative health and stability of the local stock market as well as those in surrounding countries, (2) the number of offers in the market, both at home and abroad, (3) tight monetary policy, which can prolong a recession and depress corporate profits, making it more difficult for local companies to generate the cash necessary to get involved in the privatization efforts, and (4) the perceived openness of the bidding process. Many French, for example, feel that the government has a tendency to sell major stakes in privatized companies to hard cores of friendly buyers in France which help insulate the companies from unfriendly takeovers.[45]

Shift in France to consolidation of competitors and strategic alliances with non-French companies

In 1996, the French government embarked on a new plan to move protected state-owned defense and industrial companies out of the government support mechanism by allowing consolidation among competitors inside France and then allowing the surviving companies to establish strategic alliances with similar companies in Europe. Given the deep roots of state support for national industry in France, the policy shift is not insignificant. The French government's budget deficit reduction plan has forced it to follow the policy of moving away from state-owned enterprises.[46] However, the privatization efforts have not been as extensive as advertised. The same is true with developing countries such as Venezuela, Argentina, and Mexico. Even though the governments have announced major privatization efforts, the actual experience has not been as advertised.

In most of the countries, the problem with privatization is selling the inefficient, unproductive enterprises, not those that have a chance to survive. Where permitted, the privatization process enables foreign companies to pick up assets and gain access to markets through acquisition. In addition, international managers accustomed to dealing with state-owned enterprises are finding a new breed of managers in the newly privatized enterprises with which they do business.

Transformation to a Market Economy

The demolition of the Berlin Wall and the overthrow of Eastern European communist dictatorships in 1989 renewed Western interest in doing business in countries that previously had been considered off limits. These countries were those that had had nonmarket economies (NMEs), or centrally planned economies (CPEs), or that had been commonly called the Second World or the Eastern Bloc. (The latter term was political rather than geographic. East-West trade referred to business between communist and noncommunist countries rather than to trade between the Eastern and Western Hemispheres.)

Most of the CPEs are in the process of transition to a market economy, hence the designation CEIT, as defined earlier in the chapter. In a report by the United Nations on demographic changes in CEITs, the discussion was generally grouped around the European successor states of the former USSR (Estonia, Latvia, Lithuania, Belarus, Republic of Moldova, Russian Federation, and the Ukraine), the Asian successor states of the former USSR (Armenia, Azerbaijan, Georgia, Kazkhastan, Kyrgyzstan, Tajikistan, Turkmenistan, and Uzbekistan), and other European countries (Bulgaria, Czech Republic, Hungary, Poland, Romania, Slovakia, Albania, Bosnia and Herzegovina, Croatia, Slovenia, Macedonia, and Yugoslavia). In addition, there are CPEs in other parts of the world that are going through transition, including Cuba, Vietnam, China, and North Korea.[47] And the transition is taking place at radically different rates. One could argue that Cuba and North Korea are not making any transition at all at this point. Even though there are significant demographic economic transitions taking place in these countries, there is no common pattern. In addition, data are not reliable for all countries. However, the latest data on these countries can be found in the gopher reference in note 47.

One could also argue that all countries are going through transitions of different types. For example, the statist economies of Latin America are also moving more to democracy on a political scale and are privatizing state-owned companies in order to downsize government and introduce market reforms. However, the CEITs are going through a much more significant transition from one economic system to a radically different economic system. Thus we will focus on the problems of these countries rather than all countries in transition.

The process of transformation to a market economy differs from country to country; no single formula can be applied to all. In addition, the various CEITs differ greatly in their commitment to and progress toward transformation of their centrally planned economies into market economies. At one end of the spectrum is the former German Democratic Republic (East Germany), which has been reunited with and absorbed into the German Federal Republic (West Germany), although with great difficulty. At the other end of the spectrum is Cuba, which has committed to neither reforms nor market transformation. It is unlikely Cuba will embark on transformation any time soon. Fidel Castro, Cuba's leader, said in 1989, in reference to the political liberalization and other changes within Eastern Europe, "We are witnessing sad things in other socialist countries, very sad things. We are astonished at the phenomena that we see."[48]

In the middle of the spectrum of economic transformation are the other CEITs. For example, Hungary and the Czech Republic are in the process of transformation, but Bulgaria and Romania continue to maintain that a combination of central planning and market economy is possible.[49] Poland is committed but has not had time to complete the change. China, like Bulgaria and Romania, is committed to a combination of central planning and market economy; thus it has embarked on some reforms but still adheres to communistic and central planning principles.

Why do these changes bring renewed Western interest in doing business with CEITs? The answer is partly political, partly economic. Most CEITs experienced slow economic growth during the 1970s and 1980s; consequently, the outlook for expanded commercial activities seemed bleak. However, along with reforms and

Western interest in doing business with CEITs has been renewed because of
• **Improved political relationships**
• **Prospects of economic growth**

transformation has come a thawing of Cold War tensions. With that comes the hope that governments of these countries will eliminate their trade barriers, thereby encouraging rejuvenated economic growth and increased business opportunities.

There is significant interest among MNEs in Eastern Europe HPEs and China.

Much of the recent optimism has centered around business possibilities in Eastern Europe and China. Interest in the former is due to their level of economic development, and the latter has been the focus of attention because of its huge population and rapid economic growth. These conditions help explain why McDonald's has entered Hungary, Russia, and China but not Mongolia.

China has a high growth rate.

China is a special case. Although its per capita income is only about one quarter of that of Eastern European countries, its recent economic growth rate is much higher, rivaling those of its East Asian neighbors. As noted earlier in the chapter, even the World Bank concedes that its low per capita income figures may not accurately describe the dynamic Chinese economy. Because of China's large economy and understated per capita income, there is greater market potential in that country than might seem apparent.

Political and Economic Volatility

Western business with CEITs has been compared to a light switch: It turns on and then turns off.[50] The McDonald's case illustrates how business volatility is created by changing political attitudes. McDonald's negotiations with the Soviets began in 1976 and continued without significant progress until the Soviets enacted joint venture legislation in 1987. From that point, negotiations concluded swiftly and start-up followed soon afterward.

Volatility of East-West trade has occurred when
- **CEIT actions change**
- **Different leaders come into power in the East or the West**

Sometimes volatility has resulted from unpopular actions by CEITs (such as the Soviet invasion of Afghanistan). In some cases, it may result from the ascendancy either of new political decision makers in the East or of leaders in the West who hold differing philosophies about business interactions with dictatorships and/or countries with central planning (for example, U.S. trade sanctions against Cuba).

Although relations between most CEITs and the Western industrialized countries have been more congenial since 1989, the risk of future sanctions by the West still exists.

Political volatility makes managers reluctant to expend resources.

Most companies prefer to invest their capital and human resources in endeavors that can be expected to continue for a long time. For this reason, persistent uncertainty about political relations with some CEITs causes some companies to hesitate to commit resources to business development in those countries. On the one hand, Western businesses have witnessed increased political interactions. On the other hand, they also realize that past experience shows how rapidly business can change because of politics and how it can continue to fluctuate over time.

It also is important to realize that a country's attaining a market economy does not guarantee its economic success; in fact, most of the world's developing countries currently qualify as market economies. The CEITs vary widely in terms of factors that may affect their growth, with or without a high degree of transformation. These factors include the following:

- Educational level of the population
- Quantity and distribution of natural resources
- Degree of national cohesiveness
- Access to investment capital
- Extent of existing industrial structure
- Entrepreneurial experience among the population
- Development of infrastructure

Some CEITs want to
- **Become market economies**
- **Make reforms within a central planning system**
- **Stay as they are**

Companies contemplating commercial activities in CEITs should examine development potential as well as prospects for economic transformation. The key to successful transformation to a market economy is achieving certain changes in the general economic environment, including monetary stabilization, currency convertibility, and price and trade liberalization.[51] Once a private sector appears, these economic changes are the ones that will keep the transformation process working.

The Process of Transformation

The World Bank, in its *World Development Report 1996,* entitled "From Plan to Market," described the legacy of planning and its problems. Although there were early gains in economic growth and industrialization, in the equal distribution of income, and in the welfare of people, the planning process was very unstable and inefficient, leading to a poor utilization of resources and a worsening of social indicators. "In response, most of these economies have rejected all or much of central planning and have embarked on a passage—a transition—toward decentralized market mechanisms underpinned by widespread private ownership."[52] However, the report also noted that the transition is different in different countries due to "different histories, cultures, and resource endowments."[53]

Russia's Transformation

Russian transformation is being hindered by political turmoil.

For Russia, transformation to a market economy has been difficult because the government has been trying simultaneously to change the country's economy and its political system while coming to grips with the end of an empire whose parts were politically and economically interdependent. The resulting political turmoil is exacerbated by the battle between conservatives who are afraid of moving too fast and reformers who want to install capitalism quickly through privatization and price decontrol.

Russia is trying to move to a market economy, instill democracy, and recover from the breakup of the Soviet Empire.

The Soviet economy was cumbersome, inefficient, and corrupt, but somehow it seemed to function. However, the breakup of the central Soviet government and the loss of the relationship Russia had with the other fourteen Soviet republics and the former Eastern Bloc countries resulted in the implosion of the economy. For example, in 1992, Russia's GDP fell by about 23 percent and unemployment rose from 59,000 in January to 905,000 in November. Also in 1992, prices were decontrolled. Prior to that, prices were controlled by the government and goods were distributed by means of consumers waiting in long lines, because of shortages. Price decontrol resulted in more products being brought to market, but at the cost of significantly higher prices and inflation that soared to over 1000 percent annually. Fully two thirds of the Russian people live below the poverty line. From the period of 1990–1994, the average annual growth in GDP was −10.6 percent, the average annual growth in per capita GNP from 1985–1994 was −4.1 percent, and the average annual inflation from 1984–1994 was 124.3 percent.[54] The Russian ruble, valued at 120 per U.S. dollar in early 1992, had fallen to 5683 rubles per dollar by the end of February 1997.

However, as noted earlier in the chapter, Russia is starting to make real progress in the transformation process. Although data coming from Russia look a little bleak, they are also inaccurate. Over 95 percent of Russia's shops are privately owned, and retailing now accounts for half of Russia's GDP. However, about 25 percent of the Russian economy is unrecorded, so economic activity is not as bad as it might seem. To continue the transformation process, Russia needs to stabilize the economy, enforce property rights, and reform local government. Inflation is out of control, largely because of the huge government deficit, half of which comes from subsidizing inefficient enterprises.[55]

Eastern Europe's Transformation

GDP is beginning to grow again in Eastern European countries.

In the three years following the overthrow of communism in 1989 and 1990, economic growth in Eastern Europe ground to a halt. From 1990 to 1992, GNP fell by 40 percent in Czechoslovakia, 32 percent in Hungary, and 32 percent in Poland. However, by 1992, the worst appeared to be over. Poland exhibited solid real growth in 1993 and 1994. Hungary showed a drop in real GNP in 1993, but it had real growth of 2.9 percent in 1994. The Czech Republic showed real growth in GDP of 2.6 percent in 1994 and 4.8 percent in 1995. Thus the big three in Eastern Europe—Poland, Hungary, and the Czech Republic—appear to be well on the way to positive growth.[56]

Eastern Europe's macroeconomic problems are shortages and inflation.

Its microeconomic problems arise from having invested in the wrong industries.

The process of transforming CEITs to market economies attempts to solve two types of problems that are universal in Eastern Europe: macroeconomic problems that involve shortages and inflation and microeconomic problems that involve investments in the wrong industries. As price controls ended and markets opened up all over Eastern Europe, shortages began to disappear fairly quickly. However, central planning had resulted in highly inefficient industries and the transformation of state-owned enterprises resulted in a sharp drop in production, much of which was unwanted and unnecessary anyway. Today, the output of the private sector is growing much more rapidly than that of the remaining public sector.[57]

As Eastern European countries transform, they are finding their budget deficits rising, not because of higher government expenditures, but because of weak revenue collections. Failing enterprises are not paying taxes, resulting in continuing revenue shortfalls.

China's Transformation

In 1978, China's government launched reforms designed to transform the Chinese economy on the basis of a new vision—a turning away from central planning, government ownership, and import substitution and a movement toward greater decentralization and opening up of the Chinese economy. Since then, the Chinese economy has grown to four times its size in 1978; by 2002, it is estimated to be eight times as large as in 1978.[58]

The Chinese economy is growing rapidly, but the political system is not moving toward democracy.

The Chinese approach to transformation differs significantly from those taken in Russia and Eastern Europe. The Chinese leadership is not at all interested in democratic reform. It continues to hold tight to totalitarian political control, while trying to pacify citizens with economic growth. Recently, most of such growth has been along the coast and near the special economic zones, but current reforms are rapidly moving economic changes into the much poorer interior. Privatization is not an issue, but economic activity has been decentralized swiftly. Centralized state-owned enterprises now control only half of GNP, and their share is rapidly dwindling as economic power is pushed down to the regional and local levels, resulting in what looks like a loose federation of regional economies.[59]

The Chinese economy is being rapidly decentralized but not necessarily privatized.

One major advantage China enjoys is a high rate of investment by overseas Chinese. "Today, at least 75 percent of the mainland's roughly 28,000 enterprises with significant foreign equity are financed by ethnic Chinese who live outside China. Hong Kong and Taiwan account for two-thirds [Hong Kong is the largest source of foreign investment in China]."[60] In contrast to Russia and Eastern Europe, significant foreign investment is moving into China.[61]

Overseas Chinese are major investors in China.

Keys to a Successful Transition to Market

There are several keys to a successful transition to market, including the following:

1. It is important for countries to establish the firm and persistent application of good policies, but the way this is done is partially determined by the history, geography, and culture of the country. As noted above, not every country can succeed the same way.

2. "Extensive liberalization and determined stabilization are needed for improved productivity and growth and sustaining these policies requires rapid structural change as well as institutional reform." This implies the liberalization of prices and trade regimes, hard budgets, and the entry of new businesses. A hard budget is one set by market conditions without government subsidies. In a soft budget situation, the government subsidizes the revenues of the enterprise so that expenses will always be covered. Thus the enterprise cannot go bankrupt.

3. Privatization is important, and the way it is done matters, as we will discuss below. Incentives must flow from defined property rights for a market economy to work.

4. Legal systems, financial systems, and governments must be put into place for reforms to succeed. In addition, attention must be paid to the development of human capital to cope with a market economy.[62]

Special mention must be made of five issues: the economic shocks that accompany rapid economic reform, the establishment of hard budgets, environmental damage, the development of human capital, and the privatization of state-owned enterprises.

Economic shocks   As part of bringing about a market transformation, some negative economic consequences are inevitable, at least in the short term. The basic problem is that the costs are up front, but the benefits come much later. For example, increasing efficiency through allowing foreign competition brings with it unemployment. But CEITs are not accustomed to unemployment and do not have the safety nets of fall-back compensation, retraining facilities, and job-relocation assistance that have been developed over a long period in industrial countries. In addition, price decontrol brings rapid inflation because the old prices were below the true market values. When Poland deregulated most of its prices, a standard joke among its citizens was, "We used to have long lines and empty shelves. Now we have no lines, full shelves, but no money to buy what's on the shelves."

A backlash due to short-term economic hardships may impede economic transformation.

Economic shocks are politically dangerous. Workers and consumers have high expectations for economic transformation—perhaps too high. To the extent that they are adversely affected by unemployment and higher prices (a lowering of real income), even in the short term, they may lose confidence in the elected political leadership and in the transformation process itself, thus slowing or preventing change.

Soft budgets allow government-owned enterprises to get subsidies to cover losses.

Soft budgets   A **soft budget** is a financial condition in which an enterprise spends more than it earns and the difference is met by some other institution, typically the government or a government-controlled financial institution. The CEITs all have legacies of soft budgets from the period when it was unthinkable that an enterprise would not survive. Even within an environment of transformation, pressures remain to continue soft-budget practices. Cushioned by a soft budget, a company's management has an incentive to make deals with authorities instead of effecting efficiencies that could help the company survive.

When profits don't have to be made, there are few incentives for improving efficiency.

Environmental problems will be difficult for CEITs to resolve.

Environmental damage   Environmental damage is another major concern for CEITs. Since harm to human health is the most important consequence of such damage, the two most important problems are air and water pollution. The former results from suspended metal dusts and particulate materials. The latter is exacerbated by careless disposal of toxic or nuclear waste that threatens the quality of surface and ground water in some areas.[63] The major causes of environmental pollution are heavy coal use; old technology, especially in the metallurgy industry; and low energy prices, which serve as a disincentive to save energy and raw materials.

Some argue that air pollution in the main towns and cities of Eastern Europe is no worse than in Western European cities, such as Athens, Madrid, and Milan, that have similar income levels and industrial structures. These analysts claim that environmental problems in Eastern Europe today are at the level they were in Western Europe and North America twenty to thirty years ago. In actuality, water pollution and environmental damage from inadequate nuclear waste management are far more serious in Eastern Europe today than they were in the industrial countries thirty years ago. The cost of environmental cleanup will be significant and will reduce the amount of investment capital available to transform CEITs to market economies. China is also facing environmental crisis as it modernizes its economy. Major concerns are the pollution of air, water, and farmland. Even the World Bank has warned China of the consequences of the lack of enforcement of environmental controls on all sources of pollution.

CEITs lack sufficient people who understand how to manage in a market economy.

Human capital   Many government-owned enterprises are plagued by mammoth bureaucracies that are difficult to replace. As a government eliminates central planning without also substituting knowledgeable owners to whom enterprise managers can report, there is little control over these managers' actions. Another problem, more acute in countries in which people have no memory of market operations, is that most managers have no experience in operating without a central plan that tells them what to produce and to whom to sell. They also may lack experience in controlling subordinates by hiring and firing them or by finding means of compensation as a way of motivating them. Very few of these managers understand how to read or compile financial statements, how to respond to market signals (such as changes in demand), or how to market products when there is competition and no pent-up demand, especially in Western export markets. They also may lack a strong work ethic because of their experiences with low pay and high job security. Further, egalitarian attitudes, especially in Russia and China, result in successful entrepreneurs sometimes being seen as speculators—a contemptuous label.[64]

Five objectives of privatization
- **better corporate governance**
- **speed and feasibility**
- **better access to capital and skills**
- **more government revenues**
- **greater fairness**

Privatization in CEITs   A characteristic of CEITs is the existence of large companies before the transition to market. An important dimension to the transition process, and one where foreign investors can play a role, is the privatization of large, state-owned companies. There are basically five objectives of privatization: better corporate governance, speed and feasibility, better access to capital and skills, more government revenues, and greater fairness.[65]

There are three major methods used to privatize: sale to outside owners, management-employee buyout, and equal-access voucher privatization.[66] Sale to outside owners, the method most widely used initially, leads to better corporate governance, better access to capital and skills, and more government revenue, but

Major privatization methods
- sale to outside owners
- management-employee buyout
- equal access voucher privatization

not to speed or flexibility and greater fairness. This is the process used most widely in Estonia and Hungary.

Management-employee buyout is the most used approach in Russia, Croatia, Poland, Romania, and Slovenia. This approach is relatively fast and easy to implement, but it results in employees in good companies getting vouchers with value and employees in bad companies getting vouchers worth little. In addition, the government does not raise as much revenue as would be the case in an outright sale. In Russia, privatization favors keeping insiders in control of enterprises. Each Russian citizen receives a voucher that can be used to purchase stock in former state-owned enterprises or investment funds that in turn invest in companies. Although the system appears to be a voucher system, insiders could buy up to 51 percent of their enterprise at 1.7 times book value unadjusted for inflation. In addition, investment funds could not own more than 10 percent of the shares in any one company. Further, because workers usually ended up with more power, there is more incentive to put earning into wages and bonuses than into dividends, a practice that discourages investment.[67] Eventually, insiders bought about two-thirds of the shares of 15,000 privatized firms. Outsiders obtained about 20 to 30 percent of the shares, investment funds and individual investors picked up 10 to 15 percent of the shares, and the rest went to the government.[68]

Equal-access voucher privatization is the most widely used approach, and is especially popular in the Czech Republic, Lithuania, Mongolia, and more recently, the Ukraine and Poland. Assets are spread equally among voucher holders, and the system is quick and easy to implement, but it does not raise much revenue and does not improve corporate governance. In the voucher system, vouchers are given to the general public, and they are exchanged for shares in privatizing companies. In the Czech Republic, for example, the government sold booklets of vouchers for a nominal fee, which then were used to buy shares in huge public auctions of enterprises. In two waves of privatization, the Czech government has transferred about 50 percent of the state-owned assets into private hands. However, more than two thirds of the voucher holders invested their vouchers in investment funds rather than directly in the enterprises. Many of these investment funds were controlled by banks, resulting in a concentration of ownership.[69]

Adapting to Foreign Economic Environments in the Internationalization Process

A company based in the United States is accustomed to and has devised ways to survive in the U.S. economic system. However, when such a company wants to do business in another country for the first time, it needs to find answers to questions such as the following:

1. Under what type of economic system does the country operate?
2. Is the company's industry in that country's public or private sector?

3. If it is in the public sector, does the government also allow private competition in that sector?
4. If the company's industry is in the private sector, is it moving toward public ownership?
5. Does the government view foreign capital as being in competition with or in partnership with public or local private enterprises?
6. In what ways does the government control the nature and extent of private enterprise?
7. How much of a contribution is the private sector expected to make in helping the government formulate overall economic objectives?

These questions appear simple; however, because of the dynamic nature of political and economic events, the answers are complex. Many foreign companies are still investing in Hong Kong even though Hong Kong reverted to China on July 1, 1997, and there is some uncertainty as to how China will affect the business environment of Hong Kong in the future. Hong Kong companies such as Swire are investing outside of that country because of the same uncertainty. Companies attempting to invest in Eastern Europe and the former Soviet Union are experiencing enormous difficulties because the economic environment in those countries is very different from any other in the world, and the changes taking place there are so rapid and unpredictable.

Companies intending to do business in foreign markets must be aware of their own experiences and how those have helped shape their managerial philosophies and practices. In addition, they must determine how the new environment differs from their more familiar domestic environment and decide how managerial philosophy and practice must be changed to adapt to the new conditions.

C O U N T E R V A I L I N G

F O R C E S

Small companies that do business with developing countries and CEITs potentially face the problems of inadequate financial resources, managerial expertise, and/or patience required to succeed. The resource commitment is significant, as illustrated by the McDonald's case. However, many small companies successfully trade with or invest in developing countries by exploiting a product niche. For example, before McDonald's opened its first restaurant in Moscow, a U.S. entrepreneur with limited financial resources operated a Nathan's Famous Hot Dogs mobile unit in that city. From one pushcart, he served about 1000 customers a day, and the venture was very profitable. To ensure he could always obtain needed supplies, he bought meat each day from the Central Market, where farmers sell from their private production at a significant premium over the prices offered by the state stores.[70]

Another major issue is national sovereignty. As CEITs go through the transition to market economies, they are getting a lot of advice from Western countries that are providing financial aid as well as from international organizations such as the IMF. Although the CEITs need the aid and the advice, they are trying to develop strategies that fit their unique situations and so don't always follow all the advice offered. This is especially a problem when their actions are contrary to the advice offered by aid-granting countries and organizations.

LOOKING TO THE FUTURE

The high-income countries of Western Europe are in serious economic difficulties, and it will be a few years before they begin to experience solid economic growth. Most of the current growth is in the developing countries, especially those in South and Southeast Asia. The growth rates in those regions are creating a large and relatively wealthy market that a company's management must take into account when setting a global strategy. In particular, China is rapidly becoming the economic powerhouse of Asia. Not only will it continue to be a competitor in light manufacturing and textiles, but its industrial base will improve over the next few years. When President Clinton agreed in 1996 to continue Most Favored Nation (MFN) status to China, which allows China to export products to the United States at the same low tariff rates as other countries, he basically gave U.S. companies the green light to increase their trade with that country. However, this trade could be curtailed in the future if China does not make progress in correcting human-rights abuses, controlling its proliferation of weapons, and opening its markets in order to reduce its trade surplus with the United States.

The area of real concern is Eastern Europe and the former Soviet Union. Eastern European countries are farther along in the economic transformation process than Russia is. Now that their growth rates are improving, these countries should find it easier to attract foreign capital to take advantage of cheap labor, close proximity to Western European markets, and rising standards of living. Although the current political environment in that part of the world is still too unstable for significant near-term foreign investment, it is definitely an area that companies will be watching.

WEB CONNECTION

Check out our home page for links to World Wide Web resources in economics.

Summary

- **Country analysis examines the economic strategy of the nation state.**

- **The economic system determines who owns and controls resources. In a market economy, individuals allocate and control resources; in a centrally planned economy, the government allocates and controls resources.**

- Two important societal units for a market economy are the individual and the company.

- Consumer sovereignty is the freedom of consumers to influence production.

- Economic freedom implies freedom from government constraints and legal and institutional frameworks to safeguard freedoms.

- Free countries tend to be high-income market economies, and not-free countries tend to be state capitalist and command economies.

- Governments having centrally planned economies coordinate the activities of the different economic sectors.

- Countries are classified according to three income levels: high, middle, and low. The middle- and low-income countries are often called developing countries.

- Two important components of demand are population and per capita income.

- High-income countries represent only 21 percent of the countries and 15.2 percent of the population but 79.5 percent of the GNP.

- A large and growing market is a location-specific advantage.

- As countries become more prosperous and their economies shift from low-income to high-income categories, the percentage of GDP derived from agriculture decreases and that derived from industry and services increases.

- The greatest economic growth is in the developing countries, especially those in Asia.

- High-income and developing countries are trying to privatize government-owned enterprises in order to help eliminate their budget deficits.

- Inflation has fallen in developing countries in recent years, reducing the number of countries considered to be highly inflationary.

- Significant deficits in the current account balances of countries cause trade friction, a possible renewal of inflation, pressure on currencies, and loss of investor confidence.

- Severely indebted countries, especially the poorest of the developing countries, must use a significant percentage of their export earnings to service their debt, leaving too little for development.

- Political and economic changes within the former communist countries have led to optimism in the West about doing business in those countries because political barriers may be lessened and economic growth will enhance market potential.

- In this century, political relationships between Western countries and CEITs have varied significantly, resulting in business relationships that also have fluctuated substantially. This has been especially true of trade between the United States and the former Soviet Union.

- Russia's transformation has been complicated by its transition to democracy, the breakup of the Soviet empire, and the political problems of balancing conservative efforts to retain central control over the economy and reformist efforts to move quickly to a market economy.

- Eastern European countries have approached transformation of their economies differently, and their private sectors are creating significantly more economic growth than their public sectors are.

- China's transformation has involved large infusions of capital from overseas Chinese and decentralization of economic decision making.

Case
Pizza Hut in Brazil[71]

In 1994, Pizza Hut celebrated the opening of its 10,000th restaurant worldwide by featuring the former Brazilian soccer star, Pélé, kicking an autographed soccer ball through a ceremonial ribbon to open a store in São Paulo, Brazil. This event was viewed by people in twelve countries in Europe and the United States via an international satellite broadcast. Due to changing economic conditions in Brazil, however, Pizza Hut was reexamining its strategy in 1996 to determine what changes it needed to make to be competitive in Brazil and to add value to the bottom line of its parent company, PepsiCo. Although PepsiCo announced in 1995 that it planned to invest an additional $2.1 billion in Brazil through the year 2000 for the construction of soft-drink factories and new Pizza Hut restaurants, that investment could be in jeopardy if the Brazilian economy sours.

PepsiCo, one of the largest consumer products companies in the world, was organized into three major business units in 1996; beverages, snack foods, and restaurants. Figure 4.5 identifies PepsiCo's sales and profits by division in 1995. The snack foods division, Frito-Lay, is organized around key brands, such as Fritos, Lay's potato chips, Cheetos, Doritos, and Tostitos. The restaurant division is divided into Pizza Hut, KFC, and Taco Bell. As noted in Fig. 4.5, the restaurant division is not very profitable, which resulted in the announcement in late 1996 that it would be sold off from PepsiCo.

As noted in Fig. 4.6, 71.3 percent of PepsiCo's revenues are from international operations, although beverages and snack foods are much more international than the restaurant division. PepsiCo's largest market internationally is Europe, with 9.1 percent of net sales

**Figure 4.5
PepsiCo's Net Sales
and Profits by
Divisions, 1995**

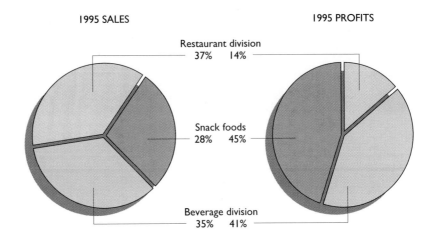

1995 SALES   1995 PROFITS

Restaurant division
37%   14%

Snack foods
28%   45%

Beverage division
35%   41%

being generated in Europe. Their next two largest markets are Mexico and Canada, which are also involved with the United States in the North American Free Trade Agreement (NAFTA), which will be discussed in Chapter 7.

Pizza Hut has more restaurant units worldwide than Taco Bell or KFC. It operates through company-owned stores, joint ventures with other partners where Pizza Hut has an equity interest in the stores, and franchises. In the case of franchises, Pizza Hut does not own an equity interest in the local stores, but it allows a local investor to own the store and pay a royalty and other fees to Pizza Hut. Operating results for the restaurant division in general and Pizza Hut in particular have been disappointing in recent years. As noted in the 1994 annual report, "There were two reasons for the decline [in Pizza Hut's volume]. First, we were less successful than usual at introducing the kind of big new products that really excite consumers and attract lots of them to our restaurants. Second, with beef prices unusually low, the hamburger chains were able to keep their prices down. That led to pretty fierce competition across most of the quick service restaurant industry."

What role will Brazil play in the growth of Pizza Hut worldwide? The three largest markets for Pizza Hut internationally are (1) the United Kingdom, (2) Canada, and (3) Australia. However, Pizza Hut's ten-year plan would put Brazil as the second or third largest market in the world. Brazil offers a number of location-specific advantages. First is its massive size. In 1993, Brazil was the fifth largest country in the world in population with 156 million people, the twelfth largest country in the world in GNP, but it only ranked 103rd in per capita income. It was also the seventh largest country in the world in land mass. Brazil is very urbanized, with São Paulo the second largest city in the world after Cairo, and Rio de Janeiro the sixteenth largest city in the world. It is ranked 42nd in the world in urbanization (76 percent), but it only ranked 175th in population density, even lower than that of the United States.

From a political standpoint, Brazil's democracy was replaced by a military dictatorship in 1964, and stayed a totalitarian state until 1984. In 1984, a new president was elected, but he died before he could take office in 1985. His vice-president, José Sarney, took office and served as president until 1990. Thus Fernando Collor de Mello took office in 1990 as the first democratically elected president since 1960. In 1994, Fernando Henrique Cardoso,

**Figure 4.6
International
Distribution of
PepsiCo's Net Sales,
1995**

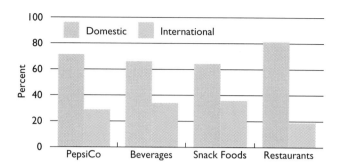

previously the finance minister, was elected president, and he took office in 1995. Thus Brazil's nascent democracy seems to be taking hold. When Cardoso took office, the Brazilian constitution did not permit the president to succeed himself, but by early 1997, President Cardoso was working hard to amend the constitution to allow him to run for a second five-year term so that his economic reforms could be put into place.

From an economic standpoint, Brazil is a land of tremendous opportunity. Historically, Brazil's governments pursued an economic policy based on import substitution and the transition from agriculture to industry. Protective tariffs and import quotas were essential to stimulate domestic industry. State-owned enterprises were established in steel, oil, infrastructure, and other industries, and they received subsidized, long-term credit to expand.

When the military took over in 1964, power was centralized from the states and from congress to the executive branch of government. As the economy began to heat up during the late 1960s and early 1970s, inflation also began to rise, averaging about 20 percent per annum. The government tried traditional means of slowing down inflation, such as raising interest rates, but the large concentration of industrial power resulted in price inflexibility, the indexing of prices above costs, and the passing on of higher interest rates as an additional cost. Due to the protection, foreign trade remained a small percentage of GDP.

The first oil shock in 1973 created problems for Brazil, because in spite of its wealth of natural resources, Brazil relies on imported oil. Economic growth expanded the demand for oil, and the rise in prices worsened Brazil's trade balance. However, import controls gave the government some breathing room. In spite of this, the government was forced to borrow money from abroad, and about 50 percent of the foreign debt was tied to state-owned enterprises. Inflation during the latter 1970s increased to an annual rate of about 40 percent, and the private sector was beginning to show significant resentment to the favoritism shown to the state-owned enterprises. The second oil shock in 1979 was accompanied by rising interest rates on foreign debt, and Brazil went into more severe shock. The economy actually fell 2 percent in 1981, and Brazil was hit by recession, devaluation of the currency, rising real interest rates, real wage reductions, and a widening federal deficit.

The newly elected governments of 1985 and 1990 focused on foreign debt, inflation, and exchange rate policies. Real per capita incomes actually fell 6 percent over the 1980s, and cumulative inflation during the 1980s reached 39,043,765 percent. Before he resigned from office in a corruption scandal, President Collor had begun to tackle Brazil's serious economic problems, but he ran out of time. However, Cardoso instituted a new economic plan while he was finance minister that slowed down Brazil's inflation and stabilized the exchange rate. Prices that had been rising 30 to 50 percent per month suddenly slowed to single-digit figures, and Cardoso's popularity soared, allowing him to win the election with 54 percent of the vote. However, Brazil continues to face serious economic and social problems. The state is still a dominant force in the economy, and privatization has been difficult. The vast gap between the rich and poor has widened in recent years, and there are problems with decent housing, clean water, and good sewage systems. However, trade restrictions have fallen, and Brazil is attracting a lot of foreign investment, both direct and portfolio.

Pizza Hut first entered Brazil in 1988 during a period of high inflation and economic instability through a franchisee who contacted Pizza Hut. At that time, Pizza Hut did not have a specific strategy for Brazil. In 1989, Pizza Hut opened a mall unit in São Paulo, and in 1991, it set up an office in Brazil dedicated to establishing a plan for Brazil. In addition to Pizza Hut, KFC is also operating in Brazil. However, the two restaurants are operating under different strategies. KFC is expanding in Brazil through unit-by-unit franchising, whereas Pizza Hut is expanding through corporate franchises. In a unit-by-unit franchise, an individual restaurant is franchised to a particular franchisee. In a corporate franchise, the corporate franchisee is given a whole territory, generally the same as a state boundary with the exception of São Paulo, and is not allowed to subfranchise (sell a franchise to someone else). The initial idea of using strong corporate franchises made sense to Pizza Hut, because they wanted franchisees with strong financial backing and experience in operating in an inflationary environment. However, the franchisees wield a great deal of power, which could affect Pizza Hut's implementation of a Brazilian strategy.

Pizza Hut establishes targets for all franchisees in terms of how they must grow the business in order to maintain the franchise. Because of its size, São Paulo is divided up into five different franchises. One of Pizza Hut's original franchisees in São Paulo, United Food Companies (UFC), also became a supplier of cheese products to the franchisees, allowing UFC to move down the value chain and the other franchisees to get access to cheese. Now Pizza Hut has diversified to other suppliers, and is importing cheese from abroad.

By 1993, UFC had established 35 stores in São Paulo, generating sales per store unit that were between 33 and 50 percent greater than at its U.S. counterparts. However, Brazil was also the only region in the world serviced solely by franchises—Pizza Hut had no equity interest in any of its stores. Management decided that it needed to own some stores in order to develop operating knowledge and expertise that it could share with its franchisees. The franchise value exists when the franchisor can make a valuable contribution to the franchisees, and Pizza Hut felt that it was lacking an important piece of operating knowledge. It was fairly easy to track the revenues and taxes of its franchisees, but it did not have a good understanding of the cost structure of the business. Therefore, Pizza Hut decided to buy UFC's 35 units in December 1993. Management soon found out that the restaurants were not very cost efficient, but they could get away with their inefficiencies due to the high prices they were charging, and the environment was beginning to change. A major aspect of the economic environment affecting Pizza Hut's profitability in Brazil was inflation. Between 1964 and 1993 when Pizza Hut bought its first 35 units, the annual increase in the consumer price index (CPI) in Brazil had been less than 20 percent only twice—in 1972 and 1973. In the 1990s, inflation was out of control, 2,938 percent increase in 1990, 441 percent in 1991, 1,009 percent in 1992, and 2,148 percent in 1993. In early 1994, the CPI was rising at the rate of 1 percent per day. Then in June 1994, the government instituted the Plan Real, and inflation began to slow down. The new currency, the Real, was pegged to the U.S. dollar, meaning that the government established an exchange rate between the Real and the dollar and would not allow the exchange rate to change as it did in the past. In addition, inflation dropped from an annual rate of 4,060 percent in the third quarter of 1994 to 33.4 percent by September 1995.

In the first six months of operations, several problems arose. The first was management culture. Store managers had been operating relatively independently without any outside control, and now they had to adopt Pizza Hut's control process, not an easy thing to do. They rebelled against the outside control and did not appreciate having to manage differently and be held accountable for their actions. Second, staff at the stores was more numerous than Pizza Hut management realized. It was easy for the original franchisee to hide costs and employees during the initial negotiations, but Pizza Hut soon found out that it had hidden costs, and it could not go back to the original owners and complain.

The third major problem was inflation, which affected business in many different ways. When the new currency came in and inflation slowed down, the stores took a big payroll hit. Although store managers had a fixed salary, they also received a bonus based on sales. Previously, the bonus was delayed 45 days, and price increases allowed stores to cover the bonuses with cheaper money, and inflated sales were immediately invested so that the store could generate interest income. However, the inflationary benefit disappeared, effectively increasing bonuses by the lost inflation—as much as 45 percent in that period. The same problem hit purchases and mall leases. In the case of purchases, Pizza Hut used to collect sales immediately, since the stores operate on a cash and carry basis, and delay the payment of supplies, thereby allowing them to pay for supplies with inflated sales revenues. However, this benefit disappeared once inflation slowed down. Mall leases are based on 6 percent of sales and are typically delayed 30 to 45 days, thus allowing them to use inflated revenues to pay for the leases. However, the drop in inflation meant that mall lease payments basically went up 30 to 45 percent.

In addition, the slowdown in inflation has made consumers more knowledgeable. When inflation was running wild, no one really knew how to compare prices. Prices were changing daily, and salaries were going up as well, so people did not have a good reference point. Now, however, people—as well as franchises—are beginning to compare prices and make more informed decisions. At approximately $19 to $20 for a medium pizza, many consumers are wondering if Pizza Hut is worth the price, given the alternatives. For example, Mr. Pizza, the largest Brazilian-brand fast-food operation in Brazil, is excited to have Pizza Hut as a competitor, because Mr. Pizza has gone from having the most expensive pizza in the market to the medium-price range.

At the same time Pizza Hut is attempting to control costs in Brazil, PepsiCo is trying to improve the profitability of its restaurant division worldwide. In November 1994, PepsiCo established PRI (PepsiCo Restaurants International) with Roger Enrico, former head of the successful Frito-Lay products division, as the head of PRI. The objective of the new PRI is to consolidate the international aspects of the restaurants in order to cut costs and improve profitability. Prior to that time, each restaurant group—Pizza Hut, KFC, and Taco Bell—had its own staffs, including human resources and finance. The same was true of each country. In Brazil, for example, Pizza Hut and KFC were relatively independent with their own local staffs. Thus PRI, which is headquartered in Dallas, is responsible for all restaurants outside of the United States and Canada. There will still be three North American restaurant divisions with the remainder consolidated in PRI. In 1995, Enrico's responsibilities were expanded when the entire restaurant division in North America and worldwide was placed under his responsibility so that he could help establish a coordinated restaurant strategy.

Beginning in 1995, Pizza Hut Brazil was faced with adapting to the new organizational structure as well as the new Brazilian operating environment. Because of the stabilization of prices and the exchange rate between the U.S. dollar and the Brazilian Real, sales in Pizza Hut's São Paulo units dropped by nearly one-half from December 1994 to December 1995, even though the number of units increased. As people perceived the relatively high prices of Pizza Hut pizzas, store traffic fell. Although Pizza Hut's target increase in volume annually in Brazil was 19 percent, it was only growing 6 percent. In order to stimulate sales, Pizza Hut attempted two different strategies. PRI told the franchisees to reduce prices by 25 percent in order to be more price competitive. McDonald's, the leading fast-food chain in Brazil, increased prices by 40 percent in January 1992 in order to catch up to inflation, but later reduced them by 20 percent and advertised the drop as a vote of confidence in Brazil. The campaign was widely successful and helped McDonald's to continue to grow. Many Pizza Hut units, on the other hand, dropped prices in the last week of October and first week of December 1995, and used the samba (a Brazilian dance of African origin) to announce the decision. However, the campaign was seen as a failure. The press covered it as a desperation move to keep pace with McDonald's, and many felt that in adopting the samba, Pizza Hut adopted a strategy very inconsistent with the U.S. brand image that it had worked so hard to cultivate. In addition, one franchisee in Rio maintained that Pizza Hut would be better off putting more money into marketing than in dropping prices. Using that strategy, he was able to increase his volume, whereas those that dropped prices found that volume initially went up but then dropped back to the previous level.

By the end of 1996, Pizza Hut was continuing to struggle worldwide, and PepsiCo announced that it was selling its restaurant division sometime in 1997. Would Pizza Hut continue its expansion in Brazil under new management, and would it be successful?

Questions

1. What are the location-specific advantages that Brazil has to offer? How do these advantages differ from those offered by other markets in Latin America?

2. Should Pizza Hut put more of its efforts in expanding in Brazil or somewhere in South East Asia? Why?

3. What dimensions of the local political and economic environment have an impact on Pizza Hut's success in Brazil in volume, revenues, and profitability? How could a change in those dimensions affect Pizza Hut's future success?

4. Why did Pizza Hut decide to purchase some stores in Brazil instead of continuing to expand through issuing franchises? What are the strengths and weaknesses of this strategy?

Chapter Notes

1. Jeffrey A. Tannenbaum, "Franchisers See a Future in East Bloc," *Wall Street Journal,* June 5, 1990, p. B1+; Erich E. Toll, "Hasabburgonya, Tejturmix and Big Mac to Go," *Journal of Commerce,* August 24, 1988, p. 1A; Tricia A. Dreyfuss, "Negotiating the Kremlin Maze," *Business Month,* Vol. 132, November 1988, pp. 55–63; Vincent J. Schodolski, "Moscovites Stand in Line for a 'Beeg Mek' Attack," *Chicago Tribune,* February 1, 1990, Sec. 1, pp. 1–2; Bill Keller, "Of Famous Arches, Beeg Meks, and Rubles," *New York Times,* January 28, 1990, p. A1+; "McDonald's," *The Economist,* Vol. 313, No. 7629, November 18, 1989, p. 34; Peter Gumbel, "Muscovites Queue Up at American Icon," *Wall Street Journal,* February 1, 1990, p. A12; Ann Blackman, "Moscow's Big Mak Attack," *Time,* February 5, 1990, p. 51; Jeffrey M. Hertzfeld, "Joint Ventures: Saving the Soviets from Perestroika," *Harvard Business Review,* Vol. 69, No. 1, January–February 1991, pp. 80–91; Celestine Bohlen, "How Do You Spell Big Mac in Russian?" *New York Times,* May 25, 1993, p. B1; Bill Essig, "Russia's Economy Shows an Appetite for U.S. Fast Food," *Wall Street Journal,* February 26, 1993, p. B2; Oleg Vikhanski and Sheila Puffer, "Management Education and Employee Training at Moscow McDonald's," *European Management Journal,* March 1993, pp. 102–107; McDonald's 1995 Annual Report, various pages; V. Snegirjov, "The Hero of Capitalist Labour," *Pravda,* July 31, 1991; Carey Goldberg, "Perestroika Pioneer Makes 'Beeg Meks' Work in Moscow," *Los Angeles Times,* August 6, 1991; "Russia Investment: McDonald's Unveils 5th Moscow Restaurant," *Economist Intelligence Unit Views Wire,* September 11, 1995, Available: NEXIS Library: General News: News: Curnws; and McDonald's fact sheets and video.

2. Bruce R. Scott, "Country Analysis," *Harvard Business School,* #382–105, March 1984.

3. Richard E. Messick, "The World Survey of Economic Freedom," *Freedom Review,* March–April 1996, pp. 7–8.

4. Ibid., p. 8.

5. *World Development Report, 1984* (Washington, D.C.: World Bank, 1984), p. 67.

6. John R. Freeman, *Democracy and Markets: The Politics of Mixed Economies* (Ithaca, N.Y.: Cornell University Press, 1989), p. 7.

7. Messick, op. cit., p. 14.

8. Michael E. Porter, *The Competitive Advantage of Nations* (New York: The Free Press, 1980), pp. 74–75.

9. Ibid., p. 86.

10. Andrew B. Abel and Ben S. Bernanke, *Macroeconomics* (Reading, MA: Addison-Wesley, 1992), p. 30.

11. The World Bank, *World Development Report 1996* (New York: Oxford University Press, 1996), p. 224.

12. Data is from *The World Bank Atlas 1996,* p. 20.

13. Ibid.

14. *World Development Report 1996,* pp. 224–225.

15. Barbara Crossette, "U.N. Survey Finds World Rich-Poor Gap Widening," *New York Times,* July 15, 1996 (international edition), p. A3. Quotes information contained in the *Human Development Report 1996,* published by the United Nations.

16. Ibid.

17. Ibid.

18. David W. Moore and Frank Newport, "People Throughout the World Largely Satisfied with Personal Lives," *The Gallup Poll Monthly,* June 1995, p. 2.

19. Richard C. Morais, "Saga of Fire and Ice," *Forbes,* October 23, 1995, p. 162.

20. "The Global Economy: A Survey," *The Economist,* October 1, 1994, p. 4.

21. Tim Carrington, "Economic Disparities Vex Developing World," *Wall Street Journal,* September 27, 1993, p. A1.

22. Joyce Barnathan and Lynne Curry, "Inflation Has China Running Scared," *Business Week,* June 14, 1993, pp. 48–49.

23. *Business America,* March 1996, pp. 11–13; Robert S. Greenberger, "June Trade Gap Narrowed, but Deficit with China Overtakes Japan's as Largest," *Wall Street Journal,* August 21, 1996, p. A3 (Western Edition); Robert S. Greenberger, "U.S. Trade Gap Hit Eight-Year High in 1996, Widened by Rise in Imports," *Wall Street Journal,* February 20, 1997, p. A2 (Western Edition).

24. *World Development Report 1996,* p. 219.

25. Ibid., pp. 190–191.

26. "States of Denial," *The Economist,* August 10, 1996, p. 57.

27. Ibid.

28. *World Development Report 1996,* pp. 220–221.

29. Ibid.

30. Ibid.

31. Ibid., p. 220.

32. "States of Denial," p. 57.

33. *World Development Report 1996,* p. 233.

34. "How to Get Good Marks, or ECUs," *The Economist,* December 14, 1991, p. 52.

35. *World Development Report 1996,* pp. 225–226.

36. Ibid., p. 191.

37. Donald Straszheim, "Economic Viewpoints," *Business Insights* (Merrill Lynch, January 1996), pp. 1–2.

38. *World Development Report 1996,* pp. 113–120.

39. International Finance Corporation. *Privatization Principles and Practice* (Washington, D.C.: IFC, 1995), p. 1.

40. Ibid.

41. Ibid., p. 9.

42. Ibid.

43. "The Perils of Privatization," *Business Week,* May 16, 1994, p. 48.
44. Barbara Casassus, "How French Privatization Could Go into Fast-Forward" *Global Finance,* March 1993, p. 59.
45. Stewart Toy and William Glasgal, "France: Investors May Be Sated," *Business Week,* May 16, 1994, p. 48.
46. Douglas Lavin, "Paris Retreats from Protected Industries," *Wall Street Journal,* July 24, 1996, p. A15.
47. United Nations Population Division, Department for Economic and Social Information and Policy Analysis. *The Demography of Countries with Economies in Transition* [on line]. Available: gopher://gopher.undp.org:70/00/ungophers/popin/wdtrends/transit.
48. "Castro Laments 'Sad Events' in Other Communist Nations," *New York Times,* November 9, 1989, p. A6; and Howard W. French, "Dreary Havana Flirts with Capitalism," *New York Times,* December 6, 1990, p. A4.
49. Paul Marer, "Roadblocs to Economic Transformation in Central and Eastern Europe and Some Lessons of Market Economies," in *United States–Soviet and East European Relations: Building a Congressional Cadre,* Dick Clark, ed. (Queenstown, MD.: Aspen Institute, 1990), pp. 17–27.
50. This term was used by R. D. Schmidt, vice chairman of Control Data, in "U.S.-USSR Trade: An American Businessman's Viewpoint," *Columbia Journal of World Business,* Vol. 18, No. 4, Winter 1983, p. 36.
51. Roman Frydman and Andrzej Rapaczynski, "Privatization in Eastern Europe: Is the State Withering Away?" *Finance & Development,* June 1993, p. 10.
52. *World Development Report 1996,* pp. 1–3.
53. Ibid.
54. Ibid., pp. 189, 191, and 209.
55. "Putting Russia Right," in "Russia's Emerging Market: a Survey," *The Economist,* April 8, 1995, pp. 16–21.
56. "East Europe Survey: More Than Half-Way There," *The Economist,* March 13, 1993, p. 9.
57. Ibid.
58. "China Survey: The Titan Stirs," *The Economist,* November 28, 1992, pp. 3–4.
59. Joyce Barnathan and Lynne Curry, "Inflation Has China Running Scared," *Business Week,* June 14, 1993, pp. 55–57.
60. Andrew Brick, in George Melloan, "China's Miracle Workers Mostly Live Elsewhere," *Wall Street Journal,* March 8, 1993, p. A11.
61. "The Overseas Chinese: A Driving Force," *The Economist,* July 18, 1992, p. 21.
62. *World Development Report 1996,* p. 5.
63. Gordon Hughes, "Cleaning Up Eastern Europe," *Finance & Development,* September 1992, pp. 17–18.
64. Jeffrey Sachs, "Poland and Eastern Europe: What Is to Be Done?" in *Foreign Economic Liberalization: Transformations in Socialist and Market Economies,* András Köves and Paul Marer, eds. (Boulder, CO: Westview, 1991) pp. 238–239; Peter Kraljic, "The Economic Gap Separating East and West." *McKinsey Quarterly,* Spring 1990, pp. 62–74; and "Now for the Acid Test," *Euromoney,* November 1990, pp. 40–47.
65. *World Development Report 1996,* p. 52.
66. Ibid.
67. Frydman and Rapaczyruski, op. cit., p. 12.
68. *World Development Report 1996,* p. 55.
69. Ibid., p. 56.
70. Richard Poe, "Guerrilla Entrepreneurs," *Success,* September 1990, pp. 34–36.
71. PepsiCo 1994 and 1995 Annual Reports; "Pepsi-Cola Wins Second Stadium Account," *Nation's Restaurant News,* August 28, 1995, p. 46; J. R. Whitaker Penteado, "Fast Food Franchises Fight for Brazilian Aficionados," *Brandweek,* June 7, 1993, pp. 20–24; "Pélé Kicks Open 10,000th Pizza Hut Outlet," *Public Relations Journal,* May 1995, p. 16; "Pizza Hut Cooks in Brazil," *Advertising Age,* April 4, 1994, p. 45; Martin Zimmerman, "The New Pepsi Challenge: Annual Profit Growth of 15%," *Buffalo News,* September 24, 1995, p. 18B; Jeanne Whalen, "PepsiCo Restaurants Cook With Enrico," *Advertising Age,* June 5, 1995, p. 4; *International Financial Statistics Yearbook, 1993;* interviews with Pizza Hut employees in Brazil.

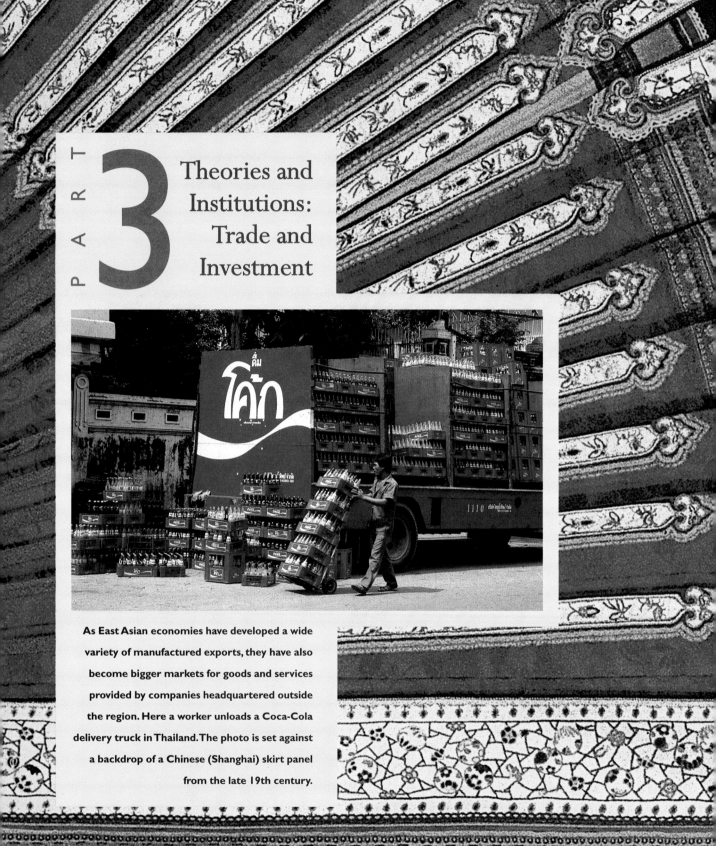

As East Asian economies have developed a wide variety of manufactured exports, they have also become bigger markets for goods and services provided by companies headquartered outside the region. Here a worker unloads a Coca-Cola delivery truck in Thailand. The photo is set against a backdrop of a Chinese (Shanghai) skirt panel from the late 19th century.

Chapter 5

International Trade Theory

A market is not held
for the sake of one person.
—African (Fulani) Proverb

Objectives

- To explain theories of trade patterns that exist in the absence of governmental trade restrictions

- To discuss how global efficiency can be increased through free trade

- To point out the underlying assumptions of trade theories

- To introduce prescriptions for altering trade patterns

- To explore how business decisions determine whether international trade takes place

Case
Sri Lankan Trade[1]

Sri Lanka, which means "resplendent land," is an island country of more than 16 million people off the southeast coast of India. Lying just above the equator, it is 270 miles long and 140 miles across at its widest point (see Map 5.1). It has a hot tropical climate with two monsoon periods, yet the central mountain region is cool enough to experience frost. Known as Ceylon from the early sixteenth century until 1972, Sri Lanka is in many ways typical of most developing countries. It has a low per capita income (about $600 per year), high dependence on a few primary products for its foreign-exchange earnings, insufficient foreign-exchange earnings to purchase all desired consumer and industrial imports, and a high unemployment rate. In many other ways, however, Sri Lanka is atypical of developing countries. On various measurements comparing the quality of life among countries, Sri Lanka ranks fairly high. Its 87-percent literacy rate is one of the highest in Asia, and its standards of nutrition, health care, and income distribution are among the highest in the Third World. Its life expectancy of 68 for males and 73 years for females is one of the highest in the developing world, and its recent population growth rate of 1.2 percent per year is one of the lowest.

Although Sri Lanka did not achieve independence from the United Kingdom until 1948, it has a long recorded history of international trade. By the middle of the third century B.C., special quarters of its capital had been set apart for "Ionian merchants." King Solomon sent his galleys to Sri Lanka to purchase gems, elephants, and peacocks with which to woo the Queen of Sheba. Sinbad and Marco Polo sailed there. Sri Lanka sent ambassadors to Claudius Caesar during the Roman Empire and later established trade links with China. One by one, the European powers came to dominate the island in order to acquire products unavailable at home. The Portuguese, for example, sought such products as cinnamon, cloves, and cardamom, and the English developed the island's economy with tea, rubber, and coconuts, which replaced rice as the major agricultural crops.

Since its independence, Sri Lanka has looked to international trade policy as a means of helping to solve such problems as (1) shortage of foreign exchange, (2) overdependence on one product and one market, and (3) insufficient growth of output and employment.

Map 5.1
Sri Lanka
The island nation of Sri Lanka lies off the southeast coast of India.

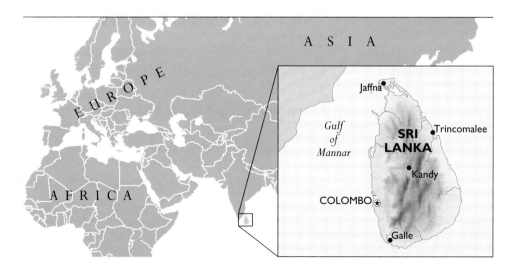

Foreign exchange is needed to buy imports. Advances in international communications and transportation have contributed to rising economic expectations among Sri Lankans, which in turn have translated into desires for foreign products or foreign machinery to produce them. These desires have grown more rapidly than have foreign-exchange earnings.

Sri Lanka also has been concerned about its overdependence on a single export product and market. Until 1975, more than half of the country's export earnings were from tea. This made Sri Lanka vulnerable in two ways. First, world demand for tea has not grown as rapidly as that for many other products, particularly manufactured ones. Therefore tea has not been as viable a means of increasing economic growth, employment, or foreign-exchange earnings as have some other products. Second, tea prices can fluctuate substantially because of a bumper crop or natural disaster in any tea-exporting country. In fact, the wholesale price of tea has changed by as much as 90 percent from one year to the next. This makes planning for long-term business or governmental projects very difficult. Because Sri Lanka is a former British colony, many Sri Lankans also have been concerned that the country cannot be politically and economically independent as long as trade centers on the British market. At the time of independence, for example, one third of Sri Lankan exports went to the United Kingdom. Sri Lanka was thus potentially vulnerable to British political demands and economic downturns.

Because of these varied but interrelated problems, Sri Lanka has attempted to reduce its reliance on traditional export products and markets and to alter its foreign trade so that sufficient foreign exchange is earned for import needs. Although these attempts have occurred throughout Sri Lanka's period of independence, the country has basically followed three different trade policies since 1960. These have reflected views of different political leaders and changes in Sri Lankan conditions. They are:

- 1960–1977 **import substitution** (seeking local production of goods and services that would otherwise be imported)
- 1977–1988 **strategic trade policy** (government actions to develop specific industries with export potential) along with import substitution
- 1988–present strategic trade policy along with openness to imports

During the 1960–1977 period, Sri Lanka sought to export more of its traditional commodities—tea, rubber, and coconuts—and to diversify its production by restricting imports in order to encourage local production, which would thus save foreign exchange. From 1977 to 1988, Sri Lanka continued to restrict imports substantially but shifted to the development of new industries that could export a part of their production and thus earn more foreign exchange. Since 1988, Sri Lanka has greatly reduced import restrictions while continuing to take an active role in developing exports. Throughout the three trade periods, Sri Lanka has become less dependent on the tea market and on sales to any single market.

Once the Sri Lankan government made the decision in 1977 to develop exports of nontraditional products, it took an active role in determining what those products should be and how to get companies to produce them for foreign markets. The export development division of the Ministry of Industries was instrumental in creating a methodology to identify appropriate products for development and promotion.

An obvious way of selecting product groups was to identify nontraditional products that were already being exported in small amounts, since such ability to export indicated the potential for growth. The export development division also sought other products that could offer Sri Lanka a potential advantage in foreign competition. They first identified products that would call for the use of semiskilled and skilled labor because labor costs in Sri Lanka were low, the labor force was fairly well educated, and unemployment and under-employment were high. The division then narrowed that group of products to include only those for which Sri Lanka had indigenous raw materials for production and packaging. This was deemed to be an important competitive indicator because it would be costly to import materials that would then have to be processed before being reexported. Finally, the division examined markets in which Sri Lanka was probably most able to sell. This examination was based on an analysis of demand in two types of markets: those in which Sri Lanka had special market concessions and therefore would experience minimal trade barriers, and those that were geographically close to Sri Lanka and could be served with minimum transport costs.

Seventeen products emerged and were ranked by export potential and expected benefits for the country. The leading items were as follows:

- Processed tea (packaged tea bags and instant tea)
- Ready-made garments (shirts, pajamas, and dresses)
- Chemical derivatives of coconut oil
- Edible fats
- Bicycle tires and tubes
- Other rubber products such as automobile tires and tubes

Other items included canvas footwear, passionfruit juice, canned pineapple, ceramicware, seafood (lobster and shrimp), handicrafts, and gems.

Identifying the most likely competitive industries encouraged some businesspeople to consider investments in new areas. In addition, the government established industrial development zones. Companies that produced in and exported their production from these zones could qualify for up to a 10-year tax holiday plus another 15 years of tax concessions, depending on the size of the investment and the number of employees. They also could defer taxes on imported goods and components until the resulting products were sold domestically. If the products were exported, there were no import taxes.

The first producers to take advantage of the incentives were textile and footwear companies that had special access to the U.S. and European markets. Since then the company base has become more diverse and includes companies making PVC film and carpets and companies entering information into computerized data banks.

Since 1988, Sri Lanka has continued to target industries that are deemed to have export potentials, such as by offering tax and investment incentives for ceramic and light engineering industries, companies doing software development, and companies using only locally derived raw materials. Sri Lanka also has encouraged the export of services, particularly earnings from its workers abroad and from foreign tourists visiting the country. For example, several hundred thousand Sri Lankans work in foreign countries and send remittances to their families. The government has encouraged visits by foreign tourists, and in 1993 announced that 60 proposed projects would increase the number of hotel rooms by 40 percent. To encourage occupancy of the new hotel rooms, Sri Lanka legalized gambling casinos and betting centers (open only to foreign nationals) in 1996. Also in 1996, the Sri Lankan government approved a British-Chinese consortium to develop the port at Galle. This would save international shipping lines about eight hours by not having to deviate to Colombo, which has already developed as a major transshipment center. What has differentiated the period since 1988 from the earlier one is the use of more open markets to determine whether companies can compete. The result has been that many companies and industries that started up when local production was protected have since gone out of existence. But the opening of the economy has permitted Sri Lanka to more easily import materials, such as bulk rubber, that allow companies in Sri Lanka to add value by processing them.

In 1995 the World Trade Organization praised Sri Lanka for trade reforms that opened its markets. Further, Sri Lanka's real GDP grew by about 5 percent per year in the 1990–1994 period in spite of a civil war and heavy military expenditures.

The move to establish new export industries has accomplished many of its objectives. Manufacturing has grown as a portion of total exports, and tea has fallen by more than half. By 1996, garments accounted for about half of total exports. Tea, although still a top export, is increasingly going out in a value-added form, such as instant tea and tea bags, which create Sri Lankan jobs and do not fluctuate in price as much as bulk tea. In addition, Sri Lanka's export markets have become more dispersed, with such countries as the United States, Saudi Arabia, Germany, and India gaining in importance. Nevertheless, the country is still vulnerable to economic and political conditions abroad. When UN trade sanctions were placed on Iraq after its 1991 invasion of Kuwait, Sri Lanka not only lost the Iraqi market, which accounted for 24 percent of its tea exports, but about 100,000 workers returned from the Middle East.

Sri Lankan trade policies have evolved in response to different objectives and conditions, both within and outside Sri Lanka. They will undoubtedly continue to evolve in the future.

Introduction

Trade theory focuses on these questions:
▸ **What products to import and export?**
▸ **How much to trade?**
▸ **With whom to trade?**

Why study trade theory? Authorities in all countries wrestle with the problems of what, how much, and with whom their country should import and export. Once they make decisions, officials enact trade policies to achieve the desired end results. These policies, in turn, affect business. They influence which products companies might be able to sell in those countries from both domestic and foreign sources. They also affect what companies can produce in given countries and where they can produce in order to serve given markets. This was demonstrated in the Sri Lanka case: Government officials in that country have created activist policies to try to achieve trade objectives. Some other countries take a more laissez-faire approach, allowing market forces to determine trading relations, on the premise that governmental policies and actions lead in practice to less optimum results for economies. Whether taking activist or laissez-faire approaches, countries rely on a shared body of trade theory.

Although some theories precede events (for example, Einstein's theory of relativity was a necessary antecedent to the atomic experiments that followed several decades later), international trade was practiced long before any trade theories had evolved. Sri Lankan trade, for example, predated recorded trade theories by more than 1500 years.

Some theories explain trade patterns that exist in the absence of governmental interference.

Two types of theories about trade are relevant to international business (see Table 5.1). The first type deals with the natural order of trade; that is, it examines and explains trade patterns under laissez-faire conditions. Theories of this type pose questions of how much, which products, and with whom a country will trade in the absence of restrictions among countries. The second type of theory prescribes governmental interference with the free movement of goods and services among countries in order to alter the amount, composition, and direction of trade. These theories have "Yes" under the question "Should government control trade?" in the table.

Some theories explain what governmental actions should strive for in trade.

Because no single theory explains all natural trade patterns and because all prescriptions are relevant to some of the actions taken by governmental policymakers, this chapter examines a variety of approaches. However, the subject of governmental interference in trade is so broad that an entire chapter is devoted to discussion of many of the specific arguments and methods (see Chapter 6). Both the descriptive

Table 5.1
Emphases of Major Theories

Theory	Description of natural trade			Prescriptions of trade relationships			
	How much is traded?	What products are traded?	With whom does trade take place?	Should government control trade?	How much should be traded?	What products should be traded?	With whom should trade take place?
Mercantilism	—	—	—	Yes	✔	✔	✔
Neomercantilism	—	—	—	Yes	✔	—	—
Absolute advantage	—	✔	—	No	—	✔	—
Country size	✔	✔	—	—	—	—	—
Comparative advantage	—	✔	—	No	—	✔	—
Factor-proportions	—	✔	✔	—	—	—	—
Product life cycle (PLC)	—	✔	✔	—	—	—	—
Country similarity	—	✔	✔	—	—	—	—
Dependence	—	—	—	Yes	—	✔	✔
Strategic trade policy	—	✔	—	—	—	✔	—

and prescriptive theories have considerable impact on international business. They provide insights about favorable market locales as well as potentially successful products. The theories also increase understanding about the kinds of governmental trade policies that might be enacted and predict how those policies might affect competitiveness.

Mercantilism

According to mercantilism, countries should export more than they import.

Why has Sri Lanka been so dependent on raw materials rather than manufactured products? Perhaps the answer lies in **mercantilism,** the trade theory that formed the foundation of economic thought from about 1500 to 1800.[2] That theory held that a country's wealth was measured by its holdings of treasure, usually in the form of gold. According to mercantilist theory, countries should export more than they import and, if successful, would receive the value of their trade surpluses in the form of gold from the country or countries that ran deficits. Nation-states were emerging during the period 1500–1800, and gold served to consolidate the power of central governments. The gold was invested in armies and national institutions that served to solidify the people's primary allegiances to the new nation with a lessening of bonds to such traditional units as city-states, religions, and guilds.

In order to export more than they imported, governments established monopolies over their countries' trade. Restrictions were imposed on most imports, and many exports received subsidies. Colonial possessions, such as Sri Lanka under British rule, were used to support this trade objective. First, they supplied many commodities that the mother country might otherwise have had to purchase from a nonassociated country. Second, the colonial powers sought to run trade surpluses with their own colonies as a further means of obtaining revenue. They did this not only by monopolizing colonial trade but also by preventing the colonies from engaging in manufacturing. Thus the colonies had to export less highly valued raw materials and import more highly valued manufactured products. Mercantilist theory was intended to benefit the colonial powers, and the imposition of regulations based on this theory caused much discontent in the British colonies and was a background cause of the American Revolution.

As the influence of the mercantilist philosophy weakened after 1800, the colonial powers seldom acted to limit the development of industrial capabilities within their colonies. However, institutional and legal arrangements continued to make colonies dependent on raw material production and to tie their trade to their industrialized mother countries. Sri Lanka, like the many other countries that have attained independence since World War II, began with such a production structure and trade pattern. Efforts to alter this pattern are discussed later in this chapter in the section on independence, interdependence, and dependence.

Running a favorable balance of trade is not necessarily a beneficial situation.

Some terminology of the mercantilist era has endured. The **favorable balance of trade,** for example, still indicates that a country is exporting more than it is importing. An **unfavorable balance of trade** indicates a trading deficit. Many of these terms are misnomers: For example, the word *favorable* implies benefit, and *unfavorable* suggests disadvantage. In fact, it is not necessarily beneficial to run a trade surplus; nor is it necessarily disadvantageous to run a trade deficit. A country that is running a surplus, or favorable balance of trade, is, for the time being, importing goods and services of less value than those it is exporting.[3] In the mercantilist period, the difference was made up by a transfer of gold, but today it is made up by holding the deficit country's currency or investments denominated in that currency. In effect, the surplus country is granting credit to the deficit country. If that credit cannot eventually buy sufficient goods and services, the so-called favorable trade balance actually may turn out to be disadvantageous for the country with the surplus.

A country that practices neomercantilism attempts to run an export surplus to achieve some social or political objective.

Recently, the term **neomercantilism** has been used to describe the approach of countries that apparently try to run favorable balances of trade in an attempt to achieve some social or political objective. For instance, a country may try to achieve full employment by producing in excess of the demand at home and sending the surplus abroad. Or a country may attempt to maintain political influence in an area by sending more merchandise to the area than it receives from it.

Absolute Advantage

So far we have ignored the question of why countries need to trade at all. Why can't Sri Lanka (or any other country) be content with the goods and services produced within its territory? In fact, many countries, following mercantilist policy, did try to become as self-sufficient as possible through local production of goods and services.

According to Adam Smith, a country's wealth is based on its available goods and services rather than on gold.

In his 1776 book, *The Wealth of Nations,* Adam Smith questioned the mercantilists' assumption that a country's wealth depends on its holdings of treasure.[4] He said instead that the real wealth of a country consists of the goods and services available to its citizens. Smith developed the **theory of absolute advantage,** which holds that different countries can produce some goods more efficiently than others; thus global efficiency can be increased through free trade. Based on this theory, he questioned why the citizens of any country should have to buy domestically produced goods when those goods could be purchased more cheaply from abroad.

Smith reasoned that if trade were unrestricted, each country would specialize in those products that resulted in a competitive advantage for it. Each country's resources would shift to the efficient industries because the country could not compete in the inefficient ones. Through specialization, countries could increase their efficiency because of three reasons:

- Labor could become more skilled by repeating the same tasks.
- Labor would not lose time in switching from the production of one kind of product to another.

- Long production runs would provide incentives for the development of more effective working methods.

A country then could use its specialized production excess to buy more imports than it could have otherwise produced. But in what products should a country specialize? Although Smith believed the marketplace would make the determination, he thought that a country's advantage would be either natural or acquired.

Natural Advantage

Natural advantage refers to climate and natural resources.

A country may have a **natural advantage** in producing a product because of climatic conditions, access to certain natural resources, or availability of an abundant labor force. The climate may dictate, for example, which agricultural products can be produced efficiently. For example, Sri Lanka's climate supports production of tea, rubber, and coconuts, and its ample labor force enables this production to be harvested and processed. Climate also is a factor in Sri Lanka's export of services because foreign tourists visit its beaches. Sri Lanka imports wheat and dairy products. If it were to increase its production of wheat and dairy products, for which its climate is less suited, it would have to use land now devoted to the cultivation of tea, rubber, or coconuts, thus decreasing the output of those products. Conversely, the United States could produce tea (perhaps in hothouses) but at the cost of diverting resources away from products such as wheat, for which its climate is naturally suited. These two countries can trade tea for wheat and vice versa more cheaply than each could become self-sufficient in the production of both. Moreover, the more diverse the climates of two countries, the more likely it will be for them to have natural advantages that favor trade with one another.

Most countries must import ores, metals, and fuels from other countries whose natural resources are plentiful. No one country is large enough or sufficiently rich in physical resources to be independent of the rest of the world except for short periods. Sri Lanka, for example, exports natural graphite but must import natural nitrates. Another natural resource is soil, which, when coupled with topography, is an important determinant of the types of products that can be produced most efficiently in different areas.

Variations in natural advantages also help to explain where certain manufactured or processed products might be best produced, particularly if transport costs can be reduced by processing an agricultural commodity or natural resource prior to exporting it. Recall that Sri Lankan authorities sought to identify industries that could use the country's primary commodities such as tea. Processing into instant tea decreases bulk and thus is likely to reduce transport costs on tea exports. Producing canned liquid tea could add weight, however, thus lessening the internationally competitive edge.

Acquired Advantage

Acquired advantage refers to technology and skill development.

Most of the world's trade today involves manufactured goods and services rather than agricultural goods and natural resources. The production location of such goods is determined largely by an **acquired advantage,** commonly in either product or process technology. An advantage in product technology refers to an ability to produce a different or differentiated product. For example, Denmark exports silver tableware, not because there are rich Danish silver mines but because Danish companies have developed distinctive products. An advantage in process technology refers to an ability to produce a homogeneous product more efficiently. For example, Japan has exported steel in spite of having to import iron and coal, the two main ingredients necessary for steel production. A primary reason for Japan's success is that its steel mills encompass new labor-saving and material-saving processes.

Rapid technological changes have created new products, displaced old ones, and altered the relative positions of countries in world trade. The most obvious examples of change are new products, such as jets and computers, which make up a large portion of international business. Products that existed in earlier periods have increased their share of world trade because of technological changes in the production process, as with automobiles, or because new uses have been found for them, as with soybeans and fish meal. Other products have been at least partially displaced by substitutes, such as artificial fibers for cotton, wool, and silk and synthetic rubber and synthetic nitrate for the natural products. Some products that were once major exports, such as natural ice, have been displaced by mechanically made products.[5] Still other products have experienced reduced growth in demand because of newly developed conservation methods. For example, thinner tin cans and finer copper wire that can carry more telephone messages simultaneously have resulted in less demand for these metals. Because most technological advances have emanated from the most industrialized (richer) countries, companies from these countries control a greater share of the trade and investment in the manufacturing sector, which has been the major growth area. Consequently, many poorer countries have had a proportionately smaller share of international business.

Resource Efficiency Example

The idea of absolute advantage in international or domestic trade can be demonstrated using two countries (or regions within one country) and two commodities. In this example, the countries are Sri Lanka and the United States, and the commodities are tea and wheat. Since we are not yet considering the concepts of money and exchange rates, we shall treat the cost of production in terms of the resources needed to produce either tea or wheat. This is a realistic treatment in that real income depends on the output of goods associated with the resources used to produce them.

Start with the assumption that Sri Lanka and the United States are the only countries and each has the same amount of resources (land, labor, and capital) that can be used to produce either tea or wheat. Let's say that 100 units of resources are available in each country (shown in Fig. 5.1). In Sri Lanka, assume that it takes 4 units to produce a ton of tea and 10 units per ton of wheat. In the United States, it

ASSUMPTIONS

Sri Lanka

1. 100 units of resources available
2. 10 units to produce a ton of wheat
3. 4 units to produce a ton of tea
4. Uses half of total resources per product when there is no foreign trade

United States

1. 100 units of resources available
2. 5 units to produce a ton of wheat
3. 20 units to produce a ton of tea
4. Uses half of total resources per product when there is no foreign trade

PRODUCTION

	Tea (tons)	Wheat (tons)
Without Trade:		
Sri Lanka (point A)	12½	5
United States (point B)	2½	10
Total	15	15
With Trade:		
Sri Lanka (point C)	25	0
United States (point D)	0	20
Total	25	20

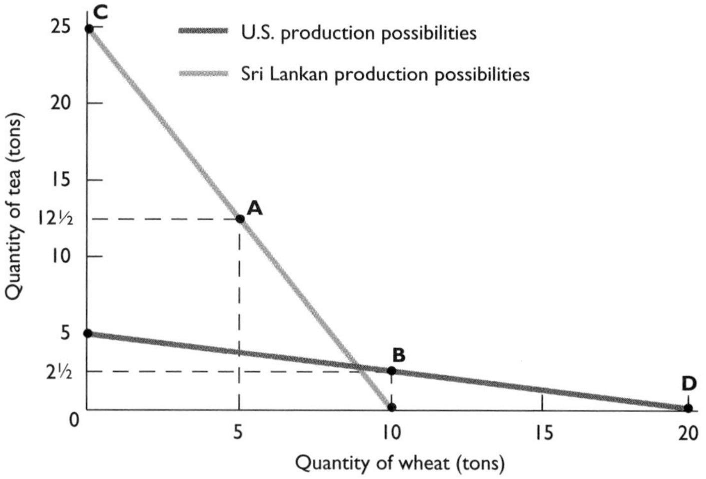

Figure 5.1
Production Possibilities with Absolute Advantage

Bigger countries differ in several ways from smaller countries. They
▸ Tend to export a smaller portion of output and import a smaller part of consumption
▸ Have higher transport costs for foreign trade
▸ Can handle large-scale production

takes 20 units per ton of tea and 5 units per ton of wheat. Sri Lanka is thus more efficient (that is, takes fewer resources to produce a ton) than the United States in tea production, and the United States is more efficient than Sri Lanka in wheat production.

Consider a situation in which the two countries have no foreign trade. If Sri Lanka and the United States each were to devote half of its resources to producing tea and half to producing wheat, Sri Lanka would be able to produce 12½ tons of tea and 5 tons of wheat (point A in Fig. 5.1), and the United States could produce 2½ tons of tea and 10 tons of wheat (point B in the figure). Since each country has only 100 units of resources, neither can increase wheat production without decreasing tea production, or vice versa. Without trade between the two countries, the combined production would be 15 tons of tea (12½ plus 2½) and 15 tons of wheat (5 plus 10). If each country specialized in the commodity for which it had an absolute advantage, Sri Lanka then could produce 25 tons of tea and the United States 20 tons of wheat (points C and D in the figure). You can see that through specialization the production of both products can be increased (from 15 to 25 tons of tea and from 15 to 20 tons of wheat). By trading, global efficiency is increased, and the two countries can have more tea and more wheat than they would without trade.

Theory of Country Size

The theory of absolute advantage does not deal with country-by-country differences in specialization; however, research based on country size helps to explain how much and what types of products will be traded.

Variety of resources   The **theory of country size** holds that countries with large land areas are more apt to have varied climates and natural resources, and therefore they generally are more nearly self-sufficient than are smaller countries. Most of the very large countries, such as Brazil, China, India, the United States, and Russia, import much less of their consumption and export much less of their production than do small countries, such as Uruguay, the Netherlands, and Iceland.[6]

Transport costs   Although the theory of absolute advantage ignored transport costs, these costs affect large and small countries differently. Normally, the farther the distance, the higher the transport costs. The average distance between the production location and markets is higher for the international trade of large countries. Assume, for example, that the normal maximum distance for transporting a given product is 100 miles because, beyond that distance, prices increase too much. Most U.S. production locations and markets are more than 100 miles from the Canadian or Mexican border. In the Netherlands, however, almost all production locations and markets are within 100 miles of its borders. Transport costs thus make it more likely that small countries will trade internationally.

Scale economies   Although land area is the most obvious way of measuring a country's size, countries also can be compared on the basis of economic size. Countries with large economies and high per capita incomes are more likely to produce goods that use technologies requiring long production runs. This is because these countries develop industries to serve their large domestic markets, and those industries tend to be competitive in export markets as well.[7] In addition, high expenditures on R&D create high fixed costs. Thus the technologically intensive company from a small nation may have a more compelling need to sell abroad than would a company with a large domestic market. In turn, this pulls resources from other industries and companies within the company's domestic market, causing more national specialization than in a larger nation.[8]

Comparative Advantage

Gains from trade will occur even in a country that has absolute advantage in all products because the country must give up less efficient output to produce more efficient output.

What happens when one country can produce all products at an absolute advantage? In 1817, David Ricardo examined this question and expanded on Adam Smith's theory of absolute advantage to develop the theory of **comparative advantage.** Ricardo reasoned that there may still be global efficiency gains from trade if a country specializes in those products that it can produce more efficiently than other products, without regard to absolute advantage.[9] Although initially this theory may seem incongruous, a simple analogy should clarify its logic. Imagine that the best physician in a particular town also happens to be the best medical secretary. Would it make economic sense for the physician to handle all the administrative duties of the office? Definitely not. The physician can earn more money by devoting all of his or her professional energies to working as a physician, even though that means having to employ a less skillful medical secretary to manage the office. In the same manner, a country will gain if it concentrates its resources on producing the commodities it can produce most efficiently. It then will buy from countries with fewer natural or acquired resources those commodities it has relinquished.

Production Possibility Example

In this example, assume that the United States is more efficient in producing both tea and wheat than Sri Lanka is. The United States thus has an absolute advantage in the production of both products. As in the earlier example of absolute advantage, again assume that there are only two countries and each country has a total of 100 units of resources available. In this example, it takes Sri Lanka 10 units of resources to produce either a ton of tea or a ton of wheat, whereas it takes the United States only 5 units of resources to produce a ton of tea and 4 units to produce a ton of wheat (see Fig. 5.2). If each country uses half of its resources in the production of each product, Sri Lanka can produce 5 tons of tea and 5 tons of wheat (point A in the figure), and the United States can produce 10 tons of tea and 12½ tons of wheat (point B in the figure). Without trade, neither country can increase its production of tea without sacrificing some production of wheat, or vice versa.

Although the United States has an absolute advantage in the production of both tea and wheat, it has a comparative advantage only in the production of wheat. This

**Figure 5.2
Production Possibilities
with Comparative
Advantage**

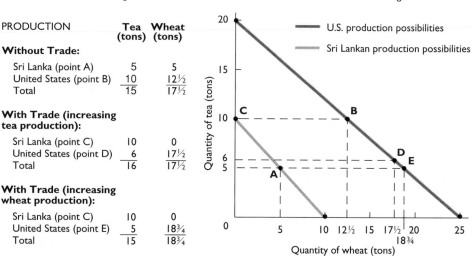

ASSUMPTIONS

Sri Lanka
1. 100 units of resources available
2. 10 units to produce a ton of wheat
3. 10 units to produce a ton of tea
4. Uses half of total resources per product when there is no foreign trade

United States
1. 100 units of resources available
2. 4 units to produce a ton of wheat
3. 5 units to produce a ton of tea
4. Uses half of total resources per product when there is no foreign trade

PRODUCTION	Tea (tons)	Wheat (tons)
Without Trade:		
Sri Lanka (point A)	5	5
United States (point B)	10	12½
Total	15	17½
With Trade (increasing tea production):		
Sri Lanka (point C)	10	0
United States (point D)	6	17½
Total	16	17½
With Trade (increasing wheat production):		
Sri Lanka (point C)	10	0
United States (point E)	5	18¾
Total	15	18¾

is because its advantage in wheat production is comparatively greater than its advantage in tea production. So, by using the same amounts of resources, the United States can produce 2½ times as much wheat as Sri Lanka but only twice as much tea. Although Sri Lanka has an absolute disadvantage in the production of both products, it has a comparative advantage (or less of a comparative disadvantage) in the production of tea. This is because Sri Lanka is half as efficient as the United States in tea production and only 40 percent as efficient in wheat production.

Without trade, the combined production would be 15 tons of tea (5 in Sri Lanka plus 10 in the United States) and 17½ tons of wheat (5 in Sri Lanka plus 12½ in the United States). By trading, the combined production of tea and wheat within the two countries can be increased. For example, if the combined production of wheat is unchanged from when there was no trade, the United States could produce all 17½ tons of wheat by using 70 units of resources (17½ tons times 4 units per ton). The remaining 30 U.S. units could be used for producing 6 tons of tea (30 units divided by 5 units per ton). This production possibility is shown as point D in Fig. 5.2. Sri Lanka would use all its resources to produce 10 tons of tea (point C in the figure). The combined wheat production has stayed at 17½ tons, but the tea production has increased from 15 to 16 tons.

If the combined tea production is unchanged from the time before trade, Sri Lanka could use all its resources on producing tea, yielding 10 tons (point C in Fig. 5.2). The United States could produce the remaining 5 tons of tea by using 25 units of resources. The remaining 75 U.S. units could be used to produce 18¾ tons of wheat (75 divided by 4). This production possibility is shown as point E in the figure. Without sacrificing any of the tea available before trade, wheat production has increased from 17½ to 18¾ tons.

If the United States were to produce somewhere between points D and E in Fig. 5.2, both tea and wheat production would increase over what was possible before trade took place. Whether the production target is an increase of tea or wheat or a combination of the two, both countries can gain by having Sri Lanka trade some of its tea production to the United States for some of that country's wheat output.

Some Assumptions of the Theories of Specialization

Full employment is not a valid assumption.

Full employment   The physician/secretary analogy we used earlier assumed that the physician could stay busy full-time practicing medicine. If we relax this assumption, then the advantages of specialization are less compelling. The physician might, if unable to stay busy full-time with medical duties, perform secretarial work without having to forgo a physician's higher income. The theories of absolute and comparative advantage both assume that resources are fully employed. When countries have many unemployed resources, they may seek to restrict imports in order to employ idle resources even though those will not be employed efficiently.

Countries' goals may not be limited to economic efficiency.

Economic efficiency objective   The physician/secretary analogy also assumed that the individual who can do both medical and office work is interested primarily in maximization of profit, or maximum economic efficiency. Yet, there are a number of reasons why physicians might choose not to work full-time at medical tasks. They might find administrative work relaxing and self-fulfilling. They might fear that a hired secretary would be unreliable. They might wish to maintain secretarial skills in the somewhat unlikely event that administration, rather than medicine, commands higher wages in the future. Countries also often pursue objectives other than output efficiency. They may avoid overspecialization because of the vulnerability created by changes in technology and by price fluctuations. In fact, a Sri Lankan journalist said, "Our unique set of cultural values cannot fit into any sort of twisted, hybrid economic culture, haphazardly devised in the name of development and economic progress."[10]

Division of gains   Although specialization brings global efficiency gains, the earlier discussion did not indicate how the increased output of tea and wheat will be divided between Sri Lanka and the United States. If both nations receive some share of the increased output, both will be better off economically through specialization and trade. However, many people, including governmental policymakers, are concerned with relative as well as absolute economic growth. If they perceive a trading partner is gaining too large a share of benefits, they may prefer to forgo absolute gains for themselves in order to prevent relative losses.[11]

Two countries, two commodities   For the sake of simplicity, Ricardo originally assumed a very simple world composed of only two countries and two commodities. Our example made the same assumption. Although unrealistic, this assumption does not diminish the theory's usefulness. Economists have applied the same reasoning to demonstrate efficiency advantages in multiproduct and multicountry situations.

Transport costs   Neither the theory of absolute advantage nor that of comparative advantage considered the cost of moving products from one country to another. However, this is not a serious limitation. Although specialization might reduce the amounts of resources necessary for producing goods, resources also are needed to move the goods internationally. If it costs more units of resources to transport the goods than are saved through specialization, then the advantages of trade are negated. For example, if tea production can be increased by one ton while leaving wheat production unchanged, we will have to divert workers from tea production to ship tea and wheat between Sri Lanka and the United States. As long as the diversion reduces output by less than what is gained from specialization (in this case, one ton of tea), there are still gains from trade.

Mobility   The theories of absolute and comparative advantage assume that resources can move freely from the production of one good to another domestically but that they are not free to move internationally. Neither assumption is completely valid. For example, a displaced steelworker in Indiana might not move easily into a

Resources are neither as mobile nor as immobile as the theories of absolute and comparative advantage assume.

software development job in California. That worker probably would have difficulty working in such a different industry and might have trouble moving to a new area. However, contrary to the theories, there is some international mobility of resources—consider the Sri Lankan workers who have gone to the Middle East.

Services   The theories of absolute and comparative advantage deal with commodities rather than services; however, an increasing portion of world trade is in services. This fact does not render the theories obsolete, however, because resources must go into producing services as well as commodities. For instance, the United States trades services for commodities and services for services. Some services that the United States sells extensively to foreign countries are education (many foreign students attend U.S. universities) and credit card systems and collections. However, the United States is a net importer of shipping services. To become more self-sufficient in international shipping, the United States might have to divert resources from their more efficient use in higher education or the production of competitive products.

Factor-Proportions Theory

According to the factor-proportions theory, factors in relative abundance are cheaper than factors in relative scarcity.

Smith's and Ricardo's theories did not help to identify the types of products that would most likely give a country an advantage. Those theories assumed that the workings of the free market would lead producers to the goods they could produce more efficiently and away from those they could not produce efficiently. About a century and a quarter later, two Swedish economists, Eli Heckscher and Bertil Ohlin, developed the **factor-proportions theory,** which held that differences in countries' endowments of labor relative to their endowments of land or capital explained differences in factor costs. These economists proposed that if labor were abundant in relation to land and capital, labor costs would be low and land and capital costs high. If labor were scarce, labor costs would be high in relation to land and capital costs. These relative factor costs would lead countries to excel in the production and export of products that used their abundant, and therefore cheaper, production factors.[12]

Land-Labor Relationship

On the basis of the factor-proportions theory, Sri Lankan authorities reasoned that their country had a competitive advantage in products that used large numbers of abundant semiskilled workers. The factor-proportions theory appears logical on the basis of casual observation of worldwide production and exports. In countries in which there are many people relative to the amount of land—for example, Hong Kong and the Netherlands—land prices are very high. (In 1996, Hong Kong had the highest annual retail rental rates in the world, averaging $8,100 a square meter.)[13] Regardless of climate and soil conditions, neither Hong Kong nor the

Netherlands excels in the production of goods requiring large amounts of land, such as sheep or wheat. These goods are produced in countries such as Australia and Canada, where land is abundant relative to the number of people. Casual observation of manufacturing proportions also seems to substantiate the theory. For example, in Hong Kong the most successful industries are those in which technology permits the use of a minimum amount of land relative to the number of people employed: Clothing production is housed in multistory factories in which workers share minimal space. Hong Kong does not compete in the production of automobiles, however, which requires much more space per worker.

Labor-Capital Relationship

Where labor is abundant in relation to capital, you might expect cheap labor rates and export competitiveness in products requiring large amounts of labor relative to capital. The opposite can be anticipated when labor is scarce. For example, Iran excels in the production of handmade carpets that differ in appearance as well as in production method from the carpets produced in industrial countries by machines purchased with cheap capital.

U.S. imports show a high intensity of less skilled labor. U.S. exports are labor-intensive compared with U.S. imports.

However, the labor-to-capital relationship in foreign trade is sometimes surprising. For example, Wassily Leontief found that the more successful U.S. exporting industries had a higher labor intensity than those that faced the most import competition.[14] Because of the presumption that the United States has abundant capital relative to labor, this surprising finding is known as the **Leontief paradox.** Several possible explanations for it have been proposed.

Production factors are not homogeneous, especially labor.

One of the most plausible is that the factor-proportions theory assumes production factors to be homogeneous. Labor skills are, in fact, very different within and among countries, since different people have different amounts and types of training and education. Training and education require capital expenditures that do not show up in traditional capital measurements, which include only plant and equipment values. If the factor-proportions theory is modified to account for different labor groups and the capital invested to train these groups, it seems to hold. If labor is viewed not as a homogeneous commodity but rather by categories, the industrial countries actually have a more abundant supply of highly educated labor (on which a high capital expenditure has been made) than of other types. Industrial country exports embody a higher proportion of professionals such as scientists and engineers; thus those countries are using their abundant production factors. Exports of less developed countries (LDCs), on the other hand, show a high intensity of less skilled labor.[15]

Technological Complexities

The factor-proportions analysis becomes more complicated when the same product might be produced by different methods, such as with either high inputs of labor or high inputs of capital. Canada produces wheat in a capital-intensive way (high level of machinery per worker) because of its abundance of low-cost capital relative to labor; in contrast, India produces wheat by using a much smaller number of machines and more of its abundant and cheap labor. When there is more than one way to produce the same output, it is the relative input cost that determines which country can produce the product more cheaply. The fact that products can be produced in different ways is another possible explanation of the Leontief paradox in that the U.S. industries facing the most competition because of cheap foreign labor are the ones that have responded most intensively by substituting machines for labor.

Technological advancements have resulted in transport cost reductions that in turn have permitted greater economies of scale. This has led to more international specialization, not only in type of product but also in type of task to produce a given product.[16] For example, a company may locate its research activities and management functions primarily in countries with a highly educated population and its production work where less skilled, and less expensive, workers can be employed.

The Product Life Cycle

According to the PLC theory, the production location for many products moves from one country to another depending on the stage in the product's life cycle.

Another theory, developed by Raymond Vernon, attempts to explain world trade in manufactured products on the basis of stages in a product's life.[17] Briefly, the theory of the **international product life cycle (PLC)** states that certain kinds of products go through a continuum, or cycle, that consists of roughly four stages—introduction, growth, maturity, and decline—and that the location of production will shift internationally depending on the stage of the cycle. The stages are highlighted in Table 5.2.

Stage 1: Introduction

The introduction stage is marked by
- Innovation in response to observed need
- Exporting by the innovative country
- Evolving product

Innovation, production, and sales in same country   New products usually are developed because there is a nearby observed need and a market for them. This means that a U.S. company is most apt to develop a new product for the U.S. market, a French company for the French market, and so on. To illustrate how this works, producers in both the United States and France observed the need for longer-term food preservation as more women worked outside the home and had less time for food shopping. In the United States, the prevalence of large kitchens and cheap electricity encouraged U.S. innovators to develop and become leaders in the production of frozen food, which could be stored in large freezer compartments. In France, however, large freezer compartments were impractical, so French innovators led in the development of food packaging (such as boxed milk) that would eliminate the need for refrigeration. Once an R&D group has created a new product, that product theoretically can be manufactured anywhere in the world, even though its sales are intended primarily for the market in which consumers' needs were first observed. In practice, however, the early production generally

Table 5.2
International Changes During a Product's Life Cycle
Overall, production and sales in LDCs grow in relative importance during a product's life cycle.

	Life cycle stage			
	Introduction	**Growth**	**Maturity**	**Decline**
Production location	• In innovating (usually industrial) country	• In innovating and other industrial countries	• Multiple countries	• Mainly in LDCs
Market location	• Mainly in innovating country, with some exports	• Mainly in industrial countries • Shift in export markets as foreign production replaces exports in some markets	• Growth in LDCs • Some decrease in industrial countries	• Mainly in LDCs • Some LDC exports
Competitive factors	• Near-monopoly position • Sales based on uniqueness rather than price • Evolving product characteristics	• Fast-growing demand • Number of competitors increases • Some competitors begin price-cutting • Product becoming more standardized	• Overall stabilized demand • Number of competitors decreases • Price is very important, especially in LDCs	• Overall declining demand • Price is key weapon • Number of producers continues to decrease
Production technology	• Short production runs • Evolving methods to coincide with product evolution • High labor and labor skills relative to capital input	• Capital input increases • Methods more standardized	• Long production runs using high capital inputs • Highly standardized • Less labor skill needed	• Unskilled labor on mechanized long production runs

occurs in a domestic location because the company wishes to use its excess capacity and because it is useful for the company to locate near the intended consumers in order to obtain rapid market feedback and to save transport costs.

Location and importance of innovation   It is useful to know where new products are developed. Indications are that more than 95 percent of the world's technology emanates from the industrial countries; thus the early manufacturing and sales of new products primarily occur in industrial countries. Many reasons account for the dominant position of industrial countries, including competition, demanding consumers, the availability of scientists and engineers, and high incomes, which permit risking expenditures on research that may or may not yield gainful results.

There is evidence that innovation is the main source of companies' competitive strength. But because innovations can be imitated, companies in the leading countries must continually develop innovations in order to stay in the forefront.[18] The innovations or improvements may come in the product itself or in the method of manufacturing or distributing the product.[19]

Many scholars argue that LDCs' lack of research capabilities hampers their development because they must compete on the basis of price by keeping wage rates low. However, work in growth theory indicates that LDCs with high levels of imports from R&D-intensive countries can gain the benefits of higher productivity by bringing in goods and services, such as the latest equipment, that incorporate the research developed elsewhere.[20]

Exports and labor   At the introduction stage of a product life cycle, a small part of the production may be sold to customers in foreign markets who have heard about the new product and actively seek it. These foreign customers are most likely to be found in countries with similar market segments—in the case of U.S. companies, in other industrial countries.

The production process is apt to be more labor-intensive in this stage than in later stages. Because the product is not yet standardized, it must be produced by a process that permits rapid changes in product characteristics, as dictated by market feedback. This implies high labor input as opposed to automated production, which is more capital-intensive. Furthermore, the capital machinery necessary to produce a product on a large scale usually develops later than product technology, only when sales begin to expand rapidly enough (Stage 2) to warrant the high development costs of the machines for the new process.

The fact that the United States excels in the development of new products, which usually are made in labor-intensive ways, helps to explain the Leontief paradox, which showed that the United States generally exports labor-intensive products. Because U.S. wage rates are known to be among the highest in the world, how can the United States compete? According to one view, this ability stems from the monopoly position of original producers, which allows them to pass on costs to consumers who are unwilling to wait for possible price reductions later. Much evidence of this behavior is based on eventual price decreases of products such as calculators and VCRs. Another explanation is that although U.S. labor is paid a high hourly wage, its education and skill levels make it adept and efficient when production is not yet standardized. When production becomes highly automated, U.S. labor becomes less competitive because unskilled labor may be quickly trained to perform highly repetitive tasks efficiently.

Stage 2: Growth

Growth is characterized by
- **Increases in exports by the innovating country**
- **More competition**
- **Increased capital intensity**
- **Some foreign production**

As sales of the new product grow, competitors enter the market. At the same time, demand is likely to grow substantially in foreign markets, particularly in other industrial countries. In fact, demand may be sufficient to justify producing in some foreign markets in order to reduce or eliminate transport charges and tariffs.

Debate over laissez-faire versus activist trade policies and independence versus dependence of countries typically is emotional because different values underlie positions.

For example, the argument for free-trade policy is based on the achievement of global economic efficiency. However, countries' goals may not be limited to economic efficiency. Further, some argue that free trade, although leading to lower costs, will not result in production locations that are optimal with respect to factor endowments because production costs are partly dependent on individual countries' standards—such as requirements for worker safety or the disposal of wastes. These standards reflect the social and environmental values of the countries' citizens. Because standards vary among countries, the costs incurred by producers vary as well. Some industries affected by import competition—for example, the U.S. electronics industry—reason that their governments should protect them because foreign producers do not have to adhere to the stringent requirements that raise production costs.[21] In another case, the EU has threatened to ban fur imports from Canada, Russia, and the United States because these countries use steel-jawed leghold traps, which not only reduce costs of trapping animals but also cause the animals great pain and a slow death.[22]

ETHICAL DILEMMAS & SOCIAL RESPONSIBILITY

Some argue that cost differences reflect not differences in efficiency but rather differences in social and environmental values. Other questions have been raised in recent years about labor conditions, such as anti-union directives in Malaysia and the use of jailed workers in China. Ethical questions are raised as to whether it is reasonable to assume that all countries should have similar standards, whether countries should limit imports of competing products because of differences in standards, and whether companies should locate production to capitalize on less stringent standards that allow them to lower their costs.

Sri Lanka tried to reduce its dependence on a single trading partner and a single product for its export earnings. A country also may be concerned about its overall trade dependence. In this context, relativists hold that it would be unethical for outsiders to interfere in a country's trade policy. In contrast, normativists argue that other countries have a duty to put pressure on a country when its trade policies cause hardship to its own citizens. For example, Bhutan pursues maximum independence in its trade policies and travel laws in order to preserve its culture. Further, all its citizens must wear traditional dress and buildings must conform with traditional architecture. Bhutan's foreign minister said that with more trade and contact, "within a year or two our value system would change."[23] But its isolation contributes to Bhutan's ranking as one of the poorest countries in the world. Because it depends heavily on foreign aid, many argue that donors should use the aid as leverage to force Bhutan to liberalize its trade policies in order to help its citizens.

Either the innovator or a competitor may begin producing abroad, but the output at this stage is likely to stay almost entirely in the foreign country with the new manufacturing unit. Let's say, for example, that the new manufacturing unit is in Japan. The output will be sold mainly in Japan for several reasons:

1. There is growth in the Japanese market.
2. Unique product variations are being introduced for Japanese consumers.
3. Japanese costs may still be high because of production start-up problems.

Because sales are growing rapidly in many markets, there are greater incentives at this level for the development of process technology. However, product technology may not yet be well developed because of the number of product variations introduced by competitors that are trying to take a leadership position by gaining market share. Thus the production process may still be characterized as labor-intensive during this stage, although it is becoming less so. The original producing country will increase its exports in this stage but face the loss of certain key export markets in which local production has commenced.

Stage 3: Maturity

In Stage 3, maturity, worldwide demand begins to level off, although it may be growing in some countries and declining in others. There often is a shake-out of producers such that product models become highly standardized, making cost a more important competitive weapon. Longer production runs become possible for foreign plants, which in turn reduce per unit cost. The lower per unit cost enables sales to increase more in LDCs.

Because markets and technologies are widespread, the innovating country no longer has a production advantage. There are incentives to begin moving plants to LDCs where unskilled but inexpensive labor can be used effectively for standardized (capital-intensive) processes. In fact, a company may establish more capital-intensive production in an LDC than it is abandoning at home because of advancements in equipment; thus it saves on labor rates *and* the number of workers employed.

Stage 4: Decline

As a product moves to the declining stage, those factors occurring during the mature stage continue to evolve. The markets in industrial countries decline more rapidly than those in LDCs as affluent customers demand ever-newer products. By this time, market and cost factors have dictated that almost all production is situated in LDCs, which export to the declining or small-niche markets in industrial countries.

Verification and Limitations of PLC Theory

Studies have found behavior to be consistent with the predictions of the PLC model for certain consumer durables, synthetic materials, and electronics.[24] However, there are many other types of products for which production movements do not take place:[25]

1. Products that, because of very rapid innovation, have extremely short life cycles, which make it impossible to achieve cost reductions by moving production from one country to another. For example, product obsolescence occurs so rapidly for many electronic products that there is little international diffusion of production.
2. Luxury products for which cost is of little concern to the consumer.
3. Products for which international transport costs are so high that there is little opportunity for export sales, regardless of the stage within the product life cycle.
4. Products for which a company can use a differentiation strategy, such as advertising, in order to maintain consumer demand without competing on the basis of price.[26]
5. Products that result when specialized knowledge is important for linking present output with the training of technical labor and the development of the next generation of technology. This seems to explain the long-term U.S. dominance of medical equipment production and German dominance in rotary printing presses.[27]

In addition, changes in technology and demand conditions might lead to all kinds of permutations. For example, microchip production began in the United States and moved largely abroad, as would be predicted by PLC theory; but then most production returned to the United States in response to further product innovations and changing market conditions.

   Regardless of the type of product, there has been an increased tendency on the part of MNEs to introduce new products at home and abroad almost simultaneously as they move from multidomestic to global strategies. In other words, instead of merely observing needs within their domestic markets, companies develop products and services to serve observable market segments that transcend national borders. In so doing, they eliminate the leads and lags that are assumed to exist as a product is diffused from one country to another. Further, companies sometimes produce abroad simply to take advantage of production economies rather than in response to growing foreign markets. Singer, for example, produces certain sewing machine models in Brazil to sell in export markets, not to supply the Brazilian market.

Trade Patterns

Country Differences

Most trade theories emphasize differences among countries in
- **Climate**
- **Factor endowment**
- **Innovative capability**

So far in this chapter, the theories explaining why trade takes place have focused on the differences among countries. These theories tend to explain most of the trade among dissimilar countries, such as trade between an industrial country and an LDC or trade between a temperate country and a tropical one. On the basis of these theories, you would expect that the greater the dissimilarity among countries, the greater the potential for trade. For example, great differences in climatic conditions will lead to highly differentiated agricultural products. Countries that differ in labor or capital intensities will differ in the types of products they can produce efficiently. And national differences in innovative abilities will affect how production of a product will move from one country to another during the product's life cycle. A number of other factors help explain global trade patterns.[28] The most important factors are described in this section.

Country-Similarity Theory

Most trade today occurs among apparently similar countries.

Observations of actual trade patterns reveal that most of the world's trade occurs among countries that have similar characteristics, specifically among industrial, or developed, countries, which have highly educated populations and are located in temperate areas of the globe. For example, the United States is the world's largest trader, and eight of the ten largest U.S. export markets are also top-ten sources for U.S. imports. Nine of the ten largest U.S. export and import partners are classified either as industrialized or newly industrialized countries.[29] Globally, all of the ten largest importers and exporters of both merchandise and services are industrialized or newly industrialized countries.[30] Thus overall trade patterns seem to be at variance with the traditional theories that emphasize country-by-country differences.

The fact that so much trade takes place among industrial countries is due to the growing importance of acquired advantage (product technology) as opposed to natural advantage (agricultural products and raw materials) in world trade (see Fig. 5.3). The **country-similarity theory** holds that once a producer has developed a

Figure 5.3
World Trade by Major Product Category as Percentage of Total World Trade for Selected Years

Source: World Trade Organization, *Annual Report 1966,* Vol. I (Geneva: World Trade Organization, 1996), p. 14.

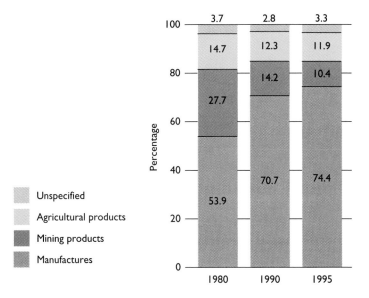

new product in response to observed market conditions in the home market, it will turn to markets that are perceived to be the most similar to those at home. In other words, consumers in industrial countries will have a high propensity to buy high-quality and luxury products, whereas consumers in lower-income countries will buy few of these products.[31] In addition, trade in commercial services, which is not included in Fig. 5.3 because of historical collection problems, was about 24 percent of the value of merchandise trade in 1995 or about 19 percent of total world trade.[32] Commercial service trade is also due to acquired advantages.

Although the markets within the industrial countries might overall have similar demands, countries also specialize in order to gain acquired advantages. Countries do this through the apportionment of their research efforts. For example, the technical efforts of the United States are strongest in mining, Japan's are in information and instruments, France's in nuclear physics, and Switzerland's in textiles.[33] Countries also do this by apportioning spending among physical items (plant and equipment), human skills, and technological development.[34] Further, those domestic industries in which there is intense competitive rivalry will probably innovate faster and develop international advantages. In addition, consumers in industrial countries want and can afford to buy products with a wide variety of characteristics. Thus companies from different countries produce different product models, and each may gain some markets abroad. This helps explain why road vehicles (automobiles and small trucks) comprise both the largest category of U.S. imports and the second largest category of U.S. exports.

The relative importance of developed countries in world trade is due, in addition to specialization, to these countries' economic size. In other words, where the value of production is high, there is more that is available to sell—both domestically and internationally. Further, where incomes are high, people buy more—from both domestic and foreign sources. In recent years as Asian developing economies have grown much more rapidly than the world's economies as a whole, their share of global imports and exports has also increased.[35] Their imports may be largely explained by country-similarity theory. In other words, growth has caused the emergence of a large consumer segment that closely resembles what is found in developed countries. Thus producers in developed countries extend sales to this segment. However, exports of the Asian developing economies are not so fully explained by this theory because so much of their new production has been in response to observed needs outside, rather than within, their home markets.

Wars and Insurrection

Military conflicts
- **Change what is produced**
- **Increase risks of international business**
- **Have a growing global effect on business**

Military conflicts disrupt traditional international business patterns as participants divert their transportation systems and much of their productive capacity to the war effort. In addition, political animosity and transport difficulties may interfere with trading channels. For example, Iraq's international trade fell sharply after its 1990 invasion of Kuwait as other countries either severed trade relations or disrupted supply lines. The composition of trade changes because of a shift from consumer goods to industrial goods that can be used in meeting military objectives. Increased global interrelationships lend far-reaching impact to today's military conflicts. A particularly notable example was the worldwide oil price increase resulting from Iraq's invasion of Kuwait.

Pairs of Trading Relationships

Trading partners are affected by
- **Distance**
- **Competitive capabilities**
- **Cultural similarity**
- **Relations between countries**
- **Business cycles**

Although the theories regarding country differences and similarities help to explain broad world trade patterns, such as between industrial countries and LDCs, they do little to explain specific pairs of trading relationships. Why, for example, will a particular industrial country buy more from one LDC than another? Why will it buy from one industrial country rather than another? Although there is no single answer to these questions that will explain all product flows, the distance between two countries accounts for many of these world trade relationships. This is especially true for products for which the transport cost is high relative to the production cost. For example, Finland is a major supplier to Russia because transport costs are cheap and fast compared to alternatives. Acer, a Taiwanese computer maker, built a plant in Finland to serve Russia because of savings compared with shipments from Asia and because Finland provided more secure storage and ease of operations than if the plant were in Russia.[36]

But transport cost is not the only factor; nor is it an insurmountable one. For example, New Zealand has favorable climatic and soil conditions for growing apples. It also has an opportunity to compete out of season in the Northern Hemisphere. However, these advantages are not unique; Chile, Argentina, and South Africa have them as well. Furthermore, these three countries have cost advantages in land, labor, and freight. Nevertheless, New Zealand was able to increase its share of global apple exports during the 1980s by increasing yields, developing new premium varieties, bypassing intermediaries to sell directly to supermarkets abroad, and consolidating efforts through a national marketing board.

Cultural similarity, as expressed through language and religion, also helps explain much of the direction of trade. Apparently importers and exporters find it easier to do business in a country they perceive as being similar. Likewise, much of the trade between specific industrial countries and LDCs is explained by historic colonial relationships; and much of the lack of trade among nations in the Southern Hemisphere is due to the absence of historic ties. Importers and exporters find it easier to continue business ties than to develop new distribution arrangements in countries in which they are less experienced.

Political relationships and economic agreements among countries may discourage or encourage trade between certain pairs of countries thus favoring some companies over others. For example, political animosities between the United States and Cuba have caused mutual trade to be almost nonexistent for about four decades and have replaced U.S. sugar imports from Cuba with imports from such countries as Mexico and the Dominican Republic. Saudi Arabia favored Boeing over Airbus Industrie with a large aircraft order largely because of unhappiness with European reluctance to provide military aid to Bosnian Muslims.[37] Trade agreements among countries, such as by the European Union (EU) to remove all trade barriers among member countries, have caused a greater share of those countries' total trade to be conducted within the group.

During economic booms, a country's imports tend to grow more rapidly than production does. The opposite occurs during periods of slow economic growth. The reason for this cyclical relationship is that consumers consider many foreign goods marginal and thus curtail imports as the economy slackens. Producers also may attempt to export only when they have surpluses and will add capacity to serve foreign markets only if demand there is sustained for a long period. This relationship affects particular markets as growth rates differ among countries. For example, during most of the 1980s, Latin American economies performed very poorly, and they took a smaller share of U.S. exports. In the 1990s, the share of U.S. exports going to Latin America increased sharply as those economies grew faster than European ones did.[38]

Independence, Interdependence, and Dependence

No country is completely dependent or independent, although some are closer to one extreme or the other.

The concepts of independence, interdependence, and dependence help to explain world trade patterns and countries' trade policies. They form a continuum, with independence at one extreme, dependence on the other, and interdependence somewhere in the middle. No countries are located at either extreme of this continuum; however, some tend to be closer to one extreme than the other.

Independence

Too much economic independence means doing without certain goods, services, and technologies.

In a situation of independence, a country would have no reliance on others for any goods, services, or technologies. However, because all countries engage in trade, no country has complete economic independence from other countries. The most recent instances of economic near-independence have been seen in the Liawep tribe, found in Papua New Guinea in 1993, and in present day Bhutan.[39] Isolation from other societies brought certain advantages to the Liaweps and Bhutanese: They have not had to be concerned, for example, that another society might cut off their supply of essential foods or tools. Of course, for both societies the price of independence is having to do without goods they could not produce themselves. A further disadvantage of independence is that it hinders a country's ability to borrow and adapt technologies already in existence; such borrowing and adaptation can add significantly to a country's economic growth rate.[40] In most countries, governmental policy has focused on achieving the advantages of independence without paying too high a price in terms of consumer deprivation. This is done by trying to forge trade patterns that are minimally vulnerable to foreign control of supply and demand.

Interdependence

One way to limit a country's vulnerability to foreign changes is through interdependence, or the development of trade relationships on the basis of mutual need. France and Germany, for example, have highly interdependent economies. Each depends about equally on the other as a trading partner; thus neither is likely to cut off supplies or markets, because the other could retaliate effectively. Such interdependence sometimes results in pressures by international companies on their governments to sustain trade relations. For example, about a third of world trade is intracompany trade—that is, companies export components and finished products between their foreign and home-country facilities—therefore, any trade cessation would adversely affect these companies. For example, Ford sources components in different countries and would be severely affected if supplies from any one were to be suddenly disrupted. Similarly, when the U.S. government proposed trade sanctions against Chinese imports because of China's human rights record, U.S. companies protested because of the export sales they would lose.

Dependence

Many developing countries have decried their dependence, realizing that they rely too heavily on the sale of one primary commodity and/or on one country as a customer and supplier. Whereas most LDCs depend on one commodity for more than 25 percent of their export earnings, Iceland is the only industrialized country with this high a dependence (on fish). And whereas about one quarter of LDCs depend on one country (almost always an industrial one) for more than half of their export earnings, Canada is the only industrialized country with this high a dependence (on the United States). Because the economies of LDCs are small, these countries tend to be much more dependent on a given industrial country than the industrial country is dependent on them. Mexico, for example, depends on the United States for over 60 percent of its imports and exports, whereas the United States depends on Mexico for less than 10 percent of its imports and exports. Thus Mexico can be much more adversely affected by U.S. policies than the United States can be affected by Mexican policies. Furthermore, LDCs primarily depend on production that competes on the basis of low-wage inputs.[41] This sort of dependence has led to a widespread belief that dependence will retard LDCs' development.[42]

Although theorists and policymakers wishing to lower dependency have proposed a number of different approaches, they all suggest that LDCs intervene in the foreign trade markets. As shown in the opening case, Sri Lanka has attempted to diversify its exports by developing nontraditional products that its policymakers believe can ultimately compete in world markets. But some LDCs see that they have little opportunity to diversify production away from a basic commodity for which there is global oversupply. For them, the best economic assurance is continued dependence on an industrial country that preferentially imports their products.[43]

Strategic Trade Policy

Given the importance of acquired advantage in world trade, it is understandable that governments have debated what their roles should be in affecting the acquired advantage of production within their borders. At the same time, it is generally acknowledged that governmental roles are seldom neutral, so even though governmental decisions and policies may not be intended to affect world trade, they nevertheless have that effect. For example, U.S. governmental efforts to improve agricultural productivity and defense capabilities have undoubtedly helped the U.S. exports of farm and aerospace products. Further, the decision to push certain capabilities may have adverse effects in other industries. For example, European airlines have argued that their governments' support for high-speed rail traffic in Europe has hurt their ability to be competitive on international routes with U.S. air carriers, which profit from not having to compete much with railroads for passenger traffic in the United States.

From the standpoint of national competitiveness, the issue revolves around the development of successful industries. Of particular importance are emerging growth industries, because they offer the possibility of high value added (because of high profits and wages) within the country in which most of the industry is headquartered. Further, by being first, there are marketing and production cost advantages that retard competition from other countries.[44] But to be internationally competitive, one must have the right resources that are needed for the targeted industry. Governments may try to alter their absolute and comparative advantages so that there is a fit, such as by importing and developing specific skills they need.

There are two basic approaches: to alter conditions that will affect industry in general, and to alter conditions to affect a targeted industry. Regardless of whether a government takes a general or specific approach, the relative competitive position of specific companies and production locations may be altered. The first approach involves altering conditions that affect factor proportions, efficiency, and innovation. For example, a country may upgrade production factors, such as by improving human skills through education, providing infrastructure (transportation, communications, capital markets, utilities), promoting a highly competitive environment so that companies are forced to make improvements, and inducing consumers to demand an ever higher quality of products and services.[45] This approach is general; that is, it creates conditions that may affect a wide variety of industries. The second, very different approach is to target specific production sectors. This approach has usually resulted in no more than small payoffs,[46] largely because of difficulty in identifying the right production sector to target. For example, a country may target a sector for which global demand never reaches expectations, such as France's support for supersonic passenger aircraft. Or, competitive conditions fail to develop, such as occurred with Thailand's support of the steel industry, which has lacked competitive costs because of poorly trained managers and rising labor costs in relation to other nearby countries.[47] Moreover, there has been a tendency for too many countries to identify the same industries, so excessive competition has led to inadequate returns.[48] Finally, relative conditions change, causing relative capabilities to change as well. For instance, Singapore successfully attracted companies in mature consumer electronics production, and was able to compete globally because of its low wages relative to productivity; however, in recent years, Singapore has been losing its competitive advantage because of its rising labor costs and has seen many companies move their production elsewhere, such as to Malaysia. Singapore is now trying to attract more research and development facilities and the production of new products that have higher profit margins.[49] Nevertheless, there are some notable successes. South Korea, for example, has been transformed in a fairly short time from a poor agricultural country to a new exporter of key manufactured products. To achieve this transformation, the South Korean government took an active role in targeting key sectors (especially steel, automobiles, and consumer electronics) to ensure that they obtained needed capital. In the case of steel, the government created a state-owned company and gave incentives for companies to acquire foreign technology and improve on it and to train workers in quality control procedures. The government also invested heavily in education to improve employee input. Not only did South Korea increase the educational attendance rate, it also increased the proportion of people studying to be scientists and engineers in institutions of higher education.[50] Regardless of whether a government takes a general or a specific approach, the relative competitive position of specific companies and production locations may be altered.

Why Companies Trade Internationally

Most trade theories are based on a national perspective, but decisions to trade are usually made by companies.

Most trade theories approach trade from a national perspective; that is, they begin with a question such as "Why should Sri Lanka trade?" Regardless of the advantages that a country may gain by trading, international trade ordinarily will not begin unless companies within the country have competitive advantages that will enable them to be viable traders. Further, these companies must perceive that there are opportunities for exporting and importing. Because companies have limited resources, they must decide whether to exploit those resources domestically or internationally. Only if they perceive that the international opportunities might be greater than the domestic ones will they divert their resources to the foreign sector. To understand why trade takes place, it is therefore useful to understand the competitive advantages and trade opportunities accruing to individual businesses.

Competitive Advantages

A recent study of a hundred industries in ten major trading nations focused on how the competitive advantage of a country is related to the companies headquartered within it. The purpose of the study was to determine why specialized competitive advantages differ among countries; for example, Italian companies have an advantage in the ceramic tile industry and Swiss companies have one in the watch indus-try. A conclusion of the study was that four conditions have been important for competitive superiority: demand; factor endowment; related and supporting indus-tries; and firm strategy, structure, and rivalry. These are shown in Fig. 5.4 in what is called the *Porter diamond*. All four of these conditions have already been discussed in the context of other trade theories, but how they combine affects the development and continued existence of competitive advantages. The framework of the diamond is, therefore, useful for understanding how and where globally competitive compa-nies develop. Usually, but not always, all four conditions need to be favorable for an industry within a country to attain global supremacy.

Both PLC theory and country-similarity theory show that new products (indus-tries) usually arise from observation of nearby need or demand. Further, start-up production usually is located near the observed market. This was the case for the modern ceramic tile industry in Italy after World War II: there was a postwar housing boom, and consumers of new housing wanted cool floors because of the hot Italian climate. The second condition of the Porter diamond—factor con-ditions (recall natural advantage within absolute advantage theory and the factor-proportions theory)—influenced both the choice of tile to meet consumer demand and the choice of Italy as the production location. Wood, for example, was less available and more expensive than tile, and most production factors (skilled labor, capital, technology, and equipment) were available within Italy on favorable terms. Although white clays had to be imported, the lack of availability of a natural resource (natural advantage) is not necessarily an insurmountable obstacle, as the earlier discussion of acquired advantage pointed out. The third condition—the

**Figure 5.4
Determinants of Global
Competitive
Advantage**

The Porter diamond shows the interaction of four con-ditions that usually need to be favorable if an industry in a country is to gain a global competitive advan-tage.

Source: Michael E. Porter, *The Competitive Advantage of Nations* (New York: Free Press, 1990), p. 72.

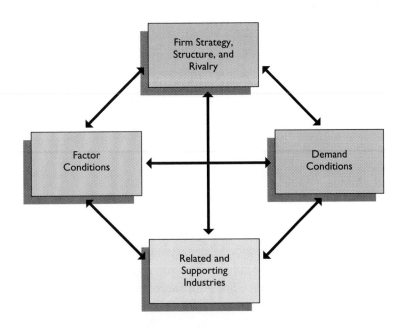

existence of nearby related and supporting industries (enamels and glazes)—was also favorable. (Recall discussions of the importance of transport costs in the theory of country size, assumptions of specialization, and limitations of PLC theory.) Thus the combination of three conditions—demand, factor endowment, and related and supporting industries—influenced companies' decisions to initiate production of ceramic tiles in postwar Italy. The ability of these companies to develop and sustain a competitive advantage required favorable circumstances for the fourth condition—firm strategy, structure, and rivalry. Barriers to market entry were low in the tile industry (some companies started up with as few as three employees), and hundreds of companies initiated production. Rivalry became intense as companies tried to serve increasingly sophisticated Italian consumers. These circumstances forced breakthroughs in both product and process technologies, which gave the Italian producers advantages over foreign producers.

Limitations of the diamond   Although the Italian tile industry illustrates the usual conditions necessary for the development of a global advantage, the existence of favorable conditions is not sufficient to guarantee that an industry will start up and develop in a given locale. Entrepreneurs may face favorable conditions for many different lines of business. In fact, comparative advantage theory holds that resource limitations may cause companies in a country not to try to compete in some industries, even though an absolute advantage may exist. For example, conditions in Switzerland would seem to have favored success if companies in that country had become players in the personal computer industry; however, Swiss companies preferred instead to protect the global positions they had already attained in such product lines as watches and scientific instruments.

A second limitation of the diamond concerns the increased openness of countries to information, production factors, supplies, and competition from abroad. Thus, the absence of any of the four conditions from the diamond domestically may not inhibit companies and industries from becoming globally competitive. First, take the existence of demand conditions. We have already discussed how observations of foreign, rather than domestic, demand conditions have spurred much of the recent growth in Asian exports. In fact, such Japanese companies as Uniden and Fujitech target their sales almost entirely to foreign markets.[51] Second, domestic factor conditions can be changed. For example, capital and managers are increasingly mobile internationally, and much of Singapore's recent global export growth of high-tech components has depended on the importation of these factors. Third, if related and supporting industries are not available locally, materials and components are now more easily brought in from abroad because of advancements in transportation and the relaxation of import restrictions. In fact, many MNEs now assemble products with parts supplied from a variety of countries. Finally, companies react not only to domestic rivals, but also to foreign-based rivals with which they compete at home and abroad. In most industries there are competitors based in various countries.[52]

Strategic Advantages of Exports

Incentives to export include
- **Use of excess capacity**
- **Reduced production costs per unit**
- **Increased markup**
- **Spread of risk**

Incentives to import include
- **Cheaper supplies**
- **Additions to product line**
- **Reduction of risk of nonsupply**

Use of excess capacity   Companies frequently have immediate or long-term output capabilities for which there is inadequate domestic demand. This excess capacity may be in the form of known reserves of natural resources or in the form of product-specific capabilities that cannot be easily diverted to producing other goods for which there might be an adequate domestic demand. Thus companies leverage their competencies by using them abroad.

As shown earlier in this chapter, small countries tend to trade more than large countries. One reason is that process technology may allow a company to produce efficiently only on a large scale, larger than the demand in the domestic market. Consider automobile production, for example: Volvo has a much greater need to export from the small Swedish market than General Motors does from the large U.S. market.

Cost reduction   Studies have shown that a company can generally reduce its costs by 20–30 percent each time its output is doubled, a phenomenon known as the **experience curve.**[53] For instance, with a 20-percent cost reduction and an initial cost of $100 per unit, the second unit produced will cost $80, the fourth $64, and so on. The reduction may come about because of several factors: covering fixed costs over a larger output, increasing efficiency because of the experience gained through producing large quantities of units, and making quantity purchases of materials and transportation. Therefore it is obvious that the market leader may garner cost advantages over its competitors. One way a company can increase output is by defining its market in global rather than domestic terms. In fact, this may give a company a **first-mover advantage** that discourages the entry of other companies in the industry. Further, many companies that are not the leaders in their domestic markets may be more active in seeking export sales in order to counter the leaders' volume advantage. For example, in Japan, Matsushita and Toyota are their industries' market leaders; however, Sony and Sanyo as followers of Matsushita and Nissan and Honda as followers of Toyota are more active in export markets.[54] However, the gains from the experience curve must be weighed against additional costs arising from exporting, such as those for product adaptation, management time, inventory increases, and more credit extension. These costs may outweigh the advantages of developing foreign markets.[55]

Greater profitability   A producer might be able to sell the same product at a greater profit abroad than at home. This may happen because the competitive environment in the foreign market is different, possibly because the product is in a different stage of its life cycle there. Thus a mature stage at home may force domestic price cutting, while a growth stage abroad may make foreign price reductions unnecessary. Greater profitability also may come about because of different governmental actions at home and abroad that affect profitability—for example, differences in the taxation of earnings or the regulation of prices. If, however, companies must divert efforts from domestic sales in order to service foreign markets, they may lack the resources to sustain their overall growth objectives.[56]

Risk spreading   By spreading sales over more than one foreign market, a producer might be able to minimize fluctuations in demand. This may come about because business cycles vary among countries and because products might be in different stages of their life cycles in different countries. For example, Donaldson Co., a U.S. manufacturer of filters, air cleaners, and mufflers, achieved record earnings in 1991 despite the fact that its two major U.S. customers, Caterpillar and Deere, were facing a recession.[57] Another factor in spreading risk through exportation is that a producer might be able to develop more customers, thereby reducing its vulnerability to the loss of a single customer or a few.

Strategic Advantages of Imports

The impetus for trade involvement may come from either the exporter or the importer. In either case, there must be both a seller and a buyer. Impetus may come from an importer because that company is seeking out cheaper or better-quality supplies, components, or products to be used in its production facilities. Or a company may be actively seeking new foreign products that complement its existing lines. These would give the importer more to sell, which also might enable it to use excess capacity in its distribution sales force.

If international procurement of supplies and components lowers costs or improves the quality of finished products, the procuring company may then be better able to combat import competition for the finished products. Or it may be able to compete more effectively in export markets. The automobile industry exemplifies global competition that depends on subcontractors, including foreign ones, to reduce production costs.[58]

An importer, like an exporter, might be able to spread its operating risks. By developing alternative suppliers, a company is less vulnerable to the dictates or fortunes of any single supplier. For example, many large U.S. steel customers, such as the automobile industry, have diversified their steel purchases to include European and Japanese suppliers. This strategy has reduced the risk of supply shortages for the U.S. automobile industry in case of a strike among steelworkers in the United States; at the same time, however, it has contributed to the problems of the U.S. steel industry.

Trade in the Internationalization Process

Export strategies and their implementation will be discussed in Chapter 17; nevertheless, it is useful to review and address companies' trade practices as they relate to their commitment to greater international involvement. Recall from Chapter 1 that export/import activities are usually the first mode companies undertake for international operations. However, as they move to deeper levels of international commitment, they usually continue importing and/or exporting as well. Thus trade is usually the one mode of foreign operations that is strategically important to companies throughout their growth internationally.

We have discussed the roles that physical distance and cultural similarity play in determining country-pairs in trading relationships. These factors also affect the choices that companies make in where to export first. In fact, small and medium-sized companies tend to limit the number of foreign countries with which they trade as compared with larger companies.[59] Thus the growth in country-diversity of operations seems to move in tandem with companies' growth in general. But company attitudes also play a role in the choice and number of countries for export activities. Those that have more ethnocentric orientations tend to concentrate more on culturally similar markets than those that have more polycentric orientations.[60]

COUNTERVAILING FORCES

When countries have few restrictions on foreign trade, companies have greater opportunities to gain economies of scale by servicing markets in more than one country from a single base of production. They also can pursue global, as opposed to multidomestic, strategies more easily. But governmental trade restrictions are very mixed from one country to another, from one point in time to another, and from one product or service to others within the same economies. Nevertheless, it is probably safe to say that trade restrictions have been diminishing, primarily because of the economic gains that countries foresee through freer trade. For example, the fastest growing LDCs have been those with the fewest import restrictions. This has allowed them to reduce costs of essential agricultural products and machinery and has given them advantages in developing exports. The area with the highest import barriers is sub-Saharan Africa, and this is the area that has lagged the most in export development and in economic growth.[61]

However, there are uncertainties as to whether the trend toward the freer movement of trade will continue. Groups worldwide question whether the economic benefits of more open economies outweigh some of the costs, both economic and noneconomic. Although the next chapter will discuss protectionist issues in detail, it is useful at this point to understand the overall issues of evolving protectionist sentiment.

One key issue involves the trade between industrial and developing countries. At the same time trade barriers are being reduced, many LDCs, where wage rates are very low, are increasing productivity more rapidly than are industrial countries.[62] The result could mean certain shifts in production to LDCs and the displacement of many jobs within industrial countries. There is uncertainty as to how fast new jobs will replace old ones in industrial countries and how much tolerance industrial countries will have for employment shifts that would be less likely to occur within protected markets.

A second key issue results from the concept of national sovereignty.[63] Separate nations exist because of differences in culture and in economic and political priorities. The more interdependent economies become because of trade, the more difficult it is for a country to maintain differences from its major trading partners. For example, two neighboring countries may differ in terms of preferences for income equality, whether to place the major tax burden on companies or individuals, how much in the way of employee safety provisions to require, and how much the environment should be protected; but such differences create production cost differences. With unrestricted trade, a country with more stringent (expensive) requirements may either have to relax those requirements or face production adjustments as products enter easily from abroad. At present there is evidence that many countries may invoke national sovereignty by preventing trade that may undermine their own priorities and objectives, even though such moves may have certain negative economic costs for them.

Companies must predict whether there will be freer or more restrictive trade in those sectors in which they operate. Restrictive trade limits their options. But uncertainty may cause them to make some decisions that are suboptimal to the actual outcome of trading relationships.

LOOKING TO THE FUTURE

If present trends continue, relationships among factor endowments (land, labor, and capital) will continue to evolve. The population growth rate is much higher in LDCs, especially those of sub-Saharan Africa, than in developed countries. Two possible consequences of this growth are continued shifts of labor-intensive production to LDCs and of agricultural production away from densely populated areas. At the same time, the finite supply of natural resources may lead to price increases for these resources (except for short respites). This may work to the advantage of LDCs because supplies in industrial countries have been more fully exploited. The World Bank predicts some major shifts among countries by the year 2020 in terms of their total output as measured by purchasing power parity. Whereas in 1992 only three of the ten largest economies were Asian countries, by 2020 the number will have ballooned to seven.[64] If this prediction is reasonably correct, Asia will account for a much larger portion of world trade.

Given the success of some Asian countries, the future is likely to bring greater efforts on the part of governments worldwide to improve trade advantages. There will be further discussions on the appropriateness of transferring successful trade policies from one country to another. For example, the collectivist approach that works so well in Japan, Taiwan, and South Korea may not be appropriate for the individualistic societies of the United Kingdom and the United States.[65]

Four factors are worth monitoring because they could cause product trade to become relatively less significant in the future:

1. There are some indications that protectionist sentiment is growing. This could prevent competitively produced goods from entering foreign countries. For example, because of public sentiment, neither major political party campaigned for freer trade in the 1996 U.S. presidential campaigns. Further, in early 1997, the United States limited Chinese textile imports for the next four years.

2. As economies grow, efficiencies of multiple production locations also grow; thus country-by-country production may replace trade in many cases. For example, most automobile producers have moved into Thailand or plan to do so as a result of Thailand's growing market size.

3. Flexible, small-scale production methods, especially those using robotics, may enable even small countries to produce many goods efficiently for their own consumption, thus eliminating the need to import those goods. For example, steel production used to take larger capital outlays that needed enormous markets before the development of efficient mini-mills that can produce on a small scale.

4. Services are growing more rapidly than products as a portion of production and consumption within industrial countries; consequently, product trade may become a less important part of countries' total trade. Further, many of the rapid-growth service areas, such as home building and dining out, are not easily tradeable; thus trade in goods plus services could become a smaller part of total output and consumption.

WEB CONNECTION

Check out our home page for links to World Wide Web resources for international trade.

Summary

- **Trade theory is useful because it helps to explain what might be produced competitively in a given locale, where a company might go to produce a given product efficiently, and whether governmental practices might interfere with the free flow of trade among countries.**

- **Some trade theories deal with the question of what will happen to international trade in the absence of governmental interference; others prescribe how governments should interfere with trade flows in order to achieve certain national objectives.**

- **Mercantilist theory proposed that a country should try to achieve a favorable balance of trade (export more than it imports) in order to receive an influx of gold. Neomercantilist policy also seeks a favorable balance of trade, but its purpose is to achieve some social or political objective.**

- **Adam Smith developed the theory of absolute advantage, which holds that consumers will be better off if they can buy foreign-made products that are priced more cheaply than domestic ones.**

- According to the theory of absolute advantage, a country may produce goods more efficiently because of a natural advantage (for example, raw materials or climate) or because of an acquired advantage (for example, technology or skills).

- The theory of country size holds that because countries with large land areas are more apt to have varied climates and natural resources, they are generally more nearly self-sufficient than smaller countries are. A second reason for this greater self-sufficiency is that large countries' production centers are more likely to be located at a greater distance from other countries, thus raising the transport costs of foreign trade.

- David Ricardo's comparative advantage theory holds that total output can be increased through foreign trade, even though one country may have an absolute advantage in the production of all products.

- Some of the assumptions of the trade theories of absolute and comparative advantage have been questioned by policymakers. These are that full employment exists, that output efficiency is always a country's major objective, that there are no transport costs among countries, that countries are satisfied with their relative gains, and that resources move freely within countries but are immobile internationally.

- The factor-proportions theory holds that a country's relative endowments of land, labor, and capital will determine the relative costs of these factors. These factor costs, in turn, will determine which goods the country can produce most efficiently.

- The international product life cycle (PLC) theory states that many manufactured products will be produced first in the countries in which they were researched and developed. These are almost always industrialized countries. Over the product's life cycle, production will tend to become more capital-intensive and will be shifted to foreign locations.

- According to the country-similarity theory, most trade today occurs among industrial countries because they share very similar market segments.

- Some LDCs are concerned that they are overly vulnerable to events in other countries because of their high dependence on one export product and/or one trading partner. As LDCs try to become more independent of the external environment, however, they face the risk that their own consumers may have to pay higher prices or do without some goods.

- **Countries seek to improve their national competitiveness by developing successful industries. They do this by altering conditions that affect industry in general or targeted industries (a strategic trade policy).**

- **Although most trade theories deal with cross-country benefits and costs, trading decisions usually are made at the company level. Companies must have competitive advantages to be viable exporters. They may seek trading opportunities in order to use excess capacity, lower production costs, or spread risks.**

Case
The Cashew[66]

The cashew tree today is best known for its nuts, which account for about 20 percent of the value of nuts produced worldwide—about equal to the value of almonds or hazelnuts. U.S. imports of cashew nuts in 1995 totaled about $245 million, about 60 percent of the world market and more than three times the imports into Europe, which is the next largest market.

The fruit of the tree (known as the cashew apple), however, drew the earliest attention. The Tupi Indians of Brazil first harvested the cashew apple in the wild. They later introduced it to early Portuguese traders, who in turn propagated the plant in other tropical countries. (See Map 5.2 for major production locations.) But attempts to grow the tree on plantations proved unsuccessful because the cashew was vulnerable to insects in the close quarters of plantations. Instead, some of the abandoned plantation trees propagated new trees in the wild where they thrived in the forests of India, East Africa, Indonesia, and Southeast Asia.

Several factors inhibited early use of the cashew nut. First, cashew fruit matures before the nut, so the fruit is spoiled by the time the nut can be harvested usefully. Second, the processing of cashew nuts is tedious and time-consuming. In the 1920s, however, a processing industry developed in India, and the nuts became more valuable than the fruit because they became so popular among Indian consumers. India maintained a virtual monopoly on cashew processing until the mid-1970s. This monopoly was due to three factors.

1. India was the largest producer of wild cashews.
2. Early demand occurred in India, meaning that any other country would have to incur added transport charges in order to reach the Indian market.
3. Most importantly, the Indian workers were particularly adept at the process technology.

Cashew nut processing was very labor-intensive and required manual dexterity and low wage rates. The nut is contained beneath layers of shell and thin skin. To remove the shell, the nut must be placed in an open fire for a few minutes and then tapped (while still hot) with a wooden hammer. If the nut is broken in the tapping, its value decreases considerably. Once the shell is removed, the nut is placed in an oven for up to ten hours, after

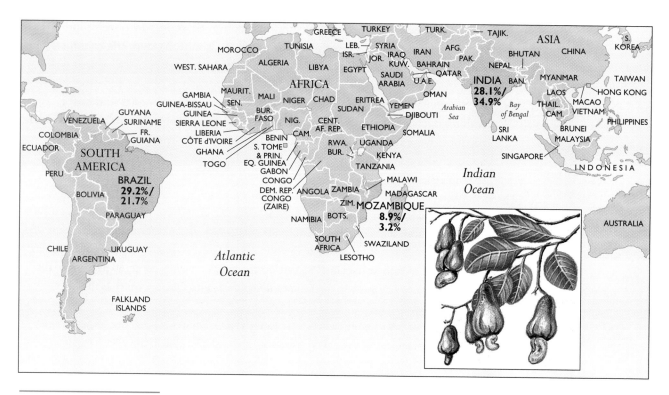

Map 5.2
Location of World's Cashew Nut and Export Supplies

The major cashew producing and exporting areas are all in the tropics. This map shows the locations of the three largest producers and exporters. The inset shows the cashew fruit and nuts. The first number shows the percentage of world production of raw nuts in the 1989–91 period. The second number shows the percentage of world exports for processed cashew nuts in the 1988–90 period.

Source: Steven Jaffee, *Private Sector Response to Market Liberalization* (Washington: World Bank, 1994).

which the skin is removed by hand while the nut is still warm. Removal is done without the use of fingernails or any sharp objects that can mark or break the surface. The nuts are then sorted and graded into twenty-four different categories by the size of the pieces. The highest grade typically sells at about four times the price of the lowest grade, which is sold almost entirely to the confectionery industry.

Through the years, several factors began to threaten India's prominence as a cashew producer. As demand for the nuts grew in the United States and the United Kingdom, a shortage developed. Because the nuts were unsuited to plantation growth, India turned to East Africa, especially Mozambique, Tanzania, and Kenya, for supplies. Those countries were experiencing high unemployment and at first were eager to sell the raw nuts.

By the 1950s, India was no longer the world's major consumer, and the East African countries began to realize that they might be able to bypass India by processing the raw nuts themselves. Cashew-processing methods were well known, so there was no technological obstacle. There was another barrier, however, that blocked early competition from East Africa. The Indian labor force worked on making handicrafts at home as children and, as a result, by the time they were employed in cashew processing, could perform delicate hand operations efficiently. Without this training, the East Africans were at a fatal disadvantage.

Although the Africans' inability to compete granted a reprieve to the Indian industry, it put them on notice that they were vulnerable to supply cutoffs. The Indian Council for Agricultural Research, the International Society for Horticultural Sciences, and the Indian Society for Plantation Crops expanded their efforts to increase India's production of raw nuts. Concomitantly, three different companies developed mechanical equipment to replace hand processing. The Sturtevant Tropical Products Institute developed a method now used by a London equipment manufacturer, Fletcher and Stewart, which cracks the shells with a steel plate. Oltremare Industria of Italy and Widmer and Ernst of Switzerland both developed shell-cutting machines. Equipment was sold to East African countries and to Brazil in the 1970s. These countries decreased their exports of raw nuts to India in order to maintain supplies for their own processing.

Three factors have kept India's hand-processing industry afloat. First, the machinery breaks many cashew nuts, so Indian processors still face little competition in the sale of higher-grade nuts. At any time, however, newer machinery might solve the breakage problem, again threatening the approximately 200 Indian processors and their 300,000 employees. Furthermore, there is increased competition for the lower-grade output. Second, Indian processors have been able to obtain increased supplies of raw nuts, partially as a result of Indian production increases. Pesticide technology now makes cashew tree plantations feasible, thus increasing the number of trees per acre. Furthermore, Indian experimentation in hybridization, vegetative propagation, and grafting and budding techniques promises to increase the output per tree to five times what it was in the wild. In addition, India has been increasing its imports of raw nuts substantially, primarily from Tanzania and Vietnam. Third, India uses fewer fertilizers than Brazil, the biggest export competitor, and the lack of fertilizer apparently gives Indian nuts a better flavor. Because its exports consist of a higher portion of higher-grade nuts and because of flavor differences, Indian exports sell for a premium in comparison with those of competitors, for example, about 15 percent more than nuts from Brazil and about 25 percent more than those from Mozambique. However, yields are usually higher in Brazil, and Brazilian processors pay only between 30 and 36 percent of the price the Indian processors pay for raw nuts. Further, because of differences in domestic demand, India typically exports about 50 percent of the raw kernels that it processes, whereas Brazil exports about 85 percent. In the 1993–1995 period, Brazil suffered crop problems, which enabled India to gain a temporary increase in global export share of processed cashew kernels.

The Indian processors were adversely affected by the thawing of the Cold War. Because India could no longer compete as well in its traditional North American and European markets for lower-grade nuts, a larger proportion of those nuts was sold during the 1980s to the Soviet Union, which became India's largest cashew nut customer in terms of tonnage. The Soviets bought the nuts at a price above world market levels, and their buying habits were believed to have a political motive. These sales decreased substantially when the Soviet Union broke up.

There is potential for an excess supply of cashew nuts, which might result from plantation techniques and improved technology in India and elsewhere. To find outlets for a possible nut glut, the All-India Coordinated Spices and Cashew Nut Improvement Project has centered on finding new markets for products from the cashew tree. The cashew apple, for example, is available in far greater tonnage than is the cashew nut. It has been discarded in the past because processors could get either fruit or nut but not both, and the nuts have been considered more valuable. Experimentation is going on to harvest both the fruit and the nut. The fruit also is being studied for commercial use in candy, jams, chutney, juice, carbonated beverages, syrup, wine, and vinegar. A second area of research is in the use of cashew nutshell liquid (oil), which was once discarded as a waste product. It is now used extensively in industrial production of friction dusts for formulation in brake linings and clutch facings. So far, however, the extraction of cashew nutshell liquid has been too costly to make the product fully competitive with some other types of oils.

Questions

1. What trade theories help to explain where cashew tree products have been produced historically?
2. What factors threaten India's future competitive position in cashew nut production?
3. If you were an Indian cashew processor, what alternatives might you consider to maintain future competitiveness?

Chapter Notes

1. Mike Levin, "Sri Lanka: Getting the Numbers Right," *Asian Business,* April 1992, pp. 40–44; "No Sri Lankan Tea for Iraq," *Wall Street Journal,* August 31, 1990, p. A8; Ramesh Venkataraman, "Sri Lanka: Bad Old Politics and Great New Economics," *Wall Street Journal,* April 4, 1991, p. A14; "Sri Lanka Investment: Inside or Outside the Free Trade Zone?" *Business Asia,* April 24, 1981, pp. 134–135; P. Murugasu, "Selecting Products for Export Development," *International Trade Forum,* October–December 1979, pp. 4–7; "United States Congress Speaks on Sri Lanka," bulletin issued by the Embassy of the Democratic Socialist Republic of Sri Lanka, Washington, April 1979; Lucien Rajakarunanayake, "Sri Lanka: Patterns of Serendipity" (Washington, D.C.: Embassy of Sri Lanka, May 1975); Colin de Silva, "Sri Lanka, the 'Resplendent Isle,' " *New York Times,* February 14, 1984, Sec. xx, p. 9; Sarath Rajapatirana, "Foreign Trade and Economic Development: Sri Lanka's Experience," *World Development,* Vol. 16, No. 10, October 1988, pp. 1143–1158; Vinita Piyaratna, "A Year of Living Optimistically," *Asian Business,* April 1993, pp. 37–38; "Foreign Investment and Trade," BBC Summary of World Broadcasts, July 3, 1996; Rohan Gunaskera, "Sri Lanka Seeks to Revive Port Fortunes," *Reuter European Business Report,* July 24, 1996; Rahul Sharma, "New Sri Lanka Government to Boost Local Industry," *Reuters World Service,* August 22, 1994; Rohan Gunaskera, "Sri Lankans Pore Over Instant Tea Exports," *Reuter Asia-Pacific Business Report,* March 24, 1996; John Zarocostas, "Sri Lanka Receives Praise for Its Trade Reforms," *Journal of Commerce,*

November 13, 1995, p. A3; and Amal Jayasinghe, "Sri Lanka to Legalise Gambling," *Financial Times,* November 7, 1996, p. 6. For up-to-date information through the Internet on Sri Lanka, the address is www.lanka.net/cgi-bin/index2.html.

2. The mercantilist period is not associated with any single writer. A good coverage of the philosophy of the era may be found in Eli Heckscher, *Mercantilism* (London: George Allen & Unwin, 1935).

3. For a discussion of the problems with running a trade surplus, see Maria Shao, William J. Holstein, and Steven J. Dryden, "Taiwan's Wealth Crisis," *Business Week,* No. 2993, April 13, 1987, pp. 46–47.

4. The book has been reprinted by various publishers. For the specific references in this chapter, the edition used was Adam Smith, *The Wealth of Nations* (New York: The Modern Library, n.d.).

5. "The Ice Trade," *The Economist,* December 21, 1991–January 3, 1992, pp. 47–48.

6. Stephen P. Magee, *International Trade* (Reading, Mass: Addison-Wesley, 1980), pp. 10–12.

7. G. C. Hufbauer, "The Impact of National Characteristics and Technology on the Commodity Composition of Trade in Manufactured Goods," in *The Technology Factor in International Trade,* Raymond Vernon, ed. (New York: Columbia University Press, 1970), pp. 145–231; Paul Krugman, "Scale Economies, Product Differentiation, and the Patterns of Trade," *American Economic Review,* December 1980, Vol. 70, pp. 950–959.

8. For a discussion of scale efficiencies, see James R. Tybout, "Internal Returns to Scale as a Source of Comparative Advantage: The Evidence," *AEA Papers and Pro-*

ceedings, May 1993, pp. 440–444; for a discussion specific to R&D, see Rachel McCulloch, "The Optimality of Free Trade: Science or Religion?" *AEA Papers and Proceedings,* May 1993, pp. 367–371.

9. David Ricardo, *On the Principles of Political Economy and Taxation,* originally published in London in 1817, has since been reprinted by a number of publishers.

10. Gaston de Rosayro, "Sri Lanka in the Doldrums," *South China Morning Post,* June 1, 1995, p. 21.

11. For a good discussion of this paradoxical thinking, see Paul R. Krugman, "What Do Undergraduates Need to Know about Trade?" *American Economic Review Papers and Proceedings,* May 1993, pp. 23–26.

12. Bertil Ohlin, *Interregional and International Trade* (Cambridge, Mass.: Harvard University Press, 1933).

13. "Hong Kong Has Priciest Rent," *Wall Street Journal,* December 4, 1996, p. A12.

14. W. W. Leontief, "Domestic Production and Foreign Trade: The American Capital Position Re-examined," *Economia Internationale,* February 1954, pp. 3–32.

15. See, for example, Anne O. Krueger, "Trade Policies in Developing Countries," in *Handbook of International Economics,* Vol. 3, Ronald W. Jones and Peter Kenen, eds. (Amsterdam: North-Holland, 1984), pp. 519–569; and Bela Balassa, *The Newly Industrialized Countries in the World Economy* (New York: Pergamon, 1981), Chapter 7.

16. Mark Casson, "Multinationals and Intermediate Product Trade," in *The Economic Analysis of the Multinational Enterprise: Selected Papers,* Peter J. Buckley and Mark Casson, eds. (London: Macmillan, 1985).

17. Raymond Vernon, "International Investment and International Trade in the Product Life Cycle," *Quarterly Journal of Economics*, May 1966, pp. 190–207; Paul Krugman, "A Model of Innovation, Technology Transfer, and the World Distribution of Income," *Journal of Political Economy*, Vol. 87, April 1979, pp. 253–266; and David Dollar, "Technological Innovation, Capital Mobility, and the Product Cycle in North-South Trade," *American Economic Review*, Vol. 76, No. 1, pp. 177–190.

18. Michael E. Porter, *The Competitive Advantage of Nations* (New York: Free Press, 1990).

19. Robert B. Reich, "The Real Economy," *The Atlantic Monthly*, Vol. 267, No. 2, February 1991, pp. 35–52.

20. David Coe, Elhanan Helpman, and Alexander Hoffmaister, "North South R and D Spillovers" (Cambridge, MA: National Bureau of Economic Research, working paper, No. 5048, 1995).

21. John M. Culbertson, "The Folly of Free Trade," *Harvard Business Review*, No. 5, September–October 1986, pp. 122–128.

22. Caroline Southey, "EU and US Head for Fur Trade Showdown," *Financial Times*, December 10, 1996, p. 6.

23. John Ward Anderson and Molly Moore, " 'Ethnic Cleansing' Charges Echo in Himalayan Bhutan," *Washington Post*, April 8, 1994, p. A1+.

24. For good summaries of the studies testing the theory as well as recent tests, see James M. Lutz and Robert T. Green, "The Product Life Cycle and the Export Position of the United States," *Journal of International Business Studies*, Winter 1983, pp. 77–93; and Alicia Mullor-Sebastian, "The Product Life Cycle Theory: Empirical Evidence," *Journal of International Business Studies*, Winter 1983, pp. 95–105.

25. Ian H. Giddy, "The Demise of the Product Life Cycle in International Business Theory," *Columbia Journal of World Business*, Spring 1978, pp. 90–97.

26. This has been argued as a factor enabling industrial countries to charge high prices to LDCs while purchasing LDC manufactured products at the lowest possible prices. See Frances Stewart, "Recent Theories of International Trade: Some Implications for the South," in *Monopolistic Competition and International Trade*, Henry Kierzkowski, ed. (Oxford, England: Oxford University Press, 1984).

27. David Dollar and Edward N. Wolff, *Competitiveness, Convergence, and International Specialization* (Cambridge, Mass.: MIT Press, 1993).

28. For a good overview of studies on this subject as well as an empirical analysis, see Rajendra K. Srivastava and Robert T. Green, "Determinants of Bilateral Trade Flows," *Journal of Business*, Vol. 59, No. 4, October 1986, pp. 623–639.

29. *Survey of Current Business*, July 1996, pp. 76–78.

30. World Trade Organization, *Focus*, Newsletter No. 10, May 1996, pp. 6–8.

31. Stefan B. Linder, *An Essay on Trade Transformation* (New York: Wiley, 1961).

32. World Trade Organization, *Annual Report 1996*, Vol. 1 (Geneva: World Trade Organization, 1996), p. 14.

33. Daniele Archibugi and Mario Planta, *The Technological Specialization of Advanced Countries* (Dordrecht, the Netherlands: Kluwer Academic Publishers, 1992), pp. 46–57.

34. Dollar and Wolff, loc. cit.

35. "The Global Economy," *The Economist*, October 1, 1994, pp. 3–46.

36. "That's Snow-biz," *The Economist*, April 13, 1996, p. 58.

37. Thomas E. Ricks and Andy Pasztor, "Saudi Arabia May Agree to Restructure $10 Billion It Owes U.S. Defense Firms," *Wall Street Journal*, January 10, 1994, p. A4.

38. Keith Bradsher, "American Exports to Poor Countries Are Rapidly Rising," *New York Times*, May 10, 1992, p. A1+; Kevin Kelly and Michael J. Mandel, "Exports Go Pfft," *Business Week*, August 3, 1992, pp. 20–21; Lucinda Harper, "Slowdown in Mexico Is Felt in the U.S.," *Wall Street Journal*, September 29, 1992, p. A2; and Al Ehrbar, "Trading Up," *Wall Street Journal*, January 18, 1993, p. A1+.

39. "New Tribe Found in New Guinea," *Herald Times* (Bloomington, Ind.), June 28, 1993, p. 1.

40. David Dollar, "What Do We Know about the Long-Term Sources of Comparative Advantage?" *AEA Papers and Proceedings*, May 1993, pp. 431–435.

41. Refik Erzan and Alexander J. Yeats, "Implications of Current Factor Proportions Indices for the Competitive Position of the U.S. Manufacturing and Service Industries in the Year 2000," *Journal of Business*, Vol. 64, No. 2, 1991, pp. 229–253.

42. For a very good survey of the literature (pro and con) on this point, see Jose Antonio Ocampo, "New Developments in Trade Theory and LDCs," *Journal of Developing Economies*, Vol. 22, No. 1, 1986, pp. 129–170.

43. "Farm Trade: Gone Bananas," *The Economist*, March 28, 1992, pp. 76–77.

44. Peter Passell, "High-tech Industry Is Hard to Help," *New York Times*, February 2, 1995, p. B5+.

45. Michael E. Porter, "The Competitive Advantage of Nations," *Harvard Business Review*, Vol. 90, No. 2, March–April 1990, p. 78.

46. Paul Krugman and Alasdair M. Smith, eds., *Empirical Studies of Strategic Trade Policies* (Chicago: University of Chicago Press, 1993).

47. Paul M. Sherer, "Thailand Trips in Reach for New Exports," *Wall Street Journal*, August 27, 1996, p. A8.

48. Richard Brahm, "National Targeting Policies, High-Technology Industries, and Excessive Competition," *Strategic Management Journal*, Vol. 16, 1995, pp. 71–91.

49. James Kynge and Elisabeth Robinson, "Singapore to Revise Trade Priorities," *Financial Times*, January 21, 1997, p. 6.

50. Alice H. Amsden, "Asia's Next Giant," *Technology Review*, May–June 1989, pp. 47–53.

51. Kiyohiko Ito and Vladimir Pucik, "R&D Spending, Domestic Competition, and Export Performance of Japanese Manufacturing Firms," *Strategic Management Journal*, Vol. 14, 1993, pp. 61–75.

52. See, for example, Lawrence G. Franko, "Global Corporate Competition in the 1990s: The Japanese Juggernaut Rolls On," University of Massachusetts/Boston College of Management, working paper, June 1995.

53. See, for example, Boston Consulting Group, *Perspective in Experience* (Boston: Boston Consulting Group, 1970); and Robert D. Buzzell, Bradley T. Buzzell, Gale Sultaw, and Ralph G. M. Sultaw, "Market Share: A Key to Profitability," *Harvard Business Review*, Vol. 58, No. 1, 1975.

54. Ito and Pucik, loc. cit.

55. For discussion of the first-mover advantage, see E. Helpman and P. Krugman, *Market Structure and Foreign Trade: Increasing Returns, Imperfect Competition, and the International Economy* (Cambridge, Mass.: MIT Press, 1985). For problems of small companies, see Jacques Liouville, "Under What Conditions Can Exports Exert a Positive Influence on Profitability?" *Management International Review*, Vol. 32, No. 1, 1992, pp. 41–54.

56. Will Mitchell, J. Myles Shaver, and Bernard Yeung, "Getting There in a Global Industry: Impacts on Performance of Changing International Presence," *Strategic Management Journal*, Vol. 13, 1992, pp. 419–432.

57. Richard C. Marais and Michael Schuman, "Hong Kong Is Just Around the Corner," *Forbes*, October 12, 1992, pp. 50–58.

58. Ulli Arnold, "Global Sourcing—An Indispensable Element in Worldwide Competition," *Management International Review*, Vol. 29, No. 4, 1989, p. 22.

59. Charlie E. Mahone, Jr., "Penetrating Export Markets: The Role of Firm Size," *Journal of Global Marketing*, Vol. 7, No. 3, 1994, pp. 133–148.

60. Aviv Shoham, Gregory M. Rose, and Gerald S. Albaum, "Export Motives, Psychological Distance, and the EPRG Framework," *Journal of Global Marketing*, Vol. 3, No. 3/4, 1995, pp. 9–37.

61. Francis Ng and Alexander Yeats, *Did Africa's Protectionist Policies Cause its*

Marginalization in World Trade? (Washington: World Bank research working paper No. 1636, 1996).

62. "The Global Economy," op. cit.

63. H. Peter Gray, "Free Trade, Economic Integration and Nationhood," *Journal of International Economic Integration,* Vol. 5, No. 1, 1990, pp. 1–12.

64. "The Global Economy," op. cit.

65. G. C. Lodge and E. F. Vogel, *Ideology and National Competitiveness* (Boston: Harvard Business School Press, 1987).

66. Data for this case were taken from "L'anacarde ou noix de cajou," *Marches Tropicaux,* June 13, 1980, pp. 1403–1405; R. J. Wilson, *The Market for Cashew Nut Kernels and Cashew Nutshell Liquid* (London: Tropical Products Institute, 1975); J. H. P. Tyman, "Cultivation, Processing and Utilization of the Cashew," *Chemistry and Industry,* January 19, 1980, pp. 59–62; Jean-Pierre Jeannet, "Indian Cashew Processors, Ltd.," ICH Case 9-378-832 (Boston: Harvard Business School, 1977); Jean-Pierre Jeannet, "Note on the World Cashew Nut Industry," ICH Case 9-378-834 (Boston: Harvard Business School, 1977); "Meanwhile, Back in Mozambique," *Forbes,* Vol. 11, No. 16, November 16, 1987, p. 110; U.S. Department of Commerce, Bureau of the Census, U.S. Imports of Merchandise International Harmonized System Commodity Classification, 1992, on CD-ROM; Steven Jaffee, *Private Sector Response to Market Liberalization: The Experience of Tanzania's Cashew Nut Industry* (Washington: World Bank, 1994); and "Cashewnuts," *Handbook of Indian Agriculture* (New Delhi: Vikas Publishing House, 1995).

Chapter 6

Governmental Influence on Trade

A little help does a great deal.
—French Proverb

Objectives

- To evaluate the rationale for governmental policies to enhance and/or restrict trade

- To examine the effects of pressure groups on trade policies

- To compare the protectionist arguments used in developed countries with those used in developing ones

- To study the potential and actual effects of governmental intervention on the free flow of trade

- To give an overview of the major means by which trade is restricted, regulated, and liberalized

- To show that governmental trade policies create business uncertainties

Case
United States–
Japanese Auto
Trade[1]

For about a quarter of a century, automobile trade has been a source of contention between the United States and Japan. Although the arguments and approaches to the problem have changed several times during this period, an underlying factor has been the large export surplus from Japan to the United States, about three quarters of which comprises trade in automobiles and parts.

Different groups have disagreed on whether U.S. governmental actions should seek to address the imbalance at all and, if so, whether emphasis should be on (a) making U.S. production more competitive with imports, (b) restricting Japanese imports by taxing or setting quantitative restrictions on them, or (c) increasing the Japanese market for automobile exports from the United States. From 1973 until the early 1990s, U.S. governmental efforts centered on restricting Japanese automotive imports. Since then, efforts have shifted toward opening the Japanese market to U.S.-produced vehicles.

The first spurt of Japanese imports was of small cars as a result of the 1973 oil shortage; however, soon after the shortage ended, U.S. consumers largely returned to Detroit's major product—large cars with rear-wheel drive. Then, in 1979 and 1980, a second oil shortage hit. The foreign share of the U.S. new-car market subsequently increased from 17 percent to 25.3 percent, most of which was held by Japan. Managers of the U.S. automakers and officials of the United Auto Workers (UAW) spoke out favoring import restrictions. As a result of this pressure, the United States and Japan negotiated a voluntary export restriction (VER). A VER is not completely voluntary, however; one country "voluntarily" limits exports of a product to another because it reasons that otherwise the other government might set even more stringent import restrictions. The first ceiling under the resultant VER was for 1.68 million cars, a figure that climbed as high as 2.3 million for 1990.

At the time of the first VER, the U.S. automakers were not holding their own in sales of the small cars that they had been producing for several years. Japanese automakers were evidently as surprised as Detroit was by the sudden shift in demand. They lacked capacity to fill U.S. orders quickly, yet many buyers were willing to wait six months for delivery of a Honda rather than purchase a U.S.-manufactured model. The reasons for this preference among U.S. consumers for Japanese automobiles were debatable. Some observers cited price differences created by labor-cost differences. Those who accepted this view largely favored the taxing of imports in order to raise their prices. Yet, on the basis of a survey of 10,000 U.S. households, imports strongly outranked domestic small cars in perceived fuel economy, engineering, and durability. People who accepted these results were opposed to limiting imports.

The initial arguments for protecting or aiding the U.S. automobile industry were voiced until the early 1990s and were based on two premises:

1. The costs of unemployment are higher than the increased costs to consumers of limiting imports.
2. U.S. production could become fully competitive with imports if actions were taken to help it overcome its temporary problems.

The first premise takes into account such factors as personal hardship for people displaced in the labor market; diminished purchasing power, which adversely affects demand in other industries; and the high taxes that would be needed to support unemployed people. A *New York Times* poll showed that 71 percent of Americans felt it was more important to protect jobs than to have access to cheaper foreign products. The second premise reflects such factors as the historical competitive capability of U.S. automakers, the possibility of scale economies for U.S. production, and the much higher productivity possible with new plants.

Some protectionists have argued that the restraints worked. GM, Ford, and Chrysler (the Big Three) were able to invest heavily in more automated plants and to trim inventory costs. A private research group reported that Ford had become more cost-efficient than Toyota or Honda at making small four-cylinder cars. In 1992, the Ford Taurus passed the Honda Accord as the top-selling automobile in the United States.

Other protectionists have argued that the allocations under the VER have been too high, thus contributing to a fall in North American employment at GM, Ford, and Chrysler. An opposing view has been that the high allocations have forced the Big Three to become more productive and innovative, thus contributing to better performance. For example, Chrysler's 1994 profits exceeded those of Japan's Big Five (Toyota, Nissan, Mitsubishi, Honda, and Mazda) combined.

Antiprotectionists have blamed the problems of U.S. automakers on poor management decisions and maintained that consumers and taxpayers should not be expected to reward the companies by paying to see them through what has been a crisis of their own making. Antiprotectionists assert that any assistance, even short-term, results in at least one of the following consequences: higher taxes because of subsidies to companies, higher prices for foreign cars (which are preferred by many consumers), or the need to buy domestic cars (which many perceive as inferior). Some antiprotectionists also have held that governmental assistance in limiting imports might result in foreign retaliation against U.S. industries that are more competitive with foreign production—Japan, for example, might curtail purchases of U.S.-made aircraft or wood products.

Antiprotectionists have argued further that U.S. consumers have had little choice except to buy more expensive cars. Because Japanese producers were not able to increase their U.S. profits by selling more cars, they did so instead by selling more luxurious models and raising prices. During the three years of the original export restraints, the price of the average Japanese import increased by $2,600; a Wharton Econometrics study attributed $1,000 of this increase to import restraints. Meanwhile, the prices of U.S.-made cars also increased. In 1975 the average vehicle bought by U.S. purchasers cost 18 weeks' earnings. This rose to 23 weeks' earnings by 1985, and 27 weeks' earnings in 1995.

Since the first restrictions were placed on Japanese automobile imports, the question of which companies and which production to protect has become more complicated. Clearly, the UAW has been primarily interested in maintaining jobs. UAW representatives were instrumental in helping to convince Japanese companies to set up U.S. operations, primarily to assemble vehicles. (Some of these operations are listed in Table 6.1.) The UAW has also been successful in pushing Japanese companies to buy more U.S.-made parts (targets have been stipulated in VER agreements) and in gaining requirements that window stickers on new cars sold in the United States show information on the location of assembly and origin of component parts. This push for "local content" runs counter to some of the policies

**Table 6.1
Japanese Automakers'
Investments in the
United States**

Year	Company
1982	Honda
1983	Nissan
1984	Toyota*
1987	Toyo Kogyo (Mazda)
1988	Mitsubishi†
1988	Toyota
1989	Subaru-Isuzu‡
1989	Honda
1992	Nissan
1993	Toyota
1996	Toyota

*Joint venture with GM for New United Motors Manufacturing
†Joint venture with Chrysler
‡Joint venture between the two companies

being pursued by some U.S. automakers. These companies are trying to produce "global" cars in order to obtain maximum economies of scale and are buying parts from countries where they can be produced more cheaply (such as die-cast aluminum parts from Italy). For example, the Ford Mondeo contained parts from many countries. Further, many automobiles sold under Big Three brand names have been made abroad by other companies. These include the Ford Festiva, made by Kia Motors in South Korea; GM's Pontiac LeMans, made by Daewoo Motors in South Korea; and Chrysler's Dodge and Plymouth Colt and Vista, made by Mitsubishi Motors in Japan (see Fig. 6.1). Toyota also sells the Toyota Cavalier in Japan, which is made by GM in the United States, and GM makes the Mitsubishi Lancer in India for sale in that market. The competitive situation is complicated by the fact that GM owns 36.7 percent of Isuzu Motors and Ford owns 33.4 percent of Mazda. In addition, Japanese-owned operations in the United States, such as Honda and Mazda, are now exporting parts and finished vehicles to Japan.

In 1995 the United States announced it would place a 100 percent tax in 30 days on the imported value of 13 models of Japanese luxury cars unless a negotiated agreement was reached to substantially cut Japan's auto trade surplus with the United States. Such a tax would effectively exclude such lines as the Lexus and Acura from the U.S. market. This was the toughest stance the United States had ever taken with Japan over automobile trade. The willingness to take such a hard line was undoubtedly influenced by the termination of the Cold War; that is to say, the United States was no longer as concerned about the cordiality of its political relations with Japan.

Whereas prior negotiations had centered on reducing Japanese automobile exports to the United States, these aimed at increasing U.S. automobile exports to Japan. (In 1995, imports, excluding those made by Japanese companies abroad, comprised only about 7 percent of the Japanese automobile market, but this market share was more than double the 3

Figure 6.1

Source: By permission of Chip Bok and Creators Syndicate.

percent in 1987.) The main reason for this change in U.S. position was that by 1995 auto production costs were much lower in the United States than in Japan, but U.S. producers enjoyed little success in selling to Japanese consumers. The Big Three argued that their difficulty stemmed primarily from government-mandated exclusive distributorship arrangements that inhibited their Japanese sales. Critics of the Big Three argued that they had not made sufficient effort to penetrate the Japanese market. For example, the Japanese drive on the left side of the road, but the Big Three were still trying to export many models with left-side steering wheels equipped for the right-side driving lanes of the United States. Further, BMW had achieved some success by creating its own sales organization, rather than trying to sell through distributors of Japanese vehicles.

Japanese authorities reacted to the U.S. announcement with statements that they would not give in. Meanwhile, representatives from the European Union, Canada, and Australia expressed concern that Japanese auto companies might divert component purchases to the United States at their expense. Newspapers reported that Japanese officials were planning counter-sanctions against U.S. goods with a high market share in Japan, such as buses, trucks, semiconductors, and computer parts. Japan also threatened to file complaints with the World Trade Organization (WTO) that the United States's proposed action was in violation of existing agreements, and most experts agreed that Japan would win its case. However, in the final minutes before expiration of the 30-day notice, the United States and Japan came to a new agreement, which included permission for 1,000 new dealerships to begin selling U.S. cars, a 25 percent increase in output of Japanese plants in the United States, and an increase of 50 percent in Japanese purchases of U.S.-made car parts.

The response by the Big Three has been mixed. Ford had already announced it would spend $180 million to convert four models to right-hand drive, and had opened 53 new sales outlets in the 18 months prior to the agreement; so the negotiations strengthened its ability to carry out efforts in the Japanese market. Chrysler announced after the negotiations that it was buying control of a distribution company for $100 million, and planned to have 500 distributors by the end of the century. However, GM, which mainly concentrated on selling Opels from its German facility, decided not to set up independent distributors. During the first full year after the agreement (1996), U.S. auto sales in Japan grew more slowly than had been forecast. This was partially due to a strengthened dollar that raised prices of U.S. products in Japan. But there were other problems as well. For example, the Ford Taurus was too long to fit in Japanese parking places, and Japanese consumers who like boxy designs did not take well to the curves on Chrysler's Neon. However, GM's sales in Japan grew by 45 percent. This increase was mainly because the Japanese think highly of European-made vehicles, thus GM's Opel from Germany not only fit the market but also became the largest selling import in Japan.

Introduction

Why study about governmental influence on trade? At some point, you may work for or own stock in a company whose performance, or even survival, may depend on governmental protectionist measures. You also are affected as consumers and taxpayers in the amounts you pay for goods and taxes.

The automobile trade case is not atypical. No country in the world permits an unregulated flow of goods and services across its borders. Restrictions commonly are placed on imports and occasionally on exports. Direct or indirect subsidies frequently are given to industries to enable them to compete with foreign production either at home or abroad. In general, governmental influence is exerted in an attempt to satisfy economic, social, or political objectives. Often these objectives conflict (for example, increased employment versus lower automobile prices). There also is much disagreement regarding the likely employment effects of trade policies—for example, employment increases for autoworkers versus possible decreases for workers in other industries if foreign countries retaliate against U.S. trade policies by restricting their imports of some U.S.-made products.

Not surprisingly, any proposal for reform of trade regulations results in heated debate among interest groups that believe they will be affected. Of course, those that are most directly affected (stakeholders) are most apt to speak up. Stakeholders whose livelihood depends on U.S. automobile production (workers, owners, suppliers, and local politicians) perceive the losses from import competition to be considerable. Workers see themselves as being forced to take new jobs in new industries, perhaps in new locales. They may experience prolonged periods of unemployment, reduced incomes, insecure work conditions, and unstable social surroundings. People threatened in this way are liable to constitute a very strong pressure group. In contrast, workers in an industry that is affected only indirectly, through retaliation, such as the aircraft industry, do not readily perceive the same threat and so are less vocal. Neither do consumers usually understand how much prices rise because of import restrictions. For example, in the United States in 1992, import restrictions resulted in the average consumer paying $360 extra for food and the average family between $200 and $420 extra for clothing. And most countries restrict trade even more than the United States does.[2] However, consumers have not been active in uniting to protest import limitations vigorously.

The Rationale for Governmental Intervention

The reasons for governmental intervention in trade may be basically classified as either economic or noneconomic. The reasons discussed in this chapter are classified this way in Table 6.2.

Unemployment

Pressure groups pose a real challenge to governmental policymakers and businesspeople. There is probably no more effective pressure group than the unemployed because no other group has the time and incentive to picket or to write letters in volume to governmental representatives.

Margin notes:

All countries seek to influence trade, and each has
• Economic, social, and political objectives
• Conflicting objectives
• Interest groups

The unemployed can form an effective pressure group for import restrictions.

Table 6.2
Rationale for Governmental Intervention in Trade

Economic rationale	Noneconomic rationale
Prevent unemployment	Maintain essential industries
Protect infant industry	Deal with unfriendly countries
Promote industrialization	Maintain sphere of influence
Improve position relative to other countries	Preserve national identity

Import restrictions to create domestic employment
• **May lead to retaliation by other countries**
• **Are less likely to be met with retaliation if implemented by small economies**
• **May decrease export jobs because of price increases for components**
• **May decrease export jobs because of lower incomes abroad**

One problem with restricting imports in order to create jobs is that other countries might retaliate. The most frequently cited example occurred in 1930 when the United States raised import restrictions to their highest levels ever. In a matter of months, other countries countered with their own restrictions, and the United States lost rather than gained jobs as its exports diminished.[3] In recent years, new import restrictions by a major country have almost always brought quick retaliation. For example, recent retaliation to U.S. import restrictions has caused more U.S. job losses than the gains in industries protected by the new restrictions.[4]

Two factors may mitigate the effects of retaliation. First, there may be less tendency to retaliate against a small country (in terms of economic power) that restricts imports. For example, Peruvian automobile import restrictions have caused no Japanese retaliation because the loss of sales by Japanese producers is too low. Second, if redistribution because of retaliation decreases employment in a capital-intensive industry but increases it in a labor-intensive industry, employment objectives may be achieved. For example, the United States limits imports of apparel, usually a labor-intensive good. Any resultant foreign retaliation against, say, U.S.-produced semiconductors, a capital-intensive good, would probably threaten fewer U.S. jobs than would be gained from maintaining apparel production. Even if there is no retaliation, the net number of jobs gained for the economy as a whole is bound to be smaller than the number of jobs in the newly protected industry. That is because import-handling jobs would be lost. For example, when the United States threatened a 100 percent tax on luxury Japanese cars, Honda estimated that 100,000 Americans worked for Acura import operations and dealerships in the United States.[5]

Imports also may help create jobs in other industries, and these industries may form pressure groups against protectionism. Consider the apparel industry in the United States. Such companies as Warnaco and Liz Claiborne joined retailers to protest textile import restrictions because they needed the variety and quality of foreign-made cloth to compete against global companies. Or consider Caterpillar Tractor, one of the largest U.S. exporters. It buys crankshafts from Germany and Japan to cut costs enough to be competitive in foreign markets.[6] Imports also stimulate exports, although less directly, by increasing foreign income and foreign-exchange earnings, which are then spent on new imports by foreign consumers.

Possible costs of import restrictions include
• Higher prices
• Higher taxes
Such costs should be compared with those of unemployment.

If import restrictions do result in a net increase in domestic employment, there still will be costs to some people in the domestic society in the form of higher prices or higher taxes. For example, the first three years of Japan's VER are estimated to have cost the United States $160,000 per job saved.[7] If protection seems permanent, the domestic industry may lag behind in technological and product development as well.

Higher prices or higher taxes must be compared with the costs of unemployment resulting from freer trade. In addition, these costs must be compared with costs of policies to ease the plight of displaced workers, such as for unemployment benefits or retraining. These tasks are challenging. First, it is hard to put a price on the distress suffered by people who must be out of work, change jobs, or move. Second, it is difficult for working people to understand that they may be better off financially if part of their taxes go to help support people whose positions were lost because of imports. Finally, it may be equally difficult to convince people to accept handouts in lieu of their old jobs.

A complicating factor is that potentially displaced workers are frequently the ones who would be least able to find alternative work. In the garment industry, for example, sewing and cutting jobs are being transferred in great numbers from industrial to developing countries. Canada is an industrial country that has been losing these jobs. Forty-one percent of its sewing and cutting workers speak English as a second language, and the record of retraining these immigrants has not been very successful because their educational level is too low compared to the needs of expanding industries.[8]

Many countries assist workers who are affected adversely by imports by supplementing their unemployment benefits. Workers often spend the funds on living expenses in the hope they will be recalled to their old jobs. Some observers argue that too little is done to retrain and relocate displaced workers. However, the reality is that these workers, especially many older ones, lack much of the educational background necessary for them to be trained in any reasonable period of time. Further, predictions of future employment needs have been far from accurate; consequently, jobs may not materialize in the industries for which training is provided.

Infant-Industry Argument

The infant-industry argument says that production becomes more competitive over time because of
• Increased economies of scale
• Greater worker efficiency

One of the oldest arguments for protectionism was presented as early as 1792 by Alexander Hamilton. The **infant-industry argument** holds that an emerging industry should be guaranteed a large share of the domestic market until it becomes efficient enough to compete against imports. The argument is still used by developing countries to support their protectionist policies. The infant-industry argument is based on the logic that although the initial output costs for an industry in a given country may be so high as to make it noncompetitive in world markets, over time the costs will decrease to a level sufficient to achieve efficient production. The cost reductions may occur for two reasons: As companies gain economies of scale, total unit costs are reduced to the levels of the competition, and as employees gain experience, they become more efficient.

Although it is reasonable to expect costs to decrease over time, they may not go down enough. Therefore two problems exist in using trade protection as a means of obtaining international competitiveness for a domestic industry. First, identifying those industries that have a high probability of reaching adulthood is difficult. Examples of industries that grew to be competitive because of governmental protection are certainly available—automobile production in Brazil and South Korea are good examples. However, in many other cases—such as automobile production in Malaysia and Australia—the industries remain in an infantile state even after many years of operation. If infant-industry protection is given to an industry that does not reduce costs sufficiently, chances are its owners, workers, and suppliers will constitute a formidable pressure group that may effectively prevent the importation of a cheaper competitive product. In fact, the protection against import competition may be a disincentive to become more efficient.

Second, even if policymakers can ascertain which industries are likely to reach productive adulthood, it does not necessarily follow that those industries should receive governmental assistance. There are, of course, many examples of entrepreneurs who endured early losses to gain future benefits, and policymakers may argue that assistance should be given only if the entry barriers to new companies are very high. Some segment of the economy must absorb the higher cost of local production during infancy. Most likely, it will be the consumer who will pay higher prices. However, a government may subsidize an industry so that consumer prices are not increased; in this case, it is the taxpayer who will absorb the burden. For the infant-industry argument to be fully viable, future benefits should exceed early costs.

Industrialization Argument

Countries seek protection to promote industrialization because that type of production
- **Brings faster growth than agriculture**
- **Brings in investment funds**
- **Diversifies the economy**
- **Brings more price increases than primary products do**

In recent years, many countries have sought protection to increase their level of industrialization, for several reasons:

1. Emphasizing industrialization will increase output more than would emphasizing agriculture.
2. Inflows of foreign investment in the industrial area will promote growth.
3. Diversification away from traditional agricultural products or raw materials is necessary to stabilize trade fluctuation.
4. The prices of manufactured goods tend to rise more rapidly than the prices of primary products do.

Countries with a large manufacturing base generally have higher per capita incomes than do countries without such a base. Since the Industrial Revolution in England in the late eighteenth century, a number of countries, such as the United States and Japan, have developed an industrial base while largely preventing competition from foreign-based production. Like the infant-industry argument, the argument favoring industrialization holds that importing cheaper products from abroad will prevent the establishment of domestic industry if free-market conditions are allowed to prevail. The industrialization argument differs from the infant-industry argument in that proponents say objectives will be achieved even if domestic prices do not become globally competitive.

Marginal agricultural returns   In many LDCs, a high portion of the population lives in rural areas, and the agricultural output per person is low. This is particularly true in economies such as those of India or Egypt, where little additional unused arable land is available. Consequently, many people may be able to leave the agricultural sector without greatly affecting such a country's agricultural output. If these surplus workers can be employed in the manufacturing sector, their output is likely to contribute a net gain to the economy because so little agricultural production is sacrificed in the process. If the cost of the domestically manufactured product is higher than that of an imported one, sales of the imported product must be restricted to ensure survival of the domestic industry. Doing this will result in either higher prices or higher taxes; nevertheless, real output should rise in the economy.

Shifting people out of agriculture is not without risk. Several problems can result:

> **When a country shifts from agriculture to industry**
> - **Output increases if the marginal productivity of agricultural workers is very low**
> - **Demands on social and political services in cities may increase**
> - **Development possibilities in the agricultural sector may be overlooked**

1. Individuals' expectations may be raised and left unfulfilled, leading to excessive demands on social and political services. Indeed, a major problem facing LDCs today is the massive migration to urban areas of people who cannot be easily absorbed. There is no work for them either because the industrialization process has proceeded too slowly or because they lack the rudimentary skills and work habits necessary for employment in manufacturing.
2. Agriculture may in fact be a better means of effecting additional output than industry is. Not all LDCs are utilizing their land fully or efficiently, nor is industrial development the only means of economic growth. The United States, Canada, and Argentina grew rapidly during the nineteenth century, in large part through agricultural exports, and they continue to profit from such exports. Australia, New Zealand, and Denmark maintain high incomes along with substantial agricultural specialization.
3. If protection is to be given to manufacturing companies, policymakers must decide on which type of industry to protect so that consumer price and tax increases are minimized.
4. Too much of a shift from rural to urban areas may reduce agricultural output in LDCs, further endangering their self-sufficiency. Interestingly, most of the world's agricultural production and exports come from the so-called industrial countries because they have highly efficient and capital-intensive agricultural sectors, which have permitted resources to move efficiently to the manufacturing sector without decreasing agricultural output.

Promoting investment inflows   Import restrictions also may increase direct investment. When the purchase of foreign-made products is restricted, foreign companies may shift production to avoid the loss of a lucrative or established market. The influx of foreign companies may hasten a country's move from agriculture to industry as well as contribute to growth by adding to the stock of capital and technology per worker employed. For example, in the opening case U.S. automobile import restrictions influenced Japanese automakers to invest in the United States. Investment inflows also may add to employment, which is an especially attractive benefit from the standpoint of most policymakers.

Diversification   Export prices of most primary products fluctuate widely. Price variations due to such uncontrollable factors as weather affecting supply or business cycles abroad affecting demand can wreak havoc on economies that depend on the export of primary products. (Thus, the diversification argument is used for countries dependent on extraction of minerals as well.) This is particularly true when an economy depends very heavily on a few commodities for employment of its population and for its export earnings. For example, the Côte d'Ivoire's exports fell by one quarter over two years when cocoa and coffee prices plummeted.[9] Because a large number of LDCs heavily depend on just one primary commodity, they frequently can afford foreign luxuries one year but are unable to afford replacement parts for essential equipment the next.

However, a greater dependence on manufacturing does not guarantee diversification or stable export earnings. Most GNPs of LDCs are small; consequently, a change may simply shift dependence from one or two agricultural products to one or two manufactured ones.

Terms of trade   The **terms of trade** constitute the quantity of imports that a given quantity of a country's exports can buy. The prices of raw materials and agricultural commodities have not risen as fast as the prices of finished products have. As a result, over time it takes more primary products to buy the same amount of manufactured goods. Further, the demand for primary products does not rise as rapidly, so most LDCs have become increasingly poorer in relation to developed countries. This condition supposedly warrants the protection of emerging manufacturing companies that use traditional raw materials and agricultural commodities by adding value to them to produce nontraditional products.[10] The declining terms of trade for LDCs have been explained in part by lagging demand for agricultural products and by changes in technology that have saved on utilization of raw materials. A further explanation sometimes offered is that because of competitive conditions, savings due to technical changes that lower production costs of primary products are largely passed on to consumers, whereas cost savings for manufactured products go to higher profits and wages.[11]

If import restrictions keep out foreign-made goods, foreign companies may invest to produce in the restricted area.

Terms of trade for LDCs may deteriorate because
- *Demand for primary products grows more slowly*
- *Production cost savings for primary products will be passed on to consumers*

Industrialization emphasizes either
• **Products to sell domestically or**
• **Products to export**

Import substitution versus export promotion   By restricting imports, a country may produce for local consumption goods it formerly imported. This is known as import substitution. In recent years, most countries have concluded that import substitution is not the best way to develop new industries through protection. If the protected industries do not become efficient, consumers may have to pay higher prices or higher taxes for an indefinite period of time to support them. In addition, because capital equipment and other supplies usually must be imported, foreign-exchange savings are minimal. These countries have witnessed the rapid growth of other countries, such as Taiwan and South Korea, which have achieved a favorable balance of payments and rapid economic growth by promoting export industries, an approach known as **export-led development.** Thus some countries are now trying to develop industries for which export markets should logically exist, such as the processing of raw materials that they currently are exporting. This change affects MNEs' operations in these countries because such companies may have to develop export markets for their foreign production rather than being able to sell it in each country of production.

In reality, it is not easy to distinguish between the two types of industrialization, nor is it always possible to develop exports. Industrialization may result initially in import substitution, yet export development of the same products may be feasible later. For example, China and India are now restricting the importation of vehicles and components so that local production captures the sales in their rapidly growing markets; however, these countries might become exporters at some time.[12] The fact that a country concentrates its industrialization activities on products for which it would seem to have a comparative advantage does not guarantee that exports can be generated. There are various trade barriers, discussed later in this chapter, that are particularly problematic to the development of manufacturing exports from nonindustrialized countries.

Economic Relationships with Other Countries

Countries are interested not only in their absolute economic welfare, but also in how well they are performing relative to other countries. Therefore, it is common for governments to impose trade restrictions in order to improve their relative positions, such as by trying to assure that they buy no more from others than others buy from them, that their export prices are sufficiently high, and that import prices are low—but not so low as to "unfairly" affect their domestic producers.

Balance-of-payments adjustments   Because the trade account is a major component of the balance of payments for most countries, governments make many attempts to modify what would have been an import or export movement in a free-market situation.

Trade restrictions may have an uneven effect on industries, but a country can choose to restrict the least essential imports.

Direct influence on trade differs from the other means of balance-of-payments adjustment (deflation of the economy or currency devaluation) primarily because of its greater selectivity. This may be either an advantage or a disadvantage compared to other adjustment mechanisms. For example, if a country is running a deficit, either a devaluation or a domestic deflation can make domestically produced goods and services less expensive than foreign ones, resulting in a widespread effect on both imports and exports as well as on such service accounts as tourism. Because of the breadth of industries affected, fairly small changes relative to other countries' prices may substantially affect payments balances, which in turn minimizes the burden of adjustment on any single industry. Direct influence on trade may, however, allow a country to choose the types of products or services to be affected. For example, in the opening case, the United States considered limitations only on luxury cars from Japan, thus limiting the number and type of consumers who would be affected and who might be politically alienated from the politicians making limitations.

Comparable access or "fairness" Many companies and industries argue that they should have the same access to foreign markets as foreign industries and companies have to their markets. From an economic standpoint, the argument is that in industries in which increased production will greatly decrease cost, either from scale economies or learning effects, producers that lack equal access to a competitor's market will have a disadvantage in gaining enough sales to be cost-competitive. This has been noted, for example, in the semiconductor, aircraft, and telecommunications industries.[13]

The argument for equal access also is presented as one of fairness. For example, the U.S. government announced it will permit foreign financial-services companies to operate in the United States, but it will rescind that permission if companies' home governments do not open their financial markets to U.S. companies. In the opening case, the U.S. government's threat to place additional restrictions on imports of luxury cars from Japan was aimed at getting market access for U.S. automobile producers. The U.S. government also restricted France Telecom and Deutsche Telekom in the U.S. telephone market because of French and German restrictions on AT&T within their markets.[14] There are at least three arguments against this fairness doctrine. First, there are advantages of freer trade, even if imposed unilaterally; thus additional restrictions may deny one's own consumers lower prices. Second, imposition of additional import restrictions to coerce other countries to reduce their restrictions may have the opposite effect. Third, negotiation of separate agreements for each of the many thousands of different products and services that might be traded is cumbersome and expensive.

Price-control objectives Countries sometimes withhold supplies from international markets in order to raise prices abroad. This supply-limiting behavior is a feature of commodity arrangements, which will be discussed in Chapter 7. In addition, a few countries hold monopoly or near-monopoly control of certain resources. To maintain control and the resulting high prices, they enforce strict

Export restrictions may
- **Keep up world prices**
- **Make it extremely costly to prevent smuggling**
- **Lead to substitution**
- **Keep domestic prices down by increasing domestic supply**
- **Give producers less incentive to increase output**
- **Shift foreign production and sales**

export regulations. However, this type of policy encourages smuggling and requires high prevention costs. For example, Colombia pays a high price to patrol its borders to try to prevent emeralds from flooding world markets. Further, export controls may be ineffective. For example, Brazil lost its world monopoly in natural rubber after a contrabandist brought rubber plants into Malaysia; it now has practically no world sales. Also, if prices are kept too high, substitutes may be developed. For example, the high price of Chilean natural nitrate led to the development of a synthetic.

A country also may limit exports of a product that is in short supply so that domestic consumers may buy it at a lower price than if foreign purchasers were allowed to bid the price up. In 1995 the European Union did this with wheat, and in 1996 Egypt with cotton.[15] The primary danger of these policies is that the lower prices at home will not entice producers to expand domestic output, whereas foreign output is expanded. This may lead to long-term market loss.

Countries also fear that foreign producers will price their exports so artificially low that they drive domestic producers out of business, resulting in a costly dislocation for workers and industries. If entry barriers are high, it is argued that the surviving foreign producers may even be able to extract monopoly profits or limit exports so that industries in their own countries will have preferential supplies. There have been allegations that Hitachi, the only producer of a key computer chip, delayed deliveries to Cray Research, the leading U.S. supercomputer producer, to give Japanese computer companies an advantage.[16] However, if there is competition among foreign producers, they probably cannot charge monopoly prices or limit exports after domestic producers are displaced. For example, low import prices have eliminated most U.S. consumer electronics production, yet U.S. prices for consumer electronics are among the world's lowest.[17] The ability to price artificially low abroad may result from high domestic prices due to a monopoly position at home or from subsidies or sponsorship policies of the home-country government.

Import restrictions may
- **Prevent dumping from being used to put domestic producers out of business**
- **Get other countries to bargain away restrictions**
- **Get foreign producers to lower their prices**

The underpricing of exports (usually below cost or below the home-country price) is often referred to as **dumping.** Most countries prohibit imports of dumped products, but enforcement usually occurs only if the imported product disrupts domestic production. If there is no domestic production, then the only host-country effect is a subsidy to consumers there. Home-country consumers or taxpayers seldom realize that they are in effect subsidizing foreign sales. The U.S. antidumping legislation is extremely controversial. Under it, a foreign company can be fined if it makes less than an 8-percent profit on its export price or if its export price is as little as 0.5 percent below its domestic price, even though currency-value fluctuations may account for a much greater difference.[18] Further, the means of comparing prices is often arbitrary. For example, the U.S. government compared the prices of new Mazda minivans in Japan with those of used ones in the United States and the prices of small New Zealand kiwis in the United States with those of large ones in New Zealand as the basis to convict companies of dumping.[19]

Trade restrictions are used to reduce prices in foreign countries by forcing other countries to bargain away their import restrictions. For example, the United States passed the Super 301 clause in its 1988 trade act. This clause permits a threat of trade retaliation to be included in negotiations in order to get other countries to reduce import barriers for U.S. exports. This clause was used in the 1995 negotiations in which Japan reduced barriers to the importation of U.S. automobiles. The danger in this mechanism is that each country may escalate restrictions rather than bargain them away.

A final price argument for governmental influence on trade is the **optimum-tariff theory,** which holds that a foreign producer will lower its prices if a tax is placed on its products. If this occurs, benefits shift to the importing country. For example, assume that an exporter has costs of $500 per unit and is selling to a foreign market for $700 per unit. With the imposition of a 10-percent tax on the imported price, the exporter may choose to lower its price to $636.36 per unit, which, with a 10-percent tax of $63.64, would keep the price at $700 for the importer. The exporter may feel that a price higher than $700 would result in lost sales and that a profit of $136.36 per unit instead of the previous $200 per unit is better than no profit at all. An amount of $63.64 per unit has thus shifted to the importing country. As long as the foreign producer lowers its price by any amount, some shift in revenue goes to the importing country and the tariff is considered to be an optimum one. There are many examples of products whose prices did not rise as much as the amount of the imposed tariff; however, it is very difficult to predict whether exporters will in fact reduce their profit margins.

Noneconomic Objectives

Much governmental action on trade is based not on economic reasoning but rather on political imperatives such as the following:

- Maintenance of essential industries (especially defense)
- Prevention of shipments to unfriendly countries
- Maintenance or extension of spheres of influence
- Conservation of activities that help preserve a national identity

In protecting essential industries, countries must
- Determine which ones are essential
- Consider costs and alternatives
- Consider political consequences

Maintaining essential industries A major consideration behind governmental action on trade is the protection of essential domestic industries during peacetime so that a country is not dependent on foreign sources of supply during war. This is called the **essential-industry argument.** On the basis of this argument, the U.S. government subsidizes domestic production of silicon so that domestic computer chip producers will not have to depend entirely on foreign suppliers.[20] This argument for protection has much appeal in rallying support for import barriers. However, in times of real crisis or military emergency, almost any product could be considered essential. Because of the high cost of protecting an inefficient industry or a higher-cost domestic substitute, the essential-industry argument should not be (but frequently is) accepted without a careful evaluation of costs, real needs, and alternatives. Once an industry is afforded protection, the protection is difficult to terminate. For example, the United States continued subsidies to mohair producers for many years after mohair was no longer essential for military uniforms.[21]

Dealing with unfriendly countries   Defense arguments often are used to prevent exports, even to friendly countries, of strategic goods that might fall into the hands of potential enemies or that might be in short supply domestically.[22] This policy may be valid if the exporting country assumes there will be no retaliation that prevents it from securing even more essential goods. Even then, it is possible that the importing country simply may find alternative supply sources or develop a production capability of its own.

Trade controls on nonstrategic goods also may be used as a weapon of foreign policy to try to prevent another country from easily meeting its economic and political objectives. For example, China tried to keep Taiwan from buying French fighter jets by announcing that French companies would be banned from bidding on a Chinese subway contract if the sale were made.[23] Another example was the international cessation of trade with Iraq after its 1990 invasion of Kuwait. Iraq's loss of oil exports was a severe economic blow, amounting to 43 percent of the combined GNPs of Iraq and Kuwait. But there were also costs to the countries imposing the sanctions. Oil prices rose, hurting LDCs especially. The United States, formerly the largest exporter to Iraq, lost sales of $1.29 billion a year; the losses were concentrated within those companies doing business in Iraq. For example, NRM-Steel had already produced equipment for an export order; the trade freeze reduced its 1990 earnings by about 20 percent.[24] But there is potential for trade gain as countries become friendlier. For example, the United States eliminated most of its export restrictions aimed at the Soviet Union once the Soviet Union broke up.

Maintaining spheres of influence   There are many examples of governmental actions on trade to support spheres of influence. Aid, credits, and purchases are frequently tied into a political alliance or even to votes within international bodies. For example, under the Caribbean Basin Initiative, the United States places low import restrictions on most products from Caribbean countries; in exchange, however, those countries must sign extradition treaties with the United States and cooperate in preventing controlled substances from entering the United States.[25] In terms of foreign aid, about 50 percent of recent outflows from the United States have gone to the Middle East and 80 percent of that to just two countries, Israel and Egypt, because of U.S. political and economic interests to maintain peace in that area. Another example is the EU's preferential treatment since 1993 of bananas from certain former colonies, such as Dominica. Guatemala, Honduras, and Mexico have argued against this treatment because of their disadvantage in selling to Europe. The United States has also complained because U.S.-based banana operators (Chiquita, Dole, and Del Monte) depend on banana supplies from countries outside the preferred area, which they sell in the EU.[26]

Threats of trade restrictions may be used to coerce governments to follow certain political actions. For example, China threatened long-term trade restrictions against Australia and New Zealand if those countries' leaders were to meet with the Dalai Lama. Further, China delayed permission for Allianz, a German insurance group, to operate in China after Germany gave a reception for the Dalai Lama.[27]

Preserving cultures and national identity   China is by far the largest consumer of rice in the world. Its pursuit of rice self-sufficiency is based partially on cultural arguments that rice farming has been a historical and cohesive force in uniting families.[28] Further, countries are held together partially through a common sense of identity that sets their citizens apart from other nationalities. To protect this separateness, countries limit foreign products and services in certain sectors. For example, Canada limits foreign publishing, cable TV, and bookselling.[29] Also, France has protected its movie industry out of fear that the English language and Anglo-Saxon culture will weaken its cultural identity. This protection has taken the form of government subsidies for film making and dubbing and limits on the percentage of foreign films that can be shown on French television.[30]

Forms of Trade Control

The previous section focused on the end objectives sought by governments when they attempt to influence exports or imports. Attaining any of the objectives depends in great part on groups at home that pressure for actions their members believe will have the most positive (or least negative) influence on them. Because the actions taken on foreign trade by one country will have repercussions abroad, retaliation from foreign governments looms as a potential obstacle to achieving the desired objectives. The choice of instruments to achieve trade goals is therefore important, since domestic and foreign groups may respond differently to them. One way to understand the types of instruments is to distinguish between those that affect quantity movements indirectly by directly influencing prices and those that affect quantity movements directly.

Another common distinction is between tariff barriers and nontariff barriers: Tariff barriers affect prices; nontariff barriers may affect either price or quantity directly. A **tariff,** or **duty,** is a governmental tax levied on a good shipped internationally. Figure 6.2 illustrates how either type of barrier affects both the price and the quantity sold, although in a different order and with a different impact on producers. Parts (a) and (b) both have downward-sloping demand curves (D) and upward-sloping supply curves (S). In other words, the lower the price, the higher the quantity demanded; the higher the price, the larger the supply made available for sale. The intersection of the S and D curves illustrates the price (P_1) and quantity sold (Q_1) without governmental interference. When a tax (tariff) raises the price from P_1 to P_2 in (a), the amount consumers are willing to buy will fall from Q_1 to Q_2. Producers don't benefit because the price increase goes to taxes rather than to them. Part (b) shows a restriction in available supply; therefore a new supply curve (S_1) is imposed. The quantity sold now falls from Q_1 to Q_2. At the lower supply, the price rises from P_1 to P_2, which reflects the intersection of the D and S_1 curves. The major difference in the two approaches is that producers raise the price in (b), which helps compensate them for the decrease in quantity sold. In (a), producers sell less *and* are unable to raise their price because the tax has already done this.

Tariffs

Tariffs may be levied
- **On goods entering, leaving, or passing through a country**
- **For protection or revenue**
- **On a per unit or a value basis**

The most common type of trade control is the tariff. If collected by the exporting country, it is known as an *export tariff;* if collected by a country through which the goods have passed, it is a *transit tariff;* if collected by the importing country, it is an *import tariff.* The import tariff is by far the most common.

Import tariffs primarily serve as a means of raising the price of imported goods so that competitively produced domestic goods will gain a relative price advantage. A tariff may be classified as protective in nature even though there is no domestic production in direct competition. For example, a country that wants to reduce the foreign expenditures of its citizens because of balance-of-payments problems may choose to raise the price of some foreign products, even though there are no close domestic substitutes, in order to curtail import consumption.

Tariffs also serve as a source of governmental revenue. Import tariffs are of little importance to large industrial countries (in fact, the EU now spends about the same to collect duties as the amount it collects[31]), but are a major source of revenue in many LDCs. This is because governmental authorities in LDCs may have more control over ascertaining the amounts and types of goods passing across their frontiers

Figure 6.2
Comparison of Trade Restrictions
In (a), the tax on imports raises the price, which decreases the quantity demanded. In (b), the quantity limit on imports decreases the supply available and raises prices. The price rise in (b) is charged by producers.

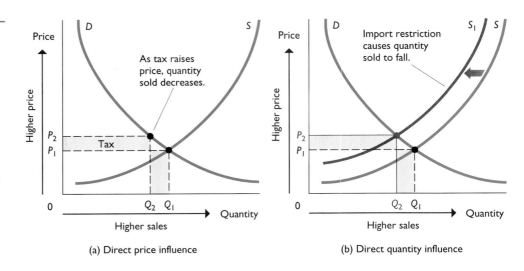

(a) Direct price influence

(b) Direct quantity influence

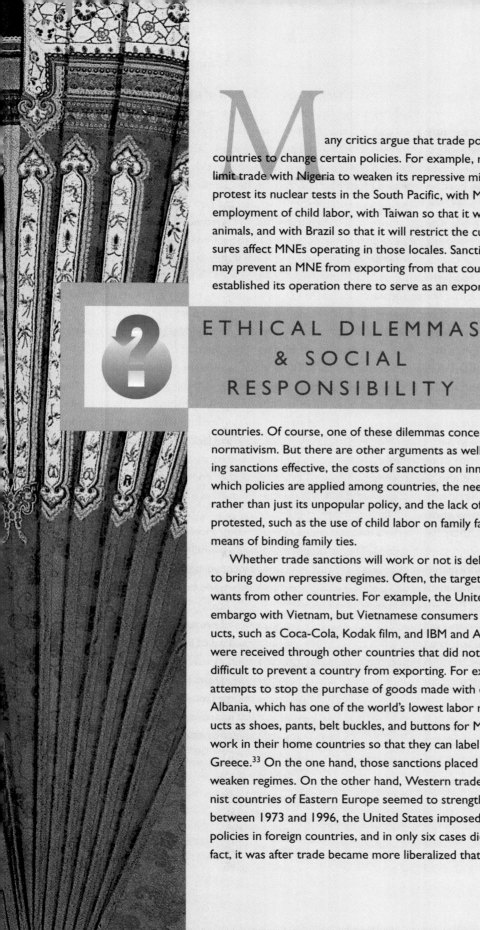

Many critics argue that trade policy should be used to pressure other countries to change certain policies. For example, recently there have been pressures to limit trade with Nigeria to weaken its repressive military dictatorship, with France to protest its nuclear tests in the South Pacific, with Malaysia so that it will prohibit the employment of child labor, with Taiwan so that it will curtail trade in parts of endangered animals, and with Brazil so that it will restrict the cutting of Amazon forests. These pressures affect MNEs operating in those locales. Sanctions against a country's overall trade may prevent an MNE from exporting from that country even though the MNE may have established its operation there to serve as an export supply point and even though it may not be engaged in the so-called undesirable practices.

ETHICAL DILEMMAS & SOCIAL RESPONSIBILITY

Although all of these causes have widespread public support, countries face dilemmas in whether to use trade policy to try to effect changes in other countries. Of course, one of these dilemmas concerns the argument of relativism versus normativism. But there are other arguments as well. These include the practicality of making sanctions effective, the costs of sanctions on innocent people, the unevenness with which policies are applied among countries, the need to look at a country's overall record rather than just its unpopular policy, and the lack of agreement about the cause being protested, such as the use of child labor on family farms which some societies value as a means of binding family ties.

Whether trade sanctions will work or not is debatable, especially if they are intended to bring down repressive regimes. Often, the targeted country manages to get what it wants from other countries. For example, the United States had a twenty-year trade embargo with Vietnam, but Vietnamese consumers were able to buy U.S. consumer products, such as Coca-Cola, Kodak film, and IBM and Apple computers because the goods were received through other countries that did not enforce the sanctions.[32] Similarly, it is difficult to prevent a country from exporting. For example, there have been widespread attempts to stop the purchase of goods made with extremely low-priced labor. However, Albania, which has one of the world's lowest labor rates, has factories making such products as shoes, pants, belt buckles, and buttons for MNEs that add just enough finishing work in their home countries so that they can label the products as being made in Italy or Greece.[33] On the one hand, those sanctions placed on South Africa and Haiti helped weaken regimes. On the other hand, Western trade embargoes against the former communist countries of Eastern Europe seemed to strengthen control by their leaders. Overall, between 1973 and 1996, the United States imposed 34 trade sanctions aimed at changing policies in foreign countries, and in only six cases did the sanctions lead to changes.[34] In fact, it was after trade became more liberalized that leaders and systems in the former communist countries were overthrown. Some proponents of trade sanctions say that it is irrelevant whether they bring about change or not. They argue that they are making a statement about policies that are important to them.

The general population, rather than the political leaders, often bear the burden of deprivation when there are trade embargoes. For example, this has occurred in Iraq where there have been widespread reports of children's deaths because of inadequate supplies of food and medicine.[35] Further, the embargoes have affected people in other countries, such as former exporters to those countries. Jordan has lost hundreds of millions of dollars in commerce because of port disruptions through UN inspections of cargo that might go to Iraq.[36] Thus critics of trade sanctions argue that, even if they are ultimately effective, the costs are too high for innocent people.

The United States considered trade sanctions in an effort to force Taiwan to curtail trade in parts of endangered animals—rhino horns and tiger bones, for example—which have been valued for centuries in that country's traditional medicine. Groups in Taiwan argued against the sanctions on grounds of fairness. They pointed out that political solidarity has caused the United States not to consider similar sanctions against China and South Korea, even though both of those countries engage heavily in the trade of endangered animals' parts as well. Further, although there are efforts to save whales, no country seeks trade sanctions against Norway, which continues whaling because whale meat has traditionally been part of the Norwegian diet.[37] Presumably, the lack of sanctions against Norway is due to its place among high-income countries and its strong record on human rights.

There is also disagreement on how to evaluate another country's practices. For example, some critics have suggested that trade policies be used as a means of pressuring Brazil to change its environmental practices—specifically to restrict the cutting of Amazon forests. Others have argued that any undesirable situation should be examined in relation to a country's overall record. They maintain that Brazil's overall environmental record—in particular, its limiting of adverse exhaust emissions by converting automobile engines to use methanol instead of gasoline—is too good to justify trade pressures.

Any of the causes that may be supported through protests or trade sanctions may themselves be controversial. For example, some critics of preserving the Brazilian rainforest argue that the trade-off is to withhold a higher standard of living for people who may live in the area.[38] Further, trade sanctions against a country may limit that country's growth because trade promotes a more efficient use of resources, and it may be easier to institute more stringent environmental rules in a growing economy than in a stagnant one. For example, growth brings resources that may be used to improve environmental awareness and commitment and to buy more environmentally effective machinery.[39]

and collecting a tax on them than they do over determining and collecting individual and corporate income taxes. Although revenue tariffs are most commonly collected on imports, many countries that export raw materials use export tariffs extensively. New Caledonia, for example, has such a tariff on nickel. Transit tariffs were once a major source of revenue for countries, but they have been nearly abolished through governmental treaties.

A tariff may be assessed on a per unit basis, in which case it is known as a *specific duty.* It also may be assessed as a percentage of the value of the item, in which case it is known as an *ad valorem duty.* If both a specific duty and an ad valorem duty are charged on the same product, the combination is known as a *compound duty.* A specific duty is easier to assess because customs officials do not need to determine a value on which to calculate a percentage. During periods of normal inflation, the specific duty will, unless changed, become a smaller percentage of the value and therefore be less restrictive to imports.

A major tariff controversy concerns industrial countries' treatment of manufactured exports from LDCs that are seeking to diversify and increase earnings by adding manufactured value to their exports of raw materials. Raw materials frequently can enter industrial countries' markets free of duty; however, if processed, those same materials usually have a tariff assigned to them. Because an ad valorem tariff is based on the total value of the product, nonindustrial countries have argued that the *effective tariff* on the manufactured portion is higher than would be indicated by the published tariff rate. For example, a country may charge no duty on coffee beans but may assess a 10-percent ad valorem tariff on instant coffee. If $5 for a jar of instant coffee covers $2.50 in coffee beans and $2.50 in processing costs, the $0.50 duty is effectively 20 percent on the manufactured portion, since the beans could have entered free of duty. This situation has made it more difficult for LDCs to find markets for their manufactured products. In addition, many of the products they are best able to produce are the ones that in industrial countries are produced by workers who are ill equipped to move easily to new employment. The result is the formation of pressure groups to keep these products out.

Another controversy concerns who bears the brunt of paying tariff costs. Some critics have claimed that in the United States, the burden falls mainly on the poor. This is largely because of restrictions on both food and textiles and apparel, which raise prices on a larger portion of expenditures by low-income families than by high-income families.[40] There is further anecdotal evidence that luxury goods are protected less than inexpensive goods. For example, mink furs, lobsters, and truffles are duty-free, whereas children's polyester sweaters, infant food preparations, orange juice, and broccoli have high tariffs. Cheaper footwear carries a higher tariff than expensive footwear.[41] However, price is only one type of burden on the poor. For example, the tariff on broccoli is imposed to ensure employment of migrant workers who plant and harvest the crops. A similar tariff on truffles would not help their employment because the United States lacks sufficient quantities of truffles to make their harvesting commercially viable.

Nontariff Barriers: Direct Price Influences

Subsidies   Although countries sometimes make direct payments to producers to compensate them for losses incurred from selling abroad, they most commonly provide other types of assistance to make it cheaper or more profitable for companies to sell overseas. For example, most countries offer their potential exporters an array of services—for example, providing information, sponsoring trade expositions, and establishing foreign contacts.[42] From an economic standpoint, service subsidies frequently are more justifiable than tariffs because they usually are designed to overcome, rather than create, market imperfections. There also are economies to be gained by disseminating information widely. Further, other countries are not likely to complain about such types of assistance. However, some observers may contend that users should be the only ones to share the costs. At any rate, export assistance is apt to result in less opposition than would import restrictions.

Other types of subsidies are more controversial, and companies frequently assert that they face unfair competition from subsidized production. There is little agreement on what a subsidy is. Did Canada subsidize exports of fish because it gave grants to fishermen to buy trawlers? Did the United Kingdom subsidize steel when the government-owned steel company had severe losses? Did the United States block some automobile imports because states made numerous concessions to convince foreign automakers to locate plants there? Recently, questions also have been raised about various governments' support of R&D and about tax programs that directly or indirectly affect export profitability. One interesting subsidy case involves commercial aircraft. The United States subsidizes Boeing and McDonnell Douglas indirectly through payments for developments in military aircraft that have commercial applications; the EU subsidizes Airbus Industrie directly. The United States and the EU have set up a bilateral agreement to allow subsidies on commercial aircraft production but to limit the amount.[43]

Other forms of governmental export assistance are foreign aid and loans. These forms are frequently "tied"—that is, the recipient must spend the funds in the donor country, making some products competitive abroad that might otherwise be noncompetitive. Tied aid is especially important in winning contracts to supply telecommunications and build railways and electric-power projects. About one third of capital goods traded worldwide are financed through tied-aid packages.[44] But some countries tie their aid more than others. For example, Japan is currently the largest foreign aid donor, and tied aid is only a little more than 20 percent of its total aid. The United States, the second largest foreign aid donor, ties over 60 percent of its aid.[45] Most industrial countries also provide repayment insurance for their exporters, thus reducing the risk of nonpayment for overseas sales. Another scheme has been to combine aid with loans so that the interest rate on paper does not look as low to competitor countries as it really is.

Customs valuation   Customs officials used to have fairly wide discretion in determining the value of an imported product for affixing an ad valorem duty. For example, if the invoice value of a shipment was $100, customs officials might use instead the domestic wholesale or retail price or even an estimation of what the product would cost if it were produced domestically. This meant that they might charge a duty on a value much higher than $100. This discretion was permitted to prevent exporters and importers from declaring an arbitrarily low price on invoices in order to avoid incurring as high a tariff as would otherwise be imposed. For example, Argentine customs authorities revalued a shipment of 2000 bicycles that were invoiced for only $1.78 each.[46] In practice, however, the discretionary powers sometimes were used as an arbitrary means of preventing the importation of foreign-made products by assessing the value too high.

Most countries now have agreed on a procedure for assessing values. First, customs officials must use the invoice price. If there is none or if its authenticity is doubtful, they then must assess on the basis of the value of identical goods. If this isn't possible, they must assess on the basis of similar goods coming in at about the same time. If this basis cannot be used, officials may compute a value based on final sales value or on reasonable cost.

The fact that so many different products are traded creates another valuation problem. It is easy (by accident or on purpose) to classify a product so that it will require a higher duty. With over 13,000 categories of products, a customs agent must use discretion to determine if silicon chips should be considered "integrated circuits for computers" or "a form of chemical silicon." A few examples should illustrate the possible problems. The U.S. Customs Service had to determine whether sport utility vehicles, such as the Suzuki Samurai and the Land Rover, were cars or trucks. They assessed the 25-percent duty on trucks instead of the 2.5-percent duty on cars, but doing this excluded the vehicles from the VER quota. Later, a federal trade court ruled them to be cars. Procter & Gamble's Duncan Hines Muffin Mix operation had to suspend production for seven weeks while awaiting a favorable ruling that the topping brought in from its Canadian plant should not be classified as sugar. In Poland, automobile parts are assessed only about half the duty assessed on automobiles. But what is an automobile part? Thousands of Poles have discovered that they can go to Germany to buy cars, dismantle them just enough so that each section can be classified as a part, and bring the sections into Poland at the lower rate of duty.[47]

Other direct price influences   Countries frequently use other means to affect prices, including special fees (for example, for consular and customs clearance and documentation), requirements that customs deposits be placed in advance of shipment, and minimum price levels at which goods can be sold after they have customs clearance.

Nontariff Barriers: Quantity Controls

A quota may
• **Set the total amount to be traded**
• **Allocate amounts by country**

Quotas The most common type of import or export restriction based on quantity is the **quota.** From the standpoint of imports, a quota most frequently limits the quantitative amount of a product allowed to be imported in a given year. The amount frequently reflects a guarantee that domestic producers will have access to a certain percentage of the domestic market in that year. For many years, the sugar import quota of the United States was set so that U.S. producers would have about half of the home market. In this case, the total quota was further allocated by country on the basis of political considerations rather than price. The consumer price of imported sugar equaled that of more expensive domestically produced sugar, since lowering the consumer price on imports could not increase the quantity of imports sold. This sort of restriction of supply usually will increase the consumer price because there is little incentive to use price as a means of increasing sales. In the case of import tariffs, the gains from price increases to consumers are received in the form of governmental revenue in the importing country. In the case of quotas, however, the gains are most likely to accrue to producers or exporters in the producing country as added per-unit profits. Windfall gains could accrue to intermediaries in the importing country if they bought at a lower, world-market price and then sold at the higher, protected domestic price.

Problems arise when quotas are allocated among countries because officials must ensure that goods from one country are not transshipped to take advantage of another country's quota. This has been a problem with Chinese- and Vietnamese-made garments that are transshipped through various countries.[48] Similarly, the product may be transformed into one for which there is no quota. For example, until completion of the GATT negotiations under the Uruguay Round, Japan did not allow rice imports but did permit imports of processed food containing rice; thus Sushi Boy, a restaurant chain in Japan, was able to import frozen sushi (which was 80-percent rice) from the United States.[49] Or a product may be transshipped as components that are not subject to the same import restrictions.[50]

Import quotas are not necessarily intended to protect domestic producers. For example, Japan maintains quotas on many agricultural products not produced in Japan. Imports are allocated as a means of bargaining for sales of Japanese exports as well as to avoid excess dependence on any one country for essential food needs, since supplies could be cut off by adverse climatic or political conditions.

Export quotas may be established to assure domestic consumers of a sufficient supply of goods at a low price, to prevent depletion of natural resources, or to attempt to raise an export price by restricting supply in foreign markets. To restrict supply, some countries have banded together in various commodity agreements (discussed in Chapter 7) that have restricted and allocated exports by producing countries of such commodities as coffee and petroleum; the intended result is to raise prices to importing countries.

A specific type of quota that prohibits all trade is known as an **embargo.** Like quotas, embargoes may be placed on either imports or exports, on whole categories of products regardless of destination, on specific products to specific countries, or on all products to given countries. Although embargoes are generally imposed for political purposes, the effects may be economic in nature. For example, the United Nations voted an embargo on Haiti in 1993 because of political animosity toward the military dictatorship in power. But the effects on Haiti were economic: The country had difficulty getting supplies, particularly oil, and it could not easily sell its products abroad.

Through "buy local" laws
• Government purchases give preference to domestically made goods
• Governments sometimes legislate preferences for domestically made goods

"Buy local" legislation   If government purchases are a large part of total expenditures within a country, the determination of where governmental agencies will make their purchases is of added importance in international competitiveness. Most governments give preference to domestic producers in their purchases of goods, sometimes in the form of content restriction (that is, a certain percentage of the product being purchased must be of local origin) and sometimes through price mechanisms (for example, a governmental agency may be able to buy a foreign-made product only if the price is at some predetermined margin below that of a domestic competitor).

There is abundant legislation worldwide that simply prescribes a minimum percentage of domestic value that a given product must have for it to be sold legally within the country. In the opening case, the local content proposed for cars sold in the United States would be, if implemented, a type of such legislated protection.

Other types of trade barriers include
• Arbitrary standards
• Licensing arrangements
• Administrative delays
• Reciprocal requirements
• Service restrictions

Standards   Countries commonly have set classification, labeling, and testing standards in a manner that allows the sale of domestic products but inhibits that of foreign-made ones. Take labels, for example. The requirement to indicate on a product where it is made is purportedly to provide information to consumers who prefer buying products from certain locales; but this adds to production costs. Further, raw materials, components, design, and labor increasingly come from a variety of countries, so most products today are of mixed origin. This leads to labeling problems. For example, Infrared Research Labs, a small U.S. manufacturer of remote-control devices, cannot use a "Made in the U.S.A." label for U.S. sales because some components brought from U.S. suppliers originate in foreign countries; however, that label is required on export sales.[51] The mixed origin also leads to contentions of protectionism. Recall in the opening case that automobile window stickers in the United States now show country-of-origin information. But in the GM/Toyota NUMMI joint venture assembly plant in the United States, the same wiring harness is listed as an import for the Toyota Corolla and as domestic for the Chevrolet Geo Prizm.[52]

The ostensible purpose of testing standards is protecting the safety or health of the domestic population. However, thwarted exporters have argued that such restrictions sometimes are imposed just to protect domestic producers. For example, more than half the value of U.S. exports to the European Union are subject to some form of EU certification, such as costly retesting after the goods arrive in Europe.[53] In some cases, the standards keep U.S. products out of the market completely, such as U.S. beef fattened with hormones, and genetically engineered corn, even though the scientific community concludes the hormones and genetic engineering pose no human health risk.[54]

Specific permission requirements   Some countries require that potential importers or exporters secure permission from governmental authorities before conducting trade transactions, a requirement known as an **import license.** To gain a license, a company may have to send samples abroad in advance. Requiring licenses may not only restrict imports or exports directly by denial of permission but also result in further deterrence of trade because of the cost, time, and uncertainty involved in the process. Similar to an import license is a **foreign-exchange control,** which is a requirement that an importer of a given product must apply to its governmental authorities to secure foreign exchange to pay for the product. As with an import license, failure to grant the exchange, not to mention the time and expense involved in completing forms and awaiting replies, constitutes an obstacle to the conduct of foreign trade.

Administrative delays and procedures   Closely akin to specific permission requirements are intentional administrative delays on entry, which create uncertainty and raise the cost of carrying inventory. For example, South Korean customs routinely take 30 days or more to clear imported merchandise, thus adding to inventory costs and making some perishables unsaleable. South Korea has also been accused of conducting more tax audits on drivers of foreign cars so that its consumers are wary of buying them. United Parcel Service suspended its ground service between the United States and Mexico because of burdensome and time-consuming Mexican customs delays at the border.[55] But correcting delays may be difficult. For example, exporters to Japan have complained that stevedore practices at Japanese ports excessively delay and add costs to their shipments; however, Japanese authorities have claimed that they have no control over the practices because they are privately run.[56]

Reciprocal requirements   In recent years, an upsurge has occurred in requirements that exporters take merchandise in lieu of money or that they promise to buy merchandise or services in the country where the sales are made. Probably 15 to 20 percent of world trade involves some type of reciprocal agreement. This is sometimes because the importer is short of foreign exchange to purchase what it wants. For example, Colombia paid for buses from Spain's ENESA with coffee, and China purchased railroad engineering services from Italy's Tecnotrade with coal.[57] More frequently, however, the arrangements involve countries with high creditworthiness that want to secure jobs and/or technical transfers as part of the transaction.[58] For example, McDonnell Douglas sold helicopters to the British government but had to agree to equip them with Rolls-Royce engines (from the United Kingdom) and to transfer much of the technology and production work to the United Kingdom.[59] These barter transactions, referred to as **countertrade,** or **offsets,** often require exporters to find markets for goods outside their lines of expertise or to engage in complicated organizational arrangements over which they lose desired control; thus many companies avoid this type of business. However, there are companies that have developed competencies in these types of arrangements. Further, there are companies that specialize in transactions of this type and that sell their services to other companies.

Restrictions on services   Trade restrictions usually are associated with governmental interference in the international movement of goods. In addition to depending on earnings from the sale of goods abroad, many countries depend substantially on revenue from the foreign sale of such commercial services as transportation, insurance, consulting, and banking. These services account for about 19 percent of the value of all international trade.[60] Nevertheless, countries engage in widespread practices that inhibit trade in services. These inhibitions come about for three main reasons:

1. *Essentiality* Countries consider certain industries to be essential because they serve strategic purposes or because they provide social assistance to important sectors of the population. Countries sometimes prohibit any private participation, foreign or domestic, in these sectors because they feel that the services should be not-for-profit. In other cases, they set price controls for private competitors and/or subsidize services given by government-owned entities, thus giving disincentives for foreign private participation. Mail, education, and hospital health services often are treated as not-for-profit sectors, where there is little foreign participation. When private participation is permitted, foreign companies may be excluded or limited in their ability to compete because countries do not want to be dependent on foreign companies for a service they consider to be essential. For example, most countries, such as the United States, restrict foreign companies from transporting cargo and passengers over their domestic routes. Some of the other service areas that are often considered to be essential and that are often protected are communications, banking, and utilities. Service companies sometimes pressure for their home-governments to negotiate deregulation abroad when their domestic markets are open and when they believe they have competitive advantages. For example, the American International Group (AIG), the largest industrial insurer in the world, has pushed the U.S. government to help open the Japanese insurance market, where foreign companies have only about 2 percent of the sales.[61]

2. *Standards*   Entry into many service professions worldwide is limited in order to assure that consumers are protected by being served only by qualified personnel. The licensing of these personnel varies by country and includes such professionals as accountants, actuaries, architects, electricians, engineers, gemologists, hair stylists, lawyers, physicians, real estate brokers, and teachers. At present, there is little reciprocal recognition in licensing from one country to another because, in fact, requirements differ substantially. This means, for example, that an accounting or legal firm from one country cannot easily do business in another country, even to service its domestic client's needs. The company must usually hire professionals within each foreign country. Or, its own accountants or lawyers must receive certification abroad. This may be very difficult because examinations will be in a foreign language and may emphasize very different materials than those in the home country. Further, there may be lengthy prerequisites for taking an examination, such as internships and courses within a local university.

3. *Immigration*   The fact that qualifications are accepted in a foreign country is no guarantee that the country will give permission for foreign personnel to work there. Simply, countries want to protect the employment of their own citizens. Given the labor-intensive and skill-specific needs of many service industries, it is necessary to get specialized personnel to the work location in a timely fashion. But governmental regulations often require that an organization search extensively for qualified personnel locally before it can even apply for work permits for personnel it would like to bring in temporarily from abroad. The delays favor local companies that can respond more rapidly to unique market needs. Such restrictions especially hamper projects involving international design and construction services.

Extent of restrictions   Countries tend to point fingers at others in terms of restrictions, yet it is difficult to calculate which country is most restrictive. Usually they are guilty of carrying out the same practices that they pressure other countries to rescind. For example, the United States pressured Japan to eliminate its citrus quotas, even though the United States was just as restrictive toward citrus imports from Brazil.[62] Table 6.3 shows some of the U.S. restrictions that the Canadian government has complained about.

From GATT to WTO

GATT was the world's major trade-liberalization organization. It
• **Set rules for negotiations**
• **Monitored enforcement**

The most important trade-liberalization activity in the post–World War II period was through the General Agreement on Tariffs and Trade (GATT) a voluntary association of countries, which began in 1947 with 23 members and grew to more than 100 members. GATT members developed a basic set of rules under which trade

Table 6.3
Selected U.S. Nontariff Barriers

Type	Examples
Subsidies	• Preferential procurement, overhead payments, and capital assistance to U.S. defense and NASA contractors • Agricultural export subsidies and promotional programs, particularly in grains and oilseeds • Low-interest loans and payment guarantees on agricultural exports
Quotas	• Sugar and dairy products import quotas
Domestic preferences	• Buy American Act and other acts favoring U.S.-produced goods in purchases by U.S. government • Set-aside programs for small, disadvantaged, minority, labor surplus, and female-owned businesses, which favor U.S. producers in government contracts • Requirements that cargo transported by water domestically must be on U.S.-built, -owned, and -manned ships
Customs and administrative procedures	• Country of origin markings that raise costs and render some products (for example, bricks) unfit for sale • Lengthy inspections and testing and limited ports of entry that cause some perishable goods to spoil
Technical and regulatory barriers	• Limited quarantine facilities for live animals • Holding of copyrighted or trademarked materials in customs 30 days to determine if there is any infringement • About 44,000 standards jurisdictions that often overlap and require testing • License requirements for milk imports and interstate milk shipments that do not permit imports • Grading, sizing, and quality and maturity standards that are different for imported horticultural products • Different distribution requirements for imported wine and beer

Source: Selected examples were taken from "Register of United States Barriers to Trade, 1992," *External Affairs and International Trade Canada,* April 1992.

and trade negotiations take place. The most recent negotiations, the Uruguay Round, began in 1986, reached agreement in 1993, and took effect in 1995. In many cases signatory countries have a lengthy period in which to comply. For example, LDCs such as Brazil and India have until 2005 before they must honor foreign patent registrations, and industrial countries will have until 2005 to phase out quotas on fabrics and clothing imports.

The biggest change from the Uruguay Round was the agreement to replace the GATT secretariat with the World Trade Organization (WTO), which has more authority to oversee trade disputes among countries. At present, both GATT and the WTO exist, and countries are members of one, both, or neither. For example, the United States terminated its GATT membership within two months of joining the WTO. It is expected that GATT will be phased out over some unspecified time period as the WTO gains more members and takes up GATT's former activities.[63]

The move to the WTO is taking place because countries are committed to freer trade, believe that the use of rounds is more cumbersome than continual activity possible with a stronger organization, and perceive a need for a stronger organization to monitor adherence to agreements.

Most-Favored-Nation Clause

To belong to GATT or the WTO, countries must adhere to the **most-favored-nation (MFN) clause.** (The U.S. Senate voted unanimously in 1996 to replace the term with **normal trade relations;** however, usage changes slowly, and references to MFN continue.)[64] This clause requires that if a country, such as the United States, grants a tariff reduction to one country, for example, a cut from 20 percent to 10 percent on wool sweaters from Australia, it must grant the same concession to all other countries. The MFN clause also applies to quotas and licenses. Although the clause initially was intended to be unconditional, countries have always made exceptions.[65] The most important exceptions are as follows:

1. LDCs' manufactured products have been given preferential treatment over those from industrial countries. For example, most industrial countries grant tariff preferences to LDCs under the Generalized System of Preferences (GSP).
2. Concessions granted to members within a trading alliance, such as the EU or the North American Free Trade Association (NAFTA), have not been extended to countries outside the alliance.
3. Countries that arbitrarily discriminate against products from a given country are not necessarily given MFN treatment by the country whose products are discriminated against. For example, the United States has not always given MFN status to China and has recently threatened to rescind it.
4. Nonsignatory countries are not always treated in the same way as those that grant concessions. For example, only countries signing GATT's Government Procurement Code, which calls for nondiscrimination against imports in government procurement, are granted automatic permission to bid on public works contracts open to foreign bids.
5. Countries sometimes stipulate exceptions based on their existing laws at the time of signing an agreement, such as Switzerland's exclusion of agricultural trade.
6. Exceptions are made in times of war or international tension. For example, the United Kingdom suspended MFN treatment of Argentina when the two countries went to war in 1982 over ownership of islands in the South Atlantic, known as The Falklands in the United Kingdom and as Islas Malvinas in Argentina.

GATT-Sponsored Rounds

GATT's most important activity was sponsoring rounds, or sessions, named for the place in which each began. These led to a number of multilateral reductions in tariffs and nontariff barriers for its members. The process of granting reductions was across the board; that is, countries may agree to lower all tariffs by a given percentage, not necessarily the same percentage for all countries, over some specified time period. Given the thousands of products traded, it would be nearly impossible to negotiate each product separately and even more difficult to negotiate each product separately with each country separately. Nevertheless, each country brought to the negotiations certain products and services and certain protective devices it considered exceptions to its own across-the-board reductions. These exceptions sometimes led to no reductions by the countries making them. For example, in the Uruguay Round, France did not eliminate protection of its film industry, nor did the United States eliminate its restrictions on shipping trade. Exceptions sometimes led to negotiated reductions in order to gain concessions from other countries. In the Uruguay Round, for example, the United States first said that its antidumping laws would not be negotiated. But because these laws are so unpopular in LDCs, the United States finally agreed to cede antidumping disputes to an international tribunal in exchange for LDCs' agreement to protect patents, trademarks, and copyrights, the nonprotection of which had been very unpopular in the United States. Such negotiations resulted in vast tariff reductions (see Fig. 6.3)—an indication not only that countries are committed to work jointly toward freer trade but also that tariffs are the easiest trade barrier to tackle.

In addition to tariff concerns, negotiating rounds have grappled with the increasingly important and complex nontariff barriers, especially in five specific areas: industrial standards, government procurement, subsidies and countervailing duties, licensing, and customs valuation. In each of these areas, conference members agreed on a code of conduct, as follows:

Figure 6.3
Progress on Tariffs
The eight GATT rounds since 1947 have reduced tariffs significantly.

*Estimated

Source: Herring in *The Christian Science Monitor* © 1993 The Christian Science Publishing Society.

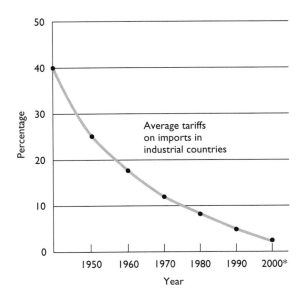

- The Agreement on Industrial Standards provides for treating imports on the same basis as domestically produced goods.
- The Agreement on Government Procurement calls for treating bids by foreign companies on a nondiscriminatory basis for most large contracts.
- The Agreement or Code of Conduct on Subsidies and Countervailing Duties recognizes domestic subsidies as appropriate policy tools whose implementation, however, should avoid any adverse impact on other countries. With the exception of agricultural products, export subsidies are prohibited. This agreement also spells out procedures regarding the possible use of countervailing duties against a second country if the first country believes its domestic companies are being harmed by the second country's subsidy.
- The Licensing Code commits members to simplifying their licensing procedures significantly and to treating both foreign and domestic companies in a nondiscriminatory manner.
- The Customs Valuation Code calls for either c.i.f. valuation (invoice value with transportation and insurance included) or f.o.b. valuation (without transportation and insurance included) and bans certain types of valuation methods, such as basing value on the selling price of the product in the importing country. (Specific customs valuation procedures were discussed in an earlier section of this chapter.)

Uruguay Round   These negotiations, which began in 1986, took more than seven years and achieved less than had been originally envisioned. The experience exemplifies the growing difficulty of reducing trade restrictions through globally oriented trade agreements. A primary problem is that less sensitive concessions have already been made and attention has moved toward services and away from products—both areas are of such high domestic sensitivity that politicians are very reluctant to yield to international pressures during negotiations. One trade concern of services is the protection of intellectual property rights, which will be discussed in Chapter 12. Other problems include:

- The fact that talks become more cumbersome as more countries engage in negotiations
- The expectation on the part of industrial countries that LDCs also should make trade concessions
- The demands by LDCs that industrial countries should import products that affect marginal workers in those countries.[66]

Nevertheless, tangible changes were made at the Uruguay Round. Virtually every participating country made concessions that politically were unpopular with its domestic pressure groups. For example, import restrictions were reduced by the United States and India on textiles, by Japan and South Korea on rice and dairy products, and by the EU on grains. Other changes concerned tariffs, quotas, subsidies, services, and settlement of disputes.[67]

Overall, the 117 nations agreed to reduce tariffs by about one third: 36 percent by industrial countries and 24 percent by LDCs. Most of the reductions by industrial countries will be on products primarily traded with each other. Quotas on textiles, finished apparel, and many agricultural products are to be eliminated; however, those on agricultural products will be replaced by tariffs of as much as several hundred percent. The ability to use VERs is greatly curtailed, to one industry per country. Subsidy reductions were agreed on for a number of agricultural products, such as grains, and for research in such goods as computer chips. LDCs agreed to open their markets for legal, accounting, and other services. They also agreed to protect patents, trademarks, and copyrights for a twenty-year period.

In some areas in which no agreement was reached, such as import restrictions on audiovisual materials and the protection of domestic shipping companies, the pact contains broad free-trade principles, which may ease the process of future negotiations. In other areas, the fact that sectors such as financial services, insurance, and telecommunications were discussed at all is a "first" and may presage future agreements.

Settlement of Disputes

There are many ways in which countries might prevent imports even after they have negotiated their freer entry. For example, they may set arbitrary health or safety standards that favor their home country production. Under GATT, countries could take trade disputes to the membership, but GATT rules necessitated unanimity for trade penalties, and no country was apt to vote against itself when there were complaints against it. Instead, the GATT Council would investigate a complaint to determine whether allegations were valid. If so, GATT had to depend on a mutual commitment to cooperate in order to make countries alter their trade practices. This approach usually worked. For example, the United States eliminated custom-user fees after the GATT Council investigated complaints from Canada and the EU, and Japan lifted quotas on eight processed-food products after complaints from the United States.

Under the WTO, there is a clearly defined dispute settlement mechanism. Countries may bring charges to a WTO panel, and countries accused of engaging in unfair trade practices may appeal. To ensure efficiency, time limits are placed on all stages of deliberations. Ultimately the panel's rulings are binding. If an offending country fails to comply with panel recommendations, its trading partners are guaranteed the right to compensation. As a final resort, the trading partners are given the right to impose countervailing sanctions against the offending country.[68] Thus far the WTO's dispute-settlement body has had a much heavier caseload than existed under the old GATT system, probably because of countries' confidence that there will be adherence to rulings. In addition, small and developing countries now have clout for the first time in dealing with trade practices in other countries.[69]

Further, by bringing cases to the panel, accused countries may agree to settle before a ruling is made. For example, South Korea agreed to extend the shelf life of meat products after the United States made a formal complaint that the short shelflife discriminated against imports. Based on the short experience thus far of the WTO system, it appears as if small countries now have more influence over trade practices of the major powers (the United States, the EU, Japan, and Canada).[70]

At this writing, it is not clear how future negotiations will be handled under the WTO. The WTO Chief said that "a new round [of negotiations] is already in the pipeline";[71] however, there has been little compulsion to embark on anything as ambitious as the Uruguay Round. At the WTO meeting in Singapore in late 1996, there seemed to be more interest in implementing earlier agreements than in reaching new ones. However, at those same meetings, a subgroup of countries representing most of the world's high technology trade agreed to remove all tariffs on computers, software, and related goods by the year 2000.[72] Thus the WTO may serve as a forum for negotiations on specific products and issues, meeting almost continuously rather than in rounds, and coming to sequential and small agreements rather than all encompassing ones at the culmination of a round.

International Business Strategy in the Internationalization Process

As companies increase their commitments to international business operations, it is not clear-cut that their strategies toward governmental trade policies change as their levels of commitment change. Rather, companies' attitudes toward trade policies differ, depending on how well they think they compete for each product from each of their production locations—with or without trade restrictions. Certainly, a company operating in many countries must deal with a more complex set of trade relationships (and potential governmental trade policies) than one operating only domestically or in a few countries. For example, a company with operations in many different countries may push for the opening of markets in one but for protection in another. However, regardless of companies' levels of international commitment, changes in governmental actions may substantially alter the competitiveness of facilities in given countries, thus creating uncertainties about which they must make decisions. These decisions affect companies that are facing import competition as well as those whose exports are facing protectionist sentiment. Further, as company capabilities change, these decisions may affect them differently. To illustrate companies' dynamic strategies, it is useful to refer to U.S.-Japanese auto trade discussed in the opening case of this chapter.

When facing import competition, companies can
- **Try to get protection**
- **Move abroad**
- **Seek other market niches**
- **Make domestic output competitive**

U.S.-Japanese Auto Trade Revisited

A U.S. automaker facing foreign competition in the United States (in this case from Japan) has a number of options:

- Pushing for import restrictions or other forms of governmental assistance
- Moving production to a lower-cost country and exporting to the United States
- Concentrating on market niches in which there is less import competition.
- Effecting internal adjustments, such as cost efficiencies, product innovations, or improved marketing

Clearly, there are substantial costs, as well as considerable uncertainty as to outcome, associated with any one of these options.

As you saw in the opening case, the U.S. automobile industry was successful in lobbying for the first option, a success attributable in part to unanimous U.S. automakers' support for import protection. The benefit of moving production abroad (the second option), such as Ford's sourcing in Mexico, could be negated if the United States afterward prohibited importation from the foreign plant. The likelihood of import restrictions in such a situation would be inversely related to the number of producers following this option. In other words, because Ford, Chrysler, and GM all went to foreign sourcing, there has been no strong coalition to push for import controls on foreign-produced components, except within labor. The Big Three also have pursued the third option in that all have arranged for foreign companies to supply their small cars, thus enabling them to concentrate more of their production efforts on larger cars, for which there is less foreign competition and where U.S. producers have demonstrated a competitive advantage. They also pursued the fourth option by instituting various cost-saving measures. In fact, these were so successful that, when combined with changed U.S. and Japanese economic conditions, automobile production costs became cheaper in the United States than in Japan. The U.S. automobile producers then pushed the U.S. government to pressure Japan to open its markets to automobile imports from the United States. It did so by threatening to put more limitations on Japanese exports of luxury cars.[73] However, cost breakthroughs are not always feasible, and when they do occur, the innovations may be short-lived as foreign competitors respond with like improvements. Further, the threat of raising trade restrictions to coerce another country to lower its restrictions may not work. A company should attempt to assess the costs and probabilities of each alternative before embarking on a program.

The potential protection of the U.S. automobile industry also created problems for Japanese companies that were exporting to the U.S. market. They could lobby against the protection, try to devise process or product technologies that would overcome the restrictive measures, or locate their production in the United States or in countries not affected by the potential protection. As was the case for domestic automakers, each option involved costs and risks. And like the U.S. companies, Japanese automakers attempted each to some extent. They lobbied with the Japanese government to take steps to counter U.S. actions. (In the case of threats to impose new tariffs only on luxury Japanese cars, the Japanese government issued a complaint with the WTO, which was withdrawn after the United States removed its threats.)[74] They developed allies, such as associations of foreign-car importers and distributors, to lobby on their behalf. They continued efforts to reduce costs in case tariffs were imposed. Before the threat of targeting luxury cars they developed capabilities for adding more luxury items so that profits might not diminish if quotas were imposed. They also negotiated arrangements to produce outside Japan, such as in Mexico and the United States, because sanctions were taken only against Japanese output.

Approaches to the International Environment

From the preceding discussion, it is clear not only that companies may take different approaches to counter changes in the international competitive environment but also that their attitudes toward protectionism are influenced by the investments they have already made to develop their international strategies.[75] Companies most apt to lose with increased protectionism are those that depend primarily on trade (whether market seekers or resource acquirers) and those that have integrated their production among different countries. Those most apt to gain are companies with single or multidomestic production facilities, such as production in the United States to serve the U.S. market and production in Mexico to serve the Mexican market. There also are differences among companies in their perceived abilities to compete against imports. In nearly half of the situations over the last sixty years in which protection has been proposed for a U.S. industry, one or more companies in the industry have been against protection. This is because they enjoy competitive advantages through such means as scale economies, relationships with suppliers, or differentiated products. They believe not only that they can compete but also that they will gain more power by having imports compete primarily against their weak domestic competitors, thus fragmenting that competition.[76]

COUNTERVAILING

FORCES

Because of difficulties in coming to global trade agreements, countries are turning more to regional approaches for trade liberalization. If they can do this successfully, companies' responses may be much more of a hybrid of global and multidomestic practices as they find opportunities to coordinate their practices on a more regional basis. For example, many automakers have pushed for longer production runs, but these runs are limited by trade restrictions. They have been better able to increase runs for the European region than they have for the world as a whole because trade barriers have been eliminated within the EU. But regional trading arrangements, discussed in the next chapter, have a history of starts and stops as countries seek to protect their own economic interests; therefore, there are uncertainties.

The discussion in Chapter 5 showed that countries attempt to become more competitive by, for example, upgrading production factors such as human skills. However, countries have objectives other than economic competitiveness that, when pursued, may harm their domestic production and economic efficiency. Several of these have been alluded to in this chapter. For example, the cessation of trade for political reasons may hurt a country's exporters, sometimes abruptly, and may cause other domestic companies to encounter supply problems. The maintenance of certain industries for strategic reasons also may cause resource utilization to be distorted, for example, by shifting production from efficient to inefficient facilities. Countries also negotiate agreements that may place their domestic companies or production at a competitive disadvantage because it is the price to pay for some other concession or expected outcome. All these actions greatly alter how companies can compete globally.

Countries prefer to act independently; however, they cede authority on trade when they perceive cooperation to be in their overall best interest. For example, countries have ceded authority to the binding dispute settlement provisions of the WTO, such as the U.S. removal of pollution standards on imported petroleum products after the WTO ruled on complaints by Venezuela and Brazil.[77] Further, there are other trade agreements. For instance, multilateral treaties, such as restrictions on ivory trade to save elephants, protect endangered species. Export control agreements prevent LDCs from acquiring technology and goods needed to produce advanced weapons. An example is the Nuclear Suppliers Group and the Coordinating Committee on Multilateral Export Controls (Cocom), which was first established to prevent such exports to communist bloc countries, some of which are now parties to the agreement.[78] However, countries are free to withdraw from agreements. For example, Iceland withdrew from the International Whaling Commission in 1992.[79]

LOOKING TO THE FUTURE

The Uruguay Round largely skirted the issue of environmental standards for products and their production. Countries with strict environmental regulations will undoubtedly consider imposing "green countervailing duties" to compensate for the cost advantages of operating where regulations are lax. Producers facing these import restrictions undoubtedly will claim that environmental standards are really a ruse to protect domestic producers. In fact, the EU has already challenged U.S. fuel efficiency standards for automobiles on these grounds.[80]

A number of issues were unresolved in the Uruguay Round. Countries effectively agreed to continue disagreeing; therefore talks will continue among small groups of WTO members. The most important of these concern trade in services—especially financial, shipping, audiovisual, and telecommunications—and subsidies for agriculture, steel, and aircraft.

Although the above examples seem to indicate a growing difficulty in bringing about freer trade, there are other more optimistic indications regarding trade growth. Global trade has been growing rapidly and should continue to do so, in part because of the movement in many countries to privatize formerly government-owned companies and to open up import markets so that domestic companies will be forced to operate more efficiently by having to compete. These movements have been especially important in Eastern Europe and in the newly industrialized countries of Asia. Even such highly protected countries as Mexico, Brazil, and Argentina have begun liberalizing imports.

WEB CONNECTION

Check out our home page for links to World Wide Web resources on GATT, the WTO, import and export subsidies, quotas, tariffs, dumping, protectionism, and other relevant topics.

Summary

- Despite the potential resource benefit of free trade, no country permits an unregulated flow of goods and services.

- Given the possibility of retaliation and the fact that imports as well as exports create jobs, it is difficult to determine the effect on employment of protecting an industry.

- Policymakers have not yet solved the problem of income redistribution due to changes in trade policy.

- The infant-industry argument for protection holds that without governmental prevention of import competition, certain industries would be unable to move from high-cost to low-cost production.

- Because industrial countries are generally more advanced economically than nonindustrial ones are, governmental interference is often argued to be beneficial if it promotes industrialization.

- Direct influence on trade is a more selective means of solving balance-of-payments disequilibrium than either changes in currency values or internal price adjustments.

- Trade controls are used to regulate prices of goods traded internationally. Their objectives include protection of monopoly positions, prevention of foreign monopoly prices, greater assurance that domestic consumers get low prices, and lower profit margins for foreign producers.

- Much of the governmental interference in international trade is motivated by political rather than economic concerns, including maintaining domestic supplies of essential goods and preventing potential enemies from gaining goods that would help them achieve their objectives.

- Many nonindustrial countries are seeking export markets within the industrialized world for their manufactured products but argue that the effective tariffs on their products are too high.

- Trade controls that directly affect price and indirectly affect quantity include tariffs, subsidies, arbitrary customs-valuations methods, and special fees.

- Trade controls that directly affect quantity and indirectly affect price include quotas, "buy-local" legislation, arbitrary standards, licensing arrangements, foreign-exchange controls, administrative delays, and requirements to take goods in exchange.

- The General Agreement on Tariffs and Trade (**GATT**) has been the main negotiating body through which countries have multilaterally reduced trade barriers and agreed on simplified mechanisms for the conduct of international trade. GATT is phasing out as countries join the World Trade Organization (**WTO**), which has better means of enforcing agreements.

- A company's development of an international strategy will greatly determine whether it will benefit more from protectionism or from some other means for countering international competition.

Case
United States–
Cuban Trade[81]

In 1996, President Clinton signed the Helms-Burton bill, which specifically provided for legal action (to seize U.S. assets) against non-U.S. companies using expropriated property in Cuba that had been owned by U.S. citizens (including Cuban exiles), the denial of U.S. visits by executives from these companies and their families, and prohibition of normal U.S. relations with any future Cuban government that includes Castro. Some proponents of the bill argued that the bill's passage would lead to reduced business relations with Cuba, a resultant weakening of the Cuban economy, and the downfall of the Castro government. Other proponents argued that the bill's passage would send a strong message of disapproval about Cuban human rights, even if the above chain of actions did not transpire.

The impetus for the bill was the shooting down of two Miami-based civilian aircraft by Cuban jets. These and other aircraft flew frequently near Cuba to look for refugee boats; however, there was conflicting evidence on whether these particular aircraft had been in Cuban territory. Prior to this incident, there was some softening of relations between the United States and Cuba, even though there had been virtually no trade between the two countries since 1961. Both the Carter and Reagan administrations had met with Castro or his intermediaries to discuss the normalization of relations between the two countries. In fact, Cuba and the United States had successfully negotiated numerous agreements, such as fly-over rights for each other's airlines, anti-hijacking procedures, an immigration accord, scholarly and athletic exchanges, and humanitarian visits. Since 1977 the two countries have had diplomatic interest sections in each other's capital. Further, in 1996 the United States permitted Cuban athletes to travel to Atlanta in charter planes for the Olympics.

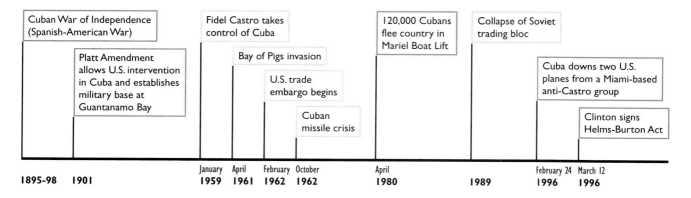

Figure 6.4
Major Events in U.S.-Cuban Relations
There have been many significant events affecting U.S.-Cuban relations during the last hundred years.

Background: The Embargo

After the Batista government was overthrown in 1959, Fidel Castro made pronouncements about exporting his type to revolution elsewhere in Latin America. The United States countered by canceling its agreements to buy Cuban sugar, and Cuba retaliated by seizing U.S. oil refineries. The oil companies then refused to supply Cuba with crude oil, and Cuba turned to the Soviet Union for supplies. Since this occurred at the height of the Cold War, when the United States and the Soviet Union had few business relations, the United States quickly severed diplomatic relations with Cuba. (Major events in U.S.-Cuban relations are shown in Fig. 6.4.)

The incidents that further strained relations during the next thirty-five years were too numerous to detail. Some were so serious that they threatened peace; others were almost ludicrous. They included the U.S. sponsorship of an invasion by exiles at the Bay of Pigs, the placement and removal of Soviet missiles in Cuba, the deployment of Cuban forces to overthrow regimes that the United States supported (such as in Nicaragua and Angola), and exposés that the CIA had tried to airlift someone to assassinate Castro and had spent thousands of dollars to develop a powder to make his beard fall out.

Initially, the United States received widespread support from other countries for an embargo on Cuba. For example, all the members of the Organization of American States except Mexico agreed in 1964 to an embargo. But, one by one, countries began trading with Cuba. In 1995 the UN General Assembly voted 117 to 3 against the U.S. embargo. Only Israel and Uzbekistan voted with the United States, and both of these countries trade with Cuba.

Opposing Viewpoints

Not all U.S. public opinion favored the Helms-Burton legislation. There was opposition based on a belief that the reprisals on foreign companies would not work to weaken Castro's political power. Further, they argued that the legislation would lead to costly retaliation and to a deepening of the U.S. immigration problem. In fact, many prominent people in the United States (including heads of major firms, senators from both parties, and labor leaders) favored normalization of U.S.-Cuban trade rather than tightening the economic noose on Cuba. They argued that the political and military danger of Cuba is no longer a reality with the end of the Cold War, that economic and political liberalization within Cuba is inevitable without massive Soviet assistance, that change in such countries as Spain and Hungary was enhanced by closer international economic contact, and that U.S. companies are losing business opportunities in Cuba while non-U.S. companies can take advantage of them.

Will the legislation work? Proponents of Helms-Burton reason that the Cuban economy is now so weak that a demoralized population will support a disgruntled military overthrow of the government if economic conditions are pushed down just a little bit lower. They point to Cuba's severe recession that pushed down GDP by nearly 35 percent between 1989 and 1993, electric outages, and a disintegrating infrastructure affecting roads, schools, and hospitals. They also cite examples of companies that have pulled out of discussions to do business in Cuba since enactment of Helms-Burton, including Cemex from Mexico and ING from the Netherlands. Meanwhile, opponents point to signs of an improved Cuban economy since 1994 due to increases in tourism (now a larger sector than sugar) and higher sugar and nickel output. Growth in GDP was 2.5 percent in 1995 and projected to be 5 percent in 1996. Prices of agricultural products have decreased and become more available, the price of the U.S. dollar dropped from 125 pesos in 1994 to about 30 in 1996, and electrical outages have almost ended. This economic improvement, they reason, will strengthen Castro, who still enjoys considerable popularity (whether or not among a majority) in Cuba. They have also cited many examples of companies that are unconcerned about Helms-Burton. For example, executives of Spain's Sol Meliá hotel chain said they would continue expanding in Cuba even if it meant relinquishing their hotel properties in Florida.

Retaliation Most major countries, such as Canada, the EU, and Mexico, have condemned Helms-Burton, so much that Clinton used a provision of the bill to allow a delay in U.S. enforcement of the provision to take legal action against foreign companies. In the meantime, the EU and Canada enacted measurements to allow their companies to take action in their courts against U.S. companies who received punitive damages against them in the United States.

Expropriation issue Expropriation of property owned by U.S. citizens has from the start been an issue in the normalization of U.S.-Cuban relations; however, Cuba has settled with other countries when they ended their embargoes. Cuba has also indicated a willingness to negotiate this with the United States. Helms-Burton makes this more complex because it addresses property that was seized from Cuban citizens who subsequently became U.S. citizens.

Immigration pressure Proponents of Helms-Burton argue that the overthrow of Castro will eliminate pressure for the United States to accept political refugees from Cuba. However, opponents counter that most pressure has come because of economic conditions in Cuba, so any success at weakening the Cuban economy will increase immigration pressure. Further, there is no assurance that a regime after Castro will be free from political repression.

U.S. business loss   Before the Castro takeover, 80 percent of Cuba's imports were from the United States. Although this level of dependency is unlikely in the future, estimates are that the amount of business currently lost by U.S. companies is substantial. One study estimated that the United States could quickly be selling $7 billion a year to Cuba if the embargo were lifted; however, Cuba's total merchandise imports for 1993 were only $1.7 billion, of which 64 percent came from only seven countries (Venezuela, 20 percent; China, 9 percent; Spain, 9 percent; Mexico, 7 percent; Italy, 4 percent; Canada, 7 percent; and France, 8 percent). Further, the 1996 estimate of FDI in Cuba was over $5 billion, none of which was owned by U.S. companies.

Human rights   Both the supporters and opponents of Helms-Burton concur that Cuba's jails hold political prisoners under deplorable conditions, though the estimates of the number of prisoners varies widely. There is also agreement that Cuba violates most of the articles in the Universal Declaration of Human Rights. On the one hand, many critics of Castro argue that the situation is getting no better. On the other hand, many people acknowledge Cuba's record in education and social welfare. For example, the Cuban life expectancy of almost 77 years now exceeds that in the United States. Further, they argue that evolutionary changes are taking place. For example, since 1993 Cubans have been allowed to be self-employed in about 100 occupations. Since 1994 farmers can basically produce and sell as they see fit, even though they cannot own the land. Cubans can now sell produce, handicrafts, and light manufactures. There is now freedom of religion and participation in municipal elections. Opponents of Helms-Burton also argue that U.S. policy has never been consistent toward countries with human rights violations and that there are a number of countries with whom the United States trades whose records are as bad as that in Cuba.

Questions

1. Should the United States seek to tighten the economic grip on Cuba? If so, how should it be done?
2. Should the United States liberalize business relations with Cuba? If so, what stipulations should be put on Cuba as a requirement for trade liberalization?
3. Assume you are Fidel Castro. What kind of business relationship with the United States would be in your best interest? What type would you be willing to accept?

Chapter Notes

1. The data for the case were taken from "U.S. Autos Losing a Big Segment of the Market—Forever?" *Business Week,* March 24, 1980, pp. 78–85; "7 of 10 Americans Agree," *New York Times,* November 6, 1980, p. A23; Leslie Wayne, "The Irony and Impact of Auto Quotas," *New York Times,* April 8, 1984, p. F1+; Rachel Dardis and Jia-Yeong Lin, "Automobile Quotas Revisited: The Costs of Continued Protection," *The Journal of Consumer Affairs,* Vol. 19, No. 2, Winter 1985,

pp. 277–292; United States General Accounting Office, *Foreign Investment: Growing Japanese Presence in the U.S. Auto Industry* (Washington: GAO/NSIAD-88-111, 1988); Doran P. Levin, "Honda Blurs Line Between American and Foreign," *New York Times,* March 14, 1990, p. A1+; Melinda Grenier Guiles, "GM Puts 'Captive Imports' to New Test," *Wall Street Journal,* September 16, 1988; "Loss Leaders," *Business Week,* March 1, 1993, p. 46; Joseph B. White, "Big Three Auto Makers Put on Display of Unity in Trade, Regulatory Matters," *Wall Street Journal,* January 11, 1993, p. A3; Neal Templin, "Ford, Chrysler Back Cap on Japan Cars; GM Balks," *Wall Street Journal,* May 15, 1992, p. A2; David Woodruff, "Why Detroit Doesn't Need the Protection It Wants," *Business Week,* February 8, 1993, p. 32; Paul Magnusson and David Woodruff, "Why Detroit Hit the Brakes," *Business Week,* February 22, 1993, p. 36; Andrew Pollack, "Japan Takes a Preemptive Step on Auto Exports," *New York Times,* January 9, 1993, p. 17; Alex Taylor III, "U.S. Cars Come Back," *Fortune,* November 16, 1992, pp. 52+; "Free Trade's Fading Champion," *The Economist,* April 11, 1992, pp. 65–66; Lee Smith, "A Dangerous Fix for Trade Deficits," *Forbes,* May 4, 1992, pp. 96–97; "US Takes Action on Two Fronts in Japan Trade War," *South China Morning Post,* May 12, 1995, p. 6 (Business); "US Targets 13 Japanese Cars for Record $45b in Tariffs," *South China Morning Post,* May 17, 1995, p. 1; Paul Ingrassia, "U.S. Auto Policy On Japan Could Drive You Crazy," *Asian Wall Street Journal,* May 30, 1995, p. 8; "Tokyo Says 'No' to Washington," *South China Morning Post,* June 7, 1995, p. 10 (Business); Merrill Goozner, "The Car Wars," *South China Morning Post,* June 22, 1995, p. 19; "Car Pact Averts Trade War," *South China Morning Post,* June 29, 1995, p. 1, 12; Andrew Pollack, "Japan Buys More U.S. Auto Parts," *New York Times,* July 14, 1995, p. C5; Haig Simonian, "Carmakers Find Their Keys," *Financial Times,* November 28, 1995, p. 17; *Averting an Automotive Trade Wreck with Japan,* Heritage Foundation Report, May 26, 1995; "International Automakers Continue Strong Export Sales of U.S.-Built Cars," *PR Newswire,* July 23, 1996; Michiyo Nakamoto, "Selling US Cars in Japan: More Than a Matter of Trade Policy," *Financial Times,* September 19, 1996, p. 6; and Valerie Reitman, "Detroit Still Seeks Right Formula in Japan," *Wall Street Journal,* January 10, 1997, p. A8; and "Clinton to Tout Success of U.S.-Japan Auto Accord," *Agence France Press,* April 12, 1996. For up-to-date information on foreign automobile companies in the United States, an Internet address is http://www.aiam.org.

2. "Guilty on All Counts," *The Economist,* August 21, 1993, quoting a GATT pamphlet, "Trade, the Uruguay Round and the Consumer."

3. James J. Kilpatrick, "How Not to Create Jobs," *Nation's Business,* March 1983, Vol. 77, No. 1, p. 5.

4. Nancy Dunne, "U.S. Shoots Itself in the Foot," *Financial Times,* August 22, 1995, p. 6, reporting on a 1995 study by the U.S. International Trade Commission, "The Economic Effects of Antidumping and Countervailing Duty (AD/CVD) Orders and Suspension Agreements."

5. "U.S. Turns Up Heat On Tokyo As List Is Due," *Asian Wall Street Journal,* May 16, 1995, p. 1.

6. John Andrew, John Helyar, and Bill Johnson, "Silver Lining," *Wall Street Journal,* February 29, 1984, p. 19; Peter Truell, "Textile Makers Demanding More Protection Threaten Hopes for Seamless U.S. Trade Policy," *Wall Street Journal,* May 16, 1990, p. A20; and Eduardo Lachica, "Alliance of Textile and Apparel Makers Splits as Senate Mulls Import-Quota Bill," *Wall Street Journal,* July 13, 1990, p. A10.

7. Robert W. Crandell, "Import Quotas and the Automobile Industry: The Costs of Protectionism," *Brookings Review,* Summer 1984, pp. 8–16.

8. Alexander Dagg, "Keeping the Jobs at Home," *Globe and Mail* [Toronto], July 3, 1990, p. 18.

9. Roger Thurow, "Ivory Coast's Reliance on Commodities Topples It from Its Role-Model Pedestal," *Wall Street Journal,* May 9, 1989, p. A16.

10. Peter F. Drucker, "The Changed World Economy," *Foreign Affairs,* Vol. 64, No. 4, Spring 1986; and Lloyd G. Reynolds, "Economic Development in Historical Perspective," *American Economic Review,* May 1980, p. 92.

11. Supportive of the premises are Raul Prebisch, *The Economic Development of Latin America and Its Principal Problems* (New York: United Nations Department of Economic Affairs, 1950); Charles P. Kindleberger, *The Terms of Trade: A European Case Study* (New York: Wiley, 1956); and W. Arthur Lewis, *Aspects of Tropical Trade, 1883–1965* (Stockholm: Almquist and Wiksells, 1969). Nonsupportive are M. June Flanders, "Prebisch on Protectionism: An Evaluation," *Econo-mic Journal,* June 1964; Theodore Morgan, "The Long-Run Terms of Trade Between Agriculture and Manufacturing," *Economic Development and Cultural Change,* October 1959; and Gottfried Haberler, "Terms of Trade and Economic Development," in *Economic Development of Latin America,* H. Ellis, ed. (New York: St. Martin's, 1961).

12. "Careering on to Asia's Highway," *Economist,* October 15, 1994, pp. 81–82.

13. Ravi Sarathy, "The Interplay of Industrial Policy and International Strategy: Japan's Machine Tool Industry," *California Management Review,* Vol. 31, No. 3, Spring 1989, pp. 132–160; David B. Yoffie and Helen V. Milner, "An Alternative to Free Trade or Protectionism: Why Corporations Seek Strategic Trade Policy," *California Management Review,* Vol. 31, No. 4, Summer 1989, pp. 111–131; and Laura D'Andrea Tyson, *Who's Bashing Whom?* (Washington: Institute for International Economics, 1993).

14. Daniel Pearl and Helene Cooper, "FCC Adopts Rules That Will Toughen Foreign Entry Into U.S. Phone Market," *Wall Street Journal,* November 29, 1995, p. A2.

15. Deborah Hargreaves, "Wheat Prices Hit 15-Year High as EU Imposes Tax on Exports," *Financial Times,* December 8, 1995, p. 1; and James Whittington, "Egypt Lifts Cotton Export Ban, *Financial Times,* February 7, 1996, p. 21.

16. John Diebold, "Beyond Subsidies and Trade Quotas," *New York Times,* November 2, 1986, p. F3.

17. Mark M. Nelson, "U.S. Is Wary of EC Import Regulations," *Wall Street Journal,* June 29, 1989, p. B1.

18. James Bovard, "No Justice in Anti-Dumping," *New York Times,* January 28, 1990, p. F13.

19. James Bovard, "Clinton's Dumping Could Sink GATT," *Wall Street Journal,* December 9, 1993, p. A14.

20. Hazel Bradford and Evert Clark, "When the Pentagon Wants Something America Doesn't Have," *Business Week,* No. 2970, October 27, 1986, p. 46.

21. "Honey, Wool and Mohair Subsidies Are Cut," *New York Times,* October 3, 1993, p. A12.

22. Eduardo Lachica, "U.S., South Korea Reach Agreement on Sale of Aircraft," *Wall Street Journal,* September 10, 1990, p. C17; John Maroff, "U.S. Export Ban Hurting Makers of New Devices to Code Messages," *New York Times,* November 19, 1990, p. A1+; Arvind Parkhe, "U.S. National Security Export Controls: Implications for Global Competitiveness of U.S. High-Tech Firms," *Strategic Management Journal,* Vol. 13, 1992, pp. 47–66; Eduardo Lachica, "U.S., 26 Other Nations to Control Exports That Could Be Used in Nuclear Bombs," *Wall Street Journal,* April 3, 1992, p. A4; and Gerald F. Seib, "Transfer of Russian Missile Technology to India Leads to U.S. Trade

Sanctions," *Wall Street Journal,* May 12, 1992, p. A6.

23. "France Confirms Sale of Fighter Jets to Taiwan," *Wall Street Journal,* January 8, 1993, p. A6.

24. Karen Pennar, "Will the Embargo Work? A Look at the Record," *Business Week,* September 17, 1990; and Eugene Carlson, "Enterprise," *Wall Street Journal,* August 29, 1990, p. B2.

25. William P. Corbett, Jr., "A Wasted Opportunity: Shortcomings of the Caribbean Basin Initiative Approach to Development in the West Indies and Central America," *Law and Policy in International Business,* Vol. 23, No. 4, 1992, p. 959.

26. Guy de Jonquières and Carolina Southey, "U.S. Files Complaint Against EU Banana Regime," *Financial Times,* September 29, 1995, p. 4; Carolina Southey, "EU Banana Rules Backed as U.S. Exports Slip," *Financial Times,* September 11, 1995, p. 4.

27. Tony Walker, "China Warns Australia over Dalai Lama Visit," *Financial Times,* September 18, 1996, p. 1.

28. "GATT 'Turns Rice Trade Barriers Into Tariffs,'" *Financial Times,* August 4, 1995, p. 27.

29. Bernard Simon, "US Accuses Canada of 'Unfair' Cultural Barriers," *Financial Times,* January 26, 1996, p. 5.

30. Alan Riding, "French Cinema Circling the Wagons," *New York Times,* September 18, 1993, p. 12; and Andrew Jack, "French Films to Get State Funds for Dubbing," *Financial Times,* January 23, 1996, p. 2.

31. Guy de Jonquières, "Report Says EU's Tariffs No Longer Cost Effective," *Financial Times,* April 15, 1996, p. 3.

32. Philip Shenon, "In Hanoi, U.S. Goods Sold But Not by U.S." *New York Times,* October 3, 1993, p. A1.

33. Neil King, Jr. "Albania Attracts Foreign Business with Cheap Labor," *Wall Street Journal,* August 5, 1996, p. A8.

34. Ted Bardacke, "American Burma Boycotts Start to Bite," *Financial Times,* February 6, 1997, p. 10, referring to a study by G. Hufbauer, Jeffrey Schott, and Kimberly Ann Elliott, *Economic Sanctions Reconsidered* (Washington: Institute for International Economics, n.d.).

35. See, for example, Michael Littlejohns, "Hunger Killing 4,500 Children a Month in Iraq," *Financial Times,* October 29, 1996, p. 7.

36. "U.S. Seeks to Assuage Jordan by Changing Monitoring of Cargo," *Wall Street Journal,* April 26, 1994, p. A22.

37. Langdon Winner, "Kill the Whales?" *Technology Review,* Vol. 97, No. 8, November–December 1994, p. 74.

38. "Technology Dilemma Over Old Cultures," *South China Morning Post,* February 20, 1995, p. 13, quoting opinions of Newt Gingrich.

39. Tun Daim Zainuddin, "Trade and Environment Inerlinked," *Asian Business,* April 1996, p. 41.

40. Warner Rose, "Protection Imposes Special Economic and Political Costs," *Washington Economic Reports* [United States Information Agency], No. 87, September 14, 1994, pp. 1–2, referring to a report by Robert L. Hetzel in *Economic Quarterly,* Spring 1994; and "Guilty On All Counts," *Economist,* August 21, 1993, p. 81.

41. James Bovard, "Our Taxing Tariff Code— Let Them Eat Lobster!" *Wall Street Journal,* March 28, 1990, p. A12.

42. F. H. Rolf Seringhaus, "The Impact of Government Export Marketing Assistance," *International Marketing Review,* Vol. 3, No. 2, Summer 1986, offers a detailed discussion of the effects. Masaaki Kotabe and Michael R. Czinkota, "State Government Promotion of Manufacturing Exports: A Gap Analysis," *Journal of International Business Studies,* 4th quarter, 1992, pp. 637–657, shows activities at the state level within the United States.

43. "Subsidise, Apologise," *The Economist,* April 4, 1992, pp. 80–82; and Asra Q. Nomani and Bushan Bahree, "Aircraft Firms Move to Delay Issue at GATT," *Wall Street Journal,* December 10, 1993, p. A3+.

44. Clyde H. Farnsworth, "U.S. Will Tie Aid to Exports in Bid to Curb the Practice," *New York Times,* May 16, 1990, p. C1, referring to a study by the National Foreign Trade Council; Robert Letovsky, "The Export Finance Wars," *Columbia Journal of World Business,* Vol. 25, Nos. 1 & 2, Spring/Summer 1990, pp. 25–35; and Gerald F. Seib, "Export-Credit Programs, Useful Tool Abroad, Can Leave Taxpayers at Home Holding the Bag," *Wall Street Journal,* June 5, 1992, p. A12.

45. Guy de Jonquières, "Tied Aid Dinosaur Defies Extinction," *Financial Times,* September 17, 1996, p. 4, referring to OECD data.

46. David Pilling, "First, Bribe Your Customs Officer," *Financial Times,* October 31, 1996, p. 6. See also, Amy Borrus, Bruce Einhorn, and Pete Engardio, "Will a Customs Dragnet Snag Big U.S. Retailers?" *Business Week,* May 25, 1992, p. 46.

47. Shoba Purushothaman, "Customs Classification Codes Confuse Importers, Who Cry 'Trivial Pursuit,'" *Wall Street Journal,* September 27, 1988, p. 38; Eduardo Lachica, "U.S. Designates Suzuki Samurai as Truck Import," *Wall Street Journal,* January 5, 1989, p. A3; Douglas Harbrecht and James B. Treece, "Tread Marks on Detroit," *Business Week,* May 31, 1993, p. 30; and Judy Dempsey, "Car Importers Take Apart Customs Regulations," *Financial Times,* June 29–30, 1996, p. 2.

48. Eduardo Lachica, "Evasion of Duties on Chinese Imports Costs U.S. Up to $300 Million a Year," *Wall Street Journal,* May 8, 1992, p. A3; Jonathan M. Moses, "Chinese Agency Indicted by U.S. in Customs Case," *Wall Street Journal,* October 10, 1992, p. A15; and John Ridding, "U.S. Clashes With Hong Kong Over Textiles Exports," *Financial Times,* June 19, 1996, p. 4.

49. Andrew Pollack, "U.S. Sushi? Tokyo Frets. Sushi Boy Says Yes," *New York Times,* September 21, 1992, p. A5; Andrew Pollack, "Japan, Relenting, Plans to Allow Import of U.S.-Made Sushi," *New York Times,* October 4, 1992, p. 4; and "Sushi Boy Went Bankrupt, Japanese Sushi Importer Fails," *Wall Street Journal,* December 15, 1993, p. A10.

50. Eduardo Lachica, "Legal Swamp," *Wall Street Journal,* June 18, 1992, p. A1+; John P. Simpson, "Rules of Origin in Transition: A Changing Environment and Prospects for Reform," *Law and Policy in International Business,* Vol. 22, No. 4, 1991, pp. 665–672; and Janet Novack, "It's Like a Big Balloon," *Forbes,* July 20, 1992, p. 48.

51. Robert Moore, "Mr. Clinton, Please Check the Label," *Wall Street Journal,* March 22, 1993, p. A14.

52. "Label or Libel," *The Economist,* September 24, 1994, pp. 67–68.

53. Erika Morphy, "Gauging Tomorrow's Standards," *Export Today,* August 1995, pp. 48–53.

54. Caroline Southey, "Hormones Fuel a Meaty EU Row," *Financial Times,* September 7, 1995, p. 2; Caroline Southey, "'No Danger' in Hormones," *Financial Times,* November 2–3, 1995, p. 2; Guy de Jonquières, "EU Defends Ban on Beef Treated With Hormones," *Financial Times,* January 13–14, 1996, p. 3; and Alison Maitland, "EU Threat to Bar US Maize," *Financial Times,* September 4, 1996, p. 10.

55. Steve Glain, "From Sausages to Autos, U.S. Products Still Face Trade Hurdles in South Korea," *Wall Street Journal,* May 31, 1994, p. A11; Julia Preston, "UPS Cancels Some Mexican Services in a Setback to Trade Pact," *New York Times,* July 13, 1995, p. C2.

56. Michiyo Nakamoto, "EU to Take Action on Japanese Port Practices," *Financial Times,* October 16, 1996, p. 7.

57. "New Restrictions on World Trade," *Business Week,* July 19, 1982, p. 119.

58. Jean-François Hennart and Erin Anderson, "Countertrade and the Minimization of Transaction Costs: An Empirical Examination," *The Journal of Law, Economics, and Organization,* Vol. 9, No. 2, 1993, pp. 290–313.

59. "McDonnell and Partner Win $4 Billion British Copter Deal," *New York Times,* July 14, 1995, p. C5.

60. World Trade Organization, *Focus,* Newsletter No. 10, May 1996, pp. 6–8; Phedon Nicolaides, "Economic Aspects of

Services: Implications for a GATT Agreement," *Journal of World Trade*, Vol. 23, No. 1, February 1989, pp. 125–236.

61. Robert Neff and Douglas Harbrecht, "U.S. Insurers Start Making Noise in Japan," *Business Week*, March 1, 1993, p. 56.

62. For a long list of inconsistencies, see James Bovard, "A U.S. History of Trade Hypocrisy," *Wall Street Journal*, March 8, 1994, p. A14.

63. Salil S. Pitroda, "From GATT to WTO: The Institutionalization of World Trade," *Harvard International Review*, Vol. XVII, No. 2, Spring 1995, pp. 46–57+.

64. "'Most Favored Nation' Bows to a More Favored Phrase," *Wall Street Journal*, September 12, 1996, p. A16.

65. Gary C. Hufbauer, "Should Unconditional MFN Be Revised, Retired, or Recast?" in *Issues in World Trade Policy*, R. H. Snape, ed. (New York: St. Martin's, 1986), pp. 32–55; and Frieder Roessler, "The Scope, Limits and Function of the GATT Legal System," *The World Economy*, Vol. 8, No. 4, September 1985, pp. 287–298.

66. Clyde H. Farnsworth, "U.S., Despite Dispute, Will Go to Trade Talks," *New York Times*, November 14, 1990, p. C1+; and Paul Magnusson, "The GATT Talks: Forget the Darn Deadline," *Business Week*, November 19, 1990, p. 51.

67. The following discussion is taken from "The Shape of the Accord," *New York Times*, December 15, 1993, p. C18; and "The Uruguay Round's Key Result," *Wall Street Journal*, December 15, 1993, p. A6.

68. Pitroda, loc. cit.

69. World Trade Organization, *Focus*, Newsletter, No. 8, January–February 1996, shows trade disputes as of March 5, 1996. Of the 18 in process, 10 were initiated by developing countries; Frances Williams, "Antagonists Queue for WTO Judgement," *Financial Times*, August 8, 1996, p. 6, shows 51 disputes during WTO's first year and a half.

70. Eduardo Lachica, "U.S. May Be Losing Its Trade-Bully Status," *Wall Street Journal*, October 13, 1995, p. A11.

71. Bhushan Bahree, "WTO's Earlier Progress on Trade May Hit Wall at Next Meeting," *Wall Street Journal*, September 26, 1996, p. A4, quoting Renato Ruggiero.

72. Helene Cooper and Bhushan Bahree, "Nations Agree to Drop Computer Tariffs," *Wall Street Journal*, December 13, 1996, p. 2A.

73. For a discussion on the protectionist activities of exporters, see Nicholas C. Williamson, Stephen R. Lucas, Benton E. Miles, and Grace E. Kissling, "Protectionist American Businesspeople and Their Firms," *Management International Review*, Vol. 36, No. 2, 1996, pp. 167–182.

74. Frances Williams, "WTO Sets Up Last Part of Legal Framework," *Financial Times*, November 29, 1995, p. 5.

75. For a discussion of changes in MNEs' lobbying efforts for protectionism, see Giles Merrill, "Coping with the 'New Protectionism': How Companies Are Learning to Love It," *International Management*, Vol. 41, No. 9, September 1986, pp. 20–26.

76. Eugene Salorio, "Trade Barriers and Corporate Strategies: Why Some Firms Oppose Import Protection for Their Own Industry," unpublished DBA dissertation, Harvard University, 1991.

77. Williams, op. cit.

78. Eduardo Lachica, "U.S., 26 Other Nations to Control Exports That Could Be Used in Nuclear Bombs," *Wall Street Journal*, April 3, 1992, p. 4; and Karen Elliott House, "We Need a Foreign Policy President," *Wall Street Journal*, November 3, 1992, p. A14.

79. Keith Schneider, "Balancing Nature's Claims and International Free Trade," *New York Times*, January 19, 1992, p. E5.

80. Timothy Noah, "Environmental Groups Say Deal Poses Threats," *Wall Street Journal*, December 16, 1993, p. A12.

81. Data for the case were taken from Alan Burchardt, "Containing Cuba" (graphic), *Indiana Daily Student* (Indiana University student newspaper, Bloomington, Indiana), August 1, 1996, p. 4; Mark Heinzl, "Canadian Will Take His Chances In Cuba," *Wall Street Journal*, July 29, 1996, p. A9; Guy de Jonquières, Stephen Fidler, and Nancy Dunne, "EU Unites Over US Measures Against Cuba," *Financial Times*, July 18, 1996, p. 6; Pascal Fletcher, "Cuban Economy 'Will Survive U.S. Sanctions,'" *Financial Times*, July 18, 1996, p. 6; Julie Wolf and Brian Coleman, "U.S. Bid to Punish Foreign Companies Trading With Cuba Gets EU Challenge," *Wall Street Journal*, July 31, 1996, p. A11; Bernard Simon, Daniel Dombey, and David White, "Cuba Embargoes Spark Protests," *Financial Times*, March 2–3, 1996, p. 3; Carla Anne Robbins and Jose de Cordoba, "Clinton Puts Cuba Lawsuits on Hold," *Wall Street Journal*, July 17, 1996, p. A10; Pascal Fletcher, "US Anti-Cuba Law Feeds Businessmen's Paranoia," *Financial Times*, July 2, 1996, p. 5; Bernard Simon and Guy de Jonquières, "Canada Retaliates Against US Law," *Financial Times*, June 18, 1996, p. 6; Pascal Fletcher, "Cuba Confident of Growth Despite US Legislation," *Financial Times*, June 18, 1996, p. 6; Lionel Barber, "Europe Vows to Act on US Anti-Cuba Law," *Financial Times*, July 16, 1996, p. 1; "The Last Caudillo," Irving Louis Horowitz and Jaime Suchlicki, "Repression Forever?" and John Train, "The Demoralized Island," *Freedom Review*, Vol. 27, No. 2, March–April 1996, pp. 18–25; Wayne S. Smith, "Cuba's Long Reform," *Foreign Affairs*, March 1996, p. 99+. For Internet information on the U.S. embargo on Cuba see: http://members.aol.com/USLAMAF/embargoinfo.html#anchor282 66. For Internet information on Cuban demographics and commerce, see: http://www.jmbco.com/cubafact.htm#SEC4

Chapter 7

Economic Integration and Cooperative Agreements

Marrying is easy, but housekeeping is hard.
—German Proverb

Objectives	• To define different forms of economic cooperation on a regional and global basis
	• To describe the static and dynamic effects and the trade creation and diversion dimensions of economic integration
	• To compare different types of regional economic integration, such as the European Union (EU), the North American Free Trade Agreement (NAFTA), and Asia-Pacific Economic Cooperation (APEC)
	• To describe the rationale for commodity agreements
	• To discuss other bilateral and multilateral treaties affecting international business

Case
Ford in Europe[1]

In 1995 Ford Motor Company was the world's second largest automaker in revenues, with the top five being General Motors (United States), Ford Motor (United States), Toyota Motor (Japan), Daimler-Benz (Germany), and Nissan Motor (Japan). (See Ford's home page for more information about Ford, including its history and its operations around the world <http:www.ford.com>.) In Europe, Ford was in fourth place with an 11.9 percent market share (Table 7.1).

Ford is composed of two major divisions: automotive and financial services. In the automotive division, Ford's operating income had begun to decline in 1989, going from a high of $6.612 billion in 1988 to a low of $3.769 billion in 1991. Even though Ford was still suffering a loss in 1992, it became profitable again in 1993, and maintained a profitable position through 1995, although profits were actually lower in 1995 than they were in 1994. Of Ford's revenues, 33.9 percent were derived from foreign sales, and 71 percent of those were in Europe. However, Ford management was not satisfied with its ability to remain competitive, given the global and technological competition it was facing, so it looked at what it could do to prepare for the future.

After the EEC [the European Economic Community, later known as the European Community (EC) and, since November 1, 1993, the European Union (EU)] was organized in 1957, many U.S. MNEs had to change their method of serving European markets. For example, some companies began producing in Europe rather than serving that market through exports, either because they feared new tariff barriers would preclude continued sales or because they thought the enlarged market would enable them to achieve the economies of scale needed for efficient production there. Some companies that were already producing in Europe began to consolidate their operations on a regional basis rather than continuing to separate them on a multidomestic basis. Another approach was to establish a regional or global headquarters for a particular line of products. Finally, companies could centralize certain functions, such as marketing, research, or sales, into a single organization.

As noted on Ford's home page on the World Wide Web, the company's first European sales branch was opened in France in 1908, with a vehicle assembly operation five years later, and a national company in 1916. The first regional company and assembly plant outside North America was established in Britain in 1911. However, Ford sold its first car in the United Kingdom in 1903, only six months after Ford was founded. A branch was opened in 1909, followed by the assembly plant in 1911. Ford did not begin operations in Germany until 1925, but an assembly plant was established only a year later.

During the next several decades, Ford's European operations operated as separate subsidiaries that reported to U.S. headquarters but did not coordinate their policies in any meaningful way. This occurred because individual countries had different environments and unique tariff and nontariff barriers to trade. Ford noted in its 1960 *Annual Report,*

> The historical patterns of trade and commerce among nations are undergoing significant changes. Trade groupings, such as the European Economic Community and the European Free Trade Association, are being established. Similar groupings are being considered in Latin America and by some of the African countries. Further changes in trade patterns

Table 7.1

Western European Automobile Market Share of New Car Sales (as a percentage), by Company, 1991–1995

Although Volkswagen is the leader of the European automobile market in terms of market share, two U.S. companies—GM and Ford—have a quarter of the market.

Company	Year				
	1991	1992	1993	1994	1995
Volkswagen	16.4%	17.5%	16.1%	15.8%	16.8%
General Motors	12.1%	12.4%	13.0%	13.1%	13.1%
PSA	12.1%	12.2%	12.2%	12.8%	12.0%
Ford	11.9%	11.3%	11.5%	11.8%	11.9%
Renault	10.0%	10.6%	10.5%	11.0%	11.1%
Fiat	12.8%	11.9%	10.3%	10.8%	10.3%

Source: Automotive News, May 27, 1996, p. 36.

have been brought about in a number of countries by government regulations that make it advantageous to manufacture locally.

The Company and its subsidiaries are responding to these trends, which bear promise of increasing competition for world automobile markets, by exploring opportunities to strengthen and to expand their international operations.

The changing environment prompted Ford to realize it could consider Europe to be one common market rather than a collection of individual markets. In 1967, Ford changed its management structure to include its European operations under one umbrella organization known as Ford Europe Incorporated. This follows the regional approach described above. Its two large U.K. and German manufacturing centers remained an important dimension of the new strategy, but they were no longer considered separate, independently operating companies. Despite nationalistic tendencies on the part of host-country management, Ford decided that, from the company's perspective, it was best to obliterate national boundaries. As the German managing director noted,

> The pooling of the two companies cut the engineering bill in half for each company, provided economies of scale, with double the volume in terms of purchase— commonization of purchase, common components—and provided the financial resources for a good product program at a really good price that we could still make money on.

Ford began designing and assembling similar automobiles throughout Europe, rather than engineering separate cars in each market, a strategy that resulted in such models as the Escort, the Capri, and the Fiesta. It also designed common components to be used in Ford automobiles. Acknowledging the importance of market size in developing this plan, one

Ford executive commented, "Neither the British nor the German company could have come up with the Capri separately, tooled it separately. Only with the whole volume of Europe in prospect did the Capri become a viable product development program."

In the mid-1980s, Ford continued its European expansion. It explored the possibility of merging its European unit with Fiat in order to allow Ford's strength in northern Europe to combine with Fiat's strength in southern Europe. However, each company was so strong and so convinced of its need to control the merged operation that the proposed merger never occurred. Ford wanted to maintain control over its global strategy, which was being developed in the United States. Fiat was controlled by the Agnelli family in Italy, and loss of control to a foreign company, especially from a country not in the EC, would have been explosive politically. Also, Fiat's management objected to being subordinate to Ford's management.

As part of Ford's evolving European strategy, its management decided to design automobiles in Germany and the United Kingdom (Ford's largest European market) and manufacture them in Belgium, Germany, Spain, and the United Kingdom. The company also entered into production and product-development agreements with other automakers such as Nissan and Volkswagen to serve the European market.

Ford's European strategy for the 1990s was being significantly influenced by two factors: Euro-recession and Japanese competition. As this chapter will discuss, a major advantage of economic integration is market expansion. However, even the large market of the EC suffered economically in the early 1990s. In the fall of 1992, Europe's slowdown turned into a full-fledged recession, and in 1993, the Western European market contracted even further. Ford not only saw sales and profits fall; it also lost market share. Further, the economic slowdown forced automakers such as Ford to lay off workers and cut back capital expenditures.

The second major influence is Japanese competition. European automakers are significantly less efficient than their American and Japanese counterparts. For example, German automakers require about 40 hours of labor to assemble a car, compared with about 30 hours for other European manufacturers and about 20 hours in Japan. Ford has upgraded its quality and lowered the amount of time it takes to manufacture a car. An MIT study determined that a Ford plant in Germany is one of the most efficient non-Japanese plants in the world; workers need just under 19 hours to build a new car, compared with 15 hours for a similar Japanese car.

The Europeans have effectively kept the Japanese out of their market. However, the drive to a more unified European market is opening up Europe to the Japanese. They will be allowed open access to the EU market by 1999. To jump European trade barriers, the Japanese have established a number of plants in Europe—primarily in the United Kingdom—to serve that market. Ford and other European automakers fear the increased access to the European market by the end this decade will give the Japanese an estimated 15 percent of the market. The Europeans are already negotiating with the Japanese to cut back on exports to Europe, and many companies want to count Japanese transplant automobiles (Japanese automobiles manufactured in Europe) as part of the allowable Japanese market share.

In 1995, Ford restructured the company and merged the North American Automotive Operations and European Automotive Operations into a single organization, Ford Automotive Operations. The major reason for the restructuring was to cut costs and be more competitive. As stated in the 1994 annual report, "We can't allow human and financial resources to be wasted duplicating vehicle platforms, powertrains and other basic components that serve nearly identical customer needs in different markets." In its 1995 annual report, Ford announced that it was reducing the number of engine and transmission combinations used worldwide and the number of basic vehicle platforms. However, Ford still intends to produce cars that suit local tastes as well as develop regional vehicles, such as the Ford Transit Van in Europe.

In addition, the regional profit centers were replaced with a product line focus. Five vehicle centers have been established within Ford Automotive Operations, "each with responsibility for worldwide development of the cars or trucks assigned to them." Four of the centers were established in North America and one in Europe. Europe will take responsibility for the development of small and mid-size cars. As part of this reorganization, 500 managers were transferred from Europe to North America or from North America to Europe.

In addition, Ford is designing cars to operate in several geographical areas, as mentioned above. An example is the Mondeo, which was designed through a collaboration of efforts between Europe and North America and launched in March 1993. North American versions of the car are the Ford Contour and Mercury Mystique, assembled in Kansas City and Cuautitlan, Mexico. The Mondeo is sold in 52 countries. The addition of the Contour and Mystique raises the number of countries selling those particular models to 78, whereas the Ford Fiesta is sold in 42 world markets. Europe provides significant market opportunity for Ford. The reduction of barriers and integration of the different country markets in Europe has caused Ford to shift its strategy from multidomestic to regional. However, changes in Ford's organizational structure will force it to integrate its European region more closely with its other regions around the world, but more especially with the United States. The merging of the North American and European Automotive divisions is the first step in that process. What will the future bring to Ford Europe?

Introduction

The Great Depression plunged the world into a period of isolation, trade protectionism, and economic chaos. In the mid- to late-1940s, countries decided greater cooperation was needed to help them emerge from the wreckage of World War II. The spirit of cooperation was designed to promote economic growth and stability. This chapter discusses some of the important forms of such cooperation, such as regional economic integration and commodity agreements.

Why do you need to understand the nature of these arrangements? Regional trading groups are an important influence on MNEs' strategy, as Ford learned. They can define the size of the regional market and the rules under which companies must operate. Companies in the initial stages of foreign expansion must be aware of the regional groups that encompass countries targeted for manufacturing locations or market opportunities. As companies proceed toward greater multinationalism, they find they must change their organizational structure and operating strategies to take advantage of regional trading groups. As noted in the opening case, Ford first shifted from a multidomestic to a regional strategy, with the establishment of Ford Europe Incorporated in 1967, soon after the formation of the EEC. However, global competitive pressures forced it to change again in 1995 by combining the North American and European Operations and giving Ford Europe the mandate to develop small and mid-size cars for the entire world. As the EU opens its markets to greater competition in 1999, auto companies, including Ford, need to be more cost-effective and competitive in a global environment. This chapter explains how such regional groups affect structure and strategy. More attention will be focused on the EU because of its size, its importance to the entire European region, and the comprehensiveness of its programs. Because it is moving far beyond the elimination of tariffs, it is a model for other regional groups to watch closely.

There are other forms of economic cooperation that cross national boundaries, such as commodity agreements. We will discuss those agreements briefly at the end of the chapter. In addition, we will discuss the United Nations. There are a number of cross-national organizations, such as the World Bank and the International Monetary Fund, and cross-national agreements, such as the Universal Copyright Convention, that are discussed in other chapters. However, the UN is an organization that crosses many different topical areas, so it will be discussed briefly in this chapter. The most important thing is to understand how these organizations and agreements affect company strategy.

Regional Economic Integration

Economic integration abolishes cross-national economic discrimination.

In the 1950s and 1960s, regional economic integration gained significant momentum. Economic integration involves the organizing of individual countries into groups that then abolish restrictions on the trade of goods and services with member countries and also may engage in other activities that promote their citizens' welfare.

Geographical proximity is an important reason for economic integration.

When we consider some of the major examples of economic integration, such as the European Union (EU) and the North American Free Trade Agreement (NAFTA), the concept of geographical proximity stands out. Neighboring countries tend to become involved in integrative activities for several reasons:

- The distances to be traversed between such countries are shorter.
- Consumers' tastes are more likely to be similar, and distribution channels can be more easily established in adjacent economies.
- Neighboring countries may have a common history, awareness of common interests, and so forth and may be more willing to coordinate their policies.[2]

Also important are ideological and historical similarities. For example, Cuba, because of its communist political and economic philosophy, was a member of the former COMECON (the Council for Mutual Economic Assistance), an association of communist countries that was disbanded when the former Soviet Union broke up.

There are four basic types of economic integration:

Major types of economic integration:
• Free-trade area—no internal tariff
• Customs union—common external tariffs
• Common market—factor mobility
• Complete economic integration

1. *Free-trade area (FTA).* Tariffs are abolished among FTA members, but each member maintains its own external tariff against non-FTA countries. An example of this level of economic integration is NAFTA.

2. *Customs union.* Levying a common external tariff is combined with the abolition of all internal tariffs. When the EEC was established, member countries decided to establish a customs union as an intermediate step toward more complete integration. When the EU negotiates at the World Trade Organization (WTO), it does so as a regional bloc, not as individual countries. In contrast, Canada, the United States, and Mexico negotiate separately at the WTO, since they are part of a free-trade area rather than a customs union.

3. *Common market.* All the characteristics of a customs union are combined with the abolition of restrictions on mobility of production factors such as labor and capital.

4. *Complete economic integration.* Fiscal and monetary policies are unified to create even greater economic harmonization.[3] This level also implies a degree of political integration. Complete economic integration is clearly the direction in which the EU is moving.

The Effects of Integration

Regional integration has political, social, and economic effects.

Regional integration has social, political, and economic effects. For example, in the social sense Canadians did not want to include liberalization of trade and investment in the film, television, and print media in the U.S.-Canada FTA because some feared Canadian culture would be undermined by U.S. culture as transmitted through movies, TV programs, and magazines. The EU and its predecessors have worked diligently to improve the social conditions of individuals within member countries. Laws relative to the environment and relationships between workers and employers are part of the more complete unification of Europe.

From a political standpoint, integration results in a partial loss of sovereignty. This concept is discussed in the Countervailing Forces section of this chapter.

With trade creation, resources shift from the least- to the most-efficient producers.

The economic aspects of integration dominate the concerns of MNEs. As noted in Chapter 6, the imposition of tariff and nontariff barriers disrupts the free flow of goods and therefore affects resource allocation. Economic integration is designed to reduce or eliminate those barriers. It produces both static and dynamic effects. Static effects result when trade barriers are reduced, giving consumers access to more new goods. As consumers purchase goods having the best quality and lowest prices, resources shift from the least efficient to the most efficient producers. This is the trade-creation aspect of integration. Production shifts from one country to another for reasons of comparative advantage, allowing consumers access to more goods at a lower price than would have been possible without integration. Companies that are protected in their domestic markets face real problems when the barriers are eliminated and they attempt to compete with more efficient producers.

With trade diversion, discrimination against outside producers diverts trade to less-efficient producers within the country or group.

Integration also may lead to trade diversion because it results in discrimination against outside producers. For example, assume U.S. companies are importing the same product from Mexico and Taiwan. If the United States enters into an FTA with Mexico but not with Taiwan, some trade will be diverted from Taiwan to Mexico to take advantage of the elimination of tariffs between Mexico and the United States. This does not mean, however, that Mexican products are any better or cheaper (in the absence of integration) than the Taiwanese goods are.

One dynamic effect of integration is that as markets grow, companies achieve economies of scale.

Dynamic effects of integration are changes in total consumption and in internal and external efficiencies that result from market growth. Reduction of trade barriers automatically increases total demand. As resources shift to the more efficient producers, these companies are able to expand output to take advantage of the larger market, which results in trade creation. This dynamic change in market size allows companies to produce goods more cheaply, since the fixed costs of production can be spread out over more units.

Efficiency increases because of competition.

Another important dynamic effect is the increase in efficiency due to increased competition. Many MNEs in Europe have attempted to grow through mergers and acquisitions in order to achieve the size necessary to compete in the larger market. For example, Ford entered into design and production agreements with other manufacturers in order to be more competitive in the European environment.

Regionalism and the Multilateral Trading System

As noted in Chapter 6, the WTO is a global response to trade barriers. When the WTO's predecessor, the General Agreement on Tariffs and Trade (GATT), was established, there were few bilateral or multilateral trading arrangements in the world. However, most of the members of the WTO now belong to one or more regional trading arrangements. Between 1948 when GATT was established and early 1997, seventy-six free-trade areas or customs unions had been established or modified, of which more than half have come in the 1990s. Most arrangements were limited in scope and focused primarily on preferential tariffs.

Concerns with regional integration
• too much diversion, too little creation
• may take precedence over multilateralism (the WTO)

Now the scope of regional integration is increasing. The concern with regional integration is that there may be more trade diversion than trade creation taking place, and regional harmonization may take the place of the multilateral trading system of the WTO. In fact, the latter issue might be the most important issue in the minds of the opponents of regional integration.[4]

The Director-General of the WTO is concerned with the conflict between liberalization, which he feels the WTO offers, and protectionism at whatever level, which he believes regional integration offers. Thus he promotes open regionalism of two forms:

Advantages of regionalism
• **tackles issues not covered by WTO**
• **fewer countries, easier, more flexible**
• **locks in trade liberalism**

1. Regionalism that ensures that rules will be consistent with the basic legal requirements of the WTO.
2. Regionalism that results in the gradual elimination of internal tariffs to trade that would be implemented at more or less the same rate and on the same timetable as the lowering of barriers to nonmembers. This is the approach being favored by Asia-Pacific Economic Cooperation (APEC) or the Southern Common Market (MERCOSUR) and points to gradual convergence of regionalism and multilateralism.[5]

Many feel that regionalism can actually help the WTO accomplish its goals in one or more of the following three ways:

1. Regionalism can lead to the liberalization of issues not covered by the WTO.
2. Regionalism, given that it typically involves fewer countries with more similar conditions and objectives, is more flexible.
3. Regional deals lock in liberalization, especially in developing countries.[6]

Regional integration
• **by type—free trade area, customs union, common market**
• **by location**
• **offers location-specific advantages to foreign investors**

Major Regional Trading Groups

There are two ways to look at different trading groups: by location and by type. There are major trading groups in every region of the world. It is impossible to cover every group in every region, so we will cover a few of the major groups in each region. However, it is important to understand that each regional group fits into one of the types defined above: free trade area, customs union, or common market. Remember, however, that a customs union is also a free trade area, and a common market is also a free trade area and customs union. In addition, these examples are representations of the hundreds of bilateral and multilateral regional groups that exist.

The regional trading groups we will discuss are classified as follows:

1. Free-Trade Area—the European Free Trade Association, the Central European Free Trade Agreement, the North American Free Trade Agreement, APEC, ASEAN, and the Asian Free Trade Area.
2. Customs Union—MERCOSUR.
3. Common Market—the Caribbean Community and Common Market, the Central American Common Market, the Andean Group, and the European Union.

Each regional group, whether it be in Africa, Asia, Europe, or Latin America, is important to the member countries. But companies look at regional economic integration from the standpoint of location-specific advantage—what does the regional group have to offer in terms of a market, a source of raw materials, or a production location? The larger and richer the new market, the more likely it is to attract the attention of the major investor countries in the world.

The European Union

The OEEC was the organization of European countries established to facilitate the implementation of the Marshall Plan.

European Evolution to Integration

World War II left in its wake economic as well as human destruction throughout Europe. To help rebuild Europe, the U.S. Congress passed the Marshall Plan, a $13-billion aid package. The sixteen-country Organization for European Economic Cooperation (OEEC) was established to facilitate utilization of the aid as well as to improve currency stability, combine economic strengths, and improve trade relations. As early as 1943, it had been noted that "European countries are too small to give their peoples the prosperity made attainable by modern conditions. They need wider markets."[7] However, the OEEC did not appear strong enough to provide the necessary economic growth. Thus further efforts at cooperation were initiated. One major school of thought held that a common market should be developed to:

- Result in the elimination of all restrictions to the free flow of goods, capital, and persons
- Allow for the harmonization of economic policies
- Create a common external tariff

Consequently, in March 1957, the European Economic Community (EEC) was established via the Treaty of Rome. Its members were Belgium, France, Italy, Luxembourg, the Netherlands, and West Germany (now Germany since the reunification with East Germany) (see Map 7.1). It expanded its membership to include Denmark, Ireland, and the United Kingdom (in 1973); Greece (in 1981); Portugal and Spain (in 1986); and Austria, Finland, and Sweden in 1995. It is considering other countries as members. The name of the EEC has changed over time to reflect even closer integration. During the 1980s, the EEC gave way to the European Community (EC), reflecting a broader sense of cooperation than merely economic. On November 1, 1993, the EC gave way to the European Union (EU) to reflect the closer cooperation resulting from the adoption of the Maastricht Treaty, which will be discussed later in this section.

European Free Trade Association

A second major school of thought rejected the notion of total European integration and favored instead a free-trade area, which would eliminate all restrictions on the

Map 7.1
European Trade and Economic Integration
Although the EU remains the dominant trading bloc in Europe, the European Free Trade Association and Central European Free Trade Association are other regional trading blocs designed to promote free trade.

EFTA is a free-trade area that does not follow the total integration approach embraced by the EU.

free flow of industrial goods among member countries, while permitting each country to retain its own external tariff structure. This approach provides the benefits of free trade among members but allows each member to pursue its own economic objectives with nonmember countries. It was especially beneficial for the United Kingdom, which had favorable trade relationships with Commonwealth countries and considered a common external tariff too restrictive of national sovereignty.

Following this line of thought, the Stockholm Convention of May 1960 created the European Free Trade Association (EFTA), which comprised seven OEEC countries that were not in the EEC: Austria, Denmark, Norway, Portugal, Sweden, Switzerland, and the United Kingdom (see Map 7.1). Iceland joined in 1970; Finland, an associate member since 1961, became a full member in 1986; and Liechtenstein joined as a full member in 1991. Denmark (in 1983), the United Kingdom (in 1983), and Portugal (in 1986) left EFTA to become full members of the EC. As of the end of 1996, EFTA was composed of Iceland, Liechtenstein, Norway, and Switzerland. By 1991, tariffs or import duties had been removed on all imports except agricultural products. In addition, a number of bilateral agreements had been signed between EFTA and other countries, primarily in Eastern Europe. The growing strength of the EU and its widening scope of integration are making it difficult for EFTA members to maintain their separate status outside of the EU. More than 50 percent of EFTA's trade is with EU countries, and EFTA can trade with EU members duty-free. However, Norway and Switzerland have both rejected membership in the EU. Norway was concerned about losing control of its fishing industry and giving away too many fishing rights to other EU countries such as Portugal in order to get better access to EU markets, so it rejected membership in the EU,

EFTA countries trade more extensively with the EU than with each other.

even though it retained membership in the EEA. Swiss citizens voted down participation in the European Economic Area and the EU because of its neutrality stance. Since the EU is working on common foreign and defense policies, Switzerland would have to accept those policies in order to join the EU.

Major EU Programs

The EEC was initially interested in the following broad categories of activity:

The EEC was intended to lead to a free flow of resources, a harmonization of policies, and a common external tariff.

- The free movement of goods through the elimination of tariff barriers
- The free movement of people, services, and capital
- The establishment of a common transportation policy

As noted in Table 7.2, the first reduction in internal tariffs occurred in 1959, and all internal tariffs had been eliminated by 1968.

CAP was established to stabilize earnings to producers and provide food for consumers.

In 1962, the Common Agricultural Policy (CAP) was established as an important element of its overall economic policy. CAP's objectives were to increase farm productivity, establish a fair standard of living for farmers, stabilize markets, ensure food security, and set reasonable consumer prices.[8] A series of tariffs and price supports were set up to achieve these objectives and to protect agricultural goods from foreign competition. The protection was intended to avoid excessive price (and therefore income) fluctuations; also the EEC believed world market prices reflected intervention by other governments.

CAP has created trade tensions between the EU countries and others, especially the United States.

CAP has affected both member and nonmember consumers and producers. Much of the EU's current budget is used to pay price supports (subsidies) to farmers. These subsidies are a significant tax burden to consumers. They also have allowed EU farmers to be competitive in world markets. Nonmember countries have found it difficult to sell to EU consumers products for which subsidies make EU farmers more competitive. Nonmembers also have had trouble competing with subsidized EU exports.[9] These subsidies have been a major source of contention in GATT negotiations, especially in the Uruguay Round (discussed in Chapter 6).

The EU's Organizational Structure

In 1967, the European Coal and Steel Community, the European Economic Community, and the European Atomic Energy Community were combined into a common institution. Informally, the group was called the European Community. Initially, the organizational structure included the Commission, the Parliament, the Council of Ministers, and the Court of Justice. It was intended that "the Commission would propose, the Parliament would advise, the Council of Ministers would decide and the Court of Justice would interpret."[10] Since that time, new institutions, such as the Court of Auditors, and other bodies, such as the European Investment Bank, the Committee of the Regions, the Economic and Social Committee, and an Ombudsman, have been added. In addition, the functions of the original

Table 7.2
European Union Milestones
From its inception in 1957, the EU has been moving toward complete economic integration.

1957	Treaty of Rome establishing the European Economic Community (EEC), or Common Market, signed. Original members were Belgium, France, Italy, Luxembourg, the Netherlands, and West Germany (effective 1/1/58).
1959	First reduction in internal tariffs.
1962	Common Agricultural Policy (CAP) established.
1967	Agreement reached on value-added tax (VAT) system; EEC changes name to European Community (EC).
1968	All internal tariffs eliminated and a common external tariff imposed.
1973	Denmark, Ireland, and the United Kingdom become members (January 1).
1979	European Parliament directly elected for the first time.
1979	European Monetary System comes into effect.
1981	Greece becomes a member (January 1).
1985	Lord Cockfield presents a white paper to the European Commission outlining 300 steps to eliminate all remaining barriers to internal trade in goods and services. This is endorsed by the member countries and becomes EC policy.
1986	Spain and Portugal become members (January 1).
1987	Single European Act (SEA) comes into effect, improving decision-making procedures and increasing the role of the European Parliament.
1992	Target date (December 31) for eliminating all trade barriers within the European Community.
1993	Treaty of Maastricht adopted by member countries (November 1); EC becomes the European Union (EU).
1995	Austria, Finland, and Sweden join the EU (January 1).
1999	Target year for the establishment of a monetary union and a common currency (the Euro).

Sources: Ernst & Whinney, *Europe 1992: The Single Market,* p. 6; *The Europa World Year Book,* 1995, Volume I (London: Europa Publications Limited, 1995), p. 143.

institutions have changed. Each of the institutions is described in detail on the EU's home page on the Internet.

The Commission initiates proposals for legislation, guards the treaties, and manages and executes Union policies.

European Commission   The Commission is composed of twenty men and women who provide the political leadership and direction of the EU. The Commission's major responsibilities are divided into three categories: initiating proposals for legislation, watching over the Union's treaties, and managing and executing Union policies and international trade relationships.[11] The members of the Commission must operate independently of their national governments and act only in the interests of the EU. The work of the Commission is carried out by the different Directorate-General offices. There are twenty-four different DG offices, each headed by a Director-General, and each with a different mission. Examples of a few of the DG's are External Relations (DG I), Competition (DG IV), and Customs and Indirect Taxation (DG XI). More specifically, DG I is responsible for international trade policy (such as the EU's trade policy with respect to the WTO), external political and economic relations with other regional trade groups such as NAFTA and APEC, and external relations in the area of nuclear energy.

The European Parliament The Parliament has become significantly stronger since its inception. Its members are directly elected by the people of the EU, and its responsibilities have been widened through the Single European Act and Treaty of the European Union of 1993. The three major responsibilities of the Parliament are legislative power, power over the budget, and supervision of executive decisions.

The Parliament has legislative power, power over the budget, and supervision of executive decisions.

Community legislation is presented to Parliament by the Commission, and Parliament must approve the legislation before it can be submitted to the Council for adoption. Parliament may approve legislation, amend it, or reject it outright. Parliament also approves the EU's budget each year and monitors spending.[12]

Council of the European Union The Council is also known as the Council of Ministers, which is composed of different ministers of the member countries. For example, when issues concerning fishing are to be discussed, the Ministers of Fishing from the different EU States come together. The Council has a tremendous amount of authority, because it can adopt Commission-proposed legislation, amend it, or ignore it. The Council has the final say in legislative matters in cooperation with Parliament.

The Council, in cooperation with Parliament, has final say over legislation.

The voting process in the Council is relatively complex. Instead of one country, one vote, the votes are allocated on the basis of population size. Germany, France, Italy, and the United Kingdom are allotted ten votes each; Spain, eight votes; Belgium, Greece, Netherlands and Portugal, five votes each; Austria and Sweden, four votes each; Ireland, Denmark and Finland, three votes each; and Luxembourg, two votes. As noted on the EU home page on the Internet, the vast majority of cases in the Council are decided by a qualified majority vote of sixty-two votes. In other cases, the qualified majority must also be cast by at least ten Member States. The more difficult areas of Common Foreign and Security Policy and cooperation in the fields of Justice and Home Affairs require unanimity in most cases.

At least twice a year, the heads of state and goverment of each member country meet as the European Council or European Summit. The European Council is important, because it sets priorities, gives political direction, and resolves issues that cannot be resolved by the Council of Ministers.[13]

The Court of Justice of the European Communities The Court of Justice ensures consistent interpretation and application of EU treaties. Cases may be

*The Court of Justice inter-
prets and applies Union
treaties.*

brought to the Court by member states, Community institutions, or individuals and companies. The Court of Justice is an appeals court for individuals, firms, and organizations fined by the Commission for infringing Treaty Law.[14]

The Single European Market

As Table 7.3 shows, in 1994 the EU had 370.2 million people and the world's second largest combined GNP, making it a formidable economic bloc. However, the early part of the 1980s was a difficult time for the EC (as it was then known). From 1970 to 1975, the EC's GDP averaged 2.7 percent growth per year, but this figure dropped to approximately 1.4 percent annually from 1980 through 1985. In contrast, the United States recorded 2.2 percent and 2.5 percent growth rates for those periods, respectively, and Japan experienced rates of 7.6 percent and 3.8 percent, respectively.[15] It was evident the EC needed more than the elimination of tariffs to achieve economic growth. A variety of nontariff barriers was keeping it from being a true common market and from enjoying the benefits of expanded market size.

*Europe 1992 was aimed at
the elimination of the
remaining barriers to the
free transfer of goods, services, and capital.*

As a result of these and other issues, the president of the Commission decided to pursue a strategy of eliminating the remaining barriers to a free and open Europe. Consequently, a white paper issued in 1985 identified 282 proposals that needed to be enacted to complete an internal market. The target date for implementation of the proposals was December 31, 1992, giving rise to the use of the phrase "Europe 1992" to refer to the elimination of the remaining barriers to trade and investment among EC members.

Once the proposals, called directives, were approved by the EC bureaucracy, they were turned over to the members' governments for passage into each

Table 7.3
Comparative Data on Five Major Trade Groups, 1994

	Population (thousands)	GDP (millions U.S. $)	Per Capita GDP (U.S. $)
APEC	2,124,634	13,474,592	6,342
ASEAN	409,909	513,073	1,252
EC	370,221	7,577,396	20,467
NAFTA	381,508	7,675,995	20,120
MERCOSUR	201,320	834,297	4,144

The countries that form the above groups are as follows:
APEC: Australia, Brunei, Canada, Chile, China, Hong Kong, Indonesia, Japan, Korea, Rep., Malaysia, Mexico, New Zealand, Papua New Guinea, Philippines, Singapore, Taiwan, Thailand, and the United States
ASEAN: Brunei, Indonesia, Malaysia, Philippines, Singapore, Thailand, and Vietnam
EU: Austria, Belgium, Denmark, France, Finland, Germany, Greece, Ireland, Italy, Luxembourg, Netherlands, Portugal, Spain, Sweden, and the United Kingdom
NAFTA: Canada, Mexico, and the United States
MERCOSUR: Argentina, Brazil, Uruguay, and Paraguay

Source: The World Book Atlas (Washington, D.C.: The World Bank, 1996).

country's national law. By the time the single market came into effect on January 1, 1993, most of the directives were ready for national approval. However, not all directives had been implemented by *all* twelve members.

Internal and External Impact of the Single European Market

It is important to understand that the Single European Market is a process, not just a date. The initiatives targeted for December 31, 1992, will take years to adopt and implement.

There are several major internal concerns about the single market, especially in the United Kingdom and Denmark. The first, expressed by the free-market side of the EU membership, is the spread of bureaucracy, centralization, overregulation, and socialism.

A second concern is the acceptance of key changes, such as the harmonization of the **value-added tax (VAT),** a tax that is a percentage of the value added to a product at each stage of the business process. Although consumers in high-tax countries might welcome the lowering of the average VAT, consumers in low-tax countries would not appreciate the increase of the average VAT. In addition, the VAT was scheduled to be simplified in 1997 by charging the VAT in the country of origin rather then the country of sale, greatly simplifying the paperwork involved in VAT rebates.[16] The VAT generated 52 percent of the EU's budget in 1994,[17] so any changes in VAT regulations have an important impact on the EU.

A third worry is the potential effect on unemployment. Although most experts believe the Single European Market will bring faster economic growth and the creation of jobs, local unions are not convinced. In northern Europe, in particular, unions are concerned that the free movement of capital will cause companies to seek lower costs in southern Europe.

A fourth concern is the possible elimination of small and medium-sized companies. This could occur for two reasons:

1. Competition due to the absence of trade barriers, which will expand the reach of large, efficient companies as they take advantage of better distribution systems
2. The wave of mergers and acquisitions taking place as companies attempt to grow in order to compete with U.S. and Japanese rivals in Europe

The major external concern regarding the Single European Market is often referred to as "Fortress Europe." Many people fear European regulations will favor European companies and exclude foreign, especially U.S. and Japanese, companies. Although that does not seem to be the case so far, foreign MNEs are adopting a variety of strategies to reserve a place in Europe. Some large MNEs—such as Ford, Coca-Cola, and IBM—are more European in terms of their geographical spread than many European companies are. The medium-sized companies currently operating in Europe are taking part in the merger-and-acquisition wave to expand their

Internal concerns about Europe 1992 include
- **The potential growth of centralization and socialism**
- **Lack of acceptance of key changes, such as tax harmonization**
- **The possible shift of jobs from northern to southern Europe**
- **The elimination of small and medium-sized companies**

An external concern regarding Europe 1992 is known as "Fortress Europe."

sizes and market shares. And those that serve Europe merely through exports are establishing offices there in order to have a physical presence within the market.[18]

Despite the appearance of a unified common market, there are still significant national differences. One study of the European strategies of twenty-two *Fortune* 500 corporations with European central offices concluded:

> Although Europe is becoming more open, differences in culture, language, and feelings of nationalism make it imperative that it not be approached as a completely homogeneous market which can be treated like any other global market. Management of American multinationals must, therefore, assess the impact of these differences on customers and consumers in determining the proper balance between global, Pan-European, and national or regional marketing strategies as they consider the European Community market integration process.[19]

The Treaty of Maastricht

Not content with the economic integration envisaged in the Europe 1992 program, EC leaders met in Maastricht, the Netherlands, in December 1991 and approved the Treaty of Maastricht. This treaty was designed to take the EC to a higher level. It is divided into two parts: economic and monetary union (EMU) and political union. EMU is designed to result in a common European currency by 1999.

The prospect of political union brings up a number of issues, such as a common European citizenship; joint foreign, defense, immigration, and policing policies; and the harmonization of social policy concerning working conditions and employees' rights. In addition, the Parliament was strengthened significantly by giving it veto power over new national laws.[20]

The Treaty of Maastricht was not easy to design because there are strong federalist tendencies in countries such as France and Germany and an abhorrence of centralized control from Brussels on the part of countries such as the United Kingdom and Denmark. Those opposing federalist tendencies included in the treaty the principle of **subsidiarity,** which implies that EU interference should occur only in areas of common concern and that most policies should be set at the national level. Further, not all countries accepted all points in the treaty.

After the euphoria that followed the signing of the treaty died down, the real work began—each country had to approve it by national referendum or parliamentary vote. By 1993, all member countries had approved the treaty.

Monetary Union

As noted above, a key element of the Maastricht Agreement was monetary union. The roots to the system began in 1979, when the **European Monetary System (EMS)** was put into place. The EMS was set up as a means of creating exchange-rate stability within the EC at that time. This system was intended primarily to facilitate trade among members by minimizing exchange-rate fluctuations. A series of exchange relationships links the currencies of most members through a parity grid. A central exchange rate is determined for the currency of each member country

European Currency Unit—a composite or basket of currencies in the EMS where each country's value is weighted according to economic strength and other factors

based on the **European Currency Unit (ECU).** The ECU is a composite or basket of currencies of those countries in the EU. Once the exchange rate is determined for the currency of each member country, a parity exchange rate is determined for each pair of currencies. For example, there is a parity rate for the French franc and the German mark, for the French franc and the Italian lira, and so on. From 1979 to 1993, bilateral exchange rates were allowed to deviate from the EMS parity rate by only 2.25 percent before the central banks of the countries involved were to intervene to protect the integrity of the central rate. The exceptions to this were the Spanish peseta and the British pound, which were permitted to fluctuate by 6 percent. However, the EMS went through several changes in 1992 and 1993; Italy and the United Kingdom dropped out of the system in 1992, and the allowed deviation from the parity rates increased from 2.25 percent to 15 percent in 1993. However, the deviation rate is 2.25 percent again.

In order to move to a common currency, the Maastricht Agreement requires the following convergence criteria:

Convergence criteria
* inflation
* long-term interest rates
* stable currency
* budget deficit as percent of GDP
* public debt as a percent of GDP

* "Inflation must be no more than 1.5 percentage points above the average of the three lowest inflation rates in Europe.
* Long-term interest rates must be no more than two percentage points higher than the average of the three lowest.
* The exchange rate must have stayed within the narrow band of the European Union's exchange-rate mechanism for two years without realignment.
* The government's budget deficit must be no more than 3 percent of GDP.
* The accumulated stock of public debt must not exceed 60 percent of GDP."[21]

The movement to EMU is expected to follow three steps:

1. A decision will be made around January 1, 1998, on which currencies qualify for a common currency, based on end-of-1997 data.

Target Date: January 1, 1999

2. Effective January 1, 1999, exchange rates would be fixed, and new European Central Bank would conduct monetary policy. At that point, "national governments, many banks and some businesses would conduct transactions in a single currency," which will be known as the "Euro."
3. At the start of 2002, new bank notes and coins will reach the general public.[22]

Key Institutions
* European Monetary Institute
* European System of Central Banks
* European Central Bank

The monetary authority that will manage the new currency is the European System of Central Banks (ESCB), which will be made up of a European Central Bank (ECB) and the national central banks of participating countries. The European Monetary Institute (EMI) was set up in 1994 to prepare the way for the establishment of the ECB and will be replaced by the ECB when the decision is made to move to economic and monetary union. The EMI is concentrating on monetary policy, strategy, procedures, and instruments.[23]

However, the movement to monetary union is not easy. As noted above, the EMS has been severely tested, especially from 1992 on. Differences in the relative strength of currencies has caused some to recommend that Europe be divided into tiers of currencies, with the strongest including countries such as Germany, Belgium, France, the Netherlands, and Luxembourg, and with the weakest including Italy, Spain, Portugal, Ireland, and Greece.[24]

Major problems
- **Instability in currency values**
- **Inability to meet convergence criteria—especially debt-related criteria**
- **Unpopularity of potential social cuts**

The biggest problem is the inability of countries to meet the convergence criteria. In 1996, for example, only one country, Luxembourg, met all three criteria of inflation, public deficit as a percent of GDP, and public debt as a percent of GDP. Although all but four countries met the inflation target, only four met the public deficit as a percent of GDP target, and only one met the public debt as a percent of GDP target.[25] The major concern is the potential impact on social programs as governments try to cut their budget deficits and eliminate debt. When the French government announced significant reductions in social benefits in 1996, labor unions called for big protests. Slow economic growth has made it impossible for governments to raise enough revenues to pay for social programs, but the general populace is not interested in social sacrifice to reach EMU.[26] In addition, it is hard to imagine that the British pound, the French franc, and the German mark could eventually go away and be replaced by the Euro. However, that is precisely the plan. And it is clear that some countries, especially Germany and France, are keen to see EMU become a reality.[27]

EU Expansion

The EU is likely to expand by accepting EFTA members.

One of the major challenges of the EU is that of expansion. There are a number of European countries interested in joining the EU, and most of them will present political and economic challenges to the EU. The first step in the expansion was the creation of the European Economic Area in 1991, the objective of which was to extend the customs union privileges of the EU to the member countries of the EFTA. With the loss of Austria, Finland, and Sweden to the EU as full members in 1995, EFTA was reduced to only four countries: Norway, Iceland, Switzerland, and Liechtenstein. The EEA agreement with the EU allows the freedom of people, goods, services, and capital to Norway, Iceland, and Liechtenstein. Switzerland is the only EFTA member not included in the EEA, because its people explicitly voted in 1991 not to join. Subsequent to the establishment of the EEA, Norway voted not to join the EU, but it remains in the EEA. Since the EAA agreement involves only three countries and the EU, it is likely to go away if and when all countries become part of the EU.

European Economic Area: EU plus Norway, Iceland, and Liechtenstein

On January 1, 1996, Turkey, with a population of 60.7 million people—larger than any country in the EU except Germany—entered into a customs union agreement with the EU. Turkey is now a part of the single European market and has adopted the EU's trade legislation and common external tariff without becoming a

Expansion
- **Turkey entered into a customs union with EU in 1996**
- **Cyprus and Malta have applied for admission**
- **Next will be countries of Central and Eastern Europe**

complete member of the EU.[28] Two other, relatively smaller countries, Cyprus and Malta, have also formally applied for membership in the EU and will probably be the next countries to join. In addition, the EU has signed numerous free trade agreements with other countries in Central and Eastern Europe, as well as with Israel. These additional agreements mean that the EU is the largest trading bloc in the world, surpassing NAFTA.

The next level of expansion is likely to include the countries of Central and Eastern Europe. As these countries adjust to new political and economic systems, they are preparing themselves to join the EU. Prior to the end of the Soviet empire, the countries of the USSR and Central and Eastern Europe were linked together in a trading relationship known as the **Council for Mutual Economic Assistance (CMEA** or also known as **COMECON**). However, the breakup of the Soviet Union and its allied countries in Eastern Europe resulted in the dissolution of CMEA in June 1991. The result was the following post-CMEA blocs: the Visegard Group (the Czech Republic, Slovakia, Hungary, and Poland); Bulgaria and Romania; the three Baltic states of Estonia, Latvia, and Lithuania; and the Commonwealth of Independent States (CIS), which is Russia and the former republics of the Soviet Union. On July 1, 1992, the **Central European Free Trade Association (CEFTA)** went into effect, with an initial membership of the Czech Republic, Slovakia, Hungary, and Poland. The goal of CEFTA is to establish a free trade area by 2000 that includes the basic trade structure of the EU.[29] Since 1992, Slovenia has been admitted to membership and several countries have applied for membership, especially Bulgaria, Romania, and the Baltic States. Even Russia has opened discussions with CEFTA.

The most likely new admissions to the EU will be the members of the CEFTA. However, this will not be an easy process. Most countries in Central and Eastern Europe are relatively poor, have fledgling democracies, and depend greatly on agriculture—as much as 20 percent of GNP, compared with only 6 percent on average in the EU. As result, the financial resources of the EU will be greatly strained. The five CEFTA countries mentioned above would add another 58 million relatively poor people. Presently, the EU provides structural funds to countries with a GDP less than 75 percent of the Union average, which these new countries would certainly fall into. And about half of the EU's budget goes to support the Common Agricultural Policy (CAP), which is basically a subsidy to farmers. Thus the new countries would end up receiving substantial transfers from the structural assistance fund and the CAP fund, putting a significant drain on the financial resources of the EU.[30]

Another problem is that of governance. The fear of the large members of the EU, such as France and Germany, is that the addition of so many new countries would weaken their control and influence. In order to address these issues, the EU began meetings in 1996 to recommend changes in its founding documents to account for the addition of new members. Estimates of total membership in the EU range from 25–30 nations by the end of the decade. That is a far cry from the original six that emerged from discussions in 1957.

Central European Free Trade Association (CEFTA)
- Began in 1992 after breakup of USSR
- Membership: Czech Republic, Slovakia, Hungary, Poland, Slovenia
- Others trying to join

Problems of Expansion
- Relatively lower income countries
- Higher dependence on agriculture
- New democracies
- Financial pressure on structural assistance fund and Common Agricultural Policy
- Governance

Other Issues

There are, of course, other issues confronting the EU besides the movement to a common currency and the enlargement of the EU beyond the current 15 member countries. There are still major political, cultural, linguistic, and economic differences among member countries, just as one would expect in any ethnically and culturally diverse a region as exists in the EU. The United Kingdom, for example, has found itself aligned against the other members of the EU in a number of issues, including the EMS and most notably the "mad cow disease" in 1995–1996 when the rest of the EU member countries voted to boycott British beef until all cattle afflicted with mad cow disease were destroyed. On the political front, the decision by U.S. President Clinton to bomb Iraq in 1996 was supported only by the United Kingdom. Other EU member countries did not agree, which created a political rift in the EU. Although the EU is trying to eliminate the barriers to the movement of people in the Union, the United Kingdom refuses to relax its passport controls because of serious internal security concerns.

Challenge to Companies: Establish a regional strategy before different national strategies

However, the EU is a tremendous market in terms of both population and income that cannot be ignored by companies. Whereas companies might have been tempted to develop a national strategy for each member country in the EU due to the differences mentioned in the preceding paragraph, they cannot be successful without first developing a regional strategy. Once a European regional strategy is established allowing a company to achieve critical mass in production, product development, and other areas of the business, the company can worry about national implementation, adaptation, and so on.

North American Free Trade Agreement (NAFTA)

NAFTA, which initially includes Canada, the United States, and Mexico, went into effect in 1994, but it originated with the Canada-U.S. Free Trade Agreement. The United States and Canada historically have engaged in various forms of mutual economic cooperation. One is the Automotive Products Trade Agreement, effective in 1965, which provides for qualified duty-free trade in specified automotive products. In the early 1980s, the two countries discussed developing free trade in specific sectors, such as steel and textiles. This discussion then was expanded to include a broader discussion of free trade, and by 1987 negotiations were being held to open up trade even more between them. The negotiations resulted in the Canada-U.S. Free Trade Agreement (FTA), which became effective January 1, 1989. The FTA was set to eliminate all tariffs on bilateral trade by January 1, 1998, although more than 85 percent of the bilateral trade was subject to tariffs of 5 percent or less even before the FTA took effect.

In February 1991, Mexico approached the United States to establish a free-trade agreement. The formal negotiations that began in June 1991 included Canada. The resulting North American Free Trade Agreement (NAFTA) was announced by the

Canadian Prime Minister and the U.S. and Mexican Presidents in August 1992 and became effective on January 1, 1994.

NAFTA has a logical rationale, in terms of both geographic location and trading importance. Although Canadian-Mexican trade was not significant when the agreement was signed, U.S.-Mexican and U.S.-Canadian trade was. The United States is the largest trading partner of both Canada and Mexico, and Canada and Mexico are the first and third most important trading partners with the United States. In 1995, Mexico was Canada's fourth largest supplier, while Mexico was Canada's thirteenth largest market. The two-way trading relationship between the United States and Canada, which reached U.S.$243.3 billion in 1995, is the largest in the world. As noted in Table 7.3, NAFTA is a powerful trading bloc with a combined population and total GNP greater than the 15-member EU. However, the addition of countries with which the EU has free trade and customs union agreements would drop NAFTA into second place. The breakdown of population, GNP, and per capita GNP for the three NAFTA members is found in Table 7.4. What is significant, especially when compared with the EU, is the tremendous size of the U.S. economy relative to those of Canada and Mexico. In addition, Canada has a much richer economy than that of Mexico, even though its population is about one-third that of Mexico.

NAFTA deals with the following areas:

- Market access—tariff and nontariff barriers, rules of origin, governmental procurement
- Trade rules—safeguards, subsidies, countervailing and antidumping duties, health and safety standards
- Services
- Investment
- Intellectual property
- Dispute settlement[31]

Mexico has made significant strides in tariff reduction since it joined GATT in 1986. At that time, its tariffs averaged 100 percent. Since then, it has reduced tariffs

---

NAFTA rationale
- **U.S.-Canadian trade is largest bilateral trade in the world**
- **The U.S. is Mexico's and Canada's largest trading partner**
- **Mexico-Canada trade is not as significant but is growing**

NAFTA calls for the elimination of tariff and nontariff barriers, the harmonization of trade rules, and the liberalization of restrictions on services and foreign investments.

Table 7.4
NAFTA Data

	Population (millions)	GNP ($ billions)	Per Capita Income ($)
Canada	29.1	569.9	19,570
Mexico	91.9	368.7	4,010
United States	260.5	6,737.4	25,860

Source: World Bank, *World Development Report 1996.* (Washington, D.C.: The World Bank, 1996), various pages.

to less than 20 percent in most cases. Under NAFTA, a tariff-reduction schedule was established for trade with Mexico that provides for a reduction of tariffs on all merchandise by the year 2008. Most of Mexico's nontariff barriers, such as import licenses, will also be eliminated during this period.[32]

NAFTA should provide the static and dynamic effects of economic integration.

NAFTA is expected to provide the static and dynamic effects of economic integration discussed earlier in this chapter. For example, Canadian and U.S. consumers are expected to benefit from lower-cost agricultural products, a static effect of economic liberalization. They also are expected to benefit from the large and growing Mexican market, which has a huge appetite for U.S. products; this benefit is a dynamic effect.

In addition, NAFTA is a good example of trade diversion. Many U.S. companies have established manufacturing facilities in Asia to take advantage of cheap labor and ship products from those facilities to the United States. It is anticipated that NAFTA members will be able to use each other rather than Asian countries as locations for trade and investment. This movement has already begun in the automobile industry: U.S. automakers such as Ford have established manufacturing facilities in Mexico to serve the U.S. market.

Rules of Origin and Local Content

Country of Origin—goods and services must originate in North America to get access to lower tariffs.

An important part of NAFTA is the concept of rules of origin and local content. Because NAFTA is a free trade agreement and not a customs union, each country has its own tariff schedule with respect to the rest of the world. Thus a product entering the United States from Canada must be accompanied by a commercial or customs invoice that identifies the origin of the product. Otherwise, an exporter from a third country would always ship the product to the country with the cheaper tariff and then re-export it to the second country duty-free.

Local Content
- the percentage of value that must be from North America for the product to be considered "North American" in terms of country of origin
- 50 percent for most products, 62.5 percent for autos

Local content refers to the percentage of the value of the export that is incurred in the NAFTA region. For example, a Ford passenger car assembled in Mexico could use parts from Canada, the United States, and Mexico, and labor and other factors from Mexico. For the car to enter Canada and the United States according to the NAFTA duty, at least 62.5 percent of its value must be generated in North America. That would not seem to be a problem for a Ford, but if the car is a Toyota using parts from Japan, it might be difficult for the car to qualify according to local content. Under the Canada-U.S. free trade agreement, the local content requirement was 50 percent for all products (which is also the local content requirement for most products under NAFTA, with the exception of autos and a few other products), but it was felt that too many non-North American manufacturers would locate in Mexico to take advantage of cheap wages and use Mexico as an export platform to the United States and Canada. Thus the local content for new autos was raised to 62.5 percent. In many respects, that was a concession to labor to get the support to pass the NAFTA agreement in the U.S. Congress.

A good example of the problems that can arise with local content rules involves Honda, which builds in North America two-thirds of the cars it sells there. In 1991, the U.S. Customs Service determined that less than 50 percent of the value of each Honda Civic being shipped into the United States from Canada originated in North America. It argued that the Civic was simply a collection of parts shipped from Japan to Canada and assembled there, and that most of the local content of the automobile was depreciation on machinery shipped to Canada from Japan.[33] Even though the agreement calls for the gradual elimination of tariffs among NAFTA members, there is still an important role for Customs officials to play, and companies have to be sure they follow local content requirements and comply with rules of origin in order to qualify for the more favorable tariffs.

Special Provisions

In spite of its free trade nature, NAFTA contains a number of special provisions that go beyond the elimination of tariffs, especially pertaining to intellectual property, workers' rights, the environment, the liberalization of regulations on trade in services, the reduction of barriers on the movement of professionals across the borders, improved standards on the flow of investments across borders, and a dispute resolution mechanism.[34]

When the agreement was drafted, opponents focused on the potential loss of jobs in Canada and the United States to Mexico as the result of cheaper wages, poor working conditions, and lax environmental enforcement in Mexico. It was felt that companies would close down factories in the North and set them up in Mexico. As a result, the labor lobby forced the inclusion of labor standards, such as the right to unionize, and the environmental lobby pushed for an upgrade of environmental standards in Mexico and the strengthening of compliance.

Rather than rely on the World Trade Organization to settle disputes or to allow the U.S. government to act unilaterally on trade issues, the agreement established a dispute resolution mechanism that allows all three countries to come to the bargaining table as peers in settling trade disputes. An example of the dispute process involved the export of cherries to be imported from the United States to Mexico. In 1991, Mexico stopped allowing cherries to be imported from the United States unless U.S. companies fumigated their cherries to destroy two specific pests, the apple maggot and the plum curculio. However, U.S. growers claimed that one of the pests did not exist in the area where the cherries are grown, and the use of methyl bromide, the fumigant Mexican officials required to be used, would harm the fruit. So they submitted the charges to a NAFTA agricultural dispute panel, which ruled in 1995 that cherries could be moved safely to Mexico without fumigation, subject to a preseason inspection by the Mexican government. The first shipment of cherries took place under the agreement in 1997.[35]

Major NAFTA Issues

In addition to those mentioned above, there are six additional major issues and concerns surrounding the agreement:

Major NAFTA provisions
- duty-free market access
- worker's rights
- the environment
- rules on trade in services and investment
- protection of intellectual property
- dispute settlement mechanism

1. The impact of the agreement on trade, investment, and jobs
2. The environment
3. National sovereignty
4. The political and economic stability of Mexico
5. The long-term stability of Canada, given the problem of Quebec separatism
6. Expansion beyond the existing membership.

- **Most trade between the United States and Canada was duty-free.**
- **U.S. tariffs on most Mexican imports were low, but tariffs on some products were quite high.**

Impact of NAFTA The test of any regional group is whether trade (and jobs) has been created. During the debates on NAFTA leading up to the ratification of the treaty, the forces in favor of NAFTA pointed out that reducing trade barriers in Mexico would result in an increase in exports, resulting in the creation of jobs. Since most trade between the United States and Canada was virtually duty-free, and since Mexico had relatively easy access to U.S. and Canadian markets, it was assumed that the major benefit would be the increase in exports to Mexico from both the United States and Canada. In some cases, U.S. tariffs on Mexican products were quite high. For example, in the late 1980s, olives carried an ad valorem tariff of 73.2 percent, brooms a tariff of 60.2 percent, and textiles a tariff of 37.5 percent. However, nearly 94 percent of Mexican products entered the United States at a tariff of 10 percent or less. Although many Canadian and U.S. firms were already investing in Mexico, it was felt that an improvement in investment rules would facilitate additional investment but would not end up with a flood of investment capital going to Mexico. Opponents, however, predicted the deindustrialization of Canada and the United States as firms moved to Mexico to take advantage of cheaper costs.

Because of geographic proximity, the three countries already trade a great deal with each other. More than 70 percent of Canada's and Mexico's trade is intrazonal. U.S. trade is more broadly distributed, but Canada and Mexico are still the U.S.'s first and third trading partners. Table 7.5 provides data on Canadian and Mexican exports from and imports to the United States. Canada/Mexico trade was relatively insignificant in 1995: Canada exported about $830 million to Mexico and imported $3.9 billion from Mexico.

The export market is important for all three countries. The U.S. government estimates that export jobs pay 13 to 16 percent more than U.S. jobs overall and that one out of every six net job increases in the United States between 1992 and 1995 came from the export sector.[36] The trade deficit with Canada increased during the first two years of the NAFTA agreement, and it was wider than in 1992 before the agreement was signed. The same is true with Mexico, although the United States had a trade surplus with Mexico in both 1992 and 1993, which turned into a huge deficit in 1995. The deficit resulted from the peso crisis that began in December 1994 and continued through 1995 and into 1996 (see the Mexican Peso case at the end of Chapter 9). The resulting collapse of the Mexican economy made it very difficult for U.S. and Canadian firms to expand sales into Mexico. However, the growth of the U.S. economy acted as a magnet for Canadian and Mexican goods,

Table 7.5
Merchandise Trade between the United States and Canada and the United States and Mexico (in $ billions)

	1993		1994		1995	
	Amount	%	Amount	%	Amount	%
Canada						
Exports to	101.2	22.1	114.8	22.8	127.6	22.1
Imports from	113.3	19.2	131.1	19.6	148.1	19.8
Balance	(12.2)		(16.3)		(20.5)	
Mexico						
Exports to	41.5	9.0	50.7	10.0	46.2	8.0
Imports from	40.4	8.8	50.1	7.5	62.4	8.3
Balance	1.0		.7		(16.2)	
Total World						
Exports to	456.8		502.5		575.9	
Imports from	589.4		668.6		749.4	

Source: Survey of Current Business. U.S. Department of Commerce. July 1996, Vol. 76., No. 7, p. 76.

Table 7.6
Hourly Compensation Costs for Production Workers in Manufacturing, in U.S. Dollars, 1995
Hourly compensation costs of manufacturing workers are significantly higher in the United States and Canada than in Mexico, where wages are also lower than in some of the newly industrialized countries in Asia.

Country	Wage
United States	$17.20
Canada	16.03
Mexico	1.51
Hong Kong	4.82
Korea	7.40
Singapore	7.28
Taiwan	5.82

Source: United States Department of Labor, Bureau of Labor Statistics, "International Comparisons of Manufacturing Hourly Compensation Costs, 1995, *News* (202-606-5654).

widening the trade deficit. It should be noted that even though the deficit widened, U.S. exports to Canada continued to grow, and U.S. exports to Mexico, while declining from 1994 to 1995, were still higher in 1995 than they were in 1993. Those in favor of the agreement will argue that the increase in exports led to the direct creation of jobs, whereas the increase in imports may lead to job displacement but not necessarily to an increase in unemployment overall if the workers are picked up by other companies. Those against the agreement argue that the increase in the deficit leads to the loss of jobs in import industries and that the fall in exports to Mexico from 1994 to 1995 resulted in layoffs in export industries, demonstrating that the job gains promised by the proponents of NAFTA did not materialize. However, the actual impact is difficult to measure.

Mexicans also are worried about losing jobs. U.S. and Canadian companies were already investing in Mexico to take advantage of cheap labor and to jump tariff barriers. In the NAFTA environment, however, the barriers will disappear, and Mexicans fear that U.S. and Canadian companies may supply the Mexican market from large manufacturing facilities in their own countries.

Although in recent years wages have been rising more rapidly in Mexico than in Canada or the United States, hourly manufacturing costs remain significantly lower in Mexico than in the other two countries (see Table 7.6). For example, hourly wages for Mexican workers in the automobile industry are higher than $1.51, but those in the maquiladora industry along the U.S.-Mexican border are lower than $1.51. In addition, Mexican wages are lower than those in the newly industrialized countries of Asia.

The Environment Some U.S. and Canadian environmentalists are convinced NAFTA will result in destruction of Mexico's environment and relaxation of U.S.

and Canadian environmental standards, as well as cause U.S. and Canadian companies to invest in Mexico because of its lax environmental standards and enforcement. The environmentalists' major concerns are air and water pollution and the use of pesticides and other chemicals in Mexican agriculture. There is a strong positive correlation between pollution and economic growth, so it may be true that pollution could worsen in Mexico if NAFTA stimulates economic growth. However, Mexican environmental standards are getting tougher and enforcement of those standards is improving. There is no evidence to support the idea that environmental standards and enforcement would lag behind as the economy grows. One could argue that NAFTA actually could force Mexico to strengthen its standards and enforcement. In addition, studies show that countries with low income levels cannot spend much money to clean up the environment, and that cleanup begins when income levels rise.

There also is some concern that if the United States and Canada were to exclude Mexican products on the grounds that they resulted from environmentally unsound production processes, Mexico could take both countries to court and charge that environmental concerns are a nontariff trade barrier. Clearly, U.S. and Canadian environmental standards must not be weakened, so a process is needed to protect them.

Finally, it is possible but highly unlikely that lax environmental standards will cause a mass migration of production facilities to Mexico. Other factors, such as market access and transport and labor costs, have greater impact on where investment flows. In addition, the cooperation that will occur through NAFTA should eliminate future environmental regulatory differences.

In terms of environmental standards, the Commission for Environmental Cooperation in Montreal was created by the North American Agreement on Environmental Cooperation and is charged with the responsibility to protect, conserve, and improve the environment. It is working on a list of environmental projects in the following areas: (1) conservation, (2), protection of human health and the environment, (3) enforcement cooperation, and (4) information and public outreach. A major area of concern is the area along the U.S./Mexico border where a number of companies have established assembly facilities. Although there is some concern about the environmental degradation by the factories themselves, by far the major concern is the impact on the basic infrastructure of the area caused by people moving in to take advantage of jobs. The NAFTA-related Border Environment Cooperation Commision and the North American Development Bank are working together to certify and finance infrastructure development projects to deal with environmental issues, especially in the area of water quality.[37]

National Sovereignty

The implementation of the original FTA between Canada and the United States was neither easy nor popular, especially in Canada. At the time the agreement was signed, Canadians were concerned about several possible effects on Canada:

- losing cultural identity,
- becoming too closely integrated with a more violent society (that of the United States),
- forfeiting independence in foreign policy, and
- becoming overwhelmed by the United States.

These issues have continued on with NAFTA. The United States is too big and powerful to be considered a completely equal partner, and this fact has created problems in the agreement. Even in the 1996 U.S. presidential campaign, there was discussion over whether or not the United States should submit to the dispute settlement mechanism and surrender U.S. sovereignty. The U.S. policy toward Cuba was also a concern since Canada and Mexico would prefer to engage in economic relations with Cuba, whereas the U.S. government would prefer to continue to put economic and political pressure on Cuba. Given the size of the U.S. economy and the importance of its foreign policy in global affairs, it is hard to imagine NAFTA extending much beyond its current reach of issues.

The Political and Economic Stability of Mexico

The political and economic crisis that began in Mexico in 1994 is one of the major criticisms of the original opponents of the agreement. During the political campaign in 1994, the representative of the ruling PRI party was assassinated. His replacement, Ernesto Zedillo, was elected President in August 1994, but the problems did not end there. The rising strength of opposition parties and politicians, charges of voter fraud and irregularities, challenges from rebels from the state of Chiapas and elsewhere, and a flourishing drug-trafficking business have forced Zedillo to focus on corruption and liberalization of the political system as well as improvement in economic performance. During the debates leading up to the signing of the agreement, many worried about trying to link too closely with a country that was not as mature politically and economically as the United States. However, one could argue that the close links between Mexico and Canada and the United States have helped Mexico weather its political and economic storms, and that long-term, Mexico will return to stability.

The Long-Term Stability of Canada

Some have argued that NAFTA is not an agreement involving three countries but that it reflects the economic realities of regions that cross national borders. For example, the agreement more closely links the west of Canada with the Pacific Northwest of the United States. The western provinces of Canada are very different from those of the center and East, and they might have more in common with contiguous western states than with each other. A major problem in Canada is the future of the French-speaking province of Quebec, which continues to argue for greater autonomy or complete separation from the rest of Canada. If Quebec is successful in becoming a new nation, it will split the east of Canada from the west of the country and will create confusion with NAFTA. Will Quebec automatically become a member of NAFTA, or will it have to apply to join?

NAFTA Expansion

When the United States began its discussions with Mexico and Canada, it perceived any resultant agreement would be part of a larger effort to pull together North, Central, and South America into an "Enterprise of the Americas." The idea was to have the United States enter into a series of bilateral trade relationships with Latin American countries that would result in a "hub and spokes" arrangement, with the United States as the hub and other countries as the spokes. Eventually, these bilateral relationships would result in one huge multilateral relationship involving the Americas. Chile was being courted as the next addition to NAFTA after the original three countries completed their negotiations and began implementation in 1994. Preliminary steps needed to prepare Chile and other Latin American countries involved lowering trade barriers and reducing or eliminating restrictions to FDI.[38]

Latin American Integration

Economic integration in Latin America has changed over the years. Two of the original examples of regional economic integration in Latin America, the Latin American Free Trade Association (LAFTA) and the Caribbean Free Trade Association (CARIFTA), changed their names to the Latin American Integration Association (ALADI) and the Caribbean Community and Common Market (CARICOM). They also changed the focus of their activities. In spite of this evolution, the initial rationale for integration remains. The post–World War II strategy of import substitution to resolve balance-of-payments problems was doomed because of Latin America's small national markets. Therefore it was felt that some form of economic cooperation was needed to enlarge the potential market size so that Latin American companies could achieve economies of scale and be more competitive worldwide.

Major Latin American Regional Groups

There are several subregional groups in Latin America that are involved in a variety of forms of cooperation. Even though their intrazonal trade is improving—intrazonal trade among ten South American countries plus Mexico improved from 15.1 percent of total imports in 1989 to 19.7 percent in 1993[39]—Latin countries still rely heavily on the U.S. market as their major export market. However, the size and scale of cooperation are increasing. Map 7.2 identifies the major trading groups in Central America—the Caribbean Community and Common Market (CARICOM) and the Central American Common Market (CACM). In 1993, 25 Caribbean countries (including the CARICOM members and Cuba) established an Association of Caribbean States to develop closer economic ties. In addition, the U.S. government established the Caribbean Initiative to give tariff concessions to Caribbean nations

**Central American
Common Market (CACM)**

Members	Date of entry	
Costa Rica	Sept.	1963
El Salvador	May	1961
Guatemala	May	1961
Honduras	April	1962
	(withdrew Jan.	1971)
Nicaragua	May	1961

**Caribbean Community and
Common Market (CARICOM)**

Participating Members	Date of entry	
Antigua and Barbuda	May	1974
Bahamas*	July	1983
Barbados	Aug.	1973
Belize	May	1974
Dominica	May	1974
Grenada	May	1974
Guyana	Aug.	1973
Jamaica	Aug.	1973
Montserrat	May	1974
St. Christopher and Nevis	May	1974
St. Lucia	May	1974
St. Vincent and the Grenadines	May	1974
Trinidad and Tobago	Aug.	1973

*The Bahamas is a member state of the community but is not a participant in the common market.

**Map 7.2
Economic Integration in Central America and the Caribbean**
Countries in Central America and the Caribbean have shifted their forms of integration from free-trade areas to common markets: the Central American Common Market (CACM) and the Caribbean Community and Common Market (CARICOM).

exporting to the United States. Many industries, including clothing and textiles, have moved manufacturing facilities offshore to the Caribbean to take advantage of the lower tariffs on products brought back into the United States.

The major trade group in South America is **MERCOSUR,** as shown in Map 7.3. MERCOSUR was established in 1991 in Brazil, Argentina, Paraguay, and Uruguay, as a subregional group of the Latin American Integration Association (ALADI). MERCOSUR is significant because of its size: the four original members generate 70 percent of the GNP of South America. By 1996, MERCOSUR had abolished tariffs on goods accounting for 90 percent of the trade between its member countries, with remaining tariffs to be abolished by 2000. Its common external tariff was implemented in January 1995, making MERCOSUR more integrated than NAFTA. In 1995, MERCOSUR and the EU signed a cooperation agreement to pave the way for a free trade accord that will be signed in 2001. This is the first major effort on the part of the EU to establish solid economic ties with Latin America.[40] In terms of expansion, Chile is likely to be the next country to join MERCOSUR. If it were also to join NAFTA, it would have built bridges with the two most significant regional groups in the Americas.

Although the Andean Common Market (ANCOM) is not as significant economically as MERCOSUR, it is the second most important regional group in South America. As noted in Map 7.3, the Andean Group has been around since 1969. However, its focus has shifted from one of isolationism and statism (placing

Map 7.3
Latin American Economic Integration
The Latin American Integration Association (ALADI) evolved from the Latin American Free Trade Association (LAFTA). The Andean Group and MERCOSUR are subgroups of ALADI designed to address special needs of member countries.

Andean Group

Members	Date of entry	
Bolivia	Nov.	1969
Chile	Sept.	1969
(withdrew	Oct.	1976)
Colombia	Sept.	1969
Ecuador	Nov.	1969
Peru	Oct.	1969
Venezuela	Nov.	1973

Latin American Integration Association (ALADI)

Members	Date of entry	
Argentina	Jan.	1981
Bolivia	Mar.	1982
Brazil	Nov.	1981
Chile	May	1981
Colombia	May	1981
Ecuador	Mar.	1982
Mexico	Feb.	1981
Paraguay	Dec.	1980
Peru	Nov.	1981
Uruguay	Mar.	1981
Venezuela	Mar.	1982

MERCOSUR

Members	Date of entry	
Argentina	Mar.	1991
Brazil	Mar.	1991
Paraguay	Mar.	1991
Uruguay	Mar.	1991

economic control in the hands of the state—the central government) to openness to foreign trade and investment.

Linkage across Groups

Summit for the Americas— goal to link together trading groups in the Americas

In December 1994, U.S. President Clinton hosted the Miami Conference, also known as the Summit for the Americas. Only Cuba was not invited. Several important initiatives took place at the conference, including the following:

- A plan was announced to form the Free Trade Area for the Americas by 2005.
- An invitation was extended to Chile by the United States, Mexico, and Canada to join NAFTA.
- The Organization of American States was given responsibility for comparing MERCOSUR, CARICOM, and other regional pacts to determine where they were similar and where significant compromises would be required.[41]

Much of the criticism of NAFTA in the United States centered on three major ethical dilemmas. The first of these concerned the closing of U.S. plants in order to move production to Mexico to take advantage of low wages. If such moves are made to increase profits rather than to preserve market share, the criticism will mount. Even though the economy began to recover in late 1993 and early 1994, job creation was weaker than it had been during previous recoveries from recessions. Total U.S. employment may rise as a result of NAFTA, but there could be job losses in certain industrial sectors and some geographical areas. On the one hand, it can be argued that a company should preserve U.S. jobs in order to sustain the country's industrial base. This is the argument of organized labor. On the other hand, it can be argued that a company must do whatever is necessary to remain competitive; otherwise, it will go out of business and stockholders will lose their investment. If moving production (and therefore jobs) to Mexico to take advantage of low wages is the best way to preserve a continuous stream of earnings, a company has an ethical obligation to its stockholders to make the move. Thus the ethical dilemma involves a choice between two different groups—employees and stockholders—and it may not be possible to pick an alternative that will bring a positive outcome for both.

ETHICAL DILEMMAS & SOCIAL RESPONSIBILITY

The second ethical dilemma involves companies' treatment of union organizers in Mexico. In early 1994, for example, Honeywell Inc. was accused of firing employees who were trying to organize a union at a Mexican manufacturing facility where workers' average pay was $1.00 per hour. Is it ethical for Honeywell or other U.S. companies to discourage union-organizing activities in a country where labor unions are not as well established or as independent as they are in the United States?

The third dilemma concerns the environmental impact of NAFTA. Some environmental interest groups charge that U.S. companies that move production to Mexico may be contributing to environmental degradation in that country or trying to take advantage of weaker environmental legislation and lax enforcement there. If the home country's environmental laws are stricter than a host country's, which laws should an MNE follow? Would it be considered imperialistic to ignore the host-country laws and apply more stringent environmental standards? Many U.S. companies with foreign investments have chosen to do that. Mattel, for example, requires a higher workplace standard for its subcontractors in China than the Chinese government does. A related question is whether one sovereign country (such as the United States) is justified in telling another (Mexico) how much and how fast to clean up its environment. This question goes beyond the ethical aspects of companies' decision making and encompasses the ethical behavior of governments and pressure groups in trying to force their standards on other countries.

The major goal, of course, would be to establish the largest free trade agreement in the world, with a population of 850 million people and a GDP of $13 trillion.[42]

What do all of these efforts mean to outside investors? Most Latin American countries demonstrate a high degree of protectionism; therefore, most foreign investors—primarily, but not exclusively, U.S. MNEs—have looked at Latin America as a series of individual national markets. However, the combination of strong economic growth and closer economic cooperation is causing many companies to rethink their strategies. In the very near future, foreign investors will be able to view Latin America as one large market that can be served by single large facilities that can achieve economies of scale. That move would help eliminate many of the inefficiencies currently existing in Latin American plants.[43]

Asian Integration Efforts

The member countries of ASEAN—Brunei, Indonesia, Malaysia, the Philippines, Singapore, Thailand, and Vietnam—have wide disparities in population and economic strength.

The first major free-trade area in Asia is the **Association of South East Asian Nations (ASEAN).** Organized in 1967, ASEAN comprises Brunei, Indonesia, Malaysia, the Philippines, Singapore, Thailand, and Vietnam (see Map 7.4). It is promoting cooperation in many areas, including industry and trade. Member countries are very protected in terms of tariff and nontariff barriers. Yet they hold promise for market and investment opportunities because of their large market size (409.9 million people) and rapid economic growth. However, the countries differ in several ways, especially population and GDP. For example, Indonesia, with 190 million people, is the world's fourth most populous country, whereas Singapore has only 2.8 million people and Brunei only 279,000. However, Indonesia has a per capita income of only $880 compared to Singapore's $23,360.

On January 1, 1993, ASEAN officially formed the ASEAN Free Trade Area (AFTA). AFTA's goal is to cut tariffs on all intrazonal trade to a maximum of 5 percent by January 1, 2008. The weaker ASEAN countries would be allowed to phase in their tariff reductions over a longer period.

In 1994, intra-ASEAN exports accounted for 25 percent of ASEAN's total exports, up from only 18 percent in 1990, and they increased to 25.4 percent of total exports in 1995.[44] However, ASEAN's largest trading partners—more so than each other—are East Asian countries, primarily Japan and NAFTA countries. In fact, some would argue that ASEAN's greatest accomplishments have been "to provide a framework for regional stability and to create a unified voice for the conduct of external relations with the rest of the world."[45]

A significant event for AFTA was the admission of Vietnam as a member in July 1995. Vietnam's membership added 72.5 million people, making it the second largest member of ASEAN after Indonesia and just above the Philippines (66.2 million). However, Vietnam's per capita income was only $190, making it clearly the poorest country in the region. The next countries scheduled for admission to

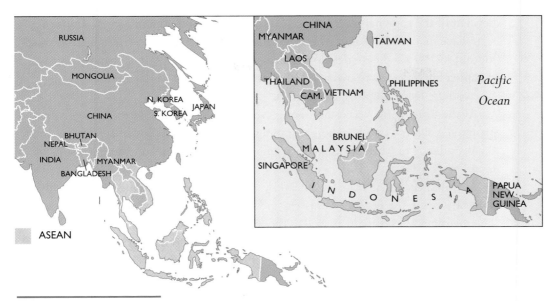

Map 7.4
The Association of South East Asian Nations

ASEAN is a regional group whose member countries have a total population greater than that of the EU or NAFTA, but their per capita GDP is smaller. However, economic growth rates of ASEAN members are among the highest in the world.

APEC comprises 18 countries that account for half of world output—including the United States, China and Japan.

APEC hopes to achieve free and open trade by 2010 (for industrial countries) and 2020 (for the rest).

ASEAN are Cambodia, Laos, and Burma (Myanmar). The latter is problematic, however, because of the oppressive military government.

APEC was formed in November 1989 to promote multilateral economic cooperation on issues of trade and investment.[46] APEC now comprises 18 countries that account for half of world output and includes the world's three largest economies: the United States, Japan, and China.[47] Table 7.3 identifies the members of APEC and their combined economic size. It includes AFTA and NAFTA, two major free trade areas, many of the major countries in East and South East Asia, Australia, New Zealand, and Chile. APEC's major objectives are to

- resist protectionist pressures and maintain the momentum of trade liberalization
- counter inward-looking regionalism elsewhere, such as in the EU and NAFTA; and
- provide ways to deal with economic conflicts on the region.[48]

Concern over the potential trade diversion of NAFTA was an important reason for the founding of APEC. By admitting NAFTA (and thus the United States) into APEC, Asian countries hoped to refocus the efforts of the United States on Asia. There was some feeling that the Clinton administration had lost a focus on Asia, and that its influence and presence, especially relative to Japan, had slipped. In addition, several trade disputes were surfacing between the United States and several countries in Asia, notably Japan and China. Thus the admission of the United States into APEC might facilitate a resolution of some of those problems.[49]

In order to accomplish its objectives, APEC leaders committed to achieve free and open trade in the region by 2010 for the industrial nations (which generate 85 percent of the regional trade) and 2020 for the rest of the members.[50] Heads of state have met annually since their first meeting in the United States (Seattle, Washington) in 1993 and have developed an aggressive agenda. Rather than rely on a complex bureaucracy to manage APEC, the host country of the annual meeting takes on the leadership responsibilities.

At the time APEC was established, ASEAN was the dominant regional economic group in Asia. As a precondition to joining, ASEAN worked out an agreement that the presidency of APEC would alternate between an ASEAN and a non-ASEAN member of APEC.

As noted above, APEC is governed by an annual Ministerial meeting, with the delegates being the Foreign Ministers and Trade Ministers of the member countries. The meetings already held as well as those planned for the future are the United States (1993), Indonesia (1994), Japan (1995), the Philippines (1996), Canada (1997), Malaysia (1998), New Zealand (1999), and Brunei (2000).

The meeting in Indonesia in 1994 was important because APEC members signed a declaration of common resolve to establish free trade and investment in the region by 2020, with the developed countries trying to meet a deadline of 2010. At the meetings in the Philippines, a Manila Action Plan (MAPA) was announced, and it is composed of Collective Action Plans (CAPs) and Individual Action Plans (IAPs) for arriving at the goals established in Indonesia.

APEC does not have a large bureaucracy as is the case with the EU, but it has two standing committees and ten working groups that report to the APEC Senior Officials who are responsible for the actions of APEC. The Senior Officials meetings are held about four times a year. The two standing committees are the Committee for Trade and Investment and the Economic Committee. The ten working groups are Trade and Investment Data, Trade Promotion, Investment and Industrial Science and Technology, Human Resource Development, Energy, Marine Resource Conservation, Telecommunications, Fisheries, Transportation, and Tourism.

APEC has the potential to become a significant economic bloc, especially given that it generates about half of the world's output and 46 percent of its merchandise trade. It is trying to establish a liberalization scheme of "open regionalism," where individual member countries can determine whether to apply the liberalization to nonmembers on an unconditional MFN basis or on a reciprocal, free trade agreement basis. The latter is the approach preferred by the United States. The key will be whether or not the liberalization process continues at the pace anticipated by the agreement in Indonesia.[51]

African Cooperation

Several forms of African integration exist, and they are not necessarily mutually exclusive. The Ivory Coast, for example, is a member of several different organizations in Africa that promote political and/or economic development. The major African groups are shown on Map 7.5:

- **Economic Community of West African States (ECOWAS)** (Benin, Burkina Faso, Cabo Verde, Gambia, Ghana, Guidea, Guinea Bissau, Ivory Coast, Liberia, Mali, Mauritania, Niger, Nigeria, Senegal, Sierra Leone, and Togo)
- **Organisation of African Unity (OAU)** (53 countries in Africa)
- **Southern African Development Community (SADC)** (Angola, Botswana, Lesotho, Malawi, Mauritius, Mozambique, Namibia, South Africa, Swaziland, Tanzania, Zambia, and Zimbabwe)

Although several groups are involved in African political and economic integration, intrazonal trade is a small percentage of Africa's total. Also, two-thirds of its internal trade is with high-income countries, primarily but not exclusively former colonial powers.

To accomplish the goals envisaged by the OAU, several regional economic groups are attempting to improve the flow of goods and capital in their region. ECOWAS is one of the oldest and strongest regional groups in Africa, with a population of 203.2 million people (although half of the population is from Nigeria). In spite of ECOWAS's efforts to improve economic coordination, it has been involved politically in trying to help resolve the conflict in Liberia. Also, the sheer size and economic strength of Nigeria keeps ECOWAS unbalanced in power.

Map 7.5
African Unity
Although there are several regional economic groups in Africa, trade among their member countries is still quite small. African countries rely heavily on trading relationships with industrial countries to absorb regional exports.

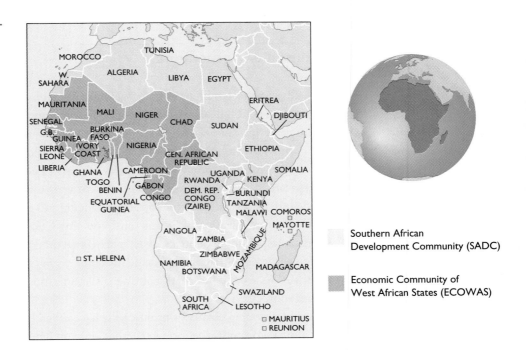

Southern African Development Community (SADC)

Economic Community of West African States (ECOWAS)

Another important group is the Southern African Development Community (SADC), with a total population of 135.7 million people. SADC was originally known as the Southern African Development Co-ordination Conference and was organized to counter the economic influence of South Africa in the region, although unsuccessfully. With the end of apartheid, South Africa and Namibia joined SADC, and the end of the civil war in Angola and Mozambique allowed SADC to focus on economic objectives, such as regional cooperation in attracting investment, in projects such as agriculture, mining, and transport, and in regional free trade and the free movement of people.[52] Other regional efforts, such as the Common Market for Eastern and Southern Africa (COMESA), have grown out of other groups and are attempting to establish an agenda to promote free trade and coordinate inward investment and development projects.

Clearly, there is considerable overlap among the African groups. Groups come and go, and membership in groups changes. Most try to cooperate in some form of economic integration, although the level of integration tends to be fairly low. In general, the countries are so poor and their economic activity so low that there is an insufficient basis for cooperation. Most African countries rely heavily on agriculture or natural resources as a major source of export revenues, so there is not much reason to lower the barriers to the primary products. Major industrial effort is fairly rare, and industries still need protection before the doors to competition are opened. However, such protection retards the development of a free-trade area. African groups also are seeking regional cooperation in other areas, such as transportation, other forms of infrastructure, and small industrial projects, as noted above. There is a strong feeling that political and economic integration must occur if African countries are to survive.

Commodity Agreements

So far this chapter has focused on how countries cooperate to reduce trade barriers, but this section deals with how countries use commodity agreements to stabilize the price and supply of selected commodities.

A commodity agreement is designed to stabilize the price and supply of a good; it takes the form of a producers' alliance or an ICCA.

A **commodity agreement** is a form of economic cooperation designed to stabilize and raise prices. Commodity agreements are of two basic types: producers' alliances and international commodity control agreements (ICCAs). Producers' alliances are exclusive memberships of producing and exporting countries. Examples are the Organization of Petroleum Exporting Countries (OPEC) and the Union of Banana Exporting Countries. ICCAs are based on cooperation between producing and consuming countries and provide for equal voting rights for both groups. Examples of ICCAs are the International Cocoa Organization and the International Sugar Organization.[53]

Commodity prices fluctuate significantly due to natural forces as well as supply and demand factors.

Most developing countries traditionally have relied on the export of one or two commodities to supply the foreign currencies from industrial countries they need for economic development. This is especially true of the African developing countries. However, commodity prices are not stable.

Both consumers and producers often prefer a stabilized pricing system that allows for predictions of future costs and earnings and thus facilitates planning. Unfortunately, many short-term factors cause price instability, leading to fluctuations in export earnings. The most important of these factors are

- Natural forces such as inclement weather and its results
- Relatively price-insensitive demand
- Relatively price-insensitive supply (in the short run)
- Business cycles in industrial countries that can cause sudden changes in demand

Changes in a commodity's price cause changes in an exporting country's total revenue as a result of shifts in demand, shifts in supply, and price elasticity of demand.

Buffer-stock systems and quota systems attempt to keep commodity prices relatively high.

A buffer-stock system is a commodity agreement by which reserve stocks of the good are bought and sold to regulate the price.

The impact price changes have on an exporting country's total revenue depends on several variables. If a price change results from a shift in demand, total revenue will move in the same direction as the change. That is, if the price rises because of an increase in demand for the commodity, total revenue also will rise. This is especially true for mineral products that are sensitive to economic activity in industrial markets. If the price change results from a shift in supply, then price and demand will move in opposite directions. That is, if the price falls because of an increase in the commodity's supply on the market, the demand will rise. Whether total revenue rises depends on the elasticity of demand, that is, the responsiveness of demand to price changes. If demand is insensitive to price changes, as is often the case with commodities, then a price rise probably will not increase total revenue, even though demand rises.

The types of commodity agreements most frequently adopted are the buffer-stock system and the quota system. A **buffer-stock system** is a partially managed system monitored by a central agency. Free-market forces are allowed to determine price within a certain range, but if the price moves outside that range, a central agency buys or sells the commodity to support the price. The signatory countries to the agreement provide funds that the buffer-stock manager can use to purchase the commodity.

Quotas influence how producing and consuming countries divide total output and sales

A **quota system** is a commodity agreement whereby producing and/or consuming countries divide total output and sales in order to stabilize the price. Quota systems have been used for such products as coffee, tea, and sugar, and such a system often is applied in conjunction with a buffer-stock system. For a quota system to work, participating countries must cooperate among themselves to prevent sharp fluctuations in supply. The quota system is most effective when a single country has a large share of world production or consumption. Two of the best examples from a production standpoint are wool, which is controlled by Australia, and diamonds, which are controlled by the DeBeers Company in South Africa.

The effectiveness of a commodity agreement depends on the strength of producers, the willingness of producers and consumers to work together, and characteristics of the commodity itself.

Not all commodity agreements work well. Countries involved in producers' alliances tend to disagree on the relevant quotas to be allotted to them, and quotas also are difficult to enforce. In the case of ICCAs, the fixing of relevant prices is the key area of contention between producers and consumers. Further, producers are rarely pleased with their import quota allotments. ICCAs work well to counter short-term price fluctuations, but they cannot solve structural market imbalances.

The type of commodity being managed also influences a commodity agreement's effectiveness. For some commodities, especially food, beverages, and agricultural raw materials, there are differences in substitutability. For example, tea can substitute for coffee, and sugar beets might substitute for cane sugar. However, not all commodities have a ready substitute. Further, if buffer stocks are to be maintained, the commodities chosen must be able to be stored at relatively low cost and must have a homogeneous market with well-defined and generally recognized grades of quality.[54]

The Organization of Petroleum Exporting Countries (OPEC)

OPEC is a producer cartel (a group of commodity-producing countries that have significant control over supply and that band together to control output and price) that is part of a larger category of energy commodities which also includes coal and natural gas. OPEC is not confined just to the Middle East; it also includes countries in Africa, Asia, and Latin America. The members of OPEC are Algeria, Gabon, Indonesia, Iran, Iraq, Kuwait, Libya, Nigeria, Qatar, Saudi Arabia, the United Arab Emirates, and Venezuela. OPEC controls prices by establishing production quotas on member countries. Producer cartels work when there is a dominant country that can control supply, and Saudi Arabia performs that role in OPEC. In 1996, Saudi Arabia had a production quota of 8 million barrels per day, compared with only 3.6 million for Iran, the country with the next largest quota.

The effectiveness of OPEC is based on several factors, such as

- political and economic conditions of member countries
- non-OPEC oil supply
- substitutes
- demand conditions
- national energy policies (of consumer nations) aimed at energy conservation
- the changing structure of the industry.[55]

The political side of OPEC has always been important. Countries with large populations are tempted to exceed quotas in order to generate more revenues for development. The invasion of Kuwait by Iraq in 1990 was due in part to Iraqi President Saddam Hussein's feeling that oil prices were depressed because Kuwait refused to accept lower production quotas.

Non-OPEC nations are also important. In the early 1970s, OPEC produced 55.5 percent of the world's oil, whereas it was only 40 percent during the early to mid-1990s. The United States, Russia, and Mexico were all producing more oil than any OPEC country except Saudi Arabia. In spite of this, OPEC's huge reserves give it tremendous control over oil prices. OPEC also was able to control the production of member countries following the Gulf War, which helped stabilize prices in the $15–20/bbl range.[56]

The United Nations

This chapter has discussed several examples of regional cooperation to demonstrate the successes and failures among the various types of integration. Obviously, when countries join together, they can accomplish a great deal. Of the numerous bilateral and multilateral organizations, treaties, and agreements, the **United Nations (UN)** is one of the most visible and extensive. Its major purposes are the following:

- To maintain international peace and security
- To develop friendly relations among countries
- To achieve international cooperation in solving international problems of an economic, social, cultural, or humanitarian nature
- To be a center for harmonizing national efforts in these areas

The UN has six major organs: the General Assembly, the Security Council, the Economic and Social Council, the Trusteeship Council, the International Court of Justice, and the Secretariat.[57] Each of these organs impacts business. As companies invest in or do business in foreign countries, political risk is a real issue. One of the major objectives of the UN is to establish peace. Although the UN's peacekeeping efforts have been criticized, it is still working hard to promote peace in the world. In addition, it is working hard to improve human rights and assist countries as they move toward self-determination and independence. Eventually, improvements in the political climate will help countries attract more investment and provide better business opportunities for companies.

The UN has established several organizations that can influence MNEs.

The UN Economic and Social Council is responsible for economic, social, cultural, and humanitarian facets of UN policy. This group organized a Commission on Transnational Corporations to secure effective international arrangements for the operations of MNEs and to further global understanding of the nature and effects of MNEs' activities. The commission has studied a variety of topics, such as transfer pricing, taxation, and international standards for accounting and reporting. The UN also has established several regional economic commissions to study economic and technological problems of different regions and to recommend ways to solve those problems.

A number of other bodies have been set up by the UN, some dealing with issues relating to MNEs. One such group is the United Nations Conference on Trade and Development (UNCTAD). UNCTAD has been especially active in dealing with relationships between developing and industrial countries regarding commodities, manufacturing, shipping, invisibles, and trade-related financing.

UNCTAD, which reports to the General Assembly through the Economic and Social Council, established four standing committees at UNCTAD VIII: commodities, poverty alleviation, economic cooperation among developing countries, and developing services sectors.[58] UNCTAD has also established three ad hoc working groups: trade, environment, and development; the role of enterprises in develop-

UNCTAD is promoting a cooperative approach between industrial and developing countries to solve economic problems.

ment; and trading opportunities in the new international trading context.[59] These working groups have direct impact on companies and their operations, especially in developing countries. It is clear that the agenda of UNCTAD has been to improve the bargaining position of developing countries vis-à-vis high-income countries in the areas mentioned above. However, it has also looked at ways to marshal the resources of high-income countries to influence developing countries and countries in transition. Groups such as the Commision on Transnational Corporations, the Intergovernmental Group of Experts on International Standards of Accounting and Reporting, and the Commission on Science and Technology for Development have been assigned to UNCTAD, making UNCTAD and its supervisory organization, the Economic and Social Council, significant organizations in terms of the impact on MNEs. The impact of the UN on environmental issues will be discussed in the next section.

The Environment

Governments, companies, and individuals are cooperating to solve serious environmental problems.

Pollution of the air, land, and sea clearly poses a threat to the future of the planet, and governments, companies, and individuals are concerned about the present and future state of the environment. Although many environmental problems are national in nature, they have cross-national ramifications and require cross-national agreements. Some of these agreements are tied to regional groups, such as the EU and NAFTA as described earlier in the chapter. These agreements tend to have a strong influence because of the commitment of group members to environmental issues. In addition, many environmental problems have a regional focus, such as the concern over water along the U.S./Mexico border. It would make sense for those issues to be tackled on a regional basis. Some agreements begin with regional groups and extend to other countries. However, these agreements still do not tackle problems on a global basis, and the major source of influence for global environmental agreements is the United Nations.

Major types of environmental degradation mentioned most often are ozone depletion, air pollution, acid rain, water pollution, waste disposal, and deforestation. Ozone depletion results from the burning of fossil fuels and the emission of ozone-depleting chemicals, such as chlorofluorocarbons (CFCs). Ozone depletion may lead to global warming and the destruction of life as a result of excessive exposure to ultraviolet radiation. The Montreal Protocol, signed in 1987, calls for the phaseout of CFCs and other ozone-depleting chemicals by the year 2006.[60] Developing countries were given more time to comply with the Montreal Protocol and were promised $250 million from the high-income countries to help pay for the transition. However, funds have been slow coming in, and this will hurt the value of the Protocol.

The UN is actively involved in environmental issues through the UN Environment Programme (UNEP), an agency of the Economic and Social Council. UNEP's four principal environmental challenges are:

- sustainable management and use of natural resources.
- sustainable production and consumption.
- a better environment for environmental health and well-being, and
- globalization trends and the environment.[61]

UNEP has become involved in a variety of environmental projects, including the management of chemicals, the transborder movements of hazardous wastes and their disposal, the protection of the marine environment from land-based activities, the Framework Convention on Climate Change (which is building on the Montreal Protocol), and the linkage of environmental and economic concerns. UNEP is very important because of its global reach in dealing with global challenges and for its ability to marshal the resources of different agencies that deal with environmental issues.[62]

The Rio Earth Summit culminated in a series of initiatives designed to solve environmental problems.

The Rio Earth Summit, held in June 1992, brought together people from around the world to discuss key environmental issues. The resulting Rio Declaration sets out fundamental principles for environmentally responsive behavior.[63] The problem with international environmental agreements is that each country is headed in its own direction, and countries differ significantly in how they deal with environmental issues. This problem is especially acute in developing countries, where some of the worst environmental damage is taking place and laws tend to be the most lax. Thus, some MNEs might be tempted to save costs by locating production facilities in countries in which environmental laws are weak.

However, many MNEs are among the world's most environmentally responsible companies; they seek to reduce costs by redesigning manufacturing processes to more efficiently use inputs. For example, Du Pont, the U.S.-based chemical company, voluntarily spends approximately $50 million a year more on environmental projects than is required by law. Its goal is zero pollution in all its activities.[64] Its management found that costs actually were reduced when production processes were designed to be more environmentally sound.

Another example of corporate responsibility is TransAlta Corporation, the Canadian energy company. TransAlta issues an environmental report in which it discusses its key environmental initiatives, including

- environment, health, and safety management
- sustainable business initiatives
- external issues, relationships, and opportunities, and
- improved decision making.

One of TransAlta's sustainable business initiatives involves uses of ash from its coal-fired thermal power plants. TransAlta discovered that ash could be substituted for cement to produce concrete and precast concrete products. The ash is valuable because of its low carbon residue, low sodium, light color, fine consistency, and moderate calcium content. Ash is cheaper than cement, and it creates carbon dioxide by displacing some of the fossil fuels, limestone, and electricity used in the production of cement.[65] This is very similar to the Du Pont program described above.

COUNTERVAILING FORCES

Economic integration can stir up a conflict between national sovereignty and the common good of member countries.

An underlying theme of this chapter's discussion is the loss of national sovereignty in the pursuit of economic and political integration. When Europeans began moving toward the Single European Market, during a time of economic expansion in Europe, loss of sovereignty was not a major issue. The one exception was the view of former British Prime Minister Margaret Thatcher that the United Kingdom could not allow the European bureaucracy to grow to the point that British sovereignty would be undermined too much. And when the Danes first rejected the Treaty of Maastricht, it was clear they did not want to lose their sovereignty to Europe's larger countries.

Germany presents another example of the conflict between self-interest and the common good. When reunification with East Germany began, all other programs—including the Single European Market—took a back seat. Clearly, Germany has been pouring billions into the former East Germany and is concerned about the impact of this fiscal stimulus on its inflation rate. Even though the rest of Europe needed lower interest rates to stimulate economic growth, Germany has maintained high interest rates to solve its own problems.

In contrast, the application of several EFTA countries to become members of the EU is an indication that maintaining national sovereignty is not as important to them as being involved in EU policy deliberations. National sovereignty versus the common good is a major issue for NAFTA as well. For example, the side agreements on labor and the environment that were developed in the United States can be seen as efforts to subordinate Mexico's sovereignty to the United States, while maintaining U.S. sovereignty over employee and environmental policies.

LOOKING TO THE FUTURE

It has been argued that the 1990s is the decade of the Triad Strategy, which takes into consideration three important areas: Asia (especially Japan), North America, and Europe (the EU, especially). Because the combined GDP of these three is so vast, companies need to develop a Triad Strategy that includes trade and investment with all of them. The liberaliza-

The Triad Strategy argues for a presence in Europe, North America, and Asia (primarily Japan).

tion of Eastern Europe probably will cause the EU's economic power to expand considerably in the 1990s. The countries that formed the republics of the former Soviet Union (with the possible exception of the Baltic states) may form a regional trading bloc to take advantage of their former economic ties. However, the Commonwealth of Independent States is not as likely to join the EU as are its former Eastern European satellites that were members of COMECON. In addition, the realization of the "Enterprise of the Americas" could considerably expand the trade and investment bases of North, Central, and South America.

Although nationalism will keep the EU from becoming a United States of Europe, significant economic harmonization will occur in the near future. However, a number of issues important to a Single European Market were not solved by December 31, 1992. Thus, Europe 1992 must be regarded as a process, not a specific date. Other key developments will be the EU's acceptance of the EFTA countries, the place of the former Soviet Union in the "European House," and the development of a common currency in 1999.

With NAFTA having taken effect in 1994, some very exciting areas of cooperation will continue to come out of the Americas. The rest of Latin America will find that economic cooperation will be essential to continued peace and prosperity. The ability of the democratically elected governments to remain in power and to develop the democratic tradition within their countries should enhance regional cooperation. A series of bilateral agreements eventually will result in a large multilateral agreement spanning the Americas.

An important issue will be the stability of commodity prices. Low commodity prices will make it difficult for exporting countries to earn enough foreign exchange to service foreign debt and to modernize. Conversely, even though most major oil-consuming countries have cut consumption as a percentage of GDP, high oil prices can have a devastating impact on their economic growth. Although the recession of the early 1990s reduced oil demand and helped hold down prices, there was fear that any significant price increase would touch off an inflationary spiral that would damage economic recovery. In 1990 it was estimated that each $1 drop in the price of a barrel of crude oil would cut the cost of gasoline in the United States by more than $2 billion per year and cut the U.S. trade deficit by $3 billion.[66] Obviously, a price increase would cause the opposite effect in the short term.

How will these trends affect management decisions? Corporate strategy must take market size into consideration, and regional integration certainly affects the size of markets. Further, as integration proceeds in Europe and in North America, companies can make production-location decisions based on economies of scale because they don't have to worry about tariff barriers. Also, as technical standards become more harmonized, companies will not have to make so many adjustments to product categories.

WEB CONNECTION

Check out our home page for links to World Wide Web resources on NAFTA, the European Union, ASEAN, the United Nations, the World Trade Organization, GATT 1994 and other relevant chapter topics.

Summary

- Efforts at regional economic integration began to emerge after World War II as countries saw benefits of cooperation and larger market sizes. The major types of economic integration are the free-trade area, the customs union, the common market, and complete economic integration.

- In its most limited form, economic integration allows countries to trade goods without tariff discrimination (a free-trade area). In its most extensive form, all factors of production are allowed to move across borders, and some degree of social, political, and economic harmonization is undertaken (complete economic integration).

- The static effects of economic integration improve the efficiency of resource allocation and affect both production and consumption. The dynamic effects involve internal and external efficiencies that arise because of changes in market size.

- Trade diversion occurs when the supply of products shifts from countries that are not members of an economic bloc to those that are.

- Once protection is eliminated among member countries, trade creation allows MNEs to specialize and trade based on comparative advantage.

- Regional, as opposed to global, economic integration occurs because of the greater ease of promoting cooperation on a smaller scale.

- The European Union (EU) is an effective common market that has abolished most restrictions on factor mobility and is harmonizing national political, economic, and social policies. As of 1993, it comprised Austria, Belgium, Denmark, Finland, France, Germany, Greece, Ireland, Italy, Luxembourg, the Netherlands, Portugal, Spain, Sweden, and the United Kingdom.

- Some of the EU's major goals are to abolish intrazonal restrictions on the movement of goods, capital, services, and labor; to establish a common external tariff; to achieve a common agricultural policy; to harmonize tax and legal systems; to devise a uniform policy concerning antitrust; and to supersede national currencies.

- By January 1, 1999, the EU hopes to unify its currencies into the Euro.

- The EU has several free-trade agreements with countries and groups of countries, making it the world's largest and richest trading bloc. The next countries that may be considered for **EU** membership are **Cyprus** and **Malta** and some countries of Eastern Europe.

- **The North American Free Trade Agreement (NAFTA) is designed to eliminate tariff barriers and liberalize investment opportunities. The inclusion of other Latin American countries would make this an even more powerful economic bloc.**

- **MERCOSUR is the major trade group in South America. Both NAFTA and the EU have made cooperation agreements with MERCOSUR.**

- **The Association of South East Asian Nations (ASEAN), a group of seven Asian countries, established a free trade area in 1993 that hopes to cut tariffs to a maximum of 5 percent by 2008.**

- **The Asia-Pacific Economic Cooperation (APEC) is a group of eighteen countries that controls half the world's output and 46 percent of the world's merchandise trade, and its goal is to reduce trade barriers and improve cooperation among the nations of the Pacific Rim.**

- **Although there are several regional economic groups in Africa, intrazonal trade is a small percentage of Africa's total.**

- **Many developing countries rely on commodity exports to supply the hard currency they need for economic development. Instability in commodity prices has resulted in fluctuations in export earnings. Commodity agreements, utilizing buffer stocks or quotas or combinations of the two, are established in the hope of stabilizing prices.**

Case
Crystal Lake
Manufacturing—A
NAFTA Dilemma[67]

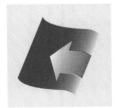

In 1996, Crystal Lake Manufacturing of Autaugaville, Alabama, was awaiting the decision of President Clinton on whether tariffs would be levied on the import of corn brooms, especially from Mexico. Depending on that decision, Crystal Lake had to decide how it was going to survive in the broom market.

The Product
The broom industry in the United States is composed of brooms that use natural fibers and brooms that use synthetic fibers. It is the natural-fibers part of the market and its relationship to U.S. trade agreements, especially the Caribbean Basin Initiative and NAFTA,

that is at issue for Crystal Lake. Corn brooms are made of stiff fiber generated from broom corn, plus the handles, wire, and so on. The principal raw material for the brooms, known as broom corn, used to come primarily from the Midwest. However, Midwest farmers stopped growing broom corn 20 years ago, and the growing of broom corn gradually moved west and then south to Mexico to take advantage of cheaper labor rates. Thus virtually all of the broom corn used by U.S. producers of corn brooms comes from Mexico.

Mexican broom-corn exporters supply the U.S. market primarily through two U.S. dealers. In addition to supplying the U.S. producers with broom corn, Mexican companies also supply broom corn to the broom industries in Honduras and Panama. U.S. producers of broom-corn brooms tend to use the two dealers in order to avoid currency risks, risks of price fluctuations, and inventory costs. In addition, the dealers can scour Mexico to find the best supplies, which tend to come from five different regions in Mexico.

The corn broom production process is very labor-intensive, using one of two different manufacturing processes. The first and most common in the United States is the "wire-bound" process, which involves the hand-winding of tufts of broom corn by workers at individual work stations using a simple winding machine operated by a foot pedal. This is the process used by Crystal Lake Manufacturing, and it takes months, sometimes years, for a worker to master the wire-bound process. An experienced worker can produce 18 to 20 brooms over an eight-hour shift. Experience is key since broom makers are paid on a piece-rate basis. Approximately 25 percent of the cost of a broom using this method is the labor cost. Skilled workers get paid about $8.00 per hour in the United States, compared with significantly lower hourly wage rates in Mexico. In 1995, the average Mexican broom cost $1.92, compared with $3.00 to $3.40 per broom for U.S.-made brooms.

The second manufacturing process is the "nailed machine-made" process, in which the broom fibers are sewn together, usually by machine. This process is less labor-intensive, but the machines are not cheap, costing about $150,000 each. It was estimated that only 16 percent pf the broom-corn brooms manufactured in the United States in 1995 used this method, and 95 percent of them were made by four companies.

Substitutes

A major issue considered by the U.S. International Trade Commission (USITC) in making a ruling to President Clinton is whether all brooms—corn brooms and synthetic brooms—should be lumped together as one product or should be considered as two products. It is clear that synthetic brooms are in direct competition to corn brooms. Even though the products have different properties, they perform the same functions. The key is that some manufacturers such as Crystal Lake produce both types, even though other manufacturers specialize in corn brooms. The significance is that diversified companies are not hurt by the fall in corn broom sales if they can offset the losses with synthetic broom sales.

Competitors

The competition in the broom industry is both domestic and foreign. The U.S. Cornbroom Task Force is composed of ten firms, one of which is Crystal Lake. Crystal Lake is one of three in the Task Force that markets a full range of cleaning supply products (corn brooms, plastic brooms, mops, and cleaning brushes) on a national basis using their own brand name. It is hard to determine the exact size of the industry, although the USITC estimates that there are fewer than eighty producers in the United States. Most of the companies, like Crystal Lake, are family-owned and relatively small. For example, Warren Manufacturing in Arcola, Illinois, and American Broom Co. in Mattoon, Illinois, employ twenty and eighteen workers, respectively. Given the competitive pressures, companies were beginning to consolidate in order to be able to supply the big accounts that dominate the retail market. Many of the companies are in very small communities where the loss of jobs could have a real impact on the local economy. For example, Autaugaville, Alabama, has a population of about 1,000 people, and Arcola, Illinois, which calls itself the Broom Capital of the World, has only 2,600 residents. One estimate put corn broom employment at about 1,500 nationwide, generating sales of about $100 million annually in 1993, and another estimate put employment at 600 nationwide in 1996.

Foreign suppliers of corn brooms to the U.S. market come principally from five countries: Mexico, Honduras, Colombia, Panama, and Hungary. Plastic brooms are sourced primarily from Brazil, Italy, and Venezuela, which accounted for more than 70 percent of the plastic broom imports in 1995.

The Breaking of the Tariff Walls

In 1992 and 1993 when NAFTA was being debated before passage, Crystal Lake management was clearly concerned about the potential impact of eliminating the 32-percent tariff on Mexican broom imports. They estimated that half the plant workers might lose their jobs as a result.

Table 7.7 provides data on shipments of corn brooms and plastic brooms by domestic and foreign producers for the five-year period ending in 1995. Foreign producers are broken into major supplier countries. Table 7.8 provides additional data on U.S. imports of corn brooms by source country for the five years ending in 1995. Finally, Table 7.9 provides information about U.S. production capacity, actual production, and capacity utilization of corn brooms for the five years ending in 1995.

Industry Response

In response to the rapid increase in corn broom imports into the United States, the U.S. Cornbroom Task Force, representing U.S. producers, filed petitions with the U.S. International Trade Commission to win protection from foreign competition. The Task Force filed petitions covered by two areas of U.S. trade law: section 302 of the North American Free Trade Agreement Implementation Act and section 202 of the Trade Act of 1974. Sections 302 and 202 set out tests for determining whether an industry is eligible for relief under the respective trade laws.

Under section 202, the Commission had to explain its decision in terms of three statutory criteria that must be satisfied in order to reach a positive determination:

Table 7.7
Broom-Corn Brooms, Plastic Brooms, and All Brooms: U.S. Producers' Shipments, U.S. Imports, by Sources, and Apparent U.S. Consumption, 1991–1995 (dozens)

Item	1991	1992	1993	1994	1995
Broom-corn brooms:					
U.S. producers' shipments	1,132,125	1,087,100	1,097,977	1,071,269	951,989
U.S. imports from:					
Mexico	157,605	104,067	123,528	195,770	388,286
Panama	43,714	38,952	51,611	107,921	62,306
Honduras	30,174	71,289	70,927	66,817	45,914
Colombia	0	4,465	10,439	13,544	24,981
Hungary	28,920	26,880	43,980	34,208	9,000
All other	39,278	7,771	36,667	26,236	16,222
Total	299,692	253,423	337,151	444,496	546,709
Apparent consumption	1,431,817	1,340,523	1,435,128	1,515,765	1,498,698
Plastic brooms:					
U.S. producers' shipments	605,676	606,067	635,616	716,897	877,844
U.S. imports from:					
Italy	333,222	442,868	305,229	351,471	361,835
Brazil	198,179	546,509	488,956	436,439	340,264
Mexico	27,355	41,428	34,715	51,085	145,347
Venezuela	119,570	84,075	125,444	105,566	120,177
All other	99,284	239,426	205,175	159,167	180,457
Total	777,610	1,354,306	1,159,518	1,103,727	1,148,080
Apparent consumption	1,383,286	1,960,373	1,795,134	1,820,624	2,025,924
All brooms:					
U.S. producers' shipments	1,737,801	1,693,167	1,733,593	1,788,166	1,829,833
U.S. imports from:					
Mexico	184,960	145,494	158,242	246,855	533,633
Italy	336,050	442,868	305,229	351,471	362,435
Brazil	198,179	546,509	488,956	436,439	342,904
Venezuela	119,570	84,075	125,444	105,566	120,177
Panama	47,121	44,767	55,063	114,542	93,849
Honduras	30,174	77,179	76,642	81,508	51,682
Colombia	312	4,465	10,439	18,709	24,981
Hungary	34,920	29,880	43,980	34,625	9,000
All others	126,016	232,492	232,675	158,509	156,129
Total	1,077,301	1,607,729	1,496,670	1,548,223	1,694,789
Apparent consumption	2,815,102	3,300,896	3,230,263	3,336,389	3,524,622

Source: U.S. International Trade Commission (USITC). *Broom Corn Brooms: Investigations Nos. TA-201-65 and NAFTA 302-1,* Publication 2984 (Washington, D.C.: USITC, August 1996), p. II–14.

1. the subject article is being imported into the United States in increased quantities;

2. the domestic industry is seriously injured or threatened with serious injury; and

3. such increased imports are a substantial cause of the serious injury or threat of serious injury.

In order to qualify for the NAFTA provision in section 302, the Commission only considers imports from a NAFTA country, and also must find that the increase in imports from a NAFTA country is a result of the reduction or elimination of a duty under NAFTA.

On July 26, 1996, the USITC Commissioners, in a split vote of 3–2, ruled as follows:

Table 7.8
Broom-Corn Brooms: U.S. Imports for Consumption, by Sources, 1991–1995

Source	1991	1992	1993	1994	1995
	Quantity (*dozens*)				
U.S. imports from:					
Mexico	157,605	104,067	123,528	195,770	388,286
Panama	43,714	38,952	51,611	107,921	62,306
Honduras	30,174	71,289	70,927	66,817	45,914
Colombia	0	4,465	10,439	13,544	24,981
Hungary	28,920	26,880	43,980	34,208	9,000
All other	39,278	7,771	36,667	26,236	16,222
Total	299,692	253,423	337,151	444,496	546,709
	Value (*1,000 dollars*)				
U.S. imports from:					
Mexico	3,129	2,173	2,356	4,070	6,695
Panama	542	491	727	1,728	1,155
Honduras	404	1,073	1,663	1,652	1,216
Colombia	0	55	149	274	460
Hungary	232	200	329	197	62
All other	216	101	228	153	192
Total	4,523	4,094	5,452	8,073	9,780
	Unit Value (*dollars per dozen*)				
U.S. imports from:					
Mexico	$19.85	$20.88	$19.07	$20.79	$17.24
Panama	12.39	12.61	14.09	16.01	18.54
Honduras	13.38	15.05	23.45	24.72	26.49
Colombia	-	12.40	14.27	20.23	18.40
Hungary	8.04	7.45	7.48	5.77	6.87
All other	5.50	12.95	6.21	5.83	11.81
Total	15.09	16.15	16.17	18.16	17.89
	Ratio to U.S. Production (*percent based on quantity*)				
U.S. imports from:					
Mexico	14.0	9.5	11.3	18.4	40.9
Panama	3.9	3.7	4.7	10.2	6.6
Honduras	2.7	6.5	6.5	6.3	5.8
Colombia	-	0.4	1.0	1.3	2.6
Hungary	2.6	2.5	4.0	3.2	0.9
All other	3.5	0.7	3.3	2.5	1.7
Total	26.7	23.2	30.7	41.8	57.7

Source: U.S. International Trade Commission (USITC). *Broom Corn Brooms: Investigations Nos. TA-201-65 and NAFTA 302-1,* Publication 2984 (Washington, D.C.: USITC, August 1996), p. II–17.

1. "broom-corn brooms are being imported into the United States in such increased quantities as to be a substantial cause of serious injury to the domestic industry producing an article like or directly competitive with the imported article; and

2. [pursuant to the NAFTA provisions] that imports of broom-corn brooms produced in Mexico account for a substantial share of total imports of such brooms and

Table 7.9
Broom-Corn Brooms: U.S. Production, Capacity, and Capacity Utilization, 1991–1995

Item	1991	1992	1993	1994	1995
Capacity (dozens)	1,457,236	1,395,886	1,402,593	1,348,810	1,349,475
Production (dozens)	1,123,134	1,094,006	1,096,656	1,063,067	948,267
Capacity utilization (percent)	70.9	73.3	72.4	72.3	64.8

Compiled from data submitted in response to Commission questionnaires.
Capacity utilization calculated using data from those firms providing both capacity and production information.

Source: U.S. International Trade Commission (USITC). *Broom Corn Brooms: Investigations Nos. TA-201-65 and NAFTA 302-1,* Publication 2984 (Washington, D.C.: USITC, August 1996), p. II–18.

contribute importantly to the serious injury caused by imports; but find that imports of broom-corn brooms produced in Canada do not account for a substantial share of total imports and thus do not contribute importantly to the serious injury caused by imports."

The Commission found that imports had increased at the expense of domestic production, especially after the NAFTA tariff reductions ensued in 1994. They found that companies were being hurt—operating income turned from a gain to a loss for a sample of U.S. producers between 1993 and 1994, and employment, hours worked, and total wages paid declined in 1995. In the case of NAFTA, the Commission looked at all possible reasons why imports went up so significantly, but nothing emerged that was more important than or as important as the tariff reductions.

As a result of their findings, the Commission recommended to President Clinton that he impose a 32-percent tariff and give broom makers four years to adjust to the new competitive landscape before tariffs are removed for good. They also recommended that the duty-free treatment of brooms by the Caribbean Basin and Andean countries be suspended.

However, two Commissioners disagreed. One of them, Commissioner Watson, argued the following against the broom-corn broom industry:

This is one of those cases where the parties disagree about nearly every issue. The petitioners argue that there is such a thing as a domestic broom-corn broom industry distinct from the broom industry generally. They also argue that industry is besieged and in danger of being swept onto the ash heap of history. They point to idled plants, increased unemployment, a loss of market share leading to lower production, and balance sheets heavily smudged by red ink. They claim that this perilous state was produced by a cascade of imports, particularly imports from Mexico.

Respondents disagree. They argue that the domestic broom-corn broom industry is but a part of a single broom industry. That industry, say respondents, is being whisked into the modern age by automation and the rapidly growing acceptance of plastic fiber as a substitute for broom corn. They bristle at the petitioners' complaints about competition and contend that what the domestic industry really needs are companies willing to try to mop up the profits to be had by investing in the equipment and training needed to increase productivity and lower the cost of production. The respondents accuse the petitioners of trying to sweep the success of such innovative American companies under the rug , and urge the Commission to peek beneath the petitioners' blanket charges to see an industry with an increasingly productive and well-paid workforce fully capable of standing upright against all competitors. The respondents acknowledge that imports of broom-corn brooms have increased, but contend that the increase is not nearly as important a source of the broom-corn broom makers' woes as is the modernization of broom manufacturing. It is certainly not, they say, the result of NAFTA's knocking a small hole in the high tariff wall built against Mexican imports.

Questions

1. How have the Caribbean Basin Initiative and the NAFTA agreements affected the market share of the U.S. corn broom industry? Be sure to analyze the data.

2. Given the impact of import competition on the corn broom industry and the recommendation of the USITC, should President Clinton allow the industry to be shielded from competition through higher tariffs? Be sure to discuss whether or not you agree with the recommendations of the USITC and the pressures you think President Clinton might have been facing in August and September of 1990 when he had to make a decision.

3. If you were a worker at Crystal Lake Manufacturing, would you be in favor of NAFTA? Why or why not? If you were the purchasing agent for brooms for Wal-Mart, would you be in favor of NAFTA? Why or why not?

4. What are the different scenarios that Crystal Lake Manufacturing could face in the future? What should be their strategies, given the different scenarios?

Chapter Notes

1. The information in this case is from the following sources: various issues of the Ford Motor Company's *Annual Report;* "Tough at the Top," *The Economist,* March 13, 1993, p. 76; Robert L. Simison, "European Auto Makers, Bracing for Downturn, Plan Big Job Cuts," *Wall Street Journal,* March 5, 1993, p. A8; Joseph B. White, "GM, Ford, Coming Out of U.S. Slump, Face Pressure from European Recession," *Wall Street Journal,* March 3, 1993, p. A3; Richard A. Melcher and John Templeman, "Ford of Europe: Slimmer, But Maybe Not Luckier," *Business Week,* January 18, 1993, pp. 44, 46; Timothy Aeppel, "Ford Reaches Fork in Road in Its European Operations," *Wall Street Journal,* October 6, 1992, p. 88; Diana T. Kurylko, "Ford Ready to Give Europe 2 New Cars a Year," *Automotive News,* June 15, 1992, pp. 3, 18; *Forbes,* July 1, 1972, pp. 22–26; *Forbes,* April 2, 1979, pp. 44–48; Roger Cohen, "Ford-Fiat: How Their Contest of Wills Prevented a 'Perfect Marriage' in Europe," *Wall Street Journal,* November 21, 1985, p. 34; Richard A. Melcher, "Ford Is Ready to Roll in the New Europe," *Business Week,* December 12, 1988, p. 60; Heidi Dawley and Keith Naughton, "Ford's Bump Odyssey in Europe," *Business Week,* November 20, 1995, p. 47; James B. Treece, Kathleen Kerwin, and Heidi Dawley, "Ford: Alex Trotman's Daring Strategy," *Business Week,* April 3, 1995, pp. 94–104; "Another New Model," *The Economist,* January 7, 1995, pp. 52–53; ". . . and Other Ways to Peel the Onion," *The Economist,* January 7, 1995, p. 52; Kevin Done, "Survey of World Car Industry," *Financial Times,* October 4, 1994, p. 2; <http://www.ford.com>.

2. Bela Balassa, *The Theory of Economic Integration* (Homewood, Ill.: Irwin, 1961), p. 40.
3. Ibid., p. 4.
4. Renato Ruggiero, "The Road Ahead: International Trade Policy in the Era of the WTO," May 28, 1996. <http://www.wto.org>
5. Ibid.
6. "Regionalism and Trade: The Right Direction?" *The Economist,* September 16, 1996, pp. 24, 27.
7. Michel-Pierre Montet, "Europe's Spiritual Origins," *International Management,* January 1989, p. 39.
8. Sanjeev Gupta, Leslie Lipschitz, and Thomas Meyer, "The Common Agricultural Policy of the EC," *Finance & Development,* June 1989, p. 37.
9. Ibid., pp. 38–39.
10. "Introduction," <http://europa.eu.int/en/eu/guide_en/intro.html>
11. "European Commission," <http://europa.eu.int/en/eu/guide_en/comm.html>
12. "European Parliament," <http://europa.eu.int/en/eu/guide_en/ep.html>
13. "Council of the European Union," <http://europa.eu.int/en/eu/guide_en/council.html>
14. "The Court of Justice of the European Communities," <http://www.cec.lu/e.guide_en/cj.html>
15. Ernst & Whinney, *Europe 1992: The Single Market,* September 1988, pp. 5–6.
16. "A Single Market," *The Economist,* October 22, 1994, p. 15 (in "The European Union Survey).
17. "Sources of EC Budget," <http://europa.eu.int/en/comm/dg10/qa/sl-17.gif>
18. John F. Magee, "1992: Moves Americans Must Make," *Harvard Business Review,* May–June 1989, pp. 78–84.
19. James R. Krum and Pradeep A. Rau, "Organizational Responses of U.S. Multinationals to EC-1992," *Journal of International Marketing,* Vol. 1, No. 2, 1993, p. 67.
20. "The Maastricht Treaty: Where's the Beef?" *The Economist,* May 1, 1993, p. 54.
21. "From Here to EMU," *The Economist,* August 5, 1995, p. 72.
22. Charles Goldsmith, "EU Ministers Adopt Three-Step Process for Single Currency, Keep 99 Deadline," *Wall Street Journal,* October 2, 1995, p. A12 (Western Edition).
23. Charles Enoch and Marc Quintyn, "European Monetary Union: Operating Monetary Policy," *Finance & Development,* September 1996, p. 28.
24. Bill Javetski and Patrick Oster, "Europe: Unification for the Favored Few," *Business Week,* September 19, 1994, p. 54.
25. Thomas Kamm and Cacilie Rohwhedder, "Many Europeans Fear Cuts in Social Benefits in One-Currency Plan," *Wall Street Journal,* July 30, 1996, p. A1 (Western Edition).
26. Thomas Kamm, "French Labor Unrest, Austerity Budget Renew Doubts about Monetary Union," *Wall Street Journal,* August 29, 1996, p. A6 (Western Edition).
27. George Melloan, "Eurocrats See the Euro as Their Holy Grail," *Wall Street Journal,* September 23, 1996, p. A21 (Western Edition).
28. John Barham and Caroline Southey, "Turkish-EU Customs Union Wins Backing from MEPs," *Financial Times,* December 14, 1995, p. 2.
29. Sandor Richter and Laszlo G. Toth, "After the Agreement on Free Trade Among Visegard Group Countries," *Russia and East European Finance and Trade,* July/August 1994, pp. 23–69.
30. "Arguments for Enlargement," *The Economist,* August 3, 1996, p. 41.
31. Linda M. Aguilar, "NAFTA: A Review of the Issues," *Economic Perspectives* (Federal Reserve Bank of Chicago, 1992), p. 14.
32. Canadian Department of Foreign Affairs and International Trade, "Canada, the North American Market and NAFTA," <http://www.dfait-maeci.gc.ca/english/trade/invest/60070b.htm; Miguel Vera Gonzalez, "Cleaning Up Customs: Part II," *Business Mexico* (American Chamber of Commerce of Mexico), April 1996; Office of the U.S. Trade Representative, "The North American Free Trade Agreement: An Overview," <http://www.ustr.gov/agreements/nafta/information/overview.html>
33. Paul Magnusson, James B. Treece, and William C. Symonds, "Honda: Is It an American Car?" *Business Week,* November 18, 1991, pp. 105–112.
34. "Preamble," http://the-tech.mit.edu/Bulletins/Nafta/00.preamble>
35. William DiBenedetto, "Mexico Says Yes to U.S. Cherries," *Journal of Commerce,* February 12, 1997: Available: NEXIS Library: GENERAL NEWS: NEWS: CURNWS
36. Office of the U.S. Trade Representative, "NAFTA and the U.S. Economy," op. cit.
37. "The North American Free Trade Agreement: An Overview," op. cit.; "NAFTA and the Environment," Office of the U.S. Trade Representative, <http://www.ustr.gov/agreements/nafta/information/environment.html>
38. "Wilson Foresees Chile in NAFTA Next Year," *Newsletter,* Canadian Consulate General, Los Angeles, April 30, 1993, p. 2.
39. "The Trade Line-Up," *The Economist,* November 26, 1994, p. 40.
40. Stephen Fidler, "Mercosur and EU to Pave Way for Accord," *Financial Times,* December 14, 1995, p. 8.
41. Laura Gaughan and Andrea Curaca Malito, "Consensus for Our Future: Free Trade in the Americas," *Business America,* December 1994, pp. 5–7.
42. "A Free Trade Agreement for the Americas," *Deloitte & Touche Review,* December 26, 1994, p. 4.
43. Geri Smith, Gail DeGeorge, and John Pearson, "Multinationals Step Lively to the Free-Trade Bossa Nova," *Business Week,* June 15, 1992, pp. 56–57, 60.
44. Joint Press Statement, the Ninth AFTA Council Meeting, Singapore, 26 April 1996, p. 1.
45. Sherry M. Stephenson, "ASEAN and the Multilateral Trading System," *Law & Policy in International Business,* January 1994, p. 439.
46. Europa World Year Book, 1996, p. 105.
47. Fred Bergsten, "The Case for APEC," *The Economist,* January 6, 1996, p. 62.
48. Ibid.
49. Jane Khanna, "Asia-Pacific Economic Cooperation and Challenges for Political Leadership," *The Washington Quarterly,* Winter 1996. Available: NEXIS Library: GENERAL NEWS: NEWS: CURNWS
50. Bergsten, op. cit.
51. <http://www.apecsec.org.sg/apecnet.html>
52. Qiu Xiaoyi, "Roundup: Southern Africa Enters New Era of Peace, Development," *Xinhua News Agency,* April 24, 1996.
53. *Encyclopedia of Public International Law,* Vol. 1 (Amsterdam: North-Holland, 1992), p. 687.
54. *Encyclopedia of Public International Law,* p. 688.
55. "International Oil Market Prospects," *Currency Profiles* (New York: Henley Centre for Economic Forecasting and Manufacturers Hanover Trust Company, December 1989) p. 6.
56. World Bank, *Commodity Markets and the Developing Countries,* May 1996, p. 36.
57. "The UN in Brief," <http://www.un.org/Overview/brief.html>
58. "How UNCTAD Works," <http://www.unicc.org/unctad/en/aboutorg/aboutorg.htm
59. Op. cit.
60. "The Air: Hot Times All Around," *Time,* October 30, 1995, p. 62.
61. "United Nations Environment Programme," <http://unep.unep.no/unep/about.htm
62. Op. cit.
63. Andrew Steer, "The Road from Rio," *Finance & Development,* September 1992, p. 20.

64. David Kirkpatrick, "Environmentalism: The New Crusade," *Fortune,* February 12, 1990, p. 48.

65. TransAlta Corporation 1995 Progress Report, *Sustainable Development.*

66. James Tanner, "Looming Shock," *Wall Street Journal,* December 10, 1990, p. A1.

67. U.S. International Trade Commission (USITC). *Broom Corn Brooms: Investigations Nos. TA-201-65 and NAFTA 302-1,* Publication 2984 (Washington, D.C.: USITC, August 1996); "Sweeping Changes Are Being Feared," *Des Moines Register,* July 31, 1996, p. 10; Barnaby J. Feder, "Tiny Industry Fears NAFTA's Reach," *New York Times,* September 24, 1993, D1; "Report to the President on Investigation No. NAFTA-302-1 (Provisional Relief Phase): Broom Corn Brooms," <http://www. usitc.gov/sec/I0513T1.htm>; Paul Magnusson, "How Many Broom-Makers Does It Take to Kill a Trade Pact?" *Business Week,* July 20, 1992, pp. 29–30; Bill Mintz and Greg McDonald, "Free-Trade Agreement: For U.S. Firms, It's a Deal Likely to Cut Both Ways," *The Houston Chronicle,* August 13, 1992, p. A–8; Paul Merrion and Sara Silver, "Broom Firms Still Bristling," *Crain's Chicago Business,* November 21, 1994, p. 15; Paul Merrion, "Trade Panel Deadlocks on Broom Makers' Appeal," *Crain's Chicago Business,* May 13, 1996, p. 45; Associated Press byline, "Tiny U.S. Broom Industry Could be Swept Away," *Los Angeles Times,* August 23, 1996, p. D-7; and Doug Thompson, "Broom Firms Seeking Tariff Get Brush Off from Clinton," *Arkansas Democrat-Gazette,* September 6, 1996, p. 1D.

Chapter 8

Foreign Direct Investment

Who moves picks up,
who stands still dries up.
—Italian Proverb

Objectives

- To explain why direct investments and portfolio investments are viewed differently by investors and governments

- To demonstrate how foreign direct investments may be acquired

- To evaluate the relationship between foreign trade and international factor mobility, especially direct investment

- To classify the major types of motivations for direct investment

- To illustrate the circumstances that lead companies to seek foreign supplies through their foreign direct investments

- To introduce the advantages of foreign direct investments

- To show the major global patterns of direct investment

Case
Bridgestone Tire
Company[1]

Although there are more than 100 tire manufacturers worldwide, a few companies are increasingly accounting for a larger portion of global sales. This sales concentration has occurred largely because automobile manufacturers prefer to place large orders with a few tire suppliers for the original equipment market (OEM) and to offer replacement tires of the same brands wherever they sell cars. Moreover, there has been a trend toward more high-tech tires that provide better handling in wet conditions and are more durable in situations where temperatures change a lot. The high-tech developments have been expensive, so only those companies with high sales can effectively recoup the developments cost. One of the major means of increasing sales has been to acquire other companies. For example, Bridgestone Tire Company from Japan acquired a controlling interest in an Indonesian tire company and all of a South African tire company in 1996. Major acquisitions by the largest tire manufacturers are shown in Map 8.1.

Bridgestone Tire Company is the world's largest manufacturer of rubber products. It ranked as the second largest company in terms of tire sales in 1994, up from fifth place in 1978. Almost all the company's sales efforts until the mid-1980s were geared toward its home market, yet its foreign sales grew, mainly through indirect exports. Indirect exports occurred because Bridgestone was a major supplier to Japanese automobile companies. Bridgestone tires were part of the original equipment on exported Japanese automobiles, so they arrived in foreign markets in which the company made little or no export effort. Direct exports also began to grow as foreign consumers wanted Bridgestone replacements on the Japanese cars they had purchased. In the mid-1980s, Bridgestone's top management believed that it was essential to grow outside of Japan, a belief based on the assumption that it would be difficult to sustain growth in Japan because exceeding the 50 percent market share Bridgestone held would be hard.

But even earlier, in 1980, Bridgestone's president had announced that the company's first priority would be to establish a manufacturing presence in the United States. Accordingly, it bought a truck-tire plant from Firestone in 1982. By 1987 one out of every ten new cars sold in the United States carried Bridgestone tires. Some dealers also carried Bridgestone tires as replacements; however, Bridgestone had only 2 percent of this larger market. Bridgestone gradually became more confident about its ability to manage and control an automobile-tire manufacturing investment in the highly competitive U.S. market. Part of this confidence derived from the company's success in three areas: with foreign manufacturing facilities in four developing countries, in Australia after buying out Uniroyal there, and with U.S. truck-tire manufacturing after 1982.

Then, in 1988, Bridgestone surprised analysts by buying Firestone's tire operations. This purchase gave Bridgestone five North American plants, which supplied about 40 percent of the tires for North American vehicles built by Ford and 21 percent of those built by GM, as well as plants in Portugal, Spain, France, Italy, Argentina, Brazil, and Venezuela.

But why should Bridgestone manufacture automobile tires in the United States? Why not continue exporting, since sales had grown by this means? Several factors had a potential negative impact on Bridgestone's export activities to the United States. First were government-imposed restrictions on tire imports. Although imports of replacement tires

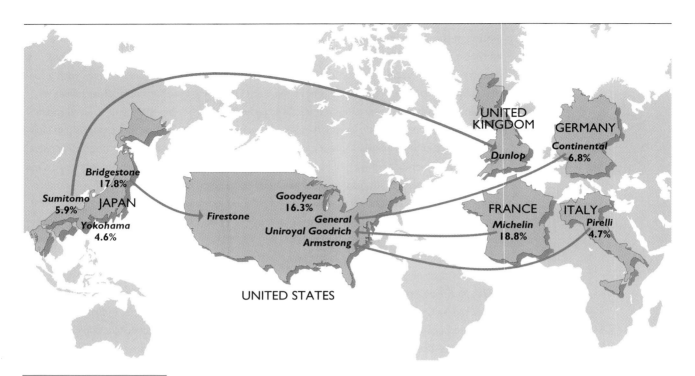

Map 8.1
Major Global Tire Producers and Their Recent Foreign Acquisitions
The percentages give the companies' 1994 global market share of tire sales. The arrows indicate the direction of recent acquisitions.

Source: Global market share figures came from *Financial Times,* January 29, 1996, p. 12.

comprised a very small part of the U.S. market, these imports could be restricted if sales of U.S.-made tires went down. Second, and more probable, was action taken against imports of Japanese automobiles, which would jeopardize the sale of original-equipment tires. The possibility of import restrictions already had led four major Japanese automakers to begin some U.S. production, and all opted for U.S.-made tires once their plants were operating. Further, in late 1987, Germany's Continental Tire, which recently had bought General Tire, announced a joint venture in the United States with two Japanese companies, Toyo and Yokohama, aimed at gaining business from the Japanese automakers' U.S. plants. If this venture proved successful, even Bridgestone's sales in Japan might be jeopardized because the automakers might prefer to buy from one global supplier. This risk was especially important with Toyota, which bought 40 percent of Bridgestone's original-equipment tires. Third, exports also might be imperiled if Japanese costs went up in relation to U.S. costs. Because of high transport costs for tires, which are bulky relative to their value, shipping them over large distances, except as part of vehicles' original equipment, usually is difficult. U.S. producers even depended on multiple U.S. plant locations in order to minimize transport costs.

Bridgestone's ability to overcome the high costs of transportation for exports was due largely to the low value of the yen relative to the U.S. dollar. Most of Bridgestone's costs were in yen, so a fall in the yen's value resulted in lower costs in terms of U.S. dollars; thus Bridgestone could absorb the costs of international transportation. When the yen strengthened, Bridgestone's dollar costs went up. By mid-1986, the strong yen put the competitive sales price below Bridgestone's break-even point. The yen strengthened even more in 1987 and 1988, making it even more difficult for the company to serve the U.S. market by exporting to it. However, the strong yen meant that Bridgestone probably would pay less in yen for an investment in the United States.

But why buy Firestone rather than starting up a new automobile-tire facility? Probably the major factor was an expectation of overcapacity in the industry brought on largely by the increased use of radial tires, which last longer than nonradials. Because Firestone already had secured a significant market share, an acquisition would add less capacity to a glutted market than a start-up operation would, and most of the output could be sold to Firestone's existing customers. In fact, one of these, GM, honored Bridgestone/Firestone as its supplier of the year in 1996 for its OEM sales to GM around the world. Moreover, Bridgestone had little experience in the United States, an environment very different from that in Japan. So the acquisition gave Bridgestone a U.S. management team that knew how to operate within the United States.

Introduction

Studying foreign direct investment (FDI) is important because production facilities abroad comprise a large and increasingly important part of international companies' activities and thus are an integral part of their strategic thrusts. In fact, FDI is now more important than trade as a vehicle for international economic transactions.[2] No one explanation or theory encompasses all the reasons for such investment.[3]

The Bridgestone case illustrates the numerous factors that influenced one Japanese company's decision to produce in a foreign country. Before deciding to invest in U.S. production facilities, Bridgestone faced a sequence of decisions. One of the first decisions was whether to serve foreign markets. The company was content with the Japanese market as long as it could expand rapidly within that market. However, once it had acquired a large and fairly stable share of a maturing market, in order to sustain growth, it had to consider either product diversification or geographical diversification—either of which would involve new risks.[4] Bridgestone chose to diversify geographically because its managers believed its competitive advantage was more specific to the production of tires than to knowledge of the Japanese market. For example, Bridgestone spends heavily on R&D and has made notable breakthroughs in both product and process technologies.[5] It first entered foreign markets through exporting and was successful at that. Nevertheless, its management felt it could not sustain an export market in the United States because of the high transport costs for tires, the possibility that the U.S. government might impose import restrictions, preferences of final or industrial consumers for a U.S.-made product, and an uncertain cost structure created by the changing yen/dollar relationship.

Bridgestone still might have chosen to license its technologies and/or its name to producers already active in the U.S. market, which would have generated revenues without the risk of operating in an alien environment. It elected not to do this for several reasons. First, Bridgestone manufactured tires for Goodyear in Japan under a license agreement, which enabled it to gain knowledge about Goodyear's technology and to use this knowledge for its own competitive advantage. Bridgestone did not want to risk competitive losses, perhaps even in the Japanese market, by sharing its own technology with another company. In fact, Goodyear terminated its license agreement with Bridgestone in 1997 because of Bridgestone's gains in competitive position.[6] Second, by this time, the perceived risk of operating in the United States was minimal because of Bridgestone's growing foreign experience, the likelihood that it could sell output to Japanese automakers with whom it had experience, and its acquisition of a company whose management had U.S. operating experience. In fact, there was risk in not operating in the United States because Toyo and Yokohama could use their U.S. presence as a means of undermining Bridgestone's Toyota connection in Japan. Third, the company felt it must be located in growth markets if it were to survive the expected consolidation in the industry.

The Bridgestone case also illustrates that FDI may be acquired in alternative ways. Neither the motives nor the methods for acquiring such investment illustrated in the case are conclusive. This chapter further examines those various motives and methods.

The growth of FDI has resulted in a heightened interest in three other questions:

1. What effect does foreign direct investment have on national economic, political, and social objectives?
2. What is, or should be, a company's pattern of investment in terms of where to operate abroad?
3. Should a company choose to operate abroad through some form other than direct investment, such as licensing?

These questions are discussed from an introductory standpoint in this chapter and explored more thoroughly in subsequent chapters: question 1 in Chapter 11 (The Impact of the Multinational Enterprise), question 2 in Chapter 13 (Country Evaluation and Selection), and question 3 in Chapter 14 (Collaborative Strategies).

The Meaning of Foreign Direct Investment

The Concept of Control

Direct investment usually implies an ownership share of at least 10 or 25 percent.

You saw in Chapter 1 that for direct investment to take place, control must follow the investment; otherwise, it is known as portfolio investment. The share of ownership necessary for control is not clear-cut. If stock ownership is widely dispersed, then a small percentage of the holdings may be sufficient to establish control of managerial decision making. However, even a 100-percent share does not guarantee control. If a government dictates whom a company can hire, what the company must sell at a specified price, and how earnings will be distributed, then it could be said that control has passed to the government. Governments frequently do impose these decisions on companies. But it is not only governments that may jeopardize the stockholders' control. If some resource the company needs in order to operate is not regulated by the company's owners, then those who control that resource may exert substantial influence on the company. Because direct investments can be difficult to identify, governments have had to establish arbitrary definitions. Usually, they stipulate that ownership of a minimum of 10 or 25 percent of the voting stock in a foreign enterprise allows the investment to be considered direct.

The Concern about Control

When foreign investors control a company, decisions of national importance may be made abroad.

Governmental concern   Why should anyone care whether an investment is controlled from abroad? Many critics of the practice are concerned that the national interest of the host country will not be best served if a multinational company makes decisions from afar on the basis of its own global or national objectives. For example, on the one hand, GM, a U.S. company, owns a 100-percent interest in Vauxhall Motors in the United Kingdom. GM's control of Vauxhall through this direct investment means that GM's corporate management in the United States is concerned directly with and makes decisions about personnel staffing, export prices, and the retention versus payout of Vauxhall's profits. This level of control concerns the British public because decisions that directly affect the British economy are being made, or at least can be made, in the United States. Private British citizens, on the other hand, own some shares of GM. Because these are not enough for control, the British citizens expend no time or effort in making management decisions for GM. Nor is the U.S. populace concerned that vital GM decisions will be made in the United Kingdom. This does not mean that noncontrolled investments are unimportant, however. They may substantially affect exchange rates (as discussed in Chapter 10), and they may play an important part in a company's financial management and strategy (as discussed in Chapter 20).

Investors who control an organization
- **Are more willing to transfer technology and other competitive assets**
- **Usually use cheaper and faster means of transferring assets**

Investor concern   Control also is very important to many companies who are reluctant to transfer certain vital resources to another domestic or foreign organization that can make all its operating decisions independently. These resources may include patents, trademarks, and management know-how, which when transferred can be used to undermine the competitive position of the original holders. This desire to deny rivals access to competitive resources is referred to as the **appropriability theory.**[7] For example, Bridgestone was hesitant to transfer either product technology, such as its SuperFiller radials, or process technology, such as its mold changeover methods, to other companies. Its management was well aware of how acquired technology can be used to competitive advantage.

In addition, operating costs may decrease and the speed of technological transfer may increase when control is retained, for several reasons:

1. The parent and subsidary are likely to share a common corporate culture.
2. The company can use its own managers, who understand its objectives.
3. The company can avoid protracted negotiations with another company.
4. The company can avoid possible problems of enforcing an agreement.

This control through self-handling of operations (internal to the organization), rather than through contracts with other companies, is often called **internalization.**[8] For example, Intel found that the transfer of technology to independent motherboard manufacturers in Taiwan was too slow, so it moved into Taiwan with its own production facility.[9]

Despite the advantages of control, many circumstances exist in which assets are transferred to noncontrolled entities, such as transferring trademarks and technology through licensing agreements. In addition, companies lack resources to control all aspects of their production, supplies, and sales, so they funnel their resources to those activities that are most important to their strategies and their performance.

Methods of Acquisition

Direct investments usually, but not always, involve some capital movement.

Foreign direct investment traditionally has been considered an international capital movement that crosses borders when the anticipated return (accounting for the risk factor and the cost of transfer) is higher overseas than at home. Although most FDIs involve some type of international capital movement, an investor may transfer many other types of assets. For example, Westin Hotels has transferred very little capital to foreign countries. Instead, it has transferred managers, cost control systems, and reservations capabilities in exchange for equity in foreign hotels.

Aside from committing nonfinancial resources, there are two other means of acquiring assets that do not involve international capital movements in a normal sense. First, funds a company earns in a foreign country may be used to establish an investment. For example, a company that exports merchandise but holds payment for those goods abroad can use settlement to acquire an investment. In this case, the company merely has exchanged goods for equity. Although this method is not used extensively for initial investment, it is a major means of expanding abroad. Initially a company may transfer assets abroad in order to establish a sales or production facility. If the earnings from the facility are used to increase the value of the foreign holdings, FDI has increased without a new international capital movement. Second, companies in different countries can trade equity. For example, KLM in the Netherlands acquired a share of Northwest Airlines in the United States by giving Northwest owners stock in KLM, a move that helped integrate the competitive strategies of the two companies.

The Relationship of Trade and Factor Mobility

Whether capital or some other asset is transferred abroad initially to acquire a direct investment, the asset is a type of production factor. Eventually, the direct investment usually involves the movement of various types of production factors as investors infuse capital, technology, personnel, raw materials, or components into their operating facilities abroad. Therefore it is useful to examine the relationship of trade theory to the movement of production factors.

The Trade and Factor Mobility Theory

Both finished goods and production factors are partially mobile internationally.

We explained in Chapter 5 that trade often occurs because of differences in factor endowments among countries. But contrary to historical treatises on trade, production factors themselves also may move internationally. Factor movement is an alternative to trade that may or may not be a more efficient allocation of resources. If neither trade nor the production factors could move internationally, a country would have to either forgo consuming certain goods or produce them differently, which in either case would usually result in decreased worldwide output and higher prices. In some cases, however, the inability to utilize foreign production factors may stimulate efficient methods of substitution, such as the development of new materials as alternatives for traditional ones or of machines to do hand work. For example, the production of synthetic rubber and rayon was undoubtedly accelerated because wartime conditions made it impractical to move silk and natural rubber, not to mention silkworms and rubber plants.

Substitution

There are pressures for the most abundant factors to move to an area of scarcity.

When the factor proportions vary widely among countries, pressures exist for the most abundant factors to move to countries with greater scarcity, where they can command a better return. Thus in countries with an abundance of labor relative to land and capital, laborers tend to be unemployed or poorly paid; if permitted, these workers will gravitate to countries that have relatively full employment and higher wages. Similarly, capital will tend to move away from countries in which it is abundant to those in which it is scarce. For example, Mexico is a net recipient of capital from the United States, and the United States is a net recipient of labor from Mexico.[10] If finished goods and production factors were both completely free to move internationally, the comparative costs of transferring goods and factors would determine the location of production. (However, as is true of trade, there are restrictions on factor movements that make them only partially mobile internationally, such as immigration restrictions in the United States that limit the legal and illegal influx of Mexican workers.)

A hypothetical example, shown in Fig. 8.1, should illustrate the substitutability of trade and factor movements under different scenarios. Assume the following:

Figure 8.1
Comparative Costs Based on Trade and Factor Mobility Assumptions: Tomatoes in the United States and Mexico
The lowest costs occur when trade and production factors are both mobile.

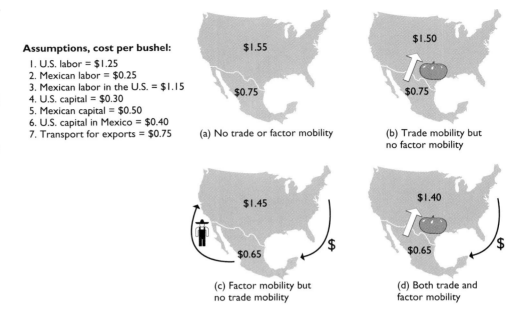

Assumptions, cost per bushel:
1. U.S. labor = $1.25
2. Mexican labor = $0.25
3. Mexican labor in the U.S. = $1.15
4. U.S. capital = $0.30
5. Mexican capital = $0.50
6. U.S. capital in Mexico = $0.40
7. Transport for exports = $0.75

(a) No trade or factor mobility

(b) Trade mobility but no factor mobility

(c) Factor mobility but no trade mobility

(d) Both trade and factor mobility

- The United States and Mexico have equally productive land available at the same cost for growing tomatoes.
- The cost of transporting tomatoes between the United States and Mexico is $0.75 per bushel.
- Workers from either country pick an average of two bushels per hour during a 30-day picking season.

The only differences in price between the two countries are due to variations in labor and capital cost. The labor rate is $20.00 per day, or $1.25 per bushel, in the United States and $4.00 per day, or $0.25 per bushel, in Mexico. The capital needed to buy seeds, fertilizers, and equipment costs the equivalent of $0.30 per bushel in the United States and $0.50 per bushel in Mexico.

If neither tomatoes nor production factors can move between the two countries (see Fig. 8.1a), the cost of tomatoes produced in Mexico for the Mexican market is $0.75 per bushel ($0.25 of labor plus $0.50 of capital), whereas those produced in the United States for the U.S. market cost $1.55 per bushel ($1.25 of labor plus $0.30 of capital). If trade restrictions on tomatoes are eliminated between the two countries (Fig. 8.1b), the United States will import from Mexico because the Mexican cost of $0.75 per bushel plus $0.75 for transporting the tomatoes to the United States will be less than the $1.55 per bushel cost of growing them in the United States.

Consider another scenario in which neither country allows the importation of tomatoes but both allow certain movements of labor and capital (Fig. 8.1c). Mexican workers can enter the United States on temporary work permits for an incremental travel and living expense of $14.40 per day per worker, or $0.90 per bushel. At the same time, U.S. capital can be enticed to invest in Mexican tomato production, provided the capital earns the equivalent of $0.40 per bushel, less than the Mexican going rate but more than the capital would earn in the United States. In this situation, Mexican production costs per bushel will be $0.65 ($0.25 of Mexican labor plus $0.40 of U.S. capital) and U.S. production costs will be $1.45 ($0.25 of Mexican labor plus $0.90 of travel and incremental costs plus $0.30 of U.S. capital). Note that each country could reduce its production costs—from $0.75 to $0.65 in Mexico and from $1.55 to $1.45 in the United States—by bringing in abundant production factors from abroad.

With free trade and the free movement of production factors (Fig. 8.1d), Mexico will produce for both markets by importing capital from the United States. According to the above three assumptions, doing this will be cheaper than sending labor to the United States. In reality, neither production factors nor the finished goods they produce are completely free to move internationally. Slight increases or reductions in the extent of restrictions can greatly alter how and where goods may be produced most cheaply.

In the United States recently, for legal reasons, capital has flowed out more freely than labor has flowed in. The result has been an increase in U.S.-controlled direct investment to produce goods that are then imported back into the United States. In fact, capital moves globally more easily than does labor. Furthermore, technology, particularly in the form of more efficient machinery, generally is more mobile internationally than labor is. Thus differences in labor productivity and costs explain much of the movement of trade and direct investment.

Complementarity of Trade and Direct Investment

Factor mobility via direct investment often stimulates trade because of the need for
- **Components**
- **Complementary products**
- **Equipment for subsidiaries**

Despite the increase in direct investment to produce goods for re-importing, companies usually send substantial exports to their foreign facilities; thus FDI usually is not a substitute for exporting.[11] In fact, about a third of world trade is among controlled entities, such as from parent to subsidiary, subsidiary to parent, and subsidiary to subsidiary of the same company. Many of the exports from parent to subsidiary would not occur if overseas investments did not exist. In these cases, factor movements stimulate trade rather than substituting for it. One reason for this phenomenon is that domestic operating units may ship materials and components to their foreign facilities for use in a finished product. For example, Coca-Cola ships concentrate to its bottling facilities abroad. Foreign subsidiaries or affiliates also may buy capital equipment or supplies from home-country companies because of confidence in their performance and delivery or to achieve maximum worldwide uniformity. A foreign facility may produce part of the product line while serving as sales agent for exports of its parent's other products. Bridgestone, for example, continued to export its automobile tires from Japan for several years while using the sales force of its U.S. truck-tire manufacturing operations to handle those imports.

Motivations for Handling International Business through Direct Investment

Recall from Chapter 1 that there are four major operating objectives that may influence companies to engage in international business:

1. To expand their sales
2. To acquire resources
3. To diversify their sources of sales and supplies
4. To minimize competitive risk

When governments are involved in direct investment, an additional motive may be to attain some political advantage. Foreign direct investment may be a means to support any of these objectives; however, other operating modes are potential alternatives to FDI. The previously discussed concepts of appropriability and internationalization help us to understand why a company may choose to self-handle its foreign operations rather than collaborating with another company to handle operations on its behalf. (Reasons *for* collaboration will be discussed in Chapter 14, Collaborative Arrangements.) However, companies may self-handle by exporting, which would seem a less risky alternative than direct investment because the company has neither to expose an investment in a foreign country nor manage within an environment less familiar than at home. The following discussion concentrates on why direct investment is chosen despite most firms considering it riskier to operate a facility abroad than at home. This discussion follows the framework on objectives for international business in general and is summarized in Table 8.1.

Market-Expansion: Investments versus Trade

Transportation

Eighteenth- and nineteenth-century trade theorists usually ignored the cost of transporting goods. More recently, location theorists have considered total landed cost (cost of production plus shipping) to be a more meaningful way of determining where production should be situated. When the cost of transportation is added to production costs, some products become impractical to ship over great distances. For example, one factor that influenced Bridgestone's decision to invest in the United States was the high cost of transporting tires relative to their production price. Many other products are impractical to ship great distances without a very large escalation in the price; a few of these products and their investing companies are newspapers (Thompson Newspapers, Canadian), margarine (Unilever, British-Dutch), dynamite (Nobel, Swedish), and soft drinks (PepsiCo, U.S.). For these companies, it is necessary to produce abroad if they are to sell abroad. When com-

Table 8.1
Motivations for FDI as an Alternative or Supplement to Trade

Sales expansion objective	Resource acquisition objective	Diversification objective	Competitive risk minimization objective	Political objective
High transport costs	Savings through vertical integration	Customer base (same motivations as for sales expansion objective)	Following customers	Influence companies, usually through factors under resource acquisition objective
Lack of domestic capacity	Savings through rationalized production		Preventing competitors' advantage	
Low gains from scale economies	Gain access to cheaper or different resources and knowledge	Supplier base (same motivations as for resource acquisition objective)		
Trade restrictions				
Barriers because of country-of-origin effects (nationalism, product image, delivery risk)	Need to lower costs as product matures			
	Gain governmental investment incentives			
Lower production costs abroad				

panies move abroad to produce basically the same products that they produce at home, their direct investments are known as **horizontal expansions.**

Excess domestic capacity
• **Usually leads to exporting rather than direct investment**
• **May be competitive because of variable cost pricing**

Lack of domestic capacity   As long as a company has excess capacity at its home-country plant(s), it may be able to compete effectively in limited export markets despite high transport costs. This might occur because fixed operating expenses are covered through domestic sales, thus enabling foreign prices to be set on the basis of variable rather than full costs. Such a pricing strategy may erode as foreign sales become more important or as output nears full plant-capacity utilization. This helps to explain why companies, even those with products for which shipping charges are a high portion of total landed costs, typically export before producing abroad.

This reluctance to expand total capacity while there is still substantial excess capacity is similar to the basis for a domestic-expansion decision. Internationally as well as domestically, growth is incremental. This process can be more readily understood by drawing a parallel of how growth may take place domestically. Most likely, a company will begin operations near the city in which its founders reside and will begin selling only locally or regionally. Eventually, sales may be expanded to a larger geographic market. As capacity is reached, the company may build a second plant in another part of the country to serve that region and to save on transport costs. Warehouses and sales offices may be located in various cities in order to assure closer contact with customers. Purchasing offices may be located near suppliers in order to increase the probability of low-cost delivery. In fact, the company may even acquire some of its customers or suppliers in order to reduce inventories and gain economies in distribution. Certain functions may be further decentralized geographically, such as by locating financial offices near a financial center. As the product line evolves and expands, operations continue to disperse. In the pursuit of foreign business, not surprisingly, growing companies eventually find it necessary to acquire assets abroad. In many ways this model of incremental expansion is becoming obsolete, however. Existing as well as new companies are becoming more prone to develop new products with a global rather than a local market segment in mind.

In large-scale process technology, large-scale production and exportation usually reduce unit landed costs by spreading fixed costs over more units of output.

In small-scale process technology, country-by-country production usually reduces unit landed costs, since transportation is minimized.

Scale economies   Costs of transportation must be examined in relation to the type of technology used to produce a good. The manufacturing of some products necessitates plant and equipment that use a high fixed-capital input. In such a situation, especially if the product is highly standardized or undifferentiated from those of competitors, the cost per unit is apt to drop significantly as output increases. Products such as ball bearings, alumina, and semiconductor wafers fall into this category. Large amounts of such products are exported because the cost savings from scale economies overcome added costs of transportation.

Products that are more differentiated benefit less by scale economies. For these types of products, transport costs may dictate smaller plants to serve national rather than international markets. This differentiation affects company production in two ways. Initially, it means an additional investment; as long as an investment is needed to serve the foreign market anyway, management might consider locating facilities abroad. Next, it may mean that certain economies from large-scale production will be lost, which may shift the least-cost location from one country to another. The more the product has to be altered for the foreign market, the more likely it is that production will be shifted abroad. Electrolux, for example, a Swedish producer of major household appliances, first entered Asian markets by exporting to them. However, it was unable to gain more than minuscule sales with its line of appliances suitable for European and North American markets; so in 1996 it launched a line of appliances aimed at these markets that included specially designed hoses to prevent rodents from chewing on them, coatings on circuit boards to discourage ants, heavy zinc coatings to prevent rust, and electrical systems that are more tolerant to erratic electric supplies. Given the number of product alterations, there was little economy of scale to be gained by exporting. Instead, Electrolux shifted production to Asia to overcome transport costs.[12]

If imports are highly restricted, companies
- **Often produce locally to serve the local market**
- **Are more likely to produce locally if market potential is high relative to scale economies**

Trade Restrictions

We have shown that, for various reasons, a government can make it impractical in many ways for companies to reach their market potential through exportation alone. Companies may find they *must* produce in a foreign country if they are to sell there. For example, many companies find export sales to China, such as of elevators, to be impractical because of Chinese trade restrictions. Such firms as

United Technologies, Schindler Holding, and Mitsubishi have made direct investments in Chinese elevator production in order to tap the growing market.[13] India
has required automobile companies to assemble within India and to use a rising
portion of parts that are made within India; thus automobile producers, such as
Hyundai, plan to increase Indian local content substantially by the early part of the
twenty-first century.[14] Such governmental trade restrictions undoubtedly favor
large companies that can afford to commit large amounts of resources abroad,
while making foreign competitiveness more difficult for very small companies,
which can only afford exportation as a means of serving foreign markets. This does
not mean that smaller companies have no FDI. Many do, such as Amsco International, a producer of sterilization equipment, and Interlake, a manufacturer of fluid-
handling products.[15] However, such companies must serve the world from a
handful of manufacturing bases rather than building plants in nearly all places in
which they have potential sales.

How prevalent are trade restrictions as an enticement for making direct investments? There is substantial anecdotal evidence of decisions by companies to locate
within protected markets, yet studies of aggregate movements of direct investment
are inconclusive regarding the importance of trade barriers.[16] Some studies have
not found import barriers to be an important enticement, perhaps because the
studies have had to rely on actual tariff barriers as the measure of restrictions. This
reliance overlooks the effects of nontariff constraints, indirect entry barriers, and
potential trade restrictions. For example, Bridgestone reacted to potential trade
restrictions rather than to the actual existence of tariffs on tires. Further, companies
sometimes will make a limited foreign investment as a means of defusing protectionist sentiments, thus prolonging their export capabilities.[17]

Import barriers almost certainly are a major enticement to direct investment,
but they must be viewed along with other factors, such as the market size of the
country imposing the barriers. For example, import trade restrictions have been
highly influential in enticing automobile producers to locate in Brazil. Similar
restrictions by Central American countries have been ineffective because of their
small markets. However, Central American import barriers on products requiring
lower amounts of capital investment and therefore smaller markets (for example,
pharmaceuticals) have been highly effective at enticing direct investment.

Removing trade restrictions among a regional group of countries also may
attract direct investment, possibly because the expanded market may justify scale
economies. Or the removal of trade restrictions may result in trade diversion, as
discussed in Chapter 7. In turn, companies may invest to take advantage of the trade
diversion. For example, the Taiwanese textile industry could export substantial
clothing products into the United States as long as it faced the same duties as producers from other countries did. The reduction of duties through NAFTA offers
tariff-saving advantages for Mexican production to serve the U.S. market that Taiwanese production does not have; so there has been some trade diversion from the
more efficient output in Taiwan to less efficient output in Mexico. Many Taiwanese

companies have reacted to NAFTA's passage by setting up factories in Mexico, and many U.S.-owned firms have shifted factories from Taiwan to Mexico.[18]

Country-of-Origin Effects

Government-imposed legal measures are not the only trade barriers to otherwise competitive goods; consumer desires also may dictate limitations. Consumers may prefer to buy domestically produced goods even when they are more expensive, perhaps because of nationalism, a belief that foreign-made goods are inferior, or the fear that service and replacement parts for imported products will be difficult to obtain.

Consumers sometimes prefer domestically produced goods because of
• Nationalism
• A belief that these products are better
• A fear that foreign-made goods may not be delivered on time

Nationalism   The impact of nationalistic sentiments on investment movements is not easily assessed; however, some evidence does exist. In many countries, promotional campaigns have been instituted to persuade people to buy locally produced goods. For example, in the United States, some manufacturers have promoted "Made in the USA" to appeal to consumers of products that have been hit with import competition; a specific example is the campaign by the American Fiber, Textiles, and Apparel Coalitions to push "Crafted with Pride in the U.S.A."[19] In addition, some Japanese companies, fearing that adverse public opinion might lead to curbs on television imports, announced they would establish U.S. production plants.[20]

Product image   The link between product image and direct investment is clearer than that between nationalism and direct investment. A product's image may stem from the merchandise itself or from beliefs concerning after-sales servicing. In tests using commodities that were identical except for the label indicating country of origin, consumers were found to view products differently on the basis of their source.[21] There are examples of eventual image changes, such as the general improvement in the image of Japanese products that occurred concomitantly with the decline in image for U.S. products. However, it may take a long time and be very costly for a company to try to overcome image problems caused by manufacturing in a country that has a lower-status image for a particular product. Consequently, there may be advantages to producing in a country that has an existing high image.

Delivery risk   Many consumers fear that service and/or replacement parts for foreign-made goods may be difficult to obtain from abroad. Industrial consumers often prefer to pay a higher price to a nearby producer in order to minimize the risk of nondelivery due to distance and strikes. For example, Hoechst Chemical of Germany located one of its dye factories in North Carolina because the textile industry in that region feared that delivery problems would plague German imports. Related to this potential problem is the global rise in **just-in-time (JIT) manufacturing systems,** which decrease inventory costs by having components and parts delivered as they are needed in production. These systems favor nearby suppliers who can deliver quickly.

Changes in Comparative Costs

A company may export successfully because its home country has a cost advantage. The home-country cost advantage depends on the prices of the individual factors of production, the size of the company's operations, the cost of transporting finished goods, any regulations on how to produce, and the productivity of the combined production factors. None of these conditions is static; consequently, the least-cost location may change over time. Recall that Bridgestone's decision to locate in the United States was based partly on the fact that Japanese costs (measured in dollars) grew much faster than U.S. costs did, largely because of a rise in the value of the yen relative to the dollar.

The concept of shifts in comparative production costs is closely related to that of resource-seeking investments. A company may establish a direct investment to serve a foreign market but eventually import into the home country from the country to which it was once exporting. Production costs are discussed in the following section on resource-seeking investments.

Resource-Acquisition Investments

Sales expansion objectives in international business imply an alternative of serving a foreign market by export or by production from a foreign direct investment. Resource acquisition objectives, however, imply a need to import from abroad; therefore, FDI is a supplement rather than an alternative to trade. Of course, one may obtain resources from abroad simply by buying them from another company; nevertheless, there are factors that favor FDI to gain these resources. The cartoon in Fig. 8.2 matches the popular image of FDI in that it is motivated mainly to take advantage of cheap labor abroad, leaving home-country workers unemployed or in lower-paid jobs. This image, though true to some extent, overlooks the fact that most FDI is market-seeking rather than resource-seeking, and that the image of many locales, such as Taiwan and Hong Kong, has outlasted the reality of their being a cheap-labor location. Further, by looking only at labor, one overlooks some of the other costs of producing abroad. For example, Quality Coils, a small maker of electromagnetic coils, moved from the United States to Mexico but had so many problems with absenteeism, low productivity, and long-distance management that it moved back home after a few years.[22] Further, there are cost advantages from direct investment that are not fully encompassed in the popular labor-oriented image.

Vertical Integration

Vertical integration is control of the different stages (sometimes collectively called a value chain) as a product moves from raw materials through production to its final

Figure 8.2

Source: Drawing Dana Fradon; ©1992 The New Yorker Magazine, Inc.

"Great. You move to Mexico, and we all end up working at McDonald's."

distribution. As products and their marketing become more complicated, there is a greater need to combine resources that are located in more than one country. If one country has the iron, a second has the coal, a third has the technology and capital for making steel and steel products, and a fourth has the demand for steel products, there is great interdependence among the four and a strong need to establish tight relationships in order to ensure that production and marketing continue to flow. One way to help assure this flow is to gain a voice in the management of one of the foreign operations by investing in it. Most of the world's direct investment in petroleum may be explained by this concept of interdependence. Since much of the petroleum supply is located in countries other than the countries having a heavy petroleum demand, the oil industry has become integrated vertically on an international basis.

Certain economies also may be gained through vertical integration. Because supply and/or markets are more assured, a company may be able to carry smaller inventories and spend less on promotion. This greater assurance also may permit considerably greater flexibility in shifting funds, taxes, and profits among countries.

Advantages of vertical integration may accrue to a company through either market-oriented or supply-oriented investments in other countries. Of the two, there have been in recent years more examples of supply-oriented investments designed to obtain raw materials in other countries. This is because of the growing dependence on LDCs for raw material supplies and the lack of resources among firms in LDCs to invest substantially abroad.

Rationalized Production

Companies increasingly produce different components or different portions of their product line in different parts of the world to take advantage of varying costs of labor, capital, and raw materials. Doing this is called **rationalized production.** For example, many Mexican plants are integrated with operations in the United

In rationalized production, different components or portions of a product line are made in different parts of the world. The advantages are
• Factor-cost differences
• Long production runs
The challenges are
• Satisfying governments that local production takes place
• Higher risk of work stoppages
• Record keeping

States. Semifinished goods are exported from the United States to Mexico for the labor-intensive portion of the production, such as sewing car seats for GM or building TV cabinets for Panasonic.[23]

Many companies shrug off the possibility of rationalized production of parts. They fear work stoppages in many countries because of strikes or a change in import regulations in just one country. As an alternative to parts rationalization, a complete product can be produced in a given country; however, only part of a company's product range is produced in that country. For example, a U.S. subsidiary in France may produce only product A, another subsidiary in Brazil only product B, and the home plant in the United States only product C. Each plant sells worldwide so that each can gain scale economies and take advantage of differences in input costs that may result in differences in total production cost. Each may get concessions to import because it can demonstrate that jobs and incomes are developed locally.

Another possible advantage of this type of rationalization is smoother earnings when exchange rates fluctuate.[24] Consider the value of the Japanese yen relative to the U.S. dollar. Honda produces some of its line in Japan and then exports this production to the United States. Honda also produces some of its line in the United States and then exports this production to Japan. If the yen strengthens, Honda may have to cut its profit margin to stay competitive on its exports to the United States. But this cut may be offset by a higher profit margin on the exports to Japan.

Access to Production Factors

A company may establish a presence in a country in order to improve its access to knowledge and other resources.

The practice of seeking abroad some input not easily or inexpensively available in the home country closely resembles vertical integration. In many cases, the move takes place because of changes in comparative costs or capabilities. For example, Mercedes-Benz has shifted some of its production to Brazil because of rising German costs.[25] Such companies as Digital Equipment have made investments in India in order to access Indian software talent.[26] In a different type of move, many foreign companies have offices in New York City in order to gain better access to what is happening within the U.S. capital market or at least to what is happening within that market that can affect other worldwide capital occurrences. With satellite telecommunications technology, information may be transferred almost instantaneously by personnel in foreign offices. The search for knowledge may take other forms as well. For example, a U.S. pharmaceutical firm may conduct in Peru research not allowed in the United States. Real examples are C.F.P. (French), which bought a share in Leonard Petroleum in order to learn U.S. marketing so as to compete better with other U.S. oil firms outside the United States, and McGraw-Hill, which has an office in Europe to allow it to uncover European technical developments.

The product life cycle theory explains why
• New products are produced mainly in industrial countries
• Mature products are more likely to be produced in LDCs

The Product Life Cycle Theory

In Chapter 5, we explained the product life cycle (PLC) theory in relation to trade and production location.[27] This theory shows how, for market and cost reasons, production often moves from one country to another as a product moves through its life cycle. During the introductory stage, production occurs in only one (usually industrial) country. During the growth stage, production moves to other industrial countries, and the original producer may decide to invest in production facilities in those foreign countries to earn profits there. In the mature stage, production shifts largely to developing countries, and the same company may decide to control operations there as well.

Governmental Investment Incentives

Governmental incentives may shift the least-cost production location.

In addition to restricting imports, countries frequently encourage direct investment inflows by offering tax concessions or a wide variety of other subsidies. This subject is discussed in greater detail in Chapter 12, but briefly, such incentives affect the comparative cost of production among countries and entice companies to invest in a particular country to serve national or international markets. Many central and local governments offer direct-assistance incentives, including tax holidays, accelerated depreciation, low-interest loans, loan guarantees, subsidized energy or transport, and the construction of rail spurs and roads to serve a plant facility. For example, South Carolina offered BMW $150 million in tax breaks and other incentives.[28]

Diversification-Oriented Investments

Companies may pursue international business, at least partially, to minimize cyclical swings in sales and profits and to reduce the dependence on a few customers or suppliers. Nevertheless, the reasons for choosing FDI as a mode of operation are no different from those we have already discussed. For example, if the diversification is sales-oriented, a company may consider exporting into new markets; however, the ability to export may be affected by such factors as high transportation costs and trade restrictions that we have already discussed. Similarly, if the objective is to diversify supplies, it may be advantageous to secure more control of the links in the value chain as discussed in the section on resource-acquisition investments.

Competitive Risk Minimization

Following Customers

Companies can keep customers by following them abroad.

Many companies sell abroad indirectly; that is, they sell products, components, or services domestically, which then become embodied in a product or service that their domestic customer exports. For example, Bridgestone sold tires to Toyota and Honda, which in turn exported fully assembled cars (including the tires) to foreign markets. In such situations, the indirect exporters commonly follow their customers when those customers make direct investments. Bridgestone's decision to make automobile tires in the United States was based partially on its desire to continue selling to Honda and Toyota once those companies initiated U.S. production.

More recently, it has followed those customers into markets in Thailand and Indonesia.[29]

Preventing Competitors' Advantage

Within oligopolistic industries (those with few sellers), several investors often establish facilities in a given country within a fairly short time.[30] For example, between 1991 and 1995, eleven different automobile companies received licenses to make investments in Vietnam.[31] Much of this concentration may be explained by internal or external changes, which affect most oligopolists within an industry at about the same time. For example, in many industries, most companies experience capacity-expansion cycles at about the same time. Thus they would logically consider a foreign investment at approximately the same time. Externally, they might all be faced with changes in import restrictions or market conditions that indicate a move to direct investment in order to serve consumers in a given country. In spite of the prevalence of these motivators, many movements by oligopolists seem better explained by defensive motives.

Much of the research in game theory shows that people often make decisions based on the "least-damaging alternative." The question for many companies is, "Do I lose less by moving abroad or by staying at home?" Assume that some foreign market may be served effectively only by an investment in the market, but the market is large enough to support only one producer. To solve this problem, competitors could set up a joint operation and divide the profits among themselves; however, antitrust laws might discourage or prevent this. If only one company establishes facilities, it will have an advantage over its competitors by garnering a larger market, spreading its R&D costs, and making a profit that can be reinvested elsewhere. Once one company decides to produce in the market, competitors are prone to follow quickly rather than let that company gain advantages. Thus the decision is based not so much on the benefits to be gained but rather on the greater losses sustained by not entering the field. In most oligopolistic industries (for example, automobiles, tires, and petroleum), this pattern helps to explain the large number of producers relative to the size of the market in some countries. Closely related to this pattern is the decision to invest in a foreign competitor's home market to prevent that competitor from using high profits obtained in that market to invest and compete elsewhere.[32]

Political Motives

Trade sometimes is driven by political motives. For example, as we discussed in Chapter 5, during the mercantilist period, European powers sought colonies in order to control those colonies' foreign trade and extend their own spheres of influence. Since the passing of colonialism, some countries continued to pursue many of the old colonial aims by encouraging their domestically based companies to control vital sectors in the economies of LDCs.[33] With the cessation of the Cold

War, this encouragement has subsided; however, governmental actions remain a potential motive for direct investment. For example, a U.S. company that controls the production of a vital raw material in an LDC can effectively prevent unfriendly countries from gaining access to the production. It also may be able to prevent local processing, dictate its own operating terms, and hold down prices on production sent to the home country. In the process of gaining control of resources, industrial nations also acquire much political control.

Control of resources is not necessarily the political reason for encouraging direct investment. For example, during the early 1980s, the U.S. government instituted various incentives designed to increase the profitability of U.S. investment in Caribbean countries that were unfriendly to Cuba's Castro regime. The incentives were designed to lure more investment to the area, thus strengthening the economies of those friendly nations and making it difficult for unfriendly leftist governments to gain control. But with the end of the Cold War, the U.S. ended investment incentives in the Caribbean region, and much investment was diverted to Mexico because of better access of output to the U.S. market through NAFTA.[34]

When governments own and control companies that operate internationally, the investments have not always been politically motivated. Countries simply may be acting in terms of any of the rational economic motives discussed earlier in this chapter.

Buy-versus-Build Decision

There are advantages and disadvantages to either acquiring an interest in an existing operation or constructing new facilities. A company must consider both alternatives carefully.

Reasons for Buying

The advantages of acquisition of an existing operation include
• Avoiding start-up problems
• Easier financing
• Adding no further capacity in the market

Whether a direct investment is made by acquisition or start-up depends, of course, on which companies are available for purchase. The large privatization programs occurring in many parts of the world have put hundreds of companies on the market, and MNEs have exploited this new opportunity to invest abroad. For example, over half the value of FDI in Central and Eastern Europe has come from privatization programs.[35] There are many reasons for seeking acquisitions. One concerns the difficulty of transferring some resource to a foreign operation or acquiring that resource locally for a new facility. One resource that is particularly difficult to acquire is personnel, especially if the local labor market is tight. Instead of paying higher compensation than competitors do to entice employees away from their old jobs, a company can buy an existing company, which gives the buyer not only labor and management but also a whole organizational structure through which these personnel may interact. Through acquisitions, a company also may gain the good will and brand identification important to the marketing of mass consumer products, especially if the cost and risk of breaking in a new brand are high. Further, a company that depends substantially on local financing rather than on the transfer of capital may find it easier to gain access to local capital through an acquisition. Local capital suppliers may be more familiar with an ongoing operation than with the foreign enterprise. In addition, an existing company sometimes may be acquired through an exchange of stock, thus circumventing home-country exchange controls.

In other ways, acquisitions may reduce costs and risks as well as provide quicker results. A company may be able to buy facilities, particularly those of a bankrupt operation, for less than it would cost to build them at current construction costs. If an investor fears that a market does not justify added capacity, as in the Bridgestone case, acquisition enables it to avoid the risk of depressed prices and lower unit sales per producer, which might result from new facilities. Finally, by buying a company, an investor avoids the high expenses caused by inefficiencies during the start-up period and gets an immediate cash flow rather than tying up funds during construction.

Reasons for Building

Companies may choose to build if
- **No desired company is available for acquisition**
- **Acquisition will carry over problems**
- **Acquisition is harder to finance**

Although acquisitions offer advantages, a potential investor will not necessarily be able to realize them. Foreign investments frequently are made where there is little or no competition, so finding a company to buy may be difficult. In addition, local governments may prevent acquisitions because they fear lessening competition or market dominance by foreign enterprises. Even if acquisitions are available, they are less likely to succeed than start-up operations.[36] One factor is that those companies that can be acquired might embody substantial problems for the investor: Personnel and labor relations may be both poor and difficult to change, ill will rather than good will may have accrued to existing brands, or facilities may be inefficient and poorly located in relation to future potential markets. Further, the managers in the acquiring and acquired companies may not work well together. For example, Bridgestone found that the Firestone operations were less efficient than it had anticipated. On top of that, Firestone initially lost the GM account, and Bridgestone had to spend heavily to modernize Firestone plants in the United States and abroad before getting the account back. Many other Japanese investors have faced problems with their U.S. acquisitions.[37] Finally, local financing may be easier rather than harder to obtain if the investing company builds facilities, particularly if it plans to tap development banks for part of its financial requirements.

Advantages of Foreign Direct Investment

Most successful domestic companies, especially those with unique advantages, invest abroad.

Direct investment makes companies more successful domestically.

Are companies profitable because they are multinational or multinational because they are profitable? Such a "chicken-or-egg" type of question has hounded direct investment theorists. On the one hand, evidence indicates that very successful domestic companies (both large and small) are most likely to commit resources to

FDI; on the other hand, ownership of FDI appears to make companies more successful domestically.[38]

Monopoly Advantages before Direct Investment

One explanation for why companies engage in FDI is that they perceive they hold some supremacy over similar companies in the countries into which they go. This edge often is called a **monopoly advantage.** The advantage results from a foreign company's ownership of some resource that is unavailable at the same price or terms to the local company. The resource may be patents, product differentiation, management skills, access to markets, or the like. Because of the increased cost of transferring resources abroad and the perceived greater risk of operating in a different environment, the company will not move unless it expects a higher return than it can get at home and a higher return than the local firm abroad makes.[39]

Large groups of companies may enjoy certain monopoly advantages, which may explain their relative ability and willingness to move abroad. For example, when capital is an integral part of a new investment, the company that can borrow in a country with a low interest rate has an advantage over the company that cannot. Prior to World War I, Great Britain was the largest source of direct investment because of the strength of the pound sterling and the resulting lower interest rates on borrowing sterling funds. From World War II until the mid-1980s, the strength of the U.S. dollar gave an advantage to U.S. firms. After that, this advantage shifted to Japanese companies.[40]

A related advantage is the relative buying power of different currencies in terms of the plant and equipment they will purchase. During the two and a half decades following World War II, the U.S. dollar was very strong, and it was perhaps overvalued in later years. As a result, by converting dollars to other currencies, U.S. companies could purchase a greater output capacity in foreign countries than they could after the dollar began to slide downward in 1971. The reverse was true for companies from such countries as Japan and Germany, which invested more heavily in the United States during the late 1970s and mid-1980s, when the yen and mark increased their purchasing power.

Currency values do not, however, provide a strong explanation for direct investment patterns. There was a two-way investment flow between the United States and Germany and between the United States and Japan when the dollar was weak as well as when the dollar was strong. Then, in the first half of the 1980s, U.S. companies did not significantly increase investment abroad, but foreign companies invested heavily in the United States despite the strong dollar. The major reasons were high real interest rates in the United States and a relatively strong U.S. economy. In the late 1980s and the early 1990s, when the dollar was weak again, direct investment flowed both to and from the United States in record amounts.[41] Therefore the currency-strength scenario only partially explains direct investment flows and must be viewed along with other motives for direct investment.

thical questions concerning direct investment activities have been widely debated. On the one hand, direct investment may lead to better global use of resources. On the other, a disproportionate share of the costs may have to be borne by only a few people. For example, transferring production from a domestic to a foreign location will cause some employees to lose their jobs, and many of them may not easily find new positions. For these employees, there is little solace in the economic gains that go to previously unemployed workers abroad or the lower consumer prices or higher earnings resulting from the foreign production. Some people argue that the plight of these newly unemployed workers is no different from the results of technological change—for example, the replacement of workers in clothes pin factories when electric clothes dryers were adopted. Thus, they should be handled no differently. Others argue that displacement due to a move abroad is different because the workers cannot move abroad to take advantage of the new opportunities there and because the change occurs within the same company. They argue that the company has an ethical obligation to ease employees' adversity by giving advance notice of the move and providing assistance, such as through training and help with job searches.

ETHICAL DILEMMAS & SOCIAL RESPONSIBILITY

Companies say that such moves are motivated by changes in external conditions over which they have no control, such as costs, taxes, market location, or regulations. For example, Acme Boots announced in 1993 that it was moving out of the United States to gain tax advantages in Puerto Rico; this move stranded its U.S. employees, some of whom had up to thirty years' service. Many critics argue that it is unethical for governments to lure companies away from existing locations by offering lucrative incentives and that it is unethical for companies to move. Do home-country governments have any ethical obligations, especially if their policies, such as environmental regulations or high tax rates, burden domestic producers disproportionately compared to foreign ones?

Rationalized production also may lead to global efficiencies through coordinated utilization of the cheap inputs of unskilled labor from LDCs and the expensive inputs of high-skilled labor and technology from industrial countries. Critics of MNEs contend that this is unethical because the process perpetuates economic distinctions between the "have" and "have not" countries. Others argue that the LDC labor would otherwise be unemployed. Do companies or governments have any ethical obligation to the unskilled laborers in their domestic markets who can find little in the way of employment?

Privatization programs recently have been stimulated by sales of enterprises to foreign investors. Is it ethical to transfer to foreign investors assets that belong to the country as a whole? Does it make any difference whether the state enterprises were profitable? In some cases, such as Argentina's sale of its national airline to Iberia of Spain, the ownership changes from domestic state ownership to foreign state ownership. Do such situations have the same ethical implications as sales to foreign private companies do?

Advantages after Direct Investment

In order to support the large-scale expenditures (such as spending for R&D) that
are necessary to maintain domestic competitive viability, companies frequently
must sell on a global basis. To do this, they often must establish direct investments
abroad. The advantage accruing to more internationally oriented companies from
spreading out some of the costs of product differentiation, R&D, and advertising is
apparent in a comparison of their profitability with that of other companies. Among
industry groups and groups of companies of similar size that spent comparable
amounts on advertising and R&D and had similar capital intensity, the more internationally oriented companies in almost every case earned more than the other
companies.[42]

Economies in various countries are in different stages of the business cycle at
different times. Companies that operate in different economies can reduce fluctuations in year-to-year sales and earnings more than can those that operate only in a
domestic environment.[43] Thus MNEs effectively reduce their operating risks.

The Strategy of Direct Investment in the Internationalization Process

Exporting to a locale usually precedes foreign direct investment there when the
output is intended to be sold primarily in the same country where the investment is
made. This is partly because of the wish to use domestic capacity before creating
new capacity abroad. But there are other factors as well. One is that companies
want a better indication that they can sell a sufficient amount in the foreign country
before committing resources for production there. Another is that foreign locations
are perceived to be riskier than domestic ones for operations because management
is not as familiar with foreign environments, where they must undertake multifunctional activities such as production and marketing. They feel that they must have
some monopolistic advantage to overcome this environmental obstacle, so the
export experience provides information on whether they actually have sufficient
product advantages and enables them to learn more about the foreign operating
environment. Once they have experience in foreign production, they are more apt
to shorten the export-experience time before they produce abroad in a new
location.

When the motive for foreign investment is to acquire resources, there is little or
no opportunity to export in order to learn about the foreign environment. However, one may question why a company chooses to invest abroad rather than simply
buy from a local company within the foreign market. Simply, there may not be a
local company with the capabilities to produce and export. Rather than transfer
capabilities to a foreign company (thus risking the development of a competitor
through appropriability or risking the higher costs to incur through the transfer),
the company may engage in internalization. The lack of being able to gain experience in the foreign country before investing there is not necessarily a greater obstacle to operating abroad successfully; there is a narrower need for environmental
knowledge because the foreign operation is only resource (production) oriented,

rather than resource *and* sales oriented. Thus, operating activities for resource-seeking investments cover fewer functions. In the case of sales-oriented investments, the export experience serves only to gain market knowledge, so neither sales nor resource-oriented investors can learn much about foreign production nuances by exporting. Resource-oriented investors, therefore, usually skip the export stage in the internationalization process.

Direct Investment Patterns

Although foreign direct investment began centuries ago, its biggest growth has occurred in recent years. During the 1980s, for example, world trade grew slightly faster than the world's gross product; however, flows of FDI grew at about three times the rate of world exports.[44] This growth resulted from several factors, particularly the more receptive attitude of governments to investment inflows, the process of privatization, and the growing interdependence of the world economy. By the mid-1990s, the global stock of FDI had reached about $2.7 trillion and included about 270,000 investments by about 39,000 companies.[45]

Country of Origin

For worldwide FDI,
- **Almost all ownership is by companies from industrial countries**
- **LDC ownership is increasing**

The developed countries account for a little over 90 percent of all direct investment outflows. This is understandable, since more companies from those countries are likely to have the resources in the forms of capital, technology, and managerial skills that enable them to invest abroad. Nevertheless, considerable recent growth has occurred in direct investment from the developing countries; their share of global FDI grew from about 2 percent in 1983 to 6 percent in 1994.[46] Today, hundreds of LDC firms, primarily from the newly industrialized countries, have FDIs; however, the holdings from individual LDC investors remain small in comparison with those of investors from industrial countries. For example, Cemex, a Mexican cement producer, is the largest foreign investor among LDCs. However, its foreign holdings are lower than those of RJR Nabisco, the 100th largest overseas investor in the industrialized world.[47]

During much of the post–World War II period, the United States was the dominant investor. However, its share has been falling as the share from other industrial countries, especially Japan, has increased. Nevertheless, in 1994 the United States still accounted for more than a quarter of all FDI ownership, and its outflow of $46 billion for that year exceeded the outflow of any other country.[48] Recently, FDI has been flowing more rapidly into the United States than from the United States; at the beginning of 1996, the book value (based on the costs when the investments were made) of direct investment within the United States was about 79 percent of the book value of U.S.-owned direct investment abroad.[49] The largest investors in the United States were the United Kingdom and Japan, accounting for about 24 and 19 percent, respectively, of FDI in the United States. The direction of recent global FDI inflows and outflows is shown in Fig. 8.3.

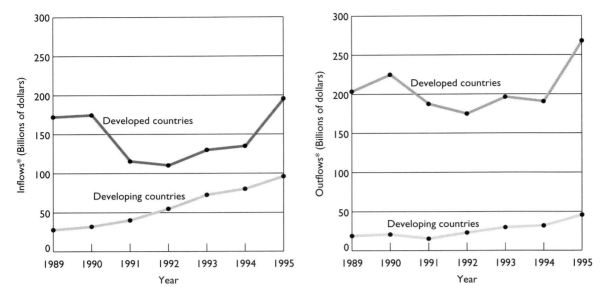

* Excludes central and eastern Europe.

Figure 8.3
Origin and Destination of Foreign Direct Investment Flows
Developing countries are both the biggest source and the destination for FDI.

Source: United Nations Conference on Trade and Development, *World Investment Report 1995: Transnational Corporation and Competitiveness* (Geneva: United Nations, 1995).

Location of Investment

The major recipients of FDI are industrial countries, which received about 83 percent of the world's total from 1986 to 1990, about 74 percent in 1991, and about 85 percent in 1995, as shown in Fig. 8.3. The small share going to LDCs has caused concern about how they will meet their capital needs. This pattern is similar to the outward flow of U.S.-owned direct investments. At the beginning of 1996, about 30 percent of such investments were in LDCs.

The interest in developed countries has resulted for three main reasons:

1. More investments have been market-seeking, and the developed countries have more income to spend.
2. Political turmoil in many LDCs has discouraged investors.
3. The industrial nations, through the OECD, are committed to liberalizing direct investment among their members, and they are parties to the Declaration on International Investment and Multinational Enterprises.[50]

Most FDI occurs in industrial countries because they have the
• Biggest markets
• Lowest perceived risk
• Least discrimination toward foreign companies

The OECD operates (with exceptions) under a principle that foreign-controlled companies should be treated no less favorably than domestic ones in such areas as taxes, access to local capital, and government procurement. The OECD member countries also have agreed on procedures through which direct investors can resolve situations that may result from conflicting laws between their home and host countries.

Economic Sector of Investment

The highest recent growth in FDI has been in services.

Trends in the distribution of FDI generally conform to long-term economic changes in the home and host countries. Over time, the portion of FDI accounted

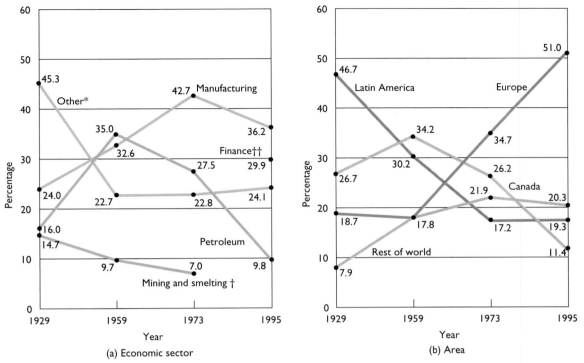

NOTE: *Includes transportation, trade, utilities, and other service industries; †Included in "Other" after 1973.
††Finance (except banking), insurance, and real estate included in "Other" before 1992.

Figure 8.4
Changing Pattern of U.S. Direct Investment Abroad by Economic Sector and Geographic Area (as percentage of value)
The largest portion of U.S. FDI is in manufacturing and in Europe.

Source: Survey of Current Business, various issues.

for in the raw materials sector that includes mining, smelting, and petroleum has declined. The portion in manufacturing, especially resource-based production, grew steadily from the 1920s to the early 1970s but has since stabilized. In the 1980s, FDI in the service sector (especially banking and finance) grew rapidly, as did FDI in technology-intensive manufacturing. By 1990, services accounted for about 50 percent of the world stock of FDI, followed by manufacturing and the primary sector.[51] Figure 8.4 shows that the U.S. sectoral distribution historically is similar to the global one.

COUNTERVAILING

F O R C E S

Direct investment is an integral means of carrying out global, multidomestic, and transnational practices. Market-seeking direct investments—those that take place because companies must produce within the markets they serve (because of high costs of transportation or trade restrictions)—generally favor multidomestic practices. Direct investments that are motivated by consumer or competitor moves are more likely to parallel global or transnational practices. Resource-seeking investments to bring about vertical integration or rationalized production usually entail global or transnational practices as well.

Direct investment, because of its implied control, permits companies to make decisions to maximize global performance. When they depend instead on licensing or foreign production contracts, the interests of their partner companies may constrain their ability to implement global practices.

Direct investments help to serve global efficiency by transferring resources to where they can be used more effectively; however, countries distort movements by restricting the inward or outward flow of direct investments and by giving incentives for companies to locate within their boundaries. Although these distortions are less important in motivating investments and their locations than political conditions and natural economic forces are, they are additional variables that managers must consider. To the extent that countries give preferential treatment to domestically headquartered or state-owned firms, the environment in which companies compete internationally is further complicated.

LOOKING TO THE FUTURE

In the near future, as in the recent past, FDI should continue to grow more rapidly than international trade or gross national products. The reasons for this growth should remain as described in this chapter. However, resource-seeking investments might grow more rapidly than market-seeking investments for two reasons: Trade restrictions on products continue to be reduced, making the use of least-cost production facilities more practical, and companies have more experience in manufacturing abroad and thus perceive less risk in integrating global production.

FDI in services also may continue to grow in relative importance for several reasons:

- The difficulty of removing protectionist barriers on service trade
- The need of service providers (such as investment bankers, advertising agencies, and insurance companies) to react quickly to the overseas needs of their clients
- The need of service companies to provide a full geographic range of activities to clients that are global

Western Europe, North America, and Japan should continue to be the major sources and recipients of FDI because of the wealth of the companies based there and the outlook for economic growth within those regions. The special trading relationship in North America and in the EU should further stimulate this growth. The former communist nations should get much more attention now that regulatory changes permit some foreign ownership and as potential investors become more optimistic about risk and opportunities there. Among LDCs also, regulatory changes should be a factor. Such countries as Argentina, Brazil, and Mexico are privatizing many state companies and allowing levels of foreign investment that have until very recently been prohibited. These moves should stimulate those countries' receipt of FDI.

WEB CONNECTION
Check out our home page for links to World Wide Web resources on multinational enterprises.

Summary

- Direct investment is the control of a company in one country by a company based in another country. Because control is difficult to define, some arbitrary minimum share of voting stock owned is used to define direct investment.

- Countries are concerned about who controls operations within their borders because they fear decisions will be made contrary to the national interest.

- Companies often prefer to control foreign production facilities because the transfer of certain assets to a noncontrolled entity might undermine their competitive position and they can realize economies of buying and selling with a controlled entity.

- Although a direct investment abroad generally is acquired by transferring capital from one country to another, capital usually is not the only contribution made by the investor or the only means of gaining equity. The investing company may supply technology, personnel, and markets in exchange for an interest in a foreign company.

- Production factors and finished goods are only partially mobile internationally. Moving either is one means of compensating for differences in factor endowments among countries. The cost and feasibility of transferring production factors rather than finished goods internationally will determine which alternative results in cheaper costs.

- Although FDI may be a substitute for trade, it also may stimulate trade through sales of components, equipment, and complementary products. Foreign direct investment may be undertaken to expand foreign markets or to gain access to supplies of resources or finished products. In addition, governments may encourage such investment for political purposes.

- The price of some products increases too much if they are transported internationally; therefore foreign production often is necessary to tap foreign markets.

- As long as companies have excess domestic capacity, they usually try to delay establishing foreign production.

- The extent to which scale economies lower production costs influences whether production is centralized in one or a few countries or dispersed among many countries.

- Because most FDIs are undertaken for the purpose of selling the output in the country in which the investments are located, governmental restrictions that prevent the effective importation of goods are a compelling force that cause companies to establish such investments.

- Consumers may feel compelled to buy domestically produced goods even though these products are more expensive. They also may demand that products be altered to fit their needs. Both of these considerations may dictate the need for a company to establish foreign operations to serve its foreign markets.

- FDI sometimes has chain effects: When one company makes an investment, some of its suppliers follow with investments of their own, followed by investments by their suppliers, and so on.

- Within oligopolistic industries, companies often invest in a foreign country at about the same time. This sometimes occurs because they are responding to similar market conditions and sometimes takes place because they wish to negate competitors' advantages in that market.

- Vertical integration is needed to control the flow of goods from basic production to final consumption in an increasingly interdependent and complex world distribution system. It may result in lower operating costs and enable companies to transfer funds among countries.

- Rationalized production involves producing different components or different products in different countries to take advantage of different factor costs.

- The least-cost production location may shift over time, especially in relation to stages of a product's life cycle. It also may change because of governmental incentives that effectively subsidize production.

- Countries may encourage domestically headquartered companies to invest abroad in order to gain advantages over other countries.

- There are advantages and disadvantages to FDI by either acquisition or start-up.

- **Monopolistic advantages help to explain why companies are willing to take what they perceive to be higher risks of operating abroad. Certain countries and currencies have had such advantages, which helps to explain the dominance of companies from certain countries at certain times.**

- **FDI may enable MNEs to spread certain fixed costs more than domestic companies can. It also may enable them to gain access to needed resources, to prevent competitors from gaining control of needed resources, and to smooth sales and earnings on a year-to-year basis.**

- **Most FDI originates from and goes to developed countries. The fastest recent growth of FDI has been in the service sector.**

Case
Cran Chile[52]

Cranberries are native to North America and were served at the first Thanksgiving dinner in 1621. The first commercial crop was hand-picked in 1817. For most of the period thereafter, almost all cranberry sales have been in the United States, and these sales have been heavily concentrated during the Thanksgiving season. Cranberries are so little known outside North America that there is no word for the fruit in most foreign languages.

The vulnerability to seasonal demand became apparent to cranberry growers in 1959, when the U.S. Secretary of Agriculture warned a few days before Thanksgiving of possible carcinogenic effects of a new pesticide sprayed on cranberries. Even though the warning proved to be unfounded, there was no market for the unsold berries. This spurred moves to find means of increasing cranberry sales during other times of the year.

Ocean Spray Cranberries, Inc., the only cooperative to be on the *Fortune* list of 500 largest U.S. industrial companies, has done most of the work to build and diversify cranberry sales. It is owned by some 750 cranberry and 150 grapefruit growers throughout the United States and Canada. Its 1994 sales of nearly $1.3 billion were about triple the sales of ten years earlier. The most notable increase in sales has come from the creation of cranberry juice, a year-round drink. In addition, Ocean Spray has worked with associations of cranberry growers to popularize recipes that will use cranberries year-round, such as cranberry chicken and cranberry-raisin pie. It has developed new products, such as Craisins— dried and sweetened cranberries that look something like red raisins. It has also worked with other companies to create products using cranberries—for example, with PepsiCo for a cranberry-raspberry lemonade, with Nabisco for a fat-free cranberry Fig Newton, and with Warner-Lambert for cranberry-flavored hard candy. Although Ocean Spray has been the dominant force behind increased cranberry sales and has about two-thirds of the U.S. market, some other companies have also become major players. For example, Seagram's Tropicana unit has a cranberry-juice cocktail under its Twister label, and Quaker Oats uses cranberries in some of its Snapple drinks. Moreover, demand has jumped as a result of studies reporting that cranberries help combat urinary tract infections.

In addition to promoting new products using cranberries, Ocean Spray began in the late 1980s to try marketing cranberry products abroad. In 1995 it projected $500 million in foreign sales by the turn of the century, a sevenfold increase in five years. These sales are being aided by grants from the U.S. Department of Agriculture's program to stimulate exports. Continued growth in domestic and foreign sales is, of course, dependent on sufficient supplies of cranberries. Supplies are a potential problem that was noted by Warren Simmons, the developer of the Pier 39 retail complex in San Francisco and the founder of the Tia Maria and Chevys Mexican Restaurants chains. In 1992 his Chevys restaurants ordered a large shipment of fresh cranberries from Ocean Spray to make cranberry margaritas, but Ocean Spray could not fill the order. Simmons investigated the shortage situation and concluded that supplies could not grow fast enough in North America to fulfill the growing demand. Figures on production are shown in Fig. 8.5.

The conclusion that there will be inadequate future supplies of cranberries from North America is based on the following factors:

1. *Regulations* Cranberries are grown in bogs, which alternatively can serve as wetlands that provide a habitat for plants and wildlife, control flooding, and serve as a natural filter for ground pollutants. As U.S. restrictions have become more stringent, it has become more difficult and costly to add more land for cultivation. For example, the application process for a three-acre expansion can cost as much as $100,000 in fees and take up to four years. Regulations are particularly severe in Massachusetts, traditionally the largest producer, and much expansion has shifted to Wisconsin and Washington. However, it may be only a matter of time before regulations in other states become as stringent as those in Massachusetts.

Figure 8.5
Annual Cranberry Production, in Millions of Pounds
Although there is an upward trend, production varies from year-to-year.

Source: Calvin Sims, "Taking Cranberries to Chile, Where They Are Really an Acquired Taste," *New York Times,* November 22, 1995, p. C13. Reprinted with permission.

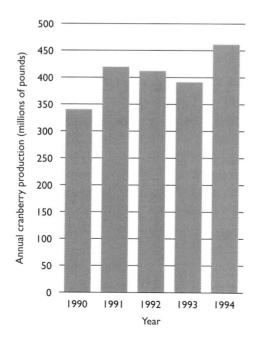

2. *Yields* Although research has been under way to increase yields, thus far it has been difficult to maintain them at accustomed levels. (An average acre yields about 150 barrels per year, at 100 pounds per barrel.) Many bogs have become less fertile because of their many years of cultivation. Further, decreases in the bumblebee population have decreased pollination and have necessitated the services of entomologists from New Zealand.

3. *Land costs* In some cranberry-growing regions, urbanization and land development have pushed land cost up so much that some areas are no longer profitable for cranberry cultivation. Further, workers cannot afford nearby accommodations from their earnings. For example, in Richmond, British Columbia, known as the "Cranberry Capital of Canada," a one-acre plot of land now costs over a half million dollars.

The aforementioned Mr. Simmons sold his Chevys Mexican Restaurants in 1992 to PepsiCo and used the proceeds to invest in foreign cranberry production. He hired one of the few horticulturists specializing in cranberries to advise him on where and how to grow berries. He chose an isolated area near Valdivia, Chile, 450 miles south of Santiago, to establish his foreign direct investment, called Cran Chile. (See Map 8.2.) This area was chosen because of the availability of fertile soil and rain, along with the absence of environment restrictions. By 1995, Simmons had invested about $20 million to begin cultivating 700 acres with 250 employees. His plans are to have 4000 acres planted by the turn of the century, when his investment will have reached about $35 million. At that time, he estimates, Cran Chile will account for 10 percent of the world's cranberry land in cultivation.

Map 8.2
Location of Cran Chile
Note that production is located far from existing markets in the United States and far from potential markets in Europe and Asia.

Because cranberry vines take four to five years to mature, it is still too early to know if Cran Chile will have good yield of high quality berries.

Another potential production problem involves the distance between Chile and cranberry processors in the United States. In 1995 Ocean Spray opened a new plant in Nevada with a computerized warehouse system, based on a just-in-time inventory system. This plant keeps an inventory of only three-week supplies, compared to customary five-week supplies. The company announced that eventually all its plants would operate that way. This will necessitate getting supplies to Ocean Spray very quickly once they are ordered—a difficult task from such a distance.

Market conditions add another uncertainty for the investment in Chile. Much of Simmons's projection for increased demand is based on a belief that he can sell to large cranberry processors (Ocean Spray, Quaker Oats, and Dole), who have projected increased sales in Asia and Europe. But the fruition of these sales may be difficult. Ocean Spray's CEO summarized this difficulty when he said, "We're introducing an unknown fruit in an unknown brand in a foreign market that's unknown to us." Ocean Spray's foreign expansion has already encountered some problems. For instance, it started selling juice in Britain in bottles, but had to change to boxes because of the British preference for rectangular packaging to save space in small refrigerators. The introduction of cranberry juice in Japan was so disappointing that the company pulled out of the market temporarily. Not even Simmons is optimistic enough to expect sales to develop in Chile, where people don't like the taste of cranberries because of their acidity.

Finally, changes in environmental regulations could affect production either in the United States or in Chile. The vice president of Decas, the largest independent handler of cranberries in the United States, spoke out in an interview about the frustration of seeing production go to Chile because of U.S. regulations. A representative of the U.S. Army Corps of Engineers, the agency responsible for administering the federal wetlands regulations, responded that no one who applied for a permit has been denied. But a permit approved in 1996 in Maine took five years to go through its hurdles. If regulations are eased in the United States or if permissions are granted more rapidly, there will be less need to depend on non-U.S. supplies. In the meantime, environmentalists have become more active in Chile. In fact, a $1 billion investment in a wood pulp plant was held up in 1996 until the company agreed not to dump waste into a river that ran into the wetlands.

In sum, Cran Chile represents a resource-seeking investment with a high risk but a potentially high return if production and marketing conditions go as Simmons anticipates. Because Chile had no cranberry production before Cran Chile's entry, the company had no way of evolving from a low commitment to a high commitment for its foreign operations.

Questions

1. What are the motivations and factors that influenced the foreign investment decision for Cran Chile? Compare these with those in the Bridgestone Tires case.
2. Do you see any ethical problems by investing where there are no environmental restrictions, such as those that make home-country investment more difficult? How

might the differences in environmental restrictions between the United States and Chile affect the future of Cran Chile?

3. Relate Simmons's process of international expansion with companies' usual internationalization process.

Chapter Notes

1. Data for the case were taken from Edward Noga, "Bridgestone," *Automotive News,* April 20, 1981, p. E10; Mike Tharp, "Bridgestone, Japan's Tire Giant, Now Seeking International Role," *New York Times,* November 21, 1980, p. D4; "Japan: Why a Tiremaker Wants a U.S. Base," *Business Week,* January 14, 1980, p. 40; Zachary Schiller and James B. Treece, "Bridgestone May Try an End Run around the Yen," *Business Week,* February 2, 1987, p. 31; Jonathan P. Hicks, "A Global Fight in the Tire Industry," *New York Times,* March 10, 1988, p. 29; Jonathan P. Hicks, "Decreasing Demand and Global Competition Propel Consolidation," *New York Times,* February 11, 1990, p. F8; Zachary Schiller and Roger Schreffler, "Why Tiremakers Are Still Spinning Their Wheels," *Business Week,* February 26, 1990, pp. 62–63; "When the Bridge Caught Fire," *Economist,* September 7, 1991, pp. 72–73; "Bridgestone/Firestone Is Named 1995 GM Supplier of the Year," *Business Wire,* May 15, 1996; Claudia H. Deutsch, "High-Tech Rubber Hits the Road," *New York Times,* July 20, 1996, p. 21+; "Bridgestone," *Jiji Press Ticker Service,* July 30, 1996; "A Come-back After Indy Wins," *Financial Times,* January 29, 1996, p. 14; "World Tyre Industry," *Financial Times,* January 29, 1996, p. 12; and Raju Narisetti and Gabriella Stern, "Goodyear Allies With a Japanese Tire Maker," *Wall Street Journal,* February 5, 1997, p. A3.

2. *World Investment Report: 1995* (New York and Geneva: United Nations Division on Transnational Corporations, 1995), p. 3.

3. Some surveys of the considerable number of explanations may be found in Jean J. Boddewyn, "Foreign and Domestic Divestment and Investment Decisions," *Journal of International Business Studies,* No. 3, Winter 1983, pp. 23–35; A. L. Calvet, "A Synthesis of Foreign Direct Investment Theories and Theories of the Multinational Firm," *Journal of International Business Studies,* Spring–Summer 1981, pp. 43–60; John H. Dunning, "Toward an Eclectic Theory of International Production," *Journal of International Business Studies,* Spring–Summer 1980, pp. 9–31;

Robert Grosse, "The Theory of Foreign Direct Investment," *Essays in International Business,* No. 3, December 1981, pp. 1–51; M. Z. Rahman, "Maximisation of Global Interests: Ultimate Motivation for Foreign Investments by Transnational Corporations," *Management International Review,* Vol. 23, No. 4, 1983, pp. 4–13; Alan M. Rugman, "New Theories of the Multinational Enterprise: An Assessment of Internalization Theory," *Bulletin of Economic Research,* Vol. 38, No. 2, 1986, pp. 101–118; and T. A. Corley, "Progress in Multinational Studies at Reading and Elsewhere, 1981–86" (Reading, England: University of Reading Department of Economics, Discussion Papers in International Investment and Business Studies, No. 120, 1989).

4. For a discussion of the effect of growth change on growth alternatives, see Briance Mascarenhas, "Strategic Group Dynamics," *Academy of Management Journal,* Vol. 32, No. 2, June 1989, pp. 333–352.

5. "A Come-back After Indy Wins," loc. cit.

6. Claudia H. Deutsch, "Goodyear and Top Rival Cut Japan Tie," *New York Times,* February 6, 1997, p. C4.

7. Internalization theory, or holding a monopoly control over certain information or other proprietary assets, builds on earlier market-imperfections work by Ronald H. Coase, "The Nature of the Firm," *Economica,* Vol. 4, 1937, pp. 386–405. It has been noted by such writers as M. Casson, "The Theory of Foreign Direct Investment," Discussion Paper No. 50 (Reading, England: University of Reading International Investment and Business Studies, November 1980); and Stephen Magee, "Information and the MNC: An Appropriability Theory of Direct Foreign Investment," in *The New International Economic Order,* Jagdish N. Bhagwati, ed. (Cambridge, Mass.: MIT Press, 1977), pp. 317–340.

8. Alan M. Rugman, *Inside the Multinationals: The Economics of Internal Markets* (New York: Columbia University Press, 1981); and David J. Teece, "Transactions Cost Economics and the Multinational Enterprise," *Berkeley Business School International Business Working Paper Series,* No. IB-3, 1985.

9. Leslie Chang, "Intel Invades Taiwan Motherboard Turf," *Wall Street Journal,* October 31, 1995, p. A18.

10. Gordon Hanson and Antonio Spilimber, *Illegal Immigration, Border Enforcement, and Relative Wages: Evidence from Apprehensions at the U.S.-Mexico Border* (Cambridge, Mass.: NBER Working Paper No. 5592, 1996), show the effect of wage differences on movement of Mexican labor to the United States.

11. Masaaki Kotabe, "Assessing the Shift in Global Market Share of U.S. Multinationals," *International Marketing Review,* Vol. 6, No. 5, 1989, pp. 20–35.

12. Neal McGratt, "New Broom Sweeps into Asia," *Asian Business,* March 1996, p. 22.

13. Joseph Kahn, "Otis Elevator Plans Expansion in China to Defend Market Share," *Asian Wall Street Journal,* May 2, 1995, p. 3.

14. Mark Nicholson, "Hyundai's $1.1 bn Indian Unit to Make 200,000 Cars a Year," *Financial Times,* January 16, 1997, p. 4.

15. Stephen Baker, Kevin Kelly, Robert D. Hof, and William J. Holstein, "Mini-Nationals Are Making Maximum Impact," *Business Week,* September 6, 1993, pp. 66–69.

16. Studies that found import barriers to be an important enticement include Sanjaya Lall and N. S. Siddharthan, "The Monopolistic Advantages of Multinationals: Lessons from Foreign Investment in the U.S.," *The Economic Journal,* Vol. 92, No. 367, September 1982, pp. 668–683; T. Horst, "Firm and Industry Determinants of the Decision to Invest Abroad," *Review of Economics and Statistics,* August 1972, pp. 258–266; John H. Dunning, *American Investment in British Manufacturing Industry* (London: Allen and Unwin, 1958); and D. Orr, "The Determinants of Entry: A Study of the Canadian Manufacturing Industries," *Review of Economics and Statistics,* Vol. 57, 1975, pp. 58–66. Those not finding import barriers to be important include R. E. Caves, M. E. Porter, A. M. Spence, and J. T. Scott, *Competition in the Open Economy: A Model Applied to Canada* (Cambridge, Mass.: Harvard University Press, 1980); and B. Balassa, "Effects of Commercial Policy on International Trade, the Location of Production and Factor Movements," in *The Interna-*

tional Allocation of Economic Activity, Bertil Ohlin, ed. (New York: Holmes & Meier, 1977).

17. Jagdish N. Bhagwati, Elias Dinopoulos, and Kar-yiu Wong, "Quid Pro Quo Foreign Investment," *American Economic Review,* May 1992, pp. 186–190.

18. Diana Solis, "Mexico's Garment Industry Is Pivotal to Plans to Boost Economy Via Exports," *Wall Street Journal,* January 19, 1993, p. A8; and James P. Miller, "Zenith Is Shifting Taiwan Jobs to Mexico, Signaling Trend in Other Manufacturers," *Wall Street Journal,* November 12, 1991, p. A4.

19. Kenneth Dreyfack, "Draping Old Glory Around Just about Everything," *Business Week,* October 27, 1986, pp. 66–67; Sherri McLain and Brenda Sternquist, "Ethnocentric Consumers: Do They 'Buy American'?" *Journal of International Consumer Marketing,* Vol. 4, Nos. 1/2, 1992, pp. 39–58.

20. "Toshiba Plans to Build Color-TV Plant in U.S.," *Wall Street Journal,* April 5, 1977, p. 43, and "Mitsubishi U.S. Unit to Assemble TV Sets in Irvine, California, Plant," *Wall Street Journal,* April 14, 1977, p. 7, show two examples of responses to nationalistic advertisements by Zenith.

21. Robert A. Peterson and Alain Jolibert, "A Meta-Analysis of Country-of-Origin Effects," *Journal of International Business Studies,* Vol. 26, No. 4, 1994, pp. 883–900.

22. Bob Davis, "Illusory Bargain," *Wall Street Journal,* September 15, 1993, p. A1+.

23. Stephen Baker, David Woodruff, and Bill Javetski, "Along the Border, Free Trade Is Becoming a Fact of Life," *Business Week,* June 18, 1990, pp. 41–42; and Lisa R. Van Wagner, "Putting Together the Pieces," *Export Today,* April 1992, pp. 10–11.

24. Sarkis Khoury, David Nickerson, and Venkataraman Sadanad, "Exchange Rate Uncertainty and Precommitment in Symmetric Duopoly: A New Theory of Multinational Production," *Recent Developments in International Banking and Finance,* Vols. IV and V, 1991; Jan Karl Karlsen and Michael H. Moffett, "On the Appropriateness of Economic or Strategic Exposure Management," Danish Summer Research Institute Paper, Copenhagen Business School, Copenhagen, Denmark, 1992.

25. Peter Gumbel, "Mercedes-Benz Plans Brazilian Facility, Continuing Move From Costly Germany," *Wall Street Journal,* September 14, 1995, p. A5.

26. Marcus Brauchli, "Bangladore Takes On Tasks a World Away," *Wall Street Journal,* January 6, 1993, p. A4.

27. Raymond Vernon, "International Investment and International Trade in the Product Cycle," *Quarterly Journal of Economics,* May 1966, pp. 191–207.

28. Krystal Miller, "BMW to Build Factory in U.S., Employ 2000," *Wall Street Journal,* June 23, 1992, p. A2.

29. "A Come-back after Indy Win," loc. cit.

30. Edward B. Flowers, "Oligopolistic Reactions in European and Canadian Direct Investment in the United States," *Journal of International Business Studies,* Fall–Winter 1976, pp. 43–55; Frederick Knickerbocker, *Oligopolistic Reaction and Multinational Enterprise* (Cambridge, Mass.: Harvard University, Graduate School of Business, Division of Research, 1973). For opposing findings, see Lall and Siddharthan, loc. cit.

31. Reginald Chua, "Vietnam's Tiny Car Market Draws Crowd," *Wall Street Journal,* January 3, 1996, p. A4.

32. E. M. Graham, "Exchange of Threat Between Multinational Firms as an Infinitely Repeated Noncooperative Game," *The International Trade Journal,* Vol. IV, No. 3, pp. 259–277.

33. Among the many treatises on this subject is Carlos F. Diaz Alejandro, "International Markets for Exhaustible Resources, Less Developed Countries and Transnational Corporations," in *Economic Issues of Multinational Firms,* Robert G. Hawkins, ed. (New York: JAI Press, 1977).

34. Larry Rohter, "Impact of NAFTA Pounds Economics of the Caribbean," *New York Times,* January 30, 1997, p. 1A+.

35. "Foreign Investment Through Privatization," *Transnationals,* Vol. 7, No. 1, March 1995, p. 2.

36. Jiatao Li, "Foreign Entry and Survival: Effects of Strategic Choices on Performance in International Markets," *Strategic Management Journal,* Vol. 16, 1995, pp. 333–351.

37. Erle Norton, "Last of the U.S. Tire Makers Ride Out Foreign Invasion," *Wall Street Journal,* February 4, 1993, p. B4; and Emily Thornton, "How Japan Got Burned In the USA," *Fortune,* June 15, 1992, pp. 114–116.

38. Mascarenhas, loc. cit.; Yui Kimura, "Firm-Specific Strategic Advantages and Foreign Direct Investment Behavior of Firms: The Case of Japanese Semiconductor Firms" (Niigata, Japan: International Management Research Institute, International University of Japan, 1988).

39. Stephen H. Hymer, *A Study of Direct Foreign Investment* (Cambridge, Mass.: MIT Press, 1976); Alan M. Rugman, "Internationalization as a General Theory of Foreign Direct Investment: A Re-Appraisal of the Literature," *Weltwirtschaftliches Archiv,* Band 116, Heft 2, 1980, pp. 365–379; and Yojin Jung, "Multinationality and Profitability," *Journal of Business Research,* Vol. 23, 1991, pp. 179–187.

40. Robert Z. Aliber, "A Theory of Direct Foreign Investment," in *The International Corporation,* Charles P. Kindleberger, ed. (Cambridge, Mass.: MIT Press, 1970), pp. 28–33; and Robert Johnson, "Distance Deals," *Wall Street Journal,* February 24, 1988, p. 1.

41. Louis Uchitelle, "Overseas Spending by U.S. Companies Sets Record Pace," *New York Times,* May 20, 1988, p. 1+; and "Investing Abroad Is Paying Off Big for U.S. Companies," *Business Week,* November 6, 1989, p. 34.

42. John D. Daniels and Jeffrey Bracker, "Profit Performance: Do Foreign Operations Make a Difference?" *Management International Review,* Vol. 29, No. 1, 1989, pp. 46–56.

43. Joseph C. Miller and Bernard Pras, "The Effects of Multinational and Export Diversification on the Profit Stability of U.S. Corporations," *Southern Economic Journal,* Vol. 46, No. 3, 1980, pp. 792–802; Alan M. Rugman, "Foreign Operations and the Stability of U.S. Corporate Earnings: Risk Reduction by International Diversification" (Vancouver: Simon Fraser University, 1974); and A. Severn, "Investor Evaluation of Foreign and Domestic Risk," *Journal of Finance,* May 1974, pp. 545–550.

44. United Nations Centre on Transnational Corporations, *World Investment Report 1991: The Triad in Foreign Direct Investment* (New York: United Nations, August 1991), p. 4.

45. U.S. State Department Briefing, September 24, 1996, with Karl Sauvant discussing UNCTAD's 1996 World Investment Report.

46. United Nations Conference on Trade and Development, *World Investment Report 1995: Transnational Corporations and Competitiveness* (Geneva: United Nations, 1995).

47. Ibid.; and R. Van Hoesel, "Multinational Enterprises from Developing Countries with Investments in Developed Economies: Some Theoretical Considerations," University of Antwerp Centre for International Management and Development, Discussion Paper #1992/E16; Guy de Jonquières, "UNCTAD Urges Phasing Out of Restrictions on Investment," *Financial Times,* December 15, 1995, p. 4.

48. United Nations Conference on Trade and Development, op. cit.

49. Jeffrey H. Lowe and Sylvia E. Bargas, "Direct Investment Positions on a Historical-Cost Basis, 1995: Country and Industry Detail," *Survey of Current Business,* July 1996, p. 45.

50. Enery Quinones Lellouche, "How OECD Governments Co-Operate on Investment Issues," *OECD Observer,* June/July 1992,

p. 10; and Marie-France Houde, "Foreign Direct Investment," *OECD Observer,* June/July 1992, pp. 9–13.

51. Ibid., p. 15.

52. Data for the case were taken from Jennifer Wolcott, "Politics Corrals Bay State Bogs," *Christian Science Monitor,* October 15, 1992, pp. 14–15; Calvin Sims, "Taking Cranberries to Chile, Where They Are Really an Aquired Taste," *New York Times,* November 22, 1995, p. C13; Joseph Pereira, "Unknown Fruit Takes On Unfamiliar Market," *Wall Street Journal,* November 9, 1995, p. B1; Rod McFarlane,

"Abuzz Over Bees: Cranberry Growers Look to Export from New Zealand for Advice on Bumblebees," *La Cross Tribune,* July 3, 1995, p. A1; Adrian Seybert, "Corporate Welfare: Even Del's Took a Taste," *Providence Journal Bulletin,* June 18, 1995, p. F1; "Striking It Rich(mond)," *Equity,* Vol. 12, No. 9, October 1994, p. 50; Amy Vreeland, "Ocean Spray Names Successor to President and Chief Executive Officer," *PR Newswire,* June 19, 1995, p. 1; "Counting Widgets: County Firms Trim Costs Via Improved Control," *Plymouth County Business Review,* Vol. 14, No. 1,

April 1995, p. 1; John Estrella, "Ocean Spray Enters Candy Industry," *Standard Times,* December 25, 1994, p. B1; John Estrella, "Ocean Spray Plans to Upgrade Plant," *Standard Times,* December 16, 1994, p. A7; William R. Long, "U.S. Businessman in Chile Works from the Ground Up," *Los Angeles Times,* February 11, 1994, p. A6; Mark Shanahan, "Proposed Cranberry Operation in Alfred Moving Slowly Through Tangle," *Portland Press Herald,* June 9, 1996, p. 1B; and Imogen Mark, "Chile Finds the Going Harder," *Financial Times,* August 16, 1996, p. 5.

4

World
Financial
Environment

The countries in Oceania have become bigger
global players in manufacturing and services;
nevertheless, they remain globally important in
the export of minerals and agricultural products.
The photo here shows an Australian salt flat,
which is set against a backdrop of a
New Zealand Maori cloak (circa 1930).

Chapter 9

Foreign Exchange

All things are
obedient to money.
—English Proverb

Objectives

- To discuss the terms and definitions of foreign exchange

- To describe how the foreign-exchange market works for immediate and long-term transactions

- To explain the role of convertibility in foreign-exchange transactions

- To illustrate how countries control foreign exchange through licensing, multiple rates, import deposit requirements, and quantity controls

- To describe how the foreign-exchange market is used in commercial and financial transactions

Case
Foreign Travels, Foreign Exchange Travails: Excerpts from the Travel Journal of Lee Radebaugh

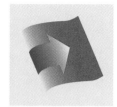

One of the most challenging parts of traveling overseas is figuring out how to deal in foreign exchange. In December 1995, I traveled to Latin America and decided to keep a journal of my adventures. I was in such a hurry to leave that I didn't even have time to check the exchange rates in the *Wall Street Journal*—something I usually do. Even though the exchange rates in the *Journal* are the selling rates (my buying rates) for transactions of $1 million or more—and I didn't plan on exchanging $1 million—I could still have used the rate to get a general idea of what to expect.

Our first stop was Chile. I decided to carry a mixture of cash and traveler's checks because you never know what you can use. The last time I had traveled to Latin America (1994) I had taken traveler's checks because I was attacked and nearly robbed in Rio de Janeiro, Brazil, in 1988, something that had not happened before nor has it happened since then, and I wanted more security since traveler's checks can be replaced. But at the airport in Buenos Aires after I left Brazil in 1994, they wouldn't cash traveler's checks—only cash. So this time I came prepared. However, I like to use credit cards, as long as the local currency is relatively stable, so that I can get a better exchange rate. Credit card companies exchange such a large volume of currency daily, that they get favorable exchange rates.

When we cleared customs in Chile, I noticed that the exchange rate was 350 pesos per dollar. I had no idea whether it was a good rate, but I decided to wait to cash in until we arrived at the hotel. We were riding with friends so we didn't need any cash yet. When we got to the hotel, I asked the woman at the front desk if she could cash $100 and she said, "Sorry. I don't have any pesos." "When will you get them?" I asked. "In about 30 minutes," she responded. No big deal because we needed to unpack and rest before having lunch. We had been flying or waiting in airports for 24 hours by then.

After a refreshing, well-deserved nap, we headed down to the front desk to get some cash. "Can you cash $100?" I asked. "Sorry. No pesos," she responded. "But there is an exchange house two blocks up the street." So off we headed. After getting lost, we finally asked directions and found a Casa de Cambio (Exchange House) down the stairs next to the metro (subway or underground train) and around a corner. To our pleasant surprise, the exchange rate was 450 pesos per dollar, and there was no service charge to convert the money. Usually when you convert currency at the airport, bank, or hotel, you have to pay a service charge on each transaction. That reduces the net amount of the currency you receive and thus worsens the exchange rate. We walked out of the Casa de Cambio with 45,000 peso—10,000 more than if we had converted at the airport.

As we walked to lunch, I tried to figure out how much things would cost. When I get foreign currency, I feel as if I'm playing Monopoly—it doesn't seem like real money. "Let's see, if I want to pay $10 for lunch, I should pay 4,500 pesos. ($10 × 450 pesos, the exchange rate I got when I traded my dollars into pesos) That's easy. But what if lunch is 7,800 pesos? How much is that? Never mind. It's more than $10 and less than $20 (between 4,500 and 9,000 pesos). I said to myself that I might have to think about this some more.

Fortunately, we didn't have to use much money because our alumni picked up all of our meals except our first lunch, and I can't remember how much lunch was. I think it was about 3,200 pesos (about $7.10) for the meal, and I couldn't figure out whether the tip was included. We left a little extra change on the table and the waiter seemed happy. I guess that meant we double-tipped him.

After two wonderful days in Santiago, we checked out of the hotel—an experience in itself. Everyone was very pleasant but the system was a little slow. The clerk said, "Do you want to keep the charges on your American Express?" "Of course," I said. I figured AMEX could get a pretty good exchange rate for my room charge for two nights of 102,000 pesos. "That will be $255," he said. "Wait," I said. "What exchange rate are you using?" "400 pesos," he replied. "That's a horrible rate," I said. "I got 450 pesos down the street." "That is not possible, Señor. Maybe you misunderstood. 405, or maybe 415, but not 450." "I know what exchange rate I got and it was 450," I replied. "That is a very good exchange rate, Señor." Yeah, right, I thought. Not only did I not get the AMEX rate, but the room cost me $127.50 per night! At my conversion rate of 450 pesos from the Casa de Cambio, I would have spent only $227 (102,000 pesos/450 pesos), saving $28. It wasn't enough to cause an international incident over, however, so I dropped the complaint and thanked him for the lovely stay. I may be back, so I don't want him to remember an ugly American.

When I got to the Santiago airport, I decided to exchange Chilean pesos for Argentinean pesos, or "Argentino" for short, so I walked up to the exchange desk and asked, "Argentino, por favor." "Sorry, we don't have Argentinean currency," the trader responded. "How about dollars?" "Okay," I said. Then I noticed that they were selling dollars for 410 pesos per dollar and buying for 430. Since I bought at 450 at the Exchange House and sold at 430 at the airport, I made $0.11 on every 1,000 pesos. If only I could have traded $1 million at that spread. . . .

When we arrived at Buenos Aires, I decided to cash at the airport. This time they accepted traveler's checks and I converted $100 for 93.95 pesos, which was a little surprising, because I read that the exchange rate was $1=1 peso. To my surprise, they charged me 5 percent to cash the traveler's checks and another 1.05 percent service fee—a total of 6.05 pesos. Because it was so expensive for everything in Buenos Aires, I quickly ran out of pesos, so I went to the American Express office the next day and they converted $100 for 99.8 pesos. Next time I'll ask before using traveler's checks. It can get confusing. Sometimes I've sold traveler's checks at a better rate than cash, and other times at a worse rate. When we left Buenos Aires, the exchange rate was the same for buying and selling—1:1. There was a $0.15 service charge, so I basically paid nothing to change currency—$100 to buy 99.8 pesos at American Express and $100 for selling 99.85 pesos (100 pesos less $0.15).

After a delay at the airport in Buenos Aires, we finally headed for São Paulo, Brazil. The currency market in Brazil has always been the haven of the black marketeer. No one ever has a clue what the real value is, and it varies by whether you cash personal checks, traveler's checks, or cash. Every hotel and shop has its own personal rate, which allows for some astute shopping.

The last time I was in Brazil (1993), the country was in the process of changing the currency to something more closely pegged to the dollar, but it was still chaotic. Taxi drivers still preferred dollars, no matter what the exchange rate. Finally, the Brazilian government succeeded in stabilizing the currency in June 1994, and the Brazilian real was fixed to the dollar (or pegged) at an exchange rate of about 1:1. When I arrived at the airport, I changed dollars into reals at R$0.9300=US $1.00. The bank didn't charge a service charge, but they sold dollars (or bought R$) for R$0.99=US $1.00. What a change from the historical value! The first time I went to Brazil, in 1964, the dollar was worth 1,200 cruzeiros, the name of the currency then. Since that time, the Brazilian currency changed names seven times: cruzeiro (1942–1967), new cruzeiro (1967–1970), cruzeiro (1970–1986), cruzado (1986–1989), new cruzado (1989–1990), cruzeiro (again!) (1990–1993), cruzeiro real (1993–1994), and real (1994–?). Every time it did, it cut three zeros off the end of the currency. Thus 1,200 cruzeiros became 1.2 new cruzeiros, and so on. At an exchange rate of 1:1, it was obviously easier to figure out how much everything cost in dollars. But everything was so expensive relative to the cost in the United States. When the Brazilian government fixed the rate at 1:1, it made the real a little too strong, so the dollar didn't have as much purchasing power as before.

The trip to Latin America was great. We worked with our alumni and recruited some great students for our MBA program. Each country provided different challenges in terms of foreign exchange, but we adjusted and can't wait to go back.

Introduction

To be effective, both MNEs and small import and export companies must understand exchange rates. The exchange rate can influence where a wholesaler or a retailer buys and sells products. It also can influence where a manufacturer acquires raw materials or components and produces products. Further, it can affect the location of capital that a company needs in order to expand. For example, in 1993 and 1994, the Japanese yen was so strong against the U.S. dollar that sales of Japanese automobiles fell significantly in comparison with those of U.S. automobiles. This occurred because the importers had to convert too many dollars into the stronger yen to pay for the imports. As the importers passed on the higher cost to the consumers, their sales began to drop. Thus many Japanese automakers shifted more of their production to the United States so that they could escape the problem of the rising yen.

For most of us on a personal level, the experiences in the opening case ring true. However, the exchange of money has become easier in many countries since 1990, as the following demonstrates:

Say I'm in Paris, it's late evening, and I need money. The bank I go to is closed, of course, but outside sits an ATM, an automated teller machine—and look what can be made to happen, thanks to computers and high-speed telecommunications. I insert my ATM card from my bank in Washington, D.C., and punch in my identification number and the amount of 1500 francs, roughly equivalent to $260. The French bank's computers detect that it's not their card, so my request goes to the CIRRUS system's inter-European switching center in Belgium, which detects that it's not a European card. The electronic message is then transmitted to the global switching center in Detroit, which recognizes that it's from my bank in

> Washington. The request goes there, and my bank verifies that there's more than $260 in my account and deducts $260 plus a fee of $1.50. Then it's back to Detroit, to Belgium, and to the Paris bank and its ATM—and out comes $260 in French francs. Total elapsed time: 16 seconds.[1]

Like this traveler, most students who study abroad quickly learn the value of the ATM.

In a business setting, there is a fundamental difference between making payment in the domestic market and making payment abroad. In a domestic transaction, only one currency is used; in a foreign transaction, two or more currencies may be used. For example, a U.S. company that exports $100,000 worth of skis to a French distributor will ask the French buyer to remit payment in dollars, unless the U.S. company has some specific use for French francs—say that it imports parts from France and can use the francs to pay the French exporter.

Assume you are a U.S. importer who has agreed to purchase a certain quantity of French perfume and to pay the French exporter 20,000 francs for it. How would you go about paying? First, you would go to the international department of your local bank to buy 20,000 francs at the going market rate. Let's assume the franc/dollar exchange rate is 5.7115 francs per dollar. Your bank then would debit your demand deposit account by $3501.71 (20,000/5.7115) plus transaction costs and give you a special check payable in francs made out to the exporter. The exporter would deposit it in a Paris bank, which then would credit the exporter's account with 20,000 francs. The transaction would be complete.

Foreign exchange includes currencies and other instruments of payment denominated in currencies.

The special checks and other instruments for making payments abroad are referred to collectively as **foreign exchange.** It is sometimes difficult to understand and relate to different currencies as you saw in the opening case. A complete understanding of foreign exchange includes knowing the global and national context in which exchange rates are set and how foreign exchange is used in international transactions. In this chapter, we focus more on the nature of the foreign exchange market than on the use of foreign exchange by companies. It is important to understand exchange rates and how foreign currencies are traded before looking at how companies use foreign exchange and protect themselves against potential foreign exchange risk. In Chapter 10, we will concentrate more on the forces that affect exchange rates. Then in subsequent chapters, we will discuss how companies use foreign exchange in a variety of settings.

Terms and Definitions

An exchange rate is the number of units of one currency needed to acquire one unit of another currency.

An **exchange rate** is the number of units of one currency that must be given to acquire one unit of another currency. For example, on March 12, 1997, it took $0.1751 to purchase one French franc. The exchange rate, then, is the link between different national currencies that makes international price and cost comparisons possible.

The **spot rate** is the rate quoted for current foreign-currency transactions. It applies to interbank transactions that require delivery of the purchased currency within two business days in exchange for immediate cash payment for that currency. This exchange process is called **settlement. Interbank transactions** are exchanges between commercial banks that collectively make up the **interbank market,** which is the market for trades that take place between such banks. The spot rate also applies to over-the-counter (OTC) transactions, which usually involve nonbank customers and require same-day settlement. The **forward rate** is a contractual rate between a foreign-exchange trader and the trader's client for delivery of foreign currency sometime in the future, after at least two business days but usually after at least one month.

The Spot Market

Most foreign-currency transactions take place between foreign-exchange traders, so the rates are quoted by the traders, who work for foreign-exchange brokerage houses or commercial banks. This is one of the confusions identified in the opening case. The rates are quoted by traders, not the buying or selling party. The traders always quote a bid (buy) and offer (sell) rate. The bid is the price at which the trader is willing to buy foreign currency, and the offer is the price at which the trader is willing to sell foreign currency. In the spot market, the **spread** is the difference between the bid and offer rates and is the margin on which the trader earns a profit on the transaction. Thus the rate quoted by a trader for the British pound might be $1.5975/85. This means the trader is willing to buy pounds at $1.5975 each and sell them for $1.5985. Obviously, a trader wants to buy low and sell high.

In this example, the foreign currency is quoted by the trader at the number of U.S. dollars for one unit of that currency. This method of quoting exchange rates is called in the United States the **direct quote.** A rate quoted in terms of the number of units of the foreign currency for one unit of the domestic currency is called the **indirect quote,** which is the inverse of the direct quote. For example,

$$\frac{£1}{\$1.5985} = 0.6256 \text{ British pounds (£) per U.S. dollar (\$)}$$

The U.S. dollar customarily is used as the base currency for international transactions; the other currency in the transaction is the quoted currency. The base currency is in the denominator in the quote; the quoted currency is in the numerator. The quote is given as the number of units of the quoted currency for one unit of the base currency.

Most large newspapers, especially those devoted to business or those having business sections, quote exchange rates daily. For example, the *Wall Street Journal* provided the direct and indirect quotes given in Table 9.1. The spot rates shown are the selling rates for interbank transactions (transactions between banks) of $1 million

The spot rate is the exchange rate quoted for transactions that require either immediate delivery or delivery within two days.

The interbank market is the foreign-exchange market among commercial banks.

The forward rate is the rate quoted for transactions that call for delivery after two business days.

The spread in the spot market is the difference between the bid (buy) and offer (sell) rate quoted by the foreign-exchange trader.

A direct quote is the number of units of the domestic currency needed to acquire one unit of the foreign currency.

An indirect quote is the number of units of the foreign currency needed to acquire one unit of the domestic currency.

Table 9.1
Exchange Rates, Wednesday, March 12, 1997

Country	U.S. $ equiv.		Currency per U.S. $	
	Wed	Tue	Wed	Tue
Argentina (Peso)	1.0012	1.0012	.9988	.9988
Australia (Dollar)	.7953	.7932	1.2574	1.2607
Austria (Schilling)	.08335	.08326	11.998	12.010
Bahrain (Dinar)	2.6525	2.6525	.3770	.3770
Belgium (Franc)	.02847	.02846	35.120	35.140
Brazil (Real)	.9450	.9492	1.0582	1.0536
Britain (Pound)	1.5985	1.6070	.6256	.6223
30-Day Forward	1.5976	1.6061	.6259	.6226
90-Day Forward	1.5960	1.6046	.6266	.6232
180-Day Forward	1.5939	1.6024	.6274	.6241
Canada (Dollar)	.7336	.7314	1.3631	1.3672
30-Day Forward	.7352	.7330	1.3602	1.3642
90-Day Forward	.7381	.7358	1.3549	1.3590
180-Day Forward	.7422	.7399	1.3474	1.3515
Chile (Peso)	.002425	.002419	412.40	413.35
China (Renminbi)	.1201	.1201	8.3253	8.3252
Colombia (Peso)	.0009410	.0009461	1062.73	1056.92
Czech. Rep. (Koruna)				
Commercial rate	.03435	.03440	29.116	29.070
Denmark (Krone)	.1540	.1539	6.4943	69.461
Ecuador (Sucre)				
Floating rate	.0002674	.0002674	3740.00	3740.00
Finland (Markka)	.1966	.1966	5.0863	5.0860
France (Franc)	.1751	.1741	5.7115	5.7450
30-Day Forward	.1754	.1744	5.7011	5.7343
90-Day Forward	.1761	.1750	5.6793	5.7134
180-Day Forward	.1751	.1740	5.7123	5.7458
Germany (Mark)	.5908	.5869	1.6925	1.7040
30-Day Forward	.5919	.5880	1.6895	1.7008
90-Day Forward	.5943	.5835	1.6826	1.7137
180-Day Forward	.5981	.5940	1.6720	1.6836
Greece (Drachma)	.003769	.003744	265.31	267.09
Hong Kong (Dollar)	.1291	.1292	7.7437	7.7427
Hungary (Forint)	.005636	.005649	177.43	177.03
India (Rupee)	.02789	.02789	35.850	35.853
Indonesia (Rupiah)	.0004168	.0004172	2399.20	2396.75
Ireland (Punt)	1.5605	1.5610	.6408	.6406
Israel (Shekel)	.2976	.2972	3.3597	3.3651
Italy (Lira)	.0005928	.0005898	1687.00	1695.50
Japan (Yen)	.008179	.008212	122.27	121.78
30-Day Forward	.008213	.008247	121.75	121.26
90-Day Forward	.008284	.008322	120.72	120.17
180-Day Forward	.008395	.008433	119.13	118.58
Jordan (Dinar)	1.4094	1.4094	.7095	.7095
Kuwait (Dinar)	3.2916	3.2949	.3038	.3035
Lebanon (Pound)	.0006464	.0006464	1547.00	1547.00
Malaysia (Ringgit)	.4041	.4044	2.4747	2.4730
Malta (Lira)	2.5974	2.5940	.3850	.3855
Mexico (Peso)				
Floating rate	.1255	.1255	7.9700	7.9650
Netherlands (Guilder)	.5250	.5214	1.9046	1.9179
New Zealand (Dollar)	.7022	.7050	1.4241	1.4184
Norway (Krone)	.1473	.1468	6.7868	6.8098
Pakistan (Rupee)	.02520	.02520	39.680	39.680
Peru (New Sol)	.3836	.3836	2.6069	2.6069
Philippines (Peso)	.03799	.03799	26.325	26.326

Table 9.1 (cont.)

Country	U.S. $ equiv.		Currency per U.S. $	
	Wed	**Tue**	**Wed**	**Tue**
Poland (Zloty)	.3244	.3241	3.0828	3.0854
Portugal (Escudo)	.005888	.005848	169.84	171.00
Russia (Ruble) (a)	.0001759	.0001760	5684.00	5683.00
Saudi Arabia (Riyal)	.2666	.2666	3.7503	3.7505
Singapore (Dollar)	.6976	.6983	1.4335	1.4320
Slovak Rep. (Koruna)	.03080	.03080	32.473	32.473
South Africa (Rand)	.2263	.2258	4.4185	4.4295
South Korea (Won)	.001140	.001138	877.25	878.65
Spain (Peseta)	.006923	.006918	144.44	144.56
Sweden (Krona)	.1300	.1311	7.6903	7.6259
Switzerland (Franc)	.6873	.6799	1.4550	1.4708
30-Day Forward	.6892	.6819	1.4509	1.4664
90-Day Forward	.6937	.6861	1.4416	1.4575
180-Day Forward	.7004	.6930	1.4277	1.4430
Taiwan (Dollar)	.03631	.03634	27.540	27.521
Thailand (Baht)	.03855	.03854	25.940	25.950
Turkey (Lira)	.00000802	.00000803	124690.00	124540.00
United Arab (Dirham)	.2723	.2723	3.6720	3.6720
Uruguay (New Peso)				
Financial	.1109	.1118	9.0150	8.9450
Venezuela (Bolivar)	.002094	.002093	477.50	477.80
SDR	1.3730	1.3765	.7283	.7265
ECU	1.1406	1.1416	—	—

Special Drawing Rights (SDR) are based on exchange rates for the U.S., German, British, French, and Japanese currencies.
Source: International Monetary Fund.
European Currency Unit (ECU) is based on a basket of community currencies.
a-fixing, Moscow Interbank Currency Exchange

Source: From *The Wall Street Journal*, March 13, 1997, p. C22. Reprinted by permission of *The Wall Street Journal*, ©1997 Dow Jones & Company Inc. All Rights Reserved Worldwide.

and more. Retail transactions, those involving individuals, provide fewer foreign currency units per dollar than interbank transactions. In addition to the spot rates for each currency, the forward rates are provided for the British pound, Canadian dollar, French franc, German mark, Japanese yen, and Swiss franc.

The cross rate is an exchange rate computed from two other exchange rates.

A final important definition that applies to the spot market is the **cross rate.** This rate is computed from two other exchange rates. Because most foreign-currency transactions are denominated in terms of U.S. dollars, it is common to see two nondollar currencies related to each other by a cross rate. As an example, let's use the indirect quotes for the Swiss franc and German mark and figure the cross rate with the franc as the quoted currency and the mark as the base currency. In Table 9.1, the spot rates for these currencies are 1.4550 francs per U.S. dollar and 1.6925 marks per U.S. dollar. The cross rate is calculated as follows:

$$\frac{1.4550 \text{ francs}}{1.6925 \text{ marks}} = 0.8597 \text{ francs per mark}$$

This means 1 mark equals 0.8597 francs. This cross rate commonly would be quoted as 85.97.

The *Wall Street Journal* publishes a cross-rate table along with the dollar-exchange rates. Table 9.2 identifies the cross rates for several key currencies. In the rows are the direct quotes for each currency. For example, starting in the Swiss franc row and going across it to the German mark column (D-mark or Deutsche mark), we find that the cross rate is 0.85968 francs per mark, which is the direct quote for Swiss francs (the number of francs for one unit of the foreign currency). In the columns are the indirect quotes for each currency. Using the same example, 0.85968 francs per mark is the indirect quote in terms of German marks (the number of units of the foreign currency for one mark). (The cross rate of 0.85968 francs per mark is slightly different from the cross rate computed above because of rounding errors and because different sources are used to compute the exchange rates.)

German and Swiss managers keep track of the cross rate because they trade extensively with each other and any material shifts in the cross rate could signal a change in the prices of goods. For example, assume a German exporter sold a product worth 100 marks to a Swiss importer for 85.97 francs (100 × .8597). If the cross rate were to change to 0.900 francs per mark, the German exporter and the Swiss importer would have to make some interesting decisions. If the exporter kept the price to the importer at 100 marks, the importer would have to come up with 90 francs (100 × .90) to buy the product. On the other hand, the exporter could lower the price to 95.52 marks so that the product would still cost the importer 85.97 francs (85.97/.90). Further, if the exporter decided to keep the price at 100 marks, the importer would have two options:

1. Increase the price to reflect the higher cost of the product and thus keep the profit margin the same as before

Table 9.2
Key Currency Cross Rates, Late New York Trading, March 12, 1997

	Dollar	Pound	SFranc	Guilder	Peso	Yen	Lira	D-Mark	FFranc	CdnDlr
Canada	1.3631	2.1789	.93684	.71569	.17103	.01115	.00081	.80538	.23866	—
France	5.7115	9.1298	3.9254	2.9988	.71662	.04671	.00339	3.3746	—	4.1901
Germany	1.6925	2.7055	1.1632	.88864	.21236	.01384	.00100	—	.29633	1.2417
Italy	1687.0	2696.7	1159.5	885.75	211.67	13.797	—	996.75	295.37	1237.6
Japan	122.27	195.45	84.034	64.197	15.341	—	.07248	72.242	21.408	89.70
Mexico	7.9700	12.74	5.4777	4.1846	—	.06518	.00472	4.7090	1.3954	5.8470
Netherlands	1.9046	3.0445	1.3090	—	.23897	.01558	.00113	1.1253	.33347	1.3973
Switzerland	1.4550	2.3258	—	.76394	.18256	.01190	.00086	.85968	.25475	1.0674
U.K.	.62559	—	.42996	.32846	.07849	.00512	.00037	.36962	.10953	.45894
U.S.	—	1.5985	.68729	.52504	.12547	.00818	.00059	.59084	.17509	.73362

2. Keep the price the same and end up with a smaller profit margin due to the higher cost of the product

If the product were especially price-sensitive, neither the exporter nor the importer would want to see the price rise in Switzerland.

The Forward Market

The spot market is for foreign-exchange transactions within two business days. However, some transactions may be entered into on one day but not completed until after two business days. For example, a French exporter of perfume might sell perfume to a U.S. importer with immediate delivery but payment not required for thirty days. The U.S. importer is obligated to pay in francs in thirty days and may enter into a contract with a trader to deliver francs in thirty days at a forward rate, the rate today for future delivery.

Thus the forward rate is the rate quoted by foreign-exchange traders for the purchase or sale of foreign exchange in the future. The difference between the spot and forward rates is known as either the **forward discount** or the **forward premium** on the contract. If the domestic currency is quoted on a direct basis and the forward rate is less than the spot rate, the foreign currency is selling at a discount. If the forward rate is greater than the spot rate, the foreign currency is selling at a premium.

As an example, let's compute the spread, or the difference between the spot and forward rates for ninety-day contracts, for British pounds and Japanese yen. Direct quotes for these currencies and the resulting points for each are given in Table 9.3. The spread in British pounds is 25 points; because the forward rate is less than the spot rate, the pound is at a discount in the ninety-day forward market. The spread in Japanese yen is only five points; because the forward rate is greater than the spot rate, the yen is at a premium in the ninety-day forward market.

The discount or premium also can be quoted in terms of an annualized percentage using the following formula:

> A discount exists when the forward rate is less than the spot rate.
>
> A premium exists when the forward rate exceeds the spot rate.

$$\text{Premium (discount)} = \frac{F_0 - S_0}{S_0} \times \frac{12}{N} \times 100$$

Table 9.3
Direct Quotes for Canadian Dollars and Japanese Yen

Rate	British pound	Japanese yen
Forward (90-day)	1.5960	0.008284
Spot	1.5985	0.008179
Points	−25	+5

where

F_0 = the forward rate on the day the contract is entered into
S_0 = the spot rate on that day
N = the number of months forward
100 is used to convert the decimal figure to a percentage (for example,
   $0.05 \times 100 = 5\%$)

Using British pounds in the formula yields

$$\text{Discount} = \frac{1.5960 - 1.5985}{1.5985} \times \frac{12}{3} \times 100 = -0.6256$$

That is, the British pound is selling at a discount of 0.6256 percent per annum under the spot rate.

Forward markets do not exist for all currencies in all countries. For example, as Table 9.1 indicates, there is no forward market in the United States for the Brazilian real. This is because a forward contract in reals generally is not available in the interbank market. Given Brazil's relatively high inflation rate, there is an excess supply of reals; thus it would be practically impossible for the interbank market to balance purchases of real contracts with sales of real contracts. The interbank market is too thin (that is, it does not have enough transactions) to warrant forward contracts. When this is the case, buyers and sellers must account for potential foreign-currency risk in some other way, such as by adjusting the selling price.

How the Foreign-Exchange Market Works

In this section of the chapter, we will provide data on different aspects of the spot and forward foreign-exchange markets, such as the size of the market, the types of transactions (spot, forward, swap, options, futures), the major countries where foreign exchange is traded, and the major currencies traded on a daily basis. Next we will look at the role of different institutions, such as banks and brokers, in trading currencies and the procedures they follow in making the trades. Finally, we will examine some of the specific nonbank markets where derivatives are traded.

Foreign-Currency Market Data

Having defined the various exchange rates and explained how they are quoted, we can examine how foreign currencies are traded. Most foreign-exchange transactions are conducted by commercial banks. The foreign-exchange market is massive (see Fig. 9.1). Worldwide foreign exchange trading in April 1995 was nearly $1.26 trillion daily, counting the "traditional" market segments of spot transactions and

Figure 9.1
Average Daily Volume in World Foreign-Exchange Markets, 1989, 1992, and 1995
The average daily volume of foreign-exchange transactions was $1.26 trillion worldwide in April 1995.

Source: Bank for International Settlements. *Central Bank Survey of Foreign Exchange and Derivatives Market Activity* (Basel: BIS, May 1996), p. 3.

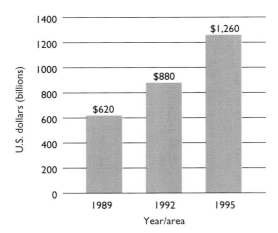

A swap is an exchange of currencies in the spot market accompanied by an agreement to reverse the transaction in the future.

An option is the right but not the obligation to trade a foreign currency at a specific exchange rate.

outright forwards and swaps, as well as over-the-counter (banks, investment banks) and exchange-traded options and futures contracts.

Of total worldwide volume in the "traditional" market segments, spot transactions were only 44 percent of total, compared with 49 percent in 1992 and 59 percent in 1989. Outright forwards and swaps were 56 percent of the market in 1995, compared with 51 percent in 1992 and only 41 percent in 1989.

All nonspot foreign-exchange instruments are collectively called **derivatives.** The **outright forward** is a forward contract that is not connected to a spot transaction. For example, an MNE might be receiving British pounds in ninety days and thus may enter into a forward contract to trade pounds for dollars in ninety days. The advantage of the outright forward is that it sets the amount of dollars that will be paid or received and establishes the cost up-front. A **swap** is a transaction involving the exchange of two currency amounts on a specific date and a reverse exchange of the same amounts at a later date. For example, a company could sell dollars for British pounds at the spot rate and agree to reverse the transaction at a specific future date at a specified exchange rate. Swaps are important, because they comprised 85 percent of all forward contracts in 1995 or 47 percent of all foreign currency transactions. Swaps tend to have a relatively short maturity: Swaps with a maturity of up to one week account on average for 71 percent of the deals, compared with only 53 percent for outright forwards.[2]

An **option** is the right but not the obligation to buy or sell a foreign currency within a certain time period (an American option) or on a specific date (European option) at a specific exchange rate (the strike price). For example, assume a company purchases an option to buy Japanese yen at 105 yen per dollar (0.00952 dollars per yen). If at the time the company wants to buy yen, the rate is 115 yen per dollar (0.00870 dollars per yen), it would not exercise the option because buying yen at the market rate would cost less than buying them at the option rate. However, if the market rate at that time is 100 yen per dollar (0.01 dollars per yen), the company would exercise the option because buying at the option rate would cost less than buying at the market rate. The option provides the company more flexibility than a forward contract would; however, the company must pay the brokerage fee and the premium regardless of whether it exercises the option. The cost of an option is not insignificant, and we will examine that cost in more detail in conjunction with a specific transaction in Chapter 20.

The **futures contract** resembles the forward contract in that it specifies an exchange rate sometime in advance of the actual exchange of currency. However, it is less flexible than a forward contract because it is for a specific currency amount and a specific maturity date; a forward contract, in contrast, can be tailor-made to fit the size of the transaction and the maturity date. Forward contracts depend on a client's relationship with a bank's foreign-exchange trader, but a futures contract can be entered into by anyone through a securities broker. We will examine futures contracts in more detail in the section on the Chicago Mercantile Exchange later in the chapter.

> A futures contract specifies in advance the exchange rate to be used, but it is not as flexible as a forward contract.

Countries and Currencies

Foreign-exchange trading occurs worldwide in an increasingly integrated way. The foreign-exchange market operates twenty-four hours a day during the business week; the only time it is silent is after the New York market closes on Friday afternoon and before the Sydney market opens on Monday morning (which would be Sunday evening New York time). Most large money-center banks have added night shifts of traders so they can trade twenty-four hours a day. Most foreign-currency transactions take place in markets as they become fully operative; thus traders must be aware of international time zones (see Map 9.1). The following explains:

> Foreign-exchange trades occur twenty-four hours a day worldwide.

> The world's communication networks are now so good, and so many countries have fairly unrestricted markets that we can talk of a single world market. It starts in a small way in New Zealand around 9:00 a.m. New Zealand time, just in time to catch the tail end of the previous night's New York market. Two or three hours later, Tokyo opens, followed an hour later by Hong Kong and Manila and then half an hour later by Singapore. By now, with the Far East market in full swing, the focus moves to the Near and Middle East. Bombay opens two hours after Singapore, followed after an hour and a half by Abu Dhabi, with Jeddah an hour behind, and Athens and Beirut an hour behind still. By this stage, trading in the Far and Middle East is usually thin and perhaps nervous as dealers wait to see how Europe will trade. Paris and Frankfurt open an hour ahead of London, and by this time Tokyo is starting to close down, so the European market can judge how the Japanese market has been trading by the way they deal to close out positions. By lunch-time in London, New York is starting to open up, and as Europe closes down, positions can be passed westward. During the afternoon in New York, trading tends to be quiet. The problem is that there is nowhere to pass a position to. The San Francisco market, three hours behind, is effectively a satellite of the New York market. Very small positions can be passed on to New Zealand banks, but the market there is extremely limited.[3]

> The largest markets for foreign exchange are in the United Kingdom, the United States, and Japan.

The largest foreign-exchange markets in 1995 were in the United Kingdom, the United States, and Japan (see Fig. 9.2). The U.K. market was important historically

Map 9.1
International Time Zones
Note that in the former Soviet Union standard time zones are advanced one hour.

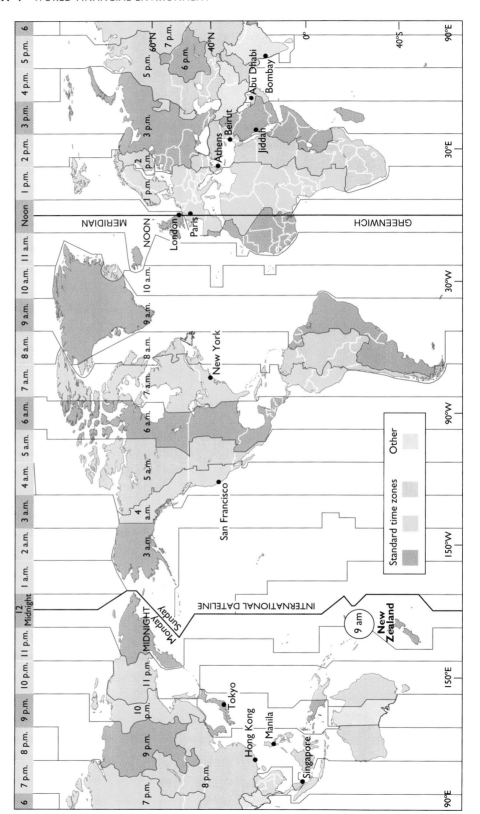

**Figure 9.2
Average Daily
Worldwide Foreign-
Exchange Volume by
Country, April 1995**
The largest volume of for-
eign-exchange transactions
occurs in the United King-
dom (London). The United
States and Japan are in sec-
ond and third place.

Source: Bank for International
Settlements. *Central Bank Survey
of Foreign Exchange and
Derivatives Market Activity* (Basel:
BIS, May 1996), p. 14.

**The U.S. dollar is the most
widely traded currency in
the world—one side of 83
percent of all transactions.**

**The top currency pair is the
dollar/deutsche mark, followed by the dollar/yen.**

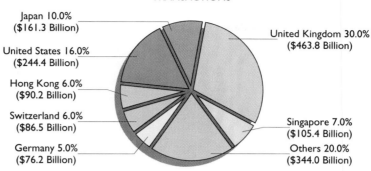

VOLUME OF FOREIGN EXCHANGE
TRANSACTIONS

Japan 10.0%
($161.3 Billion)

United States 16.0%
($244.4 Billion)

Hong Kong 6.0%
($90.2 Billion)

Switzerland 6.0%
($86.5 Billion)

Germany 5.0%
($76.2 Billion)

United Kingdom 30.0%
($463.8 Billion)

Singapore 7.0%
($105.4 Billion)

Others 20.0%
($344.0 Billion)

because it was the financial center of the former British empire. Today its importance comes from its close proximity to continental Europe and the fact that it is
the center of all U.S. dollar transactions that occur outside of the United States.

The U.S. dollar is the most important currency in the foreign-exchange market,
because it comprises one side of 83 percent of all foreign currency transactions
worldwide, as noted in Fig. 9.3. This means that since each currency trade involves
two sides (a buy and a sell), one of these sides would involve dollars 83 percent of
the time. This makes the dollar important as a vehicle for cross-trades among other
currencies. An example of a cross-trade is a situation in which a Mexican company
importing products from a Japanese exporter converts Mexican pesos into dollars
and sends them to the Japanese exporter, who converts the dollars into yen. This
cross-trade would take place instead of going directly from pesos to yen. However,
many cross-trades are now taking place directly between currencies rather than
through U.S. dollars, especially in Europe. An example might be a situation in
which a German importer trades marks for French francs rather than marks for
dollars and dollars for francs.

Another way to look at foreign-currency trades is to look at the most widely
traded currency pairs. As noted in Table 9.4, the U.S. dollar is on one side of 7 of
the top ten currency pairs, with the dollar/deutsche mark and dollar/yen trades
comprising nearly half of all currency pairs. That is the major reason why daily articles on foreign exchange in publications like the *Wall Street Journal* focus on the dol-
lar/deutsche mark, dollar/yen, and yen/deutsche mark exchange rates.

Foreign-Exchange Transactions

When a company sells goods or services to a foreign customer and receives foreign
currency, it needs to convert the foreign currency into the domestic currency. On
the import side, the company needs to convert domestic to foreign currency to pay
the foreign supplier. This activity takes place between the company and its bank.
However, there are other markets and institutions where foreign exchange is traded
(see Fig. 9.4). The client in Fig. 9.4 is the company buying or selling goods and services rather than a bank. Companies traditionally deal mostly with their banks to

Figure 9.3
Average Daily Worldwide Foreign-Exchange Transactions by Currency, April 1995
The most actively traded currencies are the U.S. dollar, the German mark, the Japanese yen, and the British pound. The largest two-way flow of currencies involves the U.S. dollar and the German mark. Because all foreign-exchange transactions involve two currencies, the total volume shown here is 200 percent.

Source: Bank for International Settlements. *Central Bank Survey of Foreign Exchange and Derivatives Market Activity* (Basel: BIS, May 1996), p. 8.

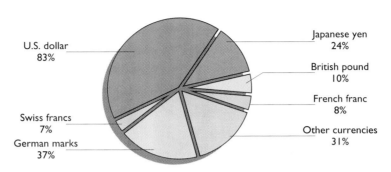

AVERAGE DAILY TRADE
BY CURRENCY

U.S. dollar
83%

Japanese yen
24%

British pound
10%

French franc
8%

Other currencies
31%

Swiss francs
7%

German marks
37%

trade foreign exchange at spot or forward. However, they could also deal with an exchange or over-the-counter (OTC) for derivatives. For example, the company could go to the Philadelphia Stock Exchange to buy or sell an option contract, and could go to the Chicago Mercantile Exchange to deal in foreign currency futures. Or the company could deal in the OTC market for derivatives by dealing with a commercial or investment bank.

Although some companies have their own trading rooms and have specialized dealers that trade foreign exchange, most of the trades take place in the bank market. Figure 9.5 illustrates how foreign exchange trades actually take place. A bank, either dealing on its own account or for a client, can trade foreign exchange with another bank (direct to the interbank counterparty) or with a broker. Well over half

Table 9.4
Reported Foreign-Exchange Market Turnover by Currency Pair in April 1995 for Spot, Outright, Forward, and Foreign-Exchange Swap Transactions

Currency Pair	Percent of Total
USD/DEM	22.3
USD/JPY	21.3
USD/GBP	6.8
USD/CHF	5.3
USD/FRF	4.5
USD/CAD	3.4
DEM/FRF	3.0
USD/AUD	2.5
DEM/JPY	2.1
DEM/GBP	1.9

Key: U.S. dollar (USD), German (Deutsche) Mark (DEM), Japanese yen (JPY), British pound (GBP), Swiss franc (CHF), French franc (FRF), Canadian dollar (CAD), Australian dollar (AUD)

Source: Bank for International Settlements. *Central Bank Survey of Foreign Exchange Derivatives Market Activity* (Basel: BIS, May 1996), p. 9.

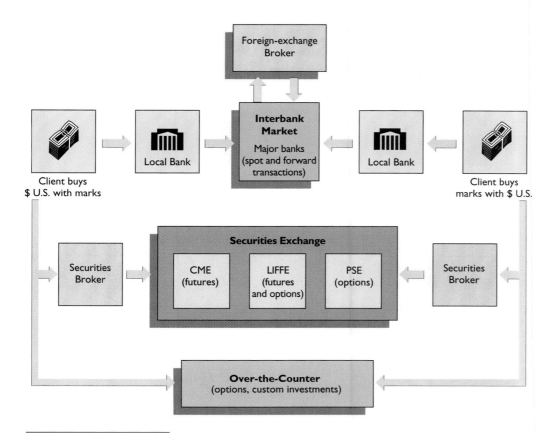

**Figure 9.4
Structure of Foreign-
Exchange Markets**

A company interested in
exchanging currency can
work with a bank, a stock
broker on a securities
exchange, or an investment
banker in the OTC market.
Banks deal with each other
in the interbank market,
primarily through foreign-
exchange brokers.

of the foreign-exchange transactions take place in the interbank market, although
the Bank for International Settlements (BIS) in Basel, Switzerland estimates that
most of this business is generated directly or indirectly by customer business, with
some the result of profit-taking by the dealers.[4]

Historically, most of the trades actually took place by telephone as a dealer in one
bank would call a dealer in another bank and execute a trade. Although some trades
also take place by telex, that market has basically dried up. The first major change in
trading that took place was the introduction of the automated dealing system by
Reuters, called Dealing 2000-1, in 1981. It was estimated in 1993 that in an average
week, 16,000 traders, engaged in 1 million conversations, used this system to execute 40 to 50 percent of foreign-exchange trades, representing 96 percent of foreign-
exchange trades that took place by computer.[5] (Reuters estimates that weekly
conversations in 1996 increased to about 1.5 million.) About 10 percent of the trades
were conducted between traders over the telephone, with the remaining 30 to 40
percent executed by brokers.[6] The Reuters system is also called a conversational
trading system, because it allows a bank to contact another bank by computer, conduct a typed conversation in English, agree to a price, and complete the transaction.[7]

As noted above, about 30 to 40 percent of the market in the early 1990s was
carried out by brokers. A foreign exchange broker is an intermediary who matches
the best bid and ask quotes of interbank traders. There are a number of brokerage
houses around the world, such as the Martin Brokers Group in London, owned by

**Figure 9.5
Foreign-Exchange
Transactions**

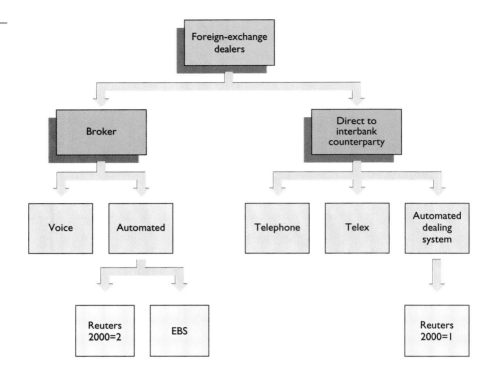

Banks deal with brokers or
in the interbank market.

Interbank trades take place
by telephone, telex (lim-
ited), or electronically.

Impact of Reuters on
foreign-exchange trading
• Dealing 2000-1: electronic
   conversational trading
• Dealing 2000-2: electronic
   broker trading

Broker Trades
• An intermediary who
   matches bid and ask
   quotes in the interbank
   market
• Voice trades—most vol-
   ume, large trades (several
   million dollars or more)
• Automated trades—com-
   puter-based trades
   Reuters or EBS

Trio Holdings, Exco, Tullett & Tokyo Forex International, and Intercapital Group.
These brokers have traditionally dealt in the market by voice, linking up interbank
traders. However, the newest technological innovation in the brokerage industry is
the introduction of automated brokering, either through Reuters's Dealing 2000-2
or EBS (Electronic Brokering System). EBS was started by a consortium of banks,
including Citibank, to respond to Reuter's domination of the foreign-exchange
trading market. Reuters has about 4,500 terminals installed worldwide, compared
with about 1,500 for EBS.

A bank gets access to the automated system by purchasing the service from
Reuters and/or EBS, paying a monthly fee, and receiving a link through telephone
lines to the bank's computers. Then the bank can use the automated system to trade
currency. The automated system is efficient, because it lists bid and ask quotes,
allowing the bank to trade immediately. The Dealing 2000-1 system requires the
bank to contact another bank and negotiate on a quote, whereas the automated broker system has quotes readily available.

In April 1995 the BIS survey noted that brokers handled 35 percent of the
foreign-exchange market activity in London, of which 30 percent was by voice and
5 percent electronic. In the United States, brokers handled 37 percent of the market, of which 24 percent was by voice and 13 percent electronic.[8]

The broker industry is in deep trouble for several reasons. Electronic brokering,
mostly in the spot market, has resulted in significant overcapacity in the voice brokerage business; highly visible losses by clients in derivatives trading has curtailed
activity; and the relative stability of exchange rates among the major markets has
slowed down market activity. Voice brokers are still used for large transactions.

Voice brokers add flexibility, contributing to the overall liquidity in the market, something even electronic brokers still prefer. For large transactions, many dealers prefer the familiarity of a trusted voice broker who can use discretion in finding a buyer or seller on the other side of the transaction. Electronic dealers are efficient but too impersonal for the large transactions. Most electronic trades are in the average $1 million to $2 million range, although occasionally a trade of $10 million to $20 million will show up. Also, the brokers are moving out of the spot market and focusing more of their efforts on derivatives, such as forwards and options. The electronic systems have focused more on spot trades, although they will probably eventually move into derivatives.[9]

Banks

A weak Japanese yen and large loan losses have hurt Japanese banks.

It used to be that only the big money center banks could deal directly in foreign exchange. Regional banks had to rely on the money center banks to execute trades on behalf of their clients. The emergence of electronic trading has changed that, however. Now even the regional banks can hook up to Reuters and EBS and deal directly in the interbank market or through brokers. However, the greatest volume of foreign exchange activity takes place with the big banks. Table 9.5 identifies the largest banks in the world in 1996. It is interesting to note that the weak Japanese yen and massive losses on loans in 1995 and 1996 have caused the Japanese banks to fall in the rankings.[10] However, that situation is not expected to last for very long. The ranking of banks in Table 9.5 is determined by using two different measures: Tier One capital and total assets. Tier One capital, as defined by BIS, covers only the core of the bank's strength—the shareholders' equity available to cover actual or potential losses.[11] It is the most important measure used to rank banks. However, the size of the bank, defined by total assets, is used in conjunction with strength to determine how solid a bank is.

Criteria for top foreign exchange traders: market, currency expertise, derivative coverage, research capabilities

However, there is more to servicing customers in the foreign-exchange market than size alone. Each year, *Euromoney* surveys banks and corporations to identify their customers' favorite banks and the leading traders in the interbank market. Criteria considered in selecting the top foreign-exchange traders include

- Ranking in specific locations, such as London, Zurich, and New York
- Capability to handle major currencies, such as the U.S. dollar and German mark
- Capability to handle major cross-trades, for example, those involving the deutsche mark and pound or the deutsche mark and yen
- Capability to handle specific currencies
- Capability to handle derivatives
- Capability to engage in research

Other factors often mentioned are price, quote speed, credit rating, liquidity, back office/settlement, strategic advice, trade recommendations, out of hours service/night desk, systems technology, innovation, and risk appraisal.[13]

Table 9.5
Largest Banks in the World

Ranking			Strength		Size
Latest	**Previous**		**Tier One Capital $m**	**$m**	**Assets rank**
1	7	HSBC Holdings London, United Kingdom (31/12/95)	21,445	351,601	13
2	8	Crédit Agricole Paris, France (31/12/95)	20,386	386,388	9
3	10	Union Bank of Switzerland Zurich, Switzerland (31/12/95)	19,903	336,188	16
4	9	Citicorp New York, NY, USA (31/12/95)	19,239	256,853	28
5	2	Dai-Ichi Kangyo Bank Tokyo, Japan (31/03/96)	19,172	498,625	4
6	11	Deutsche Bank Frankfurt, Germany (31/12/95)	18,937	503,429	1
7	4	Sumitomo Bank Osaka, Japan (31/03/96)	18,605	499,933	3
8	1	Sanwa Bank Osaka, Japan (31/03/96)	17,676	501,043	2
9	6	Mitsubishi Bank Tokyo, Japan (31/03/96)	16,667	475,010	7
10	5	Sakura Bank Tokyo, Japan (31/03/96)	15,961	478,050	6
11	3	Fuji Bank Tokyo, Japan (31/03/96)	15,443	487,341	5
12	13	BankAmerica San Francisco, CA, USA (31/12/95)	14,820	232,446	33
13	17	CS Holding Zurich, Switzerland (31/12/95)	13,751	358,734	12
14	19	ABN-Amro Bank Amsterdam, Netherlands (31/12/95)	13,372	340,642	14
15	21	Groupe Caisse d'Epargne Paris, France (31/12/95)	12,667	229,916	34
16	12	Industrial Bank of Japan Tokyo, Japan (31/03/96)	12,497	361,372	11
17	20	Swiss Bank Corp Basel, Switzerland (31/12/95)	11,733	250,566	29
18	25	National Westminster Bank London, United Kingdom (31/12/95)	11,501	260,846	27
19	23	Banque Nationale de Paris Paris, France (31/12/95)	11,453	325,250	19
20	27	Chemical Banking Corp New York, NY, USA (31/12/95)	11,436	182,926	44
21	31	Rabobank Nederland Utrecht, Netherlands (31/12/95)	11,310	182,944	43
22	14	Bank of Tokyo Tokyo, Japan (31/03/96)	11,169	237,738	32
23	29	NationsBank Charlotte, NC, USA (31/12/95)	11,074	187,298	41
24	26	Barclays Bank London, United Kingdom (31/12/95)	11,068	261,705	26
25	22	Campagnie Financière de Paribas Paris, France (31/12/95)	10,980	272,213	24

Source: The Banker, July 1996, p. 143. Reprinted with permission

For this reason, large companies may use several banks to deal in foreign exchange by selecting those that specialize in specific geographic areas, instruments, or currencies. For example, one large U.S.-based MNE uses Citibank for its broad geographic spread and wide coverage of different currencies, but it also uses Deutsche Bank for German marks, Swiss Bank Corp for Swiss francs, NatWest Bank for British pounds, and Goldman Sachs for derivatives.

One area that distinguishes between banks with broad and narrow currency coverage or that allows banks to develop niches is that of **exotic** currencies. An exotic is a currency from a developing country, such as the Russian ruble, the Malaysian ringgit, and the Mexican peso. Exotics are difficult for corporations to work with, because start-up costs are high, regulations change daily, realignments of exchange rates are common, and volatility and liquidity are very unpredictable.[14] Banks such as Citibank help their clients with exotics by cutting through the regulations on buying and selling, using local networks to manage foreign-exchange positions, dealing with difficult exchange-rate systems, working with exchange controls on investments and subsequent repatriation of capital, and getting information on potential changes in rates. The banks also help their clients manage positions and move funds. The specific financial instruments that are used, such as bills of exchange and letters of credit, are discussed in Chapter 17.

The Chicago Mercantile Exchange

The CME is the world's second-largest futures exchange and deals primarily in futures contracts for British pounds, Canadian dollars, German marks, Swiss francs, Japanese yen, and Australian dollars.

The Chicago Mercantile Exchange (CME) is the world's second-largest futures exchange, led only by the Chicago Board of Trade. It opened the International Monetary Market (IMM) in 1972 to deal primarily in futures contracts for the British pound, the Canadian dollar, the German mark, the Swiss franc, the Japanese yen, and the Australian dollar. Futures contracts have also been added in Mexican pesos, Brazilian reals, and French francs. These contracts are for specific amounts and have a specific maturity date. For example, a futures contract in Japanese yen is set by the IMM at 12.5 million yen. If you wanted to buy futures for 100 million yen, you would have to buy eight yen contracts from a broker. The contract sizes for other currencies are 125,000 German marks, 100,000 Canadian dollars, 62,500 British pounds, 125,000 Swiss francs, 100,000 Australian dollars, 500,000 new Mexican pesos, and 100,000 Brazilian reals. The "Futures Prices" section of the *Wall Street Journal* provides daily quotes on these contracts.

Even though these futures contracts have fixed maturity dates, they have a ready market. Brokers make deals on the exchange floor rather than over the telephone, as in the forward markets for banks. Futures contracts at the CME also tend to be for small amounts relative to the transactions normally encountered in the interbank market. Further, the Commodity Futures Trading Commission limits how much the futures prices may vary each day, whereas there are no such restrictions in the banking market. Finally, the CME requires a margin, or deposit.

The CME has been losing business to both the Philadelphia Stock Exchange and the over-the-counter market because of their more creative financial offerings and their ability to tailor offerings to clients. It has been estimated that CME activity in foreign-exchange futures and options is only 1 percent of the global foreign-exchange market, compared with 5 percent in 1990.[15] As a result, the CME is struggling to find its niche in the currency markets. Its major users are the managed-money funds that speculate in currency markets and smaller companies that lack the lines of credit needed to trade in the interbank market with larger companies.[16] In June 1993, the CME introduced a new type of futures contract that allowed it to compete more effectively with the banks.[17] It also joined with Reuters and the Chicago Board of Trade in 1987 to establish Globex, a 24-hour trading system that allows traders to continue trading after the exchanges close. However, most trades—even in the liquid currency market—take place in the time zones of the traders involved, so the volume of activity has been disappointing.[18]

The London International Financial Futures Exchange

The London International Financial Futures Exchange (LIFFE), which opened in September 1982, deals in futures contracts of fixed sizes in British pounds, German marks, Swiss francs, Japanese yen, and **Eurodollars,** which are dollars banked outside of the United States. This market should provide an alternative to the interbank market for avoiding foreign-exchange risk in Europe. LIFFE has become the leading overseas exchange used by speculators and money managers and investors for **hedging** their foreign-currency holdings, that is, protecting them against a loss in value.[19]

The Philadelphia Stock Exchange

The Philadelphia Stock Exchange (PSE) is the only exchange in the United States that trades foreign-currency options. The CME trades options on futures contracts rather than spot contracts. Each option is for a specific amount of currency. For example, each British pound option is for 31,250 pounds. Options against the U.S. dollar also are provided for ten currencies: the Australian dollar, the British pound, the Canadian dollar, the Dutch guilder, the European Currency Unit (ECU), the French franc, the Japanese yen, the Swiss franc, the Spanish peseta, and the Italian lira. In addition, customized currency options are available for any combination of eleven currencies (the above ten plus the U.S. dollar) for a total of 110 possible currency pairs. An example would be a Swiss franc/German mark option. For current information, see <www.phlx.com> on the Internet.

The PSE has been growing relative to the CME and Chicago Board of Trade, for several reasons. Much of the growth has come from MNEs. Although options cost more, big companies prefer them to futures (the CME instrument) because of their greater flexibility. PSE options are settled in cash, whereas CME options turn into futures contracts at maturity; corporate users therefore consider PSE options to be more convenient.[20]

Over-the-Counter Market

The over-the-counter (OTC) market has exploded in growth in recent years. Its major players are financial institutions such as Goldman Sachs (the market leader among investment banks), Merrill Lynch, and Credit Suisse First Boston (CSFB). The strength of the OTC market is the understanding these investment bankers have of investors and people who move capital. They are constantly developing new products that are individually tailored for companies and not found elsewhere. Also, the OTC market can set contracts of any size rather than in the fixed contract sizes required in the other exchanges.[21]

The strategies of the different institutions are interesting. Merrill Lynch's is "to build up a core of sophisticated customers to whom we could offer tailor-made, usually structured, products. In fact, one of [our] most important aims was to market our foreign-exchange services to other parts of Merrill Lynch—the securities business, the M&A [merger and acquisition] teams, and the asset managers." Goldman Sachs, which tends to work with the largest, most sophisticated asset managers and those corporations that run their treasury operations as profit centers, is "in the business of providing innovative product ideas and trading strategies for more sophisticated users who, in general, are looking at currencies as an asset class."[22] This market is increasingly specializing, forcing the generalists out.

Convertibility

Residents and nonresidents of a country can exchange a convertible currency for other currencies.

A key aspect of exchanging one currency for others is its convertibility. For example, although it is easy to convert U.S. dollars into Russian rubles, it has not always been easy to convert rubles into dollars. Therefore the U.S. dollar is considered freely convertible, but until recently, the Russian ruble was not.

Most countries today have nonresident, or external, convertibility. For example, all nonresidents with deposits in French banks in francs may at any time exchange all of those deposits for the currency of any other country. In other words, a U.S. exporter to France can be paid in francs and be assured that those francs can be converted to dollars or some other currency. However, not all countries permit nonresident convertibility. Lack of currency convertibility is a major problem for MNEs attempting to invest in many developing countries. For example, with limited exceptions, Peruvian enterprises are not allowed to hold foreign-exchange balances abroad and must sell foreign currency to a Peruvian bank within ten working days of receipt.[23]

Fully convertible currencies are those that the government allows both residents and nonresidents to purchase unlimited amounts of any foreign currency with. Between 20 and 25 percent of countries do not have payments restrictions, which are defined as official actions directly affecting the availability or cost of exchange or involving undue delay. All other countries have a combination of restrictions on payments for current transactions and restrictions on payments for capital transactions.[24]

A hard currency is a currency that is usually fully convertible and strong or relatively stable in value in comparison with other currencies.

Hard currencies, such as the U.S. dollar and Japanese yen, are currencies that are usually fully convertible. They also are relatively stable in value or tend to be strong in comparison with other currencies. They are desirable assets to hold. Currencies that are not fully convertible are often called **soft currencies,** or **weak currencies.**

Exchange Restrictions

Some governments impose exchange restrictions to control access to foreign exchange. The devices they use include import licensing, multiple exchange rates, import deposit requirements, and quantity controls.

Licensing

Licensing occurs when a government requires that all foreign-exchange transactions be regulated and controlled by it.

Governmental licenses fix the exchange rate by requiring all recipients, exporters, and others who receive foreign currency to sell it to the central bank at the official buying rate. A country's central bank is the institution usually empowered to establish monetary policy (these banks are discussed in greater detail in Chapter 10). It, or some other governmental agency, rations the foreign currency it acquires by selling it at fixed rates to those needing to make payment abroad for goods considered essential. An importer may purchase foreign exchange only if that importer has obtained an import license for the goods in question. An example of a government that maintains strong control over foreign exchange transactions is that of Nepal. Although individuals could not get a license to move foreign exchange out of Nepal for personal reasons, companies could exchange Nepalese currency for hard currencies to pay for imports. However, in 1996, the government found out that some business firms based in Hong Kong, Singapore, Dubai, Taiwan, and South Korea were sending invoices to Nepalese importers for more than the amount of the actual transaction so that the importers could make the excess payments to the foreign exporters and keep the difference between the real invoice and the amount paid. That allowed the importers to circumvent the foreign exchange controls established by the government of Nepal and deposit those funds out of the country.[25]

Multiple Exchange Rates

In a multiple exchange-rate system, a government sets different exchange rates for different types of transactions.

Another way to control foreign exchange is to establish more than one exchange rate. This is called a **multiple exchange-rate system.** There are several ways to determine multiple exchange rates. Some countries require a premium or discount on foreign-exchange transactions in specific industries or with specific countries. Further, if a government wants to discourage imports, it can establish a very high exchange rate for the transactions it does not favor, thereby making those imports very expensive.

Import Deposit Requirement

Some governments require an import deposit, that is, a deposit prior to the release of foreign exchange.

Another form of foreign-exchange control are advance import deposits. During the 1970s when Brazil was suffering balance of payments deficits, the government tightened the issue of import licenses and required all importers to make a one-year, interest-free deposit covering the full price of manufactured goods to be purchased from abroad. When the balance of payments situation improved, the restrictions were loosened, but that is a good example of how countries use licenses to ration scarce foreign exchange.

Quantity Controls

With quantity controls, the government limits the amount of foreign currency that can be used in a specific transaction.

Governments also may limit the amount of exchange for specific purposes. These types of controls, called **quantity controls,** often are used in conjunction with tourism. In the fall of 1996, Chinese citizens traveling abroad were allowed to convert about $1,000 of renminbi into hard currency. If they were going abroad for specific purposes, such as to study at a foreign university, they could get a certificate from the Central Bank which allowed them to take out more money. In practice, there were unofficial ways to take out even more money, and the government did not seem to be very strict in the application of the quantity restrictions. By the end of 1996, however, China had built up foreign-exchange reserves of about $100 billion, among the largest in the world, so there was not as much of a need to conserve currency as there was even five years before. Quantity restrictions can be used for other purposes as well. In 1997, for example, the government of South Africa loosened up its foreign-exchange restrictions by allowing South African companies to remove 30 million rand (about $6.8 million) to invest in factories abroad. However, the government still kept in place rules that stopped people who leave South Africa from selling their assets and taking funds with them. In addition, the government did not allow pension funds to invest abroad.[26] However, improvements in the South African economy in 1996–1997 caused the government to be optimistic about the phased removal of all foreign exchange restrictions.

The Uses of the Foreign-Exchange Market in the Internationalization Process

Commercial banks collect foreign exchange, lend foreign exchange, and buy and sell foreign exchange.

The major facilitators of foreign-exchange transactions are the international departments of the commercial banks, which perform three essential financial functions: collections, lending, and buying and selling of foreign currency. In performing collections, the bank serves as a vehicle by which payments are made between its domestic customers and foreign nationals. Lending usually takes place in the currency of the country where the bank is established, but the bank might be able to provide loans in a foreign currency if it has a branch in that country.

The purchase or sale of foreign currency is undertaken by a commercial bank for many purposes. For instance, travelers going abroad or returning from a foreign country will want to purchase or sell foreign currency. Residents of one country wanting to invest abroad also need to purchase foreign currency from a commercial bank. For example, suppose a Canadian exporter is to receive payment from a U.S. importer in U.S. dollars and wants to use the funds to make payment for raw materials purchased in Norway. The bank in this case simultaneously serves as a collector and acts as a dealer in a foreign-exchange transaction.

There are a number of reasons why companies use the foreign-exchange market. The most obvious is for transactions involving imports and exports. For example, a U.S. company importing products from an overseas supplier might have to convert U.S. dollars into a foreign currency to pay that supplier.

Companies also use the foreign-exchange market for financial transactions, such as those relating to FDI. For example, if a U.S. company decided to establish a manufacturing plant in Mexico, it would have to convert dollars into pesos to make the investment. After the Mexican subsidiary generated a profit, it would have to convert pesos to dollars to send a dividend back to the U.S. parent.

Arbitrage is the buying and selling of foreign currencies at a profit due to price discrepancies.

Sometimes companies deal in foreign exchange to make a profit, even though the transaction is not connected to any other business purpose, such as trade flows or investment flows. Usually, however, this type of foreign-exchange activity is more likely to be pursued by foreign-exchange traders and investors. One type of profit-seeking activity is **arbitrage,** which is the purchase of foreign currency on one market for immediate resale on another market (in a different country) in order to profit from a price discrepancy. For example, a trader might sell U.S. dollars for Swiss francs, the Swiss francs for German marks, and then the German marks for U.S. dollars, the goal being to end up with more dollars at the end of the process. Assume the trader converts 100 dollars into 150 Swiss francs when the exchange rate is 1.5 francs per dollar. The trader then converts the francs into 225 German marks at an exchange rate of 1.5 marks per franc and finally converts the marks into 125 dollars at an exchange rate of 1.8 marks per dollar. In this case, arbitrage yields $125 from the initial sale of $100.

Interest arbitrage is the investing in debt instruments in different countries. For example, a trader might invest $1000 in the United States for ninety days or convert $1000 into British pounds, invest the money in the United Kingdom for ninety days, and then convert the pounds back into dollars. The investor would try to pick the alternative that would be the highest-yielding at the end of ninety days.

Interest arbitrage involves investing in interest-bearing instruments in foreign exchange in an effort to earn a profit due to interest-rate differentials.

Speculators take positions in foreign-exchange markets with the major objective of earning a profit.

Foreign-exchange transactions also can be used to speculate for profit or to protect against risk. **Speculation** is the buying or selling of a commodity, in this case foreign currency, where the activity contains both an element of risk and the chance of great profit. For example, an investor could buy German marks in anticipation of the mark's strengthening against other currencies. If it does, the investor earns a profit; if it weakens, the investor incurs a loss. Speculators are important in the foreign-exchange market because they spot trends and try to take advantage of them. Thus they can be a valuable source of both supply of and demand for a currency.

As protection against risk, foreign-exchange transactions can be used to hedge against a potential loss due to an exchange-rate change. For example, a U.S. parent company expecting a dividend in British pounds in ninety days could enter into a forward contract to hedge the dividend flow. It could go to the bank and agree to deliver pounds for dollars in ninety days at the forward rate. Doing this would eliminate the risk of an unfavorable shift in the exchange rate by locking in a specific forward rate for the dividend flow.

When the British pound was under pressure in the fall of 1992, speculator George Soros was rumored to have made over $1 billion betting against the pound. Although the British government had publicly stated that it would support the pound, Soros didn't believe it. His feeling was that the European Monetary System (EMS), the system linking together the currencies of Europe (see the discussion in Chapter 7), was not working as intended, thereby creating a bias against the weak currencies. As a result of his analysis, he began selling pounds to the Bank of England at an artificially supported price. When it was clear the government could not continue its support, the bottom fell out of the market. Soros bought back his pounds at a significantly cheaper price. There is nothing illegal about what George Soros did, and most would argue that there is nothing unethical about battering a currency in order to make money. But because of the size of the foreign exchange market and the variety of instruments that can be used to trade currencies, there are plenty of opportunities for a trader to make money illegally. One of the most publicized events in the derivatives markets in recent years involved 28 year-old Nicholas Leeson and 233-year old Barings PLC. Leeson, a trader for Barings PLC, was sent to Singapore in the early 1990s to help resolve some problems Barings was having, and within a year, he was executing trades, eventually being promoted to chief trader. The problem was that he was responsible for both trading securities and booking the settlements, thus eliminating any internal control on possible fraud. In 1994, Leeson bought stock index futures on the assumption that the Tokyo stock market would rise. Unfortunately, the market fell, and Leeson had to come up with cash to cover the margin call on the futures contract.[27] However, he soon ran out of cash from Barings, so he had to figure out how to come up with more cash. One approach he used was to write options contracts and use the premium he collected on the contracts to cover his margin call. Unfortunately, he was using Barings's funds to cover positions he was taking for himself, not for clients, and he also forged documents to cover his transactions. As the Tokyo stock market continued to plunge, Leeson fell farther and farther behind and eventually fled the country, later to be caught and returned to Singapore for trial. It was estimated that Leeson generated losses in excess of $1 billion, which put Barings into bankruptcy. Eventually, Barings was purchased by the Dutch bank, ING. Leeson's activities in the derivatives market were illegal and a violation of solid internal controls policies.[28]

ETHICAL DILEMMAS & SOCIAL RESPONSIBILITY

Foreign-exchange trading generates a higher volume of transactions at a lower cost, favoring large companies over small ones.

Size and scale are important dimensions of foreign-exchange trading. The larger the foreign-exchange transaction, the lower the cost. Trades are quoted not only in terms of the specific currencies involved but also in terms of the size of the transaction. Although any bank can deal in foreign exchange, it is the size, geographical spread, and range of available currencies that cause a bank to rank above others. Time and again, corporate treasurers select specific banks because of their range of services. This is no market for the small player.

If this is the case, how do the small players survive? How can the exporter who is going to receive $50,000 in foreign currency for a sale going to make money? Must the exporter use one of the top commercial banks to be successful? Fortunately, the foreign-exchange market is available to anyone at spot. The relatively high transactions cost for small transactions will cut into the exporter's profitability, but not significantly. However, for the small exporter in a regional market, finding a local bank that understands the foreign-exchange market and can deliver the service may be difficult. The local bank will likely work through a larger money-center bank for trades, especially those involving derivatives.

Another countervailing force is global standardization versus national responsiveness. Banks like Citicorp have offices all over the world, and it is important for the branches to link themselves together for foreign exchange trades. The sheer volume of transactions allows them to offer attractive rates, as mentioned above. However, each branch must be responsive to the foreign exchange demands in their particular markets. Trading activity will take place at different times of the day simply because of time zones. Thus the market is closed down in New York when it is open and thriving in Tokyo (even though the large banks will still have limited trading going on twenty-four hours a day). Citicorp's trading in New York will take place in a different mix of currencies than will its trading in Tokyo. In London, its trading will focus more on European currencies, whereas in Tokyo its trading will focus more on Asian currencies.

LOOKING TO
THE FUTURE

Significant strides have been made and will continue to be made in the development of foreign-exchange markets. The speed at which transactions are processed and information is transmitted globally will certainly lead to greater efficiencies and more opportunities for foreign-exchange trading. For example, ten years ago, options were seldom discussed, but since 1989, the number of options transactions has jumped significantly. The options market will continue to grow in importance because of the flexibility of this type of contract, the range of products available in the OTC market, and the instability in the foreign-exchange markets—especially in Europe. Further, transactions costs will come down and companies will learn how to use options more effectively.

In addition, exchange restrictions that hamper the free flow of goods and services should diminish as governments gain greater control over their economies. A common

European currency will allow cross-border transactions in Europe to progress more smoothly. Further, under NAFTA, the Mexican government will be forced to slow inflation and stabilize the Mexican currency in order to allow trade to flow more smoothly.

Finally, technological developments may not cause the foreign-exchange broker to disappear entirely, but they will certainly cause foreign-exchange trades to be executed more quickly and cheaply. The real issue in the future is whether banks can mount a challenge to Reuters before Reuters locks up the world of foreign-exchange trade.

WEB CONNECTION
Check out our home page for links to World Wide Web resources on foreign exchange.

Summary

- A major distinction between domestic and international transactions for goods and services is that one currency is used for domestic transactions but more than one currency is used for international transactions.

- An exchange rate is the value of one currency in terms of another. The spot rate is the rate quoted by a foreign-exchange trader for current transactions; the forward rate is that quoted for a contract to receive or deliver the foreign currency in the future.

- The difference between the spot and forward rates is the discount or premium. The foreign currency is selling at a discount if the forward rate is less than the spot rate and at a premium if the forward rate is greater than the spot rate.

- Most foreign-exchange transactions occur through traders at commercial banks, with nearly half of the transactions occurring in the spot market rather than the forward market.

- Most foreign-exchange transactions take place in the interbank market rather than between banks and nonbanking institutions.

- Derivatives are swaps, outright forwards, options, and futures contracts. Swaps and forwards are the most popular, but options are growing in importance. An option is the right but not the obligation to buy or sell foreign currency.

- The world's largest foreign-exchange markets are in the United Kingdom, the United States, and Japan.

- The average daily trading volume in foreign exchange exceeds $1 trillion, and the most actively traded currencies are the U.S. dollar, the German mark, the Japanese yen, and the British pound.

- Foreign exchange is traded through brokers or with banks in the interbank market.

- Nonbank foreign-exchange trading takes place in the over-the-counter market through institutions such as Goldman Sachs and at the Chicago Board of Trade and CME (futures contracts), LIFFE, and the PSE (options).

- The most important characteristics of the banks that provide foreign-exchange services are their size, geographical spread, ability to deal in derivatives (especially options), and currency coverage.

- A convertible currency can be freely traded for other currencies. Some countries' currencies are partially convertible in that residents are not allowed to convert them into other currencies but nonresidents are.

- Some governments control foreign exchange through import licensing, multiple exchange rates, import deposit requirements, or quantity controls.

Case
Ilusión Textiles and the Mexican Peso[29]

In late 1996, the Romano family of Tizayuca, Mexico, was trying to determine how to adjust the corporate strategy of their family-owned company, Ilusión Textiles, to the changing value of the Mexican peso and changes in the Mexican economy. Ilusión, a labor-intensive textile manufacturer, produces products such as slips, camisoles, bras, and panties that are sold in the domestic and export markets. It is a second generation company that employs about 1,350 people, with blue-collar employees earning from $120 to $240 per month. As Mexico prepared to enter NAFTA, the Romanos were concerned about the impact of lowering tariffs on the future of the company. They had been growing 15 to 20 percent per year prior to the end of 1994, all from the domestic market. Given the rapid growth in the domestic market, the Romanos did not feel it was necessary to export. However, they were concerned about the possible flood of imports from Asia, so they began to invest regularly in new equipment that would increase the quality of their garments and lower costs. Much of the new equipment was imported from Italy and Germany. But then came the devaluation of the Mexican peso in 1994, and everything changed. What events led to the devaluation, and what should the Romanos do now?

The History of the Peso
In order to understand the events of 1994, it is important to go back to 1976 when the peso was devalued for the first time since its value had been set in 1955 and then to trace

its history to current times. On August 31, 1976, the Mexican peso was cut loose from its exchange rate of 12.5 pesos to the dollar, which had been established in 1955. From 1955 to 1976, the exchange rate had been maintained artificially through various mechanisms. Import controls and market intervention were used extensively to allow the peso to appear more stable than it was, thereby frustrating MNEs operating in Mexico. Many companies established manufacturing operations in Mexico only to find that the government eventually phased out their ability to import needed raw materials and components. During the 1970s, pressure began to build for a change in the peso's value. Tourism, a major source of foreign exchange, began to taper off because of rising prices resulting directly from general inflation in the economy.

Mexico began importing more than it was exporting, which resulted in an outflow of pesos. Further, exporters to Mexico preferred to convert their pesos into dollars. Governmental use of Mexico's existing dollar reserves to buy back the pesos would have depleted those reserves severely. So, instead Mexico chose to maintain its level of reserves by increasing its short-term external borrowing of dollars. However, this move would eventually have resulted in principal and interest payments that could rob Mexico of what little foreign-exchange reserves it could gather.

Because of these and other pressures, Mexican officials agreed to devalue the peso to 20.5 pesos per dollar on August 31, 1976. They hoped this devaluation would absorb some of the excess supply of pesos in the market and allow the economy to stabilize. The government also considered establishing more elaborate foreign-exchange controls so that spot transactions could be allocated according to governmental priorities. In the end, Mexico decided on devaluation rather than foreign-exchange controls because the latter would require establishing an elaborate bureaucracy to administer them.

Unfortunately, the solution to the problem was short-lived. From 1976 to mid-1981, the peso held its postdevaluation level, but inflation and other forces that had created the problems leading up to the 1976 devaluation reemerged. Imports again exceeded exports, tourism fell steadily, foreign credit became tight and expensive, and world oil prices and demand softened considerably. However, the Central Bank of Mexico steadfastly maintained that a relatively modest 15–20-percent devaluation would correct the imbalances in the economy, and officials appeared to be in no hurry to make any changes.

The situation continued to worsen. In the absence of capital controls, wealthy Mexicans spent their money abroad on consumer durables and investments that would shelter them against another devaluation. With the government's continuing to exude confidence up to the last hour, a devaluation of over 40 percent was announced on February 17, 1982, bringing the new rate to 38.50 pesos per dollar. At the same time, the government announced that it hoped to keep the exchange rate to a level of 38–43 pesos for the rest of 1982. Yet scarcely a week later, on February 26, it announced another devaluation, this time to 47.25 pesos.

The two devaluations were not successful. In August 1982, after still another devaluation, the government decided to establish two exchange rates: an official rate and a free-market rate. Unfortunately, the official rate was only 49 pesos, and the free-market rate shot up to 105 pesos. In September 1982, the government nationalized all private banks and instituted currency controls. It also established a fixed priority list for determining who would get foreign exchange.

During the 1980s, the peso continued to weaken. Its fall was fueled by inflation that averaged a low of 59.2 percent in 1984 and a high of 159.2 percent in 1987. The peso dropped to a 1983 year-end rate of 143.9 pesos per dollar. By the end of 1988, it had plummeted to 2281 pesos per dollar.

In 1988, there were two exchange markets in Mexico: the controlled market and the free market. There also were import controls and controls on access to foreign exchange. In the controlled market, importers could acquire foreign exchange for the full value of merchandise already imported for which payment had not yet been made. Full advance payment for all imports was also allowed, provided the value of the goods did not exceed US$10,000 or the payment was made through a letter of credit. For purchases that exceeded US$10,000, only 20-percent advance payment was allowed.

The Crisis of 1994

On December 1, 1988, Carlos Salinas de Gortari took office as the new president of Mexico. He speeded up the process of economic liberalization by lifting restrictions on trade and foreign investment, and he embarked on an ambitious privatization program. A major part of his new economic plan was inflation control. As inflation came down, the peso/dollar exchange rate stabilized. As noted in Fig. 9.6, the exchange rate at the end of 1992 was 3.1154 pesos per dollar (the government changed the exchange rate from 3115.4 to 3.1154 by changing the decimal place in 1993), and was 3.1059 at the end of 1993.

However, a number of things happened in 1994. As shown in Fig. 9.7, Mexico's current account balance was negative and growing from 1989 to 1994. Part of the reason for the rising deficit was the admission of Mexico into NAFTA, as discussed in Chapter 7. How-

**Figure 9.6
The Year-End
Peso/Dollar Exchange
Rate**

Source: International Monetary Fund. *International Financial Statistics.* August 1996, pp. 416–417.

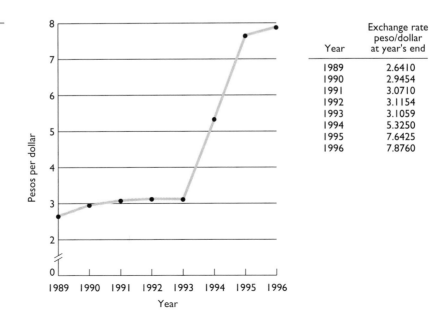

Year	Exchange rate peso/dollar at year's end
1989	2.6410
1990	2.9454
1991	3.0710
1992	3.1154
1993	3.1059
1994	5.3250
1995	7.6425
1996	7.8760

**Figure 9.7
Mexico's Current
Account Balance**

Source: International Monetary
Fund. *International Financial
Statistics.* August 1996,
pp. 418–419.

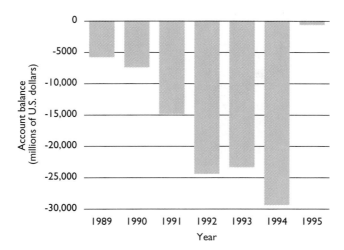

ever, much of the growth in the deficit came from net imports from non-NAFTA countries such as Germany and Japan. Mexico had no luck penetrating Japanese and German markets, leading to huge trade deficits with them.

During the 1990s, Mexico's current account deficit was being financed by portfolio investments from abroad. Large mutual funds were pouring money into Mexico to take advantage of emerging market growth potential, rising from only $289 million in 1989 to $27.9 billion in 1993. By early 1994, a large number of portfolio investors had reached their desired stocks, so the massive inflows of the prior years slowed down. In addition, interest rates began to rise in the United States, causing many investors to put their money there to receive a relatively high and stable return.

As a result, Mexico turned to its reserves to fund its deficits. As shown in Fig. 9.8, official reserves, which had been rising in the early 1990s, fell dramatically in 1994. On a quarterly basis, reserves plunged in the second and fourth quarters of 1994 before recovering in the second quarter of 1995 (see Fig. 9.9).

On the political front, Mexico held an election for President in 1994, but disaster struck early. The Institutional Revolutionary Party (PRI), which had ruled Mexico since 1929, selected its successor to Salinas, Luis Donaldo Colosio. However, in March 1994, Colosio

**Figure 9.8
Mexico's Total
Reserves, 1989–1995**

Source: International Monetary
Fund. *International Financial
Statistics.* August 1996,
pp. 416–417.

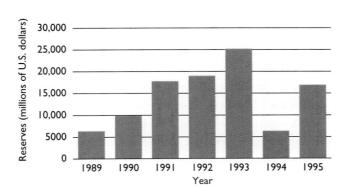

**Figure 9.9
Mexico's Quarterly
Total Reserves,
1994–1996**

Source: International Monetary
Fund. *International Financial
Statistics.* August 1996,
pp. 418–419.

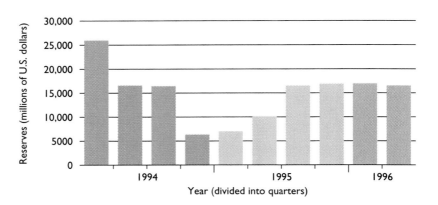

was assassinated, and foreign exchange reserves began to fall as wealthy Mexicans began moving money out of the country. Then in September 1994, PRI Secretary General Francisco Ruiz Massieu was assassinated, and President Salinas' brother was implicated in the murder (although not until February 1995, which was after the peso crisis). As if that wasn't enough, Zapatista guerrillas revolted against the leadership in Chiapas, Mexico, in early 1994, throwing politics into even greater turmoil. In this environment, Ernesto Zedillo Ponce de León was chosen to lead the PRI, was elected President, and took office on December 1, 1994.

However, a currency crisis was right around the corner, even though most experts—both foreign and domestic—were very optimistic about the future of Mexico. But there had been a major devaluation in the last year of each of the previous four presidential periods. Although the Mexican economy had opened up significantly from the previous administration, the political system was still very authoritarian and closed. In the closing days of the Salinas presidency, there was a strong debate over whether to devalue the peso, and the forces against a devaluation prevailed.

When Zedillo took office, the pressures became too great to resist, and the peso was devalued on December 20. Technically, the peso had been trading in a band with a floor of 3.4712 pesos per dollar. On December 20, the floor was lowered to 4.0016 pesos, and the market value fell to 3.96 pesos, a fall of 12.7 percent. The government announced a crawling devaluation, but on December 22, the government abandoned its efforts to support the peso, and it let it freely float. The market reacted by pushing down the peso another 15 percent. By that point, the government felt as if it had lost total control over the economy and foreign exchange markets, so it decided to let the peso continue to float and seek a true level. By the end of the year, the peso had fallen 36 percent since the devaluation and was 48 percent lower than it was at the beginning of the year. Figure 9.10 tracks the value of the peso by quarter until mid-1996.

By early 1995, Mexico was in economic crisis. The U.S. government stepped in with a loan package involving Canada, the Bank for International Settlements, and the IMF, with the United States putting up the most money. As Mexico began to tap the loan funds, the Clinton administration was severely criticized by opponents in Congress and elsewhere. But Mexico repaid most of its loans by the fall of 1996, easing most people's concerns

**Figure 9.10
The Peso by Quarter,
1994–1996**

Source: International Monetary
Fund. *International Financial
Statistics.* August 1996,
pp. 416–417.

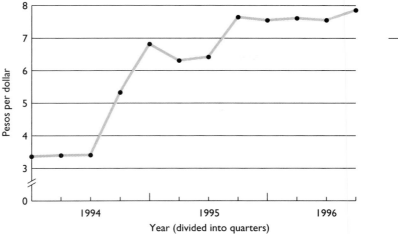

Year	Exchange rate peso/dollar at quarter
1994-I	3.3598
1994-II	3.3918
1994-III	3.4040
1994-IV	5.3250
1995-I	6.8175
1995-II	6.3092
1995-III	6.4195
1995-IV	7.6425
1996-I	7.5479
1996-II	7.6108
1996-III	7.5519
1996-IV	7.8760

about the bailout. In order to slow down inflation and attract more investment, Zedillo raised interest rates to 43.3 percent at one point. However, this caused the economy to slow down dramatically, putting a million people out of work. Many investors, both domestic and foreign, pulled their money out of the Mexican markets, causing the stock market to drop, and other companies slowed down the rate of direct investment going into Mexico.

How did these events affect Ilusión Textiles? Just before the devaluation, Ilusión had purchased capital equipment from suppliers in Germany and Italy, and probably had to pay dollars. If it had waited until early 1995, it would probably have had to come with nearly 50 percent more pesos to get the dollars. In addition, the slowdown in the Mexican economy caused sales to drop 8.9 percent by September 1995, compared with the growth of 15 to 20 percent per year prior to the devaluation. As a result, Illusión turned to export markets, as did other Mexican companies. In fact, Ilusión generated about 10 percent of its revenues from exports in 1995, up from zero in 1994, and it hoped to expand exports to 20 percent of total in 1996. For the economy as a whole, exports grew by about 28 percent in 1995 generating 25 percent of GDP, and its trade deficit turned to a surplus in 1996, and the economy began to recover.

However, more problems began to surface in late 1995, as interest rate and exchange rate volatility remained at high levels. In the August–September 1995 time frame, political conditions worsened, and the peso fell from 6.40 pesos per dollar to 8.25 pesos per dollar in a matter of days.

In 1996, the markets calmed down somewhat, as reflected in the narrowing of the bid offer spreads in the dollar/peso exchange rate. Since the peso crisis of 1994, several foreign exchange hedging derivatives were being offered, including OTC forward contracts, OTC options contracts, and Chicago Mercantile Exchange foreign exchange futures and options on futures. However, the exchange-traded instruments were relatively illiquid. Derivatives being sold in Mexico were closely monitored by the Central Bank of Mexico, and controls were being placed on derivatives dealers.

However, currency markets returned to instability in the fall of 1996. When a planned privatization of the petrochemicals arm of the state-owned oil company, Pemex, was scrapped on October 13, 1996, the value of the peso plunged to 7.73 pesos, after hovering around 7.5 pesos for most of 1996. This was disturbing, given that the Mexican economy grew by about 4 percent in 1996 after falling 6 percent in 1995, and Mexico was able to borrow funds on international capital markets again. In addition, inflation continued to trend downward, although still in double-digit figures.

Questions

1. Describe different ways that the Mexican government has instituted foreign exchange controls over the years. How successful have they been in stabilizing the peso?
2. What are some of the major factors that have affected the value of the peso since 1955? What factors would you monitor as you watch the peso over the next few years?
3. Going into the fourth quarter of 1994, many experts were still very bullish on the peso. Why do you think they were so supportive of the peso? With hindsight, what factors should have led them to believe that the peso was in trouble?
4. How has the fall in the peso affected Ilusión? How do you think it will affect them in the future?

Chapter Notes

1. Peter T. White, "The Power of Money," *National Geographic,* January 1993, p. 82.
2. Bank for International Settlements, *Central Bank Survey of Foreign Exchange and Derivatives Market Activity, 1995* (Basel, Switzerland: BIS, May 1996), pp. 18–19.
3. Julian Walmsley, *The Foreign Exchange Handbook* (New York: Wiley, 1983), pp. 7–8.
4. Bank for International Settlements, op. cit., p. 13.
5. "Banks Retaliate in Dealing-Room War," *Euromoney,* May 1993, p. 87.
6. Peter Lee, "Foreign Exchange: Bye-Bye Brokers," *Euromoney,* April 1992, p. 14.
7. Felix Salmon, "When Is a Market Like Treacle?" *Euromoney,* July 1996, p. 155.
8. Stephanie Cook, "Will Brokers Go Broke?" *Euromoney,* May 1996, p. 90.
9. Ibid. p. 92.
10. Michael Blanden, "The Mighty Are Fallen," *The Banker,* July 1996, p. 102.
11. Ibid. p. 140, discusses the determination of Tier One capital.
12. "How Investors Choose a Bank," *Euromoney,* January 1993, p. 52.
13. "Treasures Put their Views on Banks," *Euromoney,* May 1995 p. 65.
14. Euan Hagger, "Handle Exotics with Care," *Euromoney,* October 1992, p. 71.
15. Laurie Morse, "Risk and Reward: Chicago Looks to Rolling Contracts to Gather Investors," *Financial Times,* June 7, 1993, p. 19.
16. Jeffrey Taylor, "Foreign Currency Trades Slow at Merc as Firms Back Away," *Wall Street Journal,* October 20, 1992, p. C1.
17. Alice Ratcliffe, "CME Launches Novel Currency Contract on Sterling," *Reuters,* June 15, 1993.
18. Tracy Corrigan and Laurie Morse, "Trouble After Hours—Since Its Launch, the Globex Trading System Has Provoked Much Criticism," *Financial Times,* June 3, 1993, p. 17.
19. William B. Crawford Jr., "In Historic Session, London Outtrades Chicago Markets," *Chicago Tribune,* September 18, 1992, p. 3.
20. Taylor, loc. cit.
21. Ibid.
22. "The Banks' Golden Egg," *Euromoney,* May 1992, p. 78.
23. International Monetary Fund, *Exchange Arrangements and Exchange Restrictions: Annual Report 1991* (Washington, D.C.: IMF, 1991), p. 385.
24. Ibid., p. 585.
25. Gopal Sharma, "Nepal's Central Bank Sets Limits on Import Finance," *The Reuter Asia-Pacific Business Report,* December 31, 1996. Available: NEXIS Library: General News: News:Curnws.
26. Ruaridh Nicholl, "South Africa Relaxes Rules on Rand as it Seeks World Role," *The Guardian,* March 13, 1997, p. 21.
27. Leeson did not actually buy the contracts outright, but paid a certain percentage of the value of the contract, known as "margin." When the stock market fell, the index futures contract became riskier, and the broker who sold the contract required Leeson to increase the amount of the margin.
28. "The Collapse of Barings: A Fallen Star," *The Economist,* March 4, 1995, pp. 19–21; Glen Whitney, "ING Puts Itself on the Map by Acquiring Failed Barings," *Wall Street Journal,* March 8, 1995, p. B4.
29. "Hedging in Mexico," *Finance & Treasury,* May 17, 1993, p. 5; Richard Moxon, "The Mexican Peso," in *International Finance Cases and Simulation,* Robert S. Carlson, H. Lee Remmers, Christine Hekman, David K. Eiteman, and Arthur I. Stonehill, eds. (Reading, Mass.: Addison-Wesley, 1980), pp. 22–23; "Acme Do Mexico, S.A.," a case by Ingo Walter, Graduate School of Business, New York University, 1983; Lawrence Rout, "Mexican Firms

May Be Able to Get Dollars...," *Wall Street Journal,* September 3, 1982, p. 3; Lawrence Rout, "Mexicans Start Picking Up the Pieces after Last Week's 30% Devaluation," *Wall Street Journal,* February 23, 1982, p. 30; Lawrence Rout, "Mexico Seeking to Hold Peso at 38 to Dollar," *Wall Street Journal,* February 22, 1982; Lawrence Rout, "Mexico Ponders the Peso's Problems," *Wall Street Journal,* January 28, 1982, p. 27; "Mexico Eases Down the Peso," *Business Week,* August 31, 1981, p. 79; Geri Smith, Elisabeth Malkin, David Woodruff, Stanley Reed, and William Glasgall, "Mexico: Can it Cope?" *Business Week,* January 16, 1995, pp. 42–46; Geri Smith and Stephen Baker, "The Fall of Carlos Salinas," *Business Week,* March 27, 1995, pp. 53–56; Geri Smith and Stanley Reed, "Now It's Export or Die," *Business Week,* November 13, 1995, p. 116; Geri Smith, Stanley Reed, and Elisabeth Malkin, "Mexico: A Rough Road Back," *Business Week,* November 13, 1995, pp. 104–107; "Troubled Waters," *The Economist,* October 19, 1996, p. 77; Jonathan E. Heath, *The Devaluation of the Mexican Peso in 1994* (Washington, D.C.: Center for Strategic and International Studies, June 1, 1995); Euromoney, *The 1996 Guide to Emerging Market Currencies* (London: Euromoney, 1996), p. 31.

Chapter 10

The Determination of Exchange Rates

*A fair exchange
brings no quarrel.*
—Danish Proverb

Objectives

- To describe the International Monetary Fund and its role in the determination of exchange rates

- To discuss the major exchange-rate arrangements used by countries for their currencies

- To identify the major determinants of exchange rates in the spot and forward markets

- To show how to forecast exchange-rate movements using factors such as balance-of-payments statistics

- To explain how exchange-rate movements influence business decisions

Case
The Chinese
Renminbi[1]

China's currency is the renminbi, and its unit of account is the yuan. At the end of 1993, China announced it would adjust its exchange-rate system beginning January 1, 1994. After that date, rather than continuing to manage the system as a dual-track foreign-exchange system, it would allow the renminbi to float according to market forces.

The concept of a managed exchange rate as represented by the dual-track system was part of the centrally planned economy under which China has operated for decades. The People's Bank of China (PBC) is the country's central bank. The State Administration of Exchange Control (SAEC), operating under the PBC's control, is responsible for implementing exchange-rate regulations and controlling foreign-exchange transactions in accord with state policy.

The dual-track system provided for two government-approved exchange rates: the official exchange rate and the swap-market rate. Under that system, the SAEC published official exchange rates for the U.S. dollar and twenty other currencies daily. The SAEC set the official exchange rate for the renminbi based on China's balance-of-payments situation and the exchange rates of its major competitor countries, such as South Korea and Taiwan. For example, when the official rates were first set in 1986, the rate was set at 3.72 yuan per dollar; by the end of 1993, the official rate was 5.8145 yuan per dollar.

The official exchange rate was used primarily by government-owned companies. It also was used to purchase Foreign Exchange Certificates (FECs). FECs were a separate form of currency developed in 1980 for use by foreigners and foreign companies when paying for their expenses in China. However, the PBC decided to stop issuing FECs in 1994 and gradually withdraw them from circulation.

The other half of the dual-market system is the swap market, which was created in Shenzhen in 1985 for foreign and local businesses that had received official approval to exchange yuan and hard currency. The currency values in the swap market were based on supply and demand. Gradually, other swap centers, known as foreign exchange adjustment centers (FEACs), opened up; the next three were located in the Special Economic Zones of Shantou, Xiamen, and Zhuhai. In 1988, $6.2 billion in transactions occurred in the swap market, and in 1992, the volume exploded to $26 billion. By the end of 1993, there were around a hundred swap centers, one in most major cities in China. The largest was in Shanghai, which had brokers representing twenty-one Chinese financial institutions and twenty-two foreign institutions and reported 1993 trading of $5.29 billion, up 49 percent from the previous year. By the end of 1993, it was estimated that 80 percent of the hard-currency transactions in China were occurring in the swap market. At that time, the swap rate was 8.7 yuan per U.S. dollar, a significant discount over the official rate of 5.8 yuan per dollar.

In addition to the two government-approved markets—the official market and the swap market—a black market also existed. The black-market rate was at an even deeper discount than the swap rate was.

In announcing the new floating-rate system, the PBC made it clear that governmental authorities were going to continue to intervene in foreign-exchange markets and to use monetary and interest-rate policy to stabilize exchange rates. The new, floating-rate system was expected to benefit foreign MNEs that previously had had to record transactions at a variety of different exchange rates, for example, registering their foreign-currency-based capital at the official exchange rate and remitting their yuan profits at the much weaker swap rate.

As part of the move to the new exchange-rate system, the Chinese government closed the swap centers in early 1994. The swap center in Shanghai was replaced by the National Foreign Exchange Center, which is a national interbank center at which appointed banks can trade and settle foreign currencies. The remaining swap centers either became branches of the interbank system or economic information centers.

Even though the dual exchange rate system was eliminated in 1994, there were still controls on both current and capital account transactions. Since January 1994, companies in China could exchange renminbi into foreign currency to buy imports controlled by quotas if they had an import permit and an invoice. Foreign exchange for imports without quotas could be bought with just an import invoice. Foreign companies operated under different conditions than domestic companies. They could buy and sell renminbi as long as they maintained a balanced foreign exchange account, that is, as long as the demand for foreign exchange for imports was balanced off by earnings in foreign exchange from exports.

As noted in Fig. 10.1, the value of the renminbi against the U.S. dollar has risen fairly steadily since January 1, 1994. However, the real value of the renminbi has fallen because of relatively higher inflation in China than in the United States. The reason why the renminbi

**Figure 10.1
Chinese Renminbi per
U.S. Dollar, 1993–1996**

Source: Bloomberg Financial
Markets and Commodities
News: Online: Currency.

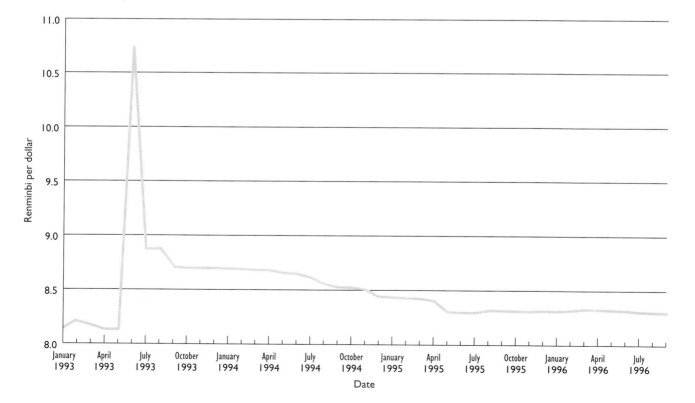

has risen instead of fallen can be traced to three factors: a strong trade surplus, an increase in inward foreign direct investment, and a steady rise in foreign exchange reserves. In Chapter 9, we looked at how the drop in reserves in Mexico was a contributing factor to that government's decision to devalue the peso. In China, however, foreign exchange reserves rose to $100 billion by the end of March 1996.

In early 1996, a national renminbi interbank market was established by electronically linking 35 cities. Prior to this event, the 35 official interbank lending centers were linked to the central bank's electronic clearing system, but not to each other. At the same time as the interbank market was established, the central bank announced that it was going to engage in open market operations by buying and selling Treasury bonds with the banks.

In November 1995, Vice-Premier Zhu Rongji announced that China would allow the renminbi to become fully convertible in 1996 on a current account (trade in goods and services) but not a capital account (investment and income flows) basis. This really caught many experts by surprise, but they also felt that China needs to liberalize its interest rate policy (interest rates are controlled by the central bank, not determined by supply and demand) and free up banks from existing restrictions. In addition, many wonder if the renminbi will continue to remain strong if China's inflation heats up some more and the trade position worsens.

Introduction

As discussed in Chapter 9, an exchange rate represents the number of units of one currency needed to acquire one unit of another currency. Although this definition seems simple, it is important that managers understand how an exchange rate initially is set and why it changes. Such understanding can help them anticipate and respond to exchange-rate changes and make decisions about situations that are influenced by those changes, such as the sourcing of raw materials and components, the location of manufacturing and assembly, and the location of final markets.

The International Monetary System

The International Monetary Fund
The Great Depression, economic isolation, and trade wars of the 1930s were followed by the global conflict of World War II. Toward the close of World War II in 1944, the major Western governments met in Bretton Woods, New Hampshire, to determine the international institutions that were needed to bring relative economic stability and growth to the free world. As a result of the meetings, the **International Monetary Fund (IMF)** and World Bank were organized in 1945.

The agreement establishing the IMF initially was signed by 29 countries; by 1996, it had been signed by 181.[2] The IMF's major objectives are

The IMF was organized to promote exchange-rate stability and facilitate the international flow of currencies.

- To promote exchange-rate stability
- To maintain orderly exchange-rate arrangements
- To avoid competitive currency devaluations
- To establish a multilateral system of payments
- To eliminate exchange restrictions
- To create standby reserves

Par value is the benchmark value of a currency, initially quoted in terms of gold and the U.S. dollar.

The **Bretton Woods Agreement,** named after the location of the 1944 conference, established a system of fixed exchange rates under which each IMF member country established a par value for its currency based on gold and the U.S. dollar. This par value became a benchmark by which the country related its currency to the other currencies of the world. Currencies were allowed to vary within 1 percent of par value (extended to 2.25 percent in December 1971), depending on supply and demand. Further moves from par value and formal changes in par value are made with the IMF's approval.

Because the U.S. dollar was strong during the 1940s and 1950s, currencies of IMF member countries were denominated in terms of gold and U.S. dollars. By 1947, the United States held 70 percent of the world's official gold reserves. Therefore, governments bought and sold dollars rather than gold. It was understood, although not formalized, that the United States would redeem gold for dollars, and the relative values of these two standards became fixed. The dollar thus became the world benchmark for trading currency.

When a country joins the IMF, it is assigned a quota related to its national income, monetary reserves, trade balance, and other economic indicators. The quota determines a country's voting power and other issues and is paid when the country joins the IMF.

The Board of Governors is the IMF's highest authority. It is composed of one representative from each member country. The number of votes a country has depends on the size of its quota. Although the Board of Governors is the ultimate authority on key matters, it delegates day-to-day authority to a 24-person Board of Executive Directors.[3]

Special Drawing Rights (SDRs)

The SDR is
- **A unit of account developed by the IMF**
- **Designed to increase international reserves**

To help increase international reserves, the IMF created the **Special Drawing Right (SDR)** in 1970. The SDR is a unit of account that was distributed to countries to expand their official reserves bases. For example, Brazil could trade some of its SDRs to the United States for dollars. The SDR initially was denominated in gold and later determined by a basket of sixteen currencies. A "basket of currencies" is the same thing as a group of currencies. That is, the value of the SDR is based on the weighted average of a group of currencies rather than on just one currency. On January 1, 1981, the IMF began to use a simplified basket of five currencies for determining valuation: The U.S. dollar made up 39 percent of the value of the SDR; the German mark, 21 percent; the Japanese yen, 18 percent; and the French franc and the

Currencies making up the SDR basket are the U.S. dollar, the German mark, the Japanese yen, the French franc, and the British pound.

British pound, 11 percent each. That is, the value of the basket is the sum of the values of the five currencies, but each one has a specific weight. These weights were chosen because they broadly reflected the relative importance of the currencies in international trade and payments. The value of the SDR can be found daily in the foreign exchange table of the *Wall Street Journal* and the *Financial Times* of London. Unless the Executive Board of the IMF decides otherwise, the weights of each currency in the valuation basket are changed every five years. This rule was determined by the Board in 1980. A new value was established in 1995 for the period 1996–2000.

The SDR is used by the IMF in its official reports.

Although the SDR was intended to serve as a substitute for gold, it has not taken over the role of gold or the dollar as a primary reserve asset. The SDR is intended eventually to become the principal reserve asset in the international monetary system.[4] The IMF uses the SDR rather than a specific national currency in most of its official reports. In addition, several countries base the value of their currency on the value of the SDR or that of a combination of the SDR and another currency.[5]

Evolution to Floating Exchange Rate

The IMF's initial system was one of fixed exchange rates. Because the U.S. dollar was the cornerstone of the international monetary system, its value remained constant with respect to the value of gold. Countries could change the value of their currency against gold and the dollar, but the value of the dollar remained fixed.

Exchange-rate flexibility was widened in 1971 from 1 percent to 2.25 percent on either side of par value.

On August 15, 1971, President Richard Nixon announced a new economic policy to force the other industrial countries to help restructure the world monetary order. The resulting Smithsonian Agreement of December 1971 had several important aspects:

- An 8-percent devaluation of the dollar (an official drop in the value of the dollar against gold)
- A revaluation of some other currencies (an official increase in the value of each currency against gold)
- A widening of exchange-rate flexibility (from 1 percent to 2.25 percent on either side of par value)

This restructuring of the international monetary system did not last. World currency markets remained unsteady during 1972, and the dollar was devalued again by 10 percent in early 1973. Major currencies began to float against each other instead of relying on the Smithsonian Agreement.

The Jamaica Agreement of 1976 resulted in greater exchange-rate flexibility.

Because the Bretton Woods Agreement was based on a system of fixed exchange rates and par values, the IMF had to change its rules in order to permit floating exchange rates. The Jamaica Agreement of 1976 amended the original rules to permit greater exchange-rate flexibility.

The move toward greater flexibility can occur on an individual-country basis as well as an overall system basis. As noted in the opening case, China adopted an official exchange rate that was significantly overvalued compared to the rates in the swap and black markets. However, the Chinese government also realized it needed to free up the currency in order to join the international community and facilitate currency trades.

Exchange-Rate Arrangements

The Jamaica Agreement formalized the break from fixed exchange rates. As part of this move, the IMF began to permit countries to select and maintain an exchange-rate arrangement of their choice, provided they communicate their decision to the IMF. Each year the countries notify the IMF of the exchange-rate arrangement they will use, and the IMF classifies each country into one of three broad categories:

1. *Pegged exchange rates.* These countries' currencies are pegged to a single currency or to a composite of currencies.
2. *Limited-flexibility arrangements.* These countries' exchange rates have displayed limited flexibility compared with either a single currency or group of currencies.
3. *More flexible arrangements.* These countries' exchange rates are fairly flexible (this category includes floating currencies such as the Chinese renminbi).[6]

Map 10.1 identifies the countries that fit in each category. Each category is subject to change each year. See the most recent issue of *International Financial Statistics* for the list of countries in each category. Table 10.1 summarizes the material provided in Map 10.1 and compares the changes in categories over three time periods: 1985, 1990, and 1996. It is interesting to note two things: the increase in the number of member countries of the IMF and the move to more flexibility from the other categories. The percentage of countries in the more flexible category (the last three categories in Table 10.1) increased from 27.5 percent in 1985 to 33.1 percent in 1990 and 56.4 percent in 1996.

It is important for MNEs to understand the exchange-rate arrangements for the currencies of countries in which they are doing business so that they can more accurately forecast trends. It is much easier to forecast a future exchange rate for a relatively stable currency that is pegged to the U.S. dollar, such as the Argentine peso, than for a currency that is freely floating, such as the Japanese yen.

Pegged Exchange Rates

Countries using this category of exchange-rate arrangements **peg,** or fix, the value of their currency to that of another currency or basket of currencies, with very narrow margins of 1 percent or less. Some countries in the latter subcategory have selected a basket of currencies that differs from that of the SDR. For example, in 1990 the Mozambique metical was "pegged to a weighted basket consisting of ten major currencies, with the weights reflecting the relative importance of these currencies in Mozambique's external transactions in goods and services."[7] (By 1996,

Table 10.1
Exchange-Rate Arrangements
Number of Countries

Classifications	1985	1990	1996
Currency pegged to	(63.1%)	(54.5%)	(35.9%)
US dollar	31	25	20
French franc	14	14	14
Other currency	5	5	9
SDR	12	6	2
Other currency composite	32	35	20
Limited Flexibility	(8.7%)	(8.3%)	(7.7%)
Flexible limited vis-à-vis single currency	5	4	4
Cooperative arrangements	8	9	10
More Flexible	(27.5%)	(32.7%)	(56.4%)
Adjusted according to a set of indicators	5	3	2
Managed floating	21	23	45
Independently floating	15	25	55
TOTAL	**149**	**156**	**181**

Source: International Monetary Fund. *International Financial Statistics* (Washington, D.C.: IMF, October 1996), p. 8. Data for 1996 is as of the end of the second quarter; data for 1985 and 1990 are year-end data. Percentages do not sum to 100 for 1985 and 1990 because of errors in IMF data.

however, Mozambique had switched to the "independently floating" subcategory, which is described below and illustrated in Map 10.1.)

Limited-Flexibility Arrangements

The limited-flexibility category of exchange-rate arrangements is divided into two subcategories. In the first, "flexibility limited in terms of a single currency," exchange rates fluctuate within a 2.25-percent margin. For example, if the government were to peg the riyal to the U.S. dollar at an exchange rate of $0.2666, the riyal would be able to strengthen by 2.25 percent to $0.2733 or weaken by 2.25 percent to $0.2599. Its central or par value would be $0.2666, and its trading range would be $0.2733–$0.2666. In reality, the riyal has historically been relatively stable against the dollar and rarely changes even the 2.25 percent. For all four countries shown on Map 10.1, the U.S. dollar is the benchmark for the currencies. The 2.25-percent margin is consistent with the Smithsonian Agreement. The second subcategory, "flexibility limited through cooperative arrangement," refers to the **European Monetary System (EMS)** as discussed in Chapter 7.

More Flexible Arrangements

Currencies of the countries with more flexible arrangements float independently, with governmental intervention to influence but not neutralize the speed of exchange-rate change. The leaders of the major industrial countries in this category

Frequent changes in a currency's value or total freedom to float according to supply and demand are the hallmarks of more flexible exchange-rate arrangements.

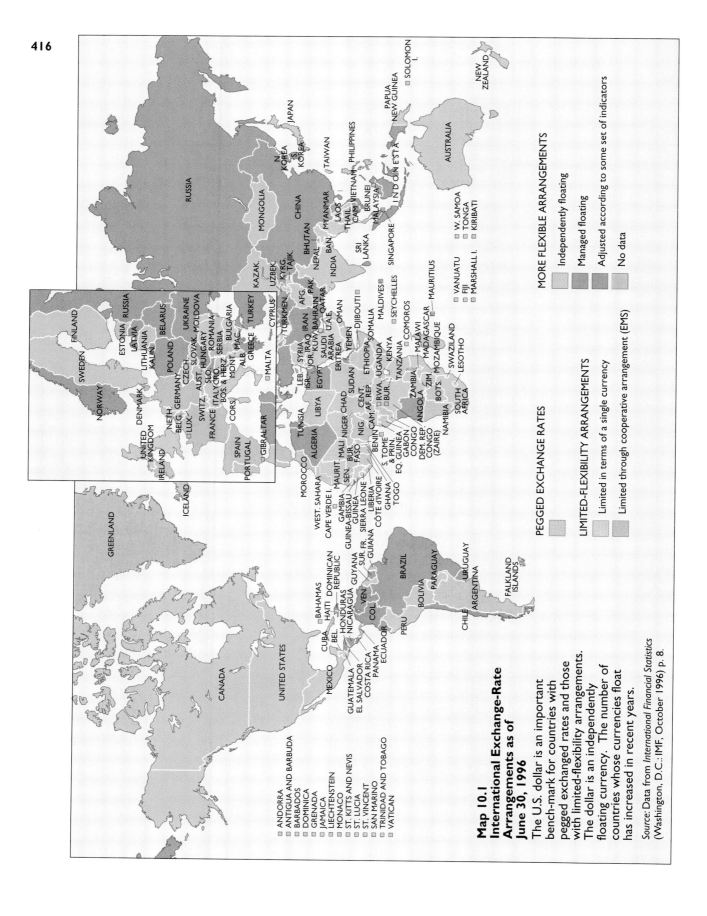

416

Map 10.1
International Exchange-Rate Arrangements as of June 30, 1996

The U.S. dollar is an important bench-mark for countries with pegged exchanged rates and those with limited-flexibility arrangements. The dollar is an independently floating currency. The number of countries whose currencies float has increased in recent years.

Source: Data from *International Financial Statistics* (Washington, D.C.: IMF, October 1996) p. 8.

PEGGED EXCHANGE RATES

LIMITED-FLEXIBILITY ARRANGEMENTS
- Limited in terms of a single currency
- Limited through cooperative arrangement (EMS)

MORE FLEXIBLE ARRANGEMENTS
- Independently floating
- Managed floating
- Adjusted according to some set of indicators
- No data

ANDORRA
ANTIGUA AND BARBUDA
BARBADOS
DOMINICA
GRENADA
JAMAICA
LIECHTENSTEIN
MONACO
ST. KITTS AND NEVIS
ST. LUCIA
ST. VINCENT
SAN MARINO
TRINIDAD AND TOBAGO
VATICAN

W. SAMOA
TONGA
KIRIBATI

VANUATU
FIJI
MARSHALL I.

meet periodically to discuss common economic issues; exchange-rate values are often on the agenda. For example, in April 1995, the Group of Seven countries, or G7 countries (Japan, Canada, the United States, France, Germany, the United Kingdom, and Italy), met and decided that they would focus more on prudent domestic policies as a way to stabilize exchange rates rather than by intervention in the markets. The reduction of inflation and budget deficits in some countries had contributed to reduction in currency volatility.[8]

As mentioned above, it is interesting to see how this category of exchange-rate arrangements has changed in the last several years, rising from 27.5 percent of the total in 1985 to 56.4 percent in 1996. Some examples of countries in the "independently floating" category are the three NAFTA countries, as well as Japan and the United Kingdom. Russia is an example of a country that recently joined the IMF and declared its currency to be independently floating but then switched to "other managed floating." Because of hyperinflation, the ruble dropped from a value of less than 10 rubles per U.S. dollar as recently as 1991 to 5456 rubles per dollar in October 1996. As Russia tries to implement the transition from a centrally planned to a market economy, its foreign-exchange market is working less than perfectly, even though the ruble is freely floating. For example, in 1993 exchange rates differed significantly from one part of the country to another. At one point, the buy/sell rate for the ruble in terms of the dollar was 1190/1270 in Moscow, 1250/1350 in Nizhiey Novgorod, and 1500/1600 in Khabarovsk. Arbitrageurs were able to convert rubles to dollars in Moscow at one rate, take the dollars to another city and convert them into rubles at a higher rate, and bring the rubles back to Moscow to convert into dollars at an even higher rate, resulting in profits of 20–40 percent, after bribes to customs officials.[9]

The final subcategory of more flexible arrangements, "adjusted according to some set of indicators," includes Chile and has always been a small category. The Chilean peso is "pegged to the U.S. dollar, at a rate adjusted at daily intervals according to a schedule established on the basis of the domestic rate of inflation during the previous month, less the estimated world rate of inflation."[10]

Black Markets

A black market will closely approximate real supply and demand for a currency.

Of the 181 IMF member countries, 55 have currencies that are independently floating. Many of the others control their currencies fairly rigidly as noted in the renminbi case. Some license foreign exchange, as noted in Chapter 9, so that neither residents nor nonresidents enjoy full convertibility. In many of these countries, a black market parallels the official market and is aligned more closely with the forces of supply and demand than the official market is. The less flexible a country's exchange-rate arrangement is, the more likely there is to be a black market. The black market exists because the government buys dollars for less than people think they are worth. According to economic theory, if the government's official rate for the currency is overvalued, the black market tends to undervalue the same currency. The true economic value is probably somewhere in between.

The black market is problematic for companies because it provides a more accurate measure of a currency's value than does the official market. This is especially important in financial reporting. For example, a U.S. company operating in China prior to elimination of the swap market in 1993 and keeping its books in renminbi would have recorded its balance sheet as well as its results at the official rate of 5.8 renminbi per dollar rather than the swap-market rate of 8.7 or the black-market rate, which may have been even higher than 8.7. Thus the company's balance sheet would have been overvalued in dollar terms. However, if the same company were to declare a dividend, it would have had to convert renminbi into dollars at the swap rate, not the official rate; the company would get about 33 percent fewer dollars at that rate. Thus the elimination of the dual-market system in China should eventually eliminate the need for a black market.

The Role of Central Banks

Each country has a central bank that is responsible for the policies that affect the value of its currency on world markets. The central bank in the United States is the Federal Reserve System (the Fed), a system of twelve regional banks. The New York Federal Reserve Bank handles the Fed's intervention in foreign-exchange markets. Intervention policies are determined by the Federal Open Market Committee. However, the Fed does not act independently of the rest of the U.S. government; in particular, the Secretary of the Treasury is legally responsible for stabilizing the dollar's value.[11] Further, the EU is planning to establish a single European currency that would replace individual national currencies; that move would require a central bank of Europe to help establish monetary policy and intervene in currency markets.

In spite of the unique nature of each country's central bank system, there is some semblance of international cooperation in the form of the **Bank for International Settlements (BIS)** in Basel, Switzerland. The BIS acts as a central banker's bank. It gets involved in swaps and other currency transactions between central banks in the major industrial countries. It also is a gathering place where central bankers discuss monetary cooperation.[12]

Central bank assets are kept in two major forms—gold and foreign-exchange reserves—but they can also be in SDRs and the country's reserve position with the IMF. The gold measure is difficult, because governments value their gold reserves at $35 per ounce officially, whereas the market price for gold is more than 10 times that amount. As a result, the IMF reports not only the national valuation of gold at its official price of $35 per ounce but also the millions of ounces of gold so that one can compute the market value. In 1996, foreign exchange reserves were 91.9 percent of total reserves for the world as a whole. However, the ratio of the major reserve assets varies by country. In the United States, 51.5 percent of reserves were in foreign exchange, and the rest was pretty evenly split among gold, SDRs, and the reserve position with the IMF. In France, only 39.5 percent of the reserves was represented by foreign exchange, and 54.3 percent was in gold. In Canada, 86.9 percent was in foreign exchange, of which 97 percent was in dollars. In Japan, 95.1

Central banks hold their assets in the form of gold and foreign-exchange reserves.

Trading on the black market involves an ethical dilemma. If a host-country government has instituted currency controls and management can't get a company's cash out of the country, is it legitimate to deal in the black market? By using the black market to convert local currency into U.S. dollars, for example, the company would be operating outside of the banking system and would not be able to send cash back to headquarters through normal banking channels. In the black market, one can obtain more local currency for hard currency but less hard currency for local currency than in the official market. However, the existence of a black market in a locale usually means that it is very difficult or even impossible to obtain hard currency there.

ETHICAL DILEMMAS & SOCIAL RESPONSIBILITY

On a personal level, it is always tempting to trade hard currency for local currency on the black market. The problem is that countries have varying attitudes—both ethical and legal—toward the black market. For example, in the late 1980s, travelers to Mozambique were warned against dealing in the black market. Because of the civil war in that country and the virtual collapse of the economy following independence, hard currency was in high demand. To discourage black-market activity by foreigners, the government was cracking down on such illegal trades. In Zimbabwe during the same period, the government permitted visitors to convert foreign currency to local currency at approved currency-exchange centers; any excess local currency could be converted back to foreign currency when the visitors left the country. However, the government emphatically warned visitors that they must prove that their transactions took place at the approved centers. Clearly, the government was discouraging currency trading on the black market. In contrast, at that time, Brazilian airport officials would meet visitors at their planes and offer to trade in currency. The Brazilian government basically looked the other way with respect to this black-market trading. The point is that it is important to be aware of the legality of black-market dealings in order to avoid making serious mistakes.

Black-market currency trading provides an illustration of the legal justification for ethical behavior, first discussed in Chapter 3. If trading on the black market is illegal, as was the case in both Mozambique and Zimbabwe, companies should avoid dealing in that market under the assumption that the law provides a clearly defined set of rules that must be followed. In countries such as Brazil, however, the law might not be the appropriate standard for regulating business activity in this context: Either the law does not deal specifically with black-market trading, or it prohibits such trading but the prohibition is not enforced. The major ethical dilemma arises in the latter case—a company might trade on the black market because of business custom even though such trading is illegal. In contrast, by following the law, managers would avoid prosecution but would sacrifice some of the company's cash flow.

percent of reserves was in foreign exchange. In Germany, only 82.5 percent was in foreign exchange, and in the United Kingdom, only 80.8 percent was in foreign exchange. As one can see, there are major differences across countries in terms of the composition of reserve assets. Because gold is valued on an official basis at only 10 percent of its market value, however, these values are somewhat distorted.[13]

Because most central banks consider gold to be the major reserve asset, their holdings remain fairly constant. Central banks are concerned primarily with liquidity to ensure they have the cash and flexibility needed to protect their countries' currencies. The mix of currencies in a country's reserves is based on its major **intervention currencies,** that is, the currencies in which the country trades the most. The degree to which a central bank actively manages its reserves to earn a profit varies by country. Generally, Asian banks, especially the Central Bank of Malaysia, are more aggressive than are European central banks or the Fed in generating reserve profits.[14]

Central banks often control the values of their countries' currencies through intervention.

European central banks played a role in the July–August 1993 currency crisis when, to prop up their currencies, many purchased or borrowed German marks from the Bundesbank (Germany's central bank) and then used the marks in currency markets to buy their own currencies, creating a demand and increasing the price. The Bundesbank sold $35 billion in marks in one day to help support other European currencies. Unfortunately, its efforts failed, and other European currencies fell in value against the mark.[15]

Government policies also change over time, depending on the particular administration in power. In the first two and a half years of the Clinton presidency, the U.S. Treasury intervened in the market by buying dollars on only 18 days, spending about $12.5 billion, compared with the Bush presidency, when in 1989 alone, the Treasury bought and sold dollars on 97 of 260 business days and sold $19.5 billion.[16] The differences in intervention reflect differences in philosophy. The Bush administration intervened heavily because it was trying to keep the dollar in a rough trading range during a period when the dollar was rising against the mark and the yen. The Clinton administration, however, intervened much more selectively, catching the market by surprise and then getting maximum publicity out of the intervention. Thus the less frequent and more subtle intervention proved to more effective and more in line with the philosophy of the Federal Reserve Board.

The Determination of Exchange Rates

Exchange rates are determined under one of three major types of exchange-rate systems: freely fluctuating, managed fixed, and automatic fixed. Factors that affect exchange rates include inflation, interest-rate differentials, and technical factors.

Demand for a country's currency is a function of the demand for that country's goods and services and financial assets.

Freely Fluctuating Currencies
Currencies that freely fluctuate respond to supply and demand conditions relatively free from government intervention. This concept can be illustrated using a

two-country model involving the United States and Japan. Figure 10.2 shows the equilibrium exchange rate in the market and then a movement to a new equilibrium level as the situation changes. The demand for yen in this example is a function of U.S. demand for Japanese goods and services, such as automobiles, and yen-denominated financial assets, such as securities. The supply of yen, which in this illustration is tied to the demand for dollars, is a function of Japanese demand for U.S. goods and services and dollar-denominated financial assets. Initially, the supply of and demand for yen in Fig. 10.2 meet at the equilibrium exchange rate e_0 (for example, 0.009 dollars per yen, or 111 yen per dollar) and the quantity of yen Q_1.

Assume demand for U.S. goods and services by Japanese consumers drops because of, say, relatively high U.S. inflation. This would result in reduced supply of yen in the foreign-exchange market, causing the supply curve to shift to S'. Simultaneously, the increasing prices of U.S. goods might lead to an increase in demand for Japanese goods and services by U.S. consumers. This in turn would lead to an increase in demand for yen in the market, causing the demand curve to shift to D' and finally leading to an increase in the quantity of yen and an increase in the exchange rate. Thus the new equilibrium exchange rate would be at e_1 (for example, 0.00917 dollars per yen, or 109 yen per dollar). From a dollar standpoint, the increased demand for Japanese goods would lead to an increase in supply of dollars as more consumers tried to trade their dollars for yen, and the reduced demand for U.S. goods would result in a drop in demand for dollars. This would result in a reduction in the dollar's price, indicating a devaluation of the dollar.

Managed Fixed Exchange-Rate Systems

In the preceding example, Japanese and U.S. authorities allowed changes in the exchange rates between their two currencies to occur in order for currencies to reach a new exchange-rate equilibrium. In fact, however, one or both countries might not want exchange rates to change. For example, assume the United States and Japan decide to manage their exchange rates. The U.S. government might not want its currency to weaken because its companies and consumers would have to pay more for Japanese products, which would lead to more inflationary pressure in the United States. The Japanese government might not want the yen to strengthen because it would mean unemployment in its export industries. But how can the governments keep the values from changing when the United States is earning too few yen? Somehow the difference between yen supply and demand must be neutralized.

A government buys and sells its currency in the open market as a means of influencing the currency's price.

In a managed fixed exchange-rate system, the New York Federal Reserve Bank would hold foreign-exchange reserves, which it would have built up through the years for this type of contingency. It could sell enough of its yen reserves (make up the difference between Q_1 and Q_3 in Fig. 10.2) at the fixed exchange rate to maintain that rate. Or the Japanese central bank might be willing to accept dollars so that U.S. consumers can continue to buy Japanese goods. These dollars would then become part of Japan's foreign-exchange reserves.

**Figure 10.2
Equilibrium Exchange
Rate**

Comparatively high inflation in the United States compared with Japan raises the demand for yen but lowers the supply of yen, increasing the value of the yen in terms of U.S. dollars. If the Japanese government wants to keep the dollar/yen exchange rate at e_0, it needs to sell yen for dollars in order to increase the supply of yen in the market and therefore decrease the exchange rate.

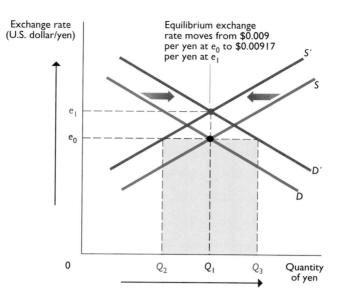

Devaluation occurs when a government reduces the value of its currency relative to that of a foreign currency.

Revaluation occurs when a government increases the value of its currency relative to that of a foreign currency.

The fixed rate could continue as long as the United States had reserves and/or as long as the Japanese were willing to add dollars to their holdings. Unless something changed the basic imbalance in the currency supply and demand, however, the New York Federal Reserve Bank would run out of yen and the Japanese central bank would stop accepting dollars because it would fear holding too many. At this point, it would be necessary to change the exchange rate so as to lessen the demand for yen.

Once a country determines that intervention will not work, it must adjust its currency's value. If the currency is freely fluctuating, the exchange rate will seek the correct level according to the laws of supply and demand. However, a currency that is pegged to another currency or to a basket of currencies usually is changed on a formal basis with respect to its reference currency or currencies. This formal change is more accurately termed a devaluation or revaluation, depending on the direction of the change. As noted earlier, if the foreign-currency equivalent of the domestic currency falls (or the domestic-currency equivalent of the foreign currency rises), then the domestic currency has been devalued in relation to the foreign currency. The opposite happens in the case of a revaluation.

The above example involved two currencies, the dollar and the yen. In many situations, however, a number of countries intervene in currency markets, sometimes in a coordinated fashion. In 1985 when the dollar was deemed to be overvalued, the finance ministers of the G-7 countries met and decided to intervene in currency markets to push down the dollar, which they did successfully. In the European Monetary System described in Chapter 7, all members can come to the support of a currency whose market value is moving too far away from its par value. It is difficult for a country to support its currency alone.

Automatic Fixed Exchange-Rate System

As with the managed fixed exchange-rate system, assume that Japan and the United States agreed to maintain fixed exchange rates by setting their domestic money supplies on the basis of the amount of reserves held by their central banks and by denominating their currency values in terms of their reserve assets. Now suppose the United States has a shortage of yen. Under an automatic fixed exchange-rate system, the United States hypothetically would sell gold to get the needed yen. However, unlike with the managed system, there would be automatic adjustments to prevent the United States from running out of gold. As the United States sold off some of its gold, its money supply, which is tied to the amount of gold it holds, would fall. This would lead to higher interest rates and lower investment in the United States, followed by increased unemployment and lower prices. Meanwhile, the increase in gold in Japan would have the opposite effect. The higher U.S. interest rates and the decrease in U.S. prices relative to the Japanese rate and prices would cause an increase in the supply of yen in the United States as funds flowed in for investment and to purchase U.S. goods and services. This would result in a strengthening of the dollar and a weakening of the yen.

This system differs from the others in that the adjustment of exchange rates does not depend on government intervention but rather on changes in the domestic money supply. A change in exchange rate for a freely fluctuating currency is more a function of the supply and demand of the currency in the foreign-exchange market than in the domestic money market. Thus, although the law of supply and demand can determine exchange rates in an open market, many governments intervene in the market to influence exchange-rate movements. Although the automatic fixed exchange-rate system is possible, it is not as widely used as freely fluctuating currencies and managed fixed exchange-rate systems.

Purchasing-Power Parity

If the domestic inflation rate is lower than that in a foreign country, the domestic currency should be stronger than that of the foreign country.

Purchasing-power parity (PPP) is the key theory that explains the relationships between currencies. In essence, it claims that a change in relative inflation must result in a change in exchange rates in order to keep the prices of goods in two countries fairly similar. According to the PPP theory, if for example, Japanese inflation were 2 percent and U.S. inflation were 3.5 percent, the dollar would be expected to fall by the difference in inflation rates. Then the dollar would be worth fewer yen than before the adjustment, and the yen would be worth more dollars than before the adjustment.

The following formula can be used to relate inflation to exchange-rate changes:

$$\frac{e_t - e_0}{e_0} = \frac{i_{h,t} - i_{f,t}}{1 + i_{f,t}}$$

where

e = the exchange rate quoted in terms of the number of units of the domestic (home) currency for one unit of the foreign currency (the direct rate)

i = the inflation rate

h indicates the home country (in these examples, the United States)

f indicates the foreign country (in these examples, Japan)

0 indicates the beginning of a period

t indicates the end of the period

The anticipated future exchange rate is given by

$$e_t = e_0 \left(\frac{1 + i_{h,t}}{1 + i_{f,t}} \right)$$

For example, assume the consumer price index (CPI) went from 100 to 103.5 in the United States and from 100 to 102 in Japan during a period when the exchange rate at the beginning of the period was 125 yen to the dollar, or 0.008 dollars per yen. The inflation rates are

$$i_{h,t} = \frac{103.5 - 100}{100} = 0.035$$

$$i_{f,t} = \frac{102 - 100}{100} = 0.02$$

Now the formula above gives

$$e_t = 0.008 \left(\frac{1 + 0.035}{1 + 0.02} \right) = 0.00812$$

The exchange rate at the end of the period is 0.00812 dollars per yen, or 123.2 yen per dollar. Thus the yen is worth more dollars, and the dollar is worth fewer yen when inflation is higher in the United States than in Japan.

A good illustration of the fallibility of the PPP theory for estimating exchange rates is the Big Mac index of currencies used by *The Economist* each year. The price of a Big Mac can be used to estimate the exchange rate between the dollar and another currency (see Table 10.2). For example, in 1996, a Big Mac cost an average of $2.36 in the United States and ¥288 in Japan. Dividing the yen price by the dollar price yields an exchange rate of 122 yen per dollar, according to the PPP theory. However, the actual exchange rate was 107 yen per dollar, so the yen was overvalued compared to the dollar. In other words, it would take more dollars to buy a Big Mac in Japan than it would in the United States. Based on the actual exchange rate, a Big Mac would cost $2.70 in Japan rather than $2.36. The overvalued yen would make it expensive for American tourists to shop in Japan, but would make the United States a bargain for Japanese tourists. There are supporters of the Big Mac index, also known as "McParity," but there are also detractors. Even though McParity may hold up in the long run, as has been shown by some studies, there are short-run problems that affect PPP:

- The theory of PPP falsely assumes that there are no barriers to trade and that transportation costs are zero.
- Prices of the Big Mac in different countries are distorted by taxes. European countries with high value-added taxes are more likely to have higher prices than countries with low taxes.
- The Big Mac is not just a basket of commodities; its price also includes nontraded costs such as rent, insurance, etc.
- Profit margins vary by the strength of competition. The higher the competition, the lower the profit margin and therefore the price.[17]

As noted in Table 10.2, the yen is overvalued by 14 percent. In the 1994 survey, however, the yen was overvalued by 64 percent. In 1995, McDonald's lowered the cost of the Big Mac in yen terms for competitive reasons. In 1994, the Big Mac cost ¥391, whereas in 1996, it cost only ¥288. In addition, the dollar gained value against most currencies, including the yen, so its purchasing power improved. Thus the relative price of goods can be altered by exchange rate changes and internal price changes. It is interesting to note that the most undervalued currency in the survey is the Chinese renminbi, which fits the discussion in the opening case where we mentioned that the renminbi was rising against the dollar, even though relatively higher inflation in China would lead one to believe that the renminbi should be falling.

Interest Rates

If the nominal interest rate in one country is lower than that in another, the first country's inflation rate is expected to be lower so that real interest rates are equal.

Although inflation is the most important long-run influence on exchange rates, interest rates are also important. For example, an article on the foreign-exchange market in the *Wall Street Journal* noted the impact of interest rates on exchange rates.

> Currency traders rushed to buy marks on Tuesday after a slew of comments by German economic and monetary officials cast doubt on the future of Europe's planned single currency. Further, Bundesbank [the German Central Bank] officials indicated the central bank isn't about to cut German interest rates. That news prompted more buying of the mark against the dollar. . . . The scenario was different against the yen. Traders, betting Japanese interest rates won't rise soon, pushed the dollar up. . . . With Japanese interest rates expected to remain low and the probability the U.S. will keep its strong dollar policy, investors will be selling the low-yielding yen for almost any other currency.[18]

Table 10.2
Big Mac Currencies: The Hamburger Standard

	Big Mac prices		Implied PPP* of the dollar	Actual dollar exchange rate 4/22/96	Local currency undervaluation (−) or overvaluation (+) (%)[†]
	Price in local currency	Price in dollars			
United States[**]	$2.36	2.36	—	—	—
Argentina	Peso3.00	3.00	1.27	1.00	+27
Australia	A$2.50	1.97	1.06	1.27	−17
Austria	Sch36.00	3.40	15.3	10.7	+43
Belgium	BFr109	3.50	46.2	31.2	+48
Brazil	Real2.95	2.98	1.25	0.99	+26
Britain	£1.79	2.70	1.32[††]	1.51[††]	+14
Canada	C$2.86	2.10	1.21	1.36	−11
Chile	Peso950	2.33	403	408	−1
China	Yuan9.60	1.15	4.07	8.35	−51
Czech Republic	CKr51.0	1.85	21.6	27.6	−22
Denmark	DKr25.75	4.40	10.9	5.85	+87
France	FFr17.5	3.41	7.42	5.13	+46
Germany	DM4.90	3.22	2.08	1.52	+37
Hong Kong	HK$9.90	1.28	4.19	7.74	−46
Hungary	Forint214	1.43	90.7	150	−39
Israel	Shekel9.50	3.00	4.03	3.17	+27
Italy	Lire4,550	2.90	1,907	1,551	+23
Japan	¥288	2.70	122	107	+14
Malaysia	M$3.76	1.51	1.59	2.49	−36
Mexico	Peso14.9	2.02	6.31	7.37	−14
Netherlands	Fl5.45	3.21	2.31	1.70	+36
New Zealand	NZ$2.95	2.01	1.25	1.47	−15
Poland	Zloty3.80	1.44	1.61	2.64	−39
Russia	Rouble9,500	1.93	4,025	4,918	−18
Singapore	S$3.05	2.16	1.29	1.41	−8
South Africa	Rand7.00	1.64	2.97	4.26	−30
South Korea	Won2,300	2.95	975	779	+25
Spain	Pta365	2.89	155	126	+23
Sweden	Skr26.0	3.87	11.0	6.71	+64
Switzerland	SFr5.90	4.80	2.50	1.23	+103
Taiwan	NT$65.0	2.39	27.5	27.2	+1
Thailand	Baht48.0	1.90	20.3	25.3	−20

*Purchasing-power parity: local price divided by price in the United States
[†]Against dollar
[**]Average of New York, Chicago, San Francisco, and Atlanta
[††]Dollars per pound

Source: From *The Economist*, 4/27/96, p. 82. © 1996 The *Economist* Newspaper Group, Inc. Reprinted with permission.

In order to understand this phenomenon, we need to understand two key finance theories: the Fisher Effect and the International Fisher Effect. The first links inflation and interest rates, and the second links interest rates and exchange rates. The **Fisher Effect** is the theory that the nominal interest rate r in a country is determined by the real interest rate R and the inflation rate i as follows:

$$(1 + r) = (1 + R)(1 + i)$$

According to this theory, if the real interest rate is 5 percent, the U.S. inflation rate is 2.9 percent, and the Japanese inflation rate is 1.5 percent, then the nominal interest rates for the United States and Japan are computed as follows:

$$r_{US} = (1.05)(1.029) - 1 = 0.08045, \text{ or } 8.045 \text{ percent}$$

$$r_J = (1.05)(1.015) - 1 = 0.06575, \text{ or } 6.575 \text{ percent}$$

Thus the difference between U.S. and Japanese interest rates is a function of the difference between their inflation rates. If their inflation rates were the same (zero differential) but interest rate was 10 percent in the United States and 6.575 percent in Japan, investors would place their money in the United States, where they could get the higher real return.

The **IFE implies that the currency of the country with the lower interest rate will strengthen in the future.**

The bridge from interest rates to exchange rates can be explained by the **International Fisher Effect (IFE),** the theory that the interest-rate differential is an unbiased predictor of future changes in the spot exchange rate. For example, the IFE predicts that if nominal interest rates in the United States are higher than those in Japan, the dollar's value should fall in the future by that interest-rate differential, which would be an indication of a weakening, or depreciation, of the dollar. That is because the interest rate differential is based on differences in inflation rates, as we discussed above. The previous discussion on purchasing power parity also demonstrated that the country with the higher inflation should have the weaker currency. Thus the country with the higher interest rate (and thus the higher inflation) should have the weaker currency. Of course, these issues reflect the long run, and anything can happen in the short run. During periods of general price stability, a country (such as Germany) that raised its interest rates is likely to attract capital and see its currency rise in value due to the increased demand. However, if the reason for the increase in interest rates is because German inflation is higher than that of its major trading partners and the German central bank is trying to reduce inflation, the German mark will eventually weaken until inflation cools down.

Although the interest-rate differential is the critical factor for a few of the most widely traded currencies, the expectation of the future spot rate also is very important. Normally, a trader will automatically estimate the future spot rate using the interest-rate differential and then adjust it for other market conditions.

How do these theories relate to the *Wall Street Journal* quotation? If the Bundesbank had lowered interest rates, investors would have moved the Deutsche mark out of Germany and put it into countries offering a higher real return. Since the Bundesbank announced that it was not going to lower interest rates, investors wanted to keep their money in Germany. In Japan, on the other hand, interest rates were so low that nobody wanted to hold yen assets. They preferred to move their money to other currencies, which would have a depressing impact on the currency.

Other Factors

Other key factors affecting
exchange-rate movements
are confidence and technical
factors, such as the release
of economic statistics.

Various other factors can cause exchange-rate changes. One important determinant in a world of political and economic uncertainty is confidence. During times of turmoil, people prefer to hold currencies that are considered safe-haven ones. For example, during the political uncertainty in Russia in 1996 because of the worsening health of President Yeltsin, money flowed into the United States and out of Germany because of the concern over the safety of Western Europe if a true crisis were to occur in Russia.

In addition to basic economic forces and confidence in leadership, exchange rates are also influenced by a number of technical factors, such as the release of national economic statistics, seasonal demands for a currency, and a slight strengthening of a currency following a prolonged weakness, or vice versa. An example of the effect of a technical factor occurred in August 1993 when the exchange-rate mechanism of the EMS changed from permitting a 2.25-percent deviation from parity rates to allowing a 15-percent deviation. Traders felt that the dollar would tend to soften as central banks in Europe repurchased the marks they borrowed from the Bundesbank to prop up their currencies.[19]

Forecasting Exchange-Rate Movements

The preceding section looked at the effect of the law of supply and demand on exchange rates, showed how governments intervene to manage exchange-rate movements, and explained how inflation and interest rates can be important determinants of exchange rates. This section identifies factors that can be monitored in order to get an idea of what will happen to exchange rates.

Managers need to be concerned with the timing,
magnitude, and direction of
an exchange-rate movement.

Because various factors influence exchange-rate movements, managers must be able to analyze those factors in order to formulate a general idea of the timing, magnitude, and direction of an exchange-rate movement. However, prediction is not a precise science, and many things can cause the best of predictions to differ significantly from reality.

Fundamental and Technical Forecasting

Fundamental forecasting
uses trends in economic
variables to predict future
exchange rates.

Technical forecasting uses
past trends in exchange rate
movements to spot future
trends.

Forecasting exchange rates can be done using either of two approaches: fundamental or technical. Fundamental forecasting involves using trends in economic variables to predict future rates. The data can be plugged into an econometric model or evaluated on a more subjective basis. Technical forecasting involves using past trends to spot future trends. Technical forecasters, or chartists, assume that if current exchange rates reflect all facts in the market, then under similar circumstances future rates will follow the same patterns.[20]

However, all forecasting is imprecise. A corporate treasurer who wants to forecast an exchange rate, say, the relationship between the British pound and the U.S. dollar, might use a variety of sources, both internal and external to the company.

Many treasurers and bankers use outside forecasters to obtain input for their own forecasts. Forecasters need to provide ranges or point estimates with subjective probabilities based on available data and subjective interpretation. Biases that can skew forecasts include the following:

- Overreaction to unexpected and dramatic news events
- Illusory correlation, that is, the tendency to see correlations or associations in data that are not statistically present but that are expected to occur on the basis of prior beliefs
- Focusing on a particular subset of information at the expense of the overall set of information
- Insufficient adjustment for subjective matters, such as market volatility
- Inability to learn from one's past mistakes
- Overconfidence in one's ability[21]

Good treasurers and bankers develop their own forecasts of what will happen to a particular currency and use fundamental or technical forecasts of outside forecasters to corroborate these. Doing this helps them determine whether they are considering important factors and whether they need to revise their forecasts in light of outside analysis. However, it is important to understand that no matter how carefully prepared a forecast is, *it is still a guess.* Forecasting includes predicting the timing, direction, and magnitude of an exchange-rate change. The timing is often a political decision, and therefore not necessarily rational or predictable. And although the direction of a change probably can be predicted, the magnitude is difficult to forecast.

For example, currency forecasting is important for Chrysler because of its foreign investments, foreign market opportunities, and foreign sourcing of components. The company uses three forecasting models. Realizing that exchange rates are difficult to forecast, it bases its short-term forecasts—one week to one month—largely on qualitative information provided by local managers. It also uses outside currency traders who specialize in short-term forecasts. Over the medium term—one to three years—Chrysler focuses more on macroeconomic indicators, especially fiscal and monetary policy. The company's long-term forecasting is more imprecise but utilizes the same indicators as for the medium-term forecasts along with structural shifts occurring in the economy.[22]

Factors to Monitor

For freely fluctuating currencies, the law of supply and demand determines market value. However, very few currencies in the world float freely without any government intervention; most are managed to a certain extent, which implies that governments need to make political decisions regarding the value of their currencies. Assuming governments use a rational basis for managing these values (an assumption that may not always be realistic), managers can monitor the same factors the governments follow in order to try to predict values. These factors are

- Capital controls
- Exchange-rate spreads
- Balance-of-payments statistics
- Foreign-exchange reserves
- GNP or GDP growth
- Government spending
- Relative inflation rates
- Money-supply growth
- Interest-rate differentials
- Trends in exchange-rate movements[23]

Most of these factors were discussed in the Mexican peso case in Chapter 9 and the Chinese renminbi case at the beginning of this chapter. However, it is good to review the importance of monitoring changes in the balance of payments as a tool to forecast exchange-rate changes. The balance of payments is a record of transactions between one country and the rest of the world. An abbreviated version of the U.S. balance-of-payments statistics is found in Table 10.3. Notice that there are several different categories of transactions. Lines 1, 5, and 9 comprise the current account balance, which is also shown as a memorandum entry on line 19. The current account includes the balance of merchandise trade (goods), services, income on investments, and unilateral transfers. Services includes items such as travel, transportation, and royalties and license fees. Income on investments (lines 4 and 8) refers to income on direct and portfolio investments, both by U.S. investors abroad (line 4) and by foreign investors in the United States (line 8). Unilateral transfers refer to foreign aid and payments by foreign workers to their families back in their home countries. If the number is positive, it means that the transaction earned foreign exchange for the United States. An export of goods, for example, results in an inflow of cash to the United States (positive). An import of goods results in an outflow of cash to a foreign exporter (negative).

The next two major categories (lines 10 and 14) are the capital accounts. In the Chinese renminbi case, we noted that controls were going to be lifted on current account transactions but not capital account transactions. Capital account transactions include changes in official reserves positions and U.S. private assets, such as direct investment. Note that the biggest changes are in private, not official, assets. An increase in foreign direct investment abroad results in an outflow of cash and is reflected as a negative transaction. On the other hand, the purchase of debt and equity securities in the United States by foreign investors—either portfolio or direct investments—results in an inflow of cash and is considered to be a positive transaction. Notice that the current account deficit is financed by a net inflow of assets from abroad (line 14 minus line 10). By studying the balance of payments

Table 10.3
Summary of U.S. International Transactions
(Millions of dollars, seasonally adjusted)

Line		1994	1995
1	Exports of goods, services, and income	840,006	969,189
2	Goods, adjusted, excluding military	502,463	575,940
3	Services	195,839	210,590
4	Income receipts on investments	141,704	182,659
5	Imports of goods, services, and income	-948,544	-1,082,268
6	Goods, adjusted, excluding military	-668,584	-749,364
7	Services	-134,097	-142,230
8	Income payments on investments	-145,863	-190,674
9	Unilateral transfers	-39,866	-35,075
10	U.S. assets abroad, net (increase/capital outflow (-))	-150,695	-307,856
11	U.S. official reserve assets, net	5,346	-9,742
12	U.S. government assets, other than official reserve assets, net	-341	-280
13	U.S. private assets, net	-155,700	-297,834
14	Foreign assets in the United States, net (increase/capital inflow (+))	285,376	424,462
15	Foreign official assets, net	40,253	109,757
16	Other foreign assets, net	245,123	314,705
17	Allocations of special drawing rights	—	—
18	Statistical discrepancy	13,724	31,548
	Memorandum:		
19	Balance on current account	-148,405	-148,154

Source: Survey of Current Business, July 1996, p. 61.

data, one can identify important trends in cash flows. For example, there was a slight improvement in the current account balance from 1994 to 1995, but there was both a doubling of direct investment abroad as well as an increase in foreign investment in the United States. In the case of Mexico, two balance of payments items were significant: the current account balance and changes in reserves.

Business Implications of Exchange-Rate Changes

Marketing Decisions

On the marketing side, exchange rates can affect demand for a company's products at home and abroad. For example, if Mexico's exports became too expensive because of its relatively high inflation, it might force down the value of its currency.

A devaluation of a currency could help the country's imports become more expensive and its exports less expensive.

Although inflation would cause the peso value of Mexican products to rise, the devaluation would mean that less foreign currency would be required to buy pesos. Thus Mexican products would remain competitive. An interesting ramification of such a peso devaluation would be the impact the cheaper Mexican goods would have on exporters from other countries. For example, the cheaper Mexican goods flooding the market in Argentina might take away market share from Italian exporters, thus affecting the Italian economy.

When a currency changes in value, exporters and importers need to decide whether to change prices.

When the U.S. dollar fell in value in 1992, foreign shoppers flocked to the United States to buy cheaper merchandise. For example, Swatch watches that cost $350–$400 overseas were selling for $80; Timberland moccasins that sold for $235 in Japan could be purchased for $120; and Sony Walkmans, which cost $100 in Italy, could be purchased for $50.[24] A related problem confronted the German electrical equipment manufacturer, Siemens AG. In the mid-1980s, when the U.S. economy was strong and the mark was rising against the dollar, Siemens simply increased its prices and passed on the exchange-rate difference to consumers. In 1992, however, when the U.S. economy was very weak, Siemens, fearing it might lose market share, hesitated to burden consumers with price increases.[25]

Production Decisions

Companies might locate production in weak-currency countries because
• Initial investment there is relatively cheap
• Such a country is a good base for inexpensive exportation

Exchange-rate changes also can affect production decisions. For example, a manufacturer in a country where wages and operating expenses are high might be tempted to locate production in a country whose currency is rapidly losing value. A foreign currency would buy lots of the weak currency, thus making the company's initial investment relatively cheap. Further, goods manufactured in that country would be relatively cheap in world markets. However, the company could accomplish the same purpose by going to any country whose currency is expected to remain weak in relation to that of the company's home country. For example, BMW made the decision to invest in production facilities in South Carolina because of the unfavorable exchange rate between the mark and the dollar. However, the company announced plans to use the facilities not only to serve the U.S. market, but also to export to Europe and other markets.[26]

Financial Decisions

Exchange rates can influence the sourcing of financial resources, the cross-border remittance of funds, and the reporting of financial results.

Finally, exchange rates can affect financial decisions, primarily in the areas of sourcing of financial resources, remittance of funds across national borders, and reporting of financial results. In the first area, a company might be tempted to borrow money where interest rates are lowest. However, recall that interest-rate differentials often are compensated for in money markets through exchange-rate changes.

In deciding about cross-border financial flows, a company would want to convert local currency into its home-country currency when exchange rates are most favorable so that it can maximize its return. However, countries with weak curren-cies often have currency controls, making it difficult for MNEs to manage the flow of funds optimally.

Finally, exchange-rate changes can influence the reporting of financial results. A simple example illustrates the impact exchange rates can have on income. If a U.S. company's Mexican subsidiary earns 1 million pesos when the exchange rate is 3.12 pesos per dollar, the dollar equivalent of its income is $320,513. If the peso depre-ciates to 4 pesos per dollar, the dollar equivalent of that income falls to $250,000. The opposite will occur if the local currency appreciates against that of the com-pany's home country.

COUNTERVAILING FORCES

Both MNEs and small companies involved in exporting and importing must consider the full range of implica-tions of exchange-rate changes on marketing, produc-tion, and financial decisions. From a marketing standpoint, it might seem that small companies would be more likely to invoice sales in their home-country's currency in order to avoid for-eign-exchange risk. However, this strategy is pursued by both large and small companies that are inexperienced in foreign sales. As companies move along the learning curve, they are more likely to consider invoicing sales in the foreign currency as a marketing strategy.

Small companies view production decisions differently than do MNEs. They are more likely to manufacture in the home-country market rather than rely on FDI in weak-currency countries as a means for manufacturing products for worldwide sale. The latter strategy is more common of large MNEs. However, small companies may subcontract pro-duction to independent manufacturers abroad in order to take advantage of lower-cost production in weak-currency countries.

The use of cross-border cash flows in the financial area is more complex for MNEs than for smaller companies. The financial flows of smaller companies are usually limited to pur-chases and sales, whereas those of MNEs involve the full range of activities—receivables and payables, dividends, royalties, management fees, and loans.

A country may give up some control over its currency to gain greater access to global markets.

Another major issue surrounding foreign exchange is the potential for some loss of sov-ereignty. As noted in the opening case, China was forced to change its exchange-rate sys-tem in an attempt to join the WTO. By creating a more open foreign-exchange system, China was admitting it needs to bring its entire economy into harmony with the world economy. In the long run, this economic openness also may affect China's political system. Another example involving partial loss of sovereignty concerns the EMS. As discussed in Chapter 7, the Treaty of Maastricht includes a significant monetary component. A major goal of the treaty is to establish a common currency called the ECU by 1999. To accom-plish this, the EU wants to set up a European central bank and to coordinate economic policies. A member country, to participate in the common currency, will have to bring its economic performance into conformity with the other members.

LOOKING TO THE FUTURE

The international monetary system has undergone significant reform in the past two decades. As CEITs undergo transition to market economies, they will experience significant pressure on their exchange rates. High inflation rates and weak demand for their currencies will lead to major devaluations. These certainly are key factors affecting the Russian ruble. In addition, former Soviet republics will need to decide whether to maintain a close relationship with the ruble or to establish a tie with a Western European currency.

The exchange-rate mechanism will continue to be an indicator of success for the EU. If EU member countries cannot better harmonize their monetary and fiscal policies, there will be no common currency by 1999.

Among countries with more flexible exchange-rate arrangements, those whose rates are adjusted according to some set of indicators or managed floating will need to gain greater control over their economies in order to move to the "independently floating" subcategory. Countries whose currencies independently float are under constant pressure to control inflation and to keep from being tempted to intervene in the markets. The greater the instability, the more likely central banks are to try intervention.

Companies will continue to face constant pressure to understand the factors influencing particular exchange rates and to adjust corporate strategy in anticipation of exchange-rate movements. This will become easier only if exchange-rate volatility diminishes, which does not appear likely to occur in the near future.

WEB CONNECTION

Check out our home page for links to World Wide Web resources for international money and finance issues. Explore the multitude of links from our "getting started" portion of the Web page; you'll find links to international organizations cited in this chapter, such as the IMF and World Bank, publications such as *The Economist*, and on-line data sources such as Bloomberg.

Summary

- **The International Monetary Fund (IMF) was organized in 1944 to promote exchange-rate stability, maintain orderly exchange-rate arrangements, avoid competitive currency devaluations, establish a multilateral system of payments, eliminate exchange restrictions, and create standby reserves.**

- **The Special Drawing Right (SDR) was instituted by the IMF to increase international reserves.**

- **The exchange-rate arrangements of countries that are members of the IMF are divided into three categories: pegged exchange rates, limited-flexibility arrangements, and more flexible arrangements.**

- Many countries that strictly control and regulate the convertibility of their currency have a black market that maintains an exchange rate that is more indicative of supply and demand than is the official rate.

- The Bank for International Settlements (BIS) in Switzerland acts as a central banker's bank. It facilitates communication and transactions among the world's central banks.

- Central banks use foreign-exchange reserves to support their countries' currencies and to earn a profit.

- The demand for a country's currency is a function of the demand for its goods and services and the demand for financial assets denominated in its currency.

- A central bank intervenes in money markets by creating a supply of its country's currency when it wants to push the value of the currency down or by creating a demand for the currency when it wants to strengthen its value.

- Devaluation of a currency occurs when formal governmental action causes the foreign-currency equivalent of that currency to fall (or that currency's equivalent for the foreign currency to rise). A depreciation occurs when a change in the same direction is permitted by the government but not formally acted on as such.

- Some factors that determine exchange rates are purchasing-power parity (relative rates of inflation), differences in real interest rates (nominal interest rates reduced by the amount of inflation), confidence in the government's ability to manage the political and economic situation, and certain technical factors that result from trading.

- Major factors managers should monitor when trying to predict the direction, magnitude, and timing of an exchange-rate change include balance-of-payments statistics, foreign-exchange reserves, relative inflation rates, interest-rate differentials, and trends in exchange-rate movements. Also, they must look at the political situation.

- Exchange rates can affect business decisions in three major areas: marketing, production, and finance.

Case
The Japanese Yen[27]

At the end of 1996, top management of Nissan, the large Japanese automaker, was trying to figure out what was going to happen to the yen/U.S. dollar exchange rate and what its pricing and production strategies should be relative to the U.S. market. Should Nissan lower prices and pick up market share, keep prices the same and earn a greater profit margin, keep producing autos and trucks in the United States, or move its production to Mexico, Southeast Asia, or back to Japan?

To appreciate Nissan's dilemma, it is important to gain a historical perspective on the yen and its value against the dollar (see Map 10.2). As recently as 1985, the yen was trading at ¥251 per dollar. By 1985, the dollar began its long slide against the yen, and by the end of 1988, a dollar was worth only ¥125.85 (see Table 10.4). However, in 1989 and early 1990, there was a period of weakening of the yen against the dollar.

The strengthening in 1989 went against conventional wisdom. Most economists felt the rate would move to ¥100 per dollar by the end of 1989, but a number of domestic and international problems subsequently tempered their enthusiasm and led to a weakening of the yen: a stock scandal that included many of Japan's top political and business leaders, the Tiananmen Square incident in China, and the reunification of East and West Germany. In addition, there was a great deal of confidence in the U.S. government's ability to manage the U.S. economy. However, there was a huge gap between dollar-denominated and yen-denominated securities that drove up the demand for dollars.

There were clearly some trouble spots in the Japanese economy. In late 1989, the stock market began to decline and inflationary pressures began to rise. In early 1990, there was open debate between the Ministry of Finance and the Bank of Tokyo over what the interest-rate policy should be. That debate drove the stock market down even further and shook investors' confidence in the Japanese government's ability to manage the economy and, therefore, the exchange rate.

Map 10.2
Japan and the Yen
The Japanese yen has strengthened significantly against the U.S. dollar since World War II. Although the yen fluctuates against the dollar daily, the year-end yen/dollar exchange rate is indicative of the movement of the yen's value over time.

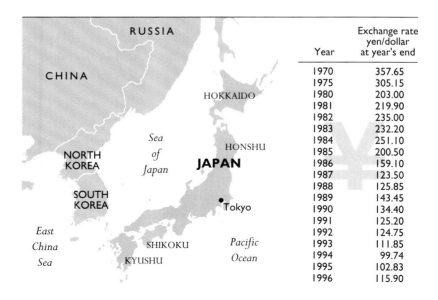

Year	Exchange rate yen/dollar at year's end
1970	357.65
1975	305.15
1980	203.00
1981	219.90
1982	235.00
1983	232.20
1984	251.10
1985	200.50
1986	159.10
1987	123.50
1988	125.85
1989	143.45
1990	134.40
1991	125.20
1992	124.75
1993	111.85
1994	99.74
1995	102.83
1996	115.90

Table 10.4
Selected Economic Data for Japan, Other Countries, and the World,
1990–1996

	1990	1991	1992	1993	1994	1995	1996Q1
Yen/dollar year-end exchange rate	134.4	125.2	124.75	111.85	99.74	102.83	106.28
Consumer Prices*							
World	21.3	12.4	11.8	19.6	23.6	11.7	8.3
Industrialized Countries	5.0	4.3	3.1	2.8	2.3	2.5	2.2
Developing Countries	104.8	48.1	45.3	51.0	64.7	27.1	18.2
Germany	2.7	3.5	4.0	4.1	3.0	1.8	1.4
Japan	3.1	3.3	1.7	1.3	.7	-.1	-.2
United Kingdom	9.5	5.9	3.7	1.6	2.5	3.4	2.8
United States	5.4	4.2	3.0	3.0	2.6	2.8	2.7
Government Bond Yields							
Germany	8.88	8.63	7.96	6.28	6.67	6.50	5.64
Japan	7.36	6.53	4.94	3.69	3.71	2.27	2.40
United Kingdom	11.08	9.92	9.12	7.87	8.05	8.26	8.08
United States	8.55	7.86	7.01	5.82	7.11	6.58	5.91
Current Account Balance	35.87	68.37	112.33	131.98	130.56	111.25	19.13

*Consumer prices reflect the change in the consumer price index over the prior year.

Source: Various issues of *International Financial Statistics* (Washington, D.C.: IMF).

Japan had once enjoyed the world's largest current-account surplus (that is, an excess of exports over imports), but since 1987 that surplus fell by one third because of a huge outflow of Japanese capital. Prices on Japanese assets, especially land and buildings, had risen dramatically, and Japanese investors found they could get a better yield on their money outside Japan.

As inflation fears began to rise in Japan, the natural response would have been to increase interest rates. The governor of the Bank of Japan decided to increase interest rates in December 1989, but the furor that ensued caused him to delay any further increases. Given that interest rates in the United States also were high at the time as a result of inflationary concerns, the demand for yen fell and the demand for dollars rose, increasing the price of the dollar in terms of yen. Although the yen was falling, the Japanese government couldn't figure out how to stop it. In the first three months of 1990, the Bank of Japan used 17 percent of its foreign-exchange reserves to sell dollars for yen, hoping to prop up the yen. The United States contributed to this effort by selling dollars for yen, but it didn't want to push the dollar down too much for fear of losing its battle against inflation. Both Japan and the United States tried to convince the governments of other countries, such as Germany and the United Kingdom, to go along with efforts to support the yen, but the U.S. government wanted those countries to use their own currencies rather than U.S. dollars. However, speculators realized that intervention would not solve the problems and that the solution lay in interest-rate policy.

By the end of the summer of 1990, many analysts were predicting that the exchange rate would be at ¥160 to the dollar by the end of the year. However, the U.S. economy began to weaken, and, as the U.S. government tried to avoid a recession, interest rates came down. The Persian Gulf War momentarily strengthened the dollar against the yen, but the economic fundamentals were more important. As Japanese interest rates rose and U.S. interest rates fell, the demand for the dollar fell, and so did the price. By the end of 1990, the exchange rate was hovering at ¥130 per dollar, after experiencing a high of 124.33 in the previous 12 months and a low of 159.79.

Relative calm reigned in 1991 and 1992 in terms of the yen/dollar exchange rate. In 1991, the rate fell gradually from ¥141 per dollar at the end of the first quarter to ¥125.2 per dollar by the end of the fourth quarter. As noted in Fig. 10.3, the dollar continued its gradual descent against the yen.

In early 1993, the yen/dollar relationship began to change. The major catalyst was the G-7 meeting in February 1993, whose agenda was expected to include a forced appreciation of the yen. On February 24, however, U.S. Treasury Secretary Lloyd Bentsen stated there would be no communique at the end of the meeting. A massive sell-off of the dollar against the yen resulted. It was felt U.S. President Clinton was using a strong yen as one way to eliminate the huge trade deficit between the United States and Japan.

By spring, several yen/dollar scenarios were being discussed, with no real consensus emerging. For example, *The Economist* Intelligence Unit expected the exchange rate to be

**Figure 10.3
Japanese Yen per
Dollar, Monthly
Exchange Rate**

Source: Bloomberg Financial
Markets and Commodities
News: Online: Currency.

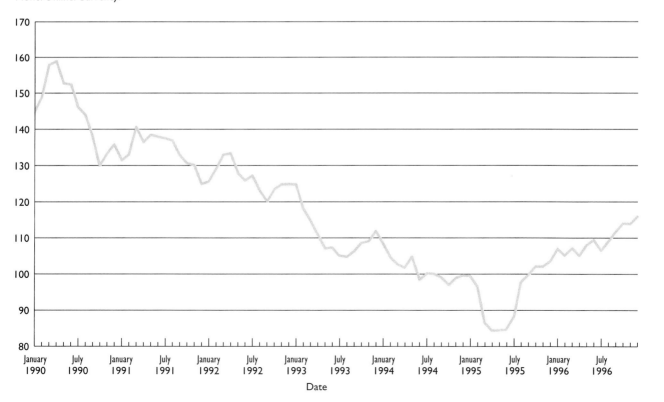

back to ¥125 per dollar within three months. Others, however, were forecasting that the yen would move to parity against the dollar and could plunge to double-digit levels.

This uncertainty created serious problems for firms. Nissan, for example, had based its financial plans for 1993 on a dollar trading at ¥120, but the rise to ¥105 by mid-June meant a $600-million drop in profits. There was a difference of opinion as to the impact of exchange rates on competitiveness. Some experts argued that Japanese exporters could not be profitable at an exchange rate of ¥115 per dollar or higher, and one expert concluded that only 80 percent of Japan's exporters could be profitable at a rate of 120 yen. Given the 1993 political crisis in Japan and the relatively weak Japanese economy, most experts did not believe the yen would rise as much as it did. However, an economically weaker Europe and a large Japanese trade surplus caused the yen to continue to strengthen against the dollar. Corporate profits had declined three years in a row as of the fiscal year ending March 31, 1993, and the stronger yen was expected to cause profits to decline for a fourth year. For consumer electronics and automobiles, for example, profits were about 6 percent of sales in 1985 but only 1 percent of sales in 1993. One economist estimated that an average exchange rate of ¥105 per dollar would cause real GNP growth to decline to 1 percent in the 1993 fiscal year and profits to fall by 33 percent.

As the Japanese economy continued to be weak, consumers became more price conscious and decided to make room for relatively cheap imports, thus creating more pressure on Japanese companies and taking away domestic cash flow that could have been used to subsidize export business.

As the yen continued to rise, Nissan found itself in a difficult position. The U.S. price of a Nissan auto sometimes rose three or four times a year during 1993–1995. However, many companies could not raise prices as fast as the yen was rising, so they were still losing profitability. At one point, U.S. autos enjoyed a $2,500 cost advantage over Nissan and other Japanese autos, and the Japanese began to lose market share. In addition, U.S. auto companies began to penetrate Japanese markets and take away market share from Nissan and the other Japanese automakers. The relatively cheap dollar also meant that U.S. automakers had a cost advantage in third-country markets, such as Germany and France. As a result, Nissan had to commit to build more autos in the United States, rely more on U.S.-manufactured auto parts, and accept much lower profit margins. In addition, Nissan had to improve its design and manufacturing operations in order to cut costs to the point of making up some of the profit margin lost by the rising yen. The Automotive Business Practices Institute of Japan estimates that the Japanese cut 15 percent of their production costs between 1994 and 1996, compared with only 10 percent by the U.S. Big Three.

However, the situation changed in mid-1995, and the dollar began to rise against the yen. From a low of ¥84.33 in 1995, the dollar climbed to over ¥110 by the end of 1996. With interest rates so low in Japan, investors were pulling their money out of yen and investing it in dollars. The Bank of Japan was keeping interest rates low in order to stimulate the economy, which had become stuck in a recession. The relatively wide spread in rates was making Japanese assets very unattractive.

However, the falling yen was certainly beneficial to Nissan. Its earnings in the United States were being translated into higher yen, and it had the choice of keeping prices the same and earning more profits or lowering prices to pick up market share. In general, Japanese automakers raised their prices by an average of only $91 a vehicle in the first half of 1996, whereas U.S. automakers raised their car and truck prices by an average of $226. However, many Japanese companies feel that an exchange rate of ¥105 is still a strong rate. As the rate moves above ¥110, however, the psychology begins to change. Not only is Nissan having trouble trying to decide what to do, but so are U.S. auto companies. Even during the time when they had a solid foreign exchange advantage over the Japanese, U.S. automakers were fighting hard to drive down costs and become more competitive. They had begun to commit resources to penetrate Japanese markets, but the strong dollar was beginning to make that impossible.

Nissan also had to worry about the future of the yen/dollar rate. Many U.S. manufacturers, including the Big Three, were lobbying the U.S. president to intervene in the market and allow the dollar to fall in order to spur exports and reduce the competitiveness of imports. If they are successful, Nissan will find the yen rising again, putting it into the same situation it was in earlier.

Questions

1. What are some of the major factors that have influenced the yen/dollar exchange rate in the past decade? Have different factors become more important at different times?

2. What are the major options available to Nissan in the weak yen environment?

3. Which approach would you recommend, and why?

4. Assume that Nissan spends an average of ¥1.875 million to manufacture a car in Japan, plus $2,600 to market and distribute the car in the United States.

    a. Assuming the exchange rate at the end of each year since 1990, what would be the impact of the exchange rate on the dollar cost of the auto?

    b. If Nissan had wanted to sell the car at the end of 1994 for the same as it could have in 1993, by how much would it have had to cut costs, given the exchange rates of the two years?

    c. If the same car were manufactured in the United States at a cost of $15,000 and 40 percent of the parts were imported from Japan, what impact would the different exchange rates have on the dollar cost?

Chapter Notes

1. "China's Financial Fix," *The Economist,* July 10, 1993, pp. 69–70; James McGregor, "Reform in China Adds to Currency Woes," *Wall Street Journal,* June 2, 1993, p. A10; "People's Republic of China," in International Monetary Fund, *Exchange Arrangements and Exchange Restrictions Annual Report 1991* (Washington, D.C.: IMF, 1991), p. 101; "China Needs Stable Currency Under Exchange Reform," *Agence France Paris,* January 31, 1994; and "China Reforms Its Foreign Exchange System," *Xinhua Foreign News Service,* December 28,

1993; Dusty Clayton, "Confusion in Wake of Move to Make Yuan Convertible," *South China Morning Post,* November 14, 1995, Business Post, p. 5; Foo Choy Peng, "China Plans Interbank Market by Next Year," *South China Morning Post,* November 15, 1995, Business Post, p. 1; Euromoney, *Emerging Market Currencies,* June 1996, p. 4; Gary M. Bennett, *China Facts & Figures Annual Handbook* (Gulf Breeze, Florida: Academic International Press, 1995), pp. 137–142; see the Bloomberg home page for the current renminbi/dollar exchange

rate <http://www.bloomberg.com/markets/wcv.html>

2. IMF Home Page: <http://www.imf.org/external/ Np/sec/memdir/members/htm>

3. See IMF home page referred to in previous note; also, see IMF, *Survey: Supplement on the IMF,* September 1996.

4. *Europa Yearbook,* 1993, pp. 72–73.

5. See IMF home page section on SDRs; also, see IMF *Survey,* April 1, 1996.

6. International Monetary Fund, *International Financial Statistics* (Washington, D.C.: IMF, October 1996), p. 8.

7. International Monetary Fund, *Exchange Arrangements and Exchange Restrictions Annual Report 1991* (Washington, D.C.: IMF, 1991), p. 331.

8. Paul Lewis, "As Summit Talks Near, A Defense," *New York Times,* June 25, 1996, p. D4.

9. Fred Kaplan, "Fortunes Being Amassed in the Black Money Trade," *We,* June 28, 1993, p. 1 (appeared originally in the *Boston Globe*).

10. International Monetary Fund, *Exchange Arrangements,* p. 97.

11. Julian Walmsley, *The Foreign Exchange Handbook* (New York: Wiley, 1983), pp. 84–90.

12. *Europa World Yearbook* (London: Europa Publication Ltd., Vol 1, 1996), pp. 113–114.

13. International Monetary Fund, *International Financial Statistics* (Washington, D.C.: IMF, February 1997), various pages.

14. Ibid., pp. 49–57.

15. Michael R. Sesit, "For Now, Central Bankers Regain Reins," *Wall Street Journal,* August 4, 1993, p. C1.

16. David Wessel, "Intervention in Currency Shrinks Under Clinton," *Wall Street Journal,* September 14, 1995, p. C1.

17. "McCurrencies: Where's The Beef?" *The Economist,* April 27, 1996. Quotes material contained in "For Here or To Go? Purchasing Power Parity and the Big Mac," *Federal Reserve Bank of St. Louis,* January 1996.

18. Betty W. Liu, "Traders Line Up for Marks as Germans Cast Doubt on Single-

Currency Plan," *Wall Street Journal,* October 30, 1996, p. C26.

19. Sesit, op. cit., p. C13.

20. "Forecasting Currencies: Technical or Fundamental?" *Business International Money Report,* October 15, 1990, pp. 401–402.

21. Andrew C. Pollock and Mary E. Wilkie, "Briefing," *Euromoney,* June 1991, pp. 123–124.

22. "Forecasting at Chrysler," *F&T Risk Advisor,* April 1993, p. 7.

23. David K. Eiteman, Arthur I. Stonehill, and Michael H. Moffett, *Multinational Business Finance,* 7th ed. (Reading, Mass.: Addison-Wesley, 1995), Chapter 5.

24. Julia Lawlor, "Weak Dollar Draws Foreign Shoppers," *USA Today,* November 18, 1992, p. B1.

25. Lindley H. Clark, Jr., and Alfred L. Malabre, "Foreign Firms' Units in U.S. Feel Pinch But Resist Raising Prices as Dollar Falls," *Wall Street Journal,* September 9, 1992, p. A2.

26. Oscar Suris, "BMW Expects U.S.-Made Cars to Have 80% Level of North American Content," *Wall Street Journal,* August 5, 1993, p. A2.

27. Most information for the case came from the following sources: "Economies on Currencies," *Euromoney,* May 1990, p. 145; Mike McNamee, "Only Higher Rates Can Half the Yen's Big Slide," *Business Week,* p. 82; "The Japanese Paradox," *The Economist,* 7 April 1990, p. 77; Steven H. Nagourney, "Yen for Trouble," *Barron's,* 26 March 1990;

International Financial Statistics, various issues; Alexei Bayer, "Watching the Yen," *Finance & Treasury,* April 26, 1993, p. 6; Michael Williams, "Japan's Global Trade Surplus Eases, But Some Say May's Fall Won't Continue," *Wall Street Journal,* June 16, 1993, p. A9; Fred R. Bleakley, "Japanese Firms Act to Lift U.S. Prices, Citing Dollar's Weakness Against Yen," *Wall Street Journal,* June 28, 1993, p. A2; Quentin Hardy and Yumiko Ono, "Yen's Run-Up, Despite Political Crisis, Underscores Japan's Trading Strength," *Wall Street Journal,* August 5, 1993, p. A9; "Bashed by the Mighty Yen," *The Economist,* June 5, 1993, p. 81; Louis Uchitelle, "No Quick Gain from Stronger Yen," *New York Times,* April 26, 1993, p. C1; Douglas Lavin, "Sales of Domestic Vehicles Rose 15.5% in Early June Amid Steady Recovery," *Wall Street Journal,* June 16, 1993, p. A2; Joseph Neu, "Time to Look at Yen/Dollar Positions," *Finance & Treasury,* March 1, 1993, p. 7; Keith Bradsher, "Falling Yen Puts Car Makers in Japan in the Driver's Seat," *New York Times,* July 15, 1996, p. A1; Jim Mateja, "The Bottom Line; Car Companies Make Some Uncommon Price Moves for '97," *Chicago Tribune,* September 29, 1996, p. 21; Ronald E. Yates, "Dollar Gain a Threat to Exports to Japan; U.S. Goods Become More Expensive to Buy with Yen," *Chicago Tribune,* October 3, 1996, p. 1; and Valerie Reitman, "The Japanese Formula: Nylon Seat Covers and a Falling Yen," *Wall Street Journal,* July 18, 1996, p. B1.

5 The Dynamics of International Business-Government Relationships

The preservation of natural habitats is receiving increased global attention because of the environmental implications of maintaining ecosystems. Many countries, especially some in Africa, have also seen potential benefits from international tourism to these areas. The inset shows a photo-safari in the Maasai Mara Game Reserve in Kenya. It is set against a backdrop of a tribal robe from Ghana.

Chapter 11

The Impact of the Multinational Enterprise

*If a little money does not go
out, great money will not
come in.*

—Chinese Proverb

Objectives

- **To examine the conflicting objectives of MNE stakeholders**

- **To discuss problems in evaluating MNE activities**

- **To evaluate the major economic impacts—balance of payments and growth—of MNEs on home (donor) and host (recipient) countries**

- **To introduce the major criticisms about MNEs**

- **To give an overview of the major political controversies surrounding MNE activities**

Case
Foreign Direct
Investment in China[1]

During the 1990s, China has received much more FDI than any other LDC. In fact, during 1993–1995 China's FDI inflow was second in the world, exceeded only by the U.S. FDI inflow. Although China's stock of FDI at the beginning of the 1990s was smaller than that of many other LDCs, in 1993 it surpassed Singapore as the largest LDC host for FDI.

In spite of the amount and growth of FDI, China has not allowed investment to enter freely. Each investment proposal is examined separately by the Chinese Ministry of Foreign Trade and Economic Cooperation (MOFTEC) or by provincial-level authorities with jurisdiction over certain types of investments. These authorities decide whether the investment is in the best interests of China, and they may disallow an FDI entry and/or negotiate with the potential investor to try to improve the benefits for Chinese stakeholders. Before a proposal reaches MOFTEC, foreign companies typically have already participated in protracted negotiations (often over several years) with Chinese companies and provincial authorities. Map 11.1 shows the provinces of China. That so much FDI has recently gone to China in spite of the arduous entry process is due to companies' strong motivations to operate in China.

Although FDI may be either market- or resource-seeking, the former seems to be the major recent motivation for entering China. A 1996 survey of about 500 Canadian companies with an established interest in China indicated that 85 percent were investing to gain access to the Chinese market. MNEs have long coveted China's potential as a market

Map 11.1
China and Its Provinces
China is the world's third largest country in area and largest in population.

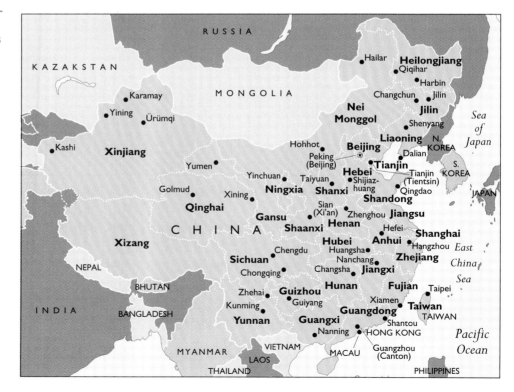

because of its large population. As early as 1971, a Monsanto spokesman summed up this allure by stating, "You just can't look at a market that size and not believe that eventually a lot of goods are going to be sold there. One aspirin tablet a day to each of those guys, and that is a lot of aspirin." In addition to China's large population of about 1.3 billion people, its purchasing power has been increasing because of economic growth. During the 1980s its increase in manufacturing output of 14.4 percent a year was the fastest rate among the world's fifty largest economies. This has translated into consumer spending. For example, between 1990 and 1995, the percentage of Chinese households with color televisions rose from 59.04 percent to 89.79 percent and those with refrigerators rose from 42.33 percent to 66.22 percent. Between 1995 and 2000 China is expected to spend over a trillion dollars on infrastructure projects including eighty dams, numerous power plants, several major highways and railroads, and subway systems in eighteen cities. Projections are that China will soon be the largest economy in the world as measured by purchasing power parity.

Chinese governmental policies limit imports by a variety of means; thus foreign companies usually find FDI to be a more feasible means than exporting to serve the Chinese market. For example, the tariffs on automotive imports run 250 percent. Further, when foreign companies bid on infrastructure projects, the winning bidder may be chosen because it offers to transfer technology to produce a high portion of the equipment within China. In effect, China practices both import substitution and export-led development trade policies. China has had a policy of promoting maximum self-sufficiency, primarily for political and cultural reasons. In addition, it is argued that the Chinese economy is potentially so large that it should be able to justify local production of almost any manufactured product.

Although market size is the main motivation for investing in China, companies have also been attracted to China because of its resources. For example, there have been substantial investments in the exploration and production of oil and coal, and almost 20 percent of U.S.-owned FDI in China is in the petroleum sector. In addition, companies have looked at China as a source of inexpensive labor, particularly as unemployed labor supplies have decreased and as labor rates have increased in some other Asian economies (e.g., Singapore, Hong Kong, and Taiwan) that no longer can be considered cheap labor sources. For example, Winsor Industrial, which was Hong Kong's largest publicly traded textile company, began moving textile production out of Hong Kong in the 1980s and shifted manufacturing from its two remaining Hong Kong plants to China in 1995. Further, by the mid-1990s many companies in the electronics industry or suppliers to it, such as Northern Telecom, Intel, and Samsung, had construction under way in China to serve both the Chinese and export markets. The largest of these was Motorola, which invested $280 million between 1992 and 1995 and whose investment is expected to reach $1.2 billion by the year 2000 for the production of semiconductor wafers, pagers, cellular phones, and other telecommunications products.

Finally, many companies have been drawn recently to China because there are few, if any, major countries in which they have not already established a strong presence. Their earlier exclusion of China from investment plans was due primarily to China's effective prohibition of foreign investment from 1949 to 1979. These were the first thirty years of communist rule in China, during which time China also traded as little as possible with other countries. Although this economic isolationism was brought in by communist rule, it was consistent with policies during much of Chinese history. China has a long history of attempted isolationism because of its fear that foreign contact will weaken it politically and pollute its culture. In "modern times," foreign countries have forced business relations with China militarily, such as in the 1839–1842 Anglo-Chinese war, the 1894–1895 Sino-Japanese war, the early 1900s Boxer Rebellion, and the 1931–1945 Japanese occupation that included the World War II period. After each of these foreign military incursions, China returned to relative economic isolationism as soon as possible after regaining its self-rule politically. Many attribute this inward-looking characteristic as an attempt to preserve cultural traditions in a society that believes in its own cultural superiority.

After Mao Zedong's death in 1976, there was a power struggle in which Deng Xiaoping emerged as the new leader of China. At this time, China, which during most of recorded history was the world's largest manufacturing country, was more than a century behind industrial countries in industrialization. In fact, it risked missing the industrial revolution altogether because it lacked infrastructure, technical know-how, and sufficient exportable products to earn the foreign exchange necessary to build its infrastructure and move forward economically. China officially condemned the grave blunder of the Cultural Revolution and began looking externally for the resources it needed. In 1979, China approved the Law on Joint Ventures Using Chinese and Foreign Investment. Concomitantly, China established special export zones (SEZs) in which foreign companies were given incentives to invest, provided that all output was exported from China. The incentives were necessary because China's political environment was so uncertain that foreign companies were wary about making investments there. Foreign companies could also establish joint ventures with Chinese companies in order to sell to the Chinese market; however, proposals to do so were scrutinized more closely and approved only if they served a top-level national priority for which China had to seek outside help. Chinese market-serving investments were generally made to improve an existing Chinese product or industry, rather than to create production of an entirely new product in China. For example, a number of joint ventures were approved in the petroleum industry, such as by Baker Marine and Dresser Industries, because future oil sales were considered a high priority for earning foreign exchange. A proposal by Beatrice Foods was approved because improvement in food preservation was a top governmental priority as China sought agricultural self-sufficiency.

Since that time, China has greatly increased its dependence on international business activities. For example, its trade (imports plus exports) as a percentage of GDP rose from 10 percent in 1978 to 38 percent in 1992. China has increased the number of SPZs. It now allows wholly foreign-owned ventures; however, these are rare because (a) foreign companies perceive that MOFTEC will view these more stringently and (b) foreign companies, rather than Chinese partners, must guide the proposal through the bureaucracy. Typically, investments are joint ventures, with the foreign partner owning 49 percent and the Chinese partner owning 51 percent. Further, China has become more active in seeking out foreign investment because Chinese companies may now look for joint venture partners on their own. Some contacts are even attempted on the Internet. For example, a recent notice read:

Shenyang Paraffin Wax Production project seeking foreign partner for the joint venture. The project has already spent about U.S. $31 million in infrastructure. An approximately U.S. $115 million of foreign investment is needed to complete the entire project. The return on the investment is forecasted at 22.24 percent.

At the same time, Chinese authorities have increased efforts and have become more adept at evaluating foreign companies' contributions to Chinese objectives. For example, Guangdong province performed appraisals in 1994 on assets brought in, such as assembly lines to make fruit chips, by 1104 foreign companies. By appraising these assets downward, foreign companies were allowed to remit smaller portions of their earnings abroad.

The attitudes toward investing in China have had their ups and downs, primarily because of political conditions that worry potential investors. For example, the 1987 removal of the moderate Hu Yaobang as party chairman, the 1989 suppression of the pro-democracy movement, and 1996 threats against Taiwan caused foreign investors to worry. However, the fact that Chinese governmental authorities did not take measures against FDI during these political events has heightened investors' optimism. Further, China's endorsement of a transition to a "socialist market economy" at the 14th Communist Party Congress in 1992 and its subsequent permissions for "experiments" in a number of service sectors by authorizing one or two foreign firms to establish joint ventures in accounting, legal services, and insurance have been seen as favorable for future business.

When considering production within China, a foreign company must first find a sponsoring Chinese organization that will approve its application to establish a representative office. The foreign company may then be assigned a Chinese company with which it negotiates. This same Chinese company may then negotiate with more than one foreign company in order to determine which will offer more in the arrangement. The following summarizes the steps needed for a joint venture approval.

1. Potential partners sign a letter of intent (not a binding contract) giving the broad outlines of a future contract.

2. The Chinese partner submits a proposal, including a preliminary feasibility study, to its immediate administrative superior, which is then passed on to provincial or national authorities, depending on the scale of the investment.

3. Once all the authorities in (2) approve, the proposed investors must complete a feasibility study that includes the type and quantity of product, target market, sales projections, equipment, infrastructure and labor requirements, and projected foreign exchange requirements.

4. The partners draft and sign a contract, while keeping authorities apprised of what their agreement will entail.

5. Agreements are presented to MOFTEC or local authorities for approval.

6. Within a month of approval (which stipulates a deadline for making the actual investment), the joint venture must register to obtain a business license. If deadlines are not met, the investor is liable for interest payments or compensation losses.

The same steps are necessary for a wholly owned investment; however, the foreign company must deal directly with all authorities, rather than having a proposed partner handle the arrangements.

Whether approval is by MOFTEC or by regional authorities depends on the priority for the particular type of investment. For example, operations that will sell all output in the export market can generally be approved at the provincial level. Further, MOFTEC prioritizes industries—those that it encourages, restricts, or prohibits. The higher the priority, the more likely that approval may be granted at the provincial level. The list of industries is quite detailed and specific. For example, the list approved in 1995 included industries within eighteen categories. Those that would serve priority needs for which China clearly lacked up-to-date technology were in the encouraged category, such as water-saving irrigation equipment production and the manufacture of complete coal gasification equipment. Those that were either low priority products or that Chinese companies already had special capabilities for were prohibited, such as the processing of teas and manufacture of blue and white porcelain. In between were restricted products, such as bicycle and sewing machine assembly and hotel operations. However, such priorities are subject to change. For example, the 1995 priorities put hotel investments lower than in the past. Further, priorities and approval points sometimes change without publicity.

In essence, China has had a love-hate relationship with FDI. It would rather be independent of other countries; however, it sees foreign companies' transfer of capital, technology, and management skills to Chinese enterprises as a means of strengthening its independence. The Chinese are enthralled by foreign modern advancements, but they fear foreign cultural contamination. Although many costs and benefits are considered by Chinese companies and by authorities when approving or rejecting investment proposals, in reality two investment benefits have been fundamental. These are the transfer of technology within a high-priority industrial sector and the generation of exports. The generation of exports earns foreign exchange to buy the ever-growing imports needed for development. The transfer of technology improves future export capabilities and increases the likelihood that Chinese companies can be globally competitive in the future without depending on partnerships with foreign companies. Such benefits to China do not always translate into achievement of the foreign investors' objectives, which tend to be more operational, such as return on investment or increase in market share. The difference in perspective creates a challenge for initiating and continuing successful FDI in China.

Introduction

As MNE managers and as national citizens, we need to understand the impact of MNEs. Companies allocate resources among countries to optimize their performance; however, this allocation is constrained and altered by governmental perceptions of the impact of MNEs. Managers must be aware of these perceptions and attempt at times to change them. As citizens, we need to argue for governmental policies that will enhance important national interests.

The opening case illustrates the ambivalence of Chinese authorities toward FDI. In other countries as well, the rapid growth of MNEs has been controversial. In fact, powerful pressure groups in both home and host countries have pushed their governments to implement policies either restricting or enhancing the movement of MNEs. These groups are sure to play an even greater role in the future expansion of international business. This chapter examines the major contentions regarding MNEs' practices and the main evidence supporting or refuting those contentions.

The primary criticism is that MNEs are inadequately concerned about national societal interests because of their global bases of operations. Further, the sheer size of many of these companies concerns the countries in which they do business. For example, the sales of GM, Exxon, and Mitsubishi exceed the GNP of such medium-sized economies as Argentina, Indonesia, Poland, and South Africa. Large MNEs such as these have considerable power in negotiating business arrangements with governments; outcomes are sometimes of greater consequence than are many treaties among countries. In fact, the executives of MNEs frequently deal directly with heads of state when negotiating the terms under which their companies may operate. But of course, as we have indicated throughout the text, not all MNEs are large.

Evaluating the Impact of the MNE

Trade-offs among Constituencies

To survive, a company must satisfy different groups, often referred to collectively as **stakeholders.** These include stockholders, employees, customers, and society at large. In the short term, the aims of these groups conflict. Stockholders want additional sales and increased productivity, which result in higher profits and larger returns going to them. Employees want additional compensation. Customers want lower prices. And society at large would like to see increased corporate taxes or corporate involvement in social functions. In the long term, all of these aims must be achieved adequately or none will be attained at all because each stakeholder group is powerful enough to cause the company's demise.

Management must be aware of these various interests but serve them unevenly at any given period. At one time, most gains may go to consumers; at another, to stockholders. Making necessary trade-offs is difficult in the domestic environment. However, abroad, where corporate managers are relatively unfamiliar with customs and power groups, the problem of choosing the best alternative is compounded; this is particularly true if dominant interests differ among countries.

The most cumbersome problem in overseas relationships is not so much one of trying to serve conflicting interests within countries but rather of handling cross-national controversies in a manner that will achieve global business objectives. Constituencies in any given country seek to fulfill their own, rather than global, objectives. For example, labor in the United States has been little concerned about the number of global jobs created by their employers, such as those created in Mexico. Instead, it has lobbied only for legislation to increase the number of jobs within the United States. Thus management's task is complicated, since decisions made in one country may have repercussions in another.

Among the many decisions managers must make are those concerning:

- Locations of production, decision making, and R&D
- Methods of acquisition and operation
- Markets to be served
- Prices to charge
- Use of profits

In the opening case, for example, many Chinese authorities were concerned about such issues. Assume a U.S. investor has production facilities in both the United States and China. Which facility will export to Venezuela? Clearly, this decision will determine where profits, taxes, employment, and capital flows will be located. Interests in either country, as well as in Venezuela, may claim that they should have jurisdiction over the sales.

Trade-offs among Objectives

The effects of an MNE's activities may be simultaneously positive for one national objective and negative for another.

An MNE's actions may affect a wide range of economic, social, and political objectives of a given country. A positive effect on one objective, such as full employment, may be concomitant with a negative effect on another objective, such as domestic control over economic matters. In other words, there may be trade-offs. A country finds it difficult to rank its objectives, since it naturally wants only benefits without costs, which is seldom possible to achieve. Despite the widespread effects of MNEs on various parts of the social system, much of the literature analyzing these companies attempts to isolate effects to a single given objective. This sometimes occurs because a solution is needed for a given problem, such as a country's balance-of-payments deficit, and sometimes because pressure groups want to win support for their positions.

In an international transaction,
- **Both parties may gain**
- **Both parties may lose**
- **One party may gain and the other lose**
- **Even when both parties gain, they may disagree over the distribution of the benefits**

In international transactions involving MNEs, people sometimes erroneously assume that if one party gains, the other must lose.[2] That may happen, but it also is possible that both parties will either gain or lose. No party would participate willingly in a cross-national transaction in the belief that the deal would harm its priorities. Controversies develop because things do not work out as anticipated, the precedence given to the objectives changes, and disagreements arise over the distribution of gains when it is acknowledged that both parties have benefited overall. The last problem is at the heart of most controversies. As described in the opening case, China has tried to encourage foreign investment while also securing more benefits from it by pushing for technology transfers that will improve its future economic situation.

Countries want a greater share of benefits from MNEs' activities.

Cause-Effect Relationships

It is extremely hard to determine whether societal conditions are caused by MNEs' actions.

The observation that two factors move in relation to each other does not prove an interconnection between them. Yet a number of recent events have been attributed to the growth in the number of MNEs and the portion of global business for which they account. Opponents of MNEs have linked them to inequitable income and power distribution, environmental debasement, and societal deprivation. Their proponents have linked them to increased tax revenues, employment, and exports. These linkages are particularly prone to arise when governments consider either restricting or encouraging FDI. Although the data presented by opponents or proponents of MNEs often are accurate and convincing, it is not certain what would have happened had MNEs not operated or not followed certain practices. Technological developments, competitors' actions, and governmental policies are just three of the variables that encumber cause-effect analysis.

Individual and Aggregate Effects

The philosophy and actions of each MNE are unique.

One astute observer has said, "Like animals in a zoo, multinationals (and their affiliates) come in various shapes and sizes, perform distinctive functions, behave differently, and make their individual impacts on the environment."[3] Thus it is difficult to make general statements about MNEs' effects. Much of the literature on the subject, from the viewpoints of both protagonists and antagonists, takes isolated examples and presents them as typical. The examples chosen usually make interesting reading because of their spectacular or extreme nature, but it is dangerous to make policies based on the exceptional rather than the usual.

Some countries have tried to evaluate MNEs and their activities individually. Although this might lead to greater fairness and better control, it is a cumbersome and costly process. Therefore, many countries apply policies and control mechanisms to all MNEs. Although doing this eliminates some of the bureaucracy, it carries with it the risk of throwing out some "good apples" along with the bad. Further, when examining foreign investments on either an individual or an aggregate basis, governments have been far from perfect in predicting future impacts. Given these caveats, this chapter will examine the major impacts of MNEs.

Potential Contributions of MNEs

Although the sheer size of many MNEs makes them suspect to stakeholders, this size gives them assets that can be used to contribute to a wide range of objectives. MNEs control a large portion of the world's capital, which can be used to increase production. They account for most of the world's exports of goods and services, thus creating access to foreign exchange for the purchase of imports. They are the major producers and organizers of technology and operating know-how, which are increasingly important in determining national competitiveness and in solving environmental problems.[4] Figure 11.1 shows the major assets of MNEs that may be used to satisfy stakeholder objectives. Nevertheless, there are controversies surrounding the impact of MNEs' use of these assets.

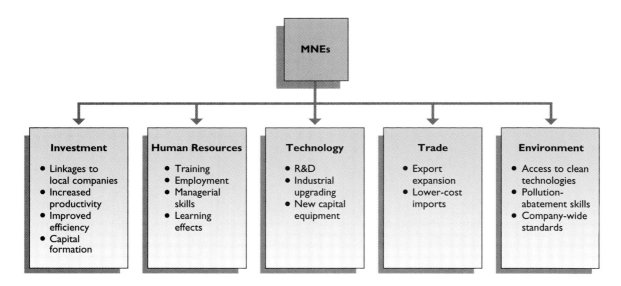

Figure 11.1
Resources and
Contributions of MNEs
By contributing directly
to investment, human
resources, technology,
trade, and the environ-
ment, the MNE contrib-
utes to host-country
objectives concerning the
items listed.

Source: Adapted from Transnational Corporations and Management Division, *World Investment
Report 1992: Transnational Corporations: Engines of Growth, An Executive Summary* (New York: United
Nations, 1992), p. 13.

One country's surplus is
another's deficit, but long-
and short-term economic
goals differ.

Economic Impact of the MNE

Balance-of-Payments Effects

Place in the economic system   Recall from the balance-of-payments discussion in
Chapter 10 that if a country runs a trade deficit, it must compensate for that deficit
by reducing its reserves or receiving an influx of capital. This influx of capital may be
from unilateral transfers (such as foreign aid), from the receipt of credit, or from the
receipt of foreign investment.[5] To put this another way, the more capital inflow a
country receives, the more it can import and the more it can run a trade deficit. The
ability to run a trade deficit is important for LDCs because they have more goods and
services available for their use than they produce themselves. The ability to use these
additional resources potentially helps them satisfy their growth objectives. FDI has
recently been crucial because global foreign aid has stagnated and private investment
flows have been accounting for a larger portion of the capital received by LDCs.[6] For
example, China has recently been a large net receiver of FDI, and it has also been
running a trade surplus. This capital accumulation has temporarily been going for the
buildup of Chinese reserves, which it holds largely in U.S. Treasury bills. This will
enable China to run trade deficits that will be necessary if China is to complete its
planned massive infrastructure development by the year 2000.

Like China, other countries attempt to regulate trade and investment movements and the capital flows that parallel those movements. They do this through
incentives, prohibitions, and other types of governmental intervention. A distinction about balance of payments is that gains are a zero sum; that is, one country's
trade or capital surplus shows up as another's deficit. If both countries were looking
only at a limited time period, then one country might justifiably be described as a

winner at the expense of the other. In fact, a country may be willing to forgo short-term surpluses in favor of long-term ones, or vice versa.

Effect of individual FDI   Two extreme hypothetical examples of the effects of FDI illustrate the need to evaluate each investment activity separately in order to determine its effect on the balance of payments. In the first example, a foreign company purchases a Haitian-owned company by depositing dollars in a Swiss bank for the former owners. No changes are made in management or operations, so profitability remains the same. However, dividends now are remitted to the foreign owners rather than remaining in Haiti, and so there is a net drain on foreign exchange for Haiti and a subsequent inflow to another country. In the second example, a foreign company purchases unemployed resources (land, labor, materials, and equipment) in Haiti and converts them to the production of formerly imported goods. Because of rising demand, all earnings are reinvested in Haiti; thus the entire import substitution results in a gain in foreign exchange.

Most investments or nonequity arrangements (such as licensing or management contracts) fall somewhere between these two simplistic and extreme examples and are not evaluated so easily, particularly when policy makers attempt to apply regulations to aggregate investment movements. There are numerous measurement difficulties, but guidelines are gradually emerging. A basic equation for making an analysis is

$$B = (m - m_1) + (x - x_1) + (c - c_1)$$

where

B = balance-of-payments effect
m = import displacement
m_1 = import stimulus
x = export stimulus
x_1 = export reduction
c = capital inflow for other than import and export payment
c_1 = capital outflow for other than import and export payment

Although the equation is simple, the problem of choosing the proper values to assign to the variables is formidable. For instance, let's try to evaluate the effect of a Honda automobile plant in the United States. To calculate the **net import change** $(m - m_1)$, we would need to know how much would be imported in the absence of the plant. Clearly, the amount that Honda produces and sells in the United States is only an indication because the selling price, product characteristics, and quality of those automobiles may be different from what would otherwise be imported. Further, some of the sales may have been at the expense of other automobile plants in the United States. The value of m_1 should include equipment, components, and materials brought in for manufacturing the product locally. For example, Honda buys many parts from suppliers who import them. The value of m_1 also should include estimates of import increases due to upward movements in national income caused by the capital inflow. For instance, if U.S. national income is assumed to rise $2 million as a result of the investment, the recipients of that income will spend some portion on imports, which is known as the **marginal propensity to import.** If this proportion is calculated to be 10 percent, imports should rise by $200,000.

The **net export effect** $(x - x_1)$ is particularly controversial because conclusions vary widely depending on the assumptions made. For the Honda example, it can be argued that a U.S. plant merely substitutes for Japanese exports and production. However, MNEs, regardless of nationality, argue that moves abroad are defensive; that is, restrictions of governments and shifts in cost advantages, such as a strong yen relative to the dollar, make foreign production inevitable. By moving abroad, MNEs pick up business that would otherwise go to foreign companies. MNEs have argued further that the investments stimulate exports of complementary products that can be sold through foreign-owned facilities. Again, we must make assumptions about the amount of these exports that could have materialized had the subsidiaries not been established.

The **net capital flow** $(c - c_1)$ is the easiest figure to calculate because of controls at most central banks. The problem with using a given year for evaluation purposes is the time lag between the outward flow of investment funds and the inward flow of remitted earnings from the investment. Thus what appears at a given time to be a favorable or unfavorable capital flow may in fact prove over a longer period to be the opposite. For example, the time it would take Honda to recoup the capital outflow is affected by its need to reinvest funds in the United States, its ability to borrow locally, and its perception of the future dollar/yen exchange rate. Given the number of variables, the capital flows will vary widely among companies and projects. A further complication arises because MNEs may transfer funds in disguised forms, such as through transactions between parent and subsidiary operations at arbitrary rather than market prices, thus misstating the real returns on the investments.

Although the equation presented above is useful for broadly evaluating the balance-of-payments effects of investments, it should be used with caution. As mentioned earlier, there are data problems. In addition, an investment movement might have some indirect effects on a country's balance of payments that are not readily quantifiable. For example, an investor might bring new technological or managerial efficiencies that are then emulated by other companies. What these other companies do may affect the country's external economic relations.

The balance-of-payments effects of FDI usually are
- **Positive for the host country and negative for the home country initially**
- **Positive for the home country and negative for the host country later**

Aggregate assumptions and responses   Fairly widespread consensus exists that MNEs' investments are initially favorable to the host country and unfavorable to the home country but that the situation reverses after some time. This occurs because nearly all investors plan eventually to remit to the parent company more than they send abroad. If the net value of the FDI continues to grow through retained earnings, dividend payments for a given year ultimately may exceed the total capital transfers required for the initial investment. The time period before reversal may vary substantially, and there is much disagreement as to the aggregate time span required.

In the case of U.S. companies' FDI, for example, more than half of the net increase in value in recent years typically has come from the reinvestment of funds earned abroad. This means that the increase in claims on foreign assets has not been coming primarily from a flow of capital to the foreign operations. It also means that the FDI's net value has become so large that the return flow of funds to the United States from foreign earnings exceeds the outward flow for increasing investment abroad.[7]

From the standpoint of home countries, restrictions on capital outflow improve short-term capital availability, but restrictions on capital outflows reduce future earnings inflows from foreign investments. Further, the restrictions may erode confidence in the economy, thus reducing capital inflows and increasing capital flight through loopholes in the regulations.[8] Consequently, the restrictions are useful only in buying the time needed to institute other means for solving balance-of-payments difficulties.

Governments also have sought to attract inflows of long-term capital as a means of developing production that will either displace imports or generate exports. The problem for investment recipients, then, is how to take advantage of the benefits of foreign capital while also minimizing the long-term adverse effects on their balance of payments. Many host countries have approached this problem by valuing new FDI only on the basis of contributions of freely convertible currencies, industrial equipment, and other physical assets, not contributions of good will, technology, patents, trademarks, and other intangibles. This valuation is then tied into regulations on the maximum repatriation of earnings. The maximum is stated as a percentage of the investment's value; by holding down the stated value, the host-country government can minimize eventual repatriation of earnings. In this respect, governments often exert strict control over the prices of equipment brought in, especially when the investor is also the equipment supplier, so that the investment value is not overstated. Recall in the opening case that China reappraised equipment brought in by foreign investors and lowered the approved value. Governments also often are interested in receiving part of the capital contribution in the form of loans and in local holdings of equity so that the future outward capital flow is reduced and has an upward limit.

Home and host countries make policies to try to improve short- or long-term effects:
- **Home countries establish outflow restrictions.**
- **Host countries impose repatriation restrictions, asset-valuation controls, and conversion to debt as opposed to equity.**

Growth and employment effects are not a zero-sum game because MNEs may use resources that were unemployed or underemployed.

Growth and Employment Effects

Unlike balance-of-payments effects, the effects of MNEs on growth and employment are not necessarily a zero-sum game among countries. Classical economists assumed production factors were at full employment; consequently, a movement of any of these factors abroad would result in an increase in output abroad and a decrease at home. Even if this assumption were true, the gains in the host country might be greater or less than the losses in the home country.

The argument that both the home and the host countries may gain from FDI rests partly on the assumption that resources are not necessarily fully employed and partly on the industry-specific and complementary nature of capital and technology. For example, a brewer, such as Anheuser-Busch, may be producing maximally for its domestic market and be limited in developing export sales because of high transportation costs. Anheuser-Busch may not easily move into other product lines or readily use its financial resources to effect domestic productivity increases. By establishing a foreign production facility, the company may be able to develop foreign sales without decreasing resource employment in the United States. In fact, it may hire additional domestic personnel to manage the international operations and receive dividends and royalties from the foreign use of its capital and technology, thus further increasing domestic income.

Home-country labor claims that jobs are exported through FDI.

Home-country losses   The United States is the home country for the largest amounts of foreign licensing and direct investment. Therefore, its policies understandably arouse some of the major critics of such outward movements. One of these critics is organized labor, which argues that foreign production often displaces what would otherwise be U.S. production. For example, a criticism of Zenith is that it shifted some production to Mexico from the United States because of NAFTA.[9] Critics also cite many examples of highly advanced technology that has been at least partially developed through governmental contracts and then transferred abroad. In fact, some U.S. MNEs are moving their most advanced technologies abroad and are even, in some cases, producing abroad before they do so in the United States. An example is Boeing's transfer of aerospace technology to China to produce aircraft parts. According to critics, if Boeing did not transfer the technology, China would purchase the products in the United States, thus increasing U.S. employment and output. These critics further argue that the technology transfer will speed the process of China's seizing control of future global aircraft sales. However, China might have bought aircraft from Airbus Industrie or developed the technology itself had Boeing not made the sale.[10]

Closely related to the question of job loss is the question of whether the outsourcing of production puts downward pressure on wages in the home country. On the one hand, there is anecdotal evidence that it does. For example, computer programmers in the United States make three to six times the monthly salary of programmers in India. Further, companies such as Texas Instruments now receive work done in India by private satellite link. So the possibility of moving more work to India has caused a recent drag on the real wages of U.S. programmers.[11] On the other hand, there is evidence that moves by companies to lower-wage countries increase the overall home-country demand and wages for skilled labor. This is because the cost savings from producing abroad increase demand for the products produced abroad, such as Nike shoes, thus increasing the need for Nike to hire more managerial personnel in the United States.[12]

Host-country gains Most observers agree that an inflow of investment by MNEs can initiate increased local development through a more optimum combination of unemployed production factors and the utilization or upgrading of resources. A company is motivated to move resources such as capital and technology abroad because the potential return is higher in an area where they are in shortage than in an area of abundance.

The mere existence of resources in a country is no guarantee they will contribute to output. MNEs may enable idle resources to be used. Oil production, for instance, requires not only the presence of underground deposits but also the knowledge of how to find them and the capital equipment to bring the oil to the surface. Production is useless without markets and transportation facilities, which an international investor may be able to supply. Access to foreign markets, particularly the investor's home market, may be particularly important to developing countries that lack the knowledge and resources necessary to sell there. An example is the sale of Mexican asparagus in the United States under the recognized Green Giant label. U.S. consumers associate the brand name with known quality; it might be prohibitively expensive for Mexican producers to gain the same brand recognition on their own.[13] Another less tangible aspect of FDI is greater resource utilization: Through exposure to new consumer products, the local labor force may develop new wants, which could encourage them to work longer and harder to acquire the additional goods and services.

MNEs' upgrading of resources may be brought about through educating local personnel to utilize equipment, technology, and modern production methods. Even such seemingly minor programs as those promoting on-the-job safety may result in a reduction of lost worker time and machine downtime. The transference of work skills increases efficiency, thereby freeing time for other activities. Further, additional competition may force existing companies to become more efficient.[14]

Host-country losses Some critics have claimed that there are examples of MNEs making investments that domestic companies otherwise would have undertaken. The result may be the displacement of local entrepreneurs and entrepreneurial drive or the bidding up of prices without additional output. Such critics argue, for example, that by their ability to raise funds in various countries, MNEs can reduce their capital cost relative to that of local companies and apply the savings either to attracting the best personnel or to enticing customers from competitors through greater promotional efforts. However, evidence for these arguments is inconclusive. MNEs frequently do pay higher salaries and spend more on promotion than local companies do, but it is uncertain whether these differences result from external advantages or represent required added costs of attracting workers and

Host countries may gain through
- **More optimal use of production factors**
- **Utilization of unemployed resources**
- **Upgrading of resource quality**

Host countries may lose if investments by MNEs
- **Replace local companies**
- **Take the best resources**
- **Destroy local entrepreneurship**
- **Decrease local R&D undertakings**

customers when entering new markets. Added compensation and promotion costs may negate any external cost advantages obtained from access to cheaper foreign capital. Additionally, in many instances, the local competition also has access to that cheaper capital.

Critics also contend that FDI destroys local entrepreneurial drive, which has an important effect on development. Since the expectation of success is necessary for the inauguration of entrepreneurial activity, the collapse of small cottage industries in the face of MNEs' consolidation efforts may make the local population feel incapable of competing. However, the presence of MNEs sometimes may increase the number of local companies in host-country markets since MNEs serve as role models that local talent can emulate.[15] Further, an MNE often buys many services, goods, and supplies locally and thus may stimulate local entrepreneurship. For example, automobile producers typically add less than half the value of an automobile at the factory, buying the remaining parts, subassemblies, and modules from suppliers.[16] In fact, true entrepreneurs will find areas in which to compete; consequently, in any country there are success stories that can be emulated.

There is considerable evidence that the lessening of dependence on FDI will lead to the deepening of local R&D activities, at least in countries that have reached a certain level of industrial development. For example, Japan, Korea, and Taiwan have been much more restrictive on FDI inflows than have Hong Kong, Malaysia, Singapore, and Thailand. The former countries spend much more on R&D as a percentage of gross domestic product than the latter ones. There is further evidence of a link between local R&D and the enhancement of a country's future competitive capability.[17] Recall from the opening case that China prefers for FDI to enter in the form of joint ventures with Chinese companies that have a base of product experience allowing them to absorb incoming technology easily. These joint ventures are contracted for a specific period of time; thus China's expectation is that Chinese companies will be able to build on the technology they absorb through independent and indigenous R&D of their own in the future.

Another argument is that investors have access to high technology abroad that they may use in their home countries. This access may prevent original developers from maintaining proprietary advantages. It may also prevent production from remaining in the country where the innovation originated as the product moves through the life cycle. For example, foreign investment, especially from Japan, has increased rapidly in high-tech industries in California's Silicon Valley. This may allow non-U.S. companies to develop competitive capacities in their home countries that are based on U.S. scientific and technical investments.[18] The ability of MNEs to make these investments may be due to a reluctance of U.S. capital suppliers to wait for potential long-term returns. As a result, there have been U.S. legislative proposals to limit foreign ownership and establish funding to assist start-up of high-tech enterprises.

Finally, critics frequently contend that MNEs absorb local capital, either by borrowing locally or by receiving investment incentives. This raises the local cost of funds and/or makes insufficient funds available to local companies. Subsidiaries have borrowed heavily in local markets and have exploited investment incentives. For example, 53 percent of the value of assets owned abroad by U.S. companies is financed by foreign debt.[19] The link to the ability of local companies to finance expansion is unclear. For MNEs to have a noticeable effect on capital availability in a country, the amount of funds diverted to those investors would have to be larger in relation to the size of the capital market than is probably the case. Further, few MNEs acquire all resources locally; the additional resources brought in usually should yield a gain for the economy.

Host countries at times have not only prohibited the entry of MNEs believed to inhibit local companies, but also restricted local borrowing by MNEs and provided incentives for them to locate in depressed areas in which resources are idle rather than scarce.

Of particular concern to many countries is the foreign purchase of local companies. The employment effects continue to be debated because of assumptions about what would have happened had the acquisition not taken place, particularly when it involves a company that is not doing well and is subsequently downsized. It is thus impossible to say for certain whether there was more or less employment because of the acquisition. For this reason, the employment effects of FDIs have been evaluated as both negative and positive.[20]

General conclusions   Clearly, not all MNE activities will have the same effect on growth in either the home or the host country; nor are the effects of MNEs' activities easily determined. Although there are dangers in attempting to categorize, the following generalizations are helpful in understanding the circumstances under which foreign investment is most likely to have a positive impact on the host country:[21]

FDI is more likely to generate growth
- **When the product or process is highly differentiated**
- **When the foreign investors have access to scarce resources**
- **In the more advanced LDCs**

1. *LDCs versus developed countries.* LDCs are less likely than developed countries to have domestic companies capable of undertaking investments similar to those in which foreign investors engage. Foreign investment in developing countries is therefore less likely to be simply a substitute for domestic investment; thus it yields more growth than if it were located in developed countries.

2. *Degree of product sophistication.* When the foreign investor undertakes to produce highly differentiated products or to introduce process technologies, it is less likely that local companies could undertake similar production on their own. The differentiation may derive from product style, quality, or brand name as well as from technology.

3. *Access to resources.* A foreign investor that has access to resources local companies cannot easily acquire is more likely to generate growth than merely to substitute for what local companies would otherwise do. Some of these resources are capital, management skills, and access to external markets.

4.   *Degree of development of the LDC.* Foreign investors are more likely to transfer technology and serve as role models for growth in the more economically advanced of the LDCs. In the least developed of these countries, the investment may have a negative impact on growth if it merely exploits cheap labor that otherwise would be subsisting.[22]

Political and Legal Impact of the MNE

Because of the size of many MNEs, there is much concern that they will undermine through political means the sovereignty of nation-states. The foremost concern is that an MNE will be used as a foreign-policy instrument of its home-country government.[23] That companies depend primarily on their home countries is illustrated by the fact that of the 100 largest companies in the *Fortune* 500 list, only 18 have a majority of their assets outside their home country and very few have a foreigner on their executive board. These companies are most internationalized in terms of their sales; however, fewer than half generate more than half their sales outside their home markets.[24] Because the home countries of most MNEs are industrial countries, it is understandable that this concern is taken most seriously in LDCs. But it is not restricted to them.

Two other sovereignty issues are raised less frequently. One is that the MNE may become independent of both the home and the host countries, making it difficult for either country to take actions considered to be in its best interests. The second is that the MNE might become so dependent on foreign operations that the host country can use it as a foreign-policy instrument against its home country or another country.

Extraterritoriality

Chapter 3 discussed extraterritoriality. Host countries generally abhor any weakening of their sovereignty over local business practices. MNEs fear situations in which home-country and host-country laws conflict, since settlement inevitably must be between governmental offices, with companies caught in the middle. Laws need not be in complete conflict for extraterritoriality to come into play. Those requiring companies to remit earnings or to pay taxes at home on foreign earnings certainly have affected foreign expansion and local governments' control over such expansion. Although extraterritoriality may result from legal differences between any two countries, and often does, the United States has been criticized the most for attempting to control U.S. companies abroad. The criticism has resulted from U.S. companies' dominance in FDI and from the extent of the U.S. government's efforts to control the companies' actions, such as through enforcement of trade restrictions and antitrust laws.

Trade restrictions   The primary focus of criticism has been the U.S. government's attempt to apply its Trading with the Enemy Act to foreign subsidiaries of U.S. companies to keep them from selling to certain unfriendly countries. Through a series of presidential orders, foreign subsidiaries have at times been prevented from making sales to such countries as Libya, Nicaragua, South Africa, and Vietnam, even though the orders violated the laws of some of the countries in which the subsidiaries were operating, such as France and Canada, which require that the sales be made. The Cuban situation has been a particularly thorny issue between Canada and the United States. Throughout most of the 1980s, the United States permitted foreign subsidiaries of U.S. companies to sell to Cuba; however, the Cuban Democracy Act of 1992 changed that. The result was adverse foreign opinion, especially in Canada, which led to discussions there on whether FDI from the United States should be limited and whether the Canada-U.S. free trade agreement should be reconsidered. And Canada was not alone in its concern. Recall the case on U.S-Cuban trade in Chapter 6. Subsidiaries of U.S. companies also were restricted from participating in the Arab boycott of Israel (now ignored by most Arab countries), even though the boycott was a foreign-policy instrument of the countries in which the subsidiaries are located.[25] A distinguishing feature of the Arab boycott of Israel was its provision for a **secondary boycott,** meaning that a company doing business with Israel was denied the ability to do business with a group of Arab countries. More recently, the United States has considered secondary boycotts against companies doing oil and gas business in Iran or Libya, a move that would be very unpopular among European governments and oil and gas companies.[26]

Antitrust laws   A second focus of criticism has been the U.S. government's antitrust actions. The United States has acted against domestic firms' foreign investments when there has been concern about possible harm to U.S. consumers.[27] At various times, the U.S. government has

- Delayed U.S. companies from acquiring facilities in foreign countries—for example, Gillette's purchase of Braun in Germany was held up
- Prevented U.S. companies from acquiring facilities in the United States that were owned by a company they were taking over abroad—for example, Gillette's purchase of a division of Sweden's Stora Kopparbergs Bergslags could not include that division's subsidiary, U.S. Wilkinson Sword
- Forced U.S. companies to sell their interests in foreign operations—for example, Alcoa's spin-off of Alcan
- Restricted entry of goods produced by foreign combines in which U.S. companies participated—for example, Swiss watches and parts
- Pressured foreign companies to allow U.S. firms to make foreign sales using technology acquired from them—for example, the British company Pilkington licensed float-glass technology to U.S. companies with the stipulation that the output could be sold only in the United States, but then permitted U.S.

companies to use the technology abroad after a suit was brought against its U.S. subsidiary[28]

The actions the companies were restrained from taking were legal in the countries in which they would have occurred. From a reverse standpoint, the United States objected to the EU's antitrust prosecution of IBM because it felt the EU did not have jurisdiction.

One cumbersome problem for U.S. companies has been the U.S. Justice Department's ambiguity regarding their relationships to other companies abroad. This ambiguity has been partially mitigated by the publication of foreign merger guidelines, including case situations illustrating how antitrust enforcement principles would be applied. Relationships that might be subject to challenge include participation in cartels to set prices or production quotas, granting of exclusive distributorships abroad, and formation of joint R&D and/or manufacturing operations in foreign countries. The United States also has signed a number of bilateral treaties with other industrialized countries that call for mutual consultation on restrictive business practices.

Key Sector Control

Political concerns include fear of
• Influence over or disruption of local politics
• Foreign control of sensitive sectors of the local economy

Closely related to the extraterritoriality issue is the fear that if foreign ownership dominates key industries, then decisions made outside of the country may have extremely adverse effects on the local economy or may exert an influence on local politics. This suggests two questions: Are the important decisions actually made outside the host countries? If so, are these decisions any different from those that would be made by local companies?

Many business decisions can and have been made centrally; examples are what, where, and how much to produce and sell and at what prices. These decisions might cause different rates of expansion in different countries and possible plant closings with subsequent employment disruption. Further, by withholding resources or allowing strikes, the MNE also may affect other local industries adversely.

Some observers argue that governments generally have more control over companies headquartered in their countries than over foreign companies' subsidiaries. Even MNEs with substantial operations abroad may have primary loyalty to their home countries. This loyalty arises because most MNEs have a majority of their assets, sales, employees, managers, and stockholders in their home countries. They depend on their home countries for most of their R&D and other innovations that enable them to compete globally. Their home-country governments have access to their global financial records and can tax them on their global earnings, which host-country governments cannot do. Further, MNEs can ask their home-country government for assistance in resolving conflicts of interest but cannot expect a foreign government to intercede on their behalf with the home-country government.[29] Given these factors, it is not surprising that in conflict situations companies tend to favor their home country's objectives over a host country's.

Political fears include the beliefs that international companies may serve as instruments of foreign policy for their home-country governments and that they also may be powerful enough to disrupt or influence local politics. The former fear is largely a carryover from colonial periods, when such companies as Levant and the British East India Company very often acted as a political arm of their home-country government. This fear has resurfaced in the case of Japanese investment in the United States. Critics have pointed out that the Japanese government and Japanese companies lobby strongly to affect U.S. government policy, such as to prevent new import restrictions on Japanese goods. Together they spend more than all political parties do for House and Senate elections, and more than the five most influential U.S. business organizations combined.[30] For example, a country that is very dependent on foreign investment may be pressured to take actions that are unpopular locally. For example, the U.S. government pressured Mexico to eliminate political dissidence in Chiapas to improve investor confidence, which meant keeping a tight lid on the politics of protest in an area of rural poor.[31]

Aside from establishing policies that generally restrict the entry of foreign investment, countries have selectively prevented foreign domination of so-called **key industries,** those that might affect a very large segment of the economy or population by virtue of their size or influence. Different countries view key industries differently. For example, NAFTA specifies that foreign investors from the three member countries generally are to be treated no less favorably than domestic investors are. But, because of different conceptions of what is "key," foreign ownership has been limited by Canada in cultural industries, by the United States in the airline and communications industries, and by Mexico in the energy and rail industries.[32] Many countries have nationalized foreign-owned mining, utility, and transportation companies. In other cases, governments have required management by local personnel in order to ensure that the industries can survive, if necessary, without foreign domination. In the United States, the President can halt any foreign investment that endangers national security, and although national security is not defined in the enabling legislation, enforcement has been extended to include economic security. In a few cases, governments have supported the development of competitive local companies to ward off foreign domination. These include consortia of computer manufacturers (for example, ICL in the United Kingdom, Telefunken and Nixdorf in Germany, and Siemens, CII, and Philips in Germany and the Netherlands) and consortia of aircraft producers (for example, Messerschmitt-Boelkow-Blohm in Germany, British Aerospace in the United Kingdom, Aeritalia in Italy, and Construcciones Aeronauticas in Spain).[33]

State-owned enterprises   When an MNE is a state-owned enterprise, the political concern about home-country control of the MNE is different only in degree. Although any MNE may in time of conflict favor home-country interests, the government-owned enterprise may be more prone to do so and do so more quickly. Government officials in the home country may be able to influence such a company more readily. Thomson Electonics, for example, a French state-owned MNE, announced it would close down its U.S. assembly operation in 1998 and move it to Mexico. Such cost-saving tactics were less possible in France because of French governmental interest in keeping jobs within France.

MNE Independence

The discussion so far has centered on the fear that MNEs are unduly influenced by their home-country governments. Many observers also fear that these companies can, by playing one country against another, avoid coming under almost any unfavorable restriction. For instance, if they do not like the wage rates, union laws, fair-employment requirements, or pollution and safety codes in one country, they can move elsewhere or at least threaten to do so. In addition, they can develop structures to minimize their payment of taxes anywhere.

This ability to play one country off against another, especially if the countries are within a regional trade agreement, is more likely to be evident when an MNE is negotiating initial permission to operate in a country. For example, Thailand and the Philippines, both members of ASEAN, vied with investment incentives to attract a GM car plant, whose output would be sold throughout the region.[34] (Similarly, foreign companies sometimes play one state against another when entering the United States.) However, the fact that companies, once operating, are generally reluctant to abandon fixed assets in one country to move abroad indicates that these charges are probably exaggerated. Further, the country from which a company moves can usually restrict importation of the goods it produces abroad under more favorable conditions.

Host-Country Captives

Critics have alleged that MNEs may become so dependent on foreign operations that they begin attempting to influence their home-country government to adopt policies favorable to the foreign countries, even when those policies may not be in the best interests of the home country. Such assertions are difficult to support because there is always disagreement on what policy actually will be in a country's "best interests." However, there certainly are many examples of lobbying efforts by MNEs seeking the adoption of policies that are more palatable to the foreign countries where they are doing business. For instance, many MNEs have lobbied against possible U.S. trade sanctions against China over its nonprotection of patents, trademarks, and copyrights because they fear that Chinese retaliation will hurt them.[35]

Bribery

No discussion of the impact of MNEs would be complete without mentioning payments to government officials. Investigations of U.S. MNEs in the 1970s and of Italian companies in the 1990s, along with much anecdotal information from various years, indicate that the practice has been widespread. MNEs as well as local companies have made payments to officials in industrial as well as developing countries.

The situation is complicated by the fact that there are cross-national differences in the rules governing payments. For example, the United States prohibits corporate payments to political parties, but most other countries do not. Also, even if two countries have similar laws on payments, one may enforce them and the other may not. The Berlin-based Transparency International assists citizens in setting up national chapters to try to fight local bribery, and it compiles an international corruption index calculated from surveys of businesspeople and journalists. The ranking of 54 countries is shown in Table 11.1.

An important motive for bribery is to secure government contracts that otherwise might not be forthcoming at all or to obtain them at the expense of competitors. For example, Foote, Cone & Belding Communications made payments to the Italian Health Ministry to obtain portions of an AIDS awareness ad campaign.[36] Another important motive is to facilitate governmental services that companies are

Table 11.1
International Corruption: A Survey of Business Perceptions

Rank	Country	Score 1996 (max = 10.00)	Score 1995 (max = 10.00)	Rank	Country	Score 1996 (max = 10.00)	Score 1995 (max = 10.00)
1	New Zealand	9.43	9.55	28	Greece	5.01	4.04
2	Denmark	9.33	9.32	29	Taiwan	4.98	5.08
3	Sweden	9.08	8.87	30	Jordan	4.89	—
4	Finland	9.05	9.12	31	Hungary	4.86	4.12
5	Canada	8.96	8.87	32	Spain	4.31	4.35
6	Norway	8.87	8.61	33	Turkey	3.54	4.10
7	Singapore	8.80	9.26	34	Italy	3.42	2.99
8	Switzerland	8.76	8.76	35	Argentina	3.41	3.24
9	Netherlands	8.71	8.69	36	Bolivia	3.40	—
10	Australia	8.60	8.80	37	Thailand	3.33	2.79
11	Ireland	8.45	8.57	38	Mexico	3.30	3.18
12	UK	8.44	8.57	39	Ecuador	3.19	—
13	Germany	8.27	8.14	40	Brazil	2.96	2.70
14	Israel	7.71	—	41	Egypt	2.84	—
15	USA	7.66	7.79	42	Colombia	2.73	3.44
16	Austria	7.59	7.13	43	Uganda	2.71	—
17	Japan	7.09	6.72	44	Philippines	2.69	2.77
18	Hong Kong	7.01	7.12	45	Indonesia	2.65	1.94
19	France	6.96	7.00	46	India	2.63	2.78
20	Belgium	6.84	6.85	47	Russia	2.58	—
21	Chile	6.80	7.94	48	Venezuela	2.50	2.66
22	Portugal	6.53	5.56	49	Cameroon	2.46	—
23	South Africa	5.68	5.62	50	China	2.43	2.16
24	Poland	5.57	—	51	Bangladesh	2.29	—
25	Czech Rep	5.37	—	52	Kenya	2.21	—
26	Malaysia	5.32	5.28	53	Pakistan	1.00	2.25
27	South Korea	5.02	4.29	54	Nigeria	0.69	—

The rank relates solely to results drawn from a number of surveys and reflects only the perception of business people who participated in these surveys. A perfect 10.00 would be a totally corrupt-free country. Same methods, but fewer countries and surveys were used to arrive at 1995 score.

Source: Financial Times, July 26, 1996, p. 3 using data from the Transparency Corruption Perception Index 1996. Reprinted with permission of FT Pictures/Graphics.

entitled to receive but that officials otherwise might delay, such as product registrations, construction permits, and import clearances. Other reported payments have been to reduce tax liabilities, to keep a competitor from operating in a specific country (by General Tire in Morocco), and to gain governmental approval for price increases (by a group of rubber companies in Mexico). Some companies have made payments because of extortion. For example, Mobil made payments to forestall the closing of its Italian refinery, and Boise Cascade, IBM, and Gillette made payments to protect the safety of their employees.

Most reported payments have been in cash, but in some cases they have included products made by the company, such as ITT's gift of a color TV set to a Belgian official. Some payments have been made directly to governmental officials by the companies; most, however, have been made via intermediaries and by diverse methods. For example, the relative of a person having influence over a purchasing decision sometimes has been put on the payroll as a consultant. In other cases, the person having influence has been paid as a middleman at a fee exceeding normal commissions. Another common practice has been to overcharge a government agency and rebate the overcharge to an individual, usually in a foreign country. One company (Pullman) even used its auditor to effect payment to a governmental official.

Bribery scandals have resulted in the replacement of chiefs of state in Honduras, Italy, and Japan. Officials have been jailed in a number of countries, including Pakistan, Iran, and Venezuela. Officials in a number of companies have resigned, been fined, or gone to jail.

In 1977, the United States passed the Foreign Corrupt Practices Act (FCPA), which makes certain payments to foreign officials illegal. One of the seeming inconsistencies in the act is that payments to officials to expedite their compliance with the law are legal, but payments to other officials who are not directly responsible for carrying out the law are not. For example, a $10,000 payment to a customs official to clear legally permissible merchandise is legal, but even a small payment to a government minister to influence the customs official is illegal.[37] The former payment is allowed because in many countries, governmental officials delay compliance of laws indefinitely until they do receive payments, even though such payments may be illegal in those countries.

Many critics of the FCPA have contended that U.S. firms lose much business because companies from many countries have not only been permitted to make bribery payments, but have also been able to take the expenses as a tax deduction. The CIA monitors bribery payments by non-U.S. companies so that the United States may put diplomatic pressure on foreign governments to stop the practices. The U.S. government has also unsuccessfully pushed other OECD countries to adopt legislation similar to the FCPA. Other countries argue that anticorruption laws might be seen as meddling in other countries' affairs.[38] However, OECD countries agreed not to allow tax deductions for overseas bribes as of 1997. The Organization of American States has also adopted a Convention Against Corruption, which calls for criminalizing bribery and the extradition of offenders.[39]

The U.S. legislation on bribery is controversial because
• **Some payments to expedite compliance with law are legal, but others are not**
• **Extraterritoriality issues emerge**
• **Business may be lost**

Although companies have been criticized for their bribes of foreign officials, attempts to stop the bribes, such as through FCPA, have been criticized on ethical grounds. One such criticism is due to the double standard for regulating payments by business versus those by governments. For example, U.S. governmental aid is frequently given as a bribe, with the understanding that the host country will grant political concessions in return. There is little effort to blame the donor when it is discovered that officials in host countries have siphoned off aid funds for themselves. Further, governments use high-level official visits and lobby aggressively for their home-based companies in order to help them gain foreign business. For example, the U.S. government has sometimes paid for ministry heads to visit the United States when a U.S. company is bidding on a contract, and has given scholarships to family members of officials that can provide business to U.S. companies.[40] A second inconsistency is that some bribes are allowed, but others are not. Further, some argue that judging the morality of bribery should be accompanied by consideration of the morality of interference with a custom that may be legally and culturally acceptable in a given country. In addition, it is sometimes argued that unethical "means" are justified to arrive at a desirable "end." For example, IBM and other U.S. companies claimed that the FCPA caused them to lose a contract for air traffic control systems in Mexico. They also alleged that their inability to make payments to Mexican authorities led to Mexico's installation of inferior technology.[41] It is debatable whether such an "end" would justify a bribe.

ETHICAL DILEMMAS & SOCIAL RESPONSIBILITY

Given the illegality of U.S. companies paying government officials abroad to get business, U.S. companies have devised legal means to ingratiate themselves with those officials. For example, the insurance company Chubb has set up an insurance program at a Chinese university and has put as board members some of the same officials who will decide the fate of Chubb's license application. Many companies, such as Hewlett-Packard in China, pay journalists to attend their news conferences, presumably so they will write favorably about the companies. So many companies pay for foreign officials to visit their plants in the United States, while simultaneously enjoying tourist attractions, that a spokesperson for the industry-funded U.S.-China Business Council said, "You'd think Disney World was a training site."[42]

In addition to extraterritoriality, there are a number of conflicting pressures on MNEs to follow certain practices abroad. For example, some governments have banned domestic sales of certain herbicides and pesticides, which some other governments have not. Most of the countries without restrictions on use are LDCs, where dangers from the use of the herbicides and pesticides are high because of the lack of consumer education and training. Also, it is legal to export from the countries that ban domestic sales.[43] If companies do export, they are accused of following dual standards of safety and contributing to poisonings in LDCs. If they refuse to export, they are accused of failing to help increase needed food supplies and/or the eradication of plants used to supply drug manufacture, such as coca plants in Peru. In addition, it is debatable how far companies should monitor the production of the goods they buy abroad or the way their exported products are used. For example, batteries contain hazardous lead, and in industrial countries, workers are required to wear outfits resembling spacesuits to work on rebuilding the batteries or processing them to re-use the lead. Yet, there is also a market to export used batteries to LDCs, such as the Philippines, where it is widely reported that workers in local companies lack safety attire and where lead fumes enter the atmosphere during the processing of the batteries. Some would argue that companies should make certain that any batteries they export are dealt with safely. Others would argue that they cannot afford to monitor conditions in a far off country and that the responsibility lies with the governments.

Finally, although there are pressures to prevent foreign companies from making payments to political parties, some companies argue that their avoidance of politics would be socially irresponsible. For example, Glaxo Wellcome, a British investor in the United States, donated to U.S. political-action committees during the 1996 U.S. elections, when such contributions became a political issue. Glaxo Wellcome's position was that it had 9,000 U.S. employees, paid U.S. taxes, and had a substantial effect on the U.S. economy; therefore, its donations were made to try to assure that policies would be in the best interest of its U.S. operations and employees.[44] If foreign-owned companies were prohibited from making payments directly to political parties, they might nevertheless be able to achieve political loyalty by paying for controversial public relations and lobbying efforts. For example, the government of Taiwan spends heavily in the United States to influence opinion leaders through academic and cultural exchange programs, and it hired Cassidy & Associates, a lobbying group, to help persuade the U.S. Congress to vote in favor of granting a visa for President Lee Teng-hui to visit Cornell University.

There is also a dual standard concerning pressures on behalf of foreign-owned companies versus pressures on behalf of foreign countries. This is particularly true concerning the U.S. foreign aid program. Critics argue that the allocation of aid is more dependent on lobbying efforts than on either advancing U.S. political interests around the world or helping countries advance their social and economic efforts. For example, Israel is by far the largest recipient of U.S. foreign aid (it receives about 20 percent), even though it is now a high-income country with a population of only about 5.6 million. This is largely because Israeli supporters raise millions of dollars of campaign funds for both Democrats and Republicans in the United States. Meanwhile, India has only 2 percent of Israel's per capita income and has almost a billion inhabitants, yet it receives only 4 percent of what Israel receives from the United States in economic and humanitarian aid.[45]

National Differences in Attitudes toward MNEs

In theory, host countries may take completely restrictive or laissez-faire positions toward MNEs. In actuality, their policies fluctuate over time but are seldom completely restrictive or completely laissez-faire. Currently, countries such as Bhutan and Cuba are close to the restrictive end, and countries such as the United States and the Netherlands are near the laissez-faire end of the continuum. However, countries between these extremes have policies with varying degrees of restrictions as they attempt to attract investment and receive the most benefit from it.

The Impact of the Multinational Enterprise in the Internationalization Process

The concern of home- and host-country stakeholders about companies' international operations increases with their international commitments. For example, home-country stakeholders are generally unconcerned when a company begins to export, but they are concerned when the company begins producing abroad because of fear that jobs and growth are being transferred. Likewise, host-country stakeholders give much more attention to foreign companies that are wholly owned direct investors than those who share ownership locally or those that are merely exporting into their market. This greater attention occurs because the company now employs local personnel, and with full ownership, the company may be able to pursue global or home-country objectives at the expense of local ones. Therefore, companies' needs to justify their operations grow in tandem with their increased international commitment.

Countries tend to be more concerned about large companies than small ones because of their greater potential impact on national economic and political objectives. But not all companies operating internationally are large. In fact, the number of new MNEs is growing at about 4,000 to 5,000 per year.[46] These are generally smaller companies with smaller foreign investments. Generally, they have to do less to justify their entry and operations. Because they are assumed to have less impact on host societies, countries often treat their entries differently. Further, many LDC governments prefer the entry of smaller companies because they may be more willing to yield to host-country wishes, increase competition because of their numbers, and supply smaller-scale technology more suited to LDC needs.[47]

The perception of a company's operations in one country may have an effect on the perception of stakeholders in other countries as well. For example, a company's confrontation with labor, tax authorities, or environmental pressure groups in one country may cause similar stakeholders in another country to be wary of the company's behavior. Further, as communications have become more rapid, negative publicity about company practices has become more extensive. As a company expands to more countries, the possibility of widescale negative perceptions about its impact increases.

Operational Impact of International Business Activities

The relationship between MNEs and societies has generated so many allegations and controversies that it is impossible to examine all of them in this chapter. A number of them deal not so much with whether international business should take place but rather with certain practices. In these cases, the targets are specific operational areas of management that, fortunately, can be examined in later chapters of this book. They are no less important than the overall areas discussed in this chapter and are listed here to illustrate the wide range of criticisms:

- In transferring technology to LDCs, MNEs set prices too high and restrict sales too stringently (Chapter 14).
- MNEs' centralization and control of key functions in their home countries perpetuate the neocolonial dependence of LDCs (Chapter 15).
- Sensitive information about countries is disseminated internationally by MNEs' global intelligence networks (Chapter 15).
- MNEs introduce superfluous products that do not contribute to social needs and that perpetuate class distinctions (Chapter 16).
- MNEs avoid paying taxes (Chapter 19).
- Through artificial transfer pricing, MNEs undermine attempts by governments to manage their countries' economic affairs (Chapter 20).
- The best jobs are given to citizens of the country in which an MNE has its headquarters (Chapter 21).
- Inappropriate technology is introduced into LDCs by MNEs (Chapter 21).
- National labor interests are undermined because of MNEs' global activities (Chapter 21).

COUNTERVAILING
FORCES

This entire chapter is essentially about countervailing forces. How do they affect a company's ability to choose a global versus a multidomestic strategy? Stakeholders, at home and abroad, seldom look specifically at the strategies MNEs follow; rather, they look at whether MNEs satisfy their interests. Fortunately for MNEs, satisfying stakeholders' interests is seldom a zero-sum situation; therefore MNEs—whether following global or multidomestic practices—usually can demonstrate positive impacts from their operations on the objectives of both home and host countries. For example, employment effects may be positive on both home and host countries, whether or not domestic and foreign operations are highly independent of each other. An MNE thus may have considerable, but not complete, latitude in deciding to produce separately for each market or to integrate its production substantially among the markets. This is because either option, if successful, will lead to employment in both the home and host countries. Furthermore, an

MNE may be able to centralize production and export into other markets because importing countries are willing to forgo local production in order to satisfy pressures from consumers.

In spite of the rivalry among countries and their desire to influence MNEs to serve their interests, countries frequently have acted cooperatively in dealing with MNEs. These dealings will be discussed extensively in Chapter 12.

LOOKING TO THE FUTURE

As long as there is nationalism, governments will try to garner a larger share of the benefits from the activities of MNEs. In the short term, most countries will probably welcome FDI. Debt problems limit the ability of LDCs to access sufficient capital, except through investment inflows. Budget- and trade-deficit problems are likely to make the United States take a positive stance toward receiving FDI. The EU probably will welcome investment inflows to attain the growth its unification is aimed at. However, in the longer term, FDI may be less welcome. Historically, the attitudes toward FDI have tended to vary, leaning toward more restrictions when economies are thriving. Yet, it is possible that if rapid growth does not occur in some LDCs and HPEs after they receive substantial FDI, they may learn to regard as models such countries as Japan and South Korea, which have grown rapidly without much FDI.

Where MNEs are controlled will continue to be an issue. Some MNEs (such as Nestlé, SKF, ABB, ICI, CPC, Coca-Cola, and Heinz) now have so many nationalities represented in their top management ranks, it is difficult to accuse them of favoring home-country interests. However, their internationalization leaves them open to the criticism of acting in their own, rather than national, interests. On the other hand, some MNEs (including Sandoz, Volvo, Michelin, Matsushita, and United Technologies) have few shares held outside their home countries and practically no foreigners in high-level corporate positions.[48]

WEB CONNECTION

Check out our home page for links to World Wide Web resources on global strategies and foreign direct investment.

Summary

- **Management must understand the need to compromise and to satisfy the conflicting interests of stockholders, employees, customers, and society at large. Internationally, the problem is more complex because the relative strengths of competing groups vary among countries. Further, satisfying interests in one country may cause dissatisfaction in another.**

- The effects of **MNEs** are difficult to evaluate because of conflicting influences on different countries' objectives, intervening variables that obscure cause-effect relationships, and differences among **MNEs'** practices. Countries are interested not only in their absolute gains or losses but also in their performance relative to other countries.

- Since a balance-of-payments surplus in one country must result in a deficit elsewhere, trade and investment transactions have been scrutinized closely for their effects. However, countries often are willing to accept short-term deficits in order to achieve a long-term surplus or other economic gains.

- The basic effects of **FDI** on a country's balance of payments theoretically can be determined, but disagreements exist about many assumptions that must be made concerning the relationship between such investment and trade. Projects differ so much that it is difficult to generalize and to make effective policies that apply to large groups of investors.

- Governments have attempted to use **FDI** to improve their balance-of-payments positions through regulating capital flows, requiring partial local ownership, limiting local borrowing by foreign investors, and stipulating that a part of capital inflows must be in the form of loans rather than equity.

- The growth and employment effects of **MNEs** do not necessarily benefit one country at the expense of another. Many of these effects are due to the relative employment of resources with and/or without the **MNEs'** activities.

- **MNEs** may contribute to growth and employment by enabling idle resources to be used, using resources more efficiently, and upgrading resources' quality.

- The factors affecting growth and employment include the location in which **MNEs** operate, product sophistication, competitiveness of local companies, governmental policies, and degree of product differentiation.

- Political concerns about **MNEs** center around the fear that they may be used as foreign-policy instruments of home-country or host-country governments or that they may avoid the control of any government.

- Extraterritoriality is the application of home-country laws to the operations of companies abroad. This sometimes leads to conflicts between home and host countries and may put an **MNE** in the untenable position of having to violate the laws of one country or the other.

- **Countries most fear foreign control of key sectors in their economies because decisions made abroad may disrupt local economic and political stability. Further, the foreign investors then may have enough power to adversely affect local sovereignty. Thus foreign ownership in key sectors of countries' economies often is restricted.**

Case
Foreign Real-Estate
Holdings in the
United States[49]

Compared to other countries, the United States has relatively few restrictions on foreign investors. Foreign control is prohibited in only a handful of industries, primarily in the areas of transportation and communication. These prohibitions have resulted because of the importance of these areas in moving essential commodities and informing the public in time of crisis. Historically, the only period in which there was a widespread concern in the United States about foreign ownership was in the late nineteenth century, when temporary prohibitions were placed on foreign ownership of agricultural land. This history does not mean that direct investment cannot be prohibited. In 1989, the United States passed legislation to prevent takeovers that, based on a case-by-case examination, would adversely affect national security. Further, the attitudes toward foreign investment in the United States, especially in land, have fluctuated widely. For example, there was much concern about foreign investment in the United States in the mid-1970s and late 1980s, but practically no concern in the early 1980s and mid-1990s. But given the changing opinions, there are always possibilities that new restrictions will be placed on foreign ownership.

The United States also has been a relatively safe place for investments. The only confiscations have been of properties held by interests from enemy countries during the two world wars and of Iranian assets when U.S. embassy personnel were held as hostages in Iran. More recently, Libyan and Kuwaiti assets were frozen but not expropriated. (The Revolutionary War could be seen as a confiscation of thirteen English investments.) No wars have been fought on U.S. land for over a hundred years; thus the loss of property through political unrest has been negligible. The low political risk, along with relatively low land prices and expected sustainable U.S. economic growth, have made the United States the largest FDI recipient in the world. A 1996 survey among leading real estate investors from outside the United States indicated that 81 percent and 77 percent felt the United States was a better place for real estate investment than Europe and Southeast Asia, respectively.

After World War II, direct investment flows went out of the United States as U.S. companies took advantage of ample resources, a strong dollar, and a welcome from foreign governments to establish facilities. In the late 1960s, the U.S. Department of Commerce established offices to lure investors to the United States, and several states began including foreign companies in their industrial promotion efforts. Although direct investment into the United States accelerated, the movement went largely unnoticed by the general public, in part because no approval by U.S. authorities was necessary before making such an investment. It was not even necessary to register anywhere that a foreign investment had been made. Many of the investors maintained a low profile and were not known, even by governmental officials, to be foreigners.

The 1973 oil embargo and the publicity about the substantial influx of direct investment to the United States during the next few years led to Congress's adopting legislation to survey the extent of FDI and practices of foreign investors in the United States. Subsequent legislation requiring foreign investors to report the establishment of a new U.S. business or acquisition of an interest in an existing U.S. business became effective in 1979. However, this has not been enough to assure people who are concerned about the foreign influx. The purchase of Rockefeller Center by Mitsubishi bolstered U.S. nationalistic feelings. A 1988 poll showed that 78 percent of people in the United States favor "a law to limit the extent of foreign investment in American business and real estate."

Some criticism of foreign investment in the United States is in response to the more stringent control of such investment in other countries. The attitude is summed up as "Why don't we treat them as harshly as they treat us?" Much of the concern, however, has focused on specific key sectors deemed vital to national interests, including banking, food, computers, high technology, oil, and coal. One area that has been singled out is real estate, especially agricultural and residential land.

The Agricultural Foreign Investment Disclosure Act of 1978 requires that agriculture land transfers to foreigners be reported. There are no reporting requirements for other types of real estate purchases by foreigners. The interest in real estate has evolved primarily because it is a sector with a historical emotional tie for Americans. The country was largely settled by landless persons who were able to better themselves economically because of the availability of free or cheap land; thus any threat of foreign control of real estate has been viewed negatively. Even after the disappearance of the western frontier, land has been valued because of the high priority placed on relatively cheap agricultural products and on housing. Numerous reports have alleged that large foreign real-estate purchases tended to inflate prices, especially in Hawaii where there has been much Japanese investment. Many in the United States fear that rising prices will put land out of reach of the average American. Some also fear that agricultural output will be exported abroad rather than being sold to Americans.

But how widespread is foreign ownership? Figure 11.2 shows that foreigners owned about $27 billion in U.S. real estate by the end of 1995. The vast bulk of this was in commercial properties by foreign institutional investors. The U.S. Department of Agriculture estimates that less than 0.5 percent of U.S. farmland is owned by foreign investors, and much of this has been acquired by foreign paper companies such as Bowater of the United Kingdom and Abitibi of Canada. Considerable publicity also has been given to foreign purchases of housing and office buildings, particularly by Japanese investors, who own about one third of the value of foreign investment in U.S. property, and especially in Miami, Honolulu, and Los Angeles (three areas in which foreign purchasers have been very active).

Although no federal restrictions have been enacted in the United States, twenty of the fifty states have restrictions on ownership of property by foreigners. Only three states (Iowa, Missouri, and Minnesota) have singled out agricultural property for special treatment. They did this in the late 1970s because of fear that foreign purchases would cause farmland prices to jump. In fact, the prices plummeted in the early 1990s, as did Japanese investment in U.S. property. By the mid-1990s, many Japanese companies had sold their

**Figure 11.2
Foreign Direct
Investment Position in
U.S. Real Estate**
As foreign ownership in
U.S. real estate grew in the
1980s, so did the criticism
of it; however, as the value
decreased in the 1990s,
the criticism of foreign
ownership also decreased.

Source: Association of Foreign
Investors in U.S. Real Estate
(AFIRE) (Washington: AFIRE,
1997).

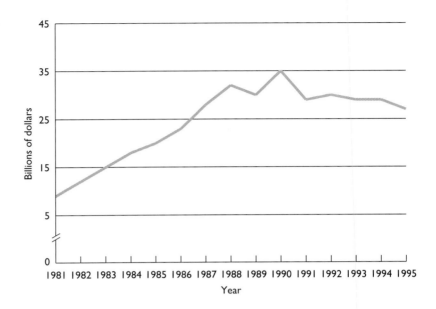

U.S. real estate investments at large losses, including Mitsubishi's ownership of Rockefeller
Center. Basically, many Japanese investors had bought near the peak of a market with rising
real estate prices, expecting that the trend would continue. U.S. landowners, real-estate
brokers, and investment bankers have since sought out foreign buyers, especially from
China, Hong Kong, and Taiwan.

Questions

1. In the interests of the United States, should federal restrictions be placed on the foreign
   acquisition of real estate?
2. If restrictions were implemented, what should they cover (for example, type of land,
   nationality of purchaser, use of land, or size of holdings)?
3. Should foreign ownership be restricted in economic sectors other than real estate?
4. What are the likely consequences if the United States does or does not place new limitations on foreign real estate investments?

Chapter Notes

1. The quotation is from Jonathan Kwitny,
   "U.S. Concerns Export Mainland-Bound
   Goods as Embargo Loosens," *Wall Street
   Journal,* March 11, 1971, p. 1. Other data
   were taken from "Motorola Invests
   US$720 Million in China Plants,"
   (http://www.idgchina.com/news/
   motorola.htm); "What's New: Canadian
   Investment in China," week of September
   2, 1996 (http://www.ccbc.com/
   investment.phtml); Paulus Chan, "Doing
   Business in China: Trade, Legal and Cultural Considerations," *Nonwovens Indus-*

   try, February 1996; "China Investment
   Opportunities" (http://www.aloha.com/
   ~uci/chinainv/500.htm); Robert F. Dodds,
   Jr., "Offsets in Chinese Government Procurement: The Partially Open Door," *Law
   and Policy in International Business,* Vol. 26,
   No. 4, June 22, 1995, p. 1119; Aimin Yan
   and Barbara Gray, "Bargaining Power,
   Management Control, and Performance
   in United States–China Joint Ventures: A
   Comparative Case Study," *Academy of
   Management Journal,* Vol. 37, December
   1994, p. 1478; Stanely Lubman, "What

   Dispute? Conflicts Between Chinese and
   Foreign Partners in Joint Ventures," *China
   Business Review,* Vol. 22, No. 3, May 1995,
   p. 46; "Guangzhou Evaluates Foreign
   Investment," *Xinhua News Agency,* Feb-
   ruary 17, 1995; Gregory E. Osland and
   Tamer S. Cavusgil, "Performance Issues in
   U.S.-China Joint Ventures," *California
   Management Review,* January 1996,
   p. 106; Cathy Chen, "Young Chinese
   Loosen the Purse Strings," *Wall Street
   Journal,* July 15, 1996, p. A8; Nicholas
   Reynolds, "End of an Era Flagged as

Garment Giant Crosses the Border," *South China Morning Post,* May 29, 1995, p. Business 3.

2. Jean J. Boddewyn and Thomas L. Brewer, "International-Business Political Behavior: New Theoretical Directions," *Academy of Management Review,* Vol. 19, 1994, pp. 119–143.

3. John H. Dunning, "The Future of Multinational Enterprise," *Lloyds Bank Review,* July 1974, p. 16.

4. John H. Dunning, "Re-evaluating the Benefits of Foreign Direct Investment," *Transnational Corporations,* Vol. 3, No. 1, February 1994, pp. 23–51, refers to these as *knowledge-based assets.*

5. See also Paul Krugman, "A Country Is Not a Company," *Harvard Business Review,* January–February, 1996, pp. 40–51.

6. Gillian Tett, "Government Aid 'At Lowest Level for 20 Years,'" *Financial Times,* February 13, 1996, p. 7, using OECD data for 1986 through 1994.

7. Nancy Dunne, "Greedy Image of U.S. Multinationals 'Overstated,'" *Financial Times,* August 10, 1995, p. 3, referring to study by Economic Strategy Institute.

8. International Monetary Fund, *International Capital Markets: Developments, Prospects and Policy Issues* (Washington: IMF, 1995).

9. Jeremy Madsen, "NAFTA Downsizing," *Multinational Monitor,* October 1995, pp. 7–8.

10. Jeff Cole, Marcus W. Brauchli, and Craig S. Smith, "Orient Express," *Wall Street Journal,* October 13, 1995, p. A1; Craig Smith and David P. Hamilton, "Price of Entry Into China Rises Sharply," *Wall Street Journal,* December 19, 1995, p. A12.

11. Keith Bradsher, "Skilled Workers Watch Their Jobs Migrate Overseas," *New York Times,* August 28, 1995, p. A1, quoting opinions of Jagdish Bhagwati.

12. Robert Feenstra and Gordon Hanson, "Foreign Investment, Outsourcing, and Relative Wages" (Cambridge, MA: National Bureau of Economic Research, Working Paper No. 5121, 1995). See also Fred R. Bleakley, "U.S. Firms Shift More Office Jobs Abroad," *Wall Street Journal,* April 22, 1996, p. A2.

13. David M. Henneberry, "U.S. Foreign Direct Investment in the Developing Nations: A Taxonomy of Host-Country Policy Issues," *Agribusiness,* Vol. 2, No. 1, 1986, p. 97.

14. Ignatius J. Horstmann and James R. Markusen, "Firm Specific Assets and the Gains from Direct Foreign Investment," *Economica,* February 1989, pp. 41–48.

15. Emilio Paguolatos, "Foreign Direct Investment in U.S. Food and Tobacco

Manufacturing and Domestic Economic Performance," *American Journal of Agricultural Economics,* Vol. 65, No. 2, May 1983, pp. 405–412.

16. "The Road Ahead," *Financial Times,* August 26, 1996, p. 16.

17. Sanjaya Lall, *Changing Perceptions of Direct Foreign Investment in Development* (Antwerp: University of Antwerp, CIMBDA discussion paper No. E19, 1995).

18. David J. Teece, "Foreign Investment and Technological Development in Silicon Valley," *California Management Review,* Vol. 34, No. 2, Winter 1992, pp. 88–106.

19. Martin Feldstein, "Outbound FDI Increases National Income," *NBER Digest,* August 1994, p. 4.

20. See, for example, Thomas Omestad, "Selling Off America," *Foreign Policy,* No. 76, Fall 1989, pp. 119–140; "Foreign Investment in the United States," Hearing before the Subcommittee on Economic Stabilization of the Committee on Banking, Finance and Urban Affairs, House of Representatives, Serial No. 101-65 (Washington, D.C.: U.S. Government Printing Office, 1989), pp. 21–23; and Edward M. Graham and Paul R. Krugman, *Foreign Direct Investment in the United States* (Washington, D.C.: Institute for International Economics, 1990).

21. U.S. Department of Commerce, *The Multinational Corporation: Studies on U.S. Foreign Investment,* Vol. 1 (Washington, D.C.: 1972), p. 61.

22. Jonghoe Yang and Russell A. Stone, "Investment Dependence, Economic Growth, and Status in the World System: A Test of 'Dependent Development,'" *Studies in Comparative International Development,* Vol. 20, No. 1, Spring 1985, pp. 98–120.

23. For a good discussion of various means of gaining political objectives through economic dependency, see Adrienne Armstrong, "The Political Consequences of Economic Dependence," *Journal of Conflict Resolution,* Vol. 25, No. 3, September 1981, pp. 401–428.

24. Winfried Ruigrok, "Why Nationality Is Still Important," *Financial Times,* January 5, 1996, p. 8, referring to 1993 data from Winfried Ruigrok and Rob van Tulder, *The Logic of International Restructuring* (London: Routledge, 1995).

25. See, for example, "Anti-Boycott Charges Are Settled by Fines for Nine Companies," *Wall Street Journal,* October 13, 1983, p. 16; and Elizabeth Weiner and Laurence J. Tell, "Out of South Africa: Divestment Hits a Snag," *Business Week,* July 6, 1987, p. 53.

26. Afshin Molavi, "Senate Targets Libya Investors," *Financial Times,* December 22, 1995, p. 5; Robert S. Greenberger and Laurie Lande, "Europeans Are Irked by Senate Move to Punish Foreign Investments in Libya," *Wall Street Journal,* December 22, 1995, p. A4; "Iran Scorns U.S. Plan to Step Up Sanctions," *Financial Times,* December 6, 1995, p. 7; Afshin Molavi and Bruce Clark, "Clinton Ready to Tighten Iran Stranglehold," *Financial Times,* November 17, 1995, p. 4.

27. Eduardo Lachica, "U.S. Decides to Enforce Antitrust Laws Against Collusion by Foreign Concerns," *Wall Street Journal,* April 7, 1992, p. C9.

28. These are but a few of the types of antitrust actions. See J. Townsend, "Extraterritorial Antitrust Revisited— Half a Century of Change," paper presented at the Academy of International Business, San Francisco, December 1983; "U.S. Seeks to Block Gillette's Purchase of Wilkinson Assets," *Wall Street Journal,* January 11, 1990, p. B6; and "U.S. Wins Accord With British on Glass Factories," *Wall Street Journal,* May 27, 1994, p. A12.

29. Yao-Su Hu, "Global or Stateless Corporations Are National Firms with International Operations," *California Management Review,* Vol. 34, No. 2, Winter 1992, pp. 107–126.

30. Pat Choate, "Political Advantage: Japan's Campaign for America," *Harvard Business Review,* Vol. 68, No. 5, September–October 1990, pp. 87–103.

31. Richard Falk, "Toward Obsolescence: Sovereignty in the Era of Globalization," *Harvard International Review,* Summer 1995, pp. 34–35+.

32. "What Is NAFTA?" *Wall Street Journal,* September 15, 1993, p. A16.

33. Tim Carrington, "Europe's Plan to Build New Fighter Plane Puts Western Firms on Cutthroat Course," *Wall Street Journal,* May 23, 1988, p. 10.

34. Edward Luce and Ted Bardacke, "Thailand and Philippines Compete for $1bn Car Plant," *Financial Times,* December 5, 1995, p. 1.

35. Richard Waters, "U.S. Big Business Fears Sanctions," *Financial Times,* May 16, 1996, p. 4.

36. Maureen Kline, "Three U.S.-Related Companies Dragged into Italian Investigation," *Wall Street Journal,* June 25, 1993, p. A7.

37. John S. Estey and David W. Marston, "Pitfalls (and Loopholes) in the Foreign Bribery Law," *Fortune,* October 9, 1978, pp. 182–188.

38. Robert S. Greenberger, "Foreigners Use Bribes to Beat U.S. Rivals in Many Deals, New Report Concludes," *Wall Street Jour-*

nal, October 12, 1995, p. 3; Robert Keatley, "U.S. Campaign Against Bribery Faces
Resistance from Foreign Governments,"
Wall Street Journal, February 4, 1994,
p. A6.
39. Nancy Dunne, "Kantor Calls for Bribery
Action," *Financial Times,* July 26, 1996,
p. 3.
40. Dana Milbank and Marcus W. Brauchli,
"Greasing Wheels," *Wall Street Journal,*
September 29, 1995, p. A1+.
41. "Mexico Asks IBM for Proof of Alleged
Bribe Request," *Wall Street Journal,* February
8, 1993. For the means-versus-end discussion, see Kent Hodgson, "Adapting Ethical
Decisions to a Global Marketplace," *Management Review,* May 1992, pp. 53–57.
42. Ibid.
43. Michael Harvey, "Marketing of Banned Pesticides and Unapproved Pharmaceuticals to
Developing Countries," *Journal of Global
Marketing,* Vol. 9, No. 3, 1996, pp. 67–93.
44. Marcus W. Brauchli, Matthew Rose, and
Jonathan Friedland, "Foreign Donors: We
Have a Stake in America, Too," *Wall Street
Journal,* October 31, 1996, p. A19.
45. Albert R. Hunt, "More Foreign Aid, but
Less for Israel," *Wall Street Journal,* March
27, 1997, p. A23.
46. John H. Dunning, "Re-evaluating the Benefits of Foreign Direct Investment," *Transnational Corporations,* Vol. 3, No. 1, February
1994, pp. 23–51.

47. Shujaat Islam, "Producing Prosperity: Multinationals in the Developing World," *Harvard International Review,* Spring 1993,
pp. 42–44.
48. William J. Holstein, Stanley Reed, Jonathan
Kapstein, Todd Vogel, and Joseph Weber,
"The Stateless Corporation," *Business
Week,* May 14, 1990, p. 103.
49. Data for the case were taken primarily
from "Foreign Share of Farms, 0.5%," *New
York Times,* January 28, 1980, p. D1; *International Report,* July 25, 1979, p. 3; "Overview
of Restrictions on Foreign Ownership of
Agricultural Land in the United States,"
unpublished report of the law offices of
Dechert Price & Rhoads, submitted to the
International Business Forum of Pennsylvania Briefing Courses, 1980; Cindy Skrzycki
and Maureen Walsh, "America on the Auc-
tion Block," *U.S. News & World Report,*
March 30, 1987, pp. 56–58; Pat Houston,
"Buy Your North 40 While It's Dirt-
Cheap," *Business Week,* April 20, 1987,
p. 92; Walter S. Mossberg, "Most Ameri-
cans Favor Laws to Limit Foreign Invest-
ment in U.S., Poll Finds," *Wall Street Journal,*
March 8, 1988, p. 28; Cynthia F. Mitchell,
"Buying America," *Wall Street Journal,* April
28, 1988, p. 1; Elisabeth Rubinfien, "The
Price Is Right," *Wall Street Journal,* June 15,
1988, p. 1+; Joan Lebow, "The Flow of
Money into Real Estate," *Wall Street Journal,*
July 24, 1989, p. B1; "Is U.S. Real Estate

Leaving the Japanese Cold?" *Business Week,*
July 23, 1990, p. 20; David Bailey, George
Harte, and Roger Sugden, "U.S. Policy
Debate Towards Inward Investment,"
Journal of World Trade, No. 26, 1992,
pp. 65–90; Rick Wartzman, "Keep Out,"
Wall Street Journal, November 2, 1992, p.
A1+; Mitchell Pacelle, "Japanese Investors
in U.S. Real Estate Finally Take Big Losses
on Soured Assets," *Wall Street Journal,* April
19, 1994, p. A2; Mitchell Pacelle, "Japan's
Banks Sell More Real Estate In U.S. at Big
Losses," *Wall Street Journal,* December 5,
1995, p. A5; "Famed Plaza on the Ropes
But Not Yet Out," *South China Morning
Post,* May 13, 1995, Business 5; Richard
Waters and Emiko Terazono, "Mitsubishi
Estate Gives Up Rockefeller Center,"
Financial Times, September 13, 1995, p. 18;
Mitchell Pacelle, "Japanese Seek to Sell
More U.S. Real Estate," *Wall Street Journal,*
June 6, 1994, p. A2; Damon Darlin,
"What's In a Name?" *Forbes,* October 9,
1995, p. 58; Viki Reath, "Foreign Investors
List D.C., Atlanta First for Real Estate,"
Washington Times October 28, 1996,
p. D13; and interview with James A. Fet-
gatter, Chief Executive of Association of
Foreign Investment in U.S. Real Estate,
February 28, 1997.

Chapter 12

International Business Negotiations and Diplomacy

*Without trouble
there is no profit.*

—African (Hausa) Proverb

Objectives	
	• To show the complementarity of interests between countries and **MNEs**
	• To illustrate negotiations between business and government in an international context
	• To trace the changing involvements of home-country governments in the settlement of **MNEs'** disputes with host governments
	• To clarify the role of public affairs and political behavior by companies in international business
	• To explain the position of companies and governments in the uneven global enforcement of intellectual property rights

Case
Saudi Aramco[1]

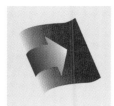

As of 1996 the ten companies holding the largest oil reserves in the world were all state-owned companies. Although there were well over a hundred companies worldwide, these ten held 77 percent of the world's oil reserves and 60 percent of global gas reserves. The giant among all these companies is Saudi Aramco, which ranks first in terms of sales and reserves and third in terms of refining. Because of concern about future global supplies of energy sources, Saudi Aramco has recently been able to use its strong reserve position in petroleum and natural gas to bolster its bargaining position when gaining FDI abroad. In other words, Saudi Aramco has been able to promise future energy supplies in exchange for permission to gain ownership on acceptable terms in foreign refining and marketing. However, the holding of supplies has not always been that advantageous in bargaining. When supplies greatly exceeded demand, petroleum producers without integrated refining and marketing operations were basically price-takers. The one exception was when OPEC was able to withhold supplies sufficiently to affect prices; however, recent lack of agreement among OPEC producers along with increased output by non-OPEC countries have influenced Saudi Aramco to secure foreign sales through international vertical integration.

The fact that Saudi Aramco is owned by the Saudi government means that it is difficult to separate Saudi Aramco's policies from those of the Saudi Arabian government. In fact, in 1995, the Aramco CEO Ali Naimi was appointed Saudi Arabia's oil minister. Further, many of Saudi Aramco's foreign deals are with state-owned oil companies, thus bringing into play the governmental interests of other countries. However, even before the Saudi government took control of Saudi Aramco (then called Aramco), the company's policies and division of earnings depended heavily on interactions among the private U.S. oil companies that owned the company, the Saudi Arabian government, and the U.S. government. As the objectives and power of these three parties evolved, so did the operations of Aramco. Reviewing some events that preceded and followed Aramco's first oil output in 1939 will help you understand these changing relationships and Saudi Aramco's recent strategy.

U.S. policy toward U.S. oil companies historically has included such objectives as ensuring sufficient and cheap oil supplies for U.S. needs and strengthening the U.S. political position in strategic areas worldwide. At least as far back as 1920, the United States realized that in the long term its domestic oil supplies would be insufficient. In the short term, however, worldwide oil supplies could not easily be sold as rapidly as they could be produced. In this environment, U.S. oil companies were in a position to serve both U.S. and Middle Eastern interests. (Map 12.1 shows the dominance of the Middle East in percentage of proven oil reserves.) In the 1920s and 1930s, the U.S. government wanted U.S. oil companies to gain concessions in the Middle East to help assure a long-term U.S. supply and to weaken the relative positions of the British and the French. The U.S. companies were welcomed in the Middle East because they offered some sales in the United States that would otherwise be impossible.

The first two companies to participate in Saudi Arabian oil production were Socal (Standard Oil of California) and Texaco, which formed a joint venture and negotiated large concessions in the 1930s. They built Saudi Arabia's first schools and compiled its first historical records. The U.S. government had no representatives there at that time, so the two

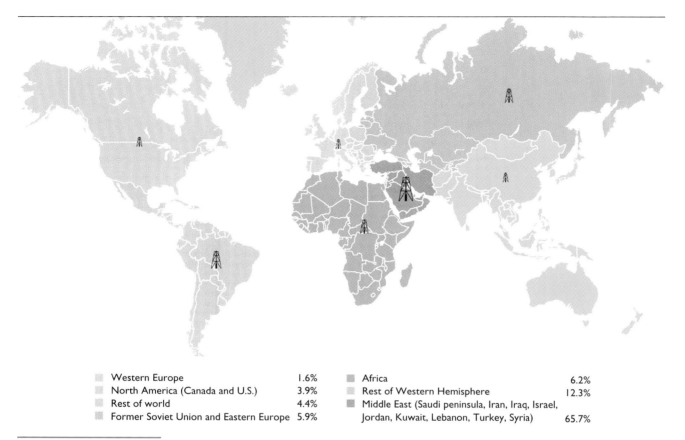

Western Europe	1.6%		Africa	6.2%
North America (Canada and U.S.)	3.9%		Rest of Western Hemisphere	12.3%
Rest of world	4.4%		Middle East (Saudi peninsula, Iran, Iraq, Israel,	
Former Soviet Union and Eastern Europe	5.9%		Jordan, Kuwait, Lebanon, Turkey, Syria)	65.7%

**Map 12.1
Regional Shares of
Proved Oil Reserves,
1993**
Note that nearly two
thirds of the world's
known reserves are in the
Middle East.

companies conducted some quasi-official diplomacy that continued throughout World War II. They organized construction of a pipeline to the Mediterranean in 1945 and received permission from the U.S. government to use steel, which was very scarce. In 1948, Exxon and Mobil joined the original companies, Socal and Texaco, in what became known as Aramco. Mobil owned 10 percent, and each of the others held a 30-percent interest.

These four companies, along with three others (Gulf, Shell, and BP), were known as the Seven Sisters. Before the 1970s, they collectively controlled such a large share of the world's oil from multiple sources that they were nearly invulnerable to the actions of any single country. By 1950, the United States was entrenched in the Cold War, and although it held military supremacy over the former Soviet Union, the Truman Administration wanted to maintain cordial relationships with strategic countries. When King Ibn-Saud demanded substantial revenue increases from Aramco, the U.S. government became directly involved in the negotiations. A plan was devised in 1951 that allowed the oil companies to maintain their ownership but pay 50 percent of Aramco's profits as taxes to Saudi Arabia. The companies then could deduct those taxes from their U.S. tax obligations so that, in effect, the increase in revenue to Saudi Arabia was entirely at the expense of the U.S. Treasury.

In 1952, Saudi Arabia learned from Iran's experience what might happen if demands on Aramco were pushed further. Iran expelled Shah Reza Pahlavi and nationalized British oil holdings. All major oil companies boycotted Iranian oil and brought the Mossadegh government to the brink of economic collapse. With CIA support, the Shah returned, and a new oil company replaced the nationalized holdings. The Seven Sisters shared 95-percent ownership of this new Iranian oil company.

When the Seven Sisters gained 95 percent of the Iranian oil holdings, the other 5 percent went to smaller, independent U.S. companies that previously had depended on the Seven Sisters for supplies. This marked the beginning of greater competition among distributors. It also meant producing countries could make agreements with the independents to gain a greater portion of the spoils. Yet as late as 1960, the producing countries were still unable to prevent the major companies from unilaterally abrogating concessions by reducing the price they paid for oil. This price decrease, which reduced the governmental revenues of petroleum-exporting countries, led to a meeting in Caracas of representatives from five oil-producing countries and the formation of the Organization of Petroleum Exporting Countries (OPEC). OPEC's purposes were to prevent oil companies from unilaterally lowering prices, to gain a greater share of oil revenues, and to move toward domestic rather than foreign ownership of the assets. At the time, however, in the early 1960s, OPEC lacked the power to flex its muscles.

Three new trends during the 1960s weakened the Seven Sisters and strengthened Saudi Arabia's position in Aramco:

1. Other oil companies were continually emerging, and they made concessions in countries previously not among the major suppliers, such as Occidental in Libya, ENI in the former Soviet Union, and CFP in Algeria. These smaller companies lacked the Seven Sisters' diversification of supplies and thus were less able to move to other supply sources if a country tried to change the terms of an agreement unilaterally.
2. Because of rapidly expanding industrial economies, oil demand was growing faster than supply; the earlier oil glut was quickly becoming an oil squeeze. No longer could even the Seven Sisters afford to boycott major supplier countries as they had earlier boycotted Iran.
3. The threat of military intervention to protect oil investors was lessening. The failure of the United States to support the abortive efforts of the British and the French to prevent the Egyptian takeover of the Suez Canal demonstrated that the major Western powers were unlikely to unify their efforts. The Soviet Union's growing strength meant there was a greater risk of a major war resulting from such intervention. The United States also was increasing its military involvement in an unpopular war in Vietnam and so was less able to lend military support to U.S. oil companies in the Middle East.

In 1970, Muammar el-Qaddafi of Libya demanded increased prices from Occidental. Since Occidental was almost completely dependent on Libya for crude oil, the company relented. Qaddafi then confronted other oil companies that no longer had sufficient alternative supplies and gained concessions from them as well. Libya's success was noted by other countries, which used OPEC to further strengthen their negotiating positions by dealing collectively with the oil companies. OPEC's Teheran Agreement of 1971 immediately increased prices. The embargo by Arab OPEC members in 1973 demonstrated that they had sufficient power to impose further economic demands. OPEC then had eleven members and controlled about 93 percent of the world's oil exports.

As the largest OPEC producer, Saudi Arabia has been able to utilize its strengths in several ways. Between 1972 and 1980, its government bought a 100-percent ownership share in Aramco operations and changed the name to Saudi Aramco. As smaller companies gained a larger share of the world oil sales and as national governments in Sweden, Germany, Japan, and France began buying directly from oil-producing countries, Saudi Arabia has increased the number of customers for its crude from the original four Aramco partners.

How has Aramco's government-owned status affected the operations of Exxon, Texaco, Socal, and Mobil in Saudi Arabia? The companies initially were able to exploit their many assets successfully in order to maintain a profitable presence in Saudi Arabia. They helped manage the Saudi oil industry because they could make contributions that the Saudis could not acquire easily from other sources. As the major employers before the Saudis' purchase of Aramco, they had demonstrated they could train Saudis, attract qualified personnel from abroad, and run an efficient operation. As Saudi Aramco expanded and moved into new activities, they continued these efforts through lucrative contract arrangements. For example, Mobil is a joint-venture partner with the Saudi government in a refinery and a petrochemical complex. The four companies also marketed crude oil exports when sales were not made directly to a foreign government. This was particularly important in the late 1980s when there was a glut due to new supplies (for example, from Mexico) and decreased demand. Further, the four oil companies provided technical assistance in finding and extracting oil.

After the Saudi government took complete ownership in Aramco, it began to replace foreign management with Saudi management until all top positions were held by Saudis. It also gradually decreased its dependence on the four former U.S.-owners. Its ability to lower this dependence was the result of several factors:

1. The number of oil companies worldwide has been growing; therefore, the Saudis have more choice in where to contract services and sell crude oil.
2. Engineering companies, such as Bechtel and Fluor, have increasingly been competing to sell management and engineering services that were once the domain of the oil companies.
3. The international boycott of Iraqi oil meant that some countries were seeking new oil supplies. Saudi Aramco, therefore, could sell directly to those countries and decrease its dependence on private oil companies to serve as intermediaries.
4. Global market growth was shifting toward east and south Asia where there were government-owned companies to whom Saudi Aramco could sell.

At the same time, Saudi Aramco has become less confident about OPEC's ability to stabilize world oil supplies and prices. Not only has there been the problem of production by non-OPEC members, but also some OPEC countries (particularly Venezuela and Nigeria) have been unwilling to cut back production or adhere to agreed-upon quotas. Saudi

Aramco has come to view captive international sales as the best way to ensure a market for Saudi crude. Its first movement was to enter into a joint venture with Texaco in 1988, buying a 50-percent interest in Texaco's refining assets and marketing system in twenty-three U.S. states. This was followed by a joint venture in South Korea with Ssangyong in 1991. In 1994 it took a 40-percent stake in Petron, the largest refiner and distributor in the Philippines. In 1996 Saudi Aramco acquired a 45-percent interest in Petrogal, Portugal's largest company and owner of three refineries and Galp, Portugal's largest chain of gasoline stations. It acquired "a minority share of less than 50 percent" in the Italian company, Erg, which owned three refineries and 2200 fuel stations in Italy. It bought a half share in the Greek Vardinoyannis oil group and announced two joint ventures in India, one with Hindustan Petroleum Oil and one with the Indian Oil Corporation. Meanwhile, Saudi Aramco was negotiating with SINOCHEM, a Chinese government-owned company for a refinery and access to the Chinese market. In addition to these foreign investments, the governments of Saudi Arabia and the United Kingdom renegotiated a $3.12 billion-a-year arms-for-oil contract whereby Saudi Aramco could cut out selling through BP and Shell as intermediaries.

Clearly, Saudi Aramco's position has evolved substantially as a result of changing supply-demand, competitive, and political conditions. Recently, the company has come closer to the stated strategy of its CEO, Abdallah S. Jum'ah "to develop a global presence in the refining and retail sectors."

Introduction

The operating terms of international companies
- **Are influenced by governments of home and host countries**
- **Shift as priorities shift and as strengths of parties change**

Chapter 11 discussed how home and host countries evaluate MNEs. Discord during such evaluation, if carried to the extreme, may result in the particular business-government relationship ending as governments refuse to grant original or continued operating permission. At the same time, companies evaluate countries and will not operate in given locales unless their terms of operations are sufficiently favorable. But countries and companies do come to agreements that, although not deemed ideal by either party, are sufficiently satisfactory to permit an evolving relationship. Thus it is useful to examine international business negotiations and diplomacy because terms of operations are highly influenced by attempts of international companies and governments to improve their own positions relative to one another.

Governmental versus Company Strength

As the Saudi Aramco case illustrates, the terms under which companies operate abroad are greatly influenced by both home- and host-country policies, and those terms change over time as governmental priorities shift and the relative strengths of the parties evolve. These strengths are affected by such factors as competitive changes, the resources the parties have at their disposal, validation by public opinion, and joint efforts with other parties.

Hierarchical View of Governmental Authority

Governments have regulations affecting international business. Companies may sometimes accept these as "givens." If so, they may comply with, circumvent, or avoid operating because of the regulations. *Compliance* occurs when the regulations don't unduly constrain a company's desired mode of operations, when benefits are sufficiently attractive in spite of regulations, and when companies feel that they cannot practically alter the regulations to their benefit. *Circumvention* occurs when companies use loopholes, legal or illegal, to bypass regulations that they find unacceptable. For example, a company's ability to control a foreign subsidiary in spite of a country's requirement for shared-ownership might be possible if the company makes a side agreement with a local partner not to vote its shares of stock. *Avoidance* is simply the reverse of compliance as a company decides not to operate in a given locale because of its regulations.[2]

Bargaining View

MNEs and host countries have mutually useful assets.

As discussed in Chapter 11, the host country and the MNE may each control assets that are useful to the other. Thus they have incentives to agree on the establishment of operations and to ensure that the operations continue functioning.

   Bargaining school theory holds that the negotiated terms for a foreign investor's operations depend on how much the investor and host country need each other's assets.[3] If either a company or a country has assets that the other strongly desires and if there are few (or no) alternatives for acquiring them, negotiated concessions may be very one-sided. For example, the Saudi Aramco case illustrated that when a few large companies dominated the extraction, processing, shipment, and final sale of an oversupply of oil, developing countries with petroleum deposits could do little but accept the terms they were offered. If a government refused the terms, a company easily could find another country that would accept a similar proposal. As the supply of oil diminished and petroleum-producing countries found alternative means for exploiting their resources, the terms of the concessions gradually evolved more in favor of those producing countries. But such shifts have not always favored countries. For example, because of slow economic growth and high unemployment, in 1996 France sought to attract more FDI. It did so by removing restrictions on foreign companies' bringing expatriate managers for senior jobs and by shortening the write-off time for equipment used in the investments.[4] Clearly, there are vast differences in bargaining strength among countries, among industries, and among companies.

Alternative sources for acquiring resources affect company and country bargaining strengths.

   The bargaining relationship between companies and governments depends very much on whether the parties see agreements as zero-sum (one party's gain equals the other party's loss) or positive-sum (both parties have net benefits) gains. In the former, relationships may conflict because one or both parties think that any concessions must be at its/their expense. In the latter, the relationship may be seen as a partnership whereby there is cooperation and interdependence.[5]

Country bargaining strength   Generally, companies prefer to establish investments in highly developed countries because those countries offer large markets and a high degree of stability. Countries such as the United States, Canada, and Germany are large recipients of foreign investment without making many concessions to the investors. In all of these countries, however, regional areas vie for investments by offering incentives. For example, several U.S. states vied to get a Mercedes plant, and Alabama ended up giving almost $300 million in tax breaks and subsidies.[6] If incentives are used, they are most appealing when they fit closely with companies' corporate strategies and when companies believe that the government has the credibility to fulfill its promises.[7] In addition, companies prefer to avoid the red tape involved in ad hoc negotiations to gain permission for investment. Although there are a few exceptions, developed countries are less likely than LDCs to examine and negotiate investment proposals on a case-by-case basis.

Company bargaining strength   Although companies have a variety of assets they can contribute to their foreign operations, some industries have traditionally enjoyed better bargaining positions than have others. For example, foreign ownership in such areas as agriculture and extractive industries is not very welcome in many countries because of historical foreign domination of these sectors and belief that the land and subsoil are public resources.

The bargain struck between the foreign investor and the host country also is influenced by the number of companies offering similar resources. For example, GM and Ford competed for rights to build sedans in China, and GM and Daewoo competed to acquire a state-owned company in Poland.[8] Foreign investors are more likely to gain a high percentage of ownership in foreign operations when they have few competitors and when they control certain types of assets. These assets include the following:[9]

- Technology. For example, IBM has been allowed 100-percent ownership of operations in a number of countries because of the local need for its unique technology. Other companies, however, have been refused the same. The French government also approved IBM's minority stake in state-owned Groupe Bull because of the company's specialized technology related to reduced instruction set computing (RISC).[10]
- Marketing expertise. For example, Coca-Cola apparently has been able to gain local consumer allies who believe its differentiated products are superior.
- Ability to export output from the foreign investment, especially when exports go to other entities controlled by the parent company. These investments gain foreign exchange that might otherwise not be forthcoming. Recall from the China case in Chapter 11 that exporters are more welcomed than companies seeking only to sell within China.

The biggest bargaining strengths for countries are
- **Large markets**
- **Political stability**

Company bargaining assets include
- **Technology**
- **Marketing expertise**
- **Ability to export output**
- **Local product diversity**

A larger extent of foreign ownership also is allowed when there is greater product diversity, probably because a variety of products offers wider future opportunities to save foreign exchange through import substitution.

Surprisingly, the amount of capital needed to set up operations has not usually affected investors' bargaining power. At least two factors play a role here:

1. A large investment may be examined much more closely than a small one because of the potential impact (positive or negative) it might have on the economy (that is, the host country wants the benefits of the capital inflow but is leery of being so dependent on foreign ownership).
2. The host-country government may be more likely to borrow funds externally to invest in large enterprises.

However, the ability to contribute large amounts of capital may improve future bargaining strengths of companies. Many LDCs have encountered debt-servicing problems since the mid-1980s, so they must depend more on FDI for their future capital needs. And the size of the potential investor may be a factor in that governments may not want to commit resources to negotiating with companies that are too small to make a substantial impact.

Joint Company Activities

Joint company activities are used by countries to strengthen national capabilities relative to strong foreign competitors and
• To spread risk
• To deal more strongly with governments

To counter production dominance by foreign companies, countries have encouraged their own manufacturers to consolidate. They have given governmental assistance for R&D and preference to their own companies in awarding governmental contracts. Two of the most notable efforts have been the development of Airbus Industrie, a consortium in Europe to compete against Boeing in aircraft production, and the development of various cooperative arrangements in Europe to counter IBM's dominance.[11] Other European cross-national efforts have occurred in such fields as consumer appliances, medical electronics, telecommunications, and television. For example, the EU's Esprit program provided $5 billion to fund electronics research, and the Eureka program, involving about 1600 companies, 99 percent of them European, was established to develop a wide range of technologies.[12]

In another approach, two or more companies from different countries band together, not so much to strengthen the initial negotiating terms but rather to improve their positions in possible later negotiations. By investing a smaller amount in a given locality, each company can invest in more countries, thus reducing the impact of loss in one. Further, in conflict situations a host government may be more hesitant to deal simultaneously with more than one home government.

Home-Country Needs

The home-country government
• Has economic objectives of its own
• Has direct political relations with the host country

The interplay between the needs of the MNE and those of the host country is not the only bargaining factor. The home-country government seldom takes a neutral position in the relationship. Like the host-country government, the home-country government is interested in achieving certain economic objectives, such as increased tax revenues and full employment. It may give incentives to or place constraints on the foreign expansion of home-based companies in order to gain what it sees as its due share of the rewards from their transactions. Recall in the Saudi Aramco case that the U.S. government gave tax concessions to oil companies to induce them to exploit foreign opportunities. However, the ability of either the home or host government to influence MNEs is tempered by the political interests and relations of the two governments.

The influence of home-country governments is illustrated by the example of France's selling off interest in its government-owned switchmaker, CGCT. The U.S. government pressured the French government to accept AT&T's bid by threatening to bar U.S. government purchases of French equipment. Germany's Chancellor personally lobbied the French Prime Minister on behalf of Siemens's bid. Caught between two foreign powers, the French government accepted the bid of a Swedish company, Ericsson.[13]

Other External Pressures

Decision makers in business and government must consider opinions of other affected groups.

The complementary nature of the assets that MNEs and countries control would seem, at first, to dictate a mutual interest in finding means to ensure that mutual benefits are pursued. Although there are pressures to do this, there also are constraints, particularly on governmental decision makers. Pressure may come from local companies with which the foreign investor is presently or potentially competing, from political opponents who seize the "external" issue as a means of inciting voters against present political leadership, or from critics who reason that more benefits may accrue to the country through alternative means. Home-country governments may respond to their local pressure groups in ways that affect relationships with other governments, causing unexpected repercussions for MNEs. For example, the United Kingdom limited imports of Indonesian T-shirts to protect its own garment industry, and the Indonesian government retaliated by denying the construction of a British-owned chemical project.[14] Companies also may face pressures from stockholders, workers, consumers, governmental officials, suppliers, and foreign groups that are concerned with their own interests rather than the achievement of worldwide corporate objectives. These pressures may result in a relationship between company and host country quite different from what might be expected on a purely economic basis. Each party should understand the types and strengths of these external groups, since they affect the extent to which either side may be able to give in on issues under discussion.

Negotiations in International Business

Terms for operations are often decided in interrelated negotiations.

Increasingly, negotiations are used as a means of deciding the terms by which a company may initiate, carry on, or terminate operations in a foreign country. At one time, negotiations prevailed only for direct investments; more recently, however, they sometimes have been extended to other operating arrangements, such as licensing agreements, debt repayment, and large-scale export sales. The following discussion highlights investment negotiations, but most of the points apply to other forms of operations as well. The negotiation process often leads to multitiered bargaining: An MNE must reach an agreement with a local company in order to purchase an interest in it, sell technology or products to it, or loan money to it. That agreement must be presented to a host-country agency that may approve, disapprove, or propose entirely new terms. The MNE may need to negotiate with its home government to gain permission to transfer technology or borrow funds. The home and host governments may negotiate regarding loans, investment guarantees, and overall economic and political relationships. These complex relationships are shown in Figure 12.1. Even when some of these parties are not directly involved in the negotiations, the participants may take their needs into consideration.

Bargaining Process

In the bargaining process, agreement occurs only if there are overlapping acceptance zones.

Acceptance zones   Before becoming involved in overseas negotiations, a manager usually will have some experience with a domestic bargaining process that is somewhat similar to that in the foreign sphere. For example, collective bargaining with labor as well as agreements to acquire or merge facilities with another company usually start with an array of proposals from both sides, just like negotiations with foreign organizations. The total package of proposals undoubtedly includes provisions that one side or the other is willing either to give up entirely or to compromise on. These are used as bargaining tokens, permitting each side to claim that it is reluctantly giving in on some point in exchange for compromise on some other

**Figure 12.1
Interrelated
Negotiations**
A complex set of interrelated negotiations may be necessary to reach agreement for foreign operating terms.

Source: From John M. Stopford and Susan Strange, *Rival States, Rival Firms,* 1991, Cambridge University Press. Reprinted with permission.

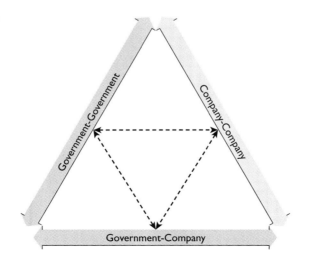

point. They also serve as face-saving devices, allowing either side to report to interested parties that it managed to extract concessions. On some points, however, it is unlikely that any compromise can be reached.

As in domestic negotiations, the outcome of foreign negotiations will depend partly on other recent negotiations or events, which serve as models. The relevant domestic model when deciding, for example, whether to give workers an additional holiday may be the economy as a whole, the industry, the local area, or recent company experience elsewhere. Abroad, what has transpired recently either between other companies and a host-country government or between similar types of companies or the same company in similar countries may serve as a common reference. Negotiations are unlikely to stray too far from that established precedent.

Finally, there are zones of acceptance and nonacceptance for the proposals presented. If the acceptance zones overlap, an agreement is possible. If zones have no overlap, positive negotiations are not possible. For example, if GM insisted on 51-percent ownership of an Indian facility but would accept up to 100 percent and the Indian government or partner insisted on 51-percent local ownership but would accept up to 75 percent, there would be no overlap of acceptance zones in which to negotiate. However, if Chrysler insisted on a "significant" interest in an Indian facility (say, 25 percent) but would take as much as it could get and the Indian government or partner required 51-percent local ownership and wanted to maximize it, there would be a wide zone that would be acceptable to both parties (for instance, 25–49 percent for Chrysler's ownership). (See Figure 12.2.) The final agreement would be based on each party's negotiating ability and strengths and on the other concessions that each made in the process. Because each side could only speculate on how far the other was willing to go, the exact amount of ownership allowed might fall anywhere within the overlapping acceptance zones. Even after an agreement is reached, whether the maximum concessions have been extracted from the parties remains uncertain.

Range of provisions   The major difference between domestic and foreign negotiations is a matter of degree. International negotiations may take much longer and may involve many provisions unheard of in the home country, such as a negotiated tax rate. Further, governments vary widely in their attitudes toward foreign investors; therefore their negotiating agendas also vary widely.

A 1995 review of 103 countries showed that 99 offer investment incentives to attract MNEs. For example, the French government contributed about $111 million, or about a quarter of the plant's cost, to attract a Mercedes-Benz facility.[15] Direct incentives that countries have offered foreign investors include tax holidays, employee training, R&D grants, accelerated depreciation, low-interest loans, loan guarantees, subsidized energy and transportation, exemption of import duties, and the construction of rail spurs and roads. Countries also provide indirect incentives, such as a trained labor force that is likely to accept employers' work conditions tranquilly.

Figure 12.2
Acceptance Zones
in Negotiating
The lined section on the top bars reading from left to right is the company's acceptance zone, and the lined section on the bottom bars from right to left is the government's. In (a), there is no overlap, but in (b) the overlap is substantial. Although this figure illustrates ownership, the same technique may be used for other points of negotiation.

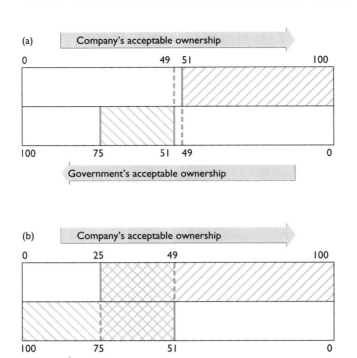

When companies negotiate to gain concessions from a foreign government, they should understand some of the problems the provisions might bring:

- Companies may face more domestic labor problems because of claims that they are exporting jobs in order to gain access to cheap labor.
- The output from the foreign facility may be subject to claims of dumping because of the subsidies given by the host government. For example, Toyota refused to accept British governmental assistance for fear other EU countries would not as readily allow its sales.
- It may be more difficult to evaluate management performance in the subsidized operation.

Finally, it should be noted that there is always a risk that promises will be broken as situations change.

Negotiations are seldom a one-way street. Companies agree to many different performance requirements aimed at improving the countries' economic and non-economic objectives that were discussed in Chapter 11, such as the balance of payments, growth, employment, and local control over important decisions. These include

* Foreign-exchange deposits to cover the cost of imports and capital repatriation
* Limits on payments for services
* Requirements to create a certain number of jobs or amount of exports
* Provisions to reduce the amount of equity held in subsidiaries
* Price controls
* Minimum levels of local input into products manufactured
* Limits on the use of expatriate personnel and on old or reconditioned equipment
* Control of prices for goods imported or exported to the parent company's controlled entities
* Demands to enter into joint ventures

Renegotiations

Agreements evolve after operations begin; the company position is usually, but not always, stronger before entry.

For early foreign investments in LDCs, it was common to obtain concessions on fixed terms for long periods or to expect that the original terms would not change. (These early investments were largely made in the commodity and utility sectors.) This situation has almost ceased to exist. Not only may the terms of operations be bargained before any operations are set up, but the same terms may be rebargained any time during start-up or after operations are under way. For example, three U.S. MNEs reached agreement with the state of Maharastra to build a $2.8 billion power plant (the largest foreign investment in India), in which Enron would own 80 percent and Bechtel Enterprises and General Electric would each own 10 percent. After investing $300 million, the government halted further work, but agreed to renegotiate the agreement. The companies lost about $250,000 per day during the renegotiations and finally agreed to use more Indian naphtha rather than Qataran natural gas to generate electricity, allow the state of Maharastra to own 30 percent of the facility, reduce Enron's ownership to 50 percent, and reduce the price of power by 22.2 percent.[16]

Generally, a company's best bargaining position exists before it makes an investment in a foreign country. Once the capital and technology have been imported and local nationals have been trained to direct operations, the foreign company is needed much less than before. Further, the company now has assets that are not easily moved to more favorable locales. The result is that the host country may be in a better position to extract additional concessions from the company. This erosion of the MNEs' bargaining strength as countries gain assets from them is known as the **theory of the obsolescing bargain.** However, a company that is aware of and responsive to the changing needs and desires of the local economy can maintain or even improve its bargaining position by offering the infusion of additional resources the host country needs. One tactic is to promise to bring in (or withhold) the latest technology developed abroad. Another is to use plant expansion or export markets as bargaining weapons. In addition, a company and country may exchange benefits, such as a company's ceding part of its ownership to local interests in exchange for guarantees on remission of its earnings.[17] A host government also may restrain from pushing too hard on established companies for fear this will make the country less attractive to other companies with which the government would like to do business.

Behavioral Characteristics Affecting Outcome

Misunderstandings may result from differences in
• **Nationalities**
• **Professions**
• **Languages**

In international negotiations, misunderstandings are a strong possibility because of cross-country cultural differences as well as possible language differences. Further, the background and expertise of governmental officials may be quite distinct from those of businesspeople; thus they face each other from different occupational cultures. In addition, the individuals involved may react on the basis of how they think their own performances are being evaluated. Finally, it is always possible that one side or the other wants to terminate bargaining but is hesitant to do so for fear of alienating future relationships with the other party.

Some cultural differences among negotiators are evident:
• **Some negotiators are decision makers; some are not.**
• **Some take a pragmatic view; others take a holistic view.**
• **Some expressions do not translate well.**

Cultural factors   In the 1930s, the humorist Will Rogers quipped, "America has never lost a war and never won a conference." Many participants and observers agree with this assessment of U.S. performance in business negotiations abroad. Much of the problem stems from cultural differences that lead to misunderstandings and mistrust across the conference table. Although this discussion cannot delineate all the possible cultural differences, the following points based on the cultural framework in Chapter 2 should indicate areas of possible misunderstanding.[18]

- Individual negotiators from some countries are more likely to have the power to make decisions than their counterparts from some other countries in part because of differences in individualism versus collectivism and differences in power distance preferences; negotiators who have the power to make decisions may lose confidence when those counterparts must reach a group decision or keep checking with their head office.
- Negotiators from low context cultures want to get to the heart of the matter quickly; negotiators from high context cultures want to spend time developing rapport and trust before addressing business details.
- Negotiators from pragmatist cultures attempt to separate the issues into small categories (getting closure on items in a linear fashion), whereas negotiators from idealistic cultures view negotiations more holistically.
- Negotiators from cultures with high trust are less prone to want to cover every possible contingency in a contract than negotiators from cultures with low trust.
- Negotiators from monochronic cultures tend to want little undivided attention to discussion of the potential contract; however, negotiators from polychronic cultures feel uncomfortable if they do not simultaneously take care of other business affairs.

- Negotiators from cultures that place a high importance on punctuality and the scheduling of time are more prone to set deadlines and then make concessions at the last minute to meet the schedules than negotiators from cultures that place less importance on punctuality and schedules. Further, they may underestimate the importance their counterparts place on the negotiations if their counterparts arrive late and don't stick to schedules.

It may be difficult for negotiators to find words to express their exact meaning in another language, which may result in occasional pauses while translators resort to dictionaries. Further, facial expressions differ by culture and, even if understood, are difficult to judge because of the time lag between the original spoken statement and its receipt in a second language. Since English is so widely understood worldwide, people with a different native language may understand quite well most of what is said in English, giving them the opportunity to eavesdrop on confidential comments and to reflect on possible responses while remarks are being translated into their language. The degree of precision in language desired by either side also may be complicated by cultural factors.

Evidence also exists that cultural factors influence whether interpreters are acceptable. For example, Saudi managers generally prefer to negotiate in English, even if their English is not very good. When interpreters are used, it is usually preferable for each side to have its own. Good interpreters help to brief their teams on cultural factors affecting the negotiation process. But even with interpreters, negotiators cannot be certain that their statements are fully understood, especially if they use slang or attempt humor that is culture-specific. This is illustrated by the experience of a U.S. politician who spoke through an interpreter in China:

> With typical American forthrightness, he said, "I'm going to tell you where I'm coming from." The interpreter said, "He'll now give you the name of his home town." Then he said, "I'm going to lay all my cards on the table." The interpreter said, "He'll play cards now." Then, making a joke, he said, "I'm not a member of any organized political party; I'm a Democrat." The interpreter said, "I think he just made a joke. Please laugh." The audience laughed and the politician knew he had their rapt attention.[19]

Negotiations may be based on
- **One's own culture**
- **The counterpart's culture**
- **Some hybrid of cultures**

The importance of cultural factors may change during renegotiations because the parties already know each other. If the relationship was amicable in the original negotiations, that quality is likely to be carried over. However, if the past relationship has been hostile, the renegotiations may be suffused by even more suspicion and obstruction than existed during the original process.[20]

Culturally responsive strategies[21]   That your counterpart comes from a country whose culture is very different from your own does not necessarily mean that he or she will behave according to that culture's norm.[22] First, the counterpart may be an exception to what one finds on average in the foreign country. Second, the counterpart may know your culture and be adapting to it. For example, one may imagine a ludicrous situation in which each side tries to act like the norm of the other culture so that roles are reversed. Therefore, it is useful to determine at the start whether you will adjust to your counterpart, have your counterpart adjust to you, or follow some form of hybrid adjustment. Figure 12.3 shows five strategic responses. The choice is highly dependent on how well you and your counterpart understand each other's culture. At one extreme, if you try to induce your counterpart to adapt to you (response 1), you need to convey that it is because of expediency rather than through lack of appreciation for the other's culture. For example, when ITT conducted merger talks with CGE of France, it did so in English and along ITT's style because the speed and success were dependent on U.S. law and investment firms. At the other extreme, you may immerse yourself in your counterpart's culture as in response 2. For example, Coca-Cola sent personnel to Cambridge to study the Chinese language and culture for a year before beginning a ten-year negotiation with a Chinese state-run organization. In response 3, both you and your counterpart agree on go-betweens, middlemen, brokers, or other intermediaries to facilitate interaction. Response 4 involves a hybrid of approaches, such as having each party speak in his or her own language or moving negotiations between the two countries. Finally, response 5 involves the conduct of negotiations different from what one might find in either culture. For example, this might occur when parties have such global experience that they have lost most elements of their home cultures.

Professional conflict   Governmental and business negotiators may start with mutual mistrust due to historic animosity or to differences in the status of their

Figure 12.3
Culturally Responsive Strategies and Their Feasibility
At each level of familiarity, a negotiator can consider feasible the strategies designated at that level and any lower level.

Source: Reprinted from "Negotiating with Romans—Part 2," by Stephen E. Weiss, *Sloan Management Review,* Spring 1994, p. 86 by permission of the publisher. Copyright 1994 by the Sloan Management Review Association. All rights reserved.

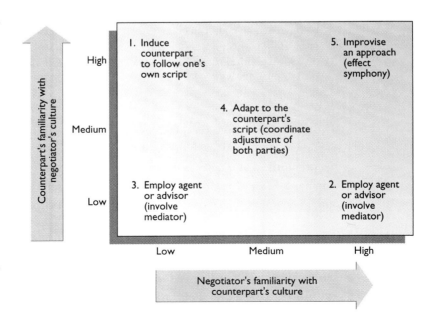

Business and governmental officials may mistrust each other and may not understand each other's objectives.

professional positions. The businesspeople may come armed with business and economic data that are not well understood by governmental officials, who may counter with sovereignty considerations that are nearly incomprehensible to the businesspeople. Thus it may take considerable time before each side understands and empathizes with the other's point of view. Even then, it is possible neither will attempt to develop a relationship designed to assure the achievement of long-term objectives. Negotiators may see their rewards as dependent on immediate results and perhaps not expect to be closely connected with longer-term problems.

The viewpoint discrepancy has been particularly evident as many LDCs have attempted to sell state-owned enterprises to foreign investors. The managers within these enterprises are suspicious of MNEs, fearful of foreign domination, and worried about their jobs after privatization.[23]

Negotiators should find some means to reinstitute future contacts.

Termination of negotiations   When one or both parties want to end serious consideration of proposals, the method of cessation can be extremely important. It may affect the negotiators' positions with their superiors. Also affected may be future transactions between the parties and their dealings with other organizations, both in that country and elsewhere in the world. Because termination is an admission of failure to achieve the original objectives, negotiators are prone to publicly blame others in order to save face. Such accusations may complicate future dealings the country or the company may have with other parties. Fearing adverse consequences from termination, negotiators sometimes drag out the process until a proposal eventually dies unnoticed. Although termination is stressful, when it is necessary, the parties should attempt to find means that allow each to save face and that avoid publicity as much as possible.

Simulation can be used to anticipate others' approach, but it is hard to simulate stress situations.

Preparation for negotiations   Role-playing is a valuable technique for training negotiators for projects requiring approval by a foreign government or agreement with a foreign company. By practicing their own roles and those of the counterpart negotiators and by researching the country's culture and history to determine attitudes toward foreign companies, a company's negotiators may be much better able to anticipate responses and plan their own actions.[24]

Choice of negotiators depends on
- **The importance of the deal**
- **The functions involved**

Using simulation presupposes that the company knows who will be negotiating for the other side. The choice of negotiators will depend on the project's importance, the functional areas being considered, and the sections of business or government involved. Commonly, MNEs use a team approach so that appropriate people with the necessary range of functional responsibilities are involved in the decision making. It also is common to use people at different organizational levels at different points in the negotiations.

One factor not easily simulated is the possible stress from being away from family and co-workers for an extended period. Because of this factor, the location of negotiations may give one side or the other an advantage in bargaining. Therefore, negotiating in your "home field" gives you an advantage because you can go home at night, eat familiar food, not have to explain your travel expense report to superiors, and more easily take care of other business at your office. If you must travel abroad for negotiations, you will likely be more alert if you arrive in time to be rested and adjust to any time changes.

Evolution of Negotiations and Diplomacy in the Internationalization Process

As with the discussion in Chapter 11, companies' need to engage in international business negotiations and diplomacy must also increase in tandem with their international commitment. For example, dealings with host governments are more apt to occur with FDI than with trade, unless the trading proposal has an unusually high potential impact on the host economy.

Because companies tend to move first to those countries most similar to their own, their early international forays need not involve as complex a set of cross-cultural relationships as those that develop later. Moreover, early commitments are more apt to be in industrial than in developing countries, and the former have usually taken a more laissez-faire attitude toward FDI; therefore, companies have less need to justify their entries. This should not imply, however, that there is no need for diplomacy in early stages of international commitment. Because of the large market attraction of industrial countries, they may sometimes be able to require complex barter or offset arrangements as a requisite for entry. Further, seemingly similar cultures may have subtle differences that hamper successful negotiations. A simple example would be English language meanings between the United Kingdom and the United States, two countries with similar cultures. For example, if a U.K. company were discussing with a U.S. company a possible import or license to manufacture a line of clothing, how would each interpret a statement that discussions should be tabled because potential customers find the designs homely? For the Britisher, the meaning would be positive—that discussions should be put on the agenda because the clothing is natural and friendly to the touch. However, for the American, the meaning would be negative—that discussions should be indefinitely delayed because the designs are unattractive in appearance.

Home-Country Involvement in Asset Protection

Historical Background

Historically most foreign investment disputes concerned expropriation, particularly in developing countries.[25] As late as the period between the two world wars, home countries ensured through military force and coercion that prompt, adequate, and effective compensation would be received by investors in cases of expropriation, a concept known as the **international standard of fair dealing.**[26] Host

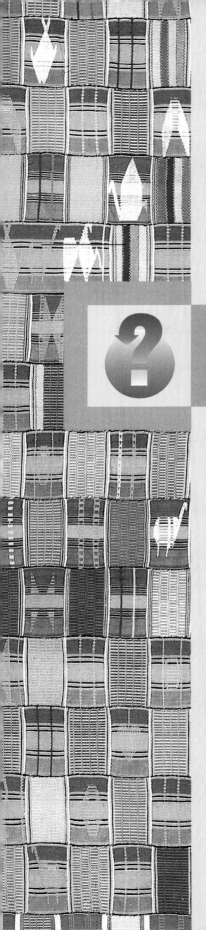

There is a long tradition of governmental help for home-country companies engaged in international business. This chapter discusses many of these efforts, which include treaties to ease the flow of resources among countries, as well as pressures on other countries to protect MNEs' tangible and intangible assets. In addition, governments establish commercial offices at home and abroad. Among other things, these offices supply trade and business information on foreign countries. What constitutes an appropriate amount of governmental assistance is argued largely in economic terms, such as whether export financing programs constitute subsidies that warrant retaliation. But there also are ethical questions about such assistance.

ETHICAL DILEMMAS & SOCIAL RESPONSIBILITY

Consider data collection and dissemination. The U.S. government collects and publishes a wide variety of data on business activities and performance in foreign countries. It then makes these data available at low cost.

As long as the information is collected openly and is available at low cost to anyone (U.S. citizens as well as foreign citizens), there seems to be no ethical question. However, there may be some point at which the method of collection, the type of information collected, or the restrictions on dissemination overstep ethical boundaries. For example, with the end of the Cold War, the U.S. Central Intelligence Agency (CIA) indicated that it was considering the collection and analysis of more business-economic data that would be shared with U.S. companies.[27] The director of the CIA said, "We do not do industrial espionage"; however, the CIA does seek to uncover situations in which foreign companies gain sales by bribing foreign officials. The French government expelled four U.S. diplomats because they reportedly sought to recruit French officials as industrial spies.[28] There have also been allegations that the CIA eavesdropped on conversations between Japanese officials and car executives during U.S.-Japanese auto trade negotiations.[29] With a yearly budget of about $30 billion and substantial high technology for information gathering, the CIA might be able to gain more competitively useful information than companies or other government agencies could. From an ethical standpoint, the following questions about such information might raise issues:

- Is it acquired by the CIA or another U.S. government agency?
- Is it collected openly or clandestinely?
- Is it in the public domain or proprietarily owned by companies?
- Is it made available to anyone or only U.S. companies?

Governmental spies are allegedly working with businesses from such countries as the United Kingdom, China, France, Israel, Japan, and South Korea.[30] Thus much of the justification for governmental spying is based on the need to be competitive with what other governments are doing.

Another area of governmental assitance is in the protection of intangible assets—such as patents, trademarks, and copyrights—which is discussed later in the chapter. Although companies lose millions of dollars in revenues from unauthorized copying, many argue that copying is justified in some circumstances because it gives poor people access to needed products that would otherwise be unavailable to them. Take books, for example. Unauthorized copies of this book are sold extensively in many LDCs at a fraction of the price of those sold legitimately, especially in Asia. These sales give no revenues to either the legitimate publisher or the authors, and the U.S. book publishing industry lost an estimated $783 million in revenues during 1995 (almost half in Asia) because of unauthorized copying.[31] Another industry where the copying of products is rampant is pharmaceuticals. For example, Argentina is the world's ninth-largest market for pharmaceuticals, and local companies routinely copy and market medicines that were developed by MNEs, such as antibiotics and anticancer agents.[32] They can sell these at a discounted price because they do not have to incur and recoup high development costs. U.S. MNEs have pressured the U.S. government to pressure foreign countries to stop the copying of both books and pharmaceuticals. If successful, MNEs will no longer lose sales; however, some consumers may be too poor to buy the legitimate version of the cut-rate copies. For example, many purchasers of copied books are students who buy texts that they could otherwise not afford because the price of a single textbook might be as much as the monthly income for a student's family. For them, the enactment and enforcement of strict copyright laws may mean a less adequate education. In the case of pharmaceuticals, the enactment and enforcement of strict patent laws may mean that some consumers will not be able to afford life-saving medicines. The ethical challenge is to assure that companies continue to develop needed products and get paid adequately for them and, at the same time, to assure that poor people can gain access to them.

countries had little to say about this standard. In conferences attended by developing countries at The Hague in 1930 and at Montevideo in 1933, participants established a treaty stating that "foreigners may not claim rights other or more extensive than nationals."[33] On the basis of this doctrine, Mexico used its own courts in 1938 to settle disputes arising from expropriation of foreign agricultural properties in 1915.[34] This same doctrine formed the precedent for later settlements and, in the absence of specific treaties, still remains largely in effect. The concept of nonintervention has been strengthened by a series of UN resolutions and by the fact that most expropriations have been selective rather than general, that is, involving a few rather than all foreign companies. In these cases, it is thought that intervention might lead to further takeovers and jeopardize settlements for the affected companies. Moreover, as host countries' priorities have shifted toward attracting FDI, rather than expropriating it, there has been less concern about home country intervention to protect investors. Instead, home governments have become more concerned that companies will receive equal legal treatment and will have their FDI approved fairly and expeditiously.[35]

Nevertheless, **dependencia theory** holds that LDCs have practically no power as host countries when dealing with MNEs. Their assets are of little importance in bargaining. Further, MNEs can enlist the loyalties of their home governments as well as of local elites in order to maintain their power. Although home-country governments no longer are as likely to resort to military intervention, they sometimes use other means to support MNEs, such as trade pressures, aid, and influence with international lending agencies. At this writing, the dependencia theory is largely out of vogue. However, some LDC leaders and political parties still hold the views;[36] consequently, those holding the views can sometimes effectively delay or prevent investments by MNEs.

The Use of Bilateral Agreements

Bilateral agreements improve climates for investments abroad.

To improve foreign-investment climates for their investors, many industrial countries have established bilateral treaties with other countries, often after long and difficult negotiations.[37] Although these agreements differ in detail, they generally provide for home-country insurance to investors to cover losses from expropriation, political violence, governmental contract abrogation, and currency control and to exporters to cover losses from nonpayment in a convertible currency. For example, the United States offers policies for small companies through the Small Business Administration and for companies in general through the Overseas Private Investment Corporation (OPIC) and Eximbank.[38] Coverage also is available through private insurers, international agencies such as the World Bank's Multilateral Investment Guarantee Agency, and some host-country governments. The home country, by approving an insurance contract, agrees to settle investors' losses on a government-to-government basis. For example, U.S. West acquired OPIC insurance to invest in the development of telecommunications projects in Russia.[39] If U.S. West suffered losses as a result of political risk, OPIC would pay U.S. West and then the U.S. government would seek settlement from Russia. Other types of bilateral agreements include treaties of friendship, commerce, and navigation as well as prevention of double taxation. All these efforts help promote factor mobility by MNEs.

Multilateral Agreements and Settlements: FDI

When MNEs are unable to reach agreement with organizations in a host country, they may agree to have a third party settle the dispute. For trade disputes, the International Chamber of Commerce in Paris, the Swedish Chamber of Commerce, and specialized commodity associations in London frequently are enlisted. Because the trade transactions are generally between private groups, these disputes do not create the type of widespread emotional environment often attendant on government-to-government or foreign-investment disputes. Government-to-government trade disputes are now largely the domain of the WTO, although allegations about unfair trade practices abroad are lodged with a company's home government, which in turn formally submits the allegations to the WTO.

A notable example of a multilateral settlement on foreign investment involved claims between the United States and Iran. This situation differed from many other attempted settlements because each country had large amounts of investments in the other's territory. In fact, when the two governments froze each other's assets, Iran had substantially more invested in the United States than the United States had in Iran. The two countries agreed to appoint three arbitrators each to an international tribunal at The Hague, and those six selected three more. Part of the assets the United States had held were set aside for the payment of arbitrated claims, and amounts have been relinquished as Iran has settled with U.S. investors on a case-by-case basis.[40]

The International Center for Settlement of Investment Disputes operates under the auspices of the World Bank and provides a formal organization to which parties can submit their disputes. Most bilateral investment treaties designate it as the arbitration center for disputes or indicate that its rules would be applicable in ad hoc arbitrations.[41] The World Bank also established the Multilateral Investment Guarantee Agency, which offers insurance against losses from expropriations, war, civil disturbances, currency convertibility, and breach of contract.

The WTO now provides an umbrella institutional framework through which it may become involved in selected aspects of investment issues and dispute settlement. Specifically, investment disputes can be linked to trade disputes, such as the prohibition of FDI that is necessary to export into a market. On a regional basis, NAFTA rules provide for investors' claims to be submitted to a tribunal.[42] The WTO has also discussed the possibility of a parallel program to settle investment disputes that are not related to trade; however, a core of LDCs is thus far opposed because of a belief that any agreement would compromise their ability to decide on development strategy and industrial policy.[43]

Multinational Agreements: IPRs

International treaties and agreements help safeguard patents, trademarks, and copyrights.

Most of the discussion in this chapter has centered on foreign direct investment; however, one of the key areas of business-government and government-to-government conflicts recently has involved intellectual property rights (IPRs), sometimes referred to as intangible assets.[44] The poet and essayist Ralph Waldo Emerson said, "If a man can write a better book, preach a better sermon, or make a better mousetrap than his neighbor, though he builds his house in the woods, the world will make a beaten path to his door." But if someone else gets hold of the design for the better book, sermon, or mousetrap, the number of people beating the way will be divided.

IPRs are associated with both industrial property, such as inventions and distinctive identifications of companies and products, and artistic property, such as books, recordings, films, and computer programs. Companies with substantial intangible assets want protection through enforceable patents, trademarks, and copyrights so that they may gain all the sales and profits as returns on the investments they made to create the property. They argue that the social benefit of protection is positive because there otherwise would be less incentive to develop new industrial and artistic property. However, critics argue that protection creates a social cost through high monopoly prices. This argument has been used, for example, to restrict the patentability of pharmaceuticals in many countries so that medicines are more affordable.

Countries differ substantially in their protection of IPRs, through laws and their enforcement. Generally, LDCs offer less protection because few of their companies create substantial intangible assets; therefore they can gain local production and low prices without making payments to companies in industrial countries. Even when two countries have similar levels of protection, their approaches differ. For example, U.S. patent applications are secret and are usually granted within two years; in contrast, Japanese applications are public and are granted in four to six years.[45] Because of different national approaches to IPRs, both companies and countries have stakes in any international agreements that are reached. The GATT agreement from the Uruguay Round provides for IPR reciprocity—granting to foreigners the same property rights available to one's own citizens.

Patents

The first major attempt to achieve cross-national cooperation in the protection of patents, trademarks, and other property rights was the Paris Convention, initiated in 1883 and periodically revised. This convention gave rise to the International Bureau for the Protection of Industrial Property Rights (BIRPI). Its main thrust is to grant reciprocity to foreigners whose countries are Convention members. A second major provision is that a registration in one country has a grace period of protection before registration must be made in other member countries. After registration, there is then a transition period of protection before the patent holder has to make use of the patent within the market. If it fails to make use, then the country may grant rights to another company. The Uruguay Round agreed for a transition period of one year in developed countries, five years in developing countries, and eleven years in the least developed countries.[46]

The three most important contemporary cross-national patent agreements are the Patent Cooperation Treaty (PCT) of the World Intellectual Property Organization (WIPO), the European Patent Convention (EPC), and the EEC Patent Convention. The PCT and EPC allow companies to make a uniform patent search and application, which is then passed on to all signatory countries.

Patent-infringement battles are both costly and complex and may take years to settle. On the international level, the rapid development of technology and the different patent rules and regulations in different countries make keeping up with patents difficult.[47] Companies are forced to change their patents from country to country to meet local needs, and patent infringement is often hard to prove. For example, a company in one country, where there is no patent protection on pharmaceuticals, could manufacture a drug patented by a company in the United States and sell it anywhere in the world. If the U.S. company were to bring suit, it would have to prove patent infringement; however, it would have difficulty getting the proof in the country without protection.

Trademarks

Companies may spend millions of dollars to develop brand names. If a brand name is not protected by a trademark, then other companies may produce under the same brand name. For example, New Zealand growers began marketing what they called Chinese gooseberries as kiwifruit in the 1960s, but neglected to register a trademark; now kiwifruit are marketed from many places.[48] Even if a brand name has a trademark, it may become generic and thus enter the public domain. "Swiss army knife" is actually a foreign trademark that has become a generic word in the United States. Because the Japanese have no name for vulcanized rubber, they call it "goodyear." Sometimes the issue of what is generic is decided in bilateral agreements. For example, the EU and the United States agreed that bourbon and Tennessee whiskey were names that could be used only by U.S. distillers, whereas Scotch whiskey, Irish whiskey, Cognac, Armagnac, Calvados, and Brandy de Jerez belong to regions of Europe.[49] One development in cross-national cooperation for trademark protection is the Trademark Registration Treaty, commonly known as the Vienna Convention. The United States, the United Kingdom, Germany, and Italy were among the industrialized countries that signed it initially; however, many countries remain as nonsignatories.

The U.S. law lies halfway between the two; trademarks can be protected for up to three years without being used as long as a company files an intention to use it. According to the Vienna Convention, a country may not require the use of a trademark as a prerequisite to obtain or maintain registration until three years after its international registration. Once the trademark has been registered internationally, each country must accept it or provide grounds for refusal within fifteen months after its registration so that the company will have sufficient time to act before the three-year period is completed. Between the time a company registers a trademark and the time it enters a foreign country, another company sometimes begins using the trademark in the foreign country. The first company using it can then delay or prevent entry of the original trademark holder. For example, in 1996 the Swedish home furnishing chain Habitat wanted to enter the Italian market; however, a small company, Galliano Habitat, won a provisional court order to prevent Habitat from using its trademark in Italy.[50]

Copyrights

Most large publishing and recording companies have extensive foreign interests and can be influenced easily by foreign competition. Without international copyright laws, a foreign producer could feasibly copy a book, software, CD, or tape and then distribute it at cut-rate prices in the country in which it was first produced. The Universal Copyright Convention (UCC) and the Berne Convention, the major cross-national agreements, honor the copyright laws of their signatory countries. In 1996, some 150 WIPO members agreed to extend copyright coverage to material on the Internet and other on-line services.[51]

Piracy

Not all countries are members of the various conventions to protect IPRs. Of those that are, some enforce the agreements haphazardly. Even if enforced, the penalties may be too small to deter violations. For example, Sterling Drug discovered in Venezuela that the maximum fines were about U.S. $12.[52] The terms *piracy* and *counterfeiting* are used to describe production without the consent of the company holding the patent, trademark, or copyright. Reports of lost sales due to piracy vary substantially; but all estimates are significant. For example, the World Health Organization estimates that 5 percent of drug trade is counterfeit, and the figure is 70 percent for drugs used in developing countries. Pirated software sales probably exceed $15 billion a year and account for more than 70 percent of the market in the Middle East, Africa, and Latin America.[53]

Piracy has occurred for several reasons:

- Cashing in on massive advertising by placing well-known trademarked labels on copies of products is tempting and has happened with almost every type of goods, from baseball caps to automobiles.[54] Fake labels even go on merchandise that the copied companies do not make; an example is the Jordache label on disco bags and caps.

- Technology allows copyrighted material such as tapes to be duplicated cheaply without loss of quality.[55]
- Some countries offer little protection for certain products. For example, when the drug company Pfizer introduced Feldene, an antiarthritic drug, to Argentina, five Argentine companies were already selling generic copies in the market.[56]
- Many people see nothing morally wrong in buying counterfeit goods. For example, the Software Publishers Association's executive director said, "It's ironic that people who would never think about stealing a candy bar from a drugstore seem to have no qualms about copying a $500 software package."[57]

What about gains or losses for consumers? Sometimes they get good-quality merchandise with a prestige label for a fraction of what the legitimate product would have cost. Some companies have even contracted counterfeiters to be legitimate suppliers. Sometimes consumers enjoy flaunting a fake product that is admittedly not of high quality and that fools no one as being genuine, such as a $15 counterfeit Rolex watch. Often, however, shoddy or even dangerous merchandise is substituted for the original goods. For example, a hundred Nigerian children died from a cough medicine, and talcum powder was found in anti-ulcer drugs sold in Europe.[58]

Various manufacturers' associations have sprung up worldwide to deal collectively with piracy. Among the deterrents that have been proposed are greater border surveillance, stiffer penalties for dealing in counterfeit goods, and cessation of aid to countries that do not join and adhere to international agreements. The World Trade Organization has taken over the international property rights administration from WIPO, and it is anticipated that enforcement will be more effective.[59] The WTO administration is the result of the Uruguay Round of GATT, which included an agreement on Trade-Related Aspects of Intellectual Property Rights (TRIPS). The TRIPS provisions cover basically all types of IPRs and require countries to agree to enforcement procedures under their national laws.[60] Further, the WTO allows countries to take trade sanctions against countries that do not protect intellectual property rights. For example, the United States has threatened Super 301 trade sanctions against countries that do not adequately protect intellectual property, and the United States threatened China with high tariff rates on a variety of Chinese merchandise because of its nonprotection of intellectual property rights. For example, pirated copies of Windows 95 were available in China and Hong Kong at a fraction of the official selling price before Microsoft even began sales.[61] Companies such as Apple Computer and Union Carbide also are successfully tracking down infringers on their own and bringing cases against them, but it is difficult to prove infringement when slight changes are made to trademarks or product models. Other companies are using high technology, such as holographic images and magnetic or microchip tags, to identify the genuine products. This has cost them millions of dollars for detecting devices.[62] Vuitton, a French luggage manufacturer, is using a withdrawal strategy—it sells registered and numbered goods only in company-owned retail outlets. Still other companies are warning the public of imitations and advising consumers on how to discern the genuine product.[63]

Role of Public Affairs

The preceding discussion dealt primarily with complaints by companies about the actions (or lack of actions) by governments to protect their assets, both tangible and intangible. But governments are also concerned with the actions of MNEs, and they have sought to deal collectively with them and to issue guidelines of expected behavior.

Codes of Conduct

Collective attitudes toward MNE activities
- **Are clarified by a number of organizations**
- **Are usually fairly vague**
- **Involve voluntary compliance**
- **May make it easier for countries to legislate**

The first widespread attempt to regulate FDI on a multilateral basis was made in 1929 by the League of Nations. Then, the attention was on foreign exploitation of the tropical commodities industry. Proposals were discarded quickly, however, with the onset of the Great Depression. Since World War II, several attempts have been made to deal with the relationship between MNEs and governments. Among these were the International Trade Organization (ITO) of 1948, which never became operative, the attempts in 1951 by the UN Economic and Social Council (ECOSOC) to regulate antitrust, and the 1961 Code for Liberalization of Capital Movements established by the Organization for Economic Cooperation and Development (OECD). It appears that none of these attempts has had much effect on MNEs' operations.

In 1975, the Center on Transnational Corporations was created at the United Nations as a result of complaints from many LDCs (the so-called Group of 77, which now comprises more than 100 LDCs). The Center collects information on MNE activities, is a forum for publicizing common complaints, and has considered the adoption of several codes of conduct for MNE activities. The OECD, which is composed of industrial countries, approved its own code in 1976. Both the codes considered by the Group of 77 and that adopted by the OECD are necessarily vague so that consensus may be reached among various countries as well as among groups within them. There have also been a number of codes dealing with specific practices, such as infant formula sales and environmental practices, or with specific areas of the world, such as employment practices in northern Mexico and in Northern Ireland.[64] In some cases, industry groups have agreed on codes, such as the International Council of Toy Makers, to provide good working conditions and avoid the use of child labor.[65] The codes also are voluntary; thus adoption does not guarantee enforcement. However, they may clarify a collective attitude toward specific MNE practices that could make it easier to pass restrictive legislation at the national level without fear that the legislation will be greatly out of step with external public opinion.

In 1995, the United States issued a voluntary code for foreign operations of U.S. companies. The code calls for companies operating abroad to provide a safe workplace, recognize the rights of workers to organize, and not use either forced or child labor in the production of their products. An interesting aspect of the code is that it asks companies to report on their activities abroad, especially to highlight their positive achievements in the workplace.[66]

Public Relations

Companies publicize good-citizenship activities, pointing out when
• **Business conduct satisfies social objectives**
• **Nonbusiness functions help society**

Many companies strongly believe that by acting as a good corporate citizen abroad, they will reduce local animosities and remove concerns that might affect their short- or long-term competitive ability. Some have even gone so far as to set their own published codes of conduct. These actions may not be sufficient, however, since employees, governmental officials, consumers, and other groups may not know or understand what the company is doing.

Because of conflicting pressures from different groups, an MNE can almost always be accused of bad behavior by someone. For instance, if it offers higher wages, it may be accused of monopolistic practices and of stimulating inflation by attracting workers from competitors. If it pays only the going wage, it may be accused of exploiting the workers. By understanding the relative power of competing groups it serves, the MNE at least may be able to emphasize practices that benefit most of the groups that are in a position to help or hurt it substantially. A good rule for serving a given group is to try to maximize benefits without excessively disrupting the local situation. Within any given economy, there usually is a range of prices, wages, and returns on investment. The MNE thus may be able to be among the leaders (for example, by offering wage rates or investment returns that are among those of the top quarter of companies) without being accused of disruptive practices, and still satisfy the groups directly involved.

The theologian Saint Augustine recounted in the fifth century that in his youth he used to pray, "Give me chastity and continence, but not yet." Like Saint Augustine, many companies try to put off public-relations efforts as long as possible. Often a company's public-relations efforts are defensive; that is, they occur in response to public criticism. Once a company is on the defensive, however, these efforts may be too little, too late. A good example of heading off potentially adverse public opinion concerned Levi Strauss. Its CEO said, "In today's world, an exposé on working conditions on *60 Minutes* can undo years of effort to build brand loyalty." To head off possible criticism about labor practices of its suppliers, the company terminated contracts in China and Peru and worked with suppliers to alter their practices in Turkey and Bangladesh. Not only did Levi Strauss prevent criticism, but the publicity about its changed policies brought the company goodwill.[67]

Companies should work to increase the number of supporters and dampen potential criticism. Opinion surveys of such interested parties as customers and workers can be conducted to allay misconceptions and anticipate criticism, thereby heading off potentially more damaging accusations. Many MNEs use advocacy publicity at home and abroad in an aggressive effort to win support for their international activities. Such publicity may take the form of newspaper and magazine ads, reports, and films showing the positive effects a company's activities have had on home- and host-country societies.

Although it may not always be possible to dispel criticism from abroad, the MNE can do several things to mitigate it. One is to consider what is important to people in the host country. Another may be as fundamental as having the parent company managers continue an existing policy. On the question of what to centralize and what to decentralize, there is much to be said for permitting local managers to determine policies concerning local customs and social matters. On such sensitive issues as employment and worker output, changes should be made only after consultation with interested parties. Headquarters personnel also may serve a useful public-relations function locally; they have higher status than local managers do and so may sometimes be better received by higher governmental authorities.

Allies through Participation

An MNE also may foster local participation designed both to reduce the image of foreignness and to develop local proponents whose personal objectives may be fulfilled by the company's continued operations. The parent company can follow policies that involve assisting the development of local suppliers from whom it purchases, establishing stock-option plans, and gradually replacing home-country personnel with local nationals. If management directly informs local union officials about possible company actions, the officials may cooperate with management rather than confront it. Carried to extremes, however, local participation can result in the host country's becoming less dependent on the foreign company. Thus the company's strategy might be to hold out some resources so that it remains needed. For instance, a centralized R&D laboratory could be in charge of new product development, whereas the local R&D facility could handle adaptations for local market and production conditions.

Some companies have taken on additional social functions to build local support. For example, Dow Chemical financed a kindergarten in Chile, Citibank participated in a reforestation program in the Philippines, and McDonald's sponsored a telethon in Australia to raise funds for disabled children. Johnson & Johnson sends Kenyans abroad to study nursing, and Sony sends Chilean music students abroad to study. Merck gives away millions of doses of a drug to fight river blindness in

The MNE might increase the number of local proponents through
- **Ownership sharing**
- **Avoiding direct confrontation**
- **Local management**
- **Local R&D**

Africa. Volvo awards an annual prize for the outstanding global innovation or discovery in the environmental field. GM publishes a public-interest report to highlight its involvement in a wide array of activities, such as environmental clean-up programs in Mexico and Eastern Europe, cancer research, AIDS education, and global celebration of Earth Day.[68]

Good corporate citizenship and the attendant publicity may not be enough to guarantee that business activity can continue. If public opinion is against foreign private ownership in general, all foreign companies lose out. For a company doing business as a key company in a key sector, criticisms may come simultaneously from so many directions that the company defense gradually loses strength. Even in these exceptional situations, a company's external affairs department may identify the worst problem areas. If this is done sufficiently in advance, the company may forestall adverse actions and establish policies to prevent or minimize losses. These policies may include decreasing new-parent obligations, selling ownership to local governments or private investors, and shifting into less visible types of local enterprises.

Occasionally, an MNE may find it advantageous to be uncompromising in its dealings with a government, even when the adversarial positions are reported publicly. It may do this because it determines it has a sufficiently strong bargaining position or because it perceives compromises will weaken its position in other countries. Even in these instances, however, the MNE should attempt to keep the government from losing face.

COUNTERVAILING FORCES

The relationships of MNEs, home governments, and host governments involve constantly shifting coalitions. These three parties would like maximum independence; however, each is limited by resources and actions taken by the others. For example, MNEs usually prefer independence in order to follow global strategies that lead them to the least-cost production locations and biggest markets. But their ability to invoke these strategies is tempered by governmental regulations on factor flows and foreign-ownership limitations. To overcome these impediments, MNEs temporarily coalesce on specific issues. For instance, a group of companies might lobby their home-country government to pressure another government to open its market and protect foreign assets there. Gaining this governmental support may require the MNEs to make concessions that limit their global strategies in other ways. To overcome those new limitations may require additional coalitions, and the results almost always necessitate new trade-offs.

Similarly, countries want independence in the form of sovereignty. But as this chapter illustrated, they sign treaties with other countries and reach agreements with MNEs in order to gain needed resources at the expense of losing some control over their domestic activities.

LOOKING TO THE FUTURE

Probably the most significant factor influencing possible change in business-government diplomacy is the end of the Cold War, which pitted the communist and noncommunist blocs against each other for nearly half a century. During that period, governments tended to influence business activities because of political-military objectives, sometimes protecting their home-based companies in order to gain or maintain spheres of influence abroad and sometimes withholding support for fear it might lead an otherwise neutral country to support the other bloc. But political schisms are not yet a thing of the past, and thus managers must continue to contend with cross-national animosities when planning international expansion strategies.

New alignments of countries based on economic factors may well replace some of the political-military rivalries of the recent past. For example, a new economic rivalry between Europe and North America may become as intense as the old political rivalry between the communist and noncommunist blocs. Companies thus may still have to satisfy national interests in their operations to the same degree as before. In the short term, it appears most countries will welcome foreign companies' operations or at least take a laissez-faire attitude toward them because of a belief that, on balance, they serve the countries' national economic interests. But there are likely to be many exceptions, for example, India and South Korea, which traditionally have not welcomed wholly owned foreign operations. Another exception centers on the privatization of state-owned enterprises, for which prospective buyers must negotiate on much more than the price. Still another exception involves negotiations in countries transforming from centrally planned to market economies, which are apt to be very long and complex.

Further, historically there have been broad swings in host-country attitudes toward private ownership, especially foreign ownership. The present welcoming of FDI could easily reverse, particularly if governments feel their own constituencies are not receiving a just share of global economic benefits. For example, Sri Lanka has passed legislation to allow the renationalization of privatized companies where new owners fail to manage them successfully, and the Socialist party in France has indicated that it might renationalize certain companies if it is returned to power.[69] Regardless of the direction national policies take, companies are likely to face ever more sophisticated governmental officials when they negotiate their operating terms abroad.

It is probably safe to say that companies headquartered in different countries will continue to become more entwined through joint ventures, licensing, contract buying, and other arrangements. Many of these companies also will continue to depend more on sales and production outside their home countries, while simultaneously bringing in more stockholders and top managers from abroad. These activities may strengthen their positions with respect to all governments but may weaken them relative to their home-country governments, which will no longer see them as representing a national interest.

Government-to-government cooperation to deal with MNEs is apt to develop slowly, at least on a global scale. There are simply too many divergent interests among countries that tend to divide them on issues of economic development, product-specific interests, and regional viewpoints. One such issue is the protection of intangibles—it pits the interests of industrial countries, which create most of the products that can be patented, trademarked, or copyrighted, against the interests of many LDCs, which do not want to pay for their use. In this area there may be more linkages to other aspects of overall economic policy, such as the cessation of trade preferences for countries that do not protect IPRs. There also may be more attempts by small groups of countries, such as those operating in trading blocs, to band together to unify or coordinate policies toward MNEs.

WEB CONNECTION
Check out our home page for links to World Wide Web resources on intellectual property rights, copyrights, patents and trademarks, and other relevant chapter topics.

Summary

- **Although host countries and MNEs may hold resources that, if combined, could achieve objectives for both, conflict may cause one or both parties to withhold those resources, thus preventing the full functioning of international business activities.**

- **Both MNE managers and host-country governmental officials must respond to interest groups that may perceive different advantages or no advantage at all to the business-government relationship. Therefore the relationship's final outcome may not be the one expected from a purely economic viewpoint.**

- **Negotiations increasingly are used to determine the terms under which a company may operate in a foreign country. This negotiating process is similar to the domestic processes of company acquisition and collective bargaining. The major differences in the international sphere are the much larger number of provisions, the general lack of a fixed time duration for an agreement, the need to agree on valuation of a company's property, and cultural differences among negotiators.**

- **The terms under which an MNE may be permitted to operate in a given country will be determined to a great extent by the relative degree to which the company needs the country, and vice versa. As the relative needs evolve over time, new terms of operation will reflect the shift in bargaining strength.**

- Generally, a company's best bargaining position is before it makes an investment. Once resources are committed to the foreign operation, the company may not be able to move elsewhere easily.

- Since international negotiations are conducted largely between parties whose cultures, educational backgrounds, and expectations differ, it is very difficult for these negotiators to understand each other's sentiments and present convincing arguments. Role-playing offers negotiators a means of anticipating responses and planning an approach to the actual bargaining.

- Historically, developed countries used military intervention and coercion to ensure that the terms agreed on between their investors and host countries would be carried out. A series of international resolutions have caused the near demise of these methods for settling disputes. Recently, developed countries have used the promise of giving or withholding loans and/or aid and the threat of trade sanctions.

- Several bilateral treaties have been established in which host countries agree to compensate investors for losses from expropriation, civil disturbances, and currency devaluation or control.

- International organizations or groups in countries not involved in a dispute are frequently used to arbitrate trade disputes among individuals from more than one country. This method has been used very rarely to settle investment disputes, however, because governments are reluctant to relinquish sovereignty over what occurs within their borders.

- International agreements have been made to protect important intangible property such as patents, trademarks, and copyrights. Since millions of dollars are often spent in the development of these assets, worldwide protection is important for their owners.

- Recently, a big problem for companies has been the pirating of intangible assets in countries that have not signed international agreements or do not actively enforce their own laws on protection of IPRs.

- Public relations may be used by companies to develop a good image, overcome a bad one, and create useful proponents for their positions. If successful, this strategy may result in better terms of operation for either side.

Case
PepsiCo in India[70]

Despite PepsiCo's operations in nearly 150 countries and territories, its chairman, D. Wayne Calloway, said, "We are still basically an American company with offshore interests. As the nineties progress, that's going to change. We'll be a truly global consumer products company." A key part of that strategy was the company's launching of an Indian snack-food and soft-drink joint venture in 1990. At that time, the company announced plans to invest $1 billion in India during the 1990s. Calloway also said, "We see ourselves as partners in India's progress. . . . We look forward to delivering the kinds of products, technologies, and marketing know-how that serve India's priorities."

The Global Competitive Situation

Two companies, Coca-Cola and PepsiCo, have dominated the global market for soft drinks. The United States has been the biggest market, with annual per capita consumption of about thirty-two cases. Analysts agree that this consumption figure is so large that almost all growth must come from building market share rather than getting people to increase consumption. Even so, the companies have promoted the consumption of soft drinks at breakfast and have added new soft-drink varieties to try to increase consumption. The fierce competition between the two companies within the United States has resulted in industry returns on assets and sales that are less than half what they have been abroad. Within the United States the two companies are close rivals. But in terms of total global sales, Coca-Cola's 47-percent share in 1990 was more than double PepsiCo's; consequently, Coca-Cola has been much stronger where profits are higher and where sales growth is expected to be much faster. For example, per capita consumption outside the United States is only about 14 percent of that in the United States; thus there is much more room to grow. In 1993, Coca-Cola earned almost 80 percent of its profits outside the United States, as opposed to only 15 percent for PepsiCo. Globally, players other than Coca-Cola and PepsiCo are small in comparison. However, some have large shares in specific country or regional markets; an example is Cadbury Schweppes in the United Kingdom.

In the soft-drink industry, it is generally conceded that there is a tremendous advantage in being first into a market. Not only is brand loyalty built up fast and difficult to change, but the early entrants gain the best bottlers/distributors. Coca-Cola preceded PepsiCo into Western Europe, Latin America, and Japan, and PepsiCo has had an uphill battle building market share in those areas. PepsiCo, however, beat Coca-Cola into the former Soviet Union in 1974 and thus dominates that market.

Because of the first-in advantage, PepsiCo has pushed hard in recent years to enter markets in which Coca-Cola is not dominant. For example, PepsiCo entered Myanmar ahead of Coca-Cola in 1990. When the United States lifted its trade embargo with Vietnam in 1994, PepsiCo began soft drink production there within hours, and Coca-Cola announced it would begin producing there as soon as concentrate and other materials could be brought into the country. In the early 1990s, both companies announced large capital investments in emerging markets and in LDCs in which the other held advantages. Some of the notable examples are shown on Map 12.2.

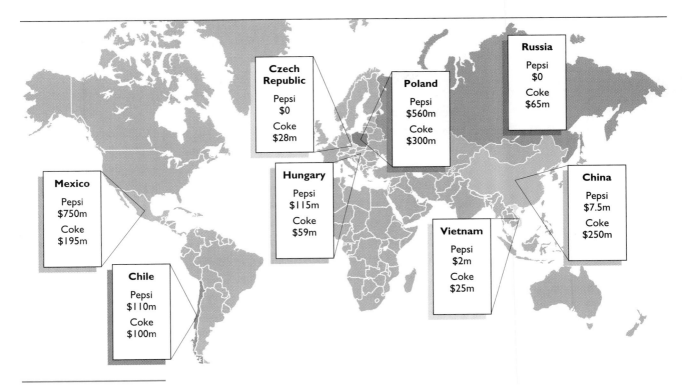

Map 12.2
Selected Capital Investment Announcements (Early 1990s): Pepsi and Coke

Note that PepsiCo and Coca-Cola are investing to counter each other's strong position in Russia and Mexico, respectively.

Source: Data were taken from company reports and appeared in Kenneth H. Hammonds, "Just What They Need," *Business Week,* August 30, 1993, p. 46.

Indian Market Potential

PepsiCo had been in the Indian market during the mid-1950s but pulled out because of lack of profitability. Coca-Cola had operated in India since 1950 but left in 1977 because of disagreements with the Indian government. Coca-Cola's departure created an opportunity for PepsiCo; however, it did not begin its three years of formal negotiations with the Indian government until 1985. After Coca-Cola's departure, an Indian company, Parle Exports, became the dominant supplier in India with its soft drink, Thums Up. By 1988, Parle Exports had estimated annual sales of about $150 million, which made up between 60 and 70 percent of the market. It also was exporting a mango pulp drink, Maaza Mango, to various markets, including the United States.

The Indian market for soft drinks has been growing rapidly. When Coca-Cola departed, annual soft-drink sales were a little over a half-billion bottles a year. By 1990, they were about 3 billion bottles a year and were expected to quadruple during the 1990s. India's population growth was expected to make it surpass China as the world's most populated country. Further, India's middle class is much larger than China's; it was estimated at 150 million people when PepsiCo entered formal negotiations with the Indian government. By 1992, this market was estimated at 300 million. Additionally, many observers have predicted that India will eventually become an economic giant; thus growing incomes should support more sales. Another indication of market potential was that India's per capita consumption of soft drinks was estimated at only 3 bottles per year in 1989, compared to 13 bottles per year in neighboring Pakistan. Coca-Cola was selling 122 bottles per capita annually in Latin America, also a low-income area.

Indian Attitude toward Foreign Investment

India's attitude was summed up by the president of the Associated Chambers of Commerce and Industry of India, who said, "The basic thing is that most of our people, in all political parties, have no concept of how the world is moving. My political friends think it's the seventeenth century and that every investment, like the East India Company, is going to come into India and take over." His reference was to the long domination of India by British, French, and Portuguese interests, which had extracted great wealth from India without returning noticeable benefit to its economy.

India has approved foreign investment on a case-by-case basis with approval necessary at the highest governmental level. By the time PepsiCo began its negotiations, the maximum equity holding allowed for foreign investors was only 40 percent of an Indian enterprise. Further, foreign companies were required to develop exports to compensate for imported equipment and components and for dividend payments.

Because of this political sensitivity, negotiations tended to be long and usually were public. Little action was apt to take place during election periods because politicians were afraid of adverse reaction if they supported the entry of foreign companies. For example, when PepsiCo began its negotiations Gillette recently had been granted approval on an investment. Gillette wanted to move into India because it has the world's highest unit razor-blade sales. Gillette spent seven years negotiating during two changes of government and finally agreed to settle for a 24-percent equity holding, to export 25 percent of its output, and not to use its name on its products. The name issue has been important to Indian authorities because of a belief that many consumers will think wrongly that a foreign-associated product is better and because a locally associated brand name would provide greater continuity if the foreign investor left the market on its own or by government decree.

Coca-Cola and IBM both left India at about the same time because of the strict operating restrictions that had come about after their initial entry. Coca-Cola objected to three governmental demands: that it reduce its equity holding from 100 to 40 percent, that it divulge its formula, and that it use dual trademarks so that Indian consumers would familiarize themselves with a local logo. Coca-Cola was particularly adamant about the latter two demands. It always had relied on the mystique of a secret formula for its promotion, and it feared an expropriation once the new trademark became accepted.

There also has been a pervading feeling among non-Indian companies that Indian competitors can and do use a great deal of influence to prevent foreign competition. Officially, the foreign company is told that its application has simply run into "political difficulties," but behind the scenes, Indian business leaders align themselves with Indian political leaders. For example, when Coca-Cola was given its directives in 1977, Ramesh Chauhan, the head of

Parle Exports, was an ally of Prime Minister Moraji Desai, and Coca-Cola executives were close to Indira Gandhi, the head of the opposition party.

The Negotiations

PepsiCo first negotiated a contingent joint-venture arrangement with two Indian companies it felt could ease the negotiation process. One of these was a division of Tata Industries, perhaps India's most powerful private company. The second was a government-owned company, Punjab Agro Industries, whose involvement gave the appearance that the public interest would be served in the venture.

Although the initial investment was only $15 million, approval had to be given at the cabinet level. There were twenty parliamentary debates, fifteen committee reviews, and 5,000 articles in the press about the proposed investment over a three-year period.

PepsiCo and its partners proposed that the new company be located in the politically volatile state of Punjab, where they enlisted the support of Sikh leaders who lobbied publicly on their behalf. They claimed that Sikh terrorism might be subdued by providing jobs and help to Punjabi farmers. The partners estimated that the investment would create 25,000 jobs in the Punjab and another 25,000 elsewhere. They also pointed out that China and the former Soviet Union had allowed entry of foreign soft-drink producers; thus India was out of step even with other socialist countries. They argued further that new technology and know-how would prevent some of the wastage of Punjabi fruits, estimated to be about 30 percent. Finally, they contended that the lack of competition with foreign companies had kept prices and profit margins artificially high so that there was little incentive for local companies to grow and distribute widely. Competitive soft-drink sales were limited primarily to the largest cities.

Opponents contended that foreign capital and imports should be restricted to those high-technology areas in which India lacked expertise, that the venture's proposed production of processed foods (such as potato chips, corn chips, fruit drinks, and sauces) would simply displace what could be made in the home, and that imported equipment would hurt India's balance of payments. Also, journalists widely reported that PepsiCo had a CIA connection aimed at undermining India's independence.

Meanwhile, in 1987 another U.S.-based company, Double-Cola, successfully terminated a secret six-year negotiation. The agreement called for the company to open three bottling plants immediately and another twenty-seven later. Double-Cola apparently had an advantage in that it was controlled by nonresident Indians in London, and the Indian Prime Minister, Rajiv Gandhi, wanted to lure investment from Indians living overseas. Double-Cola also promised to use Indian raw materials and to reinvest profits in India.

The agreement with the PepsiCo group, signed in 1988, included the following provisions:

1. The company would export five times the value of its imports, about $150 million over the first ten-year period of operations.
2. Soft-drink sales would not exceed 25 percent of the joint venture's sales.

3. PepsiCo would limit its ownership to 39.9 percent.
4. Seventy-five percent of concentrate would be exported.
5. The joint venture would establish an agricultural research center.
6. The company could sell Pepsi Era, 7-Up Era, and Miranda Era.
7. The joint venture would set up fruit and vegetable processing plants.

Aftermath and Renegotiation

Once PepsiCo's venture was approved, Coca-Cola made an application to re-enter the Indian market through production within an export processing zone. Producing in this way would allow 25 percent of output to be sold within India rather than in export markets. This proposal threatened PepsiCo because the Coca-Cola name was still well-remembered in India; cans of Coke were even smuggled in from Nepal. But after sixteen months, Coca-Cola's application was denied, leading a Coca-Cola official to say that India "doesn't follow its own rules."

In late 1989, a new prime minister, V. P. Singh, took power in a minority government. As finance minister in the mid-1980s, he had promoted liberalizing FDI. However, after taking power, he almost immediately made conflicting statements about such investment. In early 1990, the PepsiCo venture began production of snack foods and announced that soft-drink production would start up by summer. Prime Minister Singh announced the government would reexamine the PepsiCo agreement.

Several things then happened in quick succession. Because of India's strict FDI regulations, the U.S. government, without public reference to PepsiCo, threatened to impose trade sanctions against India under its Super 301 legislation. Indian governmental officials and the joint venture's management then met secretly. Subsequently, PepsiCo agreed to place a new logo, Lehar, above the Pepsi insignia. It also lobbied publicly against Super 301 sanctions against India. The U.S. government backed down. And India's Minister of Food Processing Industries announced tax breaks for food processors.

In 1991, P. V. Narasimha Rao was elected Prime Minister and launched broad economic changes, including a more welcome attitude toward FDI. A Foreign Investment Promotion Board was established, and ownership requirements were changed to allow 51-percent foreign ownership of companies. The new policies gave confidence to foreign investors, and both IBM and Coca-Cola re-entered the market. Coca-Cola announced its return in 1993 through a joint venture with Parle Exports and agreed to export three times the value of its imports; it also announced it would export plastic beverage cases to compensate for its imports of concentrate. Three years later, Indian authorities approved a $700 million expansion by Coca-Cola.

However, in 1995 political opponents of FDI garnered enough strength to cause renegotiation of the Enron power project and to harass PepsiCo. A group of 400 militant protestors smashed Pepsi bottles and burned Pepsi posters. PepsiCo's first Kentucky Fried Chicken (KFC) restaurant in Bangladore had to be protected by police because of threats, and then it was closed temporarily because of allegations of using too much monosodium glutamate, and because the chicken industry diverts available land to meat instead of traditional food production. KFC's second restaurant in New Delhi was closed for a month because two flies were found in its kitchen. Both PepsiCo's and Coca-Cola's sales were temporarily suspended because prices on bottles were smudged.

Questions

1. Did PepsiCo make too many concessions in order to enter the Indian market? Could the company have negotiated better terms?
2. In light of later events, should Coca-Cola have abandoned the Indian market in 1977?
3. From an Indian standpoint, evaluate the government's restrictions on FDI.
4. What behavioral factors might affect negotiations involving managers and government officials from the United States and India?

Chapter Notes

1. Data for the case were taken from Louis Morano, "Multinationals and Nation-States: The Case of Aramco," *Orbis,* Summer, 1979, pp. 447–468; "Saudi Takeover of Aramco Looms," *Wall Street Journal,* August 6, 1980, p. 21; Ted D'Affisio, "Aramco Long-Term Contract with Saudis May Pressure Oil Company Earnings," *The Oil Daily,* February 9, 1987, p. 3; "Aramco Has Been the Bridge Between Two Nations," *The Oil Daily,* September 18, 1989, p. B-19; Andrew Pollack, "Saudi Stake of U.S. Companies," *New York Times,* August 21, 1990, p. C1+; Gene G. Marcial, "If a Shooting War Breaks Out, Fluor Will Win," *Business Week,* December 10, 1990, p. 209; Gerald F. Seib and Peter Waldman, "Best of Friends," *Wall Street Journal,* October 26, 1992, p. A1+; "World Oil Industry: More Private Co.'s but State-Owned Co.'s Still Dominate," *Petroleum Times,* Vol. 16, No. 11, June 3, 1996, p. 8; Karen Matusic, "Saudi's Greek Refining Deal Extends Downstream Reach," *Reuter European Business Report,* March 14, 1996; Paul Mollet, "Aramco Man Gets Top Job," *Petroleum Economist,* Vol. 62, No. 9, September 1995, p. 36; Steven Swindells, "Saudi Oil Power Seen Growing in Europe," *Reuters Financial Service,* May 27, 1996; Richard J. Barnet and John Cavanaugh, *Global Dreams Imperil Corporations and the New World Order* (New York: Simon & Schuster, 1994); Joe Avancena, "Aramco Plans to Acquire Petrogal Shares," *Moneyclips,* August 31, 1996; and Neil Fullick, "Asia and Gulf Increasing Ties Because of Crude Oil," *Reuter Asia-Pacific Business Report,* September 10, 1996.

2. Jean J. Boddewyn and Thomas L. Brewer, "International-Business Political Behavior: New Theoretical Directions," *Academy of Management Review,* Vol. 19, No. 1, 1994, pp. 119–143.

3. J. Grieco, "Foreign Investment and Development: Theories and Evidence," in *Investing in Development: New Roles for Private Capital?* T. Moran, ed. (New Brunswick, N.J.: Transaction Books, 1986); and D. Encarnation, *Dislodging Multinationals: India's Strategy in Comparative Perspective* (Ithaca, N.Y.: Cornell University Press, 1989).

4. Andrew Jack, "Paris Tries to Lure Foreign Business," *Financial Times,* April 27–28, 1996, p. 2.

5. Boddewyn and Brewer, op. cit.

6. Allen R. Myerson, "O Governor, Won't You Buy Me a Mercedes Plant?" *New York Times,* September 1, 1996, sec. 3, p. 1+.

7. Thomas P. Murtha and Stephanie Ann Lenway, "Country Capabilities and the Strategic State: How National Political Institutions Affect Multinational Corporations' Strategies," *Strategic Management Journal,* Vol. 15, 1994, pp. 113–129.

8. "GM Wins Biddings for China Auto Project," *Wall Street Journal,* October 24, 1995, p. A3; and Christopher Bobinski and Kevin Done, "Daewoo Overtakes GM in Race for Polish Carmaker," *Financial Times,* August 28, 1995, p. 2.

9. For a detailed discussion of these variables, see Sushil Vachani, "Enhancing the Obsolescing Bargain Theory: A Longitudinal Study of Foreign Ownership of U.S. and European Multinationals," *Journal of International Business Studies,* Vol. 26, No. 1, 1995, p. 159.

10. Laurence Hooper, "France Chooses IBM to Bolster Groupe Bull," *Wall Street Journal,* January 29, 1992, p. A3.

11. David W. Cravens, H. Kirk Downey, and Paul Lauritano, "Global Competition in the Commercial Aircraft Industry," *Columbia Journal of World Business,* Winter 1992, pp. 47–58.

12. Thane Peterson, "Can Europe Catch Up in the High-Tech Race?" *Business Week,* October 23, 1989, p. 142+.

13. Thane Peterson, Frank J. Comes, Jonathan Kapstein, Steven J. Dryden, and John J. Keller, "The Swedes Give AT&T and the U.S. Painful Black Eyes," *Business Week,* No. 2997, May 4, 1987, pp. 44–45. For a discussion of U.S. government efforts to persuade Japan to remove its barriers to direct investment, see Marcus W. Brauchli, "U.S. to Prod Tokyo on Easing Investment," *Wall Street Journal,* November 2, 1989, p. A18.

14. John M. Stopford, "The Impact of the Global Political Economy on Corporate Strategy," (Pittsburgh: Carnegie Mellon University, Carnegie Bosch Institute working paper No. 94-7, 1994).

15. "Transparency in Incentives Policy Urged," *Transnationals,* Vol. 7, No. 2, June 1995, p. 1+.

16. Miriam Jordan, "Enron of U.S. Settles Indian Power Dispute," *Wall Street Journal,* January 9, 1996, p. A10; Allen R. Myerson, "Tentative Pact Allows Enron to Continue Project in India," *New York Times,* November 22, 1995, p. C1+; "The Mugging of Enron," *Euromoney,* October 1995, pp. 22–33; and "Enron to Drop Case Against India," *Wall Street Journal,* July 26, 1996, p. A8.

17. Vachani, loc. cit.

18. Some differences for U.S. negotiators are noted in Toshyuki Arai, "Negotiating with Japanese Corporations," *Export Today,* November–December 1992, pp. 32–35; and David L. James, "Don't Think About Winning," *Across the Board,* April 1992, pp. 49–51.

19. James, loc. cit.

20. William A. Stoever, "Renegotiations: The Cutting Edge of Relations between MNCs and LDCs," *Columbia Journal of World Business*, Spring 1979, pp. 12–13.

21. For an elaboration of this subject, see Stephen E. Weiss, "Negotiations With 'Romans'—Part 1," *Sloan Management Review*, Vol. 35, No. 2, Winter 1994, pp. 51–61; and Stephen E. Weiss, "Negotiations With 'Romans'—Part 2," *Sloan Management Review*, Vol. 35, No. 3, Spring 1994, pp. 85–99.

22. Nancy J. Adler, Richard Brahm, and John L. Graham, "Strategy Implementation: A Comparison of Face-to-Face Negotiations in the People's Republic of China and the United States," *Strategic Management Journal*, Vol. 13, No. 6, September 1992, p. 463.

23. William A. Stoever, "Why State Corporations in Developing Countries Have Failed to Attract Foreign Investment," *International Marketing Review*, Vol. 6, No. 3, 1989, pp. 62–77.

24. Julian Gresser, "Breaking the Japanese Negotiating Code: What European and American Managers Must Do to Win," *European Management Journal*, Vol. 10, No. 3, September 1992, pp. 286–293.

25. Thomas L. Brewer, "International Investment Dispute Settlement Procedures: The Evolving Regime for Foreign Direct Investment," *Law & Policy in International Business*, Vol. 26, No. 2, 1995, pp. 633–672.

26. George Schwarzenberger, "The Protection of British Property Abroad," *Current Legal Problems*, Vol. 5, 1952, pp. 295–299; Oliver J. Lissitzyn, *International Law Today and Tomorrow* (Dobbs Ferry, N.Y.: Oceana Publications, 1965), p. 77; and Gillis Wetter, "Diplomatic Assistance to Private Investment," *University of Chicago Law Review*, Vol. 29, 1962, p. 275.

27. Amy Borrus, "Why Pinstripes Don't Suit the Cloak-and-Dagger Crowd," *Business Week*, May 17, 1993, p. 39; and Jeff Cole, "Hughes Aircraft Cancels Paris Display After Warning of a French Spy Scheme," *Wall Street Journal*, April 26, 1993, p. A4.

28. Robert S. Greenberger, "Foreigners Use Bribes to Beat U.S. Rivals In Many Deals New Report Concludes," *Wall Street Journal*, October 12, 1995, p. 3.

29. William Dawkins, "Japan Angered by Claims of U.S. Spy at Car Talks," *Financial Times*, October 17, 1995, p. 1.

30. Robert Keatley, "CIA Finds a New Focus: Espionage and Bribery That Hurt U.S. Business," *Wall Street Journal*, January 15, 1994, p. A8.

31. Alice Rawsthorn, "Piracy 'Costs US Industries $14.6bn'," *Financial Times*, February 10, 1997, p. 6.

32. Johnathan Friedland, "Bristol-Myers Aims to Boost Patent Laws As Argentine Unit Sells Pirate Drugs," *Wall Street Journal*, September 23, 1996, p. A16.

33. Ian Brownlie, *Principles of Public International Law* (Oxford, England: Oxford University Press, 1966), pp. 435–436.

34. Green H. Hackworth, *Digest of International Law* (Washington, D.C.: U.S. Government Printing Office, 1942), pp. 655–661.

35. Michael A. Geist, "Toward a General Agreement on the Regulation of Foreign Direct Investment," *Law & Policy in International Business*, Vol. 26, No. 3, Spring 1995, pp. 673–717.

36. For an extensive treatise of the theory, see Robert A. Packenham, *The Dependency Movement: Scholarship and Politics in Development Studies* (Cambridge, MA: Harvard University Press, 1992). For some different national views of its validity, see Ndiva Kofele-Kale, "The Political Economy of Foreign Direct Investment: A Framework for Analyzing Investment Laws and Regulations in Developing Countries," *Law & Policy in International Business*, Vol. 23, No. 2-3, 1992, pp. 619–671; Walter T. Molano, "Lessons for Latin America," *Christian Science Monitor*, December 8, 1995, p. 18; and Stanley K. Sheinbaum, "Very Recent History Has Absolved Socialism," *New Perspectives Quarterly*, Vol. 13, No. 1, January 1996.

37. Paul Jensen, "Political Risk Coverage Eases Entry into Perilous Markets," *Export Today*, November–December 1992, pp. 39–42; and Malcolm Richard Wilkey, "Introduction to Dispute Settlement in International Trade and Foreign Direct Investment," *Law & Policy in International Business*, Vol. 2, No. 2, 1995, pp. 613–631.

38. At this writing, the future to extend OPIC is in question. See Nancy Dunne, "House Clips Wings of U.S. Overseas Investment Agency," *Financial Times*, September 13, 1996, p. 6; and Nancy Dunne, "Record Year Lifts OPIC Hopes on Reauthorization," *Financial Times*, December 6, 1996, p. 19.

39. "US West Media Group's Russian Venture Receives $200 Million Loan Facility from OPIC," *M2 Presswire*, August 16, 1996.

40. William A. Stoever, "Issues Emerging in Iranian Claims Negotiations," *Wall Street Journal*, May 7, 1981, p. 26; Carol Giacomo, "U.S., Iran Reach Agreement on Assets Disputes," *Reuters North American Wire*, November 29, 1991; and "Iranian Assets Worth Several Billion Dollars Still in U.S.," *Moneyclips*, June 25, 1994.

41. Brewer, loc. cit.

42. Brewer, loc. cit.

43. Frances Williams, "WTO Push for Investment Rules Pact," *Financial Times*, October 17, 1996, p. 4.

44. A good overview of the issues can be found in Keith E. Maskers, "Intellectual Property Rights and the Uruguay Round," *Economic Review: Federal Reserve Bank of Kansas City*, First Quarter 1993, pp. 11–26.

45. Eric Schine and Paul Magnusson, "Clay Jacobson Calls It Patently Unfair," *Business Week*, August 19, 1991, p. 48.

46. Peggy E. Chaudhry and Michael G. Walsh, "Intellectual Property Rights," *Columbia Journal of World Business*, Vol. 30, No. 2, Summer 1995, pp. 80–92.

47. Thomas J. Maronick, "European Patent Laws and Decisions: Implications for Multinational Marketing Strategy," *International Marketing Review*, Vol. 5, No. 2, Summer 1988, pp. 20–30.

48. "Jeu Zespri," *Economist*, August 10, 1996, p. 48.

49. "EU and U.S. End Drink Dispute," *Wall Street Journal*, March 29, 1994, p. A10.

50. Andrew Hill, "Habitat's Move into Italy Challenged," *Financial Times*, May 8, 1996, p. 2.

51. Frances Williams, "Welcome for Updated Rules on Copyright," *Financial Times*, December 23, 1996, p. 3.

52. Chaudhry and Walsh, loc. cit.

53. Chaudhry and Walsh, loc. cit.; and Rawsthorn, loc. cit.

54. "Car Knockoffs Spread in China," *Wall Street Journal*, November 20, 1995, p. A10; Andrea Adelson, "Retail Fact, Retail Fiction," *New York Times*, September 16, 1995; Joseph Kahn, "China's Consumers Profit by Ferreting Fake Brands," *Wall Street Journal*, January 4, 1996, p. B1.

55. Steven Erlanger, "Thailand, Where Pirated Tapes Are Everywhere and Profitable," *New York Times*, November 27, 1990, pp. B1–B2.

56. Michael G. Harvey and Ilkka A. Ronkainen, "International Counterfeiters: Marketing Success Without the Cost and the Risk," *Columbia Journal of World Business*, Vol. 20, No. 3, Fall 1985, p. 39.

57. Peter H. Lewis, "As Piracy Grows, the Software Industry Counterattacks," *New York Times*, November 8, 1992, p. 12F.

58. "Fake Drugs," *The Economist*, May 2, 1992, pp. 85–86.

59. Shenliang Deng, Pam Townsend, Maurice Robert, and Normand Quesnel, "A Guide To Intellectual Property Rights In Southest Asia and China," *Business Horizons*, November–December 1996, pp. 43–51.

60. Chaudhry and Walsh, loc. cit.

61. Simon Holberton, Tony Walker, Caroline Southey, and Ronald Van de Krol, "World's Counterfeiters Work Overtime for Windows 95," *Financial Times*, August 19–20, 1995, p. 3.

62. Louis Kraar, "Fighting the Fakes from Taiwan," *Fortune,* Vol. 107, No. 11, May 30, 1983, pp. 114–116; "Two Who Smuggled Counterfeit Computers Get Prison and Fines," *Wall Street Journal,* May 1, 1984, p. 62; and Todd Mason, "How High Tech Foils the Counterfeiters," *Business Week,* May 20, 1985, p. 119.

63. Harvey and Ronkainen, op. cit., p. 43.

64. David M. Schilling and Ruth Rosenbaum, "Principles for Global Corporate Responsibility," *Business and Society Review,* Vol. 94, Summer 1995, pp. 55–56.

65. Robert Taylor, "Code of Conduct for Toy Makers," *Financial Times,* June 4, 1996, p. 4.

66. Robert S. Greenberger, "Clinton to Unveil Voluntary Business Code," *Asian Wall Street Journal,* March 27, 1995, p. 12.

67. Robert D. Haas, "Ethics in the Third World," *Across the Board,* May 1994, pp. 12–13.

68. Belmont F. Haydel, "Description and Analysis of Johnson & Johnson's Strategic Management Process of Its Live for Life Program," paper presented at the Academy of International Business Northeast Annual Meeting, Baltimore, Md., June 5, 1989; "1992 General Motors Public Interest Report"; Michael Schroeder and Jonathan Kapstein, "Charity Doesn't Begin at Home Anymore," *Business Week,* February 25, 1991, p. 91; Elyse Tanouye,

"Merck's Drug Giveaway Hits Roadblocks," *Wall Street Journal,* September 23, 1992, p. B1; Sony Annual Report 1995; and HTTP://www.VOLVO.SE/ENVIRONMENT/PRIZE.HTM/#foundation

69. Amal Jayasinghe, "Sri Lanka May Reclaim Companies," *Financial Times,* August 8, 1996, p. 6; and David Owen, "Socialists 'Might Renationalize France Télécom'," *Financial Times,* February 10, 1997, p. 3.

70. Data for the case were taken from Subrata N. Chakravarty, "How Pepsi Broke into India," *Forbes,* November 27, 1989, pp. 43–44; Lincoln Kaye, "Pepping Up the Punjab," *Far Eastern Economic Review,* October 27, 1988, pp. 77–78; Steven R. Weisman, "Pepsi Sets Off a Cola War in India," *New York Times,* March 21, 1988, p. 28; Anthony Spaeth, "India Beckons— and Frustrates," *Wall Street Journal,* September 22, 1989, pp. R23–R25; "A Passage to India," *Panorama,* February 1989, n.p.; Barbara Crossette, "After Long Fight, Pepsi Enters India," *New York Times,* May 24, 1990, p. C2; Michael J. McCarthy, "India Gives Final Approval to Pepsi's Plans," *Wall Street Journal,* May 24, 1990, p. A5; Anthony Spaeth and Ajai Singh, "India Rejects Coca-Cola's Bid to Sell Soft Drinks, Giving Pepsi an Advantage," *Wall Street Journal,* March 16, 1990, p. B5; "Losses at PepsiCo Venture in India," *New*

York Times, February 16, 1991, p. 33; Susan Dubey, "India Clears Some Foreign Investments, Sending Bullish Signal on Reform Drive," *Wall Street Journal,* June 24, 1993, p. A8; "India Clears Venture, Includes Coke's Return," *New York Times,* June 24, 1993, p. C3; "Coke Returns to India," *Herald Times* (Bloomington, Ind.), p. B6; Joyce E. Davis and Ricardo Sookdeo, "Pepsi Opens a Second Front," *Fortune,* August 8, 1994, pp. 71–76; "PepsiCo, Coke Move Fast on Vietnam Production," *Wall Street Journal,* February 7, 1994, p. B3; Miriam Jordan, "Indian Nationalists Pick the Next Target," *Wall Street Journal,* August 8, 1995, p. A9; "KFC Outlet in India Reopens," *Wall Street Journal,* December 5, 1995, p. A12; John F. Burns, "India Effort vs. Foreign Business Upsets American Chain," *New York Times,* September 14, 1995, p. C6; "New Delhi Suspends Sales of Pepsi, Coke," *BC Cycle,* January 20, 1996; "PepsiCo Will Not Be Thrown Out of India," *Agence France Presse,* November 21, 1995; Narayan Madhavan, "Indian Leftists To Launch Campaign Against Pepsi," *Reuter Asia-Pacific Business Report,* October 15, 1995; and Miriam Jordan, "U.S. Ambassador to India Means Business," *Wall Street Journal,* July 31, 1996, p. A11.

Latin America is best known in international business for its exports of traditional agriculture and mineral products. However, service and manufacturing (including high-tech products) have been growing in importance. Here a Brazilian technician assembles solar panels. The photo is set against a backdrop of a Peruvian mantle from Paracas (circa 0-100AD).

Chapter 13

Country Evaluation and Selection

If the profits are great,
the risks are great.

—Chinese Proverb

Objectives

- To discuss company strategies for sequencing the penetration of countries and committing resources

- To explain how clues from the environmental climate can help managers limit geographic alternatives

- To examine the major variables a company should consider when deciding whether and where to expand abroad

- To overview methods and problems of collecting and comparing information internationally

- To describe some simplifying tools for determining a global geographic strategy

- To introduce how final investment, reinvestment, and divestment decisions are made

Case
Ford Motor
Company[1]

Ford is a large company by any standard—the world's fourth largest industrial company and the second largest automaker. But when it became highly involved internationally, it was still a small company. Ford began operations in 1903 and exported the sixth car it built. By 1911, the company boasted that a man could drive around the world and stop every night at a garage handling Ford parts. By 1930, Ford was manufacturing or assembling automobiles in twenty foreign countries and had sales branches in another ten. Today, Ford cars and trucks are distributed through more than 10,500 dealers in more than 200 countries and territories. Yet as large and internationally involved as Ford is, it must allocate its limited financial and human resources to maintain emphasis on those markets and production locations that are most compatible with corporate expectations and objectives.

Although foreign expansion was a stated objective at Ford's first annual meeting, the company initially was passive about where the emphasis would be. Ford's first foreign sales branches and assembly operations, in Canada, England, and France, were established because people in those countries made proposals to Ford. Ford also made international expansion decisions on a highly decentralized basis. Much of its European expansion was handled through the British operation, and its British Commonwealth expansion was implemented through the Canadian company. Where sales grew most rapidly, for example, in Argentina, Uruguay, and Brazil, Ford established assembly operations in order to save on costs of transportation by limiting the bulk of shipments. Much of Ford's early expansion, therefore, was based not on scanning the globe to choose the best locations, but rather on taking advantage of opportunities as they came along.

Ford's pattern of international activities also has been influenced by policies that the company's management considered essential. One of these stated that Ford would manufacture or assemble only at production facilities in which it had a controlling interest. The concept of control in Ford's case went beyond that of voting shares. For example, in 1930, a Ford group inspected potential production sites in China and reported to Henry Ford that the title for any Ford land purchase in China would have to be made in the name of a Chinese citizen because a foreigner couldn't own land in China. Henry Ford's response was simply, "No." In the 1950s and 1960s, Ford extended this concept of control to the point where nothing short of 100-percent ownership was acceptable. This policy further influenced Ford's geographic emphasis, causing Ford to expend resources to buy out a minority interest in its British company. It also meant abandoning production in India and Spain in 1954 because their governments insisted on sharing ownership. (Ford recommenced Spanish production in 1976. It also no longer adheres to the 100-percent ownership policy; in 1995 it bought a 20 percent interest in Jiangling Motors, a Chinese light truck manufacturer, and received Indian government approval for an automotive joint venture with Mahindra, an Indian automotive and tractor manufacturer.)

Political conditions also have helped to forge Ford's foreign-investment pattern. For example, during World War II its French facility was bombed and subsequently not replaced. Its Hungarian and Romanian assembly facilities were seized by communist governments in 1946. Not until 1977 did Ford establish a separate department to evaluate the external political environment. Changes in government regulations often have caused Ford to commit a high proportion of its resources to a given area during a given period. This occurred, for example, when Mexico required a higher portion of local content (costs incurred locally, usually as a percentage of total costs) in vehicles sold in Mexico, thus forcing Ford to increase its Mexican investment or risk losing sales there.

Despite its extended and heavy commitment to foreign operations, Ford's production and sales are highly concentrated in a few countries. Ford sells in over 200 countries and territories and has production in 30, yet Fig. 13.1 shows that over 80 percent of its unit car and truck sales and over 90 percent of its car and truck production are in only four countries. Because of Ford's heavier commitments in some countries than in others, its competitive position is much stronger in some markets than in others. In the United Kingdom and Taiwan, for example, its market shares are much higher than in France and Japan.

Ford's dependence on multiple markets and facilities has minimized year-to-year sales and profit fluctuations. This has occurred because demand and price levels move differently in various countries. For example, between 1994 and 1995, Ford sales in the United States and Canada fell by 5.3 percent and 9.6 percent, respectively, but these declines were partially offset by gains in Germany and Brazil of 5.6 percent and 22.6 percent, respectively. These data illustrate not only the positive effect of geographic diversification on the smoothing of sales, but also the importance of shifting resources in order to exploit areas of greatest profit potential.

With huge amounts of fixed assets already in place, Ford cannot easily abandon countries and then pick them up again. It can, however, compare the attractiveness of each country with actual and potential Ford operations and move toward greater emphasis on those countries that have the most promising outlooks. For example, in the late 1980s, Ford put more emphasis on the Taiwanese automobile market because that market grew faster than any of the company's more established ones. By the mid-1990s Ford announced it would expend greater relative effort until the year 2000 on manufacturing and sales facilities in India, Indonesia, South Korea, Thailand, and Vietnam. Additional export emphasis would be placed on Russia and Turkey. This change in emphasis is consistent with projections showing that the global market share for vehicle sales by all manufacturers in North America, Western Europe, and Japan will fall from 74.5 percent in 1996 to 70.4 percent in

Figure 13.1
Ford's Unit Vehicle Sales and Production
Note that Ford's production is more concentrated than its sales.

Source: Production figures are taken from *Ford Annual Report 1994.* Sales figures are taken from Ford's 10-K report of December 31, 1995.

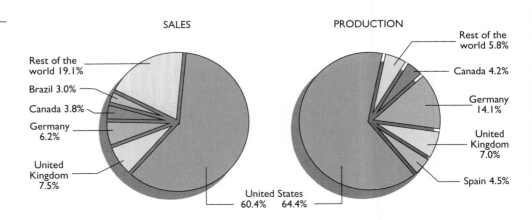

2001. Ford examines each country separately for each of its major product groups because different market conditions may have varying effects on different product groups.

Ford uses a country-comparison matrix (similar to the one shown as Fig. 13.3 and explained later in the chapter) to aid decision makers in choosing where to make strong marketing efforts. Ford ranks countries on one axis in terms of how attractive each one appears in terms of potential sales of a specific product being considered, for example, tractors, trucks, or automobiles. On the other axis, the company ranks the countries in terms of Ford's competitive capabilities for the specific markets. The resultant plotting helps narrow the focus to areas that both look attractive and seem to offer the best fit with Ford's unique capabilities. This is by no means the end of the evaluation process. The exercise does, however, enable the decision makers at Ford to concentrate on more detailed analyses of a manageable list of alternatives and to progress to interrelated decisions, such as where to locate production facilities for the chosen markets.

Introduction

In its early stages, international expansion tends to be passive.

Later expansion cannot take advantage of all opportunities.

Examining international geographic strategies is important because companies seldom have enough resources to take advantage of all opportunities. Committing human, technical, and financial resources to one locale may mean forgoing projects in other areas. Consequently, geographic alternatives are an integral part of a company's decisions on allocating resources.

We have already discussed, primarily in Chapter 1, the effect of companies' competencies on their motives for undertaking international operations. Once they have decided to undertake international operations, their location strategies should, of course, be compatible with their competencies and motives as well. Figure 13.2 repeats the framework introduced in Chapter 1 and highlights that the choice of where to operate is an overlaying tactical alternative to carry out a strategy. The figure also shows that the choice of country is affected by external influences. For example, a company should be better off by going to those countries with economic, political, cultural, and geographic conditions that permit it to utilize its competencies. Because companies' motives and competencies may differ substantially, what may be a very attractive country for one company may, at the same time, be unattractive for another. Nevertheless, the choice of foreign location should be based on the questions "Where can we best leverage our already developed competencies?" and "Where can we go to best sustain, improve, or extend our competencies?" For example, Ford's fixed costs for the development of new automobile models create competencies that may be leveraged by selling these models abroad; thus Ford identifies and emphasizes those markets that appear to offer the best sales opportunities for the types of vehicles and sales methods that Ford has already developed. At the same time, Ford has sought better design capabilities, a motive that drove it to acquire Aston Martin and Jaguar, both of which happened to be located in the United Kingdom.

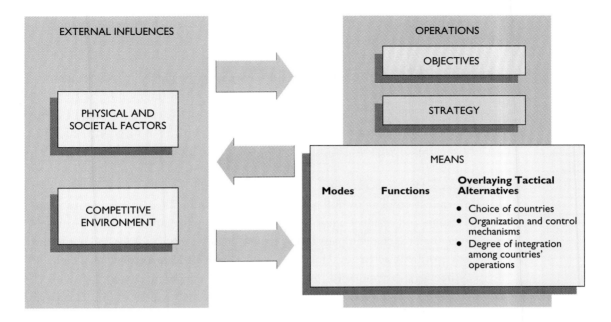

Figure 13.2
Place of Location
Decisions in
International Business
Operations
A company's choice of
countries for its operations
should be determined by
the interaction of its objectives, competencies, and
comparative environmental
fit with conditions within
different countries.

In choosing geographic sites,
a company must decide
• Where to sell
• Where to produce

Choosing Sites for Marketing and Production

Companies must determine where to market and where to produce. For example, a
U.S. company may decide to sell in Canada either by producing in Canada or by
exporting to Canada from the United States or another country. Companies also
must ascertain where to locate such specialized units as R&D departments and
regional headquarters. The answers to two questions—"Which markets should be
served?" and "Where should production be located to serve these markets?" are frequently the same, particularly if transport costs or government regulations mean
that local production is necessary for serving the chosen market. For example,
many service industries, such as hotels, construction, and retailing, must locate
facilities near their foreign customers. In other cases, sales and production may be
in different countries; for example, Ford serves the Italian market with vehicles
produced primarily in its German facilities. Nevertheless, market-location and
production-location decisions are connected.[2] If a company generates sales because
of having developed an innovative product, it must find production cost advantages,
which may be abroad, if it is to sustain a long-term competitive edge. Further, the
ability to move a product or service from one country to another is dependent on
such factors as transportation feasibility and governmental restrictions that may
favor business within a regional trading group. For example, a consortium of U.S.
power companies (Dominion Resources, General Public Utilities, Constellation
Energy, and PP&L Resources) is building a gas-fired power plant in Bolivia to serve
a section of Brazil about 600 miles away.[3] The consortium could not locate much
farther than that because of problems of transporting power over long distances.
Because of governmental restrictions, Ford can market its German-made vehicles

more easily in the rest of the EU and rationalize production more easily within the EU than it can market its U.S.-made vehicles to the EU or rationalize its U.S. production with that in the EU.

Decisions on market and production locations may be highly interdependent for other reasons. For example, a company may have excess production capacity already in place that will influence its relative capabilities to serve markets in different countries. Or it may find a given market very attractive but forgo sales there because it is unwilling to invest in needed production locations.

Overall Geographic Strategy

The determination of an overall geographic strategy must be dynamic because conditions change and results do not always conform to expectations. A plan must be flexible enough to let a company both respond to new opportunities and withdraw from less profitable activities. Unfortunately, there is little agreement on a comprehensive theory or technique for optimizing resource allocation among countries. Further, companies need to make assumptions about such widely varying factors as future costs and prices, competitors' reactions, and technology. Nevertheless, several approaches frequently are used.

A company may expand its international sales by marketing more of its existing product line, by adding products to its line, or by some combination of these two. Most companies begin by asking "Where can we sell more of our products?" instead of "What new product can we make in order to maximize sales in a given market?"[4] Therefore, in this chapter we assume that for the most part, the company has decided on its product line or product portfolio.

In essence, a company needs to decide where to operate *and* what portion of operations to place within each country where it does operate. Fig. 13.3 shows the major steps in making these decisions. The following discussion examines the major reasons for and alternatives within these steps.

Scanning for Alternatives

Recall that Ford used scanning techniques in comparing countries on the basis of broad variables. It did this so that decision makers could perform a much more detailed analysis of a manageable number of geographic alternatives that looked most promising. Scanning is useful because otherwise a company might consider too few or too many possibilities.

Risk of Overlooking Opportunities

As a company tries to optimize its sales or minimize its costs, it can easily overlook or disregard some promising options. Some locations may not be rejected; instead they may be skipped simply because managers either never think of them or decide to go where "everyone else has gone." For example, recently many U.S. companies

**Figure 13.3
Flow Chart for
Choosing Where
to Operate**

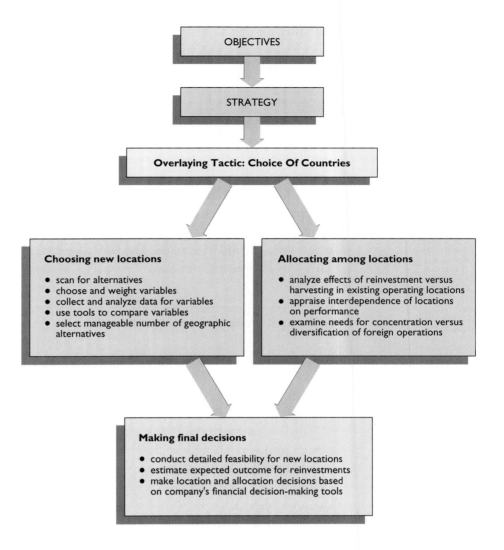

have forgone the world's fastest-growing markets in the developing countries while expanding in the more stable markets of Europe.[5]

Further, certain locales sometimes are lumped together and rejected before being sufficiently examined for expansion possibilities. Botswana, for instance, might not be considered because "Africa is too risky."[6] Or a country may be eliminated because of conditions in a nearby country, as occurred for many Latin American countries because of apprehension concerning investment there after the Cuban revolution.[7]

Risk of Examining Too Many Opportunities

A detailed analysis of every alternative might result in maximized sales or the pinpointing of a least-cost production location; however, the cost of so many studies would erode profits. For a company with 1000 products that might locate in any of

150 countries, there are 150,000 different situations to be analyzed. For each, other alternatives must be considered as well, such as whether to export or to set up a foreign production unit. Any conditions that would greatly enhance the probability of making an investment should be examined before a more detailed feasibility study is completed.

The Environmental Climate

Ford rejected certain potential investments because of its inability to gain sufficient control of the proposed operation. In any company, decision makers' perceptions of the **environmental climate** (those external conditions in host countries that could significantly affect the success or failure of a foreign business enterprise) will determine whether a detailed feasibility study will be undertaken and the terms under which a project will be initiated. The environmental analysis is key in limiting alternatives to a manageable number.

Influential Variables: Opportunities

Investment decisions are made on the basis of expected opportunities versus risks. Opportunities, in turn, are determined by revenues less costs. From a broad scanning perspective, there are variables that indicate the amount of revenue, cost factors, and risk that might be forthcoming from one country versus another.

Examining key variables helps companies
- Determine the order of entry
- Set the rates of resource allocation among countries

The factors that have the most influence on the placement of sales and production emphasis are market size, ease and compatibility of operations, costs, and resource availability. Some of these variables are more important for the sales-allocation decision; others are more important for the production-location decision; others affect both.

The ranking, or prioritizing, of countries is useful for aiding decision makers in determining the order of entry into potential markets and setting the allocation of resources and rate of expansion among the different markets. The former determination assumes a company cannot or does not want to go everywhere at once; consequently, it chooses to allocate its resources first to more desirable locations. The latter assumes a company already is selling or producing in many locales, perhaps even in all that are feasible, but wants to decide how much of its effort should be expended in one country rather than another.

Market Size

Expectation of a large market and sales growth is probably a potential location's major attraction.

Sales potential is probably the most important variable in ascertaining which locations will be considered and whether an investment will be made.[8] The assumption, of course, is that sales will be made at a price above cost; consequently, where there are sales, there will be profits.

In some cases, a company may be able to obtain past and current sales figures on a country-to-country basis for the type of product it wants to sell; in many cases, however, such figures are unavailable. Either way, management must make projections about what will happen to future sales. Such data as GNP, per capita income, growth rates, size of the middle class, and level of industrialization often are used as broad indicators of market size and opportunity.[9] Then, groups of countries may be further broken down according to such variables as dependence on private versus government spending or inflation rate.[10]

The triad market of the United States, Japan, and Western Europe accounts for about half of the world's total consumption and an even higher proportion of purchases of such products as computers, consumer electronics, and machine tools.[11] It is not surprising therefore that most MNEs expend a major part of their efforts on these areas. However, the dominance of the triad is being challenged because of the growth in certain developing countries. The World Bank forecasts (Fig. 13.4) that by the year 2020, Canada and Spain will be replaced in the top fifteen economies by Taiwan and Thailand. By that time, seven of the world's largest economies will be Asian countries, compared with only three in 1992. China is expected to surpass the United States as the world's largest economy. Developing countries will surpass the industrial countries in world output during the late 1990s. Further, the middle class is growing rapidly in many Asian countries, both in absolute numbers and in percentage of the population. For example, between 1993 and 1998, the middle class in India is projected to increase by 110 million people and from 23.5 percent to 33 percent of India's population.[12] Thus, developing countries, especially those of Asia, will command more attention by international companies as a

**Figure 13.4
Projected Economic Growth***
Note the projected gains by developing countries, particularly some in Asia.

*GDPs are calculated using purchasing price parity (PPP).
Source: From World Bank, *Global Economic Prospects and the Developing Countries 1994.* Reprinted with permission.

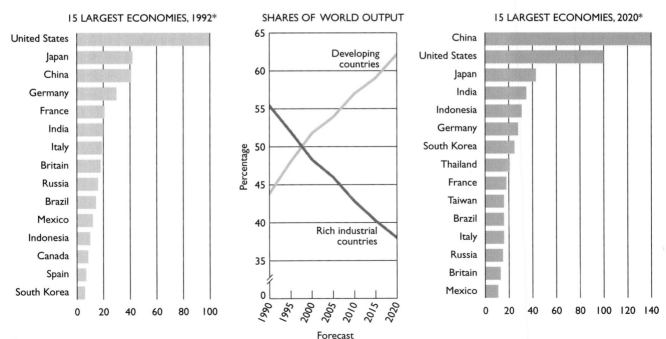

* United States = 100
Other countries = percentage of U.S.

location for both sales and production. In essence, there will be a new triad made up of North America, Europe, and East Asia.[13]

Ease and Compatibility of Operations

**Companies are highly
attracted to countries**
• **That are located nearby**
• **That share the same
  language**
• **That have market conditions similar to those in
  their home countries**

Geographic, language, and market similarities   Recall in the Ford case that earnings and vehicle sales were smoothed because of Ford's operations in various parts of the world. Investors generally prefer such smoother performance patterns.[14] Therefore, it might seem that companies would go first to those countries whose economies are least correlated with that of the home country. For example, U.S. economic cycles differ markedly from those in major Latin American countries, so you might expect U.S. companies to be motivated to smooth earnings by investing heavily in Latin America.[15] However, evidence suggests the contrary for U.S. companies, whether they go abroad in related or unrelated operations in terms of marketing systems, production technologies, or vertical or horizontal products.[16] Undoubtedly, a major basis for this anomaly is that, although foreign operations contribute to the smoothing of sales and earnings, this smoothing is not as important a reason to engage in international business as is the securement of new markets or competition-enhancing resources. The new markets and competition-enhancing resources may not be as easily found in the countries whose business cycles differ most from those in the home country.

But regardless of the industry involved, U.S. companies put more emphasis on Canada, the United Kingdom, and Mexico than would be indicated by those countries' economic size.[17] This seems to occur because decision makers prefer to go where they perceive it's easier to operate. For U.S. companies, Canada and Mexico rank high because of geographic proximity, which makes it easier and cheaper for the companies to control their foreign subsidiaries. Moreover, since the advent of NAFTA, U.S. companies encounter fewer border restrictions for their operations in Canada and Mexico than they encounter for most other locales. Also, at the early stages of international expansion, managers feel more comfortable doing business in their own language and in a similar legal system; this explains the appeal of Canada and the United Kingdom to U.S. companies. Language and cultural similarities also may lower operating costs and risks. Finally, market similarity tends to exert considerable influence on the locations of initial foreign operations. Both Canada and the United Kingdom have high per capita incomes, similar to that in the United States. Anecdotal evidence seems to indicate that companies from other countries also expand earlier and to a greater degree in those countries that are located nearby and that have market conditions similar to those in their home countries.

**There is the best chance for
a proposal to be accepted
when a location**
• **Offers size, technology,
  and other factors familiar
  to company personnel**
• **Allows a high percentage
  of ownership**
• **Permits profits to be easily
  remitted**

Fit with company capabilities and policies   After the alternatives are pared to a reasonable number, companies must prepare much more detailed feasibility studies. These studies can be expensive. Companies very often commit to locations that are far from optimal because the more time and money they invest in examining an alternative, the more likely they are to accept that project regardless of its merits, a situation known as an escalation of commitment. From the start, a feasibility study should have a series of clear-cut decision points so that sufficient information is gathered at each stage and so that, if a study is unlikely to result in an investment, it may be terminated before it becomes too costly.

One way to make the number of alternatives more manageable is to ensure that proposals fit the organization's motives, limitations, and policies. Such proposals, if presented to management decision makers, will have a higher probability of acceptance. For example, consideration may be limited to locales in which variables such as product type and plant size will be within the experience of present managers. From a policy standpoint, management may find it useful to ensure its proposal group includes personnel with backgrounds in each functional area—marketing, finance, personnel, engineering, and production. Although various factors might cause ultimate decision makers to reject a proposal once a feasibility study is completed, two stand out as sufficiently important to sway many organizations: restrictions on the percentage of ownership that can be held and the maximum allowed remittance of profits.

Local availability of resources in relation to the company's needs is another consideration. Many foreign operations require that imported resources be combined with local inputs; this requirement may severely restrict the feasibility of given locales. For example, the international company may need to find local personnel who are sufficiently knowledgeable about the type of technology being brought in. Or it may need to add local capital to what it is willing to bring in. If local equity markets are poorly developed and local borrowing is very expensive, the company may consider locating in a different country.

The fit for a particular country is important. Consider marketing capabilities, and assume that a company has developed a product in one country and successfully marketed it through mass advertising methods. Normally it is far easier and less costly to move that product into a country for which product alterations are minimal or unnecessary and where there are few advertising restrictions. Increasingly, however, companies are using a **lead country strategy,** which involves introducing a product on a test basis in a small-country market that is considered representative of a region before investing to serve larger-country markets. For example, Colgate-Palmolive used the strategy for the successful launching of its Optims shampoo.[18] On the basis of a test market in Hong Kong, Colgate-Palmolive introduced Optims throughout Asia.

Costs and Resource Availability

Costs—especially labor costs—are an important factor in the production-location decision.

So far, the discussion has centered on market-seeking operations. However, international companies also engage in the pursuit of foreign resources. The analysis is somewhat simpler for a resource that is to be transferred, such as a raw material or technology, than for a resource that will be used to make a product or component abroad for export into other markets. A company eventually must examine the costs of labor, raw material inputs, capital, taxes, and transfer costs in relation to productivity in order to determine a least-cost location. Before all this information is collected in a final feasibility study, certain indicators help decision makers narrow the alternatives to be considered.

Labor compensation is an important cost of manufacturing for most companies. However, capital intensity is growing in most industries, which reduces labor costs as a percentage of total costs and thus decreases the difference in production cost from one location to another.[19] At any rate, current labor costs, trends in those costs, and unemployment rates are useful for approximating cost differences among countries. Further, labor costs in some industries remain the critical factor for determining total cost. Labor, however, is not a homogeneous commodity. If a country's labor force lacks the specific skill levels required, a company may have to implement an expensive alternative in order to use the labor, such as training, redesigning production, or adding supervision. In the case of specialized units, such as an R&D lab, the existing availability of specific skills is almost essential.

Increasingly, it is important to be near suppliers and customers and to be in an area where the infrastructure will allow the efficient movement of supplies and finished products. And for regional headquarters, it is important to be near specialized private and public institutions such as banks, factoring firms, insurance groups, public accountants, freight forwarders, customs brokers, and consular offices, all of which handle certain international functions.

Corporate tax rates on income also affect location decisions by MNEs. For example, countries with a 1-percent lower tax rate attract up to three times more FDI from the United States. In addition, different tax rates among states affect location of FDI within the United States.[20] The difference in rates seems especially important within regional trading groups, where companies can serve the entire region from any of several countries.

Any other important costs should be added into the analysis. If precise data are unavailable, useful proxies on operating conditions may be used. For example, if a country's infrastructure is well developed and components can be easily imported, operating costs are more likely to be relatively low. If the country already turns out competitive products embodying inputs similar to those required for the production being considered, labor costs of the planned operation probably will be sufficiently low.

Companies should consider different ways to produce the same product.

The continual development of new production technologies makes cost comparisons among countries more difficult. As the number of ways in which the same product can be made increases, a company must compare, for example, the cost of producing with a large labor input in a low-wage country and that of producing with capital intensity in a high-wage country. For example, Volkswagen moved production of its Golf Syncro from Germany to Slovakia and switched from a highly automated, capital-intensive assembly line to a labor-intensive plant because the low Slovakian wages and high productivity cut costs from those in Germany.[21] A company might have to compare large-scale production to reduce fixed costs per unit by serving multi-country markets and multiple smaller-scale production units to reduce transport and inventory costs.

Because of other considerations, a company may not necessarily opt for the least-cost location. For example, BMW calculated that Mexico would be the least-cost location for North American production; however, the company chose a U.S. location because it feared that a Mexican-made vehicle would lack the same luxury image.[22] And the Japanese firm Sharp Manufacturing moved its microwave assembly from Malaysia to the United States in order to gain access to more dependable transportation facilities for export sales to Europe.[23] In both cases, the companies reasoned that lower revenues would more than negate savings from the least-cost locations. However, in another sense, the companies' decisions were least-cost. BMW did not have to incur high marketing expenses to convince U.S. consumers of Mexican quality, and Sharp could reduce inventories by using more dependable transportation linkages.

The degree of red tape is not directly measurable.

Red tape   Companies frequently compare the degrees of red tape necessary to operate in given countries. Red tape includes such things as how difficult it is to get permission to operate, to bring in expatriate personnel, to obtain licenses to produce and sell certain goods, and to satisfy government agencies on such matters as taxes, labor conditions, and environmental compliance. For example, Ukraine has thousands of government employees who have the power to block exports, ban sales, levy licensing fees, seize money from private bank accounts, and generally cause trouble for foreign businesses. Their motives range from a desire to protect friends and state-companies from competition to receiving bribes for favors.[24] The degree of red tape is not directly measurable; therefore, companies commonly have people familiar with operating conditions rate countries subjectively on this factor.

Influential Variables: Risk

Is a projected rate of return of 9 percent in Bolivia the same as a projected rate of 9 percent in France? Should return on investment be calculated on the basis of the entire earnings of a foreign subsidiary or just on the earnings that can be remitted to the parent? Does it make sense to accept a low return in one country if doing so will help the company's competitive position elsewhere? Is it ever rational to invest in a country that has an uncertain political and economic future? These are but a few of the unresolved questions that companies must consider when making international capital-investment decisions.

Risk and Uncertainty

Most investors prefer certainty to uncertainty.

Companies use a variety of financial techniques to compare potential projects, including discounted cash flow, economic value added, payback period, net present value, return on sales, return on assets employed, internal rate of return, accounting rate of return, and return on equity. The differences among these techniques is best explained in a finance course; however, the international implications of all of them are roughly the same. Given this situation, we shall refer only to return on investment as a means of explaining risk considerations in international business. Given the same expected return, most decision makers prefer a more certain to a less certain outcome. An estimated rate of **return on investment (ROI)** is calculated by averaging the various returns deemed possible for investments. Table 13.1 shows that two identical projected ROIs may have very different certainties of achievement as well as different probabilities. In the table, the certainty of a 10-percent projected ROI is higher for investment B than for investment A (40 percent versus 30 percent). Further, the probability of earning at least 10 percent is also higher for B than for A (70 percent versus 65 percent). Experience shows that most, but not all, investors will choose alternative B over alternative A. In fact, as uncertainty increases, investors may require a higher estimated ROI.

Often it is possible to reduce risk or uncertainty, such as by insuring against the possibility of nonconvertibility of funds. However, such actions are apt to be costly for a company. In the initial process of scanning to develop a manageable number of alternatives, the company should give some weight to the elements of risk and uncertainty. At the later and more detailed stage of the feasibility study, management should determine whether the degree of risk is acceptable without incurring additional costs. If it is not, management needs to calculate an ROI that includes expenditures, such as for insurance, to increase the outcome certainty of the operation.[25]

National boundaries play a role in the degree of certainty of return that investors perceive for alternative investments. As long as a company is conducting business entirely within one country, alternative investment projects fall within similar political and economic environments. Further, experience in operating within that country, as well as in operating abroad in similar countries, increases the

---

Table 13.1
Comparison of ROI Certainty
To determine the estimated ROI, (1) multiply each ROI as a percentage by its probability to derive a weighted value and (2) add the weighted values.

	ROI as percentage	Investment A		Investment B	
		Probability	Weighted value	Probability	Weighted value
	0	.15	0	0	0
	5	.20	1.0	.30	1.5
	10	.30	3.0	.40	4.0
	15	.20	3.0	.30	4.5
	20	.15	3.0	0	0.0
Estimated ROI			10.0%		10.0%

probability that the company will make accurate assessments of consumer, competitor, and government actions.[26] This is consistent with the **liability of foreignness,** a term that describes foreign companies' lower survival rate than local companies for many years after they begin operations. The probable cause of this lower survival rate is their lesser ability to predict and deal with the operating environment. However, those foreign companies that manage to overcome their early problems have comparable survival rates to those of local companies in later years.[27] The learning process also helps to explain why reinvestments or expanded investments within a country in which a company has extensive operations often are evaluated very differently than are proposed moves into a new country. (The reinvestment decision will be discussed later in this chapter.)

Competitive Risk

A company's innovative advantage may be short-lived. Even when the company has a substantial competitive lead time, the time may vary among markets. One strategy for exploiting temporary monopoly advantages is known as the **imitation lag;** to pursue this strategy, a company moves first to those countries most likely to develop local production themselves and later to other countries.[28] Local availability of technology and high international freight costs generally result in a more rapid development of local production. If technology is available in a country, local producers may start manufacturing well before foreign companies are willing to sell the technology. If freight costs are high for exports to the country, a local producer may, despite inefficiencies, be able to gain a cost advantage over imported goods.

Companies also may develop strategies to find countries in which there is least likely to be significant competition. For example, Kao, Japan's top maker of toiletries and home-cleaning products, has concentrated its international expansion in Southeast Asia because that market has been growing and because U.S. and European competitors are less entrenched there.[29] Chrysler received approval for an assembly plant in Vietnam, thinking it would be one of only four automobile manufacturers in the market; however, it changed its mind about entering the Vietnamese market after learning that twelve companies had received approval. Chrysler's decision was based on a belief that there would be too much competition relative to the size of the market.[30]

Monetary Risk

If a company's expansion occurs through direct investment abroad, access to the invested capital and the exchange rate on its earnings are key considerations. The concept of liquidity preference is a common theory that helps explain capital-budgeting decisions in general and can be applied to the international expansion decision.

Liquidity preference is the theory that investors usually want some of their holdings to be in highly liquid assets, on which they are willing to take a lower return. Liquidity is needed in part to make near-term payments, such as paying out dividends; in part to cover unexpected contingencies, such as stockpiling materials if a strike threatens supply; and in part to be able to shift funds to even more profitable opportunities, such as purchasing materials at a discount during a temporary price depression.

Sometimes companies want to sell all or part of their equity in a foreign facility so that the funds may be used for other types of expansion endeavors. However, the ability to find local buyers varies substantially among countries, depending largely on the existence of a local capital market. For example, the Mexican glass manufacturer Vitro decided to sell its U.S. subsidiary, Anchor Glass. The sale and transfer of funds to Mexico was facilitated by the U.S. capital market.[31]

Assuming a company does find a local purchaser for its foreign facility, chances are that it intends to use the funds in another country. If the funds are not convertible, the selling company will be forced to spend them in the host country. Of more pressing concern for most investors is the ability to convert earnings from operations abroad and the cost of doing so. For example, the proceeds from Vitro's sale of Anchor were easily transferred to Mexico because of the lack of U.S. capital controls. If the facility had been in a country with exchange controls, the transfer of proceeds would have been much more problematic. It is not surprising that investors may be willing to accept a lower projected ROI for projects in countries with strong currencies than for those in countries with weak currencies.

Political Risk

<aside>
Political risk may come from wars and insurrections, takeover of property, and/or changes in rules.
</aside>

Types and causes   A major concern of international companies is that the political climate will change in such a way that their operating position will deteriorate. Political actions that may affect company operations adversely are governmental takeovers of property, either with or without compensation; operational restrictions that impede the company's ability to take certain actions; and agitation that disrupts sales or causes damage to property or personnel. Although one usually thinks of political risk where the company is operating abroad, it may occur elsewhere because of the interrelationship of countries and of companies' international operations. For example, during the period of apartheid in South Africa, many foreign investors there were affected by boycotts and political sanctions taken against them outside of South Africa.

Political risk may occur for the following reasons:

1. *Opinions of political leadership* Political leaders' opinions may change over time, and the leaders may be replaced by force or election with people whose views toward business and foreign investment are much less positive. Changes may result in adverse operating regulations, such as limits on remittances or discriminatory taxes. They may breach existing contracts and/or take over the investors' property.

2. *Civil disorder* Unrest may occur because of economic conditions, human rights violations, or group animosity within the society. Further, widespread crime, such as the kidnapping of personnel, may result from inadequate police control. Conditions may result in procurement difficulties, work stoppages, shipment delays, and property damage. If carried to an extreme, the nation itself may break apart, leaving the investor to operate in a smaller market.

3. *External relations* Animosity between the host country and the foreign investor's home country may result in work-stoppage protests, forced divestment of operations, and loss of supplies and/or markets. Animosity, especially war, between the host country and any other country may result in property damage and inability to get supplies or deliver goods.

If political actions are aimed only at specific foreign investments, they are known as **micro political risks.** For example, in Peru, Cerro's mining interests and ITT's telephone company were taken over, but Cerro's manufacturing companies and ITT's hotel were not. In France, protests that disrupted operations at Euro Disney did not carry over to most other U.S.-owned facilities in France. Operations most likely to be affected by micro political risk are those that may have a considerable and visible widespread effect on a given country because of their size, monopoly position, importance to national defense, or the dependence of other industries on them. If the underlying cause of agitation is animosity between factions in the host country and the government of a foreign country, protesters may target only the most visible companies from that foreign country. There is also evidence that firms perceived to be operating in a socially irresponsive manner are more apt to face adverse political situations than are other firms.

If political actions affect a broad spectrum of foreign investors, they are known as **macro political risks.** For example, after the communist revolution in Cuba, the takeover of property was aimed at all foreign investors regardless of industry, nationality, or whether the investors' past behavior had been socially responsive or not. During the long civil war in Lebanon, foreign investment was not a target of political agitation; however, Holiday Inn lost business because of the fall in tourism. It also had its facility damaged because of being in the line of fire between east and west Beirut.

Approaches to predicting political risk   Three approaches to predicting political risk will be discussed next: analyzing past patterns, using expert opinion, and the building of models based on instability measurements.

Management can make predictions based on past patterns.

Analysis of past patterns   Companies cannot help but be influenced by what has happened in a country. However, predicting political risk on the basis of past patterns holds many dangers. Political situations may change rapidly for better or worse as far as foreign companies are concerned. For example, the perceived political risk of doing business in Vietnam improved rapidly during the early 1990s as its government sought foreign investment and trade.[32] However, the historical record of violence, expropriations, and regulation of international business is indicative of the broad climate for operations in that country. Although expropriation of property occurred frequently in the 1970s end early 1980s, it has been negligible in recent years. (The reasons for this change were discussed in Chapter 11.) Nevertheless, companies continue to worry sufficiently about takeovers so that many still seek insurance against them, such as insurance provided to U.S. companies by the Overseas Private Investment Corporation (OPIC). For example, in 1995, OPIC provided $200 million in political risk insurance for Edison Mission Energy in Indonesia as well as smaller amounts to other U.S. companies' new facilities in such countries as Poland and Georgia.[33]

Substantial variations in political risk frequently exist within countries as well. For example, except in a few countries, government takeovers of companies have been highly selective. Similarly, unrest that leads to property damage and/or disruption of supplies or sales may not endanger the operations of all foreign companies. This may be because of the limited geographic focus of the unrest. For example, there was no property damage or business disruption in Slovenia after the breakup of Yugoslavia; however, other areas in the former Yugoslavia were severely hit.

Asset takeover or property damage does not necessarily mean a full loss to investors. Most takeovers have been preceded by a formal declaration of intent by the government and a subsequent legal process to determine compensation to the foreign investor. In addition to the asset's book value, other factors must be considered in determining the adequacy of compensation. First, the compensation may earn a different return elsewhere. Second, other agreements (such as purchase and management contracts) may create additional benefits for the former investor.

Companies should
- Examine views of governmental decision makers
- Get a cross-section of opinions
- Use expert analysts

Opinion analysis   A second approach for political-risk analysis is to analyze the opinions of knowledgeable people about the situation in a country.[34] In this approach, management attempts to ascertain the evolving opinions of people who may influence future political events affecting business. The first step involves reading statements made by political leaders both in and out of office to determine their philosophies on business in general, foreign input to business, the means of effecting economic changes, and their feelings toward given foreign countries. Modern technology has improved access to press reports in foreign countries. For example, the on-line service, LEXIS-NEXIS, includes full-text reports from newspapers and television from major parts of the world and is sometimes available within hours of the original publication or broadcast. However, published statements may appear too late for a company to react.

Management should analyze the context of statements to determine whether they express true intentions or were made merely to appease particular interest groups or social classes. It is not uncommon, for example, for political leaders to make emotional appeals to the poor based on allegations that foreign business is draining wealth from the country while, at the same time, quietly negotiating entry and giving incentives to new foreign companies. Examination of the country's investment plans offers further insights into the political climate.

The second step in determining opinions and attitudes involves visits to the country in order to "listen." Embassy officials and foreign and local businesspeople are useful sources of opinions about the probability and direction of change. Journalists, academicians, middle-level local governmental authorities, and labor leaders usually reveal their own attitudes, which often reflect changing political conditions that may affect the business sector.

A more systematic method of determining opinions is to use a panel of analysts with experience in a country and have them rate categories of political conditions over different time frames. For example, these analysts might rate a country in terms of the fractionalization of political parties that could lead to disruptive changes in government in the near future or beyond. A company also may rely on commercial risk-assessment services, such as those published by *Business International, Economist Intelligence Unit, Euromoney, Political Risk Services, Bank of America World Information Services, Control Risks Information Services* (CRIS), *Institutional Investor, Moody's Investors Service, S. J. Rundt & Associates, Standard & Poor's Ratings Group,* and *Business Environment Risk Information* (BERI). [35]

Political instability does not always affect all foreign businesses in a country.

Instability assessment   A third method for predicting political risk is to build models based on instability measurements. The greater the political instability, the greater is the possibility of change in the political climate. Although political instability has been found to be a major concern of businesspeople, there is no general consensus as to what constitutes dangerous instability or how such instability can be predicted. The lack of consensus is illustrated by the diverse reactions of companies to the same political situations. For example, in the early 1990s Peru had high inflation, guerrilla warfare, political assassinations, and a fall in industrial output; yet many foreign companies perceived the time to be opportune to invest in Peru because they thought Peru's future situation would change after elections and because they thought Peruvian assets were undervalued in the market. [36] Further, different nationalities of companies may perceive risks to be different for the same locales. In a 1995 survey among 100 U.S. and U.K. companies, U.S. companies viewed the Middle East as much riskier than U.K. companies did; however, U.K. companies viewed Latin America as significantly more risky than U.S. companies did. [37] Other uncertainties include the time lag between a political event and an investor's ability to react. Further, similar symptoms of social unrest may result in different political consequences in different countries. For example, an antiregime demonstration in Iran may have different political consequences for investors than one in Mexico would. [38] At times, political parties may change rapidly with little effect on business; at other times, sweeping changes for business may occur without a change in government. Rather than political stability itself, the direction of change in government seems to be very important.

One theory holds that when there is a high and growing level of frustration within a country, that country's political leaders may try to blame foreign investors for the problems causing frustration. They may place more operational restrictions on foreign investors or take over their property. Frustration occurs when there is a difference between the level of aspirations and the level of welfare and expectations—the higher the difference, the higher the level of frustration.[39] Because frustration, aspirations, welfare, and expectations cannot be measured directly, substitutes must be used. For example, growth in urbanization, literacy, radios per capita, and labor unionization are all measurable indicators of growth in aspirations. Variables such as infant survival rate, caloric consumption, hospital beds per capita, piped water supply per capita, and income per capita are measurable indicators of welfare. Variables such as the changes in per capita income and in gross investment rates are indicators of expectations. This approach to predicting actions toward foreign investors has considerable potential, since it predicts future trends rather than looking to the past and is based on a lead time that might be sufficient for management to adjust operations in order to minimize losses.

Business Research

Information is needed at all levels of control.

Business research is undertaken to reduce uncertainties in the decision process, to expand or narrow the alternatives under consideration, and to assess the merits of existing programs. Efforts to reduce uncertainties include attempts to answer such questions as these: "Can qualified personnel be hired?" "Will the economic and political climate allow for a reasonable certainty of operations?" Alternatives may be expanded by asking "Where are possible new sources of funds or sales?" or they may be narrowed by querying "Where among the alternatives would operating costs be lowest?" Evaluation and control are improved by assessing present and past performance: "Is the distributor servicing sufficient accounts?" "What is our market share?" Clearly, there are numerous details that, if ascertained, can be useful in meeting the company's objectives.

How Much Research?

Companies should compare the cost of information with its value.

A company can seldom, if ever, gain all the information its managers would like. This is partially due to time constraints, since markets or raw materials may need to be secured before competitors gain control of them. Further, contracts that call for bids or proposals usually have deadlines. The cost of information is another factor. The larger area to be considered for international decisions compounds the number of alternatives and complexities; thus, it is useful to limit the extent of information gathering. This can be done by estimating the costs of data collection as well as the probable payoff from the data in terms of revenue gains or cost savings. In this way, a company can rank research projects on the basis of expected return from the costs of data collection.

Problems with the Data

The lack, obsolescence, and inaccuracy of data on many countries make much research difficult and expensive to undertake. Moreover, data discrepancies sometimes create uncertainties about situations. For example, official U.S. trade statistics for 1994 showed a U.S. trade imbalance with China of $30 billion; but official Chinese figures showed $7.4 billion.[40] In most industrial countries, such as the United States, governments collect very detailed demographic and purchasing data, which are available cheaply to any company or individual. (But even in the United States, GNP figures are estimated to be understated by as much as 15 percent, and the 1990 census may have missed between 4 and 6 million people.[41]) Using samples based on available information, a company can draw fairly accurate inferences concerning market-segment sizes and locations, at least within broad categories. In the United States, the fact that so many companies are publicly owned and are required to disclose much operating information enables a company to learn competitors' strengths and weaknesses. Further, companies may rely on a multitude of behavioral studies dealing with U.S. consumer preferences and experience. With this available information, a company can devise questionnaires or test-market with a selected sample so that responses should reflect the behavior of the larger target group to whom the company plans to sell. Contrast this situation to that in a country whose basic census, national income accounts, and foreign trade figures are suspect and where no data are collected on consumer expenditures. In such countries, business is conducted under a veil of secrecy, consumers' buying behavior is speculated on, market intermediaries are reluctant to answer questions, and expensive primary research may be required before meaningful samples and questions can be developed.

In 1996, twenty countries agreed to standards for collecting and publishing seventeen categories of data on the Internet. This agreement through the IMF came about because of a belief that the Mexican financial crisis of 1994 may have been averted had international financial authorities had better and more timely information about Mexico's trade, debt, and foreign exchange reserves. It is expected that other countries will join the original twenty because of embarrassment from being left out of the group.[42]

Reasons for Inaccuracies

For the most part, incomplete or inaccurate published data result from the inability of many governments to collect the needed information. Poor countries may have such limited resources that other projects necessarily receive priority in the national budget. Why collect precise figures on the literacy rate, the leaders of a poor country might reason, when the same outlay can be used to build schools to improve that rate?

Education affects the competence of governmental officials to maintain and analyze accurate records. Economic factors also hamper record retrieval and analysis, since hand calculations may be used instead of costly electronic data-processing

Inaccuracies result from
- **Inability to collect data**
- **Purposeful misleading**

systems. The result may be information that is years old before it is made public. Finally, cultural factors affect responses. Mistrust of how the data will be used may lead respondents to answer incorrectly, particularly if questions probe financial details.

Of equal concern to the researcher is the publication of information designed to persuade businesspeople to follow a certain course of action. Even if governmental and private organizations do not purposely publish false statements, many may be so selective in the data they include that false impressions are created. Therefore, it is useful for companies to consider carefully the source of such material in light of possible motives or biases.

However, not all inaccuracies are due to governmental collection and dissemination procedures. A large proportion of the studies by academicians that purport to describe international business practices are based on broad generalizations that may be drawn from too few observations, nonrepresentative samples, and/or poorly designed questionnaires.

People's desire and ability to cover up data on themselves—such as unrecorded criminal activity—may distort published figures substantially. In the United States, illegal income from such activities as drug trade, theft, bribery, and prostitution is not included in GNP figures.[43] For instance, in 1994 over 160,000 stolen automobiles were not recovered in the United States. Most of these were smuggled out of the country and into the Middle East, Eastern Europe, and Central America.[44] But they did not appear on U.S. export figures. Further, income from organized crime in 1996 was estimated at $1 trillion, which either did not appear in national income accounts or appeared in other economic sectors because of money laundering.[45]

Comparability problems arise from
- **Differences in collection methods, definitions, and base years**
- **Distortions in currency conversions**

Comparability problems   One important variable businesspeople need to consider when contrasting data from different countries is the year in which collection was done. Censuses, output figures, trade statistics, and base-year calculations are published for different periods in different countries. Thus it may be necessary for the researcher to make estimates of current figures based on projected growth rates.

There also are numerous definitional differences among countries; for example, a category as seemingly basic as "family income" may mean something different depending on the country. For one thing, such relatives as grandparents, uncles, and cousins may be included in the definition of "family." Similarly, some countries define literacy as some minimum level of formal schooling, others as attainment of certain specified standards, and still others as simply the ability to read and write one's name. Further, percentages may be published in terms of either adult population (with different ages used for adulthood) or total population. The definitions of accounting rules such as depreciation also can differ and so result in substantially altered comparability of net national product figures among countries.

Countries differ in how they measure investment inflows. Some governments record the number of foreign investment projects. Some record the value of investments in the local currency, and others value them in U.S. dollars or another major international currency. Where value of investments is used, another question is how much of the total value is recorded as "foreign investment." Some governments record the total value of the project, regardless of what portion may be locally owned or financed; some record the value of foreign capital invested; and others record the percentage of the project owned by foreign interests.[46]

Figures on national income and per capita income are particularly difficult to compare because of differences in activities taking place outside the market economy, such as within the home, and therefore not showing up in income figures. The extent to which people in one country produce for their own consumption (for example, grow vegetables, bake bread, sew clothes, or cut hair) will distort comparisons with other countries that follow different patterns.

A further problem concerns exchange rates, which must be used to convert countries' financial data to some common currency. A 10-percent appreciation of the Japanese yen in relation to the U.S. dollar will result in a 10-percent increase in the per capita income of Japanese residents when figures are reported in dollars. Does this mean that the Japanese are suddenly 10 percent richer? Obviously not, since their yen income, which they use for about 85 percent of their purchases in the Japanese economy, is unchanged and buys no more. Even if changes in exchange rates are ignored, purchasing power and living standards are difficult to compare, since costs are so affected by climate and habit. Exchange rates constitute a very imperfect means of comparing national data.[47]

External Sources of Information

Specificity and cost of information vary by source.

Throughout the discussion of opportunities, costs, and risks, we have indicated variables that may be useful for scanning or for final analysis of locational decisions. We have also indicated many of the sources of information for these variables, such as publications giving risk assessment information. However, it is impossible to include a comprehensive list of sources or explanation of anything more than a sample of sources. There are simply too many. For example, a routine search on the Internet often yields thousands of sources, and LEXIS-NEXIS gives full text citations from about 5000 sources. However, we have organized material for you in a logical way on our Web site to aid you in your research efforts. For example, if you go to our Web page and click on "Starting Points," you will find a wealth of useful links to current government sources, trade organizations, international organizations, business publications, and other sites.

The following discussion highlights the major types of information sources in terms of their completeness, reliability, and cost.

Individualized reports   In most countries, there are market-research and business-consulting companies that will conduct studies for a fee. Naturally, the quality and the cost of these studies vary widely. They generally are the most costly information source because the individualized nature restricts proration among a number of companies. However, the fact that the client can specify the information wanted often makes the expense worthwhile.

Specialized studies   Some research organizations prepare fairly specific studies that they sell to any interested company at costs much lower than for individualized studies. These specialized studies sometimes are printed as directories of companies that operate in a given locale, perhaps with financial or other information about the companies. They also may be about business in certain locales, forms of business, or specific products. They may combine any of these elements as well; for example, a study could deal with the market for imported auto parts in Germany.

Service companies   Most companies that provide services to international clients—for example, banks, transportation agencies, and accounting firms—publish reports that are available to potential clients. These reports usually are geared toward either the conduct of business in a given area or some specific subject of general interest, such as tax or trademark legislation. Since they are intended to reach a wide market of companies, these reports usually lack the specificity a company may want for making a final decision. However, much of the data give useful background information. Some service companies also offer informal opinions about such things as the reputations of possible business associates and the names of people to contact in a company.

Governmental agencies   Governments and their agencies are another source of information. Statistical reports vary in subject matter, quantity, and quality among countries. When a government or governmental agency wants to stimulate foreign business activity, the amount and type of information it makes available may be substantial. For example, the U.S. Department of Commerce not only compiles such basic data as news about and regulations in individual foreign countries and product-location-specific information in the National Trade Data Bank but also will help set up appointments with businesspeople abroad.

International organizations and agencies   Numerous organizations and agencies are supported by more than one country. These include the United Nations (UN), the World Trade Organization (WTO), the International Monetary Fund (IMF), the Organization for Economic Cooperation and Development (OECD), and the European Union (EU). All of these organizations have large research staffs that compile basic statistics as well as prepare reports and recommendations concerning common trends and problems. Many of the international development banks even help finance investment-feasibility studies.

Trade associations   Trade associations associated with various product lines collect, evaluate, and disseminate a wide variety of data dealing with technical and competitive factors in their industries. Many of these data are available in the trade journals published by such associations; others may or may not be available to nonmembers.

Information service companies A number of companies have information-retrieval services that maintain databases from hundreds of different sources, including many of those already described. For a fee, or sometimes for free at public libraries, a company can obtain access to such computerized data and arrange for an immediate printout of studies of interest.

The Internet

Printed publications are quickly becoming archives that are older than information one may find on the Internet. This is because Internet changes appear immediately, whereas changes for periodicals must be printed, disseminated, catalogued, and shelved before they are available. The amount of materials available on the Internet and World Wide Web is expanding very rapidly; however, finding these materials is still somewhat haphazard because of lags and completeness in cataloging them. Nevertheless, the Internet is bound to be of growing use in international business research.[48] For example, throughout this book, we have indicated useful Internet and Web addresses for getting up-to-date information.

Internal Generation

MNEs may have to conduct many studies abroad themselves. Sometimes the research process may consist of no more than observing keenly and asking many questions. Investigators can see what kind of merchandise is available, can see who is buying and where, and can uncover the hidden distribution points and competition. In some countries, for example, the competition for ready-made clothes may be from seamstresses working in private homes rather than from retailers. The competition for vacuum cleaners may be from servants who clean with mops rather than from other electrical-appliance manufacturers. Surreptitiously sold contraband may compete with locally produced goods. Traditional analysis methods would not reveal such facts. In many countries, even bankers have to rely more on clients' reputations than on their financial statements. Shrewd questioning may yield very interesting results. But such questioning is not always feasible. For example, Bass's Barbicon Malt with Lemon sells well in Saudi Arabia, and the company thinks, but cannot be sure, that most consumption is by women. The uncertainty is due to the fact that it cannot hold focus groups to discuss products, rely on phone books for random surveys, stop strangers on the street, or knock on the door of someone's house.[49]

Often a company must be extremely imaginative, extremely observant, or both. For example, one soft-drink manufacturer wanted to determine the market share it held relative to its competitors in the Mexican market. Management's attempts to make estimates from the points of distribution were futile because of the extremely widespread distribution. The company hit on two alternatives, both of which turned out to be feasible: The manufacturer of bottle caps was willing to reveal how many caps it sold to each of its clients, and customs would supply data on the import volume of soft-drink concentrate used by each competitor.

Tools for Comparing Countries

Environmental Scanning

International companies have become much more sophisticated in their **environmental scanning,** which is the systematic assessment of external conditions that might affect a company's operations. For example, a company might assess societal attitudes that might foreshadow legal changes. Most MNEs employ at least one executive to conduct environmental scanning continuously. The most sophisticated of these companies tie the scanning to the planning process and integrate information on a worldwide basis. Companies are most likely to seek economic and competitive information in their scanning process, and they depend heavily on managers based abroad to supply them with information.[50]

Grids

Grids are tools that
- **May depict acceptable or unacceptable conditions**
- **Rank countries by important variables**

A grid may be used to compare countries on whatever factors are deemed important. Table 13.2 is an example of a grid with information placed into three categories. Certain countries may be eliminated immediately from consideration because of characteristics decision makers find unacceptable. These factors are in the first category of variables, where country I is eliminated. Values and weights are assigned to other variables so that a country may be ranked according to attributes that are important to the decision makers. In the table, for example, country II is graphically pinpointed as high return–low risk, country III as low return–low risk, country IV as high return–high risk, and country V as low return–high risk.[51]

Both the variables and the weights will vary by product and company, depending on the company's internal situation and its objectives. The grid technique is useful even when a comparative analysis is not being done; a company may be able to set a minimum score necessary for either investing additional resources or committing further funds to a more detailed feasibility study. Grids do tend to get cumbersome, however, as the number of variables increases. Further, though they are useful in ranking, they often obscure interrelationships among countries.

Opportunity-Risk Matrix

With an opportunity-risk matrix, a company can
- **Decide on indicators and weight them**
- **Evaluate each country on the weighted indicators**
- **Plot to see relative placements**

To show more clearly the summary of data that can be illustrated on a grid, we can plot risk on one axis and opportunity on the other, a technique used by many com-

Table 13.2

Simplified Grid to Compare Countries for Market Penetration

Decision makers may choose which variables to include in the grid; this table is merely an example. Note also that decision makers may weight some variables as more important than others. Here country I is immediately eliminated because the company will go only where 100-percent ownership is permitted. Countries II and IV are estimated to have the highest return; and countries II and III are estimated to have the lowest risk.

Variable	Weight	I	II	III	IV	V
		\multicolumn{5}{c}{**Country**}				
1. Acceptable (A), Unacceptable (U) factors						
a. Allows 100-percent ownership	—	U	A	A	A	A
b. Allows licensing to majority-owned subsidiary	—	A	A	A	A	A
2. Return (higher number = preferred rating)						
a. Size of investment needed	0–5	—	4	3	3	3
b. Direct costs	0–3	—	3	1	2	2
c. Tax rate	0–2	—	2	1	2	2
d. Market size, present	0–4	—	3	2	4	1
e. Market size, 3–10 years	0–3	—	2	1	3	1
f. Market share, immediate potential, 0–2 years	0–2	—	2	1	2	1
g. Market share, 3–10 years	0–2	—	2	1	2	0
Total			18	10	18	10
3. Risk (lower number = preferred rating)						
a. Market loss, 3–10 years (if no present penetration)	0–4	—	2	1	3	2
b. Exchange problems	0–3	—	0	0	3	3
c. Political-unrest potential	0–3	—	0	1	2	3
d. Business laws, present	0–4	—	1	0	4	3
e. Business laws, 3–10 years	0–2	—	0	1	2	2
Total			3	3	14	13

panies, such as Borg-Warner.[52] Figure 13.5 is an example that is simplified to include only six countries. The grid shows that the company has current operations in four of the countries (all except countries A and E). Of the two nonexploited countries, country A has low risk but low opportunity and country E has low risk and high opportunity. If resources are to be spent in a new area, country E appears to be a better bet than country A. Of the other four countries, there are large commitments in country F, medium ones in countries C and D, and a small one in country B. In the future time horizon being examined, it appears that country F will have low risk and high opportunity. Country D's situation is expected to improve during the studied period; country C's situation is deteriorating; and country B's appears mixed (it will have better opportunity but more risk). Note that the world averages being used for comparison also shift during the period under consideration. The matrix is important as a reflection of the placement of a country *relative* to other countries.

Figure 13.5
Opportunity-Risk
Matrix
Countries above the horizontal dashed line have less risk and those to the right of the vertical dashed line have greater opportunity than the current world average. The dotted lines represent a projection of the world average for these variables in the future. Country D currently has greater than average risk; in the future it will have less risk than the projected world average.

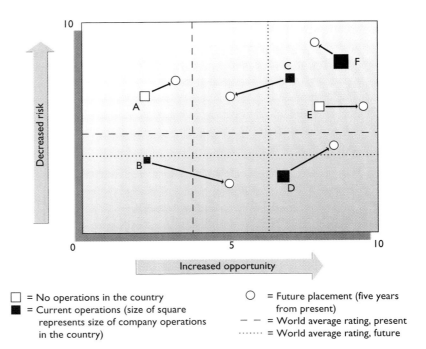

= No operations in the country
= Current operations (size of square represents size of company operations in the country)
○ = Future placement (five years from present)
– – = World average rating, present
······· = World average rating, future

But how are values plotted on such a matrix? It is up to the company to determine which factors are good indicators of risk and opportunity; the factors chosen then must be weighted to reflect their importance. For instance, on the risk axis a company might give 40 percent (0.4) of the weight to expropriation risk, 25 percent (0.25) to foreign-exchange controls, 20 percent (0.2) to civil disturbances and terrorism, and 15 percent (0.15) to exchange-rate change, for a total allocation of 100 percent. Each country then would be rated on a scale of 1 to 10 for each variable, with 10 indicating the best score and 1 the worst. The score on each variable is multiplied by the weight allocated to it. For instance, if country A were given a rating of 8 on the expropriation-risk variable, the 8 would be multiplied by 0.4 for a score of 3.2. All of country A's risk-variable scores would then be summed to give the placement of that country on the risk axis. A similar procedure would find the plot location of country A on the opportunity axis. Once the scores are determined for each country, management can determine the average scores for risk and for opportunity, thereby dividing the matrix into quadrants.

A key element of this kind of matrix, and one that is not always included in practice, is the projection of the future country location. Such a placement's usefulness is obvious if the projections are realistic. Therefore, it is helpful to have forecasts made by people who are knowledgeable not only about the countries but also about forecasting methods.

Markets shift among countries not only because of product life cycles but also because of changing conditions that may affect demand unevenly. Companies enhance their competitive capabilities by emphasizing the markets with higher growth prospects. When growth in sales prospects is due to product life cycle conditions or overall economic conditions, companies have few, if any, ethical qualms. However, some companies have been criticized for promoting potentially dangerous products more heavily abroad when domestic demand decreases. For example, the use of the pesticide DDT has been banned in the United States for environmental reasons, but U.S. companies export DDT. Also, until recently, U.S. tobacco sales were declining because of health scares and restrictions on advertising; tobacco companies have countered with heavy cigarette promotion in developing countries in which markets are growing. At the end of the Cold War, U.S. defense contractors turned more attention to foreign countries, many of which had either repressive regimes or conflicts that might escalate substantially. Relativists maintain it would be unethical to prohibit such sales. A complicating factor is that conditions abroad sometimes vary enough that product restrictions should differ.

ETHICAL DILEMMAS & SOCIAL RESPONSIBILITY

MNEs sometimes have been criticized for doing *any* business in countries with repressive regimes on the grounds that their presence strengthens those regimes. In fact, MNEs favor locations in which there is an unbelligerent workforce, and such regimes often foster this characteristic; thus, FDI often increases when a dictatorship, especially a military one, is in power. Once again, relativist versus normativist viewpoints come into play.

MNEs have justified their foreign investments largely on the grounds that those investments promote global efficiencies through low-cost production and high sales. But some moves into foreign markets are made to counteract what would otherwise be a competitor's advantage. For example, Caterpillar established operations in Japan, the home market of Komatsu, its major global competitor. This move lowered Komatsu's Japanese profits, which had been accounting for 80 percent of its worldwide cash flow, and made it more difficult for the company to expand abroad.[53] Such a move can be justified on competitive grounds but not on global efficiency grounds. Is it ethical? Would it make any difference whether Caterpillar makes a profit in Japan? What if such an action led to reduced competition in the United States?

Similarly, MNEs often respond to countries' trade restrictions by locating behind these tariff walls. In fact, they sometimes negotiate a monopoly position behind such walls in LDCs. The MNEs argue that such moves are necessary because markets would otherwise be lost; however, it is hard to justify these moves on global efficiency grounds. This brings up the dilemma of whether countries should work toward regulating FDI with global efficiency as their objective or whether each country should continue to be allowed to serve its own interests by competing for FDI.

Country Attractiveness–Company Strength Matrix

Another commonly used matrix approach highlights a company's specific product advantage on a country-by-country basis. This approach was briefly explained in the Ford case. Ford uses it for its tractor operations, for example. On the country-attractiveness scale, Ford ranks countries from highest to lowest attractiveness for tractors specifically; on the company-strength scale, it ranks its competitive strength in tractors by country. The method of performing the ranking is the same as for the opportunity-risk matrix. Ford's weighted scale for country attractiveness includes such variables as market size, market growth, price controls, red tape, requirements for local content and exports, inflation, trade balance, and political stability. Ford's weighted scale for company strength includes market share, market-share position, product fit to the country's needs, absolute profit per unit, percentage profit on cost, quality of the company's distribution in comparison with that of competitors, and the fit of the company's promotion program to the country in comparison with that of its competitors'.[54]

Figure 13.6 illustrates this type of matrix for market expansion before countries are plotted. The company should attempt to concentrate its activities in the countries that appear in the top left-hand corner of the matrix and to take as much equity as possible in investments there. In this position, country attractiveness is the highest, *and* the company has the best competitive capabilities to exploit the opportunities. In the top right-hand corner, the country attractiveness is also high, but the company has a weak competitive strength for those markets, perhaps because it lacks the right product. If the cost is not too high, the company might attempt to gain greater domination in those markets by remedying its competitive weakness. Otherwise, it might consider either **divestment** (reducing its investment) or strengthening its position through joint-venture operations with another company

**Figure 13.6
Country
Attractiveness–
Company Strength
Matrix**
Although countries are not plotted on this matrix, those that would appear closest to the top left-hand corner are the most desirable for operations and those that would be closest to the bottom right-hand corner are the least desirable.

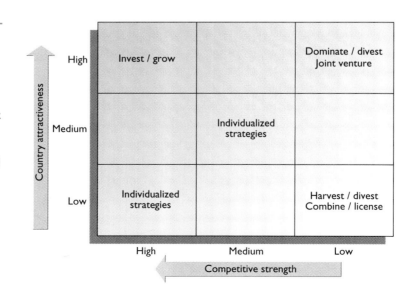

whose assets are complementary. Divestment instead of investment ordinarily should be attempted in countries in the bottom right-hand corner. Income may be "harvested" by pulling out all possible cash that can be generated while at the same time not replacing depreciated facilities. Licensing still offers potential because it may generate some income without the company's having to make investment outlays. In other areas, the company must analyze situations individually in order to decide which approach to take. These are marginal areas that require specific judgment.

Although this type of matrix may serve to guide decision making, it must be used with caution. First, it is often difficult to separate the attractiveness of a country from a company's position. In other words, the country may seem attractive because of the company's fit with it. Second, some of the recommended actions take a defeatist attitude to a company's competitive position. There are simply many examples of companies that built competitive strength in markets that had been previously dominated by a competitor or that built profitable positions without being the competitive leader. Third, a company may choose to stay in a market to prevent competitors from using their dominance there to fund expansion elsewhere.

Diversification versus Concentration Strategies

Strategies for ultimately reaching a high level of commitment in many countries are
- **Diversification—go to many fast and then build up slowly in each**
- **Concentration—go to one or a few and build up fast before going to others**
- **A hybrid of the two**

Ultimately, a company may gain a sizable presence and commitment in most countries; however, there are different paths to that position. Although any move abroad involves some geographic diversification, the term **diversification strategy** is used to describe the extreme by which the company will move rapidly into most foreign markets, gradually increasing its commitments within each of them. This can be done, for example, through a liberal licensing policy for a given product to ensure there will be sufficient resources for the initial widespread expansion. The company eventually will increase its involvement by internalizing activities that it initially contracted to other companies. At the other extreme, with a **concentration strategy,** the company will move to only one or a few foreign countries until it develops a very strong involvement and competitive position there. There are, of course, hybrids of these two strategies, for example, moving rapidly to most markets but increasing the commitment in only a few. The following subsections discuss major variables a company should consider when deciding which strategy to use.[55] (See Table 13.3.)

An increasing sales response rate favors concentration; a decreasing sales response rate favors diversification.

Growth Rate in Each Market

Fast growth favors concentration because companies must use resources to maintain market share.

When the growth rate in each market is high, a company usually should concentrate on a few markets because it will cost a great deal to maintain market share and costs per unit are typically lower for the market-share leader. Slower growth in each

Table 13.3
Product and Market Factors Affecting Choice between
Diversification and Concentration Strategies
If the conditions under "prefer diversification" exist, a company is likely to benefit by moving rapidly into many countries simultaneously; otherwise, the company might move to just one or a few foreign countries until a substantial presence is developed there.

Product or market factor	Prefer diversification if:	Prefer concentration if:
1. Growth rate of each market	Low	High
2. Sales stability in each market	Low	High
3. Competitive lead time	Short	Long
4. Spillover effects	High	Low
5. Need for product adaptation	Low	High
6. Need for communication adaptation	Low	High
7. Economies of scale in distribution	Low	High
8. Program control requirements	Low	High
9. Extent of constraints	Low	High

Source: Igal Ayal and Jehiel Zif, "Marketing Expansion Strategies in Multinational Marketing," *Journal of Marketing,* Vol. 43, Spring 1979, p. 89. Reprinted by permission of the American Marketing Association.

market may result in the company's having enough resources to build and maintain a market share in several different countries.

Sales Stability in Each Market

Recall the Ford case and the earlier description of how earnings and sales are smoothed because of operations in various parts of the world. This smoothing results from the leads and lags in the business cycles. In addition, a company whose assets and earnings base are in a variety of countries will be less affected by occurrences within a single one; for example, a strike or expropriation will affect earnings from only a small portion of total corporate assets. Further, currency appreciation in some countries may offset depreciation in others. Although we showed that such diversification is usually of secondary importance as a motive for foreign expansion, it is nevertheless an added advantage from operating abroad.

The more stable that sales and profits are within a single market, the less advantage there is from a diversification strategy. Similarly, the more interrelated markets are, the less smoothing is achieved by selling in each. For example, Ford seemingly would get less of a smoothing effect between France and Germany, because their economies are so interrelated through the EU, than between either of those two countries and the United States.

Competitive Lead Time

The longer the lead time, the more likely the company is to use a concentration strategy.

The first company to enter a market often gains advantages in terms of brand recognition and because it can line up the best suppliers, distributors, and local partners. This is called **first-in advantage** and may be difficult for followers to counteract.[56] However, so many resources may be necessary to capitalize on the first-in advantage that companies may be unable to move quickly into many markets. Thus, sequential entry is more common than simultaneous entry into multiple markets. If a company determines that it has a long lead time before competitors are likely to be able to copy or supersede its advantages, then it may be able to maintain control of the expansion by following a concentration strategy and still beat competitors into other markets.

Spillover Effects

Spillover effects are situations in which the marketing program in one country results in awareness of the product in other countries. This can happen, for example, if the product is advertised through media viewed cross-nationally, such as cable television that reaches more than one country or the Internet that can be accessed from any place in the world. In such situations, a diversification strategy has advantages because additional customers may be reached with little additional incremental cost.

Need for Product, Communications, and Distribution Adaptation

Products and their marketing may have to be altered for sale in foreign markets. The adaptation process is often costly and may lead to two factors that favor a concentration strategy. First, the additional costs may limit the resources the company has for expansion in many different markets. Second, the fixed costs incurred for adaptation cannot be as easily spread over sales in other countries as a means of reducing total unit costs. For example, Ben & Jerry's is taking a concentration strategy by moving into the British market with as rapid an increase in distribution as possible in order to cover better the high fixed costs necessary for local production and advertising of ice cream.[57]

> **Adaptation means additional costs for the company because it**
> - **May not have the resources to spread to many markets**
> - **Cannot readily gain economies of scale through diversification**

Program Control Requirements

The more a company needs to control its operations in a foreign country, the more likely it is that it should develop a concentration strategy. This is because the company will need to use more of its resources to maintain that control. Its need for more control could result for various reasons, including fear that an external arrangement will create a competitor or the need for highly technical assistance for customers.

> **Diversification often implies external arrangements that may cause control to be lost.**

Extent of Constraints

Constraints on what a company can do may be internal or external. For resource availability, for example, the higher the constraints, the more likely a concentration strategy is. If certain specialized technical personnel is the key resource needed to introduce a new product into foreign markets, a shortage of those personnel both within and outside the company will limit the number of countries into which the company can expand rapidly. Or if there are constraints on where the personnel can

> **Constraints limit resources from going to many locations simultaneously.**

be moved, the company may find it difficult to expand into many different markets rapidly. For example, Ben & Jerry's first tried to enter the United Kingdom and Russian markets almost simultaneously but quickly dissolved its Russian operation. A company manager explained the decision by saying, "We simply don't have the people and resources. We're a small company. You tie up two or three senior managers and you have a measurable effect on the company's performance."[58]

Evaluation of Investment Proposals

So far we have examined comparative opportunities on a very broad basis. At some point, a company must do a much more detailed analysis of specific projects and proposals in order to make allocation decisions. As we indicated earlier, companies use a variety of financial criteria to evaluate foreign investments.

Interdependence of Locations

The derivation of meaningful financial figures is not easy when foreign operations are concerned. Profit figures from individual operations may obscure the real impact those operations have on overall company activities. For example, if a U.S. company were to establish an assembly operation in Australia, the operation could either increase or decrease exports from the United States. Alternatively, the same company might build a plant in Malaysia to produce with cheaper labor; however, doing that would necessitate more coordination costs at headquarters.[59] Or perhaps by building a plant in Brazil to supply components to Volkswagen of Brazil, the company may increase the possibility of selling to Volkswagen in other countries. As a result of the Australian, Malaysian, or Brazilian projects, management would have to make assumptions about the changed profits in the United States and elsewhere.

The preceding discussion assumes that although overall company returns are difficult to calculate, those for the operating subsidiary are fairly easily ascertained. However, this is not the case. Much of the sales and purchases of foreign subsidiaries may be made from and to units of the same parent company. The prices charged on these transactions will affect the relative profitability of one unit compared to another. Further, the basis on which to estimate the net value of the foreign investment may not be realistically stated, particularly if part of the net value is based on exported capital equipment that is obsolete at home and useless except in the country where it is being shipped. By stating a high value, the company may be permitted to repatriate a larger portion of its earnings.

Noncomparative Decision Making

Most proposals are decided on a go–no-go basis if they meet minimum-threshold criteria.

Because companies have limited resources at their disposal, it might seem that they maintain a storehouse of foreign investment proposals that may be ranked on the basis of some predetermined criteria. If this were so, management could simply start allocating resources to the top-ranked proposal and continue down the list until no further investments were possible. This is often not the case, however. Investment proposals tend to be evaluated separately, and the decision that is made on each is commonly known as a **go–no-go decision.** This decision is usually based on a requirement that the project meet some minimum-threshold criteria. Of course, before a go–no-go decision is made, a good deal of weeding out of possible projects at various scanning and decision points has occurred.

Two major factors restricting companies from comparing investment opportunities are cost and time. Clearly, some companies cannot afford to conduct very many investigations simultaneously. Comparisons also can be restricted because feasibility studies are apt to be in various stages of completion at a given time. For example, suppose the investigation process is complete for a possible project in Australia but ongoing research is being conducted for projects in New Zealand, Japan, and Indonesia. Can the company afford to wait for the results from all the surveys before deciding on a location? The answer is, probably not. The time interval between completions probably would invalidate much of the earlier results and necessitate updating, added expense, and further delays. Another time-inhibiting problem is governmental regulations that require a decision within a given period. External time limits also may be imposed by other companies that have made partnership proposals. If no answer is forthcoming within a short period, a proposal may be made to a different potential partner.

Finally, companies must answer to both stockholders and employees. Few can afford to let resources lie idle or be employed for a low rate of return during a waiting period. This applies not only to financial resources but also to such resources as technical competence, since the lead time over competitors is reduced when a company delays a decision.

Reinvestment Decisions

A company may have to
make new commitments to
maintain competitiveness
abroad.

Most of the net value of foreign investment has come from reinvesting earnings abroad rather than from transferring new capital abroad. Decisions to replace depreciated assets or to add to the existing stock of capital from retained earnings in a foreign country differ somewhat from original investment decisions. Once committed to a given locale, a company may find it doesn't have the option of moving a substantial portion of the earnings elsewhere—to do so would endanger the continued successful operation of the given foreign facility. For example, the failure to expand might result in a falling market share and a higher unit cost than that of competitors.

Aside from competitive factors, a company may need several years of almost total reinvestment and allocation of new funds to one area in order to meet its objectives. Over time, the earnings may be used to expand the product line further, integrate production, and expand the market served from present output. Another reason for treating reinvestment decisions differently is that once there are experienced personnel within a given country, they may be the best judges of what is needed for that country; therefore, certain investment decisions may be delegated to them.

Geographic Strategy in the Internationalization Process

Ford's pattern of international expansion in the opening case is typical of many companies. In the early stages, companies may lack the experience and expertise to devise strategies for sequencing countries in the most advantageous way. Instead, they respond to opportunities that become apparent to them, and many of these turn out to be highly advantageous. As they gain more international experience, however, they actively decide which locations to emphasize for sales and production.

Further, as in the Ford case, many companies begin selling in an area very passively. A company may appoint an intermediary to promote sales for it or a licensee to produce on its behalf. If there is a demonstrated increase in sales, the company may consider investing more of its own resources. Exporting is the most common mode of initiating foreign sales. The generation of exports to a given country is an indication that sales may be made from production located in that country. However, there is little to motivate a company to shift production abroad as long as the company has production capacity to fulfill export orders, makes sufficient profits on the export sales, and perceives no threat to continue exporting.

We discussed earlier that the geographic expansion strategy is positively influenced by "nearness" in terms of geography, common language, and economic similarity. After moves to these markets, companies are then more prone to move to markets that are more dissimilar and located farther away.

Although companies expand the number of countries in which they operate over time, the speed of expansion varies widely from one company to another. The variables affecting this expansion speed were discussed in the section, "Diversification versus Concentration Strategies."

Divestment Decisions

Companies must decide how to get out of operations if
- **They no longer fit the overall strategy**
- **There are better alternative opportunities**

Companies commonly reduce commitments in some countries because those countries have poorer performance prospects than do others. For example, although Woolworth depended on its German stores for about a quarter of its operating profits, the company reasoned it should divest itself of more than 500 of those stores because of forecasted lower earnings in Germany, growth prospects in Latin America, and the need to expand its Foot Locker operations elsewhere in Western Europe.[60] First Boston moved its administration for the whole of Asia from Hong Kong to Singapore because of greater political uncertainties in Hong Kong.[61] PepsiCo withdrew from Myanmar because of concern that the poor Myanmar human rights record would affect sales in other countries.[62] In addition, Chevron announced a $2-billion downsizing of its U.S. home operation in order to increase its business abroad.[63]

Managers are less likely to propose divestments than investments.

Some indications suggest that companies might fare better by planning divestments better and by developing divestment specialists. Companies have tended to wait too long before divesting, trying instead expensive means of improving performance. Local managers, who fear losing their positions if the company abandons an operation, propose additional capital expenditures. In fact, this question of who has something to gain or lose is a factor that sets decisions to invest apart from decisions to divest. Both types of decisions should be highly interrelated and geared to the company's strategic thrust. Ideas for investment projects typically originate with middle managers or with managers in foreign subsidiaries who are enthusiastic about collecting information to accompany a proposal as it moves upward in the organization. After all, the evaluation and employment of these people depend on growth. They have no such incentive to propose divestments. These proposals typically originate at the top of the organization after upper management has tried most remedies for saving the operation.[64]

Divestments may occur by selling or closing facilities. The option of selling usually is preferred because the divesting company receives some compensation. However, a company that considers divesting because the outlook for the country's political and economic future is poor may find few potential buyers except at very low prices. In such situations, the company may try to delay divestment, hoping the situation will improve. If it does, the firm that waits out the situation generally is in a better position to regain markets and profits than one that forsakes its operation. For example, many MNEs divested their South African operations during the late 1980s primarily because of internal political unrest caused by South Africa's policy of apartheid, trade embargoes by foreign investors' home-country governments, and consumer pressure from outside South Africa. As more companies attempted to divest, there were fewer buyers that were able to buy facilities even at lower prices. By the early 1990s, the dissolution of apartheid laws brought a renewed positive outlook on South Africa's future. Companies that had remained (such as Hoechst, Crown Cork & Seal, and Johnson Matthey) were able to move much faster in the early 1990s to increase their South African business than were companies that had abandoned the market.[65] Some companies, such as Goodyear, have bought back their old properties at a price well above what they had sold them for.[66]

A company cannot always simply abandon an investment either. Governments frequently require performance contracts, such as substantial severance packages to employees, that make a loss from divestment greater than the direct investment's net value. Further, many large MNEs fear adverse international publicity and difficulty in reentering a market if they do not sever relations with a foreign government on amicable terms. During the early 1990s, several foreign investors, including Occidental Petroleum and Email and Elders, decided to take losses and leave the Chinese market, but the Chinese government made their departures slow and expensive.[67]

In the quest for competitiveness, companies with global strategies often seek least-cost production locations by moving into developing countries because of labor-cost differences. However, advantages may be short-lived for several reasons:

- Competitors follow leaders into low-wage areas.
- There is little first-in advantage for this type of production migration.
- Foreign costs rise quickly because of pressure on wage or exchange rates.

As a result, some companies, especially those with rapidly evolving technologies, seek to locate production close to product-development activities. Doing this allows for a tight linkage between product and process technologies (for example, making smaller disk drives is as much a manufacturing problem as it is a technical one), a faster market entry with new products, and unique production technologies that cannot be easily copied by competitors.[68] These factors tend to push more of a company's production into industrial countries, in which most R&D occurs. Market-seeking location decisions, whether in pursuit of global or of multidomestic strategies, also favor industrial countries for both production and sales locations. Evidence indicates that new products diffuse to developing countries slowly and incompletely.[69]

Trade barriers give companies impetus to expand sequentially by starting in those countries with the largest markets. As these barriers are removed, particularly on a regional basis, companies may more easily commence sales strategies almost simultaneously in various countries. Large markets in which there is protectionism have a greater advantage in attracting production than do large markets that can be effectively served from production locations in smaller countries with trade access to the larger markets.

LOOKING TO THE FUTURE

International geographic expansion is a two-tiered consideration: How much of a company's sales and production should be outside its home country? And how should outside sales and production be allocated among countries? As yet, no comprehensive model exists to answer these questions, and perhaps differences among companies and dynamic environmental conditions make such a model impractical. Meanwhile, companies are apt simply to place more emphasis on certain locales than on others as they see opportunities evolving. Typical of this tendency was a prediction by Procter & Gamble's CEO that more than half of that company's sales would come from abroad within the next few years, which would nearly double its foreign dependence, with sales growing more rapidly in the Far East than elsewhere.[70]

For large companies, an intriguing question is whether they are approaching an optimum ratio between domestic and foreign operations. Some data suggest they are.[71] An emphasis on more foreign business is perhaps inevitable when a company starts from a low base of international dependence. Yet the advantage of "more is better" should hold only until the company reaches some optimum combination of domestic and foreign operations. Otherwise, it would continue to improve its performance until it had no domestic operations at all—not a logical situation. If some companies are approaching their optimum positions, they can be expected to grow domestically and internationally at about the same rate in the future.

The need to allocate among opportunities because of insufficient resources is liable to play an even more important role in the near future. The opening up of Eastern Bloc economies, the global move toward privatization, and the more liberal allowance of majority ownership have combined to create more opportunities from which to choose. At the same time, companies have not increased their resource bases concomitantly to enable them to take advantage of all these new opportunities. Further, many companies in the late 1980s and early 1990s overextended their debt positions, particularly with leveraged buyouts; these debt positions might inhibit unrestricted international expansion.

Because data availability should continue to improve, global environmental scanning will assume greater importance. Companies will continue to need information because of global strategies of competitors and economic and political volatility. However, the information explosion will present new challenges as timely analysis may necessitate even greater reliance on tools that reduce the number of alternatives under consideration.

WEB CONNECTION

Check out our home page for links to World Wide Web resources on international business practices in various countries and other useful information on countries of the world.

Summary

- **Because companies seldom have sufficient resources to exploit all opportunities apparent to them, two major considerations facing companies are which markets to serve and where to locate the production to serve those markets.**

- **Market- and production-location decisions are often highly interdependent because markets often need to be served from local production, because firms seek nearby outlets for excess capacity, and because firms may be unwilling to invest in those production locations necessary to serve a desired market.**

- **Scanning techniques aid decision makers in considering alternatives that might otherwise be overlooked. They also help limit the final detailed feasibility studies to a manageable number of those that appear most promising.**

- The ranking of countries is useful for determining the order of entry into potential markets and for setting the allocation of resources and rate of expansion to different markets.

- Because each company has unique competitive capabilities and objectives, the factors affecting the geographic expansion pattern will be slightly different for each. Nevertheless, certain variables that have been shown to influence most companies are the relative size of country markets, the ease of operating in the specific countries, the availability and cost of resources, and the perceived relative risk and uncertainty of operations in one country versus another.

- The amount, accuracy, and timeliness of published data vary substantially among countries. A researcher should be particularly aware of different definitions of terms, different collection methods, and different base years for reports, as well as misleading responses.

- Sources of published data on international business include consulting firms, governmental agencies, international agencies, and organizations that serve international businesses. The cost and specificity of these publications vary widely.

- Some tools frequently used to compare opportunities in various countries are grids that rate country projects according to a number of separate dimensions and matrices on which companies may plot one attribute on a vertical axis and another on the horizontal axis, such as risk and opportunity or country attractiveness and company strength.

- Using a similar amount of internal resources, a company may choose initially to move rapidly into many foreign markets with only a small commitment in each (a diversification strategy) or to pursue a strong involvement and commitment in one or a few locations (a concentration strategy).

- The major variables a company should consider when deciding whether to diversify or concentrate are the growth rate and sales stability in each market, the expected lead time over competitors, the degree of need for product and marketing adaptation in different countries, the need to maintain control of the expansion program, and the internal and external constraints the company faces.

- Because of the interdependence of operations in different countries, it is difficult to derive meaningful financial figures to evaluate the effects or return from operations in a single country.

- Once a feasibility study is complete, most companies do not rank investment alternatives but rather set some minimum-threshold criteria and either accept or reject a foreign project based on those criteria. This type of decision results because multiple feasibility studies seldom are finished simultaneously and there are pressures to act quickly.

- Reinvestment decisions normally are treated separately from new investment decisions because a reinvestment may be necessary to protect existing resources' viability and because there are people on location who can better judge the worthiness of proposals.

- Companies must develop locational strategies for new investments and devise means of deemphasizing certain areas and divesting if necessary.

Case
Royal Dutch
Shell/Nigeria[72]

In 1997 Royal Dutch/Shell (Shell) faced the first shareholder resolution presented to any company in the United Kingdom. The resolution, which called for more public accountability of the company's Nigerian operations, was supported by a shareholder group that included eighteen public and private pension funds, five religious institutions, and an academic fund. Shell had recently made an investment decision in Nigeria to participate with a 24-percent ownership in building a $3.8 billion natural gas liquefication plant, which will be the largest investment ever made in Africa. Still pending was whether to reopen its oil fields in Ogoniland, a small 404-square-mile area of Nigeria at the delta of the Niger River, which it had closed in 1993 because of political unrest. (See Map 13.1 showing Nigeria and Ogoniland.) At the time of these investment considerations, protesters marched in Washington to urge boycotting the purchase of Nigerian oil; the European Union froze $295 million in aid to Nigeria while considering an arms sales or full embargo on business with Nigeria; the World Bank announced it would not go forward with a $100 million investment in the gas plant; various organizations in South Africa called for Shell to divest its Nigerian operations; and pressures mounted in the United Kingdom for a consumer boycott of Shell.

Nigerian Situation

Nigeria, a British colony until 1960, has a population of over 115 million, making it by far the most populous country in Africa. The country is organized into fairly autonomous states and the government has the challenge of trying to unite 250 different ethnic and linguistic groups. Ethnic conflict has at times been severe, especially in the 1966–1970 period when civil war broke out between the predominately Moslem Hausas and the predominately Christian Ibos, who seceded unsuccessfully to form the Republic of Biafra. During that period, oil companies received demands for royalty payments on Biafran oil from both the governments of Nigeria and Biafra.

Nigeria has had a series of military coups, and military rule has existed more years than civilian rule since Nigeria gained its independence. In 1997, Nigeria's central government

Map 13.1
Nigeria and Ogoniland

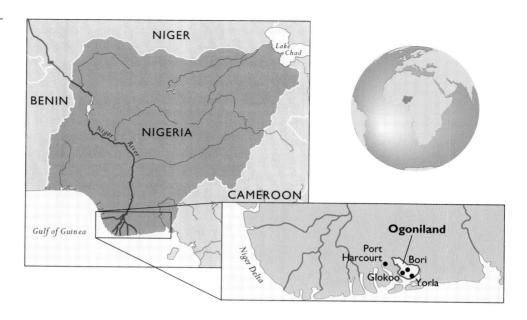

was headed by a Hausa-speaking military junta, which has sought to quell, sometimes brutally, any moves by minority groups for more autonomy.

The Nigerian National Petroleum Corporation (NNPC), a government-owned company, is a joint venture partner in all Nigerian petroleum projects. NNPC will own 49 percent of the natural gas liquefication plant in which Shell plans to invest. Oil accounts for 90 percent of Nigeria's foreign exchange earnings and for 80 percent of central government revenue. Nigeria has more foreign direct investment than any other country in Africa.

Shell in Nigeria

Shell has been a pioneer at building political risk into its decision making. In the early 1970s, Shell's planners realized that technical tools for predicting where oil might be found had become quite sophisticated; however, they reasoned that they should not make exploration location decisions only on the basis of the likelihood of finding oil at a given cost. There were many political factors that could affect the security of their ownership and of getting oil to market. They developed rating schemes to examine the underlying conditions within and between countries that could affect the security of assets and the ability to export them to their markets. These conditions were rated in a uniform manner by political specialists so that Shell's planners could plot the technical feasibility (opportunity) of securing oil on one axis and the political risk of securing that oil on the second axis. This tool served to help plan a portfolio of countries to serve as suppliers.

Shell also perfected scenario analysis to help understand conditions that might affect future global demands and supplies of petroleum and to prepare for different contingencies. One of the factors it noted was the size of a country's oil reserves did not necessarily correspond with the country's eagerness to sell the oil. For example, a country might wish to hold back supplies because it was already running a balance of payments surplus, because it could not absorb increased income efficiently into its economy, or because it expected future prices to exceed the present value of investing oil income. In this analysis, Nigeria has consistently shown up as a country willing to sell almost unlimited supplies, even though its reserves are not nearly as ample as countries such as Saudi Arabia, which is more prone to limit supplies.

However, Shell began selling in Nigeria in the late 1920s, before it developed its sophisticated tools to help deal with risk and uncertainty. In 1937, it formed a joint venture with British authorities that had exclusive rights to explore for oil. The first oil was found in 1956 in Ogoniland. Subsequently, this joint venture sold exploration rights to other oil companies; however, by 1995 Shell's operations still controlled about half of Nigeria's oil output.

Although Shell procures oil in a large portfolio of countries, the Nigerian operations are significant, as shown in Table 13.4. Analysts estimated in 1995 that if an oil embargo were placed on Nigeria, it would cost Shell about $1.6 billion a year in revenue and $150 million annually in net income.

The Ogoni Situation

The Shell joint venture includes nearly 100 oil wells, two refineries, and a fertilizer plant in Ogoniland. Revenue from these operations has traditionally gone to Nigeria's central government, and very little has been redistributed back to Ogoniland. Beginning in 1992, a group of Ogonis, led by the author Kenule Saro-Wiwa, formed the Movement for the Survival of Ogoni People (MOSOP). MOSOP began campaigning for political self-determination, a greater share of oil revenues, compensation for losses from Shell's activities, and restoration of the environment in Ogoniland. Some specific charges have been that Shell oil spills (27 incidents between 1982 and 1992) have despoiled farmlands and fishing areas, that oil flares have affected health, and that the laying of pipes destroyed freshly planted crops.

Table 13.4
Shell's Stake in Nigeria

Employees

World-wide	100,000
Nigeria	6,400*

Daily Crude Production (barrels a day)

World-wide	About 2.5 million
Nigeria	256,000

*Plus 22,000 through contracting companies.

Source: From Richard L. Hudson and Matthew Rose, "Shell Is Pressured to Scrap Its Plans For New Plant in Nigeria Amid Protests," 11/14/95. Reprinted by permission of the *Wall Street Journal,* ©1995 Dow Jones & Co., Inc. All Rights Reserved Worldwide.

Saro-Wiwa accused Shell of waging an ecological war against the Ogoni people to complete a genocide. MOSOP demonstrations have resulted in violence as the Nigerian army, using troops from other ethnic groups, have opened fire on crowds and attacked Ogoni villages. Ogonis began sabotaging Shell facilities, and the situation became so severe that Shell ceased operations in that part of Nigeria in early 1993.

Between 1992 and 1994, the Nigerian government arrested Saro-Wiwa four times, primarily for inciting and directing his supporters to violence. Shortly before his last arrest, he said, "They are going to arrest us all and execute us. All for Shell." He and eight others were held in jail nearly a year and then hanged.

Shell's Investment Dilemma

Although Shell publicly opposed the execution and wrote a letter to the Nigerian head of state requesting clemency for Mr. Saro-Wiwa, the company has been accused of not doing enough. A representative from Greenpeace, one of Shell's major critics, said, "Shell is the most powerful political actor on the Nigerian stage—both historically and currently. In Nigeria, the power doesn't come from the people, it comes from Shell. If Shell wanted to make a difference, they would." But the managing director of Shell's operation in Nigeria said, "We did not negotiate. We were not in a position to negotiate his release. We had no power to do so."

After the executions, Shell faced many, sometimes conflicting, pressures outside Nigeria. These included that it should divest all Nigerian operations, that it should cancel the natural gas plant project, that it should forgo trying to reopen operations in Ogoniland, and that it should pay all environmental and other costs in Ogoniland.

There was some precedent for Shell's giving in to outside pressure; it had recently given in to international opinion by canceling the dumping of an oil installation in the North Atlantic. But this action was practically costless and posed no threat to vital business interests. Shell's remaining in South Africa throughout the period of apartheid, while many other companies divested, is probably a better indication of its philosophy on staying in markets for the long term. Moreover, in 1996, Shell made a major oil discovery off the Nigerian coast. Thus the ability to exploit this new find could be tied to the company's investment decisions in Ogoniland.

No other foreign investors have been pressured to divest operations in Nigeria. Non-oil investments, such as those by Unilever and Standard Chartered Bank, are probably too small to be perceived as having an impact on political conditions in Nigeria. Other oil companies, such as Mobil and Chevron, operate in deep sea areas, rather than in the politically volatile area of Ogoniland.

Shell officials have indicated that they can do more for improving the lot of Nigerians, especially those in Ogoniland, by expanding in Nigeria and reopening facilities in Ogoniland. For example, by building the natural gas plant, the gas flaring problem will be eliminated. But damages to Ogoni facilities since Shell ceased operations are about $40 million. Officials indicated that they don't believe that trade sanctions are apt to work to change political leadership. They have indicated a willingness to pay for environmental damages that Shell caused, but Shell has accused Ogonis of purposely creating environmental problems in hopes of collecting compensation. Nevertheless, the former head of Shell's environmental studies group in Nigeria embarrassed the company by stating on British television that the company had ignored his group's environmental warnings. He also criticized Shell's methods of drilling, gas flaring, and waste disposal.

Questions

1. What should Shell do about reopening facilities in Ogoniland?
2. What specific political risk problems does Shell face in Nigeria? What are the underlying reasons for these problems?
3. What actions can Shell take to quell criticism about its operations in Nigeria?
4. What is the likelihood of an effective trade embargo against Nigeria? Of a consumer boycott against Shell?

Chapter Notes

1. Data for the case were taken from "Ford in Britain," *The Economist*, February 28, 1981, pp. 66–67; Gilbert D. Harrell and Richard O. Kiefer, *MSU Business Topics*, Winter 1981, pp. 5–15; Mira Wilkins and Frank Ernest Hill, *American Business Abroad: Ford on Six Continents* (Detroit: Wayne State University Press, 1964); Alan Nevins, *Ford: Expansion and Challenge: 1915–33*, Vol. II (New York: Charles Scribner's Sons, 1957); "Ford Annual Report," various years; Steven Prokesch, "Can Europe Save Ford's Future: Again?" *New York Times*, October 28, 1990, p. F1+; "Ford Around the World," *Ford International Public Affairs*, Dearborn, Michigan, various issues; and John Griffiths, "Emerging Nations Power World Vehicle Sales," *Financial Times*, May 13, 1996, p. 3; Bradley A. Stertz, "Ford Gears Up for Asian Markets," *Detroit News*, October 27, 1995, p. E3; and Katherine Yung, "Ford Steps Up Effort to Export More Vehicles," *Detroit News*, March 10, 1996, p. D3. For up-to-date information on Ford's international operations from the Internet, contact http://www.ford.com/corporate-info/international/

2. Masaaki Kotabe, "Patterns and Technological Implications of Global Sourcing Strategies," *Journal of International Marketing*, Vol. 1, No. 1, 1993, pp. 26–43.

3. "U.S. Companies to Build Electrical Plant in Bolivia," *Wall Street Journal*, September 16, 1996, p. A12.

4. Karen B. Hisey and Richard E. Caves, "Diversification Strategy and Choice of Country: Diversifying Acquisitions Abroad by U.S. Multinationals, 1978–1980," *Journal of International Business Studies*, Summer 1985, p. 52, show that between 70 and 85 percent of foreign acquisitions have been in related businesses.

5. Gene Koretz, "Where America's Bottom Line May Be Squeezed Overseas," *Business Week*, September 20, 1993, p. 22, refers to a study by Rosanne M. Cahn of First Boston Corp.

6. Yair Aharoni, *The Foreign Investment Decision Process* (Boston: Harvard University Graduate School of Business, 1966), pp. 52–53.

7. K. Fatehi-Sedeh and M. H. Safizadeh, "The Association Between Political Instability and Flow of Foreign Direct Investment," *Management International Review*, Vol. 29, No. 4, 1989, pp. 4–13.

8. John T. Harvey, "The Determinants of Direct Foreign Investment," *Journal of Post Keynesian Economics*, Vol. 12, No. 2, Winter 1989–90, pp. 260–272.

9. For overall export indicators, see Robert T. Green and Ajay K. Kohli, "Export Market Identification: The Role of Economic Size and Socioeconomic Development," *Management International Review*, Vol. 31, No. 1, 1991, pp. 37–50.

10. For a good discussion, see Ellen Day, Richard J. Fox, and Sandra M. Huszagh, "Segmenting the Global Market for Industrial Goods: Issues and Implications," *International Marketing Review*, Vol. 5, No. 3, Autumn 1988, pp. 14–27.

11. Kenichi Ohmae, "Becoming a Triad Power: The New Global Corporation," *International Marketing Review*, Autumn 1986, pp. 36–49; and "Foreign Investment and the Triad," *The Economist*, August 24, 1991, p. 57.

12. Zoher Abdoolcarim, "Middle Class, Top Dollar," *Asian Business*, Vol. 30, No. 3, March 1994, pp. 46–49.

13. Klaus Schwab and Claude Smadja, "Power and Policy: The New Economic World Order," *Harvard Business Review*, November–December 1994, pp. 40–50.

14. Raj Aggarwal, "Investment Performance of U.S.-Based Companies: Comments and a Perspective on International Diversification of Real Assets," *Journal of International Business Studies*, Spring–Summer 1980, pp. 98–104; and Rolf Buhner, "Assessing International Diversification of West German Corporations," *Strategic Management Journal*, Vol. 8, January–February, 1987, pp. 25–37.

15. Y. M. Geyikdagi and N. V. Geyikdagi, "International Diversification in Latin America and the Industrialized Countries," *Management International Review*, Vol. 29, No. 3, 1989, pp. 62–71.

16. Hisey and Caves, op. cit., pp. 58–62.

17. Irving B. Kravis and Robert E. Lipsey, "The Location of Overseas Production and Production for Export by U.S. Multinational Firms," *Journal of International Economics*, Vol. 12, May 1982, pp. 201–223, found that U.S. companies, regardless of industry, tended to enter foreign markets by going first to Canada, and then to the

United Kingdom and Mexico. Since then, aggregate foreign direct investment figures by U.S. companies indicate a continued emphasis on those three countries.

18. Christopher Power, "Will It Sell In Podunk? Hard to Say," *Business Week,* August 10, 1992, pp. 46–47.

19. Alan David MacCormack, Lawerence James Newman III, and Donald B. Rosenfield, "The New Dynamics of Global Manufacturing Site Locations," *Sloan Management Review,* Summer 1994, pp. 69–79.

20. James Hines, *Tax Policy and the Activities of Multinational Corporations* (Cambridge, MA: National Bureau of Economic Research working paper No. 5589, 1996).

21. "Volkswagen Switches Work to Low-Cost Unit in Slovakia," *Financial Times,* December 19, 1995, p. 4.

22. Robert Keatley, "Luxury-Auto Makers Consider Mexico: Its Low-Cost Labor vs. Image Perception," *Wall Street Journal,* November 27, 1992, p. A4.

23. Karen E. Thuermer, "Selecting a New Location Is a Matter of Meeting Criteria," *Export Today,* April 1993, pp. 20–23.

24. Matthew Brzezinski, "Ukraine's Bureaucrats Stymie U.S. Firms," *Wall Street Journal,* November 4, 1996, p. A14.

25. See, for example, Briance Mascarenhas, "Coping With Uncertainty in International Business," *Journal of International Business Studies,* Vol. 13, No. 2, Fall 1982, pp. 87–98; Philip J. Stein, "Should Your Firm Invest in Political Risk Insurance?" *Financial Executive,* March 1983, pp. 18–22; and Pravin Banker, "You're the Best Judge of Foreign Risks," *Harvard Business Review,* Vol. 61, No. 2, March–April, 1983, pp. 157–165.

26. For an analysis of the importance of these variables in the decision-making process, see Joseph La Palombara and Stephen Blank, *Multinational Corporations in Comparative Perspective* (New York: The Conference Board, 1977), pp. x–xii; and Gabriel R. G. Benito and Geir Gripsrud, "The Internationalization Process Approach to the Location of Foreign Direct Investments: An Empirical Analysis," in Milford B. Green and Rod B. McNaughton (eds.) *The Location of Foreign Direct Investment* (Aldershot, U.K.: Avebury, 1995), pp. 43–58.

27. Srilata Zaheer and Elaine Mosakowski, "The Dynamics of the Liability of Foreignness: A Global Study of Survival in Financial Services," Discussion Paper #213, Strategic Management Research Center, Carlson School of Management, University of Minnesota, St. Paul, Minnesota, May 1995.

28. Robert B. Stobaugh, Jr., "Where in the World Should We Put That Plant?" *Harvard Business Review,* January–February 1969, pp. 132–134.

29. Masayoshi Kanabayashi, "Japan's Top Soap Firm, Kao, Hopes to Clean Up Abroad," *Wall Street Journal,* December 17, 1992, p. B5.

30. Jeremy Grant, "Chrysler to Rethink Plans for Vietnam Plant," *Financial Times,* April 18, 1996, p. 5.

31. Leslie Crawford, "Vitro to Sell U.S. Glass Operations," *Financial Times,* August 16, 1996, p. 13.

32. Robert Greenberger, "Heading for Hanoi," *Wall Street Journal,* February 9, 1993, p. A1.

33. Ruth R. Harkin, "Testimony on Overseas Private Investment Corporation before House Appropriations Committee," in *Federal Document Clearing House Congressional Testimony,* March 28, 1996.

34. Lee C. Nehrt, "The Political Climate for Private Investment: Analysis Will Reduce Uncertainty," *Business Horizons,* June 1972, pp. 52–55; Herbert Cahn, "The Political Exposure Problem: An Often Overlooked Investment Decision," *Worldwide P & I Planning,* May–June 1972, pp. 20–22.

35. For a good discussion of the different services and their methods, see Llewellyn D. Howell and Brad Chaddick, "Model of Political Risk for Foreign Investment and Trade," *Columbia Journal of World Business,* Fall 1994, pp. 71–91; William D. Coplin and Michael K. O'Leary (eds.), *The Handbook of Country and Political Risk Analysis* (East Syracuse, NY: Political Risk Services, 1994).

36. Sally Bowen, "Foreign Money Pours Back," *Euromoney,* April 1993, pp. 120–121.

37. Stewart Dalby, "Political Worries Hit Investors," *Financial Times,* December 18, 1995, p. 4, quoting data collected by the Control Risk Group.

38. Douglas Nigh, "The Effect of Political Events on United States Direct Foreign Investment: A Pooled Time-Series Cross Sectional Analysis," *Journal of International Business Studies,* Vol. 16, No. 1, 1985, pp. 1–17; S. Desta, "Assessing Political Risk in Less Developed Countries," *The Journal of Business Strategies,* Vol. 5, No. 5, 1985, pp. 40–53; Thomas L. Brewer, "Instability in Developing and Industrial Countries: Methodological and Theoretical Issues," *Journal of Comparative Economics,* Vol. 11, 1987, pp. 120–123; and Fatehi-Sedeh and Safizadeh, loc. cit.

39. Harold Knudsen, "Explaining the National Propensity to Expropriate: An Ecological Approach," *Journal of International Business Studies,* Spring 1974, pp. 51–69.

40. Simon Holberton, "Beijing Protests Over U.S. Claims of $30bn Trade Deficit," *Financial Times,* October 9, 1995, p. 3.

41. Karen Pennar and Christopher Farrell, "Notes from the Underground Economy," *Business Week,* February 15, 1993, pp. 98–101; and Felicity Barringer, "Fed-

eral Survey Finds Census Missed 4 Million to 6 Million People," *New York Times,* April 19, 1991, p. A8.

42. Robert Chote, "Nations Rally to IMF's Statistics Standards," *Financial Times,* July 30, 1996, p. 4.

43. Maureen Kline, "Italy Goes After Tax Cheats (Again), With a Big Plan to Get Small Business," *Wall Street Journal,* November 9, 1992, p. A7.

44. Nichole M. Christian, "New Generation of Car Thieves Restructures the Business," *Wall Street Journal,* July 19, 1995, p. B1, based on a study by the National Insurance Crime Bureau.

45. Vincent Boland, "Earnings from Organised Crime Reach $1,000bn," *Financial Times,* February 14, 1997, p. 1.

46. William A. Stoever, "Methodological Problems in Assessing Developing Country Policy toward Foreign Manufacturing Investment," *Management International Review,* Vol. 29, No. 4, 1989, p. 71.

47. Steven Greenhouse, "Comparing Wealth as Money Fluctuates," *New York Times,* August 23, 1987, p. E3, discusses the problem of comparing purchasing power.

48. For a good discussion, see William L. Goffe, "Computer Network Resources for Economists," *Journal of Economic Perspectives,* Vol. 8, No. 3, Summer 1994, pp. 97–119; and John A. Quelch and Lisa R. Klein, "The Internet and International Marketing," *Sloan Management Review,* Spring 1996, pp. 60–75.

49. Tara Parker-Pope, "Nonalcoholic Beer Hits the Spot in Mideast," *Wall Street Journal,* December 6, 1995, p. B1.

50. John F. Preble, Pradeep A. Rau, and Arie Reichel, "The Environmental Scanning Practices of U.S. Multinationals in the Late 1980's," *Management International Review,* Vol. 28, No. 4, 1988, pp. 4–14.

51. This classification scheme is adapted from Carl Noble and Virgil Thornhill, "Institutionalization of Management Science in the Multinational Firm," *Columbia Journal of World Business,* Fall 1977, pp. 13–15.

52. Risk and opportunity are considered essential elements for incorporation in any portfolio analysis. See, for example, Yoram Wind and Susan Douglas, "International Portfolio Analysis and Strategy: The Challenge of the 80s," *Journal of International Business Studies,* Vol. 12, No. 2, Fall 1981, pp. 72–73; and "How Borg-Warner Uses Country-Risk Assessment as a Planning Element," *Business International,* November 9, 1979, pp. 353–356.

53. Craig M. Watson, "Counter-Competition Abroad to Protect Home Markets," *Harvard Business Review,* January–February 1982, p. 40.

54. Harrell and Kiefer, loc. cit.

55. Igal Ayal and Jehiel Zif, "Market Expansion Strategies in Multinational Marketing,"

Journal of Marketing, Vol. 43, Spring 1979, pp. 84–94.

56. Briance Mascarenhas, "Order of Entry and Performance in International Markets," *Strategic Management Journal,* October 1992, pp. 499–510.

57. Diane Summers, "Chunky Monkey Invasion," *Financial Times,* August 11, 1994, p. 7.

58. Neela Banerjee, "Ben & Jerry's Is Discovering That It's No Joke to Sell Ice Cream to Russians," *Wall Street Journal,* September 9, 1995; and Betsy McKay, "Ben & Jerry's Post-Cold War Venture Ends in Russia With Ice Cream Melting," *Wall Street Journal,* February 7, 1997, p. A12.

59. Andrew Bartmess and Keith Cerny, "Building Competitive Advantage Through a Global Network of Capabilities," *California Management Review,* Winter 1993, pp. 78–103.

60. Jeffrey A. Trachtenberg, "Woolworth Explores Sale of German Unit," *Wall Street Journal,* November 10, 1992, p. A16.

61. "A Hub to Replace Hong Kong," *Euromoney,* February 1995, pp. 80–81.

62. Ted Bardacke, "PepsiCo Joins List of Groups Quitting Burma," *Financial Times,* January 28, 1997, p. 1.

63. Frederick Rose, "Chevron to Sell Nearly a Third of U.S. Refining," *Wall Street Journal,* September 28, 1993, p. A3.

64. Jean J. Boddewyn, "Foreign and Domestic Divestment and Investment Decisions: Like or Unlike?" *Journal of International Business Studies,* Vol. 14, No. 3, Winter 1983, p. 28.

65. Elizabeth Weiner and Mark Maremont, "Business Gets Ready to March Back to Pretoria," *Business Week,* February 25, 1991, p. 53.

66. Haig Simonian, "Goodyear Buys Back South Africa Business for $121m," *Financial Times,* November 19, 1996, p. 1.

67. Julia Leung, "For China's Foreign Investors, the Door Marked 'Exit' Can Be a Tight Squeeze," *Wall Street Journal,* March 12, 1991, p. A14.

68. Bartmess and Cerny, loc. cit.

69. Mascarenhas, loc. cit.

70. Keith H. Hammonds, citing John G. Smale, "P&G's Worldly New Boss Wants a More Worldly Company," *Business Week,* October 30, 1989, pp. 40–42.

71. John D. Daniels and Jeffrey Bracker, "Profit Performance: Do Foreign Operations Make a Difference?" *Management International Review,* Vol. 29, No. 1, 1989, pp. 46–56.

72. Data for the case were taken from David Lascelles, "The Long View at Shell," *Financial Times,* November 15, 1995, p. 16; David Lascelles, Jurek Martin, and Paul Adams, "Shell 'Regrets' Execution But Continues Nigeria Strategy," *Financial Times,* November 11–12, 1995, p. 3; Paul Adams, Robert Corzine, William Lewis, and Roger Matthews, "Shell Facing New Onslaught over Nigeria," *Financial Times,* December 15, 1995, p. 3; Paul Adams, "No Doubts Over Nigeria Gas Project," *Financial Times,* November 14, 1995, p. 9; Tony Hawkins and Simon Kuper, "Foreign Investors Are in No Hurry to Divest,"

Financial Times, November 14, 1995, p. 9; David Lascelles, "Shell under Pressure as EU Toughens Stance on Nigeria," *Financial Times,* November 14, 1995, p. 18; Richard Hudson and Matthew Rose, "Shell Is Pressured to Scrap Its Plans for New Plant in Nigeria Amid Protests," *Wall Street Journal,* November 14, 1995, p. A10; Paul Adams, "Shell to Probe Niger Delta," *Financial Times,* December 18, 1995, p. 4; Simon Kuper and David Lascelles, "ANC Sanctions Threat to Shell over Nigeria," *Financial Times,* November 18–19, 1995, p. 1; Pierre Wack, "Scenarios: Uncharted Waters Ahead," *Harvard Business Review,* September–October 1985, pp. 73–89; Steve Kretzmann, "Nigeria's 'Drilling Fields'," *Multinational Monitor,* January–February 1995, pp. 8–11+; Robert Corzine and Paul Adams, "Shell Makes New Oil Find Off Nigerian Coast," *Financial Times,* March 8, 1996, p. 1; Simon Kuper, "Shell 'Ignored' Warnings on Nigerian Pollution," *Financial Times,* May 14, 1996, p. 4; and William Lewis, "Shell Faces UK First in Investors' Resolution on Ethics," *Financial Times,* February 24, 1997, p. 1+. For up-to-date information on Shell's situation in Nigeria from the Internet, see http://www.shellnigeria.com/

Chapter 14

Collaborative Strategies

*When one party is willing,
the match is half made.*

—American Proverb

- To explain the major motives that should guide companies in their choice of operational form for global business activities

- To differentiate the major operational forms by which companies may tap the potential of international business

- To describe the considerations that companies should explore when entering into international contractual arrangements with other companies

- To characterize the factors that help to explain the success and failure of collaborative arrangements

- To emphasize that companies must develop means by which to manage diverse collaborative arrangements

Case
Grupo Industrial Alfa
S.A. (GIASA)[1]

Mexican-based Grupo Industrial Alfa S.A. (GIASA), usually referred to as Alfa, announced in 1995 that its joint venture with BASF from Germany would invest $100 million (all monetary amounts in this case are in U.S. dollars) to increase the capacity of two petrochemical plants. In 1996 Alfa inaugurated a $550 million electrical cogeneration plant owned jointly with Central and Southwest from the United States. During the same year, Alfa announced it would take a 25.6-percent interest in a multibillion dollar joint venture with AT&T and GTE of the United States, Telefónica de España of Spain, and Bancomer of Mexico. At about the same time, Alfa announced a "gentlemen's agreement" to become a partner with four Mexican chemical companies (Cydsa, Grupo Vitro, Grupo Celanese, and Grupo Idesa) to buy petrochemical plants from the state-owned Pemex. Alfa is a true conglomerate with annual sales of over $2.5 billion and 1995 profits of about $220 million. In 1996 it was ranked as the fifth largest company in Mexico and twenty-fourth largest in Latin America in terms of market capitalization. Most of its business involves collaborative agreements, especially ones with foreign companies.

From its founding in 1894 until 1974, Alfa's activities were part of a family enterprise in Monterrey controlled by the Garza and Sada families. During this time, the company had been affected only slightly by foreign competition. Its major lines of business—steel, beer, and banking—included products and services not easily imported into Mexico because steel imports were restricted and the other products and services usually needed to be produced near customers. There also were prohibitions against foreign ownership in these sectors. However, although the company was relatively immune from foreign competition, its outlook was for slow growth.

In 1973, the Mexican government sought to counter foreign control of companies by enacting laws that provided for restrictions on foreign equity in new ventures and on the expansion of existing investments having large foreign ownership. The Garza and Sada families saw these Mexicanization laws as an opportunity to diversify into growth industries that foreigners from that point on would find more difficult to control. They reasoned they might be able to buy some subsidiaries from foreign companies that were unwilling to accept minority ownership. They also reasoned they were in a good position to share in collaborative arrangements with foreign companies that sought business activities involving Mexico. Further, they felt that to capitalize on these possibilities, they would be better off shedding the family image. By extending ownership beyond the family, they could raise capital by selling additional shares. Further, good professional management could be attracted to the company. In 1974, they divided the enterprise into four companies—Alfa, Cydsa, Visa, and Vitro—and went public by issuing shares in each of them. At that time, the assets of the newly formed Alfa were estimated at $315 million, of which 75 percent was in steel. Alfa's management, with help from some top international consulting groups, agreed that diversification should be based on the objectives of minimizing cyclical changes in earnings, entering growth industries, and utilizing resources for which Mexico had advantages.

Among Alfa's first moves was the acquisition of the TV production facilities and brands of three U.S. companies: Philco, Magnavox, and Admiral. Through these acquisitions, Alfa captured 35 percent of Mexico's market for TV sets as well as the right to continue using

the three trade names for sales in Mexico. By 1980, Alfa had assets of $1.9 billion, 157 sub-
sidiaries, and 49,000 employees. Two events external to Alfa contributed to its growth: the
discovery of huge oil and natural gas reserves and pro–private-enterprise government
incentives for industry, including nearly free energy. Suddenly foreign companies were rush-
ing to find ways of expanding their business in Mexico. Most expansion had to involve Mexicans. Alfa was large, had good profitability, and possessed management that had a good
reputation; thus it was in an excellent position to acquire the foreign resources it wanted.
In fact, its biggest problem was in how to choose among the many opportunities. (Map 14.1
shows some of the alliances Alfa made with foreign companies.)

Alfa established numerous Mexican companies in which it owned a majority interest,
with a foreign partner holding a minority interest. The foreign partners came from a number of countries, including Japan (Hitachi, electric motors; Yamaha, motorcycles), Canada
(International Nickel, nonferrous metal exploration), the Netherlands (AKZO, artificial
fibers), and Germany (BASF, petrochemicals). For two U.S. companies—Ford and Du
Pont—the joint-venture operations involved substantial departures from usual policies.
Ford's 25-percent interest in a Mexican plant making aluminum cylinder heads for the U.S.
and Canadian automobile markets was the first minority interest the company had ever
taken in a joint venture. Du Pont had taken minority interests before accepting 49 percent
to Alfa's 51 percent in a Mexican synthetic fibers joint venture; however, it had always managed the ventures. In this case, Alfa managed the venture because its policy was to import
technology but maintain management control.

In many of these joint-venture operations, the Mexican output has used the trademark
developed by the foreign partner. Doing this has helped the product gain Mexican consumer acceptance. For this reason, when Alfa bought 100 percent of Massey-Ferguson's
tractor operation in Mexico in 1979, it paid the Canadian company a royalty fee to use the
Massey-Ferguson trade name. In the aluminum cylinder head joint venture, Ford was
attracted not by a captive Mexican market, but rather by the lower costs of producing
components to serve the U.S. and Canadian markets. In addition to cheap energy, Mexico
offered an abundance of cheap labor and no taxes on reinvested earnings. And Alfa itself
became interested in export markets: It established a sales arrangement under which
Japan's Mitsui Trading Company would handle exports of Alfa's polyester chemicals abroad.
Total exports for Alfa reached $1.1 billion in 1995.

Alfa developed direct reduction steel production, thus bypassing the high capital costs
of blast furnaces. To transfer this patented technology to new plants in other countries
would have required substantial on-site personnel and construction assistance. Alfa lacked
both personnel that could be spared and foreign construction experience, so it transferred
the technology to four foreign engineering companies: GHH-Sterkrade (Germany),
Kawasaki Heavy Industries (Japan), and Pullman Swindell and Dravo (both from the United
States). Those companies have in turn acted as agents on behalf of Alfa and constructed
steel plants in such countries as Brazil, Indonesia, Iran, Iraq, Venezuela, and Zambia. Alfa
continues to receive fees for the use of the technology in foreign mills, and the engineering
companies receive fees for building the plants, in what are known as turnkey projects.

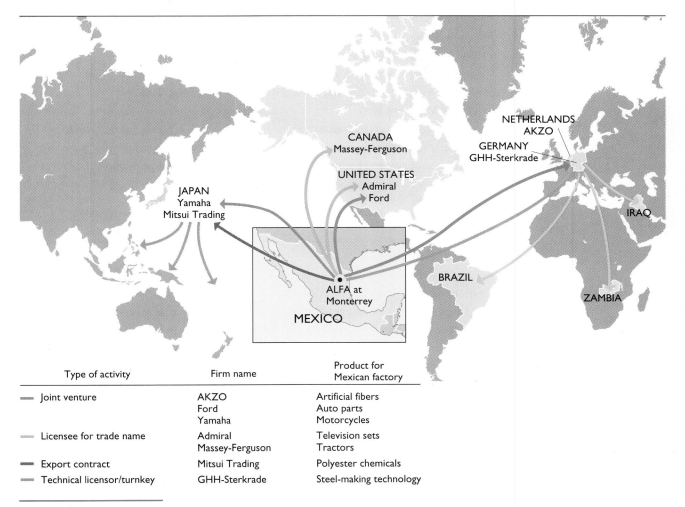

Type of activity	Firm name	Product for Mexican factory
▬▬ Joint venture	AKZO Ford Yamaha	Artificial fibers Auto parts Motorcycles
▬ ▬ Licensee for trade name	Admiral Massey-Ferguson	Television sets Tractors
▬▪▬ Export contract	Mitsui Trading	Polyester chemicals
▬ ▬ Technical licensor/turnkey	GHH-Sterkrade	Steel-making technology

Map 14.1
Alfa's International Strategic Alliances
This map shows only a sampling of the company's strategic alliances for sales and production within and outside Mexico.

For Alfa to expand and maintain management control between 1976 and 1980, it had to borrow and recruit managers outside of Mexico. Alfa ended up with debt of almost $3 billion owed to over 130 banks; about 75 percent of this was payable in U.S. dollars. Then oil prices plummeted, and the Mexican peso was devalued. Alfa lost so much money between 1980 and 1985, that it had to shut down forty of its subsidiaries and reduce the number of its employees by almost 19,000. Meanwhile, many of the foreign companies that had made agreements with Alfa in the 1970s found that their expected Mexican expansion (via joint ventures with Alfa) had been put on hold. These included, for example, BASF and Hercules. Alfa simply lacked the resources to carry out so many agreements with so many different foreign companies.

By 1987, foreign banks had converted part of Alfa's debt into a 27-percent stake in the company rather than have Alfa default. By 1989, Mexico's economy and Alfa's financial situation had turned around to such an extent that Alfa was able to buy back the foreign banks' ownership, an event hailed in the Mexican press as the "Mexicanization" of Alfa. Once again, Alfa embarked on expansion through alliances with foreign companies. Alfa also learned from its earlier dollar-debt problems; thus when Mexico's big devaluation occurred in 1994, Alfa was not adversely affected.

Although restrictions on foreign ownership in Mexico have largely been lifted, especially to investors from Canada and the United States because of NAFTA's enactment (petroleum-based industries are an exception), many foreign companies still prefer to have collaborative arrangements with Mexican companies because of the cumbersome process of dealing with the Mexican bureaucracy. Because Alfa has proven its capabilities at dealing with this bureaucracy and because it has proven its ability to manage multiple collaborative arrangements simultaneously and efficiently, foreign companies continue to seek out partnerships with it.

Introduction

International business may be conducted in various ways, as shown in Fig. 14.1 from the standpoint of market-seeking international expansion. For example, a company may produce at home or abroad. If producing abroad, the company may operate independently or it may collaborate in the production with another company. In Chapter 8, we explained the reasons for producing abroad rather than exporting and we discussed why (appropriability and internalization theories) companies would want to control foreign production through direct investment. Nevertheless, companies frequently handle much of their international operations through collaborative forms that lessen their control. The types of collaborative forms are shown in the section of Fig. 14.1 with the blue background. The truly experienced MNE with a fully global orientation usually uses most of the operational forms available, selecting them according to specific product or foreign operating characteristics. Further, the operating forms may be combined. For example, Kentucky Fried Chicken has a joint venture with Mitsubishi in Japan, which, in

**Figure 14.1
Alternative Operating
Forms for Foreign
Market Expansion**
More than one form may
be used within the same
operation. Those shaded in
blue are collaborative
arrangements.

PRODUCTION OWNERSHIP	PRODUCTION LOCATION	
	Home country	Foreign country
Equity arrangements	a. exporting	a. wholly owned operations b. partially owned with remainder widely held c. joint ventures d. equity alliances
Non-equity arrangements		a. licensing b. franchising c. management contracts d. turnkey operations

turn, franchises outlets within Japan. When collaboration is of strategic importance to one or more of the companies involved, it is known as a strategic alliance. In reality, the term *strategic alliance* often is used to describe a wide variety of collaborations, whether or not they are of real strategic importance. Collaborations involve different opportunities and problems than do trade or wholly owned direct investment; thus studying them is important.

The Alfa case illustrates the use of several different types of collaborative strategies to exploit international opportunities. Alfa established joint ventures with foreign companies, engaged in acquiring and selling process and product technology through licensing and turnkey contracts, and paid for the use of trademarks through licensing agreements.

This chapter discusses the motives for and types of collaborative arrangements, as well as the problems and methods of managing these arrangements.

Motives for Collaborative Arrangements

Companies establish collaborative arrangements for domestic operations, and their motives carry over to their international operations as well. For example, a company such as McDonald's that franchises most of its operations in the United States, also franchises most of its operations in foreign countries—and for the same reasons. In addition, companies establish collaborative arrangements abroad for other reasons. For example, in the opening case, Du Pont established a joint venture with Alfa because Mexican laws prohibited its gaining 100-percent ownership. Both the general and internationally specific reasons for collaborative arrangements are shown on Fig. 14.2. This figure also refers back to the four objectives of international business, which were introduced in Chapter 1. The strategy of using collaborative arrangements (or not) must be based on how they fit with the objectives of operating abroad and be compared with the noncollaborative arrangements of operating abroad through import/export or wholly owned direct investment.

Keep in mind that each organization participating in a collaborative agreement has its own primary objective for operating internationally and its own motive for collaborating rather than handling the operations independently. For example, Ford sought resource acquisition and Alfa sought diversification through its aluminum cylinder head joint venture. Ford's motivation for collaboration was mainly to overcome legal constraints, whereas Alfa's was to secure horizontal linkages.

Motives for Collaborative Arrangements: General

Sometimes it is cheaper to get another company to handle work, especially
- **At small volume**
- **When the other company has excess capacity**

Spread and reduce costs   To produce or sell abroad, a company must incur certain fixed costs. At a small volume of business, it may be cheaper for it to contract the work to someone else than to handle it internally. A specialist can spread the fixed costs over services to more than one company. If business increases enough,

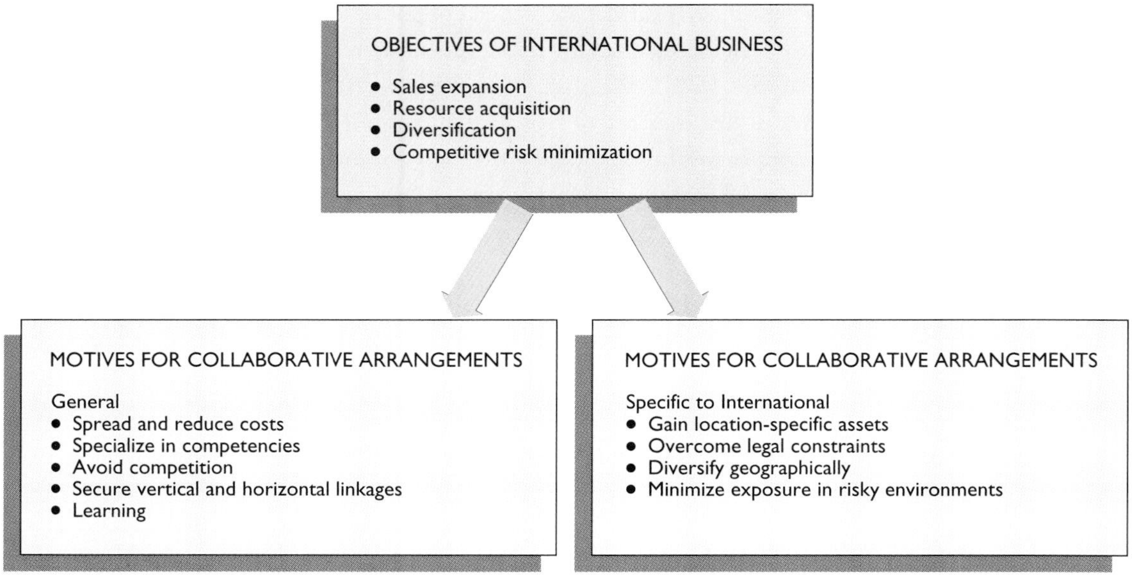

```
┌─────────────────────────────────────────────┐
│  OBJECTIVES OF INTERNATIONAL BUSINESS         │
│                                               │
│   • Sales expansion                           │
│   • Resource acquisition                      │
│   • Diversification                           │
│   • Competitive risk minimization             │
└─────────────────────────────────────────────┘
```

```
┌──────────────────────────────────────┐   ┌──────────────────────────────────────┐
│ MOTIVES FOR COLLABORATIVE ARRANGEMENTS │   │ MOTIVES FOR COLLABORATIVE ARRANGEMENTS │
│                                        │   │                                        │
│ General                                │   │ Specific to International               │
│  • Spread and reduce costs             │   │  • Gain location-specific assets       │
│  • Specialize in competencies          │   │  • Overcome legal constraints          │
│  • Avoid competition                   │   │  • Diversify geographically            │
│  • Secure vertical and horizontal      │   │  • Minimize exposure in risky          │
│    linkages                            │   │    environments                        │
│  • Learning                            │   │                                        │
└──────────────────────────────────────┘   └──────────────────────────────────────┘
```

**Figure 14.2
Relationship of
Strategic Alliances
to Companies'
International
Objectives**
Collaborative arrange-
ments may serve compa-
nies' goals, regardless of
whether they operate
internationally. In addition,
there are gains from col-
laborative arrangements
that are specific to companies' international
operations.

the contracting company then may be able to handle the activities more cheaply itself. Companies therefore should periodically reappraise the question of internal versus external handling of their varied operations.

External contracting of operations also may be lower in cost because another company may have excess production or sales capacity that can be easily utilized. Utilizing this capacity also may reduce start-up time and thus result in an earlier cash flow. Further, the contracted company may have environment-specific knowl-edge, such as how to deal with Mexican regulations and labor, that would be expen-sive for the contracting company to gain on its own. Also, contracting companies may lack the resources to "go it alone"; by pooling their efforts, they may be able to undertake activities that otherwise would be beyond their means. This is especially important for small companies.[2] But it is important for large companies when the cost of development and/or investment is very high. For example, Boeing estimates that the development cost of the next generation of 747s will cost $7 billion, an amount that strains the capabilities of even a company as large as Boeing.[3]

Cooperative ventures may, however, increase operating costs. There are addi-tional expenses involved in negotiating with another company or in transferring technology to it. Also, there usually are added headquarters costs involved in main-taining ongoing relationships with another company. Further, there may be addi-tional control costs as reports must comply to the needs of more than one company.

Licensing can yield a return
on a product that does not
fit the company's strategic
priority based on its best
competencies.

Specialize in competencies   The **resource-based view of the firm** holds that each company has a unique combination of competencies. A company may seek to improve its performance by concentrating on those activities that best fit its compe-tencies, thus depending on other firms to supply it with products, services, or sup-port activities for which it has lesser competency. For example, large, diversified companies are constantly reevaluating and altering their product lines to put their efforts where their major strengths lie. This may leave them with products, assets, or technologies that they do not wish to exploit themselves but that may be profitably transferred to other companies. For example, neither Chrysler nor Coca-Cola sees its competency to lie in the clothing business, so Murjani Merchandising has licensed the Jeep and Coca-Cola logos, which are valuable for selling a variety of merchandise.[4] However, a licensing or other collaborative arrangement has a limited time frame, which may allow a company to exploit a particular product, asset, or technology itself if at a later date its core competencies change.[5]

Avoid competition Sometimes markets are not large enough to justify entry of as many companies as would like to tap that market. Thus, various companies may band together so as not to compete. For example, AT&T and GTE originally announced separate Mexican joint ventures to compete against Telmex, the Mexican telecommunications monopoly, once that competition was opened. They merged their two joint ventures (one involving Alfa) so that they would more likely survive a shake-out in the market.[6] Companies also may combine certain resources to combat larger and more powerful competitors. For example, Daimler-Benz, China's state-run Aviation Industry General, and Samsung Aerospace formed a consortium to develop a new passenger aircraft; thus they could better compete against larger aircraft manufacturers such as Boeing and Airbus.[7]

Another example of avoiding competition involves the major aluminum producers. They have developed swap contracts that allow them to save transport costs. These companies are all vertically integrated, but not in each country in which they operate. Alcan might give Pechiney semiprocessed alumina in Canada in exchange for the same amount of semiprocessed alumina delivered to Alcan in France. Thus the companies continue to compete for sales in each market without having to compete in each market for the production of what they sell. Similarly, Ford's European plants make cars for Mazda to sell in Europe, and Mazda's Japanese factories make vehicles for Ford to sell in Japan.[8]

Secure vertical and horizontal linkages There are potential cost savings and supply assurances from vertical integration; however, companies may lack the competence or resources necessary to own and manage the full value-chain of activities. This is well illustrated in the petroleum industry. For example, recall the Saudi Aramco case in Chapter 12. Saudi Aramco has abundant oil reserves, but it lacks final distribution skills; therefore, it has established collaborative arrangements in such countries as the United States, the Philippines, and Italy for retail gas sales that assure markets for its petroleum.

Horizontal linkage may involve finished products or components. For finished products, there may be economies of scope in distribution, such as by having a full line of products to sell, which reduce the cost of sales per visit to potential customers. There may also be a better smoothing of earnings through diversification into more products. The opening case showed how Alfa has used collaborative arrangements to diversify into a broader range of products.

One of the fastest growth areas for collaborative arrangements has been with projects that are too large for any single company to handle, for example, new aircraft and communications systems. From such a project's inception, different companies (sometimes from different countries) agree to take on the high cost and high risk of developmental work for different components needed in the final product; then a lead company buys the components from the companies that did parts of the developmental work.

Gain knowledge   The motive for many companies' entries into collaborative arrangements is to learn so that their own competencies will broaden or deepen, thus making them more competitive in the future. Recall from the case on FDI in China from Chapter 11 that Chinese governmental authorities allow foreign companies to tap the Chinese market in exchange for their transference of technology to their Chinese joint venture partners.

Motives for Collaborative Arrangements: Specific to International

Gain location-specific assets   Cultural, political, competitive, and economic differences among countries create barriers for companies that want to operate abroad. When they feel ill-equipped to handle these differences, they may seek collaboration with local companies who will help manage the local operations. For example, in the opening case, AT&T's decision to team with Alfa was undoubtedly due in part to Alfa's greater ability to deal with Mexican political authorities, who are important in assuring efficient ongoing operations. In many other countries as well, foreign companies team with local companies to gain similar or other assets. For example, most foreign operations in Japan involve some type of collaboration with Japanese companies, who can help in securing distribution and a competent workforce—two assets that are very difficult for foreign companies to gain on their own in that environment. Access to distribution was the primary reason that Merck entered a joint venture with Chugai in Japan for the development and marketing of over-the-counter drugs.[9]

Overcome legal constraints   As the Alfa case showed, a company may be constrained in its choice of operating form regardless of its preferences. Some of the foreign companies discussed, such as Ford, may have preferred to wholly own the Mexican operation but were not legally permitted to do so. In addition to the outright prohibition of wholly owned operations or imports, other legal factors may influence the company's choice. These include differences in tax rates and in the maximum funds that can be remitted.

Collaboration can also be a means of protecting an asset. This may occur for two reasons. First, many countries provide very little de facto protection for foreign property rights such as trademarks, patents, and copyrights unless authorities are

Legal factors may be
- **Direct prohibitions against certain operating forms**
- **Indirect (for example, regulations affecting profitability)**

Collaboration hinders nonassociated companies from usurping the asset.

prodded consistently. To prevent pirating of these proprietary assets, companies sometimes have made collaborative agreements with local companies, which then monitor to ensure that no one else uses the asset locally. Second, some countries provide protection only if the internationally registered asset is exploited locally within a specified period. If a company does not use the asset within the country during that specified period, then whatever entity first does so gains the right to it.

Diversify geographically Not only product diversification but also geographic diversification among countries can aid a company in smoothing its sales and profits. Collaborative arrangements offer a faster initial means of entering multiple markets. In addition, if product conditions favor a diversification rather than a concentration strategy (recall the discussion in Chapter 13), there are more compelling reasons to establish foreign collaborative arrangements. However, these arrangements will be less appealing for companies whose activities are already widely extended or those that have ample resources for such extension.

Minimize exposure in risky environments There are many types of risk. However, the possibility that political or economic changes will affect the safety of assets and their earnings is often at the forefront of management's concern about foreign operations. One way to minimize loss from foreign political occurrences is to minimize the base of assets located abroad. Doing this may dictate external arrangements so that the asset base is shared by others. This move also might reduce political risk because a government may be less willing to move against a shared operation for fear of encountering opposition from more than one company. Another way to spread risk is to place operations in a number of different countries. This strategy reduces the chance that all foreign assets will be simultaneously subject to such adversity as political unrest or exchange control. As in the case of geographic diversification, the minimization in use of one's own assets permits a more rapid dispersion of operations among countries.

> The higher the perceived risk, usually the greater is the desire to operate as part of collaborative arrangements.

> External operating forms allow for greater spreading of assets among countries.

Types of Collaborative Arrangements

The forms of foreign operations differ in terms of both the amount of resources a company commits to foreign operations and the proportion of the resources located at home rather than abroad. Licensing, for example, may result in a lower additional capital resource commitment than a foreign joint venture will.

Throughout this discussion, keep in mind that there are trade-offs. For example, a decision to take no ownership in foreign production of your product, such as by licensing it to a foreign company, may reduce exposure to political risk. However, at the same time, you slow your learning about that environment, thus delaying (perhaps permanently) your reaping the full profits from producing and selling your product abroad.

> The choice of operational form may necessitate trade-offs among objectives.

Keep in mind also that when a company has a desired, unique, difficult-to-duplicate resource, it is in a good position to choose the operating form it would most like to utilize. The preferred operating form may be exporting, selling from a wholly owned direct investment, or participating in a collaborative arrangement. When there is the possibility of competition, it may have to settle on a form that is lower on its priority list; otherwise, a competitor may preempt the market.

A further constraint is in finding a desirable partner with whom to collaborate in your preferred form. For example, if the desired collaboration involves a transfer of technology, it may be impossible to find a local company that is familiar enough with the technology so that the transfer can be achieved rapidly and inexpensively. In effect, there are costs associated with transferring technology to another entity. Usually it is cheaper to transfer within the existing corporate family, such as from parent to subsidiary, than to transfer to another company (internalization theory, discussed in Chapter 8). The cost difference is especially important when the technology is complex because a subsidiary's personnel are more likely to be familiar with approaches the parent uses. For this reason, it has been noted that the higher the level of technology, the more likely it is that a company will expand abroad with its own facilities rather than contracting with another company to produce abroad on its behalf.[10]

Some Considerations

Control   The more a company deals externally, the more likely it is to lose control over decisions that may affect its global optimization, including those regarding quality, new product directions, and where output will be expanded. External arrangements also imply the sharing of revenues, a serious consideration for undertakings with high potential profits. Such arrangements also risk allowing information to pass more rapidly to potential competitors. The loss of control over flexibility, revenues, and competition is an important variable guiding companies' priorities for forms of foreign operation.

Prior expansion of the company   When a company already has operations in place within a foreign country, some of the advantages of contracting with another company to handle production or sales are no longer as prevalent. The company knows how to operate within the foreign country and may have excess capacity that can be used for new production or sales. However, much depends on whether the existing foreign operation is in a line of business or performs a function that is closely related to the product, service, or activity being transferred abroad. When there is similarity, as with production of a new type of office equipment when the company already produces office equipment, there is the highest probability that the new production will be handled internally. In highly diversified companies or where operations are limited (such as when subsidiaries only produce components for the parent), the existing foreign facility may be handling goods or functions so

Companies have a wider choice of operating form when there is less likelihood of competition.

Internal handling of foreign operations usually means more control and no sharing of profits.

dissimilar to what is being planned that it is easier to deal with an experienced external company.

Licensing

Under a **licensing agreement,** a company (the licensor) grants rights to intangible property to another company (the licensee) for a specified period, and, in exchange, the licensee ordinarily pays a royalty to the licensor. The rights may be exclusive (monopoly within a given territory) or nonexclusive. The U.S. Internal Revenue Service classifies intangible property into five categories:

1. Patents, inventions, formulas, processes, designs, patterns
2. Copyrights for literary, musical, or artistic compositions
3. Trademarks, trade names, brand names
4. Franchises, licenses, contracts
5. Methods, programs, procedures, systems, and so forth

Usually, the licensor is obliged to furnish technical information and assistance, and the licensee is obliged to exploit the rights effectively and to pay compensation to the licensor.

Major motives Frequently, a new product or process may affect only part of a company's total output and then only for a limited time. The sales volume may not be large enough to warrant establishing overseas manufacturing and sales facilities. Further, during the period of commencing operations on its own, the company faces the risk that competitors will develop improvements that will negate its advantages. As discussed earlier in this chapter, a company that is already operating abroad may be able to produce and sell at a lower cost and with a shorter start-up time. For the licensor, the risk of operating facilities and holding inventories is reduced. The licensee may find that the cost of the arrangement is less than if the development were accomplished internally.

For industries in which technological changes are frequent and affect many different products, such as chemicals and electrical goods, companies in various countries often exchange technology rather than compete with each other on every product in every market. Such an arrangement is known as **cross-licensing.** For example, DBStar from the United States and Transtar from France entered a technology-sharing, cross-licensing agreement for computer data storage whereby DBStar will sell to the North American market and Transtar will sell to the European market.[11]

Another consideration concerns the resources a company has at its disposal, of particular concern for small companies. But large ones also may be constrained. Chrysler, for example, has insufficient resources to establish its own facilities everywhere that overseas production is necessary for Jeep sales. For some of the largest markets, such as India and Australia, Chrysler has subsidiaries. For some smaller markets, such as Sri Lanka and Pakistan, it uses licensing arrangements.

LDC controversy   Given that virtually all royalties are paid to organizations in industrial countries, it is perhaps inevitable that groups within LDCs have criticized the amounts and methods of payment. Since MNEs view their technologies and trademarks as integral parts of their asset bases, it is perhaps just as inevitable that they are skeptical about transferring the use of those technologies and trademarks to other organizations.

Payment   The amount and type of payment under licensing arrangements vary widely. Each contract tends to be negotiated on its own merits. Figure 14.3 shows the major factors that determine the payment amount. In the upper left-hand box, agreement-specific factors underlie negotiated clauses that may affect the value to the licensee. For example, the value will be greater if potential sales are high, such as with long-term exclusive worldwide rights, before the asset becomes obsolete. The upper right-hand box in the figure, environment-specific factors, lists other conditions that may affect the value. For example, the licensee might pay a low amount if its government sets upper limits on payment or if other companies are vying to sell similar technology. Because neither the licensor nor the licensee can be sure of the price the other is willing to accept, the bottom of the figure illustrates how the bargaining range is based on their expectations.

Many governments of LDCs set price controls on what licensees can pay or insist on prohibitions or restrictions.[12] One thorny issue regarding sales restrictions, from the point of view of LDCs, is that licensees usually are prevented by contract from exporting; thus small-scale production spreads fixed costs inadequately, and high prices must be charged to consumers. MNEs have countered that extending sales territories would necessitate high royalties because the companies could not sell exclusive rights to parties in other countries. MNEs also have argued that the development of process technologies for small-scale production often is too costly but is done when economically feasible.

Taxes may be assessed differently depending on how payments are arranged under a licensing agreement—for example, as income or as a capital gain—thus affecting after-tax receipts. Payment also may be deferred in order to delay tax liability. Fees for using an asset may be paid in a lump sum, based either on a percentage of sales value or on a specific rate applied to usage, or on some combination of these methods.

It is common to negotiate a "front-end" payment to cover transfer costs and then follow with another set of fees based on actual or projected usage. This is done because few technologies may be moved abroad simply by transferring publications and reports. The negotiation process is itself expensive and must be followed by engineering, consultation, and adaptation. The early stages of production usually are characterized by low quality and low productivity. The substantial costs of the trans-

**Figure 14.3
Determinants of
Compensation for
International Licensing
of Technology**

The upper left-hand box lists factors in the licensing agreement that can affect the technology's value to the licensee. The upper right-hand box gives factors external to the negotiations that can affect pricing. The bottom portion shows how the bargaining range derives from the licensor's and the licensee's estimates of profits and costs.

Source: Kang Rae Cho, "Issues of Compensation in International Technology Licensing," *Management International Review,* Vol. 28, No. 2, 1988, p. 76, as adapted from Franklin R. Root and Farok J. Contractor, "Negotiating Compensation in International Licensing Agree-ments," *Sloan Management Review,* Winter 1981, p. 25.

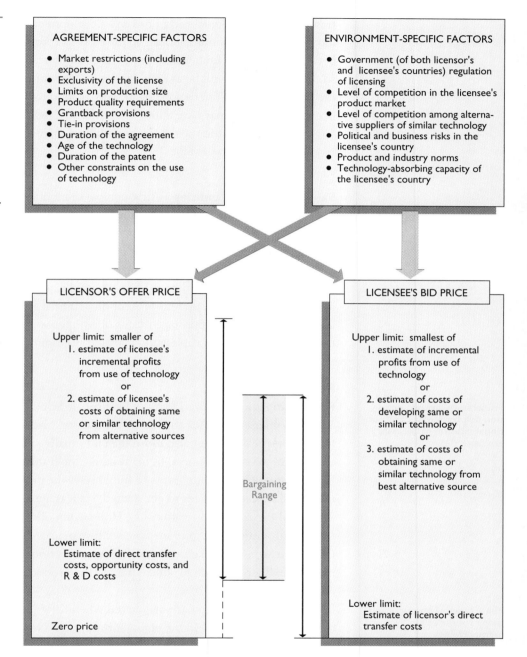

AGREEMENT-SPECIFIC FACTORS

- Market restrictions (including exports)
- Exclusivity of the license
- Limits on production size
- Product quality requirements
- Grantback provisions
- Tie-in provisions
- Duration of the agreement
- Age of the technology
- Duration of the patent
- Other constraints on the use of technology

ENVIRONMENT-SPECIFIC FACTORS

- Government (of both licensor's and licensee's countries) regulation of licensing
- Level of competition in the licensee's product market
- Level of competition among alternative suppliers of similar technology
- Political and business risks in the licensee's country
- Product and industry norms
- Technology-absorbing capacity of the licensee's country

LICENSOR'S OFFER PRICE

Upper limit: smaller of
1. estimate of licensee's incremental profits from use of technology
or
2. estimate of licensee's costs of obtaining same or similar technology from alternative sources

Lower limit:
Estimate of direct transfer costs, opportunity costs, and R & D costs

Zero price

Bargaining Range

LICENSEE'S BID PRICE

Upper limit: smallest of
1. estimate of incremental profits from use of technology
or
2. estimate of costs of developing same or similar technology
or
3. estimate of costs of obtaining same or similar technology from best alternative source

Lower limit:
Estimate of licensor's direct transfer costs

fer process increasingly are charged to the licensee so that the licensor is motivated to assure a smooth adaptation.

Technology may be old or new, obsolete or still in use at home, when it is transferred to a foreign company.[13] For example, Crown Cork and Seal held onto its three-piece manufacturing technology for cans until it developed two-piece technology; then the older technology was licensed to LDCs. Many other companies transfer technology at an early or even a developmental stage so that products are introduced almost simultaneously in different markets. For example, an alliance between AT&T and Eo licenses "personal communicator" technology to Matsushita so that the product will be available in Japan at about the same time AT&T sells it in the United States.[14] On the one hand, new technology may be worth more to a licensee because it may have a longer useful life. On the other hand, newer technology, particularly that in the development phase, may be worth less because of its more uncertain market value.

Sales to controlled entities   Although we think of licensing agreements as being collaborative arrangements among unassociated companies, many licenses are given to companies owned in whole or part by the licensor. Nearly 80 percent of licensing fees received in the United Sates are from affiliated companies.[15] A license may be needed to transfer technology abroad because operations in a foreign country, even if 100-percent owned by the parent, usually are separate companies from a legal standpoint. When there is present or potential shared ownership, a separate licensing arrangement may be a means of compensating for contributions beyond the mere investment in capital and managerial resources.

Franchising

Franchising is a specialized form of licensing in which the franchisor not only sells an independent franchisee the use of a trademark that is an essential asset for the franchisee's business, but also more than nominally assists on a continuing basis in the operation of the business. In many cases, the franchisor also provides supplies.[16] For example, Holiday Inn grants to franchisees the good will of the Holiday Inn name and support services to get started, such as appraisal of a proposed motel site. As part of the continual relationship, Holiday Inn offers reservations services and training programs to help ensure the venture's success. In a sense, a franchisor and a franchisee act almost like a vertically integrated company because the parties are interdependent and each produces part of the product or service that ultimately reaches the consumer.

Franchising is said to have originated when King John of England granted franchises to tax collectors. In the eighteenth century, German brewers franchised beer halls as distributors.[17] Today, franchising is most associated with the United States and accounts for about one third of U.S. retail sales.[18] About 75 percent of those sales are in car and truck dealerships, gasoline service stations, and soft-drink bottling. The number of foreign franchises by U.S. companies has been growing very rapidly. The most popular locations are Canada, Japan, the United Kingdom, and Australia. A 1992 survey showed that about half of U.S. franchisors without foreign units planned to grow internationally within the next five years.[19] The fastest growth areas of U.S. companies have been food and business services. Much of the impetus for foreign expansion has been the maturing of the U.S. market, thus

Franchising involves provision of a trademark and continual infusion of necessary assets.

Many types of products and many countries are involved in franchising.

allowing more growth abroad than at home. For example, McDonald's announced in 1996 that two thirds of its expansion over the next few years will be abroad.[20]

Not all franchising is by U.S. companies. Foreign-owned franchise operations are growing rapidly in the United States. Pronuptia, a French bridal wear franchisor, and food franchisors such as Wimpy's and Bake 'N' Take from the United Kingdom and Wienerwald from Germany have been among some of the earliest and most successful. There also has been a surge of foreign acquisition of franchisors based in the United States.[21] Burger King, Hardees, Holiday Inn, Howard Johnson's, Baskin-Robbins, Meineke Discount Mufflers, and Great American Cookie are U.S. franchisors that have been acquired by non-U.S. companies.

Organization A franchisor most often penetrates a foreign country by setting up a master franchise and giving that organization (usually a local one) the rights for the country or region.[22] The master franchisee then may open outlets on its own or develop subfranchisees. Royalty payments by the subfranchisees are made to the master franchisee, which then remits some predetermined percentage to the franchisor. For example, McDonald's very successful Japanese operations are handled this way.

In about 20 percent of cases, franchisors enter foreign markets by dealing directly with individual franchisees. Doing this is sometimes difficult because the franchisor may be insufficiently known to convince many local people to make investments. People are willing to make investments because the name is a guarantee of quality that can attract customers and justify joint advertising among all the franchisees using the common brand name. It therefore is common for a franchisor to enter with some company-owned outlets that serve as a showcase to attract franchisees.

Franchisors face a dilemma:
- **The more standardization, the less acceptance in the foreign country**
- **The more adjustment to the foreign country, the less the franchisor is needed**

Operational modifications Securing good locations can be a major problem.[23] Finding suppliers can be the source of added difficulties and expense. For example, McDonald's had to build a plant to make hamburger buns in the United Kingdom, and it had to help farmers develop potato production in Thailand.[24] Another concern for foreign franchise expansion has been governmental or legal restrictions that make it difficult to gain satisfactory operating permission.

Many franchise failures abroad result from the franchisor's not developing enough domestic penetration first; thus franchisors may lack sufficient cash and management depth. However, even a franchisor that is well established domestically may have difficulty in attaining foreign penetration, as evidenced by problems of Burger King in the United Kingdom, Wendy's in Australia, and Long John Silver's in Japan.[25] It is simply difficult to persuade people in a host country to invest in a venture that is not yet well known there. A dilemma for successful domestic franchisors is that their success has been largely due to three factors: product and service standardization, high identification through promotion, and effective cost controls. When entering many foreign countries, these companies may encounter various restraints that may make it difficult to conform to home-country methods. Yet the more adjustments that are made to the host-country's different conditions, the less a franchisor has to offer a potential franchisee. Franchisors' success in Japan has been due in large part to that country's enthusiastic assimilation of Western innovations; thus companies such as McDonald's have been able to copy their U.S. outlets almost exactly. Yet such food franchisors as Dunkin' Donuts and Perkits Yogurt fared poorly in the United Kingdom because it was too difficult to change certain British eating habits. However, if the companies had offered menus that were more acceptable to the British, there would have been nothing different about their product to offer a franchisee. Even in countries in which franchises have been successful, some operating adjustments usually have been necessary. For example, Kentucky Fried Chicken had to redesign its equipment and stores in Japan to save space because of higher rents. To cater to Japanese tastes, it eliminated mashed potatoes and put less sugar in its cole slaw. Pizza Hut alters its toppings by country, and in Saudi Arabia it must have two dining rooms—one for single men and one for families (single women are not allowed to go out without their families). McDonald's changed the pronunciation of its name in Japan to "MaKudonaldo" and substituted Donald for Ronald McDonald because of pronunciation difficulties among Japanese.[26]

Management Contracts

Management contracts are used primarily when the foreign company can manage better than the owners.

One of the most important assets a company may have at its disposal is management talent. The transmission of management skills internationally has depended largely on foreign investments that deploy expatriate managers and specialists to foreign countries. Management contracts are a means by which a company may use part of its management personnel to assist a foreign company for a specified period for a fee. Thus the company may gain income with little capital outlay. Contracts usually are drawn to cover three to five years, and fixed fees or fees based on volume rather than profits are most common.

Management contracts may be established when a foreign company is perceived to be able to manage an existing or new operation more efficiently than can the home-country owners. For example, the British Airport Authority (BAA) won contracts to manage the airports in Pittsburgh and Indianapolis.[27]

From the standpoint of the host country, the need to receive direct investment as a means of gaining management assistance is removed. From the standpoint of the management company, contracts help it receive income without having to make a capital outlay. A management contract may also be a means for the supplier to gain foreign experience, thus increasing its capacity to internationalize. For example, Ansett Transport Industries of Australia developed contracts to operate Air Vanuatu for the government of Vanuatu. This led to other management contracts in the South Pacific, which in turn led to Ansetts holding equity interests in Transcorp Airways (Hong Kong), Air New Zealand, Air Norway, Ladeco (Chile), and America West (United States).[28]

Turnkey Operations

Turnkey operations
• **Are most commonly performed by construction companies**
• **Are often performed for a governmental agency**

Turnkey projects involve a contract for construction of operating facilities that are transferred for a fee to the owner when they are ready to commence operations. Companies performing turnkey operations are frequently industrial-equipment manufacturers that supply some of their own equipment for the project. Most commonly, they are construction companies. They also may be consulting firms or manufacturers that decide that an investment on their own behalf in the country is infeasible.

The customer for a turnkey operation is very often a governmental agency. Many companies have chosen to perform design and construction duties, particularly where there are restrictions on foreign ownership. Recently, most large projects have been in NICs or oil-exporting countries, both of which are moving rapidly toward infrastructure development and industrialization.

One characteristic that sets this business apart from most other international business operations is the size of the contracts. Most are for hundreds of millions of dollars, and many are for billions, which means that only a few very large companies—such as Bechtel, Fluor, and Kellogg Rust—account for most of the international market. Smaller companies either are largely excluded from direct contracts, or serve as subcontractors for primary turnkey suppliers. However, even the very large companies are vulnerable because of their dependence on giant projects, which can disappear with economic downturns. For example, Fluor took heavy losses when oil prices fell and oil exporters suspended construction expansion.[29]

Contract size has prompted the companies to hire executives with top-level governmental contacts abroad. These executives can gain entry to the right decision makers to negotiate their proposals in foreign countries. The nature of these contracts also has placed importance on ceremony, such as opening a facility on a country's independence day or getting a head of state to inaugurate a facility in order to build goodwill for future contracts. For example, ABB and Companhia Brasileira de Projectos e Obras formed a joint venture to construct a turnkey dam for the government of Malaysia. They timed the signing of the $5.2 billion contract so that the Malaysian Premier could be present for the ceremony.[30] Although public relations is important, other factors—such as price, export financing, managerial and technological quality, experience, and reputation—are necessary to sell contracts of such magnitude.[31]

Payment for a turnkey operation usually is made in stages, as a project develops. Commonly, 10–25 percent comprises the down payment, with another 50–65 percent paid as the contract progresses, and the remainder paid once the facility actually is operating in accordance with the contract. Because of the long time frame between conception and completion, the company performing turnkey operations is exposed to possible currency fluctuations and so, if possible, should be covered by escalation clauses or cost-plus contracts. Because the final payment is made only if the facility is operating satisfactorily, it is important to specify very precisely what constitutes "satisfactorily." For this reason, many companies insist on performing a feasibility study as part of the turnkey contract in order not to build something that, although desired by local governmental authorities, nevertheless may be too large or inefficient. Even though a facility may be built exactly as desired, its inefficiency could create legal problems that hold up final payment.

Many turnkey contracts are for construction in remote areas, necessitating massive housing construction and importation of personnel. Projects may involve building an entire infrastructure under the most adverse conditions.

If a company holds a monopoly on certain assets or resources, such as the latest refining technology, other companies find it difficult to be competitive in building facilities. As the production process becomes known, however, the number of competitors for performing turnkey operations increases. U.S. companies have moved largely toward projects involving high technology, whereas companies from such countries as India, Korea, and Turkey can compete better for conventional projects for which low labor costs are important.[32]

Joint Ventures

A type of ownership sharing very popular among international companies is the joint venture, in which a company is owned by more than one organization. Recall from the opening case that Alfa participates in numerous joint ventures. Although a joint venture usually is formed for the achievement of a limited objective, it may continue to operate indefinitely as the objective is redefined. Joint ventures are sometimes thought of as 50/50 companies, but often more than two organizations participate in the ownership. Further, one organization frequently controls more than 50 percent of the venture. The type of legal organization may be a partnership, corporation, or some other form permitted in the country of operation. When more than two organizations participate, the resultant joint venture is sometimes called a *consortium*.

Almost every conceivable combination of partners may exist in a joint venture, including the following:

* Two companies from the same country joining together in a foreign market, such as Exxon and Mobil in Russia
* A foreign company joining with a local company, such as Sears Roebuck and Simpsons in Canada
* Companies from two or more countries establishing a joint venture in a third country, such as that of Diamond Shamrock (U.S.) and Sol Petroleo (Argentine) in Bolivia
* A private company and a local government forming a joint venture (sometimes called a mixed venture), such as that of Philips (Dutch) with the Indonesian government.

The more companies involved, the more complex the ownership arrangement will be. For example, when Australia's Hazelwood Power Station was privatized, it was

---

Joint ventures
* **Need not be 50/50 companies**
* **May involve various combinations of ownership**

bought by a British company (National Power), an Australian company (the Commonwealth Bank Group), and two U.S. companies (PacifiCorp and Destec Energy).[33] Figure 14.4 shows that as either the number of partners or the ownership sharing increases, the ease of control decreases.

Certain types of companies favor joint ventures more than others do.[34] Companies that tend to favor joint ventures include those that are new at foreign operations and those with decentralized domestic decision making, very often multi-product companies. Because these companies are accustomed to extending control downward in their organizations, it is easier for them to do the same thing internationally. There is also evidence that the incidence of entering into collaborative arrangements varies by host country. Companies are more prone to have collaborative arrangements in countries where the cultural characteristic of trust is high, apparently because host-country companies erect fewer barriers and have an open, rather than a guarded, arrangement with other companies.[35]

Equity Alliances

Equity alliances involve a cooperating companies' taking an equity position (almost always minority) in the company with which it has a collaborative arrangement. In some cases each party takes an ownership in the other. The purpose of the equity ownership is to solidify a collaborating contract so that it is more difficult to break, particularly if the ownership is large enough to secure a board membership for the

Equity alliances involve equity position to solidify collaboration.

**Figure 14.4
Control Complexity Related to Collaborative Strategy**
The more equity and the fewer partners, the more easily a company can usually control its foreign operations. Note that the non-equity arrangements may involve one or many partners.

Source: The figure was adapted from Shaker Zahra and Galal Elhagrasey, "Strategic Management of International Joint Ventures," *European Management Journal,* Vol. 12, No. 1, March 1994, pp. 83–93.

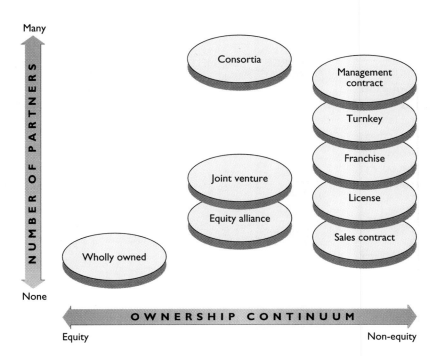

investing company. The airline industry epitomizes the use of equity alliances. This industry is discussed in depth in the ending case for this chapter.

Problems of Collaborative Arrangements

Although collaborative agreements are widespread and have many advantages, some companies avoid them when they can. Further, many have problems that lead to partners' renegotiation of new working relationships that allow agreements to continue by altering activities, ownership, or management structure.[36] In spite of new working relationships, many agreements break down or are not renewed at the end of an initial contract period. For example, in the case of joint ventures, about half break up because one or all partners is dissatisfied with the venture. In about three-quarters of break-ups, one partner buys out the other's interest so that the operation continues as a wholly owned foreign subsidiary.[37] However, Fig. 14.5 shows that joint venture divorce (and divorce from other collaborative arrangements) can follow a number of different patterns. The major strains on collaborative arrangements are due to five factors: the relative importance to the partners, differing objectives, control problems, relative contributions and appropriations, and differences in culture.[38] In spite of this emphasis on collaborative problems, we do not mean to imply that there are no success stories. There are. For example, the joint venture between Xerox (U.S.) and Rank (U.K.) has a joint venture in Japan with Fuji Photo, and both these ventures have survived and performed well.[39]

**Figure 14.5
Alternative Dissolution of Joint Ventures**
There is considerable variation in both the way that joint ventures dissolve and the outcome of the operation after the dissolution.

Source: Adapted from Manuel G. Serapio, Jr., and Wayne F. Cascio, "End Games in International Alliances," *Academy of Manage-ment Executive,* May 1996, p. 67.

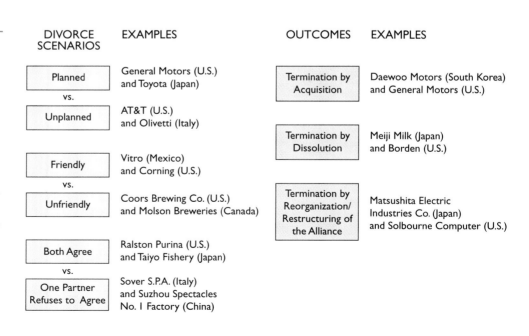

DIVORCE SCENARIOS	EXAMPLES	OUTCOMES	EXAMPLES
Planned vs. Unplanned	General Motors (U.S.) and Toyota (Japan) / AT&T (U.S.) and Olivetti (Italy)	Termination by Acquisition	Daewoo Motors (South Korea) and General Motors (U.S.)
Friendly vs. Unfriendly	Vitro (Mexico) and Corning (U.S.) / Coors Brewing Co. (U.S.) and Molson Breweries (Canada)	Termination by Dissolution	Meiji Milk (Japan) and Borden (U.S.)
Both Agree vs. One Partner Refuses to Agree	Ralston Purina (U.S.) and Taiyo Fishery (Japan) / Sover S.P.A. (Italy) and Suzhou Spectacles No. I Factory (China)	Termination by Reorganization/ Restructuring of the Alliance	Matsushita Electric Industries Co. (Japan) and Solbourne Computer (U.S.)

Relative Importance to Partners

About half of joint ventures
break down, primarily
because partners
• View the joint ventures'
  importance differently
• Have different objectives
  for the joint ventures
• Disagree on control issues
  or fail to provide sufficient
  direction
• Perceive they contribute
  more than their counterparts
• Have incompatible operating cultures

One partner may offer much closer management attention to an arrangement than the other does. If things go wrong, the active partner blames the less active partner for its lack of attention, and the less active partner blames the more active partner for making poor decisions.[40] The difference in attention may be due to the different sizes of partners. For example, if the joint venture is between a large and small company, the venture comprises a larger portion of operations for the small company than for the large one; thus the small company may take more interest in the venture. However, when companies are required to share ownership because of legal restrictions, such as in China, they may prefer partnering with companies smaller than themselves because they can more easily control the management of the operation.[41]

Differing Objectives

Although companies enter into collaborative arrangements because they presumably have complementary capabilities, their objectives may differ from the start or evolve differently over time. For instance, one partner may want to reinvest earnings for growth and the other may want to receive dividends. One may want to expand the product line and sales territory, and the other may see this as competition with its wholly owned operations. A partner may wish to sell or buy from the venture, and the other partner may disagree with the prices.

Control Problems

By sharing the assets with another company, one may lose some control on the extent or quality of the assets' use. For example, Oleg Cassini, Inc., licensed the U.S. subsidiary (Jovan) of the Beecham Group from the United Kingdom to promote and extend sales of various Cassini fragrances, cosmetics, and beauty aids worldwide. Jovan subsequently introduced Diane Von Furstenberg products instead and denied Cassini the right to license the Cassini name to other companies. Cassini sued. The case was settled when Jovan agreed to market the Cassini products; however, their sales of the products through discount stores won Cassini an award in a later suit for image injury.[42]

Some companies have well-known trademarked names that they license abroad for the production of some products that they have never produced or had expertise with. For example, the Pierre Cardin label is used by over 800 licensees in ninety-three countries to produce hundreds of different products, from clothing to sheets and clocks to deodorants. Monitoring and maintaining control of so much diversity is very difficult. Two U.S. companies, Saks Fifth Avenue and Eagle Shirtmakers, dropped sales of Pierre Cardin–labeled products because the lack of quality control on some licensees' products adversely affected the image of others.[43]

Further, in collaborative arrangements, even though control is ceded to one of the partners, both may be held responsible for irregularities. For example, in PepsiCo's KFC venture in China, the financial reporting to Chinese authorities was ceded to the Chinese partner. However, both partners were held for tax evasion as a result of underreporting income.[44] Moreover, in joint ventures and management contracts, there are gray areas as to whom employees are primarily responsible. For example, in Holiday Inn's ten-year management contract in Tibet, it was precluded from giving incentives to or disciplining its staff; consequently, there was little that could be done when waiters and waitresses took their lunch breaks all together at the same time as guests showed up for lunch.[45]

When no single company has control, the operation may lack direction. In discussing the problems of a company that was jointly owned by a U.S. organization and a Japanese one, a Sterling Drug spokesperson said, "You must decide right off the bat whether you'll control it or will put confidence in the Japanese organization."[46] This opinion is supported by studies showing that when two or more partners attempt to share in an operation's management, failure is much more likely than when one partner dominates.[47] However, studies also show that joint ventures with an even split in ownership are more likely to succeed. It is management control rather than financial control that is important; when one partner has both, the dominant company tends to overlook the other company's interests.[48]

Relative Contributions and Appropriations

One partner's capability of contributing technology, capital, or some other asset may diminish relative to its partner's capability over time. The weak link may cause a drag on the collaborative arrangement and cause dissention between the partners. Further, one partner may be suspicious that the other is taking more from the operation (particularly knowledge-based assets) than it is. In almost all collaborative arrangements, there is a danger that one's contributed assets will be used by a partner to become a competitor. (Probably the only exception would be turnkey projects to build infrastructure.) In fact, there are many examples of companies' "going-it-alone" after they have learned from and perceive no longer needing their partner. For example, Coca-Cola learned all that it needed to know from its distributorship partner, Pripps Ringes, in Norway and Sweden, and then set up its own distrbutorship operations there.[49] It is probably difficult for companies that compete head-on within their core businesses in some markets to cooperate fully for the same core business in another market. In case of joint ventures, both are apt to see substantial gains when each partner offers market expansion and technology to the other. For example, Toshiba offered Motorola access to the Japanese market, and Motorola gave Toshiba access to the U.S. market for technologies that were complementary rather than competitive.[50]

Differences in Culture

Reflecting their home-country operating environments, companies differ by nationality in how they evaluate the success of operations. For example, U.S. companies tend to evaluate performance on the basis of profit, market share, and specific financial benefits. Japanese companies tend to evaluate primarily on how an operation helps build its strategic position, particularly by improving its skills. European companies put more reliance on a balance between profitability and achievement of social objectives.[51] These differences can result in one partner's satisfaction with a collaboration concurrent with the other partner's dissatisfaction. Moreover, there are national differences in terms of the preference of nationality for a partnership company, and these preferences strongly relate to cultural compatibility. For example, British companies would least like to partner with Japanese companies, primarily because of language difficulties.[52]

In addition to national culture, differences in corporate cultures may also create problems within joint ventures. For example, one company may be accustomed to promoting managers from within the organization, whereas the other opens its searches to outsiders. One may use a participatory management style, and the other an authoritarian style. One may be entrepreneurial and the other risk-averse. For this reason many companies will develop joint ventures only after they have had long-term positive experiences with the other company through distributorship, licensing, or other contractual arrangements. Compatibility of corporate cultures also is important in cementing relationships.[53]

Collaborative Strategies in the Internationalization Process

The evolution to a different operating mode may
- **Be the result of experience**
- **Necessitate costly termination fees**
- **Create organizational tensions**

In their early stages of international development, few companies are willing to expend a large portion of their resources on foreign operations; they may not even have sufficient resources for rapid expansion abroad. Consequently, they usually move through stages of increased levels of international involvement. In the early stages, they attempt to conserve their own scarce resources and to maximize the proportion of the resources that are at home rather than abroad. This leads them to operational forms that transfer the burden of foreign commitment to outsiders. For example, Alfa's need to use resources domestically and its lack of foreign experience influenced its decision to contract with foreign engineering companies in order to transfer steel-making processes abroad. As companies and their foreign activities grow, they tend to view the foreign portions of their businesses differently. They move toward handling more operations internally and locating a larger proportion of resources abroad.[54] However, the cost of switching from one form to another—for example, from licensing to wholly owned facilities—may be very high because of having to gain expertise from and possibly pay termination fees to another company.[55]

Collaboration with a local company provides the opportunity to learn from the local partner, thus enabling the company to confidently make a deeper commitment. At the same time, the learning in one market may enable a company to enter another market at a higher level of commitment. However, the ability to carry over learning from one market to another is enhanced by cultural similarity among markets.[56]

Exporting usually precedes foreign production, and contracting with another company to handle foreign business generally precedes handling it internally. A company may be at different stages for different products and for different markets. It also may feel that differences in countries' characteristics necessitate diverse forms of involvement. Because of the multiproduct nature of most companies, varied products sold in the same country also may necessitate different stages. Further, more than one form may exist within the same operating unit. For example, a company may license technology and export to its joint venture.

Tension may develop internally as a company's international operations change and grow. For example, moving from exporting to foreign production may reduce the size of a domestic product division. Various profit centers all may perceive they have rights to the sales in a country the company is about to penetrate. Legal, technical, and marketing personnel may have entirely different perspectives on contracts. Under these circumstances, a team approach to evaluating decisions and performance may work. A company also must develop means of evaluating performance by separating those things that are controllable and noncontrollable by personnel in different profit centers.

In the internationalization process, companies usually move first to countries similar to their home country and later to dissimilar countries. Similarity between home and host countries is a two-edged sword. On the one hand, management is more confident of its ability to operate in those foreign countries whose environments it perceives to be similar to that of its home country. U.S. companies, for example, are much more likely to handle operations internally in other English-speaking countries than in non-English-speaking ones. Thus, although a firm may commence operations in both similar and dissimilar countries through contracts with other firms, it is more apt to take on a later ownership in the more similar countries. On the other hand, language and cultural differences impede communications and increase coordination costs among companies, especially if technology is being transferred. In these situations, some level of FDI may be needed so that personnel are more likely to move to the foreign locale to facilitate cross-national information flows.[57]

When collaborating with another company, a company must
- **Continue to monitor performance**
- **Assess whether to take over operations itself**
- **Work out conflicts and disputes**

Managing Foreign Arrangements

Assessment of Fit with Strategy

Any collaborative arrangement involves the combining of assets from two or more companies. We have already discussed the motivations for collaboration. If collabo-

Collaborative arrangements may allow companies to skirt the intent of government regulations; thus deciding whether to take advantage of legal loopholes involves ethical considerations. Further, one partner in a collaborative arrangement may be able to extract benefits in excess of those specified in the agreement; therefore ethical dilemmas also arise concerning partnership relations.

One legal loophole involves payments to government officials. For example, a U.S. company may not be able to sell its own output in a foreign country without paying bribes that would be illegal under the FCPA. By licensing production to a producer in that country, the U.S. company may no longer be legally culpable because the necessary bribes are paid by the local company abroad; however, the U.S. company may be ethically implicated because of knowingly fostering the bribes.

ETHICAL DILEMMAS & SOCIAL RESPONSIBILITY

There are various means by which companies sometimes are able to control a foreign operation with a minority interest. If the limit on ownership is governmentally imposed to assure domestic control, is it ethical to use these loopholes? For example, British Airways and USAir agreed to the former's purchase of a minority interest in the latter and to British Airways' having veto power over board decisions. American Airlines successfully fought the veto provision on the grounds that it violated the intent of the U.S. law requiring U.S. airlines to be domestically controlled.

Much global licensing is to entities controlled by MNEs. The price charged for licensing rights is very controversial. By varying the price, MNEs effectively may transfer more of their profits from one country to another. Home-country critics have contended that too little is charged, and thus profits are transferred to countries having low tax rates. Many of the countries having low tax rates are LDCs. They have contended the opposite, arguing that MNEs have artificially minimized their profits in LDCs in order to either move funds to countries with stronger currencies or gain certain concessions from host governments. Obviously, MNEs cannot be shifting profits simultaneously to the home and the host country; however, is it ethical for them to try to avoid exchange controls or to minimize taxes through the loophole of licensing to themselves?

All partners put resources into collaborative arrangements; however, the proportion of resources contributed and ability to extract benefits may vary among partners. This brings up the question of whether any partner should take resources from the operation that are not specified in the agreement. For example, one partner in a joint venture may transfer a scientist to the operation who, in addition to working on the venture's R&D, learns about breakthroughs that would be useful to that partner. Would it be ethical to pass this information along? Or a highly qualified manager may be hired by a joint venture. After the manager gains experience, would it be ethical for one of the partners in the venture to hire him or her away? Would the ethical issues be any different if one partner felt it was contributing more than the other relative to its income from the venture?

ration can better achieve the company's strategic objective than "going-it-alone," then the company should give little consideration to taking on duties itself. However, situations change, thus decisions need to be reassessed. For example, a company's resource base may change relative to that of other companies, making collaboration either more or less advantageous. Further, the external environment changes, such as the riskiness of or the types of operations permitted in certain locales. Because of these changes, a company needs to continually reexamine the fit between collaboration and its strategy.

Finding Compatible Partners

A company can seek out a partner for its foreign operations or it can react to a proposal from another company to collaborate with it. In either case, it is necessary to evaluate the potential partner not only in terms of the complementary or synergistic resources it can supply, but also in terms of its motivation and willingness to work with the other company. A company can identify more potential partners by monitoring journals and technical conferences. It can increase its own visibility by participating in trade fairs, distributing brochures, and nurturing contacts in the locale of potential collaboration—thus increasing the probability of being considered a partner by other companies. The proven ability to handle similar types of collaboration is a key professional qualification. For example, Alfa's track record has made it a candidate for collaboration by additional companies entering the Mexican market. Another important factor is the importance a company places on its reputation.

Negotiating Process

In technology agreements,
• Seller does not want to give information without assurance of payment
• Buyer does not want to pay without evaluating information

In addition to the points discussed in Chapter 12 about cross-national negotiations, there are some considerations unique to collaborative arrangements involving technology transfer. The value of many technologies would diminish if they were widely known or understood. Agreements historically have included provisions that the recipient will not divulge this information. In addition, some sellers have held onto the ownership and production of specific components so that recipients will not have the full knowledge of the product or the capability to produce an exact copy of it. Secrecy is an issue when companies are negotiating agreements to transfer process technology. Many times, a company wants to sell techniques it has not yet used commercially. A buyer is reluctant to buy what it has not seen, but a seller that shows the process to the potential buyer risks having the process used without payment. It has become common to set up preagreements in order to protect all parties.

Another controversial area is the degree of secrecy surrounding the financial terms of agreements. In some countries, for example, governmental agencies must approve royalty contracts. Sometimes these authorities consult with their counterparts in other countries regarding similar agreements in order to improve their negotiating position with MNEs. Many MNEs object to this procedure because they believe that contract terms are proprietary information with competitive importance and that market conditions usually dictate the need for very different terms in different countries.

Contractual Provisions

Transferring rights to an asset can create control problems, such as
• **Inadequate working of the license**
• **Poor quality of the product**

By transferring rights to another company, a company undoubtedly loses some control over the asset. A host of potential problems attend this lack of control and should be settled in the original agreement. Provision should be made for the following:

• Terminating the agreement if the parties do not adhere to the directives
• Methods of testing for quality
• Each party's obligations concerning expenditures on sales development
• Geographical limitations on the asset's use
• Which company will manage which parts of the operation related to the agreement

Contracts must be spelled out in detail, but if courts must rule on disagreements, both parties are apt to lose something in the settlement. A good example occurred with McDonald's in France. The company granted a franchise for up to 166 French stores to Raymond Dayan at less than its normal fee because of doubts the French would ever take to fast-food restaurants. Dayan, with the help of McDonald's, found very good Paris locations for fourteen stores, which he opened over a period of several years and operated successfully. However, under the franchise agreement McDonald's had the right to revoke the agreement if the company found the stores fell short of its cleanliness standards. McDonald's cancelled the agreement on these grounds. A court case resulted, and Dayan claimed that McDonald's action was simply a ruse to make him pay McDonald's usual licensing fee. He lost out on further expansion with the McDonald's trademark; but McDonald's lost something, too. When Dayan took down the McDonald's signs, he immediately replaced them with signs saying O'Keefe's Hamburgers—and he had the clientele, the know-how, and the best locations in Paris. These stores were later sold to the French firm Quick, the largest fast-food chain in France, that now operates them under the Quick logo.[58]

Many other possible conflicts can develop between companies. Contract termination and formal settlement of disputes are costly and cumbersome. If possible, it is much better for parties to settle disagreements on a personal basis. The ability to develop a rapport with the management of another company is thus an important consideration in choosing a representative.

Performance Assessment

Management also should estimate potential sales, determine whether quality standards are being met, and assess servicing requirements in order to check whether the other company is doing an adequate job. Mutual goals should be set so that both parties understand what is expected, and the expectations should be spelled out in the contract.

In addition to the continual assessment of the partner's performance in collaborative agreements, a company also needs periodically to assess whether the type of collaboration should change. For example, a joint venture may replace a licensing agreement. Further, even though a partner is doing what is expected, a company may assess that collaboration is no longer in its best interest. For example, the company may decide that it wants a wholly owned FDI so that it has greater freedom to enact measures that, although not in the best interest of the particular operation, are in the best interest of the company as a whole.

C O U N T E R V A I L I N G
F O R C E S

Over forty years ago, John Kenneth Galbraith wrote that the era of cheap invention was over and "because development is costly, it follows that it can be carried out only by a firm that has the resources associated with considerable size."[59] The statement seems prophetic in terms of the estimated billions of investment dollars needed to bring intercontinental satellite-telephone systems or a new commercial aircraft to market. Such sums are generally out of reach for companies acting alone; but governments continue to limit company size through antitrust constraints and restrictions on foreign takeovers in key sectors. Further, markets must be truly global if high development costs are to be recouped; but governments continue to generate standards, such as for high-density television, that will fragment markets globally. Thus there is a technological push toward larger investment in product and market that is countered by political constraints. One alternative is to use governmental funds to support large developmental projects; however, such support—especially for competitive prestige—seems to be waning internationally. The only other alternative is to develop strategic alliances among entities in different countries in order to get the needed investment while satisfying multiple governments. Such alliances are already developing, for example, that involving Motorola and Lockheed from the United States with British Aerospace, Deutsche Aerospace, and France's Matra Marconi for a satellite-telephone system. Government research agencies also are allying, such as those of Russia and South Africa for mining technology and those of various governments for space technology.[60]

Although some product developments require huge sums, most are much more modest. Nevertheless, companies lack all the product- and market-specific resources to go it alone everywhere in the world, especially if national differences dictate operating changes on a country-to-country basis. These situations present opportunities for alliances that employ complementary resources from different companies.

LOOKING TO THE FUTURE

As more businesses are becoming international, competition is becoming more global and more interrelated. Thus what happens competitively in one country is more likely to affect competitive viability in other countries. To expand more rapidly to meet this challenge, companies are turning increasingly to alliances with other companies. At one extreme are international mergers and acquisitions. At the other extreme are completely independent operations. The collaborative arrangements discussed in this chapter might be considered halfway houses to full merger and acquisition. These alliances may become larger and more complex. For example, we already see the development of consortia involving automobile manufacturers and their suppliers, such as the VW plant in Argentina, in which suppliers have contributed 35 percent of the fixed costs and will make parts on site and fit them directly on vehicles.[61] One prediction is that **relationship enterprises,** that is, networks of strategic alliances among big companies, spanning different industries and countries, will develop and be held together by common goals that make them act almost like a single company. Their sales may approach a trillion dollars, larger than the GDPs of all but about a half dozen countries. For example, Boeing, British Airways, TNT (an Australian parcel-delivery company), Siemens, and SNECMA (a French aero-engine manufacturer) might team up to build airports and sell their aircraft, technology, and services.[62]

Regardless of how they evolve, alliances will bring both opportunities and potential problems as companies move simultaneously to new countries and to contractual arrangements with new companies. For example, alliances must overcome differences in a number of areas:

- Societal cultures that may cause partners to perceive and interpret situations differently
- National contexts that lead to assumptions based on familiar governmental policies, institutions, and industry structures
- Corporate cultures that influence ideologies and values underlying company practices
- Strategic directions that result from partners' interests
- Management styles and organizational structures that cause partners to interface ineffectively [63]

Further, the additional operating alternatives may strain the decision-making and control processes.

WEB CONNECTION

Check out our home page for links to the World Wide Web on issues involved in selecting alternative strategies.

Summary

- Some potential advantages of collaborative arrangements, whether a company is operating domestically or internationally, are to spread and reduce costs, allow a company to specialize on its primary competencies, avoid certain competition, secure vertical and horizontal linkages, and learn from other companies.

- Some motivations for collaborative arrangements that are specific to international operations are to gain location-specific assets, overcome legal constraints, diversify among countries, and minimize exposure in risky environments.

- The forms of foreign operations differ in terms of the amount of resources a company commits and in terms of the proportion of resources committed at home rather than abroad.

- Although the form employed for foreign operations should be examined in terms of a company's strategic objectives, the choice often will involve a trade-off among objectives.

- Licensing is granting another company the use of some rights, such as patents, copyrights, or trademarks, usually for a fee. It is a means of establishing foreign production that may minimize capital outlays, prevent the free use of assets by other companies, allow the receipt of assets from other companies in return, and allow for income in some markets in which exportation or investment is not feasible.

- Franchising differs from licensing in that a trademark is an essential asset for the franchisee's business and the franchisor assists in the operation of the business on a continuing basis.

- Management contracts are a means of securing income by managing a foreign operation while providing little capital outlay. This sometimes helps the supplier to gain foreign experience, thus increasing its capacity to internationalize.

- Turnkey projects involve a contract for construction of operating facilities owned and run by someone else. Recently, these projects have been large and diverse, necessitating specialized skills and abilities to deal with top-level governmental authorities.

- Equity alliances involve a cooperative company's taking an equity position in the company with which it has a collaborative arrangement in order to solidify the collaborating contract.

- Joint ventures are a special type of ownership sharing in which equity is owned by two or more organizations. There are various combinations of owners, including local governments and private companies and two or more companies from the same or different countries.

- A common motive for jointly owned operations is to take advantage of complementary resources that companies have at their disposal.

- Problems occur in the survival of collaborative arrangements because partners place different levels of importance on and have different objectives for the venture, find a shared ownership arrangement difficult to control, worry that their partner is putting in too little or taking out too much from the operation, and misunderstand each other because of their different country or company cultures.

- Contracting for the outside management of a company's foreign business does not negate management's responsibility to ensure company resources are being worked adequately. Doing this involves constantly assessing the other company's work and evaluating new alternatives.

- Companies may use different forms for their foreign operations in different countries or for different products. As diversity increases, the task of coordinating and managing the foreign operations becomes more complex.

Case
International Airline
Alliances[64]

In 1996 Lufthansa, the world's fifth largest airline, and SAS, the world's twelfth largest, commenced a joint venture through which the two companies combine routes and sales and airport terminal services, making it the biggest air transport system in Europe. (Map 14.2 shows the home bases of the world's twenty-five largest airlines.) This alliance came shortly after Air Canada acquired 24 percent of the voting stock in Continental, and British Airways obtained 19.9 percent of the voting stock in USAir. Earlier, KLM had secured a substantial but minority equity interest in Northwest. There have been many other partial acquisitions among airlines in different countries. For example, Delta and Swissair own a stake in each other, as do Singapore Airlines and Swissair. Swissair also has an interest in Austrian Airlines and acquired a 49-percent ownership of Sabena in 1995. American Airlines has an interest in Air New Zealand, SAS in British Midland, Air France in CSA (Czech Republic), KLM in Air U.K., British Airways in Air Russia, and Iberia in VIASA (Venezuela). In addition to new ownership stakes among airlines, other recent alliances have blurred the competitive distinctions among the major international carriers.

Although airline alliances have increased recently, such alliances have been important almost from the start of international air travel. Airlines have been motivated by a

600

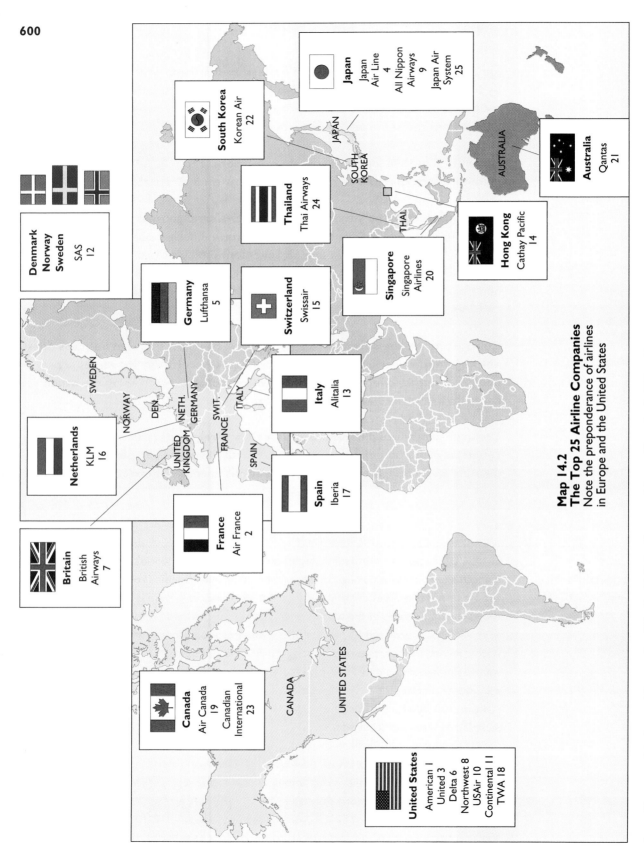

Map 14.2
The Top 25 Airline Companies
Note the preponderance of airlines
in Europe and the United States

Denmark
Norway
Sweden
SAS
12

Britain
British
Airways
7

Netherlands
KLM
16

France
Air France
2

Spain
Iberia
17

Germany
Lufthansa
5

Switzerland
Swissair
15

Italy
Alitalia
13

South Korea
Korean Air
22

Thailand
Thai Airways
24

Singapore
Singapore
Airlines
20

Japan
Japan
Air Line
4
All Nippon
Airways
9
Japan Air
System
25

Hong Kong
Cathay Pacific
14

Australia
Qantas
21

Canada
Air Canada
19
Canadian
International
23

United States
American 1
United 3
Delta 6
Northwest 8
USAir 10
Continental 11
TWA 18

Source: The names of the largest airlines are from "The Top 50 Airline Companies," *Fortune,* November 2, 1992, p. 92.

combination of regulatory, cost, and competitive factors, but their alliances have changed over time in response to evolving conditions, such as changes in the type of regulations facing airlines.

Regulatory Factors

Countries have always seen airlines as key industries; thus they have wanted domestic service that is nationally controlled. For example, the United States grants U.S.-based airlines the right to carry all passengers between domestic points, and it limits foreign ownership in U.S.-based airlines to 25 percent of voting stock and 49 percent of total equity. Many countries have ensured national control through whole or partial government ownership of airlines; examples are Iberia, KLM, Lufthansa, and Thai Airways. Many government-owned airlines are monopolies, and many lose money that is made up through governmental subsidies. Governments further protect their airlines by regulating numerous operational aspects:

- Which foreign carriers have landing rights
- Which airports and aircraft those carriers can use
- Frequency of flights
- Whether foreign carriers can fly beyond the country (For instance, the Japanese government restricted United from flying from the United States beyond Japan to Australia.)
- Overflight privileges
- Fares that may be charged

The restrictions and rights generally are agreed upon through treaties, usually to give more or less reciprocal treatment to each country's carriers but sometimes to protect the system of national ownership. For example, the International Air Transport Association (IATA) comprises nearly all the world's airlines. Given the extent of governmental ownership of airlines, governments effectively comprise the membership. Today, IATA is mainly concerned with global safety standards; however, at times it has restricted competition on routes by requiring uniform fares, meal service, and baggage allowances.

Five factors influence governments' protection of their airlines:

1. Countries believe they can save money by maintaining smaller air forces and relying on domestic airlines in times of unusual air transport needs. For example, the U.S. government used U.S. commercial carriers to help carry troops to Somalia in 1992.
2. In aviation's early days, airlines were heavily subsidized to carry mail, and governments wanted to support their own fledgling companies rather than foreign ones. This consideration has shifted somewhat because mail subsidies no longer are very important internationally. For example, they now account for less than 0.5 percent of revenues for U.S. airlines.

3. Public opinion favors spending "at home," especially for government-paid travel. Thus the maintenance of national airlines and the requirement that government-paid international travel be on those airlines are viewed as foreign-exchange savings.

4. Airlines are a source of national pride, and aircraft with the national flag symbolize a country's sovereignty and technical competence. This national identification has been especially important for LDCs, whose airlines once were largely foreign-owned. For example, the former PanAm controlled airlines in Brazil, Colombia, Mexico, Panama, and Venezuela. As soon as countries were technically and financially capable, they fostered the development of national airlines and prohibited foreign ownership.

5. Countries have worried about protecting their airspace for security reasons. This is less of a concern today because foreign carriers routinely overfly domestic territories in order to reach inland gateways. For example, many foreign carriers land international flights at Atlanta, Chicago, and Dallas. Further, overflight treaties are quite common, even among unfriendly nations. For example, Cubana overflies the United States en route to Canada, and American Airlines overflies Cuba en route to South America.

National attitudes and regulations not only give rise to separate national airlines, but they also limit airlines' expansion internationally. With few exceptions, airlines cannot fly on lucrative domestic routes in foreign countries. For example, Lufthansa cannot compete on the New York–Los Angeles route. They also cannot easily control a flight network abroad that will feed passengers into their international flights. For example, Air France has no flights to feed passengers into Chicago for connections to Paris, but American has scores of such flights; however, the situation is reversed in Paris, where Air France has a monopoly on air travel within France. Further, airlines usually cannot service pairs of foreign countries. For example, United cannot fly between Brazil and Portugal because it is a U.S. carrier. In order to tap into any of these opportunities, airlines must ally themselves via networks with carriers from other countries.

The recent increase in alliances has been due largely to the 1978 deregulation of U.S. domestic flights, allowing U.S. carriers to fly where they want and charge what they want domestically, as well as to ongoing deregulation within the EU, which allows carriers from any EU country to fly between any EU cities. For example, British Air now carries traffic between Paris and Rome, which it could not do before the deregulation began. Deregulation in the United States resulted in a shrinking number of U.S. airlines, along with business concentration—domestic and international—among a few of the survivors. Some airline analysts expect the same pattern to emerge in Europe and a few mega-carriers eventually to control most of the world's air traffic. However, this outcome is far from certain. For example, both the French and Spanish governments have recently given their national airlines substantial subsidies to make them more competitive, thus they may not be willing to become the victims of a competitive shake-out. Further, the deregulation in Europe may bring about fewer European carriers; however, the flights between Europe and the rest of the world—such as to the United States or Asia—will still remain regulated. But at any rate airlines have sought cooperative agreements to complement their route structures and other capabilities. By buying an interest in a foreign airline, even if it is a minority one because of regulations, an airline gains more assurance of a lasting relationship than it might through mere contracts.

Privatization also has been an impetus to forming alliances. For example, privatized airlines, such as British Airways and Air Canada, can no longer look to their governments for support; instead, they must find new means to be competitive internationally. Similarly, privatization in Eastern Europe and Latin America has enabled foreign carriers to take stakes in countries' airlines in those regions.

Cost Factors

Airlines have always contracted activities in locations where one company has amassed a critical mass of fixed capabilities. Costs may be spread by sharing these capabilities with other airlines. For example, KLM has long handled passenger check-in, baggage loading, and maintenance for a number of other airlines in Amsterdam. Other contracts commonly cover the use of airport gates, ground equipment such as generators, and commissary services. Airlines also sometimes sublease aircraft to each other.

When traffic on a route is low, airlines sometimes make market agreements to fly on alternate days. Or they may agree to share service in the same aircraft, which then has a dual flight designation. PanAm and Aeroflot used to do this between New York and Moscow. Air New Zealand and American do so between Honolulu and Auckland, as do Canadian International and SAS between Copenhagen and Toronto.

The high cost of maintenance and reservations systems has led to recent joint ventures. For example, Swissair, Lufthansa, and Guiness Peat Aviation are partners in a maintenance center in Ireland. United, British Airways, USAir, Swissair, Alitalia, and Air Canada share ownership in Covia, which operates and delivers the Apollo reservation system. Another reservation system, Galileo, is owned by United, British Air, Alitalia, Swissair, KLM, Olympic, Austrian Airlines, AerLingus, Sabena, and Air Portugal.

Competitive Factors

A number of airlines have established marketing agreements in order to complement their route structures. For example, USAir and Air France have blocked space on certain flights, set schedules so that flights have good connections between them, automated seat selection on the connections, and advertised the through-service. These two airlines also are partners in USAir's frequent traveler program, along with six of Air France's European competitors. Continental and SAS have gone a step further through Continental's handling of all operations in its Newark facilities. About one-third of SAS traffic from Newark to Scandinavia comes from the Continental connections. SAS also has contracted to help Continental improve its in-flight service. The joint use of facilities within alliances may be the wave of the future because it is nearly impossible to add gates at the largest airports and existing airlines own all the gates.

A problem with these marketing agreements is that the connections from one airline to another show up as separate route codes in reservations systems. These come up last on the screens of travel agents, and the agents tend to recommend the first schedules they see. Further, when passengers see that they must change airlines, they worry that they may have to make connections across great distances within ever larger airline terminals. This puts connections between two different airlines at a disadvantage relative to connections on the same airline. When KLM bought an interest in Northwest, the two airlines were able to secure the same route codes on their connecting flights. Northwest's ticket counters show KLM's logo as well. The alliance gives Northwest service to eighty European cities, whereas American serves only twelve. They have come as close as possible to a merger without actually making one. British Airways and USAir also share route codes. American Airlines and United at first vowed to fight that; however, United later was successful in making a shared route code agreement with Lufthansa.

In 1996 British Air shocked USAir by announcing its proposed alliance, negotiated secretly, with American Airlines. Even though British Air owns a minority stake in USAir, USAir at this writing is suing to block the alliance between British Air and American Airlines. It is also planning to reinstate its flights to London, which it discontinued after establishing the alliance with British Air in 1993.

Management of Alliances

An impending problem in the proliferation of alliances is the vast network of relationships. The relationships are so intertwined among so many airlines that it is difficult to determine what companies are competing, cooperating, or colluding. Management may find it increasingly hard to be cooperative, say, in joint maintenance agreements while trying to compete head-on on some routes.

Preventing full mergers may be a blessing in some ways because corporate and national cultures may be difficult to mesh. There also are structural differences. For example, pilots at Air Canada are unionized, but those at Continental are not. Analysts conclude that the problems of combining unions after PanAm's acquisition of National was a major contribution to PanAm's eventual demise. However, the lack of control is also a problem. Analysts worry that British Airways, with only a minority of voting stock in USAir, will be unable to make needed changes in that airline.

Other things simply may not mesh well in alliances. The USAir–British Airways agreement is considered synergistic because USAir is strong in the eastern United States, where most transatlantic traffic originates, and British Airways is strong in connections from London to Europe and Asia. But USAir's strength in New York is at LaGuardia Airport, which is purely domestic; therefore most connecting passengers must change airports. When Northwest and KLM allied, it was expected that KLM would help Northwest improve its service; however, the organizations could not work well in that effort.

Questions

1. Discuss a question raised by the manager of route strategy of American Airlines: Why should an airline not be able to establish service anywhere in the world simply by demonstrating that it can and will comply with the local labor and business laws of the host country?

2. The president of Japan Air Lines has claimed that U.S. airlines are dumping air services on routes between the United States and Europe because of the money they are losing. Should prices be set so that carriers make money on routes?

3. What will be the consequences if a few large airlines or networks come to dominate global air service?

4. Some airlines, such as Southwest and Alaska Air, have survived as niche players without going international or developing alliances with international airlines. Can they continue this strategy?

Chapter Notes

1. Data for the case were taken from James Flanigan, "The Strategy," *Forbes,* October 29, 1979, pp. 42–52; "Dravo Agrees to Market Type of Plant for Grupo," *Wall Street Journal,* September 23, 1980, p. 38; Hugh O'Shaughnessy, "A Hive of Private Enterprise," *Financial Times,* May 4, 1979, p. 34; Christopher Lorenz, "A Front-Runner in Mexican Industry," *Financial Times,* June 1, 1979, p. 16; "Mexico: Exporting a Cheaper Way of Making Steel," *Business Week,* June 11, 1979, p. 53; Alan M. Field, "After the Fall," *Fortune,* Vol. 135, No. 8, April 22, 1985, pp. 93–95; Keith Bradsher, "Back from the Brink, Mexico's Giant Alfa Slims Down for Hard Times," *International Management,* Vol. 41, No. 9, September 1986, pp. 65–66; Matt Moffett, "Monterrey Sides with Mexican President," *Wall Street Journal,* May 22, 1989, p. A8; Stephen Baker, "Mexico's Giants March North," *Business Week,* November 13, 1989, pp. 63–64; "Los Grandes Grupos Económicos de la Region," *America Economica,* December 1991, p. 8; Al Wrigley, "Automakers Pick Mexico Aluminum," *American Metal Market,* August 19, 1992, p. 1; "Bekaert," *Rubber World,* November 1992, p. 8; Daniel Dombey, "Increased Overseas Sales Fuel Advances at Alfa and Desc," *Financial Times,* August 1, 1995, p. 15; Paul B. Carrol, "Garza Sadas Build an Unrivaled Latin Empire," *Wall Street Journal,* December 11, 1995, p. A9; "Energy/Mining: Joint U.S.-Mexico Power Plant Opened," *Mexico Business Monthly,* Vol. 6, No. 7, August 1996; Leslie Crawford and Daniel Dombey, "Merger Plan Hits Mexico Telecoms Monopoly," *Financial Times,* April 24, 1996, p. 1+; "Grupo Alfa, BASF Mexico to Expand Petrochemical Plants," *Mexico Trade and Law Reporter,* Vol. 5, No. 9, September 1, 1995; "Alfa Profits Helped by Record Exports," *Financial Times,* January 29, 1996; Leslie Crawford and Daniel Dombey, "Mexico Gives Way to Nation-alistic Pressure: A Change of Foreign Ownership Rules Threatens the Country's Privatisation Process," *Financial Times,* April 2, 1996, p. 27; and "Top 100 Latin American Companies by Market Capitalisation," *Financial Times,* January 24, 1997.

2. Michael Selz, "Networks Help Small Companies Think and Act Big," *Wall Street Journal,* November 12, 1992, p. B2; and Joel Bleeke and David Ernst, "Sleeping with the Enemy," *Harvard International Review,* Summer 1993, pp. 12–14+.

3. Jeff Cole, "New Boeing 747s Could Cost $7 Billion to Develop," *Wall Street Journal,* November 11, 1996, p. A3.

4. Gregory A. Patterson, "Chrysler Signs Licensing Pact for Jeep Name," *Wall Street Journal,* August 30, 1988, p. 24.

5. Richard N. Osborn and C. Christopher Baughn, "Forms of Interorganizational Governance for Multinational Alliances," *Academy of Management Journal,* September 1990, pp. 503–519.

6. Crawford and Dombey, loc. cit.

7. Jeff Cole, "Europeans Gain on Boeing for a Partnership in Asia," *Wall Street Journal,* May 8, 1995, p. 2.

8. Paul Ingrassia, "Ford Nears Pact to Make Cars in Europe for Mazda in a Buy-Sell Arrangement," *Wall Street Journal,* October 28, 1991, p. A3.

9. "Merck and Chugai Form OTC Venture," *Financial Times,* September 19, 1996, p. 17.

10. Leo Sleuwaegen, "Monopolistic Advantages and the International Operations of Firms: Disaggregated Evidence from U.S. Based Multinationals," *Journal of International Business Studies,* Vol. 16, No. 3, Fall 1985, pp. 125–133; and W. H. Davidson and D. G. McFetridge, "Key Characteristics in the Choice of International Technology Transfer Mode," *Journal of International Business Studies,* Vol. 16, No. 2, Summer 1985, pp. 5–21, found evidence for this point as well as those that follow in this discussion.

11. "DBStar and Transtar Sign U.S.-European Cross-licensing Agreement," *Business Wire,* August 26, 1996.

12. Kang Rae Cho, "Issues of Compensation in International Technology Licensing," *Management International Review,* Vol. 28, No. 2, 1988, pp. 70–79; and Robert T. Keller and Ravi R. Chinta, "International Technology Transfer: Strategies for Success," *Academy of Management Executive,* Vol. 4, No. 2, 1990, pp. 33–43.

13. Ibid.

14. Louise Kehoe, "AT&T Alliances Open New Market," *Financial Times,* November 17, 1992, p. 19+.

15. John A. Sondheimer and Sylvia E. Bargas, "U.S. International Sales and Purchases of Private Services," *Survey of Current Business,* September 1994, p. 114.

16. Jerry H. Opack, "Likenesses of Licensing, Franchising," *Les Nouvelles,* June 1977, pp. 102–105.

17. John F. Preble, "Global Expansion: The Case of U.S. Fast-Food Franchisors," *Journal of Global Marketing,* Vol. 6, Nos. 1/2, 1992, p. 186, citing D. Ayling, "Franchising in the U.K.," *The Quarterly Review of Marketing,* Summer 1988, pp. 19–24; and "Franchising: A Tool for Growth in the 1980s," *Forbes,* June 7, 1982, pp. 63–72.

18. James W. Wolfe, "Is There An Overseas Franchise in Your Future?" *Export Today,* June 1992, pp. 51–52.

19. A. Kostecka, *Franchising in the Economy 1986–1988* (Washington, D.C.: U.S. Department of Commerce, February 1988), pp. 8–10; and Arthur Andersen & Co., "Franchising in the Economy: 1989–1992," n.d., p. 109.

20. Richard Gibson, "McDonald's Accelerates Store Openings In U.S. and Abroad, Pressuring Rivals," *Wall Street Journal,* January 18, 1996, p. A3.

21. Mike Connelly, "U.S. Franchising Grows Attractive to Foreign Firms," *Wall Street Journal,* December 22, 1988, p. B2; and Jeffrey A. Tannenbaum, "Foreign Franchis-

ers in U.S. on the Rise," *Wall Street Journal,* June 11, 1990, p. B2.

22. Peng S. Chan and Robert T. Justis, "Franchise Management in East Asia," *Academy of Management Executive,* Vol. 4, No. 2, 1990, pp. 75–85.

23. Joann Lublin, "U.S. Franchisers Learn Britain Isn't Easy," *Wall Street Journal,* August 16, 1988, p. 20.

24. Kathleen Deveny, John Pluenneke, Dori Jones Yang, Mark Maremont, and Robert Black, "McWorld," *Business Week,* October 13, 1986, pp. 78–86.

25. Lawrence S. Welch, "Developments in International Franchising," *Journal of Global Marketing,* Vol. 6, Nos. 1/2, 1992, p. 81–96.

26. Chan and Justis, loc. cit. For other changes by McDonald's in Europe, see Heather Ogilvie, "Welcome to McEurope: An Interview with Tom Allin, President of McDonald's Development Co.," *Journal of European Business,* Vol. 2, No. 67, July–August 1991, pp. 5–12+.

27. Michael Skapinker, "BAA Set to Operate U.S. Airport," *Financial Times,* August 1, 1995, p. 13.

28. Lawrence S. Welch and Anubis Pacifico, "Management Contracts: A Role in Internationalisation?" *International Marketing Review,* Vol. 7, No. 4, 1990, pp. 64–74.

29. David J. Jefferson, "Biggest Builder, Fluor, Sees Kuwaiti Contracts As a Mixed Blessing," *Wall Street Journal,* April 18, 1991, p. A1+.

30. "Signing of ABB Deal for Malaysia's Bakun Dam on September 30," *Agence France Presse,* September 21, 1996; and "Malaysia Signs Dam Contract," *Financial Times,* October 3, 1996, p. 7.

31. *A Competitive Assessment of the U.S. International Construction Industry* (Washington, D.C.: U.S. Department of Commerce, International Trade Administration, July 1984).

32. Joan Gray, "International Construction," *Financial Times,* April 12, 1985, pp. 13–17; and Erdener Kaynak, "Internationalization of Turkish Construction Companies," *Columbia Journal of World Business,* Winter 1992, pp. 61–75.

33. Benjamin A. Holden and Nicholas Bray, "British, Australian and Two American Firms to Purchase Utility in Australia," *Wall Street Journal,* August 5, 1996, p. A4.

34. Thomas Horst, "American Multinationals and the U.S. Economy," *American Economic Review,* May 1976, pp. 150–152; Claudio V. Vaitsos, *Intercountry Income Distribution and Transnational Enterprises* (Oxford: Clarendon Press, 1974); P. Streeten, "Theory of Development Policy," in *Economic Analysis and the Multinational Enterprise,* J. H. Dunning, ed. (London: Allen and Unwin, 1974); G. F. Kopits, "Intrafirm Royalties Crossing

Frontiers and Transfer Pricing Behavior," *Economic Journal,* December 1976; and Donald R. Lessard, "Transfer Prices, Taxes, and Financial Markets: Implications of Internal Financial Transfers within the Multinational Firm," paper presented at the New York University Conference on Economic Issues of Multinational Firms, November 4, 1976.

35. Scott Shane, "The Effect of National Culture on the Choice Between Licensing and Direct Foreign Investment," *Strategic Management Journal,* Vol. 15, 1994, pp. 627–642.

36. Linda Longfellow Blodgett, "Factors in the Instability of International Joint Ventures: An Event History Analysis," *Strategic Management Journal,* Vol. 13, No. 6, September 1992, pp. 475–481.

37. Joel Bleeke and David Ernst, "The Way to Win in Cross-Border Alliances," *Harvard Business Review,* November–December 1991, pp. 127–135.

38. There are many different ways of classifying the problems. Two useful ways are found in Manuel G. Serapio, Jr., and Wayne F. Cascio, "End Games in International Alliances," *Academy of Management Executive,* Vol. 10, No. 1, 1996, pp. 62–73; and Joel Bleeke and David Ernst, "Is Your Strategic Alliance Really a Sale?" *Harvard Business Review,* January–February 1995, pp. 97–105.

39. David Hamilton, "United It Stands," *Wall Street Journal,* September 26, 1996, p. R19.

40. Lawrence G. Franko, *Joint Venture Survival in Multinational Corporations* (New York: Praeger, 1971); and Richard H. Holton, "Making International Joint Ventures Work," in *The Management of Headquarters-Subsidiary Relationships in Multinational Corporations,* Lars Otterbeck, ed. (London: Cower, Aldershot, 1981), pp. 255–267.

41. Gregory E. Osland and S. Tamer Cavusgil, "Performance Issues in U.S.-China Joint Ventures," *California Management Review,* Vol. 38, No. 2, Winter 1996, pp. 106–130.

42. "Oleg Cassini Inc. Sues Firm Over Licensing," *Wall Street Journal,* March 28, 1984, p. 5; and "Cassini Awarded $16 Million in Fragrance Line Squabble," *Wall Street Journal,* June 2, 1988, p. 28.

43. William H. Meyers, *New York Times Magazine,* May 3, 1987, pp. 33–35+.

44. Marcus W. Brauchli, "PepsiCo's KFC Venture in China Is Fined For Allegedly False Financial Reporting," *Wall Street Journal,* July 27, 1994, p. A10.

45. Nicholas D. Kristof, "A Not-So-Grand Hotel: A Tibet Horror Story," *New York Times,* September 25, 1990, p. A4.

46. Mike Tharp, "Uneasy Partners," *Wall Street Journal,* November 8, 1976, p. 28.

47. J. Peter Killing, "How to Make a Global Joint Venture Work," *Harvard Business Review,* Vol. 60, No. 3, May–June 1982, pp. 120–127.

48. Joel Bleeke and David Ernst, "The Way to Win in Cross-Border Alliances," *Harvard Business Review,* November–December 1991, pp. 127–135.

49. Greg McIvor, "Coca-Cola Ends Link With Nordic Producers," *Financial Times,* June 20, 1996, p. 15. For factors that appear to influence the ability of foreign companies to gain knowledge about local operating conditions, see Andrew C. Inkpen and Paul Beamish, "Knowledge, Bargaining Power, and The Instability of International Joint Ventures," *Academy of Management Review,* Vol. 22, No. 1, 1997, pp. 177–202.

50. Yumiko Ono, "Borden's Messy Split with Firm in Japan Points Up Perils of Partnerships There," *Wall Street Journal,* February 21, 1991, p. B1+; and Henry W. Lane and Paul W. Beamish, "Cross-Cultural Cooperative Behavior in Joint Ventures in LDCs," *Management International Review,* Vol. 30, special issue, 1990, pp. 87–102.

51. Bleeke and Ernst, "The Way to Win in Cross-Border Alliances," loc. cit.

52. Sue Cartwright and Cary Cooper, "Why Suitors Sould Consider Culture," *Financial Times,* September 1, 1995, p. 6.

53. Bleeke and Ernst, loc. cit.; John D. Daniels and Sharon L. Magill, "The Utilization of International Joint Ventures by United States Firms in High Technology Industries," *Journal of High Technology Management Research,* Vol. 2, No. 1, 1991, pp. 113–131.

54. Seev Hirsch and Avi Meshulach, "Toward a Unified Theory of Internationalization," Working Paper 10-91 (Copenhagen: Institute of International Economics and Management, 1991); and R. T. Carstairs and L. S. Welch, "Licensing and the Internationalization of Smaller Companies: Some Australian Evidence," *Management International Review,* Vol. 22, No. 3, 1982, pp. 33–44.

55. Bent Petersen and Torben Pedersen, "Research on the Entry Mode Choice of the Firm: How Close to a Normative Theory?" Working Paper 20-92 (Copenhagen: Institute of International Economics and Management, 1992).

56. Harry G. Barkema, John H. J. Bell, and Johannes M. Pennings, "Foreign Entry, Cultural Barriers, and Learning," *Strategic Management Journal,* Vol. 17, 1996, pp. 151–166.

57. Peter J. Buckley and Mark C. Casson, "Multinational Enterprises in LDCs: Cultural and Economic Interaction," in *Multinational Enterprises in Less Developed Countries,* Peter J. Buckley and Jeremy Clegg, eds. (London: Macmillan, 1990); and Jeremy Clegg, "The Determinants of

Aggregate International Licensing Behaviour: Evidence from Five Countries," *Management International Review*, Vol. 30, No. 3, 1990, pp. 231–251.

58. "Judge Revokes License of Paris McDonald's," *International Herald Tribune* (Zurich), September 12, 1982, p. 14; Steven Greenhouse, "McDonald's Tries Paris, Again," *New York Times*, June 12, 1988, p. 1F+; and Andrew Jack, "McDonald's Makes Fast-Food Inroads on the French Palate," *Financial Times*, February 21, 1996, p. 14.

59. John Kenneth Galbraith, *American Capitalism* (Boston: Houghton-Mifflin, 1952), pp. 91–92.

60. "Beam Me Up, Scottie," *The Economist*, March 28, 1992, pp. 69–70; Neil Behrmann, "Russians, South Africans Join Forces on Mining," *Wall Street Journal*, June 17, 1992, p. C1+; Brian Coleman and Elisabeth Rubinfien, "Space Race Becomes a Joint Venture," *Wall Street Journal*, November 11, 1992, p. A8; and Richard L. Hudson, "European Phone Companies Reach Out for Partners," *Wall Street Journal*, September 30, 1993, p. B4.

61. "Alliances Forged in the Factory," *Financial Times*, November 4, 1996, p. 10.

62. "The Global Firm: R.I.P.," *The Economist*, February 6, 1993, p. 69, referring to a view of Cyrus Freidman, vice chairman of Booz, Allen & Hamilton, for a study, "The Global Corporation—Obsolete So Soon?"

63. Arvind Parkhe, "Interfirm Diversity, Organizational Learning, and Longevity in Global Strategic Alliances," *Journal of International Business Studies*, Vol. 22, No. 4, Fourth Quarter 1991, pp. 579–601.

64. Data for the case were taken from Andrea Rothman, "U.S. to World: Airline Deals Hinge on Open Skies," *Business Week*, January 11, 1992, p. 46; Christopher J. Chipello, "Midsize Air Canada Plots Survival in Industry of Giants," *Wall Street Journal*, November 12, 1992, p. B2; Andrea Rothman, Seth Payne, and Paula Dwyer, "One World, One Giant Airline Market?" *Business Week*, October 5, 1992, p. 56; "All Aboard," *The Economist*, February 29, 1992, p. 78; "Wings Across the Water," *The Economist*, July 25, 1992, p. 62; Brian Coleman, "Four European Carriers Propose Merger into Continent's Second-Largest Airline," *Wall Street Journal*, April 28, 1993, p. A3; "KLM Is Considering Allying with Swissair, SAS and Austrian Air," *Wall Street Journal*, January 28, 1993, p. A10; Agis Salpukas, "Continental Backs Air Canada's Offer to Merge Systems," *New York Times*, November 10, 1992, p. A1; Agis Salpukas, "Europe's Small Airlines Shelter under Bigger Wings," *New York Times*, November 8, 1992, p. E4; "USAir, Air France Plan Links Between Businesses," *Wall Street Journal*, September 25, 1990, p. C12; "Code Breakers," *The Economist*, November 21, 1992, pp. 78–79; Brett Pulley, "Northwest Airlines to Cut Up to 40% Fares to Europe," *Wall Street Journal*, February 1, 1993, p. C15; Agis Salpukas, "Lufthansa Drops Plan For U.S.," *New York Times*, November 3, 1992, p. C1; Robert L. Rose and Brian Coleman, "British Airways Purchases Stake in USAir Group," *Wall Street Journal*, January 22, 1993, p. A3; Wendy Zellner, William Symonds, and Andrea Rothman, "This Time, Continental May Actually Fly," *Business Week*, May 10, 1993, p. 70; Bridget O'Brian and Laurie McGinley, "Mixing of U.S., Foreign Carriers Alters Market," *Wall Street Journal*, December 21, 1992, p. B1; Bill Poling, "United, American Spar with USAir, BA over Proposed Deal," *Travel Weekly*, November 12, 1992, p. 49; Joan M. Feldman, "The Dilemma of 'Open Skies,'" *The New York Times Magazine*, April 2, 1989, p. 31+; Paula Dwyer, Andrea Rothman, Seth Payne, and Stewart Toy, "Air Raid: British Air's Bold Global Push," *Business Week*, August 24, 1992, pp. 54–61; Philippe Gugler, "Strategic Alliances in Services: Some Theoretical Issues and the Case of Air-Transport Services," paper prepared for the Danish Summer Research Institute (DSRI), Denmark, August 1992; Robert Johnson and Laurie McGinley, "Air Canada and U.S. Partner's Offer for Continental Stake Clears Hurdle," *Wall Street Journal*, January 8, 1993, p. A4; Martin Tolchin, "Shift Urged on Foreign Stakes in Airlines," *New York Times*, January 9, 1993, p. 17; Agis Salpukas, "The Big Foreign Push to Buy into U.S. Airlines," *New York Times*, October 11, 1992, p. F11; Robert L. Rose and Bridget O'Brian, "United, Lufthansa Form Marketing Tie, Dealing a Setback to American Airlines," *Wall Street Journal*, October 4, 1993, p. A4; Michael Skapinker, "BA Seeks Dismissal of USAir Lawsuit," *Financial Times*, September 22, 1996, p. 3; Robert Crandell, "When Less Really Means More," *Financial Times*, September 17, 1996, p. 17; Pierre Sparaco, "Swissair Counters Lack of Ties With EU," *Aviation Week & Space Technology*, February 13, 1995, p. 33, "SAS and Lufthansa Join Forces to Create Europe's Biggest Transport System," *South China Morning Post*, May 13, 1995, p. B5; Emma Tucker, "Commission to Approve Lufthansa-SAS Venture," *Financial Times*, January 16, 1996, p. 3; Scott McCartney, Diane Brady, Susan Carey, and Asra Q. Nomani, "U.S. Airlines' Prospects Are Grim on Expanding Access to Asian Skies," *Wall Street Journal*, September 25, 1996, p. A1; and David Owen and John Kingman, "Air France Lines Up Two US Alliances," *Financial Times*, October 17, 1996, p. 15.

Chapter 15

Control Strategies

Form your plans before sunrise.
—Indian-Tamil Proverb

Objectives

- To explain the special challenges of controlling foreign operations

- To describe the alternative organizational structures for international operations

- To show the advantages and disadvantages of decision making at headquarters and at foreign subsidiary locations

- To highlight both the importance of and the methods for global planning, reporting, and evaluating

- To give an overview of some specific control considerations affecting MNEs, such as the handling of acquisitions and the shifts in strategies to fulfill international objectives

Case
Nestlé[1]

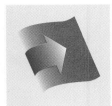

The former managing director of Nestlé, Pierre Liotard-Vogt, said, "Perhaps we are the only real multinational company existing." Although this may be something of an exaggeration, it is difficult to find other companies with such a high dependence on foreign involvement. UNCTAD's composite index on transnationality ranks Nestlé as the most international of the world's 100 largest manufacturers. The Swiss-based company was international from the start. Nestlé was formed by a 1905 merger between an American-owned company and a German-owned company. About 98 percent of Nestlé's sales are outside of Switzerland, and about half of the top management at the Vevey headquarters is non-Swiss. In 1997, Peter Brabeck, an Austrian who had worked for Nestlé in Latin America, replaced Helmut Maucher, a German, as CEO. Previously, a Frenchman, an Italian, and a Swiss who took out U.S. citizenship had held the position. Map 15.1 shows Nestlé's factories by country and percentages of sales by region.

In 1995, Nestlé's sales from 489 factories in seventy-five countries were 56.5 billion Swiss francs. With such a wide geographic spread of operations, Nestlé maintains clear-cut policies on where decisions will be made and what roles corporate and host-country managers will play.

A major responsibility of Nestlé's corporate management is to give the company strategic direction. To do this, it decides in which geographic areas and to which products it plans to allocate efforts. For example, in the 1980s, Nestlé became less dependent on chocolate and Third-World markets by placing more emphasis on culinary products and on the North American market. By the 1990s, it was placing more emphasis on LDCs, especially China. Throughout most of its history, Nestlé has concentrated on manufacturing, marketing, and wholesale distribution and has avoided vertical expansion into plantations or supermarkets. To maintain this control, its corporate management handles all acquisition decisions as well as those regarding which products will be researched at the centralized facilities in Switzerland. This decision making is handled through product groups, such as the chocolate and confectionery products group. To support these functions, each geographic group is expected to provide a positive cash flow to the parent. In fact, Nestlé tries to move almost all cash to Switzerland, where a specialized staff decides in which currencies it will be held and to what countries it will be transferred.

Headquarters also researches conditions affecting commodities and mandates amounts and prices for purchases of supplies, for example, requiring that all overseas companies contract for a supply of green coffee for, say, three to six months at some maximum price. The company is heavily dependent on introducing new products that may take several years to become profitable, so it must ensure that the more established products remain sufficiently profitable to generate needed funds. If a new product does not become profitable within a reasonable time, such as mineral water in Brazil, or if it has run its cycle of profitability, such as Libby's vegetable-canning operations, or if its development potential seems low, such as Beech-Nut's baby food, management in Switzerland decides to divest the business. Other divestments occur because certain activities of acquired companies do not fit the corporate development strategy. For example, Nestlé spun off a printing and packaging business that was part of the acquired Buitoni-Perugina operations.

Map 15.1   Locations of Nestlé Factories

Note that Nestlé's manufacturing is located in 75 different countries.

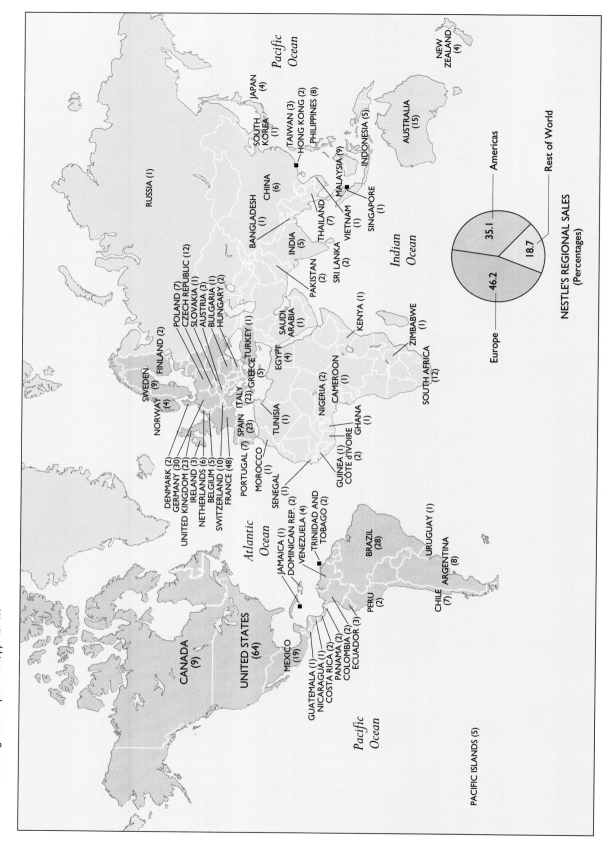

Source: Nestlé Management Report 1995, pp. 40–41.

The budget that originates from each country is the main means used to ensure that each area carries its share within the corporation. Budgets are prepared annually, revised quarterly, and subject to approval at corporate headquarters. Actual performance reports are sent to Switzerland monthly, where they are compared with the budget and the previous year's performance. The head of the country and/or area operations must explain any deviations satisfactorily or corporate management will intervene. Corporate headquarters also serves as a source of information. The successes, failures, and general experiences of product programs in one country are passed on to managers in others. For example, information on the success of a white chocolate bar in New Zealand and on a line of Lean Cuisine frozen food in the United States was disseminated this way.

Despite the centralized directives described above, Nestlé's country and/or area managers have a great deal of discretion in certain matters, especially marketing. Product research is centralized so that duplication of efforts is kept to a minimum. When a new product is developed, corporate management offers it to the subsidiaries and may urge initial trials. However, it does not force the subsidiaries to launch a new product if the subsidiary managers do not find it acceptable. If the product is introduced, local managers are fairly free to adapt it as long as corporate management does not find the changes harmful. For example, one of Nestlé's best selling products, Nescafé instant coffee, is blended and colored slightly differently from country to country.

Nestlé relies heavily not only on budgets and reports but also on information-gathering visits to local operations. The company has several policies designed to bring corporate and subsidiary management closer together. One is to alternate people between jobs in the field and jobs at headquarters. For example, the CEO of Nestlé USA spends one week of each month at Vevey. Another is to schedule meetings and training programs to bring large groups of managers together. Still another is to ensure that corporate headquarters management can converse with subsidiary management in at least French and English and preferably in German and Spanish as well. (The executive board conducts business in English.) Further, the compensation system and management style are established purposely to limit turnover among employees.

The policy of making decisions at headquarters changed in the 1980s. During that time, Nestlé became more decentralized, largely because of the management philosophy of Helmut Maucher, who became managing director in 1982. When Maucher took over, three levels of management approval were necessary even to put out a press release. He reduced the corporate staff, pushed more authority down to the operating level, and replaced twenty-five-page monthly reports with a one-page reporting form. In addition, Nestlé at one time sought to balance functional, geographic, and product viewpoints by putting different people in charge of each activity at headquarters. This meant that the heads of all activities had to agree on a decision, sometimes a slow process. To slim down the corporate staff and speed decision making, this structure was replaced under Maucher with a board of general managers that primarily represents the zones into which Nestlé divides the world.

Many company actions require new decisions on where control will be vested. Nestlé prefers to gain first-in advantages in markets; however, when this is not possible, Nestlé's policy is to expand largely through acquisition of existing companies. Acquisitions have resulted in situations that do not quite fit the established lines of responsibility. The acquisition policy is founded on the belief that it is more prudent to enter an already highly competitive market by buying an existing company and infusing resources into it than to start up a new operation. For example, in 1994 Nestlé entered the Polish market by buying Goplana, the country's second largest chocolate maker—a move that saved about two years in start-up time and did not necessitate building brand recognition. Subsequently, Nestlé has added to Goplana's product line and improved its packaging. Because acquired companies are unlikely to have the exact product and geographic basis to fit Nestlé's structure, these operations must be accommodated. For example, Nestlé acquired Libby, McNeill & Libby, a U.S. company with substantial international operations, including a subsidiary in the United Kingdom. Nestlé had to iron out not only how Libby would relate to Nestlé's existing U.S. operations but also whether the U.K. subsidiary should continue to report to Libby or report to Nestlé's European operations instead. (There was a gradual transition by which the subsidiary eventually reported to the European operations.) Later, the Libby production facilities and distribution center were closed; however, two other Nestlé divisions took on the manufacture and sale of products using the Libby name. In another case, Nestlé's acquisition of Stouffer Foods put it into hotel ownership for the first time. Because Stouffer had been highly profitable and because corporate management at Nestlé's Swiss headquarters lacked hotel experience, initially many more decisions than usual were made at the subsidiary level.

A notable Nestlé acquisition in the United States was of Carnation. Carnation initially reported directly to Switzerland instead of to North American operations, which had been established to consolidate much of the U.S. operations and to allow Swiss headquarters to spend more time on strategic planning rather than supervising day-to-day operations. Five years later, Carnation was consolidated with other U.S. food businesses in a move to save overhead expenses and to gain advantages of scale in combating such U.S. rivals as Kraft General Foods and Con-Agra.

Competitive factors have influenced Nestlé's decisions on what to emphasize. For example, its rapid growth strategy in the United States has been based in part on the realization that the company must maintain a size that is not small relative to its competitors (which have been growing internally and through acquisition). This size helps in dealing with the few large supermarket chains that account for most of Nestlé's sales.

Introduction

Control questions facing all companies:
• Where are decisions made?
• How can the company optimize globally?
• How should country units report to headquarters?

International companies have a wide variety of strategies as well as approaches for implementing those strategies. Nevertheless, many of the problems they face are very similar. The Nestlé case illustrates concerns shared by all international companies: which objectives to pursue, where decisions should be made, how foreign operations should report to headquarters, and how to ensure that global objectives are met. Behind each of these concerns is a more basic one—that of control.

Control is needed so that a company has a common direction or strategy. For example, Nestlé managers have a clear-cut understanding that, although cost and innovation are important, the company's major competitive advantage lies in the marketing of differentiated consumer products. As such, its worldwide managers concentrate on marketing aspects of the value chain, such as branding, advertising, and gaining access to distribution—rather than acquiring plantations or dairy farms to reduce costs or spending heavily on R&D to develop technically advanced products. Nestlé managers also have a clear-cut understanding of competitive entry strategies; thus they forgo situations in which they cannot acquire either first-in advantages or a company with an established brand and significant market share. The company allocates resources in order to emphasize those product and geographic markets in which it prefers to grow more rapidly, and it would seem inconceivable for a manager, in say Peru, to launch a new product in Peru or build a plant in Bolivia (Nestlé has no manufacturing in Bolivia) without considerable scrutiny and approval from corporate management in Switzerland. Concomitantly, reports to headquarters are sufficiently detailed and frequent so that adjustments can be made to meet planned objectives. Further, Nestlé's widespread global operations are organized so that country-level managers can adjust to locally specific environmental and competitive differences. At the same time, there is synergy among the worldwide operating units through exchanges of information, the sharing of fixed costs from new product development and such staff support as commodity price expertise, and the spillover advantages generally of global brands. In contrast, Prudential Securities' operations in Australia, Hong Kong, Japan, and Singapore became so independent that they moved in very different directions. The result was the company's inability to gain advantages from its multinational status, such as exchanging useful information.[2] Control is also needed so that individuals cannot make decisions that endanger the entire company. For example, Barings, a British investment bank, collapsed in 1995 after a 28-year-old futures trader in Singapore lost about $1.3 billion through speculative and fraudulent trading. Subsequent investigations showed that neither headquarters nor external auditors sufficiently understood the trader's complex dealings, and there was no clear-cut point at headquarters to control the amount of risk involved in the trading.[3]

The concept of control encompasses much more than just the ownership of sufficient voting shares to direct company policies. **Control** is the planning, implementation, evaluation, and correction of performance to ensure that organizational objectives are achieved. In essence, the primary challenge of control within an international company is the balancing of globally integrated advantages with the need to adapt to country-level differences. Several factors make control more difficult internationally than it is domestically:

Foreign control is usually more difficult because of
- **Distance**—it takes more time and expense to communicate
- **Diversity**—country differences make it hard to compare operations
- **Uncontrollables**—there are more outside stockholders and governmental dictates
- **Degree of certainty**—there often are rapid changes in the environment and data problems

1. *Distance.* In spite of the growth in e-mail and fax transmissions, many communications are still best handled by face-to-face or voice-to-voice contact. The geographic distance (especially when operations span multiple time zones) and

cultural disparity separating countries increase the time, expense, and possibility of error in cross-national communications. Inquiries and responses between headquarters and subsidiaries' managers may not be fully understood, and the time and expense of gaining verification may hinder the functioning of control systems.

2. *Diversity.* This book has emphasized the need for an MNE to adjust operations to the unique situations encountered in each country in which it operates. When market size, type of competition, nature of the product, labor cost, currency, and a host of other factors differentiate operations among countries, the task of evaluating performance or setting standards to correct or improve business functions is extremely complicated.

3. *Uncontrollables.* Performance evaluation is of little use in maintaining control unless there is some means of taking corrective action. Effective corrective action may be minimal because many foreign operations must contend with the dictates of outside stockholders, whose objectives may differ somewhat from those of the parent, and with government regulations over which the company has no short-term influence.[4]

4. *Degree of certainty.* Control implies setting goals and developing plans to meet those goals. Economic and industry data are much less complete and accurate for some countries than for others. Further, political and economic conditions are subject to rapid change in some locales. These situations impede planning, especially long-range planning, and reduce the certainty of results from plan implementation.

Although these factors make control more difficult in the international context, companies follow procedural and structural practices in an effort to ensure that foreign operations comply with overall corporate goals and philosophies. This chapter discusses five aspects of the international control process:

1. Planning
2. Organizational structure
3. Location of decision making
4. Control mechanisms
5. Special situations

Planning

Companies must mesh objectives with internal and external constraints and set means to implement, monitor, and correct.

The essence of control is to develop strategies and implement them effectively. Planning is essential in this process. A company must adapt its unique resources and objectives to different and changing international competitive situations. This is the essence of planning. Without planning, a company lacks long-range goals and means to achieve them. Without planning, it is only by luck that a company picks the best sequence and method of expansion by country. Without planning, it is also by chance that a company sets policies and practices in a given locale that result in the desired performance. Because planning has been both implicitly and explicitly discussed already, this section presents only an overview of the process.

The Planning Loop

As Fig. 15.1 shows, planning must mesh objectives and capabilities with the internal and external environments. Although we have already discussed most of the steps within Fig. 15.1—such as the need to base motives for foreign operations on companies' resources and the need to examine market and risk conditions as a prerequisite for determining where to operate—it is useful to review the steps within the context of companies' overall control frameworks. Note that the first step (A) is to develop a long-range **strategic intent,** an objective that will hold the organization together over a long period while it builds its global competitive viability.[5] Although few companies start with such an intent, most develop one as they progress toward significant international positions. Some, such as Honda and Canon, developed strategic intents to become major global competitors long before it seemed they would ever be able. The strategic intent may encompass whether and where a company wants to be a leader, such as dominating its domestic market, dominating a regional or global market, or attaining profit results without being the market leader.[6] The strategic intent may also set priorities. For example, Johnson & Johnson states that its responsibilities are to customers, suppliers and employees, the community and environment, and shareholders—in that order.[7]

The next planning step (B) is to analyze internal resources, along with environmental factors in the home country. These resources and factors affect and constrain each company differently and sometimes each product differently for the same company. Basically, the most successful companies internationally are those that find the right fit between what is needed and what they are good at.[8] For example, a small company inexperienced in foreign operations may lack financial and human resources, even though it may have unique product capabilities that indicate opportunities abroad. Unlike a larger counterpart, it may have to collaborate with another company, perhaps by licensing foreign production rather than owning facilities abroad. But it still will need to control its foreign operations through a contract with the licensee that stipulates sales targets, product characteristics, and so on. Moreover, some products benefit more than others from global rather than multidomestic production because of potential cost savings through scale economies.

Only by making an internal analysis (step B) can a company set the overall rationale for its international activities (step C). These must be examined in conjunction with the strategy for competing, such as by keeping prices low versus differentiating through brand recognition. For instance, a company competing largely on price and faced with rising domestic costs may validly pursue one of several means for

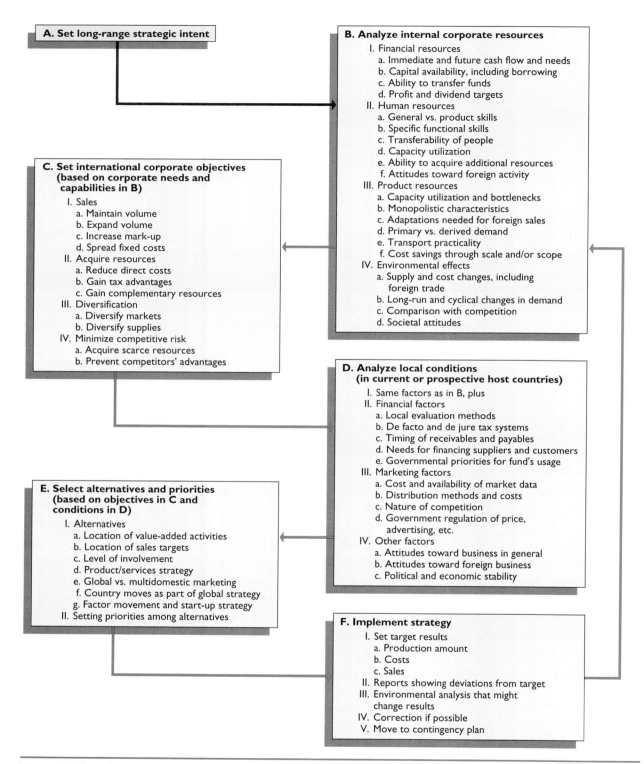

A. Set long-range strategic intent

B. Analyze internal corporate resources
  I. Financial resources
     a. Immediate and future cash flow and needs
     b. Capital availability, including borrowing
     c. Ability to transfer funds
     d. Profit and dividend targets
  II. Human resources
     a. General vs. product skills
     b. Specific functional skills
     c. Transferability of people
     d. Capacity utilization
     e. Ability to acquire additional resources
     f. Attitudes toward foreign activity
  III. Product resources
     a. Capacity utilization and bottlenecks
     b. Monopolistic characteristics
     c. Adaptations needed for foreign sales
     d. Primary vs. derived demand
     e. Transport practicality
     f. Cost savings through scale and/or scope
  IV. Environmental effects
     a. Supply and cost changes, including
        foreign trade
     b. Long-run and cyclical changes in demand
     c. Comparison with competition
     d. Societal attitudes

C. Set international corporate objectives (based on corporate needs and capabilities in B)
  I. Sales
     a. Maintain volume
     b. Expand volume
     c. Increase mark-up
     d. Spread fixed costs
  II. Acquire resources
     a. Reduce direct costs
     b. Gain tax advantages
     c. Gain complementary resources
  III. Diversification
     a. Diversify markets
     b. Diversify supplies
  IV. Minimize competitive risk
     a. Acquire scarce resources
     b. Prevent competitors' advantages

D. Analyze local conditions (in current or prospective host countries)
  I. Same factors as in B, plus
  II. Financial factors
     a. Local evaluation methods
     b. De facto and de jure tax systems
     c. Timing of receivables and payables
     d. Needs for financing suppliers and customers
     e. Governmental priorities for fund's usage
  III. Marketing factors
     a. Cost and availability of market data
     b. Distribution methods and costs
     c. Nature of competition
     d. Government regulation of price,
        advertising, etc.
  IV. Other factors
     a. Attitudes toward business in general
     b. Attitudes toward foreign business
     c. Political and economic stability

E. Select alternatives and priorities (based on objectives in C and conditions in D)
  I. Alternatives
     a. Location of value-added activities
     b. Location of sales targets
     c. Level of involvement
     d. Product/services strategy
     e. Global vs. multidomestic marketing
     f. Country moves as part of global strategy
     g. Factor movement and start-up strategy
  II. Setting priorities among alternatives

F. Implement strategy
  I. Set target results
     a. Production amount
     b. Costs
     c. Sales
  II. Reports showing deviations from target
  III. Environmental analysis that might
       change results
  IV. Correction if possible
  V. Move to contingency plan

Figure 15.1   International Planning Process
The initial step is setting the company's long-range strategic intent, followed by a loop in which short- and medium-term steps are taken to achieve the intent.

cost reduction, such as locating production where costs are lower or expanding exports to spread fixed costs.

Because each country in which the company is operating or contemplating operating is unique, local analysis is necessary (step D) before the final alternatives can be fully examined (step E). For instance, changes in local stability and market growth undoubtedly influenced Nestlé's decision to increase relative emphasis on LDCs.

The selection among the alternatives in step E determines the extent to which a company follows a global, transnational, or multidomestic strategy. These alternatives include the following:

- *Location of value-added activities*—involves the choice of where to locate each of the activities that comprise the entire value-added chain, from research to production to after-sales servicing.
- *Location of sales target*—involves the choice of country-markets in which to conduct business, and the level of activity, particularly in terms of market share.
- *Level of involvement*—involves the choice of operating through wholly owned facilities, partially owned facilities, or contract arrangements and whether the choice varies among countries.
- *Product/services strategy*—involves the extent to which a worldwide business offers the same or different products or services in different countries.
- *Marketing*—involves the extent to which a company uses the same brand names, advertising, and other marketing elements in different countries.
- *Competitive moves*—involves the extent to which a company makes competitive moves in individual countries as part of a global competitive strategy.
- *Factor movements and start-up strategy*—involves whether and the extent to which production factors are acquired locally or brought in by the company and whether the operation is made through an acquisition versus start-up.[9]

Priorities must be set among alternatives so that programs may be easily added or deleted to implement means of attaining target results (step F) as resource availability or situations change. A parent company may, for example, prefer and plan to remit dividends from one of its foreign subsidiaries back to itself; however, this may become impossible, thus management should consider what it will do with earnings if foreign-exchange controls are put into effect. Further, it must determine the alternatives that will then exist for the parent, which will have to do without the funds. It may be necessary to borrow more at home, remit more from other subsidiaries, or forgo domestic expansion or dividends. Without priorities, the company may have to make hurried decisions to accomplish its objectives even partially.

Finally, very specific objectives should be set for each operating unit, along with ways to measure both deviations from the plan and conditions that may cause such deviations. Through timely evaluation, the company can take corrective actions or at least move to contingency means to achieve the objectives. Note that there must be a constant loop from step F to step B to ensure the company is making decisions based on currently relevant situations.[10] Evaluation methods are discussed later in this chapter.

A distinction must be made between operating plans and strategic plans. Strategic plans are longer term and akin to step A, developing the strategic intent. They involve major commitments, such as what businesses the company will be in and where, and are less subject to reevaluation. Operating plans involve short-term objectives and the means to carry them out. The time horizon for operating plans is not clear-cut. For example, the chairman of Unilever pointed out the short-term needs for Unilever's consumer products (three to five years) as compared with much longer-term need for a project such as building the Anglo-French Channel Tunnel.[11] Although input for a strategic plan may come from all parts of the organization, only at an upper level can allocations be made to implement overall planned changes in geographic and product policies. Also, only those managers who have information on the company's worldwide activities, competition, and trends are in a position to make informed strategic decisions.

Uncertainty and Planning

A company's international operations have more complexity and uncertainty than its domestic ones.

The more uncertainty there is, the harder it is to plan. It is generally agreed that operations in the international sphere involve more uncertainty than do those in the domestic one because of the greater complexity of international operations. Complexity results from the greater number of operating environments (for example, having to evaluate many subsidiaries) and from different requirements for different markets in terms of the tasks performed, because products and how they are made within each subsidiary differ.[12]

Organizational Structure

No matter how good a plan is, it will achieve little unless there is an appropriate means of implementing it. Organizational structure is a necessary means of implementation that should fit the strategy being pursued. The structure defines how individuals and organizational units are grouped to carry out company activities. Such groupings are the formal structure and lines of communication. They usually involve the *major* but not the *only* lines of communication within an organization. Often the informal communications networks are very important in disseminating information within an organization. Further, such formal groupings indicate where profit and loss are counted and consolidated. The formal structure depends on many factors, including the following:

- Degree of multidomestic, global, and transnational policies employed
- Location and type of foreign facilities
- Impact of international operations on total corporate performance

Companies must establish legal and organizational structures at home and abroad to meet their objectives. These structures may differ among various foreign countries because of the unique nature of activities and different environmental requirements. Layered above the individual country organizations are additional structures that coordinate activities in multiple countries. The form, method, and location of operational units at home and abroad will affect taxes, expenses, and control. Consequently, organizational structure has an important effect on the fulfillment of corporate objectives.

Separate versus Integrated International Structures

A company's international activities may be grouped together (for example, in an international division) or integrated into the product, geographic, or functional structure the company relies on domestically. Figure 15.2 shows simplified examples of different approaches to placing foreign activity within the organizational structure. Most companies basically use one of these approaches. Note that no form is without drawbacks.

An international division
- **Creates a critical mass of international expertise**
- **May have problems getting resources from domestic divisions**

International division   Grouping international activities into their own division allows for specialized personnel to handle such diverse matters as export documentation, foreign-exchange transactions, and relations with foreign governments. It also creates a large enough critical mass that can wield power within the organization. In contrast, international operations integrated with product or functional groups may be so small in comparison to domestic business that the company gives little attention to their development. However, an international division might have to depend on the domestic divisions for product to sell, personnel, technology, and other resources. Further, because domestic division managers are evaluated against domestic performance standards, they may withhold their best resources from the international division in order to improve their own performances. Given the separation between domestic and foreign operations, this structure is probably best suited for multidomestic strategies.[13]

Part (a) of Fig. 15.2 shows an example of international division; this structure is used by such companies as Campbell Soup.[14] Although it is not popular among European MNEs, it is among U.S. MNEs.[15] One apparent reason for this difference is that U.S. companies typically depend much more on the domestic market than do European companies. Having a separate international division allows a U.S. company to gain the critical mass discussed above.

Functional divisions are popular among companies with narrow product lines.

Functional division   Parts (b), (c), and (d) in Fig. 15.2 show organizational structures in which international operations are integrated rather than handled separately. Functional divisions, like those shown in part (b) of Fig. 15.2, are popular among companies with a narrow range of products, particularly if the production and marketing methods are relatively undifferentiated among them. Most companies begin with functional structures; however, as they add new unrelated products

Figure 15.2
Placement of International Activities within the Organizational Structure
Although most companies have structures that are mixed, the five examples shown here are simplified versions of the most common types of structures for organizations that have international business activities.

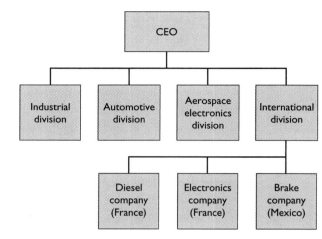

(a) International division

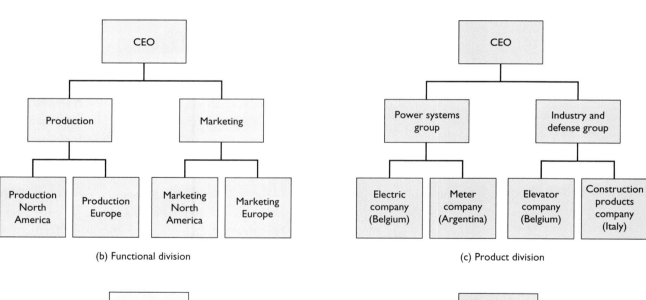

(b) Functional division

(c) Product division

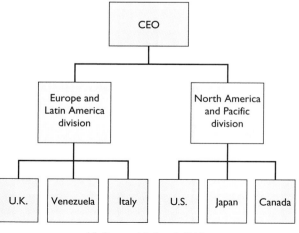

(d) Geographic (area) division

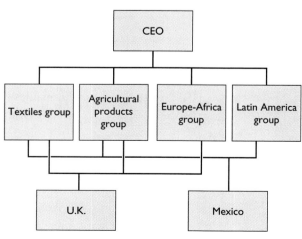

(e) Matrix

this structure becomes cumbersome. For example, in a company such as Westing-house (which produces more than 8,000 different products in such diverse areas as real-estate finance, nuclear fuel, television production, electronics systems, and soft-drink bottling), it is hard to imagine that a head of production could under-stand all the diverse needs. But many oil and mineral extraction companies, such as Exxon, use this structure. This structure is ideal when products and production methods are basically undifferentiated among countries. For example, oil compa-nies may need to differentiate methods of extraction by terrain, but not by country; thus global responsibility over production assures that each country has access to the same state-of-the-art production methods. Ford, in an attempt to narrow regional differences in automobile design (thus moving toward a global, rather than a multidomestic strategy), first returned to a global functional structure[16] and then to a global product structure.[17]

Product divisions are popular among international companies with diverse products.

Product division   Product divisions, as illustrated in (c), are particularly popular among companies that have highly diverse product groups, especially those that have become diverse primarily through acquisitions, such as Motorola. Because these groups may have little in common, even domestically, they may be highly independent of each other. As is true for the functional structure, the product divi-sion structure is well-suited for pursuit of a global strategy because both the foreign and domestic operations report to the same head, who is then able to find synergies between the two. Most likely, different product divisions will commence interna-tional operations at different times and at different rates, thus there is a probability of some duplication of international activities among the product groups—such as each having its export documentation personnel. Further, there is no formal means by which one division can learn form another's international experience. Finally, note that different subsidiaries within the same foreign country will report to dif-ferent groups at headquarters; thus a problem of this structure is that synergy may be lost within countries because of no formal lines of communication among differ-ent subsidiaries. For example, at one time in Westinghouse, one subsidiary was bor-rowing funds locally at an exorbitant rate, while another in the same country had excess cash.

Geographic divisions are popular when foreign opera-tions are large and are not dominated by a single coun-try or region.

Geographic (area) division   Geographic divisions, as shown in part (d) of Fig. 15.2, are used primarily by companies with very large foreign operations that are not dominated by a single country or area. This structure is found more com-monly among European MNEs, such as Nestlé, than among U.S. MNEs, because of the dominance of the U.S. domestic market. Recall that Nestlé can use this struc-ture because no one region dominates its operations. The structure is probably more suited to multidomestic strategies than to global strategies. Moreover, the structure is useful when maximum economies in production can be attained on a regional rather than a global basis. A drawback is possible costly duplication among areas. For example, Ford's decision to abandon its area structure was based on costly design duplication between Europe and North America.

Matrix   Because of the problems inherent in either integrating or separating foreign operations, many companies, such as Tenneco Automotive, are moving toward matrix organizations, illustrated in part (e) of Fig. 15.2. In this type of organizational structure, a subsidiary reports to more than one group (product, geographic, or functional). This structure is based on the theory that because each group shares responsibility over foreign operations, the groups will become more interdependent, exchange information, and ultimately take strategic global perspectives as they seek to exchange resources with each other. For example, product-group managers must compete among themselves to ensure that R&D personnel responsible to a functional group are assigned to the development of technologies that fall within their product domains. These product-group managers also must compete to ensure that geographic-group managers emphasize their lines sufficiently. And not only do product groups compete; functional and geographic groups also must compete among themselves to obtain resources held by others in the matrix.

Although a matrix organization requires that all major perspectives be represented in strategic decision making, it is not without drawbacks. One concerns how groups compete for scarce resources. When lower-level managers fail to agree, management above the group level must decide how to allocate the resources. This takes additional time. Further, such factors as management's faith in a specific executive or group may result in more decisions being made favoring that executive or group. As others in the organization see this occurring, they may perceive that the locus of relative power lies with a certain individual or group. Consequently, managers may divert most of their energies toward the activities that are considered most likely to be accepted, thus perpetuating the difference in relative power. This emphasis may not represent what would be the firm's best strategic direction. Consequently, these interpersonal relationships may diminish some of the advantages of the matrix organization. Or a superior may neglect control of subordinates because of assuming wrongly that someone else is overseeing them, a factor in the loss of control and demise of Barings.[18] For these reasons, some companies that adopted dual-reporting systems have gone back to conventional structures with clear lines of responsibility, including Dow Chemical, Digital Equipment, and Citibank.[19]

Dynamic Nature of Structures

A complete organizational restructure is rare enough that it gets media attention; nevertheless, a company's structure is apt to evolve as its business evolves. For example, as product lines become more diverse, the overall organization is apt to shift from a functional to a product structure. International business growth also may necessitate structural changes. When a company is only exporting, an export department attached to a product or functional division may suffice. (In most companies, departments are subordinate to divisions.) But if international operations continue to grow and are conducted via overseas production in addition to exporting, a department may no longer be sufficient. Perhaps an international division replaces the department, or perhaps each product division takes on worldwide responsibility for its own products. Most companies prefer their divisions to be of a similar size, so it may be necessary to replace an international division if it becomes too large relative to domestic divisions. For example, in the Nestlé case it would be hard to imagine a single international division handling over 95 percent of the sales.

Mixed Nature of Structures

Because of growth dynamics, companies seldom, if ever, have all their activities corresponding to the simplified organizational structures described here; most have a mixed structure. For example, a recent acquisition might report to headquarters until it can be consolidated efficiently within existing divisions. Or circumstances regarding a particular country, product, or function might necessitate that it be handled separately, apart from the overall structure. Some operations may be wholly owned, thus enabling a denser network of communications to develop than in others where there is only partial or no ownership of the foreign operations. Further, the overall structure gives an incomplete picture of divisions in the organization. For example, PepsiCo was organized by product lines (e.g., soft drinks, snacks, and restaurants) until it decided to divest its snacks and restaurant divisions, which would seem to imply that each product line was integrated globally; however, each product group had its own international division, which separated them from domestic operations.[20] Finally, although we usually think of all the divisions being headquartered in the same country, this is not necessarily the case, particularly when companies follow transnational strategies. The leadership for a particular function or product may well be located abroad because that is where the primary expertise resides and where the primary production takes place.

Evolving Structures

Because of the increase in alliances among companies, control increasingly must come from negotiation and persuasion rather than from authority of superiors over subordinates.

Network organizations   Companies have traditionally been organized as hierarchies, which are characterized by superior-subordinate relationships. However, many companies now depend heavily on networks of alliances with other companies in which it is not clear-cut that one company is the superior and the other the subordinate; therefore the management of the alliance is shared among so-called equals—a situation known as a **heterarchy.**[21] Corning is a good example of how a heterarchy works because half of its earnings come from alliances, particularly joint ventures. Formal linkages exist among the alliance partners; however, management at Corning's headquarters serves as a broker, conflict negotiator, and facilitator rather than exerting direct authority over the alliances.[22]

Many Japanese companies are linked similarly in **keiretsus,** which are organizations in which each company owns a small percentage of other companies in the group. There are long-term strong personal relationships among high-level managers in the different companies, and there are often interlocking directorships. Sometimes *keiretsus* are vertical, such as that between Toyota and its parts suppliers. Sometimes *keiretsus* are horizontal.[23] For example, the Mitsubishi group consists of core companies in which no single company predominates. The businesses are extremely diverse, including mining, real estate, credit cards, and tuna canning.[24] Typically, the core companies within a *keiretsu* buy and sell with each other only if and to the extent the transactions make business sense. However, long-term interlocking directorships and strong personal relationships among managers in core companies build common interests that do not depend on formal controls. The relationships encourage individual companies to undertake long-term and high-risk investments because they know other members of the *keiretsu* would feel morally obligated to support a core company that developed financial problems.[25]

Operations involving non-core competencies may become separate companies.

Spin-off organizations   Companies sometimes develop new products or services that do not fit easily within existing competencies. In order to enhance the creativity, innovation, and entrepreneurship necessary to bring the new product or service to its potential, the activities are spun off as separate companies in which the parent will retain some, but not necessarily all, ownership. At the same time, the spin-off permits the parent to concentrate on new learning and to use its resources elsewhere. Such U.S. companies as Johnson & Johnson, Raychem, and Thermo Electron have spun off companies that subsequently have operated almost independently. Japanese companies have historically used spin-offs, the most notable example being Todota Automated Loomworks' spin-off of newly developed automobile competencies that became Toyota Motors.[26]

Some divisions may be head-quartered in a foreign country.

Lead subsidiary organizations   The major competency for a product does not necessarily lie in the company's home country. As a result, some companies have moved the headquarters of certain divisions to foreign countries. For instance, AT&T moved its corded telephone division from the United States to France; Siemens moved its air-traffic management division from Germany to the United Kingdom; and Hyundai shifted its personal computer division from Korea to the United States. Although these divisional headquarters are still accountable to corporate headquarters, other global operations, including those in the home country, must report to them.[27]

Location of Decision Making

Centralization implies higher-level decision making, usually above the country level.

Although the organizational structure outlines who reports to whom within the MNE, it does not indicate where decisions are made within that framework. Companies must determine where decisions will be made. The higher the level within the organization at which decisions are made, the more they are considered to be centralized; the lower the level, the more they are decentralized. Whether decision making should be centralized or decentralized can be addressed from the standpoint of either the company as a whole or some part of it, such as a particular subsidiary operation. This discussion highlights the relationship of country-level operations to other parts of the MNE, such as headquarters, regional offices, or other country-level operations. For purposes of this discussion, decisions made at the foreign-subsidiary level are considered to be decentralized, whereas those made above the foreign-subsidiary level are considered to be centralized. There are opposing pressures for centralization and decentralization; consequently, policies must be adapted to each company's unique situation.

Complete centralization and complete decentralization may be thought of as the extremes. In actuality, companies neither centralize nor decentralize all decisions; instead, they vary policies according to the type of question and the particular circumstances involved. The location of decision making may vary within the same company over time as well as by product, function, and/or country. In addition, actual decision making is seldom as asymmetrical as it may appear on the surface. A manager who has decision-making authority may consult and reach consensus with other managers before exercising the authority. Putting these differences and subtleties aside, this section focuses on the rationale for locating decision control at either the corporate or the subsidiary level.

Basically, the choice of decision location should be based on a combination of three trade-offs:

- balancing pressures for global integration versus pressures for local responsiveness,
- balancing the capabilities of headquarters versus subsidiary personnel, and
- balancing the expediency versus the quality of decisions.

Pressures for Global Integration versus Local Responsiveness

Global strategy Many organizations and products lend themselves to a global strategy and decision making at the corporate level because knowledge and technology are developed in the home country and disseminated abroad. Further there may be a global performance improvement through the transference of resources internationally, economies through standardization, and synergies through systematic dealings with stakeholders. In such a situation, the performance of a particular subsidiary may suffer; however, if global gains exceed local losses, the global strategy is justified. Figure 15.3 shows in the top left-hand quadrant that such industries as engines and industrial chemicals lend themselves to global strategies because there is little need to differentiate products among countries and because economies of scale in production can greatly reduce unit costs.

Decisions on moving goods or other resources internationally are more likely to be made centrally.

Resource transference Both product and production factors—capital, personnel, or technology—may be moved from a company's operations in one country to

**Figure 15.3
Environmental Influences and Control of MNEs**
Note how the location of control (and mechanisms to implement control) are influenced by the relative strengths of forces that favor local responsiveness and forces that favor global integration.

Source: Adapted from Figures 2 and 5 and discussion in Sumantra Ghoshal and Nitin Nohria. "Horses for Courses: Organizational forms for Multinational Corporations," *Sloan Management Review,* Winter 1993, pp. 23–36.

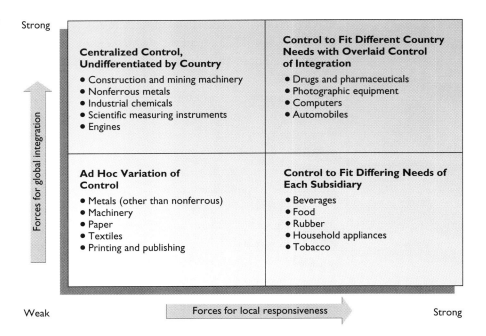

its facilities in another. For example, a company may decide to move earnings from one country to another where the projected return is higher, thus hurting the performance in one country while improving performance on a worldwide basis. Decisions involving these relationships usually are made centrally because making them requires information from all operating units and the ability to mesh the various data to achieve overall corporate objectives. Such information is usually available only at headquarters. Otherwise, reports would have to be disseminated from every unit to every other unit to determine whether a resource from one locale could be used elsewhere, and the dissemination would not guarantee that the resources would get transferred. Similarly, if exports among subsidiaries are needed to maintain a continual production flow (for example, with vertical integration or when interdependent components are needed in the company's final product), centralized control may be required to assure this flow. Another centralized decision may concern jurisdiction over exports. For example, if a company has manufacturing facilities in the United States and Germany, which facility will export to South Africa? By answering that question centrally, the company may avoid price competition among the subsidiaries and at the same time take into consideration comparative production costs, transportation costs, tax rates, foreign-exchange controls, and capacity utilization.

Global standardization usually reduces costs, but some revenue may be lost in the process.

Standardization   Worldwide uniformity of products, purchases, methods, and policies may reduce global costs substantially, even if some costs increase for a particular subsidiary. Such standardization is highly unlikely if decisions are made by each subsidiary. For example, standardizing machinery used in the production process may result in savings from quantity discounts on purchases, consolidation of mechanics' training, maintenance of manuals, and carrying of inventories of spare parts. The company may realize economies in almost any corporate activity, such as advertising, R&D, and purchase of group insurance. Product uniformity gives a company greater flexibility in filling orders when supply problems arise because of strikes, disasters, or sudden increases in demand. Production can simply be expanded in one country to meet shortages elsewhere. However, the downside of standardization is that revenue losses may exceed the gains from cost savings, for example, because some subsidiaries end up with products that do not quite fit demand. Of course, some products are more suitable to global standardization than others. GE's jet engines require no local adaptation, whereas Nestlé's food products do. Nevertheless, cost savings are usually more accurately projected than changes in revenues when instituting standardization.

Systematic dealings with stakeholders   Increasingly, the people with whom a company must deal (government officials, employees, suppliers, consumers, and the general public) are aware of what that company does in other countries in which it operates. Concessions that have been readily granted in one country may then be demanded in other countries, where they may not be afforded as easily. Suppose that for public-relations purposes, the management in one country decided to give preferential prices to the government and to establish a profit-sharing plan for employees. If the government officials and employees in another country ask for similar treatment, the result may be reduced profits if the company complies or poor public relations if it does not.

Even pricing and product decisions in one country can affect demand in other countries. With the growing mobility of consumers, especially industrial consumers, a good or bad experience with a product in one country may eventually affect sales elsewhere. This is especially true if industrial consumers themselves want uniformity in their end products. If prices differ substantially among countries, consumers may even find that they can import more cheaply than they can buy locally.

The actual and potential existence of global customers and/or competitors also may cause a company to make decisions in one country to improve performance elsewhere. For example, if a supplier gives price concessions to an automaker in Brazil, that supplier may more easily gain business in other countries in which the automaker manufactures. A company also may attack a competitor by producing and selling in the locale in which the competitor gains its major resources for competing globally.

Usually such dealings with potential global customers or competitors implies more centralized decision making because headquarters personnel are the only ones with information on all the countries where the company operates, such as information on what a global competitor is doing in one country that may have an impact elsewhere. However, the implementation to deal with the customer or competitor may shift more decision making to the subsidiary. For example, IBM's head-quarters management feared that its eroding Japanese market share would result in a spillover into other markets because Japanese competitors would have resources and confidence to fight IBM elsewhere. Decisions were pushed down to the Japa-nese subsidiary, with the result that its manufacturing capacity was substantially increased and new Japan-specific products were developed for that market.[28]

Multidomestic strategy   In some cases, cultural, legal, and economic conditions may dictate very different optimum operating practices from one country to another. For example, in the lower right-hand quadrant of Figure 15.3, the food industry usually has a weak need to integrate operations across countries because scale economies are highly offset by transportation costs. Concomitantly, it has a high need to adapt to local conditions because tastes, competitors, and distributors differ at the local level. Further, in such a situation the maximized performance of each subsidiary is assumed to maximize the company's global performance. These conditions favor a multidomestic strategy in which local management exploits local opportunities and in which knowledge is primarily developed and retained within each operating unit. Another situation favoring multidomestic control is when a subsidiary is prevented form being a full part of a global network because govern-mental protectionism isolates it from competitive threats.[29]

The more different the for-eign environment is from the home environment, the more delegation occurs. The more confidence there is in foreign managers, the more delegation occurs.

Whereas headquarters managers have information on the entire operation, lo-cal managers are usually in a better position to know what will work locally. They are normally given greater latitude when local conditions are perceived to be sig-nificantly different from those in the home country. For example, the corporate managers of a U.S. company will probably feel more competent about dictating practices to a Canadian subsidiary than to a Mexican subsidiary, since the former is presumed to parallel successful U.S. operations more closely. Yet local conditions may be more important for some functions than for others. For example, Nestlé decentralizes most of its marketing decisions because they must be adjusted to local needs; however, foreign-exchange decisions are centralized because of the impor-tance of examining global conditions.

Transnational strategies imply
- **a hybrid of multidomestic and global strategies**
- **gaining knowledge and capabilities from anywhere in the organization**
- **information flows up and down, horizontal and vertical**

Transnational strategy   The transnational company was defined in Chapter 1 and may be thought of as a company whose strategy is a hybrid in that it attempts to take advantage of the benefits of both a global and multidomestic strategy.[30] The upper right-hand quadrant of Fig. 15.3 illustrates industries that are ideal candidates for a transnational strategy because they have both a high need for global integration and a high need for local responsiveness. For example, new knowledge and capabili-ties are developed at both headquarters and at each subsidiary, both independently and jointly. These are then transferred throughout the worldwide organization. Fur-ther, assets and capabilities are dispersed unequally among operating units in differ-ent countries so that each can contribute uniquely through globally interdependent specialization. In effect, the transnational strategy attempts to gain the benefits of standardization and integration while making country decision makers an integral part of the planning and implementation.

Most of the above discussion implies that decisions are made only on a formal command-and-control basis; however, organizations are attempting to weaken the horizontal and vertical organizational partitions so that more and better information flows within the organization. In so doing, headquarters can better take advantage of the unique knowledge of the subsidiaries, and subsidiaries can better understand the global organizational needs and those conditions in other subsidiaries that can affect them. In fact, if headquarters ignores subsidiaries' viewpoints, the company may not develop the best cross-national or standardized programs. For example, Procter & Gamble (P&G) at one time allowed its country operations in Europe nearly total autonomy in adapting technology, products, and marketing approaches. To capture Europewide scale economies, P&G put one office in charge of formulating strategy for all of Europe, ignoring local knowledge, underutilizing subsidiaries' strengths, and demotivating subsidiaries' managers. P&G has since moved to greater standardization with other brand-management activities; however, this has been led by teams representing the subsidiary operations. In another case, EMI used feedback only from its home market (the United Kingdom) to decide that its central laboratory would seek to improve its CAT scanners through better image resolution. The company ignored the larger U.S. market, where a different improvement—shorter scan times—was preferred. When GE came out with a scanner that had a shorter scan time, it captured the U.S. market and got bigger scale economies than EMI did. EMI started losing money and had to accept a takeover bid.[31]

Companies have established various practices to improve the flow of information. For example, ABB has a sophisticated information retrieval system that disseminates information about and to the approximately 1,300 entities in its federation of companies. In addition, it brings together as many as 5,000 managers in meetings. This assures that upper- and lower-level managers receive the same timely information about the whole organization.[32] At 3M's European operations the company has given incentives for country units to work together to serve key accounts.[33] Ford is linking design groups in North America and Europe through videoconferencing and computer networks in the development of new automobile designs.[34]

As subsidiaries have become more interdependent, for example, because of rationalized or vertically integrated production or because of dealing with common competitors and customers, there has been a tendency for managers to initiate informal contact with their peers in the other interdependent units. Concomitantly, such companies as Digital have established ad hoc cross-cultural teams to deal with specific issues that cut across different country operations. These teams generally are composed of people chosen because of their skills and expertise, rather than position, and are made up of equals, rather than a superior with subordinates.

Therefore, the ability to reach consensus is dependent on the groups' enthusiasm and peer pressure within the groups, rather than formal procedures. The advantage is the generation of more and perhaps better ideas. The disadvantages include the time involved in deciding on the cross-unit issues and the increased potential for conflict.[35]

Ad hoc strategy   In the bottom left-hand corner are industries that gain little from global integration, while also having little need to adapt to local conditions. Companies with these characteristics may either centralize or decentralize, depending, for example, on such factors as the experience and competency of the personnel at headquarters versus subsidiaries. At the same time, the companies may mix control by function, such as decentralizing marketing while centralizing finance.

Capabilities of Headquarters versus Subsidiary Personnel

The perception of the relative competence of corporate versus local managers will influence the actions that each can pursue. Although there are rational factors affecting this perception, unrealistic attitudes may lead to excessive control being delegated to one or the other set of managers. Unrealistic attitudes include, for example, a belief that only the on-the-spot person knows the situation well enough to make a decision (polycentrism) or that corporate managers are the only individuals capable of making decisions (ethnocentrism). But there are real differences in capabilities as well. Decentralization may seem called for when the local management team is large rather than lean, local managers have worked a long time with the company, and local managers have developed successful track records.[36] These conditions change over time and will be discussed in the section "Control in the Internationalization Process."

Motivation and development   Although some decisions clearly can be made efficiently at the corporate level, this technical efficiency must be weighed against morale problems created when responsibility is taken away from local managers. When local managers are prevented from acting in the best interest of their own operation, they tend to think, "I could have done better, but corporate management would not let me." If local managers cannot participate in developing global strategies, they may lack the positive attitude to "go the extra mile" to implement global strategic decisions.[37] These managers also may lose their commitment to their jobs and thus may not gain the experience needed to advance within the company.

By giving groups of overseas employees a great deal of autonomy in certain areas, an MNE may be able to attract a higher caliber of personnel who might not want to work in its home country. For example, European scientists working at Pfizer's small U.K. laboratory have been responsible for many of Pfizer's discoveries.[38] There are many ways in which subsidiaries can have autonomy over certain activities, such as developing a specific product or technology or conducting certain market testing.

Decision Expediency and Quality

Companies must consider how long it takes to get help from headquarters in relation to how rapidly a decision must be made.

Cost and expediency   Although corporate personnel may be more experienced in advising on or making certain decisions, the time and expense involved in centralization may not justify the so-called better advice. Many decisions cannot be put off. Some headquarters' decisions could not be made effectively without face-to-face communication with subsidiary managers or on-the-spot observation. Bringing in corporate personnel may not be warranted.

More important decisions are made at headquarters.

Importance of the decision   Any discussion of location of authority must consider the importance of the particular decisions. This question is sometimes asked: How much can be lost through a bad decision? The greater the potential loss, the higher in the organization the level of control usually is. In the case of marketing decisions, for example, local autonomy is not nearly as prevalent for product design as for advertising, pricing, and distribution. Product design generally necessitates a considerably larger capital outlay than the other functions do; consequently, the potential loss from a wrong decision is higher. Further, advertising, pricing, and distribution decisions may be more easily reversed if an error in judgment is made. Rather than delineating the decisions that can be made at the subsidiary level, the company can set limits on expenditure amount, thus allowing local autonomy for small outlays while requiring corporate approval on larger ones.

Control in the Internationalization Process

Level of Importance

The more important the foreign operations, the higher in the organizational structure they report.

The more important the specific foreign operations are to total corporate performance, the higher the corporate level to which those units should report. The organizational structure or reporting system therefore should change over time to parallel the company's increased involvement in foreign activities.

At one end of the spectrum is the company that merely exports temporary surpluses through an intermediary who takes title and handles all the export details. This entire operation is apt to be so insignificant to total corporate performance that top-level management is concerned very little with it. In this case, the foreign activities should be handled at a low level in the corporate hierarchy. Anyone in the organization who knows enough about inventories and has time to discern whether orders can be filled could handle the operation.

At the other end of the spectrum is the company that has passed through intermediate stages and now owns and manages foreign manufacturing and sales facilities. Every functional and advisory group within the company undoubtedly will be involved in the facilities' establishment and direction. Because sales, investments, and profits of the foreign operations are now a more significant part of the corporate total, people very high in the corporate hierarchy are involved.

Changes in Competencies

The larger the total foreign operations, the more likely it is that headquarters has specialized staff with international expertise.
The larger the operations in a given country, the more likely it is that that country unit has specialized staff.

Small companies, especially those that are fairly new to international operations, may have little if any staff in foreign countries. Further, because they typically have narrow product lines and lean structures, they are able to get key headquarters players in different functions to work closely, both together and with foreign customers or suppliers. For example, such headquarters involvement helped CISCO, a small U.S. manufacturer of networking gear, to gain contracts with Japan's Nippon Telegraph & Telephone, and helped Pall, a small U.S.-based maker of filters, to develop extensive offshore manufacturing.[39] However, as a company's operations grow abroad, it develops a foreign management group that is capable of operating more independently of headquarters in the overseas markets. Simultaneously, corporate managers may no longer be able to deal effectively with international business operations because the company has entered so many different foreign markets; thus foreign operations tend to become more decentralized. This creates a dilemma. The subsidiary in this situation has its own capabilities, but its importance to total global performance because of its size may dictate a greater need for headquarters to intervene.[40] But as foreign operations continue to grow, people with foreign experience move into headquarters positions, and headquarters can afford staff specialists to deal with the company's multiple international operations. At that point, recentralization becomes feasible. Nevertheless, if a specific foreign country operation is very large, such as Nestlé's U.S. subsidiary, then it can afford its own specialized personnel.

Changes in Operating Forms

As the operating form evolves, so must the organizational structure.

The use of multiple operating forms, such as exporting, licensing, and joint venture, and the move from one to another may create the need to change areas of responsibility in the organization. Or it may mean that departments in the organization are not equally involved with all forms. For example, the legal department may have little day-to-day responsibility regarding exports but a great deal for licensing to the countries in which the exports are sold. Organizational mechanisms, such as joint committees and the planned sharing of information, are useful to ensure activities complement each other. It also is useful for the company to plan organizational change so as to minimize obstacles when responsibilities shift from one group to another.

A further consideration is how important the nonequity operation is to the company's overall operations. For example, if a company contracts with only one supplier for an essential component, the contract is likely to be controlled more closely and from higher in the organization than would contracts that are of less strategic importance.

Control Mechanisms

Corporate Culture

People trained at headquarters are more likely to think like headquarters personnel.

Any company has certain common values its employees share. These constitute the **corporate culture** and form a control mechanism that is implicit and helps enforce the company's explicit bureaucratic control mechanisms.[41] MNEs have more difficulty relying on a corporate culture for control because managers from different countries may have different norms pertaining to the management of operations and little or no exposure to the values and attitudes prevalent at corporate headquarters. Nevertheless, many companies encourage a worldwide corporate culture by promoting closer contact among managers from different countries. The aim is to convey a shared understanding of global goals and norms for reaching those goals.[42] Frequent transfers of managers among operations in different countries help develop increased knowledge of and commitment to a common set of values and objectives; thus fewer procedures, less hierarchical communication, and less surveillance are needed. For example, Nestlé moves management trainees around Europe so that they learn to react like Europeans rather than like any specific nationality. Matsushita brings foreign employees to Japan, partly to train them in the company culture but primarily to get Japanese employees to evolve toward a more global culture.[43]

The degree of control corporate headquarters imposes on the selection of top managers for foreign subsidiaries may dictate to a great extent how much formal control over the subsidiaries' operations the corporate personnel feel is necessary. Using home-country nationals in subsidiaries' management or even having headquarters set the standards for local managers' selection and training may be perceived as a means of assuring primary loyalty to the corporate culture rather than the subsidiary culture.[44] Such a procedure may be effective even if the operations are only partially owned or when the parent requires long-range planning assistance from the subsidiaries.[45]

Coordinating Mechanisms

Rather than changing overall structure, many companies are finding mechanisms to pull product, function, and area together.

Because each type of organizational structure has advantages and disadvantages, companies in recent years have developed mechanisms to pull together some of the diverse functional, geographic (including international), and product perspectives without abandoning their existing structures. Some of these mechanisms are as follows:

- Strengthening corporate staffs (adding or creating groups of advisory personnel) so that people with line responsibilities (decision-making authority) are required to listen to different viewpoints (whether or not they take the advice)
- Using more management rotation, such as between line and staff positions or domestic and international ones, in order to break down parochial views

- Placing international and domestic personnel in closer proximity to each other
- Establishing liaisons among subsidiaries within the same country so that different product groups can get combined action on a given issue
- Developing teams from different countries to work on special projects of cross-national importance, so that they share viewpoints
- Placing foreign personnel on the board of directors and/or top-level steering committees to bring foreign viewpoints into top-level decisions
- Giving all units credit (double counting or sharing) for business resulting from their cooperative efforts so that they are encouraged to view activities more broadly than their own units
- Basing reward systems partially on global results so that managers are committed to global as well as local performance

Companies also use staff departments (for example, legal or personnel) to centralize functions common to more than one subsidiary. For instance, at Heinz one expatriate-transfer-and-compensation policy is used by all the geographic divisions, thus minimizing duplication of effort.[46]

Reports

Headquarters needs timely reports in order to allocate resources, correct plans, and reward personnel. The decisions on the use of capital, personnel, and technology are almost continuous; consequently, reports must be frequent, accurate, and up-to-date so that these resources are efficiently used. Also, plans need to be updated in order to be realistic and to assure a high probability of meeting desired objectives. Finally, reports are needed to evaluate performance of personnel so as to reward and motivate them.

Written reports are more important in an international setting than in a domestic one because subsidiaries' managers have much less personal and oral contact with line and staff personnel above them. Thus corporate managers miss out on much of the informal communication that could tell them about the performance of the foreign operations.

Types of systems   Most MNEs use reporting systems for foreign operations that resemble those they use domestically. There are several reasons for this:

1. If the systems have been effective domestically, management often believes they also will be effective internationally.
2. There are economies from carrying over the same types of reports. The need to establish new types of reporting mechanisms is eliminated, and corporate management is already familiar with the system.
3. Reports with similar formats presumably allow management to better compare one operation with another.

MNEs' reporting systems are intended primarily to assure adequate profitability by identifying deviations from plans that indicate possible problem areas. The focus may be on short-term performance or on longer-term indicators that match the organization's strategic thrust. The emphasis is on evaluating the subsidiary rather than the subsidiary manager, although the profitability of the foreign unit is an important ingredient in the managerial evaluation.[47]

Not all information exchange occurs via formalized reports. Within many MNEs, certain members of the corporate staff spend much of their time visiting subsidiaries. Although this attention may do much to alleviate misunderstandings, there are some inherent dangers if visits are not conducted properly. On the one hand, if corporate personnel visit the tropical subsidiaries only when there are blizzards at home, the personnel abroad may perceive the trips as mere boondoggles. On the other hand, if a subsidiary's managers offer too many social activities and not enough analysis of operations, corporate personnel may consider the trip a waste of time. Further, if visitors arrive only when the corporate level is upset about foreign operations, local managers may always be overdefensive.

Management versus subsidiary performance It is generally agreed that subsidiaries should be evaluated separately from their managers so that managers are not penalized for conditions and occurrences outside their control. For example, in Chapter 13 we discussed the capital budgeting decision as it affects the allocation of operations by country. Such decisons are typically made at headquarters and are based on the outlook for operations in the area in comparison with other areas, irrespective of managerial performance. For example, a company may decide not to expand in a country because of its slow growth and risky economic and political environment while simultaneously rewarding that country's managers for doing a good job under adverse conditions. Beyond this agreement, however, companies differ significantly in what they include in managerial performance evaluations. For example, some hold managers abroad responsible for gains or losses in currency translation and others do not.[48] Factors influencing whether gains or losses are within the managers' control include whether working capital management decisions are made at headquarters versus the subsidiary level and whether there are instruments in a particular country that allow for hedging against currency value changes.

Another uncontrollable area is when centralized decisions are made that will optimize the entire company's performance. A particular subsidiary may not do as well as it might if left to operate independently. In fact, the normal profit-center records may well obscure the importance the subsidiary has within the total corporate entity.

Cost and accounting comparability Different cost structures among subsidiaries may prevent a meaningful comparison of their operating results. For example, the ratio of direct labor to sales for a subsidiary in one country may reasonably be much

Companies should evaluate managers on things they can control, but there is disagreement concerning what is within their control.

It is hard to compare countries using standard operating ratios.

higher than that for a subsidiary in another country if the former has low labor and high capital costs in relation to the latter. Chapter 19 will show that different accounting practices also can create problems. Most MNEs keep one set of books that are consistent with home-country principles and another to meet local reporting requirements.

Evaluative measurement systems   Every evaluative measurement system has shortcomings when applied internationally. Consequently, one that relies on a number of different indicators may be preferable to one that relies too heavily on one indicator. Financial criteria tend to dominate the evaluation of foreign operations and their managers. Although many different criteria are used, the most important for evaluating both the operation and its management are budget compared with profit and budget compared with sales. In addition, operations are evaluated on the basis of financial performance. Many nonfinancial criteria also are employed. The only one commonly given much weight in evaluation of operations is market-share increase. However, several are important for evaluating managers, including market-share increase, quality control, and managers' relationship with host governments.[49]

One way to overcome the problems of evaluating performance is to look at a budget agreed upon by headquarters and subsidiary managers. Doing this can help the MNE differentiate between a subsidiary's worth and its management's performance. The budget should include the goals for each subsidiary that will help the MNE achieve an overall objective.

Planning information acquisitions   This discussion has centered on information needed to evaluate the performance of subsidiaries and their management. Although this information is crucial, corporate management requires additional data, which can be categorized as follows:

- Information generated for centralized coordination, such as subsidiary cash balances and needs
- Information relating to external conditions, such as analyses of local political and economic conditions
- Information for feedback from parent to local subsidiaries, such as R&D breakthroughs
- Lateral information between related subsidiaries
- Information for external reporting needs[50]

Because information needs are so broad, companies face three problems: the cost of information relative to its value, a glut of information that is redundant, and a glut of information that is irrelevant or contradictory. To cope, companies should periodically reevaluate the documents or services they use.

The corporate philosophy on ethics relates to control issues in that if it takes a normative view of global ethics, it will need a uniform policy on a host of ethical questions. This implies two steps, the decision of what the policy is and a control system to assure compliance. Neither step necessarily parallels the location of control for other aspects of operations. An implication of normativism is that if the company decides payments to government officials are unethical, decentralized control over local marketing to governmental agencies would need to be tempered to account for this constraint. Further, managers should not be held responsible for performance that suffers through pursuit of the ethical norm.

Should a global ethical operating norm be imposed by headquarters (usually home-country personnel) or developed as a composite of varied global viewpoints? If a company's foreign operations grow as a portion of its total operations or if the location of foreign operations shifts, such a composite of

ETHICAL DILEMMAS & SOCIAL RESPONSIBILITY

ethics may have to evolve. But having an agreed-upon ethical policy does not assure compliance. For example, Johnson & Johnson's strict "credo" did not prevent employees from shredding papers related to a governmental investigation on the marketing of a drug, Retin A.[51] The essential problem is that managers are prodded to improve their performance and, under such pressure, commit infractions of the ethical policy. A company taking a relativistic view will handle ethical questions on a decentralized basis, which may lead to repercussions elsewhere, such as bad publicity. For example, after exposés of kickbacks to purchasing agents in GM's German Opel operation, GM forced the resignation of three officers, fired more than a dozen, and transferred others. It also established normative policies affecting employees at home as well as abroad. These forbade the acceptance of meals, tickets to sporting events, and most other gifts from venders.[52]

As companies have expanded operations abroad, host-country societies, particularly LDCs, have become concerned about control that leads to an ever-increasing movement of management and technical functions to the home country, leaving the menial and low-skilled jobs in the LDCs. The critics recall colonial eras in which people from the colonies were forbidden responsible positions and were dependent on the colonial powers, which controlled their destinies.[53] These critics have been particularly concerned that almost all R&D is done in industrial countries.[54] This presents dilemmas for MNEs. There are some potent arguments for centralizing most R&D in home countries. These include the availability of many people to work directly for the company, the proximity to private research organizations and universities doing related work, and the general advantages of centralized authority in reducing duplication of efforts.

Recall that in the Nestlé case, R&D on new products was done in Switzerland to reduce duplication of efforts. Nestlé did allow country operations the freedom to conduct adaptive R&D but controlled this carefully by requiring headquarters approval of the adaptations. Thus even when a company allows adaptive or new product R&D to be carried out abroad, corporate management may substantially influence it. MNEs with considerable R&D outside their home country seldom allow the foreign operations complete autonomy. Corporate management may allocate budgets, approve plans, and offer suggestions. However, subsidiaries may offer substantial input for R&D conducted centrally.[55] Because of centralized R&D, even though adaptations may be allowed at the country level, LDCs may be continually at the mercy of interests in industrial countries.

Although LDCs complain that MNEs control practices from abroad, they nevertheless assume that a company's headquarters should have enough control to assure that its subsidiaries' operations have no dire effects locally. For example, Union Carbide delegated almost all decision making and day-to-day control to management of its joint venture in Bhopal, India; however, the Indian government blamed headquarters for the deaths resulting from a chemical leak. Although an Indian government agency was responsible for making safety inspections at the facility, it was widely known that the agency was inadequately staffed. This brought up ethical questions (as well as legal ones) concerning responsibility. The Indian government, which owned 49.1 percent of the joint venture, denied responsibility because of its lack of a controlling interest and its delegation of management to Union Carbide. Union Carbide, in turn, initially claimed that responsibility rested in the joint venture. The ethical question is whether headquarters should be responsible for actions taken at the subsidiary level and whether minority stockholders should be responsible for what majority stockholders do.

Many countries have passed or are considering legislation that directly or indirectly affects the international data flow.[56] These laws have been enacted for three main reasons:

1. There is concern about individual privacy; in particular, the development and transmission of personnel data might give the company an undue advantage over the individual.
2. Local jobs will be lost if data processing and analysis are done abroad, and resource transmission will occur without payment to the country that created the resource.
3. Corporate networks may be used to pirate military and commercial data to be sent abroad.

Although most MNEs consider data-flow restrictions to be more of a potential than an actual problem, certain regulations already create barriers for them.[57] For example, some regulations require local subsidiaries to maintain copies of and monitor anything they transmit. Consequently, companies are concerned about additional costs and about competitors' acquiring proprietary information. Further, it often is difficult for an MNE to move personnel records in order to maintain centralized records, which assist in making international transfers. For example, Burroughs was unable to transfer its personnel records from Germany to other locations. But, is it ethical for MNEs to transfer the best human resources from abroad to headquarters positions? Would it be ethical to exclude these managers from high-level positions?

Another problem is the compatibility of information needed by a subsidiary and by corporate management. Even when different subsidiaries are trying to solve similar problems, their information needs may differ vastly. Consequently, corporate management may be faced with having to compare unlike data or requiring different or additional data, collection of which may be expensive. Some companies allow diversity but send copies and analyses of data to centralized databanks. For many corporate needs, standardization of what data are collected is not necessary, but standardization of coding is so that centralized personnel can compare the performance of subsidiary projects and suggest more refined models for local use.

> **Local needs for and differences in data processing create problems of compatibility.**

Aside from the problem of lack of data or of coding uniformity, an obstacle to the on-time retrieval of comparable information is the diversity among countries in data processing, especially in terms of equipment and software. Uniformity of approach may be hampered for a company by substantial cost differences in personnel, hardware, and data communications, as well as legislative requirements to buy data-processing equipment, materials, and services locally.

> **Information centers may permit a choice between centralization or decentralization.**

With expanding multinational telecommunications and computer linkages, such as the World Wide Web and Internet, managers throughout the world can share information almost instantaneously. On the one hand, this may permit more centralization, since truly global implications of policies can be examined. On the other hand, managers in foreign locations may become more autonomous because they have more information at their disposal.

Control in Special Situations

Acquisitions

> **An acquired company usually does not achieve a complete fit with the existing organization.**

As noted in the Nestlé case, a policy of expansion through acquisition can create some specific control problems. For Nestlé, some of its U.S. acquisitions resulted in overlapping geographic responsibilities as well as new lines of business with which corporate management had no experience. Another problem is that the acquiring company's criteria for evaluating performance may be different from that of the acquired company's accustomed performance criteria. For example, U.S. executives tend to focus more on profitability than market potential; whereas the opposite is true in Korean companies.[58] Thus when a U.S. company acquires a Korean company, it must communicate and implement new performance priorities. Still another problem is that existing management in an acquired firm is probably accustomed to considerable autonomy.

Attempts to centralize certain decision-making procedures or to change operating methods may result in distrust, apprehension, and resistance to change. When the acquisition is in a foreign country, resistance may come not only from the personnel but also from governmental authorities. These authorities may use a variety of discretionary means to ensure that decision making remains vested within the country.

Shared Ownership

Ownership sharing limits the flexibility of corporate decision making. For example, Nestlé shares ownership with Coca-Cola in a joint venture for the production and sale of canned coffee and tea drinks, and Nestlé has less autonomy for this operation than for those it owns wholly. Nevertheless, there are administrative devices to gain control even with a minority equity interest. These include fragmenting the remaining ownership, stipulations that board decisions require more than a majority (thus giving veto power to minority stockholders), dividing equity into voting and non-voting stock, and side agreements on who will control decision making. A company also can maintain control over some asset needed by the operation abroad, such as a patent, a brand name, or a raw material. In fact, maintaining control is a motive for having separate licensing or franchising agreements or management contracts with a foreign subsidiary.

When joint ventures are with competitors, control issues transcend the joint venture itself. Employees within the rest of the organization may have been conditioned over many years to conspire against the other organization. For example, there was a history of intense competition between Boeing and Airbus; and U.S. automotive employees have even been openly antagonistic toward people parking foreign cars in their lots. Thus, the Boeing–Airbus venture to build an 800-seat aircraft and the GM–Toyota NUMMI venture have to contend with a complex set of relationships in which cooperation is expected with the competitor under certain, but not all, situations.[59]

Changes in Strategies

Most recent changes in strategies have involved movements from multidomestic to transnational or global operations. But regardless of the type change, there will be a need for new reporting relationships, changes in the type of information collected, and a need for new performance appraisal systems.[60] For example, when Citibank moved from a multidomestic to a regional strategy within Europe, it needed to introduce interdependence among operations and to collect results not only on a country-by-country basis, but also by product and customer.[61] In addition to the practical problems of changing systems, there are human resource problems as well.

It is difficult to remove control from operations when managers are accustomed to much autonomy. Within Europe, for example, many U.S. companies owned very independent operations for decades in the United Kingdom, France, and Germany. These companies often have faced difficult obstacles when integrating these operations because the country managers perceive that integration brings personal and operating disadvantages. Managers who fear losses through a changed strategy continue to guard their autonomy and functional specialties and maintain existing allegiances.

Legal Structures

Branch versus Subsidiary

When establishing a foreign operation, a company often must decide between making that operation a branch or a subsidiary. A foreign branch is a foreign operation not legally separate from the parent company; therefore, branch operations are possible only if the parent holds 100-percent ownership. A subsidiary, however, is an FDI that is legally a separate company, even if the parent owns all of the voting stock. Because a subsidiary is legally separate, it is generally concluded that liability is limited to the assets of the subsidiary. Creditors or winners of legal suits therefore do not usually have access to other resources owned by the parent. This concept of limited liability is a major factor in the choice of the subsidiary form; otherwise, claims against a company for its actions in one country could be settled by courts in another. However, there is some evidence that the concept of limited liability will not suffice in future liability disputes. For example, after the Bhopal accident that killed more than a thousand people through a chemical leak, Union Carbide had to settle with the Indian government for damages in excess of the value of Union Carbide's 50.9-percent investment in the Indian joint venture.[62]

Because subsidiaries are separate companies, a question arises concerning which decisions the parent may be allowed to make. Generally, this does not present a problem. However, some court cases have ruled that companies were conspiring to prevent competition when the parent dictated which markets its subsidiary could serve. Another factor related to control is public disclosure. Generally, the greater the control vested by the owners, the greater the secrecy that can be maintained. In this respect, branches are usually subject to less public disclosure because they are not covered by tight local corporate restrictions.

From these examples, it should be clear that there are conflicting control advantages to either the branch or the subsidiary form. Each form also has different tax advantages and implications and may have different initiation and operating costs as well as abilities to raise capital.

Types of Subsidiaries

A company establishing a subsidiary in a foreign country usually can choose from a number of alternative legal forms. There are too many forms to list in detail in this book; however, some distinctions between them are worth mentioning. In addition to differences in liability, forms vary in terms of the following:

- Ability to transfer ownership
- Number of stockholders required
- Percentage of foreigners who can serve on the board of directors
- Amount of required public disclosure
- Whether equity may be acquired by noncapital contributions, such as goodwill

- Types of businesses (products) that are eligible
- Minimum capital required

Before making a decision, an MNE should analyze all of these differences in terms of its corporate objectives.

COUNTERVAILING FORCES

In a sense, this whole chapter is about countervailing forces. At the forefront is the complex balancing of globally integrated advantages with country-specific needs. On the one hand, technological factors and government-to-government agreements are favoring more global integration and standardization. On the other hand, the legal, cultural, economic, and political differences in norms among countries are not about to be eliminated. Therefore, the balancing act will continue. At the same time, companies are experimenting with mechanisms to handle these opposing forces. Foremost is the use of transnational strategies and various mechanisms to share multiple viewpoints and experiences from home and host countries, different functions, and different product groups. In addition, there are opposing forces for using one organizational structure versus another, centralizing versus decentralizing decision making, and choosing one legal operating form versus another. These alternatives are further complicated by ever-changing individual and operating-unit capabilities and the countervailing needs for the most rapid and best-informed decisions. No solution is without drawbacks; thus we are bound to see experimental changes as companies grapple with the continued problem. The prevailing question is, "How can we move our organization so that international operations best serve strategic intent?"

LOOKING TO THE FUTURE

As overseas sales and profits as a percentage of total sales and profits increase, there is likely to be more headquarters attention paid to foreign operations. Similarly, there will be pressures to centralize control in order to deal with the growing number of global competitors and the more homogenized needs of global consumers. The need for centralization will present more challenges for MNEs in controlling their global operations.

One challenge involves management's position in foreign facilities, where managers may see the erosion of their autonomy over marketing, production, and financial decisions. To keep those managers motivated, the company may need to include more nationalities on boards of directors and use cross-national management teams to develop practices that are globally rather than nationally oriented. But with such cross-national fertilization comes the risk of clashes between cultural traditions. For example, in work teams at Ericsson Telecom, Americans and Swedes quickly became frustrated with each other over cultural norms the two groups had developed as children. The Swedes had grown up being told that silence is golden and a good job will be recognized, whereas the Americans had learned early that class participation would improve their grades and they needed to promote themselves. The Americans viewed the Swedes as overly detached; the Swedes viewed the Americans as overly aggressive.[63] The lesson is that the human side of the organization may lag behind the need for control from a technical standpoint.

A second challenge for MNEs is a consequence of their size. A number of them already have sales larger than many countries' GDPs. To manage such organizations may require even greater decentralization and more horizontal communication among subsidiaries in different countries that are mutually dependent on parts, products, and resources. This mutual dependence among subsidiaries may in turn require new heterarchical relationships within the organizational structure.

A third challenge concerns information. On the one hand, centralized control may become easier because of faster access to information from abroad. On the other hand, this faster access may be somewhat negated by companies' limited abilities to process greater amounts of information, particularly as they increase their geographic spread of activities, product diversity, and competitive rivalries.

WEB CONNECTION
Check out our home page for links to the World Wide Web on the issue of structures of firms operating globally.

Summary

- Control is more difficult internationally because of the geographic and cultural distances separating countries, the need to operate differently among countries, the larger number of uncontrollables abroad, and the higher uncertainty resulting from rapid change in the international environment and problems in gathering reliable data in many places.

- Good planning should include environmental analysis, a long-range strategy, operating plans, and contingency strategies with inputs from both top-level and subsidiary managers.

- As a company develops international business activities, the corporate structure must include a means by which foreign operations report. The more important the foreign operations, the higher up in the hierarchy they should report.

- Whether a company separates or integrates international activities, it usually needs to develop some means by which to prevent costly duplication of efforts, to ensure that headquarters managers do not withhold the best resources from the international operations, and to include insights from anywhere in the organization that can benefit performance.

- The level at which decisions are made should depend on the relative competence of individuals, the expediency needs in relation to decision quality, and the effects the decisions will have on global and national performance.

- Even though worldwide uniformity of policies and centralization of decision making may not be best for an individual operation, overall company gains may be more than enough to overcome the individual country losses. When top management prevents subsidiaries' managers from doing their best job, however, there may be negative consequences for employee morale.

- Transnational strategies attempt to utilize competencies from everywhere in the worldwide organization.

- Many critics in LDCs argue that centralization of decision making in MNEs continues LDCs' historical dependency on industrial countries. These critics are pressuring for increased decentralization of decision making.

- The corporate culture constitutes an implicit control mechanism. It is more difficult to establish and maintain in MNEs because values differ among countries, but bringing managers together enhances the common culture.

- Timely reports are essential for control so that resources can be allocated properly, plans can be corrected, and personnel can be evaluated and rewarded.

- International reporting systems are similar to those used domestically because home-country management is familiar with them and because uniformity makes it easier to compare different operations.

- The evaluation of subsidiaries and the evaluation of their managers are separate processes; however, some of the same inputs, including financial and nonfinancial criteria, may be used for both.

- Companies sometimes find it difficult to get timely and comparable reports from foreign operating units in part because of incompatibility of data-processing systems among countries and restrictions placed on the cross-national flow of data.

- Special control problems arise for acquired operations, operations that have historical autonomy, and operations that are not wholly owned. The legal status of foreign operations may also raise control problems.

Case
GE's Tungsram Acquisition[*]

General Electric (GE), headquartered in the United States, was ranked in 1996 as the world's largest public company in terms of market capitalization. GE is organized into twelve major businesses, of which GE Lighting (GEL) has annual sales of about $3 billion. Philips Lighting, a unit of the Dutch-based Philips, and Osram, a subsidiary of the German-based Siemens, have sales about equal to those of GEL, and the three companies collectively control about 75 percent of the world market for lighting.

Since the late 1980s, GEL has included global expansion as part of its fundamental strategy because of comparative market growth expectations, antitrust inhibitions to its U.S. growth, and U.S. lighting acquisitions by Philips (Westinghouse) and Osram (Sylvania). The most important of GEL's global expansions was its acquisition of the Hungarian firm, Tungsram, that country's largest manufacturing company. From a control standpoint, GEL has been challenged to improve the performance of Tungsram and to build a global operating strategy that will encompass Tungsram and other foreign operations effectively. To meet these challenges, GEL has relied on corporate reorganization, restructuring of operations (including R&D), infusion of GE's corporate culture, and implementation of a standardized reporting system.

Tungsram

Tungsram, founded in 1896, is the world's third oldest of the major lighting companies, after only GE and Philips. The company has developed important lighting source innovations and has traditionally sold most of its production outside of Hungary. Its market position eroded during the closing era of communist rule in Hungary; nevertheless, by the late 1980s, it still ranked fifth among Europe's light source manufacturers and held about 7 percent of the European market share.

In 1987, the Hungarian government hired the consulting company, Arthur D. Little (ADL), to assess and advise on Tungsram. ADL concluded that Tungsram's cost levels were too high and its exploitation of marketing opportunities too low. Further, it was investing only 1 to 2 percent of sales as compared with 4 to 6 percent for competitors, who were also spending a higher share of sales on R&D. Nevertheless, ADL concluded that Tungsram could be turned around with restructuring help from a foreign investor who could provide capital, production technology, and management know-how.

In 1990, GE acquired 50 percent plus one share of Tungsram for $150 million. Over the next five years GE invested another $450 million, ballooning its ownership to practically 100 percent and making it the largest U.S. foreign investment through 1995 in Central and Eastern Europe.

[*]This case has been condensed by John D. Daniels from the original case by Professors Vincent A. Mabert and Paul Marer, both from the School of Business, Indiana University. It is used with permission. For a more complete discussion of the experiences in Hungary see Paul Marer and Vincent Mabert, "GE Acquires and Restructures Tungsram: The First Six Years (1990–1995)," in OECD, *Trends and Policies in Privatisation*, Vol. 111, No. 1 (Paris: OECD, 1996), pp. 149–185.

Corporate Reorganization

During the early 1990s, GEL made other foreign acquisitions, such as Thorn in the United Kingdom and Luma in Sweden. (See Map 15.2.) GEL managed these acquisitions on a multidomestic basis because it believed each country's operations differed significantly in terms of R&D, production capability, product structure, and market characteristics. However, in 1992, GE decided to move rapidly toward more control at either the regional or global level. GE reasoned that more centralization, regionally or globally, would facilitate the transfer of experience from one subsidiary to another, especially through the standardization of operations, functions, and products. In addition, GE wanted to gain a common image within and among its different product groups so that it could introduce new products more effectively into foreign markets. GEL established a European headquarters in London (GEL-London), and Tungsram lost much of the autonomy it had enjoyed until then.

GEL-London decided (a) to introduce GE brand light bulbs as a high-priced quality brand into Europe by using the yellow and blue GE logo, which was well known and carried a quality image in the United States, and (b) to continue selling under the Tungsram name, but to position Tungsram as a low-priced (value for money) brand to be promoted less than the GE brand. This created two problems. First, Europeans were unfamiliar with GE, did not consider the logo/packaging to be attractive, and had trouble reading the shapes of the letters in the logo. GE had to design a new logo for Europe. Second, although GEL-London felt the positioning of Tungsram at the low end of the market was consistent with the quality image of former Eastern bloc products, this has been a sensitive issue among Hungarians, who are proud of Tungsram's century-old tradition, scientific achievements,

**Map 15.2
GE Lighting
Subsidiaries and
Affiliates Around
the Globe, 1994**

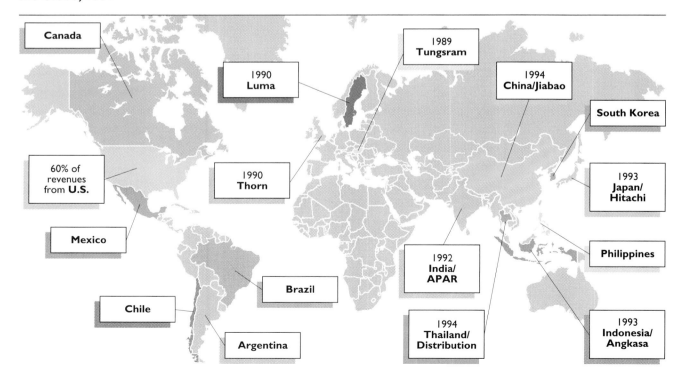

global reach, and name recognition in Europe. In 1994, about 10 percent of Tungsram's sales were in Hungary and other parts of Central and Eastern Europe, between 15 and 20 percent in the United States (under both the Tungsram and GE label), about 40 percent in Western Europe, and 30 to 35 percent in the Middle East and Asia.

Restructuring

Once the Hungarian government decided to privatize Tungsram and to allow foreign investors to bid on ownership, GE had to move fast. A closer audit after acquisition showed that many costly changes were necessary to make Tungsram competitive. For example, Tungsram's labor productivity was low due to overstaffing, bureaucratic administrative structures, and insufficient automation; thus GE reduced the labor force from nearly 20,000 in early 1990 to about 9,500 in 1993, mainly through early retirement, job relocation, voluntary separation, and a hiring freeze. The production facilities could not maintain the quality standards demanded in Western markets. Thus GE had to upgrade the telecommunication system; acquire personal computers and software; refurbish buildings; buy new equipment; and spend to improve on health, safety, and environmental standards. (Capital outlays were increased to about 10 percent of sales.) Further, the company had to write off obsolete inventories and uncollectible Soviet debts and eliminate some noncore businesses.

GEL's acquisitions resulted in R&D operations scattered among different countries. With the move away from multidomestic practices, GEL consolidated its European R&D in Hungary. By 1995, about half of GEL's professional R&D resided in Hungary and about half in the United States. Of the eight major GEL research projects under way worldwide, four were located in Hungary. Decisions on R&D priorities within GE are made centrally by a team representing all of GE's major business units. Once GEL gains approval from this team for its projects, it appoints a program manager for each project. The program manager chooses team members from a large "talent pool" located in different countries and made up of functional specialists, such as marketing and accounting personnel, as well as scientists and engineers. Thus task-oriented teams are formed and disbanded as needs change. The entire talent pool is kept informed of planned programs and projects. Individuals are encouraged to volunteer to serve as team members, but the selection is up to the program manager. Individuals who, over a period of time, are not selected to serve as team members are demoted and encouraged to leave the company. What matters is not only technical competence, but also initiative, a business sense, and the ability and willingness to work constructively with others.

Culture as Control

GE has long had a strong corporate culture, which helps unify behavior among its personnel. This culture is partially based on U.S. cultural norms, such as pride and optimism, and partially on the styles and practices of GE's top managers, such as the use of massive layoffs and quick sale of underperforming businesses.

During 1990–1991, GEL proceeded cautiously with changing the inherited corporate culture at Tungsram. One reason was GE's unfavorable experiences in France after its 1988 acquisition of a medical equipment manufacturer. GE had tried quickly to integrate the manufacturer into its U.S. division and to impose its corporate culture on the French facility. The experiment met strong resistance and prompted unfavorable publicity. However, in 1992, following the appointment of a new CEO at Tungsram, GEL decided to introduce the GE corporate culture at Tungsram more decisively and quickly. The new CEO was an American with much experience in managing GE subsidiaries abroad; thus GEL expected his managerial style and practices to reflect GE's headquarters' norm. Further, GE translated a 50-page manual, *Integrity: Code of Conduct in the Workplace,* into Hungarian and required all Tungsram employees (as it does in the United States) to pledge observance of its contents. The manual prescribes behavior to try to eliminate corruption, instructs that one must deal fairly with co-workers (regardless of nationality, gender, or creed), and requires absolute fairness in dealing with competitors and suppliers.

Many aspects of GE's culture are almost opposite to those that existed at Tungsram. For example, the norm in the United States is to be inner-directed—believing that it is up to each individual to succeed and that outside constraints can be overcome if only one tries hard enough. However, the norm in Hungary (perhaps brought about by long periods of foreign domination when there was no self-determination) is to be outer-directed— believing that uncontrollable outside forces, rather than the will of the individual, are decisive in determining outcomes. In addition, GE's use of layoffs and selloffs to improve performance contrasts sharply with the experience at Tungsram, where there is a history of paternalism. For example, from the start many Tungsram employees lived in company housing and vacationed at company resorts. Their children attended company schools. During evenings and weekends employees and their families rooted for Tungsram sport teams. The best way to get a job at Tungsram was to be recommended by a current employee; however, once employed, satisfactory work performance led to lifetime job security. Further, even the manual contradicted Hungarian norms. Because of foreign rule, Hungarians learned to survive by pretending to accept foreign mandates, which they circumvented while avoiding direct confrontation. For example, under communist rule—during which there was no legal certainty, standards were not absolute, and power was exercised arbitrarily—people became masters of finding back-door approaches to solving problems. Personal relationships and reciprocal favors were much more important than formal rules. Thus GE has tried to enforce a universal code in a culture that believes in ethical relativism.

On the one hand, GE is quite satisfied with what it has accomplished in the transfer of its corporate culture to Hungary. Tungsram's CEO said that GE is not seeking a complete eradication of cultural differences, but is working toward a degree of homogeneity that is like "a pea soup, not a stew." Several aspects of GE's efforts to bind together the separate national and corporate cultures have been those common to many multinationals, such as extensive training in language and business skills and the rotation of employees among geographic locations. On the other hand, the leader of the union at Tungsram said, "GE's [corporate] strategy is to make everyone insecure. The owner assesses us from the United States, where the structure of the economy and industrial relations are different. GE tries to employ here overseas methods, which causes conflict." Further, a *Financial Times* article said, "By comparison with some multinationals, which try to cultivate a reputation for cultural sensitivity, GE risks being accused of arrogance in its approach. . . . Those employees who find [this] difficult tend to leave."

Control by Reports

Under central planning, costs and prices were not market-determined. Enterprises were state-owned, faced no domestic competition, and could not go bankrupt. The purpose of the reporting system was to check plan fulfillment, not to control costs or to improve profits. Under GE, all units must prepare standard reports on just about all aspects of costs and operations. Everyone faces a great deal of pressure to improve on previous performance. Benchmarking—comparing performance indicators at one plant with those achieved by other plants that manufacture similar products, or with industry standards—has become an important tool of management control.

Improvement, then, has become the key word at Tungsram. Reducing labor, inventory, and scrap costs are critical to profitability. Table 15.1 shows portions of reports on a number of indicators for Tungsram's Nagykanizsa plant, the largest light-source manufacturing facility in the world. Although productivity has improved, GEL's U.S.-based production facilities were still more productive after year four, with three to four times the output per employee compared to Tungsram plants. Further, although the percentage of scrap has been reduced, scrap rates in U.S. plants were below those at the Nagykanizsa plant.

Based on reports of performance, the president of GEL-Europe set eleven specific objectives for year five in the Nagykanizsa plant, such as improving productivity by 6 percent and implementing a comprehensive supplier evaluation program. At the same time, the manager of that plant desired to improve relations with the workforce, which he thought was essential for longer term performance. The union took the position that its pay levels were not keeping up with those in other Hungarian enterprises. And even though Tungsram workers received slightly higher pay, they were expected to work much harder than people in comparable jobs did elsewhere in Hungary. The plant manager was not exactly sure whether and how he would accomplish all that his superiors expected.

Table 15.1
Tungsram: Selected Operational Data, 1990–1994

	1990	1991	1992	1993	1994
Work force (Dec.)	15,600	13,300	10,400	9,400	10,000
Production (mil PCS)	453.6	513.3	483.9	464.9	482.1
Inventory					
Raw and in-process (US$ mil)	31	25	23	21	N/A
Days supply	40	38	32	26	N/A
Finished good - Dec. (US$ mil)	17.9	17.4	28.3	24.7	N/A
Net sales of Tungsram					
and affiliates (bil HUF)	22.0	26.5	30.1	35.5	N/A
Profits/Losses (US$ mil)	-23	-15	-145	-60	50

Questions

1. After its acquisition by GE, Tungsram has gone through a change in structure and culture. What is meant by *structure* and *culture*?

2. Define *national* and *corporate cultures*. How did GE's and Tungsram's cultures differ? How did GE attempt to use its culture as a control mechanism in Hungary and elsewhere?

3. What were the pros and cons in 1992 of GEL's European operations remaining multidomestic versus becoming regional or global? What did GE decide and how did the decision affect its ability to control its subsidiaries?

4. Suppose that it is January 1996 and that you are a Hungarian (a) manager of one of Tungsram's plants in Hungary; (b) blue-collar worker employed at the plant in Nagykanizsa; (c) white-collar worker at Nagykanizsa laid off after 23 years of service; or (d) government official specializing in economic issues. What would be your thoughts about the sale of Tungsram to GE?

5. In what ways does GE attempt to gain synergy among its operations in different countries and among its different businesses?

6. What can/should GEL-Europe do to help operating units reach their objectives?

Chapter Notes

1. Data for the case were taken from "Nestlé Centralizing to Win a Bigger Payoff from the U.S.," *Business Week*, February 2, 1981, pp. 56–58; "Nestlé—At Home Abroad: An Interview with Pierre Liotard-Vogt," *Harvard Business Review*, November 1976, pp. 80–88; Robert Ball, "A Shopkeeper Shakes Up Nestlé," *Fortune*, December 27, 1982, pp. 103–106; Graham Turner, "Inside Europe's Giant Companies: Nestlé Finds a Better Formula," *Long Range Planning*, Vol. 19, No. 3, June 1986, pp. 12–19; Mark Alpert and Aimety Dunlap Smith, "Nestlé Shows How to Gobble Markets," *Fortune*, January 16, 1989, pp. 74–78; Zachary Schiller and Lois Therrien, "Nestlé's Crunch in the U.S.," *Business Week*, December 24, 1990, pp. 24–25; John Templeman, Stewart Toy, and Dave Lindorff, "Nestlé: A Giant in a Hurry," *Business Week*, March 22, 1993, pp. 50–54; Sid Astbury, "Food Maker Applies Lessons Learned from Japan," *Asian Business*, Vol. 29, No. 6, June 1993, p. 12; "Nestlé Ranked Largest Global Investor," *Transnationals*, Vol. 8, No. 1, March 1996, p. 12; Greg Steinmetz and Tara Parker-Pope, "All Over the Map," *Wall Street Journal*, September 26, 1996, p. R4; Barry B. Burr, "Limits for Business and Government," *Pensions and Investments*, October 17, 1994, p. 10; Helmut Maucher, *Leadership in Action*, (New York: McGraw-Hill, 1994); Roderick Orem and Ian Rodger, "Nestlé Prepares for Chief's Retirement by Naming Heir,"

Financial Times, November 23, 1995, p. 15; and various company reports.

2. Ahn Mi-young, Sid Astbury, David Hulme, Ian Jarrett, and Jonathan Sikes, "Why HQ Should Relax Its Grip," *Asian Business*, Vol. 30, No. 6, June 1994, pp. 46–48.

3. John Gapper and Nicholas Denton, "The Barings Report," *Financial Times*, October 18, 1995, p. 8; Sara Calian, "Rogue Trader Says Deceiving Barings Wasn't Difficult, 'Star' Status Helped," *Wall Street Journal*, February 13, 1996, p. A10; and Paul Stonham, "Whatever Happened At Barings? Part One: The Lure of Derivatives and Collapse," *European Management Journal*, Vol. 14, No. 2, April 1996, pp. 167–175.

4. William R. Fannin and Arvin F. Rodrigues, "National or Global?—Control vs. Flexibility," *Long Range Planning*, Vol. 19, No. 5, October 1986, pp. 84–88.

5. Gary Hamel and C. K. Prahalad, "Strategic Intent," *Harvard Business Review*, May–June 1989, pp. 63–76.

6. Christopher Carr, "Global, National and Resource-Based Strategies: An Examination of Strategic Choice and Performance in the Vehicle Components Industry," *Strategic Management Journal*, Vol. 14, 1993, pp. 551–568.

7. "Dusting the Opposition," *The Economist*, Vol. 335, No. 7912, April 29, 1995, p. 71.

8. Ian Turner, "Management International Organizations: Lessons from the Field," *European Management Journal*, Vol. 12, No. 4, December 1994, pp. 417–431.

9. Part of the explanation is adapted from George S. Yip, *Total Global Strategy: Managing for Worldwide Competitive Advantage* (Englewood Cliffs, NJ: Prentice-Hall, 1992).

10. For two discussions of the importance of implementation and the need to revise plans, see William G. Egelhoff, "Great Strategy or Great Strategy Implementation—Two Ways of Competing in Global Markets," *Sloan Management Review*, Winter 1993, pp. 37–50; and Lawrence Hrebeniak, "Implementing Global Strategies," *European Management Journal*, December 1992, pp. 392–403.

11. F. A. Maljers, "Strategic Planning and Intuition in Unilever," *Long Range Planning*, Vol. 23, No. 2, 1990, pp. 63–68.

12. B. Mascarenhas, "Coping with Uncertainty in International Business," *Journal of International Business Studies*, Fall 1982, pp. 87–98; Egelhoff, loc. cit.

13. G. S. Yip, P. M. Loewe, and M. Y. Yoshino, "How to Take Your Company to the Global Market," *Columbia Journal of World Business*, Winter 1988, pp. 37–48.

14. We wish to acknowledge Allen Morrison for supplying examples of companies he has found in his research that are using the different types of structures. See K. Roth, D. Schweiger, and A. J. Morrison, "Global Strategy Implementation at the Business Unit Level: Operational Capabilities and Administrative Mechanisms," *Journal of International Business Studies*, Vol. 22, No. 3, Third Quarter 1991, pp. 369–402.

15. W. G. Egelhoff, "Strategy and Structure in Multinational Corporations: An Information Processing Approach," *Administrative Science Quarterly,* Vol. 27, 1982, pp. 435–458; John D. Daniels, Robert A. Pitts, and Marietta J. Tretter, "Strategy and Structure of U.S. Multinationals: An Exploratory Study," *Academy of Management Journal,* Vol. 27, No. 2, June 1984, pp. 292–307; and Mohammed M. Habib and Bart Victor, "Strategy, Structure, and Performance of U.S. Manufacturing and Service MNCs: A Comparative Analysis," *Strategic Management Journal,* Vol. 12, 1991, pp. 589–606.

16. Paul Ingrassia and Jacqueline Mitchell, "Ford to Realign With a System of Global Chiefs," *Wall Street Journal,* March 31, 1994, p. A3.

17. Oscar Suris, "Ford to Further Revamp Global Auto Operations," *Wall Street Journal,* October 11, 1996, p. A3.

18. Gapper and Denton, loc. cit.

19. "The Discreet Charm of the Multicultural Multinational," *The Economist,* July 30, 1994, pp. 57–58.

20. Robert Frank, "Excitement Brews in Beverage Industry As Enrico's Rise at PepsiCo Stirs Market," *Wall Street Journal,* February 26, 1996, p. B8.

21. Ian D. Turner, "Strategy and Organization," *Management Update: Supplement to the Journal of General Management,* Summer 1989, pp. 1–8; and Gunnar Hedlund, "The Hypermodern MNC—A Hetarchy?" *Human Resource Management,* Spring 1986, pp. 9–35.

22. James R. Houghton, "A Chairman Reflects: The Age of the Hierarchy Is Over," *New York Times,* September 24, 1989, p. C2.

23. Vertical versus horizontal *keiretsus* are discussed in Kosaku Yoshida, "New Economic Principles in America—Competition and Cooperation," *Columbia Journal of World Business,* Winter 1992, pp. 31–44.

24. William J. Holstein, James Treece, Stan Crock, and Larry Armstrong, "Mighty Mitsubishi Is on the Move," *Business Week,* September 24, 1990, pp. 98–107.

25. Michael L. Gerlach, "The Japanese Corporate Network: A Blockmodel Analysis," *Administrative Science Quarterly,* March 1992, pp. 105–139.

26. Kiyohiko Ito and Elizabeth L. Rose, "The Genealogical Structure of Japanese Firms: Parent-Subsidiary Relationships," *Strategic Management Journal,* Vol. 15, 1994, pp. 35–51; and Michael Scott Morton, "Emerging Organizational Forms: Work and Organization in the 21st Century," *European Management Journal,* Vol. 13, No. 4, December 1995, pp. 339–345.

27. Joann S. Lublin, "Firms Ship Unit Headquarters Abroad," *Wall Street Journal,* December 9, 1992, p. B1; and Pervez Ghauri, "New Structures in MNCs Based in Small Countries: A Network Approach," *European Management Journal,* Vol. 10, No. 3, September 1992, pp. 357–364.

28. Edward E. Lucente, *Managing a Global Enterprise* (Pittsburgh: Carnegie Bosch Institute for Applied Studies in International Management, 1993), Working paper 94–2.

29. Yves Doz and C. K. Prahalad, "Controlled Variety: A Challenge for Human Resource Management in the MNC," *Human Resource Management,* Vol. 25, No. 1, Spring 1986, p. 57.

30. For a detailed examination of the characteristics of a transnational strategy, see Christopher A. Bartlett and Sumantra Ghoshal, *Managing Across Borders* (Boston: Harvard Business School Press, 1989).

31. Christopher A. Bartlett and Sumantra Ghoshal, "Tap Your Subsidiaries for Global Reach," *Harvard Business Review,* Vol. 64, No. 6, November–December 1986, pp. 87–94.

32. Christopher A. Bartlett and Sumantra Ghoshal, "Beyond the M-Form: Toward a Managerial Theory of the Firm," *Strategic Management Journal,* Vol. 14, 1993, pp. 23–46.

33. Mary Ackenhusen, Daniel Muzyka, and Neil Churchill, "Restructuring 3M for an Integrated Europe: Implementing the Change," *European Management Journal,* Vol. 14, No. 2, 1996, pp. 151–159.

34. "Ford's Reorganization," *The Economist,* January 7, 1995, pp. 52–53.

35. James McCalman, "Lateral Hierarchy: The Case of Cross-Cultural Management Teams," *European Management Journal,* Vol. 14, No. 5, 1996, pp. 509–517.

36. Donna G. Goehle, *Decision Making in Multinational Corporations* (Ann Arbor, Mich.: University Research Press, 1980).

37. W. Chan Kim and Renée A. Mauborgne, "Making Global Strategies Work," *Sloan Management Review,* Spring 1993, pp. 11–28.

38. Stephen D. Moore, "Pfizer's English Site is Research Boon, Developing Some of Firm's Major Drugs," *Wall Street Journal,* September 6, 1996, p. B8.

39. Stephen Baker, Kevin Kelly, Robert D. Hof, and William J. Holstein, "Mini-Nationals Are Making Maximum Impact," *Business Week,* September 6, 1993, pp. 66–69.

40. Nitin Nohria and Sumantra Ghoshal, "Differentiated Fit and Shared Values: Alternatives for Managing Headquarters-Subsidiary Relations," *Strategic Management Journal,* Vol. 15, July 1994, pp. 491–502.

41. See B. R. Balliga and A. M. Jeager, "Multinational Corporations: Control Systems and Delegation Issues," *Journal of International Business Studies,* Vol. 15, No. 2, Summer 1984, pp. 25–40; and Vladimir Pucik and Jan Hack Katz, "Information Control, and Human Resource Management in Multinational Firms," *Human Resource Management,* Vol. 25, No. 1, Spring 1986, pp. 121–132.

42. Nohria and Ghoshal, loc. cit.

43. Templeman et al., loc. cit.; and "The Glamour of Gaijins," *The Economist,* September 21, 1991, p. 80.

44. Samir M. Youssef, "Contextual Factors Influencing Control Strategy of Multinational Corporations," *Academy of Management Journal,* March 1975, pp. 136–145.

45. A. B. Sim, "Decentralized Management of Subsidiaries and Their Performance," *Management International Review,* No. 2, 1977, pp. 47–49.

46. C. A. Bartlett, "MNCs: Get off the Reorganization Merry-Go-Round," *Harvard Business Review,* Vol. 61, No. 2, 1983, pp. 138–146; and Robert A. Pitts and John D. Daniels, "Aftermath of the Matrix Mania," *Columbia Journal of World Business,* Vol. 19, No. 2, Summer 1984, pp. 48–54.

47. Frederick D. S. Choi and I. James Czechowicz, "Assessing Foreign Subsidiary Performance: A Multinational Comparison," *Management International Review,* Vol. 23, No. 4, 1983, p. 15.

48. Ibid., pp. 18–20.

49. Ibid., pp. 16–17.

50. George M. Scott, *An Introduction to Financial Control and Reporting in Multinational Enterprises* (Austin: Bureau of Business Research, Graduate School of Business, University of Texas at Austin, 1973), pp. 77–79.

51. "Good Grief," *The Economist,* Vol. 335, No. 7909, April 8, 1995, p. 57.

52. David Sedgwick, "GM's New Ethics Code Raises Anxiety Levels," *Crain's Small Business–Chicago,* September 1, 1996.

53. Among the many treatments of this subject are Osvaldo Sunkel, "Big Business and 'Dependencia': A Latin American View," *Foreign Affairs,* April 1972, pp. 517–531; Benjamin J. Cohen, *The Question of Imperialism—The Political Economy of Dominance and Dependence* (New York: Basic Books, 1973); and Peter Smith Ring, Stefanie Ann Lenway, and Michelle Govekar, "Management of the Political Imperative in International Business," *Strategic Management Journal,* Vol. 11, 1990, pp. 141–151.

54. Robert D. Pearce and Satwinder Singh, "Internationalisation of Research and Development Among the World's Leading Enterprises," No. 157 (Reading, England: University of Reading Discussion Papers in International Investment and Business Studies, November 1991).

55. William A. Fischer and Jack N. Behrman, "The Coordination of Foreign R&D Activities by Transnational Corporations," *Journal of International Business Studies,* Winter 1979, pp. 28–35.

56. Laura B. Pincus and James A. Belohlav, "Legal Issues in Multinational Business Strategy: To Play the Game, You Have to Know the Rules," *Academy of Management Executive,* Vol. 10, No. 3, 1996, pp. 52–61.

57. M. J. Kane and David A. Ricks, "Is Transnational Data Flow Regulation a Problem?" *Journal of International Business Studies,* Vol. 19, No. 3, 1988, pp. 477–483; and Rakesh B. Sambharya and Arvind Phatak, "The Effect of Transborder Data Flow Restrictions on American Multinational Corporations," *Management International Review,* Vol. 30, No. 3, 1990, pp. 267–289.

58. Michael A. Hitt, Beverly B. Tyler, Camilla Hardee, and Daewoo Park, "Understanding Strategic Intent in the Global Marketplace," *Academy of Management Executive,* Vol. 9, No. 2, 1995, pp. 12–19.

59. For a discussion of the difficulties of bringing competitors together, see John Hunt, *Structural and Organizational Changes in Global Firms* (Pittsburgh: Carnegie Bosch Institute for Applied Studies in International Management, 1993), Working paper 94-4.

60. Mahmoud Ezzamel, Simon Lilley, and Hugh Willmott, "The 'New Organization' and the 'New Managerial Work,'" *European Management Journal,* Vol. 12, No. 4, 1994, pp. 454–461.

61. Thomas W. Malnight, "The Transition from Decentralized to Network-Based MNC Structures: An Evolutionary Perspective," *Journal of International Business Studies,* Vol. 27, No. 1, First Quarter 1996, pp. 43–65.

62. Sanjoy Hazarika, "Bhopal Payments Set at $470 Million for Union Carbide," *New York Times,* February 15, 1989, p. 1+; and Scott McMurray, "India's High Court Upholds Settlement Paid by Carbide in Bhopal Gas Leak," *Wall Street Journal,* October 4, 1991, p. B12.

63. Michael Maccoby, *Sweden at the Edge: Lessons for American and Swedish Managers* (Philadelphia: University of Pennsylvania Press, 1991).

7 Operations: Managing Business Functions Internationally

Similar goods and services increasingly reach consumers in all parts of the world. In terms of trade and foreign investment, some of the most internationally dependent countries are those in Europe. Here advertisements for U.S., Australian, and Japanese companies vie for attention at a busy intersection (Piccadilly Circus) in the United Kingdom. The photo is set against a backdrop of a Morris embroidered panel from about 1900.

Chapter 16

Marketing

May both seller and buyer
see the benefit.
—Turkish Proverb

Objectives

- To introduce techniques for assessing market sizes for given countries

- To describe a range of product policies and the circumstances in which they are appropriate

- To contrast practices of standardized versus differentiated marketing programs for each country in which sales are made

- To emphasize how environmental differences complicate the management of marketing worldwide

- To discuss the major international considerations within each of the marketing functions: product, pricing, promotion, branding, and distribution

Case
Marks & Spencer[1]

Britain has often been called a country of shopkeepers, and Marks & Spencer (M & S) is undoubtedly the shopkeeping leader. With nearly 300 stores in the United Kingdom, M & S is that country's largest retailer; it holds 17 percent of the UK clothing market. Its Marble Arch store in London is in the *Guinness Book of World Records* as the store that takes in more revenue per square foot than any other in the world. Soft goods (clothes and household textiles) account for about 58 percent of the company's sales, and food lines account for about 42 percent.

How has M & S become so successful in the British market? Since the company's founding in 1884, its philosophy has been to sell durable merchandise at a moderate price. M & S has merchandise made to its specifications. It uses its vast buying power to induce producers to make cost-cutting investments and to compete for its business by offering low prices on merchandise to be sold under its St. Michael trademark. The goods are perceived as having excellent value and quality, so there is little need to discount prices for sales. Because M & S is so well known, it spends little on advertising, decorates its stores austerely, offers very little personal service, and provides no dressing rooms or public bathrooms. Customers receive no sales slips for small purchases, but merchandise is easily returnable.

M & S also has been successful in appealing to the nationalism of its British clientele by promoting heavily the fact that nearly all the clothing it sells originates in the United Kingdom. However, the company admits that the percentage has slipped to about four-fifths and will likely fall further as its British suppliers move more of their production abroad. Still, M & S has managed to develop an image that is as British as bed and breakfast or fish and chips. Foreign visitors to Britain usually feel they must visit an M & S store. Consequently, one of the stores has had to post warning signs to shoplifters in five languages.

M & S has experienced foreseeable barriers to continued growth in the United Kingdom. Not the least of its problems has been its high market share. Being already so dominant, M & S would have to add new products or appeal to new market segments to maintain its growth rate. The company has had trouble doing this; its attempts to move into higher-priced clothing and into a more fashion-conscious market have not been very successful. An M & S executive summed up the situation by saying, "Because the company is near saturation in the United Kingdom, its growth must be overseas." In late 1995, M & S opened an office in Shanghai to carry out studies of the Chinese market, about which a company representative said "M & S will not rush" but "it will not take long to get to a 50-store business." This opening came a day after M & S said it was looking for franchise partners in South Korea.

M & S has had mixed success abroad. Its European operations started poorly but are now successful. Its North American operations are still disappointing. Its operations in the Far East have been highly successful from the start. Overall in 1995, foreign operations accounted for 14.3 percent of M & S's sales, but only 5.7 percent of its profits. M & S opened its first stores in continental Europe in 1975, in North America in 1976, and in the Far East in 1989. In addition, M & S began exporting its St. Michael–brand merchandise and franchised stores in seventeen countries. Foreign operations and the company's dependence on them are shown on Map 16.1. Most international growth has taken place since the late 1980s.

M & S's management chose Paris and Brussels as the first locations for foreign stores. Because both cities are French-speaking, management assumed that consumer behavior would be similar in the two. Before opening stores, the company sent a team of observers to Paris for eighteen months so that product differences could be targeted to French-speaking consumers.

The team found substantial differences between French and British consumers. One was in sizes: They noted that "French girls always seem to wear a size smaller than they need with everything obviously relying on the buttons, while we [English] go for a half size too large." French women preferred longer skirts than did British women. French men's preferences, in contrast to those of British men, were for single back vents in jackets, sweaters in a variety of colors (including pastels), and jackets and slacks rather than suits. All of these differences had implications for the merchandise mix and the procurement of supplies.

Despite substantial product research, the company was not well received initially. Many fewer people entered the stores than had been anticipated. M & S management had

Map 16.1
Geographic Spread of Marks & Spencer's Operations
Although M & S has operations in twenty-four countries, over 80 percent of its business is in the United Kingdom and Ireland.

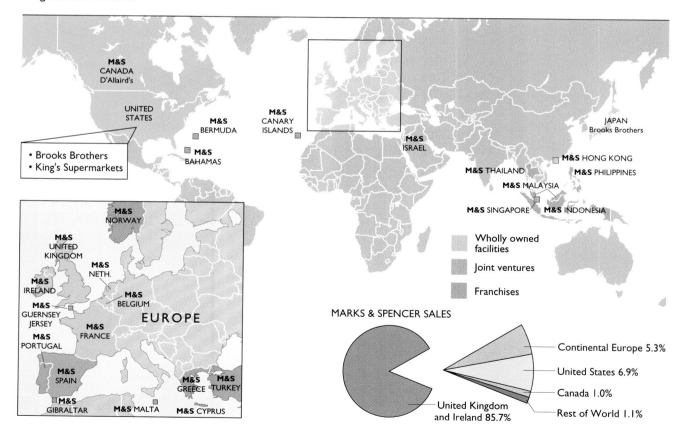

believed that because the company was so well known in the United Kingdom and so many foreign tourists visited its London stores, its reputation had preceded it. Belatedly, management learned that only 3 percent of the French had even heard of M & S or St. Michael before the continental stores were opened. Store locations exacerbated the situation. M & S wanted its first stores to be "flagships" and therefore sought to locate them on the most popular shopping streets. However, store space was at a premium on those streets. Consequently, in Paris the company had to settle for a location where most pedestrian traffic preferred the other side of the street, and in Brussels, it accepted a store with too small a frontage to give an impression of abundant merchandise inside. To entice people into the stores, M & S had to advertise more than it did in the United Kingdom; thus keeping prices low was difficult.

Another factor influencing costs was that M & S's continental stores lacked the buying power enjoyed by its U.K. stores. Initially the company contracted nearly 80 percent of its merchandise from continental sources that were unwilling to treat M & S any more favorably than other retailers already in the market. Most of the remaining merchandise came from the United Kingdom, where M & S had buying clout. Because much of the clothing was made to specifications to meet French and Belgian needs (for example, stronger thread for buttons, single-vent jackets, and pastel sweaters), the British producers had to make these items in short production runs. When initial large sales did not materialize, the British manufacturers were reluctant to keep markups very low. Even when merchandise prices were kept low, M & S found the French highly suspicious of bargains.

Another problem was that French customers were unaccustomed to the M & S stores' interior starkness and lack of service. French women insisted on trying on clothes before they bought them, even if it meant stripping down to their bras on the sales floor. A French fashion writer summed up the customer reaction to the Paris store as "not madly joyful unless of course one is as impervious to English shopping as one is to English cooking."

To attract customers to its Paris store, M & S had to make operating adjustments. The primary change surprisingly was in merchandise, the area in which the company had done so much preliminary research. In trying to copy what the continental retailers were offering in merchandise, M & S simply could not get a more durable product to customers at a sufficiently lower price to attract a mass clientele. However, the company discerned fairly quickly that there was a market segment willing to buy the more English-type merchandise for which it could exert its buying power. M & S now buys only 10 percent of its merchandise from continental sources and has differentiated itself from local competitors by capitalizing on its "Englishness." It concentrates on such items as tan and navy blue sweaters, biscuits (called crackers in the United States), English beer, and even a quiche Lorraine made in the United Kingdom. Its biggest selling food item, though, is an Indian dish, chicken tikka masala, that it first introduced in its British stores. In deference to French tastes, M & S has carpeted and put dressing rooms in its Paris store.

Not surprisingly, a large portion of the Paris store's early customers were Britishers living in France. This gradually changed as Parisians learned to like wandering through wide aisles with shopping carts and paying for all merchandise at one register. M & S became so successful that it opened additional stores in France. But customers had to be trained. For example, the French did not appreciate Christmas puddings until they learned they had to cook them. One Paris store now sells more merchandise per square meter than any other department store in France, and it is M & S's second largest store in terms of sales. About 90 percent of its business is with Parisians.

The formula of using its "Englishness" in France has also proved successful for its other operations in Europe and East Asia. However, the company does make minor product adjustments to accommodate local preferences, such as offering lighter-weight fabrics in Spain. By 1995, M & S had twenty-six stores in four continental countries (sixteen in France, three in Belgium, five in Spain through joint ventures, and two in the Netherlands). It plans to open another three in Germany so as to gain economies of scale by becoming a true mass-market retailer in Europe.

When M & S entered the Canadian market in 1976, it assumed its "Englishness" would be a greater advantage there than on the Continent. It quickly expanded to sixty stores in Canada in order to get nationwide distribution. However, Canadians found the merchandise to be dull and the stores "cold and clinical," and they did not like finding food next to clothing. Most stores were placed in downtown locations, as is the custom in the United Kingdom. However, Canadians were increasingly turning to suburban shopping centers, and only the M & S stores in those centers earned an early profit.

In deference to Canadian tastes, M & S added fitting rooms, wood paneling, mirrors, partitions between departments, and wall-to-wall carpeting. There were still complaints about the merchandise, however. A former supplier observed that M & S managers did things in Canada, such as using bigger sleeves on clothing and avoiding advertising and livelier colors in clothing, "because that's the way they did it in England."

Because the Canadian stores have continued to lose money, M & S pruned the number of stores substantially in the early 1990s. The company acquired two other Canadian clothing chains, D'Allaird's and Peoples, but sold Peoples in 1992 and D'Allaird's in 1994. When M & S first entered Canada, it had hoped those operations would serve as a springboard to enter the U.S. market. It subsequently moved into the United States in 1987 by expanding D'Allaird's into shopping malls in three cities in New York. M & S then appointed a top-level team to conduct an in-depth study of the U.S. market to determine the feasibility of setting up stores under the M & S name. One of the company's executives said, "There is nothing like M & S in the United States, and we believe there could be good potential for us." However, on the basis of the study's results, M & S decided against its Canadian approach of copying the British formula. Instead, it decided to pursue further U.S. expansion via compatible acquisitions. The first, Brooks Brothers in 1988, seemed incongruous because that retailer had a dignified image, a high level of personal service, and expensive clothes. M & S announced it would not change Brooks Brothers' successful and profitable merchandising approach. But soon thereafter, it sought to increase sales by changing some practices in order to attract less affluent customers to the stores. The company reduced the number of personnel, began replacing glass display cases with open displays, ran six-week sales instead of the customary one-week ones, and decreased the number of sizes of casual coats to simply small, medium, large, and extra-large. During the first two years, the results of the changes were disastrous as Brooks Brothers' sales and profits declined. In 1995, the M & S chairman said, "We will never justify the price we paid for Brooks Brothers. I just want to justify buying it."

The acquisition of Brooks Brothers also gave M & S that company's stores in Japan, allowing inroads to the Japanese market, where by 1992 the company had thirty-five stores. The Japanese stores are consistent with M & S's desire to build a significant presence in East and Southeast Asia. M & S has also moved recently into Hong Kong, Indonesia, Malaysia, the Philippines, Singapore, and Thailand.

In 1988, M & S bought Kings Supermarkets, a New Jersey food chain. This acquisition seemed compatible because Kings and M & S shared an operating philosophy of emphasizing perishables and upscale prepared foods. Existing management stayed on to provide U.S. marketing expertise. M & S began the following year to introduce its St. Michael lines of chilled prepared foods into the stores, while advertising them heavily and providing discount coupons in local newspapers. It began with only 18 items, prepared in the individual stores, compared with more than 2000 items in the United Kingdom, all prepared in central kitchens. Some of the U.S. items, such as chili con carne, differ from those in the United Kingdom. Because of greater distances in the United States, overnight delivery from central kitchens is not practical there. Consequently, if M & S follows its planned strategy of building a significant U.S. food presence, in-store preparation will create additional potential problems of cost and quality control.

Introduction

Domestic and international marketing principles are the same, but managers often
- **Overlook foreign environmental differences**
- **Interpret foreign information incorrectly**

The M & S case points out many of the problems a company may face internationally. Despite substantial research before beginning international operations, M & S still faced unexpected problems that inhibited rapid sales growth. Marketing principles are no different in the international arena; however, environmental differences often cause managers either to overlook important variables or to misinterpret information. M & S made mistakes regarding such important marketing variables as the target market segment, the merchandise mix, promotional needs, the degree to which products would need to be altered for the markets, and distributional differences. However, M & S has altered operations based on its experience and is now doing well in most of the foreign locations in which it operates.

Global versus national marketing programs
- **Are not an either/or decision**
- **May vary by products and decisions**

This chapter examines alternative approaches to the analysis of market potential in different countries and the selection of product, pricing, promotion, branding, and distribution strategies in international marketing. Within these areas, emphasis is placed on whether companies should follow global or multidomestic marketing strategies. These alternative approaches may be viewed as opposite ends of a spectrum. A company may move to different positions along that spectrum for any of its specific marketing programs or decisions.

Market Size Analysis

Chapter 13 explained the importance of market potential in determining a company's allocational efforts among different countries, discussed some common variables used as broad indicators for comparing countries' market potentials, and briefly introduced types of sources for collecting information on market indicators. Data must be analyzed after being collected. This section covers some techniques that can be used to estimate the size of potential markets, information that can help management decide which markets to analyze more closely and which to emphasize.

Total Market Potential

To determine potential demand, a company's management usually must first estimate the possible sales of the category of products for all companies and then estimate its own market-share potential.

Existing consumption patterns   The **input-output table** is a tool used widely in national economic planning to show the resources utilized by different industries for a given output as well as the interdependence of economic sectors. Tables featuring sectors on both the vertical and horizontal axes show the production (output) of one sector as the demand (input) of another. For instance, steel output becomes an input to the automobile industry, households, government, foreign sector, and even to the steel industry itself. Many countries publish input-output tables. By comparing these with economic projections for an economy as a whole or with plans for production changes in a given industry, management can project the total volume of sales changes for a given type of product as well as the purchases by each sector. There are three major shortcomings of this method, however:

1. For many countries, the data in the input-output tables and in plans or projections of economic changes are too sparse.
2. The assumption that the relationships among sectors and resources are fixed is questionable.
3. The tables may be many years old before they are published and readily available.

Data on other countries   The amount of sales of a product in one country may be based on the same conditions that determine sales in other countries. One such condition is per capita income: As incomes change, the demand for a product may change. For example, Korean demand for apparel, cosmetics, and automobiles has grown with increased per capita income—a trend that closely parallels the experience of industrial countries in earlier years.[2] Management thus may collect data on the consumption of a given product in countries with different per capita GNPs and then project sales at different income levels by plotting a path through which average demand changes as incomes change (see Fig. 16.1).

Reasonably good fits for many products have been found by using this method. However, so many other variables affect demand, so the analysis breaks down for some products in some countries. For example, the expenditures on food in Japan are higher than would be predicted by either population or income level because food is expensive and work habits promote eating out.[3] In India, although a small percentage of families have incomes of $30,000, those that do can usually afford to buy luxuries—such as a luxury car—that could not be bought on the same income in the United States. The reason is that prices of food and other necessities are much lower in India than in the United States.[4] Another problem with this method is that it is static. As technology and prices change, a country may change its consumption pattern much earlier or later than would be indicated by looking at a group of countries in only one time period.

Time-series analysis projects the future by examining past trends.

Time-series data   Sometimes sales follow a pattern over time. If this is the case and data are available, a company may be able to make future projections based on past values.[5] Figure 16.2 illustrates sugar consumption in the United States based on time-series data. Note that per capita consumption has fallen since 1970 because of competition from corn and low-calorie sweeteners. This drop contrasts with projections of sugar consumption shown in Fig. 16.1 based on cross-national data. The use of time-series and cross-national data also may be combined. Such analyses within an economy are useful for predicting total demand and for identifying the economic sectors generating this demand.

As income changes, product demand may change by a different percentage.

Income elasticity   A common predictive method is to divide the percentage of change in product demand by the percentage of change in income. An answer

---

**Figure 16.1
Per Capita Sugar Consumption and GNP for Selected Countries, 1989**
Plotting data on per capita sugar consumption and GNP for countries for which data are available allows construction of a line that can be used to estimate sugar consumption in countries for which data on GNP are available.

Source: UN Statistical Yearbook, 1988–89.

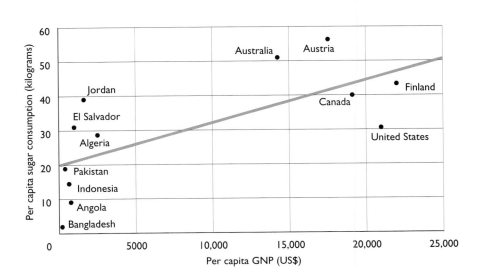

**Figure 16.2
Per Capita Sugar
Consumption in the
United States,
1899–1990**
Plotting per capita sugar
consumption over time
allows extrapolation of the
trend to make estimates
for the future.

*Source: Statistical Abstract of the
United States, Supplements 1957,
1972, and 1992.*

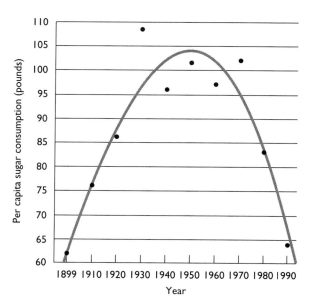

greater than 1 means the product demand is **elastic;** that is, sales are likely to increase or decrease by a percentage that is greater than the percentage by which income changes. An answer less than 1 indicates demand is **inelastic;** that is, sales are
likely to increase or decrease by a percentage that is less than the percentage change
in income. An elasticity of 1.5 would mean that a percentage change in income
would result in 1.5 times that percentage change in the demand for the specific
product. Demand for necessities, such as food, is relatively less elastic than is demand for discretionary products, such as automobiles. In other words, upward or
downward movements in income ordinarily would affect automobile sales more
than food sales.

   This tool is useful for estimating the expenditures for countries at different
income levels. For example, people in the United States spend a lower percentage
of their personal income on food than do people in LDCs. The difference is due
not to relative appetites but rather to income differences that allow people in the
United States to spend more on other types of purchases. Because a large portion of
people in LDCs are poor, a change in income level affects food consumption there
much more than it would in a higher-income country.

   As is true with any method of demand projection, income-elasticity measurements must be approached with caution, especially if a company is making projections in one country based on demand analysis in another. Differences in prices and
tastes affect consumers' demand as well. For example, because of price differences,
Italy consumes many more fruits and vegetables than Norway does, even though
Norway's per capita income is higher. Denmark and Switzerland have very similar
per capita incomes, but per capita consumption of frozen food is much higher in
Denmark because of the Danes' penchant for convenience.[6]

Demand is related to some economic or other indicator.

Regression   Regression is an important means of refining data and making predictions by uncovering relationships among variables. By using data based on the historical relationship between demand for a given product and economic or other indicators or between demand and some indicators in a given time period, a company may construct a regression equation that shows the demand (the dependent variable) based on level of the indicators (the independent variables). This technique allows for consideration of an amount of consumption not directly attributable to changes in the indicators and for the determination of the degree of correlation between the independent and dependent variables. Regression analysis thus can be used to predict demand from changes in related indicators.

Gap Analysis

The difference between total market potential and companies' sales is due to gaps:
• Usage—less product sold by all competitors than potential
• Product line—company lacks some product variations
• Distribution—company misses geographic or intensity coverage
• Competitive—competitors' sales not explained by product and distribution gaps

The tools just described may give an estimation of the market potential in various countries for a given product. Once this rough determination is made, the company must calculate how well it is doing within each market. A useful tool for scanning markets and comparing countries in this respect is **gap analysis,** which is a method for estimating a company's potential sales by identifying market segments that it is not serving adequately.[7] When a company's sales are lower than the estimated market potential for a given type of product, the company has potential for increased sales, which may result from a gap in usage, product line, distribution, or competition.

For example, the two largest Swiss chocolate companies, Nestlé and Interfood, have found very different types of gaps in different countries.[8] Consequently, they have altered their marketing programs among countries. In some markets, they have found substantial usage gaps; that is, less chocolate is being consumed than would be expected on the basis of population and income levels. Industry specialists estimate, for example, that in many countries more than 80 percent of the population has never tasted a chocolate bar. Therefore, they project that if more people in those countries can be persuaded to try chocolate bars, the companies' sales should increase with the market increase. This assumption has led the two companies to promote sales in those areas for chocolate in general.

The U.S. market shows another type of usage gap. Nearly everyone in this market has tried most chocolate products, but per capita consumption has fallen because of growing concern about weight. To increase chocolate consumption in general, Nestlé for a short time promoted chocolate as an energy source for the sports-minded. Note, however, that building general consumption is most useful to the market leader; thus Nestlé, with U.S. chocolate sales below those of Mars and Hershey, actually benefited its competitors during the short-lived campaign.

The Swiss chocolate companies also have found that they have product-line gaps in some hot climates in the market for sweetened products. By developing new products, such as chocolate products that melt less easily, they may be able to garner a larger share of that market. These companies also have found chocolate products with which they do not compete directly. Further, in some markets, such as Japan, they have not yet achieved sufficient distribution to reach their sales potentials; therefore Nestlé formed a joint venture with a Japanese cake and candy maker, Fujiya, to make Kit Kat bars and gain more distribution.[9]

Finally, there are competitive gaps—sales by competitors that cannot be explained by differences between one's own product line and distribution and those of the competitors. That is, competitors are making some additional sales because of their prices, advertising campaigns, goodwill, or any of a host of other factors. For example, in markets such as France and Germany, Nestlé and Interfood feel that most of the potential market demand is being fulfilled but that any increase in sales must come at the expense of competitors.

Product Policy

Most marketing texts categorize companies' product policies, although there is some variation in the categories they use. The treatment of these policies tends to be domestically focused. This section highlights the international application of five commonly used categories of product policies.

Production Orientation

With production orientation, companies focus primarily on production efficiency or the development of the highest-quality product. There is little analysis of consumer needs or of whether consumers will pay for differentiated products or higher quality. Although this approach has largely gone out of vogue, it is used internationally for certain cases:

- Commodity sales, especially those for which there is little need or possibility of product differentiation by country
- Passive exports, particularly those that serve to reduce surpluses within the domestic market
- Foreign-market segments or niches that may resemble the market at which the product is aimed initially

Price is the most important factor in selling many commodities.

Many raw materials and agricultural commodities, such as sugar and tin, are sold primarily on the basis of price because there is universal demand for the undifferentiated product. However, even for commodity sales, there has been a realization that marketing efforts may yield positive international sales results. For example, the promotion of the Chiquita brand on bananas has helped increase global supermarket distribution in a glutted market. In addition, oil producers, such as Petroven and Aramco, have integrated forward by buying branded gasoline-distribution operations abroad. Commodity producers also put efforts into business-to-business marketing in the form of providing innovative financing and assuring timely supplies of high quality.

Many companies begin exporting very passively. Sometimes, for unknown reasons, orders or requests for product information simply arrive from abroad. Foreign products are discovered through reports in scientific and trade journals, advertising that spills across borders, buying trips, and observations of products that others have brought into the country. At this point, companies adapt their products very little, if at all, to foreign consumers' preferences. This practice suffices for many companies that view foreign sales as an appendage to domestic sales. This type of company frequently exports only if it has excess inventory for the domestic market. In fact, fixed costs are sometimes covered from domestic sales so that lower prices are offered on exports as a means of liquidating inventories without disrupting the domestic market.[10]

A company may develop a product aimed at achieving a large share of its domestic market and then find there are market segments abroad willing to buy that product. Sometimes the product may have a universal appeal, such as French champagne. In other situations, a company may be able to target to a mass market at home and a small niche within foreign locations; an example is U.S. bourbon producers.[11] Recall that M & S first tried to sell clothing for the needs of the French mass market but later found a niche of French consumers who would buy what the company was already selling in the United Kingdom. Another situation involves sales to countries that have only a small market potential regardless of whether changes are geared to unique consumer needs. Particularly in small LDCs, MNEs may make few changes because the market size does not justify the expense to them and because competitors are apt to be other MNEs that do not make product alterations. Companies may not even adjust the voltage requirements and plugs of electrical products to local standards, instead leaving the job of conversion to local purchasers.

Sales Orientation

Internationally, sales orientation involves trying to sell abroad what the company is able to sell domestically on the assumption that consumers are sufficiently similar globally. A company may make this assumption because the distance between it and its foreign markets makes information about the foreign markets difficult to obtain. Paradoxically, the more distant a market, the less can be assumed about it.[12] This orientation differs from the production orientation because of its active rather than passive approach to promoting sales. However, there is much anecdotal evidence of foreign failures that have resulted because of assumptions that product acceptance will be the same as at home or that heavy sales efforts abroad can overcome negative foreign attitudes toward the product. Yet, there also are successful examples of

Passive sales occur when
• **Advertising spills over**
• **Foreign buyers seek new products**

The unaltered domestic product may have appeal abroad.

transferring products abroad with little or no research on foreign consumers' preferred product characteristics, particularly sales aimed at teenagers.[13]

Standardization usually reduces costs.

The greatest ability to sell the same product in multiple countries occurs when consumer characteristics are similar and when there is a great deal of spillover in product information, such as between the United States and Canada. Whether a company is exporting or has foreign production facilities, it may cut costs substantially by standardizing its products and spreading developmental costs over a larger volume of output. This usually is done on the basis of the home-country experience, since costs associated with product development, promotional programs, and distributional expertise already have been expended there. Conversely, companies may develop a new product to launch almost simultaneously in multiple countries, as Colgate-Palmolive did with Optims Shampoo.[14] Or, the standardized product may first be developed abroad, for example, Whiskas, a cat food that Mars first developed outside the United States.[15]

Customer Orientation

A customer orientation takes geographic areas as given.

In a company that operates according to sales orientation, management usually is guided by the answers to questions such as these: Should the company send some exports abroad? Where can the company sell some more of product X? That is, the product is held constant and the sales location is varied. In contrast, customer orientation involves asking: What can the company sell in country A? In this case, the country is held constant and the product is varied.

Sometimes a company wants to penetrate markets in a given country because of the country's size, growth potential, proximity to home operations, currency or political stability, or any of a host of other reasons. In the extreme of this approach, a company would move to completely unrelated products. Although an uncommon strategy, some companies have adopted it. For example, Chilena de Fosforos, a Chilean match producer, wanted to tap the Japanese market because of Japanese growth and size, competition within the Chilean market, and the promotional appeal of being able to say "We supply Japan." However, because the company was not price-competitive in Japan for matches, it began making chopsticks—a product that would utilize its poplar forest resources and wood-processing capabilities. Chilena de Fosforos now has more Japanese demand for its chopsticks than it has capacity to fulfill.[16]

As with a production orientation, a company using a customer orientation may do so passively. Increasingly, purchasing agents are setting product specifications and then seeking out contracts for the foreign manufacture of components or finished products. For example, the Hong Kong company S. T. King makes clothing to the specifications of companies such as Calvin Klein. In responding to product requests, a company may make a product that differs markedly from what it sells domestically. In such a situation, the company is less concerned about choosing product characteristics than about pricing and distributing what it is marketing abroad.

Strategic Marketing Orientation

The most common strategy
is product changes as adaptations, done by degree.

Most companies committed to continual rather than sporadic foreign sales adopt a
strategy that combines production, sales, and consumer orientations. Refusal to
make changes to accommodate the needs of foreign markets means too many sales
may be lost, especially if there are aggressive competitors willing to make desired
adaptations. Yet expertise concerning a type of product may be very important, and
companies want the products they sell abroad to be compatible with their expertise
and with their means of dealing with competitors. Companies therefore tend to
make product variations abroad without deviating very far from their experience.
For example, breweries such as Heineken, Stroh, Bass, and Lion, when faced with
restrictions against alcoholic beverages in Saudi Arabia, have turned to sales of nonalcoholic beer (marketed as malt rather than beer).[17] Products such as computers
or even coffee or tea would probably be too far from managements' areas of
expertise.

An attitude of reacting to consumers' product preferences does not necessarily
mean that a company must forgo the economies of standardization. A company may
well do market research in a number of countries in order to develop and aim a
product at a global market segment, as Canon did in developing a 35-millimeter
automatic camera. Instead of merely trying to sell a domestic product abroad, the
company designs a product to fit some global market segment, which may mean
changing what is sold domestically to correspond to the international standard.
Global products may also be possible for industrial users because the purchasers are
apt to be technically trained decision makers.

Societal Marketing Orientation

Societal marketing orientation implies that successful international marketing
requires serious consideration of potential environmental, health, social, and work-
related problems that may arise when products are sold abroad.[18] Such groups as
consumer associations, political parties, and labor unions are becoming more globally aware and may react negatively and over a long period to adverse effects of
products companies sell. Companies must increasingly consider not only how a
product is purchased but also how it is disposed of and how it might be changed to
be more socially desirable. For example, about one-third of the world's population
or approximately two billion people have no electricity in their homes. The biggest
problem is, of course, the high cost of constructing major power plants. However,
two major environmental concerns are that there will be inadequate future supplies
of fossil fuels and that too much pollution will be created by burning fossil fuels
to generate electricity. These concerns have led to high expenditures on solar
research, which have begun to yield marketable products aimed at the needs of
electricity shortages in developing countries. These include small-scale solar panels
to provide electricity to homes in Brazil, to herders' tents in Tibet, and to mobile
refrigeration units atop camels in the desert of Somalia.[19]

Reasons for Product Alteration

Legal factors   Explicit legal requirements are the most obvious reason for altering products for foreign markets. The exact requirements vary widely by country but are usually meant to protect consumers. Pharmaceuticals and foods are particularly subject to regulations concerning purity, testing, and labeling. Automobiles sold in the United States must conform to safety and pollution standards not found in many other countries.

The legal standards may be written with a domestic producer in mind. For example, Dormont Manufacturing makes hoses that hook up deep-fat fryers and the like to gas outlets. Although the hoses have gone through rigorous U.S. and Canadian approval processes and could once be sold throughout Europe, Dormont now faces country-by-country differences within Europe. For example, Italy requires that metal tubes be extendable and have no covering, whereas the United Kingdom prohibits extendability and requires a rubber coating.[20] Nevertheless, the EU has been trying to harmonize product standards on a host of products.

Legal factors are usually related to safety or health protection.

When foreign legal requirements are less stringent than domestic ones, a company may not be legally compelled to alter its products for foreign sale. However, the company will have to weigh such decisions as whether following high domestic standards abroad will raise prices and whether domestic or foreign ill will may result if those standards are not met. Some companies have been criticized for selling abroad, especially in LDCs, such products as toys, automobiles, contraceptives, and pharmaceuticals that did not meet home-country safety or quality standards.

One of the more cumbersome adjustments for companies has occurred because of different laws on packaging that are designed to protect the environment. Certain types of containers are prohibited in some countries, aluminum cans in Denmark, for example. Other countries restrict the volume of packaging materials; thus exporters of Scotch whiskey to Germany must remove the bottles from the cardboard boxes. There also are differences in national requirements as to whether containers must be reusable and whether waste materials must be recycled, incinerated, or composted.[21]

A recurring issue is to what extent it is possible to arrive at international product standards to eliminate some of the seemingly wasteful product alterations among countries. Although agreement has been reached on some products (such as the universal one for the sprocket dimensions on movie film and the nearly universal one on bar codes to identify products), other products (such as railroad gauges and power supplies and electrical socket shapes) continue to vary.[22] In reality, there is both consumer and economic resistance to standardization. For example, the conversion to the metric system on beverage containers meant U.S. consumers had to learn that 236.58 milliliters is the same as 8 fluid ounces for their soft drinks. In an economic sense, the changeover was more costly than simply educating people and relabeling. Containers had to be redesigned and production retooled so that dimensions would be in even numbers. Even for new products or those still under development, such as video-CDs, companies and countries are slow to reach agreement because they want to protect the investments they have already made.[23] At best, international standards will come very slowly.

Less apparent are the indirect legal requirements that may affect product content or demand. For example, in some countries, importing certain raw materials or components may be difficult or prohibitively expensive, forcing a company to construct an end product with local substitutes that may alter the final result substantially. Legal requirements such as high taxes on heavy automobiles also could shift sales to smaller models, thus indirectly altering demand for tire sales and grades of gasoline.

Examination of cultural differences may pinpoint possible problem areas.

Cultural factors   Consumer buying behavior is complex. It is difficult to determine in advance whether new or different products will be accepted. For example, Rubbermaid has found that most Americans like housewares in neutral blues or almond colors, but Dutch want them in white and Southern Europeans want them in red. Further, Americans prefer open-top waste baskets, and Europeans want them with tight lids.[24] Some U.S. food franchisors, such as McDonald's, have been highly successful in Japan by duplicating most of their U.S. products and means of distribution—a success attributed to the "enthusiastic assimilation" of Western ways by the Japanese. In contrast, in seemingly more similar Canada (Quebec), McDonald's had to provide cheese curds and hot gravy for french fries to create a dish called *poutine*.[25] In other cases, McDonald's has added pork burgers to its menu in Thailand because of local tastes and substituted mutton patties for beef in India because of Hindu reverence for cows.[26]

Personal incomes and infrastructures affect product demand.

Economic factors   If foreign consumers lack sufficient income, they may be able to buy insufficient quantities of the product the MNE sells domestically. The company therefore may have to design a cheaper model or perhaps sell a product that resembles an older model sold earlier in the home market. For example, in India there are practically no repeat sales for disposable products. Only about 1 percent of razor blade sales are through sales of disposable razors, and people have found means to refill disposable lighters.[27] Where consumers buy many personal items in very small quantities, such as one aspirin, one piece of chewing gum, or one cigarette, the practice usually necessitates new types of packaging.

Even if a market segment has sufficient income to purchase the same product the company sells at home, the general level of a country's economy may require that products be altered. A country's infrastructure may determine the necessary structural composition and tolerances of products. The infrastructure has other effects as well. For example, the trains connecting London with Paris and Brussels via the tunnel must be built to run on four different power supplies and three different signaling systems.[28] In another transportation example, the Japanese infrastructure for automobiles reflects crowded conditions and high land prices. Some U.S. automobile models are too wide to fit into elevators that carry cars to upper floors to be parked, and they cannot make narrow turns on back streets. On the Explorer, which does fit the Japanese infrastructure, Ford has nevertheless had to install retractable side-view mirrors to help the cars fit into tight spaces.[29] Further, in some places factory managers have to consider the low educational levels of machine operators when planning equipment purchases. Product simplification may be the result.

Alteration Costs

Cost savings due to uniformity may apply to any part of the marketing program; however, product standardization is where the greatest savings are possible. Some changes are cheap to effect yet have an important influence on demand. One such area is packaging, which is the most common alteration made by exporters.[30] For example, in Panama, Aunt Jemima Pancake Mix and Ritz Crackers are sold in cans rather than in boxes because of the high humidity—a low-cost change with a high potential payoff. Before making a decision, a company should always compare the cost of an alteration with the cost of lost sales if no alteration is made.

One strategy a company can use to compromise between uniformity and diversity is to standardize a great deal while altering some end characteristics. For example, Toyota puts its steering wheels on the left side for the U.S. market, and Ford puts steering wheels on the right for the Japanese market.[31] Also, Heinz has found that many nationalities do not like a sweet ketchup, as is preferred in the United States, so it adds spices, curry, or hot pepper, depending on the market.[32] Whirlpool sells colored refrigerators in Thailand because customers often put them in their living rooms.[33] It has also moved to the use of more common parts within its appliances sold in Europe, even though the end products look very different from each other.[34]

Extent and Mix of the Product Line

Most companies produce multiple products. It is doubtful that all of these products could generate sufficient sales in a given foreign market to justify the cost of penetrating the market. Even if they could, a company may offer only a portion of its product line, such as only some products that are sold at home. This allows sales activity to concentrate on fewer products and may sometimes be an entry strategy that reduces costs. For example, Whirlpool has entered the South Korean refrigerator market by targeting only the top 2 percent of incomes with its highest priced models in only half the colors available elsewhere. This strategy saves on translation, inventory, and promotional costs. If successful, the company may consider moving to other target segments with an expanded product line.[35] A company also must decide whether any new products need to be added to the line for sale in certain countries.

In reaching product-line decisions, the company should consider the possible effects on sales and the relative cost of having one product as opposed to a family of products. Sometimes a company finds it must produce and sell some unpopular items if it is to sell the more popular ones, such as sherry glasses to match crystal wine and water glasses. Or a company may be forced into a few short production runs in order to gain the mass market on other products. A company that must set up some foreign production in order to sell in the foreign market may be able to produce locally those products in its line that have longer production runs and import the other products needed to help sell the local production.

If the foreign market is small in relation to the domestic market, selling costs per unit may be high because of the fixed costs associated with selling. In such a situation, the company can broaden the product line to be handled, either by grouping sales of several manufacturers or by developing new products for the local market that the same salesperson can handle.[36] For example, Coca-Cola has added bar mixes in South Africa, a lemonade in Australia, a mango drink in Pakistan, a tomato juice in Belgium, and some mixed juice-based drinks in Mexico and Indonesia.

Product life cycles may differ by country in
• **Time of introduction**
• **Shape of curve**

Product-Life-Cycle Considerations

There may be differences among countries in either the shape or length of a product's life cycle. Thus a company that faces declining sales for a product in one country may be able to find a foreign market that will have growing or at least sustained sales for the product. For example, cellular phone producers, such as Ericsson and Motorola, faced a slowing growth in demand in industrial countries during the late 1980s but found that sales in some developing countries were just entering a stage of rapid growth. Foreign language versions of many U.S. television shows, such as "Let's Make a Deal" and "The Price Is Right," have successfully moved abroad after running their course in the United States. Ajax found a much longer growth period for its cleanser in Europe than in the United States because it successfully achieved a product line extension in Europe by promoting additives.[37] Volkswagen relaunched the Beetle in the Brazilian market thirty-four years after its first introduction there and seven years after Brazilian production had stopped.[38] (Safety standards prevented a relaunching in most other markets.)

Marketing in the Internationalization Process

The product policy is apt to evolve as companies increase their commitments to international operations. For example, they are apt to begin with a production or sales orientation for foreign operations; however, if their sales do not meet expectations, they are apt to analyze the legal, cultural, and economic factors that constrain their market penetration. If sales expectations justify the costs of product alterations, they will then move to a customer or strategic marketing orientation.

Companies may also limit early commitments to given foreign countries by attempting to sell regionally before moving nationally. Many products and markets lend themselves to this sort of gradual development. In many cases, geographic bar-

A company may enter a market gradually by limiting geographic coverage.

riers divide countries into very distinct markets; for example, Colombia is divided by mountain ranges and Australia by a desert. In other countries, such as Zimbabwe and Zaire, very little wealth or few potential sales may lie outside the large metropolitan areas. In still others, advertising and distribution may be handled effectively on a regional basis. For example, most multinational consumer goods companies have moved into China one region at a time. [39]

Pricing

When ranking the importance of marketing-program variables, companies generally place only product above price.[40] A price must be high enough to guarantee the flow of funds required to carry on other activities, such as R & D, production, and distribution. The proper price will not only assure short-term profits but also give the company the resources to build the other elements within its marketing mix that are necessary to achieve long-term competitive viability. Pricing is more complex internationally than domestically because of the following factors:

- Different degrees of governmental intervention
- Greater diversity of markets
- Price escalation for exports
- Changing relative values of currencies
- Differences in fixed versus variable pricing practices
- Retailers' strength with suppliers
- Strategies to counter international competitors

Governmental Intervention

Governmental price controls may
- **Set minimum or maximum prices**
- **Prohibit certain competitive pricing practices**

Every country has laws that affect the prices of goods at the consumer level, but these laws may affect different products in different ways at different times. Restrictions may prevent companies from using the strategies they consider optimal in achieving their ends. A governmental price control may set either maximum or minimum price levels. Controls against lowering prices usually are intended to prevent companies from eliminating competitors in order to gain monopoly positions. An example of this type of control is in Germany, which prohibits such items as coupons, boxtops, and giveaway articles unless these will remain a consistent policy of the company throughout the years. Germany also permits retailers to have sales only twice a year, once in the summer and once in the winter. [41] A company accustomed to relying on such devices to increase its sales at home must develop new methods in Germany. Many countries set maximum prices for many products. If costs rise, profit margins contract, sometimes resulting in an unwillingness of producers to continue selling. For example, P&G and some of its suppliers were hit hard by price controls in Venezuela. Although P&G was willing to wait out the situation while negotiating with governmental authorities, its phosphate suppliers could not afford to lower prices on the materials P&G bought for detergents. The company was forced to suspend operations until the price controls were lifted.[42] Price controls also may cause companies to lower the quality of a product; in this case they may consider changing the brand name in order to reintroduce the higher-quality product later.

The WTO permits countries to establish restrictions against any import that comes in at a price below that charged consumers in the exporting country. This makes it more difficult for companies to differentiate markets through pricing. A company might want to export at a lower price than that charged at home for several reasons. One might be to test sales in the foreign market. For example, a company may find it cannot export to a given country because tariffs or transportation costs make the price to foreign consumers prohibitively high. Yet its preliminary calculations show that by establishing foreign production, it may be able to substantially reduce the price to the foreign consumer. Before committing resources to produce overseas, the company may want to test the market by exporting so as to sell the product at the price that would be charged if it was produced locally. Nestlé tested the U.K. market in this way by exporting for a year from Canada to see if enough market would develop to justify completing a frozen-food plant to make Lean Cuisine products.[43] Shipping such dishes as spaghetti bolognese in refrigerated ships and paying customs duties made the costs of the exported products much higher than their U.K. selling prices; however, the cost of this test was small compared to the value of the information gained and the amount of Nestlé's eventual commitment. A company also may charge different prices in different countries because of competitive and demand factors. For example, it may feel that prices can be kept high in the domestic market by restricting supply to that market. Excess production then can be sold abroad at a lower price, as long as that price covers variable costs and makes some contribution to overhead.

Greater Diversity of Markets

Consumers in some countries simply like certain products more and are willing to pay more for them.

Although there are numerous ways a company can segment the domestic market and charge different prices in each segment, country-to-country variations create even more natural segments. For example, few sea urchins or tuna eyeballs can be sold in the United States at any price, but they can be exported to Japan, where they are considered delicacies.[44] Levi's manages to sell jeans in Europe for more than twice the U.S. price.[45] In some countries, a company may have many competitors and thus little discretion regarding its prices. In others, it may have a near monopoly due either to the stage in the product life cycle or to government-granted manufacturing rights not held by competitors. In near-monopoly situations, a company may exercise considerable pricing discretion, using any of the following:

- A skimming strategy—charging a high price for a new product by aiming first at price-inelastic consumers and progressively lowering the price

- A penetration strategy—introducing a product at a low price to induce a maximum number of consumers to try it
- A cost-plus strategy—pricing at a desired margin over cost

Country-of-origin stereotypes also limit pricing possibilities. For example, exporters in LDCs often must compete primarily on the basis of price because of negative perceptions about their products' quality.[46] But there are dangers in lowering prices in response to adverse stereotypes because a lower price may reduce the product image even further.

The total cost of a product to the consumer will be more than the sales price if there are additional charges because of buying on credit. How consumers view these additional charges may affect total demand as well as the sales price they are willing to pay. The tax treatment of interest payments as well as attitudes toward debt affect whether consumers will pay in cash or by credit. For example, the Japanese have been much more reluctant than Americans to rely on consumer credit. Thus in Japan it is less possible than it is in the United States to use credit payments as a means of inducing the sale of goods.

Price Escalation in Exporting

If standard markups are used within distribution channels, lengthening the channels or adding expenses somewhere within the system will further increase the price to the consumer. For example, assume the markup is 50 percent and the product costs $1.00 to produce. The price to the consumer would be $1.50. However, if production costs were to increase to $1.20, the 50-percent markup would make the price $1.80, not $1.70 as might be expected. In export sales, price escalation occurs for two reasons:

1. Channels of distribution are usually longer because of greater distances and because of the need to contract with organizations that know export procedures and/or how to sell in the foreign market.
2. Tariffs are an additional cost that may be passed on to consumers.

There are several implications of price escalation. Many seemingly exportable products turn out to be noncompetitive abroad. Further, to become competitive in exporting, a company may have to sell its product to intermediaries at a lower price in order to lessen the amount of escalation.

Currency Value and Price Changes

For companies accustomed to operating with one relatively stable currency, pricing in highly volatile currencies can be extremely troublesome. Pricing decisions should be made to assure sufficient funds are received so that the company can replenish its inventory and still make a profit. Otherwise, it may be making a "paper profit" while liquidating itself; that is, what shows on paper as a profit may result from the company's failure to adjust for inflation while the merchandise is in stock. The company must consider not only inflation's effect on prices but also the possibility its income taxes will be based on the paper profits rather than on real profits. Table 16.1 illustrates a pricing plan to make a target profit (after taxes) of 30 percent on replacement cost. The company that does not use a similar plan may quickly lack sufficient funds to operate. The longer the collection period, the more important it is for the company to use a graduated pricing model. For example, Peruvian inflation in the late 1980s forced P&G to raise its detergent prices 20–30 percent every two weeks. P&G also eliminated its sixty-day free credit to retailers and began charging interest on fifteen- to thirty-day payments.[47]

Two other pricing problems occur because of inflationary conditions:

1. The receipt of funds in a foreign currency that, when converted, buy less of the company's own currency than had been expected
2. The frequent readjustment of prices necessary to compensate for continual cost increases

---

Table 16.1

Effect of Tax and Inflation on Pricing

The pricing structure for sales or collections at the end of the year is calculated as follows: Replacement cost is cost plus inflation until collection, or $1000 + 0.36(1000) = 1360$; income after taxes is profit goal times replacement cost, or $0.30(1360) = 408$. Income after taxes is 60 percent of taxable income; thus taxable income may be calculated as $408 \div 0.6$, or 680; tax is $0.4(680) = 272$; sales price is original cost (1000) plus taxable income (680); markup on replacement is sales price (1680) less replacement cost (1360), or 320.

Assume: Cost at beginning is 1000
36% inflation
40% tax rate
30% profit goal on replacement cost after taxes

If sold and collected at beginning of year		If sold and collected at end of year	
Cost	1000	Replacement cost	1360
Markup	500	Markup on replacement	320
Sales prices	1500	Sales price	1680
− Cost	1000	− Original cost	1000
Taxable income	500	Taxable income	680
Tax @ 40%	200	Tax @ 40%	272
Income after taxes	300	Income after taxes	408

In the first case, the company sometimes (depending on competitive factors and governmental regulations) can specify in sales contracts an equivalency in some hard currency. For example, a U.S. manufacturer's sale of equipment to a company in Uruguay may specify that payment be made in dollars or in pesos at an equivalent price, in terms of dollars, at the time payment is made. In the second case, frequent price increases make it more difficult for the company to quote prices in letters or catalogues. Perpetual price rises may even hamper what would otherwise be a preferred distribution method. For example, price increases in vending machine sales are frequently difficult to effect because of the attendant need to change machines and to come up with coins or tokens that correspond to the desired percentage increase in price.

Currency-value changes also affect pricing decisions for any product that has potential foreign competition. For example, when the U.S. dollar is strong, non–U.S.-made goods can be sold more cheaply in the U.S. market. In such a situation, to be competitive U.S. producers may have to accept a lower profit margin. When the dollar is weak, however, foreign producers may have to adjust their margins downward.

When companies sell similar goods in multiple countries, price differences among them must not exceed by much the cost of bringing the goods in from a lower-priced country, or spillover in buying will occur. Soft-drink manufacturers can easily vary their prices by a large percentage from country to country because the transportation costs relative to the product's price render large-scale movements across borders impractical. However, with higher-priced items, consumers can feasibly buy abroad and import. For example, about 20 percent of South Korea's car imports enter the country through overseas purchases and are then sold through unofficial distributors at prices below those offered by official distributors in South Korea.[48] The handling of goods through unofficial distributors is known as the **gray market,** and such handling can undermine the longer-term viability of the distributorship system or upset the balance of capacity utilization among plants. Thus companies may try to keep prices fairly close among countries in order to prevent such movements from taking place. Further, the cosmetic company Nu Skin entered the U.K. market in 1995 and saw that a gray market was developing from that market to other countries in Europe. In order to control its European distribution, Nu Skin moved very rapidly into markets in other European countries.[49]

Fixed versus Variable Pricing

Export prices, particularly to foreign distributors, are often negotiated. Small companies, especially those from LDCs, frequently give price concessions too quickly, thereby limiting their ability to negotiate on a range of marketing factors that affect their costs:

- Discounts for quantity or repeat orders
- Deadlines that increase production or transportation costs

There are country-to-country differences in
- **Whether manufacturers set prices**
- **Whether prices are fixed or bargained in stores**
- **Where bargaining occurs**
- **How sale prices can be used**

- Credit and payment terms
- Service
- Supply of promotional materials
- Training of sales personnel or customers[50]

Table 16.2 shows ways in which an exporter may deal more effectively in price negotiations.

The extent to which manufacturers can or must set prices at the retail level varies substantially by country. For instance, in India, soft drinks must have the prices put on the containers by the bottlers.[51] There also is substantial variation in whether, where, and for what products consumers bargain in order to settle on an agreed price. For instance, in the United States it is common to bargain for automobiles, real estate, and large orders of industrial supplies, but not for grocery items. In contrast, in Guatemala one bargains in native markets but not in supermarkets

---

Table 16.2
Preparations for Price Discussions
Note that the suggested approach for exporters is to delay a pricing commitment while discussing a whole package of other commitments.

Importer's reaction to price offer	Exporter's possible response
1. The initial price quoted is too high; a substantial drop is required.	Ask the buyer what is meant by too high; ask on what basis the drop is called for; stress product quality and benefits before discussing price.
2. Better offers have been received from other exporters.	Ask for more details on such offers; find out how serious such offers are; convince the buyer that the exporter has a better offer.
3. A counteroffer is required; a price discount is expected.	Avoid making a better offer without asking for something in return, but without jeopardizing loss of interest; when asking for something in return, make a specific suggestion, such as "If I give you a 5% price discount, would you arrange for surface transport including storage costs?"
4. The price of $___ is my last offer (the importer specifies a lower price).	Avoid accepting such an offer immediately; find out the quantities involved; determine if there will be repeat orders; ascertain who will pay for storage, publicity, after-sales service, and so on.
5. The product is acceptable, but the price is too high.	Agree to discuss details of the costing; promote product benefits, reliability as a regular supplier, timely delivery, unique designs, and so on.
6. The initial price quoted is acceptable.	Find out why the importer is so interested in the offer; recalculate the costing; check competition; contact other potential buyers to get more details on market conditions; review the pricing strategy; accept a trial order only.

Source: Claude Cellich, "Negotiating Strategies: The Question of Price," *International Trade Forum,* April–June 1991, p. 12.

for food, and fixed prices for automobiles are the norm. Bargaining is much more prevalent in purchases from street vendors in India than in Singapore, whereas bargaining in high-priced specialty stores is more frequent in Singapore than in India.

Retailers' Strength with Suppliers

Recall that one of Marks & Spencer's advantages in the United Kingdom is its ability, because of its size in the market, to convince suppliers to offer them low prices. Thus, M & S can usually undercut its competitors' prices at home. However, M & S had no advantage over other retailers in the French market. Similarly, Wal-Mart has lacked the same buying clout in Mexico that it has in the United States, thus making it hard to compete on the basis of being the lowest cost retailer. [52]

Countering International Competitors

Remember that one of the four objectives of international operations is to minimize competitive risk. When a company enters a market defensively to prevent a competitor from gaining global advantages within that market, pricing decisions are an integral part of achieving that objective. For example, P&G was concerned about the possible U.S. entry of the large Japanese consumer-products company, Kao. By selling detergent at a low price in the Japanese market, P&G forced Kao to freeze its prices below P&G's for twelve years and delayed its entry into the United States. [53] A company also may face the same industrial consumer in more than one market; therefore the paint price to Toyota in Mexico may well affect the paint company's ability to sell to Toyota in other countries.

Promotion

Promotion is the process of presenting messages intended to help sell a product or service. The types and direction of messages and the method of presentation may be extremely diverse, depending on the company, product, and/or country of operation.

The Push-Pull Mix

Push is more likely when
• **Self-service is not predominant**
• **Product price is a high portion of income**
• **Advertising is restricted**

Promotion may be categorized as push, which involves direct selling techniques, or pull, which relies on mass media. An example of push is door-to-door selling of encyclopedias; an example of pull is magazine advertisements for a brand of cigarettes. Most companies use combinations of both strategies. For each product in each country, a company must determine its total promotional budget as well as the mix of the budget between push and pull.

Several factors necessitate differences in the relative mix of push and pull among countries:

- Type of distribution system
- Cost and availability of media to reach target markets
- Consumer attitudes toward sources of information
- Price of the product relative to incomes

Generally, the more tightly controlled the distribution system, the more likely a company is to emphasize a push strategy because a greater effort is required to get distributors to handle a product. This is true, for example, in Belgium, where distributors are small and highly fragmented, forcing companies to concentrate on making their goods available.[54] Also affecting promotion is the amount of contact between salespeople and consumers. In a self-service situation, in which there are no salespersons to whom customers can turn for opinions on products, it is more important for the company to advertise through mass media or at the point of purchase.

Because of diverse national environments, promotional problems are extremely varied. For example, in rural India over half the population is illiterate, and only one-third of households have television sets. Colgate-Palmolive reaches this audience to sell toothpaste with half-hour infomercials from video vans that travel through the countryside.[55] In many countries, government regulations pose an even greater barrier. For example, Scandinavian television has long refused to accept commercials. A less obvious effect of government on the promotional mix is the direct or indirect tax many countries place on advertising.

France and the United States present an interesting contrast of cultural factors that affect the push-pull mix.[56] U.S. homemakers spend more time watching television and reading magazines, and they rely more on friends and advertising before purchasing a new product. In contrast, French homemakers spend more time shopping, examining items on shelves, and listening to the opinions of retailers. Therefore it has been easier to presell U.S. homemakers, whereas in France discounts to distributors and point-of-purchase displays have been more effective.

Finally, the amount of consumer involvement in making a purchase decision varies by country because of income levels. When a product's price relative to consumers' income is high, the consumer usually will want more time and information before making a decision. Information is best conveyed in a personal selling situation where two-way communication is fostered. In LDCs, more products usually have to be pushed because incomes are low in relation to price.

Standardization of Advertising Programs

The economies from using the same advertising programs as much as possible, such as on a global basis or among a group of countries with shared consumer attributes, are not as great as those from product standardization. Nevertheless, they can be significant.

In addition to reducing costs, standardization may be implemented to improve the quality of advertising at the local level (since local agencies may lack expertise),

Advantages of standardized advertising include
- **Some cost savings**
- **Better quality at local level**
- **Rapid entry to different countries**

to prevent internationally mobile consumers from being confused by different images, and to speed the entry of products into different countries. For example, Coca-Cola's ads showing people singing in twelve different languages was a truly standardized campaign that reached 3.8 billion viewers in 131 countries.[57] But standardized advertising usually means a program that is recognizable from market to market rather than one that is identical in each. For example, Coca-Cola's print advertisements for the United States and France used the same concept of "refreshment" and showed young people who had been playing sports. In the United States, the slogan was "Coke is it!" and the ad showed a baseball player in action. In France, the slogan was "*Un Coca-Cola pour un sourire*" ("A Coca-Cola for a smile") and the ad showed soccer players. Some of the problems that hinder complete standardization of advertising relate to translation, legality, and message needs.

Standardization usually implies using the same advertising agency globally; however, companies may differentiate campaigns among countries even if they use the same agency everywhere. By using the same agency, companies such as IBM, Colgate, and Tambrands have found that they can take good ideas in one market and quickly introduce them into other markets. However, some companies, such as Blockbuster and Procter & Gamble, prefer to use more than one agency in order to keep the agencies in a state of perpetual competition and to cover one agency's weak spots by drawing on the ideas of another agency.[58]

Translation   When media reach audiences in multiple countries, such as MTV programs aired throughout most of Europe, ads in those media cannot be translated. However, when a company is going to sell in a country with a different language, translation is usually necessary. For example, Wal-Mart encountered considerable ill will when it sent circulars to Quebec in English only instead of in French or a combination of French and English.[59] In contrast, to market its motorcycles abroad, Harley-Davidson published its magazines in foreign languages and staged beer-and-band rallies.[60] The most visible problem in translation is dubbing, because words on an added sound track never quite correspond to lip movements. Dubbing problems can be avoided by using actors who do not speak, along with a voice and/or print overlay in the appropriate language. Levi Strauss has done this for its jeans ads.[61] The voice and/or print overlay may be advantageous even when using the ad in different countries with the same language because of different spellings of the same words and the difficulty of understanding accents from another country.[62]

On the surface, translating a message would seem to be easy; however, some messages, particularly those involving a play on words, simply don't translate. One example is a Kellogg's U.S. ad: "What are you eating?" "Nut n' Honey." The number of ludicrous but costly mistakes companies have made attest to translation difficulties. Sometimes what is an acceptable word or direct translation in one place is obscene, misleading, or meaningless in another. For example, one company described itself as an "old friend" of China; however, it used the character for "old" that meant former instead of long-term.[63] Even within the same language, words can have different meanings in different countries. For example, United Airlines showed Paul Hogan, star of the *Crocodile Dundee* films, in the Australian outback on the cover of its inflight magazine. The caption was "Paul Hogan Camps It Up," which in Australian slang means "flaunts his homosexuality."[64] Another problem is in choosing the language when more than one is used within the country. For example, in Haiti a company might use Creole to reach the general population but French to reach the upper class.[65]

Legality   What is legal in one place may not be elsewhere. The differences result mainly from varying national views on consumer protection, competitive protection, promotion of civil rights, standards of morality, and nationalism. A few examples illustrate the vast differences that exist. In terms of consumer protection, policies differ on the amount of deception permitted, what can be advertised to children, whether warnings must be given of possible harmful effects, and the extent to which ingredients must be listed. The United Kingdom and the United States allow direct comparisons with competitive brands (for example, Pepsi versus Coca-Cola), whereas the Philippines prohibits them. Only a few countries regulate sexism in advertising. However, an interesting twist on sexism is South Korea's ban on advertising cigarettes to women. This ban has led Philip Morris to aim its Virginia Slims at men in Korea, even though the same brand is targeted at women in the United States.[66] Advertising of some products (for example, contraceptives and feminine-hygiene products) has been restricted in some locales because of rationales based on morality and good taste. Elsewhere, restrictions have been placed on ads that might prompt children to misbehave or people to break laws (for example, advertising automobile speeds that exceed the speed limit) and those that show barely clad women. New Zealand banned a Nike ad in which a rugby team tackles the coach, as well as a Chanel ad in which the model said to her male lover before kissing him, "I hate you. I hate you so much I think I'm going to die from it darling." In both cases, the ads were deemed to threaten violence.[67] Finally, nationalism and/or union contracts in several countries have caused them to restrict the use of foreign words, models, or themes in advertisements. A number of countries restrict the entry of foreign-produced films, tapes, mats, and other advertising materials through import duties, quotas, or embargos.[68]

Message needs   An advertising theme may not be appropriate everywhere because of national differences in how well the product is already known and perceived, who will make the purchasing decision, and what appeals are most important. Recall from the discussions of gap analysis and product life cycles how product-knowledge conditions vary. For example, American Express's U.S. campaign "Do You Know Me?" is aimed at gaining market share from other credit cards. However, in Europe the company needed to build credit-card usage.[69] Because

Japanese consumers perceive that their products are of good quality, advertisers within Japan concentrate more on image than on messages emphasizing quality.[70] Whether purchasing decisions for specific products are made by the husband, wife, or jointly varies among countries; therefore, companies need not only to place ads where the right decision-makers will see them, but also to use messages that may appeal differently to men and women.[71] The importance of different appeals may be affected by differences in economic or cultural factors. For example, a theme for selling Green Giant frozen vegetables in the United States is convenience; however, this theme could not be used in Japan because Japanese mothers take pride in the amount of time they take to prepare a meal. Instead, Green Giant uses an appeal that the frozen vegetables allow the opportunity to prepare the families' favorite foods more often. Green Giant also advertises canned corn according to the main way it is eaten in different countries—as a hot side-dish in the United States, a pizza topping in the United Kingdom, a cold addition to salads in France, an after-school treat in Japan, and a topping for ice cream in South Korea.[72]

Branding

MNEs must make four major branding decisions:

1. Brand versus no brand
2. Manufacturer's brand versus private brand
3. One brand versus multiple brands
4. Worldwide brand versus local brands[73]

Only the last of these is substantially affected by the international environment.

Some companies, such as Coca-Cola, have opted to use the same brand and logo globally. Doing this gives the product instant recognition and may save some promotional costs. Some other companies, for example, Nestlé, have associated many of their products under the same family of brands, such as the Nestea and Nescafé brands, in order to share in the goodwill that they have developed. Yet, there are a number of problems in trying to use uniform brands internationally.

Language Factors
One problem is that names may carry a different association in another language. For example, GM thought its Nova model could easily be called the same in Latin America, since the name means "star" in Spanish. However, people started pronouncing it "*no va,*" which is Spanish for "it does not go." Coca-Cola tries to use global branding wherever possible but discovered that the word "diet" in Diet Coke had a connotation of illness in Germany and Italy; consequently, the brand is called Coca-Cola Light outside the United States. Mars hesitated for years to change the

name of its Marathon candy bar in Britain to Snickers in order to create an internationally known brand because of the closeness in pronunciation to "knickers," a British term for women's underwear.[74] And Mars has encountered problems in standardizing names for other candy bars because of longstanding product alterations. For example, the company has both Mars and Milky Way bars in both the United States and Europe. The Mars bar in Europe is the same as a Milky Way in the United States. The U.S. Mars bar is unlike any candy bar the company has in Europe, and the Milky Way in Europe is unlike any the company has in the United States.[75]

Unilever has successfully translated the brand name for its fabric softener, while leaving its brand symbol, a baby bear, intact on the packaging. The U.S. name "Snuggle" is "Kuschelweich" in Germany, "Cajoline" in France, "Coccolino" in Italy, and "Mimosin" in Spain. But "Snuggle" did not quite convey the same meaning in English-speaking Australia, where Unilever uses "Huggy."[76]

Pronunciation presents other problems, because a foreign language may lack some of the sounds of a brand name or the pronunciation of the name may have a different meaning from the original. For example, McDonald's uses Donald McDonald in Japan because the Japanese have difficulty pronouncing the letter R. Marcel Bich dropped the H from his name when branding Bic pens because of the fear of mispronunciation in English. Perrier's popular French soft drink, Pschitt, has an unappetizing meaning when pronounced in English.

Different alphabets present still other problems. For example, brand names in English are judged by whether the name sounds appealing, whereas, brand names in Mandarin and Cantonese are judged on their visual appeal as well. Such companies as Coca-Cola, Mercedes-Benz, and Boeing have taken great effort to assure not only that the translation of their names is pronounced roughly the same as in English, but also that the brand name is meaningful. For example, Coca-Cola is pronounced Ke-kou-ke-le in Mandarin and means tasty and happy. Further, companies have sought names that are considered lucky in China, such as a name with eight strokes in it and displayed in red rather than blue.[77]

Acquisitions
Much international expansion takes place through acquisition of companies in foreign countries that already have branded products. For example, when Nestlé acquired Carnation, the Carnation name was so well known in the United States that it was kept as an addition to the canned-milk brands Nestlé promotes elsewhere. When Whirlpool, virtually unknown by consumers in Europe, acquired the appliance business of Philips, the brand name Philips-Whirlpool was used. In 1998, the Philips name will be dropped; by then Whirlpool expects to be well known.[78] Sunbeam has continued to use acquired brand names in Italy (Rowenta, Oster, Cadillac, Aircap, and Stewart) because they are well known and enjoy goodwill; however, Sunbeam has found that stretching the promotional budget over so many brands means that promotions are not as effective as they might be.[79]

Country-of-Origin Images

Images of products are affected by where they are made.

Companies should consider whether to create a local or a foreign image for their products. The products of some countries, particularly developed countries, tend to have a higher-quality image than do those from other countries. But images can change. Consider that for many years various Korean companies sold abroad under private labels or under contract with well-known companies. Some of these Korean companies, such as Samsung, now emphasize their own trade names and the quality of Korean products.[80]

There also are image differences concerning specific products from specific countries. For example, the French company BSN-Gervais Dannone brews Kroenenbourg, the largest-selling bottled beer in Europe, and the company's director general frankly admits that the Kroenenbourg trademark "sounds German."[81] Also, Czechs associate locally made products with poor quality, and so P&G has added German words to the labels of detergents it makes in the Czech Republic.[82]

In an innovative effort to create a British ice cream flavor along the lines of its American Cherry Garcia, Ben & Jerry's ran a contest for the best name and flavor. Cool Britannia won out over such entrants as Minty Python, Grape Expectations, Choc Ness Monster, and The Rolling Scones.[83]

Generic and Near-Generic Names

If a brand name is used for a class of product, the company may lose the trademark.

Companies want their product names to become household words but not so much so that trademarked brand names can be used by competitors to describe similar products. In the United States, the names Xerox and Kleenex are nearly synonymous with copiers and paper tissues but have remained proprietary brands. Some other names, such as cellophane, linoleum, Swiss army knives, and cornish hens, have become generic, or available for anyone to use.

In this context, companies sometimes face substantial differences among countries that may either stimulate or frustrate their sales. For example, Roquefort cheese and champagne are proprietary names in France but generic in the United States, a situation that impairs French export sales of those products. Also, international sales of U.S., Canadian, Irish, and Japanese whiskeys are hindered by the fact that in much of the world, whisky is a synonym for Scotch whisky.

Distribution

Companies may have to devise ways to help distributors so that they give attention to the companies' products.

A company may accurately assess market potential, design products or services for that market, and promote to probable consumers; however, it will have little likelihood of reaching its sales potential if the goods or services are not conveniently available to customers. One aspect of this problem is getting goods to where people want to buy them. For example, does a man prefer to buy hair dressing in a grocery store, barber shop, drugstore, or some other type of outlet?

riticisms have been leveled at MNEs for introducing and promoting products that are not aimed sufficiently at the needs of LDCs. For example, pharmaceutical companies are criticized because they spend very little on antimalarial research as compared with research on diseases more prevalent in industrial countries, even though malaria results in more fatalities.[84] Further, so-called superfluous products and luxury goods are criticized for shifting spending away from necessities and contributing to the enhancement of elitist class distinctions.[85] For example, critics have questioned making soft drinks available to consumers who lack funds for pharmaceuticals. This criticism has been answered largely by arguments that consumers should make their own choices and by showing the

ETHICAL DILEMMAS & SOCIAL RESPONSIBILITY

positive side effects of seemingly unnecessary products. For example, soft-drink companies have argued that they are responsible for introducing the sanitary bottling operations essential for other industries, such as pharmaceuticals. Further, Coca-Cola once test marketed a soft drink in Brazil with vitamins added, and Quaker Oats introduced a high-protein and low-cost drink aimed at poor Colombians; however, neither Coca-Cola nor Quaker Oats were able to garner enough sales to sustain those products. Yet critics question if this is sufficient justification. But even if products reach only affluent customers, companies may be criticized. For example, Benetton has been criticized for opening hard-currency-only shops for tourists in Cuba and North Korea because they are an affront to the local population who are economically and legally prohibited from buying the merchandise.[86]

There are also questions as to whether companies have a similar ethical responsibility in industrial countries, in which consumers are more likely to have the educational level necessary to make informed choices. For example, as the Japanese economy has become more open, consumption of food additives, sugar, beef, and dairy products in Japan has grown to the point that diet-related heart disease, strokes, protein anemia, diabetes, and cancer have increased markedly.

MNEs also have been criticized for advertising products to people who are not equipped to understand those products' implications or their own needs. The most famous case involved sales of infant formula in LDCs, where infant mortality increased because the rate of bottle feeding increased over that of breast feeding. Because of low incomes and poor education, mothers frequently overdiluted formula so that it was no longer nutritious and gave it to their babies in unhygienic conditions. Critics argued that increased bottle feeding resulted from heavy promotion of formula. Companies countered by claiming increased bottle feeding resulted from factors other than promotion of formula—specifically, the rise in the number of working mothers and a resultant general trend toward fewer products and services being made in the home. The promotion, they argued, persuaded people to give up their "home brews" in favor of the most nutritious breast milk substitute available. Regardless, the World Health Organization overwhelmingly passed a voluntary code for restricting formula promotion in developing countries. The company hardest hit by criticism was Nestlé because it had the largest market share in LDCs and because organizing a boycott against it was easy because of its name-identified products. In 1984, the company agreed to cease advertising that could discourage breast feeding, limit free formula supplies at hospitals, and ban personal gifts to health officials.[87] Despite these events, governments have been slow and reluctant to prohibit infant formula promotion. For example, in Taiwan fewer than 10 percent of babies are breast-fed, but its government did not restrict formula promotion until 1993 and then only on TV advertisements.[88] In the absence of regulations, how far companies should go to protect consumers is unclear.

When consumers boycott a company, some argue that it is unethical to give in to the pressure groups that have taken a stand on some issue. Perhaps the most notable recent example of this controversy concerns the abortion pill., RU 486. It was developed by the French company, Roussel Uclaf, which was acquired by the German company, Hoechst. Hoechst, fearful of adverse publicity, forbade the sale of RU 486 except in the three countries (the United Kingdom, France, and Switzerland) where Roussel Uclaf had already begun sales. The French health ministry has insisted that the product remain on sale on the grounds that it is "the moral property of women." Yet, in 1997, U.S. anti-abortion activists took out full-page newspaper advertisements urging U.S. consumers not to use Allegra, a recently launched Hoechst anti-hayfever treatment because of the continued sales of RU 486 outside the United States.[89] Thus, Hoechst faces ethical criticism, regardless of what it does.

Distribution is the course—physical path or legal title—that goods take between production and consumption. In international marketing, a company must decide on the method of distribution among countries as well as the method within the country where final sale occurs. We already have discussed many considerations for distribution, including the distribution channels to move goods among countries, how the title to goods gets transferred, and the operating forms for foreign-market penetration. This section does not review these aspects of distribution; it discusses distributional differences and conditions within foreign countries that an international marketer should understand.

Difficulty of Standardization

Different systems   Within the marketing mix, distribution is one of the most difficult functions to standardize internationally, for several reasons. Each country has its own distribution system. This usually is difficult to change because it has evolved over time and reflects the country's cultural, economic, and legal environments. Some of the factors that influence how goods will be distributed in a given country are the attitudes toward owning one's own store, the cost of paying retail workers, labor legislation differentially affecting chain stores and individually owned stores, legislation restricting the operating hours and size of stores, the trust that owners have in their employees, the efficacy of the postal system, and the financial ability to carry large inventories. For example, Hong Kong supermarkets, compared to those in the United States, carry a higher proportion of fresh goods, are smaller, sell smaller quantities per customer, and are located more closely to each other (see Table 16.3).

A few other examples should illustrate how distribution norms differ. Finland has few stores per capita because general-line retailers predominate there, whereas Italian distribution is characterized by a very fragmented retail and wholesale structure. In the Netherlands, buyers' cooperatives deal directly with manufacturers; in Japan, there are cash-and-carry wholesalers for retailers that do not need financing or delivery. In Germany, mail-order sales are very important; however, in Portugal, they aren't.

How do these differences affect companies' marketing activities? One soft-drink company, for example, has targeted most of its European sales through grocery stores; however, the method for getting its soft drinks to those stores varies widely. In the United Kingdom, one national distributor has been able to gain sufficient coverage and shelf space so that the soft-drink company can concentrate on other aspects of its marketing mix. In France, a single distributor has been able to get good coverage in the larger supermarkets but not in the smaller ones; consequently, the soft-drink company has been exploring how to get secondary distribution without upsetting its relationship with the primary distributor. In Norway, regional distributors predominate; thus the soft-drink company has been challenged to get them to cooperate sufficiently that national promotion campaigns will be effective.

Table 16.3
Sociocultural Elements of Supermarket Technology in the United States and Hong Kong
Different conditions (columns 2 and 3) with respect to sociocultural elements (column 1) have caused supermarkets in Hong Kong to sell a high proportion of fresh foods, to handle customers more frequently, to sell in low quantities, and to be located closer to competitors.

Sociocultural elements	United States	Hong Kong
Dietary habits	Like meats Used to frozen foods	Like seafood and meats Used to fresh foods
Shopping patterns	Objective to save time Infrequent	Objective to preserve freshness of food More frequent
Living conditions	Better conditions Spacious	Conditions not as good Crowded
Size of refrigerator	Bigger	Smaller
Availability of car	More available	Less available
Population density	Less dense	Very dense
Urbanization	Low	High

Source: From "Development of Supermarket Technology: The Incomplete Transfer Phenomenon" by Suk-ching Ho and Ho-fuk Lau, *International Marketing Review*, Spring 1988, p. 27. Reprinted with permission.

In Belgium, the company could find no acceptable distributor, so it has had to assume that function itself.

Choosing Distributors and Channels

Distribution may be handled internally
- **When volume is high**
- **When there is a need to deal directly with the customer due to the nature of the product**
- **When the customer is global**
- **To gain a competitive advantage**

Internal handling   When sales volume is low, it usually is more economical for a company to handle distribution by contracting with an external distributor. By doing so, however, it may lose a certain amount of control. Management should reassess periodically whether sales have grown to the point that they can be effectively handled internally.

Circumstances conducive to the internal handling of distribution include not only high sales volume but also the following:

- When the product has the characteristic of high price, high technology, *or* need for complex after-sales servicing (such as aircraft), the producer probably will have to deal directly with the buyer. The producer may simultaneously use a distributor within the foreign country that will serve to identify sales leads.

- When the company deals with global customers, especially in business-to-business sales, such as an auto-parts manufacturer that sells original equipment to the same automakers in multiple countries, such sales may go directly from the producer to the global customer.
- When the company views its main competitive advantage to be its distribution methods, such as some food franchisors, it eventually may franchise abroad but maintain its own distribution outlet to serve as a "flagship." Amway, Avon, and Tupperware are examples of companies that have successfully transferred their house-to-house distribution methods from the U.S. to their operations abroad. Matsushita, which sells in Japan largely within its 20,000 corner shops containing only its products, plans to establish a network of 3,000 retail outlets in China.[90] Dell Computer has successfully handled its own mail-order sales in Europe.[91]

Some evaluation criteria for distributors include their
- **Financial capability**
- **Connections with customers**
- **Fit with a company's product**
- **Other resources**

Distributor qualifications   A company usually can choose from a number of potential distributors. Common criteria for selecting a distributor include

- Its financial strength
- Its good connections
- Extent of its other business commitments
- Current status of its personnel, facilities, and equipment [92]

The distributor's financial strength is important because of the potential long-term relationship between company and distributor and because of the assurance that money will be available for such things as maintaining sufficient inventory. Good connections are particularly important if sales must be directed to certain types of buyers, such as governmental procurement agencies. The amount of other business commitments can indicate whether the distributor has time for the company's product and whether it currently handles competitive or complementary products.[93] Finally, the current status of the distributor's personnel, facilities, and equipment indicates not only its ability to deal with the product but also how quickly start-up can occur.

Spare parts and service are important for sales.

Spare parts and repair   Consumers are reluctant to buy products that may require spare parts and service in the future unless they feel assured these will be readily available in good quality and at reasonable prices. The more complex and expensive the product, the more important after-sales servicing is. When after-sales servicing is important, companies may need to invest in service centers for groups of distributors that serve as intermediaries between producers and consumers. Earnings from sales of parts and after-sales service sometimes may match that of the original product.

Distributors choose what
they will handle. Companies
• May need to give
  incentives
• May use successful products as bait for new ones
• Must convince distributors
  that product and company
  are viable

Gaining distribution   Companies must evaluate potential distributors, but distributors must choose which companies and products to represent and emphasize. Both wholesalers and retailers have limited storage facilities, display space, money to pay for inventories, and transportation and personnel to move and sell merchandise; therefore they try to carry only those products that have the greatest profit potential. In many cases, distributors are tied into exclusive arrangements with manufacturers that prevent new competitive entries. For example, there are about 25,000 Japanese outlets that sell only Shiseido's cosmetics, 13,000 that sell only Toshiba products, and 11,000 that sell only Hitachi products.[94] A company that is new to a country and wants to introduce products that some competitors are already selling may find it difficult to convince distributors to handle its brands. Even established companies sometimes may find it hard to gain distribution for their new products, although they have the dual advantage of being known and of being able to use existing profitable lines as "bait" for the new merchandise.

A company wanting to use existing distribution channels may need to analyze competitive conditions carefully in order to offer effective incentives for those distributors to handle the product. It may need to identify problems distributors have in order to gain their loyalty by offering assistance. For example, Coca-Cola has held seminars for mom-and-pop stores abroad on how to operate more efficiently and to compete with larger distributors.[95] Companies alternatively may turn to several other possibilities, including offering higher margins, after-sales servicing, and promotional support, any of which may be offered on either a permanent or introductory basis. The type of incentive should also depend on the comparative costs within each market. In the final analysis, however, incentives will be of little help unless the distributors believe a company's products are viable. The company therefore must sell the distributors on its products as well as itself as a reliable company.

Hidden Costs

When companies consider launching products in foreign markets, they must consider what final consumer prices will be in order to estimate sales potential. Because of different national distribution systems, the cost of getting products to consumers varies widely from one country to another. Five factors that often contribute to cost differences in distribution are infrastructure conditions, the number of levels in the distribution system, retail inefficiencies, size and operating-hours restrictions, and inventory stock-outs.

In many countries, the roads and warehousing facilities are so poor that getting goods to consumers quickly, at a low cost, and with minimum damage or loss en route is problematic. For example in Nigeria, Nestlé has had to build small warehouses across the country instead of depending on a central warehouse that one would expect based on the country's area. Roads are in such poor condition that travel is slow and trucks are prone to breakdowns. Further, because of crime,

Nestlé uses armed guards on its trucks and allows them to travel only during day-light hours.[96] Differences in infrastructure create additional operating adjustments. For example, Domino's Pizza, which depends on call-in orders and quick deliveries for its competitive advantage, faces a different situation in Iceland because most people don't own phones. It has contracted with local establishments, such as drive-in movie theaters, so that drivers can borrow cellular phones to call Domino's. In Japan, it has had to install large wall maps and ask detailed questions of callers because houses are not numbered sequentially.[97] Many countries have multitiered wholesalers that sell to each other before the product reaches the retail level. For example, national wholesalers sell to regional ones, who sell to local ones, and so on. This sometimes occurs because wholesalers are too small to cover more than a small geographic area. Japan is an example of such a market: There are, on average, 2.21 wholesale steps between producer and retailer in Japan, compared with 1.0 in the United States and 0.73 in France. Because each intermediary adds a markup, product prices are driven up. However, such overall figures obscure differences by product. For example, fresh food passes through much longer and complex chan-nels than such products as electronic goods.[98]

In some countries, particularly LDCs, low labor costs and a basic distrust by owners of all but family members result in retail practices that raise consumer prices. A typical situation involves counter service rather than self-service. In the former case, a customer waits to be served and shown merchandise. If the customer decides to purchase what is shown, the customer is given an invoice to take to a cashier's line in order to pay. Once the invoice is stamped as paid, the customer must go to another line to pick up the merchandise after presenting the stamped invoice. This procedure is followed for purchases as small as a pencil. The additional personnel add to retailing costs, and the added time people must be in the store means fewer people can be served in the given space. In contrast, most retailers in some (mainly industrialized) countries have equipment that improves the efficiency of handling customers and reports, such as electronic scanners, cash registers linked to inventory control records, and machines connecting purchases to credit card companies.

Many countries, such as France, Germany, and Japan, have laws to protect small retailers. These effectively limit the number of large retail establishments and the efficiencies they bring to sales.[99] Many countries also limit operating hours as a means of protecting employees from having to work late at night or on weekends. At the same time, the limit keeps retailers from covering the fixed cost of their space over more hours, thus these costs are passed on to consumers. Further, stores cannot use longer opening hours as a competitive advantage. For example, 7-Eleven stores in Sweden cannot sell a full range of goods between midnight and six a.m.[100] Where retailers are typically small, as is true of grocers in Spain, there is little space to store inventory. Wholesalers must incur the cost of making small deliveries to many more establishments and sometimes may have to visit each retailer more fre-quently because of stock outages.

COUNTERVAILING

F O R C E S

One trend that is most likely to have an impact on the future of international marketing is the continued improvement in transportation and communications, which influences global awareness of products and life-styles. Thus a continued trend toward standardized marketing programs on a worldwide basis is likely. This does not mean, however, that MNEs will be able to narrow their product lines or promotional activities. Instead, they may have to differentiate further in order to satisfy people's needs according to demographic, sociographic, and psychographic variables that cut across national boundaries. For example, companies may well find themselves defining a market segment as finely as "females, age 26 to 30, working, unmarried, three to four years of college, high achievement motivation, affiliated religiously, with low dogmatic personalities." As discretionary income increases, not only do exotic products become so commonplace that they lose their attractiveness but also more products and services compete with each other (for example, cars, travel, jewelry, and furniture compete for the same discretionary spending). Thus increased segmentation probably will be necessary.

Greater standardization also does not imply that companies can disregard national differences. As companies from industrial countries have increasingly embraced the concept of global standardization, there is some evidence that they are losing market niches to companies from NICs that are more willing to make adaptations.

LOOKING TO
THE FUTURE

Most projections are that disparities between the "haves" and "have-nots" will grow rather than diminish in the foreseeable future, both within and among countries. This probably will mean a simultaneous growth in affluent and poor market segments. Globally, the affluent sector will have the means of purchasing more goods and services and will not be likely to forgo purchases because of antimaterialistic sentiments. Because of rising educational levels within this sector, more of its members will be knowledgeable about slight differences in the end utility of products. It will be less possible to segment along national lines to reach these consumers.

The rise in affluence and leisure of the "haves" probably will result in changes in where they spend their money. As these consumers take at least a part of productivity increases in the form of leisure, they will spend a proportionately larger amount of their incomes on entertainment, sports clothes and equipment, organizational memberships, and travel. In addition, they probably will spend more on services than on products.

At the other extreme will be growing numbers of poor people who will have little disposable income to spend on nonnecessities. MNEs will face increasing pressures to develop standardized products to fit the needs of these people and to produce goods by labor-intensive methods so as to employ more of them. Accomplishing this will create operational problems because of conflicting competitive pressures to differentiate products and to cut costs through capital-intensive methods.

Despite the growing proportions of "haves" and "have-nots," the actual numbers of people moving out of poverty levels and into middle income levels is projected to increase.

This is largely because of population and income growth in many LDCs, especially in Asia. Such a shift will likely mean growth in sales of many products in LDCs for which there is a mature market in industrial countries, such as for telephones and household appliances. Further, with increased access to the Internet, customers will be able to purchase goods from anywhere in the world. In the process, companies will find it more difficult to charge different prices in different countries. But they will more effectively be able to cut out middlemen in the distribution of their products. For example, Japanese consumers already purchase more than half their international airline tickets over the Internet. This enables them, for example, to purchase a Seoul–Los Angeles ticket with a stop in Tokyo and then not use the Seoul–Tokyo portion because a Tokyo–Los Angeles ticket is much more expensive. Estimates for 1995 were that about seven million computers (about half in the United States) were connected to the Internet, with Internet sales of over $400 million—up from $20 million a year earlier and expected to exceed $1 billion in 1996.[101]

What products and services are likely to enjoy the major growth markets? It is generally agreed that data generation and storage will continue to be a major growth area during the next few decades. It also is probable that among the market-growth leaders will be companies making breakthroughs in process technologies to improve productivity, such as lasers, optics, and robotics, and those making breakthroughs in energy conservation, such as solar photovoltaics, fuel cells, and coal conversion.

WEB CONNECTION
Check out our home page for links to marketing resources on the **World Wide Web.**

Summary

- Although the principles for selling abroad are the same as those for selling domestically, the international businessperson must deal with a less familiar environment, which may change rapidly.

- Tools for broadly assessing foreign demand for products include analysis of consumption patterns, estimates based on what has happened in other countries, studies of historical trends, income elasticity, regression, and gap analysis. Some problems with these tools include changes in taste and technology that render observations from the past and observations from other countries invalid for specific countries.

- A standardized approach to marketing means maximum uniformity in products and programs among the countries in which sales occur. Although this approach minimizes expenses, most companies make changes to fit country needs in order to increase sales volume.

- A variety of legal and other environmental conditions may call for altering products in order to capture foreign demand. In addition to determining when products should be altered, companies also must decide how many and which products to sell abroad.

- Because of different demand characteristics, a product may be in a growth stage in one country and in a mature, or declining, stage in another. Companies can usually exert more control over pricing during the growth stage.

- Government regulations may directly or indirectly affect the prices companies charge. International pricing is further complicated because of fluctuations in currency values, differences in product preferences, and variations in fixed versus variable pricing practices.

- For each product in each country, a company must determine not only its promotional budget but also the mix between push and pull. The relationship between push and pull promotions should depend on the distribution system, cost and availability of media, consumer attitudes, and the product's price relative to incomes.

- Major problems for standardizing advertising in different countries involve translation, legality, and message needs.

- Global branding is hampered by language differences, expansion by acquisition, national images, and laws concerning generic names.

- Distribution channels vary substantially among countries. The differences may affect not only the relative costs of operating but also the ease of making initial sales.

Case
Avon[102]

Avon, which commenced operations in 1886, is now one of the world's largest manufacturers and marketers of beauty and related products. About 62 percent of its 1995 sales of $4.5 billion were in cosmetics, fragrances, and toiletries, with the rest in gift and decorative items, apparel, and fashion jewelry and accessories. The company is headquartered in the United States, but about 65 percent of its sales, 59 percent of its assets, and 75 percent of its employees are outside the country. It has direct investments in 41 countries and sells in another 84 through licensing, franchising, and distributor arrangements. Map 16.2 shows the location of Avon's direct investments and its breakdown of sales by region.

Avon moved into the Canadian market in 1914. Its next foreign market entry was not until 1954, when it entered the Venezuelan market. Since then, its international expansion has accelerated, and growth in foreign sales has exceeded the growth in U.S. sales. In fact, it

Developing markets

Established markets

NET SALES BY REGION

European region
16%

United States
35%

Pacific region
16%

Americas
33%

**Map 16.2
Avon's Foreign Direct
Investment and
Breakdown of Sales
by Region**
Most of Avon's sales are
international. Those countries in the developing
markets category are
where Avon expects most
future growth to occur.

Source: Avon 1995 Annual Report.

entered 14 new countries between 1990 and 1996. The emphasis on foreign operations
has resulted from several factors that have slowed U.S. growth potential. First, there is little
or no usage gap remaining in the United States for cosmetics, fragrances, and toiletries.
Even if there were, only 5.4 percent of the world's women live in the United States and
Canada. Second, Avon's U.S. sales have relied on independent salespersons (almost always
women working part-time), who are usually referred to as "Avon ladies" or "Avon representatives." They make direct sales to households by demonstrating products and giving
beauty advice. They then place sales orders with Avon and deliver orders to the customers
once they receive them. But as more U.S. women have entered the workforce full-time,
they have become less receptive to door-to-door salespersons, have less time to spend on
makeup demonstrations, want to receive their purchases immediately, and are less willing
to work as Avon ladies. Third, the recent popularity in the United States of the so-called
"grunge" look (one that spurns glamour) has further slowed sales growth potential.

Concomitantly, many foreign markets have been ideal for Avon's growth. For example,
the lack of developed infrastructure in the rural areas of such countries as Brazil, China,
and the Philippines deters women from leaving their homes to shop for cosmetics. But in
these countries, Avon ladies reach consumers in some of the most remote areas, such as
by canoe in the Amazon region of Brazil, despite the dangers of piranhas, poisonous snakes,
and black caimans. (At year-end 1995, Avon had 206,000 active representatives in Brazil—a
number that exceeded the membership in all of Brazil's armed forces.) In transitional
economies, Avon's market entry has coincided with pent-up demand from the period of

centrally planned economic policies. (Avon entered Hungary in 1990, and by the end of 1992 also had direct investments in Poland, the Czech Republic, and Slovakia.) In rapid-growth economies, such as Chile and Malaysia, there has been a growing middle class that can afford Avon's products. In all of the aforementioned countries, there are ample labor supplies of potential Avon ladies.

Product lines vary by country, primarily because they are geared to the needs of specific markets. For example, Avon sells a skin cream, Sol & Cor, only in the Brazilian market. The cream provides a combination of moisturizer, sunscreen, and insect repellent. The company also sells creams in parts of Asia to lighten the complexion, but the desire for skin lightening is too small elsewhere to justify marketing efforts.

Avon representatives sometimes sell abroad products that Avon does not handle in the United States. By offering a wider array of products, the average order per household can potentially be increased. For example, Avon has licensed the right to sell Crayola products in Brazil and Disney products in Mexico. Avon and *Reader's Digest* are collaborating in Canada, Brazil, Australia, France, and New Zealand; Avon representatives sell *Reader's Digest* publications, and *Reader's Digest* includes Avon inserts with its subscriptions.

Because of Avon's extensive distribution abroad, it is often approached to become a partner for manufacturers who lack sales experience in a particular country. For example, Avon was approached by the British firm Betterware, and the two companies now have a joint venture in Mexico for the production and sale of plastic products for the home. This joint venture uses the same basic system of independent representatives that Avon employs in Mexico, but the joint venture has its own representatives apart from those selling Avon products.

When new products are developed for a given country, information is disseminated to Avon facilities in other countries. For example, Avon-Japan developed emulsion technologies to produce lotions and creams with lighter textures and higher hydration levels, and the process is now used in many of the countries where Avon operates. Avon also has a Far East office in Hong Kong that sources goods from nine countries and issues about 2000 supplier contracts for about 600 new products per year. The office finds sources of products for country groups, tests and handles quality assurance, and designs and develops new products. For example, the office buys gift items for the U.S. market and lingerie for European markets.

In addition to developing products for specific markets, Avon has recently emphasized standardized products using global brands for products that have a broad appeal to women of many nationalities. One of these has been a family of skin-protection products using the Anew brand. The first to use alpha hydroxy acid, these products have become the market leader in virtually every country in which they are sold. Some other global brands are Rare Gold and Far Away fragrances. Through standardized products and local branding, Avon can create a uniform global image of quality and, at the same time, effect cost savings from uniform ingredients and packaging. Global branding also helps inform consumers that the company is global. This helps sales in countries such as Thailand, where consumers prefer not to buy products made by local companies. Between 1993 and 1995, Avon's worldwide share of sales from the globally standardized products with global brands grew from 11 percent to 22 percent.

Global standardization of products and brands is complicated when Avon enters new markets by making acquisitions. For example, in 1996 Avon acquired Justine, a well-respected and prestige direct seller of beauty products in South Africa. Because Justine held the second largest market share within South Africa, Avon wanted to capitalize on the recognition and goodwill Justine had built. So Avon plans to maintain the Justine products and brands and aim them at the high end of the market. Meanwhile, Avon will use Justine's marketing expertise to launch a separate line of Avon products aimed at the mid-range of the market. Avon will also recruit its own sales force of 10,000 representatives to augment the 10,000 sales representatives selling Justine products.

Although Avon prominently displays its name on most of its products worldwide, most of its brand names differ among countries. Instructions are printed in local languages, but the brand names themselves are sometimes in the local language and sometimes not. English or French brand names are often used because of the high-quality image associated with the United States and France for beauty products. For example, Rosa Mosqueta (in Spanish), Revival (in English), and Renaissage (in French) are brand names for Avon skin care products in Chile, Argentina, and Japan, respectively. In each case, the Avon logo appears prominently on the products' containers as well.

Each country operation sets its own prices to reflect local market conditions and strategic objectives. The prices are subject to change for each sales campaign. Avon runs a new campaign with different special offers every two weeks in the United States and every three weeks abroad. The shortness of campaigns is helpful for adjusting prices in highly inflationary economies. However, during Brazil's hyper-inflationary period in the early 1990s, Avon chose not to raise prices as much as the inflation rate. This decision lowered Avon-Brazil's profit performance, but allowed for the recruitment of more representatives and the building of market share and consumer loyalty. The strategy paid off after mid-1994, when the Brazilian governmental policies stabilized inflation. When the Mexican peso devalued in late 1994, the company took the same approach it had taken in Brazil.

Avon's major promotion is through the brochures used for each of its campaigns and delivered to potential customers by the Avon ladies. The company prints about 600 million copies of the brochures in fifteen languages, dwarfing the circulation of any magazine or commercial publication. Additionally, Avon relies on both print and television advertising.

The basic aim of Avon's promotion is the same throughout the world—to promote its products and image, increase the number of customers served, and recruit new representatives. However, the specific needs and execution of the promotion differ among markets. For example, in 1996 Avon's ads in the U.S. and Canada used the theme "Just Another Avon Lady" to show that women in all walks of life use Avon. In Germany, the ads sought to change Avon's image of being old-fashioned. In Japan, where more than 2000 cosmetic companies compete and Avon is not a leading competitor, the company sought consumer awareness of its name. In the Philippines, Avon used a top entertainer and fashion model to counter similar ads by Revlon and Max Factor.

Avon seeks to develop a global image of being a company that supports women and their needs. It sponsored "The Olympic Women" exhibit at the Atlanta Olympics, where many women competed under the sponsorship of various Avon subsidiaries. Avon publicizes how being an Avon lady heightens the role of women. For example, its publicity has shown how civil war in El Salvador caused casualties and disabled men, leaving women with little education to head households; however, by being Avon ladies, they can earn income while continuing their duties at home. The company also gives annual *Women of Enterprise Awards* to leading women entrepreneurs. Avon's activities and publicity have generated further favorable publicity in media reports, such as a 20-page article in *Veja,* a weekly Brazilian magazine. Perhaps Avon's biggest social responsibility project involves its work internationally in fighting breast cancer. Avon ladies disseminate information about breast cancer along with their promotion brochures and sell pins to raise money for local needs, such as mammography machines in Venezuela and a public awareness TV commercial in Malaysia. Such work has not gone unnoticed, and Avon has received many publicity-generating awards, such as the 1996 Gilda's Club Corporate Vision Award.

Avon has used a variety of means to enter foreign markets, not only acquisition and start-up, but also wholly owned direct investments (such as in Mexico), joint ventures (such as in Turkey), licensing of its technology and trademark (such as in Egypt), and sales to distributors (such as in Costa Rica). The degree of commitment is based primarily on the potential market size of the country; however, Avon sometimes clusters a group of countries into a region and serves that region from one of the countries. For example, Avon uses Guatemala to manufacture and create brochures that are shipped to the rest of Central America. In addition, Avon has manufacturing plants in fewer countries than it has direct investments; thus the company is actively engaged in exporting from numerous locations. Within Europe, Avon relies on its manufacturing plants in the United Kingdom, Italy, and Germany to supply other countries.

Avon's basic distribution method is duplicated in foreign countries, which means it sells to independent representatives who have taken orders from customers they have visited. However, there are some substantial variations in distribution among the countries where Avon products are sold. To begin with, not all of Avon's distribution abroad is door-to-door. In Russia, during decades of communist rule, women became wary of knocks on the door—a discomfort that persists—so representatives sell at work or through personal networks. In India, sales are made similarly because door-to-door transactions are associated with old-newspaper and old-clothes buyers. In parts of Brazil, many upscale customers are cloistered in apartments that are virtually inaccessible to salespeople because of security entrances. Avon-Brazil advertises on television and offers an 800 number to reach that clientele.

A drawback of direct selling is that customers cannot obtain a product whenever they want it; they must wait until they are visited by a representative to place an order and then must wait again to receive the merchandise. In response to this drawback, Avon-Malaysia opened a retail outlet in Malaysia in 1990. Called a *beauty boutique,* customers can buy Avon products there and receive as much personal attention as when they buy at home. Moreover, representatives can go to the boutique to obtain products immediately, rather than waiting for their orders to be filled. The concept proved so successful that by 1993, the company had eight boutiques in Malaysia and began franchising Avon stores that distribute only Avon products to top-selling representatives. By the end of 1995, the company had 35

Malaysian boutiques to augment sales through its 25,000 representatives. The Malaysian concept has since been duplicated in Chile.

In an interesting departure from the Malaysian experience, Avon-Argentina opened a "Beauty Center" in 1995 in an upscale suburb of Buenos Aires. In addition to selling products, as in Malaysia, this center provides customers with a wide variety of services, such as hair styling and manicures. The center also serves to build an upscale image among customers who would normally shop at retail outlets and/or buy imported products. This same approach is now followed in Mexico and Venezuela as well.

In some countries, particularly LDCs, getting merchandise to consumers in rural areas is a major challenge. Mail systems are unreliable, and personal delivery to representatives is expensive. Because of this problem, Avon-Philippines pioneered a system of branch selling. Instead of delivering orders to the homes of district managers who in turn would arrange delivery to representatives, as in the United States, Avon-Philippines has established franchise centers that stock merchandise. Nearly 100 franchise managers visit the centers and pick up merchandise for the representatives in their district. This saves the representatives from making arduous treks, sometimes two hours by bus. Since 1991, the centers have experimented with more retail-like services. For example, they have wide aisles, shopping carts, and scanners at check-out so that the franchise managers can fill and pay for their orders quickly. The concept of the franchise centers has since been adapted by Avon in other countries, such as China and Indonesia.

In the preceding discussion, successful practices in one country have been copied in other countries. To encourage the transfer of know-how, Avon brings marketing personnel from different countries together to share what they call "best practices." They also promote competition among countries, such as contests for best brochure cover and best color cosmetics advertisement.

Avon anticipates that international operations will account for the bulk of its growth in the foreseeable future. Although its foreign expansion has been aggressive, Avon products are still not available to over half the world's women. Avon classifies the countries in which it sells as either developing markets or established markets. It expects most of its future growth to be in the former, which are shown in pink on Map 16.2 In addition, in 1996, Avon was considering entry into four new countries: Bulgaria, Romania, Ukraine, and Vietnam.

Questions

1. Among the product policies described in the chapter, how would you classify that of Avon?
2. As economies develop, will Avon have to de-emphasize its direct selling methods? What alternatives might it consider?
3. In the trade-off between globalization and national responsiveness, do you believe Avon has the right mix?
4. Some critics argue that products such as cosmetics and toiletries are superfluous to the needs of poor consumers, yet Avon is actively trying to sell to these consumers. How might Avon answer those critics?

Chapter Notes

1. Data for the case were taken from "M & S Getting Their French Lessons Right," *The Times* (London), August 2, 1976, p. 16; Barbara Crossette, "British Store Shapes Up for Parisians," *New York Times*, June 28, 1975, p. 14; "St. Michael Spreads the Gospel," *Economist*, September 1977, pp. 68–69; "Super Supermarkets," *The Accountant*, June 26, 1980, pp. 981–983; Alan Freeman, "Marks & Spencer Canada Adheres to Parent's Principles Despite Losses," *Wall Street Journal*, August 4, 1981, p. 39; Margaret de Miraval, "British Influence Aiding French Department Stores," *Christian Science Monitor*, July 7, 1983, p. 15; "Marks & Spencer Tries Yet Again," *Financial Times*, April 25, 1985, p. 16; Mina Williams, "St. Michael Chilled Foods Introduced in Kings Stores," *Supermarket News*, December 11, 1989, p. 1+; Stephen Dowdell, "Marks & Spencer Buys Kings in First U.S. Food Venture," *Supermarket News*, August 15, 1988, p. 1+; Steven Weiner, "Low Marks, Few Sparks," *Forbes*, September 18, 1989, pp. 146–147; Isadore Barmash, "Brooks Brothers Stays the Course," *New York Times*, November 23, 1990, p. C1; John Thornhill, "A European Spark for Marks," *Financial Times*, July 13, 1992, p. 12; Mike Sheridan, "British Values," *Sky*, October 1992, pp. 69–74; Stephanie Strom, "A Quiet Updating for Brooks Bros.," *New York Times*, November 9, 1992, p. C1; Maureen Whitehead, "International Franchising—Marks & Spencer: A Case Study," *International Journal of Retail and Distribution Management*, Vol. 19, No. 2, March–April 1991, pp. 10–12. Craig R. Whitney, "Seducing France With Watercress Sandwiches," *New York Times*, May 19, 1995, p. A4; Tara Parker-Pope, "Marks & Spencer Takes Its Lumps Abroad," *Wall Street Journal*, May 24, 1995, p. A10; Neil Buckley, "Marks and Spencer Dips Toe Into China," *Financial Times*, October 12, 1995, p. 7; Merrill Lynch Capital Markets Report, Marks & Spencer, November 16, 1995; "Marks & Spencer to Sell Chain in Canada," *Daily News Record*, March 7, 1996, p. 7; and "Channel Crossing," *Women's Wear Daily*, April 13, 1995, p. 12.

2. Michael Schuman, "U.S. Companies Crack South Korean Market," *Wall Street Journal*, September 11, 1996, p. A14.

3. "Food Spending Dominates in Japan," *Wall Street Journal*, March 4, 1991, p. A6.

4. Miriam Jordan, "In India, Luxury Is Within Reach of Many," *Wall Street Journal*, October 17, 1995, p. A15, referring to studies by the National Council for Applied Economic research, a New Delhi think tank.

5. Houston H. Stokes and Hugh Neuburger, "The Box-Jenkins Approach—When Is It a Cost-Effective Alternative?" *Columbia Journal of World Business*, Winter 1976, pp. 78–86.

6. Joann S. Lublin, "Slim Pickings," *Wall Street Journal*, May 15, 1990, p. A20.

7. J. A. Weber, "Comparing Growth Opportunities in the International Marketplace," *Management International Review*, No. 1, 1979, pp. 47–54.

8. "Chocolate Makers in Switzerland Try to Melt Resistance," *Wall Street Journal*, January 5, 1981, p. 14.

9. Yumiko Ono, "Japanese Treating Themselves to More Imported Chocolate," *Wall Street Journal*, January 5, 1990, p. A4.

10. Bruce Siefert and John Ford, "Are Exporting Firms Modifying Their Product, Pricing and Promotion Policies?" *International Marketing Review*, Vol. 6, No. 6, 1989, pp. 53–68, discuss these points.

11. For a discussion of niche strategy, see James Leontiades, "Going Global—Global Strategies vs. National Strategies," *Long Range Planning*, Vol. 19, No. 6, December 1986, pp. 96–104. For details on the bourbon example, see Christopher Power and Robert Neff, "Sweet Sales for Sour Mash—Abroad," *Business Week*, July 1, 1991, p. 62.

12. Sigurd Villads Troye and Van R. Wood, "A Conceptual Perspective of International Marketing: Meeting the Educational Challenges of the 1990s and Beyond," *1989 International Management Symposium* (Monterrey, CA: Monterrey Institute of International Studies, 1989), pp. 84–95.

13. Shawn Tally, "Teens: The Most Global Market of All," *Fortune*, May 16, 1994, pp. 90–97.

14. Christopher Power, "Will It Sell in Podunk? Hard to Say," *Business Week*, August 10, 1992, pp. 46–47.

15. Michael J. McCarthy, "More Companies Shop Abroad for New Product Ideas," *Wall Street Journal*, March 14, 1990, p. B1+.

16. Matt Moffett, "Learning to Adapt to a Tough Market, Chilean Firms Pry Open Door to Japan," *Wall Street Journal*, June 7, 1994, p. A10.

17. Tara Parker-Pope, "Nonalcoholic Beer Hits the Spot in Mideast," *Wall Street Journal*, December 6, 1995, p. B1+.

18. Troye and Wood, loc. cit.

19. Julie Edelson Halpert, "Harnessing the Sun and Selling It Abroad," *New York Times*, June 5, 1996, p. C1+; Caspar Henderson, "The Solar Revival," *Financial Times*, July 3, 1996, p. 8; and Jenny Gregory, *Financing Mechanisms for Renewable Energy Systems: A Guide for Development Workers* (London: IT Publications, 1996).

20. Timothy Aeppel, "Europe's 'Unity' Undoes a U.S. Exporter," *Wall Street Journal*, April 1, 1996, p. B1.

21. "Abolishing Litter," *The Economist*, August 22, 1992, pp. 59–60; and Philippe Bruno and Bernd Graf, "The New EC Environmental Framework for Packaging," *Export Today*, March 1993, pp. 17–23.

22. See *Financial Times*, October 13, 1995, for special section on international standards.

23. "Discjockeying," *The Economist*, January 28, 1995, p. 60; and Michiyo Nakamoto and Alice Rawsthorn, "Electronics Rivals End Battle Over Format of Video Discs," *Financial Times*, September 16–17, 1995, p. 1.

24. Raju Narisetti, "Can Rubbermaid Crack Foreign Markets?" *Wall Street Journal*, June 6, 1996, p. B1.

25. G. Pierre Goad, "In the U.S., They'll Probably Try Renaming It McGlop or Big Muck," *Wall Street Journal*, March 8, 1990, p. B1.

26. Dan Biers and Miriam Jordan, "McDonald's in India Decides the Big Mac Is Not a Sacred Cow," *Wall Street Journal*, October 14, 1996, p. A11.

27. Miriam Jordan, "Marketing Gurus Say: In India, Think Cheap, Lose the Cold Cereal," *Wall Street Journal*, October 11, 1996, p. A7.

28. Charles Batchelor, "Difficulties With Diversity," *Financial Times*, October 13, 1995, p. 2.

29. Andrew Pollack, "Gulliver's Japanese Travels," *New York Times*, July 7, 1995, p. 17+.

30. Siefert and Ford, loc. cit.

31. "Ford Begins to Sell Right-Hand Drive Tauruses in Japan," *Wall Street Journal*, February 28, 1996, p. 36.

32. Gabriella Stern, "Heinz Aims to Export Taste for Ketchup," *Wall Street Journal*, November 20, 1992, p. B1+.

33. Rahul Jacob, "The Big Rise," *Fortune*, Vol. 129, No. 11, May 30, 1994, pp. 74–90.

34. Marcia Berss, "Whirlpool's Bloody Nose," *Forbes*, March 11, 1996, pp. 90–92.

35. Michael Schuman, "U.S. Companies Crack South Korean Market," *Wall Street Journal*, September 11, 1996, p. A14.

36. Susan P. Douglas and C. Samuel Craig, "Evolution of Global Marketing Strategy: Scale, Scope and Synergy," *Columbia Journal of World Business*, Vol. 14, No. 3, Fall 1989, p. 54.

37. Stephen Baker, Sally Gelston, and Jonathon Kapstein, "The Third World Is Getting Cellular Fever," *Business Week,* April 16, 1990, pp. 80–81; "Dinosaur Brands," *Adweek's Marketing Week,* June 17, 1991, p. 17; and Robert La Franco, "Long-lived Kitsch," *Forbes,* February 26, 1996, p. 68.

38. "The Bugs from Brazil," *The Economist,* August 21, 1993, p. 54.

39. Sally D. Goll, "Few Retailers In China Carry Modern Goods," *Asian Wall Street Journal,* April 11, 1995, p. A1+.

40. Saeed Samiee, "Pricing in Marketing Strategies of U.S.- and Foreign-Based Companies," *Journal of Business Research,* Vol. 15, No. 1, February 1987, pp. 17–30.

41. Daniel Benjamin, "Germany Considers Legalizing The Ancient Art of Haggling," *Wall Street Journal,* July 19, 1994, p. B1.

42. Alicia Swasy, "Foreign Formula," *Wall Street Journal,* June 15, 1990, p. A7; and "Venezuela Sets Price Controls," *Wall Street Journal,* January 11, 1994, p. A10.

43. Mark Alpert and Aimety Dunlap Smith, "Nestlé Shows How to Gobble Markets," *Fortune,* Vol. 119, January 16, 1989, p. 76.

44. Andrea C. Rutherford, "Sea Urchin Industry Is Threatened By Its Own Growth," *Wall Street Journal,* July 11, 1992, p. B2; and "Japanese Snap Up Eye of Tuna," *Wall Street Journal,* April 7, 1994, p. A10.

45. Nina Munk, "The Levi Straddle," *Forbes,* January 17, 1994, pp. 44–45.

46. Luis V. Dominguez and Carlos G. Sequeira, "Strategic Options for LDC Exports to Developed Countries," *International Marketing Review,* Vol. 8, No. 5, 1991, pp. 27–43.

47. Swasy, loc. cit.

48. Robin Bulman, "Auto Dealerships in Korea See Red Over Gray Market," *Journal of Commerce,* September 5, 1996, p. 1A.

49. Nicholas Hall & Company, *European Cosmetics Market,* March 1, 1996.

50. Claude Cellich, "Negotiating Strategies: The Question of Price," *International Trade Forum,* April–June 1991, pp. 10–13.

51. "New Delhi Suspends Sale of Pepsi, Coke," *BC Cycle,* January 20, 1996.

52. Bob Ortega, "Wal-Mart Is Slowed By Problems of Price and Culture in Mexico," *Wall Street Journal,* July 29, 1994, p. A1.

53. Alicia Swasy and Jeremy Mark, "Japan Brings Its Packaged Goods to U.S.," *Wall Street Journal,* January 17, 1989, p. B1.

54. Seymour Banks, "Cross-National Analysis of Advertising Expenditures: 1968–1979," *Journal of Advertising Research,* Vol. 26, No. 2, April–May 1986, p. 21.

55. Miriam Jordan, "In Rural India, Video Vans Sell Toothpaste and Shampoo," *Wall Street Journal,* January 10, 1996, p. B1+.

56. Robert T. Green and Eric Langeard, "A Cross-National Comparison of Consumer Habits and Innovator Characteristics," *Journal of Marketing,* July 1975.

57. Kevin Goldman, "Prof. Levitt Stands By Global-Ad Theory," *Wall Street Journal,* October 13, 1992, p. B7.

58. "A Passion for Variety," *The Economist,* November 30, 1996, pp. 68–71.

59. "Wal-Mart Again Runs Into Language Law Trouble," *Wall Street Journal,* June 14, 1994, p. A4.

60. Kevin Kelly and Karen Lowry Miller, "The Rumble Heard Round the World: Harleys," *Business Week,* May 24, 1993, pp. 58–60.

61. Ken Wells, "Selling to the World," *Wall Street Journal,* August 27, 1992, pp. A1+.

62. Harold M. Spielman, "Local Partnerships: The Strategic Asset in Multicultural Research," *Journal of Advertising Research,* Vol. 35, No. 1, January–February 1995.

63. Rene White, "Beyond Berlitz: How to Penetrate Foreign Markets through Effective Communications," *Public Relations Quarterly,* Vol. 31, No. 2, Summer 1986, p. 15.

64. John R. Zeeman, "What United Airlines Is Learning in the Pacific," speech before the Academy of International Business, Chicago, November 14, 1987.

65. Michael Christie, "Marketing Overseas: When Translating Isn't Enough," *Export Today,* March 1995, pp. 16–17.

66. Namjo Cho, "Korean Men Take a Drag on Virginia Slims," *Wall Street Journal,* January 14, 1997, p. B10.

67. Sally D. Goll, "New Zealand Bans Reebok, Other Ads It Deems Politically Incorrect for TV," *Wall Street Journal,* July 25, 1995, p. A12.

68. Jean J. Boddewyn, *Barriers to Trade and Investment in Advertising: Government Regulation and Industry Self-Regulation in 53 Countries* (New York: International Advertising Association, 1989).

69. John Marcom, Jr., "American Express's Ads in Europe Seek to Leap Borders," *Wall Street Journal,* April 1, 1988, p. 16.

70. "The Enigma of Japanese Advertising," *The Economist,* August 14, 1993, pp. 59–60.

71. John B. Ford, Michael S. LaTour, and Tony L. Henthorne, "Perceptions of Marital Roles in Purchase Decision Processes: A Cross-Cultural Study," *Journal of the Academy of Marketing Science,* Spring 1995, pp. 120–131.

72. Tara Parker-Pope, "Custom-Made," *Wall Street Journal,* September 26, 1996, p. R22.

73. Sak Onkvisit and John J. Shaw, "The International Dimension of Branding: Strategic Considerations and Decisions,"

74. Steven Prokesch, " 'Eurosell' Pervades the Continent," *New York Times,* May 31, 1990, p. C1+.

75. E. S. Browning, "In Pursuit of the Elusive Euroconsumer," *Wall Street Journal,* April 23, 1992, p. B1.

76. Shlomo Maital, "Transnational Teddies," *Across the Board,* Vol. 26, No. 10, October 1989, pp. 15–18.

77. Bernd H. Schmitt, "Language and Visual Imagery: Issues of Corporate Identity in East Asia," *Columbia Journal of World Business,* Winter 1995, pp. 28–36.

78. "But Will It Wash?" *The Economist,* July 13, 1991, p. 70.

79. Myron M. Miller, "Sunbeam in Italy: One Success and One Failure," *International Marketing Review,* Vol. 7, No. 1, 1990, pp. 68–73.

80. "Marketing Korean as Korean," *Business Korea,* Vol. 3, No. 5, November 1985, p. 41.

81. William H. Flanagan, "Big Battle Is Brewing as French Beer Aims to Topple Heineken," *Wall Street Journal,* February 22, 1980, p. 16. For some Japanese examples, see Yumiko Ono, "Japan Eats Up 'U.S.' Food Never Tasted in America," *Wall Street Journal,* April 4, 1990, p. B1+.

82. E. S. Browning, "Eastern Europe Poses Obstacles for Ads," *Wall Street Journal,* July 30, 1992, p. B6.

83. Tara Parker-Pope, "Minty Python and Cream Victoria? Ice Creams Leave Some Groaning," *Wall Street Journal,* July 3, 1996, p. B1.

84. "Limited Imagination," *The Economist,* September 28, 1996, pp. 80–85.

85. Donald G. Howard, "Developing a Defensive Product Management Philosophy for Third World Markets," *International Marketing Review,* Vol. 5, No. 1, Spring 1988, pp. 31–40.

86. "Benetton Opens a Havana Boutique Aimed at Tourists; Exile Groups Protest," *Wall Street Journal,* January 26, 1993, p. A10.

87. "Boycott against Nestlé over Infant Formula to End Next Month," *Wall Street Journal,* January 27, 1984. p. 19; and Alix M. Freedman, "Advertising," *Wall Street Journal,* April 25, 1989, p. B6.

88. "Baby-Formula TV Ads in Taiwan," *Wall Street Journal,* February 24, 1993, p. A8.

89. Andrew Jack, Bruce Clark, and Daniel Green, "Boycott Forces Hoechst to Drop Abortion Pill," *Financial Times,* April 9, 1997, p. 1+.

90. Michiyo Nakamoto, "Matsushita Plans Network of 3,000 Shops Across China," *Financial Times,* September 29, 1995, p. 1.

91. Patrick Oster and Igor Reichlin, "Breaking Into European Markets by Breaking the Rules," *Business Week,* January 20,

73. (*continued*) *International Marketing Review,* Vol. 6, No. 3, 1989, pp. 22–34.

1992, pp. 88–89; Jack G. Kaikati, "Don't Crack the Japanese Distribution System—Just Circumvent It, *Columbia Journal of World Business,* Summer 1993, pp. 35–45; Tony Jackson, "Tupperware Decides It's Time to Party on Its Own," *Financial Times,* December 5, 1995, p. 20; Paulette Thomas, "U.S. Cosmetics Makers Market American Look to World's Women," *Asian Wall Street Journal,* May 5, 1995, p.10.

92. For aspects of contractual considerations see Kojo Yelpaala, "Strategy and Planning in Global Product Distribution—Beyond the Distribution Contract," *Law & Policy in International Business,* Vol. 25, 1994, pp. 839–944.

93. See for example, "The International Supplier Selection: The Relevance of Import Dependence," *Journal of Global Marketing,* Vol. 9, No. 3, 1996, pp. 23–45.

94. "Taking Aim," *The Economist,* April 24, 1993, p. 74; and John Fahy and Fuyuki Taguchi, "Reassessing the Japanese Distribution System." *Sloan Management Review,* Winter 1995, pp. 49–61.

95. Bert Rosenbloom, "Motivating Your International Channel Partners," *Business Horizons,* Vol. 33, No. 2, March–April 1990, pp. 53–57.

96. Greg Steinmetz and Tara Parker-Pope, "All Over the Map," *Wall Street Journal,* September 26, 1996, p. R4+.

97. Parker-Pope, loc. cit.

98. Fahy and Taguchi, loc. cit.

99. Andrew Jack, "Carrefours Up Sharply But Hits at Government," *Financial Times,* February 29, 1996, p. 14; Bob Davis, Peter Gumbel, and David P. Hamilton, "Red-Tape Traumas," *Wall Street Journal,* December 14, 1995, p. A1; John Griffiths, "Too Many Car Dealers in Europe," *Financial Times,* October 22, 1996, p. 2; and "A Matter of Convenience," *The Economist,* January 25, 1997, pp. 60–62.

100. Hugh Carnegy, "Swedish 7-Eleven Stores Lose Some of Their Convenience," *Financial Times,* March 29, 1996, p. 1.

101. Kenichi Ohmae, "Letter From Japan," *Harvard Business Review,* May–June 1995, pp. 154–163; and John A. Quelch and Lisa R. Klein, "The Internet and International Marketing," *Sloan Management Review,* Spring 1996, pp. 60–75.

102. *Avon Annual Report* for 1995; "Acquisition of Upscale Direct Seller Opens Doors for Avon in South Africa," *Outlook,* May–June 1996, p. 4; "Big Hit in Small Markets," *Outlook,* January–February 1996, p. 6; "A Steady Stream of Suitors, *Outlook,* January–February 1996, p. 14; Paulette Thomas, "U.S. Cosmetics Makers Market American Look to World Women," *Asian Wall Street Journal,* May 8, 1995, p. 20; "Boutiques of Beauty," *Outlook,* November–December 1995, pp. 11–13; "The Fundamentals in the Asia Pacific Region," *Outlook,* September–October 1995, p. 4; "Thai Journalists Take a Global Look at Avon," *Outlook,* September–October 1995, p. 5; "Reaching More Women Every Year," *Outlook,* September–October 1995, p. 7; "Branching Out in the Philippines," *Outlook,* September–October 1995, pp.10–13; "Resource in the East," *Outlook,* September–October 1995, p. 14; "The Changing Face of Avon," *Outlook,* July–August 1996, pp. 14–20; "Argentina Center Pampers Women," *Outlook,* September–October 1996, p. 7; "Avon Emerges in Russia," *Outlook,* September–October 1996, pp. 10–15; Rasul Bailay, "Avon Tries Twist On Sales Technique for Push Into India," *Wall Street Journal,* July 2, 1996, p. B8; "Brazil Bounces Back," *Outlook,* March–April 1995, pp. 8–13; James Brooke, "In the Amazon, Guess Who's Calling?" *New York Times,* July 7, 1995, p. A4; and Veronica Byrd and Wendy Zellner, "The Avon Lady of the Amazon," *Business Week,* October 24, 1994, p. 93+.

Chapter 17

Export and Import Strategies

*There may be trade
and none able to do it.*

—Chinese Proverb

Objectives

- To identify the key elements of export strategies

- To compare direct and indirect selling of exports

- To discuss the role of several types of trading companies in exporting

- To show how freight forwarders help exporters with the movement of goods and the accompanying documentation

- To identify the methods of receiving payment for exports and the financing of receivables

- To identify key elements of import strategies

Case
Grieve Corporation[1]

As noted in the Chinese proverb on the preceding page, it is not always easy to engage in trade, especially for small companies. The top fifty U.S. exporters generate about 30 percent of U.S. merchandise exports, and their shipments are bigger on average than are the shipments of smaller exporters. However, there are an estimated 100,000 U.S. companies engaged in export activity, and most of them are small, as is Grieve Corporation (only 125 employees) of Round Lake, Illinois, near Chicago.

As recently as 1992, Grieve Corporation manufactured laboratory and industrial ovens, furnaces, and heat processing systems only for the U.S. market. Whenever a customer moved overseas, the company would continue to supply that customer with product, but eventually this market would begin to erode. After a while, the customer would source locally. The company had not considered exports proactively for three main reasons:

1. *The nature of its product.* Industrial ovens and furnaces are rather large and bulky and also relatively expensive. Top management assumed the product's size would make shipping costs so high that Grieve would price itself out of the market. For example, one shipment of a fully automated conveyorized system to the Philippines overseas entailed shipping costs of $40,999.
2. *Doubts about its success abroad.* Grieve is a small business, and top management assumed it could not be successful internationally. Managers were so busy doing all that needed to be done in the domestic market with a relatively thin management structure that they just didn't have time to think strategically about the international market.
3. *Concern about competition.* More seasoned exporters from Germany, Japan, and the United Kingdom offered relatively fierce competition. Even within the United States, the company had strong competition from local producers in markets outside the Chicago area.

However, Grieve realized that something had to be done. It was losing customers overseas to local suppliers, and it was beginning to experience competition from abroad. Top management realized it needed to combat the competition or lose the market entirely. In addition, Grieve Corporation had to make shipments to both California and Connecticut, its number 1 and number 2 markets, and they had to contend with location competition and high transportation costs, so they decided that the international market might not be so bad. In 1992, Patrick J. Calabrese, Grieve's president, attended a one-day seminar featuring the U.S. ambassadors to the ASEAN countries. He left that seminar convinced there might be strong market opportunities in one of the world's fastest-growing regions. However, he was not familiar with the market, and the company had no sales offices or representatives in the ASEAN countries. He also was concerned about the British, German, and Japanese competition already entrenched in that market.

Grieve's marketing staff decided to sample potential interest in Asia by advertising in trade publications circulating in Southeast Asia, such as the *Asian Industrial Reporter,* the *Asian Literature Showcase,* and the *World Industrial Reporter.* To learn more about the market, Calabrese worked with a representative of the Chicago office of the International Trade

Administration of the U.S. Department of Commerce's U.S. & Foreign Commercial Service. This office helped him plan a trip to Asia by arranging for interpreters at each stop on his itinerary and meetings with U.S. embassy personnel. His trip was intended primarily to determine market potential and identify possible agents. Calabrese had received inquiries from some distributors that were familiar with Grieve's product line but he had not pursued them. However, Calabrese's staff had begun filing correspondence by country rather than by company name, so it was relatively easy to locate potential distributors and customers along with the leads provided by Commerce. In addition to these distributors, Calabrese used the U.S. Department of Commerce's Agent/Distributor Service to identify several other possible distributors. After researching their product lines, Calabrese narrowed the list to the most likely candidates. He then developed company literature for each country and price lists for the product line. All of this information was forwarded in advance to the potential agents. In addition, Calabrese sent a detailed questionnaire to potential distributors, figuring that those who were really interested would fill out the questionnaire, and those who weren't would not. This was a good way to gauge interest before incurring the cost of a visit.

The trip was a big success for Grieve. Interviews were held with twenty-eight potential agents over twenty-eight days, and exclusive agents were signed up in each country. Calabrese lined up both an interpreter and a driver for each country so that he wouldn't have to worry about either issue. This saved a lot of time trying to find a cab or relying on the potential distributor to help with transportation. In addition, the interpreter could give an evaluation of the company as well. After visiting each potential distributor and before selecting the exclusive distributor, Calabrese would meet with the Commercial Officer and the interpreter and gain their input in the final selection. Each agent then completed a training session that familiarized the agent with Grieve and its products. The company subsequently placed firm orders through several of these new agents. It also identified several trade shows at which its products could be displayed. In order to facilitate the business side of the visits, Calabrese arranged for a small suite in each hotel so that he could make detailed notes on each distributor as well as send faxes back to the home office. This turned out to be very valuable, because when a particular agent or distributor did not work out, Calabrese could return to his original reports to find another suitable partner.

Calabrese quickly learned that he had to cut shipping costs. So Grieve redesigned its packaging to be more compact. In addition, it began shopping among freight forwarders to find the best rates, which varied depending on the forwarder's experience and its relationship with a particular steamship company.

Calabrese also learned how important it was for him to visit potential customers in Asia personally rather than relying on a sales manager. He said:

> The one thing that I found is that almost to an individual [Asian customers] are very keen on a personal association. If I were to give anybody advice, I would never send a second-level individual. Never send a marketing manager or sales manager; I would send a top manager. If your company isn't too large to prohibit it, I would send the president or chairman. On the other end, you are talking to the owner of a small distributor or the president of a small manufacturing company and you've got to meet them on an equal

level. My limited experience is they are very cognizant of this; in other words, they are pretty much attuned to a president talking to a president. They also like to feel secure that they are dealing with someone who can make decisions.

Another thing I found is that potential customers want to feel that you are financially secure and that you have sufficient funding to continue to work with them for a period of years, because it takes some time and some money on our end to get these people going.

Follow-up is incredibly important. I heard all kinds of stories about American businessmen who would come over and spend a day and talk to potential customers and leave catalogues. Then the first time the potential customers would send a fax asking for information, they didn't hear from them for two weeks, and that just turns them right off.

Although Grieve faces high transport costs and significant competition from foreign companies as it works to penetrate foreign markets, top management is optimistic. The company has a good product. As Calabrese pointed out, "Our strength is that we are selling engineered products, using our forty-five years of expertise to build something for them." Calabrese's experience was very successful in two different ways. The first is the increase in foreign sales from zero to over $1,000,000 within three years. Half of the sales came from the five new agents appointed in Southeast Asia, and the rest came from renewed interest in foreign sales by the home office. The second benefit was what Calabrese learned about doing business overseas, in addition to the points mentioned in the quote above. They are:

1. Know your product well. Many people who go to Asia from the United States know very little about their own product. In some cases, potential agents who have studied company brochures know more about the product than the company representative.
2. Learn about the competitive situation in the foreign market and the potential sale for your products.
3. Advertise in the local market before going there in order to determine the interest level and to build contacts.
4. Work hard. Too many foreign visitors want to spend a lot of time playing golf or seeing the sights.
5. Build a strong response base back home. Most foreigners complain about poor factory backup, lengthy delays in getting correspondence answered, and delays in getting quotations.
6. Arrange for your own transportation and don't rely on the potential representative to solve your problems for you. That shows a lack of understanding of the local environment.
7. Provide someone at the home office who can be the principal contact for the representative. They need someone who will answer questions and provide assistance.
8. Learn the customs and business etiquette of the countries you visit. Once again, the U.S. Department of Commerce can provide assistance in this area.
9. Have the authority to make decisions and commit the company. If you are going to meet with the top person in the representative organization, be responsible yourself.

Calabrese obviously learned a great deal from his initial foray overseas. In 1995, Grieve shipped products to seventeen countries all over the world. This new way of doing business has created some challenges, but it also has helped Grieve be more successful and profitable.

Introduction

As the Grieve case demonstrates, successful exporting is a complex process. A company either makes what it sells or sells what it makes. Once it has identified the product it wants to sell, it must explore market opportunities, a process that involves a significant amount of market research that may or may not be supported by the home-country government. Next, it must develop a production strategy, prepare the goods for market, determine the best strategy for getting the goods transported to market, sell the product, and receive payment. All of these steps require careful planning and preparation. The Grieve case demonstrated that a company has limited capabilities. Without a separate export staff, it must rely on specialists such as freight forwarders to move goods from one country to another, agents or distributors to sell the products, banks to collect payment, and, often, the government to identify market opportunities and potential distributors.

As noted in Chapter 14, there are many different forms that companies can choose from when determining a strategy for entering foreign markets. In this chapter we will focus primarily on the export strategy, drawing from strategic concepts discussed in Chapter 14, but we will also discuss imports from the perspective of companies that import final products for the consumer, such as Toyota USA's import of autos into the United States for U.S. consumers. The strategic use of foreign sourcing as part of an overall production strategy, such as the import of parts into the United States by Nissan to assemble autos for the U.S. market, will be discussed in Chapter 18. In addition, this chapter flows logically from Chapter 16 on marketing, since much of what we will discuss deals with elements in the marketing mix, especially channels of distribution.

Characteristics of Exporters

Research conducted on the characteristics of exporters has resulted in two basic conclusions:

1. The probability of being an exporter increases with company size.
2. Export intensity is not positively correlated with company size. Export intensity refers to the percentage of total revenues coming from exports. The greater the percentage of exports to total revenues, the greater the intensity.

The first conclusion is based on the idea that small companies can grow in the domestic market and avoid undertaking the risks of exporting, but large companies

> The probability of a company's being an exporter increases with the size of the company.
>
> Export intensity is not positively correlated with company size.

must export if they are to increase sales.[2] The exceptions are small high-tech or highly specialized companies that operate in market niches with a global demand and small companies that sell expensive capital equipment.[3] In a study of Canadian companies, the two conclusions above were confirmed, but the author found that firm size was not the most important factor in determining the propensity to export, number of countries served, and export intensity. Factors such as the risk profile of management and industry factors were as important as size.[4]

A good example of this idea in operation is found in the United States. As noted in Table 17.1, the largest exporters in the United States in terms of export revenues are also among the elite of the Fortune 1000 largest industrial companies. It used to be that the top 50 exporters were primarily among the top 100 companies in the United States, but that is changing. Only 30 of the top 50 in 1994 were among the top 100 industrial companies, although all of the top 50 exporters are among the top 500 U.S. industrials. However, there are some differences among the top U.S. exporters. The top exporter is General Motors with $16.1 billion in exports. Most of GM's exports were intracompany transfers of components from the United States to manufacturing facilities in foreign locations rather than sales to final consumers. It is estimated that intracompany sales make up one quarter of all U.S. exports.[5] However, GM ranked only thirty-eighth as a percentage of total revenues at 10.4 percent. Boeing, the number three exporter in sales dollars was number one in exports as a percentage of total revenues with 54 percent. It is interesting to note that the second largest exporter as a percentage of total revenues is Novell, the Utah software company, at 43 percent of total sales. However, Novell only ranked 44 on the list in terms of sales dollars generated from exports.[6]

U.S. trade data confirm that smaller exporters make smaller shipments (approximately $25,000 per shipment), and bigger exporters make bigger shipments (approximately $40,000 each). As Fig. 17.1 shows, shipments worth $100,000 and up accounted for 56 percent of the total dollar value of exports; however, they accounted for only 5 percent of the total number of shipments.[7] Thus 95 percent of export shipments but only 44 percent of export volume comes from approximately 94,000 small U.S. exporters.

The largest exporters in the United States also are among the largest industrial corporations.

Smaller exporters make smaller shipments; larger exporters make larger shipments.

Figure 17.1
Export Shipments of Various Sizes as Percentages of Total Dollar Value of Exports
Out of a total dollar value of $420 billion, over half is accounted for by large shipments valued at $100,000 or higher.

Source: SED's Bureau of Census, © Copyright 1992, Trade Data Reports, Inc.

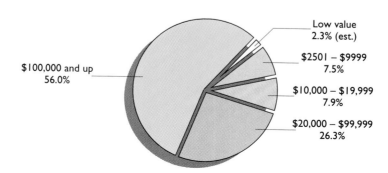

Total value of exports = $420 billion

Table 17.1
Top Fifty U.S. Exporters

1994 Rank	Company	Major export products	U.S. exports 1994 (millions of dollars)	Percent of total revenues	Rank
1	General Motors (Detroit)	Motor vehicles and parts, locomotives	16,127.1	10.4	38
2	Ford Motor (Dearborn, Mich.)	Motor vehicles and parts	11,892.0	9.3	43
3	Boeing (Seattle)	Commercial aircraft	11,844.0	54.0	1
4	Chrysler (Highland Park, Mich.)	Motor vehicles and parts	9,400.0	18.0	16
5	General Electric (Fairfield, Conn.)	Jet engines, turbines, plastics, med. sys., locomotives	8,110.0	12.5	33
6	Motorola (Schaumburg, Ill.)	Communications equipment, semiconductors	7,370.0	33.1	5
7	IBM (Armonk, N.Y.)	Computers and related equipment	6,336.0	9.9	40
8	Philip Morris (New York)	Tobacco, beer, food products	4,942.0	9.2	44
9	Archer Daniels Midland (Decatur, Ill.)	Protein meals, vegetable oils, flour, alcohol, grain	4,675.0	41.1	3
10	Hewlett-Packard (Palo Alto)	Measurement, computation, commun. prod. and sys.	4,653.0	18.6	14
11	Intel (Santa Clara, Calif.)	Microcomputer components, modules, systems	4,561.0	39.6	4
12	Caterpillar (Peoria, Ill.)	Engines; turbines; constr., mining, and agr. machinery	4,510.0	31.5	7
13	McDonnell Douglas (Berkeley, Mo.)	Aerospace products, missiles, electronic systems	4,235.0	32.1	6
14	E.I. Du Pont De Nemours (Wilmington, Del.)	Chemicals, polymers, fibers, specialty products	3,625.0	10.4	39
15	United Technologies (Hartford)	Jet engines, helicopters, cooling equipment	3,108.0	14.7	25
16	Eastman Kodak (Rochester, N.Y.)	Imaging products	2,600.0	15.4	22
17	Lockheed[1] (Calabasas, Calif.)	Aerospace products, missiles, electronic systems	2,079.0	15.8	21
18	Compaq Computer (Houston)	Computers and related equipment	2,018.0	18.6	15
19	Raytheon (Lexington, Mass.)	Electronic systems, engineering and constr. projects	1,867.0	18.6	13
20	Digital Equipment (Maynard, Mass.)	Computers, software, related equipment	1,830.7	13.6	28
21	Allied Signal (Morris Township, N.J.)	Aircraft and automotive parts, chemicals	1,818.0	14.2	27
22	Minnesota Mining & Mfg. (St. Paul)	Ind., elec., health care, consumer, and imaging prod.	1,755.0	11.6	34
23	Westinghouse Electric (Pittsburgh)	Power sys., radars, office furn., transport refrig.	1,613.0	17.5	18
24	Dow Chemical (Midland, Mich.)	Chemicals, plastics, consumer specialties	1,575.0	7.9	47
25	Merck (Whitehouse Station, N.J.)	Health products	1,572.5	10.5	37
26	IBP (Dakota City, Nebr.)	Fresh, frozen beef, pork, related byproducts	1,549.6	12.8	31
27	Weyerhaeuser (Feaere Way, Wash.)	Pulp, newsprint, paperboard, logs, lumber	1,540.0	14.8	24
28	Textron (Providence)	Aircraft, automotive systems and products	1,441.0	14.9	23
29	International Paper (Purchase, N.Y.)	Pulp, paperboard, wood products	1,421.0	9.5	42
30	Xerox (Stamford, Conn.)	Copiers, printers, processing services and supplies	1,291.0	7.2	48

(cont.)

[1]Figures do not reflect merger between Lockheed and Martin Marietta, March 15, 1995

Table 17.1 (cont.)

1994 Rank	Company	Major exports	U.S. exports 1994 (millions of dollars)	Percent of total revenues	Fortune 1000 revenues rank
31	Rockwell Intl. (Seal Beach, Calif.)	Electronics, auto parts, high-speed printing presses	1,280.0	11.4	35
32	Abbott Laboratories (Abbott Park, Ill.)	Drugs, diagnostic equipment	1,231.5	13.5	29
33	Union Carbide (Danbury, Conn.)	Chemicals, plastics	1,198.0	24.6	9
34	FMC (Chicago)	Armored military vehicles, chemicals	1,150.0	28.4	8
35	Deere (Moline, Ill.)	Farm, industrial, and lawn- and grounds-care equipment	1,144.0	12.7	32
36	Sun Microsystems (Mountain View, Calif.)	Computers and related equipment	1,123.4	24.0	10
37	Unisys (Blue Bell, Pa.)	Computers and related equipment	1,075.6	14.5	26
38	Georgia-Pacific (Atlanta)	Pulp, building products, containerboard, paper	1,020.0	8.0	46
39	Cummins Engine (Columbus, Ind.)	Diesel engines, related products	1,004.0	21.2	11
40	Alcoa (Pittsburgh)	Aluminum products	988.0	9.5	41
41	Dresser Industries (Dallas)	Compressors, drilling fluids, drill bits	938.7	17.6	17
42	Monsanto (St. Louis)	Food ingredients, herbicides, chemicals, pharmaceuticals	900.0	10.9	36
43	Bristol-Myers Squibb (New York)	Pharmaceuticals, health care products, medical devices	867.0	7.2	49
44	Novell (Orem, Utah)	Computer software	860.0	43.0	2
45	Exxon (Irving, Texas)	Petroleum, chemicals	834.0	0.8	50
46	Microsoft (Redmond, Wash.)	Computer software	787.0	16.9	19
47	Honeywell (Minneapolis)	Building, industrial, and aviation control systems	780.0	12.9	30
48	Occidental Petroleum (Los Angeles)	Chemicals	756.0	8.0	45
49	Ingersoll-Rand (Woodcliff Lake, N.J.)	Industrial machinery	743.0	16.5	20
50	General Dynamics (Falls Church, Va.)	Battle tanks and related support services	722.0	19.5	12
Totals			$150,761.1		

In addition, the data support the conclusion that export intensity is not positively correlated with company size. The general assumption is that small companies have limited resources, lack the scale economies in manufacturing that would allow them to export, and perceive a high risk to exporting. However, many of the larger exporters have a small percentage of exports to total sales (see Table 17.1). Thus, although several studies have shown some correlation between company size and initiation of export activity, they do not support the fact that smaller companies do not export or that larger ones continue to rely more on exports.[8]

Grieve is a perfect example illustrating these concepts. Although considered a small company in terms of total sales, its export revenues are significant and are the key to its survival. It must export in order to maintain its market share abroad and its competitive position in the United States relative to foreign suppliers.

Getting accurate current data on exporters is very difficult, because those data are not systematically collected and analyzed on an annual basis. The U.S. Department of Commerce will conduct a census of exporters in 1997, and that will help update the figures provided above. But there are estimates that about 10 percent of all companies with fewer than 100 employees export and that about 15 percent of all companies with fewer than 500 employees export. The USDC also estimates that there are about 135,000–150,000 U.S. companies that export annually, whereas Federal Express places that number closer to 300,000 companies.[9] However, it is sufficient to realize that there is a large number of both large and small firms involved in exporting around the world.

Export Strategy

Entry mode depends on ownership advantages of the company, location advantages of the market, and internalization advantages of integrating transactions within the company.

Demand in foreign countries can be serviced in various ways. The choice of entry mode is a function of different factors, such as the ownership advantages of the company, location advantages of the market, and internalization advantages of integrating transactions within the company.[10] Ownership advantages relate to specific assets and are a function of company size, international experience, and ability to develop differentiated products. For example, Boeing trades on its ownership advantage through the development of sophisticated aircraft; doing the same would be difficult for a new entrant to the market to duplicate. Location advantages of the market are a combination of market potential (the size and growth potential of the market) and investment risk. For example, Southeast Asia possesses location advantages, being one of the world's fastest-growing regions; this was a major reason why Grieve decided to explore that area as an export market. Internalization advantages refer to the benefits of holding onto specific assets or skills within the company and integrating them into its activities rather than licensing or selling them. For example, Grieve Corporation could have explored licensing its technology to manufacturers in Southeast Asia but preferred to maintain control over its technology and serve Southeast Asia through exports from its own U.S. plants.

Companies that have lower levels of ownership advantages either do not enter foreign markets or use low-risk strategies such as exporting.

In general, companies that have lower levels of ownership advantages either do not enter foreign markets or use low-risk entry modes such as exporting. Exporting also requires a lower level of investment than do other modes, such as foreign investment, but it offers a lower risk/return alternative. Exporting allows significant management operational control but does not provide as much marketing control, since the exporter is farther from the final consumer and often must deal with independent distributors abroad that control many of the marketing functions.[11]

Strategic considerations affect the choice of exporting as an entry mode.

However, the choice of exporting as an entry mode is not just a function of these ownership, location, and internalization advantages. It also is a function of the company's overall strategy. This is illustrated by the following questions, which any company must consider before it decides to enter the export market:

- What does the company want to gain from exporting?
- Is exporting consistent with other company goals?
- What demands will exporting place on its key resources—management and personnel, production capacity, and financing—and how will these demands be met?
- Are the expected benefits worth the costs, or would company resources be better used for developing new domestic business?[12]

These are strategic questions that must take into account global concentration, synergies, and strategic motivations. Global concentration refers to the fact that many global industries have only a few major players, and a company's strategy for penetrating a particular market might be a function of what competitors are doing. Global synergies arise when the company's specific inputs, such as R&D, marketing, or manufacturing, are shared by its subunits worldwide. Global strategic motivations refer to the reasons why a company might want to enter a market. For example, it might enter a market in a specific country as a means of combating a competitor in that market, not just because of specific market or profit potential.[13]

Exporting occurs for several good reasons. Raw materials must be exported to the manufacturer, components to the assembly operation, and finished goods to foreign distributors and consumers. Sometimes this process occurs within the confines of a vertically integrated company, allowing the exporter to sell directly to the next level through an intracompany transaction. In many cases, however, the sale is to an outsider, and the exporter may sell directly to the buyer or indirectly through an intermediary.

Factors Favoring Exportation

The most common means by which companies begin international activity is through exporting. Even those with sizable foreign contractual arrangements and investments usually continue to export to achieve their overall objectives.

Exporting
- **Expands sales**
- **Achieves economies of scale in production**
- **Is less risky than FDI**
- **Allows the company to diversify sales locations**

Companies get involved in exporting primarily to increase sales revenues. This is true for service companies as well as manufacturers. Many of the former, such as advertising and public accounting firms, export their services to meet the needs of clients working abroad. Grieve, a manufacturer, exported products to clients that had moved abroad. Companies that are capital- and research-intensive, such as biotechnology and pharmaceutical companies, must export in order to spread their capital base over a larger sales volume.

Export sales also can be a means of alleviating excess capacity in the domestic market. In addition, some companies export rather than invest abroad because of the perceived high risk of operating in foreign environments. Finally, many export to a variety of different markets as a diversification strategy. Since economic growth is not the same in every market, broadly based exports allow a company to take advantage of strong growth in one market to offset weak growth in another. For example, Grieve is developing markets in Southeast Asia to expand its sales base and diversify its markets from strictly U.S. sales.

Stages of Export Involvement

Many companies begin exporting by accident rather than by design. Consequently, they tend to encounter a number of unforeseen problems. They also may never get a chance to see how important exports can be. For these reasons, developing a good export strategy is important.

As Fig. 17.2 shows, export involvement can be divided into three broad phases:

1. Pre-engagement phase
2. Initial phase
3. Advanced phase[14]

As companies move from initial to advanced exporting, they tend to export to more countries and expect exports as a percentage of total sales to grow.

These stages are not based on company size but rather on degree of export involvement—both large and small companies can be at any stage. In fact, more new companies are exporting sooner in their own life cycle because of the increased awareness of international business and international experience of a new generation of entrepreneurs and managers. In addition, the ability to generate sales on the Internet is one reason why companies are exporting faster. As a company establishes a home page, Internet surfers from all over the world can have instant access to the company's product line and even initiate sales directly. An example is Mity-Lite, a small U.S. company that manufactures and sells a variety of lightweight tables and chairs. Their home page (http://www.mitylite.com) provides a lot of text and visual information (including video clips) of the product line, as well as information about how to order products. There is a separate international section that provides information about distributors in different countries and information on how to order products for countries where there is no distributor.

**Figure 17.2
Phases of Export
Development**
As companies gain greater
expertise and experience
in exporting, they diversify
their markets to countries
that are farther away or
have business environ-
ments that differ from that
of their home country.

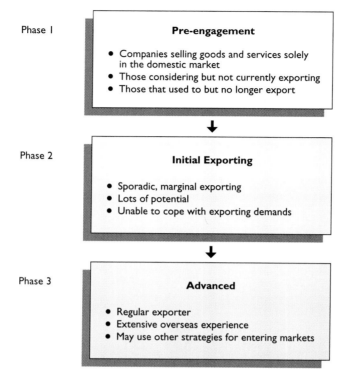

Phase I

Pre-engagement

- Companies selling goods and services solely
  in the domestic market
- Those considering but not currently exporting
- Those that used to but no longer export

Phase 2

Initial Exporting

- Sporadic, marginal exporting
- Lots of potential
- Unable to cope with exporting demands

Phase 3

Advanced

- Regular exporter
- Extensive overseas experience
- May use other strategies for entering markets

Potential Pitfalls

To understand the important elements in an export strategy, it is important first to
identify the major problems that exporters often face. Aside from problems that are
common to international business in general and not unique to exporting, such as
language and other culturally related factors, the following mistakes are among
those most frequently made by companies new to exporting:

1. Failure to obtain qualified export counseling and to develop a master international marketing plan before starting an export business
2. Insufficient commitment by top management to overcome the initial difficulties and financial requirements of exporting
3. Insufficient care in selecting overseas agents or distributors
4. Chasing orders from around the world instead of establishing a base of profitable operations and orderly growth
5. Neglecting export business when the U.S. market booms
6. Failure to treat international distributors on an equal basis with their domestic
   counterparts
7. Unwillingness to modify products to meet other countries' regulations or cultural preferences
8. Failure to print service, sales, and warranty messages in locally understood
   languages

9. Failure to consider use of an export management company or other marketing intermediary when the company does not have the personnel to handle specialized export functions
10. Failure to consider licensing or joint-venture agreements (This factor is especially critical in countries that have import restrictions.)[15]

These mistakes do not necessarily reflect the major problems that exporters themselves are concerned about, although there is some overlap. The list of export-related problems given in Fig. 17.3 focuses more on the procedural issues that managers face once their companies become involved in exporting.

Designing an Export Strategy

Designing an export strategy involves the following steps:

In designing an export strategy, a company must
- **Assess export potential**
- **Get expert counseling**
- **Select market or markets**
- **Set goals and get the product to market**

- *Assess the company's export potential by examining its opportunities and resources.* It would not be smart to commit to exporting if the company does not have the production capacity to deliver the product.
- *Obtain expert counseling on exporting.* Most governments provide assistance for their domestic companies, although the extent of commitment varies by country. For U.S. companies, the best place to start is with the nearest International Trade Administration (ITA) office. Such assistance is invaluable in helping an exporter get started. In the Grieve case, for example, Calabrese used a lot of information provided by the U.S. government to learn about Asian markets. Other government agencies also assist exporters. As a company's export plan increases in scope, it probably will want to secure specialized assistance from banks, lawyers, freight forwarders, export management companies, export trading companies, and others.
- *Select a market or markets.* This key part of the export strategy may be done passively or actively. In the former case, the company learns of markets by responding to requests from abroad that result from trade shows, advertisements, or articles in trade publications. A more active approach is that taken by Grieve's Calabrese, who selected Southeast Asia as an area for export development as a result of a seminar he attended featuring the U.S. ambassadors to the ASEAN countries. A company also can determine the markets to which products like its own are currently being exported. For example, in the U.S. setting, *U.S. Census Trade Statistics* identifies the markets for different classifications of exports, and the National Trade Data Bank (NTDB) provides specific industry reports for different countries. The NTDB is updated monthly, so potential exporters can get the most recent studies. Similar forms of assistance are found in other countries. The NTDB can also be accessed through the Internet by searching the home page of the International Trade Administration of the U.S. Department of Com-

EXPORT-RELATED PROBLEMS

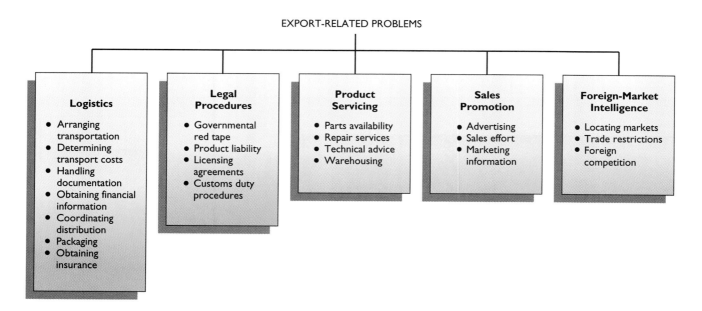

Figure 17.3
Export-Related
Problems
The five major categories
of export-related problems
are logistics, legal procedures, product servicing,
sales promotion, and
foreign-market intelligence.

Source: From "State Government
Promotion of Manufacturing
Exports: A Gap Analysis,"
Masaaki Kotabe and Michael R.
Czinkota, *Journal of International
Business Studies,* Vol. 23, No. 4,
Fourth Quarter 1992, p. 651.
Reprinted with permission.

merce. There is an access charge, but you can find out more information by searching <http://www.ita.doc.gov/uscs/uscsntdb.html>. That site describes the NTDB and explains how you can access it from government statistics.

- Regardless of how the company obtains market information, it is important that it pick a market or markets in which to concentrate a push strategy. Because national markets differ, the company should focus on a few key markets rather than try to develop global expertise all at once. Often, the initial markets are geographically close to the company's home country or are in countries that closely resemble the home country culturally. For both of these reasons, Canada, Mexico, and the United Kingdom are important to U.S. exporters. Once the primary, secondary, and tertiary markets have been determined, the company needs to research each to determine their major economic trends.

- *Formulate an export strategy.* This step usually involves considering the following factors: the company's export objectives, both immediate and long term; specific tactics the company will use; a schedule of activities and deadlines that will help the company achieve its objectives; and the allocation of resources to accomplish the different activities.

- *Determine how to get the goods to market.*

It is important that a company organize its exporting efforts. Table 17.2 provides a sample business plan a company can use to establish a specific export strategy. It requires the company to understand its expertise in export procedures as well as to gauge the availability of corporate resources to support exporting.

Table 17.2
An Export Business Plan
When establishing an export business plan, management needs to assess the company's strengths, determine one or two markets for initial concentration, and commit time and resources to developing personnel and supporting the export activities.

I.   **Executive summary**
    A. Key elements of the plan
    B. Description of business and target markets
    C. Brief description of management team
    D. Summary of financial projections
II.   **Business history**
    A. History of company
    B. Products/services offered and their unique advantages
    C. Domestic-market experience
    D. Foreign-market experience
    E. Production facilities
    F. Personnel—international experience and expertise
    G. Industry structure, competition
III.   **Market research**
    A. Target countries
        1. Primary
        2. Secondary
        3. Tertiary
    B. Market conditions in target countries
        1. Existing demand
        2. Competition
        3. Strengths and weaknesses of the economy—barriers to entry, etc.
IV.   **Marketing decisions**
    A. Distribution strategies
        1. Indirect exporting
        2. Direct exporting
        3. Documentation
        4. Direct investment, strategic alliances
    B. Pricing strategy
    C. Promotion strategy
V.   **Legal decisions**
    A. Agent/distributor agreements
    B. Patent, trademark, copyright protection
    C. Export/import regulations
    D. ISO 9000
    E. Dispute resolution
VI.   **Manufacturing and operations**
    A. Location of production facilities for exports
    B. Capacity of existing facilities
    C. Plans for expansion
    D. Product modification necessary to adapt to local environment
VII.   **Personnel strategies**
    A. Personnel needed to manage exports
    B. Experience and expertise of existing personnel
    C. Training needs of existing personnel
    D. Hiring needs in the short term and long term
VIII. **Financial decisions**
    A. Pro forma financial statements and projected cash flows assuming export activity
    B. Identification of key assumptions
    C. Current sources of funding—private and bank funding
    D. Financial needs and future sources of funding
    E. Tax consequences of export activity
    F. Potential risk and sources of protection
IX.   **Implementation schedule**

Export Intermediaries

A company that either exports or is planning to export must decide whether certain essential activities are to be handled by its own staff or through contracts with other companies. The following functions must be carried out:

1. Stimulate sales, obtain orders, and do market research
2. Make credit investigations and perform payment-collection activities
3. Handle foreign traffic and shipping
4. Act as support for the company's overall sales, distribution, and advertising staff

Companies use external specialists for exporting before developing internal capabilities.

Performing these functions can be costly and can require expertise a company doesn't have. Thus most companies initially use external specialists and/or intermediary organizations to assume some or all of these functions, although a company later may develop in-house capabilities to perform them. Specialists are useful for such duties as preparing export documents, preparing customs documents in the importing country, and identifying the best means of transportation. And most companies can benefit at some time from using an intermediary organization. Some of these act as agents on behalf of the exporter, and some take title to the goods and sell them abroad. Others are involved in certain specialized aspects of the export process; for example, a freight forwarder is responsible for moving the products from the domestic to foreign markets.

Companies may market their products either directly or indirectly through external specialists or intermediary organizations.

A company that is determining whether to market a product directly using its own staff or indirectly using external specialists and/or intermediary organizations must consider company size, nature of the product, previous export experience and expertise, and business conditions in the selected foreign markets.[16]

Direct Selling

Direct selling involves sales representatives, agents, distributors, or retailers.

In Chapter 16, we discussed channels of distribution in foreign markets. In this section, we will focus more specifically on channels of distribution for exporters. Exporters undertake **direct selling** to give them greater control over the marketing function and to earn higher profits. When selling direct, a manufacturer normally sells to retailers, but it may sell to a sales representative or agent operating on a commission basis or to a foreign distributor who takes title to the product and earns a profit on the final sale to the consumer.

A sales representative usually operates on a commission basis.

A distributor is a merchant who purchases the products from the manufacturer and sells them at a profit.

A **sales representative** resembles a manufacturer's representative in the United States. The representative usually operates either exclusively or nonexclusively within an assigned market and on a commission basis, without assuming risk or responsibility. For example, Grieve's agents operated on an exclusive basis in their respective markets. A **distributor** in a foreign country is a merchant that purchases the products from the manufacturer and sells them at a profit. Distributors usually carry a stock of inventory and service the product. They also typically deal with retailers rather than end users in the market.

Companies should consider the following points about each potential foreign sales representative or distributor:

- The size and capabilities of its sales force
- Its sales record
- An analysis of its territory
- Its current product mix
- Its facilities and equipment
- Its marketing policies
- Its customer profile
- The principals it represents and the importance of the inquiring company to its overall business
- Its promotional strategies[17]

Foreign retailers are outlets primarily for consumer goods and can be serviced by traveling salespeople or by catalogs or trade fairs. Sales of products manufactured to specification, however, are made directly to the end user. This practice is more common in industrial marketing than in consumer marketing.

A company that has sufficient financial and managerial resources and decides to export directly rather than working through an intermediary must set up a solid organization. This organization may take any number of forms ranging from a separate international division, to a separate international company, to full integration of international and domestic activities. Whatever the form, there commonly is an international sales force separate from the domestic sales force because of the different types of expertise required in dealing in foreign markets.

Indirect Selling

In **indirect selling,** the exporter deals through an indirect intermediary, which is another domestic company, before entering the international marketplace. That intermediary may act as a **commission agent** for the manufacturer and not take title. The commission agent usually acts on behalf of the foreign buyer and tries to find a specific product at the cheapest price. The agent is paid a commission by the foreign purchasing agent. An indirect intermediary also may purchase a product from the manufacturer and sell it abroad.

The two major types of indirect intermediaries are the **export management company (EMC)** and **export trading company (ETC).** EMCs and ETCs sometimes act as agents operating on a commission and sometimes take title to the merchandise and earn income through the margin. However, the terms EMC and ETC are sometimes used interchangeably, especially for the smaller intermediaries. The larger intermediaries, however, are almost always referred to as Export Trading

Commission agents work for the buyer.

EMCs provide export services for a specific exporter or group of exporters.

Companies or simply trading companies, since they typically deal with both exports and imports. We will discuss those intermediaries below.

Export Management Companies

An EMC usually acts as the export arm of a manufacturer, although it also can deal in imports, and often uses the manufacturer's own letterhead in communicating with foreign sales representatives and/or distributors. The EMC's primary function is to obtain orders for its clients' products through the selection of appropriate markets, distribution channels, and promotion campaigns. It collects, analyzes, and furnishes credit information and advice regarding foreign accounts and payment terms. The EMC also may handle documentation, arrange transportation (including the consolidation of shipments to reduce costs), set up patent and trademark protection in foreign countries, and counsel and assist in establishing alternative forms of doing business, such as licensing or joint ventures.[18]

EMCs operate on a contractual basis, usually for two to five years, and provide exclusive representation in a well-defined foreign territory. The contract specifies pricing, credit and financial policies, promotional services, and basis for payment. An EMC might operate on the basis of a commission for sales (unless it takes title to the merchandise) and a retainer for other services. EMCs usually concentrate on complementary and noncompetitive products so that they can present a more complete product line to a limited number of foreign importers.

EMCs in the United States are mostly small, entrepreneurial ventures that tend to specialize by product, function, or market area.

In the United States, most EMCs are small, entrepreneurial ventures that tend to specialize by product, function, or market area. Although EMCs perform an important function for companies that need their expertise, a manufacturer that uses an EMC may lose control over foreign sales. Thus the manufacturer needs to balance the desire for control with the cost of performing the export functions directly.[19]

Rizzo Co. of Scottsdale, Arizona, is an example of an intermediary that takes title to products. The company basically purchases manufactured goods and sells them worldwide. In many respects, Rizzo Co. is another domestic customer for the manufacturer. It takes title to the goods and demands a two-year exclusive agreement to export the goods, promising in return to not represent competing products in the assigned foreign market. Then Rizzo take all of the risk and earns the return in export markets. On the other hand, Last Concepts of Phoenix, Arizona, acts more as an agent in the market. Last Concepts locates foreign customers for a manufacturer, negotiates prices, ensures that the goods meet requirements for warranties and labeling, assists in getting export licenses, arranges the services of freight forwarders, and manages the letter of credit process with the customer's bank. In return, Last Concepts charges a fee or commission for its services.[20]

Export Trading Companies

ETCs tend to operate on the basis of demand rather than supply.

ETCs resemble EMCs but operate more on the basis of demand than of supply. ETCs are like independent distributors that match up buyers and sellers. ETCs find out what foreign customers want and then identify different domestic suppliers for the products. Rather than representing a manufacturer, an ETC looks for as many manufacturers as it can find to supply overseas customers.

In the fall of 1982, the U.S. government enacted the Export Trading Company Act, which removed some of the antitrust obstacles to the creation of ETCs in the United States. It was hoped that ETCs would lead to greater exports of U.S. goods and services.

Four major types of ETCs were identified in the U.S. legislation:

1. Newly formed ETCs that receive antitrust certification
2. ETCs organized by state and local governments
3. ETCs created by commercial banks
4. ETCs initially organized by U.S. companies to handle their own exports

The first type consists of business enterprises that would like to cooperate for foreign sales but have difficulty cooperating for domestic sales because of antitrust concerns. The U.S. government set strict guidelines on how companies qualify for exemption from antitrust considerations: Cooperation must not lessen competition in the United States. One example of the second type, ETCs organized by state and local governments, is the Port Authority of New York and New Jersey. This ETC, known as XPORT, courts smaller companies that produce high-technology products that have an export potential. Most large money-center banks have applied for permission to establish the third type of ETC. These applications must be approved by the Federal Reserve Board before the bank can start export operations. Many of the banks concentrate on customers in their geographical market and in parts of the world in which they already have a good banking network.

The fourth type of ETC consists of those initially set up by U.S. companies to handle their own export business. Many of these have expanded to include products produced by other companies.

However, the ETC concept has not really taken hold in the United States. Because the U.S. market is so huge, companies have tended to develop their own channels of distribution rather than hire someone else and allow them to capture the margins from distributing products. In addition, many ETCs developed in countries where they were established by the government, and the U.S. government has tended to let companies act on their own. It has worked well for undifferentiated products such as agricultural products but not for differentiated products that require significant individual attention. In the United States, differentiated products are handled best by EMCs that specialize in those products.

Non-U.S. Trading Companies

Unlike the U.S. trading companies, which tend to be small and medium sized, some of the largest companies in the world in terms of sales are trading companies from other countries. Table 17.3 lists the largest trading companies in the world

ETCs can be formed by
- **Competitors and be exempt from antitrust laws**
- **State and local governments**
- **Money-center banks**
- **Major corporations**

Table 17.3
Top Global Trading Companies 1995

Rank	Company	Country	Global 500 rank	1995 Revenue ($millions)
1	Mitsubishi	Japan	1	184,365
2	Mitsui	Japan	2	181,519
3	Itochu	Japan	3	169,165
4	Sumitomo	Japan	5	167,531
5	Marubeni	Japan	6	161,057
6	Nissho Iwai	Japan	11	97,886
7	Tomen	Japan	21	67,756
8	Nichimen	Japan	35	50,842
9	Kanematsu	Japan	37	49,838
10	Veba Group	Germany	42	46,280
11	Samsung	South Korea	67	35,060
12	Viag	Germany	94	29,260
13	Hyundai	South Korea	127	23,221
14	Preussag	Germany	179	18,759
15	Toyota Tsusho	Japan	209	16,928
16	SHV Holdings	Netherlands Antilles	230	16,170
17	Kawasho	Japan	270	14,063
18	LG International	South Korea	304	13,189
19	Cofco	China	338	12,305
20	Sumikin Bussan	Japan	359	11,894
21	Nittetsu Shoji	Japan	395	11,091

according to sales. It is also interesting to note that the biggest trading companies are also the biggest companies in the world from all industries. Although nine of the top ten trading companies in the world are from Japan, there are also trading companies from Germany, South Korea, the Netherlands Antilles, and China. Note that no U.S. trading companies are in the ranking, which draws from the top 500 companies in the world.

Japanese trading companies are known as *sogo shosha.*

The **sogo shosha,** the Japanese equivalent word for trading company, can trace its roots back to the late nineteenth century, when Japan embarked on an aggressive modernization process. At that time, the trading companies were referred to as *zaibatsu,* large, family-owned businesses composed of financial and manufacturing companies usually held together by a large holding company. These companies were very powerful, so U.S. General Douglas MacArthur broke them up after World War II and made many of their activities illegal.

The *sogo shosha* initially took the primary role of acquiring raw materials for Japan's industrialization process and then finding external markets for its goods. When these trading companies were first organized after World War II, their primary functions were handling paperwork for import and export transactions, financing imports and exports, and providing transportation and storage services. However, their operations expanded significantly to include investing in production and processing facilities, establishing fully integrated sales systems for certain products, expanding marketing activities, and developing large bases for the integrated processing of raw materials.[21]

An example of the type of activities that the Japanese trading companies get involved in is the joint purchase by Itochu Corporation and Arco of the western U.S. coal operations of Coastal States Energy Company. Although Itochu will hold a 35-percent equity interest in the coal operations, located primarily in Utah (U.S.), it will use its marketing expertise in Japan and elsewhere in the Pacific Rim to sell the coal.[22]

The Japanese trading companies are part of the larger corporate relationships known as **keiretsu.** Korean trading companies are part of the large Korean business groups called *chaebol.* Although the Korean trading companies were modeled after their Japanese counterparts, there are some differences. The Japanese trading companies, also known as *sogo shosha,* are relatively loosely linked to the rest of the *keiretsu,* whereas the companies in the *chaebol* are relatively tightly linked to each other, with a high degree of intercompany transactions with each other and with the trading companies. The *sogo shoshas* are not only more loosely linked to their *keiretsus,* but they are also more professionally managed, with the *chaebol* still very dependent on family patriarchs. The Japanese trading companies are very big in commodities and are heavily involved in triangular trading; for example, a Japanese company may sell Latin American commodities to the U.S., whereas the Korean companies derive about 70 percent of their revenues from Korean exports.[23] However, the *chaebol* are trying hard to challenge the *sogo shosha* in the trading company market.

Piggyback Exports

Sometimes an exporter can use another exporter as an intermediary. For example, a company may agree to supply products to a foreign distributor even though it does not produce the entire range of products. Then it might look for other manufacturers to fill the gaps in the product line. In this way, the second manufacturer becomes an exporter indirectly by using the first exporter's distribution channels.

Toys 'R' Us uses a variation on this idea. Many of the companies that supply products to Toys 'R' Us are not directly involved in exporting toys to other countries. However, when Toys 'R' Us began establishing stores overseas, it offered many of the same products as in its U.S. stores. Thus some suppliers became exporters through their continued relationship with Toys 'R' Us overseas. In its Japanese stores, for example, Toys 'R' Us initially provided a mixture of roughly two-thirds Japanese toys and one-third imports, including Huffy bikes, Mattel's Barbie dolls, and Tonka trucks.[24]

Foreign Freight Forwarders

Dealing in air and ocean transportation involves a number of institutions and documentation with which the typical exporter does not have expertise. This is true

Japanese trading companies are the world's largest companies in terms of sales.

Keiretsu—a Japanese business group that usually contains a trading company (also known as sogo shosha) as members of the group.

Chaebol—Korean business groups that are similar to keiretsu and also contain a trading company as part of the group

Piggyback exports are products exported by a company through another manufacturer's channels of distribution.

A foreign freight forwarder is an export or import specialist dealing in the movement of goods from producer to consumer.

even if the manufacturer is exporting components to a foreign subsidiary controlled by a common parent company. To assist in the documentation and transport of goods from one country to another, companies usually employ the services of a **freight forwarder,** known as the travel agents of cargo. Even export management companies and other types of trading companies often use the specialized services of foreign freight forwarders.

On average, the foreign freight forwarder is the largest export intermediary in terms of value and weight handled; however, the services offered are more limited than those of an EMC. The freight forwarder manages the movement of cargo from origin to destination. Once a foreign sale has been made, the freight forwarder acts on behalf of the exporter in obtaining the best routing and means of transportation based on space availability, speed, and cost. This process involves getting the products from the manufacturing facility to the air or ocean terminal and then overseas. The forwarder secures space on planes or ships and necessary storage prior to shipment, reviews the letter of credit, obtains export licenses, and prepares necessary shipping documents. It also may advise on packing and labeling, purchase transportation insurance, repack shipments damaged en route, and warehouse products, which saves the exporter the capital investment of warehousing.

The freight forwarder's compensation usually is a percentage of the shipment value, paid by the exporter, with a minimum charge dependent on the number of services provided. The forwarder also receives a brokerage fee from the carrier. Despite these costs, using a freight forwarder still is usually less costly for an exporter than providing the service internally, particularly since most companies find it difficult to utilize a traffic department full-time and to keep up with shipping regulations. The forwarder also provides the advantages of being able to get space more easily because of its close relationship with carriers and to consolidate shipments in order to obtain lower rates.

Freight forwarders can also operate on the import side as customs brokers, which will be discussed later in the chapter. The important thing to understand at this point is that a freight forwarder can assist in both exports and imports. The four leading international freight forwarders in the United States are Air Express International, Expeditors International of Washington, Fritz Co., and the Hasper Group. Expeditors International, located in Seattle, Washington, has 103 offices worldwide to service its clients, and it combines freight forwarding with customs processing. By having offices in different countries, freight forwarders can handle both the export and import sides more easily. Sometimes freight forwarders almost act as the outsourcers of the logistics function of a company. For example, Air Express International manages the entire inventory and distribution of an Intel plant in Malaysia.[25]

Freight forwarders, especially the smaller ones, sometimes specialize in terms of mode used (such as surface freight, ocean freight, and air freight) and geographical area served. Increasingly, however, the freight forwarders are multimodal providers, involved in truck, rail, and air freight, for example.[26] The movement

The typical freight forwarder is the largest export intermediary in terms of value and weight handled.

across different modes from origin to destination is known as *intermodal transportation.*

Air and Ocean Freight

Of total global trade, 99 percent calculated by *weight* moves by ocean, but 34 percent calculated by *value* is shipped by air.[27] Although ocean freight is the cheapest way to move merchandise, it also is the slowest. Thus even though it still dominates global trade, its position is eroding somewhat. Ocean freight rates are based on space first, and weight second. Rate schedules also differ depending on the ports involved and the direction the goods travel. For example, different rates apply to shipments from the United States to Germany and to shipments from Germany to the United States. Forwarders help manufacturers get the best contract and help prepare the products for export. Exporters can load merchandise in a container for shipment overseas, or they can rely on a freight forwarder to consolidate their shipment with others in order to fill a container. As mentioned in the opening case, Grieve's president believes in getting quotes from different freight forwarders when booking space on cargo ships. Even large companies compare rates with those offered by freight forwarders. The person who handles the export of Shell Oil Co.'s nonhazardous lubricating oils and greases negotiates rates with the steamship lines himself, but if the forwarders' steamship line rates are lower, he will use them instead. Sometimes the freight forwarders do more volume on certain lanes and thus get better rates than he can negotiate.[28]

Three trends favor the air-freight business: more frequent shipments, lighter-weight shipments, and higher-value shipments.[29] As companies attempt to lower carrying costs (inventory storage) and move to just-in-time inventory management, they must rely on quick and timely delivery of merchandise. Air freight is much more effective in accomplishing these objectives than is ocean freight.

Documentation

Freight forwarders also can help exporters fill out documents related to exporting. These documents differ from those used in domestic transportation, and most manufacturers need a freight forwarder to determine which are needed and how to complete them. One of these documents is an **export license.** Each country determines whether domestic products or products transshipped through its borders can be exported to certain countries. In the United States, an exporter needs to check with the U.S. Department of Commerce to determine if its products can be shipped under a general license or if they must be exported under an individually validated license (IVL). For example, exports of certain high-tech products might be restricted for national security reasons, so an exporter must apply for an IVL to determine whether the exportation is permitted.

Of the many documents that must be completed, some of the most important (excluding financial documents, which are discussed in the next section) are as follows:

- A *pro forma invoice* is an invoice, like a letter of intent, from the exporter to the importer outlining the selling terms, price, and delivery if the goods are actually shipped. If the importer likes the terms and conditions, it will send a purchase order and arrange for payment, such as issuing a letter of credit. At that point, the exporter can issue a commercial invoice.[30]
- A *commercial invoice* is a bill for the goods from the buyer to the seller. It contains a description of the goods, the address of buyer and seller, and delivery and payment terms. Many governments use this form to assess duties.
- A *bill of lading* is a receipt for goods delivered to the common carrier for transportation, a contract for the services rendered by the carrier, and a document of title.[31]
- A *consular invoice* sometimes is required by countries as a means of monitoring imports. The consular invoice can be used to monitor prices of imports and to generate revenue for the embassies that issue the consular invoice.
- A *certificate of origin* indicates where the products originate and usually is validated by an external source, such as the chamber of commerce. It helps countries determine the specific tariff schedule for imports.
- A *shipper's export declaration* is used to monitor exports and to compile trade statistics.
- An *export packing list* itemizes the material in each individual package, indicates the type of package, and is attached to the outside of the package. The list is used by the shipper or freight forwarder and sometimes by customs officials to determine the nature of the cargo and whether the correct cargo is being shipped.[32]

Export Financing

Financial issues related to exporting:
- **Product price**
- **Method of payment**
- **Financing of receivables**
- **Insurance**

Four major issues relate to the financial aspects of exporting: the price of the product, the methods of payment, the financing of receivables, and insurance.

Product Price

Product pricing of exports involves many of the same factors that must be considered in domestic pricing.

Export pricing is influenced by:
- **Exchange rates**
- **Transportation costs**
- **Duties**
- **Multiple channels**
- **Insurance costs**
- **Banking costs**

As noted in Chapter 16, there also are some differences. A major consideration is how the price takes exchange rates into consideration. If the exporter bills in the home-country currency, the importer absorbs the foreign-exchange risk and must decide whether to pass on any exchange-rate differences to the consumer. If the exporter bills in the currency of the importer's country, the foreign-exchange risk falls on the exporter. Another difference between domestic and export pricing is that price escalation results because of transportation costs, duties, multiple wholesale channels in the importing countries, cost of insurance, and banking costs.

Finally, the price may depend on dumping laws in the importing country. Recall from Chapter 6 that dumping refers to the sale of exports below cost or below what they are sold for in the domestic market. In 1993, when the Japanese yen rose significantly against the U.S. dollar, U.S. automakers threatened to ask for dumping sanctions from the U.S. government unless Japanese automakers increased their prices to reflect the increased import costs. An exporter must be aware of the dumping laws in each foreign market and the degree to which these laws are enforced.

Methods of Payment

The flow of money across national borders is complex and requires the use of special documents. Foreign trade usually is financed on credit. Exporters rarely get paid right away because of collection and foreign-exchange problems.

In descending order in terms of security to the exporter, the basic methods of payment for exports are

- Cash in advance
- Letter of credit
- Draft or bill of exchange
- Open account
- Other payment mechanisms, such as consignment sales or countertrade

When an individual or a company pays a bill in a domestic setting, they typically use a check. This is also known as a *draft,* also called a *bill of exchange.* A draft is an instrument in which one party (the drawer) directs another party (the drawee) to make a payment. The drawee can either be a company like the importer or a bank. In the latter case, the draft would be considered a bank draft. If the exporter requests payment to be made immediately, the draft is called a *sight draft.* If the payment is to be made later, for example, thirty days after delivery, the instrument is called a *time draft.* A time draft is obviously more flexible to the importer and more risky to the exporter. A time draft drawn on a bank and bearing the bank's promise to pay at a future date is known as a *banker's acceptance.* Often, the draft is accompanied by documents which contain information about the shipment. Banks assist in establishing and collecting a draft and usually charge the exporter a modest fee that ranges from about one-eighth to one-quarter percent of the value of the draft, with a minimum of $35–$75 and a maximum of $150–$200.

With a bill of exchange, it is always possible the importer will not be able to make payment to the exporter at the agreed-upon time. A **letter of credit (L/C),** however, obligates the buyer's bank in the importing country to honor a draft presented to it, provided the draft is accompanied by the prescribed documents. A documentary letter of credit stipulates that payment will be made by the bank on the basis of the documents, not on the terms of the sale. However, the exporter still needs to be sure that the bank's credit is valid as well. A common mistake for people new to international business is to ship merchandise on a false letter of credit. Either the letter of credit can be forged, or it can be issued on a nonexistent bank.

The exporter, even with the added security of the bank, still needs to rely on the importer's credit because of possible discrepancies that could arise in the transaction. A letter of credit does not eliminate foreign exchange risk if the sale is denominated in a currency other than that of the exporter's country. However, a letter of credit denominated in the exporter's currency means the exporter incurs no risk of loss as a result of possible exchange-rate fluctuations. As with a draft, a letter of credit may be issued at sight or time. Even in the case of a letter of credit drawn with a sight draft, it may take two or three days for the cash to clear, so the exporter's collecting bank might be able to extend immediate credit to the exporter. In addition, the exporter might try to discount the letter of credit (sell it to someone else at less than face value) in order to get instant access to cash.

When an exporter requires a letter of credit, the importer is responsible for arranging for it at the importer's bank. Figure 17.4 explains the relationships among the parties to a letter of credit.

A letter of credit can be revocable or irrevocable. A **revocable letter of credit** is one that can be changed by any of the parties involved. However, both exporter and importer may prefer an **irrevocable letter of credit** (see Fig. 17.5), which is a letter that cannot be canceled or changed in any way without the consent of all parties to the transaction. With this type of L/C, the importer's bank is obligated to pay and is willing to accept any drafts (bills of exchange) at sight, meaning these drafts will be paid as soon as the correct documents are presented to the bank. As noted above, an L/C can also be issued at time. It is important to note that all the conditions on the letter of credit—such as the method of transportation and the description of the merchandise—must be adhered to precisely by the exporter; otherwise, the letter of credit will not be paid without approval of all parties to an elimination of the discrepancies. The L/C in Fig. 17.5 is a hard-copy typed L/C, but many

A revocable letter of credit may be changed by any of the parties to the agreement.

An irrevocable letter of credit requires all parties to agree to a change in the documents.

Figure 17.4
Letter-of-Credit Relationships
A letter of credit guarantees the exporter that the importer's bank will pay for the imports. The credit relationship exists between the importer and the importer's bank (the opening bank). A confirmed letter of credit has an added guarantee from the exporter's bank: If the importer's bank defaults, the exporter's bank must pay.

Source: Adapted from *Export and Import Financing Procedures* (Chicago: The First National Bank of Chicago), p. 22.

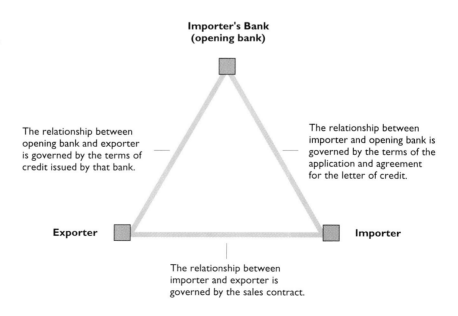

Importer's Bank (opening bank)

The relationship between opening bank and exporter is governed by the terms of credit issued by that bank.

The relationship between importer and opening bank is governed by the terms of the application and agreement for the letter of credit.

Exporter   **Importer**

The relationship between importer and exporter is governed by the sales contract.

**Figure 17.5
An Export Letter
of Credit**
A letter of credit is a precisely worded document whose terms must be adhered to in order for the exporter to receive payment.

Source: First Security Bank, N.A. Reprinted with permission.

First Security Bank.

IRREVOCABLE DOCUMENTARY CREDIT	ISSUED IN SALT LAKE CITY, UTAH ON <u>24 OCT 1996</u>

MAIL TO

BENEFICIARY	APPLICANT	ADVISING BANK
XYZ COMPANY	ABC COMPANY	FIRST SECURITY TRADE SERVICES LTD.
HONG KONG	123 ANY STREET	NEW HENRY HOUSE, 3RD FLOOR
	ANY TOWN, UT 99999	10 ICE HOUSE STREET CENTRAL
		HONG KONG

TRANSSHIPMENTS PERMITTED
PARTIAL SHIPMENTS PERMITTED

AMOUNT
USD $257,000.00
TWO HUNDRED FIFTY SEVEN THOUSAND
AND 00/100 UNITED STATES DOLLARS

<u>DATE AND PLACE OF EXPIRY</u>
15 MAR 1997, HONG KONG

WE HEREBY ISSUE OUR IRREVOCABLE DOCUMENTARY CREDIT

CREDIT AVAILABLE WITH <u>ANY BANK</u> BY <u>NEGOTIATION</u> OF DRAFT AT <u>30 DAYS B/L DATE</u> DRAWN ON <u>FIRST SECURITY BANK OF UTAH, N.A.</u> FOR 100 PERCENT OF INVOICE AMOUNT.

SHIPMENT FROM: <u>HONG KONG</u>   SHIPMENT TO: <u>U.S. WEST COAST PORT</u>

NO LATER THAN: <u>01 MAR 1997</u> COVERING SHIPMENT OF <u>GENERAL MERCHANDISE</u> FOB <u>HONG KONG</u>
WHEN ACCOMPANIED BY THE FOLLOWING DOCUMENTS:

- 2 SIGNED COMMERCIAL INVOICES IN ORIGINAL AND 1 COPY
- 2 PACKING LISTS IN ORIGINAL
- 1 CERTIFICATE OF ORIGIN IN ORIGINAL
- FULL SET PLUS 1 COPY OF CLEAN ON BOARD OCEAN B/L'S MARKED FREIGHT COLLECT

<u>CONSIGNED TO:</u>   ABC COMPANY
                          1234 SOUTHWEST LANE
                          SALT LAKE CITY, UT 84111
<u>NOTIFY:</u>   FORWARDING COMPANY, INC.
                          AMELIA EARHART DRIVE
                          SALT LAKE CITY, UT 84104

SPECIAL CONDITIONS:
- DOCUMENTS MUST BE PRESENTED TO PAYING/NEGOTIATING BANK WITHIN 21 DAYS AFTER THE DATE OF SHIPMENT HOWEVER WITHIN VALIDITY OF LETTER OF CREDIT.
- DOCUMENTS MUST BE PRESENTED IN ONE MAIL.
- INSURANCE COVERED BY BUYER.
ALL CHARGES EXCEPT THE OPENING BANK'S CHARGES ARE FOR THE ACCOUNT OF THE BENEFICIARY.

NOTE THAT WE WILL ASSESS A DISCREPANCY FEE OF USD40.00 ON EACH PRESENTATION OF DOCUMENTS CONTAINING DISCREPANCIES.

<u>REIMBURSEMENT INSTRUCTIONS:</u>   <u>CONFIRMATION INSTRUCTIONS:</u>
VIA REGISTERED MAIL TO: WITHOUT ADDING YOUR CONFIRMATION.
FIRST SECURITY BANK OF UTAH, N.A.
INTERNATIONAL DEPARTMENT
41 EAST 100 SOUTH
P.O. BOX 30004
SALT LAKE CITY, UT 84130

WE HEREBY ENGAGE WITH DRAWERS, ENDORSERS, AND BONA FIDE HOLDERS THAT DRAFTS DRAWN AND NEGOTIATED IN CONFORMITY WITH THE TERMS OF THIS CREDIT WILL BE DULY HONORED ON PRESENTATION AND THAT DRAFTS ACCEPTED WITHIN THE TERMS OF THIS CREDIT WILL BE DULY HONORED AT MATURITY. EACH DRAFT MUST BE ENDORSED ON THE REVERSE THEREOF BY THE NEGOTIATING BANK. THE AMOUNT OF EACH DRAFT MUST BE ENDORSED ON THE REVERSE OF THIS CREDIT BY THE NEGOTIATING BANK.

THE NUMBER OF THE CREDIT AND THE NAME OF OUR BANK MUST BE QUOTED ON ALL DRAFTS REQUIRED. IF THE CREDIT IS AVAILABLE BY NEGOTIATION, THE AMOUNT OF EACH DRAWING MUST BE ENTERED ON THE REVERSE OF THIS CREDIT BY THE NEGOTIATING BANK.

THIS CREDIT IS SUBJECT TO THE UNIFORM CUSTOMS AND PRACTICE FOR DOCUMENTARY CREDITS, 1993 REVISION, INTERNATIONAL CHAMBER OF COMMERCE, PUBLICATION NO. 500.

AUTHORIZED SIGNATURE(S)

*First Security Bank - Financial Services Division - 41 East 100 South - Salt Lake City, Utah 84111
Telephone (801) 246-5334 - SWIFT Address: FSBUUS55*

---

banks are now issuing L/C's electronically. They can establish an L/C system template on the customer's system that allows them to submit the L/C to the bank, and the bank can then transfer the L/C electronically to the overseas supplier.

A letter of credit transaction may involve a confirming bank in addition to the parties mentioned above. With a **confirmed letter of credit,** the exporter has the guarantee of an additional bank, sometimes in the exporter's home country, some-

A confirmed irrevocable letter of credit adds an obligation to pay for the exporter's bank.

times in a third country. It rarely happens that the exporter establishes the confirming relationship. Usually, the opening bank seeks the conformation of the L/C with a bank with whom they already have a credit relationship. If this letter of credit is irrevocable, none of the conditions can be changed unless all four parties to it agree in advance.

An exporter occasionally may sell on **open account.** This means the necessary shipping documents are mailed to the importer before any payment from or definite obligation on the part of the buyer. Releasing goods in this manner is somewhat unusual because the exporter risks default by the buyer. An exporter ordinarily sells under such conditions only if it successfully conducted business with the importer for an extended time. This is generally the arrangement used when the importer and exporter are related entities.

Financing Receivables

A cash-flow analysis can help an exporter determine if it has sufficient working capital to carry it from production through collection. The increased distances and time involved in exportation can create cash-flow problems for the exporter. This is especially true if the exporter extends payment through a time draft.

Because exporting is risky, banks often are unwilling to provide funding for it. This is a major problem for small exporters that do not have the working capital to sustain themselves over the long timeline between production and payment. They complain that banks will not fund small needs for working capital arising from exporting but provide funding readily to domestic clients that are greater credit risks. Small exporters need to find a way to get access to funds or guarantee their export revenues so that banks will lend them working capital.

There are many funding sources that companies can access, both public and private.[33] Other than banks, companies can get access to funds through their customers, factoring or forfaiting. Factoring is the discounting of a foreign account receivable that does not involve a draft. The exporter transfers title of their foreign accounts receivable to a finance company that specializes in factoring for a cash discount from the face value.[34] Forfaiting is similar to factoring in that the forfaiting company purchases receivables or promissory notes of the foreign buyer at a discount. Typically, these instruments are longer term.[35]

In addition, exporters can apply for guarantees from government agencies in order to get banks to loan them money until they can collect on their receivables. For example, the Ex-Im Bank (Export Import Bank of the U.S.) is an independent federal agency that supports the export of U.S. goods and services through loan guarantees and insurance programs.[36] Ex-Im Bank offers four programs:

- Working Capital Guarantees
- Export Credit Insurance
- Guarantees of Commercial Loans to Foreign Buyers
- Direct Loans for Foreign Buyers[37]

Ex-Im Bank provides direct loans to importers or guarantees to financial institutions.

The working capital guarantees cover 90 percent of the principal and interest on commercial loans to creditworthy small and medium-sized companies. With the guarantees, lenders can provide funds on a single project or revolving credit basis. Export credit insurance policies protect against both political and commercial risks of a foreign buyer defaulting on payment. The insurance helps exporters finance receivables more easily by assigning the proceeds of the policy to the lender. Guarantees of commercial loans to foreign buyers of U.S. goods or services cover 100 percent of principal and interest against political and commercial risks of nonpayment. Direct loans can also be made to foreign buyers of U.S. goods.[38]

The SBA guarantees long-term financing of loans by financial institutions to small exporters.

Another example of how governments can fund exports is the Small Business Administration (SBA) of the United States. The SBA operates an Export Working Capital Program (EWCP) and a facilities-and-equipment loan program. Small business can borrow up to $1.25 million in combining the two types of loans. The EWCP is a combined effort of the SBA and the Ex-Im Bank. The EWCP loans have a maturity of up to three years at rates of up to 2.25 percent above prime. Loans of $833,333 or less can be made by the SBA, whereas loans in excess of that amount can be funded by the Ex-Im Bank. The SBA can guarantee up to 80 percent of loans of $100,000 and less and up to 75 percent of loans above $100,000, up to a maximum guarantee of $750,000.[39]

Countertrade

Countertrade refers to any one of a number of different arrangements by which goods and services are traded for each other.

Countertrade often takes place because of a foreign-exchange shortage.

Sometimes countries have so much difficulty generating enough foreign exchange to pay for imports that they need to devise creative ways to get the products they want. Although this shortage of foreign exchange is associated primarily with historically planned economies (HPEs) and developing countries, it also can affect industrial countries. For example, Canada and Australia found they had to enter into special agreements with McDonnell-Douglas to pay for military aircraft they wanted to purchase. Thus, both companies and governments often are forced to resort to creative ways of settling payment, many of which involve trading goods for goods as part of the transaction. **Countertrade** refers to any one of several different arrangements by which goods and services are traded for each other, on either a bilateral or a multilateral basis. More specifically, it is defined as "a practice whereby a supplier commits contractually—as a condition of sale—to reciprocate and undertake certain specified commercial initiatives that compensate and benefit the buyer."[40]

It is difficult to know how big the countertrade market is. Estimates range from 20 percent of all world trade[41] to 40 percent of the world's economy.[42] In addition, some articles claim that countertrade is increasing, whereas some claim that it is decreasing. The increase in countries with freely floating currency markets, as discussed in Chapter 10, is evidence that there is less need for countertrade than in previous years, but good countertrade data are hard to find. There are several types of countertrades, but the three most widely used are barter, buybacks, and offset.[43]

Barter

Barter occurs when goods are traded for goods.

Barter, the oldest form of countertrade, is a transaction in which goods are traded for goods of equal value without any flow of cash. Many problems attend the negotiating of a barter agreement. Nevertheless, there are recent examples of successful bartering. For example, in 1994, Paul Johnson, Managing Director of New Zealand-based Clendon Wool, shipped a woolscouring machine worth $1.8 million to Kazakhistan and received $2 million in Kazakh wool, as illustrated in Fig. 17.6. In this case, Clendon Wool was able to use the wool directly and the Kazakh exporter was able to use the woolscouring machine. In early 1994, however, Johnson completed a barter transaction with Kazakhistan by selling Hungarian busses to pay for the wool.[44]

Although the countertrade transactions often take place between the two major parties to the transaction, there are also barter firms that act as an intermediary between the exporter and importer, often taking title to the goods received by the exporter for a price, or selling the goods for a fee and/or a percentage of the sales value. For example, a commodity broker will purchase the goods from the company at a discounted price, often 20 percent of the total value of the contract.[45] This puts great pressure on exporters to make sure that the merchandise they receive in the transaction has enough value to cover the export as well as the discount.

Buybacks involve counterdeliveries that are related to, or originate from, the original export. An example would be where a company exports capital equipment to a country to be used in a mining operation and receives as payment minerals which they can sell on world markets. Another example was where PepsiCo pro-

Figure 17.6
A Barter Transaction
Clendon Wool ships a woolscouring machine to Kazakhistan in return for Kazakh wool. The machine cost $1.8 million, but was worth $2 million, resulting in a good profit for Clendon Wool.

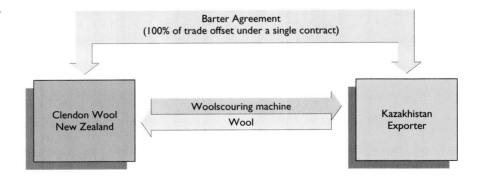

A major area of concern for some companies is the exportation of hazardous substances, especially pesticides and chemicals. Generally, companies should accept the ethical norms of a host country for products that are exported to it; however, regulations concerning pesticides are more lax in many developing countries than they are in industrial countries. Thus exporting pesticides or harmful chemicals that are illegal in a company's home country but not in the host country raises an ethical dilemma. There is a major argument over the concept of prior informed consent (PIC), which would require each exporter of a banned or restricted chemical to obtain through its home-country government the express consent of the importing country to receive the banned or restricted substance. Countries favoring the PIC concept argue that many developing countries are not adequately informed of the danger of certain chemicals and therefore need the assistance of industrial countries. Those against PIC argue that this principle infringes on the national sovereignty of importing countries and replaces their ethical norms with those of the exporting country.[46]

ETHICAL DILEMMAS & SOCIAL RESPONSIBILITY

Governments often control the export of so-called sensitive technology to certain countries. Before the Iron Curtain fell in 1989, Toshiba shipped to the former Soviet Union sensitive technology that could be used in submarine warfare. The company transshipped products through different ports in order to disguise the sale and shield itself from prosecution. However, this illegal activity was eventually uncovered. Another example of the exportation of sensitive technology involves the arming of Saddam Hussein prior to the Persian Gulf War. A British company was found guilty of exporting a large gun, disguised as industrial pipes, that could be used as an offensive weapon. The company lied about the nature of the export but eventually was found out. In addition, German companies were guilty of selling to Libya chemicals that could be used in chemical warfare. In these cases, documents were falsified to keep the authorities from finding out the transactions' true nature.

Sometimes shippers lie to freight forwarders about the nature of their products. One freight forwarder was working with a company that was shipping large drums to Sweden by air. The forwarder asked the shipper if the drums contained hazardous materials, and the shipper said no. In fact, unfortunately, the drums contained a very toxic material. This substance leaked through the drum and ate through the bottom of a 747 just as it was landing in Sweden.

vided Pepsi syrup to state-owned bottling plants in Russia and received Stolichnya vodka which it marketed in the west.

Offset Trade

Another type of countertrade, called **offset trade,** is becoming increasingly important. Offsets are most often used for big ticket items, such as defense sales and civilian aircraft sales. Offset arrangements are usually one of three types:

- Direct offsets include any business that relates directly to the product being sold; generally, the foreign vendor seeks local contractors to joint venture or coproduce certain parts.
- Indirect offsets include all business unrelated to the product being sold; generally the vendor is asked to buy a country's goods or invest in an unrelated business, or;
- A combination of direct and indirect offsets.[47]

Some of the most common offset practices in military sales include coproduction, licensed production, subcontractor production, overseas investment, and technology transfer. Each of these involves direct offsets. Examples of indirect offsets might include assisting in the export of unrelated products from the host country or generating tourist revenues for the host country.

A good example of how a company might have to deal with offset trade involves McDonnell-Douglas and the sale of F-18A fighter aircraft to Canada in 1980. This sale was to net McDonnell-Douglas nearly $3 billion, a significant amount of money for one transaction. Over the eight-year period specified for delivery dates, Canada would average imports of several hundred million dollars per year. Given the weakness of the Canadian dollar in relation to the U.S. dollar at the time of the sale, this significant increase in imports concerned the Canadian government. Consequently, the negotiations for the sale of the aircraft involved not only the technical capabilities of the F-18As and their cost but also the industrial benefits that McDonnell-Douglas could promise the Canadian government. The Canadian offset agreement covered fifteen years with a three-year grace period. The total program commitment of $2.9 billion was covered from the following three areas: aerospace and electronics, advanced technology, and diversified activities. The aerospace and electronics area, the most important of the three, involved designated production, coproduction, technology transfer, and joint R&D. The diversified activities portion of the offset agreement involved investment/technology development, export development, and tourism development.

Figure 17.7 shows how a complex transaction such as the F-18A sale to Canada might be structured. As noted in the figure, the transaction involves the primary exporter, the importing government, and other secondary exporters and importers.

Whether companies become involved in the complexities of offset trade depends mainly on the strength of demand for their products, whether they have

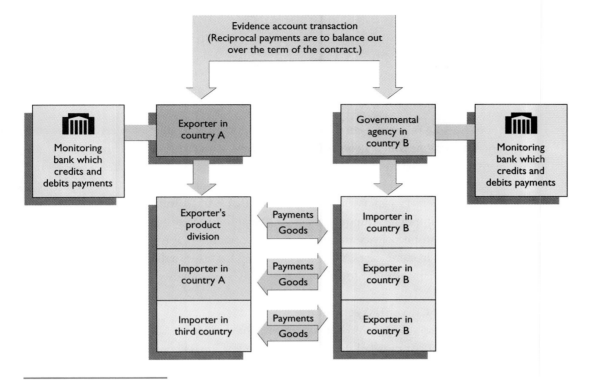

Figure 17.7
An Offset Transaction
In this form of counter-trade, the exporter (in country A) is required to find ways for the importing country (country B) to earn foreign exchange to pay for the exports.

Source: From Pompiliu Verzariu, *Countertrade, Barter, Offsets,* © 1985, New York: McGraw-Hill, p. 32. Reprinted with permission.

Importers need to be concerned with procedural and strategic issues.

alternative sources of supply, and the extent of foreign-exchange problems in the buying country. In any case, offset trade results primarily from foreign-exchange shortages and is a good example of how companies and governments can compensate for such a shortage through creative business transactions.

The Import Strategy

There are two different types of considerations for potential importers: procedural and strategic. Procedural considerations relate more to the rules and regulations of the customs agency of a country. Strategic issues refer to the long-term reasons why a company would rather buy products from foreign than domestic sources. In this chapter, we are considering the import of goods and services for resale in the domestic market. However, there is another side of importing—the import of parts and components to be used in the domestic manufacturing process. This could be a function of outsourcing—purchasing parts and components from an unrelated party abroad—or setting up your own facilities abroad and importing parts and components in an integrated manufacturing process. These issues will be covered in Chapter 18.

The following procedural steps must be considered by an importer once a foreign source for products has been determined:

- Ship the products to the importing country by air, land, or ocean
- Clear customs
- Pay the exporter
- Store the products until they can be sold
- Sell the products and collect payment

Importing requires a certain degree of expertise in dealing with institutions and documentation, which a company may not have acquired. Consequently, the company may elect to work through an **import broker.** The import broker is a person who obtains various governmental permissions and other clearances before forwarding necessary paperwork to the carrier that is to deliver the goods from the dock to the importer. Import brokers in the United States are certified as such by the U.S. Customs Service to perform the functions necessary to bring products into the country. In some cases, personnel working for intermediaries such as public accounting firms, freight forwarders, and EMCs are certified as import brokers.

An import broker is an intermediary that helps an importer clear customs.

The Role of Customs Agencies

When importing goods into any country, a company must be totally familiar with the customs operations of the importing country. In this context, "customs" refers to the country's import and export procedures and restrictions, not its cultural aspects. The primary duties of the U.S. Customs Service, for example, are "the assessment and collection of all duties, taxes, and fees on imported merchandise, the enforcement of customs and related laws, and the administration of certain navigation laws and treaties." As a major enforcement organization, it "combats smuggling and frauds on the revenue and enforces the regulations of numerous other Federal agencies at ports of entry and along the land and sea borders of the United States."[48] An importer needs to know the way to clear goods, the duties that must be paid, and the special laws that exist.

Customs agencies assess and collect duties and ensure import regulations are adhered to.

On the procedural side, when merchandise reaches the port of entry, the importer must file documents with customs officials in which a tentative value and tariff classification are assigned to the merchandise. The U.S. government has over 10,000 tariff classifications, and approximately 60 percent of them are subject to interpretation; that is, a particular product could fit more than one classification. Then customs officials examine the goods to determine whether there are any restrictions on their importation. If there are none, the importer pays the duty and the goods are released. The amount of the duty depends on the product's country of origin, the type of product, and other factors.[49]

A broker or other import consultant can help an importer minimize import duties by doing the following:

- *Valuing products in such a way that they qualify for more favorable duty treatment.* Different product categories have different duties. For example, finished goods typically have a higher duty than do parts and components.

- *Qualifying for duty refunds through drawback provisions.* Some exporters use in their manufacturing process imported parts and components on which they paid a duty. In the United States, the drawback provision allows exporters to apply for a refund of 99 percent of the duty paid on the imported goods, provided the goods are used in the manufacture of goods that are exported.
- *Deferring duties by using bonded warehouses and foreign trade zones.* Companies do not have to pay duties on imports stored in bonded warehouses and foreign trade zones until the goods are removed for sale or used in a manufacturing process.
- *Limiting liability by properly marking an import's country of origin.* Because governments assess duties on imports based in part on the country of origin, a lower duty on an import may be had by ensuring that the import's country of origin is accurate. For example, in the United States, if an article or its container is not properly marked when it enters the country, a marking duty equal to 10 percent of the customs value of the article is assessed.[50]

Drawback provisions are an important part of the U.S. tariff code because they encourage domestic manufacturing by allowing U.S. companies to use foreign components in the manufacturing process without having to include the duty paid on the merchandise in costs and sales prices. A direct identification drawback is permitted on imported merchandise that is actually used to manufacture goods for export, provided the imported goods are not used for final consumption in the United States and are exported within five years of the import date. Sometimes domestic merchandise is substituted for merchandise that was imported for eventual export, in which case substitution drawback is permitted for duties on the imported merchandise.

Documentation

When a shipment arrives at a port, the importer must file specific documents with the port director in order to take title to the shipment. Some of the documents relate directly to customs and determine whether or not the importer has the right to bring the products into the country. These documents are of two different types: those that determine whether customs will release the shipment, and those that contain information for duty assessment and statistical purposes.[51] The specific documents required by customs vary by country but include an entry manifest, a commercial invoice, and a packing list. For example, the commercial invoice, prepared by the exporter, contains information such as the port of entry to which the merchandise is destined, information on the buyer and seller, a detailed description of the merchandise, the purchase price of the item and the currency used for the sale, and the country of origin.

Many small companies also are successful exporters.

COUNTERVAILING

FORCES

The export strategy outlined in this chapter is based on the perspective of a company's efforts to penetrate foreign markets through goods or services manufactured or developed in the home country. However, many exports are intracompany in nature. For example, Ford might manufacture carburetors in Italy, export them to a Ford assembly plant in Germany, and export the final product—automobiles—to consumers in Belgium. Such intracompany shipments tend to fulfill a global strategy of production, assembly, and sales to the consumer. This strategy is investigated in more detail in Chapter 18. However, when Grieve is determining how to sell its ovens in different world markets, it examines each market separately and tries to ascertain how to adapt its product to consumer's needs in each country.

An article on mini-nationals, that is, companies with average sales of $600 million, pointed out that successful exporters in this size category must keep focused—they must concentrate on being number one or number two in technology niches they have developed.[52] This competitive strategy applies to countries as well. Some of the industrial and newly industrializing countries of Asia—such as Hong Kong, Japan, Korea, Singapore, and Taiwan—have grown rapidly through exporting. They have established fiscal and monetary policies and provided direct governmental assistance in promoting exports, thus creating jobs and significant wealth. Japan's huge trade surplus with the rest of the world—especially with the United States and Europe—has created considerable ill will, which in turn has resulted in pressure on Japan to correct its trade imbalance. In response to this pressure, some companies have voluntarily reduced their exports in order to help the Japanese government improve the country's relations with the rest of the world.

Multilateral trade groups such as the EU and NAFTA are designed to eliminate tariff and nontariff barriers in order to spur exports. However, exporters still find numerous trade barriers that keep them from selling their products in foreign markets. Countries are challenged to continue their cooperation in reducing trade restrictions so that exporters can increase their access to markets and operate in a more stable and predictable environment.

LOOKING TO
THE FUTURE

Exporting continues to differ among countries in terms of its importance in generating GDP and, therefore, jobs. When the global economy is growing and barriers come down, exports tend to increase. When the world is in an economic slowdown, nontariff barriers to trade combine with low demand to slow the rate of export growth. Thus any predictions of export activity are directly tied to predictions of economic growth. And future economic growth is tied to efforts to reduce trade barriers. Examples of these efforts are the EU and NAFTA. When barriers to trade rise, exporters from large countries such as the United States pull back their exporting efforts and focus on domestic markets.

Advances in transportation and communications will continue to facilitate export growth and make it easier for companies to get involved in global activity. One example of advances in communication is electronic data interchange, the electronic movement of information. As freight forwarders continue to automate, they become able to transmit documents electronically, which will reduce border delays in getting goods to market. Also, advances in communications will allow shippers to track shipments more accurately so that they can predict when the shipments will arrive in port to be claimed by the importer.

An area in which companies probably will receive little relief in the next few years is governmental assistance, especially in the financial area. Most industrial countries have serious federal budget deficits, a result of economic slowdown and reduced tax receipts, and so have been forced to privatize and cut governmental services. One of those areas affected will be exports. In the United States, for example, cutbacks in funding to the Department of Commerce, the SBA, and Ex-Im Bank have made it more difficult for exporters to get assistance, especially access to loan guarantees. This situation will not improve soon; thus pressure will continue on the small exporter to penetrate markets alone.

WEB CONNECTION
Check out our home page for links to resources on exporting and importing.

Summary

- The probability of a company's becoming an exporter increases with company size, but the extent of exporting does not directly correlate with size.

- *Fortune*'s top fifty exporters account for 30 percent of U.S. exports; smaller companies tend to have smaller-sized shipments on average than do larger ones.

- Companies new to exporting (and also some experienced exporters) often make many mistakes. One way to avoid those is to develop a comprehensive export strategy that includes an analysis of the company's resources as well as of market opportunities.

- Companies get involved in exporting to increase sales revenues, utilize excess capacity, and diversify markets.

- As a company establishes its export business plan, it must assess export potential, obtain expert counseling, select a market or markets, formulate its strategy, and determine how to get its goods to market.

- Exporters may deal directly with agents or distributors in a foreign country or indirectly through export management companies or other types of trading companies.

- Trading companies can perform many of the functions for which manufacturers lack the expertise. In addition, exporters can use the services of other specialists, such as freight forwarders, to facilitate exporting. These specialists can help an exporter with the complex documentation that accompanies exports.

- There are three major issues that relate to the financial aspects of exporting: the price of the product, the method of payment, the financing of receivables, and insurance.

- Export prices are a function of domestic pricing pressures, the impact of exchange rates, and price escalation due to longer channels of distribution, tariffs, and so forth.

- In descending order in terms of security, the basic methods of payment for exports are cash in advance, letter of credit, draft, open account, and other payment mechanisms such as consignment sales or countertrade.

- A letter of credit is a financial document that obligates the importer's bank to pay the exporter.

- Governmental agencies in some countries, such as the Ex-Im Bank in the United States, provide assistance in terms of direct loans to importers, bank guarantees to fund exporters' working-capital needs, and insurance against commercial and political risk.

- Countertrade refers to any one of several different arrangements by which goods and services are traded for each other, on either a bilateral or a multilateral basis. Barter involves trading goods for goods. Buybacks involve counterdeliveries that are related to the original export, such as the receipt of minerals in exchange for the export of mining equipment. Offsets involve an obligation by the exporter to help the importer earn foreign exchange or the transfer of technology or production to the importing country.

- Importers need to be concerned with strategic issues (why import rather than buy domestically) and procedural issues (what are the steps that need to be followed to get goods into the country).

- Customs agencies assess and collect duties and ensure that import regulations are adhered to.

Case
Sunset Flowers of New Zealand, Ltd.[53]

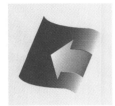

After eighteen months of residing in the United States, John Robertson, a New Zealander, glances frequently at a map of the United States on his wall, wondering when he will get the time and resources to travel into the various metropolitan areas of the central, southern, and eastern states. Through such travel, he believes, he can gain an improved appreciation of the characteristics of the markets for fresh-cut flowers, an item that he began importing into the United States from New Zealand during his summer "vacation" from school.

In August, Robertson and his family left New Zealand for Seattle so he could study for his MBA degree at the University of Washington. A month earlier, he had resigned from his job and leased their house and small farm. On completion of the degree, the Robertsons intended to return to New Zealand, where John would seek employment in a senior management position with a company involved in exporting.

New Zealand is a country the size of Oregon with a population of 3 million. The relatively small size of its population base coupled with its distance from world markets (see Map 17.1) inhibits its ability to establish an industrial base competitive with those of the world's leading industrial countries. Therefore New Zealand depends heavily on world trade, importing fuel and manufacturing products and gaining most of its foreign exchange through exports of agricultural produce. Its f.o.b. exports average around 22 percent of its GDP, compared with the U.S. figure of 8 percent (f.o.b. stands for "free on board," which includes the cost of the product to the city of export but excludes international shipping costs). To hold its place in the world economy, New Zealand lobbies hard to remove the restrictions imposed on imported agricultural products by the EU, Japan, and the United States. Along with this campaign, efforts are being made to diversify into horticultural products such as fresh flowers and fruit.

Immediately prior to leaving New Zealand, Robertson had worked for almost four years as the financial manager of a company involved in growing, wholesaling, and exporting live ornamental trees and shrubs. To sell its products on world markets, the company used agents, including two based in the United States, one in Japan, and one in Europe. The agents were paid retainers and typically provided services for several exporters. The experience gained from working for this company provided Robertson with a background in the procedures necessary for exporting. It also gave him insight into the problems that exporters face when trying to compete in foreign markets, where control over representation is hindered by distance and lack of knowledge of business procedures.

It was while working for this company that Robertson was introduced to cut-flower products. The Robertsons raised enough money to purchase a farm and then became acquainted with their neighbors, the Pratts, who were first-class horticulturalists. The Pratts had developed a new variety of the Leucadendron plant that yielded a beautiful, red leaflike flower, which the Robertsons and Pratts felt could be exported successfully.

During their first year of production, the Robertsons and Pratts formed a new entrepreneurial venture. They exported their yield through an established export company whose principal line of business was exporting fresh fruit and vegetables. The company had a large market share of this business and also had assumed a significant share of the exports

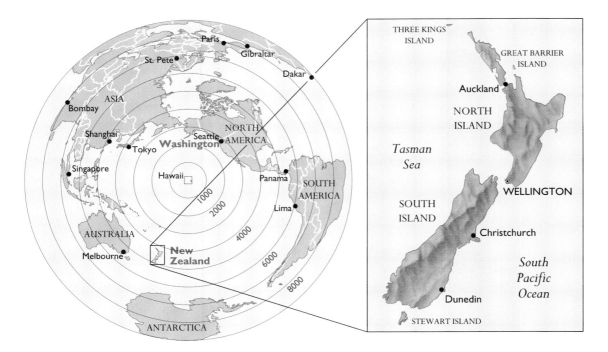

Map 17.1
New Zealanders' View of the World
New Zealand is an industrial country that is one of only two OECD members in the Southern Hemisphere. The great distance from this country to major world markets, such as the United States, is an important barrier that an exporter such as Sunset Flowers of New Zealand needs to overcome.

of cut flowers from New Zealand. The New Zealand cut-flower export industry was small and, with the exception of trade in orchids, immature. Export companies provided the many part-time cut-flower growers with the marketing infrastructure that they themselves were unable to put together.

As the harvesting season progressed, the returns paid to the venture by the exporter declined until they reached a point at which production levels of 10,000 stems or fewer became only marginally profitable. Gary Pratt and John Robertson met with the exporter to discuss the trends. The exporter explained that price was a function of volume and that the lower prices resulted from the increased volumes of cut flowers being placed on world markets. Export market returns were substantiated by documentation.

Pratt and Robertson were not convinced by the explanation. However, they knew little about world markets for fresh-cut flowers, and they could only speculate as to the reasons for the price movements. As there were no other established cut-flower export companies to turn to, the only way to research the matter seemed to be to do so themselves. Robertson's going to the United States for his MBA studies presented the opportunity to carry out some research there.

During his first semester of school, Robertson had little time to do research. At the end of the winter quarter, when he picked up a sample cart of Leucadendron flowers consigned by Pratt to him at Sea-Tac Airport, his ideas on how to approach the market were not yet defined. He took the flowers home and, on inspection, found that they had kept well in transit and their quality was good.

In the six days remaining before school began again, Robertson decided to concentrate on researching the production and shipping costs associated with the product, production forecasts, import procedures, the basic structure of the U.S. cut-flower industry, and market reaction to the Leucadendron.

When he had picked up the samples from the airport, Robertson had been told by airline officials that if he was going to undertake imports of invoice value greater than $250, he would have to engage the services of a customs broker. Presuming such brokers to be the experts on import procedures, he made an appointment with one. The broker was most helpful. Imported cut flowers had to be inspected by the U.S. Department of Agriculture (USDA) on arrival. Once given clearance, duty was assessed at the rate of 8 percent on f.o.b. value. The broker would arrange for these clearances through the USDA and the U.S. Customs Service. The broker would charge a fee for such services. Robertson learned that this fee is fixed for shipments regardless of size but varies among brokers; the broker with whom the meeting was held charged $50 per shipment. The broker also volunteered to arrange for freight forwarding companies to handle transportation to foreign markets.

As Robertson prepared his market strategy, he consulted numerous U.S. publications that helped him get a feel for the U.S. market. In addition, he asked Pratt to mail him a copy of a market-research publication funded by the New Zealand Export-Import Corporation that included research on the U.S. flower market. From that publication, he learned that the major agricultural exports from New Zealand in order of importance were kiwi fruit, apples, berryfruit, processed kiwi fruit, flowers and plants, squash, frozen vegetables, onions, and other products.

Robertson finally contacted a Seattle wholesaler who was willing to place a large order for flowers, provided he was given exclusive rights to distribute the flowers in Washington State. Robertson was pleased with the reaction from the wholesaler but was aware that he had made the approach with insufficient preparation. Had he underpriced the product? Was the wholesaler's credit sound? Were exclusive rights typically given in this industry, and should he have conceded them? Was the reaction one that is normal when a new product is shown to a market? Would repeat orders be placed? In addition to these market-related issues, there were administrative and organizational issues to consider. What should be his role in the marketing chain? Should he act as an agent taking a commission or buy from Pratt and resell the product? What form of organization should he establish?

Questions

1. What were the issues that Robertson had to consider in developing his strategy for exporting flowers from New Zealand to the United States?
2. What were the intermediaries that Robertson used, and what roles did they play?
3. What did Robertson have to worry about in terms of import procedures?
4. What role should Robertson play in the marketing chain, and why?

Chapter Notes

1. "Exporting Pays Off," *Business America,* May 17, 1993, p. 19; and interview with Mr. Patrick J. Calabrese, president of Grieve Corporation.

2. Andrea Bonaccorsi, "On the Relationship Between Firm Size and Export Intensity," *Journal of International Business Studies,* Vol. 23, No. 4, Fourth Quarter 1992, p. 606.

3. Ibid.

4. Jonathan L. Calof, "The Relationship Between Firm Size and Export Behavior Revisited," *Journal of International Business Studies,* Vol. 25, No. 2, Second Quarter 1994, pp. 367–387.

5. Therese Eiben, "U.S. Exporters Keep on Rolling," *Fortune,* June 14, 1993, p. 130.

6. James Aley, "New Lift for the U.S. Export Boom," *Fortune,* November 13, 1995, pp. 74 and 76.

7. Leslie Stroh, "The Fact Sheet: Fishing Where the Trout Are," *Clearinghouse on State International Politics,* Vol. 3, No. 5, July 1993, p. 3.

8. Hans-George Gemunden, "Success Factors of Export Marketing: A Meta-Analytic Critique of the Empirical Studies" in *New Perspectives on International Marketing,* S. J. Paliwoda, ed. (London: Routledge, 1991); S. Tamer Cavusgil, "Organizational Characteristics Associated with Export Activity," *Journal of Management Studies,* Vol. 21, No. 1, pp. 3–22; and Michael R. Czinkota and Wesley J. Johnston, "Exporting: Does Sales Volume Make a Difference?" *Journal of International Business Studies,* Vol. 14, Spring–Summer 1983, pp. 147–153.

9. Conversation with Marti Dougin of the Small Business Administration and Leslie Stroh at *The EXPORTER* magazine.

10. John H. Dunning, "The Eclectic Paradigm of International Production: Some Empirical Tests," *Journal of International Business Studies,* Vol. 19, Spring 1988, pp. 1–31.

11. Sanjeev Agarwal and Sridhar N. Ramaswami, "Choice of Foreign Market Entry Mode: Impact of Ownership, Location and Internalization Factors," *Journal of International Business Studies,* Vol. 23, No. 1, First Quarter 1992, pp. 2–5.

12. U.S. Department of Commerce, *A Basic Guide to Exporting,* January 1992, p. 1-1.

13. W. Chan Kim and Peter Hwang, "Global Strategy and Multinationals' Entry Mode Choice," *Journal of International Business Studies,* Vol. 23, No. 1, First Quarter 1992, pp. 32–35.

14. Leonidas C. Leonidous and Constantine S. Katsikeas, "The Export Development Process: An Integrative Review of Empirical Models," *Journal of International Business Studies,* Vol. 27, No. 3, Third Quarter 1996, pp. 524–525.

15. "Ten Most Common Mistakes of New-to-Export Ventures," *Business America,* April 16, 1984, p. 9.

16. TransNational, Inc., *A Basic Guide to Exporting* (Washington, D.C.: U.S. Department of Commerce, September 1986), p. 17.

17. U.S. Department of Commerce, op. cit., pp. 4–6.

18. Philip MacDonald, *Practical Exporting and Importing,* 2nd ed. (New York: Ronald Press, 1959), pp. 30–40; and TransNational, Inc., op. cit., p. 17.

19. "Basic Question: To Export Yourself or To Hire Someone To Do It for You?" *Business America,* April 27, 1987, pp. 14–17.

20. Frank G. Long, "Compare Before Choosing Export Management Firm," *Arizona Business Gazette,* January 18, 1996, p. 10.

21. Marubeni Corporation, *The Unique World of the Sogo Shosha* (Tokyo: Marubeni Corporation, 1978), p. 14.

22. "Arco, Itochu Units to Purchase Coastal's Utah Coal Operations," *PR Newswire,* October 24, 1996. Available in Lexis Nexis: News/Curnws.

23. Assif Shameen, "Playing Korea's Recovery: The Trading Companies May Be One Way to Do It," *Asiaweek,* September 20, 1996, p. 66. Available in Lexis Nexis: News/Curnws.

24. Robert Neff, "Guess Who's Selling Barbies in Japan Now?" *Business Week,* December 9, 1991, pp. 72–76.

25. Erick Schonfeld, "Greasing the Wheels of World Trade," *Fortune,* October 28, 1996, p. 228.

26. Helen Richardson, "Freight Forwarder Basics: Contract Negotiation," *Transportation & Distribution,* May 1996. Available in Lexis Nexis: News: Curnws.

27. E. J. Miller, "Trends Bode Well for Air," *Distribution,* July 1992, p. 36.

28. Richardson, op. cit.

29. Ibid.

30. Richardson, op. cit.

31. Philadelphia National Bank, *International Trade Procedures* (Philadelphia, 1977), p. 30.

32. U.S. Department of Commerce, *A Basic Guide to Exporting,* pp. 12-2 and 12-3.

33. See <http://www.tradeport.org/ts/t-expert/finance/sources>

34. <http://www.tradeport.org/ts/t-expert/finance/sources/private.html>

35. Ibid.

36. <http://www.israeltrade.com/VI/VI7.html>

37. *Export-Import Bank of the United States General Information* (Washington, D.C.: Ex-Im Bank, September 1996), p. 2. See also <http://www.exim.gov>

38. Ibid.

39. <http://www.sbaonline.sba.gov/business_finances/FinancingYourBusiness.html>

40. Pompiliu Verzariu, "Trends and Developments in International Countertrade," *Business America,* November 2, 1992, p. 2.

41. <http://www.i-trade.com/inforsrc/aca/ctover1.html>

42. Cyndee Miller, "Worldwide Money Crunch Fuels More International Barter," *Marketing News,* March 2, 1992, p. 5.

43. American Countertrade Association, "Forms of Countertrade," <http://www.i-trade.com/infosrc/aca/ctover6.html>

44. Charles Oliver, "When Barter Is the Only Way," *Corporate Finance,* April 1995, p. 23: Available: NEXIS Library: General News: News: Curnws.

45. Ibid.

46. Tom L. Beauchamp and Norman E. Bowie, *Ethical Theory and Business,* 4th ed. (Englewood Cliffs, N.J.: Prentice-Hall, 1993), pp. 514–515.

47. American Countertrade Association, "Forms of Countertrade," op. cit.

48. U.S. Department of the Treasury, *Importing into the United States* (Washington, D.C.: Superintendent of Documents, U.S. Government Printing Office, May 1984), p. 28.

49. Robert P. Schaffer, "Maximize Your Import Profits . . . Minimize Your Customs Duties," *Review* (New York: Price Waterhouse).

50. Ibid.; and U.S. Department of the Treasury, U.S. Customs Service, *Importing into The United States* (Washington, D.C.: U.S. Government Printing Office, September 1991), p. 41.

51. U.S. Department of the Treasury, op. cit., p. 7.

52. Stephen Baker, Kevin Kelly, Robert D. Hof, and William J. Holstein, "Mini-Nationals Are Making Maximum Impact," *Business Week,* September 6, 1993, pp. 66–69.

53. Adapted from Harry R. Knudson, "Sunset Flowers of New Zealand, Ltd.," *Journal of Management Case Studies,* Winter 1985, Volume 1, No. 4. Reprinted with permission.

Chapter 18

Global Operations Management and Sourcing Strategies

Right mixture
makes good mortar.
—English Proverb

Objectives

- To gain an overview of the different dimensions of a global operations management strategy

- To describe different manufacturing configurations

- To examine how quality can affect a company's operations management strategy

- To study outsourcing, purchasing, and supplier relations

- To show how important global design is to the manufacturing process

Case
Black & Decker
(B&D)[1]

Black & Decker (B&D), once known almost exclusively as a manufacturer of power tools for professionals, designs, manufactures, and markets products in two major divisions: consumer and home improvement products and commercial and industrial products. As noted in Fig. 18.1, the consumer and home improvement products segment is composed of six major divisions generating 86 percent of B&D's revenues: power tools, accessories, outdoor products, household products, security hardware, and plumbing products. The commercial and industrial products division specializes in fastening systems and glass container-making equipment. The power tools segment, which sells products under the three key brand names of Black & Decker, DeWALT, and Elu, drives the revenues and profitability of the company. Figure 18.2 illustrates how the domestic side of B&D's business still drives revenues and profitability, but also how the global side is becoming increasingly important.

In the 1970s, before broadening its base to include a larger segment of the household market, B&D was flying high. It had captured a large share of the world's power-tool market, and financial analysts were betting strongly on its future. By 1981, however, the picture began to change. Earnings had begun to slip, and a worldwide recession caused a significant downturn in the power-tools segment of B&D's business, which was its bread and butter. Other events in the world economy added to B&D's problems. For example, a strong U.S. dollar eroded the company's competitive position in export markets and made it vulnerable to foreign competition from companies such as Japan's Makita Electric Works Ltd. and Germany's Bosch. Makita adopted a global strategy for its products that allowed it to become the world's lowest-cost producer of power tools. It decided that consumers in different countries really did not need significantly different products. Then it combined its cost advantage with aggressive marketing and took advantage of the yen's relative weakness compared to the U.S. dollar and of B&D's problems to make serious inroads in the power-tools market. By the late 1970s and early 1980s, Makita was able to nearly equal B&D's 20 percent market share in professional tools worldwide.

Figure 18.1
Black & Decker's
Business Segments

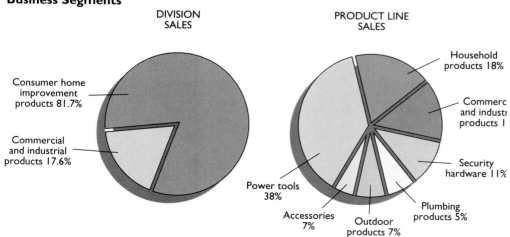

**Figure 18.2
Black & Decker's
Geographic Segments**

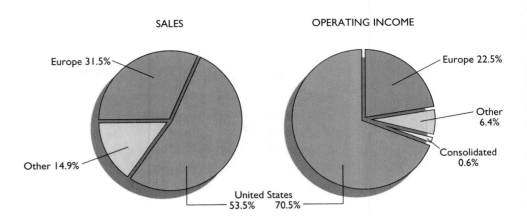

SALES

OPERATING INCOME

Europe 31.5%

Europe 22.5%

Other 6.4%

Consolidated 0.6%

Other 14.9%

United States
53.5%   70.5%

B&D's problems were partly a result of its own strategy. By 1982, it operated twenty-five manufacturing plants in thirteen countries on six continents. It had three operating groups in addition to its Maryland headquarters. Each group had its own staff; this led to duplication and overstaffing. In addition, individual B&D companies, such as B&D of West Germany, operated autonomously in each of the more than fifty countries in which the company sold and serviced products. The parent company's philosophy had been to let each country company adapt products and product lines to fit its market's unique characteristics: The Italian company produced power tools for Italians, the British company made power tools for Britons, and so on.

As a result, companies in different countries did not communicate well with each other. Successful products in one country often took years to introduce in others. For example, the highly successful Dustbuster, introduced in the United States in the late 1970s, did not make it to Australia until 1983. When efforts were made to introduce B&D home products into European markets, the European managers balked. Despite stagnating sales, B&D still held a large percentage of the European power-tool market in the early 1980s—over 50 percent on the Continent and 80 percent in the United Kingdom. In fact, the B&D name is so well known in the United Kingdom that people refer to home improvement projects as "Black & Deckering." The managers felt that home appliances and products were uniquely American and would not do well outside of the United States.

Meeting the tailor-made specifications of different markets resulted in inefficient utilization of design centers. At one point eight design centers around the world had produced 260 different models of motors, even though B&D needed fewer than 10 models. Plant capacity utilization was low, employment levels were high, and output per employee was unacceptable. Further, B&D had begun to stagnate in new product development.

B&D's consumer-tool and professional-tool product lines operated in two different product groups. However, the groups did not work together to develop new product lines. It appeared the company had decided to concentrate on its top lines and sell them aggressively. Thus Makita was able to spot a market niche that it could exploit—mid-priced tools.

As B&D moved into the mid-1980s, management realized it had to do something. One of the first things new CEO Nolan Archibald did was establish a global strategy. He then surrounded himself with the personnel necessary to effect it. His strategy included selling the same basic products worldwide with relatively minor modifications. Consequently, B&D had to improve its designs and reduce the number of parts per product.

Archibald's strategy also called for a cut-and-build program. Under this program, 3000 of the company's 23,000 employees were let go between 1985 and 1987, resulting in the closing of five plants worldwide and the downsizing of several others. This move enabled B&D to concentrate production in fewer plants, thus increasing economies of scale. At the same time, the sales force was almost doubled and the new-product and engineering departments were increased.

Acquisitions also became an important part of B&D's new global strategy. One area in which the Japanese had not made significant inroads was the housewares and small-appliances market. Japanese consumers were not fond of those items, so Makita and other competitors had not established a strong home market to use as an export base. B&D was having trouble introducing its own line of housewares because of its image as a power-tool manufacturer. As a result, B&D acquired the small-appliances division of GE in 1984 to give it more shelf space in housewares and also a large enough line of products to provide economies of scale in manufacturing.

In April 1989, B&D acquired Emhart Corporation, the worldwide manufacturer of such leading brands as Kwikset door locks and hardware, Price Pfister faucets, True Temper lawn and garden products, Molly bolts, POP rivets, and other consumer and commercial products. However, the added debt created problems, and B&D's management had to look for ways to cut costs and service the debt.

Operations Management Strategies

B&D operates 47 manufacturing facilities worldwide. As noted in Map 18.1, B&D has manufacturing facilities in the United States, Europe, Latin America, and Asia. Those facilities supply products for the domestic markets where they are located as well as for markets worldwide. This is a marked departure from the old B&D, which had manufacturing facilities that basically serviced their respective domestic markets.

Manufacturing is an important element in B&D's overall strategy. One of the key strategies of the power tools division is to reduce costs by modernizing and streamlining manufacturing. As noted earlier, significant improvements were made in manufacturing during Archibald's earlier years, and they have continued. In 1995, for example, two foreign plants were closed down and production shifted to other countries. One facility in Brazil was shut down and another opened up in 1996 as part of B&D's strategy to improve manufacturing performance. In the household products division, a major strategy for the future is to improve profitability by streamlining manufacturing and reducing overhead expense. In addition, B&D is continuing to implement *kaizen* (continuous improvement process) to improve manufacturing flexibility, product quality, and costs.

Sometimes external factors can influence the location of production and assembly operations, as noted in Chapter 13. For example, Makita, one of B&D's key competitors, has shifted a substantial amount of production overseas to cope with the rising value of the

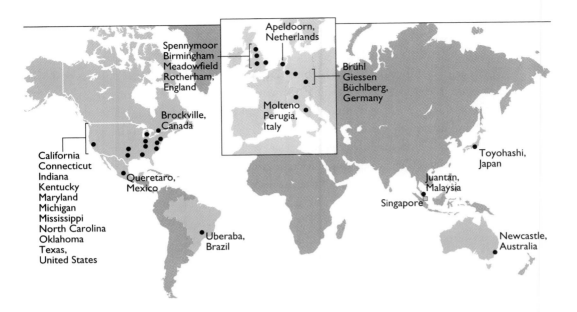

**Map 18.1
Location of Black &
Decker's
Manufacturing
Facilities**

yen and increasing production costs in Japan. This is especially true for its mass-produced, general-purpose power tools. Much of this expansion is taking place in Asia, where Makita is close to a rapidly expanding market. B&D is expanding in Asia as well, through its own subsidiaries as well as through joint ventures in China and India.

A second important part of B&D's operations management strategy is the improvement of product design. B&D introduces new products at a rapid rate; its product managers have worldwide responsibility for B&D products, allowing them to push products into new markets more quickly. B&D's product development process involves cross-functional teams composed of engineering, manufacturing, marketing, finance, and other skills, including key suppliers. Not only does B&D want to increase the number of new products, but it also wants to accelerate the development process. Product development activities for the consumer and home improvement products segment take place in three U.S. locations as well as in Slough, England; Spennymoor, England; Brockville, Canada; Civate, Italy; Idstein, Germany; and Croydon, Australia. A new design and engineering center was also opened in Singapore in 1995. The commercial and industrial products division develops new products at its domestic locations as well as at its three foreign locations: Birmingham, England; Giessen, Germany; and Toyohashi, Japan.

Quality is a key issue for B&D as well. One of the reasons why B&D lost market share to Makita in the 1980s was because its reputation for quality was slipping. A survey conducted among vendors and distributors about top power tools suppliers indicated that quality and depth of line are the primary characteristics of top line suppliers. Thus B&D has had to focus much more on quality. For example, two of its divisions received ISO certification for quality in 1995. The household products division received ISO 9002 certification of quality systems in manufacturing at all company-owned facilities, and the security hardware division achieved ISO 9001 certification of quality systems in design and manufacturing at several European facilities.

Introduction

There are a number of keys to Black & Decker's current and future success that are discussed in this chapter, including manufacturing strategy and configuration; a focus on quality; outsourcing, purchasing, and supplier relations; materials management and inventory systems; and product design, which also includes a discussion on global research and development.

The Black & Decker example focuses on the more traditional manufacturing sector, but the services sector of the economy is increasingly important. The use of operations management instead of production or manufacturing management in the title of this chapter is designed to broaden the discussion to include the services sector. Operations management, more broadly defined, "refers to the direction and control of the processes that transform inputs into finished goods and services."[2] Figure 18.3 illustrates the differences between the manufacturing and services sectors. Although Fig. 18.3 intimates that the services sector primarily services local markets, there are elements of the sector that are very international, such as banking and other financial services, public accounting, law, tourism, and transportation. Thus the concepts we discuss in this chapter are just as relevant for the services sector as for manufacturing.

Global Manufacturing Strategies in the Internationalization Process

MNEs are involved in fairly sophisticated forms of production sharing in which they may produce and/or assemble components in one or several countries for worldwide markets. In the simplest form of production sharing, production occurs in the home country and goods are exported to final markets. Alternatively, an MNE could produce in different countries in order to serve those particular markets or third-country markets. However, during the past decade intermediate goods, such as components, are increasingly being produced in many countries and shipped to

**Figure 18.3
Continuum of
Characteristics of
Manufacturing and
Service Organizations**

Source: Adapted from Lee J. Krajewski and Larry P. Ritzman, *Operations Management,* 4/e, 1996, Addison-Wesley Longman. Reprinted with permission.

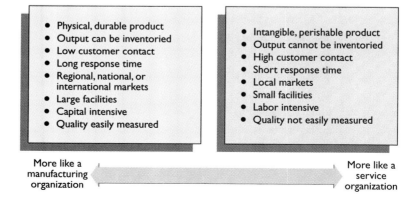

other countries for assembly and sale. The production and exporting functions are much more complex than they used to be under the simpler forms.

For each particular market an MNE serves, the strategy of global sourcing implies that it needs to determine where parts and components will be manufactured and where the final products will be assembled. This was one of the first problems that Archibald had to solve when he took over the leadership of B&D.

Global sourcing implies that companies need to determine where parts and components will be manufactured and where final products will be assembled.

Historically, companies tend to operate initially on a country-by-country basis. However, as they become more globally oriented, they find they can develop a definite competitive advantage by coordinating and integrating their operations across national borders.[3]

Similar problems occur in the services sector. Novell, the U.S.-based developer of network software, has to develop and manufacture its software. In the early years, Novell developed its software at its Provo, Utah, facilities. However, it is now developing some software in India. The operations in India are not just entering code sent by satellite from Utah, they are also initiating projects and carrying them through to completion.

As an MNE establishes its manufacturing strategy, it must do so in the context of its competitive strategy. Competitive strategies are based on the following priorities:

Five elements of the competitive strategy that affect the manufacturing strategy:
- **Efficiency/cost**
- **Dependability**
- **Quality**
- **Flexibility**
- **Innovation**

- Efficiency/cost—reduction of manufacturing costs
- Dependability—degree of trust in a company's products and its delivery and price promises
- Quality—performance reliability, service quality, speed of delivery, and maintenance quality of the product(s)
- Flexibility—ability of the production process to make different kinds of products and/or to adjust the volume of output
- Innovation—ability to develop new products and ideas[4]

For example, cost-minimization strategies and the drive for global efficiencies tend to force MNEs to establish economies of scale in manufacturing, often by producing in areas with low-cost labor. On the other hand, the need for responsiveness or flexibility because of differences in national markets results in regional manufacturing to service local markets. As a company's competitive strategies change, so do its manufacturing strategies. In addition, MNEs may adopt different strategies for different product lines, depending on the competitive priorities of those products. This was one of the dilemmas B&D faced in the mid-1980s because it had always operated on the basis of local flexibility and yet it was losing market share because of high costs. This loss argued for a move to economies of scale in manufacturing.

The manufacturing strategy needs to take into account different activities. Of these, the most important are as follows:

Manufacturing activities are
- **Location and scale**
- **Choice of process**
- **Control of the system**
- **Degree of vertical integration relative to outsourcing**
- **Coordination of R&D**
- **Licensing of technology**

- Location and scale of the manufacturing facilities
- Choice of manufacturing process

- Control of the production system, including the assignment of activities to plants in a multiplant network
- Degree of vertical integration relative to outsourcing of each manufacturing facility
- Coordination of R&D units
- Licensing of technology[5]

International Manufacturing Configurations

MNEs differ from smaller companies involved in international business in their sheer scale and geographic reach. There are three basic philosophies MNEs consider as they establish a global manufacturing strategy—that is, the pattern of decisions in manufacturing activities. Some MNEs have followed a multidomestic approach in which they manufacture products close to their customers, using country-specific manufacturing facilities to meet local needs—the old B&D approach. A variation on this approach is to use regional manufacturing facilities to serve customers within a specific region. Others have centralized manufacturing and offer a selection of standard, lower-priced products to different markets.[6] In reality, MNEs choose a combination of these approaches depending on their product strategies.

Although MNEs must integrate their worldwide operations if they are to be globally competitive, there are a variety of international manufacturing configurations (IMC) that relate to different manufacturing strategies. These are the major types of IMCs:

- Home-country production with limited or extensive exporting
- Autonomous regional plants designed to serve the needs of specific foreign markets
- Combination of regional and global focus (configurations involving local or regional assembly of globally produced parts and components)
- Coordinated global focus (configurations involving international dispersal of stages of the production process to low-cost regions, with final assembly taking place at different locations)
- Centers of excellence where production takes place in different locations not because of a proximity to country or regional markets but in order to take advantage of specialization of production for certain products. An example would be Hoechst, the German chemical company, which has selected sites in the United States for R&D and production in biotechnology, both because of the U.S. market and in order to take advantage of other location-specific advantages of the United States, such as a favorable climate for biotechnology research.

These different configurations are not mutually exclusive but are often used simultaneously, depending on competitive demands.

In each of these configurations, the MNE is trying to balance conflicting objectives that relate to its product strategy. One product strategy is technology-driven. In this case, the plant-location strategy would be to position the plant in a high-income country that has a large market. This is basically a country-specific strategy. Although the parent company would influence manufacturing decisions, most would be made at the local level, unless there were significant intracompany transfers of components.[7]

If the product strategy is marketing-intensive, the key is to operate a marketing program that includes good product quality and prompt delivery. In this case, several manufacturing facilities are located close to local markets and controlled by local management. The company would adopt a country-specific or regional manufacturing strategy.

If the product strategy is low-cost, the manufacturing strategy is to use large-scale manufacturing to reduce unit costs or to rely on manufacturing in cheap-labor countries if labor is a significant component of total cost. There is significantly more central control in this situation than with a marketing-intensive strategy.[8] However, the low-cost strategy is a little misleading, because cost minimization is central to any manufacturing strategy. As noted in the B&D case, a major strategy of the power tools division is to reduce costs by modernizing and streamlining manufacturing. The Makita example in the case also pointed out that Makita's high-end manufacturing is continuing to be done in Japan, whereas the mass-produced, low-end products are being manufactured elsewhere in Asia where costs are lower.

Manufacturing systems:
- **Single plant**
- **Multiple plants**
- **Manufacturing interchange**
- **Rationalization**

A company may choose one of many manufacturing systems. For example, it could try to serve all markets from one plant. However, transportation charges and tariffs could make this system infeasible. In addition, the scale of production may be so large in this case that the marginal cost of production would be higher than if smaller plant sizes were used to achieve economies of scale. A company also may specialize production by product or process so that a particular plant produces a product or range of products or produces all products using a particular process and serves all markets (rationalization). Or it may have several plants specializing in the same product or process so that it has a larger geographical spread. The process of manufacturing interchange involves plants producing a range of components and interchanging them so that all plants assemble the finished product for the local market. Obviously, there is no one best way to set up the production process. For a particular product or line of products, a company may use a single-plant strategy and depend on exports to serve world markets. This would be essentially a worldwide product and production strategy. For other products or groups of products, a multiplant strategy such as rationalization or manufacturing interchange may be best.

Offshore manufacturing often is done in low-cost locations and followed by importation into the home market.

Offshore manufacturing—manufacturing outside of the borders of a particular country—is a form of production sharing that has provided a useful means to avoid losing market share to low-cost foreign competitors. Worldwide, it escalated sharply in the 1960s and 1970s in the electronics industry as one company after another set up production facilities in the Far East, principally in Taiwan and Singapore. Those locations were chosen because of low labor costs, availability of cheap materials and components, and proximity to markets. Even the athletic shoe market left the United States for Korea. As wages rose in Korea, however, manufacturing began to shift to other low-cost countries, such as Indonesia, Malaysia, and Thailand.

Market conditions also can affect offshore production sharing strategies. As B&D's operations in Europe continued to falter in the early 1990s due to the European recession, B&D found it had to close down some plants and cut back production in others. This move favored using U.S. production facilities to serve world markets for many products.

Recall from Chapter 7 that Mexico has become one of the most important centers for offshore production for U.S. companies through maquiladora operations. Under the Mexican maquiladora concept, U.S.-sourced components are shipped to Mexican border facilities duty-free and assembled by Mexican workers; the goods then are re-exported to the United States or other foreign markets under favorable tariff provisions. U.S. duties are levied on the imports only to the extent of the value added in Mexico. The benefits of establishing a maquiladora operation are especially strong for companies for which 30 percent or more of the product cost is labor. This condition applies to fewer and fewer companies because the average labor percentage for most products manufactured in the United States is less than 20 percent.

Maquiladora operations benefited greatly from the peso devaluations of 1994 and 1995. Although the overvaluation of the peso prior to the devaluation hurt the competitiveness of Mexican exports, the December 1994 devaluation had the effect of reducing the average hourly wage for maquiladora workers from $2.61 in 1994 to $1.80 in 1995. As a result, maquiladora exports increased in 1995 over the rate of the prior year, and new investments are expected to escalate.[9] Maquiladora operations directly employ about 650,000 workers in Mexico, so the employment impact is important to Mexico.[10] In addition, the NAFTA agreement will gradually allow maquiladoras to supply the domestic Mexican market, whereas they were initially allowed to export only. Although offshore manufacturing occurs worldwide, the Mexican example illustrates how factors such as government policies and exchange rates can affect location decisions.

> A maquiladora is an operation in Mexico to which components are shipped from the United States duty-free for assembly and the goods re-exported to the United States.

Plant Location

Selecting the number of plants and their locations depends on complex factors, such as transportation costs, duties on components versus those on finished goods, need for closeness to the market, foreign-exchange risk, economies of scale in the production process, technological requirements, and national image. In addition, a company's decision as to the specific location within a country for manufacturing is a function of external factors (such as market size and local government incentives) and internal strategic factors (such as the relative importance of product lines, location of markets, importance of cost, the improvement over time of knowledge of the country, and the perceptions of changes in risks).[11]

An example of location issues, which is actually covered in more depth in Chapter 13, is the selection of Thailand by General Motors as the site of its first major plant in Southeast Asia. GM picked Thailand over the Philippines because "there are more auto suppliers, the labor climate is better, the economic growth is faster and the utilities are more dependable than the Philippines." They also picked Thailand because of "its proximity to other growing Asian markets, such as Vietnam."[12] This reemphasizes the importance of establishing regional plants to service specific foreign markets. Because of transportation costs, localization demands, tariffs, and manufacturing costs, it does not make sense for GM to service the entire world through one huge manufacturing facility in the United States.

Layout Planning

The manufacturing configuration is partly a function of how the manufacturing process will take place. One would assume that there is an optimal way to manufacture a product that everyone will use, or at least that each manufacturing unit in the same company would manufacture products the same way. But the manufacturing process is not so simple. Take automobiles, for example. If you were to tour a Toyota facility in Japan and one in Thailand, you would notice striking differences in how the auto is assembled. In Japan, the auto assembly plant is highly automated, whereas in Thailand, it is very labor-intensive. The same is true of Volkswagen in Germany versus Volkswagen in Brazil.

Another example involves a Chinese brewery that is a joint venture between San Miguel, the Philippines-based brewery, and Bada, a local brewery from Hebei Province in China. The equipment they are using for the brewing of beer in China is used equipment purchased from Romford Brewery, a British brewery. Many factories in industrial countries are upgrading facilities to become globally competitive and are selling their equipment to manufacturers in developing countries that can offset old equipment with cheaper labor and operating costs. This has even given rise to companies that specialize in selling new and secondhand machinery to developing countries.[13]

Other issues that can affect the design of a plant include the cost of land. A plant that focuses on repetitive or continuous production will be designed differently from one that focuses on low-volume, high-variety production. However, plants using a product layout that facilitates repetitive or continuous production can be designed differently in different parts of the world. Swire Coca-Cola, a Hong Kong-based company, has bottling facilities in many locations in the world, including Salt Lake City, Utah, and Hong Kong. The Salt Lake facility is similar to many high-volume plants, with all operations taking place on one level and the product moving continuously from start to finish. In Hong Kong, however, the assembly plant is a high-rise building where the process moves from one floor to the next. The key in any layout strategy is to make economic decisions about the physical arrangement of economic activity centers within a facility.[14] The layout strategy, though basically replicable in different facilities worldwide, may have to be adjusted for factors such as production technology and location.

Quality

As noted in the B&D case, quality is a key issue in global manufacturing. It is also important in the services industry. No one wants to buy computer software that has so many bugs in it that it is too frustrating to use. However, the need to get product to market means that many software manufacturers will get a product to market even before the errors are corrected and then rely on users to help find the errors so that the developer can correct them. In the airline industry, service is a key. Some airlines, such as Singapore Air, have developed a worldwide reputation for excellence in service. That is a distinct competitive advantage in attracting the business traveler especially.

Quality has many dimensions. In the automobile industry, it involves issues such as fit and finish. In Brazil, Volkswagen inspectors expect locally manufactured autos to live up to the standards of German consumers. However, they have found that Brazilian consumers have become as discriminating as German consumers, so they need to pay attention to indicators that are significant to Brazilians. Quality can mean zero defects, an idea perfected by Japanese manufacturers who refuse to tolerate defects of any kind. Before the strong emphasis on zero defects, U.S. companies operated according to the premise of **acceptable quality level.** This premise implied there was an acceptable level of bad quality. It held that unacceptable products would be dealt with through repair facilities and service warranties. This type of environment required buffer inventories, rework stations, and expediting. The goal was to push through products as fast as possible and then deal with the mistakes later.[15]

> **TQM is designed to eliminate all defects and to ensure customer satisfaction.**

The Japanese approach to quality is **total quality management (TQM).** TQM is the process that a company follows in order to achieve quality. It stresses three principles: customer satisfaction, employee involvement, and continuous improvements in quality.[16] The center of the entire process, however, is customer satisfaction. TQM does not mean "cheap," since some things a company must do to achieve high quality may be expensive. The goal of TQM is to eliminate all defects.

The difference between the two approaches centers on the attitude toward quality. In a Western setting, quality is a characteristic of a product that meets or exceeds engineering standards. In Japan, quality means that a product is "so good that the customer wouldn't think of buying from anyone else."[17]

TQM is a process of continuous improvement at every level of the organization. It implies that the company is doing everything it can to achieve quality at all stages of the process, from customer demands, to product design, to engineering. If management accounting systems are focused strictly on cost, they will preclude measures that could lead to higher quality. The key is to understand the company's overall strategy. TQM does not utilize any specific production philosophy or require the use of other techniques such as a just-in-time system for inventory delivery. TQM implies a proactive strategy. Although benchmarking, determining the best processes used by the best companies, is an important part of TQM, using the best practices of other companies is not intended to be a goal. TQM implies that a company will try to be better than the best.

Executives who have adopted the zero-defects philosophy claim that long-run production costs decrease as defects decrease. There are three dimensions to TQM (see Fig. 18.4):

1. Determine the percentage of production that makes it all the way through the production process without rework. Many companies do not even keep track of this statistic, but it is a crucial one for the Japanese, who are trying to eliminate all defects.
2. Determine the impact of an increase in quality and a decrease in defects on manufacturing costs.
3. Consider in capital-equipment purchase decisions how new equipment would save manufacturing costs and result in improved quality and fewer defects.[18]

The continuous improvements process is also known as *kaizen,* and it involves identifying problems and enlisting employees at all levels of the organization to help eliminate the problems. The key is to make continuous improvement a part of the daily work of every employee.

ISO 9000

Numerous awards are presented each year to recognize quality, such as the Deming Award and the Malcolm Baldrige National Quality Award. However, even more important than awards is certification. As part of the effort to establish the Single

ISO 9000 is a European set of quality standards intended to promote quality at every level of an organization.

THREE DIMENSIONS TO TQM

**Figure 18.4
Dimensions of Total Quality Management**
The goal of TQM is to eliminate all defects through a process of continuous improvement at every level of the organization. This approach is favored by many Japanese companies.

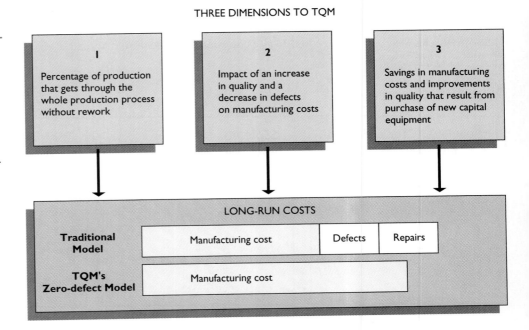

European Market, the EU, through the International Standards Organization in Geneva, established the ISO 9000 guideposts, which became effective in 1987. ISO 9000 is intended to promote the idea of quality at every level of an organization. Initially, it was designed to harmonize technical norms within the EU. Now, it is an important part of business operations throughout Europe and has been adopted in over seventy countries worldwide, including the United States.

Basically, under ISO 9000, companies must document how workers perform every function that affects quality and install mechanisms to ensure that they follow through on the documented routine. ISO 9000 certification involves a complex analysis of management systems and procedures, not just a quality-control standard. Rather than judging the quality of a particular product, ISO 9000 evaluates the management of the manufacturing process. Procedures must be followed in twenty domains, from purchasing to design to training. A company that wants to be ISO-certified must fill out a report and then be certified by a team of independent auditors.[19] The process can be expensive and time-consuming—certifying a company with a hundred employees costs about $20,000 and takes anywhere from six to eighteen months. Each site of a company must be separately certified. The certification of one site cannot cover the entire company. In the B&D case, for example, it was noted that the security hardware division had received ISO 9001 certification of quality systems in design and manufacturing at several European locations, not all locations. However, the household products division noted that it had achieved ISO 9002 certification of quality systems in manufacturing at all company-owned facilities. Although ISO certification is becoming an important consideration for companies expecting to do business in the EU, it is not the solution to all quality issues, as noted in Fig. 18.5.

ISO 9001 is the most comprehensive and detailed standard in the series of ISO standards. It is used when the site has to assure conformance to specific requirements for design, development, production, installation, and servicing. ISO 9002 is directed to sites not dealing with design and after-market service and therefore is

**Figure 18.5
ISO 9000 Certification:
An Important Edge?**

DILBERT is reprinted with permission of United Feature Syndicate, Inc.

Dilbert® by Scott Adams

intended to assure conformance to specific requirements for production and installation. ISO 9003 focuses on final inspection of products (or services) and testing.

The guidelines provide interpretation of the standards for particular industries: The ISO 9004 Quality Management System describes the philosophy behind the standards by providing guidelines for developing and implementing a quality system. It describes the primary elements of a quality system: product and service requirements, organization and control, customer satisfaction, customer/product responsibility, and system guidance. ISO 9004-2 focuses on the service industry. ISO 9004-3 describes what a software company must account for in connection with development, supply, and maintenance in order to comply with a standard (usually 9001).

U.S. companies that operate in Europe are becoming ISO-certified in order to maintain access to the European market. For example, when Du Pont lost a major European contract to an ISO-certified European company, it decided to become certified. By doing so, not only was Du Pont able to position itself better in the European market; it also benefited from the experience of going through ISO certification and focusing on quality in the organization.[20] Although Du Pont lost a European contract because it was not ISO-certified, some European companies will not do business with a certified company if its suppliers are not also ISO-certified. Thus some U.S. companies are working hard to get their suppliers ISO-certified.

> **Non-European companies operating in Europe need to become ISO-certified in order to maintain access to that market.**

Global Sourcing, Purchasing, and Supplier Relations

> **Global sourcing and production strategies need to include consideration of location and stage in the production process.**

From an international standpoint, the global sourcing and production strategies can be better understood by looking at Fig. 18.6. This figure illustrates the basic options available by country (the home country or any foreign country) and by stage in the production process (sourcing of raw materials and/or components and the manufacture and assembly of components and final products).

For example, Ford assembles cars in Hermosillo, Mexico, and ships them into the United States. The cars are designed by the Japanese company Toyo Kogyo Co. (Mazda) and use some Japanese parts. Ford can purchase components manufactured in Japan and ship them to the United States for final assembly and sale in the U.S. market, or it can have Japanese- and U.S.-made components shipped to Mexico for final assembly and sale in the United States and Mexico. For Mexican assembly, some of the components come from the United States, some from Japan, and a small percentage from Mexico. If the components are manufactured in Japan, many of the raw materials are probably imported. When Ford decided to manufacture the Escort in Europe, it utilized the global sourcing of components from plants in fifteen different countries for final assembly in the United Kingdom and Germany. Figure 18.7 illustrates how that was accomplished.

Figure 18.6
Global Sourcing and Production Strategy
Companies have many possibilities for sourcing raw materials and assembling them into final goods to serve worldwide markets. For example, a U.S. company could source components in the United States, assemble them in Mexico, and export the final product back to the United States or to other countries.

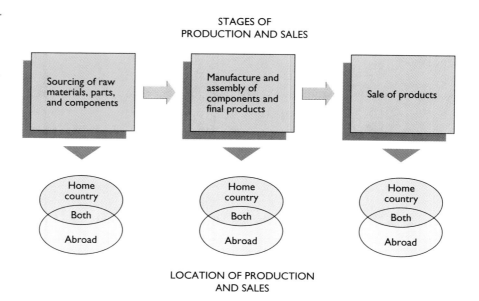

STAGES OF
PRODUCTION AND SALES

LOCATION OF PRODUCTION
AND SALES

An expansion of Fig. 18.6 would show sixty-four different combinations for manufacturing components and assembling them into final products for different markets. This expanded model would account for the facts that components can be manufactured internally in the company or purchased from external (unrelated) manufacturers and that final assembly also can be done internally or by external companies. Manufacture of components and final assembly may take place in the company's home country, the country in which it is trying to sell the product, a developed third country, or a developing third country.[21]

Before components can be manufactured, raw materials must be procured. The least complicated way of sourcing inputs is to obtain them from domestic sources. Using domestic sources enables companies to avoid numerous problems, including those connected with language differences, long distances and/or lengthy supply lines, exchange-rate fluctuations, inventory levels, wars and insurrections, strikes, politics, tariffs, and complex transportation channels. However, for many companies domestic sources may be unavailable or more expensive than foreign sources. For example, in Japan, foreign procurement is critical, since nearly all of that country's uranium, bauxite, nickel, crude oil, iron ore, copper, and coking coal and approximately 30 percent of its agricultural products are imported. Japanese trading companies came into being expressly to acquire the raw materials necessary to fuel Japan's manufacturing.

Why are MNEs increasingly sourcing components on a global basis? One could argue that standard location theory explains the most important factors in determining where to source: barriers to trade, factor costs, transportation costs, exchange-rate stability, etc.[22] Companies that pursue global sourcing strategies do so if they expect to achieve dramatic and immediate improvement in four critical areas:

Using domestic sources for raw materials and components allows a company to avoid problems with language differences, distance, currency, political problems, and tariffs, among others.

The major reasons for global sourcing are to lower costs and to improve quality.

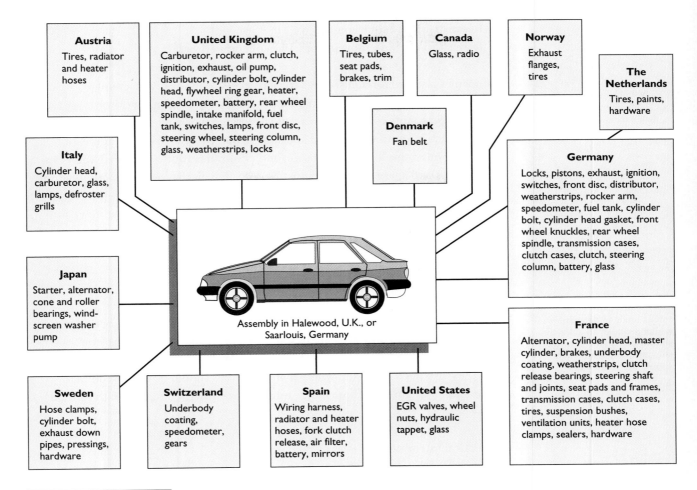

Figure 18.7
The Global Component Network for Ford's European Manufacturing of the Escort
Ford assembles Escorts in only two facilities in Europe, but parts and components used in the automobiles come from all over the world.

Source: World Development Report 1987 (New York: Oxford University Press, 1987), p. 39.

1. Cost reduction
2. Quality improvement
3. Increased exposure to worldwide technology
4. Delivery and reliability improvements[23]

The major cost reduction factors are less expensive labor, less restrictive work rules, and lower land and facility costs.[24] However, there are other reasons to source abroad:

- To strengthen the reliability of supply by supplementing domestic with foreign suppliers
- To gain access to materials only available abroad, possibly because of technical specifications or product capabilities
- To gain access to high product quality[25]
- To combat the introduction of competition to the domestic supply base
- To establish a presence in a foreign market

- To satisfy offset requirements
- To react to offshore sourcing practices of competitors[26]

Companies also use foreign sources to gain access to innovative technology being developed overseas. By locking up a supplier, they can keep competitors away. Also, using foreign suppliers gives them access to foreign markets.

However, in some ways global sourcing is more expensive than domestic sourcing. For example, transportation and communication are more expensive and brokers and agent fees often must be paid. Given the longer length of supply lines, it often takes more time to get components from abroad, and lead times are less certain. This increases the inventory-carrying costs and makes it more difficult to use JIT. If imported components come in with errors and need to be reworked, the cost per unit will rise, and some components may have to be shipped back to the supplier.

Make or Buy Decision

MNEs struggle with deciding which production activities should be carried on inside the company and which are best to outsource, that is, to source from other firms not part of the company's operations (the make or buy decision). In the latter case, they also need to decide whether the activities should be carried on in the home market or abroad. Three major models have emerged to deal with sourcing issues:

1. Vertical integration
2. Arms-length purchases from outside suppliers
3. Japanese *keiretsu* relationships with suppliers[27]

Manufacturers need to select one or a combination of these approaches, and global parts manufacturers need to develop a strategy for supplying MNE customers based on a strictly arm's-length arrangement or on a more closely tied *keiretsu*-style relationship. In deciding whether to outsource, MNEs should focus on those components that are critical to the product and that they are distinctively good at making. They should outsource components when suppliers have a distinct comparative advantage, such as greater scale, fundamentally lower-cost structure, or stronger performance incentives. They also should use outsourcing as a means of generating employee commitment to improving manufacturing performance.[28]

Strategic subsystems are those that

- Have a high impact on what customers perceive as the most important product attributes, including cost
- Require highly specialized design and manufacturing skills and specialized physical assets, for which there are very few, if any, capable independent suppliers

- Involve technology that is relatively fluid and in which there is a significant likelihood of gaining a clear technological lead[29]

For these subsystems, an MNE needs to determine the design and manufacturing capabilities of potential suppliers relative to its own. If the supplier has a clear advantage, management needs to decide what it would cost to catch up to the best suppliers and whether it would make sense to do so.

Japanese manufacturers tend to outsource more than U.S. manufacturers do.

There are clearly some differences in the degree to which Japanese and American companies outsource. In Japan, companies with fewer than fifty employees account for 23 percent of the value of manufacturing industry shipments, compared with only 12 percent in the United States. This difference is largely due to a higher degree of outsourcing to smaller parts suppliers—69 percent of total output is outsourced by Japanese manufacturers versus 58 percent for U.S. manufacturers.[30]

The difference is even more pronounced in the automobile industry. Toyota directly produces only 20 percent of the value of its cars, compared with 70 percent for GM and 50 percent for Ford. Chrysler has become more like Toyota: It produces only 30 percent of the value of the cars it sells.[31]

Many of the suppliers, especially in the auto industry, are among the largest companies in the world. The top fifty auto suppliers generate $224 billion in combined sales annually. Some of the suppliers, such as GM's Delphi Automotive Systems, supply other auto manufacturers as well. And these suppliers are becoming increasingly international themselves, with number one Delphi moving aggressively into Asia and Latin America, number two Bosch of Germany moving into North America and wanting to move into Asia, and number three Japanese Nippondenso (the key supplier to Toyota), selling to all markets and with huge operations in the United States. A major goal of Ford Automotive Components is to generate 50 percent of its sales from overseas business.[32] The big suppliers initially expand abroad to service their major client, but then they start picking up independent business in the new market. As noted above, these suppliers are from all over the world. Although the United States dominates as the home country to nineteen of the top fifty suppliers, the top ten are from the United States (5), Japan (3), and Germany and the Netherlands (one each).

Supplier Relations

In 1990 when Honda was designing the 1994 Accord, it sent engineers to thirty-three key subcontractors in Japan and twenty-eight in the United States, which together make parts that represent 60–70 percent of the car's value. The purpose of the visits was to reduce manufacturing costs by obtaining suggestions on parts designs. As a result of supplier inputs and other efforts at cost control, Honda was able to reduce the cost of components and not increase the price of the new model.[33] This example illustrates the Japanese approach to value-adding partnership: A group of independent companies work together to manage the flow of goods and services along the entire value-added chain.[34]

MNEs can vertically integrate, source through independent suppliers, or develop close linkages with suppliers.

If an MNE decides it must outsource rather than integrate vertically, it must determine how to work with suppliers. For example, Toyota pioneered the Toyota Production System to work with unrelated suppliers. Toyota sends a team of manufacturing experts to each of its key suppliers to observe how the supplier organizes its factory and makes its parts. Then the team advises on how to cut costs and boost quality. In 1987, Toyota approached Bumper Works, a small 100-person factory in Illinois, and asked its management to design and manufacture a bumper that would meet Toyota's rigid specifications. After demonstrating that it could satisfy Toyota, Bumper Works became the sole supplier for that company's U.S. facilities. However, Toyota expected annual price reductions, higher-quality bumpers, and on-time deliveries. Toyota helped Bumper Works determine how to change the dies used in its metal-stamping process so that it could provide the flexibility that Toyota required for different types of bumpers.

It is common for Toyota to identify two suppliers for each part and have the suppliers compete aggressively with each other. The supplier that performs the best gets the most business. However, both suppliers know that they will have an ongoing relationship with Toyota and will not be dumped easily.[35]

Japanese companies tend to have closer relationships with their suppliers than U.S. companies do.

This is a good example of the close relationships that Japanese companies develop with their suppliers. It is very different from the arm's-length relationship that U.S. companies tend to have with their suppliers. Further, Toyota has been able to reduce the number of supplier relationships it develops. For example, for its British operations, Toyota relies on about 150 parts suppliers, compared with the 500–1000 suppliers typical for other European automakers.[36]

A contrasting approach is that used by GM. The auto parts industry in the United States employs about 600,000 people and generates sales of more than $100 billion annually. GM alone accounts for about $30 billion in purchases from U.S. auto parts companies each year. In 1991, however, GM lost $7.5 billion and as a result embarked on a strategy of improving quality and cutting costs—to be implemented largely through supplier relations. The company also announced that its in-house parts operations would be subject to the same competitive pressures as outside suppliers. GM's president, John F. Smith, Jr., the former head of the company's European operations, brought Ignacio Lopez from Europe to work on supplier relations. Even though GM had already made an arrangement with its suppliers to reduce costs by 3 percent, 2 percent, and 2 percent over three years, Lopez made it clear that contracts would be renegotiated. In one case, he sought new bids on a multimillion-dollar contract twice in three weeks. And he informed suppliers that they would have to rebid contracts that they had already been awarded for the 1993 model year. (Lopez eventually defected to Volkswagen.)

In order to help suppliers, GM has offered to send its own engineering consultants to seek ways to boost productivity. These manufacturing teams, called Purchased Input Concept Optimization with Suppliers (PICOS), are intended to help suppliers identify waste, install lean production techniques, and cut costs in any way

possible. Although this use of teams is similar to Toyota's, suppliers have less confidence in GM's production skills. They also are concerned about the lack of stability
of the company's supplier relations. Further, smaller suppliers are afraid that they
will lose GM's business entirely. Others fear that if GM focuses mainly on price,
that policy will destroy the potential for long-term partnerships—the cornerstone
of Japanese supplier relationships. [37]

The Purchasing Function

The link between the outsourcing decision and supplier relationships is the purchasing agent. Just as companies go through stages of globalization, so do purchasing
agents and the purchasing function. The four phases in the internationalization of
the procurement process are:

1. Domestic purchasing only
2. Foreign buying based on need
3. Foreign buying as part of procurement strategy
4. Integration of global procurement strategy. [38]

The final phase occurs when the company realizes greater benefits from integration
and coordination of purchasing on a global basis. The second and third phases
assume a domestic company becoming involved in foreign purchasing in different
degrees, but the fourth phase is more applicable to the MNE. The integration phase
is similar to the centralization/decentralization dilemma. Rather than allow each
individual subsidiary to make all purchasing decisions, there is some degree of centralization of all or some of the purchasing decisions.

There are five major sourcing strategies that companies pursue as they move
into phases 3 and 4 above:

1. Assign domestic buyer(s) for international purchasing
2. Use foreign subsidiaries or business units
3. Establish international purchasing offices
4. Assign design, building, and sourcing to a specific business unit(s)
5. Integrate and coordinate worldwide sourcing. [39]

Black & Decker provides a good example of the stages and strategies of global
sourcing. When B&D began to restructure in the mid-1980s, purchasing was as
affected as manufacturing. At that time, purchasing was decentralized to the plant
level with little coordination or ability to leverage large purchasing decisions.
Sometimes, purchasing agents worked against each other. B&D had experimented
with purchasing in the 1960s, but the experiment was a disaster. The centralization

of purchasing decisions had slowed decision making down to a crawl. But decentralization did not make sense, given that B&D wanted to rationalize design and manufacturing. The head of purchasing adopted a strategy of centralizing key purchasing decisions for all plants and then letting local management make the other purchasing decisions.

Key commodities for which centralization made sense had one of the following criteria:

1. High dollar volume
2. Small supplier base
3. Strategic importance
4. Importance of and significance to quality
5. High technical content

When B&D purchased General Electric's housewares business, it purchased a significant amount of expertise overseas, especially in Singapore. That allowed it to establish purchasing centers in different parts of the world. By having on-site personnel in these locations, it could better understand the purchasing conditions in those locations and did not have to go through intermediaries to make purchases.[40] In addition, allowing on-site personnel to make purchasing decisions can be important in countries where there are local content requirements. As mentioned in Chapter 7, there is a 50-percent local content rule in NAFTA (62.5 percent for autos), so it would be difficult to centralize purchasing decisions outside of the NAFTA region and still be able to comply with local content requirements.

Once B&D decided to centralize its key buying decisions, it had to develop a strategy for working with suppliers. The cornerstones of its buying policy are:

- Dominant supplier strategy—one dominant supplier for each major commodity (the supplier may get 70 percent or more of the business);
- Long-term agreements—two to five years;
- Centralization of key commodities—working with a centralized purchasing group rather than with purchasing agents all over the world;
- International buying—focusing on suppliers from all over the world.[41]

Many of the supplier alliances are strategic in nature and involve more than just the purchasing of inputs. The traditional relationships are characterized by low commitment, limited information sharing, and contractual agreements. The newer alliances involve providing more information about order quantities and timing, upcoming design changes, long-range plans, and so on.[42] As noted in the Toyota example, they may also involve process technology assistance. The key is to develop a good match of expectations between supplier and buyer.

A s the Ethical Dilemmas features in Chapters 3, 7, and 8 noted, there are major ethical issues involved in locating production in foreign countries, especially with respect to labor costs and health and safety standards. When quality is an important dimension of the production process, companies are less likely to move production to low-wage countries or to use processes that are potentially harmful to employees. Achieving high quality and zero defects requires a relatively skilled workforce—not one that is low in skills and education level and operates in sweatshop conditions.

A utilitarian view of ethical conduct argues that the worth of actions or practices is determined by their consequences. That is, an action or practice is right if it leads to the

ETHICAL DILEMMAS & SOCIAL RESPONSIBILITY

best possible balance of good consequences and bad consequences for all parties affected.[43] A good example illustrating this view is found in this chapter's discussion of supplier relations. When an MNE such as Toyota develops close relationships with its suppliers, both parties become exposed to significant risk. In working with a supplier, Toyota requires a full understanding of that supplier's manufacturing capabilities and financial position. This requirement is difficult for non-Japanese companies because they are not used to providing such detailed information to customers. Toyota takes a hard-line approach to improving quality and driving down costs, but in turn it provides its suppliers with a stable business relationship. It shares development information with a supplier's competitors but not in such a way as to damage its relationship with the supplier. Even though it is in Toyota's self-interest to keep costs as low as possible in order to maximize its competitiveness within the industry, the company also has an ethical obligation to treat its suppliers fairly. As long as Toyota maintains a stable business relationship with suppliers and helps them become more competitive as manufacturers, its actions result in a positive utilitarian outcome.

In contrast, some of GM's supplier relations have been far less positive. When GM requires suppliers to enter into contractual agreements and then tears up the contracts and forces the suppliers to renegotiate, it is acting in its own self-interest and to the suppliers' detriment. Given the negative impact on the suppliers, one could argue that GM's actions do not constitute positive ethical conduct according to the utilitarian view. Following the departure of its head of purchasing for Volkswagen, it will be interesting to see how GM's supplier relations evolve. As Toyota increases its production in the United States to take advantage of the relatively cheap dollar, it will form more relationships with U.S. auto parts manufacturers—providing a basis for comparison with GM's tactics. In the face of this competition, GM may find that it has to adjust its supplier relations or lose some suppliers to Toyota.

Inventory Systems

The greater the interchange of products and components, the more difficult the inventory-control process is. The problems of distance and time and the uncertainty of the international political and economic environment can make it difficult to determine correct reorder points. For example, if a manufacturer in a country with a weak currency regularly imports inventory from a country with a strong currency, management may want to stockpile inventory in anticipation of a devaluation, despite large carrying costs and the risk of damage or pilferage. Another reason for stockpiling inventory is the perceived risk that political chaos or legislation will slow down imports. Rapidly changing international events can ruin a smoothly running inventory-control system.

In recent years, much press has been given to **just-in-time (JIT) inventory management,** a system fine-tuned by the Japanese and becoming increasingly popular among U.S. manufacturers as a part of total quality control. The JIT system is based on the idea that raw materials, parts, and components must be delivered to the production process just in time to be used so that companies do not carry large inventories. Lower inventory levels save financing and storage costs. However, the use of JIT means that parts must have few defects and must arrive on time to be used.

Foreign sourcing can create big risks for companies that use JIT, since interruptions in the supply line can cause havoc. JIT implies that inventories must be small; however, foreign sourcing almost always requires large inventories in order to counteract these risks.

Major problems occur because of distance, language and/or cultural differences, and transportation economics. More specifically, the effects of international sourcing on JIT manufacturing include

- Frequency of shipment
- Inventory policy
- Supplier reaction capability
- Quality
- Communication
- Sole sourcing
- Supplier delivery performance
- Flexibility[44]

Distance, especially transportation time, causes uncertainty or variability in supply lines. This means that the supplier has to find an intermediary warehouse from which to supply the buyer, which increases the cost; or the buyer has to purchase a larger stock of inventory, which increases the cost. If the demand of the buyer is large enough on a consistent basis, it is easier for the supplier to fill a container when sending products by ocean freight. Another option is for the buyer to consoli-

A JIT system delivers inputs to production as they are needed and lowers cost through higher quality and lower storage costs.

date shipments of several suppliers into one container, or for the supplier to fill a container for several buyers, thus filling the supply line faster and more cheaply. If the good is small enough and valuable enough, such as computer software, the supplier can use air freight and nearly eliminate the transportation time problem.[45]

Inventory policy is related to frequency in that the less frequent the delivery, the more likely the need to store inventory somewhere. Since JIT requires delivery just as the inventory is to be used, some concession must be made for inventory arriving from foreign suppliers. Sometimes that means adjusting the arrival time to a few days before use rather than immediately when it is to be used. Kawasaki, U.S.A. carries a minimum of three days' inventory on parts coming from Japan, with an average inventory of five days.[46]

Supplier capability refers to the ability of the supplier to react to changes in the buyer's schedule. About the only way to do that is through air freight.[47] Ocean freight is simply too slow a channel of distribution, because once the inventory arrives at the port, it must be transported by truck or train to the buyer. Even with the speed of ocean delivery that is taking place now, the delivery time is still too slow.

Quality of inventory is important, because inventory with significant amounts of defects will create problems with JIT. If the buyer has to purchase more because of expected defects, there will not only be the waste of the bad inventory, but there will also be higher carrying costs. Nike contracts out the manufacture of shoes to China, but it also has a Nike team on hand at the factories in China to ensure high-quality manufacturing. The geographic distance between buyer and supplier, language differences, and cultural differences can increase the time it takes to educate suppliers on how to supply products of high quality.[48]

JIT typically implies sole sourcing in order to get the supplier to commit to the stringent delivery and quality requirements inherent in JIT. However, some argue that global sourcing has too many risks to permit only one supplier. That means cultivating either another supplier in the same country or a supplier in the country of the buyer. Either way, the buyer runs the risk of not being able to get volume pricing from the supplier. Thus buyers may use a sole supplier for all but critical inputs for which there are few readily available substitutes. Then it is best to cultivate solid secondary suppliers.[49]

Foreign Trade Zones

FTZs are special zones designated by a government where tariffs can be delayed or avoided.

In recent years, **foreign trade zones (FTZs)** have become more popular as an intermediate step in the process between import and final use. Often, the final use is for export; however, these zones also are good for making use of foreign sourcing. As noted above, one of the problems with JIT is the length of the supply line when relying on global sourcing, possibly causing either the buyer or the supplier to stockpile inventory somewhere until it is needed in the manufacturing process. One place to stockpile inventory is in a warehouse in an FTZ. FTZs are areas in which domestic and imported merchandise can be stored, inspected, and manufactured free from formal customs procedures until the goods leave the zones. The zones are intended to encourage companies to locate in the country by allowing them to defer duties, pay less duties, or avoid certain duties completely.[50]

FTZs can be general-purpose zones or subzones. A general-purpose zone usually is established near a port of entry, such as a shipping port, a border crossing, or an airport, and usually consists of a distribution facility or an industrial park. A subzone generally is physically separated from a general-purpose zone but is under the same administrative structure. Since 1982, the major growth in FTZs has been in subzones rather than general-purpose zones, although the latter must be established before the former. For example, the major growth in subzones in the United States has been in the automobile industry, especially in the Midwest.[51] In fact, 60 percent of all subzone activity in the United States is connected with that industry. These zones are available to foreign-owned as well as domestic companies. During trade negotiations between Japan and the United States in 1994, U.S. negotiators threatened to withdraw subzone eligibility for Japanese automakers if the Japanese government did not make progress in helping the United States reduce its trade deficit with Japan. It was hoped that the Japanese automakers would pressure their government. Subzone activity is spreading to other industries, especially shipbuilding, pharmaceuticals, and home appliances, and becoming more heavily oriented to manufacturing and assembly than was originally envisioned.[52]

FTZs are used worldwide. For example, in Japan, they are being established for the benefit of foreign companies exporting products to that country. Japanese zones serve as warehousing and repackaging facilities at which companies can display consumer goods for demonstration to Japanese buyers.[53]

In the United States, FTZs have been used primarily as a means of providing greater flexibility as to when and how customs duties are paid. However, their use in the export business has been expanding. The exports for which these FTZs are used fall into one of the following categories:

- Foreign goods transshipped through U.S. zones to third countries
- Foreign goods processed in U.S. zones, then transshipped abroad
- Foreign goods processed or assembled in U.S. zones with some domestic materials and parts, then re-exported
- Goods produced wholly of foreign content in U.S. zones and then exported
- Goods produced from a combination of domestic and foreign materials and components in U.S. zones and then exported
- Domestic goods moved into a U.S. zone to achieve export status prior to their actual exportation[54]

An example of how an FTZ can be used occurs at a subzone in Texas, where a Coastal Corp. subsidiary refines imported oil. If the subsidiary exports the refined oil products, it pays no duty at all. If it sells the products domestically, it saves over $250,000 a year in interest on duties postponed until the products leave the zone.[55]

Smith Corona established an FTZ in order to import parts and components into the United States duty-free for its typewriter-manufacturing facilities. The U.S.

Customs code provides that duties apply to parts but not to a final product.[56] Therefore Smith Corona's imported parts and components were subject to duty, but the imported finished typewriters of its major competitors in the United States—Brother, Panasonic, and others—were not.[57] Since establishing the FTZ, Smith Corona imports parts and components into the zone and assembles them into typewriters there. The finished typewriters then are officially imported into the United States duty-free.

Kawasaki, U.S.A. became an FTZ in order to speed up the delivery of parts from Japan to its assembly operations in the United States. By becoming an FTZ, Kawasaki bypassed Customs and had the parts delivered directly to its assembly operations. In addition, Kawasaki did not have to pay duties on the inventory until the final goods left the zone. Not only did Kawasaki speed up delivery of parts by five days, but it also improved its cash flow.[58]

Product Design

International companies attempt to coordinate product design and get input from design facilities in different countries.

As noted earlier, Black & Decker has established several design centers around the world, and it tries to coordinate the design process with manufacturing, engineering, and marketing. Two additional examples of companies using global design strategies are found in the automobile industry: Honda and Ford. The new Honda Accord introduced in 1993 was developed by three design teams, one each from Japan, Germany, and the United States. Honda's reliance on the U.S. market and its alliances with automakers in Great Britain and South Korea had forced its engineers to consider engineering and marketing issues globally. In June 1990, Honda kicked off its new Accord project by bringing together the three design teams. The design teams were strongly competitive, although they borrowed ideas from each other. Each team presented full-scale models to top management. Honda's president and chief designer chose the Japanese model. In rejecting the American model, the president said, "We don't want a car with American taste. We want Honda taste well-fitted to the American market."[59]

The interchange of ideas between design and manufacturing engineers helps reduce costs and increase quality.

After the design was selected, the cooperation continued. U.S. production engineers and their families were moved to Japan for two to three years at an expense of $500,000 to Honda. This exchange of ideas occurred two years sooner than is normally the case. The objective of bringing together production and design engineers from both countries so soon was to identify product designs that would cause problems at Honda's Marysville, Ohio manufacturing facility, which would build the new Accord. For example, by making a single design change, the facility saved $1 million, the cost it would have incurred to modify its assembly equipment. In addition, American marketers and engineers were able to get design changes that reflected the U.S. market.

Cross-national differences in consumer tastes and preferences argue for decentralized product design.

Ford is the first automaker to coordinate its worldwide design teams through a single international network. Its design sites are located in six countries and coordinated by a corporate design organization in Michigan (see Map 18.2). By linking

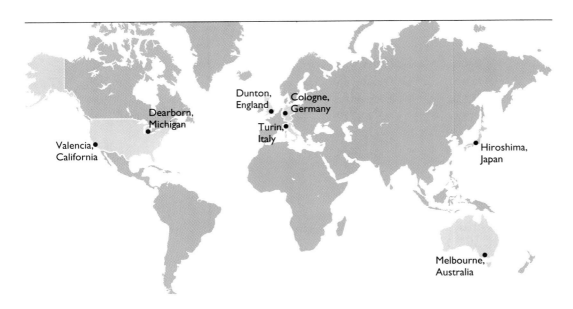

Map 18.2
Ford's Design Centers
Ford coordinates its worldwide design facilities through a sophisticated computer network.

Source: Julie Edelson Halpert, "Technology: One Car Worldwide, with Strings Pulled from Michigan," August 29, 1993, p. 7. Copyright © 1993 by The New York Times Company. Reprinted with permission.

production and design engineers with suppliers, Ford hopes to cut its new-car lead time to twenty-four months, down from the current U.S. industry average of fifty-four months. Using three-dimensional images created with computer software developed by Utah-based Evans & Sutherland, Ford designers can transmit images from England to Michigan for feedback and revisions. The revised images then can be sent to Italy, where a clay model of the car is sculpted. The entire process takes a matter of a few hours and is a function of design software, faster computer hardware, networking software, satellite links, undersea cables, and land lines.[60]

Critics of Ford's design network argue that consumer tastes vary too much by country for companies to rely on global designs. Their strategy is to create products and processes that are unique to each country or region, requiring a more decentralized approach to R&D. Thus different companies in the same industry, competing with each other for global market share, have different points of view on how to coordinate R&D worldwide.

COUNTERVAILING

FORCES

An issue touched on only indirectly in this chapter is company size. In discussing outsourcing by Japanese manufacturers, we noted that many Japanese suppliers are small. However, some suppliers—especially U.S. suppliers—have become large MNEs in their own right and are establishing components factories worldwide to supply their customers.

Another dimension of scale involves the size of manufacturing operations abroad. When an MNE employs a technology-driven product strategy, the key manufacturing strategy is flexibility to change products and processes quickly to take advantage of market trends. In this case, manufacturing facilities tend to start out small and grow as markets

An important countervailing force is the difference in the size of manufacturing operations abroad.

grow. With a marketing-intensive product strategy, manufacturing facilities tend to be located in or near local markets in order to respond more quickly to market needs. The size of the manufacturing facility is directly correlated to the size of the market and the degree to which the MNE uses the facility to serve markets nearby.

With a low-cost product strategy, for which the manufacturing strategy is to achieve economies of scale, the MNE tends to establish manufacturing facilities on a regional basis or in large markets (such as the United States) and to use large-scale operations. When the low-cost strategy is accomplished by using low-cost labor, MNEs are usually manufacturing mature products and components, so the scale is not very large. Thus you can see that product strategy can have an important impact on the location and size of manufacturing facilities.

Company and country strategies often conflict in the area of employment.

Company and country strategies often conflict in the area of employment. If the company uses a single-plant strategy with the home country as the plant's location, it will generate jobs in compatibility with the desires of the home-country government. However, if the company adopts a multidomestic or regional manufacturing strategy, then jobs will be lost in the home-country market. In addition, if it adopts a single-plant strategy that is compatible with a low-cost product strategy, then the plant may well be located in a country with low labor costs. In this case, the company's strategy will not be consistent with the home country's, and unemployment may ensue. The problem is that the company must adopt whatever manufacturing strategy is consistent with its product strategy, and it cannot make full employment in the home country a strategic objective. If it does, it runs the risk of going out of business altogether.

Most host countries prefer to have R&D facilities located locally rather than have all R&D take place abroad.

Another important issue relates to the centralization or decentralization of R&D, discussed earlier in this chapter. There are clear strategic differences between MNEs and countries concerning the location of R&D facilities. Although MNEs can benefit from the decentralization of such facilities, individual countries will always argue for local R&D facilities in order to develop products for global markets and to attract and retain a domestic scientific community. There also are tax implications of R&D location. For example, the IRS requires U.S. companies to allocate R&D expenditures to revenues from foreign sources. However, foreign governments are not inclined to allow the reallocation of U.S.-based expenses to revenues generated in their countries. This sets up a key conflict between governments.

LOOKING TO THE FUTURE

In establishing manufacturing facilities to serve worldwide markets, MNEs started with large home-market plants and exported to foreign markets. As the importance of those markets increased, companies needed to establish manufacturing facilities abroad, almost in a multidomestic approach. Now, however, they are finding that they need much stronger control over manufacturing operations worldwide in order to take advantage of market differences and to drive down costs.

Improvements in communications technology will continue to facilitate the flow of information worldwide. This will be especially helpful in the design of new products. As the design time is cut down, MNEs will be able to get new products to market much more quickly.

An important trend is the movement of MNEs away from vertical integration and toward outsourcing as a way to cut costs. This movement will continue to accelerate, and MNEs will be forced to develop closer relationships with suppliers in order to increase quality and reduce costs.

WEB CONNECTION

Check out our home page for links to resources on foreign trade zones, maquiladoras, and other relevant chapter topics.

Summary

- Operations management refers to the direction and control of the processes that transform inputs into finished goods and services.

- Both manufacturing companies and service companies need to determine where goods and services are going to be produced.

- A competitive manufacturing strategy is based on efficiency/cost, dependability, quality, flexibility, and innovation.

- Major types of manufacturing configurations are home country with exporting, autonomous regional plants, combination of regional and global focus, and coordinated global focus.

- Offshore manufacturing, including the maquiladora operations in Mexico, is an example of production sharing.

- Layout planning is a function of the process technology and skill sets of workers.

- Quality in manufacturing implies zero defects, the attitude that the goods are of such high quality that the consumer wouldn't think of buying anything else.

- Total quality management (TQM) is continuous improvement that leads to zero defects.

- ISO 9000 is a European set of quality standards intended to promote quality at every level of an organization.

- Global sourcing and production strategies need to include consideration of location and stage in the production process.

- **A major challenge for companies is to develop strong, mutually beneficial relationships with suppliers. Distance and communications problems make this difficult for global suppliers.**

- **MNEs strive for the integration of a global procurement strategy for key materials.**

- **Just-in-time (JIT) inventory flow is complicated when global sourcing is used because of the distance, time, and uncertainty of materials flows.**

- **Foreign trade zones can be used to store inventory until it is needed in the production process.**

- **MNEs need to coordinate design worldwide to enhance product innovation and drive down product and manufacturing costs.**

Case
Applied Magnetics Malaysia (AMM)[61]

It was early winter near the end of 1992, but you wouldn't know it by the weather. It was the same weather all year around—hot. You could work up a sweat just walking from the car to the plant. M. Ganesan, managing director of Applied Magnetics Malaysia (AMM) in Pinang (see Map 18.3), was addressing a group of managers and a researcher from the Universiti Malaya: "We need to get ISO-certified and to establish a TQM environment. But we lack the effective team cooperation that both of these projects critically need." As managing director, Ganesan holds the highest management position in AMM, similar to the position of CEO in a U.S. company. He had come up through the management ranks of Motorola Malaysia in Kuala Lumpur and had made an impressive reputation for himself as an innovative go-getter and problem solver, qualities that prompted AMM to offer him the managing directorship.

AMM is a division of Applied Magnetics (AM), a $344.4-million U.S. company at the end of fiscal year 1996 that is a leading independent supplier of magnetic recording heads for both disk and tape drives for the data-storage segments of the worldwide computer industry. Its goal is "to be the world's best supplier of high-quality magnetic recording heads, where customer satisfaction is the primary measure of performance."

AM operates in seven countries and employs a total of about 5,500 employees, of whom approximately 800 are located in California, 4,500 are located in Asia, and approximately 200 are located in Ireland. AM's production facility in Malaysia has been facing potential labor shortages issues, as many disk drive and component manufacturers have expanded their production facilities in Malaysia and compete for the supply of labor in that country. To protect against potential future labor shortages, AM opened a manufacturing facility in Beijing, China in fiscal 1995. Its major facilities are in China, Ireland, Malaysia, Singapore, South Korea, and the United States. However, it conducts substantially all of its production assembly and test operations in its facilities in Korea, Malaysia, and Singapore. In addition, the company leases office space and manufacturing facilities in China. The princi-

**Map 18.3
Malaysia and Its
Workforce**
One of the fastest-growing
countries in Southeast
Asia, Malaysia is a favored
location for foreign
investment.

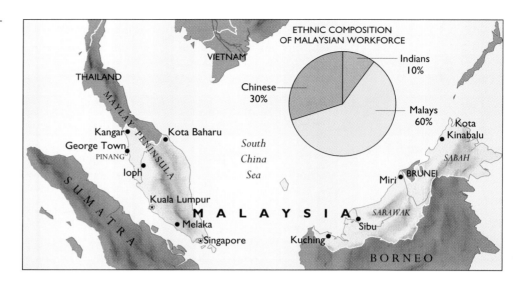

pal competitive factors in the markets that AM serves are price, technological sophistication, product performance and quality, product availability, and responsiveness to customers.

AMM manufactures very technical products—read/write heads for hard-disk drives for
the microcomputer market and semiconductor wafers. The Malaysian workforce seems to
be well suited to the manufacture of this type of product due to strong skills, high quality
and efficient performance in production, use of high technology in production, and relatively cheap wages, which is why many U.S. high-tech companies have relocated to Malaysia.

AMM uses the JIT inventory management strategy that it learned from its U.S. counterpart. Although the strategy isn't implemented perfectly, it's getting there. Interestingly, in
Malaysia only a few U.S. plants, and none of the Japanese plants, have implemented JIT, primarily because (according to the Japanese) they have had difficulty with organizing effective
work teams. The United States is the second-largest investor in Malaysia, following Japan.
The Japanese plants, and most of the other plants, tend to be based on Material Requirements Planning (MRP). MRP is a computerized information system developed specifically to
aid in managing dependent demand inventory and scheduling replenishment orders.

AMM has organized its production area into numerous production "lines" in an attempt
to implement the lessons learned from management's experience at Motorola. These lines
are a series of tables laid out in the sequence of the production process. They use table-
space-defined KANBANs, where each KANBAN takes the form of a tape-defined location
on the table rather than a card or a box. The KANBAN system was developed to control
the flow of production through a factory as part of the JIT system. In AMM's case, when
parts are used up in the table-defined space, the parts need to be replenished, which
implies that production of the parts needs to occur. However, Ganesan was concerned:

> We also need to get our production lines balanced. There are large differences between
> capacity and workload on many of our lines. These differences are causing workload ineffi-

ciency, bottlenecks, and employee frustration. Some employees feel they are getting overworked when compared with their counterparts. I'm not sure which aspect is more important, the line balancing or the teaming.

AMM needs to integrate into the international marketplace. Specifically, the company is trying to make its mark in Europe. However, the European market has developed the ISO 9000 quality standards for all international suppliers. To effectively serve this marketplace, AMM needs to be ISO-certified. Of the several classifications within this certification, AMM is specifically focusing on ISO 9002 certification, which focuses on manufacturers.

AMM also is forward-looking in that it sees ISO-certification as only a stepping stone toward a total continuous quality improvement program. Management is hoping to implement TQM and the "Total Quality Control Philosophy" of the AM corporate office, based on TQM principles. For ISO certification, or even more importantly, for TQM to function effectively, teaming is critical.

Senior Quality Assurance Engineer Ridzwan Raja said, "We need to get the teaming working first. It's the teams that come up with the ideas that help in the line-balancing process. A large part of the problem behind our ineffective teaming is the cross-cultural mixture of employees within our factory." Like Ganesan, Raja is Malaysian born and a Malaysian citizen, although of Indian descent. However, unlike Ganesan, who has maintained his Hindu faith, Ridzwan Raja recently converted from the Hindu faith to the Muslim faith and has changed his name to Raja Mohan, although his business cards still reflect his Hindi name.

AMM's workforce, like that of most Malaysian companies, was composed of about 60 percent Malays, 30 percent Chinese, and 10 percent Indians, all of which are Malaysian-born and Malaysian citizens (see Map 18.3). However, each group has its own culture and religion, and outside the workplace, each tends to be culturally isolated. AMM also had a few expatriates, such as Ken Lanshe, a quality manager, who was from corporate headquarters in the United States.

Raja went on to explain:

> What happens is that we will organize a team of employees based on the project we want the team to accomplish, selecting which employees would be the most appropriate. Then, when the team meets together, only that employee with the highest status will speak. Status can be defined by number of years on the job, job position, or even age. Somehow, status is nonverbally defined. Everyone just seems to know which individual has the most status. Out of respect for that individual, all the remaining members of the team will subordinate their comments to the ranking team member. No one will offer anything creative or innovative except this one individual.

Sri Shan, another quality manager, added:

> Even if we carefully organize our team so that all the members of the team have relatively equal status, thereby allowing everyone to comment freely, we still have problems, isn't it. What happens is that no one is willing to criticize anyone else. They only pat each other on the back, la. How can we get them to improve if they are afraid to comment, la?

(The words "isn't it" and "la" are used in Malaysia to add emphasis, like the Canadian "ey.")

In Malaysia, it is considered bad taste to demean someone's "face." People should always try to respect and positively influence someone else's "face." This becomes especially important when mixing cultures. Cross-cultural understanding is often very weak, and employees look at each other as strangers, to some extent, not wanting to put themselves or their cultures in a bad light. The presence of the different ethnic groups mentioned above has created tensions in Malaysian society. Malays make up the most powerful group in Malaysian politics, but the Chinese control much of the nation's economy. Social, economic, and political differences between the Chinese and Malays have led to friction and—sometimes—violence between members of the two groups. After violent clashes in the early 1980s, those from different cultures, especially the Malay Bumi-Putras ("People of the Land" who are Muslims) and the Chinese, tend to "walk on eggs" when interacting with each other. No one wants the issues to pop out into the open again; they prefer to keep them "hidden."

The problem is that the company can't wait until it has the teams working in order to balance the production process. The balancing is an operations research process and requires the use of mathematical models. Once the line has been balanced as much as possible, then the team can start improving the process flow by eliminating the waste, which is part of the production process. The line balancing and the team building should go on simultaneously, since one involves the development of the employees and the other can be worked on by the operations research group.

From the standpoint of multi-ethnic work groupings, it is important to teach the employees to criticize the function, not the person. It also is important for members of the work group to become socially comfortable with each other. They need to be given opportunities to spend time together outside the work setting. Often the best ideas and suggestions occur during these informal settings. A social strategy of this nature takes longer to implement but has worked effectively in other U.S.-based, team-oriented companies functioning in Malaysia.

Another teaming strategy that has been effective is defining a set of goals that can be used as a measurement tool and a motivation tool for the teams. Often, the ineffectiveness of teams derives from their lack of understanding of what is needed and how to satisfy this need. No one wants to volunteer a suggestion or idea that may turn out to be off the mark.

"Training and cross training of team members would help a lot in the implementation of these suggestions," commented Lanshe. "If employees understand each other's job functions better, they would be more willing to offer suggestions and less concerned about making themselves look bad."

A consultant to AMM suggested the following:

Malaysians need to start looking at the benefits of their cultural mix. This mix offers them the opportunity to look at problems through several different perspectives. The synergy of this type of mix can make Malaysian industry leading-edge. Back in my home of the United States, we have teaming problems too, but nothing compared to the complexity that you are experiencing. However, in spite of its complexity the Malaysian culture offers enormous synergistic benefits, if you can only learn to cash in on them.

Ganesan wrapped up by saying, "We need to achieve the Total Quality Control Philosophy as stated by our corporate office. We need to do this through JIT, ISO certification, and TQM, all of which require effective teaming. We also need to work towards a greatly improved balance in our production process."

Questions

1. Describe AM's product and manufacturing strategies.
2. Discuss the cultural dimensions affecting AMM and their impact on AMM's ability to achieve its objectives in terms of quality and production scheduling.
3. How can culture influence manufacturing strategy and international manufacturing configurations?

4. Why do you think AM has a manufacturing facility in Malaysia? What advantages might Malaysia offer over another offshore site? Given the unique challenges AMM faces, under what conditions should AM move these facilities elsewhere?

Chapter Notes

1. Roy Furchgott, "Dateline: Towson, Md.," *The Houston Chronicle,* February 7, 1993; several issues of Black & Decker's *Annual Report;* Bill Saporito, "Black & Decker's Gamble on 'Globalization,' " *Fortune,* May 14, 1984, p. 40+; Christopher S. Eklund, "How Black & Decker Got Back in the Black," *Business Week,* July 13, 1987, pp. 86–90; "How Black & Decker Forged a Winning Brand Transfer Strategy," *Business International,* July 20, 1987, pp. 225–227; Mary Lu Carnevale, "Black & Decker Goes to Full-Court Press," *Wall Street Journal,* November 10, 1988, p. A8; and Stuart Flack, "All Leverage Is Not Created Equal," *Forbes,* March 19, 1990, p. 39; Black & Decker, Form 10K, 1995; Tetsuo Sato, "Japan's Power Tool Industry's Overseas Development Advances Further," *Japan 21st,* June 1996, Vol. 41, No. 6, p. 27; Jerry Brady, "Lessons Learned from the Brink of Disaster," *Washington Business Journal,* May 17, 1996, Vol. 15, No. 1, p. 63; George M. Fodor, "Quality, Depth Earn Top Kudos," *Industrial Distribution,* January 1995, Vol. 84, No. 1, p. 22; Matthew Schifrin, "Cut and Build Archibald," *Forbes,* September 23, 1996, pp. 44–48.
2. Lee J. Krajewski and Larry P. Ritzman. *Operations Management: Strategy and Analysis,* 4th ed. (Reading, MA.: Addison-Wesley Longman Publishing Company, 1996), p. 3.
3. Michael E. Porter, ed., *Competition in Global Industries* (Boston: Harvard Business School Press, 1986).
4. S. C. Wheelwright, "Reflecting Corporate Strategy in Manufacturing Decisions," *Business Horizons,* Vol. 21,

February 1978; S. C. Wheelwright, "Manufacturing Strategy: Defining the Missing Link, *Strategic Management Journal,* Vol. 5, 1984, pp. 77–91; and Frank DuBois, Brian Toyne, and Michael D. Oliff, "International Manufacturing Strategies of U.S. Multinationals: A Conceptual Framework Based on a Four-Industry Study," *Journal of International Business Studies,* Vol. 24, No. 2, Second Quarter 1993, pp. 313–314; Robert H. Hayes, Steven C. Wheelwright, and Kim B. Clark, *Dynamic Manufacturing* (New York: Free Press, 1988), pp. 10–11.
5. Robert Stobaugh and Piero Telesio, "Match Manufacturing Policies and Product Strategy," in *Transnational Management,* Christopher A. Bartlett and Sumantra Ghoshal, eds. (Homewood, Ill.: Richard D. Irwin, 1992), pp. 760–768.
6. Michael E. McGrath and Richard W. Hoole, "Manufacturing's New Economies of Scale," *Harvard Business Review,* May–June 1992, p. 94.
7. Stobaugh and Telesio, op. cit., p. 765.
8. Stobaugh and Telesio, op. cit., pp. 767–768.
9. "Maquiladoras Take on a New Life," *Deloitte & Touche Review,* August 21, 1995, p. 3.
10. "Mexico's Maquiladora Industry Expanded 24 Percent," <http://www.latino.com/biz/mexmaq.html>
11. Paul M. Swamidass, "A Comparison of the Plant Location Strategies of Foreign and Domestic Manufacturers in the U.S.," *Journal of International Business Studies,* Second Quarter 1990, p. 302.
12. Gabriella Stern, "GM Is Expected to Pick Thailand as Site for First Major Plant in Southeast Asia," *Wall Street Journal,* May 16, 1996, p. A2.

13. Andrew Taylor, "Third World Looks to First World Cast-Offs," *Financial Times,* January 16, 1996, p. 5.
14. Krajewski and Ritzman, op. cit., p. 398.
15. Robert H. Hayes, Steven C. Wheelwright, and Kim B. Clark, op. cit., p. 17.
16. Krajewski and Ritzman, op. cit., p. 140.
17. Gerhard Plenert, "TQM—Clearing Away the Confusion to Find Out What's Compatible and What's Not," *PORG Newsletter,* Second Quarter, 1991 (Provo, UT: BYU Productivity and Quality Research Group).
18. Robert S. Kaplan, "Measuring Manufacturing Performance: A New Challenge for Managerial Accounting Research," *The Accounting Review,* Vol. 58, No. 4 (October 1983), pp. 690–691.
19. Jonathan B. Levine, "Want EC Business? You Have Two Choices," *Business Week,* October 19, 1992, p. 58.
20. Mary Saunders, "U.S. Firms Doing Business in EC Have Options in Registering for ISO 9000 Quality Standards," *Business America,* June 14, 1993, p. 7.
21. Masaaki Kotabe and Glen S. Omura, "Sourcing Strategies of European and Japanese Multinationals: A Comparison," *Journal of International Business Studies,* Spring 1989, pp. 120–122.
22. Paul M. Swamidass and Masaaki Kotabe, "Component Sourcing Strategies of Multinationals: An Empirical Study of European and Japanese Multinationals," *Journal of International Business Studies,* Vol. 24, No. 1, First Quarter 1993, p. 84.
23. Robert M. Monczka and Robert J. Trent, "Global Sourcing: A Development Approach," *International Journal of Purchasing and Materials Management,* Spring 1991, p. 3.

24. Mark L. Fagan, "A Guide to Global Sourcing," *The Journal of Business Strategy,* March–April 1991, p. 21.
25. Ibid., p. 22.
26. Monczka and Trent, op. cit.
27. Alan S. Blinder, "A Japanese Buddy System That Could Benefit U.S. Business," *Business Week,* October 14, 1991, p. 32.
28. Ravi Venkatesan, "Strategic Sourcing: To Make or Not To Make," *Harvard Business Review,* November–December 1991, p. 98.
29. Ibid., pp. 101–102.
30. John McMillan, "Managing Suppliers: Incentive Systems in Japanese and U.S. Industry," *California Management Review,* Summer 1990, p. 38.
31. Russell Johnston and Paul R. Lawrence, "Beyond Vertical Integration—The Rise of the Value-Adding Partnership," *Harvard Business Review,* July–August 1988, p. 98.
32. Lindsay Chappell, "50 Top Suppliers Vie to Be World Champs," *Automotive News,* July 8, 1996, p. 1.
33. Karen Lowry Miller, Larry Armstrong, and David Woodruff. "A Car Is Born," *Business Week,* September 13, 1993, p. 68.
34. Johnston and Lawrence, op. cit., p. 94.
35. Joseph B. White, "Japanese Auto Makers Help Parts Suppliers Become More Efficient," *Wall Street Journal,* September 10, 1991, p. 1.
36. Ibid., p. 10.
37. Zachary Schiller, David Woodruff, Kevin Kelly, and Michael Schroeder, "GM Tightens the Screws," *Business Week,* June 22, 1992, p. 30.
38. Monczka and Trent, op. cit., pp. 4–5.
39. Robert M. Monczka and Robert J. Trent, "Worldwide Sourcing: Assessment and Execution," *International Journal of Purchasing and Materials Management,* Fall 1992, pp. 17–18.
40. "Black & Decker," *Purchasing,* September 29, 1988, pp. 48–49, 56.
41. Ibid., p. 47.
42. F. Ian Stuart and David McCutcheon, "Problem Sources in Establishing Strategic Supplier Alliances," *International Journal of Purchasing and Materials Management,* Winter 1995, p. 4.
43. Tom L. Beauchamp and Norman E. Bowie, *Ethical Theory and Business,* 4th Edition (Englewood Cliffs, N.J.: Prentice-Hall), pp. 21–22.
44. Shawnee K. Vickery, "International Sourcing: Implications for Just-in-Time Manufacturing," *Production and Inventory Management Journal,* Third Quarter, 1989, p. 67.
45. Ibid., p. 67.
46. Ibid., pp. 67–68.
47. Ibid., pp. 68–69.
48. Ibid., p. 69.
49. Ibid., p. 70.
50. Sonia Nazario, "Boom and Despair," *Wall Street Journal,* September 22, 1989, p. R26.
51. David D. Weiss, "Foreign Trade Zones: Growth Amid Controversy," *Chicago Fed Letter,* Number 48, August 1991, pp. 1–2.
52. Peter Tirschwell, "Subzones: Vehicle of Choice?" *Journal of Commerce and Commercial,* August 2, 1993.
53. "World Becomes Smaller as Japan, Central Europe Catch Zone Fever," *The Journal of Commerce and Commercial,* October 1991, p. 6B.
54. John J. DaPonte, Jr., "Foreign-Trade Zones and Exports," *American Export Bulletin,* April 1978.
55. Ken Slocum, "Foreign-Trade Zones Aid Many Companies But Stir Up Criticism," *Wall Street Journal,* September 30, 1987, p. 1.
56. Ibid.
57. Peter Trischwell, "Subzones: Vehicle of Choice?" *Journal of Commerce and Commercial,* May 15, 1992, p. 12B.
58. Vickery, op. cit., p. 68.
59. Miller, Armstrong, and Woodruff, op. cit., p. 67.
60. Julie Edelson Halpert, "One Car, Worldwide, with Strings Pulled from Michigan," *New York Times,* August 29, 1993, p. F7.
61. This case was created by Professor Gerhard Plenert of Brigham Young University based on his experiences in Malaysia in 1992–93. Reprinted with permission. Information also was found in Applied Magnetics' 1992 and 1995 *Annual Reports* and 1993 *Prospectus.*

25. Ibid., p. 22.

26. Monczka and Trent, op. cit.

27. Alan S. Blinder, "A Japanese Buddy System That Could Benefit U.S. Business," *Business Week*, October 14, 1991, p. 32.

28. Ravi Venkatesan, "Strategic Sourcing: To Make or Not To Make," *Harvard Business Review*, November–December 1991, p. 98.

29. Ibid., pp. 101–102.

30. John McMillan, "Managing Suppliers: Incentive Systems in Japanese and U.S. Industry," *California Management Review*, Summer 1990, p. 38.

31. Russell Johnston and Paul R. Lawrence, "Beyond Vertical Integration—The Rise of the Value-Adding Partnership," *Harvard Business Review*, July–August 1988, p. 98.

32. Lindsay Chappell, "50 Top Suppliers Vie to Be World Champs," *Automotive News*, July 8, 1996, p. 1.

33. Karen Lowry Miller, Larry Armstrong, and David Woodruff. "A Car Is Born," *Business Week*, September 13, 1993, p. 68.

34. Johnston and Lawrence, op. cit., p. 94.

35. Joseph B. White, "Japanese Auto Makers Help Parts Suppliers Become More Efficient," *Wall Street Journal*, September 10, 1991, p. 1.

36. Ibid., p. 10.

37. Zachary Schiller, David Woodruff, Kevin Kelly, and Michael Schroeder, "GM Tight-

ens the Screws," *Business Week*, June 22, 1992, p. 30.

38. Monczka and Trent, op. cit., pp. 4–5.

39. Robert M. Monczka and Robert J. Trent, "Worldwide Sourcing: Assessment and Execution," *International Journal of Purchasing and Materials Management*, Fall 1992, pp. 17–18.

40. "Black & Decker," *Purchasing*, September 29, 1988, pp. 48–49, 56.

41. Ibid., p. 47.

42. F. Ian Stuart and David McCutcheon, "Problem Sources in Establishing Strategic Supplier Alliances," *International Journal of Purchasing and Materials Management*, Winter 1995, p. 4.

43. Tom L. Beauchamp and Norman E. Bowie, *Ethical Theory and Business*, 4th Edition (Englewood Cliffs, N.J.: Prentice-Hall), pp. 21–22.

44. Shawnee K. Vickery, "International Sourcing: Implications for Just-in-Time Manufacturing," *Production and Inventory Management Journal*, Third Quarter, 1989, p. 67.

45. Ibid., p. 67.

46. Ibid., pp. 67–68.

47. Ibid., pp. 68–69.

48. Ibid., p. 69.

49. Ibid., p. 70.

50. Sonia Nazario, "Boom and Despair," *Wall Street Journal*, September 22, 1989, p. R26.

51. David D. Weiss, "Foreign Trade Zones: Growth Amid Controversy," *Chicago Fed Letter*, Number 48, August 1991, pp. 1–2.

52. Peter Tirschwell, "Subzones: Vehicle of Choice?" *Journal of Commerce and Commercial*, August 2, 1993.

53. "World Becomes Smaller as Japan, Central Europe Catch Zone Fever," *The Journal of Commerce and Commercial*, October 1991, p. 6B.

54. John J. DaPonte, Jr., "Foreign-Trade Zones and Exports," *American Export Bulletin*, April 1978.

55. Ken Slocum, "Foreign-Trade Zones Aid Many Companies But Stir Up Criticism," *Wall Street Journal*, September 30, 1987, p. 1.

56. Ibid.

57. Peter Trischwell, "Subzones: Vehicle of Choice?" *Journal of Commerce and Commercial*, May 15, 1992, p. 12B.

58. Vickery, op. cit., p. 68.

59. Miller, Armstrong, and Woodruff, op. cit., p. 67.

60. Julie Edelson Halpert, "One Car, Worldwide, with Strings Pulled from Michigan," *New York Times*, August 29, 1993, p. F7.

61. This case was created by Professor Gerhard Plenert of Brigham Young University based on his experiences in Malaysia in 1992–93. Reprinted with permission. Information also was found in Applied Magnetics' 1992 and 1995 *Annual Reports* and 1993 *Prospectus*.

Chapter 19

Multinational Accounting and Tax Functions

Even between parents and children, money matters make strangers.

—Japanese Proverb

Objectives

- To examine the major factors influencing the development of accounting practices in different countries and the worldwide harmonization of accounting principles

- To explain how companies account for foreign-currency transactions and translate foreign-currency financial statements

- To describe the impact of accounting methods on the evaluation of foreign operations

- To investigate the U.S. taxation of foreign-source income

- To examine some of the major non-U.S. tax practices and to show how international tax treaties can alleviate some of the impact of double taxation

Case
The Coca-Cola
Company[1]

A Coke is a Coke is a Coke no matter where on the planet you drink it. But a Coke Light can be a Diet Coke and a Mellow Yellow can be a Lychee Mello. Fanta is a dozen different things—Peach in Botswana, passion fruit (what else?) in France, and flower-flavored in Japan (huh?). Other countries have their own flavors—only Italy can pour a Beverly (and some travelers who've tried it are just fine with that).

That little quote from Coca-Cola's home page on the Internet (the quote changes each day) describes the global dimension of Coca-Cola, the U.S.-based company with the number 2 brand in the world, just behind McDonald's.

Between 1886, when Atlanta pharmacist J. S. Pemberton mixed up his first batch of Coca-Cola, and 1995, Coca-Cola's worldwide revenues increased from only $50 to more than $18 billion. Prior to 1995, Coca-Cola operated three divisions: soft drinks international, soft drinks U.S., and foods. In 1995, however, Coca-Cola changed its organizational structure by combining the U.S. and international soft drinks business and forming five regional groups headed by a group president: North America; Africa; Greater Europe; Latin America; and Middle and Far East and Canada. The foods division is still separate from the beverages division and yields about 9 percent of Coca-Cola's revenues. In 1995, however, the foods division operated at a loss. In this sense, Coca-Cola is far less diversified than PepsiCo, its major competitor in the soft-drink industry, which has three product divisions: beverages, restaurants (KFC, Taco Bell, and Pizza Hut), and snack foods. In 1997, however, PepsiCo announced that it was planning to spin off its restaurant division and retain only the beverages and snack foods divisions. According to its 1995 *Annual Report,* Coca-Cola is the world's largest manufacturer, marketer, and distributor of soft-drink concentrates and syrups, both of which it sells to bottling and canning operations. It also manufactures fountain/post-mix soft-drink syrups, which it sells to fountain wholesalers and some fountain retailers. Further, Coca-Cola has substantial equity investments in numerous soft-drink bottling and canning operations, and it owns and operates certain bottling and canning operations outside the United States. In its foods division, Coca-Cola processes and markets citrus and other juice and juice-drink products, primarily orange juice. It is the world's largest marketer of packaged citrus products.

The company averages a 47-percent worldwide market share in flavored carbonated soft drinks: Its market share is 42 percent in the United States and about half internationally. In terms of total sales, Coca-Cola has four of the world's top five carbonated soft drinks: Coca-Cola and Coca-Cola Classic (number 1), Diet Coca-Cola and Coca-Cola Light (number 3), Fanta (number 4), and Sprite (number 5). Diet Coke is called Coke Light in many countries because the word "diet" has a connotation of illness in Germany and Italy. Coca-Cola is the worldwide market leader in the three largest carbonated soft-drink segments: cola (61 percent of the world market), orange (32 percent), and lemon-lime (36 percent).

As Fig. 19.1 shows, Coca-Cola's domestic revenues and profits are only 29 percent and 18 percent of total revenues and profits, respectively. Although the United States is its largest market in terms of revenues, the EU is a close second. As a result of strong price

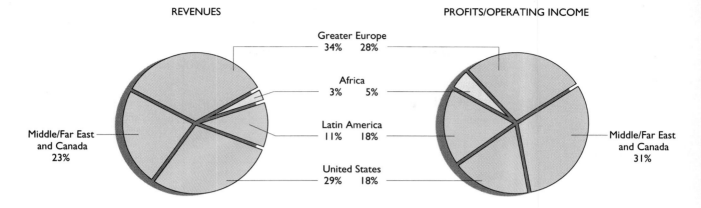

REVENUES   PROFITS/OPERATING INCOME

Greater Europe
34%   28%

Africa
3%   5%

Latin America
11%   18%

Middle/Far East
and Canada
23%

United States
29%   18%

Middle/Far East
and Canada
31%

**Figure 19.1
Coca-Cola's Revenues
and Profits by
Geographical Area**
Coca-Cola generates 71
percent of its revenues and
82 percent of its profits
outside the United States.
Greater Europe is the
largest foreign market in
terms of revenues but
ranks second to the Middle
and Far East markets in
terms of profits.

competition in the United States, however, both the EU and the Pacific and Canadian
regions are more profitable.

Coca-Cola truly operates worldwide. The Coca-Cola brand is sold in more than 195
countries, Diet Coke/Coke Light in 117 countries, Fanta in 164 countries, and Sprite in 164
countries. The company continues to expand internationally because of market growth and
potential. Although the average annual growth rate of unit case volume for Coca-Cola in
the five years ending in 1995 was only 4 percent in the United States, it was 6 percent
worldwide, compared with an industry growth rate of only 3 percent. Coca-Cola's largest
market growth was in China (40 percent), East Central Europe (21 percent), Middle East
(17 percent), and Argentina and Chile (13 percent). The United States leads the world with
average per capita consumption of 343 servings of Coca-Cola's carbonated soft drinks
(each serving equals one 8-ounce drink). The international average is only 54 servings; in
China, for example, per capita consumption is only 4 servings per year.

Given its international growth, foreign exchange is a major issue for Coca-Cola. Balance
sheets and income statements for all of the countries in which it operates must be translated from the foreign currencies into U.S. dollars so that they can be combined with Coca-
Cola's domestic dollar results.

One of Coca-Cola's key strategies has been its investment in bottling companies worldwide. In 1986, Coca-Cola purchased several poorly performing U.S. bottlers and combined
them with its own network of bottlers, forming a new company called Coca-Cola Enterprises (CCE). Coke then took CCE public but retained a 49-percent interest in the company. In 1995, CCE had $6.8 billion in revenues and $9 billion in assets, compared with $18
billion in revenues and $15 billion in assets for Coke. Coke then proceeded to sell many of
its foreign bottlers to CCE and use CCE to acquire other bottlers worldwide. In addition,
Coca-Cola has an ownership interest in other bottlers outside of the United States, such as
Coca-Cola Amatril Limited of Australia, which operates in 16 countries. In each of these
cases, Coke owns less than 50 percent of the bottling company. This is significant, because
if Coke owned more than 50 percent of the bottling companies, it would have to add the
balance sheets (including debt) and income statements of the bottlers to Coke's own balance sheet and income statement (known as the consolidation of accounts). When Coke

spun off the bottlers in 1986, it got rid of billions of dollars in debt and removed a low-return, cash-hungry business from its books. Now all it has to do is keep the value of its investments on its balance sheet (see Table 19.1). Basically, that investment account is only increased by new investments and Coke's equity interest in the income of the bottlers, and decreased by the sale of bottlers.

In the mid-1980s, Coca-Cola's management saw that its international operations were increasing significantly and that the nature of its business had changed since its last account-

Table 19.1
Coca-Cola Balance Sheet

The Coca-Cola Company and Subsidiaries		
Consolidated Balance Sheets		
December 31 (in millions except share data)	**1995**	**1994**
Assets		
Current		
Cash and cash equivalents	$1,167	$1,386
Marketable securities	148	145
	1,315	1,531
Trade accounts receivable, less allowances of $34 in 1995 and $33 in 1994	1,695	1,470
Finance subsidiary receivables	55	55
Inventories	1,117	1,047
Prepaid expenses and other assets	1,268	1,102
Total Current Assets	5,450	5,205
Investments and Other Assets		
Equity method investments		
Coca-Cola Enterprises Inc.	556	524
Coca-Cola Amatil Limited	682	694
Other, principally bottling companies	1,157	1,114
Cost method investments, principally bottling companies	319	178
Finance subsidiary receivables and investments	351	255
Marketable securities and other assets	1,246	1,163
	4,311	3,928
Property, Plant and Equipment		
Land	233	221
Buildings and improvements	1,944	1,814
Machinery and equipment	4,135	3,776
Containers	345	346
	6,657	6,157
Less allowances for depreciation	2,321	2,077
	4,336	4,080
Goodwill and Other Intangible Assets	944	660
	$15,041	$13,873

Table 19.1
Coca-Cola Balance Sheet, cont.

December 31 (in millions except share data)	1995	1994
Liabilities and Share-Owners' Equity		
Current		
Accounts payable and accrued expenses	$2,894	$2,564
Loans and notes payable	2,371	2,048
Current maturities of long-term debt	552	35
Accrued taxes	1,531	1,530
Total Current Liabilities	7,348	6,177
Long-Term Debt	1,141	1,426
Other Liabilities	966	855
Deferred Income Taxes	194	180
Share-Owners' Equity		
Common stock, $.25 par value		
Authorized: 2,800,000,000 shares		
Issued: 1,711,839,497 shares in 1995; 1,707,627,955 share in 1994	428	427
Capital surplus	1,291	1,173
Reinvested earnings	12,882	11,006
Unearned compensation related to outstanding restricted stock	(68)	(74)
Foreign currency translation adjustment	(424)	(272)
Unrealized gain on securities available for sale	82	48
	14,191	12,308
Less treasury stock, at cost (459,540,663 shares in 1995; 431,694,661 shares in 1994)	8,799	7,073
	5,392	5,235
	$15,041	$13,873

Source: Coca-Cola, *Annual Report 1995*, pp. 50–51.

ing manual was written. It needed a comprehensive, easy-reference accounting manual to help it maintain strong financial controls over its operations. Management felt that a better accounting manual would help the company acquire reliable information about units all over the world in order to help local subsidiaries operate at peak efficiency and generate corporate-wide reports consistently.

In addition, after Robert Goizueta became CEO, he became concerned about the poor financial information he was getting. He also noticed that the company, in effect, was going out of business because it was investing equity capital at 16 percent but earning only 8–10 percent on some of its investments. He decided to evaluate the company's performance by type of business worldwide. Across the top of his financial chart, he identified Coca-Cola's lines of business. Down the side, he listed key financial measures, such as cash-flow reliability, capital requirements, etc. But to make the concept work, Goizueta needed reliable information from operations worldwide.

A team consisting of a project manager and three senior accountants worked for eight months to develop an entirely new accounting manual. A universal chart of accounts was set up so that each account in the balance sheet and income statement would be shown consistently by Coca-Cola subsidiaries around the world. Based on the chart of accounts, the team wrote definitions of each account and developed policies and procedures governing the use of each and the flow of information into the financial statements. A separate section was written describing how to translate financial statements from local currencies into U.S. dollars. Drafts of the report were given to audit, legal, and tax managers for their comments, and other field accounting managers were asked for their input before a final policy was completed.

Introduction

The accountant is essential in providing information to financial decision makers.

Managers cannot make good decisions without the availability of adequate and timely information regarding accounting and taxation. Although accounting and information systems specialists provide the information, all managers need to understand which data are needed and the problems specialists face in gathering that data from around the world. The accounting and finance functions of any MNE such as Coca-Cola are very closely related. Each relies on the other in fulfilling its own responsibilities. The financial manager of any company, whether domestic or international, is responsible for procuring and managing the company's financial resources. That manager relies on the accountant to provide the information necessary to manage financial resources. It is also interesting to note that Doug Ivester, President and Chief Operations Officer of Coca-Cola and heir-apparent to Roberto Goizueta, comes from an accounting background. He was hired from the public accounting firm of Ernst & Young (then Ernst & Whinney), where he was the managing partner of the Coca-Cola audit. After serving as chief financial officer, he moved into top management and has been responsible for developing and implementing many of Coca-Cola's key strategies.

The actual and potential flow of assets across national boundaries complicates the finance and accounting functions. The MNE must learn to cope with differing inflation rates, exchange rate changes, currency controls, expropriation risks, customs duties, levels of sophistication, and local requirements.

The controller of an international company must be concerned about different currencies and accounting systems.

A company's accounting or controllership function is responsible for collecting and analyzing data for internal and external users. As noted in Chapter 15, foreign managers and subsidiaries are usually evaluated based on data provided by the controller's office. Reports must be generated for internal consideration, local governmental needs, creditors, employees, stockholders, and prospective investors. The controller must be concerned about the impact of many different currencies and inflation rates on the statements as well as being familiar with different countries' accounting systems.

Factors Influencing the Development of Accounting around the World

Both the form and the substance of financial statements are different in different countries.

One problem that an MNE such as Coca-Cola faces is that accounting standards and practices vary around the world; for example, financial statements in the United Kingdom do not look the same as those in the United States. Note the balance sheet of the British company Cable & Wireless in Table 19.2 to see how different it is from that of Coca-Cola in Table 19.1. Coke's balance sheet is in a balance format of assets = liabilities + share-owners' equity, whereas the balance sheet for Cable & Wireless is in an analytical format of fixed assets + current assets − current liabilities = net current assets − noncurrent liabilities = capital and reserves. The Cable & Wireless balance sheet is in reverse liquidity in comparison with Coke's balance sheet (fixed assets before current assets). Also, some terms are different, such as inventory for Coca-Cola and stocks for Cable & Wireless; share-owners' equity for Coca-Cola, and capital and reserves for Cable & Wireless; and receivables and payables for Coca-Cola, and debtors and creditors for Cable & Wireless. In addition, Coca-Cola only presents a set of consolidated financial statements, whereas Cable & Wireless provides both company (meaning parent company) and group (consolidated) financial statements. Some observers argue that this is a minor matter, a problem of form rather than substance. In fact, however, the substance also differs, in that assets are measured differently and income is determined differently in different countries.

A good example of this involves Montedison, the Italian chemical and agro-industrial giant, which was sued by the U.S. Securities and Exchange Commission (SEC) over Montedison's accounting practices. Because Montedison wanted to raise capital in the United States, it had to comply with U.S. accounting practices. However, the SEC claimed that Montedison falsified its U.S. regulatory filings through "extensive and long-term efforts to conceal hundreds of millions of dollars of payments that, among other things, were used to bribe politicians in Italy and other persons." The problem was not just the bribes themselves but the recording of the bribes as a bad loan, which affected the truthfulness of their financial statements.[2] These disclosures resulted in a scandal not only in the United States, but also in Italy.

Generally accepted accounting principles are those established in each country that must be followed by companies in generating their financial statements.

These variations put the MNE in a difficult position because it needs to prepare and understand reports generated according to the local accounting standards as well as prepare financial statements consistent with **generally accepted accounting principles (GAAP)** in the home country in order to provide information for home-country users of financial statements. Each country develops its own GAAP, which are the accounting standards recognized by the profession as being required in the

Table 19.2
Cable & Wireless plc Balance Sheets

		Balance Sheets			
		Group		**Company**	
at 31 March	Note	1996 £m	1995 £m	1996 £m	1995 £m
Fixed assets					
Tangible assets	15	5,338	4,941	143	125
Investments	16	1,287	697	1,947	1,252
		6,625	5,638	2,090	1,377
Current assets					
Stocks	17	87	117	–	–
Debtors—due within one year	18	1,013	882	242	229
—due after more than one year	18	254	211	43	43
Current asset investments	19	–	36	–	29
Short-term deposits	20	924	882	86	437
Cash at bank and in hand	20	117	109	7	4
		2,395	2,237	378	742
Creditors: amounts falling due within one year	21				
Loans and obligations under finance leases		419	321	12	18
Other creditors		1,838	1,424	366	304
		2,257	1,745	378	322
Net current assets		138	492	–	420
Total assets less current liabilities		6,763	6,130	2,090	1,797
Creditors: amounts falling due after more than one year	22				
Convertible bonds		138	150	138	150
Other loans and obligations under finance leases		1,551	1,190	467	253
Other creditors		150	33	11	11
Provisions for liabilities and charges					
Deferred taxation	23	155	130	24	19
Other provisions	24	50	90	17	13
		2,044	1,593	657	446
		4,719	4,537	1,433	1,351
Net assets					
Capital and reserves					
Called up share capital	25	555	549	555	549
Share premium account	26	429	387	429	387
Associated undertakings	26	(128)	(67)	–	–
Profit and loss account	26	2,403	2,470	449	415
Equity shareholders' funds		3,259	3,339	1,433	1,351
Equity minority interests		1,460	1,198	–	–
		4,719	4,537	1,433	1,351

Source: Cable & Wireless plc, *Annual Report,* 1996, p. 49.

preparation of financial statements for external users. Each country's GAAP is a function of the factors discussed in the following sections. The more the GAAP differs from country to country, the more costly and difficult it is for an MNE to generate financial statements.

Accounting Objectives

Accounting is basically a process of identifying, recording, and interpreting economic events, and its goals and purposes should be clearly stated in the objectives of any accounting system. According to the Financial Accounting Standards Board (FASB), the private-sector body that establishes accounting standards in the United States, financial reporting should provide information useful in the following areas:

- Investment and credit decisions
- Assessment of cash-flow prospects
- Evaluation of enterprise resources, claims to those resources, and changes in them[3]

The users of these data identified by the board are primarily investors and creditors, although other users might be considered important. The **International Accounting Standards Committee (IASC),** a standard-setting organization composed of professional accounting organizations from over eighty countries, includes employees as well as investors and creditors as critical users. Also named as users of this information are suppliers, customers, regulatory and taxing authorities, and many others.

Although the question of whether there should be a uniform set of accounting standards and practices for all classes of users worldwide, or even for one class of users, has been discussed widely, no consensus has been reached. To understand the different accounting principles and how they affect an MNE's operations, you must be aware of some of the forces leading to the development of accounting practices internationally (see Fig. 19.2). Although all the factors shown in the figure are important, they vary in importance by country. For example, investors are an important source of influence in the United States and the United Kingdom, but creditors—primarily banks—are more important in Germany and Switzerland. Also, taxation is a major source of influence on accounting standards and practices in Japan and France, but it is less important in the United States. Certain international factors also are important, such as former colonial influence and foreign investment. For example, most former members of the British Commonwealth have an accounting system similar to the United Kingdom's; former French colonies use the French model, and so forth.

Cultural Differences

A major source of influence on accounting standards and practices is culture. Of special interest to international investors are the differences in measurement and

The FASB sets accounting standards in the United States.

The IASC is an international private-sector organization that sets accounting standards.

Critical users of information are creditors, investors, and employees. Additional users are suppliers, customers, and regulatory and tax authorities.

Equity markets are an important source of influence on accounting in the United States and the United Kingdom. Banks are more influential in Germany and Switzerland, and taxation is a major influence in Japan and France.

Former colonial relationships influence accounting.

Culture influences measurement and disclosure practices.
Measurement—how to value assets
Disclosure—the presentation of information and discussion of results

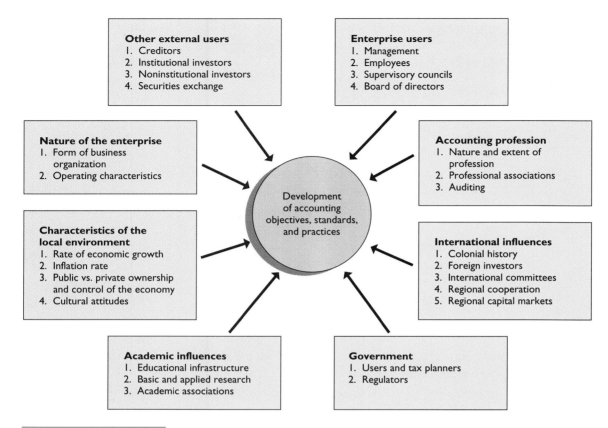

**Figure 19.2
Environmental
Influences on
Accounting Practices**
The importance of any of
these environmental influ-
ences on accounting prac-
tices varies by country.

Source: Lee H. Radebaugh, "Environmental Factors Influencing
the Development of Accounting
Objectives, Standards, and Practices—The Peruvian Case," *The
International Journal of Accounting,*
Fall 1975, p. 41.

Secrecy and transparency
refer to the degree to which
corporations disclose information to the public.

Optimism and conservatism
refer to the degree of caution companies display in
valuing assets and recognizing income.

disclosure practices among countries. Measurement refers to such issues as how to
value assets, including inventory and fixed assets. Disclosure refers to the presentation of information and discussion of results in documents that are prepared for
external users of financial data, such as the annual report.

Figure 19.3 depicts the possible locations of the accounting practices of various
groupings of countries in a matrix of the cultural values of secrecy/transparency
and optimism/conservatism. With respect to accounting, secrecy and transparency
refer to the degree to which companies disclose information to the public. Countries such as Germany, Switzerland, and Japan tend to have less disclosure (illustrating the cultural value of secrecy) than do the United States and the United Kingdom—Anglo-Saxon countries—which are more transparent or open with respect
to disclosure. This is illustrated by the more extensive footnotes in reports of the
Anglo-Saxon countries than is the case elsewhere.

Optimism and conservatism (in an accounting, not a political, sense) refer to the
degree of caution companies exhibit in valuing assets and recognizing income—an
illustration of the measurement issues mentioned above. More conservative countries from an accounting point of view tend to understate assets and income,
whereas optimistic countries tend to be more liberal in their recognition of
income. The problem with comparing this cultural value is that accounting is
inherently conservative, so we are really looking at the degree of conservatism.

Figure 19.3
Cultural Differences in Measurement and Disclosure for Accounting Systems
Anglo-Saxon countries (such as the United Kingdom and the United States) have accounting systems that tend to be more transparent and optimistic. Systems in Germanic countries, in contrast, tend to be secretive and conservative.

Source: Lee H. Radebaugh and Sidney J. Gray, *International Accounting and Multinational Enterprises*, 4th ed. (New York: John Wiley & Sons, 1997), p. 82.

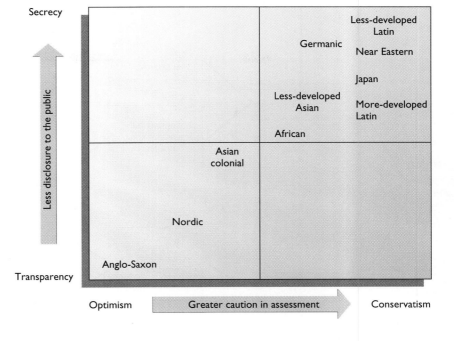

British companies are very optimistic in recognizing income, and U.S. companies are slightly less optimistic. Japanese companies are even less optimistic than U.S. ones.

For example, German companies are funded primarily by banks, and banks are concerned with liquidity. Therefore German companies tend to be very conservative in recording profits—which keeps them from paying taxes and declaring dividends—while piling up cash reserves that can be used to service their bank debt. In contrast, U.S. companies want to show optimistic earnings in order to attract investors. Generally, British companies tend to be more optimistic in earnings recognition than U.S. companies, but U.S. companies are significantly more optimistic than other European companies and Japanese ones. In a very subjective crossnational comparison of earnings that sets the index of earnings of U.S. companies equal to 100, British earnings are at an index level of 125, German earnings are at a level of 87, and Japanese earnings are at 66.[4] Thus there are significant worldwide differences in accounting standards and practices that affect earnings measures.

Classification of Accounting Systems
Although accounting standards and practices differ significantly worldwide, systems used in various countries can be grouped according to common characteristics. Figure 19.4 illustrates one approach to classifying accounting systems. This scheme does not attempt to classify all countries but simply illustrates the concept using several developed Western countries.

In the figure, accounting systems are initially divided into macro-uniform and micro-based systems. Macro-uniform systems are shaped more by governmental influence than are micro-based systems. Except for Sweden's system, macro-uniform systems are influenced by tax law or just a strong legal system. These sys-

Macro-uniform accounting systems are shaped more by governmental influence, whereas micro-based systems rely on pragmatic business practice.

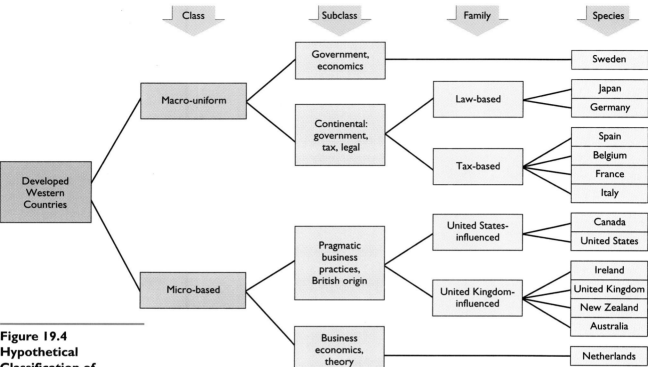

**Figure 19.4
Hypothetical
Classification of
Accounting Systems of
Developed Western
Countries**
Accounting systems can be
classified as macro-uniform
or micro-based depending
on how important govern-
mental influence is.

Source: From C. W. Nobes, "A
Judgmental International Classification of Financial Reporting
Practices," *Journal of Business
Finance and Accounting,* Spring
1983, p. 7. Reprinted with
permission.

Major reporting issues:
• **Language**
• **Currency**
• **Financial statements (balance sheet, income state-
ment, statement of cash
flows)**
• **Financial statement
format**
• **Extent of footnote disclosures**
• **Underlying GAAP on
which the financial statements are based**

tems also tend to be more conservative and secretive about disclosure. Micro-based
systems, except for that of the Netherlands, include features that support pragmatic
business practice and have evolved from the British system. The U.S. system is
closer to the macro-uniform systems than is the British system, however, because of
the strong influence of the Securities and Exchange Commission (SEC), a federal
government agency that regulates securities offerings within the United States.

The bottom line is that MNEs need to adjust to different accounting systems
around the world. Thus the accounting function is made more complex and costly
to perform. An MNE's parent company must gather data from far-flung subsidiaries
and affiliates and convert those data into a format consistent with the home country's preferred accounting system.

The financial statements of a country include not only the statements themselves, but also the accompanying footnotes. Thus the financial statements of one
country differ from those in another country in six major ways:

• Language
• Currency
• Financial statements (balance sheet, income statement, statement of cash flows)
• Financial statement format
• Extent of footnote disclosures
• Underlying GAAP on which the financial statements are based

A company wishing to provide financial information for investors throughout the world needs to deal with all six issues. If the company does not want to list and trade its equity securities (stocks in the United States, shares in the United Kingdom, as noted in Tables 19.1 and 19.2) outside of its home country, it probably will not do anything special for foreign investors. If it wishes to list on a foreign stock exchange, however, its disclosures must conform with the requirements of the exchange. In addition, the company may wish to voluntarily disclose information over and above what is required in order to attract investors.

London tends to be the major country where companies will list first outside of their home country. However, the United States is also increasing the number of foreign listings at a rapid pace. Thus a company listing in London or New York will translate the financial statements from their home language to English. However, they will typically keep the numbers in the home currency rather than translate everything into dollars. In Table 19.2, for example, Cable & Wireless provides its balance sheet in British pounds (£). But since Cable & Wireless also has listed securities in the United States, it provides information in its footnotes in U.S. dollars and British pounds (see Table 19.3). However, that is the only information it provides in dollars.

As noted above, the major financial statements that a company provides its investors are the balance sheet, the income statement, and the statement of cash flows. Most countries require the balance sheet and income statement, but not all require a statement of cash flows. However, that is becoming more common. Foreign corporations that want to list in New York must provide a statement of cash flows since that is required for U.S. companies as well. However, foreign registrants may also provide more information than is required by the local exchange. For example, in Table 19.2 we noted that Cable & Wireless provides both parent company and group (consolidated) financial statements. That is common for a British company but not for a U.S. company.

Financial statement format is not a big issue, but it can be confusing to read a balance sheet prepared in an analytical format, as is the case with Cable & Wireless, when you are used to seeing a balance sheet in the balance format, as is the case with Coca-Cola. A major area of difference is the nature of footnotes. Footnote disclosures in the United States tend to be the most comprehensive in the world. When a foreign corporation simply lists but does not trade its securities in the United States, it is allowed to use the footnote disclosures that are prepared in its home country. When it wants to trade securities in the United States, however, it must prepare the same extensive footnotes that a U.S. company must provide.

Major approaches to dealing with accounting and reporting differences:
- **Mutual recognition**
- **Reconciliation to local GAAP**
- **Recast financial statements in terms of local GAAP**

Finally, the most problematic area is that of differences in underlying GAAP. The biggest barrier to raising capital in different countries is dealing with the accounting requirements of each country. Some countries care more about those differences than others. In Germany and the Netherlands, for example, the principle of mutual recognition applies. That means that a foreign registrant that wants to list and trade securities on the local exchange need only provide information prepared according

Table 19.3
Additional Information for U.S. Investors, Cable & Wireless plc 1996

The effects of these differing accounting principles are as follows:			
	1996 US$m	1996 £m	1995 Restated £m
Net income as reported under UK GAAP	931	607	252
US GAAP adjustments:			
Amortisation of goodwill	(31)	(20)	(17)
Goodwill written off in respect of sale of subsidiary undertakings	5	3	21
Capitalisation of interest	3	2	1
Deferred tax – full provision	(47)	(31)	(86)
– tax effect of other US GAAP reconciling items	11	7	(4)
Pension costs	(10)	(7)	13
Restructuring costs	(33)	(21)	22
Other	5	3	(4)
Minority interests	5	3	10
Net income under US GAAP	839	546	208
Earnings per share under US GAAP	$0.37	24.2p	9.4p
Earnings per ADR* under US GAAP	$1.11	72.6p	28.2p

The effect on shareholders' equity of the difference between
UK GAAP and US GAAP is as follows:

	1996 US$m	1996 £m	1995 Restated £m
Shareholders' equity as reported under UK GAAP	5,003	3,259	3,339
US GAAP adjustments:			
Goodwill	1,477	962	409
Capitalisation of interest	310	202	200
Deferred tax – full provision	(1,210)	(788)	(755)
– tax effect of other US GAAP reconciling items	(165)	(108)	(86)
Proposed final dividend	237	154	137
Pension costs	(32)	(21)	(15)
Restructuring costs	7	5	22
Unrealistic gains on equity securities	81	53	39
Other	(28)	(18)	(15)
Minority interest	176	115	92
Shareholders' equity under US GAAP	5,856	3,815	3,367

An exchange rate of US$ 1.5348 has been used to translate £ to US$. Such translations are for convenience only and should not be constructed as representations that the £ amounts have been converted into US$ at that or any other rate.
*Computed on the basis that one American Depositary Receipt (ADR) represents three ordinary shares.

Source: Cable & Wireless plc, *Annual Report* 1996, p. 85.

to the GAAP of the home country. However, other exchanges, like the U.S. exchanges, require foreign registrants to either reconcile their home country financial statements with the local GAAP or provide financial statements that are prepared in accordance with local GAAP. This information is provided in Form 20-F, which must be filed with the Securities and Exchange Commission. In Table 19.3, for example, Cable & Wireless reconciles its British net income and shareholders' equity to U.S. GAAP net income and shareholders' equity. This is included at the end of its footnotes. Other companies, however, prepare their actual financial statements according to U.S. GAAP when listing on a U.S. exchange and thus do not have to provide a footnote reconciliation. This is more common with Japanese companies.

Harmonization of Differences

Despite the many differences in accounting standards and practices, a number of forces are leading to harmonization:

Major forces leading to harmonization:
- **Investor orientation**
- **Global integration of capital markets**
- **MNEs' need for foreign capital**
- **Regional political and economic harmonization**
- **MNEs' desire to reduce accounting and reporting costs**

- A movement to provide information compatible with the needs of investors
- The global integration of capital markets, which means that investors have easier and faster access to investment opportunities around the world and therefore need financial information that is more comparable
- The need of MNEs to raise capital outside of their home-country capital markets while generating as few different financial statements as possible
- Regional political and economic harmonization, such as the efforts of the EU, which affects accounting as well as trade and investment issues
- Pressure from MNEs for more uniform standards to allow greater ease and reduced costs in general reporting in each country and in reporting to be used by investors in the parent company's country

The EU is harmonizing accounting in order to promote the free flow of capital.

Impelled by these developments, some countries and organizations are working to harmonize accounting standards on a regional as well as an international level. Regionally, the most ambitious effort is taking place in the EU. The European Commission is empowered to set directives, which are orders to member countries to bring their laws into line with EU requirements within a certain transition period. The initial accounting directives addressed the type and format of financial statements, the measurement bases on which the financial statements should be prepared, the importance of consolidated financial statements, and the requirement that auditors must ensure that the financial statements reflect a true and fair view of the operations of the company being audited.

Other countries in Europe, including those of Eastern Europe and the former Soviet Union, are following the lead of the EU.

The EU's influence is being felt beyond the borders of its members. The EFTA and Eastern European countries are attempting to adopt EU accounting directives in preparation for becoming members. In addition, Eastern European countries and those of the former Soviet Union are moving from centrally planned to market economies, and they need an accounting system that will aid in the transition. The EU directives provide some guidance in this area.

Even though the EU has improved the comparability of financial statements, the directives do not cover many important issues. In addition, some directives allow options, and member countries interpret the directives differently. Thus EU companies listing outside of their home countries must still provide two sets of financial statements—the home country statements and a reconciliation. In order to enhance the harmonization process, the EU has decided to put its weight behind the International Accounting Standards Committee (IASC). The reason for choosing the IASC is that the EU can influence standards since it is represented on the IASC, and it also avoids funding and developing a competing standards-setting body.[5]

The International Accounting Standards Committee (IASC), organized in 1973 by the professional accounting bodies of Mexico and several primarily industrial countries, has worked toward harmonizing accounting standards. IASC member countries are shown on Map 19.1. The organization comprises 119 professional accounting organizations representing 86 countries. Initially, the IASC wanted to develop standards that would have rapid and broad acceptance; thus it seemed to focus mostly on improved disclosure. More recently, it has been interested in tackling some more substantive issues.

The IASC has no legislative mandate like that of the EU, so it must rely on goodwill for acceptance of its standards. However, a number of countries have used the standards as models for their own legislation. For example, Singapore has successfully adopted IASC standards. Other countries have modified the standards as appropriate for their own national settings.

The most significant development for the IASC is an agreement with the International Organization of Securities Commissions (IOSCO) to complete a core set of accounting standards that would be acceptable to IOSCO and thus to national securities regulators, including the SEC in the United States. The goal is to approve the core set of standards by March 1998. That would allow companies to list on any exchange in the world as long as they prepared their financial statements according to the core set of standards.[6] In the first step of the process, the IASC examined its original standards and revised them to eliminate alternative treatments and tighten up the regulations. As an example of wider recognition of the revised IASC standards, the U.S. SEC allows foreign registrants to provide cash flow statements prepared according to International Accounting Standard (IAS) #7 rather than have to use the relevant U.S. standard. The goal of IOSCO is to extend that concept to a broader core of standards, reducing the cost and speeding up the process of cross-border listings.

Transactions in Foreign Currencies

A major accounting problem for international business arises from operating in different currencies. In addition to eliminating or minimizing foreign-exchange risk, a company must concern itself with the proper recording and subsequent accounting of assets, liabilities, revenues, and expenses that are measured or denominated in foreign currencies. These transactions can result from the purchase and sale of goods and services as well as the borrowing and lending of foreign currency.

Map 19.1 Membership of the International Accounting Standards Committee

The IASC membership consists of 119 accountancy bodies from 86 countries. For example, the members from the United States are the American Institute of Certified Public Accountants, the National Association of State Boards of Accountancy, and the Institute of Management of Accountants, the Institute of Internal Auditors. The IASC board is made up of representatives of accountancy bodies from twelve countries, the Nordic Federation of Public Accountants, and up to four other organizations with an interest in financial reporting.

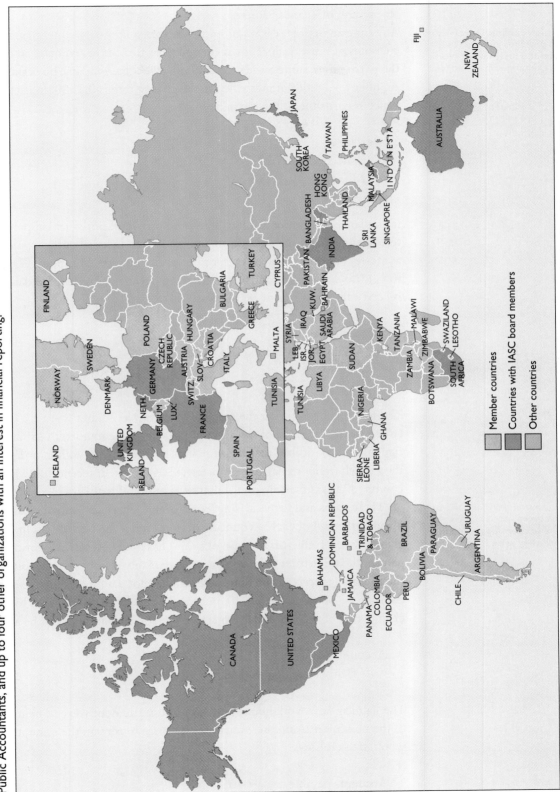

See <http://www.ifac.org/MemberBodies.html>for list of member countries of IASC (Same as membership of International Federation of Accountants–IFAC)

Recording of Transactions

Any time an importer is required to pay for equipment or merchandise in a foreign currency, it must trade its own currency for that of the exporter in order to make the payment. Assume Sundance Ski Lodge, a U.S. company, buys skis from a French supplier for 28,000 francs when the exchange rate is 0.1900 dollar per franc. Sundance records the following in its books:

Purchases	5320	
Accounts payable		5320
FF28,000 @ $0.1900		

If Sundance pays immediately, there is no problem. But what happens if the exporter extends thirty-days' credit to Sundance? The original entry would be the same as above, but during the next thirty days, anything could happen. If the rate changed to 0.1800 dollar per franc by the time the payment was due, Sundance would record a final settlement as follows:

Accounts payable	5320	
Gain on foreign exchange		280
Cash		5040

The merchandise stays at the original value of $5320, but there is a difference between the dollar value of the account payable to the exporter ($5320) and the actual number of dollars that the importer must come up with in order to purchase the French francs to pay the exporter ($5040). The difference between the two accounts ($280) is the gain on foreign exchange and is always recognized as income.

These gains and losses arising from foreign-currency transactions must be recognized at the end of each accounting period even if the payable (in the case of a purchase) or receivable (in the case of a sale) has not been settled. For most U.S. companies, this adjustment is made monthly. For the example above, assume the end of the month has arrived and Sundance still has not paid the French exporter. The skis continue to be valued at $5320, but the payable has to be updated to the new exchange rate of 0.1800 dollar per franc. The journal entry would be as follows:

Accounts payable	280	
Gain on foreign exchange		280

The liability now would be worth $5040. If settlement were to be made at the end of the next month and the exchange rate were to remain the same, the final entry would be as follows:

Accounts payable	5040	
Cash		5040

If the U.S. company were an exporter and anticipated receiving foreign currency, the corresponding entries (using the same information as in the example above) would be as follows:

Accounts receivable	5320	
Sales		5320

Cash	5040	
Loss on foreign exchange	280	
Accounts receivable		5320

In this case, a loss results because the company received less cash than if it had collected its money immediately.

Correct Procedures for U.S. Companies

The FASB requires foreign-currency transactions of U.S. companies to be recorded at the original spot exchange rate and subsequent gains and losses on foreign-currency receivables or payables to be taken to the income statement.

The procedures that U.S. companies must follow to account for foreign-currency transactions are found in Financial Accounting Standards Board (FASB) Statement No. 52, "Foreign Currency Translation," which the board adopted in December 1981. Statement No. 52 requires companies to record the initial transaction at the spot-exchange rate in effect on the transaction date and record receivables and payables at subsequent balance-sheet dates at the spot-exchange rate on those dates. Any foreign-exchange gains and losses that arise from carrying receivables or payables during a period in which the exchange rate changes are taken directly to the income statement.[7]

Procedures vary in other countries, however. For example, some countries recognize transactions losses but not gains. Other countries allow a loss that occurs from a major devaluation to adjust the value of the underlying asset rather than be taken directly to income. The IASC pretty much follows the procedure required in the United States, but it allows a company to write up the value of an asset by the amount of a foreign-exchange loss resulting from a one-time devaluation of the currency as described above. As more countries move to a freely floating exchange-rate system, as discussed in Chapter 10, there are fewer examples of major devaluations occurring. One example that occurred recently, however, is the devaluation of the Mexican peso in 1994. According to IASC guidelines, a Mexican importer of capital equipment that suffered a foreign-exchange loss due to the December devaluation could have increased the carrying value of the equipment by the amount of the loss rather than take that entire loss to the income statement immediately.

Translation of Foreign-Currency Financial Statements

Even though U.S.-based MNEs receive reports originally developed in a variety of different currencies, they eventually must end up with one set of financial statements in U.S. dollars in order to help management and investors get an aggregate

Translation is the process of restating foreign-currency statements into U.S. dollars.

Consolidation is the process of combining financial statements of different operations into one statement.

view of worldwide activities in a common currency. The process of restating foreign-currency financial statements into U.S. dollars is known as **translation.** The combination of all of these translated financial statements into one is known as **consolidation,** as discussed in the Coca-Cola case.

Translation in the United States is a two-step process:

1. The foreign-currency financial statements are recast into statements consistent with U.S. GAAP.
2. All foreign-currency amounts are translated into U.S. dollars.

FASB Statement No. 52 describes how companies must translate their foreign-currency financial statements into dollars.

Translation Methods

The functional currency is the currency of the primary economic environment in which the entity operates.

Statement No. 52 allows either of two methods to be used to translate financial statements: the current-rate method or the temporal method. The method the company chooses depends on the **functional currency** of the foreign operation, which is the currency of the primary economic environment in which that entity operates. For example, one of Coca-Cola's largest operations outside the United States is in Japan. The primary economic environment of the Japanese subsidiary is Japan, and the functional currency is the Japanese yen. The FASB identifies several factors that are examined to determine whether the parent's currency or the foreign operation's currency is used the most, and thus is the functional currency. Among the major factors are cash flows, sales prices, sales market data, expenses, financing, and intercompany transactions. For example, if the cash flows and/or expenses are primarily in the foreign operation's currency, that is the functional currency. If they are in the parent's currency, that is the functional currency.

The current-rate method is used when the local currency is the functional currency.

The temporal method is used when the parent's reporting currency is the functional currency.

If the functional currency is that of the local operating environment, the company must use the **current-rate method.** The current-rate method provides that all assets and liabilities are translated at the current exchange rate, which is the spot exchange rate on the balance sheet date. All income statement items are translated at the average exchange rate, and owners' equity is translated at the rate in effect when capital stock was issued and retained earnings were accumulated. For example, Coca-Cola states in its *Annual Report* that it distributes its products in more than 195 countries and uses approximately 48 functional currencies. In Germany and the United Kingdom, the functional currency would be the mark and the pound, respectively, because Coca-Cola's primary operating environments would be the local environments. Thus Coca-Cola would use the current-rate method to translate the financial statements of operations in Germany and the United Kingdom from marks and pounds to dollars.

Although the spot rate is used for translation purposes, which spot rate does a company select when multiple exchange rates exist? In general, the exchange rate used to translate foreign-currency financial statements is the rate that must be used for dividends sent back to the parent company. In some countries, this exchange rate also is called the *financial rate*.

If the functional currency is the parent's currency, the MNE must use the **temporal method.** The temporal method provides that only monetary assets (cash, marketable securities, and receivables) and liabilities are translated at the current exchange rate. Inventory and property, plant, and equipment are translated at the historical rate, that is, the exchange rate in effect when the assets were acquired. In general, net income also is translated at the average exchange rate, but cost of goods sold and depreciation expenses are translated at the appropriate historical exchange rate.

Figure 19.5 summarizes the selection of translation method, depending on the choice of functional currency. As explained above, if the functional currency is the local currency of the foreign subsidiary (also referred to sometimes a the *foreign currency*), the current rate method is used. If the functional currency is the reporting currency of the parent company, the temporal method is used.

Tables 19.4 and 19.5 show a balance sheet and income statement developed under both approaches in order to compare the differences in translation methodologies. Some of the key assumptions are as follows:

$1.5000	Historical exchange rate when fixed assets were acquired and capital stock was issued
$1.6980	Current exchange rate on December 31, 1996
$1.5617	Average exchange rate during 1996
$1.5606	Exchange rate during which ending inventory was acquired
$1.5600	Historical exchange rate for cost of goods sold

Also, the beginning balance in retained earnings for both methods is assumed to be $40,000. The British pound was falling in value between the time when the fixed assets were acquired and the end of the year, so the balance sheet reflects a negative

**Figure 19.5
Selection of Translation
Methology**

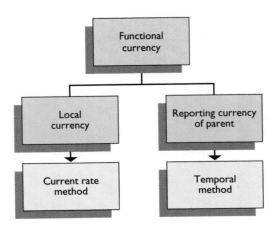

Table 19.4
Balance Sheet, December 31, 1996

	Pounds	Temporal Method		Current-rate Method	
		Rate	Dollars	Rate	Dollars
Cash	20,000	1.6980	33,960	1.6980	33,960
Accounts receivable	40,000	1.6980	67,920	1.6980	67,920
Inventories	40,000	1.5606	62,424	1.6980	67,920
Fixed assets	100,000	1.5000	150,000	1.6980	169,800
Accumulated dep.	(20,000)	1.5000	(30,000)	1.6980	(33,960)
Total	180,000		284,304		305,640
Accounts payable	30,000	1.6980	50,940	1.6980	50,940
Long-term debt	44,000	1.6980	74,712	1.6980	74,712
Capital stock	60,000	1.5000	90,000	1.5000	90,000
Retained earnings	46,000	*	68,652	*	77,481
Accum. trans. adj.					12,507
Total	180,000		284,304		305,640

*Retained earnings is the sum of all income earned in prior years and translated into dollars and this year's income. There is no single exchange rate used to translate retained earnings into dollars.

accumulated translation adjustment under the current-rate method. This is consistent with the idea that assets were losing value in a weak currency.

Disclosure of Foreign-Exchange Gains and Losses

A major difference between the two translation methods is the recognition of foreign-exchange gains and losses. Under the current-rate method, the gain or loss is called an accumulated translation adjustment and is taken directly to the balance sheet as a separate line item in owners' equity. Under the temporal method, the

> With the current-rate method, the translation gain or loss is taken to owners' equity.

Table 19.5
Income Statement, 1996

	Pounds	Temporal method		Current-rate method	
		Rate	Dollars	Rate	Dollars
Sales	230,000	1.5617	359,191	1.5617	359,191
Expenses					
CGS	(110,000)	1.5600	(171,600)	1.5617	(171,787)
Depreciation	(10,000)	1.5000	(15,000)	1.5617	(15,617)
Other	(80,000)	1.5617	(124,936)	1.5617	(124,936)
Taxes	(6,000)	1.5617	(9,370)	1.5617	(9,370)
	24,000		38,285		37,481
Transl. gain (Loss)			(9,633)		
Net income	24,000		28,652		37,481

With the temporal method, the translation gain or loss is taken to income.

gain or loss is taken directly to the income statement and thus affects earnings per share. For example, Coca-Cola Company recorded a negative accumulated translation adjustment balance of $424 million on December 31, 1995. This is illustrated in Table 19.1, in the owners' equity portion of the balance sheet for Coca-Cola for 1995. In its *Annual Report,* Coca-Cola also disclosed that it recognized in "other income" a foreign-exchange loss of $21 million in 1995. Although part of the gain shown in the table came from foreign-currency transactions, a portion of it came from the company's use of the temporal method of translation for some of its operations.

Performance Evaluation and Control in the Internationalization Process

Major performance evalua-
tion financial measures:
• **Budgets**
• **Profits**
• **Return on investment (ROI)**

Chapter 15 discussed some of the reports MNEs use as part of the control process. Table 19.6 identifies the major financial measures these companies use to evaluate foreign subsidiaries and their managers. Budgets, profits, and return on investment (ROI) dominate the list. It is interesting to note how currency translation can affect the financial ratios. Using the information in Tables 19.4 and 19.5, it is possible to compute the ROI (net income/total assets) in British pounds, U.S. dollars under the current-rate method, and U.S. dollars under the temporal method. The ROI is 13.3 percent in pounds. However, in dollars it is 12.3 percent using the current-rate method but only 10.1 percent using the temporal method. Net income is lower and total assets are higher under the temporal method than under the current-rate method in this example. When evaluating subsidiaries' results, managers need to be sure to compare like measures.

Table 19.6
Measures Used to Evaluate Foreign Subsidiaries and Their Managers

Financial measure	Percentage of the sixty-four MNEs using each measure	
	Foreign subsidiary	Foreign-subsidiary managers
Return-on-investment (ROI)	74	67
Profits	78	66
Budgeted ROI compared to actual ROI	66	64
Budgeted profit compared to actual profit	86	87
Other measures	36	36

Source: From Wagdy M. Abdallah and Donald E. Keller, "Measures Used to Evaluate Foreign Subsidiaries and Foreign Subsidiary Managers," *Management Accounting,* October 1985, p. 27. Reprinted with permission of the Institute of Management Accountants.

Transfer Prices

A transfer price is a price on goods and services sold by one member of a corporate family to another.

A major impediment to performance evaluation is the extensive use of transfer pricing in international operations. A **transfer price** is a price on goods and services sold by one member of a corporate family to another, such as from a parent to its subsidiary in a foreign country. Because the price is between related entities, it is not necessarily an **arm's-length price,** that is, a price between two companies that do not have an ownership interest in each other. The assumption is that an arm's-length price is more likely than a transfer price to accurately reflect the market.

Companies establish arbitrary transfer prices primarily because of differences in taxation between countries. For example, if the corporate tax rate is higher in the parent company's country than in the subsidiary's country, the parent will set a low transfer price on products it sells the subsidiary in order to keep profits low in its country and high in the subsidiary's country. The parent also will set a high transfer price on products sold to it by the subsidiary.

Arbitrary transfer pricing affects performance evaluation.

Companies also set arbitrary transfer prices for competitive reasons or because of restrictions on currency flows. In the former case, if the parent ships products at a low transfer price to the subsidiary, the subsidiary will be able to sell the products to local consumers for less, thus improving its competitive position. In the latter case, if the subsidiary's country has currency controls on dividend flows, the parent can get more hard currency out of the country by shipping in products at a high transfer price or by receiving products at a low transfer price. Because prices are manipulated for reasons other than market conditions, arbitrary transfer pricing makes evaluating subsidiary and management performance difficult. In addition, the tax authorities of a country (such as the Internal Revenue Service in the United States) can audit the transactions of an MNE to determine whether the prices were made on an arm's-length basis. If not, they can assess a penalty and collect back taxes from the company.

Budgets

Budgets may be established in the local currency, the parent currency, or both.

The most important financial measure is the budget. MNEs must determine the appropriate currency in which the budget should be prepared: the local currency of the country in which the subsidiary is established or the reporting currency of the parent company (the parent currency). Using the local currency is advantageous because the subsidiary's management operates in that currency and it is more indicative of the overall operating environment than is the parent currency. Another argument for using the local currency is that the exchange rate is something over which local management has no control, so it would not be wise to have a key uncontrollable item as part of the budgeting and evaluation process.

On the other hand, it is often difficult for top management in the parent's country to understand budgets generated in different currencies. This is especially true for a geographically diverse company such as Coca-Cola. Translating the budget into the parent currency enables top management to compare the performance of subsidiaries from all over the world and forces the subsidiaries' managers to think in terms of the parent currency.

Arbitrary transfer pricing can create legal and ethical problems. In the United States and many other countries, companies are expected to establish transfer prices on an arm's-length basis. Doing this ensures that taxes are paid on profits based on market decisions. However, when companies manipulate profits in order to minimize global tax payments and maximize cash flows, they may be breaking the law. Laws in this regard are much more rigid in Canada, France, Germany, the United Kingdom, and the United States. The U.S. government, for example, requires that companies use an arm's-length price on intracompany transactions between the United States and foreign countries; otherwise, the IRS will allocate profits between the two taxing jurisdictions. Sometimes foreign companies underinvoice shipments to the United States in order to minimize customs payments. In that case, the U.S. Customs Service can fine them and force them to correct the invoice so that the proper duty is paid.

ETHICAL DILEMMAS & SOCIAL RESPONSIBILITY

Some countries, such as Italy, Japan, and Korea, are less interested in rigid transfer-pricing policies. Others, such as Ireland, Puerto Rico, and a few other tax-haven countries, have no transfer-pricing policies. Thus an MNE needs to determine whether it is ethical to transfer profits to low-tax countries through arbitrary transfer-pricing policies. By shifting profits to a low-tax country, the MNE is not harming tax collection in that country, but it is harming tax collection in the high-tax country from which the profits are shifted. In trying to maximize cash flows, management of an MNE is likely to assume that ethical means legal. If there are no legal requirements for transfer-pricing policies in a particular country, management is likely to assume that the absence of law implies permission to pursue the company's self-interest.

In some cases, an MNE might take advantage of transfer-pricing policies to transfer cash out of weak-currency developing countries. If a developing country has currency controls and does not allow cash to be shipped out in the form of dividends, a company might be tempted to charge a high transfer price on a product shipped to the country as a way of getting cash out. Doing this also results in lower taxable income in the developing countries and lower tax payments, which creates a problem for developing countries that desperately need hard currency. Such behavior by MNEs could be construed as unethical. Further, if a country has laws that establish the need for market-based transfer prices, the actions could be construed as illegal. It is doubtful that an MNE's home country would encourage the use of market-based transfer prices, because a high price on exports to developing countries would result in greater taxable income in the home country.

Budgets and final results can be translated into dollars at the actual exchange rate when the budget was set, a projected exchange rate, or the actual rate at the end of the period.

Generally, the budget is translated into the parent currency and then compared with final results. However, there are many different exchange rates that can be used for establishing the budget and monitoring results. Table 19.7 identifies nine different combinations for establishing the budget and monitoring results using three different exchange rates:

- The actual exchange rate in effect when the budget was established
- A projected, or forecasted, rate that is a prediction of what the exchange rate is expected to be during the period being budgeted
- The exchange rate actually in effect when performance takes place

Of the possibilities identified in the table, the ones most likely to be used are A-3, P-2, and P-3. The advantage of P-2 and P-3 is that management is forced to forecast the exchange rate for budget purposes. Although this is very difficult to do, it is helpful for management in attempting to determine where the company might be at the end of the forecasting period. The difference between P-2 and P-3 is that under P-2, there is no foreign-exchange variance, only an operating variance, whereas under P-3, the foreign-exchange variance is the difference between the forecasted and actual exchange rates. For A-3, the foreign-exchange variance is the difference between the rate in effect when the budget was made and the actual rate at the end of the period. For both A-3 and P-3, performance is measured at the actual exchange rate at the end of the period.

Taxation

Tax planning influences profitability and cash flow.

Tax planning is crucial for any business, since taxes can profoundly affect profitability and cash flow. This is especially true in international business. As complex as

Table 19.7
Possible Combinations of Exchange Rates for the Budget Process

Rate used for determining budget	Actual at time of budget	Projected at time of budget	Actual at end of period
	Rate used to track performance relative to budget		
Actual at time of budget	A-1	A-2	A-3
Projected at time of budget	P-1	P-2	P-3
Actual at end of period (through updating)	E-1	E-2	E-3

Source: From Donald R. Lessard and Peter Lorange, "Currency Changes in Management Control: Resolving the Centralization/Decentralization Dilemma," *The Accounting Review,* 52, July 1977, p. 630. Reprinted with permission.

domestic taxation seems, it is relatively simple compared to the intricacies of international taxation. The international tax specialist must be familiar with both the home country's tax policy relating to foreign operations and the tax laws of each country in which the international company operates.

Taxation has a strong impact on several choices:

- Location of the initial investment
- Legal form of the new enterprise, such as branch or subsidiary
- Method of financing, such as internal versus external sourcing and debt versus equity
- Method of setting transfer prices[8]

This section examines taxation for the company with international operations, emphasizing U.S. tax policy because of the nature and extent of U.S. FDI. However, as any country finds domestic companies generating more and more foreign-source income, it must decide on the principles of accounting for that income. Therefore principles of taxation that U.S.-based MNEs face at home and abroad are, or could be, applicable to companies domiciled in other countries.

When a domestic company decides to sell its products internationally, it can do so directly through exportation of goods and services (including licensing agreements, management contracts, and so on), through foreign branch operations (a legal extension of the parent), and/or through foreign corporations in which it holds an equity interest that may vary from a small percentage to complete ownership.

Exports of Goods and Services

Many companies, such as public accounting firms, advertising agencies, banks, and management consulting firms, deal in services rather than products. Many manufacturing industries also find it easier and more profitable to sell expertise, such as patents or management services, than to sell goods. Generally, payment is received in the form of royalties and fees, and this payment usually is taxed by the foreign government. Because the sale of services is made by the parent, the sale also must be included in the parent's taxable income.

> An FSC can be used by a U.S. exporter to shelter some of its income from taxation.

> The FSC must be engaged in substantial business activity.

To gain tax advantages from exporting, a U.S. company can set up a **foreign sales corporation (FSC)** according to strict IRS guidelines. To qualify as an FSC, a company must be engaged in the exporting of either merchandise or services, such as engineering or architectural services. Also substantial economic activity must occur outside the United States. An FSC cannot be a mailbox company in Switzerland that simply passes documents from the United States to the importing country. It must engage in advertising and sales promotion, processing customer orders and arranging for delivery, transportation, determination and transmittal of final invoices or statements of account and receipt of payments, and the assumption of credit risk.[9] If a foreign corporation qualifies as an FSC, a portion of its income is exempt from U.S. corporate income tax. Also, any dividends distributed by the FSC to its parent company are exempt from U.S. income taxation as long as that income is foreign trade income.

Foreign Branch

Foreign branch income (or loss) is directly included in the parent's taxable income.

A foreign branch is an extension of the parent company rather than an enterprise incorporated in a foreign country. Therefore any income generated by the branch is taxable immediately to the parent, whether or not cash is remitted. However, if the branch suffers a loss, the parent is allowed to deduct that loss from its taxable income, thus reducing its overall tax liability.

Foreign Subsidiary

Tax deferral means that income is not taxed until it is remitted to the parent company as a dividend.

Income earned from a foreign corporation is either taxable or tax-deferred, that is, not taxed until it is remitted to the U.S. investor. Which tax status applies depends on whether the foreign corporation is a controlled foreign corporation and whether the income is active or passive. These factors are discussed next.

A **controlled foreign corporation (CFC)** is any foreign corporation that meets the following two tests:

In a CFC, more than 50 percent of the voting stock is held by U.S. shareholders.

1. More than 50 percent of its voting stock is held by "U.S. shareholders."
2. A "U.S. shareholder" is any U.S. person or company that holds 10 percent or more of the CFC's voting stock.

Table 19.8 shows how this might work. Foreign corporation A is a CFC because it is a wholly owned subsidiary of a U.S. parent company. Foreign corporation B also is a CFC because U.S. persons V, W, and X each own 10 percent or more of the voting stock, which means they qualify as U.S. shareholders and their combined voting stock is more than 50 percent of the total. Foreign corporation C is not a CFC because, even though U.S. persons V and W qualify as U.S. shareholders, their com-

Table 19.8
Determination of Controlled Foreign Corporations
A controlled foreign corporation must have U.S. shareholders holding more than 50 percent of the voting shares.

Shareholder	Percentages of the voting stock		
	Foreign corporation A	Foreign corporation B	Foreign corporation C
U.S. person V	100%	45%	30%
U.S. person W		10	10
U.S. person X		20	8
U.S. person Y			8
Foreign person Z		25	44
Total	100%	100%	100%

bined stock ownership is only 40 percent. U.S. persons X and Y do not qualify as U.S. shareholders because their individual ownership shares are only 8 percent each.

If a foreign corporation qualifies as a CFC, the U.S. tax law requires the U.S. investor to divide the foreign-source income into two categories: active income, and Subpart F (or passive) income. **Active income** is income derived from the active conduct of a trade or business, such as from sales of products manufactured in the foreign country. **Subpart F income,** which is specifically defined in Subpart F of the U.S. Internal Revenue Code, is income from sources other than those connected with the active conduct of a trade or business. Subpart F income includes these major types:

- *Holding company income*—primarily dividends, interest, rents, royalties, and gains on sale of stocks
- *Sales income*—income from foreign sales corporations that are separately incorporated from their manufacturing operations, and the product is manufactured outside of and sold for use outside of the CFC's country of incorporation and the CFC has not performed significant operations on the product
- *Service income*—income from the performance of technical, managerial, or similar services for a company in the same corporate family as the CFC and outside the country in which the CFC is organized

Subpart F income usually derives from the activities of subsidiaries in tax-haven countries such as the Bahamas, the Netherlands Antilles, Panama, and Switzerland, as well as Hong Kong. The tax-haven subsidiary may act as an investment company, as a sales agent or distributor, as an agent for the parent in licensing agreements, or as a holding company of stock in other foreign subsidiaries, which are called grandchild, or second-tier, subsidiaries, as shown in Fig. 19.6. In the latter role, its

Active income is that derived from the active conduct of a trade or business.

Passive income usually is derived from operations in a tax-haven country.

A tax-haven country is one with low taxes or no taxes on foreign-source income.

**Figure 19.6
A Tax-Haven
Subsidiary as
a Holding Company**
A parent company can shelter income from U.S. income taxation by utilizing a tax-haven subsidiary located in a low-tax country, such as Hong Kong.

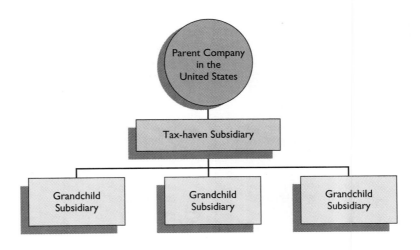

purpose is to concentrate cash from the parent's foreign operations into the low-tax country and to use the cash for global expansion.

Figure 19.7 illustrates how the tax status of a subsidiary's income is determined. All non-CFC income—active and Subpart F—earned by the foreign corporation is deferred until remitted as a dividend to the U.S. shareholder (the parent company in this example). In contrast, a CFC's active income is tax-deferred to the parent, but its Subpart F income is taxable immediately to the parent as soon as it is earned by the CFC. If the income is earned by a foreign branch, it is immediately taxable to the parent company, whether it is active or Subpart F. There is an exception, however. If the foreign-source income is the lower of $1 million or 5 percent of the CFC's gross income, none of it is treated as Subpart F income. Or, if the foreign-source income is subject to a tax liability at least 90 percent of the U.S. tax liability, none of it is subject to U.S. tax.

Tax Credit

The IRS allows a tax credit for corporate income tax paid to another country.

Every country has a sovereign right to levy taxes on all income generated within its borders. Problems arise when companies are owned by foreigners or are branches of foreign companies. This is an important issue for U.S. companies because of the magnitude of U.S. FDI.

A tax credit is a dollar-for-dollar reduction of tax liability and must coincide with the recognition of income.

A U.S. parent that defers recognition of active income until a dividend is declared to it gets credit for a portion of income taxes paid. For example, if 50 percent of the income of the foreign subsidiary is distributed as a dividend to the parent, the parent can claim no more than 50 percent of the tax as a creditable tax. Branch income cannot be deferred, but all branch foreign income taxes are eligible for inclusion in the tax credit. Credit also is allowed for taxes (called withholding taxes) paid by the parent to the foreign government on dividends paid by the foreign corporation to the parent.

Figure 19.7
Tax Status of Active and Subpart F Income from Foreign Subsidiaries of U.S. Companies
Different rules regarding the tax status and deferrability of income are in effect for CFCs, non-CFCs, and foreign branches.

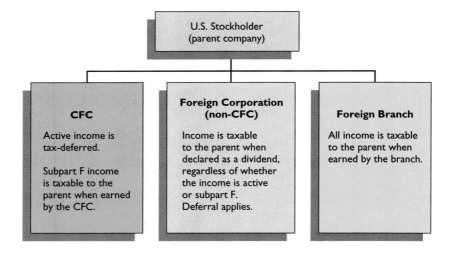

The total tax credit is subject to an upper limit—what
the tax would have been in
the United States.

After a U.S. company adds up its eligible credits, it finds that it is constrained by an upper limit imposed by the IRS. The upper limit is what it would have paid in taxes on that income in the United States. For example, if the foreign-source income is $1 million and the applicable U.S. tax rate is 35 percent, the upper limit is $350,000. If the tax credits exceed $350,000, the company can carry the excess credits back two years and recompute its tax burden or carry them forward five years and try to use them. If the credits total less than the upper limit, the company is allowed the full amount.

In reality, the computation of tax credits is significantly more complex. Foreign-source income must be divided into separate categories, or baskets: overall and passive. The overall category basically contains active income and probably will generate excess credits. The passive category basically contains Subpart F income and probably will use up all of its available credits and then some.

Taxation of U.S. Citizens Abroad

There are unique problems associated with compensating U.S. personnel working abroad. A company usually must offer employees a significant salary to entice them to move abroad. The total compensation usually consists of the base salary plus additional compensation in the form of a housing allowance, a hardship allowance, an education allowance for children, a cost-of-living differential, and so on. These additional allowances can escalate an employee's total compensation significantly and subject it to a higher income tax in the foreign country as well as in the United States.

U.S. citizens working abroad
can exclude $70,000 of their
income from U.S. taxation.

The U.S. policy of taxing such foreign income has changed significantly through-out history. The more lenient the tax treatment, the easier it is to send employees abroad. Under current law, U.S. expatriates (that is, U.S. citizens working abroad) are allowed to exclude up to $70,000 of their foreign-source income from U.S. taxation. This income is taken off the top; that is, income at higher marginal tax rates is excluded first, and the taxpayer ends up paying tax on income in the lowest tax brackets.[10]

U.S. employees working
abroad can claim a housing
exclusion for housing
expenses in excess of a base
amount determined by the
IRS.

In addition to the foreign earned-income exclusion, an expatriate may elect to claim a housing exclusion. Housing expenses in excess of a base amount determined by the IRS can be excluded from the determination of income for tax purposes.

An expatriate might receive a significant amount of income that could be taxed by foreign and U.S. authorities. Income taxes paid to foreign governments can be treated as a credit or deduction, similar to the way in which corporate taxes are treated. However, companies sending expatriates abroad generally must make up the difference between what the expatriate would have paid in taxes in the United States and what must be paid because of the foreign assignment. The difference in tax liability is usually a result of the higher compensation earned by the expatriate as a result of allowances for housing, hardship, cost of living, etc. That tax-equalization practice can be quite expensive for the company.

An example of the tax equalization problem involves the People's Republic of China. Any Hong Kong person who works more than 90 days in China must pay China income taxes in addition to what he or she pays in the home country. However, Americans and Singaporeans operated in a 183-day time frame because of tax treaties signed with the Chinese government. It is hoped that this will be extended to Hong Kong managers at some point. But managers who stay in China long enough, whether it be 90 or 183 days, must deal with double taxation. Most U.S. and European companies establish tax equalization agreements to ensure that employees are no worse off than they would have been in the home country. Usually, the employee pays home-country tax on the income, which is deducted from income, and the employer pays the Chinese tax. Since tax rates in Hong Kong are only 15 percent, compared with 25 percent in the People's Republic of China, the tax difference can be significant.[11]

Non-U.S. Tax Practices

Problems with different countries' tax practices are related to
* **Lack of familiarity with laws**
* **Loose enforcement**

Differences in tax practices around the world often cause problems for domestic companies operating overseas. Lack of familiarity with laws and customs can create confusion. In many countries, tax laws are loosely enforced. In others, taxes generally are negotiated between the tax collector and the taxpayer, if they are ever paid at all.

Variations among countries in GAAP can lead to differences in the determination of taxable income. This in turn may affect the cash flow required to settle tax obligations. For example, in France companies can depreciate assets very quickly and take additional depreciation for certain assets. In Sweden, companies can reduce the value of inventories, which tends to reduce taxable income.

In the separate entity approach, each taxable entity is taxed when it earns income.

Taxation of corporate income is accomplished through one of two approaches in most countries: the separate entity, or classical, approach, or the integrated system. In the **separate entity approach,** which is used in the United States, each separate unit—company or individual—is taxed when it earns income. For example, a corporation is taxed on its earnings and stockholders are taxed on the distribution of earnings (dividends). The result is double taxation.

An integrated system tries to avoid double taxation of corporate income through split tax rates or tax credits.

Most other industrial countries use an **integrated system** to eliminate double taxation. The British give a dividend credit to stockholders to shelter them from double taxation. In Germany, a split-rate system provides for a lower corporate income tax rate to be applied to distributed profits, since the stockholders are taxed also. A German stockholder must increase the value of the dividend by including the corporate tax that was paid and then pay the tax based on the individual tax rate. However, the stockholder is allowed to take a tax credit equal to what the corporation paid.

Countries also have unique systems for taxing the earnings of the foreign subsidiaries of domestic companies. Some, such as France, use a territorial approach and therefore tax only domestic-source income. Others, such as Germany and the

United Kingdom, use a global approach; that is, they tax the profits of foreign branches and the dividends received from foreign subsidiaries. The United States is the only country to tax unremitted earnings in the form of Subpart F income.

Value-Added Tax

A **value-added tax (VAT)** has been used since 1967 by most Western European countries. A VAT is computed by applying a percentage rate on total sales less any purchases from other business entities that have already paid the VAT. As the name implies, VAT means that each independent company is taxed only on the value added at each stage in the production process. For a company that is fully integrated vertically, the tax rate applies to its net sales because it owned everything from raw materials to finished product.

With a value-added tax, each company is taxed only on the value added to the product.

The VAT rates vary significantly among European countries despite efforts by the EU toward harmonization among its members. However, the EU is narrowing differences in rates for like categories of goods. The VAT does not apply to exports, since the tax is rebated (or returned) to the exporter and thus is not included in the final price to the consumer. This practice results in an effective stimulus for exports.

Tax Treaties: The Elimination of Double Taxation

The purpose of tax treaties is to prevent double taxation or to provide remedies when it occurs.

The primary purpose of tax treaties is to prevent international double taxation or to provide remedies when it occurs. The United States has active tax treaties with more than thirty countries. The general pattern between two treaty countries is to grant reciprocal reductions on dividend withholding and to exempt royalties and sometimes interest payments from any withholding tax.

The United States has a withholding tax of 30 percent for owners (individuals and corporations) of U.S. securities that are from countries with which it has no tax treaty. However, interest on portfolio obligations and on bank deposits is normally exempted from withholding. When a tax treaty is in effect, the U.S. rate on dividends generally is reduced to 15 percent and the tax on interest and royalties either is eliminated or is reduced to a very low level.

An example is a protocol to the 1980 tax treaty between the United States and Canada, which took effect on January 1, 1996, and which accomplishes three things:

(1) Reduces the withholding rate on dividends paid to a corporation owning 10 percent or more of the voting stock of the payor to 6 percent for payments in 1996, and 5 percent thereafter
(2) Reduces the withholding rate on interest to 10 percent
(3) Reduces the tax resulting from the imposition of both U.S. estate tax and Canadian income tax on transfers at death[12]

Several treaties and protocols were signed between the United States and foreign countries with an effective date of January 1, 1996, and they were very similar. In those treaties involving the reduction of withholding rates on dividends, the rate was typically 5 percent, although the rate for Portugal was 15 percent in some cases, 10 percent in others.

Planning the Tax Function

Companies should set up
* **Branches in early years to recognize losses**
* **Subsidiaries in later years to shield profits**

Because taxes affect both profits and cash flow, they must be considered in the investment as well as the operational decision process. When a U.S. parent company decides to set up operations in a foreign country, it can do so through a branch or a foreign subsidiary. If the parent expects the foreign operations to show a loss for the initial years of operation, it should begin with a branch, since the parent can deduct branch losses against its current year's income. As the operations become profitable, the company should switch to a foreign subsidiary. If tax deferral applies to the subsidiary's income, then the income of the subsidiary will not be taxed until a dividend is declared.

Debt and equity financing both have tax ramifications.

Tied in with the initial investment decision as well as with continuing operations is the financing decision. Both debt and equity financing affect taxation. If loans from the parent are used to finance foreign operations, the repayment of principal is not taxable, but the interest income received by the parent is taxable. Also, the interest paid by the subsidiary is generally a business expense for that entity, which reduces taxable income in the foreign country. Dividends are taxable to the parent and are not a deductible business expense for the subsidiary. One reason why international finance subsidiaries are set up outside the United States is to escape withholding tax requirements.

An MNE aiming to maximize its cash flow worldwide should concentrate profits in tax-haven or low-tax countries. This can be accomplished by carefully selecting a low-tax country for the initial investment, setting up companies in tax-haven countries to receive dividends, and carrying out judicious transfer pricing. Whenever possible, the parent company should utilize the 5-percent rule. This rule provides that if the parent has a profitable operating subsidiary in a relatively low-tax country, it can accumulate Subpart F income there without worrying about U.S. taxes, provided that income does not reach 5 percent of total subsidiary income. For example, because of its low-tax status and membership in the EU, Ireland can be used as both a manufacturing center to supply the EU with goods and a tax-haven country. The Subpart F income provisions require complicated tax planning, but opportunities still exist. Tax law is very involved, and a company needs the counsel of an experienced tax specialist.

C O U N T E R V A I L I N G

F O R C E S

Although there are forces for harmonization of both accounting and taxation, national sovereignty is a major stumbling block. Accounting standards and practices are a function of each country's unique environment. As noted in this chapter, capital markets have a strong influence in countries such as the United States and the United Kingdom, whereas banks have a strong influence in countries such as Germany and Japan. Because of these differences, harmonizing accounting standards and practices worldwide is very difficult. Even the IASC is composed of organizations of accountants, such as the American Institute of Certified Public Accountants, rather than standards-setting bodies, such as the Financial Accounting Standards Board.

National sovereignty is a major stumbling block to harmonization of accounting standards and practices.

Some countries, such as Germany, prefer the principle of mutual recognition rather than harmonization. Under this principle, the securities regulators of one country are willing to accept a foreign company's financial statements, provided those statements are prepared according to the GAAP of the company's home country. However, the SEC has rejected this principle and instead requires foreign companies to adhere to U.S. GAAP in order to file in the United States. Thus the major forces of harmonization—the globalization of stock markets and the global interest of investors—directly conflict with national sovereignty, as both the German and the U.S. examples show.

The principle of mutual recognition means that securities regulators of one country are willing to accept a foreign company's financial statements if those statements are prepared according to the GAAP of the company's home country.

The international harmonization of taxation is even more difficult because of the political nature of taxes. Although the EU has tried to narrow tax differences among its members in order to improve the flow of capital, it has not eliminated all differences. NAFTA deals only with trade issues and does not even refer to tax harmonization.

LOOKING TO THE FUTURE

Although accounting standards differ significantly by country, the differences are beginning to narrow. As capital markets become increasingly integrated and as companies increasingly move to list their stock on different national stock exchanges, accounting differences will continue to decrease. The stock exchanges will become an increasingly more important force in harmonizing accounting standards.

It is hard to predict what will happen in taxation, since tax policy is subject to the whim of governments. Certainly tax differences among countries in the EU will narrow in the years to come. Harmonization should take place in the determination of taxable income and the tax rates themselves. MNEs will need to be more creative in their tax planning worldwide as they seek to operate in such a way as to minimize their tax liabilities.

WEB CONNECTION

Check out our home page for links to accounting resources on the World Wide Web.

Summary

- **In performing its finance and accounting functions, an MNE must cope with differing inflation rates, exchange-rate changes, currency controls, risk of expropriation, customs duties, levels of sophistication, and local reporting requirements.**

- **A company's accounting or controllership function is responsible for collecting and analyzing data for internal and external users.**

- Some of the major factors that influence the development of accounting standards and practices are finance and capital markets, taxation, legal systems, inflation, former colonial influence, and culture.

- Culture can have a strong influence on the accounting dimensions of measurement and disclosure. The cultural values of secrecy and transparency refer to the degree of disclosure of information. The cultural values of optimism and conservatism refer to the valuation of assets and the recognition of income. Conservatism results in the undervaluation of both assets and income.

- Financial statements differ in terms of language, currency, financial statements, formats, footnotes, and underlying **GAAP**.

- Stock exchanges may permit mutual recognition or require reconciliation to local **GAAP**.

- The major forces for harmonization of accounting standards and practices are global investors and global capital markets.

- The **EU** is engaged in the most effective regional effort to harmonize accounting.

- The **IASC** is a global organization of public accountants from different countries that is trying to harmonize accounting standards.

- When transactions denominated in a foreign currency are translated into dollars, all accounts are recorded initially at the exchange rate in effect at the time of the transaction. At each subsequent balance-sheet date, recorded dollar balances representing amounts owed by or to the company that are denominated in a foreign currency are adjusted to reflect the current rate.

- The translation of financial statements involves measuring and expressing in the parent currency and in conformity with parent country's **GAAP** the assets, liabilities, revenues, and expenses that are measured or denominated in a foreign currency.

- According to **FASB** Statement No. 52, the financial statements of foreign companies are translated into dollars by using the current-rate or temporal method. According to the more widely used current-rate method, all balance-sheet accounts except owners' equity are translated into dollars at the current exchange rate in effect on the balance-sheet date. All income statement accounts are translated at the average exchange rate in effect during the period.

- **Foreign-exchange gains and losses arising from foreign-currency transactions are entered on the income statement during the period in which they occur. Gains and losses arising from translating financial statements by the current-rate method are entered as a separate component of owners' equity. Gains and losses arising from translating according to the temporal method are entered directly on the income statement.**

- **International tax planning has a strong impact on the choice of location for the initial investment, the legal form of the new enterprise, the method of financing, and the method of setting transfer prices.**

- **Tax deferral means that income earned by a subsidiary incorporated outside the home country is taxed only when it is remitted to the parent as a dividend, not when it is earned.**

- **A CFC must declare its Subpart F income as taxable to the parent in the year it is earned, whether or not it is remitted as a dividend.**

- **A tax credit allows a parent company to reduce its tax liability by the direct amount paid to foreign governments on dividends declared by a subsidiary to the parent as well as by the amount of the corporate income tax paid by the subsidiary to the foreign government.**

- **Policies of countries vary as to what is taxable income and how taxes are assessed. The United States taxes each separate unit (the separate entity approach), whereas most other industrial countries use an integrated system in which double taxation of dividends is minimized or eliminated.**

- **The purpose of tax treaties is to prevent international double taxation or to provide remedies when it occurs.**

Case
Daimler-Benz
and a U.S. Listing[13]

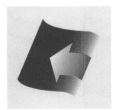

In 1993, Daimler-Benz management decided to adjust its financial reporting in order to list shares of stock as American Depositary Receipts (ADRs), also known as American Depositary Shares, on the New York Stock Exchange (NYSE). This decision resulted from months of negotiations between Daimler-Benz, the NYSE, and the SEC.

An ADR is a negotiable certificate issued by a U.S. bank in the United States to represent the underlying shares of stock, which are held in a custodian bank. ADRs are sold, registered, and transferred in the United States in the same way as any share of stock.

Daimler-Benz is the large German MNE best known for its vehicles division, Mercedes-Benz. In 1992, Daimler-Benz saw profits fall by 25 percent from the previous year, and prospects for the future were not bright. The company relied historically on strong profits for cash flow, and thus its management realized that it would have to look to other sources of cash to fund future growth.

One way to raise cash is to borrow funds. Only 22.8 percent of the assets of Daimler-Benz in 1992 were funded by equity. Daimler-Benz has relied more on debt financing from banks—especially Deutsche Bank, the large German bank—than on equity financing. This strategy is typical of Germanic countries, such as Germany and Switzerland, and countries heavily influenced by the German tradition, such as Japan. When West Germany decided to absorb East Germany into a reunified country, there was a tremendous need on the part of the German government for money to fund the venture. Thus a significant amount of debt capital was pulled into the public sector, and interest rates rose to counter the inflationary effects of heavy governmental spending. Debt financing consequently became scarce and costly.

An alternate means of raising cash is to issue shares of stock. Daimler-Benz is a major player in the German stock market. In 1992, 11.5 percent of all shares traded on the eight German stock exchanges were Daimler-Benz shares, and 90 percent of Daimler-Benz share activity took place on the German exchanges, primarily Frankfurt but also Berlin, Bremen, Düsseldorf, Hamburg, Hanover, München, and Stuttgart. About one third of Daimler-Benz's shares are held by approximately 400,000 stockholders, one half of whom live outside of Germany. Of the remaining shares, 28 percent are owned by Deutsche Bank, 25 percent by Mercedes AG Holding, and about 14 percent by the Emirate of Kuwait.

To gain access to non-German capital, Daimler-Benz has actively traded its shares in other markets, although such trading has made up only 10 percent of share activity. The company has been listed in Switzerland since the 1980s (Basel, Geneva, and Zurich), in Tokyo since September 1990, in Vienna since February 1991, and in Paris since October 1991. In addition, its shares are listed on the London Stock Exchange. Although Daimler-Benz had offered unlisted ADRs through the Bank of New York, until 1993 it had avoided the largest stock market in the world, the NYSE.

Why has Daimler-Benz avoided the NYSE for so many years? The major reason is the difference in accounting standards. The SEC has held fast to the idea that foreign companies must adhere to U.S. GAAP if they want to list in the United States. German companies tend to be much more conservative than are U.S. companies in reporting earnings and information in general. Company law is the predominant influence on accounting in Germany. The legal system in Germany is highly codified and prescriptive, since it is based on the Roman law system rather than the Anglo-Saxon common law system used in the United States and the United Kingdom. The tax laws also strongly influence the extent to which annual accounts form the basis for tax accounts. Thus any allowance or deduction claimed for tax purposes must be charged in the annual accounts.

The accounting tradition in Germany gives preference to the information needs of creditors and tax authorities. There is a very conservative approach to valuation in Germany, with strict application to historical cost accounting. Consistent with the emphasis on creditor interests, there also is a much more prudent interpretation of historical-cost accounting principles than usually occurs in the United States or the United Kingdom. To protect creditors, the law also requires German corporations to create a legal reserve. Depreciation rates are determined by the tax rules, and accelerated methods are widely used. With respect to inventories, the lower-of-cost-or-market rule is used but conservatively applied.

Provisions for future losses or expenses are a very important aspect of accounting in Germany. Traditionally, such provisions have been used to smooth or reduce profits. In good years, provisions may be made against the probability that the current results are unlikely to be maintained into the future; in bad years, these provisions will be called upon. This undervaluation of assets and overstatement of expenses and liabilities gives rise to hidden reserves that allow German companies to retain cash in the business to protect creditors, cash that is not available to stockholders because of the conservative determination of profits. Financial information is generally reported only annually, and footnote disclosures tend not to be extensive, leading to the charge that German financial statements are not very transparent.

When Daimler-Benz announced on March 25, 1993, that it was nearing an agreement with the SEC on the nature of its financial reporting for U.S. listing, it declared DM4 billion ($2.45 billion) in hidden reserves as an extraordinary profit on its 1992 balance sheet. These hidden reserves emerged as a result of applying uniform valuation methods throughout the company; different accounting methods had been used for different subsidiaries, so there was no uniformity in accounting. Since 1992, however, results have been provided on a uniform basis. The hidden reserves will be retained as an internal cash reserve rather than used for investment purposes. Daimler-Benz does not provide quarterly earnings reports and provides divisional results only annually. Even annual results are provided much later than would be the case for a U.S. company: 1992 results were not disclosed to the public until May 1993, and the results by division were not disclosed even then. This will have to change in order for Daimler-Benz to list in the United States. Another change in reporting, to be consistent with SEC requirements, is the need for a statement of cash flows divided into operating, investing, and financing activities, something that Daimler-Benz had not done prior to its 1992 *Annual Report.*

As the company's management negotiated with the SEC, it had two major options: It could offer one set of financial data to U.S. investors that meets SEC regulations and another set to German investors, or it could combine its financial data into one package acceptable to both groups. The German, U.S., and U.K. offices of KPMG Peat Marwick, a global public accounting firm, worked with Daimler-Benz to determine how results would be presented within the SEC's Form 20-F (the filing required for foreign companies listing in the United States).

Daimler-Benz issued a sponsored ADR on October 5, 1993, and is hoping that eventually 10 percent of its shares will be traded on the NYSE. Because of Daimler-Benz's high share price of DM760 (approximately $467) on October 5, ten ADRs equaled one share in order to make the price of the ADR more similar to share prices of other blue-chip companies in the United States. Other global service firms played an important role. For example, Citibank is the depositary bank for the ADR, and Deutsche Bank Capital Corporation of New York and Goldman, Sachs & Co. acted as investment bank advisors. The U.S.-based international law firm of Skadden, Arps, Slate, Meagher & Flom advised Daimler-Benz on matters relating to the registration and listing of the shares, and KPMG, mentioned above, prepared and audited the accounts to make sure that they conformed with U.S. GAAP.

Form 20-F includes a lot of information that provides insight into the differences between German and U.S. accounting practices and shows how difficult it is for an international investor to make investment decisions. Daimler-Benz provides financial information in German marks. This information was also provided in the annual report. As stated in the 1995 Annual Report,

> With the listing of Daimler-Benz stock on the New York Stock Exchange, we are obligated to file an annual report on Form 20-F with the Securities and Exchange Commission (SEC). Much of the information contained in this report is taken from our annual report; however, additional data and financial information are provided that were determined on the basis of U.S. accounting principles. Since there are substantial differences, especially in net income and stockholders' equity, the reconciliations are required to convert certain financial data from the German consolidated financial statements to the values calculated using the U.S. GAAP.

Table 19.9 contains reconciliation data provided by Daimler-Benz in Form 20-F and the *Annual Report.* Form 20-F identifies the major differences between German and U.S. GAAP that influenced the numbers in the table. The major difference is appropriated retained earnings—provisions, reserves, and valuation differences. According to German GAAP, accruals or provisions may be recorded for uncertain liabilities and loss contingencies. The amount of such accruals or provisions represents the anticipated expense to the company. Application of German GAAP may also lead to higher accrual balances and reserves for possible asset risks than are allowed under U.S. GAAP. In addition, other significant differences arise from accounting for goodwill and business combinations, deferred taxes, pensions, securities, and financial instruments.

Questions

1. What are some of the differences in philosophy and practice between German and U.S. accounting?
2. Why did Daimler-Benz decide to list ADRs on the NYSE?
3. Do you think Daimler-Benz would prefer that the SEC allow mutual recognition of accounting practices in approving listings on the NYSE? Explain.
4. Was the SEC right in requiring Daimler-Benz to provide a reconciliation to U.S. GAAP as a precondition to listing on the NYSE? Explain.
5. In 1996, Daimler-Benz was considering switching from German to U.S. GAAP for its external reporting. What would be the costs and benefits of doing so?

Table 19.9
Reconciliation of Consolidated Net Income/Loss and Stockholders' Equity to U.S. GAAP

- in millions of DM -	1995	1994
Consolidates net (loss) income in accordance with German HGB (Commercial Code)	**(5,734)**	895
+/- Changes in appropriated retained earnings:		
provisions, reserves and valuation differences	(640)	409
	(6,374)	1,304
Additional adjustments		
+/- Long-term contracts	(9)	53
Goodwill and business acquisitions	(2,241)	(350)
Deconsolidation of MBL Fahrzeug-Leasing GmbH & Co. KG	369	(652)
Pensions and other postretirement benefits	(219)	(432)
Foreign currency translation	52	(22)
Financial instruments	49	633
Securities	238	(388)
Other valuation differences	(215)	232
Deferred taxes	2,621	496
Consolidated net (loss) income in accordance with U.S. GAAP		
before cumulative effect of a change in accounting principle	(5,729)	874
Cumulative effect of change in accounting for certain investments in debt and equity		
securities as of January 1, 1994, net of tax of DM 235 million	–	178
Consolidates net (loss) income in accordance with U.S. GAAP	**(5,729)**	(1,052)
Net (loss) income per share in accordance with U.S. GAAP	DM (111.67)	DM 21.53
Net (loss) income per American Depositary Share[1] in accordance with U.S. GAAP	DM (11.17)	DM 2.15
Stockholders' equity in accordance with German HGB	**13,842**	20,251
Appropriated retained earnings:		
provisions, reserves and valuation differences	5,604	6,205
	19,446	26,456
Additional adjustments		
+/- Long-term contracts	253	262
Goodwill and business acquisitions	(559)	1,978
Deconsolidation of MBL Fahrzeug-Leasing GmbH & Co. KG	(283)	(652)
Pensions and other postretirement benefits	(2,469)	(2,250)
Foreign currency translation	115	63
Financial instruments	1,058	1,013
Securities	525	27
Other valuation differences	(1,073)	(336)
Deferred taxes	5,847	2,874
Shareholders' equity in accordance with U.S. GAAP	**22,860**	29,435

1) Corresponds to one tenth of share of stock of DM 50 par value.

Source: Daimler-Benz, *Annual Report* 1995, p. 49.

Chapter Notes

1. Sources for the case were the 1989 *Annual Report* of the Coca-Cola Company; Timothy K. Smith and Laura Landro, "Profoundly Changed, Coca-Cola Co. Strives to Keep on Bubbling," *Wall Street Journal*, April 24, 1986, p. 1; Andrew L. Nodar, "Coca-Cola Writes an Accounting Procedures Manual," *Management Accounting*, October 1986, pp. 52–53; "Assessing Brands: Broad, Deep, Long and Heavy," *The Economist*, November 16, 1996, pp. 72, 75; Patricia Sellers and Patty de Llosa, "How Coke is Kicking Pepsi's Can," *Fortune*, October 28, 1996; <http://www.cocacola.com> The quote above was from November 21, 1996.

2. Jeffrey Taylor, "Italy's Montedison Is Sued by SEC Over Past Scandal," *Wall Street Journal*, November 22, 1996, p. A4.

3. Financial Accounting Standards Board, *Statement of Financial Accounting Concepts No. 1—Objectives of Financial Reporting by Business Enterprises* (Stamford, Conn.: FASB, 1979), paragraphs 34–54.

4. Lee H. Radebaugh and Sidney J. Gray, *International Accounting and Multinational Enterprises*, 3rd ed. (New York: John Wiley, 1993), p. 473.

5. "EU Puts Weight Behind IASC," *IASC Insight*, March 1996, pp. 1 and 3.

6. "Fast Track for IASC," *IASC Insight*, July 1996, p. 1.

7. Financial Accounting Standards Board, *Statement of Financial Accounting Standards No. 52: Foreign Currency Translation* (Stamford, Conn.: FASB, December 1981), pp. 6–7.

8. Albert J. Radler, "Taxation Policy in Multinational Companies," in *The Multinational Enterprise in Transition*, A. Kapoor and Philip D. Grub, eds. (Princeton: Darwin Press, 1972), p. 30.

9. Prentice-Hall, *A Complete Guide to the Tax Reform Act of 1984* (Englewood Cliffs, N.J.: Prentice-Hall, 1984), pp. 1791–1805.

10. Arthur Andersen & Co., *U.S. Taxation of Americans Abroad*, 4th ed. (Chicago: Arthur Andersen & Co., S.C., 1991).

11. Nisha Gopalan, "Beijing May Ease Double-Tax Trap," *South China Morning Post*, November 17, 1996, p. 12.

12. "U.S. Tax Treaty Developments," *Deloitte & Touche Review*, February 5, 1996, p. 5.

13. Timothy Aeppel, "Daimler Says Mercedes Has Operating Loss," *Wall Street Journal*, May 7, 1993, p. A11; Timothy Aeppel, "Daimler-Benz Discloses Hidden Reserves of $2.45 Billion, Seeks Big Board Listing," *Wall Street Journal*, March 25, 1993, p. A10; "Daimler Plays Ball," *The Economist*, March 27, 1993, p. 76; Herbert Fromme, "Daimler Drives into Trouble," *World Accounting Report*, May 1993, pp. 2–3; Bernhard Harling, corporate communications of Daimler-Benz North America Corporation, New York; Christopher Parkes, "Daimler to Make New York Debut in October," *Financial Times*, July 28, 1993, p. 23; Radebaugh and Gray, op. cit., pp. 91–93 and 386–390; Anita Raghavan and Christi Harlan, "Daimler-Benz's Listing Is Likely to Draw More Foreign Firms to the U.S. Market," *Wall Street Journal*, March 31, 1993, p. A4; and Daimler-Benz *Annual Report*, 1996.

Chapter 20

The Multinational Finance Function

To have money is a good thing;
to have a say over the money
is even better.

—Yiddish Proverb

Objectives

- To describe the multinational finance function and how it fits in the MNE's organizational structure

- To show how companies can acquire outside funds for normal operations and expansion

- To discuss the major internal sources of funds available to the MNE and show how these funds are managed globally

- To explain how companies protect against the major financial risks of inflation and exchange-rate movements

- To highlight some of the financial aspects of the investment decision

**Case
LSI Logic Corp.**[1]

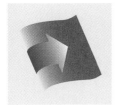

In the late 1970s, Wilfred Corrigan, the British-born chairman and president of Fairchild Camera & Instrument Corp., sold Fairchild to Schlumberger Ltd. Approximately one year later, in November 1980, he started LSI Logic Corp., a manufacturer of custom-made microchips based in Malpitas, California. Although Corrigan's idea of manufacturing custom-made microchips sounded unconventional at the time, he was able to use his track record at Fairchild to convince some U.S. venture capitalists to invest nearly $7 million in the new company in January 1981.

The company began with only four employees, but because Corrigan had solved two key issues—the nature of the product and the initial infusion of cash—there was a solid foundation for growth. He next had to decide how LSI Logic should service its customers worldwide and how and where it would raise capital to keep expanding.

From his experience at Fairchild, Corrigan knew that a producer of microchips had to think globally in terms of the location of production and the consumer. He quickly decided that in order to be successful, he needed to concentrate on three key geographic areas—Asia, Europe, and the United States. He called this his "global triad strategy," defining the triad more specifically as Japan, Western Europe, and North America (see Map 20.1). His key organizational strategy was to incorporate companies in the producing and consuming countries that would be jointly owned by LSI Logic and local investors, with LSI Logic holding the controlling interest. Although the operations in each country would be relatively independent of each other, they would be linked by technology, money, and management. This setup would encourage the synergy of interdependence while permitting local freedom in meeting the demands of the market.

Once Corrigan got operations under way, he began to look for more cash. The key was to find the right amount, at the right price, with the least number of problems. In February 1982, LSI Logic turned to Europe in search of venture capital, which was found in a Euro-

**Map 20.1
Triad Strategy for
LSI Logic Corp.**
LSI Logic's global business and financing strategy focused on three of the world's largest markets: North America, Western Europe, and Japan.

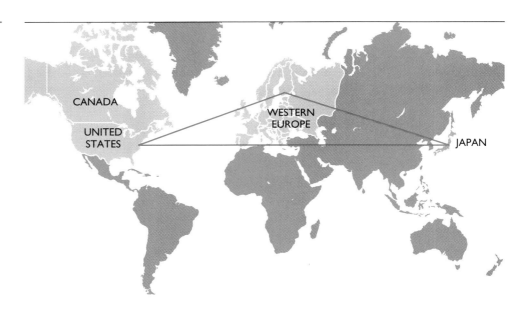

pean investing community hungry for U.S. high-tech stock. The company subsequently was able to raise $10 million, mostly—but not exclusively—in the United Kingdom. At this point, LSI Logic was growing rapidly. In May 1983, Corrigan took the company public in the United States and raised over $162 million, an average of $21 a share. That demonstrated the size of the appetite in the United States for stock in new high-tech companies.

Despite the European and U.S. successes, Corrigan still had not been able to raise capital in Japan. However, he learned that the Japanese brokerage house Nomura Securities had purchased large blocks of LSI stock for its clients in Japan. Encouraged by this information, Corrigan traveled to Japan to meet with Nomura officials and to try to decide what LSI Logic's next move should be. As a result of the visit, Corrigan decided the time was right for starting operations in Japan. Following the strategy he had used elsewhere, he established a Japanese subsidiary of LSI Logic (called LSI Logic Corp. K.K.), of which the parent company owned 70 percent and twenty-five Japanese investors together owned 30 percent. The new investment was just right for LSI Logic—it gained access not only to the Japanese consumer market but also to the Japanese capital market. As a Japanese company, LSI Logic Corp. K.K. and its manufacturing affiliate, Nihon Semiconductor Inc., could establish lines of credit with Japanese banks, and did so at only 6 percent, compared with 9 percent in the United States at the time.

When business in Japan was under way, Corrigan once more turned his attentions to Europe. He planned to set up a new European company and needed to decide on its structure. The company could be set up as a European company, or it could be set up as a branch of the U.S. parent that would use U.S. capital and be totally controlled and protected by the parent. Corrigan decided on the former and consequently used Morgan Stanley & Co., the large U.S.-based securities firm, to set up LSI Logic Ltd. Corrigan was convinced that by setting up a European company, he would be able to get more money by selling shares at a higher price than would be possible otherwise and that LSI Logic Ltd. would be better placed to serve European customers than would a branch of the parent company. The parent company retained an 82-percent ownership share in the new company and sold the rest in a private offering to European investors, one of which was the venture-capital arm of five German banks.

In 1985 and again in 1987, Corrigan returned to European capital markets; both times LSI Logic floated a bond issue. The first issue of $23 million was put together by Swiss Bank Corp., one of the world's largest banks. The second, a bond issue with securities convertible into common stock, was floated by Morgan Stanley and Prudential-Bache Capital Funding. LSI Logic was attracted to the Eurobond market for two main reasons: a decent price (lower interest rates than were being offered in the United States), and a quicker time frame. Because the company was issuing the bonds in Europe and so didn't have to worry about the more onerous regulations of the SEC, it was able to get the offering together and out to the investing public faster.

By 1995, LSI was generating $1.27 billion in revenues from sales worldwide. It is considered the world leader in the design, production, and sale of advanced custom semiconductors. LSI also employed about 4,000 workers worldwide in 1995, with manufacturing facilities in the United States, Japan, and the Far East. Management and control of LSI's manufacturing operations are performed by the company's Hong Kong affiliate. The predicted increase in chip sales to Asia between now and the end of the decade prompted LSI to establish a regional headquarters in Singapore in 1996.

Because of its worldwide operations, LSI is heavily exposed to exchange rate changes. A substantial portion of the cost of LSI's manufacturing operations is denominated in Japanese yen. In addition, LSI purchases a significant amount of its raw materials and components from foreign suppliers. International sales are usually denominated in the local currency instead of U.S. dollars, which creates more foreign exchange risk for the company. Because of its foreign exchange exposures, LSI enters into hedging transactions to minimize exposure to currency rate fluctuations. LSI also has borrowings and operating lease obligations denominated in yen, which totaled approximately 25 billion yen as of December 31, 1995. These borrowings and lease obligations were secured by assets in Japan, and Japanese cash flows are used to cover the liabilities.

LSI is a good example of companies that have to use foreign capital markets to raise funds and that also must deal with foreign exchange risk. It is not an MNE in the same sense that Coca-Cola is, but it still has to deal with foreign markets in order to survive.

Introduction

Why do you need to understand the nature of capital markets, cash management, and financial risk? Having a good product idea is not sufficient for success. MNEs need to get access to capital markets in different countries in order to finance expansion. Even though U.S. capital markets are the world's largest and most significant, many companies still choose to raise money in the markets in which they plan to expand.

The small company involved only tangentially in international business may be concerned primarily about the functions of the foreign-exchange section of its commercial bank and not global capital markets. However, the MNE investing and operating abroad usually is concerned about access to capital in local markets as well as in the large global markets. This chapter examines external sources of funds available to companies operating abroad, internal sources of funds that often arise from intercompany links, global cash management, risk-management strategies, and international dimensions of the capital investment decision.

The Finance and Treasury Functions in the Internationalization Process

One of the most important people on the management team, crucial to a company's success, is the vice president of finance, also known as the chief financial officer (CFO). The functions of the CFO are often divided into the controllership and treasury functions. The responsibilities of the controller were discussed in Chapter

19. This chapter focuses on the most important global responsibilities of the CFO's treasury side.

The corporate finance function deals with the acquisition of financial resources and their allocation among the company's activities and projects. Acquiring resources (financing) involves generating funds either internally (within the company) or from sources external to the company at the lowest possible cost. Allocating resources (investing) involves increasing stockholders' wealth through the allocation of funds to different projects and investment opportunities.[2]

The CFO's job is more complex in a global environment than in the domestic setting because of forces such as foreign-exchange risk, currency flows and restrictions, different tax rates and laws pertaining to the determination of taxable income, and regulations on access to capital in different markets.

MNEs clearly are looking for capital worldwide in order to ensure their long-term ability to survive. They may issue stock or borrow money in foreign markets for parent-company needs, or they may raise capital to fund subsidiaries in foreign countries. The choice between debt and equity funding is complex. The company's capital structure, or capitalization, is the permanent financing of its assets through long-term debt, capital stock, and retained earnings. Its leverage is the ratio of the book value of total debt to total assets. The CFO is responsible for ensuring that the total cost of capital (both debt and equity) is as low as possible.

The CFO must determine the degree to which a firm leverages its assets, which varies from country to country. Country-specific factors are a more important determinant of a company's capital structure than is any other factor. Even though leveraging is often perceived as the most cost-effective route to capitalization, it may not be the best approach in all countries, for two major reasons. First, excessive reliance on long-term debt increases financial risk and so requires a higher return for investors. Second, foreign subsidiaries of an MNE may have limited access to local capital markets, making it difficult for the MNE to rely on debt to fund asset acquisition.[3] In a study of foreign subsidiaries of U.S. MNEs, it was found that the debt/asset ratio of those studied averaged 0.54. The debt/asset ratio on average for companies in a few countries was as follows: the Netherlands (0.32), Brazil (0.37), Australia (0.49), Mexico (0.51), Canada (0.52), England (0.64), Japan (0.65), and Germany (0.69).[4]

In addition, different tax rates, dividend remission policies, and exchange controls may cause a company to rely more on debt in some situations and more on equity in others. The debt/equity ratio of the MNE will be a weighted average of the debt/equity ratios of all entities in its corporate structure. German, Japanese, and Swiss companies traditionally have relied on debt financing because of its relatively better availability compared to equity financing and because of low interest rates. However, a rise in interest rates and an improvement in equity markets in recent years have prompted them to consider changing their mix of debt and equity financing. It is important to understand that the different debt and equity markets discussed in this chapter have different levels of importance for companies worldwide.

External Sources of Funds

An MNE that needs to raise capital through debt markets has a number of options. Obviously, the local debt market is the first source that a company will tap. But there are other markets as well. LSI Logic, for example, floated a Eurobond issue in European capital markets, and also borrowed Japanese yen to fund operations in Japan, and in 1993 borrowed Deutsche marks in Germany to fund operations there. Thus companies can tap international banks for local currency borrowings or Eurodollar borrowings, as well as the longer term bond markets. Debt capital is available on a short-term or long-term basis, and is priced on a fixed or floating rate basis. The next several sections will cover different approaches to borrowing money internationally, and will also cover the issuing of equity to users outside a company's home country.

Local Debt Markets

After the initial investment, the parent company usually prefers to have the foreign subsidiary become self-sufficient through retained earnings and straight debt rather than relying on it for additional infusions of capital in order to survive.

Because each country has different business customs, MNEs must not attempt to impose the same operating procedures in all countries. For example, Caterpillar Tractor was accustomed to operating through one bank for all of its transactions. However, when it first entered Brazil, it quickly realized that the country's tight credit market required a different operating procedure. So it opened accounts at several Brazilian banks, thus enabling it to tap several different credit sources. Caterpillar liked this Brazilian policy so much that it exported it back to the United States.

Although domestic and international markets are becoming more and more like a single market—at least among industrial countries—local markets still are influenced a great deal by internal political and economic pressures. For example, Brazil's high inflation rates have made it difficult for MNEs to get access to funds on a consistent, ongoing basis. Further, interest rates are usually very high in order to ensure a real return for the lending institutions. Occasionally, the Brazilian government has excluded the subsidiaries of foreign-owned companies from the domestic credit markets in order to encourage those companies to bring in hard currency from abroad.[5]

Sometimes, foreign companies' subsidiaries can obtain credit easier than local companies can because of the former's access to hard currency. They can enter into **back-to-back loans** during periods when interest rates are high or credit is frozen. A back-to-back loan is one that involves a company in country A with a subsidiary in country B and a bank in country B with a branch in country A. For example, the Italian subsidiary of a U.S. food company gained access to Italian loans when its U.S. parent provided dollars to the U.S. branch of an Italian bank. Under that condition, the Italian bank lent money to the Italian subsidiary of the U.S. parent:

In a back-to-back loan, the parent company in country A deposits cash in the local branch of a bank from country B, and the bank from country B loans funds to the parent's subsidiary in Country B.

> A dollar deposit is made in the United States with a branch of a leading Italian bank. At the same time, the equivalent amount in lira is lent by the bank to the company's Italian subsidiary as a seven-year loan. The loan will be repaid in full to the bank at the end of the loan period. Once the loan is terminated, the parent will withdraw its deposit plus interest. The subsidiary pays Italian prime [the prime interest rate]. Every six months, the exchange rate is adjusted if it varies more than 5 percent from the contracted rate. Thus, the subsidiary shoulders the exchange risk.[6]

A good example of how an MNE can utilize local debt and equity markets for its operations was discussed in the Euro Disney case in Chapter 1. When Euro Disney was initially capitalized, the project cost 24 billion French francs (about $4.4 billion), and the funding came from both debt and equity sources. Disney purchased 49 percent of the capital stock at only 10 francs per share, compared with a price of 72 francs per share to other stockholders. Operating losses in 1992 and 1993 caused the price of the stock to fall, so Euro Disney could not raise additional funds through issuing capital stock. The operating losses prevented Euro Disney from generating enough cash to service existing debt and to expand. Most of the debt—21 billion francs—had been raised from French banks by Euro Disney, not by Disney. Thus Disney had limited its own exposure by having its subsidiary raise funds from local French banks, with the debt to be serviced by franc revenues in France. In addition, this debt was not guaranteed by Disney, so the immediate exposure was limited to Euro Disney and the French banks, as well as the French government, which had backed some of the loans. Apparently, NCR also took advantage of local capital markets by borrowing Japanese yen through its subsidiary in Japan.

Eurocurrencies

A Eurocurrency is any currency banked outside of its country of origin.

The Eurocurrency market is an important source of debt financing for the MNEs. A **Eurocurrency** is any currency that is banked outside of its country of origin. Eurodollars, which constitute a fairly consistent 65–80 percent of the Eurocurrency market, are dollars banked outside of the United States. Dollars held by foreigners on deposit in the United States are not Eurodollars, but dollars held at branches of U.S. or other banks outside of the United States are. Smaller Eurocurrency market segments exist for Japanese yen (Euroyen), German marks (Euromarks), and other currencies, such as British pounds (Eurosterling), French francs, and Swiss francs.

London is the key center of the Eurocurrency market.

The **Eurocurrency market** is a market whose transactions take place worldwide.[7] Large transactions occur in Asia (Hong Kong and Singapore), Canada, and the Caribbean (the Bahamas and the Cayman Islands), as well as in London and other European centers. However, London is the key center for this market, with nearly 20 percent of all Eurocurrency transactions taking place there. Luxembourg is the center for Euromark deposits, and Brussels and Paris are the centers for Eurosterling deposits.[8]

The major sources of Eurocurrencies are

- Foreign governments or individuals who want to hold dollars outside of the United States
- Multinational corporations that have cash in excess of current needs
- European banks with foreign currency in excess of current needs
- Countries such as Germany, Japan, and Taiwan that have large balance-of-trade surpluses held as reserves.

The demand for Eurocurrencies comes from sovereign governments, supranational agencies such as the World Bank, companies, and individuals. Eurocurrencies exist partly for the convenience and security of the user and partly because of cheaper lending rates for the borrower and better yield for the lender.

The Eurocurrency market is a wholesale rather than a retail market, which means that transactions tend to be very large. Public borrowers such as governments, central banks, and public-sector corporations tend to be the major players. MNEs are involved in the Eurodollar market; for example, as will be noted in the closing case, NCR borrowed heavily there. However, nearly four fifths of the Eurodollar market is interbank; that is, the transactions occur between banks. The Eurocurrency market exists for savings and time deposits rather than demand deposits. That is, institutions that create Eurodollar deposits do not draw down those deposits into a particular national currency in order to buy goods and services.

> **A Eurocredit** is a type of loan that matures in one to five years.

The Eurocurrency market is both short- and medium-term. Short-term borrowing has maturities of less than one year. Anything over one year is considered a **Eurocredit,** which may be a loan, line of credit, or other form of medium- and long-term credit, including **syndication,** in which several banks pool resources to extend credit to a borrower.

> **Syndication** occurs when several banks pool resources to make a large loan in order to spread the risk.

> **LIBOR** is the interest rate that banks charge each other on Eurocurrency loans.

A major attraction of the Eurocurrency market is the difference in interest rates compared with those in domestic markets. Because of the large transactions and the lack of controls and their attendant costs, Eurocurrency deposits tend to yield more than domestic deposits do, and loans tend to be relatively cheaper than they are in domestic markets. Traditionally, loans are made at a certain percentage above the **London Inter-Bank Offered Rate (LIBOR),** which is the deposit rate that applies to interbank loans within London. How much above LIBOR the interest rate charged to a borrower is depends on the credit-worthiness of the customer and must be large enough to cover expenses and build reserves against possible losses. However, the Eurocurrency market's unique characteristics mean that the borrowing rate usually is less than it would be in the domestic market. Most loans are variable-rate, and the rate-fixing period generally is six months, although it may be one or three months.

International Bonds

Many countries have very active bond markets available to domestic and foreign investors. Even though the domestic bond market dominates total bond issues, with the U.S. market offering the best opportunities, the international bond market still fills an important niche in financing.

Foreign Bonds, Eurobonds, and Global Bonds

Foreign bonds are sold outside of the country of the borrower but in the currency of the country of issue.

The international bond market can be divided into foreign bonds, Eurobonds, and global bonds. **Foreign bonds** are sold outside of the borrower's country but are denominated in the currency of the country of issue. For example, a French company floating a bond issue in Swiss francs in Switzerland would be selling a foreign bond. Foreign bonds typically make up about 18 percent of the international bond market. They also have creative names, such as Yankee bond (issued in the United States), Samurai bond (issued in Japan), and Bulldog bond (issued in England).

Eurobonds are sold in countries other than the one in whose currency the bond is denominated.

A **Eurobond** is usually underwritten (placed in the market for the borrower) by a syndicate of banks from different countries and sold in countries other than the one in whose currency the bond is denominated. A bond issue floated by a French company in German marks in London, Luxembourg, and Switzerland is a Euro-bond. Eurobonds make up approximately 75 percent of the international bond market.

A global bond is registered in different national markets according to the registration requirements of each market.

The **global bond,** introduced by the World Bank in 1989, is a combination of domestic bond and Eurobond in that it must be registered in each national market according to that market's registration requirements. It also is issued simultaneously in several markets, usually those in Asia, Europe, and North America. Global bonds are a small but growing segment of the international bond market.

Global bond issues are becoming increasingly popular. In the nine months ending September 1996, $509 billion in global bonds had been issued, compared with $465 billion for the entire 1995 year.[9] An example of a global bond issue involves the Korean Development Bank (KDB). In 1996, the U.S. investment banks of J.P. Morgan and Merrill Lynch arranged a $500 million global bond issue simultaneously in the North American, European, and Asian markets, and distribution of the bonds reflected significant demand across all three regions. The interest rate was based on seven-year U.S. Treasury yields and reflected the tightest-ever spread (the difference between the yields on the global bond and the yield on a U.S. Treasury bill of the same maturity) on a Korean debt issue.[10]

The international bond market is an attractive place to borrow money. For one thing, it allows a company to diversify its funding sources from the local banks and bond market and in maturities that might not be available in the domestic markets. In addition, the international bond markets tend to be less expensive than local bond markets. However, not all companies are interested in global bonds or Eurobonds. Asian companies, for example, tend to rely on their domestic banks more because of the ready availability of cheap debt. In addition, the companies and banks tend to develop a cozier relationship than might be the case with Western companies and banks.[11] However, there are still good opportunities to use the international bond markets.

The Eurobond Market

Although the Eurobond market is centered in Europe, it has no national boundaries. Unlike most conventional bonds, Eurobonds are sold simultaneously in several financial centers through multinational underwriting syndicates and are purchased by an international investing public that extends far beyond the confines of the countries of issue.

Eurobonds were first issued in 1963 as a means of avoiding U.S. tax and disclosure regulations. They are typically issued in denominations of $5000 or $10,000, pay interest annually, are held in bearer form, and are traded over the counter (OTC), most frequently in London.[12] Any investor who holds a bearer bond is entitled to receive the principal and interest payments. In contrast, for a registered bond, which is more typical in the United States, the investor is required to be registered as the bond's owner in order to receive payments. Obviously, there is more secrecy attached to a bearer bond. An OTC bond is traded with an investment bank rather than on a securities exchange, such as the London Stock Exchange.

Occasionally, Eurobonds may provide currency options, which enable the creditor to demand repayment in one of several currencies and thereby reduce the exchange risk inherent in single-currency foreign bonds. More frequently, however, both interest and principal on Eurobonds are payable to the creditor in U.S. dollars.

The European Currency Unit (ECU) has become an interesting "currency" of lending in the Eurobond market. Based on a basket composed of the currencies of the EU member countries, the ECU at one time accounted for nearly 10 percent of all international bond issues.[13] The ECU bond enables a borrower to diversify into different currencies and to use cash flows from different countries in which it has operations to pay back the investors. However, uncertainty about European monetary integration has caused ECU bonds to be less attractive.

> Eurobonds are typically issued in denominations of $5000 or $10,000, pay interest annually, are held in bearer form, and are traded over the counter.

> Some Eurobonds have currency options, which allow the creditor to demand repayment in one of several currencies.

> The ECU bond is based on a basket of currencies of the countries that are EU members.

Equity Securities

Another source of financing is the equity-capital market. Nine of the world's ten largest stock exchanges in terms of market capitalization (the total number of shares of stock listed on the exchange times the market price per share) are in what are considered developed countries (including Hong Kong). South Africa is the largest emerging market and ranks number 9. The world's three largest stock exchanges are the New York Stock Exchange (NYSE), Tokyo Stock Exchange, and London Stock Exchange (LSE). It is interesting to note that from 1987 to 1989, the

> The three largest stock markets in the world are in New York, Tokyo, and London.

stock market in Japan was larger than that of the United States, but the U.S. market was 1.86 times greater than the Japanese market in 1995.[14]

A major trend recently has been the increasing importance of stock markets in emerging nations. In 1986, the market capitalization of these emerging-country markets was only 3.6 percent of the total; by 1995, it was 10.7 percent (see Fig. 20.1). The emerging-country markets also are among the world's highest-performing. Map 20.2 identifies the ten largest emerging-country stock exchanges and the ten largest developed-country stock exchanges.

Emerging markets have gone through some rough times in recent years. The crash of the Mexican peso in December 1994 sent shock waves through most emerging markets, especially those in Latin America. However, the markets began to recover again in late 1995. Now other factors are influencing the growth of emerging markets. One is the level of interest rates in the United States. As long as interest rates are low—long-term U.S. treasury bonds below 7 percent—U.S. investors will look outside of the United States for investment opportunities.[15] In 1996, due to low U.S. interest rates, it was not uncommon for investment advisors to recommend that an individual's equity portfolio be composed of about 50 percent foreign equity. That, of course, leads to an increase in demand for emerging market securities, helping drive the growth in the market. Another factor causing emerging markets to grow is the rising privatization of government-owned enterprises as countries move to reduce budget deficits. This is an issue in industrial countries as well, especially the countries in the EU that are trying to meet the strict requirements to join the new common currency. Privatization of government-owned enterprises, such as Deutsche Telecom, is giving rise to activity in Euroequity markets, which will be discussed in more detail below.

The Euroequity Market

Another significant event in the past decade is the creation of the **Euroequity market,** the market for shares sold outside the boundaries of the issuing company's home country. Prior to 1980, few companies thought of offering stock outside the

---

Emerging-country stock markets are an important source of funds and are growing on average more rapidly than are the developed-country stock markets.

The Euroequity market is the market for shares sold outside the boundaries of the issuing company's home country.

**Figure 20.1
Growth of
Emerging-Country
Stock Markets**
The market capitalization of emerging-country stock markets rose from 2.5 percent of the world's total in 1983 to 7 percent in 1992.

Source: International Finance Corporation, *Emerging Stock Markets Factbook 1996* (Washington, D.C.: IFC, 1996), pp. 16–17.

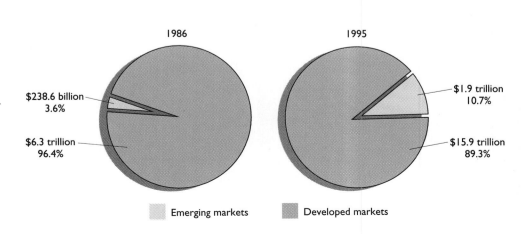

1986

1995

$238.6 billion
3.6%

$1.9 trillion
10.7%

$6.3 trillion
96.4%

$15.9 trillion
89.3%

Emerging markets   Developed markets

Map 20.2   Market Capitalization (in billions of U.S. dollars), 1995

Stock markets in the industrial countries far surpass those in developing countries in terms of market capitalization. Note that almost 43 percent of the world's market capitalization is in U.S. stock markets.

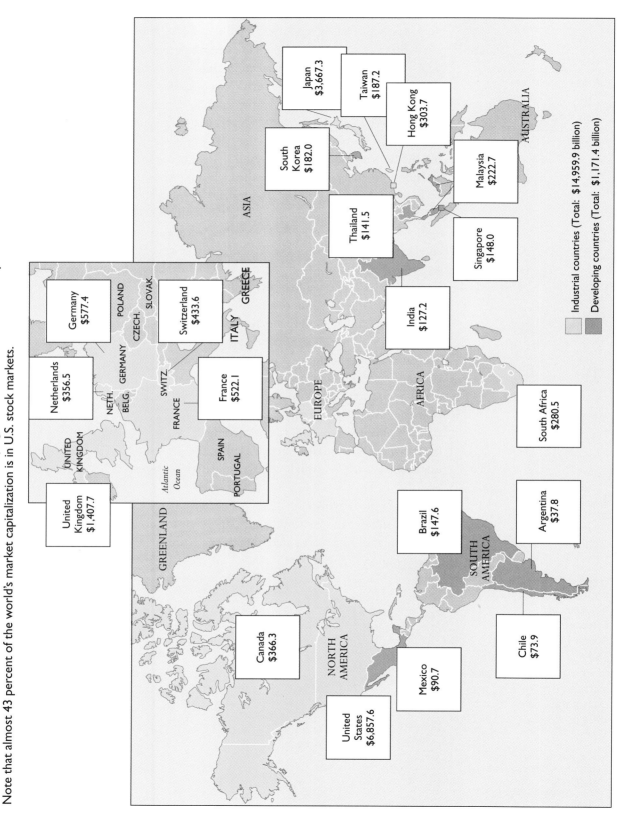

Japan
$3,667.3

Taiwan
$187.2

Hong Kong
$303.7

South Korea
$182.0

Malaysia
$222.7

Thailand
$141.5

Singapore
$148.0

India
$127.2

Germany
$577.4

Switzerland
$433.6

Netherlands
$356.5

France
$522.1

United Kingdom
$1,407.7

South Africa
$280.5

Brazil
$147.6

Argentina
$37.8

Canada
$366.3

Mexico
$90.7

United States
$6,857.6

Chile
$73.9

Industrial countries (Total: $14,959.9 billion)

Developing countries (Total: $1,171.4 billion)

ASIA

AUSTRALIA

EUROPE

AFRICA

GREENLAND

NORTH AMERICA

SOUTH AMERICA

Atlantic Ocean

POLAND

CZECH.

SLOVAK.

GERMANY

GREECE

ITALY

SWITZ.

FRANCE

NETH.

BELG.

SPAIN

PORTUGAL

UNITED KINGDOM

national boundaries of their headquarters country. Since then, hundreds of companies worldwide have issued stock simultaneously in two or more countries.

In some cases, companies list on only one foreign exchange. It is expensive to list on foreign exchanges and so companies often list on one big one, such as the NYSE or the LSE. However, some companies list on several different exchanges, especially if they have foreign investments in several countries and are trying to raise capital in those countries. For example, AT&T lists its stock on exchanges in Brussels, Geneva, London, Paris, and Tokyo, in addition to the United States. Deutsche Bank of Germany lists on eight different exchanges, including Brussels, London, Paris, Tokyo, and several exchanges in Germany.[16]

The U.S. market is important for U.S. and foreign companies looking for equity capital and is popular for Euroequity issues partly because of the size of the market and the speed with which offerings are taken. For example, the large pension funds in the United States can buy large blocks of stock at relatively low transaction costs. Pension-fund managers regard foreign stocks as a good form of portfolio diversification.

The most popular way for a Euroequity to get a listing in the United States is to issue an ADR as Daimler-Benz did (see the closing case in Chapter 19). ADRs are traded like shares of stock, with each one representing some number of shares of the underlying stock; for example, ten ADRs equal one share of Daimler-Benz stock.

The listings of foreign shares in the United States have increased dramatically in recent years. For example, the most actively traded stock in 1992 in the United States was Glaxo Holdings, a British pharmaceuticals giant; more than 569 million shares changed hands on the NYSE through ADRs. In 1992, ADRs worth $125 billion were traded in the United States, a 33-percent increase over 1991. By mid-1993, 1000 different ADRs were available to U.S. investors.[17]

The United States is not the only market for Euroequities. A much larger percentage of the total shares traded on the London Stock Exchange belong to foreign companies than is true for the NYSE, even though the total trading volume in the United States is quite large. Total world market capitalization in 1995 was $17.787 trillion, total trades equaled $11.666 trillion, and 38,864 companies were publically listed. It is hard to know how many companies are listed in Euroquity markets, but the New York Stock Exchange estimates that worldwide trading of foreign shares was $5 trillion in 1995. In the U.S. market alone, trading in 234 listed non-U.S. issues grew 33 percent in 1995, compared with an increase in overall trading of 19 percent.[18] Teléfonos de Mexico was the NYSE's most actively traded stock in 1994 and 1995 and was in the top ten in 1996.[19]

Many foreign corporations try to raise capital in the United States, but they don't want to list on an exchange. Such is the case with several Russian companies. By September 1996, six Russian companies had issued Level I ADRs, which allow them to sell shares to qualified institutional investors over the counter (OTC) rather than on an exchange. One advantage of the Level I ADR is that the company

An ADR is a negative certificate issued by a U.S. bank and representing shares of stock of a foreign corporation.

does not have to make U.S.-style financial disclosures. However, the huge Russian company, LUKoil, wants to move from Level I to Level III. A Level III ADR would allow LUKoil to issue new capital in the United States but would require financial statements prepared according to U.S. GAAP (as discussed in Chapter 19) and audited by a Western auditing firm.[20] A Level II ADR allows a company to list its shares on a U.S. exchange, thus facilitating trades, but not issue new capital.

Offshore Financial Centers

Offshore financial centers are cities or countries that provide large amounts of funds in currencies other than their own. Generally, the markets in these centers are regulated differently, and usually more flexibly, than the domestic markets are. These centers provide an alternative, and usually cheaper, source of funding for MNEs so that they don't have to rely strictly on their own national markets. In essence, offshore financial centers are the locations for Eurocurrency trading of all types and maturities and have one or more of the following characteristics:

- A large foreign-currency (Eurocurrency) market for deposits and loans (that in London, for example)
- A market that is a large net supplier of funds to the world financial markets (that in Switzerland, for example)
- A market that is an intermediary or pass-through for international loan funds (those in the Bahamas and the Cayman Islands, for example)
- Economic and political stability
- An efficient and experienced financial community
- Good communications and supportive services
- An official regulatory climate favorable to the financial industry, in the sense that it protects investors without unduly restricting financial institutions[21]

These centers can be considered as operational centers, where extensive banking activities are carried out, or booking centers, where little actual banking activity takes place but where transactions are recorded in order to take advantage of secrecy and low (or no) tax rates. London is an example of an operational center; the Cayman Islands is an example of a booking center. Although there are many offshore financial centers, the seven most important are Bahrain (for the Middle East), the Caribbean (servicing mainly Canadian and U.S. banks), Hong Kong, London, New York, Singapore, and Switzerland.

London is a crucial center because it offers a variety of services and has a large domestic as well as offshore market. The Caribbean centers (primarily the Bahamas, the Cayman Islands, and the Netherlands Antilles) are essentially offshore locations for New York banks. Switzerland has been a primary source of funds for decades, offering stability, integrity, discretion, and low costs. Singapore has been the center for the Eurodollar market in Asia (sometimes referred to as the Asiadollar market) since 1968, thanks to its strategic geographic location, its strong worldwide telecommunications links, and a variety of governmental regulations that have facilitated the flow of funds. Hong Kong is critical because of its unique status with respect to China and the United Kingdom and its geographic proximity to the rest of the Pacific Rim. Bahrain, an island country in the Persian Gulf, is the financial center of petrodollars (dollars generated from the sale of oil) in the Middle East.

Offshore financial centers are good locations for establishing finance subsidiaries that can raise capital for the parent company or its other subsidiaries. They allow the finance subsidiaries to take advantage of lower borrowing costs and tax rates.

Internal Sources of Funds

Funds are working capital, or current assets minus current liabilities.

A company that wants to expand operations or needs additional working capital can look not only to the debt and equity markets, but also to sources within itself. For an MNE, the complexity of internal sources is magnified because of the number of its subsidiaries and the diverse environments in which they operate. Although the term *funds* usually means cash, it is used in a much broader sense in business and generally refers to working capital, that is, the difference between current assets and current liabilities.

Sources of internal funds:
- **Loans**
- **Dividends**
- **Intercompany receivables and payables**
- **Investments through equity capital**

Figure 20.2 illustrates a situation involving a parent company with two foreign subsidiaries. The parent, as well as the two subsidiaries, may be increasing funds through normal operations. These funds may be used on a company-wide basis. One possible way is through loans: The parent can loan funds directly to one subsidiary or guarantee an outside loan to the other.

Equity capital from the parent is another source of funds for the subsidiary. Funds also can go from subsidiary to parent. The subsidiary could declare a dividend to the parent as a return on capital or could loan cash directly to the parent. If the subsidiary declared a dividend to the parent, the parent could lend the funds back

**Figure 20.2
Internal Sources of
Working Capital
for MNEs**
There are many ways in which MNEs can use internal cash flow to fund worldwide operations.

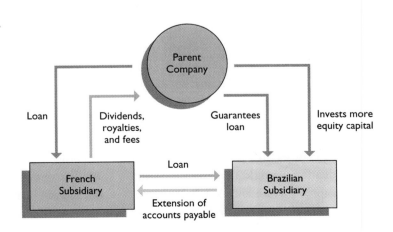

to the subsidiary. The interest payment to the parent would be additional foreign-source income. There may be a withholding tax on the interest payment, which would reduce the cash flow to the parent. However, if the withholding tax is less than the tax on dividends, local management might be happy with the lower tax outflow.[22]

Intercompany financial links become extremely important as MNEs increase in size and complexity. Goods as well as loans can travel between subsidiaries, giving rise to receivables and payables. Companies can move money between and among related entities by paying quickly (leading payments) or can accumulate funds by deferring payment (lagging payments). They also can adjust the size of the payment by arbitrarily raising or lowering the price of intercompany transactions in comparison with the market price. (This strategy, called transfer pricing, was discussed more fully in Chapter 19.)

Thus cash is generated from debt and equity markets both domestically and overseas, from operations, and from internal sources. The problems of managing cash globally are complex. International cash management is complicated by differing inflation rates, changes in exchange rates, and governmental restrictions on the flow of funds.

Global Cash Management

Effective cash management is a chief concern of the MNE. The following three questions must be answered to ensure effective cash management:

1. What are the local and corporate system needs for cash?
2. How can the cash be withdrawn from subsidiaries and centralized?
3. Once the cash has been centralized, what should be done with it?

The MNE must collect and pay cash in its normal operational cycle, and then it must deal with financial institutions, such as commercial and investment banks, in generating and investing cash.

Cash budgets and forecasts are essential in assessing a company's cash needs.

Before any cash is remitted to a control center, whether on a regional or a head-quarters level, local cash needs must be properly assessed through cash budgets and forecasts. Because the cash forecast projects the excess cash that will be available, the manager also will know how much cash can be invested for short-term profits.

Dividends are a good source of intercompany transfers, but governments often restrict their free movement.

Once local needs have been adequately provided for, the cash manager must decide whether to allow the local manager to invest the excess cash or to have it remitted to a central cash pool. If the cash is centralized, the manager must find a way of making the transfer. A cash dividend is the easiest way to distribute cash, but governmental restrictions may reduce the effectiveness of this means. For example, foreign-exchange controls may prevent the company from remitting as large a dividend as it would like. In some countries, the size of the dividend may be tied to the capital invested in the local operation. Cash also can be remitted through royalties, management fees, and repayment of principal and interest on loans.

Many developing countries with large foreign debt, such as Brazil, have made transferring money abroad difficult for companies operating within them because they want to curtail the outflow of foreign exchange. For example, one U.S. company with large operations in Brazil used dividends, loan repayments, and sales commissions to transfer funds out of Brazil. The Brazilian operation was treated as a manufacturing facility, and all export sales were made by a sales subsidiary of the U.S. parent. When the manufacturing facility was established in Brazil, it was financed primarily through debt rather than equity. The parent could get more cash out of Brazil by paying off principal and interest than it could by paying a dividend, which was subject to such large taxes. When foreign sales were made, the Brazilian manufacturer was permitted to pay a commission to the sales company in the United States, which allowed it to transmit more funds abroad. However, the Brazilian government constantly tried to lower the amount of the commission, whereas the parent company tried to increase it.

Multilateral Netting

An important cash-management strategy is netting cash flows internationally. For example, an MNE with operations in four European countries could have several different intercompany cash transfers resulting from loans, the sale of goods, licensing agreements, etc. In Fig. 20.3 for example, there are seven different transfers among the four subsidiaries. Table 20.1 identifies the total receivables, payables, and net position for each subsidiary. Rather than have each subsidiary settle its accounts independently with subsidiaries in other countries, many MNEs are establishing cash-management centers in one city (such as Brussels) to coordinate cash flows among subsidiaries from several countries. Figure 20.4 illustrates how each subsidiary in a net payable position transfers funds to the central clearing account. The manager of the clearing account then transfers funds to the accounts of the net receiver subsidiaries. Thus in this example only four transfers need to take place. The clearing account manager receives transactions information and computes the net position of each subsidiary at least monthly. Then the manager orchestrates the

> Multilateral netting enables companies to reduce the amount of cash flow and move cash more quickly and efficiently.

Figure 20.3
Multilateral Cash Flows
Multilateral cash flows in the absence of netting require each subsidiary to settle intercompany obligations.

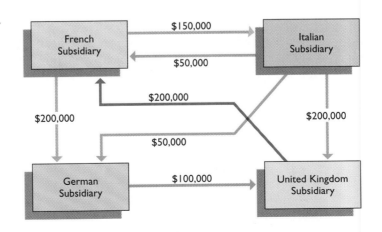

Table 20.1
Net Positions of Subsidiaries in Four Countries (in dollars)
Net positions show total receivables less total payables

Subsidiary	Total receivables	Total payables	Net position
French	250,000	350,000	(100,000)
German	250,000	100,000	150,000
Italian	150,000	300,000	(150,000)
U.K.	300,000	200,000	100,000

settlement process. The transfers take place in the payor's currency, and the foreign-exchange conversion takes place centrally.

Executives who set up cross-currency cash pooling systems often have multiple goals that include:

- Optimizing the use of excess cash
- Reducing interest expenses and maximizing interest yields
- Reducing costly foreign exchange, swap transactions and intercompany transfers
- Minimizing administrative paperwork
- Centralizing and speeding information for tighter control and improved decision making[23]

The multilateral netting process has several major advantages:

- Savings in foreign-exchange conversion costs, since the central manager can effect large exchanges
- Savings of transfer charges and commissions, again due to the large size and smaller number of transactions
- Quicker access to the funds

Figure 20.4
Multilateral Netting
Multilateral netting allows subsidiaries to transfer net intercompany flows to a cash center, or clearing account, which disburses cash to net receivers.

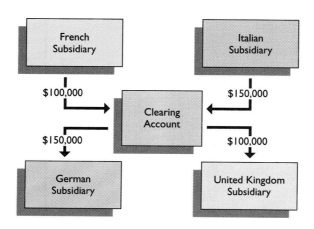

It sometimes can take five days for funds to be exchanged through wire transfer, so netting allows the company to get access to the cash much faster. Electronic transfers also enable the company to standardize and streamline payment routes and banking channels.[24]

Even though there are significant benefits to netting activities, experts estimate that only 50 percent of the *Fortune* 1000 companies actually use netting techniques.[25] One reason is that for netting to work, companies need to establish custom software that not only does the netting at the corporate netting center but also allows subsidiaries to link to the netting center to automatically upload receivables and payables data so that the work does not have to be done manually. Netting also becomes more economically feasible the more subsidiaries and currencies involved. An example of the savings that come from netting involves the U.S. company, Du Pont. "Starting slowly with only the wholly-owned subsidiaries, the company recorded a $2 million savings the first year attributable to netting. Webber Lee, the regional Du Pont treasurer based in Singapore, says the Asia Pacific region includes some 13 countries and approximately 40 entities which currently participate in a netting arrangement."[26]

Coordination Centers

Regional finance-coordina-tion centers can be used to centralize cash-management strategies and practices.

The netting process just described is one of the functions that a regional finance-coordination center can perform. Other functions of such a center are:

- Centralization of financial transactions, including foreign-exchange dealings, pooling, and reinvoicing
- Centralization of administration, accounting, data processing, and information gathering and dissemination
- Advertising, insurance, and reinsurance
- Auxiliary services such as planning[27]

Europe is currently a favored location for these centers. Belgium (especially Brussels) is popular because it levies virtually no taxes on those operations and offers low rents and salaries, compared with European standards.

Financial-Risk Management

Major financial risks arise from inflation and exchange-rate changes.

Global cash-management strategy focuses on the flow of money for specific operating objectives. Another important objective of an MNE's financial strategy is to protect against the risks of investing abroad. The strategies that it adopts to do this may involve the internal movement of funds as well as the use of one or more of the foreign-exchange instruments described in Chapter 9, such as options and forward contracts.

In examining the risks encountered in international business, companies must consider the nature of a risk, the circumstances under which it can occur, the implications for the company, and the best defense against it. Major categories of risks are currency, commercial, and political. Currency risks include inflation and exchange-rate changes. Commercial risks arise from the problems of extending and receiving credit and the difficulties of collection or payment of accounts in different currencies. Political risks are extensive and include trade relations and expropriations.

Inflation

Inflation occurs in varying degrees in nearly every country in which MNEs operate. It can erode the value of financial assets and make financial liabilities more attractive, although the attractiveness of liabilities is softened somewhat by the high interest rates that often accompany loans in countries with high inflation.

High inflation rates often bring a variety of problems that influence the way MNEs operate. The following are the most important:

- Accelerated depreciation or devaluation of the local currency or a maxidevaluation
- Tighter capital controls and import restrictions
- Scarcer credit and higher borrowing costs
- A buildup of accounts receivable and lengthening of collection periods
- Price controls to help bring inflation under control
- Economic and political chaos and labor unrest
- Capital flight
- Greater difficulty in evaluating the performance of foreign subsidiaries[28]

Many companies faced with price controls need to get around them through imaginative product development and pricing strategies. This may involve slight product or packaging modifications and/or brand-name changes in order to effect price increases. Frequently, however, MNEs are so brand-conscious that they refuse to exploit this strategy. For example, Coca-Cola would never consider changing its product name in order to get a price increase. The importance of the brand name outweighs any advantage to be gained by changing it.

One multinational cosmetics company operating in Brazil during a high inflation period in the past got around price controls by changing the container size of a brand-name product to a smaller container while listing the product at a significantly higher price. However, in order to attract sales it would sell the product for considerably less than list price. Then it could increase the price according to inflationary trends up to the upper price limit established by price-control authorities. A major problem the company faced was trying to estimate inflation correctly. If it predicted inflation at 200 percent and priced accordingly, it would be in serious trouble if inflation actually was 500 percent because it would have underpriced its products and sold them for less than the replacement cost of raw materials. On the other hand, if inflation ran at less than 200 percent, it risked pricing itself out of the market.

Financial managers need to assess
- The nature of a financial risk
- Circumstances under which it can occur
- Its implications for the company
- Defensive strategies

High inflation is often accompanied by a weak currency.

Price controls can be circumvented by
- Modifying product strategies
- Reintroducing products with different brand names
- Changing packaging

ETHICAL DILEMMAS & SOCIAL RESPONSIBILITY

Cash-flow management gives rise to numerous ethical dilemmas. Many critics question the practice of setting up subsidiaries in tax-haven countries, especially when the legitimate use of offshore centers turns into illegal activity as a result of the underreporting of revenues or the overstating of expenses. MNEs have been known to transfer money illegally into tax-haven countries so that it can be used to pay bribes. This practice became common knowledge in the United States with the investigation of the Watergate break-in during the presidency of Richard Nixon. The secrecy possible in tax-haven countries makes them natural locations in which to hide cash for illegal purposes. However, not all use of tax havens is illegal. Although the governments of high-tax countries may criticize domestic companies that shelter income in tax-haven countries, those companies are simply taking advantage of differences in tax rates and are not necessarily acting unethically.

Many think that even when investing cash to yield a high return, MNEs should be concerned about the nature of investments. For example, prior to the all-race elections in South Africa in 1994, many pension-fund managers had eliminated from their portfolios the securities of South African companies and of foreign companies doing business in South Africa. Activists had put a lot of pressure, especially during the 1970s, on pension-fund managers for local and state governments, demanding that they get rid of South African investments. More recently, activists have argued that the U.S. government should impose sanctions against China because of human-rights violations by that country's government. However, there have been no attempts to boycott U.S. companies that do business in China or to pressure pension-fund managers to get rid of investments related to that country. An example of a value-based investment practice is that of Muslim-owned banks, which do not invest in business activities that are inconsistent with the tenets of Islam, such as the manufacture of alcoholic beverages.

Another ethical criticism of MNEs is that they are able to use their size and power to extract favorable borrowing terms in developing countries, leaving little capital for local companies and forcing them to pay higher rates than the MNEs pay.[29] However, this is true primarily of large MNEs, rather than medium-sized or small ones. Many smaller MNEs are not able to access local capital markets any differently than domestic companies do. Large MNEs that bring capital into a locale instead of getting it from local sources are behaving more ethically from the viewpoint of the host country. However, MNEs often employ local borrowing as a strategy for hedging against possible future losses, as Disney did when building Euro Disney. Further, it is easier to repay local-currency loans with local-currency revenues than it is to convert local-currency revenues into foreign currency to pay off foreign-currency loans.

In countries with high inflation, payables should be
stretched out, receivables
collected quickly, and excess
cash repatriated or invested.

It is evident that a company operating in an inflationary environment needs to manage receivables and payables carefully. Receivables must be collected on a timely basis through a well-trained credit and collection department and a sophisticated and reliable reporting system.[30] Once receivables are collected, idle cash should be kept at a minimum. Funds should be remitted to the parent cash pool, as described earlier in this chapter, or invested in income-producing assets that provide a return in excess of inflation.

Exchange-Rate Changes

If all exchange rates were fixed in relation to one another, there would be no foreign-exchange risk. However, rates are not fixed, and currency values change frequently. Instead of infrequent one-way changes, currencies fluctuate often and both up and down. A change in the exchange rate can result in three different exposures for a company: translation exposure, transaction exposure, and economic exposure.

Translation exposure arises
because, as the exchange
rate changes, the dollar
value of the exposed asset or
liability changes.

Translation exposure   Foreign-currency financial statements are translated into the reporting currency of the parent company (assumed to be U.S. dollars for U.S. companies) for a number of reasons, as noted in Chapter 19. Exposed accounts—those translated at the balance sheet rate or current exchange rate—either gain or lose command over dollars. For example, assume a subsidiary of a U.S. company operates in Mexico and has 900,000 pesos in a bank account there. If the Mexican peso, weakened by inflation, were to depreciate in relation to the dollar from 7.9 pesos per dollar to 8.5 pesos per dollar, the subsidiary's bank account would drop in value from $113,924 to $105,882 as a result of the depreciation.

The combined effect of the exchange-rate change on all exposed assets and liabilities is either a gain or a loss. However, whether the foreign-currency financial statements are translated according to the temporal method or the current-rate method, the gain or loss does not represent an actual cash-flow effect. For example, the cash in the Mexican bank is only translated, not converted, into dollars.

Transaction exposure arises
because the receivable or
payable changes in value as
the exchange rate changes.

Transaction exposure   Denominating a transaction in a foreign currency represents foreign-exchange risk because the company has accounts receivable or payable in foreign currency that must be settled eventually. For example, assume a U.S. exporter delivers merchandise to a British importer at a total price of $500,000 when the exchange rate is 1.5000 dollars per pound. If the exporter were to receive payment in dollars, there would be no immediate impact on the exporter if the dollar/pound exchange rate changed. If payment were to be received in pounds, however, the exporter could be exposed to a foreign-exchange gain or loss. For example, with the exchange rate at 1.5000 dollars per pound, the sale would be carried on the exporter's books at $500,000, but the underlying value in which the sale is denominated, as explained in Chapter 19, would be 333,333 pounds. If the rate moved to 1.4000 dollars per pound by the time the receivable was collected, the exporter would receive 333,333 pounds, but that payment would be worth $466,666, a loss of $33,334. This would be an actual cash-flow loss to the exporter.

For example, the Mexican distributors of Novell, a U.S.-based software company, were greatly affected by the peso devaluation of 1994. Since Novell invoiced its software sales in dollars, it had no foreign-exchange risk, but the distributors in Mexico did, because they were selling the software in pesos but paying Novell in dollars. When the peso devalued in December 1994, it took more pesos to convert into dollars to pay Novell, and the distributors could not come up with enough cash to pay Novell.

Economic exposure   Economic exposure arises from, for example, the pricing of products, the sourcing and cost of inputs, and the location of investments. The economic impact on the company is difficult to measure, but that impact is crucial to its long-run viability. Pricing strategies have both an immediate and a long-term impact. For example, the inventory sold to the British importer probably was sold to final users before the exchange rate changed, but future sales would be affected by the rate change. Assume the exporter sold its most recent shipment of $500,000 at an exchange rate of 1.5000 dollars per pound for a cost to the importer of 333,333 pounds. If the British pound were to weaken to 1.4000 dollars per pound, the exporter would have two choices. The first alternative is to continue to sell the product to the British importer for $500,000, which would now cost the importer 357,143 pounds. At the higher price, the importer might lose market share. Or the importer could absorb the cost increase in its profit margin and continue to sell the product for a total of 333,333 pounds. The second alternative is to sell the inventory to the importer for fewer dollars so that the pound equivalent is still 333,333 pounds. At the new exchange rate, the sale price would have to be $466,666. Thus the exporter would end up with the lower profit margin. Exporters and importers must always determine the impact of a price change on volume.

Because of the strengthening yen, many Japanese companies have moved production facilities offshore, including to the United States, in order to avoid their high costs and take advantage of low-cost locations.

Exposure-Management Strategy

To protect assets adequately against risks from exchange-rate fluctuations, management must

- Define and measure exposure
- Organize and implement a reporting system that monitors exposure and exchange-rate movements
- Adopt a policy assigning responsibility for hedging exposure
- Formulate strategies for hedging exposure

Defining and measuring exposure   Most MNEs will be subject to all three types of exposure: translation, transaction, and economic. To develop a viable hedging strategy, a company must be able to forecast the degree of exposure in each major currency in which it operates. Because the types of exposure differ, the actual exposure by currency must be kept separate. For example, the translation exposure in Brazilian cruzeiros should be kept separate from the transaction exposure because the transaction exposure will result in an actual cash flow, whereas the translation exposure may not. Thus the company may adopt different hedging strategies for the different types of exposure.

Exchange-rate movements are forecasted using in-house or external experts.

A key aspect of measuring exposure involves forecasting exchange rates that apply to the identified exposure. Estimating future exchange rates is similar to fortune telling: Approaches range from gut feelings to sophisticated economic models, each having varying degrees of success. Whatever the approach used, a company should estimate ranges within which it expects a currency to vary over the forecasting period. Some companies develop in-house capabilities to monitor exchange rates, using economists who also try to obtain a consensus of exchange-rate movements from the banks with whom they deal. Their concern is to forecast the direction, magnitude, and timing of an exchange-rate change. Other companies contract out this work.

The reporting system should utilize both central control and input from foreign operations.

A reporting system   Once the company has decided how to define and measure exposure and estimate future exchange rates, it must design, organize, and implement a reporting system that will assist in protecting it against risk. To achieve this, substantial participation from foreign operations must be combined with effective central control. Foreign input is important in order to ensure the quality of information being used in forecasting techniques. Because exchange rates move frequently, the company must obtain input from those who are attuned to the pulse of the foreign country. In addition, the maximum effectiveness of hedging techniques will depend on the cooperation of personnel in the foreign operations.

Central control of exposure is needed to protect resources more efficiently. Each organizational unit may be able to define its own exposure, but the company also has an overall exposure. To set hedging policies on a separate-entity basis might not take into account the fact that exposures of several entities (that is, branches, subsidiaries, affiliates, and so on) could offset one another.

Management of an MNE should devise a uniform reporting system to be used by all units. The report should identify the exposed accounts the company wants to monitor, the exposed position by currency of each account, and the different time periods to be covered. Exposure should be separated into translation, transaction, and economic components, with the transaction exposure identified by cash inflows and outflows over time.

The time periods to be covered depend on the company. One possibility is to look at long-term as well as short-term flows. For example, staggered periods (thirty, sixty, and ninety days; six, nine, and twelve months; or two, three, and four years) could be considered. The reason for the longer time frame is that operating commitments, such as plant construction and production runs, are fairly long-term decisions.[31]

Once each basic reporting unit has identified its exposure, the data should be sent to the next organizational level for preliminary consolidation. That level may be a regional headquarters (for Latin America or Europe, for example) or a product division, depending on the company's organizational structure. The preliminary consolidation enables the region or division to determine exposure by account and by currency for each time period. The resulting reports should be routine, periodic, and standardized to ensure comparability and timeliness in formulating strategies. Final reporting should be at the corporate level, where corporate exposure can be determined and strategies identified to reflect the best interests of the company as a whole.

Centralized exposure-management policy permits economies of scale and the specialization of experts.

A centralized policy It is important for management to decide at what level hedging strategies will be determined and implemented. To achieve maximum effectiveness in hedging, a policy should be established at the corporate level. Having an overview of corporate exposure and the cost and feasibility of different strategies at different levels in the company, the corporate treasurer should be able to design and implement a cost-effective program for exposure management. As the company grows in size and complexity, it may have to decentralize some decisions in order to increase flexibility and speed of reaction to a more rapidly changing international monetary environment. However, such decentralization should stay within a well-defined policy established at the corporate level. Some companies run their hedging operations more as profit centers and nurture in-house trading desks. Most MNEs, however, are very traditional and conservative in their approach, preferring to cover exposure (enter into a hedging strategy that minimizes losses due to exposed positions) rather than to extract huge profits or risk huge losses.

Hedging strategies can be operational or contractual.

Formulating hedging strategies Effective management of foreign-exchange risk involves deciding which risks are important and then establishing a management structure that can manage the risk. Once a company has identified its level of exposure and determined which exposure is critical, it can hedge its position by adopting numerous strategies, each with cost/benefit implications as well as operational implications. The safest position is a balanced position in which exposed assets equal exposed liabilities. Achieving this involves operational strategies to hedge exposure, the principal ones being balance-sheet management and leads and lags in the transfer of funds. In addition, companies can enter into a number of contractual obligations to hedge exposure, such as forward-exchange contracts and currency options.

Operational strategies include
- **Using local debt to balance local assets**
- **Taking advantage of leads and lags for intercompany payments**

To reduce exposure through operational strategies, management must determine the working capital needs of a subsidiary. Although it may be wise to collect receivables as fast as possible in an inflationary country in which the local currency is expected to depreciate, the company must consider the competitive implications of not extending credit.

In reality, working-capital management under exchange risk assumes that currency values move in one direction. A weak-currency country generally (although not always) suffers from inflation. The approach to protecting assets in the face of currency depreciation also applies to protection against inflation. Inflation erodes the purchasing power of local currency, whereas depreciation erodes the foreign currency equivalent. In the weak-currency situation, subsidiaries' cash should be remitted to the parent as fast as possible or invested locally in something that appreciates in value, such as fixed assets. Accounts receivable should be collected as quickly as possible when they are denominated in the local currency and stretched out when denominated in a stronger currency. Liabilities should be treated in the opposite manner.

A policy for inventory is difficult to determine. If inventory is considered to be exposed, it should be kept at as low a working level as possible. However, because its value usually increases through price rises, it can be a successful hedge against inflation and exchange-rate moves. If the inventory is imported, it should be stocked before a depreciation, since it will cost more local currency after the change to purchase the same amount in foreign currency. When price controls are in effect or there is strong competition, the subsidiary may not be able to increase the price of inventory. In this case, inventory can be treated in the same way as cash and receivables. These principles can be reversed when an appreciation is predicted, that is, keep cash and receivables high and liquidate debt as rapidly as possible. The safest approach is to keep the net exposed position as low as possible.

The use of debt to balance exposure is an interesting strategy. Many companies have adopted a "borrow locally" strategy, especially in weak-currency countries. One problem with this strategy is that interest rates in weak-currency countries tend to be quite high, so there must be a trade-off between the cost of borrowing and the potential loss from exchange-rate variations. For example, Coca-Cola has a strategy whereby at least half of its net exposed asset position in foreign countries is offset by foreign currency borrowings.[32] B&D also uses local borrowings to hedge a net exposed asset position, but each exposure is considered on a case-by-case basis rather than automatically covered with local borrowing.[33]

Protecting against loss from transaction exposure becomes very complex. In dealing with foreign customers, it is always safest for the company to denominate the transaction in its own currency. Alternatively, it could denominate purchases in a weaker currency and sales in a stronger currency. If forced to make purchases in a strong currency and sales in a weak currency, it could resort to contractual measures or try to balance its inflows and outflows through more astute sales and purchasing strategies.

Another operational strategy, known as leads and lags, often is used to protect cash flows among related entities, such as a parent and its subsidiaries. The **lead strategy** involves collecting foreign-currency receivables before they are due when the foreign currency is expected to weaken and paying foreign-currency payables before they are due when the foreign currency is expected to strengthen. With a **lag**

A lead strategy involves collecting or paying early.

A lag strategy involves collecting or paying late.

strategy, a company delays collection of foreign-currency receivables if that currency is expected to strengthen and delays payables when the currency is expected to weaken. In other words, a company usually leads into and lags out of a hard currency and leads out of and lags into a weak currency.

Leads and lags are much easier to use among related entities when a central corporate financial officer can spot the potential gains and implement a policy. There are two problems with a lead or lag strategy. First, it may not be useful for the movement of large blocks of funds. If there are infrequent decisions involving small amounts of money, it is easy to manage the system, but as the number, frequency, and size of transactions increase, it becomes difficult to manage. Second, as mentioned earlier in this chapter, leads and lags are often subject to governmental control, since currency movements impact a country's balance of payments.

Sometimes an operational strategy means shifting assets overseas to take advantage of currency changes. When the yen strengthened against the U.S. dollar, for example, Toyota shifted more of its manufacturing into the United States to take advantage of the cheaper dollar. As long as the yen was strong, it was difficult to export from Japan to the United States, so the companies could service U.S. demand through production in the United States.

Forward contracts can be used to establish a fixed exchange rate for future transactions.

In addition to the operational strategies just mentioned, a company may hedge exposure through contractual arrangements, using derivatives such as forward contracts and options. The most common approach is to use a forward contract. For example, assume a U.S. exporter sells goods to a British manufacturer for 1 million pounds, with payment due in ninety days. The spot exchange rate is 1.5000 dollars per pound, and the forward rate is 1.4500 dollars per pound. At the time of the sale, it is recorded on the books of the exporter at $1.5 million, and a corresponding receivable is set up for the same amount. However, the exporter is concerned about the exchange risk. The exporter can enter into a forward contract, which will guarantee that the proceeds of the receivable can be converted into dollars at a rate of 1.4500 dollars per pound, no matter what the actual future exchange rate is. This move will yield $1.45 million, for a cost of protection of $50,000. Or the exporter could wait until the receivable is collected in ninety days and gamble on a better rate in the spot market. If the actual rate at that time is 1.4700 dollars per pound, the exporter will receive $1.47 million, which is not as good as the initial receivable of $1.5 million but is better than the forward yield of $1.45 million. On the other hand, if the dollar strengthens to 1.4000 dollars per pound, the exporter would be much better off with the forward contract. Each company has a risk profile, and they have to adopt a hedging strategy consistent with that profile. For example, some companies are willing to tolerate a certain degree of risk and do not want to enter into the expense to hedge that risk. Other companies may tolerate less risk and are thus willing to incur the cost of a hedge in order to get rid of the risk.

Currency options can be utilized to assure access to foreign currency at a fixed exchange rate for a specific period of time.

The foreign-currency option is a relatively recent foreign-exchange instrument. It is more flexible than the forward contract because it gives its purchaser the right, but not the obligation, to buy or sell a certain amount of foreign currency at a set exchange rate within a specified amount of time. For example, assume a U.S. exporter decides to sell merchandise to a British manufacturer for 1 million pounds when the exchange rate is 1.5000 dollars per pound. At the same time, the exporter goes to Goldman Sachs, its investment banker, and enters into an option to deliver pounds for dollars at an exchange rate of 1.5000 dollars per pound at an option cost of $25,000. (Alternatively, the company could use the Philadelphia Stock Exchange to get access to options, but the investment bank usually provides greater flexibility at lower cost for large clients.) That means that whether or not the exporter exercises the option, having it costs $25,000. When the exporter receives the 1 million pounds from the manufacturer, it must decide whether to exercise the option. If the exchange rate is above 1.5000 dollars per pound, it will not exercise the option, because it can get a better yield by converting pounds at the market rate. The only thing lost is the $25,000 cost of the option, which is like insurance. On the other hand, if the exchange rate is below 1.5000 dollars per pound, say at 1.4500, the exporter will exercise the option and trade pounds at the rate of 1.5000. The proceeds will be $1.5 million less the option cost of $25,000.

Historically, companies have preferred to use a forward contract when the amount and timing of the future cash flow are certain. Where there is high uncertainty, they prefer the flexibility of an option. Although options can be more expensive than forward contracts, especially in a highly volatile market, they sometimes can be very useful. Their flexibility has prompted corporate treasurers to use options increasingly since the mid-1980s.

Examples of Foreign-Exchange Strategies

There is a difference of opinion as to the importance of hedging foreign-exchange risk.[34] A hedging strategy is a mixture of operating and financial hedges and differs by the type of exposure—translation, transaction, economic. As noted in the opening case, LSI Logic sources many of its products in Japan. When the Japanese yen fell in the spring of 1995, LSI had to cut costs in its Japanese operations to counteract the negative effect on earnings when it translated its sales in yen back into dollars for accounting purposes.[35] Some companies change prices as exchange rates change. Kyocera, the Japanese ceramic chip manufacturer, had to increase its prices in the United States as the Japanese yen rose in value. Canon, Inc., the Japanese manufacturer of printers, has stated that when the Japanese yen weakens, it has to lower prices because of pressure from dealers. Their products compete directly with Hewlett-Packard, and the dealers feel that a lower price will help them become more competitive.[36]

In addition to adjusting price, many companies enter into derivative contracts to hedge exposures. Hewlett-Packard protects profit margins on foreign orders by buying options or forward purchase contracts for dollars, yen, and other currencies.[37] A foreign order is usually denominated in the currency of the seller, so H-P purchases derivatives from foreign-exchange traders to set their cost in dollars in advance.

Given the bad press that derivatives have generated in recent years (see the Barings example in Chapter 9), companies are careful to describe how they use derivatives. In its 1995 annual report, Coca-Cola explains its use of derivatives as follows:

> With approximately 82 percent of our 1995 operating income generated outside the United States, weakness in one particular currency is offset by strengths in others.
>
> Most of our foreign currency exposures are managed on a consolidated basis, which allows us to net certain exposures and thus take advantage of any natural offsets. We use forward exchange contracts to adjust the currency mix of our recorded assets and liabilities, which further reduces our exposure from adverse fluctuations in exchange rates. In addition, we enter into forward exchange and swap contracts and purchase options to hedge both firmly committed and anticipated transactions, as appropriate, and net investments in certain international operations.
>
> "We use primarily liquid spot (spot contracts that are widely and easily traded), forward, option and swap contracts. Our Company does not enter into leverage or structured contracts. Additionally, we do not enter into derivative financial instruments for trading purposes. As a matter of policy, all of our derivative positions are used to hedge underlying economic exposures by mitigating certain risks such as changes in currency, interest rates and other market factors on a matched basis. Gains or losses on hedging transactions are offset by gains or losses on the underlying exposures being hedged."[38]

Thus Coca-Cola uses a mix of operating and financial strategies, primarily hedging its transactions exposure, but also translation exposures (hedging of net investments) for some of its foreign operations. It is careful to point out that all of its hedges are for operating purposes, not speculation (trading purposes).

Financial Aspects of the Investment Decision

The parent company needs to compare the net present value or internal rate of return of a foreign project with that of its other projects and with that of others available in the host country.

The parent company must compare the net present value or internal rate of return of a foreign project with that of its other projects and that of others available in the host country. Discounted cash flows often are used to compare and evaluate investment projects. Several aspects of capital budgeting are unique to foreign project assessment:

- Parent cash flows must be distinguished from project cash flows. Each flow contributes to a different view of value.
- Parent cash flows often depend on the form of financing. Thus cash flows cannot be clearly separated from financing decisions.

- Remittance of funds to the parent must be explicitly recognized because of differing tax systems, legal and political constraints on the movement of funds, local business norms, and differences in how financial markets and institutions function.
- Cash flows from subsidiaries to parent can be generated by an array of nonfinancial payments, including payment of license fees and payments for imports from the parent.
- Differing rates of national inflation must be anticipated because of their importance in causing changes in competitive position and thus in cash flows over time.
- The possibility of unanticipated exchange-rate changes must be considered because of their potential direct effects on the value of cash flows to the parent, as well as their indirect effects on the competitive position of the foreign subsidiary.
- Use of segmented national capital markets may create an opportunity for financial gains or may lead to additional financial costs.
- Use of loans subsidized by the host-country government complicates both capital structure and the ability to determine an appropriate weighted average cost of capital for discounting purposes.
- Political risk must be evaluated because political events can drastically reduce the value or availability of expected cash flows.
- Terminal value (the value of the project at the end of the budgeting period) is more difficult to estimate because potential purchasers from the host, home, or third countries or from the private or public sector may have widely divergent perspectives on the value of the project.[39]

Management must view cash flows from two perspectives: the total flows available to the local operations, and the cash available to the parent. The outflows to the parent are important to consider in light of the original investment made, especially if the investment was made with the parent's funds. Finally, the company must analyze foreign political and exchange risks. The best approach is for it to adjust forecasted cash outflows to different estimates representing different levels of risk.

COUNTERVAILING

F O R C E S

To optimize the flow of funds worldwide, the MNE must determine the proper parent-subsidiary relationship with respect to the finance function. In addition, the finance function needs to be broken down into different elements, such as foreign-exchange risk management and long-term and short-term financing decisions, because the parent-subsidiary relationship may depend on the specific decision being considered.

The MNE needs to deter-
mine the proper parent-
subsidiary relationship for
the finance function.

Types of parent-subsidiary
relationships:
• **Complete decentralization
  at the subsidiary level**
• **Complete centralization
  at the parent level**
• **Varying degrees of
  centralization**

Parent-subsidiary relationships are typically viewed as being of three types:

1. Complete decentralization at the subsidiary level
2. Complete centralization at the parent level
3. Varying degrees of decentralization, typically through regional financial centers[40]

However, general organizational structure complicates the choice of parent-subsidiary relationships. For example, if a company is organized along product lines as well as by geographic regions, does the finance function flow through the product chain of command or the regional one?

Some argue for decentralization of the finance function because country environments are so unique that they need to be treated differently. For example, in the 1980s when Argentina's annual inflation rate rose to 5000 percent, a U.S. pump manufacturing company with an Argentinean subsidiary found that it was generating lots of cash that it was able to invest at high interest rates. It was earning so much interest income that its net income actually exceeded sales. The company's U.S. management was having a difficult time understanding the problems of the local environment, so it gave local management the responsibility for managing liquid assets, to the great benefit of the company.

If an MNE's management regards overseas operations as a portfolio of independent businesses—basically a multidomestic strategy—the parent-subsidiary relationship is likely to be more informal, with very simple financial controls. If management thinks of overseas operations as appendages of the parent company, the financial control systems are likely to be much tighter, with information and excess cash being shipped back to the parent. Finally, if management treats overseas operations as delivery pipelines to a unified global market—a global strategy—financial controls are likely to be tight, but only so that financial resources can be used on a global basis as needed.[41]

In a decentralized situation, in which the subsidiary is relatively independent of the parent, the parent receives reports but generally issues only minor guidelines, especially when foreign sales comprise a small part of total sales and when the parent staff is relatively unfamiliar with the foreign environment. In a centralized situation, the parent staff dominates planning and decision making, and the subsidiary carries out orders. The idea behind this approach is that the more sophisticated parent staff understands the intricacies of moving funds across national boundaries in order to serve the needs of the whole company at the greatest profit.

An argument for decentralization is that country environments are so unique that
they need to be treated
differently.

However, truly global companies try to achieve high levels of sophistication at both parent and subsidiary levels. Because of this dual expertise, the parent staff is better suited to coordinate system activities and to monitor results, whereas the subsidiary staff is better able to act within specified guidelines. To maintain close proximity to foreign financial-information sources, many companies have organized regional financial decision-making centers. The parent staff continues to issue guidelines for decision making and coordinates the entire system, but financial organization and management functions are turned over to the regional organizations.

LOOKING TO THE FUTURE

It is difficult to forecast trends in global capital markets because of rapid economic changes worldwide. As world trade increases and global interdependence rises, the velocity of financial transactions also must increase. Financial markets will continue to be dominated by the world's largest—New York, Tokyo, and London. However, the action increasingly will take place in the emerging nations within Eastern Europe, Latin America, and Southeast Asia. As fund managers continue to diversify their portfolios to include securities of emerging countries and as investment advisors continue to recommend that their clients diversify their portfolios away from domestic to global funds, the interest in emerging-country markets will continue to rise. This will clearly benefit investors through high returns and also will help the emerging nations in capital formation.

Two events will significantly influence the cash-management and hedging strategies of MNEs in the future: the information and technology explosion, and the growing number and sophistication of hedging instruments (financial derivatives such as options and forwards). The information explosion will continue to enable companies to get information more quickly and cheaply. In addition, the advent of electronic data interchange (EDI) will allow them to transfer information and money instantaneously worldwide. Companies will significantly reduce paper flow and increase the speed of delivery of information and funds, enabling them to manage cash and to utilize intercompany resources much more effectively. Consequently, companies will be able to reduce not only the cost of producing information, but also interest and other borrowing costs.

The growing number and sophistication of financial derivatives, along with the growing expertise of providers and users of those instruments, should allow companies to identify and hedge their exposure much more effectively. Companies that previously did not hedge certain types of exposure will find that the availability of derivatives will increase and their cost will decrease, making risk protection much more possible.

Also, the centralization and regionalization of cash and exposure management will increase, not decrease, even though local finance staff will become much more sophisticated. The sheer volume of transactions and the resulting economies argue for more, not less, centralization. The speed and sophistication of communication should allow companies to manage assets much more quickly than in the recent past.

WEB CONNECTION

Check out our home page for links to finance resources on the World Wide Web.

Summary

- **The corporate finance function deals with the acquisition of financial resources and their allocation among the company's present and potential activities and projects.**

- Country-specific factors are the most important determination of the capital structure of a company.

- Local debt markets, which vary dramatically from country to country because of local business customs and practices, are important sources of funds for MNEs.

- A Eurocurrency is any currency banked outside of its country of origin, but primarily dollars banked outside the United States.

- A Eurobond is a bond issue sold in a currency other than that of the country of issue. A foreign bond is one sold outside the country of the borrower but denominated in the currency of the country of issue. A global bond is one issued simultaneously in North America, Asia, and Europe according to the listing requirements of each market.

- Although the three largest stock markets in the world are in New York, Tokyo, and London, the markets in emerging countries in Asia, Eastern Europe, and Latin America are among the world's most dynamic.

- Euroequities are shares listed on stock exchanges in countries other than the home country of the issuing company.

- Offshore financial centers such as Bahrain, the Caribbean, Hong Kong, London, New York, Singapore, and Switzerland deal in large amounts of foreign currency.

- The major sources of internal funds for an MNE are dividends, royalties, management fees, intercompany loans, loans from parent to subsidiaries, purchases and sales of inventory, and equity flows from parent to subsidiaries.

- Global cash management is complicated by differing inflation rates, changes in exchange rates, and governmental restrictions on the flow of funds. A sound cash-management system for an MNE requires timely reports from affiliates worldwide.

- Management must protect corporate assets from losses due to inflation and exchange-rate changes. Exchange rates can influence the dollar equivalent of foreign-currency financial statements, the amount of cash that can be earned from foreign-currency transactions, and a company's production and marketing decisions.

- **Foreign-exchange risk management involves defining and measuring exposure, setting up a good monitoring and reporting system, adopting a policy to assign responsibility for exposure management, and formulating strategies for hedging exposure.**

- **Forward contracts can lock the company into a specific exchange rate for future obligations, which could result in gains or losses, depending on what happens to the actual exchange rate. However, a forward contract eliminates exchange-rate uncertainty for the company.**

- **Foreign-currency options give the purchaser the option to buy or sell foreign currency in a certain amount, at a fixed exchange rate, during a specified time period. An option is more expensive than a forward contract but is more flexible.**

- **When deciding to invest abroad, a company must consider its optimal debt/equity ratio, evaluate local currency and parent currency rates of return, identify cash flows unique to the foreign investment, calculate a multinational cost of capital, and offset foreign political and exchange risks.**

Case
NCR's Risk-
Management
Strategy[42]

In 1997, NCR embarked on a new phase of its existence, which began in 1884 when John H. Patterson founded the National Cash Register Company, maker of the first mechanical cash register. The new NCR, which was acquired by AT&T in 1991 and was subsequently spun off from AT&T at the end of 1996, is divided into four major business groups:

- Computer Systems Group
- Communications Industry Business Unit
- Financial Systems Group
- Retail Systems Group

The Computer Systems Group develops, manufactures, and markets computer systems. The other three groups represent specific industries targeted by NCR.

NCR generated $8 billion in revenues in 1995, the smallest of the AT&T groups (the new AT&T generated $51 billion in revenues, and Lucent Technologies generated $21 billion in revenues). However, NCR is the most international of the group, generating over 50 percent of its revenues abroad, whereas AT&T as a whole generated only 10.9 percent of total revenues from abroad. NCR has 37,900 employees worldwide, 19,000 of whom are in the United States. It also has 1100 offices and 31 development and manufacturing locations in more than 130 countries. Its top five countries in revenues are Japan, Germany, Switzerland, the United Kingdom, and France.

NCR's leadership team is divided into product groups, geographic areas (Americas Region, Asia/Pacific Region, and Europe & Middle East/Africa Region), and functional areas (such as Global Human Resources, Corporate Strategy, and Finance & Administration). The role of the leadership team is to set the vision, mission, and direction for NCR.

Effective July 1, 1996, Earl C. Shanks was hired away from Farley Industries Inc. and named as the head of the company's treasury functions. He reports directly to Per-Olof Loof, head of the Financial Systems Group and member of NCR's leadership team. This was an important appointment, because in 1991 when AT&T acquired NCR, virtually all of NCR's treasury functions were transferred to AT&T. Thus Shanks's mission is to rebuild the treasury group from zero. He is responsible for creating a global organization which will manage the company's worldwide cash flows and foreign-exchange risk, establish adequate borrowing facilities, and establish and implement finance and investment objectives and strategies for pension assets and benefits.

Until NCR issues its 1996 annual report, it is impossible to know how important each of the geographic areas is.

In 1990, the last year NCR issued an annual report before the merger, it noted that transfer pricing between geographic divisions is done at market prices. It also emphasized how interdependent its units are: "The methods followed in developing the geographic area data require the use of estimation techniques and do not take into account the extent to which NCR's product development, manufacturing, and marketing depend upon each other. Thus, the information may not be as indicative of results as it would be if the geographic areas were independent organizations."

Similar breakdowns are not found in the AT&T *Annual Report,* since foreign revenues are only 10.9 percent of total revenues. AT&T provides revenues, operating income, and identifiable assets for only two geographic segments: United States and other geographic areas. FASB Statement No. 14 does not require the disclosure of geographic segment data if foreign revenues, earnings, and identifiable assets are less than 10 percent of total revenues. However, AT&T's *Annual Report* mentions that foreign revenues in its segment disclosures include only revenues from foreign-based operations. Revenues from all international activities, including the foreign-segment revenues and those from international telecommunications services and export sales, provided 26.2 percent of consolidated revenues in 1995. AT&T had hoped to generate 50 percent of its revenues from abroad by the turn of the century. However, NCR, with nearly 60 percent of its revenues coming from abroad, is clearly more global than AT&T in general.

Prior to the merger, NCR took advantage of foreign capital markets to borrow money. In its 1990 *Annual Report,* NCR reported notes payable totaling $182 million, classified as short-term borrowings from banks, mainly denominated in foreign currencies. NCR also included long-term obligations denominated in Eurodollars (which will be explained more fully in this chapter) and in Japanese yen.

If AT&T uses foreign capital markets, it does not disclose much information. AT&T's 1995 *Annual Report* describes its debt obligations but does not disclose whether any are in a foreign currency. The annual report mentions, however, that a consortium of lenders provides revolving credit facilities to AT&T and AT&T Capital. Both AT&T and AT&T Capital maintain lines of credit with different consortiums of primary foreign banks. In addition, AT&T lists its stock on exchanges in Brussels, Geneva, London, Paris, and Tokyo, in addition to several in the United States, so it is gaining access to equity capital abroad.

Figure 20.5 identifies the geographic segment revenues for the old NCR. There are some differences in organizational structure for the new NCR, as noted at the beginning of the case. Under the old NCR structure, the Latin America/Middle East/Africa geographic segment generated about 4.8 percent of total revenues for NCR, and it encompassed a politically and economically volatile region of the world. This segment was essentially a marketing unit that bought products at a discount from the company's production and development units and then sold the products in its own regions. To focus corporate resources and expertise internationally, the unit performed its own currency-risk management in coordination with corporate treasury staff.

The objective of NCR's risk-management strategy was to neutralize economic exposure from foreign-currency fluctuations, first through operational strategies and second with foreign-exchange contracts. To illustrate how significant those contracts were, on December 31, 1990, NCR had $1.271 billion in outstanding forward contracts, of which 60 percent were in European currencies and 40 percent were in Pacific currencies. There were no contracts in Latin American currencies, because those financial markets were not developed enough for forward contracts.

From an organizational standpoint, NCR put a lot of responsibility on the shoulders of group management. Each geographic unit had a group vice president and finance director responsible for the overall risk-management strategy of the group, subject to the approval of top management and corporate treasury. Each of the eight regions that composed the Latin America/Middle East/Africa group had a general manager and a finance director. Once the risk-management strategy had been determined, the execution of the strategy was left to the local level, where market conditions vary considerably.

Foreign-Exchange Risk Management in the Old NCR

It is hard to know how the new NCR will deal with foreign exchange risk management, but we can get a general idea by looking at how NCR dealt with that issue prior to being

Figure 20.5
NCR's 1990 Revenues by Geographic Area
Less than half (40.2 percent) of NCR's 1990 revenues were from the United States, and only 4.8 percent were from the volatile regions of Latin America, the Middle East, and Africa. Europe (34 percent) and the Pacific (21 percent) were fairly significant sources of revenue. The Pacific region includes Australasia, the Far East, and Canada.

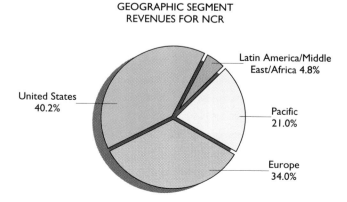

GEOGRAPHIC SEGMENT
REVENUES FOR NCR

Latin America/Middle East/Africa 4.8%

United States 40.2%

Pacific 21.0%

Europe 34.0%

acquired by AT&T, and how AT&T dealt with those issues in the intervening years before spinning off NCR.

Prior to 1991, NCR was organized differently than it is now on a geographic basis, as noted in Fig. 20.5. However, it was still considered one of the world's premier MNEs in terms of the amount of foreign to total revenues. Although the new NCR has an Americas division that includes North America and Latin America, the old NCR had a Latin America/Middle East/Africa geographic region that encompassed the world's most volatile regions at the time.

Foreign-Exchange Risk Management under AT&T

Foreign-exchange exposure was greater under AT&T than it was for NCR, but international was a smaller part of its total business, so AT&T started with little real expertise in the area. As AT&T began to expand its foreign revenues, both in terms of exports and imports as well as foreign direct investment, it had to develop policies and procedures for managing exposures. When AT&T acquired NCR, it permitted NCR to retain its foreign currency risk-management responsibilities for foreign operations, but philosophical conflicts arose over the best way to deal with exposures. For example, NCR felt it was important to hedge balance sheet as well as cash flow exposures, whereas AT&T did not feel inclined to hedge balance sheet exposures. In its 1995 annual report, AT&T discussed its general philosophy for hedging foreign-exchange exposures:

> We enter into foreign currency exchange contracts, including forward, option and swap contracts, to manage our exposure to changes in currency exchange rates, principally Canadian dollars, Deutsche marks, pounds sterling and Japanese yen. Some of the contracts involve the exchange of two currencies, according to the local needs of foreign subsidiaries. The use of these derivative financial instruments allows us to reduce our exposure to risk that the eventual dollar net cash inflows and outflows, resulting from the sale of products to foreign customers and purchases from foreign suppliers, will be adversely affected by changes in exchange rates. Our foreign exchange contracts are designated for firmly committed or forecasted purchases and sales. These transactions are generally expected to occur in less than one year. For firmly committed sales and purchases, gains and losses are deferred in other current assets and liabilities. These deferred gains and losses are recognized as adjustments to the underlying hedged transactions when the future sales and purchases are recognized, or immediately if the commitment is canceled. Gains or losses on foreign exchange contracts that are designated for forecasted transactions are recognized in other income as the exchange rates change.

Questions

1. Compare LSI Logic's use of international capital markets to fund expansion with that of AT&T. Which strategy is NCR more likely to follow? Why?

2. Prior to being acquired by AT&T, NCR hedged both transaction and translation exposures. What types of exposure did AT&T hedge? Which strategy do you think NCR should pursue?

3. Given the type of company NCR is, describe how you think it should organize its foreign-exchange risk management function. Be sure to draw on the answer to question 2 in establishing a foreign-exchange risk management strategy.

Chapter Notes

1. LSI Logic, *Annual Report, 1992*; Ken Siegmann, "An American Tale of Semi-Success: How American Chip Companies Regained Lead," *The San Francisco Chronicle*, December 20, 1993, p. B1; Udayan Gupta, "Raising Money the New-Fangled Way," in "Global Finance & Investing: A Special Report," *Wall Street Journal*, September 18, 1987, p. 14D; Nick Arnett, "LSI Lands Former NEC Chief to Head Affiliated Company," *Business Journal* (San Jose), January 14, 1985, p. 17(1); and "LSI Gets a Circuit-Supply Pact," *Wall Street Journal*, January 6, 1987, p. 7; "LSI Logic Sets Up in Singapore," *Electronic Buyer's News*, October 21, 1996, p. 14; LSI Logic 1995 Form 10K; <http://www.lsilogic.com>

2. Alan C. Shapiro, *Modern Corporate Finance* (New York: Macmillan, 1988), p. 1.

3. "Theory versus the Real World," *Finance & Treasury*, April 26, 1993, p. 1.

4. Ibid., p. 2.

5. Rodrigo Briones, "Latin American Money Markets," in *International Finance Handbook*, Abraham M. George and Ian H. Giddy, eds. (New York: Wiley, 1983), p. 4.9.4.

6. "Italy," in *Financing Foreign Operations* (New York: Business International Corporation, June 1990), p. 13.

7. Bank for International Settlements, *63rd Annual Report* (Basel, Switz.: BIS, June 14, 1993), p. 99.

8. "The Euromarkets," in *Financing Foreign Operations* (New York: Business International Corporation, May 1990), p. 1.

9. "Exchange Changes," *The Economist*, October 5, 1996, p. 7.

10. "The Korean Development Bank Completes $500 Million Global Bond Issues through J.P. Morgan and Merrill Lynch," *Business Wire*, November 7, 1996: Available: NEXIS Library: General: News: Curnws.

11. "An Offer They Can Refuse," *Euromoney*, February 1995, p. 76.

12. Anant Sundaram, "International Financial Markets," in *Handbook of Modern Finance*, Dennis E. Logue, ed. (New York: Warren, Gorham, Lamont, 1994), pp. F3–4.

13. Ibid., p. 2.

14. International Finance Corporation, *Emerging Stock Markets Factbook 1996*. (Washington, D.C.: IFC, 1996), pp. 16–17.

15. Bernard Wysocki Jr., "Some Painful Lessons on Emerging Markets," *Wall Street Journal*, September 18, 1995, p. A1.

16. Maximo Eng and Francis A. Lees, "Eurocurrency Centers," in *International Finance Handbook*, Abraham M. George and Ian H. Giddy, eds. (New York: Wiley, 1983), pp. 3.6.3 and 3.6.4.

17. Steven Ramos, "Making Foreign Shares More Marketable," *Forbes*, July 19, 1993, p. 188.

18. NYSE, *The Exchange*, Vol. 3, No. 1, January 1996, p. 3.

19. NYSE, *The Exchange*, Vol. 3, No. 6, September 1996, p. 1.

20. Betsy McKay, "Moscow Starts Trading on the Hudson," *Wall Street Journal*, September 9, 1996, p. A14.

21. "How the Heavyweights Shape Up," *Euromoney*, May 1990, p. 56.

22. Robert K. DeCelles and Anthony G. Alexandrou, "Relaxed U.S. Interest Allocation Rules Open Up Intercompany Debt for Foreign Funding," *Business International Money Report* (New York: Business International Corporation, February 6, 1989), pp. 34–35, 39.

23. Henri Waszkowski, "New Cash Pooling Systems Cut Transaction Fees, Optimize Use of Excess Cash," *Corporate Cashflow Magazine*, December 1995: Available: Nexis: Library: General: News: Curnsw.

24. William J. Bokos and Anne P. Clinkard, "Multilateral Netting," *Journal of Cash Management*, June–July 1983, pp. 24–34.

25. "Corporations Taking Hold of Foreign Exchange Risk," *Treasury Manager's Report*, July 19, 1996: Available in NEXIS: Library: News: Curnws.

26. Ibid.

27. Bill Millar, "What Is a BCC?" *Business International Money Report* (New York: Business International Corporation, March 6, 1989), p. 67.

28. "Financial Strategies in Risky Markets," *Financing Foreign Operations* (New York: Business International Corporation, January 1987), pp. 1–2.

29. Richard T. De George, *Business Ethics*, 3rd ed. (New York: Macmillan, 1990), p. 403.

30. "Financial Strategies in Risky Markets," pp. 2–5.

31. Helmut Hagemann, "Anticipate Your Long-Term Foreign Exchange Risks," *Harvard Business Review*, March–April 1977, p. 82.

32. Bill Millar, "How Coca-Cola's Treasury Manages a Giant's Global Finances," *Business International Money Report* (New York: Business International Corporation, September 25, 1989), p. 311.

33. Susan Arterian, *Business International Money Report* (New York: Business International Corporation, December 18, 1989), p. 405.

34. See the following articles for pros and cons: Thomas E. Copeland and Yash Joshi, "Why Derivatives Don't Reduce Foreign Exchange Risk," *Risk Management*, July 1996, p. 76+; Zar Amrolia, "Why FX Risk Must Be Hedged," *Corporate Finance*, August 1996, pp. 9–10.

35. Don Clark, "Silicon Valley Manufacturers Are Seen as Beneficiaries of the Dollar's Rise," *Wall Street Journal*, September 12, 1995.

36. Ibid.

37. Ibid.

38. Coca-Cola, *1995 Annual Report*, p. 43.

39. David K. Eiteman and Arthur I. Stonehill, *Multinational Business Finance*, 6th ed. (Reading, Mass.: Addison-Wesley, 1992), pp. 493–494.

40. Sidney M. Robbins and Robert B. Stobaugh, *Money in the Multinational Enterprise* (New York: Basic Books, 1973), pp. 37–48.

41. Christopher A. Bartlett and Sumantra Ghoshal, *Managing Across Borders* (Boston: Harvard University Press, 1989), pp. 48–53.

42. Nilly Landau, "Volatility Is the Common Thread," *Finance & Treasury*, May 10, 1993, pp. 5–6; NCR, 1990 *Annual Report*; and AT&T, 1995 *Annual Report*; <http://www.ncr.com/fact_sheet.html>; "NCR Appoints Earl C. Shanks Vice President and Treasurer," *Edge*, June 17, 1996: Available in NEXIS: News: Curnws.

Chapter 21

Human Resource Management

If the leader is good,
the followers will be good.
—Philippine Proverb

Objectives

- To explain the unique qualifications of international managers

- To evaluate the specific issues that occur when managers are transferred internationally

- To examine alternatives for recruitment, selection, compensation, and development of international managers

- To discuss how national labor markets can affect optimum methods of production

- To describe diversities in labor policies and practices on a country-to-country basis

- To highlight some major international pressures on how **MNEs** deal with labor worldwide

- To examine the effect of transnational operations on collective bargaining

Case
Dow's International Management Development[1]

Dow Chemical, a U.S.-based company with over half its revenues abroad, celebrated its 100th birthday in 1997. Less than a year earlier, William Stavropoulos, who had formerly served as president of both Dow Latin America and Dow U.S.A., replaced the Bulgarian-born former head of Dow's European division, Frank P. Popoff, as CEO. Popoff replaced Italian-born Paul Oreffice as CEO in 1992, who had replaced Hungarian-born Zoltan Merszei as COO in 1979. A majority of Dow's top management committee includes managers who were either non-U.S. born or who have had considerable foreign experience.

This placement of foreign-born and/or internationally experienced persons at the helm of the company might suggest the process of multinationalization. For example, Peter Drucker, a leading management authority, stated that a truly multinational company "demands of its management people that they think and act as international businessmen [businesswomen] in a world in which national passions are as strong as ever." A company whose top management includes people from various countries and with varied country experiences presumably is less likely to place the interests of one country above those of others and supposedly will have a more worldwide outlook. Whether this is true is debatable. However, the experience of working abroad under some very different environmental conditions is very useful for grasping some problems that are not as prevalent in a purely domestic context. In 1990, Paul Oreffice described the importance of foreign experience at Dow:

> Our chief financial officer is Cuban, our treasurer is Brazilian, the next man at the top is Italian, and after him comes a Chilean. Native-born Americans seem to have fallen behind in Treasury simply because of the wider experience that financial people from other countries have had all over the world.

In 1994, Popoff reiterated the importance of this experience when he said "Dow is an organization that wants to be ever more global in an environment where globalization is part and parcel of how the industry operates."

To make international operations an integral part of the company's total commitment, Dow had to gain a dedication to international business from a broad spectrum of managers. The company estimates that it took about twenty years to bring this about. Until 1954, only about 6 percent of Dow's business was abroad, and of that, over 80 percent was from its one foreign subsidiary in Canada. The attitude in the late 1950s was expressed by a company historian:

> As for the overseas operations, a majority of the veterans regarded them as a sideline. The foreign market was all right as a place for getting rid of surplus products, but the only truly promising market was in the United States. They questioned the idea of the company becoming too deeply involved in countries whose politics, language, culture, monetary controls, and ways of doing business were strange to them.

Some of Dow's younger managers did not share this ethnocentric attitude, but dramatic steps were needed to convert the majority of managers to an international outlook. One method employed by the company's president in 1958 was to give international responsibilities to people who were widely perceived to be destined for top-level positions in the company. C. B. Branch, who was managing Dow's fastest-growing department, was appointed head of foreign operations. Herbert "Ted" Dow Doan, who at 31 was already a member of the board of directors, went to Europe on a fact-finding mission. (Ted Doan's father and grandfather both had been Dow presidents.) Both Branch and Doan quickly went on to become presidents of Dow. Thus the importance of international operations became readily apparent to the company's managers.

Although the discussion so far emphasizes the importance of international exposure for top-level managers in MNEs, this is not the only management consideration. Companies also must attract and retain high-quality personnel within each country in which they operate. These are largely local personnel. To attract them, Dow feels it must give people from all over the world the same opportunity to reach the top levels within their own specialties. Local needs also change as corporate strategies evolve. For instance, Dow had to hire many more non-U.S. scientists and technicians in the 1980s when the company was strengthening R&D in Europe and Asia.

Companies also must transfer people to foreign locations when qualified local managers are not readily available. When Dow sends managers to foreign operations, what qualifications should they have? Robert Lundeen, a former Dow chairman who had served twelve years as president of the Pacific division and three years as president of the Latin American division, gave some indication of his philosophy. After speaking about the obvious technical needs, he said, "When I worked in Asia, I observed that many Americans seemed to delight in their insularity, and that attitude hurts the ability of the United States to do business in foreign countries."

For many years, Dow had difficulty in convincing people to take foreign assignments because of bad experience in repatriating them to acceptable positions. Dow has reacted to this problem by

- Sending some of its best people abroad so that "everybody will want them when they come back"
- Assigning higher-level supervisors to serve as "godfathers" by looking after the transferred employees' home-career interests
- Providing each transferee with a written guarantee of a job at the same or higher level on return from the foreign assignment

Because many managers have difficulty adjusting to foreign locations, Dow holds a briefing session with each prospective transferee to explain transfer policies and to provide an information package compiled by personnel in the host country. This is followed by a meeting between the transferee and that person's spouse and a recently repatriated employee or spouse to explain the emotional issues involved in the move's early stages. The couple is also given the option of attending a two-week language and orientation program.

Introduction

The Dow case highlights one company's experience in dealing with some international aspects of its personnel policies. Dow's international human resource efforts are more comprehensive than one finds within most other MNEs.[2] In fact, its human resource policies in general are more developed than one finds in most other MNEs. For example, the company has invested heavily in developing the management of its global intellectual assets, which include human capital (the knowledge that each individual has and generates) and organizational capital (the knowledge that has been captured/institutionalized within the structure, processes, and culture of the organization).[3] Although companies have taken various approaches to international human resource management, most agree on the importance of having qualified personnel in order to achieve foreign growth and operational objectives. For instance, at a roundtable discussion of chief executives on how the world is changing and what, if anything, management can do to keep change under control, the chairman of Unilever said, "The single most important issue for us has been, and will continue to be, organization and people."[4]

The need to have highly qualified people to staff the organization cannot be overemphasized. Any company must determine its personnel needs, hire people to meet those needs, motivate them to perform well, and upgrade their skills so that they can move to more demanding tasks. Several factors make the management of international human resources different from such management at the domestic level:

- *Different labor markets.* Each country has a different mix of available workers and a different mix of labor costs. MNEs may gain advantages by accessing these various human resource capabilities. For example, GM's Mexican upholstery operation employs low-cost production workers, and IBM's Swiss R&D facility hires skilled physicists. Whether companies seek resources or markets abroad, they may produce the same product differently in different countries, for example, substituting hand labor for machines because of diverse labor markets.

- *International mobility problems.* There are legal, economic, physical, and cultural barriers to overcome when moving workers to a foreign country. Yet MNEs benefit from moving people, especially when labor market differences result in shortages of needed skills at an acceptable cost. In such situations, companies often must develop special recruitment, training, compensation, and transfer practices.

- *National management styles and practices.* Attitudes toward different management styles vary from country to country; norms among management practices and labor-management relations testify to this. These differences may strain relations between headquarters and subsidiary personnel or make a manager less effective when working abroad than when working at home. At the same time, the experience of working with different national practices offers some opportunities for transferring successful practices from one country to another.

- *National orientations.* Although a company's goals may include attaining global efficiencies and competitiveness, its personnel (both labor and management) may emphasize national rather than global interests. Certain personnel practices can help overcome national orientations; other operating adjustments may be necessary when such orientations prevail.

- *Strategy and control.* Specific country operations vary in terms of their importance for global corporate success, integration with operations in other countries, dependence on headquarters for resources, and need for national responsiveness. Further, these variances may change over time. Management qualifications and styles need to parallel the needs of these different operations so that overall global strategy may more likely be achieved.

This chapter emphasizes these points, differentiating between managerial and labor personnel.

Management Qualifications and Characteristics

Headquarters–Subsidiary Relationship

Management must consider country and global needs.

International staffing is two-tiered: First, the subsidiary level must employ persons who are equipped to conduct the activities within the countries in which the company is operating. Second, people at corporate and/or regional headquarters must be equipped to coordinate and control the company's various worldwide and regional operations. These two staffing dimensions are closely related, particularly since headquarters personnel usually choose and evaluate those who direct the subsidiaries. Both headquarters and subsidiary personnel must be sufficiently aware of and willing to accept trade-offs between the need to adapt to local environmental differences and the need to gain global efficiencies.

Headquarters-subsidiary relationships are affected by
- **Polycentrism versus ethnocentrism**
- **Benefits of independence**

The balance of power for these trade-offs is complex and depends on such factors as the company's philosophy (for example, polycentric versus ethnocentric) and on how much its operations in different countries may benefit from independence as opposed to interdependence. There is much less need to impose standard human resource practices or a corporate culture abroad when a company's strategy is multidomestic and its foreign subsidiaries are a federation of highly independent operations than when its strategy is global or transnational and its foreign operations are internationally interdependent.[5] Regardless of where between these extremes the company lies, it may face dilemmas because the technology, policy, and managerial style it has developed in one place may be only partially applicable elsewhere. International managers, at headquarters and in subsidiaries, are responsible for introducing (or not introducing) practices to a country.

Matching Style to Operations

Where there is a need for cross-border integration, whether between headquarters and subsidiaries or among subsidiaries, feeling-type managers (those concerned with how their decisions will affect others, particularly others' feelings) are apt to be more effective than thinking-type managers (those concerned with processing information analytically and impersonally). The reason is that the collaborative nature of integration requires a high level of cooperation; thus, cooperation is enhanced by understanding and considering the feelings of people who can expedite or retard the integration.[6]

Similarly, when MNEs follow a multidomestic strategy, there is little need or possibility to transfer human resource competencies from one unit to another. Thus the operation in Singapore might work independently to develop human resource practices that deal effectively with labor shortages and high worker mobility; however, information on such practices would not be transferred to units of the company in other countries. In a global strategy, the company would attempt to transfer its home country policies and practices to its foreign units because it feels that such policies are generalizable outside the parent country. In a transnational strategy, the company would attempt to transfer policies from anywhere to anywhere that they may improve performance.[7]

There is also a need to manage in a style that subordinates will accept. Recall from Chapter 2 that there are different national norms in terms of employee preference, such as between authoritarian versus participatory styles and individualism versus collectivism in the workplace. Although any country has successful managers whose styles vary widely, there is substantial anecdotal evidence of a better chance of success when managerial actions are congruent with subordinates' preferences and expectations.[8]

Top-Level Duties Abroad

Top managers in subsidiaries usually have broader duties than do managers of similar-sized home-country operations.

Subsidiary management   Although foreign subsidiaries usually are much smaller than their parents, their top managers often have to perform top-level management duties. This usually means having responsibility for a wide variety of functions and spending more time on the job; on external relations with the community, government, and general public; and on outside business meetings. Managers with comparable profit or cost responsibility in the home country may be performing middle-management tasks there and lack the breadth of experience necessary for a top-level management position in a foreign subsidiary.

Corporate managers abroad
• **Deal at top levels in many countries**
• **Experience the rigors of foreign travel**
• **Face difficulties if they have risen entirely through domestic divisions**

Headquarters travel   The corporate staff charged with responsibility for international business functions must interact frequently with very high-level authorities in foreign countries, for example, in negotiations for new or expanded plants, in the sale of technology, and in the assessment of monetary conditions. Their tasks are in many ways even more difficult than those of the subsidiary managers since they must be away from home for extended and indefinite periods while seeking the confidence and rapport of officials in many foreign countries rather than in just one. Further, during the first few days in many foreign locations they suffer *jet lag,* a condition in which one's biological clock tells the body the wrong time to sleep, eat, and feel alert or drowsy; this clock can adjust by only one or two hours a day.[9] Even if headquarters personnel are not faced with the rigors of foreign travel, they may be ill at ease with the foreign aspects of their responsibilities if their rise to the corporate level has been entirely through work in domestic divisions.

Communication Problems

International communications are complex and more likely to be misunderstood than domestic ones are.

Interpretation   International managers must communicate well to ensure that the intent of messages between headquarters and subsidiary operations is understood. Although technology, such as e-mail and faxes, now enables messages to reach foreign destinations almost instantaneously, these messages are not always perfect substitutes for face-to-face or voice-to-voice messages. Yet companies rely on the technology internationally because of distance that impairs travel for face-to-face meetings and different time zones that complicate voice-to-voice transmissions.

Communication difficulties are further compounded when managers' native languages differ, or even if they come from different countries whose language is the same because accents and vocabulary may differ. Corporate communications, directives, and manuals may be translated, which takes time and expense. If they are not, the content may be understood perfectly abroad, but the comprehension time may be longer because people read more slowly in a second language. Likewise, communication problems may force a manager working abroad to work harder to do the same quality work as home-country counterparts.[10] Although these inherent inefficiencies are often overlooked by the parent, subsidiary management is held responsible.

Cultural differences color intents and perceptions of what is transmitted and received in formal communications; thus international managers may assume erroneously that foreigners will react the same way as their compatriots to such things as decision-making and leadership styles. This is a particular problem when various nationalities are grouped, such as on a team project. Some of these differences may be lessened through the development of a common corporate culture. A corporate culture may help little, however, when managers must work internationally in the growing number of cooperative business activities that include not just different nationalities but also different companies, such as joint ventures and licensing agreements.[11]

Use of English   Today, English is the international language of business because so much international business is conducted by companies from and in English-speaking countries. Further, when people learn a second language, English has become the most common choice worldwide. Managers cannot be expected to learn all the languages in every country in which their companies operate. Thus business between, for example, Mexico and Brazil or between Italy and Saudi Arabia may be conducted in English. Even some MNEs from non–English speaking countries have adopted English as their official language.[12]

A working knowledge of the host country's language nevertheless can help transplanted managers of a subsidiary adapt to the country as well as gain acceptance by its people. It also helps them assess potential changes in the external environment because they can read local newspapers and talk to nationals about politics and other conditions. Further, English may be spoken by upper-level managers but not necessarily by the staff, customers, and suppliers with whom the transplanted manager comes in contact. However, even those who are fully fluent in a local or common language should consider employing good interpreters when attempting serious discussions, such as negotiations with governmental officials.

Which foreign language should be learned by a native English speaker who wants a successful international business career in the twenty-first century? The choice depends largely on where one's employer does business and on one's geographic work preference.

Isolation

A foreign-subsidiary manager must be able to work independently because many staff functions are eliminated abroad to reduce the costs of duplication. At headquarters, a manager can get advice from specialists by walking to the next office or floor or making a few telephone calls. The subsidiary manager, however, ends up relying much more heavily on his or her personal judgment.

Headquarters personnel traveling abroad also can face problems of isolation, with the added element of being isolated in their personal lives. They are apt to miss family celebrations of their own holidays because they are on assignment abroad where those holidays are not celebrated.[13] Further, international trips are apt to be longer than domestic trips are because of the greater distances and the difficulty of returning home for weekends. As one international executive commented humorously:

> Often you won't be able to plan in advance when you are leaving on business or when you will return. Being present at birthdays, school plays, anniversaries, family reunions, and other events may become the exception instead of the rule. While you're away, mortgage payments will probably be due, the MasterCard bill will arrive, the furnace will fail, your child will get chicken pox, the IRS will schedule a full audit, the family car will be totaled, and your spouse will sue for divorce.[14]

International Managerial Transfers

Some Definitions

Managers are commonly categorized as **locals** (citizens of the countries in which they are working) or **expatriates** (noncitizens). Expatriates are either **home-**

country nationals (citizens of the country in which the company is headquartered) or **third-country nationals** (citizens neither of the country in which they are working nor of the headquarters country). Locals or expatriates may be employed in the company's home country or in its foreign operations.

Expatriates: A Minority of Managers

Most managerial positions in both headquarters and foreign subsidiaries are filled by locals rather than expatriates. The one exception is for project management in some LDCs, such as Saudi Arabia, where there is an acute shortage of qualified local candidates.

Foreign managerial slots are difficult to fill because
- Many people don't want to move
- There are legal impediments to using expatriates

Mobility   Many people enjoy the excitement of living and working in a foreign country, but many others do not want to work in a foreign country, particularly if an assignment is perceived to be very long-term or permanent. However, some nationalities (Americans, Australians, British, and Dutch) are more willing to accept foreign assignments than are others (French, Germans, Italians, Spanish, and Swiss).[15] The most common reason for rejecting a foreign assignment is the negative effect on family lifestyle, such as unacceptable living conditions, inadequate educational opportunities for children, and the need to be near aged parents. Career considerations are also important, for two reasons: In many companies, a foreign assignment takes one outside the corporate mainstream for advancement; the spouse can rarely get a permit to work in a comparable job abroad.[16] If the couple is not married, the "significant other" may not even be able to get permission to live in the foreign location. There are also legal impediments for people willing to accept overseas assignments, such as licensing requirements that prevent the use of foreign-trained accountants and lawyers and immigration restrictions that cause delays and uncertainties in filling positions. In many cases, companies have had to set up special operating units to employ people who cannot or will not work where a company would prefer; for example, R&D labs and regional staff offices have been established abroad when personnel refused to move to the country where global headquarters is located.

Local managers may help sales and morale.

Local needs   The greater the need for local adaptations, the more advantageous it is for companies to use local managers, since they presumably understand local conditions better than expatriates would.[17] The need to adapt may arise because of unique environmental conditions, barriers to imports, or the existence of strong local competitors or large customers.

When there is animosity toward foreign-controlled operations, local managers may be perceived locally as "better citizens" because they presumably put local interests ahead of the company's global objectives. This local image may play a role in employee morale as well, since many subsidiary employees prefer to work for someone from their own country.[18]

Incentives to local personnel   The possibility of advancement provides an incentive to local employees to perform well; without this incentive, they may seek employment elsewhere. Practices that keep the best-qualified people, regardless of nationality, from top positions in foreign subsidiaries and at corporate headquarters may be even more damaging to employee motivation.

Reasons for Using Expatriates

Although expatriate managers comprise a minority of total managers within MNEs, companies employ expatriates because of their competence to fill positions, their need to gain foreign experience, and their ability to control operations according to headquarters' preferences. In fact, we do not have precise figures on the number of expatriates; however, the U.S. State Department estimates that there are about 2.6 million Americans abroad, excluding those connected with governmental or military service.[19] These numbers include families of expatriates as well as people, such as retirees, who are not working abroad for companies. Nevertheless, they exclude non-Americans who are working for non-U.S. MNEs and third-country nationals with U.S. MNEs. Considering that most expatriates spend only a few years abroad and are then replaced by new expatriates, the number of managers with expatriate experience is probably in the millions.

Competence   Companies use expatriate managers primarily when they cannot find qualified local candidates. This is partly a function of the particular country's level of development; thus expatriates constitute a much smaller portion of subsidiary managers in industrial than in developing countries. It also is a function of the need to infuse new home-country developments abroad. For example, when new products or new production methods are to be transferred, especially in start-up operations, there usually is a need to transfer home-country personnel to subsidiaries or subsidiary personnel to the home country until the operation is running smoothly.

Management development   MNEs transfer foreigners to their home country or regional operations and home-country nationals to foreign subsidiaries to train them to understand the overall corporate system.[20] In companies with specialized activities only in certain countries (for example, extraction separated from manufacturing or basic R&D separated from applied R&D), long-term foreign assignments may be the only means of developing a manager's integrative competence. These moves also enhance a manager's ability to work in a variety of social systems and are therefore valuable training for ultimate corporate responsibility, involving both domestic and foreign operations.

The move of expatriates into top-level corporate positions has been slow, however, even though an increasing number of companies have become highly dependent on their foreign operations. For example, only about a quarter of CEOs at the largest U.S. companies have worked outside the United States, and only about 10 percent of large U.S. companies have foreigners either as board members or in high corporate positions.[21] (Dow therefore represents a small minority of companies.) There are obvious international perspectives that former expatriates and foreigners can bring to a company. The founder of Compaq Computer said, "As more and more companies are forced to be global, you are going to see more mixing of nationalities at the top."[22]

People transferred from headquarters are more likely to know corporate policies.

People transferred to headquarters learn the headquarters' way.

Control   MNEs use transfers and visits to subsidiaries to control the foreign operations and coordinate organizational development. These goals are accomplished because the people who are transferred are used to doing things the headquarters way and because frequent transfers let them increase their knowledge of the company's global network.[23] Further, foreign nationals may spend time at worldwide or regional headquarters, thereby giving a foreign perspective to the company's global direction. Through the greater interchange brought about by moves of both home- and host-country nationals, a new hybrid corporate culture, or at least an understanding and acceptance of global corporate goals, can develop as a means of controlling the company's operations. In fact, there is evidence of a new cadre of expatriates who neither carry their home-country values everywhere they go, nor go native. Instead, they are developing a global management culture.[24]

A company that follows a more global strategy needs to use more expatriates for control purposes. They generally are or become more familiar with the complexities of the corporate system and tend not to see their own personal development in terms of what happens only in the country to which they are assigned.[25]

The use of expatriates for control is affected by the type of ownership of foreign operations. For example, an expatriate transferred abroad by a joint-venture partner may be in an ambiguous situation, not knowing for sure whether he or she represents and should report to both partners or just the partner making the transfer. Nevertheless, many companies with local partners insist on using their own personnel for positions in which they fear local personnel will make decisions in their own, rather than the joint venture's, best interest. For example, expatriates are commonly found as financial officers in Chinese joint ventures to assure that money is not spent on non–business-related items.[26]

Home-Country versus Third-Country Nationals

Most advances in technology, product, and operating procedures originate in the home country and are later transferred into foreign operations. Because the use of expatriates in foreign facilities is dictated in part by a desire to infuse new methods, personnel with recent home-country experience (usually home-country nationals) are apt to have the desired qualifications.

Third-country nationals may know more about
• **Language**
• **Operating adjustments**

However, third-country nationals sometimes might have more compatible technical and personal adaptive qualifications than do home-country expatriates. For example, a U.S. company used U.S. personnel to design and manage a Peruvian plant until local managers could be trained. Years later, the company decided to manufacture in Mexico using a plant that more closely resembled the Peruvian operations than its U.S. operations in terms of size, product qualities, and factor inputs. The company's Spanish-speaking Peruvian managers were adaptive and were used effectively in the planning, start-up, and early operating phases in Mexico. When companies establish lead operations abroad, such as headquarters for a product division or a country operation that is larger than that in the home country, third-country nationals are more likely to have the competencies needed for the foreign assignments.

Some Individual Considerations for Transfers

Job-ability factors are a necessary attribute.

Technical competence   Unless a foreign assignment is clearly intended for training an expatriate, local employees will resent someone coming in from a foreign country (usually at higher compensation) who, they feel, is no more qualified than they are. The opinions of corporate decision makers, expatriate managers, and local managers all confirm that job ability factors, usually indicated by past job performance that is not necessarily international, are determinants of success in overseas assignments.[27] Although various other skills are important for success in an overseas assignment, the expatriate must know the technical necessities of the tasks as they are performed in the home country and must be able to adapt to foreign variations, such as scaled-down plants and equipment, varying standards of productivity, lack of efficient infrastructure and internal distribution, nonavailability of credit, and restrictions on type of communications media selected. The expatriate also must be fully aware of corporate policies so that foreign decisions are compatible with them. For these reasons, managers usually have several years' work experience with a company before being offered a foreign assignment.

Adaptiveness   Although some companies rely only on technical competence as the criterion in the selection of expatriates for transfer, three types of adaptive characteristics are important for an expatriate's success when entering a new culture:

1. Those needed for self-maintenance, such as being self-confident and able to reduce stress
2. Those related to the development of satisfactory relationships with host nationals, such as flexibility and tolerance
3. Cognitive skills that help one to perceive correctly what is occurring within the host society[28]

Family adaptation is important.

An expatriate who lacks any of these may not be able to function effectively. Unfortunately, as is true with most behavorial characteristics, adaptability characteristics are assessed imperfectly. At an extreme, the expatriate may leave, either by choice or by company decision.

Recent surveys indicate that less than 10 percent of expatriates fail to complete their assignments abroad—a much lower rate than had been found in earlier studies and one that appears to be no higher than one finds in domestic assignments.[29] Nevertheless, because the relocation cost for each expatriate averages between two and three times the expatriate's annual salary, the cost of the turnover is high.[30] In addition, there is a high cost in lost performance.[31] An international move may greatly disrupt a family's current way of living, especially since many transfers send people to countries very different from their own, and a major reason for failure in a foreign assignment is the family's inability to adjust.[32] A move means new living and shopping habits, new school systems, and unfamiliar business practices. In addition, close friends and relatives—the personal support system—are left behind. However, some individuals do enjoy and adapt easily to a foreign way of life; MNEs should use them if possible. Some companies even maintain a core international group of employees who are the only ones assigned abroad.

Fixed-term versus open-end assignments are viewed differently.

A distinction must be made between a foreign assignment of fixed duration and one that is open-ended. Many more people can cope with a position abroad if they know that they will return home after a specific time period.

Expatriates may meet with local prejudice.

Local acceptance   Expatriates may encounter some acceptance problems regardless of who they are. For example, it usually takes time for managers to gain recognition of their personal authority, and expatriates may not be there long enough to achieve this. Local employees may feel that the best jobs are given to overpaid foreigners. Expatriates may have to make unpopular decisions in order to meet global objectives. Or local management may have had experiences with expatriates who made short-term decisions and then left before dealing with the longer-term implications.[33] If negative stereotypes are added to these attitudes, the expatriate may find it very difficult to succeed. Certain individuals may encounter insurmountable problems when dealing as an expatriate with employees, suppliers, and customers, for example, a Jewish manager in Libya, a very young manager in Japan, or a female manager in Saudi Arabia. The U.S. Civil Rights Act of 1991 extended the nondiscrimination provisions of the earlier civil rights law to cover the employment of U.S. citizens abroad, except where foreign law prohibits the employment of a certain class of individual. Because most discrimination problems abroad are cultural rather than legal, companies face challenges in handling the requirements of this act.[34]

But do companies overreact to these acceptance problems? Consider stereotypes of women: They should not give orders to men, they are temperamental, their place is in the home, clients will not accept them, employees will not take them seriously, they don't have the stamina to work in harsh areas, they will not be given work permits, they don't want to upset their husbands' careers. Partly because of these stereotypes, MNEs have given very few expatriate positions to women, especially to foreign women in the companies' home countries. Yet women have succeeded as expatriates in such male-dominated places as India, Japan, and Thailand because they were seen in the workplace first as foreigners and then as women.[35] This should not imply that the successful women confronted no problems. They have faced discrimination outside the workplace, such as in banks and immigration offices, and have encountered sexist remarks that, although deemed totally inoffensive locally, would be unacceptable elsewhere. They have used such coping devices as giving off the "right signals" through attire and demeanor, have adapted communication styles that would not seem abrasive, and have simply accepted that cultural norms are different.[36] Suggestions to improve the acceptability of women as expatriates may be applied as well to other groups. These include selecting very well-qualified older, mid-career women who could command more authority, giving a clear title and job position, disseminating in advance information concerning the person's high qualifications, placing expatriate women in locations where there are already some local women in management positions, and establishing longer than normal assignments in order to develop role models for acceptance.[37]

Securing a successful foreign assignment   Although the above discussion highlights why some people do not adjust to or want a foreign assignment, most expatriate assignments are successful from the standpoint of both the expatriates themselves and the organizations they represent. Further, many students seem more concerned about getting foreign assignments than avoiding them. In reality, the chances of being offered a foreign assignment soon after graduation are small. Companies generally want people to prove themselves domestically before transferring them abroad; therefore, a work record demonstrating technical competence and knowledge of the company's policies and practices is probably the major prerequisite to becoming an expatriate. Once this prerequisite is met, an employee may gain an edge over other candidates by additionally demonstrating a knowledge of the language and environment where the foreign assignment is located.

A person can do a number of things to help adjust to foreign locations, including learning the language and associating with support groups abroad, such as religious groups and expatriate associations. Information from people who have worked in the locale and who have positive rather than negative memories of it can alleviate adjustment difficulties.

Post-Expatriate Situations

Coming home can require adaptation in many areas, including
- **Financial**
- **Job**
- **Social**

Repatriation problems   About 12 percent of returning expatriates leave their companies within one year of repatriation.[38] Problems with repatriation arise in three general areas: personal finances, readjustment to home-country corporate structure, and readjustment to life at home. Expatriates are given many financial benefits to encourage them to accept a foreign assignment. While abroad, they may live in the best neighborhoods, send their children to the best private schools, employ domestic help, socialize with the upper class, and still save more money than before the move. But this life style is lost on their return home. Returning expatriates often find that many of their peers have been promoted above them in their absence, that they now have less autonomy in the job, that they are "little fish in a big pond," and that they now have less in common with their friends than before the foreign assignments. Some suggestions for smoothing the reentry include providing ample advance notice of when the return will occur, maximum information about the new job, housing assistance, and a reorientation program, as well as requiring frequent visits to headquarters and using a formal headquarters mentor to look after the manager's interests while that person is abroad.[39]

Career movements   The significance of an overseas assignment to one's career may be positive, neutral, or negative. This variation is confirmed in studies of career paths of top executives and by the opinions of repatriated employees.[40] However, past career paths and opinions may not reflect the future. For example, Gerber Products has traditionally used few expatriates but is now increasing the number substantially. Its CEO said, "Foreign assignments will be emphasized in the future as part of normal career development."[41] Whether the experience is positive, negative, or neutral depends on individual differences and such factors as the company's commitment to foreign operations, the integration between domestic and international activities, and the communications linkages between headquarters and subsidiary personnel.

For companies with a very high commitment to global operations, multicountry experience may be as essential as multifunctional and multiproduct experience in reaching upper-echelon organizational levels. The Dow case illustrates such a situation. Nevertheless, some companies with a high international commitment so separate foreign and domestic operations that they function almost as two separate companies. If the domestic business dominates, there may be not only little interchange of personnel between domestic and foreign operations but also little advancement of personnel with international experience to top-level positions.

In any case, very few people reach the top rungs of large companies, with or without foreign work experience. Some companies, particularly those with international divisions, depend heavily on a cadre of specialists who may either rotate between foreign locations and international headquarters assignments or spend most of their careers abroad. Although not reaching the top management levels of the parent, they can reach plateaus above most domestic managers in terms of compensation and responsibility. Many people with a penchant for international living do not aspire to anything different. For example, after stints in Singapore and London, a Morgan Stanley expatriate in India said, "I still don't want to go back to the U.S. It's a big world—lots of things to see."[42]

Within some companies, foreign assignments carry a high career risk, regardless of corporate executives' statements to the contrary. This type of situation may arise for two reasons. First, there may be little provision to fit someone into the domestic or headquarters organization on repatriation. One's old office simply does not stay vacant while one is abroad for several years; a repatriated employee cannot easily bump his or her replacement. Holding a position available while an employee is abroad is particularly difficult when the foreign assignment is of indefinite length, and such open-ended assignments are a significant portion of the total; at Hewlett-Packard such assignments constitute 25 percent of foreign transfers, for example.[43] Second, some "out of sight, out of mind" may come into play. A General Dynamics executive said he would never have known about domestic openings if a friend had not kept him apprised of the organization's promotional pipeline.[44] Reentry is further complicated if the expatriate is on lengthy assignment in a location where older technologies and corporate policies are practiced.

When repatriated employees have career problems, it becomes more difficult to convince other people to take foreign assignments. Very few companies follow Dow's example and make written guarantees that repatriated employees will come back to jobs at least as good as those they left. (However, companies do not guarantee future positions to their domestic managers either.) Some companies simply explain the career risk and compensate employees so highly that they are enticed to become expatriates. Others integrate foreign assignments into career planning and are developing mentor programs to look after the expatriates' domestic interests.[45]

Foreign nationals who are transferred to headquarters sometimes confront a different problem. If the assignment is a promotion from a manager's subsidiary post rather than part of a planned rotation, then the move to headquarters may be permanent. For example, the Brazilian head of a Brazilian subsidiary may have performed so well that the MNE wants to give that manager multicountry responsibility at the corporate offices in New York or Frankfurt. Because the manager would not be able to return to Brazil without taking a demotion, he or she might refuse the transfer.

Expatriate Compensation

MNEs must pay enough to entice people to move but must not overpay.

If a U.S. company transfers its British finance manager, who is making $50,000 per year, to Italy, where the going rate is $60,000 per year, what should the manager's salary be? Or if the Italian financial manager is transferred to the United Kingdom, what pay should be offered? Should the compensation be in dollars, pounds, or lira? Whose holidays should apply? Which set of fringe benefits should apply? These are but a few of the many questions that must be solved when a company moves people abroad; therefore, it is not surprising that the most oft-mentioned problem by MNEs in developing an international workforce is in dealing with differing pay levels, benefits, and perks.[46] On the one hand, the company must keep costs down; on the other, it must maintain high employee morale.

The amount and type of compensation necessary to entice a person to move to another country vary widely by person and locale. Company practices also vary widely in terms of compensation for differences. Companies with very few expatriate employees may work out a foreign compensation package on an individual basis. As international activities grow, however, it becomes too cumbersome to handle each transfer in this way. As long as consistency is sought in transfer policy, some people inevitably will receive more than would be necessary to entice them to go abroad. Overall, the package may multiply the compensation cost in comparison with what the expatriate had been making domestically. Table 21.1 illustrates a typical package.

Cost of living   Most people who move to another country encounter cost-of-living increases (sometimes called a goods-and-services differential), primarily because their accustomed way of living is expensive to duplicate in a new environment. Habits are difficult to change. For example, Westerners pay dearly in some parts of Asia to rent accommodations with Western bathrooms and kitchens. Knowledge of the local country is a second consideration. Food and housing may sometimes be obtained at higher than the local rate because expatriates may not know the language well, where to buy, or how to bargain for reductions. Housing costs also vary substantially because of crowded conditions that raise land prices as well as shortages of domiciles that are acceptable to expatriates. Some recent estimates are shown in Figure 21.1.

Living is more expensive abroad because
- **Habits change slowly**
- **People don't know how and where to buy**

MNEs use various cost-of-living indexes and
- **Increase compensation when foreign cost is higher**
- **Do not decrease compensation when foreign cost is lower**
- **Remove the differential when the manager is repatriated**

Table 21.1
Typical First-Year Cost for a U.S. Expatriate (Married, Two Children) in Tokyo, Japan
An expatriate's cost to the company may be several times what it would be for the same employee in his or her home country.

Direct compensation costs	
Base salary	$100,000
Foreign-service premium	15,000
Goods and services differential	73,600
Less: U.S. housing norm*	(15,400)
U.S. hypothetical taxes	(17,200)
Company-paid costs	
Schooling (two children)	15,000
Annual home leave	4,800
Housing*	150,000
Japanese income taxes†	84,000
Transfer/moving costs	38,000
Total company costs	$447,800

*Assumes company rents housing in its name and provides to expatriate. If company pays housing allowance instead, Japanese income taxes (and total costs) will be about $65,000 higher.
†Note that Japanese income taxes will increase each year as some company reimbursements, most notably for taxes, become taxable.

Source: Organization Resources Counselors, Inc.

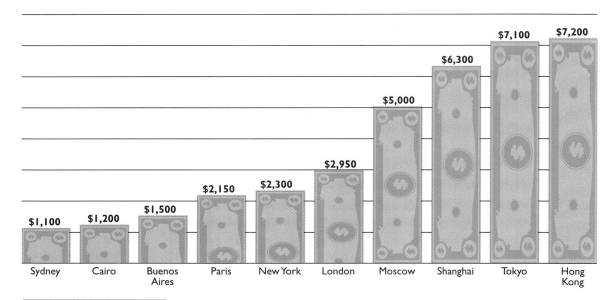

**Figure 21.1
Comparative
Apartment Costs
(July 1, 1995)**
The amounts are average
monthly rents in U.S. dollars for the type of two-
bedroom apartment that
an expatriate would rent in
each city.

Source: Associates for
International Research, Inc.
as appearing in *New York Times,*
July 9, 1995, p. 4E.

Most companies raise salaries by a differential to account for higher foreign-country costs. After the expatriate returns home, the differential is removed. A few companies reduce the cost-of-living differential over time, reasoning that as expatriates become better assimilated, they should be able to adjust more to local purchasing habits, for example, by buying vegetables from a native market instead of using imported packaged goods. When moves are to areas with a lower cost of living, few companies reduce an employee's pay because doing so might adversely affect the employee's morale; thus expatriates may receive a windfall.

Companies rely on estimates of cost-of-living differences, even though the differences do not fit everyone's situation perfectly. Some commonly used sources of such estimates are the U.S. State Department's cost-of-living index published yearly in *Labor Developments Abroad,* the *U.N. Monthly Bulletin of Statistics,* and surveys by the *Financial Times, P-E International, Business International,* and the International Monetary Fund *Staff Papers.* In using any of these, companies must determine which items are included in order to adjust omitted ones separately. Some items commonly handled separately are housing, schooling, and taxes. Differences in inflation and exchange rates may quickly render surveys and indexes obsolete; thus cost-of-living adjustments must be updated frequently.

The ultimate objective of cost-of-living adjustments is to ensure that expatriates' after-tax income will not suffer as a result of a foreign assignment. Because taxes are usually assessed on the overseas premiums in addition to the base salaries, the premiums must be adjusted even further upward if the foreign tax rate is higher than the home country's.

**A transfer is more attractive
if employees see it as an
advancement.**

Job-status payment   Some employees may not accept a position abroad unless it is considered a promotion, and most people consider a promotion without a pay increase inequitable. Expatriates compare their compensation with that of other managers in both the foreign country and their home country. Thus where the going rate for the job is higher than that in the home country, companies also will normally raise an expatriate's salary temporarily while the person is working abroad.

Foreign-service premiums and hardship allowances   There are bound to be things expatriates will have to do without when living abroad. Such sacrifices range from nuisance to hardship. For example, expatriates may miss certain foods, a holiday celebration, television in the native language, or following particular sports results. Or their children may have to attend school away from home, perhaps even in another country. There also is the problem of adjusting to a new culture; such adjustments may cause adverse psychological effects and social frustrations. Further, in some countries, domestic help is deemed essential for expatriates because of unavailability of babysitters, unsanitary conditions that require more housework, such as boiling water and soaking vegetables, and security considerations that dictate always having someone in the residence.[47] Consequently, companies frequently give expatriates foreign-service premiums just for being posted in a foreign location. This practice appears to be dropping off, however, especially in so-called world capitals, in which there is assumed to be little deprivation and to which it is not difficult to get people to transfer.[48] Further, the hardships from foreign assignments are decreasing as advances in transportation and communication enable expatriates to keep in closer contact with people in their home countries, as the openness of economies allows them to buy familiar products and services, and as the general level of housing, schooling, and medical services increasingly meet expatriates' needs.

But few would deny that living conditions in certain locales still present particularly severe hardships, such as harsh climatic or health conditions or political insurrection or unrest that places the expatriate and family in danger. For instance, expatriate personnel in such MNEs as Goodyear, Eastman Kodak, and Sanyo have been targeted for kidnapping and armed assault.[49] Consequently, companies have had to not only rethink their hardship allowances but also purchase ransom insurance, provide training programs on safety for expatriates and families, pay for home alarm systems and security guards, and spend management time in considering their legal liability for handling employee safety issues. But even where conditions are less severe, expatriates may encounter living conditions that are substandard (or better) than what they had at home. The Corporate Resources Group publishes a yearly Quality-of-Living Report that compares the major cities of the world on 45 key quality factors, such as political, social, economic, sociocultural, natural environment, education, public services, health conditions, and recreation.[50]

Finally, a hardship may occur because of potential changes in total family income and status. In the home country, all members of the family may be able to work. Many companies now provide spouses of expatriates with job-search assistance, often through networks with other companies. For example, Eastman Kodak finds employment for about 25 percent of spouses.[51] However, people other than the transferred employee are seldom given permission to work in a foreign country. So the spouse (or live-in companion) of an expatriate may either have to give up well-paying and satisfying employment or be separated from the partner for long periods. Some companies increase the expatriate's compensation, and about one third of large U.S. companies assist couples with commuter marriages. For example, Stride Rite transferred a manager to Taiwan, while her husband continued working in the United States. Stride Rite paid for all their telephone calls to each other plus seven trips a year to reunite.[52]

Choice of currency   An expatriate's salary is usually (but not always) paid partly in local currency and partly in the currency of the expatriate's home country. This procedure allows the expatriate to save money in the home country and often to forgo host-country taxes on the home-country portion of income. Other factors that influence the preference for payment in home-country or host-country currency include whether hard-currency expenditures can be charged to the local operation, whether exchange control exists, and whether the expatriate can receive more local currency by exchanging the hard currency through a free market.

> Salaries usually are paid in a mixture of home- and host-country currencies.

Remote areas   Many large-scale international projects are in areas so remote that MNEs would get few people to transfer there if the companies did not create an environment more like that at home or make other special arrangements. For example, Lockheed Aircraft set up its own color TV broadcasting station in Saudi Arabia for its expatriates there. Also, INCO built schools, hospitals, churches, supermarkets, a golf course, a yacht club, a motel, and a restaurant for its expatriates in Indonesia.[53]

> MNEs may have to provide more fringe benefits to employees in remote areas.

Expatriates in remote areas often are handled very differently from employees elsewhere. To attract the large number of people necessary for construction and start-up, MNEs usually will offer fixed-term contract assignments at high salaries and hire most people from outside the company. Some people are attracted to these assignments and are willing to undergo difficult living conditions because they can save money at a rate that would be impossible to achieve at home.

Complications of nationality differences   As companies employ expatriates from both home and third countries, compensation issues have become very complex. There is no consensus among companies on how to deal with most of these. For example, salaries for similar jobs vary substantially among countries, as do the relationships of salaries within the corporate hierarchy. For example, in 1992 the head of human resources at an Italian company made about 37 percent more than that person's counterpart in a U.S. company; however, the typical U.S. CEO made 55 percent more than the typical Italian CEO. The method of payment also varies substantially. Long-term incentives, such as options on restricted stock, are popular in the United States but not in Germany. However, German managers often receive compensation that U.S. managers do not, such as housing allowances and partial payment of salary outside Germany, neither of which is taxable. Further, in the trade-off between longer hours for more pay versus fixed pay for fewer hours, Americans prefer the former and Germans the latter. When sending people of different nationalities abroad to work, companies disagree on how to calculate home-country base incomes and whether to use a standard means of adjusting those incomes. However, there is nearly a consensus to maintain expatriates on their home-country retirement systems because of the complexities involved in standardization and the need to protect people in the locales in which they are most apt to retire.[54]

Management Recruitment and Selection

College Recruitment

College recruitment is used at home and abroad, but the biggest need abroad is for higher-level managers.

MNEs recruit through universities at home and abroad to find capable nationals of the countries in which they have foreign operations. They also recruit home-country nationals, usually to work for several years in their domestic operations until they have gained technical experience and knowledge of the corporate culture.

Management Inventories

Foreign personnel are not easily encompassed in information inventories because foreign operations may not be wholly owned.

Some companies have centralized personnel record systems, which include data on home- and foreign-country nationals. These data include not only the usual technical and demographic data but also information on adaptive capabilities such as foreign-language qualifications, willingness to accept foreign assignments, and results of company-administered tests. However, a company may encounter problems in bringing foreign managers into the system; if the company owns less than 100 percent of the foreign facility, the other stockholders may complain. Moreover, there is a growing criticism of the inclusion in personnel records of data that are considered to be private, such as results from personality tests.[55]

Adaptability Assessment

Companies usually know more about their employees' technical capabilities than about their adaptive ones; thus they must focus on measuring adaptability for foreign-transfer purposes. For example, people who have successfully adjusted to domestic transfers or have previous international experience are more likely to adapt abroad. In addition, some companies use a variety of testing mechanisms as assessment aids. One is the Early Identification Program, which assesses an individual's match with different environments. Many other tests assess personality traits that indicate a willingness to change basic attitudes. These include the Minnesota Multiphasic Personality Inventory, the Guilford-Zimmerman Temperament Survey, and the Allport-Vernon Study of Values.[56]

A few companies include spouses in tests and extensive interviews because a foreign assignment is usually more stressful for the spouse than for the transferred employee.[57] For example, a foreign assignment is generally (in most cases) an advancement for the husband, but the wife must start at the bottom in developing new social relations and learning how to carry out the day-to-day management of the home. The separation from friends, family, and career often makes her very lonely so that she turns to her husband for more companionship. But the husband may have less time because of his new working conditions. This may lead to marital stress which, in turn, affects work performance. Interviewers thus look not only at likely adaptiveness but also at whether the marriage is strong enough to weather the stress and not impede performance of employment duties.[58]

Tests' ability to predict success in foreign assignments is not very high.

Although some companies follow a rigorous procedure of selecting and training people cross-culturally for foreign assignments, the adjustment and performance of their expatriates have been mixed. Nevertheless, the evidence supports a positive relationship between vigorous procedures and adjustment and performance.[59]

The Help of Local Companies

Acquisitions and joint ventures secure staff but the staff may be
• **Inefficient**
• **Hard to control**

One way to staff foreign operations is by buying an existing foreign company and using the personnel already employed; however, companies should consider the possible efficiency problems of acquisitions. Companies also may tie in closely with local companies in the expectation that the latter will contribute personnel to the operation as well as hire new personnel. In countries such as Japan, where the labor market is tight and people are reluctant to move to new companies, the use of a local partner may be extremely important. However, if a local partner handles staffing arrangements, the employees may see their primary allegiance to that partner rather than to the foreign investor.

International Development of Managers

The Needs

To carry out global operations, companies need people with a variety of specialized skills; therefore, programs to develop managers internationally must be tailored to some extent to specific individuals and situations.[60] There is, however, agreement on two developmental needs:

1. Top executives must have a global mindset that is sufficiently free of national prejudices and sufficient knowledge about the global environment that they can exert the leadership necessary to attain a global mission.
2. Operating personnel, particularly those with direct international responsibility, must be able to effect a proper balance in well-being between corporate and national operations.

Preemployment Training

There is an increase in international studies in universities.

Managers need to be trained to understand how operating differences are brought about by international business activities. Managers with direct international responsibilities need specialized skills; those with indirect responsibilities need generalized skills. Business schools are increasing their international offerings and requirements, but there is no consensus as to what students should learn to help prepare them for international responsibilities. Two distinct approaches are to convey specific knowledge about foreign environments and international operating adjustments and to train in interpersonal awareness and adaptability. The former may tend to remove some of the fear and aggression that are aroused when dealing with the unknown. However, the understanding of a difference does not necessarily imply a willingness to adapt to it, particularly to a cultural difference. The Peace Corps uses sensitivity training, which is designed to develop attitudinal flexibility.[61] Although either approach generally helps a person adjust relative to those who lack training, there appears to be no significant difference in the effectiveness of the two approaches.[62]

Postemployment Training

Postemployment training may include
• **Environment-specific information**
• **Adaptiveness training**
• **Training by an unaffiliated company abroad**

Many employees may continue to place domestic performance objectives above global ones or feel ill-equipped to handle worldwide responsibilities as they move up in their organizations. To counter this, a company can train those people who are about to take a foreign assignment, such as through language and orientation programs. Or it could include international business components in external or internal programs for employees that may or may not work abroad. Examples of internal programs are those at PepsiCo International and Raychem, which bring foreign nationals to U.S. divisions for periods of six months to a year; IBM's regional training centers, in which managers from several countries are gathered for specific topics; P&G's training on globalization issues; and GE's, Motorola's, and Honda of America's programs to teach foreign languages and cultural sensitivity.[63] Sometimes a company will train employees and families from an unaffiliated company, including those from abroad, as a means of amortizing training costs and broadening backgrounds of attendees.[64]

Transferees may find it difficult even to know which questions to ask; thus the most common predeparture training takes the form of an informational briefing. Topics covered typically include cultural differences, job design, compensation, housing, climate, education, health conditions, home sales, taxes, transport of goods, job openings after repatriation, and salary distribution. A suggestion is to follow predeparture training with cultural training about six months after arrival in a foreign country so that expatriates may relate better to issues covered.[65]

Human Resource Management in the Internationalization Process

A company's international human resources efforts should complement its level of international development and grow with its international commitment. Dow is an

MNE already highly dependent on and committed to international operations. Its international human resource needs are more extensive than those of a company that merely exports or imports a small portion of its output or supplies. Such a company's primary need is for personnel that are technically trained or knowledgeable about trade documentation, foreign-exchange risk, and political-economic conditions that may affect trade flows. An MNE such as Dow shares this need but also needs a multinational workforce and managers who can integrate this workforce effectively.

As a company moves to foreign production, it must consider how to staff, motivate, and compensate its foreign workforce. The norms in these human resource activities vary substantially from one country to another because of economic, cultural, and legal conditions. Some of the major differences are discussed in the next section.

Labor-Market Differences

External Reference Points

MNEs should look to existing operations as references for planning manpower needs in new operations abroad.

Typically, a company setting up a new foreign operation is duplicating, perhaps on a small or slightly altered scale, a product, process, or function being performed at home. Past experience will have shown company officials which type and how many employees are needed for the size of operation being built. The company probably will have descriptions for each type of job to be filled and from past experience will know which types of people ideally fit into specific positions.

The Production Method

MNEs may shift labor or capital intensities if relative costs differ.

There is some danger in a company's attempting to duplicate organizational structures and job descriptions abroad, particularly in LDCs. Labor-saving devices that are economically justifiable at home, where wage rates are high, may be more costly than labor-intensive types of production in a country with high unemployment rates and low wages. Using labor-intensive methods also may ingratiate the company with governmental officials, who must cope with the host country's unemployment. Because of differences in labor skills and attitudes, the company also may find it advantageous to simplify tasks and use equipment that would be considered obsolete in a more advanced economy.

International Labor Mobility

There is pressure for labor to move from high-unemployment and low-wage areas to places of perceived opportunities.

Cause   At the same time that most LDCs and the countries of Eastern Europe have faced critical unemployment problems, many industrialized countries, underpopulated oil-producing countries, and newly industrialized countries of Asia have been short of workers to run facilities. A great deal of pressure for increased immigration has resulted, which in turn has been tempered by legal restrictions to minimize the economic and social problems for the countries absorbing large numbers of immigrants. These restrictions, in spite of illegal immigration and sizable minority groups in many countries, have resulted in less dependence today on labor migration than in earlier generations.[66]

There is incentive to hire immigrant workers because they often will work for a fraction of what domestic workers with comparable skills will demand. This is especially true of illegal immigrants who cannot afford to return to their own countries. It is also true within the European Union, where workers may move legally from one country to another in response to wage rate differences. For example, as of 1995 about 100,000 construction workers from other EU countries (mainly Britain, Ireland, and Portugal) were working in Germany at considerably less than the wage for German labor.[67] In other cases, companies have sought specialists from abroad. For example, Computer Consulting Services, a small U.S.-based software company, has brought in 90 percent of its computer consultants from abroad. Alternatively, Software Services International has exported much of its software work to India.[68]

Reliable figures on the amount of international migration are unavailable because so many immigrants are illegal and therefore undocumented. However, the fragmentary evidence is rather startling. Estimates for the early 1990s indicate that about 1 million immigrants a year entered the United States and about half a million a year went to Western Europe.[69] Remittances home from workers from such countries as Egypt, Jordan, Pakistan, and the Republic of Yemen exceed the value of exports from those countries.[70]

Companies are less certain of labor supply when they depend on foreign laborers because
- **Countries become restrictive**
- **Workers return home**
- **Turnover necessitates more training**

Workforce stability problem Migrant workers in many countries have permission to stay for only short periods, for example, three to six months for New Zealand's workers from Fiji and Tonga. In many other cases, workers leave their families behind in the hope of returning home after saving sufficient money while working in the foreign country; this creates workforce uncertainty for employers. In the mid-1970s, for example, France had a net loss in its workforce as large numbers of Spanish workers returned home, and in the late 1980s, the United States had a net loss of Korean scientists and engineers. Another uncertainty is the extent to which governmental authorities will restrict the number of foreign workers. All industrial countries are pressured to expel foreign workers in order to protect job opportunities for domestic workers or to promote a more homogeneous culture. Even if cutbacks are accomplished during a slack period in the economy, during which a company may switch to using local rather than foreign workers, the company then may face the costly process of training workers who may leave as soon as the economy improves.

MNEs must build infrastructure to operate in remote areas.

Employment adjustments MNEs' ability to mobilize capital, technology, and management has fed the demand for migrant workers in remote parts of the world. To operate facilities where minerals are located or in previously unoccupied areas of oil-producing countries, companies have had to import many foreign workers. When doing this, they have had to construct housing and infrastructure and to develop social services to serve the new population. Even in populated areas, housing shortages might prevent the influx of temporary workers if a company did not make housing provisions.

The influx and use of foreign workers create additional workplace problems. For example, in parts of Western Europe today, certain nationality groups are relegated to less complex jobs because their language makes training them difficult. A result has been the development of homogeneous ethnic work groups at cross-purposes with other groups in the organization, as well as the emergence of go-betweens who can communicate with management and labor.

Labor Compensation

Importance of Differences

Labor-cost differences among companies and countries sometimes lead to competitive advantages and can influence where companies will establish production facilities. The amount of compensation people receive depends on their estimated contributions to the business, supply of and demand for particular skills ("going wage") in the area, cost of living, government legislation, and collective-bargaining ability. The methods of payment (salaries, wages, commissions, bonuses, and fringe benefits) depend on customs, feelings of security, taxes, and governmental requirements. Both the amount and method of payment are affected by a country's culture. For example, within a highly individualistic society such as the United States, there is a preference for compensation to be based on proportional contribution—the result being a heavy reliance on bonuses and a high disparity in incomes within the organization. In a more collectivist society, such as China, there is a preference for more egalitarian allocations, regardless of contributions.[71]

MNEs usually pay slightly better than do their local counterparts in lower-wage countries, although the salary is still less than what would be paid in higher-wage countries. Some factors leading to higher wages paid by MNEs relate to their management philosophies and structures: The typical management philosophy, particularly in contrast to that of local, family-run companies, often is to attract high-level workers by offering higher relative wages. In addition, techniques that lead to greater efficiencies allow for higher employee compensation. Further, when a company first comes into a country, experienced workers may demand higher compensation because they have doubts about whether the new operation will succeed.

MNEs may need to pay more than local companies to entice workers from existing jobs.

Fringe Benefits

Fringe benefits vary substantially among countries.

Fringe benefits differ radically from one country to another. Direct-compensation figures therefore do not accurately reflect the amount a company must pay for a given job in a given country. The types of benefits that are either customary or have been required also vary widely. In Japan, for example, workers in large companies commonly receive such benefits as family allowances, housing loans and subsidies, lunches, children's education, and subsidized vacations; thus fringe benefits make up a much higher portion of total compensation in Japan than in the United States. Also common in many countries are benefits such as end-of-the-year bonuses of up to three-months' pay, housing, payments based on the number of children, long vacations, and profit sharing.

In many countries, it is impossible or expensive to lay off workers.

Job-security benefits   In many countries, firing or laying off an employee may be either impossible or very expensive, resulting in unexpectedly higher costs for a company accustomed to the economies that can result from manipulating its employment figures. In the United States, for example, layoffs are not only permitted but have grown to be expected when demand falls seasonally or cyclically. In many countries, however, a company has no legal recourse except to fire workers—and then perhaps only if it is closing down its operations—at which time it must pay high severance compensation.[72] To curtail operations in such countries, a company must come to an agreement with its unions and the government on such issues as extended benefits and the retraining and relocation of workers. At the same time, unemployment benefits are low in the United States compared with those in Western Europe, so there is more incentive for unemployed U.S. workers to find new jobs.[73]

Workers or the company may be responsible for on-the-job injuries.

Liability for injuries   Company, worker, or third-party neglect may lead to various types of worker or company injuries. The worker may be injured physically from, for example, negligent driving by transport workers, faulty maintenance of equipment, and/or lack of safety equipment. The company may be injured monetarily from, for example, careless handling of cash, embezzlement of funds, and breakage of product and equipment. There are widespread variances in the extent to which workers or companies are held responsible for injuries.[74] The determination of responsibility should influence how companies handle these contingencies. The amount and allocation of expenditures for insurance, training, and safety equipment thus vary substantially by country.

How to compare   Too often, compensation expenses are compared on a per-worker basis, which may bear little relationship to the total employment expenditure. People's abilities and motivations vary widely; consequently, it is the output associated with cost that is important. Seemingly cheap labor actually may raise the total compensation expenditure because of the need for more supervision, added training expenses, and adjustments in the method of production. For example, Quality Coils, a small U.S. company, moved some operations to Mexico because hourly wages were only about one third of what it paid in Connecticut. However, the company later returned to Connecticut because of high absenteeism and low productivity in Mexico.[75] Further, if labor turnover is high, there is a continual need to retain a workforce.[76]

Labor-Cost Dynamics

Differences among countries in amount and type of compensation change; salaries and wages (as well as other expenditures) may rise more rapidly in one locale than in another. Therefore, the relative competitiveness of operations in different countries may shift. For example, in the 1980s Korean workers made hundreds of thousands of shoes for Nike and Reebok; however, as Korean labor costs grew, most of these jobs shifted to China and Indonesia.[77] But the process of comparing costs is complex. An example will illustrate shifting capabilities. Assume U.S. productivity per worker in manufacturing increased by 2.8 percent, and hourly compensation rates went up by 10.2 percent. The result was a unit labor-cost increase of 7.2 percent (1.102 divided by 1.028). Meanwhile, in the United Kingdom productivity increased by 5.9 percent and hourly compensation by 16.2 percent, amounting to a unit labor-cost increase of 9.7 percent (1.162 divided by 1.059). This meant that labor costs were rising more rapidly in the United Kingdom than in the United States in terms of local currencies. But if the pound depreciated substantially in relation to the dollar, the unit labor cost measured in dollars could actually have become more favorable in the United Kingdom than in the United States.

Comparative Labor Relations

In each country in which an MNE operates, it must deal with a group of workers whose approach will be affected by the sociopolitical environment of the country and by the traditions and regulations concerning collective bargaining.

Sociopolitical Environment

There are striking international differences in how labor and management view each other. When there is very little mobility between the two groups and a marked class difference exists, considerable labor strife may result. Labor may perceive itself as involved in a class struggle, even though it may have been gaining in real and relative terms for some time.

In such countries as Brazil, Switzerland, and the United States, labor demands are largely met through an adversarial process between the directly affected management and labor. Unions in the United States negligibly influence members' vote in political elections. In contrast, labor groups in many countries vote largely in blocs, resulting in a system in which demands are met primarily through national legislation rather than collective bargaining with management. Because of few U.S. legislative restrictions, management in the United States has more discretion over such human resource functions as hiring, firing, and educational certification than does management in most of Western Europe.[78] Such mechanisms as strikes or slowdowns to effect changes also may be national in scope. In this situation a company's production or ability to distribute its product may be much more dependent on the way labor perceives conditions in the whole country.

The use of mediation by an impartial party to try to bring opposing sides together varies as well. In Israel, it is required by law; in the United States and the United Kingdom, it is voluntary. Among countries that have mediation practices, attitudes toward it are diverse; for example, there is much less enthusiasm for it in India than in the United States.[79] Not all differences are settled either through changes in legislation or through collective bargaining. Other means are the labor court and the government-chosen arbitrator. For example, in Austria wages in many industries are arbitrated semiannually.[80]

Although the means of settling labor disputes vary widely, union membership as a portion of the total workforce has been falling in most countries. This is illustrated in Fig. 21.2.

The reasons for the decline in union membership are several:

* Increase in white-collar workers as a percentage of total workers
* Increase in service employment in relation to manufacturing employment
* Rising portion of women in the workforce
* Rising portion of part-time and temporary workers
* Trend toward smaller average plant size
* Decline in the belief in collectivism among younger workers[81]

In spite of the overall decrease in union membership, the unions in Scandinavia, Austria, and Belgium have maintained their strength. This is attributed to their forging of cooperative relationships with large companies (such as Sweden's ABB, Electrolux, and Volvo) to improve corporate competitiveness and to share in the rewards from the results.

**Figure 21.2
Changes in Union
Membership in
Selected Industrial
Countries**

Source: Organisation for Economic Cooperation (OECD) and Development appearing in *Financial Times,* August 14, 1995, p. 10. Reprinted with permission of FT Pictures/Graphics.

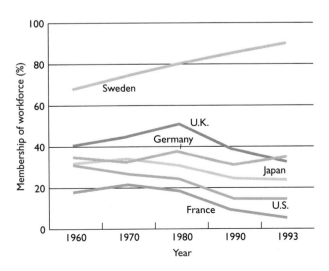

Union structure can be
• National versus local
• Industry versus company
• One versus several for the
  same company

Union Structure

Companies in a given country may deal with one or several different unions. A union itself may represent workers in many different industries, in many different companies within the same industry, or in only one company. If it represents only one company, the union may represent all plants or just one plant. Although there are diversities within countries, one type of relationship is most prevalent within most countries. For example, unions in the United States tend to be national, representing certain types of workers (for example, airline pilots, coal miners, truck drivers, or university professors). Thus a company may deal with several different national unions. Each collective-bargaining process usually is characterized by a single company on one side rather than an association of different companies that deals with one of the unions representing a certain type of worker in all the companies' plants. In Japan, one union typically represents all workers in a given company and has only very loose affiliations with unions in other companies. This allegedly explains why Japanese unions are less militant than those in most other industrialized countries: They seldom strike, and when they do, they may stop working for only a short period of time or may continue working while wearing symbolic arm bands. Because of the workers' closer affiliation with the company, Japanese union leaders are hesitant to risk hurting the company's ability to compete in world markets.[82] In Sweden, bargaining tends to be highly centralized in that employers from numerous companies in different industries deal together with a federation of trade unions. In Germany, employers from associations of companies in the same industries bargain jointly with union federations, although there has been a recent tendency for companies and their workers to use legal loopholes to negotiate separate agreements.[83]

Protection from Closures and Redundancy

Workers' takeover of plants
has been done to publicize
their plight.

In response to proposed layoffs, shifts in production location, and cessation of operations, workers in many countries have physically moved into plants to prevent the transfer of machinery, components, and finished goods. They have even continued to produce until they ran out of raw materials and components and then sold the output on the streets in order to prolong their ability to occupy the plants. The results of these efforts have been mixed, sometimes preventing the plant's closing and other times not.

Prior notification of plant
closings has been legislated
in some countries.

The fact that workers will go so far to try to prevent a plant from closing indicates how important this issue is in some countries, particularly those in Western Europe where prenotification has been negotiated or legislated almost everywhere. The Western European situation contrasts with that in Canada and the United States, where few contracts require employers to give more than a week's notice of closure.

The lifetime-employment custom in Japan offers some contrasts to labor practices in North America and Western Europe. Some Japanese employees, usually skilled male workers in large companies, enjoy lifetime employment. In turn, these

Critics have argued that MNEs have too often established capital-intensive rather than labor-intensive production methods, thus not contributing fully to decreasing unemployment in LDCs. **Appropriate technology** is the technology that best fits the factor endowment where it is used; however, the term usually is used to mean technology that is more labor-intensive than would be cost-effective in an industrial country.

Ethical dilemmas arise whether or not a labor-saving production method is more economical. For example, in India machine-made textiles are less expensive to produce than hand-woven ones are. However, hand-woven textiles employ about 7.5 million people in India, and their production represents a strong cultural value of self-reliance.[84] As the country's production of machine-made textiles has increased (some by MNEs), the number of unemployed weavers and reports of starvation deaths among them have increased. On the one hand, critics have argued that the hand-loom industry should be subsidized and that on ethical grounds, companies should not establish production that will cause unemployment. On the other hand, others argue that the perpetuation of inefficient production merely condemns workers and their descendants to lifetimes of drudgery.

ETHICAL DILEMMAS & SOCIAL RESPONSIBILITY

The evidence is very mixed on whether MNEs alter production to the extent that is cost-feasible. There are undoubtedly engineering biases toward duplicating facilities built to save labor in industrialized countries. Management control systems also may heavily emphasize output per person, which is more relevant to production needs in industrialized countries. Further, many governmental authorities within LDCs want showcase plants as symbols of modernization. However, case studies point to substantial alterations by MNEs, such as using human labor instead of mechanized loading equipment, because of local costs and availabilities.[85]

But when labor is substituted for capital, the productivity of the labor is low, so wages are low. Some companies, nevertheless, have been heavily criticized for their labor rates relative to the price of their end products and what they pay celebrities to advertise them. For example, Nike pays Indonesian workers a little over two dollars a day, while selling some of the shoes for over $100 and paying sports figures, such as André Agassi, millions of dollars to advertise them.[86] Companies have been further criticized for having merchandise produced in so-called sweatshops; however, there is disagreement among companies, unions, and human rights groups who have tried to develop a voluntary code of conduct for the apparel industry on what constitutes a sweatshop. For example, some contend that it is sufficient for companies to pay the local minimum or prevailing wage, but others argue for paying wages high enough to meet basic needs. Some contend that employees should be required to work no more than 48 hours per week, and others argue for a 60-hour-per-week standard.[87]

MNEs also are criticized for exploiting women in many LDCs, where they have had less formal education than men have, have been trained since childhood in tasks requiring manual dexterity, and are willing to accept lower wages than men will. Their qualifications are thus ideal for certain labor-intensive activities. Without the constraints of sex-discrimination legislation, companies advertise openly that they want female workers. Governments even encourage the practice. For example, Malaysia has advertised "the manual dexterity of the Oriental female" within its investment-promotion programs. But the ethical issue is broader. As women have been enticed into the workplace in LDCs, sometimes living in company-provided dormitories, critics argue that social costs have increased because of resultant instability within the family unit and increase in unemployment among the traditional male heads of households. Companies argue that these practices make more jobs and income available and that the employment gives women more independence from their traditional subservient roles.

As another example, some critics contend that the hiring of children by MNEs in lower-income countries is unethical because the practice denies children access to the education needed for their future development. The International Labor Organization (ILO) estimates that a quarter of all children between five and fourteen in lower-income countries are engaged in economic activity; in Africa, the figure is one out of three.[88] One critic said:

> Whether child labor is practiced in a host country or not, the obligation of a multinational corporation not to hire children as full-time, permanent laborers is transnational. This duty cannot be waived by appealing to cultural practices, traditions, or even shared beliefs.[89]

But what if the choice isn't between working and education? For many of the poor children in these countries, there is no opportunity for education, whether or not they work. Without the opportunity for work, many may join the legions of abandoned street children, such as those in Guatemala City who sniff glue to kill hunger pains and steal just enough to subsist. Relatedly, Bangladesh criticized a proposed U.S. law that would restrict the importation of child-made products, arguing that such a law could force thousands of children into begging or prostitution. The ILO agrees that the threat of trade sanctions might endanger rather than protect children.[90] Nevertheless, some private groups, such as Fifa, the world football's governing body, have adopted codes of not using or selling merchandise made by child labor.[91] UNICEF acknowledges the need for children to work in poverty situations, but has called for the elimination of child labor that is hazardous or exploitative.[92]

employees voluntarily switch companies less frequently than do their counterparts in North America and Europe. Other Japanese workers are considered temporaries. The number of temporaries is large, constituting about 40 percent of the workforce even in a large company such as Toyota. In addition, there are many part-time workers. When business takes a downturn or when labor-saving techniques are introduced, Japanese companies keep the lifetime employees on the payroll by releasing the temporary workers, reducing the variable bonuses of lifetime employees, and transferring workers to other product divisions.[93]

Lifetime employment in Japan
- **Is a dual system**
- **Helps institute certain efficiency measures**

There is some evidence, although inconclusive, that this system has enabled Japanese companies to introduce automated systems more effectively than companies elsewhere can because unionized employees have little concern about job security. It also has helped Japanese companies to spend heavily on training because the lifetime employees have a strong moral commitment to stay with their employers. The temporary workers have tolerated the system because of the labor shortage that has existed during recent decades in Japan and because many are women who, because of culture, are disinclined to engage in adversarial behavior.[94]

Codetermination

Some MNEs seek labor-management cooperation through sharing of leadership.

Particularly in Northern Europe, labor participates in the management of companies, a process known as **codetermination.** Most commonly, labor is represented on the board of directors, either with or without veto power.

Despite some voluntary moves toward codetermination, most existing examples have been mandated by legislation, such as that in Germany. These moves have been dictated not only by the philosophy of cooperative leadership but also by the feeling that labor has risks and stakes in the organization just as stockholders do. Because of a belief that the interests of blue-collar workers and white-collar workers differ, some effort has been made to ensure each group is represented. Although there are some early examples of workers deterring investment outflows, acquisitions, and plant closures, codetermination apparently has had little effect on either the types of decisions reached by companies or the speed with which those decisions have been reached. One reason given for this minimal effect is that workers are so divided in terms of what they want that it is hard for their representatives to take strong stances on issues. Where layoffs have been necessary, foreign workers have been given less protection than citizens have.[95]

For example, in Germany workers elect representatives to serve on the company's works' council.[96] This council makes decisions on social matters (such as employee conduct, hours of work, and safety), and when disputes arise between the council and the company's labor director, they are settled by arbitration. In economic and financial matters, the council is provided information and consulted in decisions. However, the workers do not have the greater strength on the council. Although the stockholders and workers have an equal number of representatives, the chairman (elected by stockholders) has the tie-breaking vote. The works' council and the unions have different responsibilities. Collective bargaining takes place between employer associations and the unions and covers all workers within a German state or part of that state. The companies in the employer associations vary in size and ability to cover different possible wage rates, so the negotiated annual wage rates are minimums and can be negotiated upward at the company level. But the unions are barred by law from negotiating at the company or plant level; this is the task of the works' council, whose members are mostly union members.

Team Efforts

In some countries, work teams have been emphasized in order to foster a group cohesiveness and involve workers in multiple rather than a limited number of tasks. In terms of group cohesiveness, it is not uncommon for a portion of the compensation to be based on the group output so that peer pressure is created to reduce absenteeism and increase efforts. In terms of worker involvement in multiple tasks, workers may rotate jobs within the group to reduce boredom and to develop replacement skills to use when someone is not present. Practices that allow workers' groups to control their own quality and repair their own equipment also have been included. The team concept has been adapted to the particular cultures of workers in different countries. For example, quality circles in Japan involve small groups of workers concentrating on very focused problems. GE tried introducing the concept in the United States but found it too constricting for U.S. workers. Now it has meetings on nonfocused issues that involve very large groups of workers, who may suggest broad changes involving significant investment. GE accepts most of the suggestions and also recognizes individual contributions.[97]

International Pressures on National Practices

The ILO monitors labor conditions worldwide.

In 1919, the International Labor Organization (ILO) was set up on the premise that the failure of any country to adopt humane labor conditions is an obstacle to other countries that want to improve their conditions. Several associations of unions from different countries also support similar ideals. These include various international trade secretariats representing workers in specific industries, for example, the International Confederation of Free Trade Unions (ICFTU), the World Federation of Trade Unions (WFTU), and the World Confederation of Labour (WCL).[98] Through these organizations' activities and the general enhancement of communications globally, people increasingly are aware of differences in labor conditions among countries. Among the newsworthy reports have been legal proscriptions against collective bargaining in Malaysia and wages below minimum standards in Indonesia. The ILO also has brought attention to the prevalence of child labor in LDCs. Once such conditions have been noted, there has been pressure for changes through economic and political sanctions from abroad.

The most noteworthy example of these efforts involved pressures by various groups on MNEs operating in South Africa. For example, through church groups, resolutions were presented to stockholders proposing that companies cease, cut back, operate on a nondiscriminatory basis, or report more fully on their South African operations. These pressures led to a large exodus of FDI from South Africa in the late 1980s, the 1991 repeal of apartheid laws, and the subsequent return of many foreign companies.

Another area influencing MNE labor practices has been codes of conduct on industrial relations issued by the OECD and the ILO. Another is the Social Charter, a nonbinding statement of intent by EU heads of government. Although the codes and charter are voluntary, they may signal future transnational regulations of MNE activities. Trade unions have been anxious to get interpretations of the guidelines and make them legally enforceable.

Multinational Ownership and Collective Bargaining[99]

MNE Advantages

Labor may be at a disadvantage in MNE negotiations because the
- **Country bargaining unit is only a small part of MNE activities**
- **MNE may continue serving customers with foreign production or resources**

Product and resource flows   If, during a strike in one country, an MNE can divert output from facilities in other countries to the consumers in the country in which the strike is occurring, there is less pressure due to lost revenues for the MNE to reach an agreement. Further, since the operations in a given country usually comprise a small percentage of an MNE's total worldwide sales, profits, and cash flows, a strike in that country may have minimal effect on the MNE's global performance. The MNE's geographic diversification therefore is argued to be to its advantage when bargaining with labor in a given country. Some analysts contend an MNE simply may hold out longer and be less affected in a strike situation than a domestic company would be.

MNE limitations come from capacity, legal restrictions, shared ownership, integrated production, and differentiated products.

Several factors moderate the MNE's ability to continue supplying customers in the struck country. The MNE may divert output to other markets only if it has excess capacity and only if an identical product is produced in more than one country. If these two conditions are present, the MNE still would confront the cost and trade barriers that led to the initial establishment of multiple production facilities. If the struck operation is only partially owned by the MNE, partners or even minority stockholders may be less willing and able to sustain a lengthy work stoppage. Further, if the idle facilities normally produce components needed for integrated production elsewhere, then a strike may have far-reaching effects. For example, because of a strike at one GM facility in the United States, GM's Mexican plants could not get parts needed for assembly operations; however, because of Mexican laws against layoffs, GM had to maintain its Mexican workers on the payroll, thus adding pressure on GM to reach an agreement.[100] Thus there appear to be advantages of international diversification for the collective-bargaining process, but only in limited circumstances.

MNEs may threaten workers with the prospect of moving production abroad.

Production switching   There are documented examples of threats by companies to move production units to other countries if labor conditions and demands in one country result in changes in the least-cost location of production. For example, Daimler-Benz secured worker concessions in Germany for wages below the nationally agreed-upon level for the industry after its management procured agreements that French, Czech, and British workers would produce for less than the German industry level.[101] But such threats are not limited to international operations. When GM announced that either a plant in Michigan or one in Texas would be closed, the Texans flouted the union and agreed to cut costs by moving to three shifts without overtime pay.[102] Further, production shifts may be inevitable as the least-cost location changes, regardless of labor actions.

Even domestic companies face threats of losing jobs to workers abroad.

Although sometimes production shifts would seem more plausible when a company has facilities in more than one country, at other times they would seem more plausible when facilities in different countries are owned by different companies. For example, a Korean company producing only in Korea and exporting to the Canadian market may not worry much about what happens as a result to employment at a competitor's Canadian-owned plant in Canada. However, if the Canadian and Korean facilities were both owned by the same MNE, management would have to weigh the cost-saving advantages of moving its production location against the losses in terms of cutting back at existing facilities, creating bad will, and becoming vulnerable through decreased diversification.

Labor claims it is disadvantaged in dealing with MNEs because
- Decision making is far away
- It is hard to get full data on MNEs' global operations

Structural problems   Observers often contend it is difficult for labor unions to deal with MNEs because of the complexities in the location of decision making and the difficulties involved in interpreting financial data. It often is assumed that when the real decision makers are far removed from the bargaining location, at home-country headquarters, for example, arbitrarily stringent management decisions will result. Conceivably, the opposite might happen, particularly if the demands abroad seem low in comparison with those being made at home. In reality, labor relations usually are delegated to subsidiary management.

The question of interpreting MNEs' financial data is complex because of disparities among managerial, tax, and disclosure requirements in home and host countries. Labor has been particularly leery of the possibility that artificial transfer pricing may be used to give the appearance that a given subsidiary is unable to meet labor demands. These concerns seem to place an overreliance on a company's ability to pay rather than on the seemingly more important going wage rates in the industry and geographic area. Although MNEs may have more complex data, at least one set of financial statements must satisfy local authorities. This set should be no more difficult to interpret than that of a purely local company. In terms of transfer pricing, it is very doubtful that MNEs set artificial levels to aid in collective-bargaining situations. To understate profits in one place would imply overstating elsewhere, which would negate the advantage, unless changes were made to reflect different contract periods. Tax authorities would not be likely to approve sudden price changes before contract negotiation. Further, any decision to set artificial prices also would have to consider income taxes, tariffs, and opinions of minority stockholders.

Labor Responses and Initiatives

Information sharing   The most common form of cooperation among unions in different countries is exchanging information, which helps them refute company claims as well as cite precedents from other countries when bargaining issues seem transferable. The information exchange is carried out by international confederations of unions representing different types of workers and ideologies, by trade secretariats composed of unions in a single industry or in a complex of related industries, and by company councils that include representatives from an MNE's plants around the world.[103] There are now European work councils (EWCs) representing employees throughout a company's operations within the European Union. Through the EWC, the company informs and consults with employees on such issues as its corporate strategies so that global changes do not occur unexpectedly, leaving employees with little time to react.[104]

Assistance to foreign bargaining units   Labor groups in one country may support their counterparts in other countries in several ways. These include refusing to work overtime when that output would supply the market normally served by striking workers' production, sending financial aid to workers in other countries, and presenting demands to management through other countries. For example, French workers pledged to disrupt work at Pechiney in support of striking workers in the company's U.S. facilities.[105] However, this type of support is still extremely rare. There are more examples of refusals to cooperate in these matters than of successful collaborations.

Simultaneous actions   There have been a few examples of simultaneous negotiations and strikes. But labor's cooperation across borders is a problem because of national differences in terms of union structures and demands. The percentage of workers in unions is much higher in some countries than others; for example, it is much higher in Belgium than in the Netherlands. About half of organized workers in France and Portugal belong to communist unions that do not get along with unions representing the bulk of workers elsewhere in Europe. In addition, both wage rates and workers' preferences differ widely. For instance, Spanish workers are more willing to work on weekends than are German workers. Further, there undoubtedly has been a growing nationalism among workers as their fear of foreign competition has grown.

National approaches   Unions' conflicts with MNEs have been primarily on a national basis. There is little enthusiasm on the part of workers in one country to incur costs to support workers in another, since they tend to view each other as competitors. Even when labor in one country helps labor in another, it may have its own interests in mind. For example, a union representing U.S. tomato pickers helped its Mexican counterpart to win a stronger contract—thus dissuading the Campbell Soup Company from moving operations to Mexico.[106] Even in Canada and the United States, which have long shared a common union membership, there has been a move among Canadian workers to form unions independent of those in the United States. One Canadian organizer summed up much of the attitude by saying, "An American union is not going to fight to protect Canadian jobs at the expense of American jobs." The logic is that international unions will adopt policies favoring the bulk of their membership, which in any joint Canadian-U.S. relationship is bound to be American.[107]

National legislation in some countries has provided for worker representation on boards of directors, regulated the entry of foreign workers, and limited imports and foreign investment outflows. It is probable that most future regulations will be at the national rather than international level.

COUNTERVAILING FORCES

Managers are challenged to break down nationalistic barriers that impair the achievement of global corporate cultures and integrated global strategies. To balance a company's global and national needs, managers must be neither too ethnocentric nor too polycentric (recall the discussion in Chapter 2). MNEs are challenged to find managers who are committed to the operations at which they work, to the parent company if they happen to be working in a foreign subsidiary, and to the company's global well-being. However, even a dual allegiance (local operation and parent company) is rarely found.

Expatriate managers may be classified into one of four categories, as shown in Fig. 21.3: free agent, heart at home, going native, and dual citizen.[108] There are two types of "free agent." The first consists of people whose commitment to career is higher than their commitment to either the parent company or the foreign operation where they are working. They often are highly effective, but they will move with little warning from one company to another in foreign assignments, may serve their own short-term interests at the expense of the company's long-term ones, and do not want to return to their home country. The second type of "free agent" includes people whose careers have plateaued at home and who take a foreign assignment only for the paycheck. The "heart at home" type is overly ethnocentric and is usually eager to be repatriated. When there is a need for strong headquarters control, this type of person may be very effective. The "going native" type learns the local way of doing business very well and wants to stay in the foreign location and be left alone by headquarters. This type of person may be very appropriate for situations in which multidomestic practices are followed. The "dual citizen" type has a clear understanding both of why he or she is needed there and of local realities that may cause operations to deviate from home-country practices. This person usually finds mechanisms by which to

**Figure 21.3
Allegiance of
Expatriate Managers**
The "dual citizen" type of
manager is most effective
at balancing global and
local needs; however, each
of the other types can be
very effective for spe-
cific types of foreign
operations.

Source: Reprinted from "Serving
Two Masters: Managing the Dual
Allegiance of Expatriate
Employees," by J. Stewart Black
and Hal B. Gregersen, *Sloan
Management Review,* Summer
1992, p. 62, by permission of the
publisher. Copyright 1992 by the
Sloan Management Review
Association. All rights reserved.

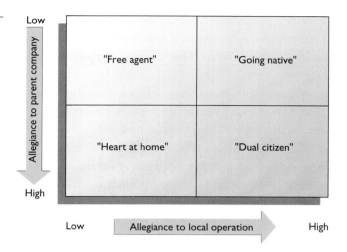

work out differences between headquarters and subsidiary and is overall the most effective
type of expatriate manager.

To counterbalance a "heart at home," the company may send younger managers abroad
and do everything possible to facilitate cultural adjustment. To counterbalance "going
native," the company may send people abroad who have strong ties to the company, limit
their time away from headquarters, keep in close contact with them (perhaps through a
mentor program), and provide them with assistance in repatriation. In either situation, the
international transfer should be handled so that the expatriate understands why he or she
is being sent to the post, how the performance will be measured, the objectives of the parent company and local unit, and the location of control. These suggestions also may be
applied to other than expatriate employees. For example, local managers in foreign subsidiaries may be less apt to be a "heart at home" if they have closer contact with headquarters and see their own future as tied more to global than to local interests. To accomplish
increased interactions, more cross-national interchange may be necessary, although the
traditional problems of cost and governmental regulations continue to impede these
interchanges.

**LOOKING TO
THE FUTURE**

As capital and technology continue to become more mobile,
among countries and among companies, human resource
development should account increasingly for competitive dif-
ferences. Consequently, the access to and retention of ever more qualified personnel
should gain in importance. This does not mean there will be a lack of employee mobility. In
fact, the highly skilled, highly valued worker will likely be more difficult to retain in the
future.[109]

Personal adaptation probably will be a continuing problem. The head of international
human resources at Campbell Soup Company said, "There is too much emphasis on executives' technical abilities and too little on their cultural skills and family situation."[110] This

does not mean that technical skills will be less important to success in foreign assignments but rather that this dimension is already well understood and taken into account. But management still knows far too little about the identification and training of successful personnel for overseas assignments. Further, such factors as two-career families and international terrorism may make managers even more reluctant to accept foreign assignments.

Demographers are nearly unanimous in projecting that populations will grow much faster in LDCs (China being an exception) than in industrial countries, at least up to the year 2030.[111] At the same time, in industrial countries the number of elderly people as a percentage of the population will grow, as will the need to be educated for more years to get the so-called "better jobs" and the tendency to retire at earlier ages. Overall, these industrial-country trends indicate that there will be fewer people to do the productive work within society. Adjustments may come about in any of several ways or combinations of them, and each way has a number of social and economic consequences. MNEs must adapt their production to these changing conditions.

One reaction might be to encourage immigration to industrial countries from LDCs, which neither have now generated nor are expected to generate enough jobs for their potential workers. In Canada, the United States, and parts of Western Europe there has been a fairly long-term entry of foreign workers, both legally and illegally. During the late 1980s, both Italy and Japan had to seek foreign workers, perhaps for the first time ever. Such movements generate assimilation costs within receiving countries and, if they involve highly qualified personnel, charges of a brain drain from LDCs. Further, in economic downturns, foreign workers are likely to be blamed for unemployment. If such movements develop, companies will have to spend more efforts on paperwork required for work permits and develop means of incorporating different groups into the workforce.

Another potential reaction is a continued push toward adoption of robotics and development of other labor-saving equipment. Although this may help solve some of the shortages in industrial countries, average work-skill levels may increase so much that less educated members of the workforce may be either unemployable or forced to take lesser-paying jobs in the service sector. Gaps between haves and have-nots thus may widen, and unemployment problems of LDCs will not be solved. If this scenario occurs, companies may be pressured to shift technology away from labor-saving development and toward natural resource-saving and new product development.

A third possible reaction is the acceleration of industry migration to LDCs to tap ample supplies of labor. At the same time, LDCs may seek ways to reverse their brain drains, which would have the result of shifting production away from industrial countries. For example, India is already attempting to do this for the approximately 15 million overseas Indians, many of whom are highly educated and skilled.[112] India is doing this primarily by offering investment incentives and high-interest bank accounts to overseas Indians. Such moves would enhance the international division of labor but may amplify the distinctions between developed countries and LDCs and the dilemma of what to do with marginal workers in industrial countries. Companies sourcing more heavily in LDCs will have to expend more efforts on logistics to ensure that supplies flow among countries. They also will have to concern themselves more with efforts to minimize the political and monetary risks of operating in LDCs.

WEB CONNECTION
Check out our home page for links to human resource management resources on the World Wide Web.

Summary

- The tasks of international managers differ from those of purely domestic managers in several ways, including needing to know how to adapt home-country practices to foreign locales and being more likely to deal with high-level governmental officials.

- The top-level managers of foreign subsidiaries normally perform much broader duties than do domestic managers with similar cost or profit responsibilities. They must cope with communications problems between corporate head-quarters and the subsidiaries, usually with less staff assistance.

- MNEs employ more local than expatriate managers because the locals understand regional operating conditions and may focus more on long-term operations and goals. Doing so also demonstrates that opportunities are available for local citizens, shows consideration for local interests, avoids the red tape of cross-national transfers, and usually is cheaper.

- MNEs transfer people abroad in order to infuse technical competence and home-country business practices, to control foreign operations, and to develop managers.

- MNEs that transfer personnel abroad should consider how well the people will be accepted, how to treat them when the foreign assignment is over, and how well they will adapt.

- When transferred abroad, an expatriate's compensation usually is adjusted because of hardship and differences in cost of living and job status.

- Companies frequently acquire personnel abroad by buying existing companies. They also may go into business with local companies, which then assume most staffing responsibilities.

- Two major international training functions are to build a global awareness among managers in general and to equip managers to handle the specific situations entailed in a foreign assignment.

- **When setting up a new operation in a foreign country, a company may use existing facilities as guides for determining labor needs. However, it should adjust to compensate for different labor skills, costs, and availabilities.**

- **For some areas, a substantial portion of the labor supply is imported, which creates special stability, supervision, and training problems for companies operating there.**

- **Because of the enormous variation in fringe benefits, direct-compensation figures do not accurately reflect the amount a company must pay for a given job. In addition, job-security benefits (no layoffs, severance pay, etc.) add substantially to compensation costs.**

- **Although per-worker comparisons are useful indicators of labor-cost differences, it is the output associated with total costs that is relevant for international competitiveness. These costs may shift over time, thus changing relative international competitive positions.**

- **A country's sociopolitical environment will determine to a great extent the type of relationship between labor and management and affect the number, representation, and organization of unions.**

- **Codetermination is a type of labor participation in a company's management and usually is intended to cultivate a cooperative rather than an adversarial environment.**

- **In recent years, there have been efforts to get companies to follow internationally accepted labor practices regardless of where they are operating or whether the practices conflict with the norms and laws of the countries in which they are operating.**

- **MNEs often are blamed for weakening the position of labor in the collective-bargaining process because of those companies' international diversification, threats to export jobs, and complex structures and reporting mechanisms.**

- **Cooperation between labor groups in different countries in conflicts with MNEs is minimal. Strategies include information exchanges, simultaneous negotiations or strikes, and refusals to work overtime if the intent is to compensate for a striking company in another country.**

Case
Office Equipment Company (OEC)

In 1997, the managing director (a U.S. national) of the Office Equipment Company (OEC) in Lima, Peru (see Map 21.1), announced suddenly that he would leave within one month. The company had to find a replacement. OEC manufactures a wide variety of small office equipment (such as copying machines, recording machines, mail scales, and paper shredders) in eight different countries and distributes and sells products worldwide. It has no manufacturing facilities in Peru but has been selling and servicing there since the early 1970s. OEC first tried selling in Peru through independent importers but quickly became convinced that in order to make sufficient sales it needed to have its own staff there. Despite Peru's political turmoil, which at times has bordered on being a full-scale civil war, OEC's operation there (with about 100 employees) has enjoyed good and improving sales and profitability.

OEC is constructing its first factory in Peru that is scheduled to begin operations in early 1999. This factory will import components for personal computer printers and assemble them locally. Peru offers an abundant supply of cheap labor, and the assembly operation will employ approximately 150 people. The government will allow up to 10 percent of the output to be sold locally. By assembling locally and then exporting, OEC expects to be able to ward off trade restrictions on the other office equipment it imports for sale within Peru. This plant's construction is being supervised by a U.S. technical team, and a U.S. expatriate will be assigned to direct the production. This director will report directly to OEC's U.S. headquarters on all production and quality-control matters but will report to the managing director in Peru on all other matters, such as accounting, finance, and labor relations.

OEC, by policy, will replace the exiting managing director with an internal candidate. The company employs a combination of home-, host-, and third-country nationals in top positions in foreign countries, and managers commonly rotate among foreign and U.S. locations. In fact, it has been increasingly evident to OEC that international experience is an important factor in deciding who will be appointed to top corporate positions. The sales and service facility in Peru reports to a Latin American regional office located in Coral Gables, Florida. A committee at this office, charged with selecting the new managing director, quickly narrowed its choice to five candidates.

Tom Zimmerman   A thirty-year OEC veteran, Zimmerman is well versed in all the technical and sales aspects required in the job. He has never worked abroad for OEC but has visited various of the company's foreign facilities as part of sales teams. He is considered competent and will retire in about four and a half years. Neither he nor his wife speaks Spanish. Their children are grown and living with their own children in the United States. Zimmerman currently is in charge of an operation that is about the size of that in Peru after the new factory begins operating. However, Zimmerman's present position will become redundant because the operation he heads is being merged with another.

Brett Harrison   Harrison, 40, has spent fifteen years at OEC. Considered highly competent and capable of moving into upper-level management within the next few years, he has

PERU

Population
    22.3 million
Monetary unit
    New sol
Major languages
    Spanish
    Quechua
    Aymara
Largest city
    Lima
Major industrial areas
    Arequipa
    Chimbote
    Cuzco
    Iquitos
    Lima
    Talara

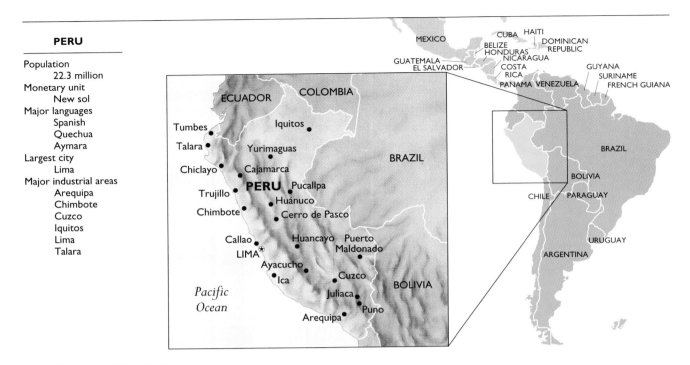

Map 21.1
Peru

never been based abroad but has worked for the last three years in the Latin American regional office and frequently travels to Latin America. Both he and his wife speak Spanish adequately, and their two children, ages 14 and 15, are just beginning to study the language. His wife holds a responsible marketing position with a pharmaceuticals company.

Carolyn Moyer   Moyer joined OEC twelve years ago after getting her MBA from a prestigious university. At 37, she has already moved between staff and line positions of growing responsibility. For two years, she was second in command of a product group that was about the size of the newly expanded one in Peru. Her performance in that post was considered excellent. Currently, she works on a planning staff team. When she joined OEC, she indicated her interest in eventual international responsibilities because of her undergraduate major in international affairs. She has recently expressed interest in international duties because of a belief it will help her advancement. She speaks Spanish well and is unmarried.

Francisco Cabrera   Cabrera, 35, currently is an assistant managing director in the larger Mexican operation, which produces and sells for the Mexican market. A Mexican citizen, he has worked for OEC in Mexico for all his twelve years with the company. He holds an MBA from a Mexican university and is considered to be a likely candidate to head the Mexican operation when the present managing director retires in seven years. He is married with four children (ages 2 to 7) and speaks English adequately. His wife does not work outside the home or speak English.

Juan Moreno   At 27, Moreno is assistant to the present managing director in Peru. He has held that position since joining OEC upon his U.S. college graduation four years ago. Unmarried, he is considered competent, especially in employee relations, but lacking in experience. He had been successful in increasing OEC's sales, in part because he is well connected with local families who can afford to buy new office equipment for their businesses.

Questions

1. Which candidate should the committee choose for the assignment, and why?
2. What problems might each candidate encounter in the position?
3. How might OEC go about minimizing the problems that each candidate would have in managing the Peruvian operations?
4. Calculate an estimated compensation package for each candidate based on the following additional information:

- Present annual salaries: Zimmerman, US$70,000; Harrison, US$75,000; Moyer, US$65,000; Cabrera, M$124,000; Moreno, S57,000
- Exchange rates: $1 = M$3.1 (Mexican pesos); $1 = S1.9 (Peruvian new sols)
- U.S. Department of State cost-of-living index based on items covering 35 percent of income for a family of one, 40 percent for a family of two, 45 percent for a family of four, and 50 percent for a family of five or more: Washington, D.C. = 100; Lima = 86; Mexico City = 77
- U.S. Department of State foreign-service premiums for Peru: hardship = 15 percent; danger = 15 percent
- Housing allowance (nontaxable): single = US$12,100; family = US$15,000
- Schooling allowance: age 6–12 = US$5000; age 13–18 = US$9000
- Average tax rates: Mexico = 20 percent; United States = 25 percent; Peru = 30 percent

---

Chapter Notes

1. The data for the case were taken from Edwin McDowell, "Making It in America: The Foreign-Born Executive," *New York Times*, June 1, 1980, Section 3, p. 1+; Don Whitehead, *The Dow Story* (New York: McGraw-Hill, 1968); "Lundeen Urges More Aid for Universities," *Chemical Marketing Reporter*, Vol. 224, No. 19, November 7, 1983, p. 3+; Paul L. Blocklyn, "Developing the International Executive," *Personnel*, Vol. 66, March 1989, pp. 44–47; "Globesmanship," *Across the Board*, Vol. 27, Nos. 1, 2, January–February 1990, pp. 24–34; William Storck, "Dow Chemical Changes Executive Lineup," *Chemical and Engineering News*,

September 14, 1992, p. 5; "Popoff on Challenges for Dow and for the Industry," *Chemical Week*, May 18, 1994, pp. 26–28; and Susan J. Sinsworth, "Issues Management Is Central to Frank Popoff's Globalization Strategy," *Chemical Engineering News*, Vol. 72, No. 21, May 23, 1994, pp. 25–29.
2. Gary R. Oddou and Mark E. Mendenhall, "Succession Planning for the 21st Century: How Well Are We Grooming Our Future Business Leaders?" *Business Horizons*, January–February 1991, pp. 26–34.
3. Gordon Petrash, "Dow's Journey to a Knowledge Value Management Culture,"

European Management Journal, Vol. 14, No. 4, August 1996, pp. 365–373.
4. "Globesmanship," *Across the Board*, Vol. 27, Nos. 1, 2, January–February 1990, p. 26, quoting Michael Angus.
5. Daniel Ondrack, "International Transfers of Managers in North American and European MNEs," *Journal of International Business Studies*, Vol. 16, No. 3, Fall 1985, pp. 1–19; and John M. Hannon, Ing-Chung Huang, and Bih-Shiaw Jaw, "International Human Resource Strategy and Its Determinants: The Case of Subsidiaries in Taiwan," *Journal of International Business Studies*, Vol. 26, No. 3, Third Quarter 1995, pp. 531–554.

6. Kendall Roth, "Managing International Interdependence: CEO Characteristics in a Resource-Based Framework," *Academy of Management Journal,* Vol. 38, No. 1, 1995, pp. 200–231.

7. Sully Taylor, Schon Beechler, and Nancy Napier, "Toward An Integrative Model of Strategic International Resource Management," *Academy of Management Review,* Vol. 21, No. 4, 1996, pp. 959–985, discusses these in the context of multidomestic and a combination of global and transnational strategies.

8. See, for example, Martin J. Gannon, "Overcoming Culture Shock," *Export Today,* Vol. 10, No. 4, 1994, pp. 12–16.

9. Katarzyna Wandycz, "Resetting the Internal Clock," *Forbes,* August 30, 1993, p. 74.

10. Bob Masterson and Bob Murphy, "Internal Cross-Cultural Management," *Training and Development Journal,* Vol. 40, No. 4, April 1986, pp. 56–60.

11. Peter Lorange, "Human Resource Management in Multinational Cooperative Ventures," *Human Resource Management,* Vol. 25, No. 1, Spring 1986, pp. 133–148; Wayne E. Cascio and Manuel G. Serapio, Jr., "Human Resources Systems in an International Alliance: The Undoing of a Done Deal?" *Organizational Dynamics,* Winter 1991, pp. 63–75; and Heinz-Dieter Meyer, "The Cultural Gap in Long-Term International Work Groups: A German-American Case Study," *European Management Journal,* Vol. 11, No. 1, March 1993, pp. 93–101.

12. Jean Ross-Skinner, "English Spoken Here," *Dun's Review,* March 1977, pp. 56–57; and David A. Weeks, *Recruiting and Selecting International Managers,* Report No. 998 (New York: The Conference Board, 1992).

13. Jonathan Kaufman, "On the Road Again," *Wall Street Journal,* November 19, 1996, p. A1+.

14. David C. Waring, "Doing Business Overseas," *Cornell Enterprise,* Fall–Winter 1988, p. 29.

15. Robert Taylor, "Companies Cut Back Overseas Transfer Benefits," *Financial Times,* July 18, 1996, p. 1, reporting a survey by Monks Partnership, an independent remuneration adviser.

16. Weeks, loc. cit.

17. For a good example of IBM in Korea, see Edward E. Lucente, *Managing a Global Enterprise* (Pittsburgh: Carnegie Bosch Institute for Applied Studies in International Management, 1993), Working Paper No. 94-2.

18. Dafna N. Izraeli, Moshe Banai, and Yoram Zeira, "Women Executives in MNC Subsidiaries," *California Management Review,* Vol. 23, No. 1, Fall 1980, pp. 53–63; Yves Doz and C. K. Prahalad,

"Controlled Variety: A Challenge for Human Resource Management in the MNC," *Human Resource Management,* Vol. 25, No. 1, Spring 1986, pp. 55–57; and Peter Coy and Neil Gross, "When the Going Gets Tough, Yanks Get Yanked," *Business Week,* April 26, 1993, p. 30.

19. Barry Newman, "Expat Archipelago," *Wall Street Journal,* December 12, 1995, p. A1+.

20. Anders Edström and Jay R. Galbraith, "Alternative Policies for International Transfers of Managers," *Management International Review,* No. 2, 1977, pp. 13–14; and Asya Pazy and Yoram Zeira, "Training Parent-Country Professionals in Host-Country Organizations," *Academy of Management Review,* Vol. 8, No. 2, 1983, pp. 262–272.

21. Joann S. Lublin, "More U.S. Companies Venture Overseas for Directors Offering Fresh Perspectives," *Wall Street Journal,* January 27, 1992, p. B1; Joann S. Lublin, "Foreign Accents Proliferate in Top Ranks as U.S. Companies Find Talent Abroad," *Wall Street Journal,* May 21, 1992, p. B1; and Judith Rehak, "For U.S. Corporations, the Modern Day Byword Is 'Globalize or Die'," *International Herald Tribune,* September 3–4, 1994, p. 15, referring to a 1993 survey by the National Foreign Trade Council.

22. Ibid.

23. Anders Edström and Jay R. Galbraith, "Transfer of Managers as a Coordination and Control Strategy in Multinational Organizations," *Administrative Science Quarterly,* June 1977, pp. 248–261; and A. B. Sim, "Decentralized Management of Subsidiaries and Their Performance," *Management International Review,* No. 2, 1977, p. 48.

24. Alfred Jaeger, "Organization Development and National Culture: Where's the Fit?" *Academy of Management Review,* Vol. 11, No. 1, 1986, pp. 178–190; "The Elusive Euro-Manager," *The Economist,* November 7, 1992, p. 83; and Newman, loc. cit.

25. Anders Edström and Peter Lorange, "Matching Strategy and Human Resources in Multinational Companies," *Journal of International Business Studies,* Fall 1984, pp. 125–137; Stephen J. Kobrin, "Expatriate Reduction and Strategic Control in American Multinational Corporations," *Human Resource Management,* Vol. 27, No. 1, Spring 1988, pp. 63–75; and Louis Uchitelle, "Only the Bosses Are American," *New York Times,* July 24, 1989, p. 21+.

26. Ingmar Bjorkman and Annette Schaap, "Outsiders in the Middle Kingdom: Expatriate Managers in Chinese-Western Joint Ventures," *European*

Management Journal, Vol. 12, No. 2, 1994, pp. 147–153.

27. Michael G. Duerr and James Greene, *The Problems Facing International Management,* Managing International Business, No. 1 (New York: National Industrial Conference Board, 1968), p. 18; see also Richard D. Hays, "Behavioral Determinants of Success-Failure among U.S. Expatriate Managers," *Journal of International Business Studies,* Spring 1971, pp. 40–46; Martine Gertsen, "Intercultural Competence and Expatriates," Working Paper No. 1, 1990, Copenhagen School of Economics and Business Administration, Institute of International Economics and Management; Moran, Stahl & Boyer, Inc., *International Human Research Management* (Boulder, Colo.: Moran, Stahl & Boyer, 1987); and Weeks, loc. cit.

28. J. Stewart Black and Mark Mendenhall, "Cross-Cultural Training Effectiveness: A Review and a Theoretical Framework for Future Research," *Academy of Management Review,* Vol. 15, No. 1, January 1990, p. 117; and Mark Mendenhall and Gary Oddou, "The Dimensions of Expatriate Acculturation: A Review," *Academy of Management Review,* Vol. 10, No. 1, January 1985, pp. 39–47.

29. Windham International and National Foreign Trade Council, *Global Relocation Trends: 1994 Survey Report,* November 1994, based on a survey of 103 companies, mainly based in the United States, found that 92 percent of expatriates finish their foreign assignments. Erika Morphy, "Expatriate Gains," *Export Today,* February 1997, pp. 38–41, referred to a report by the Employee Relocation Council that about 90 percent of international assignments are successful.

30. Jack Anderson, "The Survey's In: Although Costly, Good Expatriate Executives Are Sound Investments," *International Herald Tribune,* September 3–4, 1994, p. 15, referring to a study by the Confederation of Business and Industry and Ernst & Young of 600 MNEs; and Meg G. Birdseye and Jon S. Hill, "Individual, Organizational/Work and Environmental Influences on Expatriate Turnover Tendencies: An Empirical Study," *Journal of International Business Studies,* Vol. 26, No. 4, Fourth Quarter 1995, pp. 787–813.

31. Philip R. Harris and Robert L. Moran, *Managing Cultural Differences* (Houston: Gulf, 1979), p. 164; J. Stewart Black and Gregory K. Stephens, "The Influence of the Spouse on American Expatriate Adjustment and Intent to Stay in Pacific Rim Overseas Assignments," *Journal of Management,* Vol. 15, No. 4, 1989, pp. 529–530; and Alicia Kitsuse, "At

Home Abroad," *Across the Board,* September 1992, pp. 34–39.

32. Karen Dawn Stuart, "Teens Play a Role in Moves Overseas," *Personnel Journal,* March 1992, pp. 72–78. PHH Relocation estimated that for 1995, the top three locations for U.S. transfers were Mexico, Chile, and Belgium in "At Home Abroad," *Wall Street Journal,* February 2, 1996. A survey by Windham International of 138 companies indicated that the expected biggest relocations for 1996 would be China, India, and Mexico in "China Blues," *Wall Street Journal,* March 19, 1996, p. A1.

33. Izraeli et al., loc. cit.

34. Patricia Feltes, Robert K. Robinson, and Ross L. Fink, "American Female Expatriates and the Civil Rights Act of 1991: Balancing Legal and Business Interests," *Business Horizons,* March–April 1993, pp. 82–86.

35. Mariann Jelinek and Nancy J. Adler, "Women: World Class Managers for Global Competition," *Academy of Management Executive,* Vol. II, No. 1, February 1988, pp. 11–19; Jolie Solomon, "Women, Minorities and Foreign Postings," *Wall Street Journal,* June 2, 1989, p. B1; and Weeks, loc. cit.

36. R. I. Westwood and S. M. Leung, "The Female Expatriate Manager Experience," *International Studies of Management & Organization,* Vol. 24, No. 3, 1994, pp. 64–85; and Sully Taylor and Nancy Napier, "Working in Japan: Lessons from Women Expatriates," *Sloan Management Review,* Spring 1996, pp. 76–84.

37. Izraeli et al., loc. cit. For some suggestions on how women may make themselves more acceptable, see Gladys L. Symons, "Coping with the Corporate Tribe: How Women in Different Cultures Experience the Managerial Role," *Journal of Management,* Vol. 12, No. 3, 1986, pp. 379–389; and Marlene L. Rossman, *The International Businesswoman* (New York: Praeger, 1986).

38. Windham International and National Foreign Trade Council, loc. cit.

39. David M. Noer, "Integrating Foreign Service Employees to Home Organization: The Godfather Approach," *Personnel Journal,* January 1974, pp. 45–50; William F. Cagney, "Executive Reentry: The Problems of Repatriation," *Personnel Journal,* September 1975, pp. 487–488; J. Alex Murray, "Repatriated Executives: Culture Shock in Reverse," *Management Review,* November 1973, pp. 43–45; Philip R. Harris, "Employees Abroad: Maintain the Corporate Connection," *Personnel Journal,* Vol. 65, No. 8, August 1986, pp. 107–110; Oddou and Mendenhall, loc. cit.; and Jodi Zurawski, "Plan for Expatriates:'Welcome Home' before

They Say 'Bon Voyage,' " *Human Resources Professional,* Summer 1992, pp. 42–44.

40. Oddou and Mendenhall, loc. cit., found that foreign assignments helped careers in 29 percent of cases. Moran, Stahl & Boyer, as reported in the *New York Times,* June 17, 1990, Sec. 3, p. 1, found that of the MNEs studied, 44 percent perceived foreign assignments as being advantageous or essential to careers, whereas 56 percent viewed them as immaterial or detrimental.

41. Patrick Oster, Neil Gross, Sunita Wadekar Bhargava, and Elizabeth Lesly, "The Fast Track Leads Overseas," *Business Week,* November 1, 1993, pp. 64–65.

42. Newman, loc. cit.

43. Amanda Bennett, "What's an Expatriate?" *Wall Street Journal,* April 21, 1993, p. R5.

44. Claudia H. Deutsch, "Getting the Brightest to Go Abroad," *New York Times,* June 17, 1990, p. C1.

45. Ibid. Most indications are that these involve a minority of companies; however, Weeks, loc. cit., found the inclusion of international experience in succession plans of 61 percent of large companies.

46. Bennett, loc. cit., referring to a study by Organizational Resources Counselors involving 45 companies.

47. "Domestic Help for Expatriates," *Wall Street Journal,* September 9, 1991, p. A10.

48. Taylor, loc. cit.; and Judith Rehak, "Overseas Fat Cats Face Tough Order. Slim Down," *International Herald Tribune,* May 11–12, 1996, p. 17.

49. Patrick M. Reilly and Joann S. Lublin, "Should Business Negotiate With Terrorists?" *Wall Street Journal,* September 20, 1995, p. B1; Amon Cohen, "Destination Danger," *Financial Times,* June 17, 1996, p. 14; Joel Millman, "Sanyo Executive Released Unharmed By Kidnappers in Mexico After 8 Days," *Wall Street Journal,* August 20, 1996, p. A12; Jonathan Dahl, "Psst . . . Private Tips Safeguard Business Trips," *Wall Street Journal,* August 5, 1996; and Craig Torres, "Mexico City Crime Alarms Multinationals," *Wall Street Journal,* October 29, 1996, p. A16.

50. "Thinking of Relocating?" *World Executive's Digest,* April 1995, p. 23.

51. Gilbert Fuchsberg, "As Costs of Overseas Assignments Climb, Firms Select Expatriates More Carefully," *Wall Street Journal,* January 9, 1992, p. B1.

52. Joann S. Lublin, "Spouses Find Themselves Worlds Apart as Global Commuter Marriages Increase," *Wall Street Journal,* August 19, 1992, p. B1+.

53. "Global Report," *Wall Street Journal,* July 11, 1977, p. 6; and Barry Newman, "Mine over Matter," *Wall Street Journal,* August 25, 1977, p. 1.

54. Bennett, loc. cit.; Amanda Bennett, "Managers' Incomes Aren't Worlds Apart," *Wall Street Journal,* October 12, 1992, p. B1; Richard Morais et al., "The Global Boss' Pay: Where and How the Money Is," *Forbes,* June 7, 1993, pp. 90–98; Linda Bell and Richard Freeman, *Why Do Americans and Germans Work Different Hours?* (Cambridge, MA: National Bureau of Economic Research Working Paper No. 4804, 1994); and Jack Anderson, "For Expatriates, a Barrage of Barriers," *International Herald Tribune,* September 24–25, 1994, p. 15.

55. Frances Williams, "Protect Workers' Privacy, Says ILO," *Financial Times,* October 8, 1996, p. 5.

56. Rosalie L. Tung, "Selection and Training of Personnel for Overseas Assignments," *Columbia Journal of World Business,* Vol. 16, No. 1, Spring 1981, p. 72; Canadian International Development Agency (CIDA), "Going Abroad with CIDA"; Bureau of Naval Personnel, *Overseas Diplomacy: Guidelines for United States Navy: Trainer* (Washington, D.C.: U.S. Government Printing Office, 1973); M. H. Tucker, D. Raik Rossiter, and M. Uhes, *Improving the Evaluation of Peace Corps Training Activities,* Vol. 3 (Denver: Center for Research and Education, June 4, 1973); and J. Stewart Black, "Work-role Transitions: A Study of American Expatriate Managers in Japan," *Journal of International Business Studies,* Vol. 19, 1988, pp. 277–294.

57. Weeks, loc. cit., found that 32 percent of companies interview families and 16 percent use psychological tests for either the employee or the employee and family.

58. Michael G. Harvey, "The Executive Family: An Overlooked Variable in International Assignments," *Columbia Journal of World Business,* Spring 1985, pp. 84–92; and Black and Stephens, loc. cit.

59. Black and Mendenhall, op. cit., pp. 118–119; and J. Stewart Black, Mark Mendenhall, and Gary Oddou, "Toward a Comprehensive Model of International Adjustment: An Integration of Multiple Theoretical Perspectives," *Academy of Management Review,* March–April 1991.

60. Christopher A. Bartlett and Sumantra Ghoshal, "What Is a Global Manager?" *Harvard Business Review,* September–October 1992, pp. 124–132.

61. R. Lynn Barnes, "Across Cultures: The Peace Corps Training Model," *Training and Development Journal,* Vol. 39, No. 10, October 1985, pp. 46–49.

62. P. Christopher Earley, "Intercultural Training for Managers: A Comparison of Documentary and Interpersonal Methods," *Academy of Management Journal*, Vol. 30, No. 4, December 1987, pp. 685–698.

63. F. T. Murray and Alice Haller Murray, "SMR Forum: Global Managers for Global Businesses," *Sloan Management Review*, Vol. 27, No. 2, Winter 1986, pp. 75–80; Joann S. Lublin, "Younger Managers Learn Global Skills," *Wall Street Journal*, March 31, 1992, p. B1; and Bob Hagerty, "Trainers Help Expatriate Employees Build Bridges to Different Cultures," *Wall Street Journal*, June 14, 1993, p. B1.

64. Alicia Kitsuse, "At Home Abroad," *Across the Board*, September 1992, pp. 34–39; and Yoram Zeira and Asya Pazy, "Crossing National Borders to Get Trained," *Training and Development Journal*, Vol. 39, No. 10, October 1985, pp. 53–57.

65. Kitsuse, loc. cit., referring to suggestions by Stewart Black.

66. Vincent Cable, "The Diminished Nation-State: A Study In The Loss Of Economic Power," *Daedalus*, Vol. 124, No. 2, 1995, pp. 22–53.

67. "Foreign Workers In Germany," *The Economist*, April 22, 1995, pp. 67–68.

68. Brent Bowers, "Tapping Foreign Talent Pool Can Yield Lush Growth," *Wall Street Journal*, March 23, 1992, p. B2.

69. Igor Reichlin, Sabrina Kiefer, Charles Hoots, and Jacek Dobrowlski, "Long Days, Low Pay, and a Moldy Cot," *Business Week*, January 27, 1992, pp. 44–45; and Michael J. Mandel, Christopher Farrell, Dori Jones Yang, Gloria Lau, Christina Del Valle, and S. Lynne Walker, "The Immigrants," *Business Week*, July 13, 1992, pp. 114–122.

70. R. Aggarwal and I. Khera, "Exporting Labor: The Impact of Expatriate Workers on the Home Country," *International Migration*, Vol. 25, No. 4, 1987, pp. 415–424.

71. Chao C. Chen, "New Trends in Rewards Allocation Preferences: A Sino-U.S. Comparison," *Academy of Management Journal*, Vol. 38, No. 2, 1995, pp. 408–428.

72. "In Europe, Cash Eases the Pain of Getting Fired," *Business Week*, March 16, 1992, p. 26; and Greg Steinmetz, "Americans, Too, Run Afoul of Rigorous German Rules," *Wall Street Journal*, February 2, 1996, p. A6.

73. Roy B. Helfgott, "Labor Market Models in Europe and America and Unhappiness with Both," *Business Horizons*, Vol. 39, No. 2, March–April 1996, pp. 77–84.

74. Felice Morgenstern, "The Civil Liability of Workers for Injury or Damage Caused in Their Employment," *International Labour Review*, May–June 1976, pp. 317–328.

75. Bob Davis, "Illusory Bargain," *Wall Street Journal*, September 15, 1993, p. A1+.

76. "Asia's Costly Labour Problems," *The Economist*, September 21, 1996, p. 62.

77. Steve Glain, "Korea Is Overthrown as Sneaker Champ," *Wall Street Journal*, October 7, 1993, p. A12.

78. Chris Brewster, "Towards a 'European' Model of Human Resource Management," *Journal of International Business Studies*, Vol. 26, No. 1, First Quarter 1995, pp. 1–21.

79. Joseph Krislov, "Supplying Mediation Services in Five Countries: Some Current Problems," *Columbia Journal of World Business*, Vol. 18, No. 2, Summer 1983, pp. 55–63.

80. Frances Bairstow, "The Trend Toward Centralized Bargaining—A Patchwork Quilt of International Diversity," *Columbia Journal of World Business*, Spring 1985, pp. 75–83.

81. Robert Taylor, "Challenge Facing Endangered Species," *Financial Times*, August 14, 1995, p. 10; and "Adapt or Die," *The Economist*, July 1, 1995, p. 54.

82. Masayoshi Kanabayashi, "Japan's Unions, Anxious to Avoid Fight, Again Likely to Accept a Modest Pay Raise," *Wall Street Journal*, February 9, 1984, p. 31.

83. Bairstow, loc. cit.; and Greg Steinmetz, "Hire Standard," *Wall Street Journal*, October 17, 1995, p. 1A+.

84. Edward A. Gargan, "As Hand Looms of India Fall Silent, the Country's Social Fabric Frays," *New York Times*, October 7, 1992, p. A4.

85. For a good survey of the various studies, see Peter Enderwick, *Multinational Business & Labor* (New York: St. Martin's Press, 1985), pp. 55–58.

86. "Workers Foot the Bill: Nike," *South China Sunday Morning Post* (Agenda Section), March 5, 1995, p. 1.

87. Steven Greenhouse, "Voluntary Rules on Apparel Proving Elusive," *New York Times*, February 1, 1997, p. 1+.

88. Frances Williams, "ILO Gives Warning on Child Labour Boycotts," *Financial Times*, November 2, 1995, p. 8.

89. Thomas Donaldson, "Can Multinationals Stage a Universal Morality Play?" *Business and Society Review*, Spring 1992, pp. 51–55.

90. Williams, loc. cit.

91. "Child Labour Code Agreed," *Financial Times*, September 5, 1996, p. 4.

92. United Nations Children's Fund, *The State of the World's Children* (Oxford: Oxford University Press, 1977).

93. Eamonn Fingleton, *Blindside: Why Japan Is Still on Track to Overtake the U.S. by the Year 2000* (New York: Houghton Mifflin, 1995).

94. Panos Mourdoukoutas and S. N. Sohng, "The Japanese Industrial System: A Study in Adjustment to Automation," *Management International Review*, Vol. 27, No. 4, 1987, pp. 46–55; John Hoerr and Wendy Zellner, "A Japanese Import That's Not Selling," *Business Week*, February 26, 1990, pp. 86–87; Masayoshi Kanabayashi, "Bucking Tradition," *Wall Street Journal*, October 11, 1988, p. 1+; Masayoshi Kanabayashi, "Japanese Workers Aren't All Workaholics," *Wall Street Journal*, May 8, 1989, p. A10; and D. H. Whittaker, *Managing Innovation: A Study of British and Japanese Factories* (Cambridge, Eng.: Cambridge University Press, 1990).

95. For early operational problems, see "Sweden: Worker Participation Becomes the Law," *Business Week*, June 21, 1976, pp. 42–46; G. McIsaac and H. Henzler, "Co-Determination: A Hidden Noose for MNCs," *Columbia Journal of World Business*, Winter 1974, pp. 67–74; and M. Warner and R. Peccei, "Worker Participation and Multinationals," *Management International Review*, No. 3, 1977, pp. 93–98. For recent evidence on overall effects, see Wolfgang Scholl, "Codetermination and the Ability of Firms to Act in the Federal Republic of Germany," *International Studies of Management & Organization*, Vol. XVII, No. 2, Summer 1987, pp. 27–37; and Giuseppe Benelli, Claudio Loderer, and Thomas Lys, "Labor Participation in Corporate Policy-making Decisions: West Germany's Experience with Codetermination," *Journal of Business*, Vol. 60, No. 4, October 1987, pp. 553–575.

96. Much of the information on codetermination in Germany is taken from Trevor Bain, "German Codetermination and Employment Adjustments in the Steel and Auto Industries," *Columbia Journal of World Business*, Vol. 18, No. 2, Summer 1983, pp. 40–47.

97. Amal Kumar Naj, "Shifting Gears," *Wall Street Journal*, May 5, 1993, p. A1.

98. "Child-Worker Abuses in Third World Draw Fire of Labor Group," *Wall Street Journal*, June 8, 1988, p. 26.

99. Unless otherwise noted, information in this section is taken largely from the following treatises: Gerald B. J. Bomers and Richard B. Peterson, "Multinational Corporations and the Industrial Relations: The Case of West Germany and the Netherlands," *British Journal of Industrial Relations*, March 1977, pp. 45–62; Duane A. Kujawa, "Collective Bargaining and Labor Relations in Multinational Enterprise: A U.S. Policy Perspective," paper presented at New York University Conference on Economic Issues of Multinational Firms, November 1976; Duane Kujawa, "U.S. Manufacturing Investment

in the Developing Countries: American Labour's Concerns and the Enterprise Environment in the Decade Ahead," *British Journal of Industrial Relations,* Vol. 19, No. 1, March 1981, pp. 38–48; and Roy B. Helfgott, "American Unions and Multinational Enterprises: A Case of Misplaced Emphasis," *Columbia Journal of World Business,* Vol. 18, No. 2, Summer 1983, pp. 81–86.

100. Neil Templin, "GM Strike Hits Mexican Output As Talks on Settlement Resume," *Wall Street Journal,* March 20, 1996, p. A3.

101. Steinmetz, loc. cit.

102. Gregory A. Patterson, "New Rules," *Wall Street Journal,* March 6, 1992, p. A1.

103. Martin C. Seham, "Transnational Labor Relations: The First Steps Are Being Taken," *Law and Policy in International Business,* Vol. 6, 1974, pp. 347–354.

104. D. Van Den Bulcke, *The European Works Council: A New Challenge for Multinational Enterprises* (Antwerp: University of Antwerp Centre for International Management and Development Discussion Paper No. 1996/E/26, 1996); and Robert Taylor, "Unions to Join Works Council at Philip Morris," *Financial Times,* January 30, 1996, p. 1.

105. David Moberg, "Like Business, Unions Must Go Global," *New York Times,* December 19, 1993, p. F13.

106. Moberg, loc. cit.

107. Douglas Martin, "A Canadian Split on Unions," *New York Times,* March 12, 1984, p. D12.

108. J. Stewart Black and Hal B. Gregersen, "Serving Two Masters: Managing the Dual Allegiance of Expatriate Employees," *Sloan Management Review,* Summer 1992, pp. 61–71, covers the typologies of expatriates.

109. For a good discussion of the changing power of employees, see Frank P. Doyle, "The Changing Workplace: People Power: The Global Human Resource Challenge for the 1990s," *Columbia Journal of World Business,* Vol. 25, Nos. 1 and 2, Spring–Summer 1990, pp. 36–45.

110. Blocklyn, op. cit., p. 44, quoting Roger Herod.

111. For a short summary, see Kenneth H. Bacon, "The Outlook," *Wall Street Journal,* June 6, 1988, p. 1.

112. James Kynge, "India Seeks to Reverse Its Brain Drain," *Financial Times,* June 27, 1996, p. 4.

Glossary

Absolute advantage: A theory first presented by Adam Smith, which holds that because certain countries can produce some goods more efficiently than other countries can, they should specialize in and export those things they can produce more efficiently and trade for other things they need.

Acceptable quality level: A concept of quality control whereby managers are willing to accept a certain level of production defects, which are dealt with through repair facilities and service centers.

Accounting: The process of identifying, recording, and interpreting economic events.

Acquired advantage: A form of trade advantage due to technology rather than the availability of natural resources, climate, etc.

Acquired group memberships: Affiliations not determined by birth, such as religions, political affiliations, and professional and other associations.

Acquisition: The purchase of one company by another company.

Active income: Income of a CFC that is derived from the active conduct of a trade or business, as specified by the U.S. Internal Revenue Code.

Ad valorem duty: A duty (tariff) assessed as a percentage of the value of the item.

Administratively guided market economy: An economic system in which there is a great deal of cooperation among government, management, and workers to achieve growth and full employment with low job turnover on a nonmandated basis.

ADR: *See* American Depositary Receipt.

AFTA: *See* ASEAN Free Trade Area.

ALADI: *See* Latin American Integration Association.

American Depositary Receipt (ADR): A negotiable certificate issued by a U.S. bank in the United States to represent the underlying shares of a foreign corporation's stock held in trust at a custodian bank in the foreign country.

American system: *See* U.S. terms.

Andean Group (ANCOM): A South American form of economic integration involving Bolivia, Colombia, Ecuador, Peru, and Venezuela.

Appropriability theory: The theory that companies will favor foreign direct investment over such non-equity operating forms as licensing arrangements so that potential competitors will be less likely to gain access to proprietary information.

Appropriate technology: Technology that best fits the local factor endowment; often used to mean a more labor-intensive technology than would be cost-efficient in a developing country.

Arbitrage: The process of buying and selling foreign currency at a profit resulting from price discrepancies between or among markets.

Area division: *See* Geographic division.

Arm's-length price: A price between two companies that do not have an ownership interest in each other.

Arrangement Regarding International Trade in Textiles: An agreement among governments establishing rules on textile trade; also known as the Multifibre Arrangement (MFA).

Ascribed group memberships: Affiliations determined by birth, such as those based on gender, family, age, caste, and ethnic, racial, or national origin.

ASEAN: *See* Association of South East Asian Nations.

ASEAN Free Trade Area (AFTA): A free-trade area formed by the ASEAN countries on January 1, 1993, with the goal of cutting tariffs on all intrazonal trade to a maximum of 5 percent by January 1, 2005.

Association of South East Asian Nations (ASEAN): A free-trade area involving the Asian countries of Brunei, Indonesia, Malaysia, the Philippines, Singapore, and Thailand.

Back-to-back loan: A loan that involves a company in Country A with a subsidiary in Country B, and a bank in Country B with a branch in Country A.

Balance of payments: Statement that summarizes all economic transactions between a country and the rest of the world during a given period of time.

Balance-of-payments deficit: An imbalance of some specific component within the balance of payments, such as merchandise trade or current account, that implies that a country is importing more than it exports.

Balance-of-payments surplus: An imbalance in the balance of payments that exists when a country exports more than it imports.

Balance of trade: The value of a country's exports less the value of its imports ("trade" can be defined as merchandise trade, services, unilateral transfers, or a combination of these).

Balance on goods and services: The value of a country's exports of merchandise trade and services minus imports.

Bank for International Settlements (BIS): A bank in Basel, Switzerland that facilitates transactions among central banks, effectively the central banks' central bank.

Bargaining school theory: A theory holding that the negotiated terms for foreign investors depend on how much investors and host countries need each other's assets.

Barter: The exchange of goods for goods instead of for money.

Base currency: The currency whose value is implicitly 1 when a quote is made between two currencies; for example, if the cruzeiro is trading at 2962.5 cruzeiros per dollar, the dollar is the base currency and the cruzeiro is the quoted currency.

Basic balance: The net current account plus long-term capital within a country's balance of payments.

Bid (buy): The amount a trader is willing to pay for foreign exchange.

Bill of exchange: *See* Commercial bill of exchange.

Bill of lading: A document that is issued to a shipper by a carrier, listing the goods received for shipment.

BIRPI: *See* International Bureau for the Protection of Industrial Property Rights.

BIS: *See* Bank for International Settlements.

Black market: The foreign-exchange market that lies outside the official market.

Body language: The way people move their bodies, gesture, position themselves, etc., to convey meaning to others.

Bonded warehouse: A building or part of a building used for the storage of imported merchandise under supervision of the U.S. Customs Service and for the purpose of deferring payment of customs duties.

Booking center: An offshore financial center whose main function is to act as an accounting center in order to minimize the payment of taxes.

Branch (foreign): A foreign operation of a company that is not a separate entity from the parent that owns it.

Brand: A particular good identified with a company by means of name, logo, or other method, usually protected with a trademark registration.

Bretton Woods Agreement: An agreement among IMF countries to promote exchange-rate stability and to facilitate the international flow of currencies.

Broker (in foreign exchange): Specialists who facilitate transactions in the interbank market.

Buffer-stock system: A partially managed system that utilizes stocks of commodities to regulate their prices.

Bundesbank: The German central bank.

Buy local legislation: Laws that are intended to favor the purchase of domestically sourced goods or services over imported ones, even though the imports may be a better buy.

Buybacks: Counterdeliveries related to, or originating from, an original export.

CACM: *See* Central American Common Market.

Canada-U.S. Free Trade Agreement: An agreement, enacted in 1989, establishing a free-trade area involving the United States and Canada.

Capital account: A measure of transactions involving previously existing rather than currently produced assets.

Capital market: The market for stocks and long-term debt instruments.

Capitalism: An economic system characterized by private ownership, pricing, production, and distribution of goods.

Caribbean Community and Common Market (CARICOM): A customs union in the Caribbean region.

CARICOM: *See* Caribbean Community and Common Market.

Caste: A social class separated from others by heredity.

CEFTA: *See* Central European Free Trade Association.

Central American Common Market (CACM): A customs union in Central America.

Central bank: A governmental "bank for banks," customarily responsible for a country's monetary policy.

Central European Free Trade Association (CEFTA): An association which went into effect on July 1, 1992 with an initial membership of the Czech Republic, Slovakia, Hungary, and Poland, and whose goal is to establish a free trade area that includes the basic trade structure of the EU by the year 2000.

Centralization: The situation in which decision making is done at the home office rather than the country level.

Centrally planned economy (CPE): *See* Command economy.

Certificate of origin: A shipping document that determines the origin of products and is usually validated by an external source, such as a chamber of commerce; it helps countries determine the specific tariff schedule for imports.

CFC: *See* Controlled foreign corporation.

Chicago Mercantile Exchange: The largest commodity exchange in the world, dealing primarily in agricultural products, U.S. treasury bills, coins, and some metals.

CIA: The Central Intelligence Agency, a U.S. governmental agency charged with gathering intelligence information abroad.

Civil law system: A legal system based on a very detailed set of laws that are organized into a code; countries with a civil law system, also called a codified legal system, include Germany, France, and Japan.

Civil liberties: The freedom to develop one's own views and attitudes.

COCOM: *See* Coordinating Committee on Multilateral Exports.

Code of conduct: A set of principles guiding the actions of MNEs in their contacts with societies.

Codetermination: A process by which both labor and management participate in the management of a company.

Codified legal system: *See* Civil law system.

Collaborative arrangement: A formal, long-term contractual agreement among companies.

COMECON: *See* Council for Mutual Economic Assistance.

Command economy: An economic system in which resources are allocated and controlled by government decision.

Commercial bill of exchange: An instrument of payment in international business that instructs the importer to forward payment to the exporter.

Commercial invoice: A bill for goods from the buyer to the seller.

Commission agent: A type of intermediary that sells a manufacturer's goods for commission without taking title.

Commission on Transnational Corporations: A United Nations agency that deals with multinational enterprises.

Commodities: Basic raw materials or agricultural products.

Commodity agreement: A form of economic cooperation designed to stabilize and raise the price of a commodity.

Common Agricultural Policy (CAP): An EU policy aimed at free trade, price supports, and modernization programs in agriculture.

Common law system: A legal system based on tradition, precedent, and custom and usage, in which the courts interpret the law based on those conventions; found in the United Kingdom and former British colonies.

Common market: A form of regional economic integration in which countries abolish internal tariffs, use a common external tariff, and abolish restrictions on factor mobility.

Communism: A form of totalitarianism initially theorized by Karl Marx in which the political and economic systems are virtually inseparable.

Comparable access: A protectionist argument that companies and industries should have the same access to foreign markets as foreign industries and companies have to their markets.

Comparative advantage: The theory that there may still be global efficiency gains from trade if a country specializes in those products that it can produce more efficiently than other products.

Compound duty: A tax placed on goods traded internationally, based on value plus units.

Concentration strategy: A strategy by which an international company builds up operations quickly in one or a few countries before going to another.

Confirmed letter of credit: A letter of credit to which a bank in the exporter's country adds its guarantee of payment.

Conservatism: A characteristic of accounting systems that implies that companies are hesitant to disclose high profits or profits that are consistent with their actual operating results; more common in Germanic countries.

Consolidation: An accounting process in which financial statements of related entities, such as a parent and its subsidiaries, are combined to yield a unified set of financial statements; in the process, transactions among the related enterprises are eliminated so that the statements reflect transactions with outside parties.

Consortium: The joining together of several entities, such as companies or governments, in order to strengthen the possibility of achieving some objective.

Consular invoice: A document that covers all the usual details of the commercial invoice and packing list, prepared in the language of the foreign country for which the goods are destined, on special forms obtainable from the consulate or authorized commercial printers.

Consumer-directed market economy: An economy in which there is minimal government participation while growth is promoted through the mobility of production factors, including high labor turnover.

Consumer price index: A measure of the cost of typical wage-earner purchases of goods and services expressed as a percentage of the cost of these same goods and services in some base period.

Consumer sovereignty: The freedom of consumers to influence production through the choices they make.

Continental terms: *See* European terms.

Control: The planning, implementation, evaluation, and correction of performance to ensure that organizational objectives are achieved.

Controlled foreign corporation (CFC): A foreign corporation of which more than 50 percent of the voting stock is owned by U.S. shareholders (taxable entities that own at least 10 percent of the voting stock of the corporation).

Convertibility: The ability to exchange one currency for another currency without restrictions.

Coordinating Committee on Multilateral Exports (COCOM): An agreement among Western industrial nations to limit militarily useful exports to communist countries; disbanded in 1991 after the former Soviet Union broke up.

Copyright: The right to reproduce, publish, and sell literary, musical, or artistic works.

Corporate culture: The common values shared by employees in a corporation, which form a control mechanism that is implicit and helps enforce other explicit control mechanisms.

Correspondent (bank): A bank in which funds are kept by another, usually foreign, bank to facilitate check clearing and other business relationships.

Cost-of-living adjustment: An increase in compensation given to an expatriate employee when foreign living costs are more expensive than those in the home country.

Council for Mutual Economic Assistance (CMEA or COME-CON): A regional form of economic integration that involved essentially those communist countries considered to be within the Soviet bloc; terminated in 1991.

Council of Ministers: One of the five major institutions of the EU; composed of one member from each country in the EU and entrusted with making major policy decisions.

Countertrade: A reciprocal flow of goods or services valued and settled in monetary terms.

Country analysis: A process of examining the economic strategy of a nation state, taking a holistic approach to understanding how a country, and in particular its government, has behaved, is behaving, and may behave.

Country-similarity theory: The theory that a producer, having developed a new product in response to observed market conditions in the home market, will turn to markets that are most similar to those at home.

Country size theory: The theory that larger countries are generally more self-sufficient than smaller countries.

Court of Justice: One of the five major institutions of the EU; composed of one member from each country in the EU and serves as a supreme appeals court for EU law.

CPE (centrally planned economy): *See* Command economy.

Creolization: The process by which elements of an outside culture are introduced.

Cross-licensing: The exchange of technology by different companies.

Cross rate: An exchange rate between two currencies used in the spot market and computed from the exchange rate of each currency in relation to the U.S. dollar.

Cultural relativism: The belief that behavior has meaning and can be judged only in its specific cultural context.

Culture: The specific learned norms of a society, based on attitudes, values, and beliefs.

Culture shock: A generalized trauma one experiences in a new and different culture because of having to learn and cope with a vast array of new cues and expectations.

Current-account balance: Exports minus imports of goods, services, and unilateral transfers.

Current-rate method: A method of translating foreign-currency financial statements that is used when the functional currency is that of the local operating environment.

Customs duties: Taxes imposed on imported goods.

Customs union: A form of regional economic integration that eliminates tariffs among member nations and establishes common external tariffs.

Customs valuation: The value of goods on which customs authorities charge tariffs.

Debt-service ratio: The ratio of interest payments plus principal amortization to exports.

Decentralization: The situation in which decisions tend to be made at lower levels in a company or at the country-operating level rather than at headquarters.

Deferral: The postponing of taxation of foreign-source income until it is remitted to the parent company.

Democracy: A political system that relies on citizens' participation in the decision-making process.

Democratic socialism: The belief that economics and politics are so closely connected that the voters should rely on their elected governments to control the economic system.

Dependencia theory: The theory holding that LDCs have practically no power when dealing with MNEs as host countries.

Dependency: A state in which a country is too dependent on the sale of one primary commodity and/or too dependent on one country as a customer and supplier.

Derivative: A foreign-exchange instrument such as an option or futures contract that derives its value from some underlying financial instrument.

Derivatives market: Market in which forward contracts, futures, options, and swaps are traded in order to hedge or protect foreign-exchange transactions.

Devaluation: A formal reduction in the value of a currency in relation to another currency; the foreign-currency equivalent of the devalued currency falls.

Developing country: A poor country, also known as a Third-World country or a less developed country.

Direct foreign investment: *See* Foreign direct investment.

Direct identification drawback: A provision that allows U.S. firms to use imported components in the manufacturing process without having to include the duty paid on the imported goods in costs and sales prices.

Direct investment: *See* Foreign direct investment.

Direct quote: A quote expressed in terms of the number of units of the domestic currency given for one unit of a foreign currency.

Direct selling: A sale of goods by an exporter directly to distributors or final consumers rather than to trading companies or other intermediaries in order to achieve greater control over the marketing function and to earn higher profits.

Directive: A proposed form of legislation in the EU.

Discount (in foreign exchange): A situation in which the forward rate for a foreign currency is less than the spot rate, assuming that the domestic currency is quoted on a direct basis.

Distribution: The course—physical path or legal title—that goods take between production and consumption.

Distributor: A merchant in a foreign country that purchases products from the manufacturer and sells them at a profit.

Diversification: A process of becoming less dependent on one or a few customers or suppliers.

Diversification strategy: A strategy by which an international company produces or sells in many countries to avoid relying on one particular market.

Divestment: Reduction in the amount of investment.

Drawback: A provision allowing U.S. exporters to apply for refunds of 99 percent of the duty paid on imported components, provided they are used in the manufacture of goods that are exported.

Dumping: The underpricing of exports, usually below cost or below the home-country price.

Duty: A governmental tax (tariff) levied on goods shipped internationally.

Economic Community of West African States (ECOWAS): A form of economic integration among certain countries in West Africa.

Economic exposure: The foreign-exchange risk that international businesses face in the pricing of products, the source and cost of inputs, and the location of investments.

Economic integration: The abolition of economic discrimination between national economies, such as within the EU.

Economic system: The system concerned with the allocation of scarce resources.

Economics: A social science concerned chiefly with the description and analysis of the production, distribution, and consumption of goods and services.

Economies of scale: The lowering of cost per unit as output increases because of allocation of fixed costs over more units produced.

ECOWAS: *See* Economic Community of West African States.

ECU: *See* European Currency Unit.

EEC: *See* European Economic Community.

EEC Patent Convention: An important cross-national patent convention that involves the members of the EU.

Effective tariff: The real tariff on the manufactured portion of developing countries' exports, which is higher than indicated by the published rates because the ad valorem tariff is based on the total value of the products, which includes raw materials that would have had duty-free entry.

EFTA: *See* European Free Trade Association.

Elastic (product demand): A condition in which sales are likely to increase or decrease by a percentage that is more than the percentage change in income.

Electronic data interchange (EDI): The electronic movement of money and information via computers and telecommunications equipment.

Embargo: A specific type of quota that prohibits all trade.

EMC: *See* Export management company.

EMS: *See* European Monetary System.

Entente Council: A regional economic group in Africa that includes the nations of Benin, Burkina Faso, Côte d'Ivoire, Niger, and Togo.

Enterprise of the Americas: A proposed series of bilateral trade relationships between the United States and Latin American countries, based on a "hub and spokes" concept and eventually resulting in one huge multilateral relationship involving the Americas.

Entrepôt: A country that is an import/export intermediary; for example, Hong Kong is an entrepôt for trade between China and the rest of the world.

Environmental climate: The external conditions in host countries that could significantly affect the success of a foreign business enterprise.

Environmental scanning: The systematic assessment of external conditions that might affect a company's operations.

EPC: *See* European Patent Convention.

Equity alliance: A situation in which a cooperating company takes an equity position (almost always a minority) in the company with which it has a collaborative arrangement.

Essential-industry argument: The argument holding that certain domestic industries need protection for national security purposes.

ETC: *See* Export trading company.

Ethnocentrism: A belief that one's own group is superior to others; also used to describe a company's belief that what worked at home should work abroad.

Eurobond: A bond sold in a country other than the one in whose currency it is denominated.

Eurocredit: A loan, line of credit, or other form of medium- or long-term credit on the Eurocurrency market that has a maturity of more than one year.

Eurocurrency: Any currency that is banked outside of its country of origin.

Eurocurrency market: An international wholesale market that deals in Eurocurrencies.

Eurodollars: Dollars banked outside of the United States.

Euroequity market: The market for shares sold outside the boundaries of the issuing company's home country.

Europe 1992: Legislation enacted by the EU and designed to eliminate most key barriers to trade of goods and services by December 31, 1992.

European Commission: One of the five major institutions of the EU; composed of a president, six vice presidents, and ten other members whose allegiance is to the EU and serving as an executive branch for the EU.

European Community (EC): The predecessor of the European Union.

European Council: One of the five major institutions of the European Union; made up of the heads of state of each of the EU members.

European Currency Unit (ECU): A unit of account based on a currency basket composed of the currencies of the members of the EU.

European Economic Community (EEC): The predecessor of the European Community.

European Free Trade Association (EFTA): A free-trade area among a group of European countries that are not members of the EU.

European Monetary System (EMS): A cooperative foreign-exchange agreement involving most of the members of the EU and designed to promote exchange-rate stability within the EU.

European Parliament: One of the five major institutions of the EU; its representatives are elected directly in each member country.

European Patent Convention (EPC): A European agreement allowing companies to make a uniform patent search and application, which is then passed on to all signatory countries.

European terms: The practice of using the indirect quote for exchange rates.

European Union (EU): A form of regional economic integration among countries in Europe that involves a free-trade area, a customs union, and the free mobility of factors of production that is working toward political and economic union.

Exchange rate: The price of one currency in terms of another currency.

Eximbank: *See* Export-Import Bank.

Exotic currencies: The currencies of developing countries; also called *exotics*.

Expatriates: Noncitizens of the country in which they are working.

Experience curve: The relationship of production-cost reductions to increases in output.

Export-Import Bank (Eximbank): A U.S. federal agency specializing in foreign lending to support exports.

Export-led development: An industrialization policy emphasizing industries that will have export capabilities.

Export license: A document that grants government permission to ship certain products to a specific country.

Export management company (EMC): A company that buys merchandise from manufacturers for international distribution or sometimes acts as an agent for manufacturers.

Export packing list: A shipping document that itemizes the material in each individual package and indicates the type of package.

Export tariff: A tax on goods leaving a country.

Export trading company (ETC): A form of trading company sanctioned by U.S. law to become involved in international commerce as independent distributors to match up foreign buyers with domestic sellers.

Exports: Goods or services leaving a country.

Exposure: A situation in which a foreign-exchange account is subject to a gain or loss if the exchange rate changes.

Exposure draft: The first draft of an accounting standard, which is open to comment by parties other than the IASC.

Expropriation: The taking over of ownership of private property by a country's government.

External convertibility: *See* Nonresident convertibility.

Externalities: External economic costs related to a business activity.

Extraterritoriality: The extension by a government of the application of its laws to foreign operations of companies.

Factor mobility: The free movement of factors of production, such as labor and capital, across national borders.

Factor-proportions theory: The theory that differences in a country's proportionate holdings of factors of production (land, labor, and capital) explain differences in the costs of the factors and that export advantages lie in the production of goods that use the most abundant factors.

FASB: *See* Financial Accounting Standards Board.

Fatalism: A belief that events are fixed in advance and human beings are powerless to change them.

Favorable balance of trade: An indication that a country is exporting more than it imports.

FCPA: *See* Foreign Corrupt Practices Act.

FDI: *See* Foreign direct investment.

Fees: Payments for the performance of certain activities abroad.

Financial Accounting Standards Board (FASB): The private-sector organization that sets financial accounting standards in the United States.

FIRA: *See* Foreign Investment Review Act.

First-in advantage: Any benefit gained in terms of brand recognition and lining up of the best suppliers, distributors, and local partners because of entering a market before competitors do.

First-mover advantage: A cost-reduction advantage due to economies of scale attained through moving into a foreign market ahead of competitors.

First-World countries: The nonsocialist industrialized countries.

Fisher Effect: The theory about the relationship between inflation and interest rates; for example, if the nominal interest rate in one country is lower than that in another, the first country's inflation should be lower so that the real interest rates will be equal.

Fixed price: A method of pricing in which bargaining does not take place.

Flexible exchange rate: An exchange rate determined by the laws of supply and demand and with minimal governmental interference.

Floating currency: A currency whose value responds to the supply of and demand for that currency.

Foreign bond: A bond sold outside of the borrower's country but denominated in the currency of the country of issue.

Foreign Corrupt Practices Act (FCPA): A law that criminalizes certain types of payments by U.S. companies, such as bribes to foreign governmental officials.

Foreign direct investment (FDI): An investment that gives the investor a controlling interest in a foreign company.

Foreign exchange: Checks and other instruments for making payments in another country's currency.

Foreign-exchange control: A requirement that an importer of a product must apply to governmental authorities for permission to buy foreign currency to pay for the product.

Foreign freight forwarder: A company that facilitates the movement of goods from one country to another.

Foreign investment: Direct or portfolio ownership of assets in another country.

Foreign Investment Review Act (FIRA): A Canadian law intended to limit foreign control of that country's economy.

Foreign sales corporation (FSC): A special type of corporation established by U.S. tax law that can be used by a U.S. exporter to shelter some of its income from taxation.

Foreign trade zone (FTZ): A government-designated area in which goods can be stored, inspected, or manufactured without being subject to formal customs procedures until they leave the zone.

Forward contract: A contract between a company or individual and a bank to deliver foreign currency at a specific exchange rate on a future date.

Forward discount: *See* Discount.

Forward premium: *See* Premium.

Forward rate: A contractually established exchange rate between a foreign-exchange trader and the trader's client for delivery of foreign currency on a specific date.

Franchising: A specialized form of licensing in which one party (the franchisor) sells to an independent party (the franchisee) the use of a trademark that is an essential asset for the franchisee's business and also gives continual assistance in the operation of the business.

Free-trade area (FTA): A form of regional economic integration in which internal tariffs are abolished, but member countries set their own external tariffs.

Freight forwarder: *See* Foreign freight forwarder.

Fringe benefit: Any employee benefit other than salary, wages, and cash bonuses.

FSC: *See* Foreign sales corporation.

FTZ: *See* Foreign trade zone.

Functional currency: The currency of the primary economic environment in which an entity operates.

Functional division: An organizational structure in which each function in foreign countries (e.g., marketing or production) reports separately to a counterpart functional group at headquarters.

Futures contract: A foreign-exchange instrument that specifies an exchange rate, an amount of currency, and a maturity date in advance of the exchange of the currency.

G-7 countries: *See* Group of 7.

GAAP: *See* Generally accepted accounting principles.

Gap analysis: A tool used to discover why a company's sales of a given product are less than the market potential in a country; the reason may be a usage, competitive, product line, or distribution gap.

GATT: *See* General Agreement on Tariffs and Trade.

General Agreement on Tariffs and Trade (GATT): A multilateral arrangement aimed at reducing barriers to trade, both tariff and non-tariff ones; at the signing of the Uruguay round, the GATT was designated to become the World Trade Organization (WTO).

Generalized System of Preferences (GSP): Preferential import restrictions extended by industrial countries to developing countries.

Generally accepted accounting principles (GAAP): The accounting standards accepted by the accounting profession in each country as required for the preparation of financial statements for external users.

Generic: Any of a class of products, rather than the brand of a particular company.

Geocentric: Operations based on an informed knowledge of both home and host country needs.

Geographic division: An organizational structure in which a company's operations are separated for reporting purposes into regional areas.

Geography: A science dealing with the earth and its life, especially with the description of land, sea, air, and the distribution of plant and animal life.

Global bond: A combination of domestic bond and Eurobond that is issued simultaneously in several markets and must be registered in each national market according to that market's registration requirements.

Global company: A company that integrates operations located in different countries.

Global sourcing: The acquisition on a worldwide basis of raw materials, parts, and subassemblies for the manufacturing process.

Globally integrated company: *See* Global company.

Go–no-go decision: A decision, such as on foreign investments, that is based on minimum-threshold criteria and does not compare different opportunities.

Grandchild subsidiary: An operation that is under a tax-haven subsidiary; also called a second-tier subsidiary.

Grantback provisions: Stipulations requiring that licensees provide licensors with the use of improvements made on the technology originally licensed.

Grass-roots campaign: A method of influencing governmental action from the bottom up.

Gray market: The handling of goods through unofficial distributors.

Gross domestic product (GDP): The total of all economic activity in a country, regardless of who owns the productive assets.

Gross national product (GNP): The total of incomes earned by residents of a country, regardless of where the productive assets are located.

Group of 7 (G-7): A group of developed countries that periodically meets to make economic decisions; this group consists of Canada, France, Germany, Italy, Japan, the United Kingdom, and the United States.

GSP: *See* Generalized System of Preferences.

Hard currency: A currency that is freely traded without many restrictions and for which there is usually strong external demand; often called a freely convertible currency.

Hardship allowance: A supplement to compensate expatriates for working in dangerous or adverse conditions.

Hedge: To attempt to protect foreign-currency holdings against an adverse movement of an exchange rate.

Heterarchy: An organizational structure in which management of an alliance of companies is shared by so-called equals rather than being set up in a superior-subordinate relationship.

Hickenlooper Amendment: A U.S. act requiring cessation of aid to a country that nationalizes assets of U.S. citizens or has moved to abrogate contracts without taking appropriate means of settlement within a reasonable period of time.

Hierarchy of needs: A well-known motivation theory stating that there is a hierarchy of needs and that people must fulfill the lower-order needs sufficiently before they will be motivated by the higher-order ones.

High-context culture: A culture in which most people consider that peripheral and hearsay information are necessary for decision making because they bear on the context of the situation.

High-need achiever: One who will work very hard to achieve material or career success, sometimes to the detriment of social relationships or spiritual achievements.

High-value activities: Activities that either produce high profits or are done by high-salaried employees such as managers.

Historically planned economy (HPE): The World Bank's term for Second-World countries in transition to market economies.

History: A branch of knowledge that records and explains past events.

Home country: The country in which an international company is headquartered.

Home-country nationals: Expatriate employees who are citizens of the country in which the company is headquartered.

Horizontal expansion: Any foreign direct investment by which a company produces the same product it produces at home.

Host country: Any foreign country in which an international company operates.

HPE: *See* Historically planned economy.

Hyperinflation: A rapid increase (at least 1 percent per day) in general price levels for a sustained period of time.

IASC: *See* International Accounting Standards Committee.

Idealism: Trying to determine principles before settling small issues.

Ideology: The systematic and integrated body of constructs, theories, and aims that constitute a society.

IFE: *See* International Fisher Effect.

ILO: *See* International Labor Organization.

IMF: *See* International Monetary Fund.

Imitation lag: A strategy for exploiting temporary monopoly advantages by moving first to those countries most likely to develop local production.

Import broker: An individual who obtains various governmental permissions and other clearances before forwarding necessary paperwork to the carrier that will deliver the goods from the dock to the importer.

Import deposit requirement: Governmental requirement of a deposit prior to the release of foreign exchange.

Import licensing: A method of governmental control of the exchange rate whereby all recipients, exporters, and others who receive foreign exchange are required to sell to the central bank at the official buying rate.

Import substitution: An industrialization policy whereby new industrial development emphasizes products that would otherwise be imported.

Import tariff: A tax placed on goods entering a country.

Imports: Goods or services entering a country.

In-bond industry: Any industry that is allowed to import components free of duty, provided that the components will be re-exported after processing.

Independence: An extreme situation in which a country would not rely on other countries at all.

Indigenization: The process of introducing elements of an outside culture.

Indirect quote: An exchange rate given in terms of the number of units of the foreign currency for one unit of the domestic currency.

Indirect selling: A sale of goods by an exporter through another domestic company as an intermediary.

Individually validated license (IVL): A special export license under which certain restricted products need to be shipped.

Industrialization argument: A rationale for protectionism that argues that the development of industrial output should come about even though domestic prices may not become competitive on the world market.

Inelastic (product demand): A condition in which sales are likely to increase or decrease by a percentage that is less than the percentage change in income.

Infant-industry argument: The position that holds that an emerging industry should be guaranteed a large share of the domestic market until it becomes efficient enough to compete against imports.

Infrastructure: The underlying foundation of a society, such as roads, schools, and so forth, that allows it to function effectively.

Input-output table: A tool used widely in national economic planning to show the resources utilized by different industries for a given output as well as the interdependence of economic sectors.

Intangible property: *See* Intellectual property rights.

Integrated system: A system for taxation of corporate income aimed at preventing double taxation through the use of split rates or tax credits.

Intellectual property rights: Ownership rights to intangible assets, such as patents, trademarks, copyrights, and know-how.

Interbank market: The market for foreign-exchange transactions among commercial banks.

Interbank transactions: Foreign-exchange transactions that take place between commercial banks.

Interdependence: The existence of mutually necessary economic relations among countries.

Interest aggregation: The collection of interests in the political system.

Interest arbitrage: Investing in debt instruments in different countries and earning a profit due to interest-rate and exchange-rate differentials.

Interest articulation: The process by which politicians, individuals, businesses, and interest groups make their desires known in the political process.

Interest rate differential: An indicator of future changes in the spot exchange rate.

Internalization: Control through self-handling of foreign operations, primarily because it is less expensive to deal within the same corporate family than to contract with an external organization.

International Accounting Standards Committee (IASC): The international private-sector organization that sets financial accounting standards for worldwide use.

International Bureau for the Protection of Industrial Property Rights (BIRPI): A multilateral agreement to protect patents, trademarks, and other property rights.

International business: All business transactions involving private companies or governments of two or more countries.

International division: An organizational structure in which virtually all foreign operations are handled within the same division.

International Fisher Effect (IFE): The theory that the relationship between interest rates and exchange rates implies that the currency of the country with the lower interest rate will strengthen in the future.

International Labor Organization (ILO): A multilateral organization promoting the adoption of humane labor conditions.

International Monetary Fund (IMF): A multigovernmental association organized in 1945 to promote exchange-rate stability and to facilitate the international flow of currencies.

International Monetary Market (IMM): A specialized market located in Chicago and dealing in select foreign-currency futures.

International Organization of Securities Commissions (IOSCO): An international organization of securities regulators that wants the IASC to establish more comprehensive accounting standards.

International standard of fair dealing: The concept that investors should receive prompt, adequate, and effective compensation in cases of expropriation.

International Trade Administration (ITA): A branch of the U.S. Department of Commerce offering a variety of services to U.S. exporting companies.

Intervention currencies: The currencies in which a particular country trades the most.

Intrazonal trade: Trade among countries that are part of a trade agreement, such as the EU.

Investment Canada: A Canadian act whose intent is to persuade foreign companies to invest in Canada.

Invisibles: *See* Services.

IOSCO: *See* International Organization of Securities Commissions.

Irrevocable letter of credit: A letter of credit that cannot be canceled or changed without the consent of all parties involved.

Islamic law: A system of theocratic law based on the religious teachings of Islam; also called Muslim law.

ISO 9000: A quality standard developed by the International Standards Organization in Geneva that requires companies to document their commitment to quality at all levels of the organization.

IVL: *See* Individually validated license.

Jamaica Agreement: A 1976 agreement among countries that permitted greater flexibility of exchange rates, basically formalizing the break from fixed exchange rates.

JIT: *See* Just-in-time system.

Joint venture: A direct investment of which two or more companies share the ownership.

Just-in-time (JIT) system: A system that decreases inventory costs by having components and parts delivered as they are needed in production.

Keiretsu: A corporate relationship linking certain Japanese companies, usually involving a noncontrolling interest in each other, strong high-level personal relationships among managers in the different companies, and interlocking directorships.

Key industry: Any industry that might affect a very large segment of a country's economy or population by virtue of its size or influence on other sectors.

Labor market: The mix of available workers and labor costs available to companies.

Labor union: An association of workers intended to promote and protect the welfare, interests, and rights of its members, primarily by collective bargaining.

LAFTA: *See* Latin American Free Trade Association.

Lag strategy: An operational strategy that involves delaying collection of foreign-currency receivables if the currency is expected to strengthen or delaying payment of foreign-currency payables when the currency is expected to weaken; the opposite of a lead strategy.

Laissez-faire: The concept of minimal governmental intervention in a society's economic activity.

Latin American Free Trade Association (LAFTA): A free-trade area formed by Mexico and the South American countries in 1960; it was replaced by ALADI in 1980.

Latin American Integration Association (ALADI): A form of regional economic integration involving most of the Latin American countries.

Law: A binding custom or practice of a community.

Lead country strategy: A strategy of introducing a product on a test basis in a small-country market that is considered representative of a region before investing to serve larger-country markets.

Lead strategy: An operational strategy that involves collecting foreign-currency receivables early when the currency is expected to weaken or paying foreign-currency payables early when the currency is expected to strengthen; the opposite of a lag strategy.

Lead subsidiary organization: A foreign subsidiary that has global responsibility (serves as corporate headquarters) for one of a company's products or functions.

Learning curve: A concept used to support the infant industry argument for protection; it assumes that costs will decrease as workers and managers gain more experience.

Leontief paradox: A surprising finding by Wassily Leontief that overall U.S. exports were less capital-intensive and more labor-intensive than U.S. imports.

Less developed country (LDC): *See* Third-World country.

Letter of credit: A precise document by which the importer's bank extends credit to the importer and agrees to pay the exporter.

Liability of foreignness: Foreign companies' lower survival rate than local companies for many years after they begin operations.

LIBOR: *See* London Inter-Bank Offered Rate.

License: Formal or legal permission to do some specified action; a governmental method of fixing the exchange rate by requiring all recipients, exporters, and others that receive foreign exchange to sell it to the central bank at the official buying rate.

Licensing agreement: Agreement whereby one company gives rights to another for the use, usually for a fee, of such assets as trademarks, patents, copyrights, or other know-how.

Licensing arrangement: A procedure that requires potential importers or exporters to secure permission from governmental authorities before they conduct trade transactions.

Lifetime employment: The Japanese custom that workers are effectively guaranteed employment with the company for their working lifetime and that workers seldom leave for employment opportunities with other companies.

LIFFE: *See* London International Financial Futures Exchange.

Liquidity preference: A theory that helps explain capital budgeting and, when applied to international operations, means that investors are willing to take less return in order to be able to shift the resources to alternative uses.

Lobbyist: An individual who participates in advancing or otherwise securing passage of legislation by influencing public officials before and during the legislation process.

Local content: Costs incurred within a given country, usually as a percentage of total costs.

Locally responsive company: Synonym for *multidomestic company*.

Locals: Citizens of the country in which they are working.

London Inter-Bank Offered Rate (LIBOR): The interest rate for large interbank loans of Eurocurrencies.

London International Financial Futures Exchange (LIFFE): An exchange dealing in futures contracts for several major currencies.

London Stock Exchange (LSE): A stock exchange located in London and dealing in Euroequities.

Low-context culture: A culture in which most people consider relevant only information that they receive firsthand and that bears very directly on the decision they need to make.

Maastricht (Treaty of): The treaty approved in December 1991 that was designed to bring the EU to a higher level of integration and is divided into Economic and Monetary Union (EMU) and political union.

Macro political risk: Negative political actions affecting a broad spectrum of foreign investors.

Management contract: An arrangement whereby one company provides management personnel to perform general or specialized management functions to another company for a fee.

Manufacturing interchange: A process by which various plants produce a range of components and exchange them so that all plants assemble the finished product for the local market.

Maquiladora: An industrial operation developed by the Mexican and U.S. governments in which U.S.-sourced components are shipped to Mexico duty-free, assembled into final products, and re-exported to the United States.

Marginal propensity to import: The tendency to purchase imports with incremental income.

Market capitalization: A common measure of the size of a stock market, which is computed by multiplying the total number of shares of stock listed on the exchange by the market price per share.

Market economy: An economic system in which resources are allocated and controlled by consumers who "vote" by buying goods.

Market environment: The environment that involves the interactions between households (or individuals) and companies to allocate resources, free from governmental ownership or control.

Matrix: A method of plotting data on a set of vertical and horizontal axes, in order to compare countries in terms of risk and opportunity.

Matrix structure: An organizational structure in which foreign units report (by product, function, or area) to more than one group, each of which shares responsibility over the foreign unit.

Mentor: A person at headquarters who looks after the interests of an expatriate employee.

Mercantilism: An economic philosophy based on the beliefs that a country's wealth is dependent on its holdings of treasure, usually in the form of gold, and that countries should export more than they import in order to increase wealth.

Merchandise exports: Goods sent out of a country.

Merchandise imports: Goods brought into a country.

Merchandise trade account: The part of a country's current account that measures the trade deficit or surplus; its balance is the net of merchandise imports and exports.

MERCOSUR: A major subregional group composed of Argentina, Brazil, Paraguay, and Uruguay, which spun off from ALADI in 1991 with the goal of setting up a customs union and common market.

MFA: *See* Multifibre Arrangement.

MFN: *See* Most-favored-nation clause.

Micro political risk: Negative political actions aimed at specific, rather than most, foreign investors.

Middle East: The countries on the Arabian peninsula plus those bordering the eastern end of the Mediterranean; sometimes also including other adjacent countries, particularly Jordan, Iraq, Iran, and Kuwait.

Ministry of International Trade and Industry (MITI): The Japanese governmental agency responsible for coordinating overall business direction and helping individual companies take advantage of global business opportunities.

Mission: What the company will seek to do and become over the long term.

Mission statement: A long-range strategic intent.

Mixed economy: An economic system characterized by some mixture of market and command economies and public and private ownership.

Mixed venture: A special type of joint venture in which a government is in partnership with a private company.

MNE: *See* Multinational enterprise.

Monochronic culture: A culture in which most people prefer to deal with situations sequentially (especially those involving other people), such as finishing with one customer before dealing with another.

Monopoly advantage: The perceived supremacy of foreign investors in relation to local companies, which is necessary to overcome the perceived greater risk of operating in a different environment.

Most-favored-nation (MFN) clause: A GATT requirement that a trade concession that is given to one country must be given to all other countries.

Multidomestic company: A company with international operations that allows operations in one country to be relatively independent of those in other countries.

Multifibre Arrangement (MFA): *See* Arrangement Regarding International Trade in Textiles.

Multilateral agreement: An agreement involving more than two governments.

Multilateral Investment Guarantee Agency (MIGA): A member of the World Bank Group that encourages equity investment and other direct investment flows to developing countries by offering investors a variety of different services.

Multinational corporation (MNC): A synonym for *multinational enterprise*.

Multinational enterprise (MNE): A company that has an integrated global philosophy encompassing both domestic and overseas operations; sometimes used synonymously with multinational corporation or transnational corporation.

Multiple exchange-rate system: A means of foreign-exchange control whereby the government sets different exchange rates for different transactions.

Muslim law: *See* Islamic law.

National responsiveness: Readiness to implement operating adjustments in foreign countries in order to reach a satisfactory level of performance.

Nationalism: The feeling of pride and/or ethnocentrism focused on an individual's home country or nation.

Nationalization: The transfer of ownership to the state.

Natural advantage: Climatic conditions, access to certain natural resources, or availability of labor, which gives a country an advantage in producing some product.

Need hierarchy: *See* Hierarchy of needs.

Neomercantilism: The approach of countries that apparently try to run favorable balances of trade in an attempt to achieve some social or political objective.

Net capital flow: Capital inflow minus capital outflow, for other than import and export payment.

Net export effect: Export stimulus minus export reduction.

Net import change: Import displacement minus import stimulus.

Netting: The transfer of funds from subsidiaries in a net payable position to a central clearing account and from there to the accounts of the net receiver subsidiaries.

Network organization: A situation in which a group of companies is interrelated, and in which the management of the interrelation is shared among so-called equals.

Newly industrializing country (NIC): A Third-World country in which the cultural and economic climate has led to a rapid rate of industrialization and growth since the 1960s.

Nonmarket economy: *See* Command economy.

Nonmarket environment: Public institutions (such as government, governmental agencies, and government-owned businesses) and non-public institutions (such as environmental and other special-interest groups).

Nonpublic institutions: Special-interest groups, such as environmentalists.

Nonresident convertibility: The ability of a nonresident of a country to convert deposits in a bank to the currency of any other country; also known as external convertibility.

Nontariff barriers: Barriers to imports that are not tariffs; examples include administrative controls, "Buy America" policies, and so forth.

Normal quote: Synonym for *direct quote.*

North American Free Trade Agreement (NAFTA): A free-trade agreement involving the United States, Canada, and Mexico that went into effect on January 1, 1994 and will be phased in over a period of fifteen years.

OAU: *See* Organization of African Unity.

Obsolescing bargain (theory of): The premises that a company's bargaining strength with a host government diminishes after the company transfers assets to the host country.

OECD: *See* Organization for Economic Cooperation and Development.

OEEC: *See* Organization for European Economic Cooperation.

Offer rate: The amount for which a foreign-exchange trader is willing to sell a currency.

Official reserves: A country's holdings of monetary gold, Special Drawing Rights, and internationally acceptable currencies.

Offset: A form of barter transaction in which an export is paid for with other merchandise.

Offset trade: A form of countertrade in which an exporter sells goods for cash but then helps businesses in the importing country find opportunities to earn hard currency.

Offshore financial centers: Cities or countries that provide large amounts of funds in currencies other than their own and are used as locations in which to raise and accumulate cash.

Offshore manufacturing: Manufacturing outside the borders of a particular country.

Oligopoly: An industry in which there are few producers or sellers.

OPEC: *See* Organization of Petroleum Exporting Countries.

Open account: Conditions of sale under which the exporter extends credit directly to the importer.

Operational centers: Offshore financial centers that perform specific functions, such as the sale and servicing of goods.

OPIC: *See* Overseas Private Investment Corporation.

Opinion leader: One whose acceptance of some concept is apt to be emulated by others.

Optimism: A characteristic of an accounting system that implies that companies are more liberal in recognition of income.

Optimum-tariff theory: The argument that a foreign producer will lower its prices if an import tax is placed on its products.

Option: A foreign-exchange instrument that gives the purchaser the right, but not the obligation, to buy or sell a certain amount of foreign currency at a set exchange rate within a specified amount of time.

Organization of African Unity (OAU): An organization of African nations that is more concerned with political than economic objectives.

Organization for Economic Cooperation and Development (OECD): A multilateral organization of industrialized and semi-industrialized countries that helps formulate social and economic policies.

Organization for European Economic Cooperation (OEEC): A sixteen-nation organization established in 1948 to facilitate the utilization of aid from the Marshall Plan; it evolved into the EU and EFTA.

Organization of Petroleum Exporting Countries (OPEC): A producers' alliance among twelve petroleum-exporting countries that attempt to agree on oil production and pricing policies.

Organizational structure: The reporting relationships within an organization.

Outright forward: A forward contract that is not connected to a spot transaction.

Outsourcing: The use by a domestic company of foreign suppliers for components or finished products.

Overseas Private Investment Corporation (OPIC): A U.S. government agency that provides insurance for companies involved in international business.

Over-the-counter (OTC) market: Trading in stocks, usually of smaller companies, that are not listed on one of the stock exchanges; also refers to how government and corporate bonds are traded, through dealers who quote bids and offers to buy and sell "over the counter."

Par value: The benchmark value of a currency, originally quoted in terms of gold or the U.S. dollar and now quoted in terms of Special Drawing Rights.

Parliamentary government: A form of government that involves the election of representatives to form the executive branch.

Passive income: Income from investments in tax-haven countries or sales and services income that involves buyers and sellers in other than the tax-haven country, where either the buyer or the seller must be part of the same organizational structure as the corporation that earns the income; also known as Subpart F income.

Patent: A right granted by a sovereign power or state for the protection of an invention or discovery against infringement.

Patent cooperation treaty: A multilateral agreement to protect patents.

Peg: To fix a currency's exchange rate to some benchmark, such as another currency.

Penetration strategy: A strategy of introducing a product at a low price to induce a maximum number of consumers to try it.

Philadelphia Stock Exchange (PSE): A specialized market dealing in select foreign-currency options.

Piggyback exporting: Use by an exporter of another exporter as an intermediary.

Piracy: The unauthorized use of property rights that are protected by patents, trademarks, or copyrights.

Planning: The meshing of objectives with internal and external constraints in order to set means to implement, monitor, and correct operations.

PLC: *See* Product life cycle theory.

Pluralistic societies: Societies in which different ideologies are held by various segments rather than one ideology being adhered to by all.

Political freedom: The right to participate freely in the political process.

Political risk: Potential changes in political conditions that may cause a company's operating positions to deteriorate.

Political science: A discipline that helps explain the patterns of governments and their actions.

Political system: The system designed to integrate a society into a viable, functioning unit.

Polycentrism: Characteristic of an individual or organization that feels that differences in a foreign country, real and imaginary, great and small, need to be accounted for in management decisions.

Polychronic culture: A culture in which most people are more comfortable dealing simultaneously with all the situations facing them.

Porter diamond: A diagram showing four conditions— demand, factor endowments, related and supporting industries, and firm strategy, structure, and rivalry—that usually must all be favorable for an industry in a country to develop and sustain a global competitive advantage.

Portfolio investment: An investment in the form of either debt or equity that does not give the investor a controlling interest.

Positive-sum gain: A situation in which the sums of gains and losses, if added together among participants, is positive, especially if all parties gain from a relationship.

Power distance: A measurement of preference for consultative or autocratic styles of management.

PPP: *See* Purchasing-power parity.

Pragmatism: Settling small issues before deciding on principles.

Premium (in foreign exchange): The difference between the spot and forward exchange rates in the forward market; a foreign currency sells at a premium when the forward rate exceeds the spot rate and when the domestic currency is quoted on a direct basis.

Pressure group: A group that tries to influence legislation or practices to foster its objectives.

Price escalation: The process by which the lengthening of distribution channels increases a product's price by more than the direct added costs, such as transportation, insurance, and tariffs.

Prior informed consent (PIC): The concept of requiring each exporter of a banned or restricted chemical to obtain, through the home-country government, the expressed consent of the importing country to receive the banned or restricted substance.

Privatizing: Selling of government-owned assets to private individuals or companies.

Product division: An organizational structure in which different foreign operations report to different product groups at headquarters.

Product life cycle (PLC) theory: The theory that certain kinds of products go through a cycle consisting of four stages (introduction, growth, maturity, and decline) and that the location of production will shift internationally depending on the stage of the cycle.

Production switching: The movement of production from one country to another in response to changes in cost.

Promotion: The process of presenting messages intended to help sell a product or service.

Protestant ethic: A theory that there is more economic growth when work is viewed as a means of salvation and when people prefer to transform productivity gains into additional output rather than into additional leisure.

Pull: A promotion strategy that sells consumers before they reach the point of purchase, usually by relying on mass media.

Purchasing power: What a sum of money actually can buy.

Purchasing-power parity (PPP): A theory that explains exchange-rate changes as being based on differences in price levels in different countries.

Push: A promotion strategy that involves direct selling techniques.

Quantity controls: Government limitations on the amount of foreign currency that can be used for specific purposes.

Quota: A limit on the quantitative amount of a product allowed to be imported into or exported out of a country in a year.

Quota system: A commodity agreement whereby producing and/or consuming countries divide total output and sales in order to stabilize the price of a particular product.

Quoted currency: The currency whose value is not 1 when an exchange rate is quoted by relating one currency to another.

Rationalization: *See* Rationalized production.

Rationalized production: The specialization of production by product or process in different parts of the world to take advantage of varying costs of labor, capital, and raw materials.

Reciprocal quote: The reciprocal of the direct quote; also known as the *indirect quote*.

Regression: A statistical method showing relationships among variables.

Reinvestment: The use of retained earnings to replace depreciated assets or to add to the existing stock of capital.

Relationship enterprises: Networks of strategic alliances among big companies, spanning different industries and countries.

Renegotiation: A process by which international companies and governments decide on a change in terms for operations.

Repatriation: An expatriate's return to his or her home country.

Representative democracy: A type of government in which individual citizens elect representatives to make decisions governing the society.

Resource-based view of the firm: A perspective that holds that each company has a unique combination of competencies.

Return on investment (ROI): The amount of profit, sometimes measured before and sometimes after the payment of taxes, divided by the amount of investment.

Revaluation: A formal change in an exchange rate by which the foreign-currency value of the reference currency rises, resulting in a strengthening of the reference currency.

Reverse culture shock: The encountering of culture shock when returning to one's own country because of having accepted what was encountered abroad.

Revocable letter of credit: A letter of credit that can be changed by any of the parties involved.

Rio Declaration: The result of the Rio Earth Summit, which sets out fundamental principles of environmentally responsive behavior.

Rio Earth Summit: A meeting held in Rio de Janeiro in June 1992 that brought together people from around the world to discuss major environmental issues.

ROI: *See* Return on investment.

Rounds: Conferences held by GATT to establish multilateral agreements to liberalize trade.

Royalties: Payments for the use of intangible assets abroad.

SADC: *See* Southern African Development Community.

SADCC: *See* Southern African Development Co-ordination Conference.

Sales representative (foreign): A representative that usually operates either exclusively or nonexclusively within an assigned market and on a commission basis, without assuming risk or responsibility.

Sales response function: The amount of sales created at different levels of marketing expenditures.

SDR: *See* Special Drawing Right.

Second-tier subsidiaries: Subsidiaries that report to a tax-haven subsidiary.

Second-World countries: Socialist countries, often referred to as historically planned economies, centrally planned economies, or communist countries.

Secondary boycott: The boycotting of a company that does business with a company being boycotted.

Secrecy: A characteristic of an accounting system that implies that companies do not disclose much information about accounting practices; more common in Germanic countries.

Secular totalitarianism: A dictatorship not affiliated with any religious group or system of beliefs.

Securities and Exchange Commission (SEC): A U.S. government agency that regulates securities brokers, dealers, and markets.

Separate entity approach: A system for taxation of corporate income in which each unit is taxed when it receives income, with the result being double taxation.

Service exports: International received earnings other than those derived from the exporting of tangible goods.

Service imports: International paid earnings other than those derived from the importing of tangible goods.

Services: International earnings other than those on goods sent to another country; also referred to as invisibles.

Services account: The part of a country's current account that measures travel and transportation, tourism, and fees and royalties.

Settlement: The actual payment of currency in a foreign-exchange transaction.

Shipper's export declaration: A shipping document that controls exports and is used to compile trade statistics.

Sight draft: A commercial bill of exchange that requires payment to be made as soon as it is presented to the party obligated to pay.

Silent language: The wide variety of cues other than formal language by which messages can be sent.

Single European Act: A 1987 act of the EU (then the EC) allowing all proposals except those relating to taxation, workers' rights, and immigration to be adopted by a weighted majority of member countries.

Smithsonian Agreement: A 1971 agreement among countries that resulted in the devaluation of the U.S. dollar, revaluation of other world currencies, a widening of exchange-rate flexibility, and a commitment on the part of all participating countries to reduce trade restrictions; superseded by the Jamaica Agreement of 1976.

Social market economy: An economic system in which there is heavy governmental spending and high taxation to pay for such social services as health care, education, subsidized housing for the poor, and unemployment benefits but the prices of products are determined by supply and demand rather than by government fiat.

Society: A broad grouping of people having common traditions, institutions, and collective activities and interests; the term *nation-state* is often used in international business to denote a society.

Soft budget: A financial condition in which an enterprise's excess of expenditures over earnings is compensated for by some other institution, typically a government or a state-controlled financial institution.

Soft currency: *See* Weak currency.

Sogo shosha: Japanese trading companies that import and export merchandise.

Sourcing strategy: The strategy that a company pursues in purchasing materials, components, and final products; sourcing can be from domestic and foreign locations and from inside and outside the company.

Southern African Development Community (SADC): An organization endeavoring to counter the economic influence of South Africa in the region by focusing on economic objectives, such as regional cooperation in attracting investment.

Sovereignty: Freedom from external control, especially when applied to a body politic.

Special Drawing Right (SDR): A unit of account issued to countries by the International Monetary Fund to expand their official reserves bases.

Specific duty: A duty (tariff) assessed on a per-unit basis.

Speculation: The buying or selling of foreign currency with the prospect of great risk and high return.

Speculator: A person who takes positions in foreign exchange with the objective of earning a profit.

Spillover effects: Situations in which the marketing program in one country results in awareness of the product in other countries.

Spin-off organization: A company now operating almost independently of the parent because its activities do not fit easily with the parent's existing competencies.

Spot market: The market in which an asset is traded for immediate delivery, as opposed to a market for forward or future deliveries.

Spot rate: An exchange rate quoted for immediate delivery of foreign currency, usually within two business days.

Spread: In the forward market, the difference between the spot rate and the forward rate; in the spot market, the difference between the bid (buy) and offer (sell) rates quoted by a foreign-exchange trader.

Stakeholders: The collection of groups, including stockholders, employees, customers, and society at large, that a company must satisfy to survive.

Stereotype: A standardized and oversimplified mental picture of a group.

Strategic alliance: An agreement between companies that is of strategic importance to one or both companies' competitive viability.

Strategic intent: An objective that gives an organization cohesion over the long term while it builds global competitive viability.

Strategic plan: A long-term plan involving major commitments.

Strategy: The means companies select to achieve their objectives.

Subpart F income: Income of a CFC that comes from sources other than those connected with the active conduct of a trade or business, such as holding company income.

Subsidiarity: A principle that implies that EU interference should take place only in areas of common concern and that most policies should be set at the national level.

Subsidiary: A foreign operation that is legally separate from the parent company, even if wholly owned by it.

Subsidies: Direct or indirect financial assistance from governments to companies, making them more competitive.

Substitution drawbacks: A provision allowing domestic merchandise to be substituted for merchandise that is imported for eventual export, thus allowing the U.S. firm to exclude the duty paid on the merchandise in costs and in sales prices.

Super 301: A clause in U.S. tariff legislation permitting U.S. trade negotiators to threaten more restrictive import regulations to get other countries to lower their restrictions against U.S.-made products or services.

Swap: A simultaneous spot and forward foreign-exchange transaction.

Syndication: Cooperation by a lead bank and several other banks to make a large loan to a public or private organization.

Tariff: A governmental tax levied on goods, usually imports, shipped internationally; the most common type of trade control.

Tax treaty: A treaty between two countries that generally results in the reciprocal reduction on dividend withholding taxes and the exemption of taxes or royalties and sometimes interest payments.

Tax-haven countries: Countries with low income taxes or no taxes on foreign-source income.

Tax-haven subsidiary: A subsidiary of a company established in a tax-haven country for the purpose of minimizing income tax.

Technology: The means employed to produce goods or services.

Technology absorbing capacity: The ability of the recipient to work effectively with technology, particularly in relation to the need for training and equity in the recipient in order to effect a transfer.

Temporal method: A method of translating foreign-currency financial statements used when the functional currency is that of the parent company.

Terms of trade: The quantity of imports that can be bought by a given quantity of a country's exports.

Theocratic law system: A legal system based on religious precepts.

Theocratic totalitarianism: A dictatorship led by a religious group.

Theory of country size: The theory which holds that countries with large land areas are more apt to have varied climates and natural resources, and therefore, generally are more nearly self-sufficient than smaller countries.

Third-country nationals: Expatriate employees who are neither citizens of the country in which they are working nor citizens of the country where the company is headquartered.

Third-World countries: Developing countries or those not considered socialist or nonsocialist industrial countries.

Tie-in provisions: Stipulations in licensing that require the licensee to purchase or sell products from/to the licensor.

Time draft: A commercial bill of exchange calling for payment to be made at some time after delivery.

Time series: A statistical method of illustrating a pattern over time, such as in demand for a particular product.

TNC: *See* Transnational corporation.

Tort: A civil wrong independent of a contract.

Total quality management (TQM): The process that a company uses to achieve quality, where the goal is elimination of all defects.

Totalitarianism: A political system characterized by the absence of widespread participation in decision making.

TQM: *See* Total quality management.

Trade diversion: A situation in which exports shift to a less efficient producing country because of preferential trade barriers.

Trade Related Aspects of Intellectual Property Rights (TRIPS): A provision from the Uruguay round of trade negotiations requiring countries to agree to enforce procedures under their national laws to protect intellectual property rights.

Trademark: A name or logo distinguishing a company or product.

Transaction exposure: Foreign-exchange risk arising because a company has outstanding accounts receivable or accounts payable that are denominated in a foreign currency.

Transfer price: A price charged for goods or services between entities that are related to each other through stock ownership, such as between a parent and its subsidiaries or between subsidiaries owned by the same parent.

Transit tariff: A tax placed on goods passing through a country.

Translation: The restatement of foreign-currency financial statements into U.S. dollars.

Translation exposure: Foreign-exchange risk that occurs because the parent company must translate foreign-currency financial statements into the reporting currency of the parent company.

Transnational: (1) An organization in which different capabilities and contributions among different country-operations are shared and integrated; (2) multinational enterprise; (3) company owned and managed by nationals from different countries.

Transnational corporation (TNC): A company owned and managed by nationals in different countries; also may be synonymous with multinational enterprise.

Transparency: A characteristic of an accounting system that implies that companies disclose a great deal of information about accounting practices; more common in Anglo-Saxon countries (United States, United Kingdom).

Triad strategy: A strategy proposing that an MNE should have a presence in Europe, the United States, and Asia (especially Japan).

TRIPS: *See* Trade Related Aspects of Intellectual Property Rights.

Turnkey operation: An operating facility that is constructed under contract and transferred to the owner when the facility is ready to begin operations.

Underemployed: Those people who are working at less than their capacity.

Unfavorable balance of trade: An indication of a trade deficit—that is, imports are greater than exports.

Unilateral transfer: A transfer of currency from one country to another for which no goods or services are received; an example is foreign aid to a country devastated by earthquake or flood.

Unit of account: A benchmark on which to base the value of payments.

United Nations (UN): An international organization of countries formed in 1945 to promote world peace and security.

United Nations Conference on Trade and Development (UNCTAD): A UN body that has been especially active in dealing with the relationships between developing and industrialized countries with respect to trade.

Universal Copyright Convention: A multilateral agreement to protect copyrights.

Unrequited transfer: *See* Unilateral transfer.

U.S.–Canada Free Trade Agreement: *See* Canada-U.S. Free Trade Agreement.

U.S. shareholder: For U.S. tax purposes, a person or company owning at least 10 percent of the voting stock of a foreign subsidiary.

U.S. terms: The practice of using the direct quote for exchange rates.

Value-added tax (VAT): A tax that is a percentage of the value added to a product at each stage of the business process.

Value chain: The collective activities that occur as a product moves from raw materials through production to final distribution.

Variable price: A method of pricing in which buyers and sellers negotiate the price.

VAT: *See* Value-added tax.

VER: *See* Voluntary export restrictions.

Vertical integration: The control of the different stages as a product moves from raw materials through production to final distribution.

Visible exports: *See* Merchandise exports.

Visible imports: *See* Merchandise imports.

Voluntary export restraint (VER): A negotiated limitation of exports between an importing and an exporting country.

Weak currency: A currency that is not fully convertible.

West African Economic Community: A regional economic group involving Benin, Burkina Faso, Côte d'Ivoire, Mali, Mauritania, Niger, and Senegal.

Western hemisphere: Literally the earth's area between the zero and 180th meridian, but usually indicates the continents of the Americas and adjacent islands, excluding Greenland.

WIPO: *See* World Intellectual Property Organization.

World Intellectual Property Organization (WIPO): A multilateral agreement to protect patents.

World Trade Organization (WTO): A voluntary organization through which groups of countries negotiate trading agreements and which has authority to oversee trade disputes among countries.

WTO: See World Trade Organization.

Zaibatsu: Large, family-owned Japanese businesses that existed before World War II and consisted of a series of financial and manufacturing companies usually held together by a large holding company.

Zero defects: The elimination of defects, which results in the reduction of manufacturing costs and an increase in consumer satisfaction.

Zero-sum gain: A situation in which one party's gain equals another party's loss.

Company Index and Trademarks

Name Index

Subject Index